Praise for *AI Systems Performance Engineering*

AI systems are moving incredibly fast through intense research and development, and are filled with multiple layers of complexity. Chris breaks down this complexity and explains it in a way we can all benefit from, providing a singular reference that will set a standard for years to come.

—*Chris Lattner, CEO at Modular*

Understanding how LLMs work is just the beginning. Getting the most out of them through model and hardware optimization is what separates good practitioners from great ones. Chris's book is the missing reference manual that shows you how.

—*Sebastian Raschka, PhD, ML/AI researcher and author of bestselling book* Build a Large Language Model from Scratch *(Manning, 2024)*

The breadth here is insane—CUDA kernels, distributed training, PyTorch compiler internals, disaggregated inference, all in one place. Chris pulled together stuff that's usually scattered across a million blog posts and papers. This is an excellent encyclopedia of ML systems.

—*Mark Saroufim, PyTorch engineer at Meta and founder of GPU MODE Community*

Taming AI systems at scale is one of the immense challenges of our time. Chris Fregly has written the definitive field guide for this new frontier. He masterfully connects the dots from the silicon all the way up to the application, providing the full-stack wisdom that every AI engineer needs to turn raw compute into efficient, high-performance models.

—*Harsh Banwait, director of product at Coreweave*

This book is an exceptional resource for anyone looking to immerse themselves in modern ML systems engineering. Its focus on the details of state-of-the-art projects like vLLM and llm-d demonstrates a deep understanding of inference optimization techniques and the transformative power of open source software.

—Michael Goin, vLLM maintainer and principal engineer at Red Hat

This book is a definitive guide for AI engineers who refuse to settle for default performance. Whether you're tuning CUDA kernels, scaling LLM inference, or orchestrating AI agents across GPUs, this book gives you the surgical tools and system-level clarity to efficiently run modern AI workloads. Read it, use it and you will redefine how you build, scale, and think about modern AI systems. *AI Systems Performance Engineering* is a master key to unlocking AI performance.

—Arpitha Srinivas, AI systems performance engineer at the world's leading manufacturer of high-performance and high-efficiency AI servers

AI Systems Performance Engineering brilliantly connects GPU hardware architecture with modern AI workload optimization, combining rigorous low-level tuning with high-level system design. Spanning GPU memory bandwidth optimization, KV cache management, batching strategies, and multi-GPU inference, the book delivers insights forged in real-world production. Chris brings clarity to complex topics like Nsight profiling, transformer attention tuning, and distributed scaling, making it a must-read for performance engineers bridging hardware, systems, and AI.

—Amer Ather, cloud and ML performance engineer at Netflix

The most comprehensive and up-to-date guide on building modern-day AI systems. A must-read for every AI/ML developer and practitioner.

—Chaim Rand, AI/ML algorithm engineer

This is the go-to reference for anything AI-performance related. Chris's latest book is packed full of content that helps me in my day-to-day activities of optimizing and tuning AI workloads. He covers all of today's AI systems performance issues—and provides solutions that are invaluable to every company trying to put AI into production.

—Antje Barth, member of technical staff at Amazon AGI

There is no other book in this field that even comes close to *AI Systems Performance Engineering*. Each chapter demonstrates deep expertise and could easily be a standalone book. The content feels so fresh and evergreen, and very easy to digest.

—Suman Debnath, ML systems engineer at Anyscale

A tour-de-force that is essential reading for performance engineers who are working with the latest AI-based applications.

—*Adrian Cockcroft, OrionX.net (former head of cloud infrastructure at Netflix and VP of engineering at AWS)*

This is the book I was waiting for. It ties together the scattered, vast, and fast-moving world of AI systems performance engineering into one clear, modern resource.

—*Madison Kanna, AI engineer at Baseten*

As AI becomes the foundation of modern computing, understanding accelerator architectures and their ecosystems is no longer optional—it's a strategic imperative. Chris distills extraordinary technical depth into a clear and accessible narrative. For anyone engineering or leading at hyperscale, this book is the essential starting point.

—*Omer Zaki, VP of AI infrastructure at Oracle*

Today's AI is a system problem where one has to co-optimize the software for the hardware fabric to achieve peak performance. Chris peels back the curtain to showcase the different levels of the AI software and hardware stack that modern AI workloads run on.

—*Abdul Dakkak, head of GenAI at Modular*

AI Systems Performance Engineering

Optimizing Model Training and Inference Workloads with GPUs, CUDA, and PyTorch

Chris Fregly

O'REILLY®

AI Systems Performance Engineering

by Chris Fregly

Copyright © 2026 Flux Capacitor, LLC. All rights reserved.

Published by O'Reilly Media, Inc., 141 Stony Circle, Suite 195, Santa Rosa, CA 95401.

O'Reilly books may be purchased for educational, business, or sales promotional use. Online editions are also available for most titles (*https://oreilly.com*). For more information, contact our corporate/institutional sales department: 800-998-9938 or *corporate@oreilly.com*.

Acquisitions Editor: Nicole Butterfield
Development Editor: Angela Rufino
Production Editor: Kristen Brown
Copyeditor: nSight, Inc.
Proofreader: Piper Content Partners

Indexer: Sue Klefstad
Cover Designer: Susan Brown
Cover Illustrator: José Marzan Jr.
Interior Designer: David Futato
Interior Illustrator: Kate Dullea

November 2025:   First Edition

Revision History for the First Edition

2025-11-11:   First Release
2026-01-16:   Second Release
2026-03-13:   Third Release

See *http://oreilly.com/catalog/errata.csp?isbn=9798341627789* for release details.

979-8-341-62778-9

[LSI]

Table of Contents

Preface

In the vibrant streets of San Francisco, where innovation is as common as autonomous vehicle traffic on US Route 101, we find ourselves surrounded by an amazing world of artificial intelligence. Rapid advancements in AI are redefining our daily lives in every aspect. Over the last 20 years, we've experienced recommendation engines (2000s), AI assistants (2010s), and fully autonomous vehicles (2020s). The 2030s are going to be even more exciting, as AI is progressing extremely quickly and with massive societal influence.

My personal journey into the fast-moving AI systems performance engineering field was driven by a curiosity to understand the delicate balance and codesign between cutting-edge hardware, highly optimized software, and clever algorithms that power such complex systems and impactful use cases. This realization inspired me to dive deep into the realm of "full-stack" AI performance engineering. I wanted to understand how multiple components like processors, memory architectures, network interconnects, operating systems, and software frameworks all work together in harmony. The complexity of these interactions presented the challenges—and opportunities—that fueled my desire to dive deep and explore this unique combination of technologies.

This book is a realization of my explorations throughout the years as a hands-on ML and AI performance engineer. I created this book for engineers, researchers, practitioners, and enthusiasts who are eager to understand the underpinnings of AI systems performance at all levels. Readers might be building AI applications, optimizing neural network training strategies, or designing and managing scalable inference servers, or they may simply be fascinated by the mechanics of modern AI systems. Overall, this book provides the insights that bridge theory and practice across multiple disciplines.

The reader of this book likely has a foundational understanding of neural networks and a basic familiarity with Python and ML. However, even without these fundamentals, a curious reader can follow the multidimensional codesign performance narrative rooted in the first principles across hardware, software, and algorithms. I promise there is something in this book for every type of reader—and I guarantee every reader will learn a few new things in these pages.

Throughout the chapters, we examine the evolution of hardware architectures, dive into the nuances of software optimization, and explore real-world case studies that highlight the patterns and best practices of building both high-performance and cost-efficient AI systems. Each section is designed to build upon the last, covering everything from foundational concepts to advanced applications.

Conventions Used in This Book

The following typographical conventions are used in this book:

Italic
: Indicates new terms, URLs, email addresses, filenames, and file extensions.

`Constant width`
: Used for program listings, as well as within paragraphs to refer to program elements such as variable or function names, databases, data types, environment variables, statements, and keywords.

`Constant width bold`
: Shows commands or other text that should be typed literally by the user.

`Constant width italic`
: Shows text that should be replaced with user-supplied values or by values determined by context.

> This element signifies a tip or suggestion.

> This element signifies a general note.

Using Code Examples

Supplemental material (code examples, exercises, etc.) is available for download at *https://github.com/cfregly/ai-performance-engineering*.

If you have a technical question or a problem using the code examples, please send email to *support@oreilly.com*.

This book is here to help you get your job done. In general, if example code is offered with this book, you may use it in your programs and documentation. You do not need to contact us for permission unless you're reproducing a significant portion of the code. For example, writing a program that uses several chunks of code from this book does not require permission. Selling or distributing examples from O'Reilly books does require permission. Answering a question by citing this book and quoting example code does not require permission. Incorporating a significant amount of example code from this book into your product's documentation does require permission.

We appreciate, but generally do not require, attribution. An attribution usually includes the title, author, publisher, and ISBN. For example: "*AI Systems Performance Engineering* by Chris Fregly (O'Reilly). Copyright 2026 Flux Capacitor, LLC, 979-8-341-62778-9."

If you feel your use of code examples falls outside fair use or the permission given above, feel free to contact us at *permissions@oreilly.com*.

O'Reilly Online Learning

O'REILLY® For more than 40 years, *O'Reilly Media* has provided technology and business training, knowledge, and insight to help companies succeed.

Our unique network of experts and innovators share their knowledge and expertise through books, articles, and our online learning platform. O'Reilly's online learning platform gives you on-demand access to live training courses, in-depth learning paths, interactive coding environments, and a vast collection of text and video from O'Reilly and 200+ other publishers. For more information, visit *https://oreilly.com*.

How to Contact Us

Please address comments and questions concerning this book to the publisher:

O'Reilly Media, Inc.
141 Stony Circle, Suite 195
Santa Rosa, CA 95401
800-889-8969 (in the United States or Canada)
707-827-7019 (international or local)
707-829-0104 (fax)
support@oreilly.com
https://oreilly.com/about/contact.html

We have a web page for this book, where we list errata and any additional information. You can access this page at *https://oreil.ly/AI-SysPerfEng*.

For news and information about our books and courses, visit *https://oreilly.com*.

Find us on LinkedIn: *https://linkedin.com/company/oreilly-media*.

Watch us on YouTube: *https://youtube.com/oreillymedia*.

Acknowledgments

Although I'm the sole author of this book, this effort builds on the work of many practitioners and academics who have dedicated their lives to these topics. I am indebted to the awesome folks whose research and innovations have paved the way for the topics covered in this book. Their contributions helped shape the content and depth of this work. I'd like to thank the end-to-end reviewers (Adrian Cockroft, Antje Barth, Arpitha Moorthy, Chaim Rand, Fabrizio Milo, Simon Zamarin, Suneeta Mall, and Todd Bezenek) as well as many part-time reviewers who greatly improved the overall quality of this book. You challenged me and my understanding of these complex topics. And your insights are embedded in every page of this book.

I'd especially like to thank Mark Saroufim from Meta. He and his successful GPU Mode community (*https://oreil.ly/_SMa7*) helped me realize the need for this type of deep technical content covering hardware-software co-design across PyTorch, CUDA, and GPUs. I know how much work goes into maintaining and growing a large community for advanced topics such as these.

And to my close family (Ann Marie, Meredith, Tommy, and Conor), whose continuous support kept me writing through the night and into the early morning hours, I extend much heartfelt gratitude. Apologies if I wasn't always "present" while visiting you over the past year...I was down in the basement researching, coding, and writing!

And in a somewhat peculiar way, I'd like to also thank my car, Little Red Whiting Hood (Figure P-1). You are a complex, multidisciplinary system of highly tuned hardware and software. I've had you since I started this San Francisco journey more than 15 years ago. Every time I drive you, you remind me why I became an engineer. In relative GPU generations, you would be the NVIDIA Ampere A100—a timeless classic built by multidisciplinary engineers using the highest-performance components available at that time. And while you were originally designed for air cooling (Luftkühlung), you understand that water cooling (Wasserkühlung) is required for maximum performance. Your creator has stubbornly and relentlessly pushed your physical engineering limits generation after generation. Your turbos are like Tensor Cores, which get both moody and hot when pushed too hard. I'll never get rid of you.

And as the lyrics in the classic Phish song, "Contact," say:

> I woke up one morning in November
> And I realized I love you
> It's not your headlights in front
> Your tailpipe, or the skylight above you
> It's the way you cling to the road
> When the wind tries to shove you
> I'd never go driving away
> And come back home without you

Thanks for encouraging me to embrace mechanical sympathy, Little Red!

Figure P-1. Dashboard of a high-performance, mechanically sympathetic Porsche 911 Turbo named "Little Red Whiting Hood" (white exterior, red interior)

As we continue to push the frontiers of artificial intelligence and supercomputing, the knowledge in this book aims to inspire, educate, and empower the reader. The exploration through the complexities of *AI Systems Performance Engineering* is not just a technical exploration—it's a reminder of human ingenuity, the need to understand our surroundings, and a desire to continuously improve through technology and innovation. There are few people in this world who understand the fundamentals of codesigning hardware, software, and algorithms for maximum performance and efficiency. After reading this book, you will be one of them!

Chris Fregly
San Francisco, California

## CHAPTER 1

Introduction and AI System Overview

In late 2024, a small startup in China called DeepSeek.AI stunned the AI community by training a *frontier* large language model (LLM) without access to the latest, state-of-the-art NVIDIA GPUs at the time. Due to export restrictions, DeepSeek's engineers could not obtain top-tier NVIDIA Blackwell (B200, B300, etc.) or Hopper (H100, H200, etc.) GPUs, so they resorted to locally available, export-compliant alternatives at the time, including the NVIDIA H800 GPU. They used custom kernels and advanced optimization techniques such as model distillation to squeeze out maximum performance from these less capable GPUs.

Despite these limitations, DeepSeek.AI trained their DeepSeek-R1 model and achieved reasoning capabilities near the performance of leading frontier models that were trained on the most capable NVIDIA chips at the time. This case underscores that practitioners and researchers skilled in AI systems performance engineering can get the most out of their available hardware—no matter the constraints.

For example, DeepSeek's engineers treated communication bandwidth as a *scarce resource*, optimizing every byte over the wire to achieve what many thought impossible on that infrastructure. They scaled out to thousands of these constrained GPUs—connected with limited-bandwidth interconnects—using novel software and algorithmic optimizations to overcome these limitations.

Contrast DeepSeek's approach with the "brute force" path taken by the largest AI frontier labs in the United States and Europe. These labs continue to pursue larger compute clusters and larger models. Model sizes have exploded from millions to billions and now to trillions of parameters. And while each 10× increase in scale has unlocked qualitatively new capabilities, they require tremendous cost and resources.

For instance, training OpenAI's GPT-4 (2023) reportedly cost an estimated ~$100 million, while training Google's Gemini Ultra (late 2023) is estimated at a staggering ~$191 million. This demonstrates the need for resource efficiency going forward as these models scale up in size and cost.

DeepSeek claims that their model was trained for less than $6 million (*https://oreil.ly/ENITx*) in compute—an order of magnitude lower than models like GPT-4 and Gemini Ultra. At the same time, DeepSeek's model performance results are comparable to far more expensive closed-model systems on the benchmarks they report.

And while there is some doubt as to the validity of the $6 million claim—and what exactly it includes (e.g., just a single training run) or excludes (e.g., experimentation and the model-development pipeline)—the announcement briefly shocked the US financial markets, including NVIDIA's stock, which dropped (*https://oreil.ly/EdnK_*) ~17% in a single day based on this news. This was caused by concerns that DeepSeek's efficiency innovations would somehow require less NVIDIA hardware (*https://oreil.ly/jK5O6*) in the future. While this market reaction was a bit overblown—and NVIDIA stock recovered in subsequent trading sessions—it demonstrates the significant financial impact that breakthroughs in AI efficiency can have on global financial markets.

Beyond model training, DeepSeek boasts significant inference efficiency gains through novel hardware-aware algorithmic improvements to the transformer architecture that powers most modern, frontier LLMs. DeepSeek has clearly demonstrated that clever AI systems performance engineering optimizations can upend the economics of ultrascale AI model training and inference. These optimizations are covered throughout the rest of the book.

The takeaway is a profound realization that, at these scales, every bit of performance squeezed out of our systems could translate to millions, or even billions, of dollars saved. Every bottleneck eliminated can have an outsized impact on training throughput and inference latency. This, in turn, reduces cost and increases overall end-user happiness. In short, AI systems performance engineering isn't just about speed—it's about making the previously impossible both possible and affordable.

In Chapter 1, we embark on an in-depth exploration of the AI systems performance engineer—a role that has become pivotal in the era of large-scale artificial intelligence. This chapter serves as a comprehensive guide to understanding the multifaceted responsibilities and the critical impact of this profession on modern AI systems.

We begin by tracing the evolution of AI workloads, highlighting the transition from traditional computing paradigms to the demands of contemporary AI applications. This context sets the stage for appreciating the necessity of specialized performance engineering in AI.

The chapter then dives into the core competencies required for an AI systems performance engineer. We examine the technical proficiencies essential for the role, including a deep understanding of hardware architectures, software optimization techniques, and system-level integration. Additionally, we discuss the importance of soft skills such as problem solving, communication, and collaboration, which are vital for navigating the interdisciplinary nature of AI projects.

A significant portion of the chapter is dedicated to the practical aspects of the role. We explore how performance engineers analyze system bottlenecks, implement optimization strategies, and ensure the scalability and reliability of AI systems. Real-world scenarios and case studies are presented to illustrate these concepts, providing tangible examples of challenges and solutions encountered in the field.

Furthermore, we discuss the tools and methodologies commonly employed by performance engineers, offering insights into performance testing, monitoring, and benchmarking practices. This includes an overview of industry-standard tools and how they are applied to assess and enhance system performance.

By the end of Chapter 1, readers will have a thorough understanding of the AI systems performance engineer's role, the skills required to excel in this position, and the critical importance of performance engineering in the successful deployment and operation of AI systems. This foundational knowledge sets the stage for the subsequent chapters, where we dive deeper into specific techniques, technologies, and best practices that define excellence in AI performance engineering.

The AI Systems Performance Engineer

The AI systems performance engineer is a specialized role focused on optimizing the performance of AI models *and* the underlying systems they run on. These engineers ensure that AI training and inference pipelines are fast, cost-efficient, and performant—as well as reliable and highly available. As the scale increases, the AI systems performance engineer becomes even more critical.

An AI systems performance engineer commands top salaries—and for very good reasons. Our work has a clear impact on the bottom line. We blend expertise across hardware, software, and algorithms. We must understand low-level OS considerations, memory hierarchies, networking fundamentals, and multiple languages like Python and C++, as well as different AI frameworks and libraries such as PyTorch, OpenAI's Triton, and NVIDIA's Compute Unified Device Architecture (CUDA).

On any given day, an AI systems performance engineer might be examining low-level GPU kernel efficiency, optimizing OS thread scheduling, analyzing memory access patterns, increasing network throughput efficiency, or debugging distributed training algorithms. Key responsibilities of an AI systems performance engineer include benchmarking, profiling, debugging, optimizing, scaling, and managing resources efficiently. And while performance engineers may specialize in a combination of hardware, software, and algorithms, the point is that these specializations need to be codesigned together (see Figure 1-1). As such, it's good to understand their trade-offs and how they affect one another.

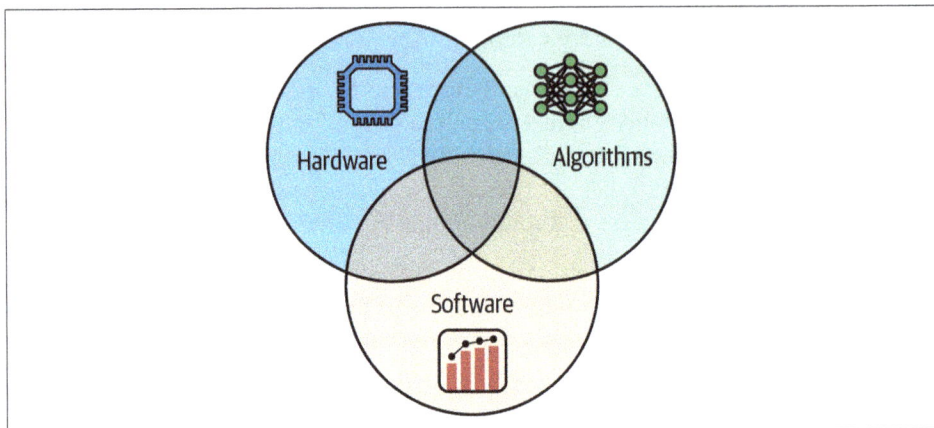

Figure 1-1. Codesigning hardware, software, and algorithms

Benchmarking and Profiling

Benchmarking and profiling involve measuring latency, throughput, memory usage, and other performance metrics for AI models under various workloads, including training and inference. To identify bottlenecks, we must iteratively use NVIDIA Nsight Systems and NVIDIA Nsight Compute together with the PyTorch profiler. Combined, these tools help pinpoint bottlenecks and track performance over time at different levels of the stack as we continue to improve overall performance of our AI system.

> It's important to set up automated performance tests to catch regressions, reductions in performance, early in the development cycle.

Debugging and optimizing performance issues requires that we trace performance issues to their root cause, whether it's a suboptimal CUDA kernel, an unnecessary communication overhead, or an imbalance in our training or inference workload.

In one case, we may want to use more efficient matrix operations that take advantage of the latest NVIDIA Transformer Engine (TE) hardware optimized for modern LLMs that use the transformer (*https://oreil.ly/Q4C0U*) architecture. In another case, we can improve the software framework by configuring a higher degree of parallelism for our "embarrassingly parallel" inference workload. In yet another case, we may try to improve the transformer's attention algorithm (*https://oreil.ly/Eaj5b*) by implementing better memory management and reducing the amount of memory moved in and out of GPU RAM relative to the number of GPU computations required.

Even minor code tweaks can produce major wins. For example, maybe a data preprocessing step written in Python is holding up an entire training pipeline. You can remove that bottleneck by reimplementing the code in C++ or use NVIDIA cuPyNumeric (*https://oreil.ly/z1_8B*), a drop in NumPy replacement, that can distribute array-operation workloads across both CPUs and GPUs.

Scaling Distributed Training and Inference

Scaling small research workloads to larger production workloads on ultrascale clusters will ensure that as we move from 8 GPUs to 80,000 GPUs, the system will scale with minimal overhead and loss of efficiency. This requires optimizing communication using NVIDIA Collective Communications Library (NCCL, pronounced "nickel") for distributed collectives like all-reduce commonly seen in training runs. In addition, the NVIDIA Inference Xfer Library (NIXL) provides high throughput, low latency, and point-to-point data movement across GPU memory and storage tiers for distributed inference. This communication can be between GPUs either on a single node or across thousands of nodes. They also optimize communication and collective aggregation operations like all-reduce, all-to-all, and all-gather, which are used extensively during model training and inference.

You may want to place data cleverly across nodes using data, tensor, and pipeline parallelism. Or you may need to redesign the workload to use tensor parallelism or pipeline parallelism because the model is so large that it doesn't fit onto a single GPU. Perhaps you are using a *mixture of experts* (MoE) model and can take advantage of expert parallelism.

Managing Resources Efficiently

It's important to optimize how models utilize resources like CPU cores, GPU memory, interconnect bandwidth, and storage I/O. This can involve many efforts such as ensuring GPUs are fed with data at full throttle, pinning threads on specific CPU cores, reducing context-switch overhead, orchestrating memory usage, and avoiding out-of-memory (OOM) errors on GPUs when training and inferencing with large models. Techniques like GPU virtualization (e.g., NVIDIA's Multi-Instance GPU [MIG]) can partition GPU resources for better overall utilization when full GPU power isn't needed for a job.

Cross-Team Collaboration

Cross-team collaboration is absolutely critical for AI systems performance engineers. It's important to work hand in hand with researchers, data scientists, and application developers—as well as infrastructure teams, including networking and storage.

Improving performance might require modifying model code, which involves coordination with researchers. Or you may want to deploy a new GPU driver to improve efficiency, which requires the infrastructure team.

Often, performance improvements span multiple teams. For instance, updating the CUDA driver or CUDA version for bug fixes and efficiency will involve careful coordination with DevOps, infrastructure, and support teams. And improving model code for performance involves close work with researchers. The performance engineer sits at the intersection of these multidisciplinary domains and speaks the language of AI, computer science, and systems engineering.

Transparency and Reproducibility

In performance engineering, it's vital to measure everything and trust data, not assumptions. By publishing your work, others can learn, reproduce, and build upon your findings.

One notable aspect of DeepSeek's story is how openly they shared their infrastructure optimizations. During DeepSeek's Open-Source Week (*https://oreil.ly/01O69*) in February 2025, they released a suite of open source GitHub repositories, including FlashMLA (*https://oreil.ly/BKy9W*), DeepGEMM (*https://oreil.ly/NzRsU*), DeepEP (*https://oreil.ly/FmRyz*), expert parallelism load balancer (*https://oreil.ly/7u0dr*) (EPLB), DualPipe (*https://oreil.ly/d2ReA*), and Fire-Flyer File System (*https://oreil.ly/haIQx*) (3FS). Each project was production-tested and aimed at squeezing the most performance from their hardware. These projects are described in the DeepSeek-V3 Technical Report (*https://oreil.ly/lE-4h*).

FlashMLA is their optimized attention kernel written in CUDA C++. DeepGEMM provides an FP8-optimized matrix multiplication library that reportedly outperforms many vendor kernels on both dense and sparse operations. Deep Experts Parallelism (DeepEP) is their highly tuned communication library for mixture-of-experts (MoE) models. EPLB implements a redundant expert strategy that duplicates heavily loaded experts to handle the additional load. DualPipe is a bidirectional pipeline parallelism algorithm that overlaps the forward/backward computation and communication phases to reduce pipeline bubbles. And 3FS is their high-performance distributed filesystem, reminding us that every layer needs to be optimized—including the filesystem—to get the most performance out of our AI system.

By open sourcing these projects (*https://oreil.ly/5WAIN*) on GitHub during their February 2025 "Open-Source Week," DeepSeek not only demonstrated the credibility of their claims by allowing others to reproduce their results but also contributed back to the community. This transparency allows other developers to benchmark, reproduce, and learn from their methods, including overlapping communication with DeepEP/DualPipe pipeline parallelism and saturating NVMe SSD/RDMA bandwidth with 3FS.

Open efforts like DeepSeek's Open Infra Index (*https://oreil.ly/qNUqk*) provide valuable baselines and tools. They provide real-world performance measurements on various AI hardware setups and encourage apples-to-apples comparisons and reproducibility. Similarly, the MLPerf (*https://oreil.ly/ZU2hI*) open benchmark suite provides a standard for reproducibly comparing training and inference performance across hardware and software setups.

Industry benchmarks such as MLPerf have quantified these kinds of codesigned optimizations across hardware generations. In MLPerf Training (*https://oreil.ly/Ao1l8*) v5.0 (2025), a Blackwell-based NVIDIA GB200 NVL72 system produced up to 2.6× higher training throughput per GPU over an equivalent Hopper system, as shown in Figure 1-2. In MLPerf Inference (*https://oreil.ly/V-jze*) v5.0 (2025), the Blackwell NVL72 achieved about 3.4× higher inference throughput per GPU over an equivalent Hopper cluster due to higher per-GPU performance and the much larger NVLink domain. These results were reported by NVIDIA as shown in Figure 1-3.

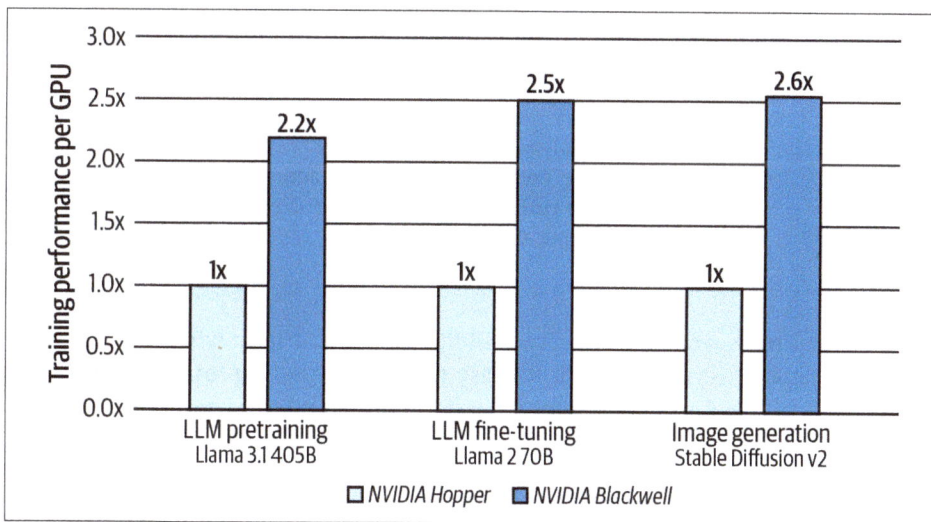

Figure 1-2. NVIDIA-derived per-GPU MLPerf Training v5.0 comparison from published GB200 NVL72 versus Hopper submissions (source: https://oreil.ly/Ao1l8)

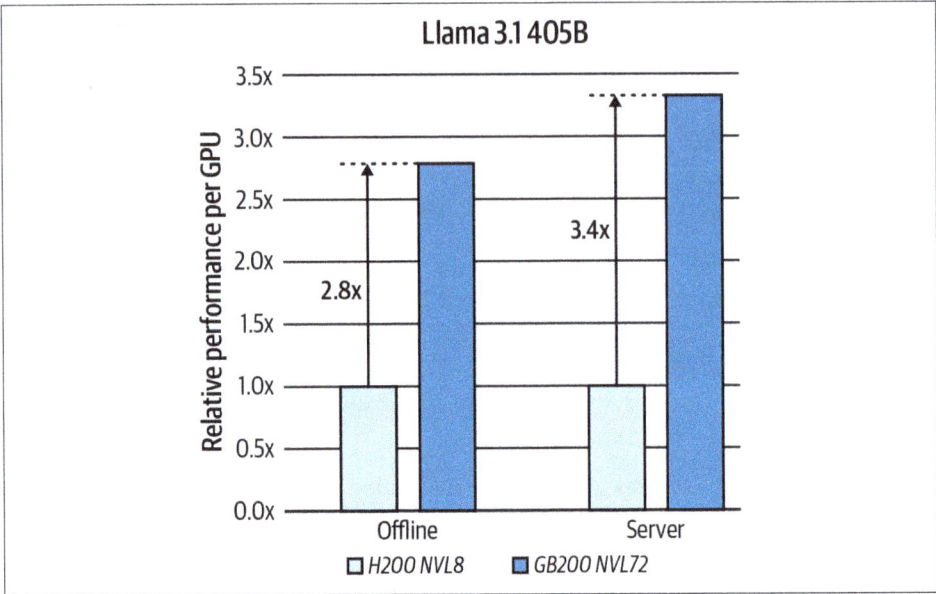

Figure 1-3. NVIDIA-derived per-GPU MLPerf Inference v5.0 comparison from published GB200 NVL72 versus Hopper submissions (source: https://oreil.ly/V-jze)

In later chapters, we'll reference some of these open benchmarks to support various performance tuning concepts. For instance, when discussing GPU kernel optimizations, we will reference DeepSeek's published profiles showing how their custom kernels achieved near-peak memory bandwidth utilization on NVIDIA GPUs.

> When we cite MLPerf results, remember that MLPerf cautions that per-GPU results are not a primary metric across platforms. Use system-level, end-to-end throughput as the correct basis for comparison. Consider per-GPU numbers only as component-level indicators.

Experimental transparency and reproducibility are critical in moving the field of AI performance engineering forward. It's easy to fall into the trap of anecdotal "vibe" optimizations ("We did X and things felt faster"). Instead, I'm advocating for a rigorous, scientific approach that develops hypotheses, measures the results with reproducible benchmarks, adjusts to improve the results, reruns the benchmarks, and shares all of the results at every step.

DeepSeek Scales to ~680-Billion Parameter Models Despite US Export Hardware Restrictions in China

Sometimes systems-performance innovations are born from necessity. As mentioned, DeepSeek found itself constrained to using only NVIDIA's H800 GPUs due to US export restrictions. The H800 is an export-compliant variant of the Hopper GPU. Compared to the H100, it reduces NVLink interconnect bandwidth and FP64 performance while keeping HBM capacity and bandwidth largely similar.

For context, an NVIDIA H100 provides about 900 GB/s NVLink interconnect bandwidth per GPU, while H800 provides about 400 GB/s bandwidth per GPU. This makes inter-GPU data transfers slower and ultimately limits multi-GPU scalability. Additionally, while the H100 offers 3.35 TB/s of memory bandwidth, the H800's limited throughput means that data transfers are much slower. This threatens to bottleneck distributed training jobs and limit scalability efficiency.

DeepSeek set out to train a massive ~680-billion-parameter MoE language model, called DeepSeek-V3, in this heavily constrained environment. This MoE model uses only about 37 billion active parameters per input token—rather than all ~680 billion at once.

With this architecture, only a fraction of the model is activated at any given time. This helps manage computational load—even with the compact H800 setup. Specifically, for each token, DeepSeek-V3 uses 1 shared expert plus 8 router-selected experts (out of 256 experts) for a total of 9 active experts per token, as shown in Figure 1-4.

We'll cover MoEs in more detail in the upcoming chapters. But just know that, to work around the environment limitations, DeepSeek implemented a novel DualPipe parallelism algorithm that carefully overlaps computation and communication to mask the H800's inherent weaknesses.

By designing custom CUDA kernels to bypass some of the default NCCL communication collectives, DeepSeek was able to coordinate data transfers in tandem with ongoing computations. This keeps the GPUs efficiently utilized despite their reduced interconnect bandwidth. This kind of communication/computation overlap is a theme we will revisit throughout the rest of the book.

This innovative engineering paid off, as DeepSeek-V3 was trained to completion at a fraction of the GPU time (and cost) of similarly sized frontier models from OpenAI, Meta, DeepMind, and others. This is a fraction of the resources that many assumed were necessary to train a model of this scale using a more capable cluster.

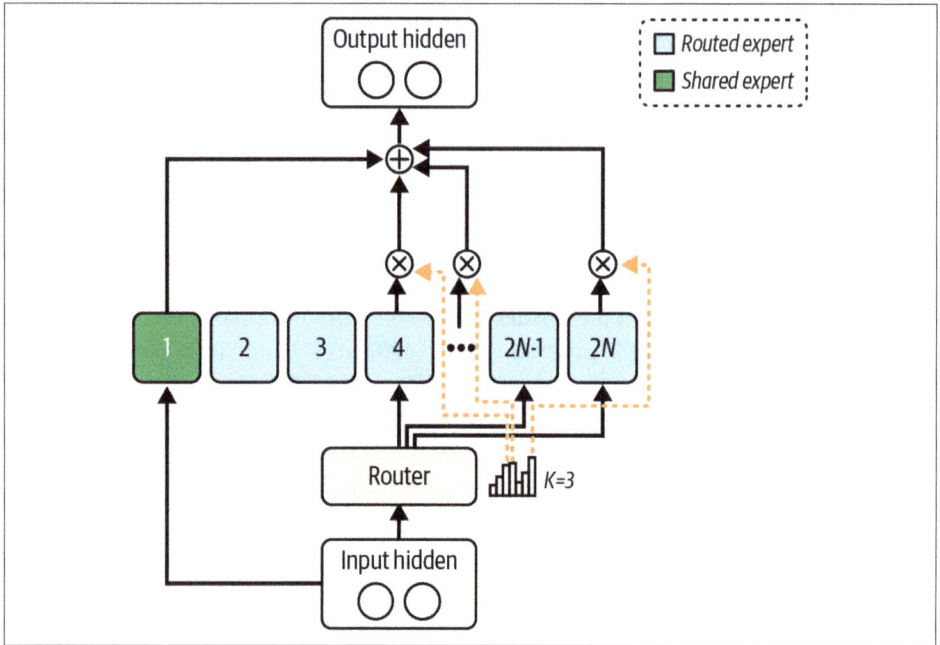

Figure 1-4. DeepSeek-V3's expert routing

DeepSeek reports (*https://oreil.ly/lE-4h*) that its open source models are comparable to closed source frontier models from OpenAI and Anthropic on the benchmarks they publish for language understanding, reasoning, and coding-style tasks. This supports the core point that open models can rival closed models despite hardware constraints.

Building on the DeepSeek-V3 model, the team then created DeepSeek-R1, which is its specialized reasoning model built similarly to OpenAI's o1 and o3 series (*https://oreil.ly/sVim6*) of reasoning models. These models use a traditional staged-pipeline training approach that includes cold-start data, supervised fine tuning (SFT), rejection sampling, and reinforcement learning (RL).

In addition, DeepSeek created DeepSeek-R1-Zero, which used a novel training approach that emphasized RL over SFT. This technique used minimal supervised data and instead focused on using RL with chain-of-thought reasoning data. This approach reduced training cost and time and underscored that smart software and algorithm design can overcome hardware bottlenecks.

The lessons learned are that large, sparsely activated MoE models can be effectively scaled even on limited memory and compute budgets. Novel training schedules and low-level communication/computation overlap optimizations can overcome hardware limitations, as demonstrated by the enormous return on investment (ROI) of DeepSeek's efforts.

The ROI is clear, as DeepSeek's unconventional approach brought about huge efficiencies and created a series of powerful models at much lower training cost and time. By extracting every ounce of performance from NVIDIA's H800 GPU—even under the constraints of reduced communication bandwidth—the team delivered GPT-4-level model performance for millions of dollars less. Additionally, DeepSeek saved even more money by not requiring as much human-labeled data during R1's fine-tuning stage for reasoning.

In short, smart software and algorithm design overcame brute-force hardware limitations. This enabled DeepSeek to develop large-scale AI models on a tight cost and hardware budget.

Toward 100-Trillion-Parameter Models

100-trillion-parameter models are an aspirational milestone for AI and are often compared against the estimated 100 trillion synaptic connections in the human neocortex. Each synaptic connection is equivalent to a model parameter. Achieving a model of this size is theoretically possible, but it demands an extraordinary amount of resources—and money. Scaling to 100-trillion-parameter models by brute force would be impractical for all but the absolute wealthiest organizations.

As a rough order of magnitude, a dense 100-trillion-parameter model trained on about 29 trillion tokens is often approximated with the dense-transformer heuristic $C \approx 6ND$, which gives about 1.74×10^{28} ($6 \times 1e14 \times 2.9e13$) FLOPs. Larger token counts scale this linearly. And while sparse (MoE) activations can reduce effective compute, it's not enough to train ultrascale models. Consistent with this book's theme, practical training of massive models requires effective codesign of hardware, software, and algorithms.

While the optimizations discussed in this book can be applied to smaller models and cluster sizes, I will continue to revisit the 100-trillion-parameter model to enforce the idea that we can't just throw hardware at the scaling problem. We need clever software and algorithmic innovations that are codesigned with hardware, including compute, networking, memory, and storage.

Such explosive growth in training cost is driving a search for new AI systems and software engineering techniques to increase performance, reduce cost, and make extreme-scale AI feasible with limited compute resources, power constraints, and money. Researchers are always exploring novel techniques to reduce the effective compute requirements.

One prominent idea is to use sparsity and, specifically, MoE models. Sparse models like MoEs are in contrast to traditional dense models like the common GPT-series large language models (LLMs) made popular by OpenAI. In fact, there is public speculation that some frontier models like OpenAI's proprietary GPT-series and o-series reasoning models are based on the MoE architecture.

Sparse models like MoEs activate only parts of the model for each input token. By routing each input token through only a subset of its many internal "experts," the FLOPS per token stays roughly constant even as total parameters grow. Such sparse models prove that scaling to multi-trillion-parameter models is done without an equivalent explosion in computation cost. Additionally, since these models use fewer active parameters during inference, request-response latencies are typically much lower for MoE models compared to their dense equivalents. These are crucial insights toward training and serving 100-trillion-parameter-scale models.

DeepSeek-V3 (base model) and -R1 (reinforcement-learning-based reasoning variant) are great examples of MoE efficiency. They contain ~680 billion total parameters with about 37 billion active per input token. DeepSeek's technical report and public write-ups describe an MoE with 1 shared expert and 8 selected experts out of 256 per token, which yields about 9 active experts and roughly 37 billion active parameters per token. This makes DeepSeek-V3 and -R1 much more resource-efficient than similarly sized dense large language models. Another example is Google's Switch Transformer (*https://oreil.ly/X4pRK*) MoE from 2021. This 1.6-trillion-parameter MoE model achieved the same accuracy as a dense model with only a fraction of the computation. It was trained 7× faster than a comparable dense approach.

In addition to massive compute requirements, memory is also a major bottleneck. For example, a 100-trillion-parameter model would require approximately 200 TB of GPU memory to load FP16 weights (100 trillion parameters × 2 bytes). This is roughly three orders of magnitude larger than the addressable 180 GB HBM capacity of a single NVIDIA Blackwell B200 GPU.

To load only the weights, a 100-trillion-parameter model would require approximately 1,110 B200 GPUs (180 GB each) or about 695 B300 GPUs (288 GB each). And this doesn't include memory needed to store activations, optimizer states, KV cache, and serving/training workspace overhead. These would further increase the total memory required.

For context, a typical B200 GPU compute node contains just 8 B200 GPUs. To use these, you would require ~125 GPU nodes just to load the model with a B200, and ~86 GPU nodes to load the model with a cluster of Ultra B300 GPU compute nodes (8 B300 GPUs per node).

Additionally, loading training data also becomes extremely difficult since feeding such a model with data fast enough to keep all of those GPUs busy is nontrivial. In particular, communication overhead between the GPUs grows significantly as the 100-trillion-parameter model is partitioned across 1,000 B200 GPUs or 700 B300 GPUs. Training a single model could consume millions of GPU-hours and megawatt-hours of energy. This is an enormous amount of cost—and energy consumption—to scale out large enough to train and serve a 100-trillion-parameter model.

The era of 100-trillion-parameter AI will force us to completely rethink system design to make training and deployment practical at this scale. Hardware, algorithms, and software all need to coevolve to meet this new frontier.

NVIDIA's "AI Supercomputer in a Rack"

To meet the challenges of ultrascale computing, NVIDIA has built a new class of AI supercomputers specifically aimed at trillion-parameter-scale workloads. Some examples include the NVIDIA Grace Blackwell GB200 NVL72 in 2024 and the GB300 NVL72 Ultra, which uses Blackwell Ultra GPUs with 288 GB HBM3e per GPU and maintains a 72-GPU NVLink domain with about 130 terabytes per second aggregate bandwidth.

Vera Rubin VR200 (2026) and Feynman (2028) systems continue this trend of exascale supercomputers condensed into a single data center rack. In fact, NVIDIA refers to these NVL rack systems (e.g., NVL72, NVL144, NVL576) as "AI supercomputers in a rack"—and for good reason.

Each GB200/GB300 NVL72 rack integrates 36 Grace Blackwells connected through NVLink with NVSwitch, providing the rack scale switching fabric. Each Grace Blackwell Superchip is a combination of one NVIDIA Grace CPU (with 72 CPU cores) and two NVIDIA Blackwell GPUs for a total of 36 Grace CPUs and 72 Blackwell GPUs—hence, the "72" in the name "NVL72."

If you haven't guessed already, the NVL in NVL72 stands for *NVLink*. This helps remind you that the GPUs in this system are interconnected using NVLink. Just in case we forget!

Each Grace Blackwell board connects to other boards using NVSwitch, the on-rack NVLink switch network. This way, all 72 GPUs can communicate with one another at full NVLink 5 bandwidth of 1.8 TB/s bidirectional per GPU (18 × 100 GB/s links). Across the rack, the NVLink Switch System provides about 130 TB/s aggregate GPU to GPU bandwidth within one NVL72 domain.

Effectively, the NVL72's internal fabric unifies all 72 Grace Blackwell GPUs into one high-speed cluster. As such, frameworks like PyTorch for training and vLLM for inference can use the single NVLink domain for efficient data tensor pipeline and expert parallelism. CUDA Unified Memory can migrate or remotely access pages across NVLink when needed. However, remote memory has distinct latency and bandwidth that should be treated as nonuniform. When relying on managed allocations across Grace and Blackwell, prefer explicit prefetch using `cudaMemPrefetchAsync` and `cudaMemAdvise` to reduce page-fault stalls.

More details are provided on the compute, memory, and interconnect hardware details of this supercomputer in upcoming chapters. For now, let's analyze the overall performance specifications of this AI supercomputer as a whole in the context of modern generative AI models.

A full GB200 NVL72 rack can theoretically reach about 1.44 exaFLOPS for FP4 and about 720 petaFLOPS for FP8 with 2 to 1 structured sparsity. It provides roughly 13.5 TB (13,824 GB = 192 GB per GPU × 72 GPUs) of HBM3e across the 72 GPUs and around 30 TB total when counting Grace CPU memory in the same NVLink domain.

NVLink provides pooled access across the 72 GPUs, and CUDA Unified Memory can migrate or remotely access pages over NVLink, but remote access has different performance, and the rack does not behave as a single uniform memory device.

In short, the GB200 NVL72 is a self-contained 72 GPU 1.44 exaFLOPS 30 TB memory system with about 120 to 132 kW rack power, depending on vendor configuration and cooling. It's truly an AI supercomputer that can train and serve multi-trillion-parameter models in a single rack.

By combining these racks to form ultrascale clusters, you can support massive multi-trillion-parameter models. Even better, you can provision these racks and rack clusters with a few clicks (and quite a few dollars!) using your favorite cloud provider, including Amazon Web Services (AWS), Google Cloud Platform (GCP), Microsoft Azure, CoreWeave, Lambda Labs, and many others.

> While this book focuses heavily on the Grace Blackwell generation of NVIDIA chips, the optimization principles discussed are derived from many previous generations of NVIDIA hardware. And these optimizations will continue to apply and evolve to many future NVIDIA chip generations to come, including Vera Rubin (2026), Feynman (2028), and beyond. This roadmap continues the pattern of doubling performance, memory, and integration with each new GPU generation.

Throughout the book, you will learn how each generation's innovation in compute, memory, networking, and storage will contribute to more AI scaling in the form of ultrascale clusters, multi-trillion-parameter models, high-throughput training jobs, and extreme-low-latency model inference servers. These innovations are fueled by hardware-aware algorithms that enforce the principles of mechanical sympathy and hardware-software codesign discussed in the next section.

Mechanical Sympathy: Hardware-Software Codesign

Mechanical sympathy is a term originally coined by software engineer Martin Thompson, who was drawing an analogy to the British Formula One champion Jackie Stewart (*https://oreil.ly/_xHIB*), who intimately understood his cars' mechanical details. In computing, it refers to writing software that is deeply aware of the hardware it runs on. In the AI context, it means codesigning algorithms hand in hand with hardware capabilities to maximize performance.

Real-world experience has shown that even minor tweaks in GPU kernels or memory access patterns can produce outsized gains. A classic example is FlashAttention (*https://oreil.ly/0okGm*), a novel algorithm that reimplements the transformer attention mechanism in a hardware-aware way.

FlashAttention "tiles" GPU computations, which minimizes the number of reads and writes issued to the GPU's memory. FlashAttention significantly reduces memory movement and speeds up attention computation. Replacing the default transformer attention mechanism/algorithm with FlashAttention produces a 2×–4× speedup in training and inference for long sequences while also reducing the overall memory footprint.

This kind of change reduces what used to be a major bottleneck (attention) down to a fraction of overall runtime. FlashAttention became the default in many libraries almost overnight because it let models handle longer sequences faster and more efficiently. Since FlashAttention, many new attention algorithms have emerged, including DeepSeek's Multi-Head Latent Attention (MLA).

DeepSeek's MLA algorithm—implemented as an NVIDIA GPU kernel and open sourced in 2025—is another example of hardware-software codesign, or mechanical sympathy. Similar to FlashAttention, MLA restructures the attention computations to better utilize NVIDIA's memory hierarchy and dedicated GPU "Tensor Cores." These optimizations allowed MLA to exploit the constrained H800 GPUs' architecture, achieving higher throughput at a fraction of the cost—surpassing even FlashAttention's performance on those same H800 systems.

This entire book is effectively a study in mechanical sympathy. We will see countless cases where new hardware features—or hardware constraints, as in the case of DeepSeek—inspire novel new software and algorithmic techniques. Conversely, we'll see where new software algorithms encourage new hardware innovations.

For instance, the rise of transformer models and reduced-precision quantization (e.g., FP8/FP4) led NVIDIA to add specialized hardware like the Transformer Engine and dedicated reduced-precision Tensor Cores for faster matrix-math computation units. These hardware innovations, in turn, enable researchers to explore novel numeric optimizers and neural-network architectures. This, then, pushes hardware designers even further, which then unlocks even newer algorithms, etc. It's a virtuous cycle!

Modern GPUs use the latest Transformer Engine with FP4 support and microscaling. Combined with the latest generation NVLink, these features increase attention throughput primarily through faster Tensor Core math, higher memory bandwidth, and improved Special Function Units (SFUs.) For instance, the exponential computation unit (*https://oreil.ly/ewGjA*) is specifically designed to accelerate the softmax operation used heavily by the transformer's attention algorithm—a key part of today's LLM models. With the popularity of transformers, softmax latency had become a bottleneck on previous GPUs, given that it's critical to the transformer attention mechanism.

> By improving special function throughput and fast math pipelines with modern GPUs, NVIDIA demonstrates mechanical sympathy and hardware-software-algorithm codesign in its best and purest form. They work directly with researchers and practitioners to address and reduce the bottlenecks of modern LLM algorithms (e.g., attention) running on their hardware.

This tight interplay—GPUs and AI algorithms coevolving—is the heart of mechanical sympathy in AI. These codesign innovations can happen only with close collaboration between the hardware companies (e.g., NVIDIA and Advanced RISC Machine [ARM]), AI research labs (e.g., OpenAI and Anthropic), and AI systems performance engineers (e.g., us!).

Measuring "Goodput" Useful Throughput

When operating clusters of hundreds, thousands, or millions of GPUs, it's important to understand how much of the theoretical hardware capability is actually performing useful work. Traditional throughput metrics like FLOPS and device utilization are misleadingly high, as much of the time is likely spent on stalled communication, idling computation, or failed job restarts. This is where the concept of "goodput" comes in—as described by Meta as "effective training-time ratio" in a 2025 paper (*https://oreil.ly/NpG3o*).

NVIDIA calls the theoretical hardware maximum the *speed of light*, as you may have seen in NVIDIA blogs, documentation, webinars, and conference talks.

In simple terms, goodput measures the throughput of useful work completed (number of tokens processed or inference requests completed) per unit time—discounting everything that doesn't directly contribute to model training or inference. It's effectively the end-to-end efficiency of the system from the perspective of productive model training or inference. Goodput can then be normalized by the cluster's maximum possible throughput to produce a percent efficiency value.

For example, suppose a node with 8 GPUs can process 100,000 tokens in 10 seconds. In this case, its goodput is 10,000 tokens per second. If each GPU in the node can achieve a peak theoretical throughput of 1,500 tokens per second, or 12,000 tokens per second across all 8 GPUs, the node's efficiency is 83.3% (0.833 = 10,000 achieved throughput/12,000 peak throughput).

Meta's AI infrastructure team highlighted the importance of goodput in the "Revisiting Reliability" paper. The paper introduces the *effective training time ratio metric* and shows how preemptions resource fragmentation and failures reduce realized training time even when headline utilization is high. In this paper, Meta's team analyzes how preemptions, hardware faults, and network congestion reduce realized throughput.

In other words, while the cluster appeared to be 100% utilized, 70%–75% of the compute was lost due to overheads like communication delays, suboptimal parallelization, data delays, or failure recovery. Additionally, Meta's analysis showed that, at scale, issues like job preemptions, network hotspots, and unrecoverable faults were major contributors to lost goodput.

For example, imagine a training job that could theoretically process 1,000 samples/second on ideal hardware, but due to a poor input pipeline and excessive synchronization, it achieves only 300 samples/second of actual training throughput. We'd say that the job is running at 30% goodput. The remaining 70% capacity is essentially wasted.

Identifying these gaps and closing them is a core part of our work. For instance, if GPUs are waiting on data loading from storage, we might introduce caching or async prefetch. If they're idling during the gradient synchronization step of our model training process, we likely want to overlap the GPU computation (e.g., calculating the gradients) with the communication between GPUs (e.g., synchronizing the gradients). Our goal is to turn wasted, inefficient cycles into useful work.

This gap between theoretical and realized performance is the value proposition of the AI systems performance engineer role. Our mission is to drive that goodput number as high as possible—ideally increasing it closer to 100%—by attacking inefficiencies and reducing cost at every level of the stack, including hardware, software, and algorithms.

> Investments in AI systems performance engineers consistently generate returns well above cost. Consider a performance engineer helping to achieve a 20% boost in cluster efficiency. This can reduce hardware costs by millions of dollars in large-scale AI environments.

By focusing on goodput, we are optimizing what truly matters—the amount of useful training done per dollar of cost and per joule of power. Goodput is the ultimate metric of success—more so than raw FLOPS or device utilization—because it encapsulates how well hardware, software, and algorithms are harmonized toward the end goal of training AI models faster and cheaper.

Improving goodput requires a deep understanding of the interactions between the hardware (e.g., CPUs, GPUs, network topologies, memory hierarchies, storage layouts), software (e.g., operating system configurations, paged memory, I/O utilization), and algorithms (e.g., transformer architecture variants, attention mechanism alternatives, and different caching and batching strategies).

This broad and deep understanding of multiple disciplines—including hardware, software, and algorithms—is why AI systems performance engineers are so scarce today. This is also why I'm writing this book! Next is the roadmap and methodology that maps out the rest of this book.

Book Roadmap and Methodology

How will we approach the optimization of 100-trillion-parameter AI systems? This book is organized to take you from the hardware fundamentals up through the software stack and algorithmic techniques—with an emphasis on hands-on analysis at each level. Here is a breakdown of the rest of the book.

Chapter 2 provides an in-depth look at NVIDIA AI system hardware, including the GB200/GB300 NVL72 "AI supercomputer in a rack," which combines Grace Blackwell Superchip design with the NVLink network to create performance/power characteristics of an AI supercomputer.

Chapters 3–5 will then cover OS-level, networking, and storage optimizations for GPU-based AI systems. These optimizations include CPU and memory pinning, as well as Docker container and Kubernetes orchestration considerations, including network I/O and storage configurations for GPU environments.

Chapters 6–12 discuss NVIDIA CUDA programming fundamentals and CUDA-kernel optimizations that are essential for developing novel hardware-aware algorithms. Such popular algorithms include FlashAttention and DeepSeek's MLA. These algorithms target the resource-intensive attention mechanism of the transformer architecture, which dominates today's generative AI workloads.

With NVIDIA hardware and CUDA software context in hand, we'll dive into distributed communication optimizations, including training and serving ultralarge models efficiently. We'll examine strategies to minimize communication, such as overlapping computation with communication—a pattern that applies to many layers of the AI system stack.

Chapters 13 and 14 discuss PyTorch-specific optimizations, including the PyTorch compiler stack and OpenAI's Python-based Triton language and compiler for custom GPU kernels. These compilers lower the barrier for developing novel CUDA kernels, as they don't require a deep understanding of C++ typically required to develop CUDA kernels. These chapters also discuss distributed parallelization techniques for model training, including data parallelism (DP), fully sharded data parallelism (FSDP), tensor parallelism (TP), pipeline parallelism (PP), context parallelism (CP), and mixture-of-experts (MoE). We will show how multi-trillion-parameter models are split and trained across many GPUs efficiently. And we will discuss techniques for memory optimization during ultrascale model training, including activation checkpointing, sharding optimizer states, and offloading to larger CPU memory. These techniques are vital when model sizes exceed the physical GPU hardware limits.

Chapters 15–19 focus on software and algorithmic innovations for high-throughput, low-latency model inference and agentic AI systems. This includes disaggregated prefill and decode, which is now supported in NVIDIA Dynamo and community stacks with key-value (KV) cache movement over UCX with GPUDirect RDMA, NCCL point-to-point, or framework-provided transports. We also discuss the widely used model serving engines, including vLLM, SGLang, and NVIDIA TensorRT LLM. We then cover the NVIDIA Dynamo distributed inference framework, which integrates with these engines and includes NIXL for low-latency KV cache transfer in disaggregated prefill decode setups.

We'll also look at leveraging the Grace CPU in the NVL72 for preprocessing, co-running smaller "draft" models for high-performance inference algorithms such as speculative decoding, and efficient request routing and batching to maximize overall throughput of the inference system. We will also explore model compression and acceleration techniques such as 4-bit quantization, knowledge distillation to teach smaller "student" models from wiser "teacher" models, sparsity and pruning, and the use of specialized TensorRT kernels. There is a heavy focus on disaggregated prefill-decode and adaptive techniques to dynamically tune a system at runtime.

Chapter 20 describes modern efforts to use AI-assisted tools to optimize kernel and AI system performance. The chapter also includes case studies on training and serving multi-billion- and multi-trillion-parameter models efficiently. It also covers emerging trends for self-improving AI system optimizations and agents. This helps to paint a picture of where 100-trillion-parameter-scale AI systems are headed—and how to position ourselves for the future of AI systems performance engineering.

The Appendix provides a checklist of common performance-optimization and cost-saving tips and tricks to apply to your own AI system. This is a summary of actionable optimizations and efficiency gains discussed throughout this book.

In short, this book implements a hands-on and empirical methodology to apply performance optimizations. We will frequently analyze actual runs, case studies, benchmark results, and profiling data to understand bottlenecks and verify improvements. By the end of the book, you should grasp the principles of optimizing ultralarge AI systems—as well as gain some practical experience with tools to apply those optimizations on ultrascale, multi-GPU, multinode, and multirack AI systems like the NVIDIA GB200/GB300 NVL72 AI supercomputer in a rack—or similar AI systems now and in the future.

Key Takeaways

The following qualities collectively define the role of the AI systems performance engineer, whose expertise in merging deep technical knowledge with strategic, profile-driven optimizations transforms raw hardware into cost-effective, high-performance AI solutions:

Measure goodput
> Look beyond raw FLOPS or utilization. Instead, measure the ratio of time the GPU spends performing useful work (e.g., forward/backprop computations) versus waiting on data or other overhead. Use NVIDIA Nsight Systems/Compute or PyTorch profiler to measure this ratio. Strive to improve this ratio, as goodput focuses on effective, useful GPU utilization.

Prefer skillful engineering optimizations instead of brute-force spending
> More hardware isn't a silver bullet. Clever software and system optimizations can bridge the gap when hardware is limited, enabling results that would otherwise require far more expensive infrastructure. We saw this with DeepSeek's achievement. By optimizing communication and hardware usage, their engineers trained a frontier model on restricted H800 GPUs (with limited interconnect bandwidth) at a fraction of the cost. The DeepSeek model matched the performance of frontier

models trained on far more powerful hardware. In other words, skillful engineering outperformed brute-force spending.

Look for order-of-magnitude impact with incremental optimizations
At scale, even a small-percentage efficiency gain can save millions of dollars. Said differently, small inefficiencies such as redundant computations and slow data pipelines can silently increase costs as the system scales.

Approach performance tuning with a profile-driven mindset
Use data and profiling tools to guide optimizations. Use profilers to identify the true bottlenecks—whether it's compute utilization, memory bandwidth, memory latency, cache misses, or communication/network delays. Then apply targeted optimizations for that bottleneck.

Maintain a holistic view
Improving AI systems performance spans hardware, including the GPU, CPU, memory, and network—as well as software such as algorithms and libraries. A weakness in any layer can bottleneck the whole. The best performance engineers consider hardware-software codesign: sometimes algorithm changes can alleviate hardware limits, and sometimes new hardware features enable new algorithms.

Stay informed on the latest hardware, software, and algorithms
Modern AI hardware and software are evolving rapidly. New capabilities such as unified CPU-GPU memory, faster interconnects, and novel numerical-precision formats can change the optimal strategies. A good performance engineer keeps an eye on these and updates their mental models accordingly to eliminate bottlenecks quickly. Additionally, the MLPerf benchmark (*https://oreil.ly/ZU2hI*) suites are a great resource to understand AI hardware performance for various models.

Conclusion

This introductory analysis underscores that optimizations are not optional at large scale—they are absolutely necessary. It is the difference between a system that works and one that is utterly impractical. Traditional approaches, whether in hardware or algorithms, break down at this scale. To push forward, we need both advanced hardware and smart software techniques.

It's clear that AI models are pushing physical resource limits. Hardware is racing to keep up with new model architectures and algorithms. And performance engineers are the ones in the driver's seat to ensure that all this expensive machinery is actually delivering results.

We have demonstrated that the role of the AI systems performance engineer is gaining more and more importance. Simply throwing money and hardware at the problem is not enough. We need to co-optimize everything—model architectures, algorithms, hardware, and system design—to push toward the next leaps in AI capability.

As an AI systems performance engineer, your job is multidisciplinary, complex, and dynamic. You will dive into GPU profiling one day, network topology the next day, and perhaps algorithmic complexity the following day. This is a role for a "full-stack" performance geek who loves to squeeze out every drop of available performance from both hardware and software.

In essence, an AI systems performance engineer's mantra is "mechanical sympathy." We deeply understand the machinery—both hardware and software—so that we can tailor efficient solutions that exploit the entire stack's performance capabilities to the fullest.

As we saw earlier, a 100-trillion-parameter model is well beyond the reach of today's hardware—even an exascale system would require several millennia of GPU time for one training run. This is clearly impractical, underscoring why we need both advanced hardware and clever software optimizations to ever reach this scale.

In the coming chapters, we will demonstrate how to break down the components of an AI system from processors to memory to interconnects to software frameworks—and learn how to optimize each component in a principled way. We'll study concrete case studies where making small changes brings about huge performance and cost improvements. Doing so, we will help create a mental model for reasoning about performance optimization along multiple dimensions.

By the end of this journey, you as a reader and practitioner will be equipped with knowledge of today's best practices as well as an engineering mindset to tackle tomorrow's challenges. You will have an arsenal of techniques to push AI systems to their limits—now and in the future. For AI systems performance engineers, the mandate is clear. We must learn from these innovations and be ready to apply aggressive optimizations at every level of the stack.

Now, with the context established, let's dive into the hardware components of modern AI systems, including the CPUs, GPUs, memory technologies, network fabrics, and storage mechanisms. By studying the components that underpin contemporary AI supercomputers, you will learn the fundamentals that provide the foundation of subsequent deep dives into optimization techniques in later chapters.

AI System Hardware Overview

Imagine condensing a supercomputer's worth of AI hardware into a single rack. NVIDIA's latest architecture does exactly that. In this chapter, we dive into how NVIDIA fused CPUs and GPUs into powerful *superchips* and then wired dozens of them together with ultrafast interconnects to create an AI supercomputer-in-a-box. We'll explore the fundamental hardware building blocks—the Grace CPU and Blackwell GPU—and see how their tight integration and enormous memory pool make life easier for AI engineers.

Then we'll expand outward to the networking fabric that links 72 of these GPUs as if they were one machine. Along the way, we'll highlight the leaps in compute performance, memory capacity, and efficiency that give this system its superpowers. By the end, you'll appreciate how this cutting-edge hardware enables training and serving multi-trillion-parameter models that previously seemed impossible.

The CPU and GPU Superchip

NVIDIA's approach to scaling AI starts at the level of a single, combined CPU + GPU superchip module. Beginning with the Hopper generation, NVIDIA started packaging an ARM-based CPU together with one or more GPUs in the same unit, tightly linking them with a high-speed interface. The result is a single module that behaves like a unified computing engine.

The first implementation of the superchip was Grace Hopper (GH200), which pairs one Grace CPU with one Hopper GPU. Next came the Grace Blackwell (GB200) Superchip, which pairs one Grace CPU with two Blackwell GPUs in the same package. The Grace CPU sits in the center of the module, surrounded by two Blackwell GPU dies, as shown in Figure 2-1.

Figure 2-1. NVIDIA Grace Blackwell Superchip module containing one Grace CPU (center) and two Blackwell B200 GPUs (top left and right) on a single module with a shared unified memory space and connected by a custom high-speed link called NVLink-C2C (chip-to-chip)

In a traditional system, the CPU and GPU have separate memory pools and communicate over a relatively slow bus (like PCIe), which means data has to be copied back and forth. NVIDIA's superchip eliminates that barrier by connecting the CPU and GPUs with a custom high-speed link called NVLink-C2C (chip-to-chip).

NVLink-C2C provides up to ~900 GB/s between the Grace CPU and the Blackwell GPUs in GB200 Superchips. By comparison, PCIe Gen5 x16 (Blackwell B200) is about 64 GB/s per direction, and PCIe Gen6 x16 (Blackwell Ultra B300) is about 128 GB/s per direction. NVLink-C2C's interconnect speed is an order of magnitude faster than typical PCIe. And, importantly, it is cache-coherent.

Cache coherency means the CPU and GPU share a coherent, unified memory architecture. As such, they always see the same values. In practice, the Grace CPU and Blackwell GPUs on a superchip can all access one another's memory directly as if it were one huge memory pool. The GPU can read or write data stored in the CPU's memory, and vice versa, without needing explicit copies. This unified memory architecture is often called Unified CPU-GPU Memory or Extended GPU Memory (EGM) by NVIDIA, and it effectively blurs the line between CPU memory and GPU memory.

Each Grace Blackwell Superchip carries a tremendous amount of memory. The Grace CPU comes with hundreds of gigabytes of LPDDR5X DRAM attached, and each Blackwell GPU has its own high-speed, high-bandwidth memory (HBM) stacks.

In the GB200 Superchip, the Grace CPU provides up to ~480 GB of LPDDR5X at up to ~500 GB/s, and the two Blackwell GPUs together contribute up to ~384 GB of HBM3e memory (192 total GB per GPU). In total, a GB200 Superchip exposes roughly ~900 GB of memory of coherent, unified memory accessible by the GPUs and CPUs in a unified address space.

To put it simply, each superchip has nearly a terabyte of fast, unified memory at its disposal. This is a game changer for giant AI models. In older systems, a single GPU might be limited to < 100 GB of memory, which meant models larger than that had to be partitioned or offloaded to slower storage. Here, a GPU can seamlessly utilize the CPU's memory as an extension.

If a neural network layer or a large embedding table doesn't fit in the GPU's local HBM, it can reside in the CPU's memory, and the GPU will still be able to work with it across NVLink-C2C. From a programmer's perspective, the unified virtual address space and coherence simplify correctness. However, for performance, one should explicitly manage placement and memory movement using techniques such as asynchronous prefetch and staged pipelines. Accessing LPDDR5X using NVLink-C2C has higher latency and roughly an order-of-magnitude lower bandwidth than accessing HBM directly.

GPU memory is still much faster and closer to the GPU cores than CPU memory—you can think of the CPU memory as a large but somewhat slower extension. Accessing data in LPDDR5X isn't as quick as HBM on the GPU. It's on the order of 10× lower bandwidth and higher latency. A smart runtime will keep the most frequently used data in HBM and use the CPU's LPDDR5X for overflow or less speed-critical data. The key point is that overflow no longer requires going out to NVMe SSD or across a network.

The GPU can fetch from CPU RAM at perhaps 900 GB/s (450 GB/s per direction), which, while slower than HBM, is much faster than fetching from NVMe SSD storage. This flexibility is critical, as it means a model that is, say, 500 GB in size (too large for a single GPU's HBM) can still be placed entirely within one superchip module with access to a combined 192 (180 usable) GB in HBM and ~500 GB of CPU memory. This model can run without partitioning the model across multiple GPUs. The GPU would just transparently pull the extra data from CPU memory when needed.

In essence, memory size ceases to be a hard limit for fitting ultralarge models, as long as the total model fits within the combined CPU + GPU memory of the superchip. Many researchers have faced the dreaded "out of memory" errors when models don't fit on a GPU—this architecture is designed to push that boundary out significantly.

NVIDIA Grace CPU

The Grace CPU itself is no sloth. It's an ARM Neoverse V2 CPU custom-designed by NVIDIA for bandwidth and efficiency. Its job in the superchip is to handle general-purpose tasks, preprocess and feed data to the GPUs, and manage the mountain of memory attached to it. It runs at a modest clock speed but makes up for it with huge memory bandwidth—up to ~500 GB/s to its LPDDR5X memory—and lots of cache, including over 100 MB of L3 cache.

The philosophy is that the CPU should never become a bottleneck when shoveling data to the GPUs. It can stream data from storage or perform on-the-fly data transformations like tokenization or data augmentation—feeding the GPUs through NVLink-C2C very efficiently. If part of your workload is better on the CPU, the Grace cores can tackle that and make the results immediately accessible by the GPUs.

This is a harmonious coupling in which the CPU extends the GPU's capabilities in areas where GPUs are weaker, like random memory accesses or control-heavy code. And the GPUs accelerate the number-crunching where CPUs can't keep up.

The low-latency link between the CPU and GPUs means they can trade tasks without the usual overhead. For example, launching a GPU kernel from the CPU can happen much faster than on a traditional system, since the command doesn't have to traverse a slow PCIe bus. The CPU and GPU are essentially on the same board. This is similar to calling a fast local function versus a slower remote function. Next, let's talk about the Blackwell GPU, the brute-force engine of the superchip.

NVIDIA Blackwell "Dual-Die" GPU

Blackwell is NVIDIA's codename for this GPU generation, and it represents a significant leap over the previous Hopper (H100) GPUs in both compute horsepower and memory. The Blackwell B200 and B300 "Ultra" GPU are not single chips. Instead, they use a multichip module (MCM) design with two GPU dies placed in a single module. As such, Blackwell is called a *dual-die* GPU (see Figure 2-2).

> While this section dives into the details of the dual-die architecture, the rest of the book will refer to Blackwell's two combined GPU dies collectively as just the "Blackwell GPU."

This *chiplet* approach splits what would normally be one enormous GPU into smaller GPU dies—linking them together with a superfast, on-package die-to-die interconnect. Why do this? Because a single monolithic die is limited by manufacturing because there's a limit to how large you can make a chip on silicon. By combining two physical GPU dies into a single module, NVIDIA can double the total transistor budget for the module.

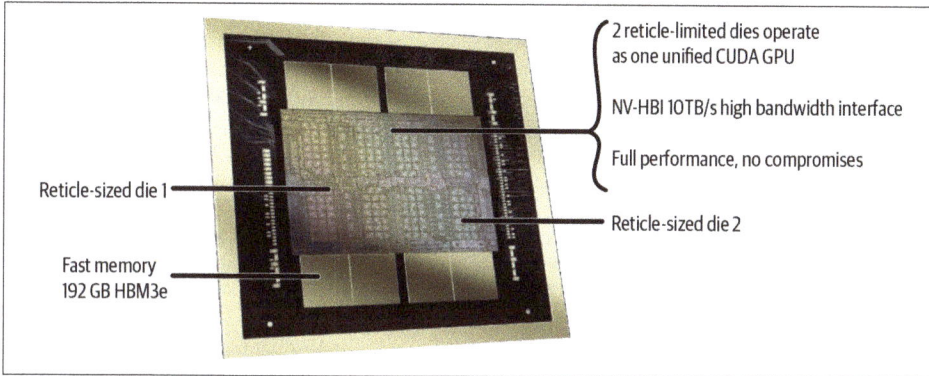

Figure 2-2. Blackwell dual-die multichip module (MCM) design

For the Blackwell B200 MCM, each GPU die has about 104 billion transistors and 96 GB HBM3e memory. The combined GPU module has around 208 billion transistors and 192 (180 usable) GB total memory per B200 GPU. By comparison, the Hopper H100 GPU had ~80 billion transistors and 80 GB HBM3 (versus Blackwell's HBM3e) memory. As such, Blackwell's B200 more than doubles transistor count and ~2.4× increases memory size.

Blackwell's two GPU dies communicate using a specialized, high-speed 10 TB/s die-to-die interconnect called NV-HBI (High-Bandwidth Interface). This lets the two GPU dies in the module function as a single unified GPU. The software layer running on top of it sees only a single GPU.

From the system's perspective, a Blackwell GPU is one single module, or device, with a large pool of memory (192 [180 usable] GB HBM3e) and a ton of execution units, but under the hood it's two chips working in tandem. NVIDIA's software and scheduling ensure that work is balanced across the two GPU dies and memory accesses are coherent. This allows developers to largely ignore this complexity, as they appear as one GPU, as NVIDIA intended.

Each Blackwell B200 GPU module has 192 (180 usable) GB of HBM3e memory combined across the two GPU dies (96 GB each) and divided into 8-Hi stacks. An 8-Hi HBM3e stack is built by vertically stacking eight DRAM dies—each 3 GB—for a total of 24 GB per stack.

The B200 GPU uses eight of these stacks (four per die) to provide 192 (180 usable) GB (192 GB = 8 stacks × 24 GB per stack) of on-package memory. This increases the per-GPU stack count and capacity compared to the previous generation Hopper GPUs—and gives more headroom for model parameters, activations, gradients, and input data.

> Only 180 GB of the 192 GB HBM3e memory is usable per B200 due to error correcting code (ECC), system firmware usage, manufacturing limitations, and other issues that prevent the chip from exposing the full 192 GB. As such, we'll reference 180 GB instead of the full 192 GB for the Blackwell B200 available memory.

The memory is also faster, as Blackwell's B200 HBM3e has an aggregate bandwidth up to roughly 8 TB/s per GPU. For comparison, the Hopper uses the previous generation HBM3, which delivers ~3.35 TB/s per GPU. As such, Blackwell's memory bandwidth throughput is roughly 2.4× higher than Hopper's.

Feeding data at 8 terabytes per second, the Blackwell GPU cores are kept busy crunching on huge matrices without frequently stalling to wait for data. NVIDIA also beefed up on-chip caching, as Blackwell has a total of 126 MB of L2 cache (63 MB per die). This cache is a small but ultrafast memory on the GPU that holds recently used data.

By increasing the L2 cache size by more than 2.5× compared to Hopper's 50 MB L2 cache, Blackwell can keep more of the neural network weights or intermediate results on chip, avoiding extra trips out to HBM. This again helps ensure the GPU's compute units are seldom starved for data.

Next, let's show how the Blackwell GPU is paired with a dedicated set of reduced-precision Tensor Cores—as well as transformer-optimized hardware and software APIs from NVIDIA called the Transformer Engine. Frameworks, like PyTorch and inference engines like vLLM, support these optimizations by using libraries like CUDA, CUTLASS, and OpenAI's Triton, which we talk about in later chapters.

> Remember that the rest of this book refers to Blackwell's dual-die GPU as just the "Blackwell GPU."

NVIDIA GPU Tensor Cores and Transformer Engine

Speaking of compute units, Blackwell introduces enhancements specifically aimed at AI workloads. Central to this is NVIDIA's Tensor Core technology and the Transformer Engine (TE). Tensor Cores are specialized units within each streaming multiprocessor (SM) of the GPU that can perform matrix multiplication operations at very high speed.

Tensor Cores were present in prior generations, but Blackwell's Tensor Cores support even more numerical formats, including extremely low-precision ones like 8-bit and 4-bit floating point. The idea behind lower precision is simple. By using fewer bits to represent numbers, you can perform more operations at the same time—not to mention your memory goes further since fewer bits are used to represent the same numbers. This assumes that your algorithm can tolerate a little loss in numerical precision. These days, a lot of AI algorithms are designed with low-precision numerical formats in mind.

NVIDIA pioneered the TE to automatically adjust and use mixed precision in deep learning where critical layers use higher precision (FP16 or BF16) and less critical layers use FP8. TE automatically optimizes the balance of precision with the goal of maintaining the model's accuracy at the lower precision.

In the Hopper generation, the TE first introduced FP8 support, which doubled the throughput versus FP16. Blackwell takes it one step further by introducing NVIDIA FP4 (NVFP4), a 4-bit floating-point format that uses half the number of bits of FP8. FP4 is so small that it can potentially double the compute throughput of FP8. Figure 2-3 shows the relative speedup of FP8 and FP4 compared to FP16.

An entire NVL72 rack (72 GPUs) has a theoretical Tensor Core throughput over 1.4 exaFLOPS (that's 1.4×10^{18}) in 4-bit precision. This is a mind-boggling number that puts this single rack in the realm of the world's fastest supercomputers—albeit at low FP4 precision. Even if real-world workloads don't always hit that peak, the capability is there, which is astonishing.

Modern GPUs use a TE that adds NVFP4 support together with improved scaling and calibration. In practice, you adopt TE by using its kernels and modules in frameworks such as PyTorch. This way, FP8 and NVFP4 are applied when they preserve accuracy. This is not a fully automatic per-layer decision in all frameworks.

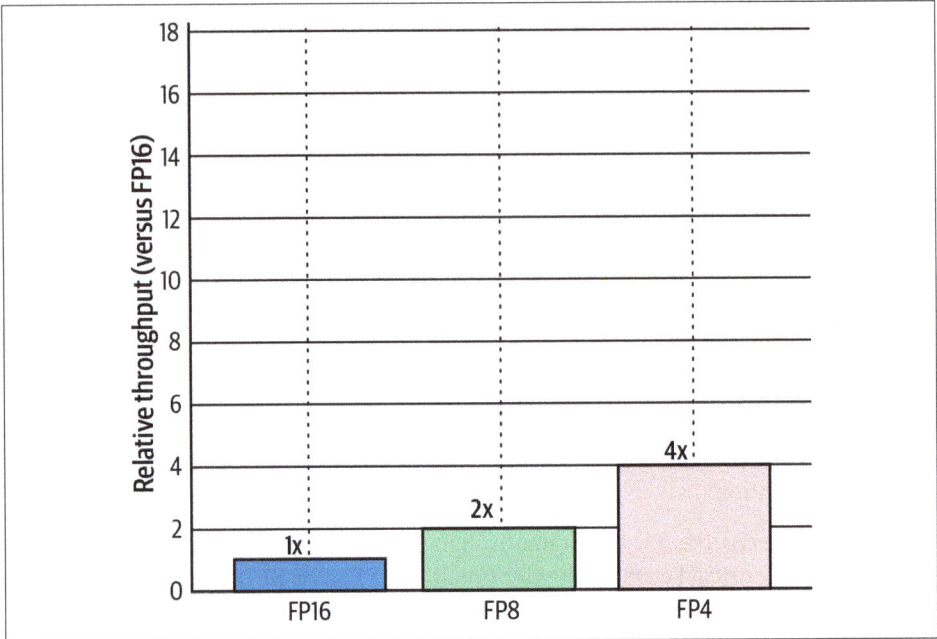

Figure 2-3. Relative speedup of FP8 and FP4 compared to FP16

Advanced techniques include dynamically changing the precision for each layer of a neural network during training and inference. The goal is to use the lowest precision that will still preserve model accuracy for each of those layers. For example, the TE might keep the first layers of a neural net in FP16 since early layers can be sensitive to noise. But, based on heuristics, it could decide to use FP8 or FP4 for later layers that are more tolerant—or for giant embedding matrices where high precision isn't as critical.

All of this can happen under the hood in NVIDIA libraries and AI frameworks like PyTorch. As a user, you just enable mixed precision, and the result is a huge speedup that essentially comes "for free." We'll discuss mixed precision in Chapter 9, but just know that many LLMs today use mixed precision for this reason. These reduced precisions improve training speed compared to FP16 and FP32—and reduce accuracy loss. Blackwell was built to make FP8 and FP4 accessible and efficient.

These reduced-precision formats reduce memory usage as well. Using FP4 halves the memory needed per parameter compared to FP8 (and FP8 halves FP16 memory usage), meaning you can pack an even larger model into the GPU's memory.

NVIDIA has effectively bet on AI's future being in lower precision arithmetic and has given Blackwell the ability to excel at it. This is especially critical for inference serving of massive models, where throughput (tokens per second) and latency are paramount.

To illustrate the generational leap forward from Hopper to Blackwell, NVIDIA reported an H100-based system could generate only about 3.4 tokens per second per GPU for a large 1.8-trillion-parameter MoE model—with over 5 seconds of latency for the first token. This is too slow for interactive use.

The Blackwell-based system (NVL72) ran the same model with around 150 tokens per second per GPU and a low first-token latency of ~50 milliseconds. That is roughly 30× the real-time throughput improvement over the Hopper generation. The NVL72 allowed this massive model to serve real-time responses—opening it up to many more low-latency use cases.

This speedup came from raw FLOPS, the combination of faster GPUs, lower precision (FP4) usage, and the NVLink interconnect keeping the GPUs fed with data. It underscores how a holistic design that spans across both compute and communication can translate into real-world performance gains.

In essence, Blackwell GPUs are more powerful, smarter, and better fed with data than their predecessors. They chew through math faster, thanks to Tensor Cores, TE, and low precision. Additionally, the system architecture ensures that data is made available quickly thanks to huge memory bandwidth, large caches, and NVLink.

Before moving on, let's quickly discuss the hierarchy inside the GPU, as this is useful to understand performance tuning later.

Streaming Multiprocessor, Threads, and Warps

Each Blackwell GPU, like its predecessors, consists of many streaming multiprocessors (SMs). Think of these like the "cores" of the GPU, as shown in Figure 2-4.

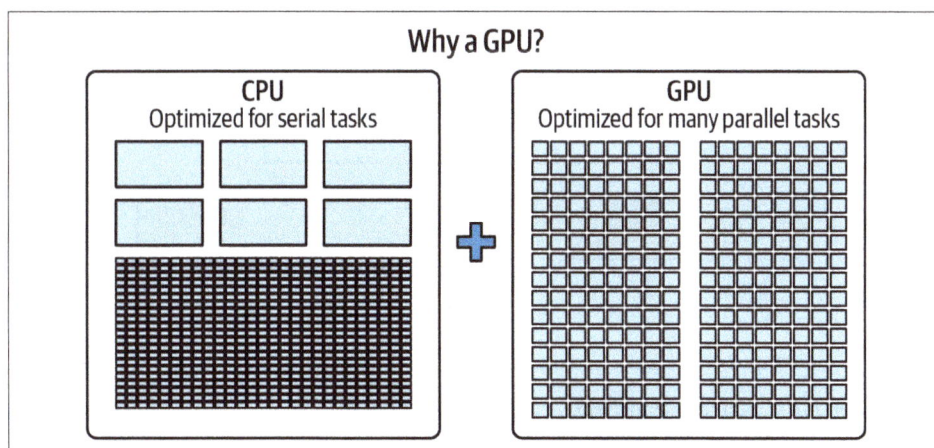

Figure 2-4. Comparing CPU cores to GPU cores (source: https://oreil.ly/003EH, https://oreil.ly/Z25Tf)

Each SM contains a bunch of arithmetic units (for FP32, INT32, etc.), Tensor Cores for matrix math, load/store units for memory operations, and some special function units for things like transcendental math. The GPU also has its own small pool of superfast memory, including registers, shared memory, and L1 cache.

An SM executes threads in fixed-size groups known as *warps*, with each warp containing exactly 32 threads that execute the exact same instructions in lockstep. This is called the single instruction, multiple threads (SIMT) execution model.

SMs execute many active warps in parallel to help cover the latency of a thread waiting on data accessed from global memory. Consider an SM having dozens of warps (hundreds of threads) in flight concurrently. If one warp is waiting on a memory fetch, another warp can run. This is called *latency hiding*. We will revisit latency hiding throughout the book. This is a very important performance-optimization tool to have in your tuning toolbox.

A high-end GPU like Blackwell will have hundreds of SMs. Each SM is capable of running thousands of threads concurrently. This is how we get tens of thousands of active threads onto a single GPU. All those SMs share a 126 MB L2 cache, as we mentioned earlier, and share the memory controllers that connect to the HBM. The memory hierarchy contains registers (per thread) → shared memory (per thread block, on each SM) → L1 cache (per SM) → L2 cache (shared across all SMs on the GPU) → HBM memory (off chip), as shown in Figure 2-5.

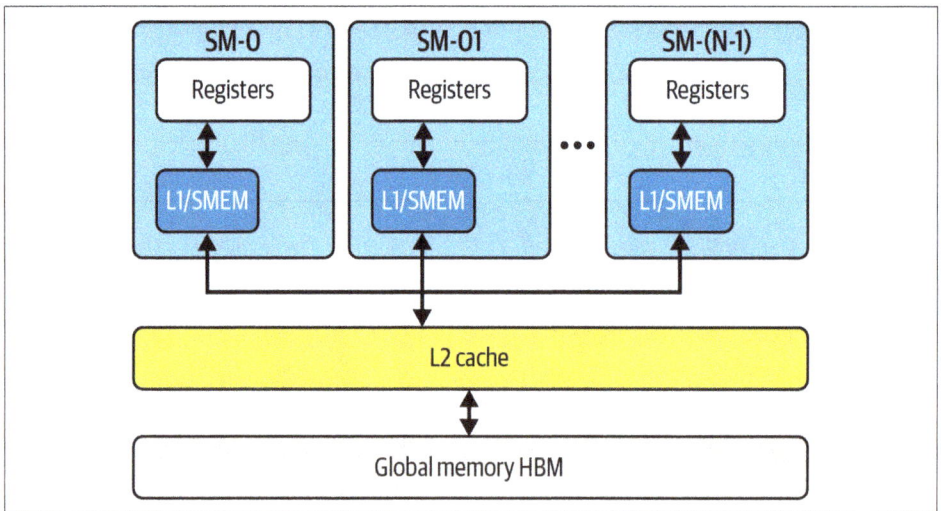

Figure 2-5. GPU memory hierarchy

For best performance, data needs to stay as high in that hierarchy as possible. If every operation went out to HBM even at 8 TB/s, the GPU would stall too often due to the increased latency of accessing off-chip memory. By keeping reusable data in SM local memory or L2 cache, the GPU can achieve enormous throughput. The Blackwell architecture's doubling of cache and bandwidth is aimed exactly at keeping the GPU beast fed and happy.

As performance engineers, we'll see many examples where a kernel's performance is bound by compute as well as memory traffic and throughput. NVIDIA clearly designed Blackwell so that, for many AI workloads, the balance between FLOPS and memory bandwidth is well-matched.

Blackwell's design balances compute and memory so that for many AI kernels the GPUs can keep computing with minimal stalls. In practice, well-optimized dense math operations can reuse data from on-chip memory to approach peak FLOPS without being severely memory bound.

All of this means that, given well-optimized code, the GPUs will often be busy computing rather than waiting on data. Note that certain operations like huge reductions or random memory accesses can still be memory bound, but the updated GPU, memory, and interconnect hardware make this a bit less of an issue.

Ultrascale Networking Treating Many GPUs as One

Packing two GPUs and a CPU into a superchip gives us an incredibly powerful node. The next challenge is connecting many of these superchips together to scale out to even larger model training.

NVIDIA provides a large rack configuration using GB200/GB300 Superchips called the NVL72 system. NVL72 stands for a system with 72 Blackwell GPUs—and 36 Grace CPUs—all interconnected with NVLink. This is essentially an AI supercomputer in a single rack.

The GB200/GB300 NVL72 is built as 18 compute nodes in which each node contains two GB200/GB300 Superchips for a total of four Blackwell GPUs + two Grace CPUs per compute node, as shown in Figure 2-6.

Figure 2-6. A 1U compute tray within the GB200/GB300 NVL72 rack with two Grace Blackwell Superchips (source: developer.nvidia.com (https://oreil.ly/V0TqY))

Here, each superchip module has one Grace CPU and two Blackwell GPUs (each B200 is a dual-die MCM). The NVL72 has 18 of these trays linked together. By connecting the 18 compute nodes together, the GB200/GB300 NVL72 links 72 Blackwell GPUs (18 nodes × 4 GPUs) and 36 Grace CPUs (18 nodes × 2 CPUs) together to form a powerful, unified CPU-GPU cluster.

The interesting thing about the NVL72 is that every GPU can talk to any other GPU through the NVLink Switch fabric at very high speed within a single NVLink domain. NVIDIA achieved this using a combination of NVLink 5 connections on the GPUs and a dedicated switch silicon called NVSwitch.

NVLink and NVSwitch

Each Blackwell GPU exposes 18 NVLink 5 ports. Aggregate bidirectional NVLink bandwidth is 1.8 TB/s per GPU (18 NVLink links × 100 GB/s bidirectional) with the NVL72 wiring all ports to the NVLink Switch System. Each NVLink switch tray delivers 144 NVLink ports at 100 GB/s. Across the nine trays, each GPU's 18 NVLink 5 links are wired one per NVSwitch chip so the 72 GPUs are fully connected at full bisection bandwidth. The aggregate bidirectional NVLink 5 bandwidth is 1.8 TB/s per GPU (18 NVLink links × 100 GB/s bidirectional).

This is double the per-GPU NVLink bandwidth of the previous generation used by Hopper GPUs. The Hopper H100 uses 18 NVLink 4 ports but runs at half the speed of NVLink 5. Inter-GPU latency over NVLink is in the single-digit microsecond range.

The GPUs are cabled in a network through NVSwitch chips. NVSwitch is essentially a switching chip similar to a network switch, but it's built specifically for NVLink. This means any GPU can reach any other GPU through one switch stage in the NVLink Switch System at full bisection bandwidth. This one-stage property holds true within a single NVL72 rack because each GPU uses its 18 NVLink links to connect to the 18 NVSwitch chips, enabling a path through a single switch. Figure 2-7 shows an NVLink Switch tray used in NVL72.

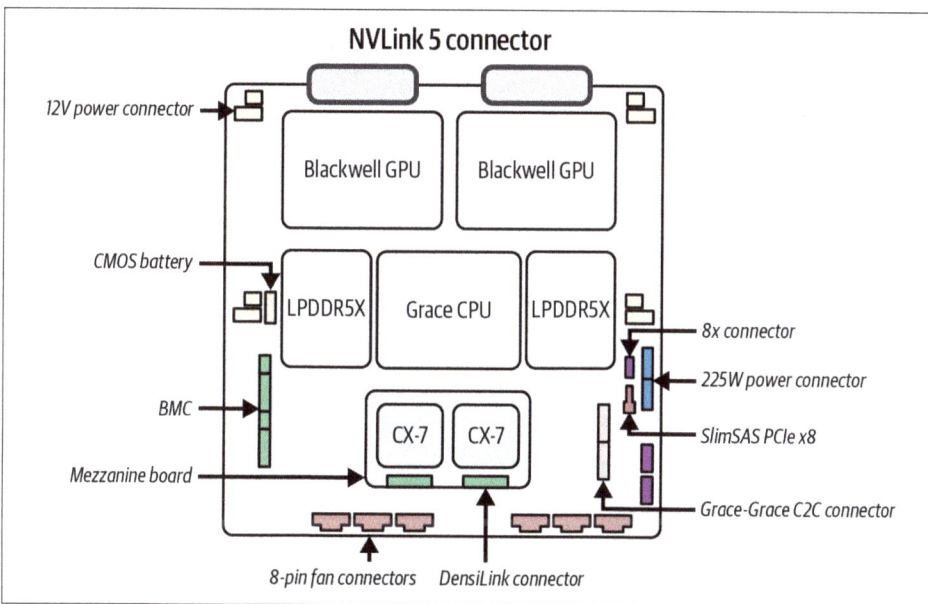

Figure 2-7. One NVLink Switch tray inside the NVL72 (source: https://oreil.ly/h7seG)

Each switch tray contains two NVSwitch chips and multiple high-speed ports. The NVL72 rack comprises 9 such switch trays and 18 compute trays, as shown in Figure 2-8.

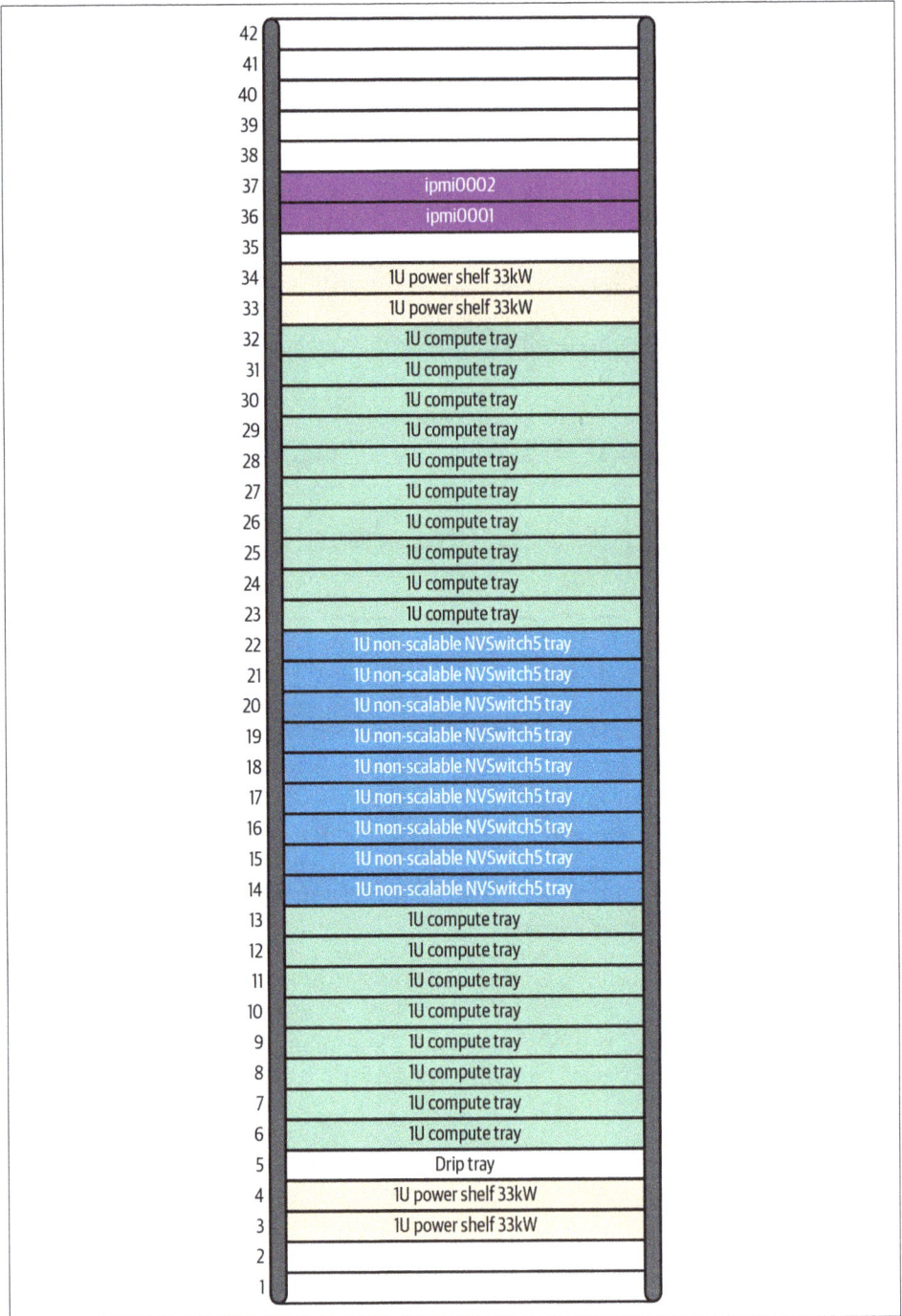

42	
41	
40	
39	
38	
37	ipmi0002
36	ipmi0001
35	
34	1U power shelf 33kW
33	1U power shelf 33kW
32	1U compute tray
31	1U compute tray
30	1U compute tray
29	1U compute tray
28	1U compute tray
27	1U compute tray
26	1U compute tray
25	1U compute tray
24	1U compute tray
23	1U compute tray
22	1U non-scalable NVSwitch5 tray
21	1U non-scalable NVSwitch5 tray
20	1U non-scalable NVSwitch5 tray
19	1U non-scalable NVSwitch5 tray
18	1U non-scalable NVSwitch5 tray
17	1U non-scalable NVSwitch5 tray
16	1U non-scalable NVSwitch5 tray
15	1U non-scalable NVSwitch5 tray
14	1U non-scalable NVSwitch5 tray
13	1U compute tray
12	1U compute tray
11	1U compute tray
10	1U compute tray
9	1U compute tray
8	1U compute tray
7	1U compute tray
6	1U compute tray
5	Drip tray
4	1U power shelf 33kW
3	1U power shelf 33kW
2	
1	

Figure 2-8. NVSwitch System of nine trays inside an NVL72 rack (source: https://oreil.ly/h7seG)

Since each of the 9 switch trays contains two NVSwitch chips, the total is 18 NVSwitch chips in the NVL72 system. The network is arranged as a full crossbar such that every GPU is connected to every NVSwitch, and every NVSwitch is connected to every GPU. This provides a high-bandwidth path between any pair of GPUs.

Each switch tray exposes 144 NVLink ports to fully connect the 18 NVLink links on each GPU. Concretely, each GPU uses its 18 NVLink links to connect to the 18 NVSwitch chips (one link to each switch). This means any GPU can reach any other GPU in one hop (GPU → NVSwitch → GPU), with enormous bandwidth along the way. Figure 2-9 shows the full NVL72 architecture with 72 fully connected GPUs (36 GB200 superchips) and 18 NVSwitches.

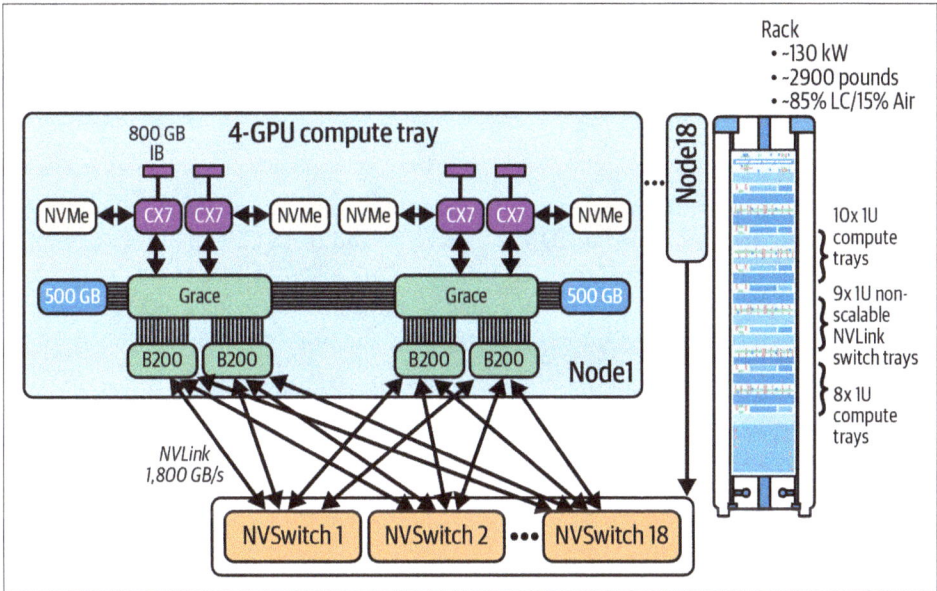

Figure 2-9. Each GPU connects to each NVSwitch (one link for each switch)

The aggregate bisection bandwidth across the entire 72-GPU network is about 130 TB/s within an NVL72 rack. For perspective, that is many times higher than even a top-end InfiniBand cluster of similar scale. The design exposes a fully connected, high-bandwidth fabric with a global address space across GPUs. This allows efficient collectives and one-sided operations while preserving explicit software control over synchronization and consistency.

Multi-GPU Programming

From a programming model standpoint, one GPU can directly access another GPU's memory over NVLink using peer-to-peer and partitioned global address space (PGAS) models such as NVIDIA SHMEM (NVSHMEM), NVIDIA's GPU-accelerated OpenSHMEM implementation. There is a global address space, but GPU caches are not globally coherent across GPUs. Only the CPU–GPU path over NVLink-C2C is cache coherent. Software stacks such as NCCL and NVSHMEM provide the synchronization and ordering required for correct multi-GPU access. Combined, hardware cache coherency and software synchronization techniques allow the NVL72 to be seen as essentially one big GPU.

Remote direct memory access (RDMA) is a network technology that enables direct, zero-copy memory transfers between hosts across InfiniBand and RDMA over Converged Ethernet (RoCE) transports. Optional remote atomic operations are defined by the InfiniBand Trade Association (IBTA) (*https://oreil.ly/eNn4x*) for InfiniBand and RoCE.

GPUDirect RDMA (*https://oreil.ly/hTqV-*), NVIDIA's implementation of the RDMA protocol, enables network interface controllers (NICs) (*https://oreil.ly/Cn3_B*) to register GPU memory and perform RDMA directly to and from GPU memory using the nvidia-peermem (*https://oreil.ly/mp58A*) driver. This allows GPUs to exchange data and execute atomic operations across nodes without involving the CPU. This allows NICs to perform direct DMA to and from GPU memory without staging through host RAM.

Remote atomics and one-sided operations across nodes are provided by upper-layer libraries such as NVSHMEM, which implement these semantics over RDMA transports. Note that GPUDirect RDMA supplies the direct data path rather than the atomic APIs themselves. Distributed training and inference workloads need to synchronize and exchange information frequently across many GPUs.

Traditionally, the GPUs are in different compute nodes and racks. As such, synchronization can happen over relatively slow network links like InfiniBand and Ethernet. This is often the bottleneck when scaling across many GPUs to support large AI models.

With an NVL72 system, those exchanges happen over NVLink and NVSwitch at a superfast pace. This means you can scale your training job or inference cluster up to 72 GPUs with minimal communication overhead. And since the GPUs spend far less time waiting for data from one another, overall throughput scales near-linearly up to 72 GPUs.

In contrast, consider scaling the same job across a similarly sized 72-GPU H100 cluster of nine separate compute servers—each with eight Hopper H100 GPUs. This configuration requires InfiniBand, which will create network bottlenecks that greatly reduce the cluster's scaling efficiency.

Let's analyze and compare the NVL72 and 72-GPU H100 clusters using concrete numbers. Within a single NVL72 rack, GPU-to-GPU bandwidth is up to 1.8 TB/s per GPU (bidirectional aggregate), and latency is on the order of 1–2 microseconds for a small message on the order of kilobytes. Large messages take longer and are typically bandwidth-limited. Across a conventional InfiniBand network, bandwidth per GPU might be more like 20–80 GB/s—depending on how many NICs and their speed—and latency is likely 5–10 microseconds or more.

The NVL72 network offers substantially higher per-GPU bandwidth and lower latency than host-NIC fabrics. Specifically, NVLink 5 provides about 1.8 TB/s of aggregate bandwidth per GPU, whereas modern host NICs provide about 50–100 GB/s per port at 400–800 Gb/s line rates. All of this decreases collective-operation overhead down from tens of percent down to just a few percent.

In practical terms, collective overhead is substantially lower within an NVLink-connected NVL72 system versus a traditional node-to-node fabric, but the exact fraction of iteration time is workload-dependent. For example, NVIDIA reported (*https://oreil.ly/_br-i*) that a 1.8-trillion-parameter MoE model improved from about 3.4 tokens per second per GPU with over 5 seconds time to first token on H100 to about 150 tokens per second per GPU with roughly 50 ms time to first token on GB200 NVL72. This speedup is largely due to eliminating inter-GPU communication bottlenecks inside the NVL72 rack in addition to Blackwell's higher compute throughput.

Within a single NVL72 rack, communication is so fast that communication bottlenecks become low priority as they are almost completely eliminated, whereas communication in traditional InfiniBand and Ethernet clusters is often the primary bottleneck and needs careful optimization and tuning at the software level.

In short, you should design and implement software that exploits the NVL72 configuration by keeping as much of the workload's communication inside the rack ("intra-rack") as possible to take advantage of the high-speed NVLink and NVSwitch hardware. Use the slower InfiniBand- or Ethernet-based communication between racks ("inter-rack") only when absolutely necessary to scale beyond the NVL72's compute and memory resources.

In-Network Aggregations with NVIDIA SHARP

Another hardware-enabled optimization is in-network collective offload with mechanisms including both NVLink and InfiniBand Scalable Hierarchical Aggregation and Reduction Protocol (SHARP) (*https://oreil.ly/3RVob*). These paths have different enablement approaches, topology constraints, and supported-collective behaviors.

NVLink SHARP (NVLS) provides collective offload support for SHARP-enabled NVSwitch domhey ains. For these SHARP-enabled NVSwitch systems, the practical benefit is that supported collectives can shift some reduction/replication work into the switch fabric. This way, endpoints move less data and spend less time stalled on communication.

Figure 2-10 visualizes how NVLink Switch System racks provide in-network reductions using SHARP engines integrated directly into the NVSwitch ASICs to offload reductions and other collectives in-network.

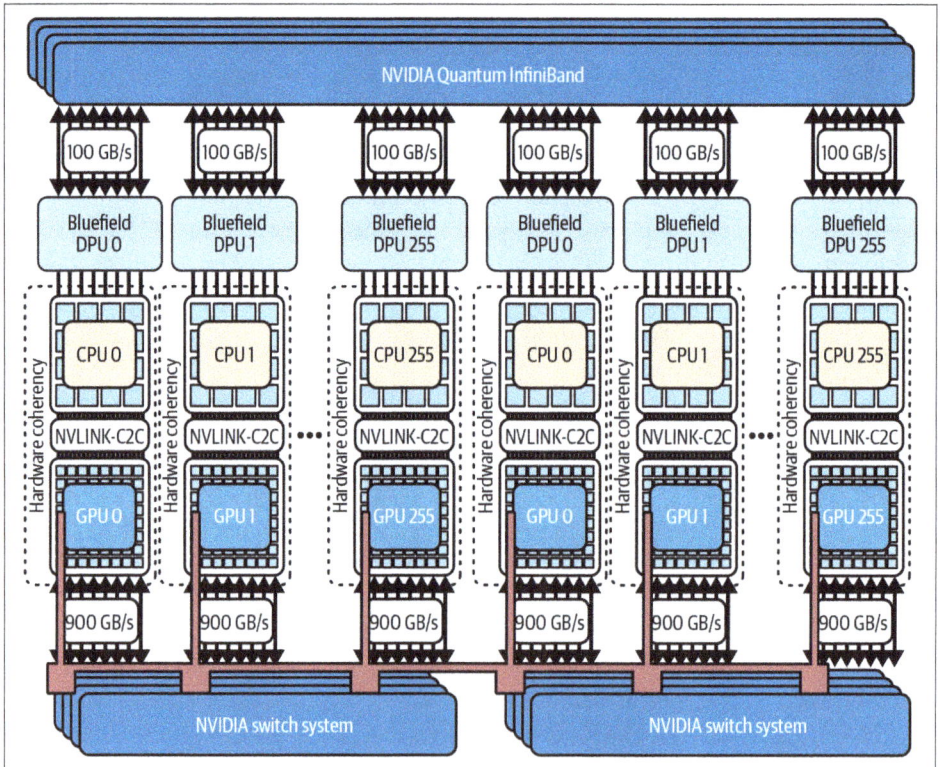

Figure 2-10. In-switch collective offload inside NVSwitch domains using NVLink SHARP (NVLS) reduction engines

In addition, InfiniBand SHARP provides in-network reduction for SHARP-enabled InfiniBand fabrics. It's typically used with NCCL's CollNet collective path. On Infini-Band fabrics, SHARP plays a similar role, but at the network-switch level.

The NVSwitch fabric combines partial results without the data needing to funnel through the GPUs. By offloading collective computations from the GPUs to the switch hardware itself, SHARP allows the GPUs to focus on more complex computations, lowers collective latencies, reduces the overall volume of data traversing the network, and increases system efficiency.

SHARP's increased efficiency means that during distributed training, the heavy lifting of aggregating gradients or synchronizing parameters is handled by the NVSwitch's dedicated SHARP engines. The result is much more efficient scaling across both intra-rack and inter-rack configurations.

With SHARP, you'll see near-linear performance improvements even as the number of GPUs grows. This in-network computing capability is especially critical for training ultralarge models, where every microsecond saved on collective operations can translate into substantial overall speedups.

SHARP is one of the most impactful innovations that NVIDIA received during their 2019–2020 acquisition of Mellanox. You should explore SHARP if you are not currently using it. SHARP can significantly reduce latency and traffic for collectives and often improves scaling efficiency for communication-bound training.

Multirack and Storage Communication

Next, let's discuss how an NVL72 rack talks to another NVL72—or to an external storage system like a shared filesystem. As we have shown, inside the NVL72 rack, NVLink covers all GPU-to-GPU traffic. But outside the rack, it relies on more traditional networking hardware.

Each compute node in NVL72 is equipped with high-speed Network Interface Cards and a Data Processing Unit (DPU). A DPU offloads, accelerates, and isolates networking, storage, security, and management tasks from the host CPU. By running these operations directly on the NIC, DPUs reduce CPU overhead and latency.

In the NVL72 design, the BlueField-3 DPU handles line-rate packet processing, RDMA, and NVMe over Fabrics (oF) operations. NVMe-oF is a protocol variant of NVMe that extends storage across network fabrics. As such, the DPU moves data directly between the network, storage, and GPU memory without CPU involvement. This maximizes overall system throughput and efficiency.

GB200/GB300 NVL72 racks integrate with Quantum-X800 InfiniBand or Spectrum-X800 Ethernet fabrics. The compute trays commonly use four ConnectX-8 800 Gb/s

NICs per node for high external bandwidth. BlueField-3 DPUs are used where in-network acceleration or offload is required for storage, security, and control-plane tasks.

With four 800 Gb/s NICs, it is 3.2 Tbit/s per compute node and about 57.6 Tbit/s per rack (57.6 Tbit/s = 3.2 Tbit/s per node × 18 nodes). While this throughput is eye-popping, remember that when you exit the rack, you still need an ultrafast network. This way, multirack scaling isn't bottlenecked at the rack boundary. NVIDIA calls these multirack deployments *AI factories*. And they've made sure that the NVL72 can plug into a larger network fabric using these four NICs per node.

The BlueField-3 DPU in each node helps offload networking tasks like RDMA, TCP/IP, and NVMe SSD storage access. This makes sure the Grace CPU isn't bogged down managing network interrupts. The DPU essentially serves as a smart network controller, moving data directly between NICs and GPU memory using NVIDIA's GPUDirect RDMA software. This does not require staging data through host memory or using any CPU cycles.

BlueField DPUs avoid CPU involvement, which is especially useful when streaming large datasets from a storage server for large-scale training jobs. Specifically, the DPU can handle the transfer and deposit data directly into GPU memory—while the CPU focuses on other tasks like data preprocessing.

In addition to providing performance-offload capabilities, the DPU supports secure multitenancy. It isolates network traffic for different jobs and users—acting as a smart firewall/switch on the node.

When scaling out to multiple NVL72 racks, NVIDIA uses Quantum-series InfiniBand switches. Multiple NVL72 racks can be interconnected using these InfiniBand switches to form a large cluster of NVL72 racks.

For example, an 8-rack NVL72 totaling 576 GPUs is connected as one NVLink 5 domain using the NVLink Switch System. InfiniBand or Ethernet is then used to connect that NVLink domain to other domains (e.g., other NVL72 racks) or to external storage (though the performance for cross-rack InfiniBand or Ethernet communication will be lower than the intra-rack NVLink/NVSwitch communication).

In short, InfiniBand and Ethernet NICs such as NVIDIA's ConnectX and BlueField DPU are typically used alongside NVLink. These provide high-bandwidth connectivity between racks and also offload protocols using in-network computing on DPUs.

Preintegrated Rack Appliance

Because NVL72 is such a complex system, NVIDIA delivers it as a preintegrated rack "appliance" in a single cabinet. It comes assembled with all 18 compute nodes, all 9 NVSwitch units, internal NVLink cabling, power distribution, and a cooling system.

The idea is that an organization can order this as a unit that is ready to go when it arrives. One simply connects the rack to facility power, hooks up the water cooling interfaces, connects the InfiniBand cables to your network, and powers it on.

The system is essentially ready for use out of the box, requiring only minimal setup to begin running AI workloads. There is no need to individually cable 72 GPUs with NVLink, as NVIDIA has already done this inside the rack for you. Even the liquid cooling setup is self-contained, as we'll discuss soon.

This appliance approach accelerates deployment and ensures that the system is built correctly and validated by NVIDIA. The rack also includes its NVIDIA Base Command Manager cluster-management software—as well as the Simple Linux Utility for Resource Management (SLURM) and Kubernetes for cluster-job scheduling and orchestration.

In short, the NVL72 rack is designed to be dropped into your environment and ready to run production AI workloads right out of the box. It doesn't need any manual installation or complex configuration.

Co-Packaged Optics: Future of Networking Hardware

As networking data throughput rates climb to 800 Gbit/s, 1.6 Tbit/s, and beyond, NVIDIA has begun integrating silicon photonics and co-packaged optics (CPO) into its networking hardware. This includes the Quantum-X800 InfiniBand and Spectrum-X800 Ethernet platforms. These platforms ship with 800 Gb/s end-to-end connectivity and in-network computing features (e.g., SHARP). With CPO, the optical transmitters are integrated right next to the switch silicon. This drastically shortens electrical pathways, enabling even higher bandwidth links between racks, reducing power draw, and improving overall communication efficiency.

In practical terms, technologies like CPO are paving the way to connect hundreds and thousands of racks (AI factories) into a single unified fabric in which inter-rack bandwidth is no longer the bottleneck. Such optical networking advancements are crucial to the high-performance, inter-rack bandwidth needed to ensure that the network can keep up with the GPUs at ultrascale.

To summarize, inside an NVL72 rack, NVIDIA uses NVLink and NVSwitch to create a blazingly fast, all-to-all connected network between 72 GPUs. These interconnects are so fast and uniform that the GPUs effectively behave like one unit for many collective operations. Beyond the rack, high-speed NICs (e.g., InfiniBand or Ethernet) connect the rack to other racks or to storage, with DPUs to manage data movement efficiently.

The NVL72 is an immensely powerful standalone system and a basic building block for larger AI supercomputers or *AI factories*. The concept of an AI factory, a large-scale AI data center composed of multiple such racks, is now becoming reality.

NVIDIA partners with OEM and system vendors like HPE and Supermicro to supply the GB200 NVL72 systems. NVIDIA's hardware and network roadmaps are squarely aimed at enabling the AI factory vision. In short, the NVL72 shows how far codesign can go as the GPU, networking, and physical-rack hardware are built hand in hand to scale to thousands and millions of GPUs as seamlessly and efficiently as possible.

Compute Density and Power Requirements

The NVL72 rack is incredibly dense in terms of compute, which means it draws a very high amount of power for a single rack. A fully loaded NVL72 can consume up to ~130 kW of power under max load. This is more than 2× NVIDIA's previous generation AI rack, which consumed around 50–60 kW. Packing 72 bleeding-edge GPUs—and all the supporting hardware—into one rack pushes the limits of what data center infrastructure can handle.

To supply 130 kW to the NVL72 rack, you can't just use a single standard power feed. Data centers will typically provision multiple high-capacity circuits to feed this kind of power. For instance, a data center can deploy two fully independent power feeds. In this case, each feed is sized to carry the entire rack load in case of a failure on one of the feeds.

If one feed goes offline, the remaining circuit can support the full 130 kW draw to avoid a blown circuit. This kind of redundancy is important protection. Otherwise, the power interruption could halt your multimonth training job.

Within the rack, power is distributed to the power supplies of each 1U compute node. The power is converted from AC to DC for the local electronics. Each compute node in the NVL72 contains two Grace Blackwell Superchips, which together consume on the order of 6 kW. With 18 compute nodes, the total power consumed is ~110 kW. The NVSwitch trays, network switches, air cooling, and water cooling pumps account for ~20 kW for a total of 130 kW consumed by the entire NVL72 rack.

The current used at a typical data center in voltages (e.g., 415 V 3-phase AC) is massive, so everything is engineered for high amperage. Operators have to carefully plan to host such a rack, which often requires dedicated power distribution units (PDUs) and careful monitoring. Power transients are also a consideration, as 72 GPUs, when ramping from idle to full power, could rapidly draw tens of kW of power in just milliseconds. A good design will include capacitors or sequencing to avoid large voltage drops.

The system might stagger the GPU boost clocks by tiny intervals so they don't all spike at exactly the same microsecond, smoothing out the surge. These are the kind of electrical engineering details that go into making a 130 kW rack manageable.

It's not far-fetched to call this NVL72 rack, at the cutting edge of high-density compute, a mini power substation. Eight of these racks combined for 576 GPUs would draw nearly 1 MW of power (8 racks × 130 kW per rack), which is the entire capacity of a small data center! The silver lining is that although 130 kW is a lot in one rack, you are also getting a lot of work done per watt.

If one NVL72 replaces several racks of older equipment, the overall efficiency is better. But you definitely need the infrastructure to support that concentrated power draw. And any facility hosting the NVL72 racks must ensure they have adequate power capacity and cooling, as we will discuss next.

Liquid Cooling Versus Air Cooling

Cooling 130 kW in one rack is beyond the reach of traditional air cooling. Blowing air over 72 GPUs that each can dissipate ~1,200 watts would require hurricane-like airflow and would be extremely loud and inefficient—not to mention the hot air exhaust would be brutal. As such, liquid cooling is the only practical solution for the NVL72 rack running at this power density.

The NVL72 is a fully liquid-cooled system. Each Grace Blackwell Superchip module and each NVSwitch chip has a cold plate attached. A cold plate is a metal plate with internal tubing that sits directly on the component. A water-based coolant liquid flows through the tubing to carry away heat. All these cold plates are linked by hoses, manifolds, and pumps that circulate the coolant throughout the system.

Typically, the rack will have quick-disconnect couplings for each node so you can slide a server in or out without spilling the coolant. The rack then has supply and return connections to the external facility's chilled water system. Often, there's a heat exchanger called a Coolant Distribution Unit (CDU) either built into the rack or immediately next to it. The CDU transfers heat from the rack's internal coolant loop to the data center's water loop.

The facility provides chilled water at 20–30°C. The water absorbs the heat through the heat exchanger. The warmed-up water is then pumped back into the chillers or cooling towers to be cooled again. In modern designs, they might even run warm water cooling, in which chilled water comes into the system at 30°C and leaves at 45°C. The water can then be cooled by evaporative cooling towers without active refrigeration, improving overall efficiency. The point is, water, or a liquid coolant, can carry far more heat per unit of flow than air, so liquid cooling is vastly more effective when running at high watts in small spaces.

By keeping the GPU and CPU temperatures much lower than they would be with air, liquid cooling reduces thermal GPU throttling. The GPUs can sustain their maximum clocks without hitting temperature limits. Also, running chips cooler improves reliability and even efficiency since power leakage is lower when running at lower temperatures.

The NVL72 keeps GPU temps in the 50–70°C range under load, which is excellent for such power-hungry devices. The cold plates and coolant loops have been engineered very carefully to allow each GPU to dump 1,000 W and each CPU to dump 500 W into the system. In addition, the coolant flow rate has to be sufficient to remove that heat quickly. A rough estimate shows on the order of 150–200 liters per minute at a 10–12°C water temperature rise to dissipate about 130 kW.

The system undoubtedly has sensors and controls for coolant temperature, pressure, and leak detection. If a leak is detected from its drip or pressure-loss sensors, the system can shut down or isolate that section quickly. It's recommended to use self-sealing connections—and perhaps a secondary containment tray—to minimize the risk of leaking fluids.

This level of liquid cooling in racks was once exotic, but it is now the standard for these large-scale AI clusters. Companies like Meta, xAI, and Google are adopting liquid cooling for their AI clusters because air cooling simply cannot support the large amount of power drawn from these systems.

So while an NVL72 requires more facility complexity, including liquid-cooling loops, many data centers are now built with liquid cooling in mind. The NVL72 rack, with its built-in internal liquid cooling, can be connected directly to the cooling loop.

One side effect of the internal liquid cooling is the weight of the rack. The NVL72 rack weighs on the order of 3,000 lbs (1.3–1.4 metric tons) when filled with hardware and coolant. This is extremely heavy for a rack, as it's roughly the weight of a small car but concentrated on a few square feet of floor. Data centers with raised floors have to check that the floor can support this load, measured in pounds per square foot. Often, high-density racks are placed on reinforced slabs or supported by additional struts. Moving such a rack requires special equipment such as forklifts. This is all part of the deployment consideration, as you're installing an AI supercomputer, which comes with its unique physical and logistical challenges.

NVIDIA also integrates management and safety features in the form of a rack management controller that oversees things like coolant pumps, valve positions, and power usage, and monitors every node's status. Administrators can interface with it to do things like update firmware across all nodes, or to shut down the system safely.

All these considerations illustrate that the NVL72 was codesigned with data center infrastructure in mind. NVIDIA worked on the compute architecture in tandem with system engineers who figured out power delivery and cooling, and in tandem with facility engineers who specified how to install and run these things. It's not just about fast chips—it's about delivering a balanced, usable system.

The payoff for this complexity is huge. By pushing the limits of power and cooling, an enormous, amount of compute is concentrated into a single rack and translates to a large amount of compute-per-watt. Yes, 130 kW is a lot of power, but per GPU or per trillion FLOP (TFLOP), it's actually efficient compared to spreading the same GPUs across multiple racks with less efficient cooling.

Performance Monitoring and Utilization in Practice

When you have a machine this powerful, you want to make sure you're getting the most out of it. Operating an NVL72 effectively requires careful monitoring of performance, utilization, and power. NVIDIA provides tools like Data Center GPU Manager (DCGM) that can track metrics on each GPU for things like GPU utilization percentage, memory usage, temperature, and NVLink throughput.

As a performance engineer, you'd keep an eye on these during training runs and inference workloads. Ideally, you want your GPUs to be near 100% utilized most of the time during a training job. If you see GPUs at 50% utilization, that means something is keeping them idle for half the time. Perhaps there is a data loading bottleneck or a synchronization issue.

Similarly, you can monitor the NVLink usage. If your NVLink links are saturating frequently, communication is likely the culprit. The BlueField DPUs and NICs have their own statistics that are monitored to ensure that you're not saturating your storage links when reading data. Modern systems like the NVL72 expose this telemetry.

Power monitoring is also crucial. At ~130 kW, even a small inefficiency or misconfiguration can waste a lot of power and money. The system likely lets you monitor power draw per node or per GPU. Administrators might cap the power or clocks of GPUs if full performance isn't needed, to save energy.

NVIDIA GPUs allow setting power limits. For instance, if you're running a smaller job that doesn't need every last drop of performance, you could dial down GPU clocks to improve efficiency—measured in performance per watt—and still meet your throughput requirement. This could save kilowatts of power in the process. Over weeks of training, this can translate to significant savings and cost efficiency.

Sharing and Scheduling

Another aspect is sharing and scheduling workloads on the NVL72. Rarely will every single job need all 72 GPUs. You might have multiple teams or multiple experiments running on subsets of GPUs. Using a cluster scheduler like SLURM or Kubernetes with NVIDIA's plugins, you can carve out, say, 8 GPUs for one user, 16 GPUs for another user, and 48 GPUs for yet another user—all within the same rack.

Furthermore, NVIDIA's Multi-Instance GPU (MIG) feature lets you split a single physical GPU into smaller GPUs partitioned at the hardware level. For example, one Blackwell GPU with 180 GB of GPU memory could be split into smaller chunks to run many small inference jobs concurrently.

Each Blackwell GPU supports up to seven fully isolated MIG instances. This allows one physical GPU to be partitioned into up to seven smaller GPUs with dedicated memory and SMs. MIG sizes are fixed by product generation. We will dive into the details of MIG partitions in the next chapter.

In practice, with such a large GPU, MIG might be used for inference scenarios where you want to serve many models on one GPU. The presence of the BlueField DPU also enables secure multitenancy as the DPU can act as a firewall and virtual switch. This isolates network traffic for different jobs and users. This means an organization could safely let different departments or even external clients use partitions of the system without interfering with one another—similar to how cloud providers partition a big server for multiple customers with secure multitenant isolation.

From a cost perspective, a system like NVL72 is a multimillion dollar asset, and it could consume tens of thousands of dollars in electricity per month. So you really want to do as much useful work, or goodput, as possible. If it sits idle, that's a lot of capital and operational cost wasted. This is why monitoring utilization over time is important. You might track GPU hours used versus available hours.

If you find that the system is underutilized, you might want to consolidate workloads or offer it to additional teams for more projects. Some organizations implement a chargeback model where internal teams use their own budget to pay per GPU-hour of usage. This encourages efficient use and accounts for electricity and depreciation costs. Such transparency ensures that people value the resource.

ROI of Upgrading Your Hardware

One might ask if it's worth investing in this bleeding-edge hardware. When analyzing the return on investment (ROI), the answer often comes down to performance per dollar. If NVL72 can do the work of, say, four older-generation racks, it might actually save money long-term, both in hardware and power. Earlier in the chapter, we discussed how one Blackwell GPU could replace 2–3 Hopper GPUs in terms of throughput. This means if you upgrade, you might need fewer total GPUs for the same work.

Let's analyze a quick case study. Suppose you currently have 100 H100 GPUs handling your workload. You could potentially handle it with 50 Blackwell GPUs because each is more than twice as fast (or more, using FP8/FP4). So you'd buy 50 instead of 100 GPUs. And even if each Blackwell costs more than an H100, buying half as many could be cost-neutral or better. Power-wise, 100 H100s might draw 70 kW, whereas 50 Blackwells might draw 50 kW for the same work. This is a notable power savings.

Over a year, that power difference saves tens of thousands of dollars. Additionally, fewer GPUs means fewer servers to maintain, which means less overhead in CPUs, RAM, and networking for those servers, providing even further savings. All told, an upgrade to new hardware can pay for itself in 1–2 years in some cases—especially if you have enough work to keep them busy 24 hours a day.

The math obviously depends on exact prices and usage patterns, but the point is that the ROI for adopting the latest AI hardware can be very high for large-scale deployments. Besides the tangible ROI, there are soft benefits like using a single powerful system instead of many smaller ones that can simplify your system architecture. This simplification improves operational efficiency by lowering power consumption and reducing network complexity.

For example, not having to split models across multiple older GPUs due to memory limits can simplify software and reduce engineering complexity. Also, having the latest hardware ensures you can take advantage of the newest software optimizations and keep up with competitors who also upgrade. Nobody wants to be left training and serving models at half the speed of rivals. Upgrading will improve your performance while simultaneously enabling larger models, faster iterations, and quicker responses.

Running an NVL72 effectively is as much a software and management challenge as it is a hardware feat. The hardware gives you incredible potential, but it's up to the engineers to harness the full power of the hardware by monitoring performance, keeping utilization high, and scheduling jobs smartly.

The good news is NVIDIA provides a rich software stack to monitor and improve performance, including drivers, profilers, container runtimes, and cluster orchestration tools. Throughout the rest of the book, we'll see how to optimize software to fully utilize systems like the GB200/GB300 NVL72. For now, the takeaway is that when you're given an AI system with exaFLOPS-scale performance in a box, you need equally advanced strategies to make every flop and every byte count.

A Glimpse into the Future: NVIDIA's Roadmap

At the time of writing, the Grace Blackwell NVL72 platform represents the state-of-the-art in AI hardware. But NVIDIA is already preparing the next leaps. It's worth briefly looking at NVIDIA's hardware roadmap for the coming few years, because it shows a clear pattern of scaling. NVIDIA intends to continue doubling down on performance, memory, and integration.

Blackwell Ultra and Grace Blackwell Ultra

NVIDIA's Blackwell Ultra (B300) and corresponding Grace Blackwell Ultra Superchip (GB300) are a drop-in upgrade to the NVL72 architecture. Each Blackwell Ultra B300 GPU has approximately 50% more memory capacity (288 GB) than the B200 (180 GB)—as well as 1.5× higher AI compute performance and larger on-die accelerators specifically designed for attention operations and reduced precision (e.g.,

NVFP4). This translates to the Blackwell B300 producing 45-50% higher inference throughput than the B200.

A 72-GPU rack of GB300s consists of 36 Grace Blackwell Ultra modules (2 GPUs + 1 CPU each), ~20.7 TB of HBM (72 × 288 GB), and ~18 TB of DDR (36 × 500 GB). Combined, this is ~38 TB of fast memory per GB300 NVL72 rack. And the intra-rack NVLink and NVSwitch networks in the GB300 NVL72 Ultra use the same NVLink 5 generation as the GB200 NVL72.

In short, the GB300 is an evolutionary upgrade to the GB200, as it uses the same architecture. However, it has more of everything, including more SMs, higher memory, and faster clocks.

Vera Rubin Superchip (2026)

Codenamed after the female astronomer whose work provided evidence of dark matter, the Vera Rubin Superchip (VR200) is the next major architecture step. Vera is the ARM-based CPU successor to the Grace CPU, and Rubin is the GPU architecture successor to Blackwell. NVIDIA continues the superchip concept by combining one Vera CPU with two Rubin GPUs in a single module (VR200) similar to the Grace Blackwell (GB200/GB300) configuration.

The Vera CPU uses TSMC's 3nm semiconductor process with more CPU cores and faster LPDDR6 memory running at approximately 1 TB/s. The Rubin GPU supports higher GPU high-bandwidth memory (HBM) running at approximately 13–14 TB/s.

NVLink is also expected to move to its sixth generation, NVLink 6, which would double the CPU-to-GPU and GPU-to-GPU link bandwidth. There's also speculation that the Vera Rubin could allow more nodes per rack—or more racks per NVLink domain —to scale beyond the 576 GPU limit of the eight-rack GB200/GB300 NVL72 cluster.

The bottom line is that the Vera Rubin generation is yet another ~2× jump in most metrics, including more cores, more memory, more bandwidth, and more TFLOPS. Rubin GPUs increase SM counts to ~200 SMs per die. This could further add efficiency improvements. They could also integrate new features like second-generation FP4 or even experimental 2-bit precisions, though that's just speculation at this point.

Another especially interesting possibility is that because Rubin's 288 GB HBM RAM is still a bottleneck for large AI models, NVIDIA might incorporate some second-tier memory for GPUs directly in the GPU module. For instance, they may place some LPDDR memory directly on the base of the GPU module to act as an even larger, but slower, memory pool for the GPU—separate from Vera's CPU DDR memory.

If this happens, a single GPU module could have ~550 GB (288 GB HBM + 256 GB LPDDR) of total cache-coherent, unified memory. This would further blur the line between CPU and GPU memory, as GPUs would have a multitier memory hierarchy of their own. Whether this happens with the Rubin GPU generation or not, it's a direction to keep an eye on.

Overall, the Vera Rubin and Vera Rubin Ultra racks deliver 5× the performance of a GB200/GB300 NVL72. They also run at 5× the power—nearly 600 kW per rack. The VR200/VR300 NVL system comes with a massive amount of total GPU HBM per rack across all of the Rubin GPUs (288 GB HBM per GPU) plus tens of TB of CPU memory. And NVLink 6 within the rack incurs less communication overhead than NVLink 5.

Rubin Ultra and Vera Rubin Ultra (2027)

Following the pattern, an "Ultra" version of Rubin (R300) and Vera Rubin arrives a year after the original release. One report suggests that NVIDIA might move to a four-die GPU module by then. This would combine two dual-die Rubin packages and put them together to yield a quad-die Rubin GPU. This R300 Rubin Ultra GPU module has four GPU dies on one package and 16 HBM stacks totaling 1 TB of HBM memory on a single R300 GPU module. The four dies together double the cores of the dual-die B300 module.

In particular, the Vera Rubin NVL144 system has 144 of those dies across the rack. This is 36 superchip modules of four dies each. There is also a Vera Rubin NVL576 configuration that will have 4× the GPU count with multidie packages in the complete system.

By 2027, each rack could be pushing 3–4 exaFLOPS of compute performance and a combined 165 TB of GPU HBM RAM (288 GB HBM per Rubin GPU × 576 GPUs). While these numbers are still a bit speculative, the trajectory toward ultrascale AI systems with a massive number of exaFLOPS for compute and terabytes for GPU HBM RAM is clear.

Feynman GPU (2028) and Doubling Something Every Year

NVIDIA has code-named the post-Rubin generation as Feynman, which is scheduled for a 2028 release. Details are scarce, but the Feynman GPU will likely move to an even finer 2 nm TSMC process node. It will likely use HBM5 and include even more DDR memory inside the module. And perhaps it will double the number of dies from four to eight.

By 2028, it's expected that inference demands will surely dominate AI workloads—especially as reasoning continues to evolve in AI models. Reasoning requires hundreds or thousands of times more inference-time computation than previous, nonreasoning models. As such, chip designs will likely optimize for inference efficiency at scale, which might include more novel precisions, more on-chip memory, and on-package optical links to improve NVLink's throughput even further.

NVIDIA seems to be doubling something every generation, every year if possible. One year they double memory, another year they double the number of dies, another year they double interconnect bandwidth, and so on. Over a few years, the compound effect of this doubling is huge. NVIDIA's aggressive trajectory can be seen in how each generation doubles something significant. For instance, Blackwell introduced dual GPU dies (two dies per module instead of one), NVLink bidirectional bandwidth per link doubled from ~900 GB/s to ~1.8 TB/s, and per-GPU memory increases from 180 GB in Blackwell to ~288 GB in the Blackwell Ultra generation. Rubin and Feynman further increase compute, memory, and bandwidth.

NVIDIA repeatedly talks about AI factories where the racks are the production lines for AI models. NVIDIA envisions offering a rack as a service through its partners so companies can rent a slice of a supercomputer rather than building everything themselves. This trend will likely continue as the cutting-edge hardware will be delivered as integrated pods that you can deploy. And each generation allows you to swap in new pods to double your capacity, increase your performance, and reduce your cost.

For us as performance engineers, what matters is that the hardware will keep unlocking new levels of scale. Models that are infeasible today might become routine in a few years. It also means we'll have to continually adapt our software to leverage things like new precision formats, larger memory pools, and improved interconnects. This is an exciting time as the advancement of frontier models is very much tied to these hardware innovations.

Key Takeaways

The following innovations collectively enable NVIDIA's hardware to handle ultralarge AI models with unprecedented speed, efficiency, and scalability:

Integrated superchip architecture
    NVIDIA fuses ARM-based CPUs (Grace) with GPUs (Hopper/Blackwell) into a single superchip, which creates a unified memory space. This design simplifies data management by eliminating the need for manual data transfers between CPU and GPU.

Unified memory architecture
    The unified memory architecture and coherent interconnect reduce the programming complexity. Developers can write code without worrying about explicit data movement, which accelerates development and helps them focus on improving AI algorithms.

Ultrafast interconnects
    Using NVLink (including NVLink-C2C and NVLink 5) and NVSwitch, the system achieves extremely high intra-rack bandwidth and low latency. This means

GPUs can communicate nearly as if they were parts of one large processor, which is critical for scaling AI training and inference.

High-density, ultrascale system (NVL72)

The NVL72 rack integrates 72 GPUs in one compact system. This consolidated design supports massive models by combining high compute performance with an enormous unified memory pool, enabling tasks that would be impractical on traditional setups.

Advanced cooling and power management

NVL72 relies on sophisticated liquid cooling and robust power distribution systems and operates at around 130 kW per rack (130 kW = 18 nodes × 6 kW per node + ~20 kW NVSwitch/cooling/overhead). This amount of cooling and power are essential for managing the high-density, high-performance components and ensuring reliable operation.

Significant performance and efficiency gains

Compared to previous generations such as the Hopper H100, Blackwell GPUs offer roughly 2–2.5× improvements in compute and memory bandwidth. This leads to significant improvements in training and inference speeds—up to 30× faster inference in some cases (*https://oreil.ly/_br-i*) that use Blackwell's FP4 Tensor Cores and Transformer Engine—as well as potential cost savings through reduced GPU counts.

Modern software stack support

NVIDIA's software and frameworks continue to evolve to fully utilize their latest hardware and support the latest codesigned system optimizations. This includes unified memory management and native FP8/FP4 precision support. As such, engineers can utilize the system's full performance with minimal code changes.

Future-proof roadmap

NVIDIA's development roadmap (including Blackwell Ultra, Vera Rubin, Vera Rubin Ultra, and Feynman) promises continual doubling of key parameters like compute throughput and memory bandwidth. This trajectory is designed to support ever-larger AI models and more complex workloads in the future.

Conclusion

The NVIDIA NVL72 system—with its Grace Blackwell Superchips, NVLink fabric, and advanced cooling—exemplifies the cutting-edge of AI hardware design. In this chapter, we've seen how every component is codesigned to serve the singular goal of accelerating AI workloads. The CPU and GPU are fused into one unit to eliminate data transfer bottlenecks and provide a gigantic, unified memory.

Dozens of GPUs are wired together with an ultrafast network so they behave like one colossal GPU with minimal communication delay. And the memory subsystem is expanded and accelerated to feed the voracious appetite of the GPU cores. Even the power delivery and thermal management are pushed to new heights to allow this density of computing.

The result is a single rack that delivers performance previously seen only in multirack supercomputers. NVIDIA took the entire computing stack—chips, boards, networking, cooling—and optimized it end to end to allow training and serving massive AI models at ultrascale.

But such hardware innovations come with challenges, as you need specialized facilities, careful planning for power and cooling, and sophisticated software to utilize them fully. But the payoff is immense. Researchers can now experiment with models of unprecedented scale and complexity without waiting weeks or months for results. A model that might have taken a month to train on older infrastructure might train in a few days on NVL72. Inference tasks that were barely interactive (seconds per query) are now a real-time (milliseconds) reality. This opens the door for AI applications that were previously impractical, such as multi-trillion-parameter interactive AI assistants and agents.

NVIDIA's rapid roadmap suggests that this is just the beginning. The Grace Blackwell architecture will evolve into Vera Rubin and Feynman and beyond. As NVIDIA's CEO, Jensen Huang, describes (*https://oreil.ly/wQbFu*), "AI is advancing at light speed, and companies are racing to build AI factories that can scale to meet the processing demands of reasoning AI and inference time scaling."

The NVL72 and its successors are the core of the AI factory. It's the heavy machinery that will churn through mountains of data to produce incredible AI capabilities. As performance engineers, we stand on the shoulders of this hardware innovation. It gives us a tremendous raw capability, as our role is to harness this innovation by developing software and algorithms that make the most of the hardware's potential.

In the next chapter, we will transition from hardware to software. We'll explore how to optimize the operating systems, drivers, and libraries on systems like NVL72 to ensure that none of this awesome hardware goes underutilized. In later chapters, we'll look at memory management and distributed training/inference algorithms that complement the software architecture.

The theme for this book is codesign. Just as the hardware was codesigned for AI, our software and methods must be codesigned to leverage the hardware. With a clear understanding of the hardware fundamentals now, we're equipped to dive into software strategies to improve AI system performance. The era of AI supercomputing is here, and it's going to be a thrilling ride utilizing it to its fullest. Let's dive in!

## CHAPTER 3

OS, Docker, and Kubernetes Tuning for GPU-Based Environments

Even with highly optimized GPU code and libraries, system-level bottlenecks can limit performance in large-scale AI training. The fastest GPU is only as good as the environment feeding it data and instructions. In this chapter, we explore how to tune the operating system and container runtime to let GPUs reach their full potential.

We begin by exploring the foundational GPU software stack. We then dive into key CPU and memory optimizations such as NUMA affinity and hugepages. These ensure that data flows efficiently from storage through the CPU to the GPU. In parallel, we discuss critical GPU driver settings like persistence mode, Multi-Process Service (MPS), and Multi-Instance GPU (MIG) partitions. These help maintain maximum GPU utilization by reducing overhead and synchronizing resources effectively.

Using solutions like the NVIDIA Container Toolkit, Container Runtime, Kubernetes Topology Manager, and Kubernetes GPU Operator, you can create a unified and highly optimized software stack for GPU environments. These solutions enable efficient resource allocation and workload scheduling across single-node and multinode GPU environments—and ensure GPU capabilities are fully utilized.

Along the way, you'll build intuition for why these optimizations matter. In essence, they minimize latency, maximize throughput, and ensure your GPUs are constantly fed with data and operating at their peak performance. The result is a robust, scalable system that delivers significant performance gains—and a high goodput percentage—for both training and inference workloads.

Operating System

The operating system (OS) is the foundation that everything runs on. GPU servers typically run a Linux distribution such as Ubuntu Server LTS or Red Hat with an updated kernel that supports the latest GPU hardware. The NVIDIA driver installs kernel modules that create device files like `/dev/nvidia0`, `/dev/nvidia1`, and `/dev/nvidia2`—one for each GPU. The driver also creates `/dev/nvidiactl` for driver control operations, `/dev/nvidia-uvm` for unified virtual memory, and `/dev/nvidia-modeset` for mode-setting and buffer management.

The OS manages CPU scheduling, memory, networking, and storage—all of which should be tuned for high GPU throughput. As such, the OS should be configured to avoid interfering with GPU tasks. For example, GPU nodes should disable swapping or set `vm.swappiness` to 0 to avoid any OS-initiated memory swapping that could interfere with GPU workloads. Part of our job as performance engineers is to adjust these OS settings to set the GPUs up for maximum performance.

A GPU-focused server might want to run additional daemons, or background processes, such as the NVIDIA Persistence Daemon to keep the GPU driver and hardware context loaded and ready—even when no GPU jobs are running. In addition, the Fabric Manager manages GPU interconnect topology. And the NVIDIA Data Center GPU Manager (DCGM) monitors GPU system health metrics.

NVIDIA Software Stack

Running a multi-petaFLOP GPU cluster involves more than just writing high-level PyTorch, TensorFlow, or JAX code. There is a whole software stack underpinning GPU operations, and each layer can affect performance. Figure 3-1 shows a common set of frameworks, libraries, compilers, runtimes, and tools used to develop and productionize modern LLM workloads, including PyTorch, cuDNN, cuBLAS, CUTLASS, CUDA C++, `nvcc`, and the CUDA Runtime API (e.g., CUDA tools, driver, etc.).

In addition, the NVIDIA GPU and CUDA ecosystem embraces Python libraries and allows you to create CUDA kernels in Python using frameworks like OpenAI's Triton (*https://oreil.ly/-dYst*) domain-specific language (DSL) and NVIDIA's Warp (*https://oreil.ly/C9jue*) framework—as well as NVIDIA's CUDA Python (*https://oreil.ly/m_Fc_*), cuTile, and CUTLASS (*https://oreil.ly/L46r_*) libraries.

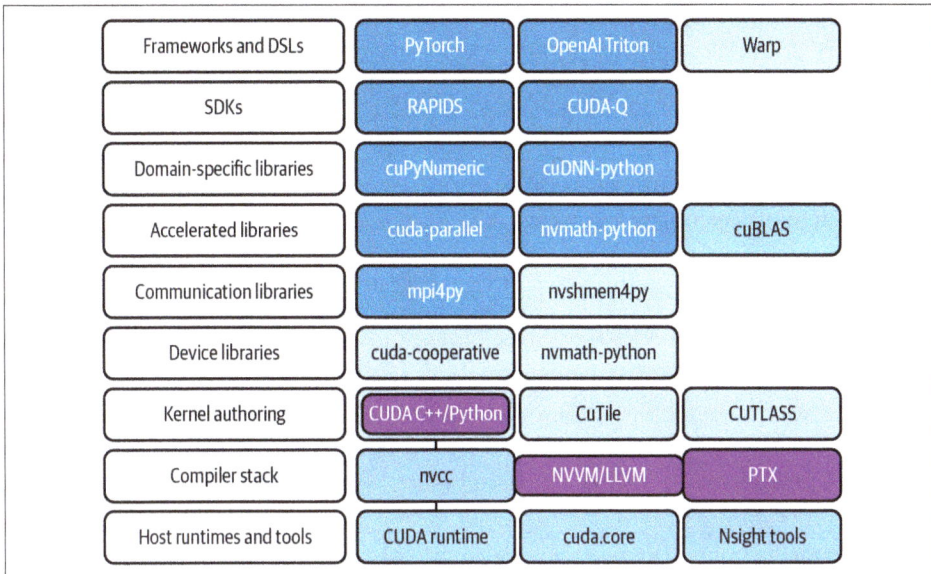

Figure 3-1. Common set of frameworks, libraries, compilers, runtimes, and tools used to develop and productionize modern LLM workloads

GPU Driver

At the base is the NVIDIA GPU driver, which interfaces between the Linux OS and the GPU hardware. The driver manages low-level GPU operations, including memory allocation on the device, task scheduling on GPU cores, and partitioning the GPU for multitenant usage.

The GPU driver turns on the GPUs' features and keeps the hardware fed with work. It's important to keep the NVIDIA driver up-to-date. New driver releases often unlock performance improvements and support the latest GPU architectures and CUDA features.

Tools such as `nvidia-smi` come with the driver and allow you to monitor temperatures, measure utilization, query error-correcting code (ECC) memory status, and enable different GPU modes like persistence mode.

CUDA Toolkit and Runtime

On top of the driver sits the CUDA Runtime and libraries called the CUDA Toolkit. The toolkit includes the CUDA compiler, `nvcc`, used to compile CUDA C++ kernels. When compiled, CUDA programs link against the CUDA runtime (`cudart`). The CUDA runtime communicates directly with the NVIDIA driver to launch work and allocate memory on the GPU.

Additionally, the CUDA Toolkit provides many optimized libraries: cuDNN for neural network primitives, cuBLAS for linear algebra, NCCL for multi-GPU communication, etc. As such, it's critical to use the latest CUDA Toolkit version that supports your GPU's compute capability (CC) since an up-to-date toolkit has the latest compiler optimizations and libraries specific to your GPU. We will cover the CUDA compiler and programming model—as well as CUDA (and PyTorch) optimizations—in more detail in the upcoming chapters.

CUDA Forward and Backward Compatibility Across GPU Hardware Generations

An important feature of NVIDIA's GPU programming model is its compatibility across hardware generations. When you compile CUDA code, the resulting binary includes virtual, or intermediate, PTX code as well as physical device code (e.g., ARM, x86, GPU instructions), as shown in Figure 3-2.

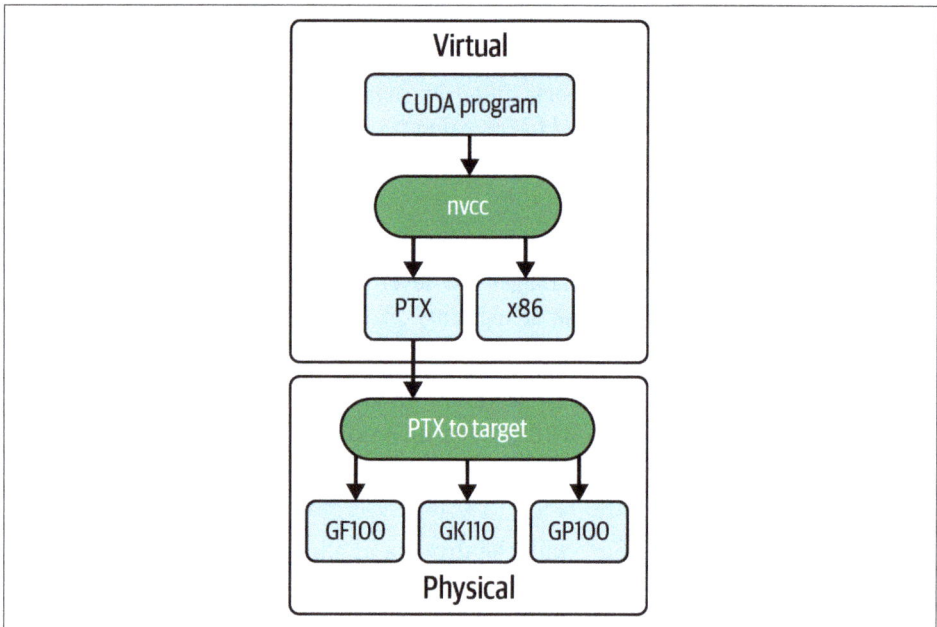

Figure 3-2. Using nvcc to compile a CUDA program into PTX—and ultimately the low-level instructions for the GPU target device

This allows newer GPUs to just-in-time (JIT) compile the PTX so your program runs on future architectures—and allows newer GPUs to execute older binary code for prior architectures. This compatibility is achieved through NVIDIA's *fatbinary* model, which contains PTX for future-proofing and *CUBIN*, or architecture-specific CUDA device code binaries, for known architectures.

CUBIN is the architecture-specific binary produced by `nvcc` for specific SM targets using the `-cubin` option. It contains compiled GPU streaming assembler (SASS) instructions for a given NVIDIA architecture. It's packaged into a fatbinary (a.k.a "fatbin") for loading by the CUDA driver at runtime. Unlike PTX, which is a virtual ISA representation used for forward compatibility via JIT compilation on newer architectures, CUBIN binary files allow direct execution on known GPU architectures. In practice, include both PTX and relevant native CUBINS in fatbinaries. PTX provides forward compatibility, while CUBINS provide fast native load on known SM targets.

C++ and Python CUDA Libraries

While most CUDA toolkit libraries are C++, NVIDIA's current Python-facing options include CUDA Python (e.g., low-level driver and runtime access); cuPyNumeric, CuTe DSL (*https://oreil.ly/IWXK4*), cuTile, and CuPy for array programming; and NVIDIA Warp for authoring GPU kernels in Python. CUTLASS is a C++ templated library used under the hood by libraries such as cuBLAS rather than a Python library.

While most of the CUDA Toolkit libraries are C++ based, more and more Python-based libraries are emerging from NVIDIA that are prefixed with "Cu" and built upon the C++ toolkit. For instance, cuTile and cuPyNumeric are Python libraries launched in early 2025. They are targeted at lowering the barrier to entry for Python developers to build applications for NVIDIA GPUs using CUDA.

cuTile is a Python library designed to simplify working with large matrices on GPUs by breaking them into smaller, more manageable submatrices called *tiles*. It provides a high-level, tile-based abstraction that makes it easier to perform block-wise computations, optimize memory access patterns, and efficiently schedule GPU kernels.

By dividing a large matrix into tiles, cuTile helps developers take full advantage of the GPU's parallelism without needing to manage low-level details manually. This approach can lead to improved cache usage and overall better performance in applications that require intensive matrix computations.

cuPyNumeric is a drop-in replacement (`import cupynumeric as np`) for the popular `numpy` Python library that utilizes the GPU. It provides nearly the same functions, methods, and behaviors as NumPy, so developers can often switch to it with minimal changes to their code. Under the hood, cuPyNumeric leverages CUDA to perform operations in parallel on the GPU. This leads to significant performance gains for compute-intensive tasks such as large-scale numerical computations, matrix operations, and data analysis.

By offloading work to the GPU, cuPyNumeric accelerates computation and improves efficiency for applications handling massive datasets. Its goal is to lower the barrier for Python developers to harness GPU power without having to learn a completely new interface, making it a powerful drop-in alternative to NumPy for high-performance computing.

Another notable Python-based programming model is OpenAI's open source Triton language and compiler. Triton is a Python DSL that allows writing custom GPU kernels in Python. While not an NVIDIA library, Triton complements CUDA by allowing developers to write high-performance kernels directly in Python.

We cover Triton and various Triton-based optimizations in a later chapter, but just know that Triton reduces the need for handwritten CUDA C++ in many cases. And it's integrated into PyTorch's compiler backend to automatically optimize and fuse GPU operations for better performance. Let's now turn the discussion to PyTorch.

PyTorch and Higher-Level AI Frameworks

Some popular Python-based frameworks built on CUDA are PyTorch, TensorFlow, JAX, and Keras. These frameworks provide high-level interfaces for deep learning while leveraging the power of NVIDIA GPUs. This book primarily focuses on PyTorch's compilation and graph optimization features, including the `torch.compile` stack.

The PyTorch compiler stack consists of TorchDynamo, AOT Autograd, and a backend like TorchInductor or Accelerated Linear Algebra (XLA), which automatically capture and optimize your models. TorchInductor is the most common backend, and it uses OpenAI's Triton under the hood. Triton fuses kernels and performs kernel autotuning for your specific GPU and system environment, as we'll cover in Chapter 14.

When you perform operations on PyTorch tensors using GPUs, they are moved from the CPU to the GPU in what appears to be a single Python call. However, this single call is actually translated into a series of calls to the CUDA runtime utilizing various CUDA libraries, as shown in Figure 3-3.

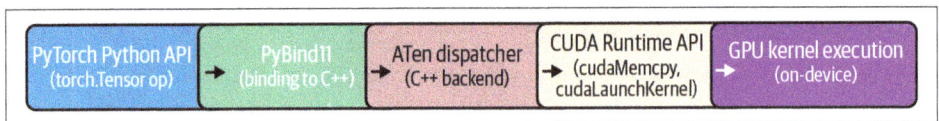

Figure 3-3. Flow from PyTorch code to GPU device

When you perform matrix multiplications, for example, PyTorch delegates these tasks to libraries such as cuBLAS. cuBLAS is part of the CUDA Toolkit and optimized for GPU execution. Behind the scenes, PyTorch ensures that operations like forward and backward passes are executed using low-level, optimized CUDA functions and libraries.

In short, PyTorch abstracts away the complexity of direct CUDA programming, allowing you to write intuitive Python code that ultimately calls highly optimized CUDA routines, delivering both ease of development and high performance. We will discuss CUDA programming and optimizations in Chapters 4 and 5—as well as PyTorch optimizations in Chapter 9.

All of these components—OS, GPU Driver, CUDA Toolkit, CUDA libraries, and PyTorch—must work together to create the ideal GPU-based development environment. When a researcher submits a training job, the scheduler reserves nodes, the OS provides the GPU devices and memory allocations using the NVIDIA driver, and the container provides the correct software environment (including the optimized, hardware-aware CUDA libraries). The user code (e.g., PyTorch, TensorFlow, JAX) uses these CUDA libraries, which ultimately communicate with the driver and hardware.

The optimizations described in this chapter are designed to make each layer of this stack as efficient as possible. They will help the GPUs stay busy with actual useful training and inference work—instead of the GPU waiting on the CPU, waiting for memory or disk I/O, or waiting on other GPUs to synchronize.

A well-tuned system ensures that models split across dozens of GPUs are not bottlenecked by I/O or OS overhead. System-level tuning is often overlooked in favor of model optimizations, but system-level optimizations can yield substantial performance gains. In some cases, you can get double-digit percentage improvements with small tweaks to your OS-level configuration. At the scale of a big AI project, this can save tens or hundreds of thousands of dollars in compute time.

Configuring the CPUs and OS for GPU Environments

One of the most common reasons that GPUs don't reach full utilization is that the CPU isn't keeping them fed with useful work. In a typical training loop, the CPU is responsible for preparing the next batch of data, including loading the data from disk, tokenizing the data, transforming it, etc. In addition, the CPU is responsible for dispatching GPU kernels and coordinating between threads and processes.

If these host-side tasks are slow—or if the OS schedules them poorly—the expensive GPU can find itself idle, twiddling its transistors and waiting for the next task or batch of data. To avoid this, we need to optimize how the CPU and OS handle GPU workloads.

These optimizations include setting the CPU affinity to avoid cross-NUMA-node traffic so the right cores handle the right data, using memory-allocation strategies to avoid NUMA penalties and applying OS-level changes to eliminate unnecessary latency. This way, the GPU is never starved for data. Part of this involves isolating background daemons and OS tasks on their own cores—and away from the cores that feed the GPUs, which we'll discuss next.

NUMA Awareness and CPU Pinning

Modern server CPUs have dozens of cores and are often split into multiple NUMA nodes. A *NUMA node* is a logical grouping of CPUs, GPUs, network interface controllers (NICs), and memory that are physically close to one another. Being aware of the system's NUMA architecture is important for performance tuning. Accessing resources within a single NUMA node is faster than accessing resources in other NUMA nodes.

For example, if a process running on a CPU in NUMA node 0 needs to access a GPU in NUMA node 1, it will need to send data across an internode link, which will incur higher latency. In fact, memory access latency can nearly double when crossing to the other NUMA nodes.

> On Grace-based superchips such as GH200 and GB200, the CPU and GPU are linked by NVLink-C2C, which provides coherent CPU-to-GPU memory access at up to ~900 GB/s between Grace and its paired accelerator. Linux still treats CPU DRAM as CPU NUMA memory and GPU HBM as device memory. As such, you should continue to bind CPU threads to the local Grace CPU and respect data locality, even though coherence reduces software overheads.

On many dual-socket systems, remote memory access latency can be significantly higher than local memory access. In one experiment (*https://oreil.ly/9YSst*), local NUMA node memory access latency is ~80 ns compared to remote (cross-node) memory access latency of ~139 ns. This is roughly a 75% increase in latency, which is a huge difference in access speed between local and remote NUMA node memory access.

By binding a process to a CPU on the same NUMA node as its GPU, we can avoid this extra overhead. For instance, you can use `numactl --cpunodebind=<node> --membind=<node>` to bind both CPU threads and memory allocations to the GPU's local NUMA node. You'll learn more about this in a bit. The key idea is to keep CPU execution and memory access local to the GPU that it's serving.

While Linux includes basic NUMA balancing, it's usually not sufficient for performance-critical AI workloads. By default, processes
may be migrated across NUMA nodes. This will lead to additional
latency caused by remote memory accesses. As such, it's important
to explicitly bind processes and memory to the same NUMA node
as the local GPU. You can do this using numactl, taskset, or
cgroups, as we'll show in a bit.

To explicitly specify NUMA-affinity, you need to "pin" processes or threads to specific CPUs that are connected to the same NUMA node as the GPU. This type of CPU
affinity is called *CPU pinning*. Suppose you have eight GPUs in a node, with four
GPUs connected to NUMA node 0 and the other four to NUMA node 1.

If you launch eight training processes, one per GPU, you should bind each training
process to a CPU core—or set of CPU cores—connected to the same NUMA node as
the GPUs. In this case, GPUs 0–3 are connected to NUMA node 0 and GPUs 4–7s are
connected to NUMA node 1's cores, as shown in Figure 3-4.

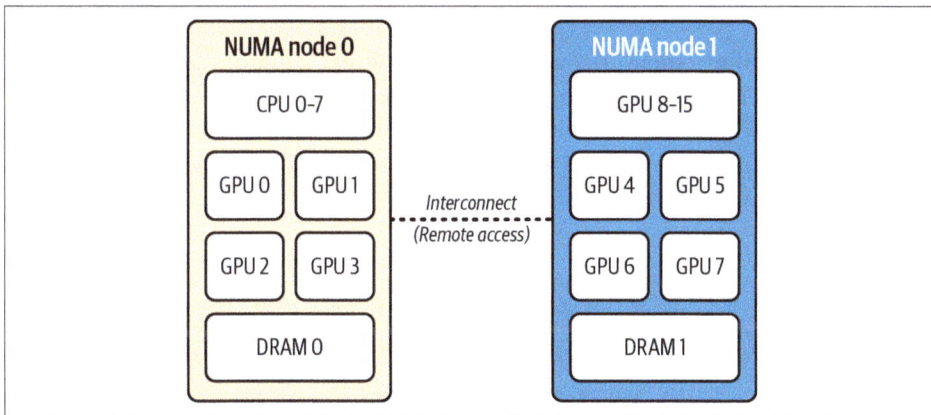

*Figure 3-4. Eight GPUs in a node, with four GPUs connected to NUMA node 0 and the
other four to NUMA node 1*

This way, when a CPU process wants to feed data to GPU 4, it should be running on a
CPU connected to NUMA node 1 since GPU 4 is connected to NUMA node 1. Linux
provides tools to do this, including numactl --cpunodebind=<node> --membind=
<node>, which launches a process pinned to the given NUMA node.

You can also use taskset to pin processes to specific core IDs. Here is an example
using numactl to bind the train.py script to a CPU running in the same NUMA
node 1 as GPU 4:

```
numactl --cpunodebind=1 --membind=1 \
    python train.py --gpu 4
```

This assumes we know the NUMA node ID and that we are binding the script to only one GPU. Binding the `train.py` to multiple GPUs to an unknown NUMA node is a bit more complicated. The following script dynamically queries the topology using `nvidia-smi` topo and binds the script to GPUs using the local NUMA node:

```bash
#!/bin/bash
for GPU in 0 1 2 3; do
  # Query NUMA node for this GPU
  NODE=$(nvidia-smi topo -m -i $GPU \
          | awk '/NUMA Affinity/ {print $NF}')

  # Launch the training process pinned to that NUMA node
  numactl --cpunodebind=$NODE --membind=$NODE \
    bash -c "CUDA_VISIBLE_DEVICES=$GPU python train.py --gpu $GPU"
done
```

Here, we use `topo` `-m` to get both CPU and NUMA affinities. We then extract the single-node ID from the NUMA Affinity column. Finally, we bind both `--cpunodebind` and `--membind` to that node to ensure your process's threads *and* memory allocations stay local to the GPU's NUMA domain.

Many deep learning frameworks also let you set thread affinities programmatically. For instance, PyTorch's DataLoader exposes `worker_init_fn` so you can set CPU affinity for each worker process during initialization, as shown here:

```python
import os
import re
import glob
import subprocess
import psutil
import ctypes
import torch
import torch.distributed as dist
from torch.nn.parallel import DistributedDataParallel as DDP
from torch.utils.data import DataLoader, Dataset
from functools import partial

# Optional: NVML is preferred for GPU↔NUMA mapping
try:
    import pynvml as nvml  # pip install nvidia-ml-py3
    _HAS_NVML = True
except Exception:
    _HAS_NVML = False

# --- libnuma for memory binding
_libnuma = ctypes.CDLL("libnuma.so")
if _libnuma.numa_available() < 0:
    raise RuntimeError("NUMA not available on this system")
_libnuma.numa_run_on_node.argtypes = [ctypes.c_int]
_libnuma.numa_set_preferred.argtypes = [ctypes.c_int]
```

```python
def parse_physical_cpu_list(phys_str: str):
    """Parse '0-3,8-11' -> [0,1,2,3,8,9,10,11]."""
    cpus = []
    if not phys_str:
        return cpus
    for part in phys_str.split(','):
        part = part.strip()
        if not part:
            continue
        if '-' in part:
            start, end = map(int, part.split('-'))
            cpus.extend(range(start, end + 1))
        else:
            cpus.append(int(part))
    return cpus

def get_numa_cpus_for_node(node: int):
    """Read /sys/devices/system/node/node{node}/cpulist."""
    path = f"/sys/devices/system/node/node{node}/cpulist"
    with open(path, "r") as f:
        return parse_physical_cpu_list(f.read().strip())

def get_numa_cpus_and_memory():
    """Return (current_cpu_mask, preferred_node) from numactl --show."""
    out = subprocess.run(["numactl", "--show"],
        capture_output=True, text=True).stdout
    phys = re.search(r"physcpubind:\s*([\d,\-\s]+)", out).group(1)
    cpus = parse_physical_cpu_list(phys)
    node = int(re.search(r"preferred node:\s*(-?\d+)", out).group(1))
    return cpus, node

def get_gpu_numa_node(device: int) -> int:
    """
    Determine NUMA node for a GPU (prefer NVML; fall back to sysfs;
    final fallback to current preferred node).
    """
    # NVML path (preferred)
    if _HAS_NVML:
        try:
            nvml.nvmlInit()
            props = torch.cuda.get_device_properties(device)
            pci = props.pci_bus_id  # '0000:03:00.0' or '00000000:03:00.0'
            # Normalize to 8-hex-digit domain if needed for NVML
            try:
                domain, bus, devfn = pci.split(':')
                if len(domain) < 8:
                    domain = domain.rjust(8, '0')
                pci8 = f"{domain}:{bus}:{devfn}"
            except ValueError:
                pci8 = pci
            try:
                handle = nvml.nvmlDeviceGetHandleByPciBusId_v2(pci8)
```

```python
        except AttributeError:
            handle = nvml.nvmlDeviceGetHandleByPciBusId(pci8)

        # Direct NUMA ID if driver exposes it
        try:
            numa_id = nvml.nvmlDeviceGetNUMANodeId(handle)
            if isinstance(numa_id, int) and numa_id >= 0:
                return numa_id
        except Exception:
            pass

        # Derive from NVML CPU affinity
        cpu_count = psutil.cpu_count(logical=True)
        elems = (cpu_count + 63) // 64
        mask = nvml.nvmlDeviceGetCpuAffinity(handle, elems)
        cpus = []
        for i, m in enumerate(mask):
            m = int(m)
            for b in range(64):
                if m & (1 << b):
                    cpu_id = i * 64 + b
                    if cpu_id < cpu_count:
                        cpus.append(cpu_id)
        # Build CPU→NUMA map from sysfs and choose majority node
        cpu2node = {}
        for node_path in sorted(glob.glob("/sys/devices/system/node/node*")):
            node_id = int(os.path.basename(node_path).replace("node", ""))
            with open(os.path.join(node_path, "cpulist"), "r") as f:
                for c in parse_physical_cpu_list(f.read().strip()):
                    cpu2node[c] = node_id
        counts = {}
        for c in cpus:
            n = cpu2node.get(c)
            if n is not None:
                counts[n] = counts.get(n, 0) + 1
        if counts:
            return max(counts.items(), key=lambda kv: kv[1])[0]
    except Exception:
        pass

# sysfs fallback
try:
    props = torch.cuda.get_device_properties(device)
    pci = props.pci_bus_id
    sysfs_path = f"/sys/bus/pci/devices/{pci}/numa_node"
    with open(sysfs_path, "r") as f:
        val = int(f.read().strip())
        return val if val >= 0 else 0
except Exception:
    pass

# last resort: current preferred node
```

```
        _, node = get_numa_cpus_and_memory()
        return node if node >= 0 else 0


def set_numa_affinity(node: int):
    """Bind current process to CPUs and memory of the given NUMA node."""
    cpus = get_numa_cpus_for_node(node)  # IMPORTANT: CPUs of target node
    psutil.Process(os.getpid()).cpu_affinity(cpus)
    _libnuma.numa_run_on_node(node)
    _libnuma.numa_set_preferred(node)
    print(f"PID={os.getpid()} bound to NUMA node {node} (CPUs={cpus})")
    return cpus


def _worker_init_fn(worker_id: int, node: int, cpus: list):
    """Reapply binding in each DataLoader worker (no CUDA calls here)."""
    psutil.Process(os.getpid()).cpu_affinity(cpus)
    _libnuma.numa_run_on_node(node)
    _libnuma.numa_set_preferred(node)
    print(f"Worker {worker_id} (PID={os.getpid()}) bound to NUMA node {node}")

 # ----- Example usage below -----
class MyDataset(Dataset):
    def __len__(self): return 1024
    def __getitem__(self, idx): return torch.randn(224*224*3, device='cpu')

def main():
    # DDP setup
    dist.init_process_group(backend="nccl", init_method="env://")
    device = torch.cuda.current_device()

    # Determine GPU's NUMA node and bind this process
    gpu_node = get_gpu_numa_node(device)
    cpus = set_numa_affinity(gpu_node)

    # Build dataloader with closure-based worker_init_fn
    dataset = MyDataset()
    init_fn = partial(_worker_init_fn, node=gpu_node, cpus=cpus)
    dataloader = DataLoader(
        dataset,
        batch_size=32,
        num_workers=4,
        pin_memory=True,
        persistent_workers=True,   # reduces worker respawn churn
        worker_init_fn=init_fn,
        prefetch_factor=2,
    )

    # Model and DDP
    model = torch.nn.Linear(224*224*3, 10, bias=True).to("cuda")
    ddp_model = DDP(model, device_ids=[device], static_graph=True)

    for batch in dataloader:
        batch = batch.to("cuda", non_blocking=True)
```

```
            out = ddp_model(batch)
            # ... loss, backward, optimizer ...

if __name__ == "__main__":
    main()
```

This script binds the main training process and each DataLoader worker process to the GPU's local NUMA node to prevent cross-NUMA memory access. In the DataLoader, we pass a closure-based worker_init_fn that reapplies the precomputed NUMA binding inside each worker. And we do this without touching any CUDA APIs in the worker.

At startup, the process uses NVML to map the current GPU to its NUMA node and CPU-affinity mask. When available, we read the node directly via nvmlDeviceGet NUMANodeId. Otherwise, we derive it from the GPU's CPU-affinity mask (nvmlDevice GetCpuAffinity). If NVML is unavailable or does not expose the node, we fall back to the kernel's sysfs entry at /sys/bus/pci/devices/<PCI_ID>/numa_node. As a last resort, we use the process's current preferred node.

We then compute the CPU list for that node from /sys/devices/system/node/node<N>/cpulist and apply CPU affinity to those cores with psutil. We also bind all future allocations to that node using libnuma (numa_run_on_node + numa_set_preferred).

Because some launchers, container runtimes, or kernels do not reliably propagate NUMA policy to children, we explicitly reapply and verify the binding in every forked worker. It's not safe to rely on inheritance alone.

Remember to set pin_memory=True and use non_blocking=True on H2D copies so that page-locked host buffers stay on the correct NUMA node. Prefer persis tent_workers=True to avoid re-forking workers and losing their affinity between epochs. And do not call torch.cuda.* in worker_init_fn. Instead, pass the GPU index using a closure or environment variable.

The result is that data preparation and batch loading happen entirely in local memory. This way, your GPUs stay busy and never need to pause for a remote-NUMA hop. With this code, you get robust, topology-aware affinity on any Linux server with libnuma and numactl (*https://oreil.ly/wAIRC*) installed.

By default, numactl applies its CPU and memory policy to a process and is documented to inherit that policy to all forked children. In practice, however, threads spawned by Python frameworks or exec'd subprocesses don't always pick up the same settings on every kernel or Linux distribution. When using framework-managed worker processes, you should explicitly reassert the CPU and memory policy inside of each worker.

With a superchip architecture like Grace Blackwell (and Vera Rubin), the CPU and GPU are coherent using NVLink-C2C. However, Linux still models CPU DRAM and GPU HBM as separate pools. Binding CPU threads to the local CPU NUMA node still remains beneficial for locality.

In practice, pinning can eliminate unpredictable CPU scheduling behavior. It ensures that a critical thread such as a data-loading thread for your GPU doesn't suddenly get migrated by the OS to a core on a different NUMA node in the middle of training or inferencing. In practice, it's possible to see 5%–10% training throughput improvements just by eliminating cross-NUMA traffic and CPU core migrations. This also tends to reduce performance jitter and variance.

Many high-performance AI systems evaluate CPU simultaneous multithreading (SMT), or *hyperthreading* as it's often called—and sometimes disable it for more predictable per-core performance, but the benefit is workload-dependent. These systems may also reserve a handful of cores exclusively for OS background tasks by setting the isolcpus kernel parameter to isolate them from the general scheduler. You can also use Kubernetes CPU isolation for system daemons. This ensures that the remaining cores are dedicated entirely to training and inference threads and doing useful work.

It's important to note that for integrated CPU-GPU superchips like NVIDIA's Grace Blackwell, many of the traditional concerns about CPU-to-GPU data transfer are alleviated because the CPU and GPU expose a coherent shared virtual address space over NVLink-C2C, while CPU DRAM and GPU HBM remain distinct memory pools. This means that issues like cross-NUMA delays are minimized, and the data can flow more directly between the CPU and GPU.

It's not a coincidence that NVIDIA tackled the CPU-to-GPU bottleneck by combining the CPU and GPU onto a single superchip such as the Grace Blackwell architecture. In this design, the CPU and GPU even share a unified, coherent memory using NVLink-C2C at up to 900 GB/s, which minimizes data transfer overhead. Expect NVIDIA to continue addressing system bottlenecks with more of these types of hardware innovations codesigned with the needs of software and algorithms.

Even with the tightly coupled CPU-GPU superchip architecture, it's still important to optimize the stack by ensuring that the hardware and software are configured properly so that the integrated system operates at peak efficiency. Even in these tightly coupled architectures, you want to minimize any unnecessary delays in data handling to keep the GPU fully utilized. This includes configuring hugepages, using efficiency prefetching, and pinning memory, as you will see in the next sections.

NUMA-Friendly Memory Allocation and Memory Pinning

By default, a process will allocate memory from the NUMA node of the CPU it's currently running on. So if you pin a process to NUMA node 0, its memory will naturally come from NUMA node 0's local RAM, which is ideal. However, if the OS scheduler migrates threads—or if some memory was allocated before you did the pinning—you could end up with the nonideal scenario in which a process running in NUMA node 0 is using memory from NUMA node 1. In this case, every memory access has to hop to the other NUMA node, negating the benefit of CPU pinning.

To avoid this, the `numactl --membind` option forces memory allocation from a specific NUMA node, as mentioned in an earlier section. In code, there are also NUMA APIs or even environment variables that can influence this configuration. The general rule is to keep memory close to the CPU, which is close to the GPU. That way the chain of data movement from memory to CPU to GPU is all within a single NUMA node. Here is the same example as before but with `--membind=1` to force memory allocation from the preferred NUMA node that includes NUMA node 1:

```
numactl --cpunodebind=1 --membind=1 python train.py --gpu 5 &
```

It's important to note that when you launch a process under `numactl`, both its CPU (`--cpunodebind`) and memory policies (`--membind`) are applied to that process and inherited by all of its child processes. As such, any worker subprocesses forked by your training script will automatically use the same NUMA memory binding. However, they must be created using a fork-based model. If you switch to a spawn start method, or otherwise `exec` a new program, those child processes do not inherit the parent's memory policy.

In addition, pinned memory, also called *page-locked memory*, is essential for efficient and direct GPU access. When memory is pinned, the OS won't swap or move it. This leads to faster direct memory access (DMA) transfers. Copying data from pinned host memory to GPU can be 2–3× faster than from regular pageable memory since the GPU or NIC can perform DMA directly.

> You can test the data-transfer bandwidth between CPU memory and GPU memory using `bandwidthTest --memory=<pinned or pageable>` from the installed CUDA utilities.

In fact, this is the basis of NVIDIA's GPUDirect technologies such as GPUDirect RDMA, which allows NICs like InfiniBand to directly exchange data with GPU memory. Similarly, GPUDirect Storage (GDS) allows NVMe drives to stream data into GPU memory without extra CPU overhead.

Deep learning frameworks provide options to use pinned memory for data loaders. For example, PyTorch's `DataLoader` has a flag `pin_memory=True`, which, when true, means the batches loaded will be placed in pinned RAM, as shown in Figure 3-5.

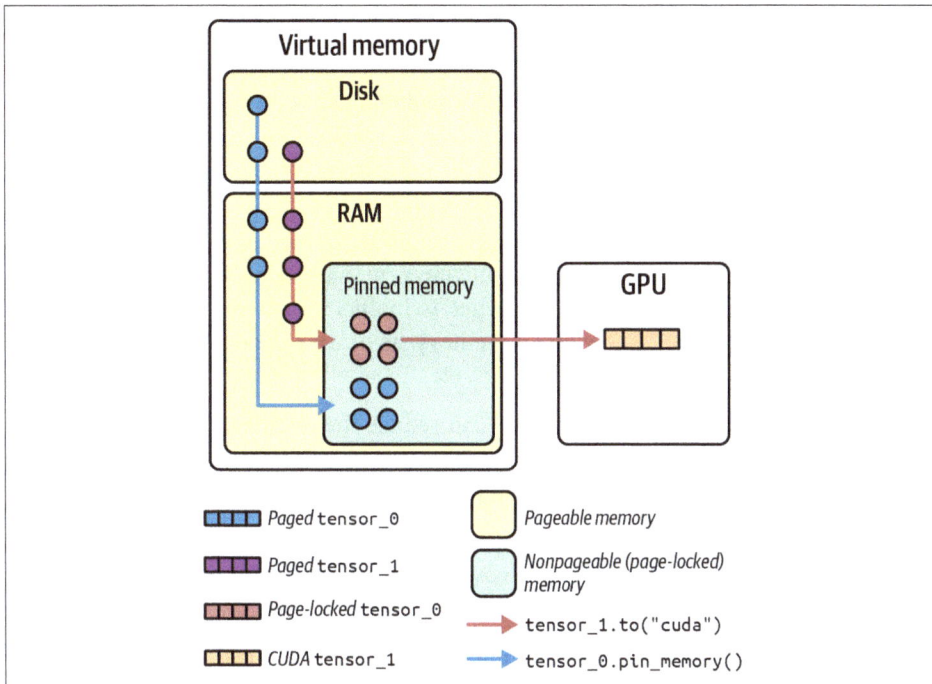

Figure 3-5. Pinned memory (aka page-locked or nonpageable) is a type of memory that cannot be swapped out to disk

Memory pinning speeds up `tensor.to(device)` transfers primarily because page-locked host memory enables efficient DMA and better overlap of host-to-device copies with GPU work. With pageable memory, the runtime may need extra staging or synchronization which reduces overlap.

In practice, `pin_memory=True` often improves throughput. However, the exact gain depends on the workload, batch size, and host-memory behavior. Memory pinning is especially beneficial when you are using large batch sizes or when H2D copies are on the critical path.

In short, you should make sure that your data loader uses pinned memory (e.g., `pin_memory=True` in PyTorch `DataLoader`) and that GPUDirect RDMA and GDS are enabled for supported hardware. This will reduce data transfer latency.

It's important to note that the OS has a limit on how much memory a user can lock (pin). This is set with the `ulimit -l <max locked memory>` command. In container-ized environments, you can adjust the container's security context and Docker

`--ulimit memlock` setting accordingly. This way, the container can lock sufficient memory.

> If you plan to use large, pinned buffers, ensure the `ulimit` value is high—or set it to unlimited. Otherwise the allocation might fail. Typically, one sets it to unlimited for large AI workloads and high-performance computing (HPC) applications.

Transparent Hugepages

In addition to pinning memory and binding it to NUMA nodes, we should talk about transparent hugepages (THPs). Linux memory management typically uses 4 KB pages, but managing millions of tiny pages is inefficient when you have processes using tens or hundreds of gigabytes of memory, as in the case of deep learning datasets, prefetched batches, model parameters, etc.

Hugepages—2 MB or even 1 GB pages—can reduce the overhead of virtual memory management by making memory chunks bigger. The main benefits are fewer page faults and less pressure on the translation lookaside Buffer (TLB).

The TLB is a cache that the CPU uses to map virtual addresses to physical ones. Fewer, larger pages means the TLB can cover more memory with the same number of entries, reducing misses.

Hugepages typically produce modest gains—often on the order of ~3%–5% throughput improvement. They do this by reducing page-fault overhead and TLB pressure. Enabling THP is a simple win on most systems since the kernel will automatically back large allocations with 2 MB pages. In scenarios with very large memory pools (e.g., preallocated pinned buffers for I/O), you may also consider explicit hugepages using `vm.nr_hugepages` or `hugetlbfs` for more deterministic performance.

> Remember that, when using large, pinned memory regions, you should raise the `ulimit -l` setting (max locked memory) to a high value or `unlimited`. If this limit is too low, your attempt to pin memory can fail, leading to fallback on swappable memory—or out-of-memory (OOM) errors.

It's important to note that THP's background compaction can introduce unpredictable pauses that are disastrous for latency-sensitive LLM inference workloads. Linux is configured by default to use THP to automatically allocate 2 MB pages whenever possible. This is often sufficient, but it's worth testing for your workload.

You can disable THP, but you will need to manually allocate and control hugepages. This will incur extra complexity, but it might be needed for low-latency workloads like inference. With THP disabled, your system will avoid stalls caused by kernel-driven defragmentations.

> The modern consensus is to enable THP for most GPU-based training workloads in which throughput is important and to disable THP completely (`transparent_hugepage=never`)—or use `madvise`—for workloads like inference in which latency is important. This is also true for distributed training workloads in which many ranks (GPUs) allocate memory simultaneously.

Beyond CPU/memory pinning and hugepages, there are a few other OS-level tweaks worth mentioning. These include thread scheduling, virtual memory management, filesystem caching, and CPU frequency settings, which we'll cover in the next few sections.

Scheduler and Interrupt Affinity

On a busy system, you want to make sure that important threads such as data-pipeline threads aren't interrupted frequently. Linux by default uses the Completely Fair Scheduler (CFS) that works well for most cases.

But if you have a very latency-sensitive thread that feeds the GPU with data, for example, you could consider using real-time first in, first out (FIFO) or round-robin (RR) priority scheduling for that thread. This would make sure that the high-priority thread runs without being preempted by normal-priority threads.

However, use this with caution, as real-time threads can starve other processes if not managed properly. In practice, however, if you've pinned your threads to dedicated cores, you often don't need to mess with real-time thread priorities, but it's worth keeping an eye on.

Another option is to isolate cores or create separate CPU partitions to further reduce interruptions on these dedicated compute resources. To do this, you can use `cset`, kernel parameters like `isolcpus` and `nohz_full`, or cgroup `cpuset` isolation. With isolation, the OS scheduler leaves those CPU cores for you to use as you wish.

> cgroup CPU and memory affinity is strongly recommended in production environments. Using these, each AI workload is isolated on its own physical cores and memory regions. This will prevent cross-workload contention and NUMA penalties. Tools like `cpuset` cgroups or container runtimes (`docker --cpuset-cpus`) should be used to enforce this.

You can assign each device's hardware interrupts to cores on the same NUMA node. This will prevent cross-node interrupt handling that would otherwise incur extra latency and evict useful cache lines on a remote node. For example, if your GPU or NIC on NUMA node 0 raises an interrupt, you'd bind it to a core on node 0 so that no other node handles it. Without this binding, a CPU on a different NUMA node might process the interrupt. This would force cache coherency traffic and cross-node communication.

In practice, performance-sensitive systems often disable the default `irqbalance` daemon or run it with bespoke rules. The other option is to manually set each interrupt's affinity mask using `/proc/irq/*/smp_affinity`. By pinning every GPU and NIC interrupt to the nearest cores, you guarantee that those device interrupts are always serviced on the optimal NUMA node.

In short, the combination of dedicated cores, appropriate scheduling priorities, and NUMA-aware hardware interrupt bindings can help minimize jitter for data loading threads that are feeding the GPUs.

Virtual Memory and Swapping

It goes without saying, but you should always try to avoid memory swapping. If any part of your process's memory gets swapped to disk, you will see a catastrophic, multiple-orders-of-magnitude slowdown. GPU programs tend to allocate a lot of host memory for data caching. If the OS decides to swap some data out of memory and onto disk, the GPU will experience huge delays when it needs to access that data.

We recommend setting `vm.swappiness=0`, which tells Linux to avoid swapping except under extreme memory pressure. It effectively isolates your training job's memory with cgroup limits to prevent any swapping.

> You should use cgroups v2 through Docker or Kubernetes to pin memory and CPUs to the AI process. This will enforce NUMA affinity and no-swap policies in containerized environments.

You can also use `sudo swapoff -a` to temporarily disable all swap devices and files until the next reboot. Just make sure you have enough RAM for your workload—or put limits to prevent overcommit. Otherwise, the OOM killer may reap the process. Monitor swap usage using `vmstat` or `free -m` to make sure swap stays at zero.

Another related setting is `ulimit -l`, as mentioned earlier for pinned memory. If you want to prevent memory from swapping, you should set that limit high or you may experience excessive memory swapping. Again, typically one sets this limit to unlimited for large AI workloads that utilize a lot of memory.

Filesystem Caching and Write-Back

A best practice for large training jobs is to write frequent checkpoints to disk in case you need to restart a failed job from a known good checkpoint. During checkpointing, however, huge bursts of data might fill up the OS page cache and cause stalls.

For storage, you can adjust `vm.dirty_ratio` and `vm.dirty_background_ratio` to tune the page-cache size for buffering writes. For example, with multi-GB checkpoints, using a higher dirty ratio lets the OS batch more data in RAM before flushing to disk. This will smooth out large checkpoint writes and reduce stalls in your training loop.

Another option is to perform checkpointing in a separate thread. A more recent option in PyTorch is to write distributed checkpoint partitions from nodes across the cluster. In this case, the checkpoint partitions will be combined when the checkpoint is loaded after a failed-job restart.

In latency-sensitive training workflows, it's best to bypass the page cache entirely. For example, open checkpoint files with `O_DIRECT` or use Linux's `io_uring` for asynchronous I/O to avoid page-cache stalls. After writing each checkpoint, call `posix_fadvise` (`fd, 0, 0, POSIX_FADV_DONTNEED`) to immediately drop those pages from cache and prevent memory pressure on subsequent iterations.

CPU Frequency and C-states

By default, many compute nodes will run CPUs in a power-saving mode, which either downclocks a CPU or puts it to sleep when it's idle. This helps save energy and reduce heat and lowers the cost. During model training, the CPUs might not always be 100% utilized as the GPUs are churning through the final batches of their dataset. However, these power management features could cause extra latency when the system wakes the CPUs up again when new work arrives.

For maximum and consistent performance, AI systems often configure the CPU frequency governor to "performance" mode, which keeps the CPU at max frequency all the time. This can be done using `cpupower frequency-set -g performance` or in the Basic Input/Output System (BIOS).

Likewise, disabling deep C-states can keep cores from going into a low-power sleep state. CPU C-states are power-saving modes defined by the system's ACPI specification. When a CPU core is idle, it can enter a C-state to save energy. The deeper the C-state, the more power is saved but the longer it may take for the core to wake up when work arrives. Disabling deeper C-states can remove excessive latency spikes. C0 is active; everything above C0 represents a deeper state of sleep.

In practice, many server BIOS/UEFI (Unified Extensible Firmware Interface) offer a high-performance profile that automatically sets the CPU governor to "Performance" and disables deep C-states.

Essentially, we can trade a bit of extra power draw for more responsive CPU behavior. In a training scenario where GPUs are the big power consumers, a bit more CPU power usage is usually fine if it keeps the GPUs fed. For example, if a data loader thread sleeps while waiting for data and the CPU goes into the deep C6 state, significant portions of the CPU are powered down to maximize energy savings.

If the CPU enters a deeper sleep state, it might take a few microseconds to wake up. While this is not a long time, many microseconds can add up and can cause GPU bubbles if not managed properly. *Bubbles* are periods of time when the GPU is waiting for the CPU to resume data processing. By keeping the CPU ready, we reduce such hiccups. Many BIOSes for servers have a setting to disable C-states—or at least limit them.

You should always turn off anything in your system that might introduce unpredictable latency, such as excess context switching, CPU frequency scaling, and memory-to-disk swapping. The result should be that your CPUs deliver data to the GPUs as fast as the GPUs can consume it, without the OS scheduling things on the wrong core or taking CPU cycles away at the wrong time.

Tune Host CPU Memory Allocator

On a well-tuned GPU server, CPU usage may not be very high since GPUs handle most of the computation. However, CPU usage should remain steady and in lockstep with GPU activity. The CPUs must stay busy preparing each incoming batch while the current batch is being processed by the GPU.

Proper CPU-to-GPU handoff is crucial for sustaining high GPU utilization. By tuning your host's memory allocator (`jemalloc` or `tcmalloc`), you can eliminate unpredictable pauses in data preparation. This will keep GPUs running at their peak—except for intentional synchronization points.

After tuning, you should see each GPU's utilization hover near 100% and drop only at required synchronization barriers. The GPUs should never stall for data due to CPU-side delays. With `jemalloc`, you can shard allocations into per-CPU arenas (`narenas`), enable `background_thread` for off-path purging, and lengthen `dirty_decay_ms/muzzy_decay_ms` so that freed pages aren't immediately returned to the OS. This will minimize lock contention and fragmentation.

You can tune `jemalloc` with the `MALLOC_CONF` environment variable as follows:

```
export MALLOC_CONF="narenas:8,dirty_decay_ms:10000,muzzy_decay_ms:10000
,background_thread:true"
```

Similarly, `tcmalloc` benefits from tuning the `TCMALLOC_MAX_TOTAL_THREAD_CACHE_BYTES` and `TCMALLOC_RELEASE_RATE` environment variables. These will provide larger per-thread caches so that small allocations avoid global locks and syscalls—keeping CPU threads ready to feed the GPU with low, predictable latency. You can do this as follows:

```
export TCMALLOC_MAX_TOTAL_THREAD_CACHE_BYTES=$((512*1024*1024))
export TCMALLOC_RELEASE_RATE=16
```

In short, optimizing the allocator can reduce allocator overhead and fragmentation. This will keep CPU threads consistently fast and avoid unexpected stalls feeding the GPU. Experiment with these environment variables and tune them for your specific workload and environment.

GPU Driver and Runtime Settings for Performance

We've optimized the CPU side, but there are also important settings for the GPU driver and runtime that can affect performance—especially in multi-GPU and multi-user scenarios. NVIDIA GPUs have a few knobs that, when tuned properly, can reduce overhead and improve how multiple workloads share a GPU.

Next, we'll cover GPU persistence mode, the partitions of MPS, MIG, and a few other considerations like clock settings, ECC memory, and out-of-memory behavior.

GPU Persistence Mode

By default, if no application is using a GPU, the driver may put the GPU into a lower-power state and unload some of the driver's context. The next time an application comes along and wants to use the GPU, there's a cost to initialize it. This can take on the order of a second or two for the driver to spin everything up.

GPU initialization overhead can negatively impact performance for workloads that periodically release and reacquire the GPU. For instance, consider a training cluster where jobs are starting and stopping frequently. Or a low-volume inference cluster that has to wake up the GPU every time a new inference request arrives. In both of these cases, the overhead will reduce overall workload performance.

Persistence mode (*https://oreil.ly/FSuik*) is enabled by running the `nvidia-persistenced` daemon. This keeps the GPU driver loaded and the hardware in a ready state even when no application is active. This requests that the system not fully power down the GPU when idle, which prevents power gating. Persistence keeps the GPU awake so that the next job has zero startup delay. This is generally recommended for long-running and latency-sensitive workloads. You can enable the persistence daemon at boot time using the following command:

```
systemctl enable nvidia-persistenced
```

> In Kubernetes environments, the NVIDIA GPU Operator can be configured to enable persistence mode on all GPUs automatically.

On AI clusters, it's common to just enable persistence mode on all GPUs at server boot time. This way, when a job begins, the GPUs are already initialized and can start processing immediately. It won't make your actual compute any faster, as it doesn't speed up the math operations, but it shaves off job-startup latency and prevents cold start delays.

GPU persistence mode also helps with interactive usage, as without persistence, the first CUDA call you make after some idle time might stall while the driver reinitializes the GPU. With persistence on, that call returns quickly.

The only downside of persistence is a slightly higher power draw when idle since the GPU stays in a higher readiness state. But, for most data center GPUs, this is an acceptable trade-off for better performance consistency. Once GPU persistence mode is set by an admin with sudo access, you can enjoy the benefits and move on to tackle other optimizations.

MPS

Normally, when multiple processes share a single GPU, the GPU's scheduler time-slices between them. For example, if two Python processes each have some kernels to run on the same GPU, the GPU might execute one process's kernel, then the other process's kernel, and so on. If those kernels are short and there's an idle gap between them, the GPU can end up underutilized as it's doing "ping-pong" context switches and not overlapping the work.

NVIDIA's MPS is a feature that creates a sort of umbrella under which multiple processes can run on the GPU concurrently and without strict time-slicing. With MPS, the GPU can execute kernels from different processes at the same time as long as the GPU resources (streaming multiprocessors [SMs], Tensor Cores, etc.) are available. MPS essentially merges the contexts of the processes into one scheduler context. This way, you don't pay the full cost of switching and idling between independent processes.

When is MPS useful? For model training, if you normally run one process per GPU, you might not use MPS. But if you have scenarios like running many inference jobs on one big GPU, MPS is a game changer. Imagine you have a powerful GPU or GPU cluster, but your inference job—or set of multiple inference jobs—doesn't fully use it.

For instance, consider running four separate inference jobs on one 40 GB GPU, each using 5–10 GB and only 30% of GPU compute. By default, each inference job gets a time-slice, so at any moment, only one job's work is actually running on the GPU. That leaves the GPU 70% idle on average.

If you enable MPS for these inference jobs, the GPUs can interleave their work so that while one job is waiting on memory, another job's kernel might fill the GPU, etc. The result is higher overall GPU utilization. In practice, if two processes each use 40% of a GPU, with MPS you might see the GPU at 80%–90% utilization serving both.

For instance, two training processes that each would take one hour on their own—on the same GPU, running sequentially—can run together with MPS. In this case, they would finish in a bit more than one hour total in parallel instead of two hours sequentially. The speedup from MPS can approach a near-doubling when kernels and memory bandwidth from concurrent clients complement one another. To visualize, imagine Process A and Process B each launching kernels periodically without MPS. The GPU schedule might look like A-B-A-B with gaps in between while each one waits, as shown in Figure 3-6.

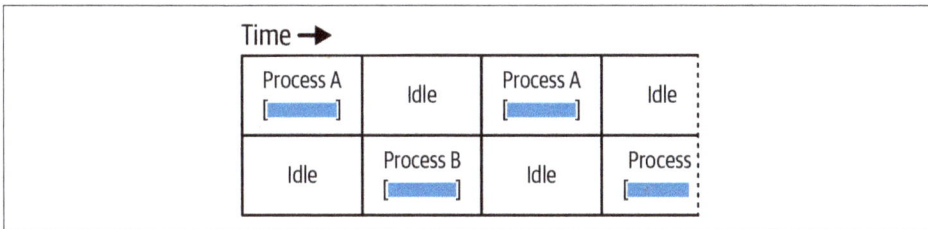

Figure 3-6. GPU alternates between running Process A's kernels and Process B's kernels and creates idle gaps in which one process is waiting while the other is active

With MPS, the schedule overlaps A and B so that whenever A isn't using some parts of the GPU, B's work can use them simultaneously, and vice versa. This overlapping eliminates idle gaps, as shown in Figure 3-7.

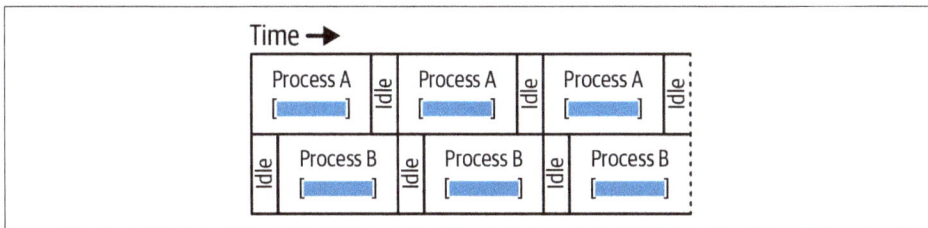

Figure 3-7. Reducing idle gaps for processes A and B using MPS

Setting up MPS involves running an MPS control daemon (`nvidia-cuda-mps-control`), which then launches an MPS server process that brokers GPU access. On modern GPUs, MPS is more streamlined as clients (the processes) can talk directly to the hardware with minimal interference from the compute node itself.

Typically, you start the MPS server on a node—often one per GPU or one per user—and then run your GPU jobs with an environment variable that connects them to MPS. All jobs under that server will share the GPU concurrently.

Another feature of MPS is the ability to set an active thread percentage per client. This limits how many SMs (GPU cores, essentially) a client can use. This can be useful if you want to guarantee quality of service (QoS) where two jobs, for example, each get at most 50% of the GPU's execution resources. In this case, you can set `CUDA_MPS_ACTIVE_THREAD_PERCENTAGE=50` to cap a client to about 50% of SM execution capacity. If not explicitly set, the jobs will just compete and use whatever GPU resources they can.

Note that MPS does not partition GPU memory, so all processes will share the full GPU memory space. MPS is mainly about compute sharing and scheduling. The issue is that one process could request a massive amount of GPU RAM, cause an OOM error on the GPU, and result in terminating all of the other processes running on the GPU. This is very disruptive. Also, if one program saturates the GPU 100% on its own, MPS won't magically make it go faster, as you can't exceed 100% utilization. It's beneficial only when individual jobs leave some slack that others can fill.

Another limitation of MPS is that, by default, all MPS clients must run as the same Unix user since they share a context. In multiuser clusters, this means MPS is usually set up at the scheduler level such that only one user's jobs share a GPU at a time. Otherwise, you can configure a system-wide MPS that's shared by all users, but understand that the jobs are not isolated from a security standpoint.

Modern NVIDIA drivers support multiuser MPS so that processes from different Unix users can share a single MPS server. This improves usability but does not provide memory isolation. Prefer MIG when strong isolation is required. One specific alternative to MPS is a feature for time-slicing GPUs in Kubernetes. Time-slicing on Kubernetes allows the device plugin to schedule different pods on the same GPU by time. For instance, if you configure a single GPU with a time-slicing replication factor of four, four pods on that GPU can each receive a time share.

Kubernetes time-slicing is sort of an automated time-sharing algorithm that doesn't require MPS. However, this doesn't overlap execution. Instead, it just switches more rapidly than the default driver would. Time-slicing may be useful for interactive workloads where you prefer isolation at the cost of some idle time. For high-throughput jobs, overlapping with MPS or splitting the GPU with a MIG is usually better than fine-grained time-slicing, as discussed next.

MIG

Modern GPUs can be partitioned at the hardware level into multiple instances using MIG. MIG is a form of virtualization but done in hardware. This way, the overhead is very low—maybe a few percent—due to the loss of some flexibility.

If one instance is idle, it can't lend its resources to another, as they are hard partitioned. MIG allows a GPU to be sliced into as many as seven smaller logical GPUs—each with its own dedicated portion of memory and compute units, or SMs, as shown in Figure 3-8.

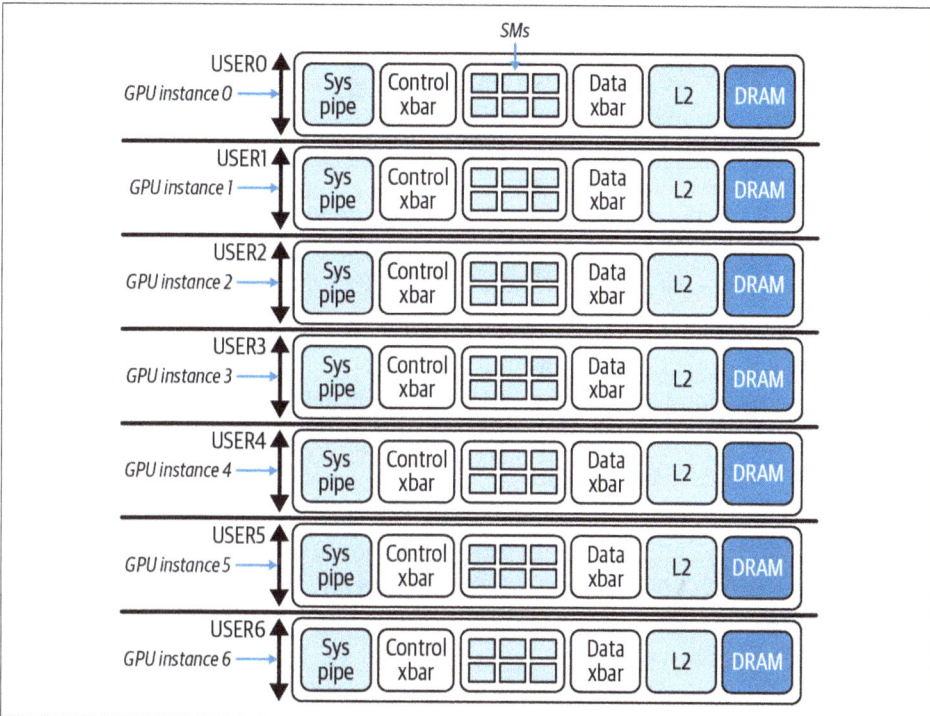

Figure 3-8. A single physical GPU partitioned into seven MIG instances (adapted from the NVIDIA MIG User Guide)

By convention, NVIDIA's MIG profile naming uses the prefix <X>g to denote the number of compute slices between 1 (min) and 7 (max) on modern GPUs. Each slice number represents a number of SM groups allocated to that partition. Each SM group is roughly a 1/7 slice of the total number of SMs.

If a GPU has 132 SMs, each 1/7 slice represents 132 SMs × 1/7 = ~19 SMs in a group. As such, 1g represents ~19 SMs, 2g represents ~38 SMs, all the way up to 7g, which represents the total of ~132 SMs.

In contrast, and somewhat confusingly, the suffix <Y>gb specifies the exact amount of HBM GPU RAM in gigabytes that is reserved for that profile. The MIG profile values are fixed for each GPU generation and type and listed in the NVIDIA documentation (*https://oreil.ly/FsPEx*). For the Blackwell B200, some of the MIG profile values are shown in Table 3-1.

Table 3-1. MIG Profiles for Blackwell B200 (source: https://oreil.ly/FsPEx)

Profile name	Fraction of memory	Fraction of SMs	L2 cache size	Copy engines	Number of instances
MIG 1g.23gb	1/8	1/7	1/8	2	7
MIG 1g.45gb	2/8	1/7	2/8	2	4
MIG 2g.45gb	2/8	2/7	2/8	3	3
MIG 3g.90gb	4/8	3/7	4/8	6	2
MIG 4g.90gb	4/8	4/7	4/8	8	1
MIG 7g.180gb	Full	Full	Full	16	1

The table also shows the number of hardware units, copy engines, and L2 cache fractions for each profile. These fixed profiles align with the GPU's hardware memory controllers such that each memory slice maps to contiguous HBM channels.

This two-part scheme separates compute capacity (number of SM groups) from memory capacity (total GB). Administrators can choose combinations of MIG profiles. The sum of allocated SMs and HBM does not need to exactly match the full GPU capacity. However, certain combinations are constrained by hardware partitioning. They cannot invent new slice sizes, for instance.

Administrators can enable or disable only the supported MIG profiles (e.g., 1g.23gb, 2g.45gb, 4g.90gb, etc.) on each GPU using tools like nvidia-smi -mig or using the NVIDIA Kubernetes GPU Operator's nvidia.com/mig.config config map. Reconfiguring MIG requires draining workloads and invoking MIG's dynamic reconfiguration capability to apply the changes.

Once a GPU is in MIG mode, modern GPUs can create and destroy MIG partitions dynamically without rebooting the entire system. You can adjust MIG instances on the fly after draining existing workloads, but to enable or disable MIG mode itself on a GPU, a reset of that GPU is needed.

Each MIG instance acts like a separate GPU from the perspective of software since it has its own memory, its own SMs, and even separate engine contexts. The benefit of MIG is strong isolation and guaranteed resources for each job. If you have multiple users or multiple services that need only, say, 10 GB of logical GPU memory each, you can pack them onto one physical GPU without them interfering with one another's memory or compute.

Jobs can request MIG devices specifically, but you have to be careful to schedule in a way that uses all slices. For instance, if you have a 7-slice setup and a job takes only 1 slice, the other 6 should be packed with other jobs, or you're leaving a lot idle. It's possible to configure certain nodes in your cluster to use MIG for small inference jobs, for example, and configure other nodes for non-MIG workloads for large training jobs.

One important operational note is that, in order to use MIG, you typically configure it at the system level—or at least at the node level. The GPU has to be put into MIG mode, the slices created, and the GPU reset. Once these happen, the slices appear as separate devices to the system—each with their own unique device ID.

If you're not using all of the available MIG slices because of poor upfront planning, you'll end up wasting resources by leaving them fragmented and unused. It's important to plan partition sizes upfront to match your workloads—and adjust the partition sizes when the workload changes. You will need to reset the GPUs to pick up the change.

For large-scale model training jobs and inference servers that span many GPUs, MIG is typically not useful since we want access to the full set of GPUs. On the other hand, for multitenant, small-model inference servers that can run smaller GPU partitions, MIG and its isolation features could be useful.

> With current MIG deployment guidance (including R570-era behavior), cross-GPU MIG P2P remains unsupported (*https:// oreil.ly/37-9-*). In addition, CUDA IPC across GPU instances is unsupported, and NCCL is not supported with MIG. Same-GPU MIG-instance peer paths may be supported, but confirm your training/inference topology does not depend on cross-GPU peer communication before enabling MIG for distributed workloads.
>
> This can reduce distributed training throughput. Large-scale training jobs (and sparse MoE expert inference systems) require massive GPU-to-GPU communication. As such, they are typically not good candidates for MIG. Instead, communication between GPU MIG instances must travel through either the host or network fabric.

In short, enable MIG only when you need to run multiple independent jobs on the same GPU with strong isolation. Do not use MIG for large-scale distributed training or inferencing that spans GPUs, as you want access to the full power of the GPUs and their fast interconnects.

In our context of large transformer-based model training and inferencing, we will leave MIG off. But it's good to know that this feature exists. Perhaps a cluster might dynamically switch modes and run MIG during the day when lots of small training or inferencing experiments are happening, then turn MIG off at night to run big training jobs that use whole GPUs.

> The Kubernetes device plugin will list MIG devices as resources like `nvidia.com/mig-1g.23gb` in the case of a 1/7 GPU slice with a total 23 GB for the slice.

GPU Clock Speeds and ECC

NVIDIA GPUs have something called GPU Boost, which automatically adjusts the core clock within power and thermal limits. Most of the time, you should let the GPU just do its thing. But some users like to lock the clocks for consistency so that the GPU always runs at a fixed maximum frequency. This way, run-to-run performance is stable and not subject to variations in power or temperature.

Fixing the clock is extremely important when performing benchmarks since later runs may be throttled due to excessive heat. If you do not account for this, you may inadvertently interpret the poor results of later runs incorrectly since the GPUs of these subsequent runs may be throttled due to excessive heat caused by previous runs.

Specifically, NVIDIA's GPU Boost will vary the core clock up or down to stay within power/thermal limits. Locking the clock at the max stable frequency using `nvidia-smi -lgc` to lock the core clock and `-ac` to lock the memory clock. This will make sure the GPU runs at a constant frequency—and prevents the GPU's Boost default functionality from downclocking in later runs.

> This is mostly relevant during benchmarking to achieve deterministic and reproducible results. For everyday training and inferencing, it's recommended to leave auto-boost on unless you notice significant performance variance and GPU throttling.

Locking the clocks is something to be aware of if you're chasing the last bit of determinism and consistency. Typically, however, leaving the GPU in the default auto-boost mode is fine.

Some teams purposely underclock the GPUs to reduce heat—especially if they are running very long jobs and don't want to suffer the eventual thermal slowdown over time. Data center GPUs typically have enough temperature headroom—as well as proper air and liquid cooling—so that you don't need to do this, but it's good to know that it's an option.

Another approach is to use `nvidia-smi -pl` to set a power limit slightly below the maximum thermal design power (TDP) of the GPU. TDP is the maximum amount of heat, measured in watts, that a GPU can generate under sustained load. This dictates the amount of heat that must be dissipated to prevent overheating.

If you set the power limit below TDP, the GPU Boost will auto-adjust clocks below the thermal throttle point. This can reduce peak heat generation, prevent throttling, and incur minimal performance impact.

ECC memory on GPUs is another consideration. ECC ensures that if there's a single-bit memory error caused by cosmic rays, for example, the memory can be corrected on the fly. And if there's a double-bit error, the error is detected and will throw an error to the calling code. ECC is usually enabled by default on NVIDIA data center GPUs.

Disabling ECC can free up a small amount of memory since ECC requires extra bits for error checking. This might yield a marginal performance gain by reducing the overhead associated with on-the-fly error checking, but typically just a few percent. However, turning off ECC also removes critical memory-error protection, which can lead to system instability or undetected data corruption.

For NVIDIA's data center GPUs, including Hopper and Blackwell, ECC comes enabled by default and is intended to remain enabled to ensure reliable, error-corrected computation and data integrity. For long training or inference jobs on huge models, a single memory error could crash the job completely or, even worse, silently corrupt your model without a warning.

It's recommended to always keep ECC on for any serious AI workload. The only time you'd possibly consider turning it off is in a research setting where you are fine with taking the risk because you need that extra sliver of memory for your model to fit into your limited-memory GPU cluster.

Toggling ECC mode requires resetting the GPU and likely restarting jobs that are currently running on that GPU. So it's not a toggle that you want to switch frequently. Keep ECC on for stability and reliability. The peace of mind outweighs the negligible speedup of turning ECC off.

GPU Memory Oversubscription, Fragmentation, and Out-of-Memory Handling

Unlike CPU RAM, by default there is no such thing as GPU "swap" memory. If you try to allocate more GPU memory than available, you will get an unfriendly OOM error along with an even-unfriendlier process crash. There are a couple of mechanisms to mitigate this issue: allow memory to grow dynamically, embrace unified memory across CPU and GPU, and utilize memory pools and caching allocators.

By default, some frameworks (e.g., TensorFlow) grab all of the available GPU memory at startup to avoid fragmentation and improve performance. If you don't know this, it can be very bad in scenarios where you are sharing the GPU. PyTorch, by default, allocates GPU memory only as needed.

TensorFlow has an option (`TF_FORCE_GPU_ALLOW_GROWTH=true`) to make it start small and dynamically grow the GPU memory usage as needed—similar to PyTorch. However, neither PyTorch nor TensorFlow lets you allocate more memory than the GPU has available. But this lazy allocation plays nicer in multitenant scenarios because two processes won't both try to simultaneously allocate the maximum available GPU memory from the start.

CUDA's Unified Memory system lets you allocate memory without predefining whether it resides on the CPU or GPU. The CUDA Runtime handles moving pages as needed. Modern NVIDIA GPUs like Hopper and Blackwell include hardware support for on-demand paging using the Page Migration Engine (PME).

PME automatically migrates memory pages between GPU memory and host CPU RAM when the GPU runs low on available memory. However, while PME provides flexibility, relying on it can introduce performance penalties compared to having enough GPU memory for your workload.

This GPU-to-CPU memory offloading can be slow, however, since CPU memory I/O is slower than GPU high-bandwidth memory (HBM) I/O, as we learned in Chapter 2. This mechanism is mostly a convenience for practitioners trying to run models that don't fit into GPU RAM.

For performance-critical workloads, you generally want to avoid relying on unified memory oversubscription where possible. It's there as a safety net instead of outright crashing your script, but your job will run slower when GPU memory is oversubscribed.

Libraries like PyTorch use a caching allocator so that when you free GPU memory, it doesn't return the memory to the OS immediately. Instead, it keeps it to reuse for future allocations. This avoids memory fragmentation and the overhead of asking the OS to repeatedly allocate the same block of memory.

You can configure PyTorch's allocator using environment variables like `PYTORCH_ALLOC_CONF` (formerly `PYTORCH_CUDA_ALLOC_CONF`) to set a max pool size. We'll cover optimizations to PyTorch's memory-allocation mechanism in a later chapter.

If you run into the GPU OOM error, which you surely will at some point, it's likely caused by memory fragmentation or excessive memory caching. You can try to clear the cache using PyTorch's `torch.cuda.empty_cache()`, but it almost always means your workload legitimately needs that much memory.

PyTorch also provides tools like `torch.cuda.memory_stats()` and `torch.cuda.mem ory_summary()` to help diagnose fragmentation by showing allocated versus reserved memory. NVIDIA's Nsight Systems also shows GPU memory usage patterns to help identify memory leaks, long-lived allocations that correlate with leaks, CPU-GPU interconnect activity, and GPUDirect Storage timeline tracing. Additionally, the Nsight Compute profiler provides low-level kernel analysis, including occupancy, throughput, and NVLink usage. We'll cover all of these in the upcoming chapters.

Docker provides the `--gpus` flag to select and expose GPUs to a container, but it does not support setting a GPU memory limit. If you need hard isolation for GPU memory or compute, use MIG to partition the device or use Multi-Process Service (MPS) with active thread percentage for fair sharing. Configure limits in Kubernetes using MIG resources like `nvidia.com/mig-2g.45gb` when you require strict partitioning.

In multitenant nodes, this could be useful to isolate jobs. In a single-job-per-GPU situation, it's not common to set a memory limit, as you want to let the job use as much of the GPU memory as it can get.

In general, running out of GPU memory is something you can manage at the application level. For instance, you can reduce the data batch size, model weight precision, or even the model parameter count, if that's an option.

A best practice is to monitor GPU memory usage with `nvidia-smi` or NVML APIs during model training and inferencing. If you're close to the memory limit, consider workarounds like reducing batch size, using activation checkpointing for training, or other techniques to lower memory usage.

Also, you should ensure that your CPU memory isn't being swapped, as this would indirectly hurt your GPU utilization and goodput because each time your GPU tries to fetch something from the CPU host, but the host memory page has been swapped to disk, your performance will be bottlenecked by the much slower disk I/O. So it's important to combine these memory-reduction best practices with the earlier advice about pinning memory, increasing the `ulimit`, and disabling swappiness, etc.

In short, it's recommended to always keep the GPU driver loaded instead of unloading the GPU driver between jobs. This is similar to GPU persistence mode but at a deeper level. Some clusters are configured to unload the driver when no jobs are running in order to free OS kernel memory and for security. However, if you do that, the next job has to pay the cost of reloading the GPU driver and, if MIG is used, reconfiguring MIG slices.

It's recommended to keep the driver and any MIG configuration persistent across jobs. The only time you want to unload the GPU driver is for troubleshooting or upgrading the driver. As such, cluster admins often set up the system so that the NVIDIA driver modules are always present once the machine boots.

Container Runtime Optimizations for GPUs

Many AI systems use orchestration tools and container runtimes to manage the software environment. Kubernetes and Docker are popular in AI infrastructure. Using containers ensures that all dependencies, including CUDA and library versions, are consistent. This avoids the "but it works on my machine" problem. Containers introduce a bit of complexity and a tiny amount of overhead, but with the right configuration, you can get near bare-metal performance for GPU workloads using containers.

A container running on a node is not a traditional virtual machine (VM). In contrast to VMs, containers share the host OS kernel so that CPU and memory operations perform at near-native speed. And with the NVIDIA Container Toolkit, GPU access from within a Docker container is direct and does not incur overhead.

> For modern GPUs running with the latest NVIDIA Container Toolkit, GPU performance within a properly configured environment is virtually identical (< 2% difference) to running the code directly on the bare-metal host outside of the container. In fact, Red Hat OpenShift and Kubernetes were used in the MLPerf Inference v5.0 results, which demonstrates (*https://oreil.ly/xPJv4*) that modern containers and orchestration configuration do not compromise efficiency or latency.

NVIDIA Container Toolkit and CUDA Compatibility

One challenge when using containers with GPUs is making sure that the CUDA libraries inside the container match the driver on the host. NVIDIA solves this through their Container Toolkit and base Docker images. The host provides the NVIDIA driver, which, remember, is tightly integrated with the kernel and hardware. Inside the container, you typically find the CUDA runtime libraries of a certain version.

The general rule is that the host's NVIDIA driver version must be at least as recent (*https://oreil.ly/4Zr0e*) as the minimum driver version required by the CUDA version inside the container. For CUDA 13.x, the minimum required Linux host driver branch is R580 or newer. For CUDA 12.x, the minimum required Linux host driver branch is R525 or newer. Using a newer CUDA runtime with an older driver will cause the CUDA initialization to fail.

> Each new CUDA version requires a minimum NVIDIA driver version. Always consult NVIDIA's official compatibility matrix (*https://oreil.ly/JxcTd*) and upgrade the host driver when you update the CUDA toolkit.

For Docker and Kubernetes environments, the simplest approach is to use NVIDIA's official base Docker images from the NVIDIA GPU Cloud (NGC) or DockerHub image repositories. These images (e.g., `nvcr.io/nvidia/pytorch` or similar) bundle the proper versions of the CUDA runtime, cuDNN, NCCL, etc. In addition, these Docker images list the minimum required CUDA driver, depending on the CUDA version. This way, you get support for the latest hardware without dependency headaches.

NVIDIA Container Runtime

Alternatively, NVIDIA's container runtime can actually inject the host driver libraries into the container at runtime, so you don't even need to ship the NVIDIA driver inside the image. Instead, you just rely on the host's driver. Again, this works because the container isn't fully isolated like a traditional VM. Docker containers are allowed to use host devices, volumes, and libraries.

Inside the container, your application uses the CUDA runtime libraries, such as `libcudart.so` from the container image, while the NVIDIA Container Toolkit injects the host's driver libraries such as `libcuda.so` and `libnvidia-ml.so` at container start. The host driver libraries are invoked directly on the host so that everything just works.

The split between CUDA runtime libraries (container) and NVIDIA Container Toolkit (host) is supported as long as the host driver meets the minimum version required by the CUDA Toolkit in the image. If you were to mismatch and try to use a newer CUDA version in the container with an old driver on the host, you'd likely get an error. It's important to match the CUDA and driver versions.

The key takeaway is that there is no hypervisor or virtualization layer involved when using containers for GPUs. The container is sharing the host kernel and driver directly, so when a kernel launches on the GPU, it's as if it launched from the host.

In other words, you aren't losing performance to Docker-based virtualization—unless you are using something like VMware or Single Root Input/Output Virtualization (SR-IOV) virtual GPUs, which is a special scenario that requires some tuning. With Docker plus NVIDIA, it's basically the equivalent of bare metal performance.

The NVIDIA Container Toolkit works with containerd and Podman as well, not only Docker. This is relevant for modern Kubernetes environments that use containerd as the default container runtime.

Avoiding Container Overlay Filesystem Overhead

The main difference when running in a Docker container versus running directly on the host might be in I/O. Containers often use a union filesystem that transparently overlays multiple underlying filesystems, like the host filesystem and the container filesystem, into a single, unified view.

In a union filesystem such as OverlayFS, files and directories from multiple sources will appear as if they belong to one filesystem. This mechanism is especially useful for containers, where the read-only filesystem from the base image layer is combined with a writable container layer.

There is some overhead when using an overlay filesystem, however. This extra latency arises because the filesystem must check multiple underlying layers—both read-only and writable—to determine which version of a file should be returned. The additional metadata lookups and the logic for merging these layers can add a small amount of overhead compared to reading from a single, simple filesystem.

Furthermore, there is overhead when writing to the copy-on-write (CoW) mechanism used by the overlay. CoW means that when you modify a file in the read-only layer (e.g., the base image), the file must first be copied to the writable layer. The write then happens to the copied writable file—instead of the original, read-only file. As mentioned earlier, reading a modified file requires looking at both the read-only and writable layers to determine which is the correct version to return.

Model training often involves heavy I/O operations when reading datasets, loading a model, and writing model checkpoints. To work around this, you can mount a host directory—or network filesystem—into the container using bind mounts.

Bind mounts bypass the overlay and therefore perform similarly to disk I/O directly on the host. If the host filesystem is something like an NVMe SSD or an NFS mount, you get the full performance of that underlying storage device. We purposely do not package a multi-terabyte dataset inside the image. Instead, we bring the data in through the mounts.

For example, if your training data is on `/data/dataset` on the host, you'd run the container with `-v /data/dataset:/mnt/dataset:ro`, where *ro* means read-only mount. Then your training script reads from `/mnt/dataset`. This way, you're reading directly from the host filesystem.

In fact, it's a best practice to avoid heavy data reads/writes against the container's writable layer. Instead, mount your data directory and output directory from the host into the container. You want to ensure that I/O is not bottlenecked by the overhead of the container's CoW mechanism.

Reduce Image Size for Faster Container Startup

Container startup times can be quite a bit slower if the image is huge and needs to be pulled over the network. But in a typical long-running training loop, a startup time of a few minutes is negligible compared to the hours, days, or months of training time. It's still worth keeping images reasonably slim by not including unnecessary build tools or temporary build files. This saves disk space and improves container startup time.

Some HPC centers prefer Singularity (Apptainer) over Docker, because it can run images in user space without a root daemon. It also uses the host filesystem directly and tends to have virtually zero overhead beyond what the OS already has.

In either case, Docker or Apptainer (formerly Singularity), studies and benchmarks have shown that once properly configured, these container solutions measure only a couple percent difference between running a container or directly on the host. Essentially, if someone gave you a log of GPU utilization and throughput, it would be difficult to tell from the log alone whether the job ran in a container or not.

Kubernetes for Topology-Aware Container Orchestration and Networking

Kubernetes (also known as K8s) is a popular container orchestrator for AI training and inference. The NVIDIA device plugin for Kubernetes (*https://oreil.ly/Z6sST*) is a lightweight component that advertises GPU hardware (`/dev/nvidia0`, `/dev/nvidiactl`, etc.) to the scheduler. It mounts those device nodes into your pods when you request `nvidia.com/gpu` under `resources.limits` and optionally under `resources.requests`, if you want to set both explicitly. This way, when you deploy a container on Kubernetes with this device plugin, Kubernetes takes care of making the GPUs available to the container. The device plugin is topology aware, as well. This means it can prefer to allocate multiple GPUs from the same NVLink Switch or the same NUMA node for a given pod.

The NVIDIA Kubernetes GPU Operator (*https://oreil.ly/ljnkp*) automates the installation and lifecycle of all NVIDIA software, including driver libraries, the NVIDIA Kubernetes device plugin mentioned previously, and the NVIDIA Container Toolkit. It's also responsible for node labeling using NVIDIA's GPU Feature Discovery (*https://oreil.ly/d8M6Q*) to label each GPU with its NUMA node and NVLink/NVSwitch ID. The scheduler can then use these labels to intelligently allocate GPUs to jobs. The GPU Operator also implements GPU monitoring using DCGM.

When using Kubernetes to orchestrate GPU-based containers, you want it to allocate resources to containers in a manner that is aware of the hardware topology, including the NUMA node and network bandwidth configurations. However, by default,

Kubernetes is not topology-aware. It treats each GPU as a resource but doesn't know if GPU 0 and GPU 1 are on the same NUMA node or if they use the same NVLink interconnect. This could make a big difference.

Consider an 8-GPU server with two sets of 4 GPUs—each connected by NVLink. If you request 4 GPUs from Kubernetes for a job, it would be ideal if K8s gave you four GPUs that are all interconnected with NVLink, as they can share data faster. However, if Kubernetes picks four arbitrary GPUs spread anywhere in the system, your job might be allocated two GPUs from one NVLink domain and two GPUs from a different NVLink domain.

Allocating GPUs without topology awareness will introduce slow interconnects (e.g., InfiniBand or Ethernet) into the GPU-to-GPU route. This can cut your inter-GPU bandwidth in half. In this case, Kubernetes would ideally allocate four GPUs that are all interconnected by NVLink and use the same NUMA node rather than four that span different racks and NUMA domains.

For instance, consider NVIDIA's NVL72 rack built on NVLink 5 interconnects, which connects 72 GPUs into a single high-bandwidth domain with a combined ~130 TB/s throughput inside the rack (72 GPUs * 1.8 TB/s per GPU). In this configuration, if a Kubernetes scheduler isn't topology aware, it might place a multi-GPU job across different NVLink domains—or even outside the NVL72 group. Allocating GPUs to a job without respecting the system's topology would negate the benefits of the NVL72's massive intra-rack bandwidth.

To avoid resource contention, you should try to either reserve the resources that you need or request the entire node for your job. For the container/pod placements, you should align pods with CPU affinities and NUMA nodes using the Kubernetes Topology Manager component (*https://oreil.ly/RzPI7*) to bind the container's CPUs to the same NUMA node as the GPUs that the container was allocated. Let's discuss this next.

Orchestrating Containers with Kubernetes Topology Manager

Kubernetes Topology Manager can provide detailed topology information. For example, it can detect that GPU 0 is connected to NUMA node 0, NVLink domain A, and PCIe bus Z. The Kubernetes scheduler can then use this information to allocate containers to GPUs in an optimal way for efficient processing and communication.

Topology-aware GPU scheduling is still maturing. In many clusters, administrators explicitly label nodes using Kubernetes labels to capture the GPU and system topology. These labels ensure that multi-GPU pods land on servers whose GPUs share the same NVLink interconnect or reside within the same NUMA domain.

For our purposes, if you're running multi-GPU jobs in Kubernetes, make sure to enable topology-aware scheduling. This typically involves configuring `--topology-manager-policy` to `best-effort`, `restricted`, or, in some cases, `single-numa-node`. This policy configuration helps multi-GPU and CPU + GPU workloads achieve lower latency by avoiding remote memory access. This complements the OS-level NUMA tuning.

Also, be sure to use the latest NVIDIA GPU device plugin and NVIDIA Kubernetes GPU Operator, mentioned in the previous section, as these are topology aware and support packing multi-GPU pods onto GPUs that are connected to the same NUMA node. These help optimize performance by minimizing cross-NUMA-node communication and reducing latency in multinode GPU workloads.

On NVLink-5 NVL72 systems, a single rack-level NVLink domain provides up to 130 TB/s of aggregate bidirectional GPU-to-GPU bandwidth, equivalent to about 1.8 TB/s per GPU. When scheduling collective-heavy training, prefer placements that keep traffic inside the fast NVLink domain before crossing the slower network fabric.

Job Scheduling with Kubernetes and SLURM

In multinode deployments, job schedulers are essential for maximizing resource utilization across all nodes. Commonly, the Simple Linux Utility for Resource Management (SLURM) is used for training clusters, while Kubernetes is typically favored for inference clusters. However, hybrid solutions have emerged that integrate SLURM with Kubernetes. The open source Slinky project (*https://oreil.ly/D-s1i*) is an example solution to simplify cluster management across training and inference workloads.

These systems handle the allocation of GPUs to jobs and coordinate the launch of processes across nodes. If a training job requests 8 nodes with 8 GPUs per node, the scheduler will identify eligible nodes and start the job using tools like `mpirun` or container runtimes such as Docker. This way, each process is aware of all available GPUs in the job. Many clusters also rely on well-tested Docker repositories like NVIDIA's NGC Docker repository to guarantee a consistent software environment—including GPU drivers, CUDA toolkits, PyTorch libraries, and other Python packages—across all nodes.

With SLURM, similar issues exist. SLURM has the concept of "generic resources" for GPUs, and you can define that certain GPUs are attached to certain NUMA nodes or NVLinks/NVSwitches. Then in your job request, you can ask for GPUs that are, say, connected to the same NUMA node.

If not properly set, a scheduler might treat all GPUs as identical and provide nonideal allocations for your multi-GPU container requests. Proper configuration can avoid unnecessary cross-NUMA-node and cross-NVLink GPU communication overhead.

SLURM supports scheduling MIG partitions as distinct resources as well. This can be useful for packing multiple jobs onto one GPU. This is analogous to how Kubernetes can schedule GPU slices using the Kubernetes device plugin. Next, we'll discuss how to use MIG slices with Kubernetes.

Slicing a GPU with MIG

When you enable NVIDIA's MIG mode, introduced in an earlier section, a single physical GPU is sliced into smaller, fixed, and hardware-isolated partitions called MIG instances. Next is an example Kubernetes pod configuration for two of the `nvidia.com/mig-2g.45gb` MIG slices (this configuration assumes that the NVIDIA Kubernetes device plugin (*https://oreil.ly/ktnuE*) is configured to recognize MIG devices on each node):

```
resources:
  limits:
    nvidia.com/mig-2g.45gb: "2"
```

Here, the configuration specifies running a pod on a node with at least two free `2g.45gb` instances on one GPU; in other words, 2 slices in which each slice is 2/7 of the SMs (2g). If a GPU has a total of 132 SMs, each is 2/7 × 132 SMs = ~38 SMs. Multiply this by 2), and the pod is allocating a total of ~76 SMs. The total memory allocation is 45 GB of GPU RAM.

Note that the scheduler cannot split these across GPUs or nodes. Kubernetes will schedule the pod only if a single node can provide both partitions. This is because pods cannot span multiple nodes. If no single node has two free `2g.45gb` slices available for a total of 76 SMs and 45 GB of GPU RAM (as calculated previously), the pod remains in a Kubernetes `Pending` (unscheduled) state and therefore won't run—even if other nodes collectively have enough MIG capacity.

This constraint highlights the importance of planning your MIG sizes according to typical workload needs. For instance, if many jobs request `2g.45gb` slices, you might configure each GPU to host three `2g.45gb` instances—among its seven possible slices—so that two such instances can co-reside on one GPU for a single pod.

> This single-node constraint can cause pods to never run—even if the combined MIG resources can be found across different nodes of the cluster. The request can be satisfied only if the requested MIG resources are available on a single node.

An administrative drawback with MIG is that switching a GPU between MIG mode and normal (non-MIG) mode requires resetting the GPUs—or rebooting the compute node. So it's not something the scheduler can easily do dynamically per job.

However, you usually create MIG partitions in advance and leave the configuration running for some period of time.

In a Kubernetes environment, the NVIDIA Kubernetes GPU Operator's MIG Manager can automatically configure and preserve MIG partitions on nodes. This way, the MIG slices remain active across reboots and driver reloads. In Kubernetes, treat MIG partitioning as an explicit lifecycle operation managed by the MIG Manager policy. And always validate post-boot state before scheduling.

You can label one K8s node with "mig-enabled" and another as "mig-disabled" and let the scheduler place jobs/pods accordingly. This is more of an operational detail, but it's good to know that MIG is a truly static partition—and not a product of a dynamic scheduler.

> Persistence mode is recommended when using MIG so that the MIG configuration remains active on the GPU even if no jobs are running. This way, the GPU doesn't have to keep rebuilding the slices before running each periodic job.

Optimizing Network Communication for Kubernetes

When you run multinode GPU workloads using containers with Kubernetes, the pods need to talk to one another. In Kubernetes, by default, pods have their own IP, and there might be an overlay network or network-address translation (NAT) between pods on different nodes. This can introduce complications and additional overhead.

Often, the simplest solution for GPU clusters is to use host networking for these performance-sensitive jobs. That means the container's network is not isolated, as it uses the host's network interface directly. To enable this in Kubernetes, you set host Network: true on the pod specification. In Docker, you could run with --network=host.

Using host networking allows a container to access the InfiniBand interconnect exactly as the host does—without any additional translation or firewall layers. This is particularly useful for MPI jobs because it eliminates the need to configure port mappings for every MPI rank.

However, if host networking is not an option due to security policies, you must ensure that your Kubernetes container network interface (CNI) and any overlay network can handle the required traffic. In such cases, you may need to open specific ports for NCCL bootstrap and data exchange. Prefer setting Linux ephemeral port policy via net.ipv4.ip_local_port_range (e.g., cluster sysctl policy) and use NCCL_SOCKET_IFNAME to bind the intended interfaces. This is the most robust way to control bootstrap behavior across Kubernetes and container networking layers.

When operating over an overlay network, it's critical that latency remains low and operations run in kernel space. Also, make sure that no user-space proxies throttle traffic between nodes. These factors can significantly impact performance.

When using a Kubernetes environment and you want to enable RDMA, consider installing the Kubernetes RDMA device plugin (*https://oreil.ly/ZcGE3*) from Mellanox. This plugin exposes InfiniBand and GPUDirect RDMA endpoints on the pods interface to enable low-latency, zero-copy networking.

> If you have InfiniBand or RoCE networking, remember to enable GPUDirect RDMA in the NVIDIA driver if your NIC supports it. This allows GPUs to directly exchange data with the NIC—bypassing the CPU for internode communication. This is essential for maintaining high performance in a multinode environment.

Reducing Kubernetes Orchestration Jitter

Running an orchestrator like Kubernetes means there are some background processes running on every node (e.g., the Kubernetes "kubelet"), container runtime daemons, and (ideally) monitoring agents. While these services consume CPU and memory, the consumption is on the order of a few percent of a single core. So they won't steal noticeable time from a GPU-based training job, which uses these cores for data loading and preprocessing.

However, if the training job is running on a node that is also running an inference workload, you may experience some jitter, or unpredictable variation, in the execution timing and throughput. This is common in any multitenancy situation, though. If another container on the same machine unexpectedly uses a lot of CPU or I/O, it will affect your container—whether training or inference—by competing for the same resources.

> Homogeneous workloads such as all training or all inference are much easier to debug and tune from a system's perspective than a heterogeneous mix of both training and inference.

Improving Resource Guarantees

To safeguard against resource contention, Kubernetes lets you define resource requests and limits for pods. For example, you can specify that your training job requires 16 CPU cores and 64 GB of RAM. Kubernetes reserves requested resources for scheduling, but exclusive CPU core assignments require a CPU Manager `static` policy with `Guaranteed` pods and non-fractional (integer) CPU requests. Without this, CPU time sharing can still occur even when requests/limits are set.

These limits are enforced using Linux cgroups, so if your container exceeds its allocation, it can be throttled or even terminated by the OOM killer. It's common practice to use resource requests—and optionally the CPU Manager feature to pin cores—to ensure that performance-critical jobs get exclusive access to the necessary CPU resources so that other processes cannot steal CPU time from your reserved cores.

Another source of jitter is background kernel threads and interrupts, as we discussed in Chapter 2 in the context of using interrupt request (IRQ) affinity. Similar to Kubernetes, if other pods are using the same network or disks as your job, the other pods might cause a lot of interrupts and extra kernel work on the compute nodes that host your job. This will cause jitter and affect your job's performance.

Ideally, a GPU node is fully dedicated to your job. However, if it's not, you should ensure that the node is carefully partitioned using Linux cgroup controllers for I/O and CPU so that other workloads don't interfere.

Fortunately, Kubernetes supports CPU isolation, which ensures that pods get the dedicated CPU cores and memory they request—and prevents other pods from being scheduled on the same CPU core as yours. This avoids extra overhead from context switching and resource contention.

> In practice, performance-sensitive Kubernetes jobs should request all of the CPUs and GPUs of a given node so that nothing else interferes or contends with the jobs' resources. Easier said than done, but this is the ideal job configuration from a performance and consistency standpoint.

Memory Isolation and Avoiding the OOM Killer

Memory interference can also occur if not properly limited. Kubernetes provides first-class memory isolation support (using Linux cgroups). However, a greedy container, if unconstrained, could allocate too much memory on the host. This would cause the host to swap some of its memory to disk.

If an unbounded container uses too much memory on the host, the infamous Linux "OOM killer" will start killing processes—and potentially your Kubernetes job—even if your job wasn't the one using too much memory.

The OOM killer uses heuristics when deciding which pods to kill. Sometimes it decides to kill the largest running pod, which is likely your large training or inference job holding lots of data in CPU RAM to feed the GPUs. To avoid this, you can purposely not set strict memory limits on training or inference containers. This way, they can use all available memory, if needed.

With proper monitoring and alerting, you can ensure the job doesn't try to over-allocate beyond what you expect. If you do set a memory limit, make sure it's above what you actually expect to use. This provides a bit of headroom to avoid getting killed by the OOM killer three days into a long-running training job.

> In Kubernetes, a Pod with no requests/limits is treated as `BestEf fort` and is the most likely to be evicted. To obtain `Guaranteed` QoS, every container must set `requests == limits` for both CPU and memory. Setting a high limit alone will result in a `Burstable` QoS, not `Guaranteed`.

Dealing with I/O Isolation

As of this writing, Kubernetes does not offer native, first-class I/O isolation out of the box, unfortunately. While Linux does support I/O controls using cgroup controllers, Kubernetes itself does not automatically enforce I/O limits in the same way it does for CPU and memory.

If you need to ensure that heavy I/O workloads on a GPU node don't interfere with one another, you might need to manually configure I/O controls at the node level. This can involve adjusting the cgroup v2 I/O controller or using other OS-level configurations to partition I/O resources. In short, while Kubernetes prevents CPU contention through scheduling and resource requests, I/O isolation usually requires additional, manual tuning of the underlying Linux system.

It's important to note that, inside a container, some system settings are inherited from the host. For instance, if the host has CPU frequency scaling set to performance mode, the container will inherit that setting. But if the container is running in a virtualized environment such as a cloud instance, you might not be able to change these settings.

It's a good idea to always ensure that the host machine is tuned since containers can't change kernel parameters like hugepage settings or CPU governor limits. Usually, cluster admins set these parameters and settings through the base OS image. Or, in a Kubernetes environment, they might use something like the NVIDIA GPU Operator to set persistence mode and other `sysctl` knobs on each node.

Key Takeaways

Here is a list of key takeaways from this chapter, including optimizations across the operating system, driver, GPU, CPU, and container layers:

Data and compute locality is critical
   Ensure that data is stored and processed as close to the computation units as possible. Use local, high-speed storage such as NVMe SSD caches to minimize latency and reduce reliance on remote filesystems or network I/O.

Implement NUMA-aware configuration and CPU affinity

Optimize CPU-to-GPU data flow by aligning processes and memory allocations within the same NUMA node. Pin the CPU with tools like `numactl` and `taskset` prevents cross-node memory access. This will lead to lower latency and improved throughput.

Maximize GPU driver and runtime efficiency

Fine-tune the GPU driver settings, such as enabling persistence mode to keep GPUs in a ready state. Consider features like Multi-Process Service (MPS) for overlapping work from multiple processes on a single GPU. For multitenant environments, explore MIG partitions to isolate workloads effectively.

Prefetch and batch data effectively

Keep the GPUs fed by prefetching data ahead of time and batching small I/O operations into larger, more efficient reads. Leverage prefetching mechanisms like PyTorch's DataLoader `prefetch_factor` (along with `num_workers`) to load multiple batches in advance.

Pin memory when data loading

Combining data prefetching with memory pinning using PyTorch's DataLoader `pin_memory=True` uses pinned CPU memory (page-locked, not swappable to disk) for faster, asynchronous data transfers to the GPU. As a result, data loading and model execution can overlap, idle times are reduced, and both CPU and GPU resources are continuously utilized.

Optimize memory transfers

Leverage techniques such as pinned, page-locked memory and hugepages to accelerate data transfers between the host and GPU. This helps reduce copy over-head and allows asynchronous transfers to overlap with computations.

Overlap communication with computation

Reduce the waiting time for data transfers by overlapping memory operations like gradient synchronization and data staging with ongoing GPU computations. This overlap helps maintain high GPU utilization and better overall system efficiency.

Tune and scale the networking stack

In multinode environments, use RDMA-enabled networks (e.g., InfiniBand/Ethernet), and tune network settings such as TCP buffers, MTU, and interrupt affinities to maintain high throughput during distributed training and inference.

Use containerization and orchestration for consistency

Use container runtimes like Docker with the NVIDIA Container Toolkit and orchestration platforms like Kubernetes with the NVIDIA GPU Operator and device plugin so that the entire software stack—including drivers, CUDA libraries, and application code—is consistent across nodes. These solutions help align CPU-GPU affinities and manage resource allocation based on hardware topology.

Eliminate container runtime overhead

While containers increase reproducibility and ease of deployment, ensure that CPU and GPU affinities, host networking, and resource isolation are correctly configured to minimize any container overhead.

Use orchestration and scheduling best practices

Robust container orchestrators like Kubernetes are essential components for ensuring efficient resource allocation. Advanced scheduling techniques—such as the Kubernetes Topology Manager—help ensure that GPUs with fast interconnects are clustered together.

Strive for flexibility through dynamic adaptability and scaling

The orchestration layer distributes work and dynamically manages workload segmentation across nodes. This flexibility is crucial for both scaling up training tasks and ensuring efficient runtime in inference scenarios where data loads and request patterns vary widely.

Tune continuously and incrementally

System-level optimizations are not one-and-done. Regularly monitor performance metrics; adjust CPU affinities, batch sizes, and prefetch settings as workloads evolve; and use these small improvements cumulatively to achieve significant performance gains.

Reduce bottlenecks across the stack

The ultimate goal is to ensure that all components, from the OS and CPU to the GPU driver and runtime, work in harmony. Eliminating bottlenecks in one layer, such as CPU memory allocation or driver initialization, unlocks the full potential of the GPUs, which directly translates to faster training, lower costs, and more efficient resource usage.

Together, these strategies work to minimize data transfer friction, reduce wait times, and ensure that your hardware is used to its fullest potential for efficient training and inference.

Conclusion

This chapter has demonstrated that even the most advanced GPUs can be hindered by inefficiencies in their surrounding environment. A well-tuned operating system, container runtime, cluster orchestrator, and software stack form the backbone of high-performance AI systems. By aligning data with compute through NUMA-aware pinning and local storage solutions, overlapping communication with computation, and fine-tuning both the host system and GPU drivers, you can reduce latency and increase throughput.

Think of your entire system as a precision-engineered sports car where each component (CPU, memory, GPU, network, containers, orchestrators, and programming stack) must work seamlessly together to deliver maximum performance. Small tweaks, such as enabling persistence mode or optimizing CPU scheduling, may seem minor on their own, but when combined and scaled across a large GPU cluster, they can lead to substantial savings in time and cost. These optimizations ensure that GPUs are consistently operating near their peak efficiency when training massive transformer models and running complex inference pipelines.

As the field evolves and models continue to grow, the importance of system-level tuning will only increase. The techniques discussed in this chapter empower performance engineers and system architects to leverage every bit of hardware potential. This enables faster iteration cycles and more cost-effective AI deployments. Ultimately, a deeply optimized system accelerates research and makes cutting-edge AI applications more accessible to a broader audience.

Finally, remember that while the hardware and software stack may seem like an unmanageable amount of interconnected knobs and switches, small tweaks can translate into significant savings in time and cost. By continuously monitoring performance metrics and incrementally refining each layer of the stack, you can transform potential bottlenecks into opportunities for efficiency gains. Let the data guide you, and you will unlock the full potential of your AI system.

## CHAPTER 4

Tuning Distributed Networking Communication

In today's AI landscape, the need for seamless and low-latency data movement between GPUs, storage, and network interfaces is a must. In this chapter, we cover NVIDIA Magnum IO (e.g., NCCL, GPUDirect RDMA, GDS) for training and NIXL for disaggregated inference. We'll discuss these in the context of modern GPUs and clusters like the NVL72. You'll learn how these libraries—and their underlying supported hardware—form the critical fabric needed for ultrascale AI systems.

In large-scale systems, even the fastest GPUs can be hindered by inefficient communication and data transfer from memory and disk. We discuss strategies for speeding up data transfers, proper data sharding techniques, how to work directly with fast storage subsystems, and advanced patterns for overlapping communication and computation on GPUs. Overlapping communication and computation is a common pattern that we revisit frequently throughout our journey on AI systems performance engineering.

We explore the importance of overlapping communication and computation using components of NVIDIA's IO acceleration platform called Magnum IO (*https://oreil.ly/wyBGj*), which includes NCCL (*https://oreil.ly/1fI7h*), GPUDirect RDMA (*https://oreil.ly/PLZiQ*), and GPUDirect Storage (GDS) (*https://oreil.ly/m_YbJ*). We demonstrate how to use these libraries to lower communication latency, reduce CPU overhead, and maximize throughput across all layers of a multi-node, multi-GPU AI system.

High-level AI frameworks like PyTorch can use these low-level libraries to overlap computation with communication. Integrating these technologies into your AI system represents a holistic approach to accelerating communication and data pipelines for both training ultrascale models and scaling distributed inference servers to power applications with billions of users.

All of these optimizations ensure that every component is tuned for peak performance. Performance engineers need to carefully configure and tune the network and storage fabric to maintain a high level of GPU utilization and "goodput" (useful throughput).

Overlapping Communication and Computation (Pipelining)

Overlapping communication and computation, or *pipelining*, plays a key role in building efficient training and inference systems at scale. In these environments, it's important to keep GPUs busy and spend less time waiting for data.

The main idea is to ensure that data transfers occur concurrently with ongoing computations so that when one task finishes, the results needed for the next stage are already in progress or have been delivered. Modern frameworks such as PyTorch support asynchronous operations so that collective communication (e.g., all-reduce of gradients) can run alongside compute tasks. This reduces idle GPU time (see Figure 4-1)—and improves overall system throughput.

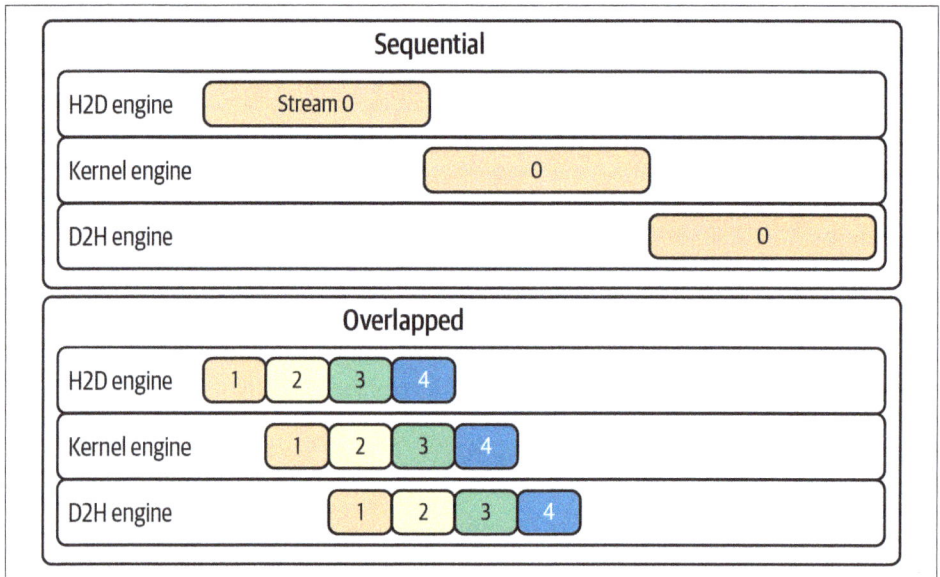

Figure 4-1. Overlapping host-to-device (H2D) and device-to-host (D2H) communication with computation on multiple CUDA streams 0–3

CUDA-based libraries exploit the power of multiple CUDA streams. While one stream executes compute-heavy matrix multiplications, another handles communication tasks such as aggregating gradients. As each layer of a neural network finishes its computation, the previous layer's outputs are already on their way for aggregation or further processing. This overlapping ensures that the system produces results without unnecessary waiting periods and maintains a steady flow of data.

Increasing the amount of compute performed between communication events can further minimize the relative overhead of communication. When the system processes larger batches of data, it performs more computation before needing to stop and exchange information.

In distributed training, for instance, this appears as gradient accumulation, where updates from several minibatches are combined into a single synchronization step. By reducing the frequency of communication events, the system lowers the overhead of each exchange and boosts overall throughput.

Another technique that supports seamless overlap between computation and communication is compression. Compression reduces the volume of data that needs to be transferred. For example, if a model compresses its gradients before sending them, the network moves a smaller amount of data. This reduces transfer time and eases congestion.

The shorter transfer time means that the communication phase is less disruptive to the computation phase. Although compression does not directly cause overlap, it shortens the window during which data moves across the network and allows computational work to continue in parallel more effectively.

Modern deep learning frameworks also split large tensor communications into smaller buckets to facilitate overlap. Frameworks like PyTorch automatically divide large gradients or activation tensors into several buckets that are transmitted as soon as they become available. Rather than waiting for an entire layer's gradients to be ready, for instance, portions of them can begin their all-reduce immediately.

By tuning bucket sizes and scheduling these transfers appropriately, one can achieve a higher degree of overlap and prevent communication delays from stalling the compute pipeline. Tools such as the PyTorch profiler and NVIDIA Nsight Systems offer insight into whether your computation and communication are overlapping, allowing engineers to adjust these parameters for maximal efficiency.

By combining larger batch sizes, gradient accumulation, asynchronous transfers, compression, and bucketing into one cohesive strategy, large, distributed AI models can overcome network limitations and reduce idle time. This design minimizes synchronization events while achieving high throughput and optimal GPU utilization.

The outcome of these optimizations is a training system that reduces overall training and inference time and makes more efficient use of available hardware resources. Engineers are freed from reinventing low-level networking routines and can focus on innovating model architectures and tuning higher-level parameters, rather than coding intricate data transfer mechanisms.

Asynchronous Execution with Streams

Achieving overlap fundamentally relies on asynchronous execution. GPUs support multiple streams, or queues of operations, that can execute concurrently or overlap if they target different resources. One stream can handle compute kernels such as matrix multiplies, while another stream handles communication such as data copies and all-reduce calls.

By assigning work to different streams and using nonblocking operations, communication can happen in the background. For example, an all-reduce operation can be launched to a separate stream without waiting for completion.

Meanwhile, the default stream proceeds with further computations on independent data. This requires that communication libraries such as NCCL use nonblocking calls that return control immediately. By doing this, the programmer ensures proper synchronization when needed.

In practice, AI frameworks hide most of this complexity. PyTorch's `DistributedData Parallel` automatically installs hooks on the backward pass so that each gradient bucket triggers an asynchronous NCCL all-reduce on a dedicated communication CUDA stream, while the default CUDA stream continues computing gradients for subsequent layers.

> We will dive deeper into CUDA streams in a later chapter, but just know that they are useful for overlapping communication and computation—and avoiding unnecessary synchronization points in your code.

This interleaving of computation and communication with CUDA streams creates a steady wave, or cascading pipeline, of work that hides communication latency and keeps the GPU busy at all times. To maintain proper overlapping, avoid unnecessary synchronization points with `torch.cuda.synchronize()` or inadvertently triggering a full device sync by moving tensors to the CPU with `torch.Tensor.item()`. If you do need to measure the overall iteration time, place a single synchronization at the very end of the iteration to wait for all outstanding GPU work to finish without disrupting the ongoing pipeline.

Reducing Communication Frequency and Volume

As noted, performing more work per communication step can increase overlap and efficiency. Gradient accumulation during model training is one such technique. Instead of all-reducing gradients for every single minibatch, you accumulate gradients over a few minibatches, sum them locally, and then do one all-reduce. This effectively trades off memory to store the unreduced gradients for fewer synchronization points.

Consider accumulating four minibatches; you cut the all-reduce frequency by 4×. This allows more computations to happen in between synchronizations. The downside is that your effective batch size increases. This can affect model convergence and memory usage. You can often find a sweet spot that creates a good balance between communication frequency, memory usage, and convergence.

Another approach to reduce communication volume is compressing or quantizing the data exchanged. Techniques like gradient compression can reduce the amount of data sent in each communication without significantly impacting model quality. Less data to send means faster transfers and more opportunity to hide those transfers behind computation. The extreme of this is sparsification. When using sparsity, you send only a fraction of the gradients. This typically requires algorithmic changes to preserve accuracy, however.

Bucketing, as implemented in PyTorch's Distributed Data Parallel (DDP) communication mechanism, also reduces per-call overhead by grouping many small tensors into larger messages. However, bucket sizing is a trade-off. Very large buckets maximize bandwidth utilization but delay the start of communication since you wait for more gradients to accumulate before kicking off the all-reduce. Very small buckets start transfers earlier but incur more overhead due to many small NCCL calls.

As of this writing, the default bucket size in PyTorch DDP is 25 MB. This is a balance that overlaps well in most cases. However, if you have a model with very large layers, you might increase this to reduce overhead. If you have a model with many small layers, you might actually benefit from smaller buckets to start communication sooner. Ultimately, achieving maximal overlap may require profiling different bucket sizes to see which yields the best iteration time.

Achieving Maximal Overlap in Practice

To see the benefit of overlapping communication with computation, let's run through an example that compares two scenarios in which one performs gradient communication synchronously after all computation with no overlap, and one where communication is overlapped with computation such as DDP. We'll simulate a simple distributed training step with two GPUs to illustrate the difference.

Suppose we don't use DDP's built-in overlap and instead implement distributed training manually such that each process computes all gradients locally, then performs an all-reduce on those gradients at the end of the backward pass. This will mimic the unoptimized, nonoverlapping scenario since communication happens only after all computation is done. We can simulate this using PyTorch's distributed primitives, disabling DDP's hooks, and explicitly calling `dist.all_reduce` after `loss.backward()`.

In the code that follows, we launch two processes on gpu/rank 0 and gpu/rank 1 on a single node, in this case, with a simple model. We'll run a forward and backward pass, then manually average gradients across the two processes:

```python
import torch
import torch.nn as nn
import torch.optim as optim
import torch.distributed as dist
import torch.multiprocessing as mp

# A simple model with multiple layers to produce multiple gradients
class MultiLayerNet(nn.Module):
    def __init__(self, size):
        super().__init__()
        self.fc1 = nn.Linear(size, size)
        self.fc2 = nn.Linear(size, size)
        self.fc3 = nn.Linear(size, 1)
    def forward(self, x):
        x = torch.relu(self.fc1(x))
        x = torch.relu(self.fc2(x))
        return self.fc3(x)

def train_no_overlap(rank, world_size):
    dist.init_process_group("nccl", init_method="env://",
                            world_size=world_size, rank=rank)
    torch.cuda.set_device(rank)

    # Each rank synthesizes its own data
    # (avoid sending big tensors via spawn)
    batch_size = 256
    data = torch.randn(batch_size, 1024, device=rank)
    target = torch.randn(batch_size, 1, device=rank)

    model = MultiLayerNet(data.size(1)).to(rank)
    optimizer = optim.SGD(model.parameters(), lr=0.01)

    # Forward + backward (manual, no overlap)
    output = model(data)
    loss = nn.functional.mse_loss(output, target)
    loss.backward()

    # Synchronous gradient all-reduce after backward
    for p in model.parameters():
        dist.all_reduce(p.grad, op=dist.ReduceOp.SUM)
```

```
                    p.grad /= world_size

            optimizer.step()
            dist.destroy_process_group()

    if __name__ == "__main__":
        import torch.multiprocessing as mp
        mp.set_start_method("spawn", force=True)
        world_size = min(2, torch.cuda.device_count() or 1)
        if world_size > 1:
            mp.spawn(train_no_overlap, args=(world_size,), nprocs=world_size,
                    join=True)
        else:
            train_no_overlap(0, 1)
```

In this code, each process computes gradients for MultiLayerNet independently. After loss.backward(), we explicitly perform an all-reduce for each parameter's gradient to average them. This is effectively what DDP does internally, but here we wait and do it after the entire backward pass has finished—rather than doing the all-reduce concurrently during the backward pass.

If we were to time this iteration, the all-reduce operations would add directly to the iteration time since it's not overlapping with any other steps. For example, say the forward and backward computations together take 10 ms and the gradient all-reduces take 12 ms. The total iteration time would be roughly 22 ms in this approach. In contrast, a fully overlapped implementation might achieve a total time closer to the max of these values, or 12 ms in our case. This is possible since the all-reduce communication can be almost completely hidden under the computation.

In practice, if we profile this no-overlap case with a tool like Nsight Systems, we would see all the backward computation kernels for fc1, fc2, and fc3 execute first, and only after they complete do we see NCCL all-reduce kernels for each gradient. There is a clear separation in which compute happens first, then communication. During the communication phase, the GPUs would be idle aside from the NCCL work since no further computations are happening.

Now let's use PyTorch's DDP to perform the same operation with overlap. DDP will hook into the backward pass and overlap gradient reduction with backward computation. The code is similar, but we simply wrap the model with DistributedData Parallel and let it handle synchronization:

```
import torch
import torch.nn as nn
import torch.optim as optim
import torch.distributed as dist
import torch.multiprocessing as mp

class MultiLayerNet(nn.Module):
    def __init__(self, size):
```

```
            super().__init__()
            self.fc1 = nn.Linear(size, size)
            self.fc2 = nn.Linear(size, size)
            self.fc3 = nn.Linear(size, 1)
        def forward(self, x):
            x = torch.relu(self.fc1(x))
            x = torch.relu(self.fc2(x))
            return self.fc3(x)

    def train_ddp(rank, world_size):
        rank = int(os.environ.get("LOCAL_RANK", rank))
        torch.cuda.set_device(rank)
        dist.init_process_group("nccl", init_method="env://",
                            world_size=world_size, rank=rank)
        torch.cuda.set_device(rank)

        model = MultiLayerNet(1024).to(rank)
        ddp_model = nn.parallel.DistributedDataParallel(model, device_ids=[rank])
        optimizer = optim.SGD(ddp_model.parameters(), lr=0.01)

        # Each rank makes its own data
        batch_size = 256
        data = torch.randn(batch_size, 1024, device=rank)
        target = torch.randn(batch_size, 1, device=rank)

        output = ddp_model(data)
        loss = nn.functional.mse_loss(output, target)
        loss.backward()  # DDP overlaps gradient all-reduce on background stream
        optimizer.step()
        dist.destroy_process_group()

    def main():
        world_size = min(2, torch.cuda.device_count() or 1)
        mp.set_start_method("spawn", force=True)
        if world_size > 1:
            mp.spawn(train_ddp, args=(world_size,), nprocs=world_size, join=True)
        else:
            print("Only one GPU present; running DDP demo with world_size=1")
            train_ddp(0, 1)

    if __name__ == "__main__":
        main()
```

With the DDP overlapping approach, the code is simpler since we rely on `Distribu
tedDataParallel` to handle gradient synchronization rather than writing it ourselves.
When `loss.backward()` is called, DDP's internal reducer splits the gradients into
buckets and launches NCCL all-reduce operations as soon as each bucket is ready on
a separate CUDA stream. For instance, it might all-reduce the `fc3.weight` and
`fc3.bias` gradients immediately after they are computed since those are from the last
layer and are computed last in the backward pass, while the `fc1` and `fc2` gradients

from earlier layers will have already been all-reduced by the time we reach the end of the backward pass.

If the model is very small such that all gradients fit into one bucket, DDP might do only one all-reduce at the end, which wouldn't overlap much. But with larger models and bigger batch sizes, there will be multiple buckets and significant overlap—showing even more impressive performance gains from this technique.

Profiling the DDP case would show NCCL all-reduce kernels interleaved with backward compute kernels. So instead of a clear two-phase split, we'd see a sawtooth pattern in the timeline with some compute happening, then some NCCL communication happening, then compute, and so on.

Key signs of good overlap are that the total iteration time is lower than the sum of compute + comm times, and the GPU is rarely idle waiting for communication because the all-reduces happen during the compute, as shown in Table 4-1.

Table 4-1. The benefit of overlap

Metric	No overlap (manual sync)	Overlap (DDP)	Notes
Total backward + comm time	100% (baseline)	~70% of baseline	e.g., 30% faster per iteration due to overlap (illustrative)
Comm start time	After backward complete	During backward	In DDP, comm begins midway through backward
GPU idle during comm phase	Yes—after backward, GPUs wait during all-reduce	Minimal—comm runs while other layers still computing	DDP hides most of the latency
SM (GPU) utilization	Lower (some cycles where SMs idle during comm)	Higher (continuous activity)	Overlap keeps GPU busy more consistently
Overlap achieved (% of comm covered by compute)	0% (serial execution)	~50% (or more)	Rough estimate: larger models or batches can overlap more

> Note: The numeric values in all metrics tables are illustrative to explain the concepts. For actual benchmark results on different GPU architectures, see the GitHub repository (*https://github.com/ cfregly/ai-performance-engineering*).

In this example, overlapping communication with computation yields roughly a 30% iteration time improvement in our example workload. In larger training jobs, the gains would be more substantial since larger models create more potential for communication bottlenecks. PyTorch `DistributedDataParallel` uses 25 MiB buckets by default. This way, it launches an all-reduce for each bucket as soon as it is ready. Tuning `bucket_cap_mb` can help increase overlap for your specific model topology, but larger buckets increase latency for the last bucket.

The takeaway is that a well-tuned DDP should overlap most of the gradient communication with computation. Often the only portion of communication that cannot be overlapped is the tail end, or the last gradient bucket, if it happens to finish after the last compute. Research efforts (*https://oreil.ly/DAmDl*) are ongoing to even overlap the optimizer step with communication or to use techniques like tensor partitioning to achieve further overlap, but PyTorch's DDP's default overlap strategy is often described as *wait-free backpropagation* (WFBP), which bucketizes gradients and launches reductions as soon as each bucket is ready.

It's worth noting that certain coding patterns can inadvertently eliminate overlap. For instance, if you perform any operation that forces a synchronization between backward and the next iteration, you will stall the computation until all communications are done.

> Avoid operations that inadvertently move tensors from the GPU to the CPU (e.g., calling .item() on a tensor) until you're sure that all asynchronous GPU work is finished. Otherwise, you will force a synchronization, stall the computation, and slow down your training or inference workload. This typically happens when adding print() or log() statements for debugging. These can be disastrous for performance.

You should move such operations to a separate stream if possible. Also, manual calls to torch.cuda.synchronize() should be minimized and used only for accurate benchmarking—or when required for correctness. Otherwise, they will serialize GPU work and negatively impact performance. DDP's design and PyTorch's operations are already asynchronous and handle dependencies correctly. Explicit synchronization is rarely needed in user code.

In summary, overlapping computation and communication is one of the most effective techniques for distributed performance engineering. Properly utilized, it can significantly reduce training time by hiding communication latencies behind useful work.

In the following sections, we'll explore the software and hardware infrastructure that makes this possible and how to ensure you're getting the maximum overlap on modern systems. Next, we will overview NVIDIA's Magnum IO stack, which includes technologies that make overlapping of compute and communication possible.

NVIDIA Magnum IO Optimization Stack

Magnum IO (*https://oreil.ly/h62IL*), NVIDIA's overarching I/O acceleration platform, brings together a range of technologies to speed up data movement, access, and management across GPUs, CPUs, storage, and network interfaces. There are four key components of the Magnum IO architecture spanning storage, network, in-network computing, and I/O management, as shown in Figure 4-2.

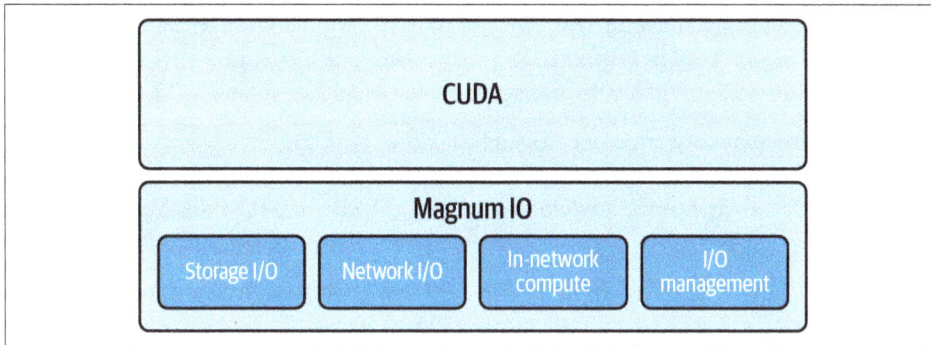

Figure 4-2. Four components of NVIDIA's Magnum IO acceleration platform

Here is a description of the four components in Figure 4-2:

Storage I/O
This is implemented by technologies such as NVIDIA GPUDirect Storage (GDS) (*https://oreil.ly/UshxS*) and BlueField SNAP (*https://oreil.ly/NWwDh*). These let GPUs access storage including NVMe SSDs directly without unnecessary copies through host CPU memory. We'll dive deeper into GDS in Chapter 5.

Network I/O
This includes technologies like GPUDirect RDMA (*https://oreil.ly/PLZiQ*), NCCL (*https://oreil.ly/1fI7h*), NVSHMEM (*https://oreil.ly/gb7TB*), UCX (*https://oreil.ly/webTn*), and HPC-X (*https://oreil.ly/fzD1D*) (MPI/SHMEM software bundle) to enable direct, high-speed data transfers between GPUs across nodes, bypassing the CPU for internode communication.

In-network compute
SHARP performs in-network reductions inside Quantum-class InfiniBand switches. The reduction arithmetic happens in the switch silicon. BlueField DPUs offload networking and can host control services such as the Subnet Manager and the SHARP Aggregation Manager. When the NCCL RDMA SHARP plugin is enabled and the fabric has SHARP firmware and an active Aggregation Manager, eligible collectives can be offloaded to the IB switches, reducing host and GPU overhead. We will cover NVIDIA SHARP in more detail in a bit.

Ethernet-based GPU clusters rely on technologies like RoCEv2 for RDMA but generally lack features like SHARP. This is one of the reasons that many ultrascale AI systems use InfiniBand or similar high-performance interconnects instead of Ethernet. SHARP provides a significant performance boost and should be utilized when available.

I/O management

Tools like NVIDIA NetQ (*https://oreil.ly/L0LZO*) and Unified Fabric Manager (UFM) (*https://oreil.ly/ipWHb*) fall in this category, providing real-time telemetry, diagnostics, and lifecycle management for the data center's I/O fabric.

These components work together through flexible APIs and SDKs that hide much of the low-level complexity. Magnum IO's goal is to maximize end-to-end throughput for large-scale AI and data analytics workloads. Magnum IO continues to evolve alongside new hardware.

Magnum IO now integrates support for NVLink Switch network domains, which enables intra-rack GPU communication at fabric scale. It also leverages advancements in InfiniBand (Quantum-2 and Quantum-X800 families) and Ethernet (Spectrum-X) to further reduce communication overhead.

Throughout this chapter, we will dive into several of these components such as RDMA for network transfers, NCCL for collectives, NIXL for inference data movement, and GDS for efficient data loading. Additionally, we will see how to profile and tune each of them. Let's dive right into it!

High-Speed, Low-Overhead Data Transfers with RDMA

RDMA is a technology optimized for low-latency, high-throughput data transfers. RDMA works by allowing direct memory-to-memory communication between devices without burdening the CPU with unnecessary data-copy operations. In a nutshell, RDMA bypasses much of the traditional kernel network stack and allows a NIC to directly read/write application memory. This avoids CPU involvement in each packet and reduces context switches and buffer copies. Prefer RDMA paths where available and verified. And always confirm (and continuously reconfirm) with logs and microbenchmarks that the RDMA data path is active.

In container environments like Docker and Kubernetes, ensure the container has direct access to the host's InfiniBand devices (e.g., /dev/infiniband). Otherwise, NCCL may silently fall back (*https://oreil.ly/KMG9t*) to TCP sockets instead of GPU-Direct RDMA—and without any obvious errors to highlight the degradation. This results in throughput dropping from tens of GB/s to only a few Gb/s, with no obvious error messages.

A related container pitfall arises when the container's GID assignments don't match the host, as in some "rdma-shared" Docker images. This prevents GPUDirect registration and uses CPU-driven RDMA copies instead of using true GPU-based RDMA.

> Always verify that it is true GPUDirect RDMA. Confirm that the kernel module is loaded with `lsmod | grep nvidia_peermem`, and check `dmesg` for initialization. For an end-to-end check, run NCCL with `NCCL_DEBUG=INFO` to confirm NET/IB paths and use RDMA perftests with `--use_cuda` to validate GPU-to-GPU transfers. Verifying will help prevent stealthy (*https://oreil.ly/SIGy5*) performance degradations.

The reduced throughput would show up in the profiler as an order-of-magnitude reduction in throughput. But you have to be aware of this possibility and continuously monitor your system for these types of subtle fallbacks.

NVIDIA's RDMA implementation for GPUs is called GPUDirect RDMA. GPUDirect RDMA lets an RDMA-capable NIC such as InfiniBand and RDMA over Converged Ethernet (RoCE) (*https://oreil.ly/o6YJp*) perform direct memory access (DMA) to and from the GPU's device memory across two servers—bypassing host CPU and system RAM entirely. A data transfer with RoCE is shown in Figure 4-3.

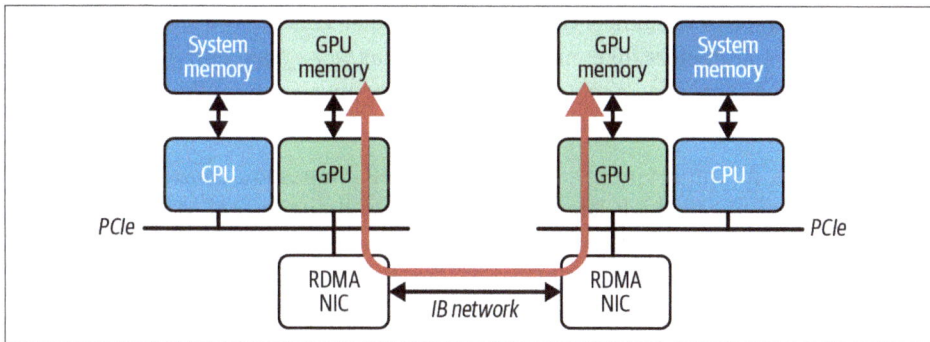

Figure 4-3. GPU-to-GPU direct data transfer with RoCE

By registering GPU buffers with the NIC, GPUDirect RDMA enables one-sided RDMA reads and writes between remote GPUs. This minimizes both latency and CPU overhead in multinode training.

RDMA is supported inherently by InfiniBand and also by some high-speed Ethernet networks through RoCE. With RoCE, you get RDMA-like zero-copy transfers over Ethernet, assuming the network gear supports RDMA and is properly configured for it. Using RDMA with RoCE usually requires a properly configured system with the necessary drivers, including NVIDIA OFED for InfiniBand/RoCE.

The performance difference between using RDMA versus standard TCP/IP networking can be huge. For example, a modern InfiniBand link might provide latency on the order of a few microseconds for a small message, whereas standard TCP over Ethernet might incur 5–10× higher latency.

For large transfers that are network-bandwidth-bound, RDMA on InfiniBand can sustain very high throughput on the order of hundreds of Gbps. In contrast, a typical TCP/IP network might be limited by kernel overhead and NIC speed—often 100 Gbps or less unless using 200–400 Gbps Ethernet with RDMA capabilities. TCP/IP networks also incur more overhead.

In distributed deep learning, large-message throughput tends to matter more than tiny message latency since gradients are large, for instance. Both high bandwidth and low latency keep the protocol efficient—and the GPUs busy.

If you only have Ethernet available, you should use the highest bandwidth and lowest-latency configuration possible. For instance, 200+ Gbps Ethernet with RDMA (RoCE) will perform much better for all-reduce traffic than a basic 10–25 Gbps TCP network. At a minimum, ensure you are using jumbo frames such as MTU 9000. Enabling this configuration for your cluster network, data transfers will send fewer large packets instead of many small ones. This reduces CPU overhead and improves efficiency similarly to how larger disk block sizes improve sequential disk throughput.

Also, it's important to tune the TCP stack for a similar reason. You should verify that Linux `sysctl` parameters like `net.core.rmem_max`/`wmem_max` and the autotuning ranges `net.ipv4.tcp_rmem`/`tcp_wmem` are set high enough to fully utilize a high-bandwidth link.

And, of course, it's important to use a modern TCP congestion control algorithm to improve throughput on high-latency links. On a well-engineered, dedicated cluster network with no external internet traffic, the default CUBIC (*https://oreil.ly/Oj-tR*) congestion control typically performs adequately since it's engineered to avoid congestion.

> For any high latency-bandwidth links, consider using a modern TCP congestion algorithm like Bottleneck Bandwidth and Round-trip propagation time (BBR (*https://oreil.ly/qnlRG*)) and adjust buffer sizes to ensure full utilization. Always validate that the default settings are not limiting throughput. Use tools like `sysctl net.ipv4.tcp_congestion_control` to inspect and tune the setting.

In cloud or hybrid environments, be cautious of whether you truly have a controlled high-speed connection. For example, if you use AWS EC2 instances with Elastic Fabric Adapter (EFA), you get something similar to InfiniBand-level RDMA between instances deployed in the same "placement group." But if you try to run a multinode training or inference job that spans both an on-premises data center and the cloud without direct connectivity, your traffic will likely traverse the public internet. This will introduce unpredictable latency and congestion.

> Always ensure your multinode setup is on a properly configured, high-performance, low-congestion network. Work directly with your cloud provider to understand every hop in the network architecture.

Even when using RDMA, the CPU is not completely out of the picture. The host still sets up RDMA transfers and handles communication-completion events. Therefore, proper CPU affinity is important. Remember to pin the network interrupt handling—or polling threads—to a CPU core on the same NUMA node as the NIC and, ideally, the GPU as well. For example, if an InfiniBand host channel adapter is on NUMA node 0, bind its interrupt CPU affinity cores to node 0. This reduces cross-NUMA traffic and latency for control operations.

Tuning Multinode Connectivity

For distributed, multinode training with GPUs, it is crucial to ensure that the network is not a bottleneck. This involves using the right communication and networking technologies as previously described—as well as configuring these technologies properly. Here are some tips to adopt and pitfalls to avoid:

Understand the topology
Use `nvidia-smi topo -m` to get a basic GPU interconnect view, but for NVSwitch- and NVLink-based systems, it's recommended to also use `nvidia-smi nvlink` or Nsight Systems to understand multihop switch fabric connectivity.

Leverage NVLink Switch domains if available
The multinode NVIDIA's GB200 and GB300 NVL72 rack solutions connect up to 72 GPUs in a single NVLink domain using NVLink Switch, which provides extremely low per-hop latency—on the order of a few hundred nanoseconds. The GB200 NVL72 architecture provides up to ~130 TB/s of all-to-all bandwidth with submicrosecond latencies across all GPUs in the rack. If your cluster includes such infrastructure, make sure your jobs are placed within the same NVLink domain to fully utilize this ultrafast interconnect. This can significantly reduce the need for slower InfiniBand and Ethernet communication between nodes. Fortunately, modern InfiniBand switches such as NVIDIA's Quantum series provide up to 800 Gb/s per link and in-network computing features. However,

NVLink's massive intra-rack bandwidth and < 1μs latency are preferred. Keep traffic on NVLink/NVSwitch whenever possible.

Use RDMA whenever possible

If running on InfiniBand or RoCE-capable hardware, make sure your communication library, such as NCCL, is actually using RDMA. NCCL will automatically use GPUDirect RDMA if available. But if RDMA is misconfigured or unsupported, NCCL may silently fall back to TCP. One red flag for this is if you notice that during all-reduce operations, GPU utilization drops and CPU utilization spikes. This indicates that the CPU is copying data for communications.

Aggregate bandwidth with multiple NICs if available

Some servers have multiple network interfaces (NICs). NCCL can stripe traffic across multiple NICs (called *multirail*) to increase bandwidth. But you may need to set some environment variables like `NCCL_NSOCKS_PERTHREAD` and `NCCL_SOCKET_NTHREADS` to optimize this. We'll discuss these in more detail in a bit. Just make sure that each NIC is on a different subnet and that NCCL can discover both. With proper setup, using two 800 Gbps NICs in parallel, for instance, gives an aggregate of 1.6 Tbps for NCCL traffic. And four such NIC links (e.g., two dual-port NICs) can achieve ~3.2 Tbps.

Utilize optimized "direct NIC" mode when available

Favor high-bandwidth, multirail NIC configurations that give each GPU or small groups of GPUs sufficient dedicated network bandwidth. Physically, NICs attach using PCIe to the host CPU or to a DPU. With modern GPU systems, NCCL supports GPU-initiated networking with InfiniBand GPUDirect Async (IBGDA) and the direct NIC path, as shown in Figure 4-4. This lets the GPU drive full-bandwidth RDMA without CPU intervention.

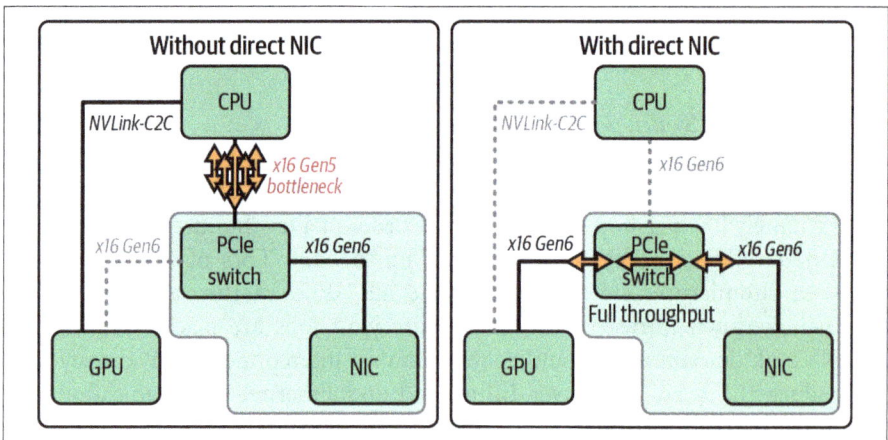

Figure 4-4. Bypassing CPU bottlenecks with direct connectivity between GPUs and NICs

Check for misconfigurations

A common pitfall is a mismatch in network configuration that causes a fallback to a slower path. If RDMA is not working due to a misconfiguration, for instance, NCCL might be using TCP on a 100 Gbps Ethernet network but getting only a fraction of that due to kernel overhead. Even worse, if the cluster's high-speed network is misidentified, traffic might go over a slower management network running only 10 Gbps Ethernet without the user realizing. Tools like NCCL's debugging output and network interface counters (`ibstat`, `ifstat`) can help verify which interface is being used more heavily. For modern systems with large 200–400 Gbps paths, dropping to 10 Gbps would cause a severe bottleneck.

Multinode Communication Pitfalls

Scaling training across multiple nodes in a cluster introduces a new class of pitfalls. Here we highlight a few common issues and demonstrate how to fix them with concrete examples.

Pitfall #1: Using a CPU-bound Gloo backend instead of NCCL

PyTorch's distributed framework supports multiple backends for communication. For multi-GPU training, NCCL is the preferred backend for NVIDIA GPUs, but there is also a fallback backend called Gloo, which uses CPUs and TCP sockets. If one mistakenly initializes `ProcessGroup` with Gloo for GPU training—or if NCCL fails to initialize and it falls back to Gloo, the training will still function correctly but all cross-GPU communication will go through the CPU and Ethernet stack. This results in extremely slow performance.

Unfortunately, it's fairly common to accidentally use this misconfiguration since the code appears to work normally and not crash. It just runs an order of magnitude slower and requires either a profiler or careful log analysis to detect. In summary, always specify NCCL for multi-GPU, CUDA-based training to utilize high-performance GPU collectives. In modern PyTorch, when a backend is omitted, the selection is inferred by device type (`nccl` for CUDA tensors, `gloo` for CPU tensors). However, it's recommended to always be explicit. This way, you improve reproducibility and debugging clarity.

Let's illustrate this with code. We'll simulate two processes running on gpu/rank 0 and gpu/rank 1 on two different "nodes" connected with an 800 Gb/s (100 GB/s) Infini-Band interconnect and perform a large all-reduce of a tensor. First, we intentionally use the Gloo backend (CPU bound) for PyTorch distributed communication as shown here:

```
# dist_allreduce.py

#!/usr/bin/env python
```

```python
import os
import argparse
import torch
import torch.distributed as dist

def main():
    parser = argparse.ArgumentParser(description="Multi-node Gloo all-reduce")
    parser.add_argument(
        "--data-size",
        type=int,
        default=1024 * 1024 * 100,  # 100M floats ≈ 400 MB
        help="Number of elements in the tensor",
    )
    args = parser.parse_args()

    # Initialize the default ProcessGroup over env://
    # (uses MASTER_ADDR, MASTER_PORT, etc.)
    dist.init_process_group(backend="gloo", init_method="env://")

    rank = dist.get_rank()
    world_size = dist.get_world_size()

    # Allocate a large CPU tensor (Gloo is CPU-bound)
    tensor = torch.ones(args.data_size,
        dtype=torch.float32, device="cpu")

    # Warm up and barrier
    dist.barrier()

    # All-reduce (sum) across all ranks
    dist.all_reduce(tensor, op=dist.ReduceOp.SUM)

    # Barrier
    dist.barrier()

    ...

    dist.destroy_process_group()

if __name__ == "__main__":
    main()
```

In this code, we intentionally chose backend="gloo". The tensor (400 MB) is allocated on the CPU for each rank (device="cpu") because Gloo is CPU-bound. When
you use Gloo, collectives operate on CPU memory and communicate over TCP. If
you instead attempt GPU tensors with Gloo, PyTorch will stage through the CPU and
be limited by that path. Either way, the result is far slower than NCCL on GPUs. This
is inefficient compared to letting GPUs talk directly using RDMA.

In the preceding code, we intentionally chose `backend="gloo"`. If you attempt `dist.all_reduce()` with a Gloo process group, the run will either fall back to host-staged paths or fail depending on the build. This defeats the point of measuring GPU collectives.

Running this code with proper timing would yield the following:

```
Rank0: All-reduce of 400.0 MB took 200.00 ms (2 GB/s)
```

For 400 MB of data, 200 ms is quite slow since this is 2 GB/s aggregated throughput—far below expectations or 100 GB/s for our 800 Gb/s InfiniBand hardware that we're using in this example. This indicates a lot of extra overhead incurred on the CPU path. We confirm this by profiling the CPU utilization, which, in this case, is near 100%.

Let's change the backend to NCCL and see the difference. We simply set `back end='nccl'` and ensure the environment is configured to allow GPU-direct communication. Assuming NCCL is properly configured, this code will use direct GPU-to-GPU communication. The improvement is dramatic. Running the updated code with timing would show something like the following:

```
Rank0: All-reduce of 400.0 MB took 4.00 ms (100 GB/s)
```

Here, we see 4 ms for 400 MB, which is 100 GB/s. This is two orders of magnitude faster—and running at the line rate limit of our 800 Gb/s InfiniBand hardware. This is far better than the 2 GB/s we saw earlier with Gloo. This demonstrates how crucial it is to use NCCL for GPU multinode communication. Using the wrong backend can degrade performance significantly. In short, use `backend="nccl"` so that collectives run on the GPU with GPUDirect RDMA when available.

> You can verify the backend in PyTorch by calling `torch.distributed.get_backend()`.

From a GPU's perspective, NCCL's all-reduce collective is done by the GPU using direct memory access to the other GPU's memory. As such, the GPU stays busy doing communication. Either the SMs will be executing some network-copy kernels or the GPU's DMA engines will be active. In contrast, with Gloo, the GPU was essentially idle during the communication since the CPU was involved and the GPU had to wait for data to travel through the CPU's memory buffers over TCP instead of InfiniBand.

In a production cluster environment with multiple NICs, you should explicitly set `NCCL_SOCKET_IFNAME=ib0` so that NCCL's initial TCP handshake runs over the InfiniBand host channel adapter (HCA). This ensures it bootstraps correctly and then hands off to GPUDirect RDMA on the fastest path. Otherwise, you may see failed connections or, worse, silently fall back to a much slower interface. Be sure that all nodes can reach one another over the selected interconnect.

Pitfall #2: Mismatched NCCL versions

If you run PyTorch's bundled NCCL (e.g., `torch.cuda.nccl.version() == ()`) against a different version of the system-installed `libnccl`, you will hang the system. Or worse, you will silently fall back to a slower implementation. This can be difficult to detect. Make sure you have alignment by matching `nvidia-nccl-cu*` packages or rebuilding PyTorch against the system NCCL and avoid these compatibility pitfalls (*https://oreil.ly/2ptHR*).

Pitfall #3: TCP port exhaustion during NCCL bootstrap

NCCL uses ephemeral TCP ports for its out-of-band setup, and if your OS's `net.ipv4.ip_local_port_range` is too narrow, you can exhaust available ports, causing failed or stalled handshakes. It's recommended that you widen your port range in `/proc/sys/net/ipv4/ip_local_port_range` (e.g., `50000 51000`) to avoid hidden bootstrap failures (*https://oreil.ly/6JXVI*). Note that modern NCCL versions have improved bootstrap handling, but it's still best to proactively set a broad port range on large clusters.

Pitfall #4: Insufficient network bandwidth or misconfigured NICs

Another multinode pitfall is simply not having enough network bandwidth for the amount of data being synced—or not using all of the available interfaces. This pitfall becomes more common as GPU clusters scale. For example, saturating a single 400 Gbps link per node is easy with Blackwell GPUs.

When profiling your workload under these unfortunate conditions, you will observe that scaling to multiple nodes significantly slows down training. In other words, the "per-GPU throughput" will drop. In this case, check the network links.

It's often useful to monitor the network throughput using `nvidia-smi dmon`, for instance, to collect NVLink/PCIe/Network statistics. You can also use built-in tools like `ethtool -S <iface>` or `ip -s link show <iface>` for byte/packet counters, or launch interactive monitors such as `iftop` or `nload` to watch live NIC throughput.

You can also try to utilize multiple interfaces, if available. If you're saturating an 800 Gbps (100 GB/s) InfiniBand link, for instance, and your job needs more network throughput, consider enabling NCCL's multi-NIC support—assuming that you have multiple NICs. Make sure that `NCCL_NSOCKS_PERTHREAD` and `NCCL_SOCKET_NTHREADS` are tuned, as these tune NCCL's socker/TCP transport path.

In cases with multiple NICs, increasing these environment variable values from their platform-dependent defaults can help utilize both NICs. For example, if you have two NICs, you might set `NCCL_NSOCKS_PERTHREAD=2` and keep `NCCL_SOCKET_NTHREADS=2` (since 2 threads × 2 sockets = 4 total connections per process). However, do not arbitrarily increase these values. Remember that the product of threads and sockets should not exceed 64 per NVIDIA guidance (*https://oreil.ly/bnv7N*) since more threads mean more CPU usage.

`NCCL_NSOCKS_PERTHREAD` and `NCCL_SOCKET_NTHREADS` are useful when socket transport is in use, but they are not the primary tuning knobs for RDMA/InfiniBand data paths. For IB/RDMA tuning, focus on fabric health and NCCL IB settings such as `NCCL_IB_HCA`, `NCCL_IB_GID_INDEX`, and related transport policies.

> Increase these thread-related settings stepwise (e.g., 2 → 4 → 8), and continuously measure the throughput. Too many threads will contend for resources and potentially diminish returns. Always validate configuration changes with NCCL debug and performance-profiling tools.

Pitfall #5: Straggler nodes or processes

In multinode training, the slowest node, or GPU, will determine the overall pace because synchronization needs to wait for every node and GPU to respond. If one machine has a slower network link, or is overloaded with other tasks, it will slow down the entire job.

To avoid stragglers, it's important to use homogeneous hardware and dedicated cluster resources for each training job, if possible. This way, your environment is predictable. If you're running in a cloud environment, for instance, mixing different instance types or using different switch fabrics can introduce variability.

Using monitoring tools like NVIDIA's DCGM or InfiniBand counters on each node can help spot if one node has degraded performance due to NIC link flapping or GPU thermal throttling. Modern monitoring tools like PyTorch's `torch.distributed.monitored_barrier` and NCCL's asynchronous error handling should be used to detect these types of issues quickly.

Pitfall #6: GPU memory fragmentation under UCX/RDMA

PyTorch's caching allocator holds onto GPU memory across iterations. In distributed settings using UCX/RDMA, these long-lived allocations can exhaust registration pools or fragment memory, causing sporadic allocation failures or performance cliffs. Monitoring `torch.cuda.memory_reserved()` versus `memory_allocated()` helps surface these edge cases (*https://oreil.ly/XFyri*):

```python
import torch
import torch.distributed as dist
import os
import time

def log_mem(iteration):
    reserved = torch.cuda.memory_reserved()
    allocated = torch.cuda.memory_allocated()
    print(f"[Iter {iteration:02d}] Reserved: {reserved/1e9:.3f} GB, "
          f"Allocated: {allocated/1e9:.3f} GB")

def run(rank, world_size):
    # Standard DDP / UCX init
    dist.init_process_group(backend="nccl", init_method="env://")
    rank = int(os.environ["LOCAL_RANK"])
    torch.cuda.set_device(rank)

    # Pre-allocate a big buffer that UCX will register once and hold
    big_buffer = torch.empty(int(2e8), device=rank)  # ~0.8 GB
    log_mem(0)

    for i in range(1, 11):
        # Simulate per-iteration tensor allocations of varying size
        small = torch.randn(int(1e7), device=rank)  # ~40 MB
        medium = torch.randn(int(5e7), device=rank) # ~200 MB

        # Free them explicitly to return to allocator cache
        del small, medium
        torch.cuda.synchronize()

        # Log memory after freeing
        log_mem(i)

        # Barrier so all ranks print in sync
        dist.barrier()
        time.sleep(0.1)

    dist.destroy_process_group()

if __name__ == "__main__":
    run(0, 1)
```

The output code show how the reserved memory grows each iteration as the caching allocator holds onto freed blocks. This speeds up future allocations. However, it never returns them to the OS or UCX registration pool. Allocated memory drops back to zero after each free, since no live tensors remain:

```
[Iter 00] Reserved: 0.800 GB, Allocated: 0.800 GB
[Iter 01] Reserved: 1.040 GB, Allocated: 0.000 GB
[Iter 02] Reserved: 1.240 GB, Allocated: 0.000 GB
...
[Iter 10] Reserved: 1.240 GB, Allocated: 0.000 GB
```

To mitigate this situation, be sure to upgrade to the latest CUDA runtime. You can also try using `torch.cuda.empty_cache()` as a last resort to recover from fragmentation issues. However, `empty_cache()` is not a long-term solution. Some long-term solutions include tuning the allocator, tracking down the issue, and fixing it.

Let's summarize multinode pitfalls as follows: always use NCCL for GPU communication, ensure RDMA/high-speed network is active, utilize all available bandwidth (multiple NICs if possible), use the latest NCCL that ships with CUDA to inherit the latest fixes, and watch out for any configuration that would cause a fallback to slower communication. In the next sections, we focus on NCCL specifics and how to optimize intranode and internode GPU communication.

NCCL for Distributed Multi-GPU Communication

NVIDIA NCCL is a many-to-many communication library for operations, called *collectives*, used by groups of GPUs to share data. NCCL underpins most multi-GPU training workloads in NVIDIA's ecosystem.

NCCL provides optimized implementations of collective communication operations like all-reduce, all-gather, broadcast, and reduce-scatter that scale from a few GPUs to many thousands and, someday, millions. When performing model training and inference across multiple GPUs, data such as model weights, gradients, and activations must be exchanged quickly to keep the GPUs busy. NCCL is the library that orchestrates these exchanges efficiently.

During distributed training, each GPU computes gradients on its portion of data. NCCL is then used to perform an all-reduce of these gradients across all GPUs such that each GPU updates the model weights with the averaged gradients.

During distributed inference, GPUs need to exchange activations and other intermediate results.

In the inference case, some frameworks use NCCL's send() and recv(), but many deployments prefer transports exposed using UCX or specialized libraries like NIXL for lower tail latency and better overlap.

NCCL is optimized for NVIDIA GPUs and supports communication over various interconnects such as PCIe, NVLink, NVSwitch, InfiniBand, and TCP sockets. It will automatically choose the fastest path available between any two GPUs.

Complementing NCCL is the newer NVIDIA Inference Xfer Library (NIXL), which is optimized for inference and point-to-point transfers like KV cache movement.

NIXL provides pluggable storage backends, including POSIX files and GPUDirect Storage (GDS). Object-store support such as Amazon S3 is provided through its object-store plugin and is deployment-dependent. These plugins move KV cache fragments between the memory hierarchy and the storage backends when appropriate. We'll cover NIXL in depth in a bit—as well as in future chapters focused on tuning inference workloads.

> Many inference deployments now favor NIXL for these point-to-point transfers due to its lower latency, as described later. However, NCCL send() and recv() are still available, as well. However, they are not as optimized as NIXL for minimal latency. In practice, large-scale inference workloads prefer NIXL for one-to-one transfers due to its lower overhead and latency, whereas NCCL send/recv is used more rarely when custom integration is needed.

Topology Awareness in NCCL

Topology awareness plays a major role in NCCL's performance. NCCL detects how GPUs are physically connected and optimizes its communication pattern accordingly. For example, in a system of fully connected NVLink and NVSwitches, every GPU will communicate with every other GPU using these high-speed interconnects.

While NCCL can use a simple pattern communication like ring all-reduce to communicate with each link equally, it will automatically use a topology-aware hierarchical communication pattern to maximize communication performance. For systems with multiple NUMA node domains, for instance, NCCL might first do an intranode reduce, then a cross-node reduce, then an intranode broadcast, which is effectively a hierarchical all-reduce. The goal is to maximize traffic over the fastest interconnects.

Concretely, consider a topology in which GPUs 0–1 share an NVLink connection and GPUs 2–3 share another NVLink connection. However, any communication between the 0–1 pair and the 2–3 pair must go over a lower PCIe interconnect. In this case, NCCL's hierarchy algorithm will perform the reduce collective on each NVLink-connected pair first, then do a reduce exchange across the PCIe link with one GPU from each pair, then distribute the data within each pair again. This way, the slow PCIe link handles only a fraction of the data.

NCCL will usually choose the most performant approach when it detects such topologies. However, in some cases, the automatic detection might not activate, for instance, if the topology choices are comparable—or if the message sizes are small, etc. It is possible to override NCCL's algorithm selection with the environment variable NCCL_ALGO (e.g., NCCL_ALGO=NVLS,NVLSTree,Tree,Ring,PAT, etc.), but generally

NCCL does a good job of automatically choosing the best path based on the topology. Manual override is usually only for specific situations like troubleshooting, research experiments, and more.

To illustrate topology effects on NCCL, consider a scenario with four GPUs on a system with two PCIe switches (GPUs 0–1 on one switch, 2–3 on another). A naive all-reduce using a single ring over all four GPUs would end up passing a lot of data over the PCIe interswitch link. This would be a major communication bottleneck. In contrast, a hierarchical approach with two separate rings of 0–1 and 2–3 combined with an exchange between one GPU from each ring/pair would reduce the communication pressure. In practice, NCCL would choose this communication pattern under the hood if it detects the slower link in the topology.

A quick experiment with profiling tools can reveal if NCCL is topology-optimized. Using Nsight Systems or NCCL traces, you will see multiple NCCL CUDA kernels when hierarchy is used. For instance, you would see some intragroup all-reduce kernels and some intergroup kernels. We will also see performance differences. For example, the nonoptimized, topology-unaware algorithm will achieve on the order of tens of GB/s per GPU because one stage of the all-reduce goes over the slower PCIe link, whereas the topology-aware algorithm can achieve hundreds of GB/s per GPU by utilizing NVLink fully and minimizing PCIe usage.

Consider a naive approach: GPUs waiting on the PCIe interconnect measuring only 60% SM utilization and a total iteration time of 100 ms without overlap. In this case, many warps are stalled on memory access since they are waiting for data transfers running over the slow PCIe interconnect. In the topology-aware approach, however, SM utilization jumps to 90%, and total iteration time drops by 30% from 100 ms down to 70 ms—showing far fewer memory stall cycles. This indicates that the GPUs were much more fully utilized with less waiting for data since transfers were happening over NVLink instead of PCIe, as shown in Table 4-2.

Table 4-2. Key GPU performance metrics before and after applying topology-aware NCCL and compute–communication overlap optimizations

Metric	Before (no overlap)	After (with overlap)
SM busy	60%	90%
Memory stall warps	High	Much lower
Iteration time	100 ms (no overlap)	70 ms (with overlap)

In summary, topology awareness can make or break the performance of scaling multi-GPU systems. A rule of thumb is to keep as much communication as possible on the fastest interconnect available—likely NVLink/NVSwitch for intranode communication—and minimize transfers over slow paths such as PCIe and inter-NUMA node links.

If your multi-GPU job isn't scaling on one node, first verify that traffic isn't being forced over slow paths. And remember that GPUs have only a fixed number of direct NVLink lanes. For instance, each Blackwell GPU in a GB200/GB300 NVL72 system supports 18 NVLink 5 links at ~100 GB/s each for a total of ~1.8 TB/s of GPU-to-GPU bidirectional aggregate. This is double the previous generation's 900 GB/s.

Communicating between devices that aren't directly paired can drop you back to fewer lanes—or even PCIe. If data needs to cross NUMA domains, your throughput will drop significantly. In an NVL72 rack, all 72 Blackwell GPUs are part of a single NVLink Switch domain. Within an NVL72 rack, any GPU can reach any other GPU in a single NVSwitch stage at full bisection bandwidth. The GPU domain provides uniform all-to-all connectivity with NVLS support.

NCCL's hierarchy algorithm should automatically pick the highest-bandwidth routes, but you should confirm this in your profiling. If you still hit a bandwidth wall, constrain your job to a tightly connected subset of GPUs.

For instance, four GPUs on the same NUMA node or within a single NVSwitch island is much better than spanning all eight GPUs across slower links. The extra synchronization overhead over those limited or indirect links will often outweigh the benefit of using the additional devices.

It's also worth mentioning that the NVIDIA superchips blur the line between CPU and GPU memory. They offer extremely fast CPU-GPU interconnects on the order of 900 GB/s NVLink-C2C between CPU and GPU in a Grace Blackwell Superchip, for instance. This allows the CPU memory to act as a high-speed extension of GPU memory.

This means that even if some part of the all-reduce involves the CPU or system memory, it may still be as fast as older GPU-GPU links. The key takeaway is to optimize your intranode communication by using the fastest paths available—and minimize usage of slow paths.

Tools like NVIDIA Nsight Systems—or NCCL's own traces with NCCL_DEBUG=INFO and NCCL_TOPO_DUMP_FILE=<path>—will show if NVLink paths are being utilized fully.

NCCL Communication Algorithms

Internally, NCCL can employ different communication algorithms depending on the size of data, number of GPUs, and topology. The primary algorithms NCCL uses for collectives are Ring, Tree, CollNet, and Parallel Aggregated Tree (PAT), among others. Let's dive into each of these:

Ring

In the ring all-reduce, GPUs are logically arranged in a ring. Each GPU sends data to its neighbor and receives data from its other neighbor in a pipelined fashion. For an all-reduce, each chunk of the data will circulate around the ring, accumulating partial sums. The ring algorithm has the nice property that it perfectly balances network load such that each GPU sends and receives exactly the same amount of data. It is bandwidth-optimal, as each rank (and each ring link in steady state) transfers a total of $(2 \times$ data_size $\times$ (num_gpus $- 1) \div$ num_gpus) bytes in an all-reduce collective. Equivalently, each step transfers (data_size $\div$ num_gpus) bytes. The downside is latency. The total time scales with the number of GPUs since the data has to traverse all hops. Ring is often great for large messages because, when you send very large messages, the time spent actually moving bytes far outweighs the cost of actually starting the transfer. This is known as a *bandwidth-dominated workload*.

Tree and NVLSTree

In the tree algorithm, reductions and broadcasts are done in a tree structure using the spanning tree algorithm. An all-reduce in the tree algorithm is implemented as a reduce to the root followed by a broadcast. A tree can complete an all-reduce in O(log N) steps for *N* GPUs—as opposed to O(N) for the ring. As such, a tree algorithm provides lower latency for smaller messages. However, it may not fully utilize all links for large messages because not all GPUs transmit all the time. Some GPUs are leaves of the tree and send only one time up the tree, for instance. NCCL's tree algorithm is optimized and often used for smaller message sizes in which the total time is dominated by the transfer-startup latency. This is known as a *latency-dominated workload*—in contrast to the ring algorithm's bandwidth-dominated use case for large messages. Using NVLSTree will enable NVLink SHARP offload.

CollNet (hierarchical collectives across nodes)

CollNet is NCCL's hierarchical collective path that combines fast local-domain aggregation with cross-group exchange. It combines these two collective strategies to optimize communication at different scales (*https://oreil.ly/p7in1*). The CollNet algorithms are designed for environments where the network can actively assist with collective operations. When supported by technologies such as NVIDIA SHARP, parts of the reduction can be executed directly within the network fabric. This reduces the volume of data that must traverse the network and lowers end to end communication latency.

First, it groups GPUs that share a fast local interconnect, such as all GPUs in a single node or within an NVSwitch island. CollNet then applies a high throughput algorithm such as a ring or local tree to aggregate the data within each group of GPUs. One designated leader GPU from each group participates in the second level tree reduction across groups. This minimizes the number of cross group communication rounds. By layering a local reduction on top of a global tree exchange, CollNet delivers both low latency for internode transfers and high bandwidth for intranode traffic. This makes it especially effective at reducing network load in very large, multinode GPU clusters.

NCCL implements CollNet through multiple variants. CollNet Direct supports dense communication among GPUs within a node. CollNet Chain organizes GPUs into an ordered sequence, performing the reduction in one direction and distributing the result in the reverse direction.

Parallel aggregated tree (PAT)

PAT is NCCL's pipelined hybrid of ring and tree algorithms. As soon as one segment of the tensor has been reduced across its tree of GPUs, the next segment simultaneously begins its own tree reduction in a staggered, round-robin manner. This overlap of successive reduction phases lets PAT keep links saturated and achieve bandwidth close to a pure ring all-reduce. At the same time, it bounds transfer-startup latency to $O(\log N)$ per segment, similar to the tree algorithm. In practice, PAT splits a large message into multiple chunks, launches a tree-based reduce-scatter on chunk 1, then immediately issues the same on chunk 2, and so on. This interleaves so that there is always work in flight. The result is near–ring-level throughput for large data transfers plus tree-level latency advantages for smaller segments. It's best-of-both-worlds approach.

As when choosing any communication algorithm, the choice of NCCL algorithm typically comes down to message size and topology. Small messages (on the order of 10s of megabytes) favor tree algorithms since there are fewer steps. Large messages favor ring algorithms because they provide better bandwidth utilization.

By default, NCCL will automatically choose the best algorithm for a given collective operation, message size, and topology. NCCL supports symmetric memory optimizations and low-latency kernels that reduce all-reduce latency for small and medium messages on NVLink-connected systems. In some cases, this reduction has been measured (*https://oreil.ly/3Lcnh*) up to ~7.6× for small and medium messages on NVLink-connected systems. These improvements, alongside algorithms like PAT, further decrease communication overhead on systems like the NVL72.

NCCL continues to evolve its communication strategies to be topology aware. For instance, NCCL can utilize NVSwitch's hardware multicast for one-hop broadcasts within an NVLink domain. This is ideal for situations in which you need to send identical data, such as updated model weights, to all GPUs at once.

NCCL also utilizes the latest hardware advancements. On InfiniBand fabrics, NCCL can use SHARP through the NCCL RDMA SHARP plugin on supported deployments. On supported NVSwitch systems, NCCL can also use NVLink SHARP (NVLS) for in-switch collective offload.

Additionally, NCCL implements the PAT algorithm, which combines ringlike throughput with treelike latency, as mentioned earlier. This algorithm divides large messages into chunks, inspects the physical GPU and switch topology layout, and uses this information to interleave reduce-scatter and all-gather phases across different CUDA streams appropriately. This takes full advantage of the network topology to balance the best of both worlds: treelike latency and ringlike bandwidth when the hardware and network support it.

By default, NCCL's communicator initialization automatically inspects the message size, interconnect topology, and GPU generation to automatically pick the fastest algorithm and protocol combination for each collective and topology. However, if profiling your workload reveals suboptimal communication, such as unexpectedly high cross-node latency, you can override the communication algorithm on a case-by-case basis by setting the `NCCL_ALGO` environment variable (e.g., `NCCL_ALGO=NVLSTree,PAT`). This will force NCCL to use a particular algorithm on that communicator. If setting this variable in code, make sure to do it before calling `ncclCommInitRank()`.

Distributed Data Parallel Strategies

In practice, large-scale training and inferencing of multi-billion- and multi-trillion-parameter models requires a combination of parallelism strategies, including data parallel, tensor model parallel, pipeline parallel, expert parallel, context parallel, etc. These are required to scale your training clusters linearly and not waste GPU resources with excessive overhead.

The key is to overlap communication with computation at every level. This includes using NCCL for all-reduce and NIXL for one-to-one transfers. Using these mechanisms, you can scale to thousands and millions of GPUs with high efficiency.

Other techniques like gradient accumulation and activation checkpointing are also critical at ultrascale to manage the memory footprint without sacrificing throughput.

When scaling to multiple GPUs on a single node, PyTorch offers both data-parallel (split the data) and model-parallel (split the model) approaches at the framework level. We'll cover these in more detail in a later chapter, but for now, let's compare two of the most basic data-parallel strategies from a systems performance standpoint: `nn.DataParallel` (DP) and `torch.distributed.DistributedDataParallel` (DDP).

It's important to understand their differences as choosing the wrong one can severely impact performance:

Data parallelism (DP)

DP is an easy-to-use API that involves a single process, or single Python thread, controlling multiple GPUs. The module automatically splits each input batch across the available GPUs. It then performs forward passes on each split, gathers the outputs back to the main GPU, and computes the aggregated loss. Finally, during the backward pass, it gathers gradients back to the main GPU, averages them, and broadcasts back to the others.

In DataParallel, the entire training loop is single-process. This makes it simpler to integrate since there is no need to launch multiple processes. Even though DP uses multithreading, it is limited by Python's GIL (Global Interpreter Lock) for launching operations on different devices. As such, DP does not scale well beyond 2–4 GPUs because the single Python thread becomes a bottleneck and the GPU utilization suffers. Additionally, the gradient gathering step in DP is synchronous and does not overlap with computation. This means it behaves similarly to our "no overlap" scenario described earlier.

Fully sharded data parallelism (FSDP)

FSDP avoids full model replicas by sharding activations, gradients, and parameters across GPUs, greatly reducing memory overhead. For ultrascale models, FSDP is often combined with other parallelism strategies like tensor parallel and pipeline parallel.

> We'll talk about FSDP—and other ultrascale training techniques like expert parallelism—in Chapter 13. This section will focus on DP and DDP to establish the foundation for the additional complexity discussed in later chapters.

Distributed Data Parallel (DDP)

DDP uses one process per GPU device and relies on NCCL to communicate gradients. Like most simple data parallel strategies (FSDP being the exception), each process has its own copy of the model.

During the backward pass, gradients are exchanged, or all-reduced, directly among GPUs. This all-reduce communication is typically overlapped with the backward computation, which is ideal, as we discussed earlier.

DDP avoids the GIL issue entirely by using separate processes. And NCCL's efficient C++ kernels handle communication. The result is that DDP nearly always outperforms DP for multi-GPU training. In fact, PyTorch developers recommend (*https://oreil.ly/ylal4*) using `DistributedDataParallel` over `DataParallel` for any serious multi-GPU work because DP's Python threading, limited by the dreaded GIL, often becomes a bottleneck.

Let's revisit the example from earlier, but in the context of comparing DP and DDP on a single node. We will use a simple model and measure a single training step with DP and DDP.

In this scenario, we use DataParallel to wrap a model so that PyTorch splits each input batch and uses two GPUs. We'll time a single training iteration:

```python
# before_dataparallel.py

import torch
import torch.nn as nn
import torch.optim as optim

# Dummy model and dataset
class SimpleNet(nn.Module):
    def __init__(self, input_size, hidden_size):
        super(SimpleNet, self).__init__()
        self.linear1 = nn.Linear(input_size, hidden_size)
        self.relu = nn.ReLU()
        self.linear2 = nn.Linear(hidden_size, 1)
    def forward(self, x):
        return self.linear2(self.relu(self.linear1(x)))

# Setup model and data
input_size = 1024
hidden_size = 256

model = SimpleNet(input_size, hidden_size)

model.cuda()  # move model to GPU 0, it will also replicate to GPU 1

model = nn.DataParallel(model)    # utilize 2 GPUs (0 and 1 by default)

optimizer = optim.SGD(model.parameters(), lr=0.01)
data = torch.randn(512, input_size).cuda()   # batch of 512 on GPU0
target = torch.randn(512, 1).cuda()          # target on GPU0

# Run a single training step
output = model(data)                          # forward (DP splits data internally)
loss = nn.functional.mse_loss(output, target)
loss.backward()                               # backward (DP gathers grads to GPU0)
optimizer.step()
```

Here, the forward pass of `nn.DataParallel` splits the input tensor (matrix) of shape [512,1024] into two tensors of size [256,1024]. One tensor is sent to GPU 0 and one is sent to GPU 1. Both GPU 1 and GPU 2 contain replicas of the same model using `model.cuda()` in the preceding code.

Technically, the model was initially only on GPU 0, but when `for
ward` is called for the first time, DP automatically copies the model
to GPU 1—and any other GPUs involved—before executing the
computation.

Then `DataParallel` launches the forward pass on GPU 0 and GPU 1 in parallel using
one thread per GPU to enqueue each replica's computation. However, because these
threads share the single Python process and contend for our nemesis, GIL, the
kernel-launch calls occur sequentially in Python. Fortunately, the enqueued GPU
work runs on the device concurrently.

After the forward pass, `DataParallel` gathers all per-GPU outputs onto the primary
device (GPU 0) for loss calculation. During the backward pass, it similarly collects
and sums gradients from all replicas onto GPU 0, broadcasts the aggregated gradients
from GPU 0 back to the remaining GPUs (GPU 1 in this case), then runs the optimizer step.

A couple things to highlight in this example with `DataParallel`. GPU 0 bears the
extra burden of gathering and summing all gradients. Moreover, each gradient reduction (GPU 1 → GPU 0 and back) is performed synchronously—blocking further
work on the backward pass. This design incurs two key penalties. First, the Python
controller thread must serialize kernel launches on each device, which adds CPU-side
overhead. Second, because gradient aggregation isn't overlapped with ongoing computation, GPU 0 can become a performance bottleneck. Let's now compare how
`DistributedDataParallel` addresses these issues.

After switching to `DistributedDataParallel`, we start one process per GPU using
`torch.multiprocessing.spawn`, for example. Each process holds its own complete
model replica and works on a separate slice of the batch. In the next example, the
batch size is 256. With two processes running, the effective total batch size remains at
512, which matches the DataParallel setup for a fair comparison:

```python
# after_ddp.py

import os, time
import torch
import torch.nn as nn
import torch.optim as optim
import torch.distributed as dist
import torch.multiprocessing as mp

class SimpleNet(nn.Module):
    def __init__(self, input_size, hidden_size):
        super(SimpleNet, self).__init__()
        self.linear1 = nn.Linear(input_size, hidden_size)
        self.relu = nn.ReLU()
        self.linear2 = nn.Linear(hidden_size, 1)
```

```python
    def forward(self, x):
        return self.linear2(self.relu(self.linear1(x)))

def train_ddp(rank, world_size):
    rank = int(os.environ.get("LOCAL_RANK", rank))
    torch.cuda.set_device(rank)
    dist.init_process_group("nccl",
        init_method="env://",
        world_size=world_size, rank=rank)
    model = SimpleNet(input_size=1024,
        hidden_size=256)

    model.cuda(rank)

    ddp_model =
        nn.parallel.DistributedDataParallel(model,
            device_ids=[rank])
    optimizer = optim.SGD(ddp_model.parameters(),
        lr=0.01)

    # Each process gets its own portion of data
    batch_size = 256
    data = torch.randn(batch_size, 1024).cuda(rank)
    target = torch.randn(batch_size, 1).cuda(rank)

    # Run one training iteration
    output = ddp_model(data)
    loss = nn.functional.mse_loss(output, target)
    loss.backward()
    optimizer.step()

    dist.destroy_process_group()

if __name__ == "__main__":
    main()
```

You can run this using the `torchrun` launcher (or your cluster's MPI/SLURM/ Kubernetes integration) and setting the `MASTER_ADDR` and `MASTER_PORT` environment variables. Running the following script, you will see output like the following (note: these results are workload and hardware specific and will not necessarily match your results):

```
# Environment (common gotchas)
export NCCL_DEBUG=INFO
export NCCL_ASYNC_ERROR_HANDLING=1
export NCCL_SOCKET_IFNAME=ib0        # use your HCA (e.g., ib0, ib1)
# Optional: for multi-rail IB, set NIC ordering
# so ranks use distinct rails.

# Local bring-up, 2 GPUs
torchrun --standalone --nproc-per-node=2 after_ddp.py
```

```
# SLURM (example)
srun --ntasks=$WORLD_SIZE --gpus-per-task=1 --nodes=$NNODES \
    --cpus-per-task=8 python after_ddp.py

### Output: ###

DDP step took 30.00 ms
```

While your exact number will vary, the DDP iteration is significantly faster than DP. In this case, DDP is 33% faster than DP even though they're both processing the same amount of overall data.

The improvement comes from multiple factors. First, each process handles half the batch without Python GIL contention, so they truly run in parallel. Next, the gradients are all-reduced using NCCL, which overlaps communication with the backward computation. Additionally, there is no extra copying of gradients to a single aggregation GPU (e.g., GPU 0) and back. Also, each GPU's gradients are directly exchanged and averaged in place. Last, the communication work is spread across all GPUs that participate in this all-reduce collective rather than burdening a single GPU responsible for aggregating data—among many other things.

In our example, DDP required 30 ms to complete versus DP's 45 ms. In larger models, the gap will be even bigger—especially as you scale to thousands of GPUs. DP might actually degrade superlinearly when scaling beyond 2–4 GPUs because the main thread becomes overwhelmed. DDP, on the other hand, tends to scale well to the number of GPUs, limited mostly by communication bandwidth and not by CPU or single-GPU overhead.

To sum up, one should always prefer `DistributedDataParallel` over `DataParallel` for multi-GPU training—plain and simple. The PyTorch team explicitly recommends (*https://oreil.ly/ylal4*) this because of the performance and scalability benefits. The only situation where DP might be acceptable is for quick prototyping on 2 GPUs where ease of use is valued and performance is secondary.

If you care about training throughput, it takes only a few lines to switch from `Data Parallel` to `DistributedDataParallel`. You can do this even on one node with multiple GPUs. By spawning one process per GPU (e.g., `torch.multiprocessing.spawn`), each process holds its own model replica and data partition.

Under the hood, DDP uses asynchronous NCCL all-reduces to overlap gradient communication with computation and avoids Python GIL contention entirely. This results in much better GPU utilization and faster end-to-end iteration times. For these reasons, performance-minded engineers on multi-GPU systems almost always favor `DistributedDataParallel` over `DataParallel`.

NCCL Communicator Lifecycle and Environment Gotchas

While NCCL abstracts most low-level details, how we use NCCL in our code can still affect performance. Additionally, NCCL has many environment variables (*https://oreil.ly/bnv7N*) to control its behavior. Misconfiguring these variables can degrade performance or even cause hangs.

In this section, we cover common pitfalls related to NCCL communicators and environment settings. We also show how to diagnose and avoid these issues.

Pitfall #1: Creating NCCL communicators too often

A NCCL communicator represents a group of GPUs, or ranks, that can communicate collectively. Creating a communicator with either C++'s `ncclCommInitRank` in C++ or PyTorch's `torch.distributed.init_process_group` is an expensive operation. Initializers require that all ranks exchange information with one another, including unique IDs, network addresses, etc. They also set up rings/trees and allocate buffers.

If your code repeatedly initializes NCCL communicators, you'll pay a heavy cost each time. Consider a system with 32 GPUs. If you create 32 separate NCCL communicators, one per rank, this could require 2–3 minutes as opposed to 2–3 seconds (or quicker). Communicator initialization can have worse-than-linear scaling with number of ranks because it often requires all-to-all handshakes and coordination among the many GPUs.

In PyTorch's DDP, this is handled for you. You simply call `init_process_group` once at the start of your program and DDP will create one communicator for all processes. This is subsequently used for all collectives at each iteration.

To illustrate the cost of creating NCCL communicators on every iteration, here is a PyTorch example where someone naively initializes and destroys a NCCL process group every iteration of training:

```python
import torch
import torch.distributed as dist
import torch.multiprocessing as mp

def run(rank, world_size):
    rank = int(os.environ.get("LOCAL_RANK", rank))
    device = torch.cuda.device(rank)
    for i in range(5):  # simulate 5 iterations
        # This naive approach re-initializes NCCL each
        # iteration. THIS IS EXTREMELY SLOW AND NOT RECOMMENDED!!!
        dist.init_process_group("nccl", init_method="env://",
                                world_size=world_size, rank=rank)
        # do a tiny all-reduce to simulate some work
        tensor = torch.ones(1).cuda(rank)
        dist.all_reduce(tensor)
        if rank == 0:
```

```
        print(f"Iter {i} done")
    dist.destroy_process_group()
```

If you run this, you will notice it's extremely slow even though the all-reduce is trivial because most of the time is spent in `init_process_group` and `destroy_process_group`. In a real scenario with more ranks, the cost multiplies.

Since the `init_process_group` call is designed to be called once at startup, you should avoid any design that reinitializes it on every iteration. The fix is to initialize once outside the loop, as shown here:

```python
import torch
import torch.distributed as dist
import torch.multiprocessing as mp
import os

def run(rank, world_size):
    # Pin GPU
    rank = int(os.environ.get("LOCAL_RANK", rank))
    device = torch.cuda.device(rank)

    # Initialize NCCL communicator once
    dist.init_process_group(
        backend="nccl",
        init_method="tcp://127.0.0.1:45678",
        world_size=world_size,
        rank=rank
    )

    # Simulate 5 training iterations
    for i in range(5):
        tensor = torch.ones(1, device=rank)
        dist.all_reduce(tensor)

    # Cleanup once at the end
    dist.destroy_process_group()

if __name__ == "__main__":
    world_size = 2
    mp.spawn(run, args=(world_size,), nprocs=world_size)
```

By moving the communicator setup and teardown out of the loop, you eliminate the 48 ms initialization overhead incurred each iteration. This reduces total iteration time by over 98%, as shown in Table 4-3.

Table 4-3. Impact of avoiding repeated communicator init/destroy on per-iteration time

Metric	Before (per iter)	After (per iter)
init_process_group + destroy	48.0 ms	0 ms
dist.all_reduce (1-element tensor)	0.5 ms	0.5 ms
Total iteration time	48.5 ms	0.5 ms

The tiny all-reduce itself remains at 0.5 ms, but previously it was completely dominated by the frequent initialization cost. In real multinode scenarios with more ranks, the savings will multiply. Initializing once is a clear performance best practice.

Pitfall #2: Do not create and destroy NCCL communicators on every iteration

Because NCCL communicator initialization is so expensive, be careful not to accidentally create new NCCL communicators when defining subgroups of processes for model parallelism and pipeline parallelism. Instead, create the subcommunicators once at the beginning using PyTorch's `torch.distributed.new_group()` and reuse these communicators. Never create and destroy communicators on every iteration.

If you need to create multiple communicators because, for instance, you have a dynamic runtime membership scenario or a staged initialization, NCCL provides a C++ API to initialize multiple communicators together using `ncclGroupStart()`, `ncclCommInitRank(...)`, and `ncclGroupEnd()`. This will greatly reduce overhead.

> As of this writing, PyTorch does not support fully dynamic membership changes at runtime without a full communicator teardown. All ranks must invoke creation and destruction calls in lockstep to prevent hangs.

Pitfall #3: Avoid overtuning or disabling NCCL features with environment variables

NCCL has many environment variables such as `NCCL_BUFFSIZE`, `NCCL_NSOCKS_PERTH READ`, `NCCL_P2P_LEVEL`, `NCCL_SHM_DISABLE`, etc. It's usually best to leave them at their defaults unless you have a specific reason. Better yet, set their values to their current defaults to be explicit and not rely on defaults! Be sure to review the release notes and adjust the values accordingly.

> While `NCCL_BUFFSIZE` can be increased to improve bandwidth for large all-reduce operations, it must be sized carefully. Setting it too high can cause GPU memory pressure or force smaller models to evict their working sets. Start at 4 MB and increase stepwise. Monitor GPU memory usage as you increase this value.

A common mistake is to disable features while debugging and forget to reenable them in production. For example, never leave peer-to-peer (P2P) or shared-memory transports turned off in production.

Disabling direct P2P GPU copies with `NCCL_P2P_DISABLE=1` might help isolate a problem during troubleshooting, but it will drastically reduce intranode performance if left enabled. This is because it forces all intranode traffic to go through CPU host-staged intermediate buffers instead of GPU-direct NVLink links. This adds extra hops and CPU work that can increase latency from a few microseconds to tens of microseconds and cut bandwidth from hundreds of GB/s down to tens of GB/s.

Use `NCCL_P2P_DISABLE=1` only when diagnosing an issue. Remember to reenable P2P with `NCCL_P2P_DISABLE=0` (or remove the environment variable altogether) when you're done debugging.

Likewise, leaving shared-memory exchanges disabled (`NCCL_SHM_DISABLE=1`) would force NCCL to not use shared memory for intranode communication. This causes a fallback to network or host-mediated copies, which incurs additional kernel-driver overhead and context switches that further increase latency and throttle throughput.

Change performance-critical environment variables only briefly during debugging. And don't forget to set them back to production settings before returning to normal operations.

Another variable is `NCCL_DEBUG`. Setting `NCCL_DEBUG=INFO` or `DEBUG` is useful to log NCCL operations, as logs can hint at issues like falling back to Ethernet, for instance. But additional logging does incur overhead. Don't run at `DEBUG` level in production; use it when needed. For performance reasons, however, you may want to lower the setting to `WARN` (default) or even just `VERSION`. This would silence everything except the NCCL version but will make things difficult to debug when the time comes—and it will! To tune performance, some of the useful variables include the following:

NCCL_NSOCKS_PERTHREAD and NCCL_SOCKET_NTHREADS (Socket/TCP transports). These tune NCCL's Socket/TCP transport path, so they are relevant when Socket transport is in use. If you are using multiple NICs, first validate whether NCCL is actually on Socket or RDMA transport, then tune the corresponding transport-specific controls. If you have, say, two NICs with Socket transport, you might set `NCCL_NSOCKS_PERTHREAD=2` so that each thread handles two sockets for a total of four connections allowed. Defaults vary by platform and build, but what matters is that the product of `NCCL_NSOCKS_PERTHREAD` and `NCCL_SOCKET_NTHREADS` must not exceed 64 per NVIDIA guidance (*https://oreil.ly/bnv7N*).

This 64 limit is NCCL's built-in maximum for the total number of TCP socket connections allowed per communicator. It's defined as the product of `NCCL_SOCKET_NTHREADS` * `NCCL_NSOCKS_PERTHREAD`. It's designed to bound CPU and network resource usage—and avoid exceeding operating-system and hardware limits.

NCCL_MIN_NCHANNELS and NCCL_MAX_NCHANNELS. These control how many subrings NCCL may use since NCCL splits data across multiple rings to use multiple NVLinks in parallel, if possible. It's recommended to leave these values as default. On GPU systems with NVSwitch, NCCL will auto-tune the number of channels based on topology and message size. Additionally, NCCL creates the same number of subrings as channels to match the number of concurrent hardware links. Each channel corresponds to one CUDA block used for communication. As such, a higher number of channels will require more GPU resources.

NCCL_TOPO_FILE. You can set this variable with a topology file for the system to guide NCCL to make wise decisions. This is useful in complex networks or cloud environments where NCCL might not detect the topology correctly. To capture what NCCL detects at runtime, set NCCL_TOPO_DUMP_FILE to an output path and inspect the generated file.

NCCL_MNNVL_ENABLE. Enable NVIDIA multi-node NVLink (MNNVL). This is designed for high-speed communication in systems with support for multi-node NVLink switches (e.g., NVL72 GB200/GB300).

NCCL_SHARP_DISABLE. This setting controls the usage of SHARP for in-network aggregation. We will discuss SHARP in a bit. By default, if SHARP is available and the job is configured to use it, NCCL will enable it. You can disable SHARP explicitly by setting NCCL_SHARP_DISABLE=1 for A/B testing and troubleshooting.

In summary, use environment defaults unless you have evidence that a specific tunable will help. And if you do change these values, make sure to document them and continuously monitor that their effects are still beneficial when upgrading to newer hardware and NCCL versions.

Pitfall #4: Verify CPU-GPU NUMA-node affinity for NCCL threads

NCCL launches background CPU threads for network polling and kernel dispatch. When you start multiple processes with torch.multiprocessing or Message Passing Interface (MPI), each process inherits a CPU affinity mask that may target all cores or only a subset if bound with tools such as taskset or numactl.

NCCL normally assigns its threads to the cores nearest the GPUs they serve, but if the process is pinned to a narrow set of cores, it may collapse all NCCL threads onto a single core and suffer from poor scheduling and low throughput. To prevent this, set the environment variable NCCL_IGNORE_CPU_AFFINITY=1 so that NCCL ignores the inherited CPU affinity mask and freely spreads its worker threads across the cores in the local NUMA domain. The recommended approach is to bind each GPU process to the CPU cores for its NUMA domain and then set `NCCL_IGNORE_CPU_AFFINITY=1` so that NCCL can fine-tune thread placement within those cores.

Consider a compute node with two NUMA node domains and eight GPUs. If the GPUs 0–3 are attached to the first CPU and devices 4–7 are attached to the second CPU, you would bind ranks 0–3 to the first set of CPU cores and ranks 4–7 to the second set of CPU cores. Next, you would set `NCCL_IGNORE_CPU_AFFINITY=1` to ignore the inherited CPU affinity mask.

> In practice, using `numactl` or setting `CUDA_DEVICE_ORDER` and `CUDA_VISIBLE_DEVICES` can help enforce this binding. PyTorch's launch utilities handle much of this automatically, but it's good to verify.

You can also specify an explicit topology file (*https://oreil.ly/DlOjT*) to further reduce latency and improve throughput. If you prefer not to pin processes manually, you can rely on MPI runtime binding or job scheduler options such as SLURM `--cpu-bind` to ensure each rank lands on the correct cores.

Pitfall #5: Resist the temptation to ignore NCCL warnings and errors

NCCL prints many logs if logging is judiciously enabled. In those logs, there could be warnings about falling back to slower PCIe bandwidth, for instance. These are important warnings to address.

If you see logs like "unable to enable P2P, falling back to copy," don't ignore these! They often indicate suboptimal conditions. If you see this warning, it means that NCCL was unable to establish direct GPU P2P between two GPUs. Perhaps because they're on different PCIe root complexes with no support. This means that data transfers will be much slower, as they must travel through host CPU memory buffers.

Warnings could prompt you to rearrange which GPUs are used in a process. The solution would be to ensure that GPUs that need to talk to one another are on the same NUMA node or using a different pairing schema. Another example is the `NCCL INFO NET/Socket: using Ethernet interface eth0` warning, which tells you which interface was picked. If that's not the highest-performing interconnect, you might need to set `NCCL_SOCKET_IFNAME` explicitly. For instance, you can set `NCCL_SOCKET_IFNAME=ib0` so the bootstrap handshake uses the intended fabric. You should track down why this is not being automatically set to the fastest interface. This is likely a larger issue.

Pitfall #6: NCCL communicator hangs, errors, or shuts down completely

Occasionally, if a process crashes or one GPU rank hits an error, NCCL communicators might hang the other ranks since the collectives won't complete. Unfortunately this is quite common in large-scale clusters given the relatively high frequency of GPU failures at scale, as described by Meta (*https://oreil.ly/z8QKu*) in Table 4-4.

Table 4-4. Root-cause categorization of unexpected interruptions during a 54-day period of Llama 3 405B pretraining (source: https://oreil.ly/z8QKu)

Component	Category	Interruption count	% of Interruptions
Faulty GPU	GPU	148	30.1%
GPU HBM3 memory	GPU	72	17.2%
Software bug	Dependency	54	12.9%
Network switch/cable	Network	35	8.4%
Host maintenance	Unplanned Maintenance	32	7.6%
GPU SRAM memory	GPU	19	4.5%
GPU system processor	GPU	17	4.1%
NIC	Host	7	1.7%
NCCL watchdog timeouts	Unknown	7	1.7%
Silent data corruption	GPU	6	1.4%
GPU thermal interface and sensor	GPU	6	1.4%
SSD	Host	3	0.7%
Power supply	Host	3	0.7%
Server chassis	Host	2	0.5%
IO expansion board	Host	2	0.5%
Dependency	Dependency	2	0.5%
CPU	Host	2	0.5%
System memory	Host	2	0.5%

Enabling `NCCL_ASYNC_ERROR_HANDLING=1` can improve resiliency by allowing NCCL to abort on errors asynchronously, but this may incur a slight overhead. PyTorch sets this by default in recent versions when you use `init_process_group`. However, it's a good idea to keep explicitly setting this value for clarity and reproducibility.

For PyTorch deployments, prefer configuring `TORCH_NCCL_ASYNC_ERROR_HANDLING` explicitly (PyTorch-level behavior), and use `NCCL_ASYNC_ERROR_HANDLING` where you need direct NCCL-level control.

> Never rely on default values. Always be explicit! Default values can sometimes change from version to version—and they are extremely hard to debug when they change. Setting these values explicitly during initialization avoids version-dependent behavior. Keep these values explicit in runbooks to avoid ambiguity across framework and NCCL version changes.

It's important to treat NCCL as a high-performance engine that just works. But be mindful of how you initialize and use NCCL. Initialize once, pin CPUs appropriately, use the environment variable to adjust affinity if needed, and be cautious with environment variables and their defaults.

Also, one should always review NCCL release notes when upgrading. New versions often bring optimizations—especially when new networking hardware emerges. And always test after upgrading NCCL as default settings and performance might change. Typically, NCCL performance improves with each new version. But default values may sometimes change, which would require retuning your system if you have not explicitly pinned the NCCL environment variables.

Profiling and Debugging NCCL

NCCL supports asynchronous error handling and failover for cases like network errors. To enable asynchronous error handling, set the environment variable `NCCL_ASYNC_ERROR_HANDLING=1`. And when debugging NCCL, make sure to also enable `NCCL_DEBUG=WARN` or `INFO`. This way, you can check for common issues like unmatched ranks or socket misconfigurations.

Also available to debug NCCL is the NCCL profiler plugin API (*https://oreil.ly/Xz2kE*). This API lets you monitor the internal timeline of GPU communications and pinpoint any lagging device or bottleneck in the system. The NCCL profiler plugin API is designed to address performance issues that become increasingly difficult to diagnose as GPU clusters scale up.

The NCCL profiler plugin can be dynamically loaded via the `NCCL_PROFILER_PLUGIN` interface and integrated by tools that support it. The `NCCL_PROFILER_PLUGIN` environment variable governs the loading and initialization of this plugin in a manner similar to other NCCL plugins.

NVIDIA created this flexible API to simplify the integration of third-party profiling tools (e.g., PyTorch Kineto (*https://oreil.ly/Rwwwh*)) with NCCL and ensure that complex communication activities are monitored and captured in a clear, hierarchical, and low-overhead manner during runtime execution. PyTorch's Kineto can also gather NCCL activity using CUPTI and NVTX if the NCCL plugin is not enabled.

> The NCCL profiler plugin is bundled with NVIDIA's tools and third-party profilers like the PyTorch/Kineto profiler. Use it to give timeline views of all-reduce operations.

Once loaded, the NCCL profiler plugin configures an event activation mask, which is a 32-bit integer where each bit corresponds to a distinct NCCL event like group events, collective events, point-to-point events, and various proxy-related operations. This structure creates a natural hierarchy of events to help represent detailed performance information in a meaningful way and pinpoint issues quickly.

The NCCL profile plugin API defines five function callbacks. The `init` callback sets up the plugin by providing an opaque context and establishing which events should be profiled. The `startEvent` callback receives an event descriptor from NCCL and allocates a new event object, returning an opaque handle that NCCL uses for further operations.

The `stopEvent` callback marks the completion of an event so that its resources can be recycled. The `recordEventState` callback allows the plugin to update events as they transition through different states. The `finalize` callback releases all resources associated with the profiler context once profiling is complete.

In-Network SHARP Aggregation

When using advanced network hardware that supports in-network computing, such as NVIDIA's Scalable Hierarchical Aggregation and Reduction Protocol (SHARP), additional performance gains can be realized by offloading parts of collective operations to the network itself.

InfiniBand SHARP is an in-network reduction technology used with Quantum-class InfiniBand switches, and uses the NCCL RDMA SHARP plugin.

Related but different, NVLink SHARP (NVLS) is an NVSwitch-domain collective offload mechanism that is supported by certain NVLink systems. NVLS offloads collectives within the NVSwitch fabric. In modern NVLink Switch domains (e.g., NVL72), NVLS accelerates collectives and enables efficient all-to-all and broadcast across the domain (e.g., 72-GPU NVL72 domain).

In practical terms, SHARP enables collectives such as all-reduce to be partially offloaded and computed by supported network hardware and the fabric. As data from multiple GPUs flows into the switch, it will reduce/aggregate (e.g., sum) the data and share the partially reduced result. This saves each GPU from having to redundantly transfer many intermediate results between other GPUs. This reduces the overall amount of data that each GPU must handle, which reduces latency for large MPI and NCCL collectives.

Specifically, for a ring reduce-scatter operation, each GPU normally receives $B(n-1)/n$ bytes across $(n-1)$ hops. With in-network reduction, the switch aggregates and returns only B/n to each GPU. this results in a $1/(n-1)$ per-endpoint receive versus full-ring.

For an all-gather operation, hardware multicast with NVLS lets each GPU send its B/n segment once while the network replicates it. This reduces the sender's volume by

$1/(n-1)$ versus the full ring. And when you overlap a multicast all-gather with an in-network reduce-scatter, the end-to-end phase time can drop by ~1/2 for bandwidth-bound phases since the network performs the aggregation and replication work instead of the endpoints. In this case, the effective wall time for a shard exchange is the max of the two operations instead of the sum.

In short, NVLS results in less data per endpoint and fewer serialized hops. This produces higher effective bandwidth and shorter stalls during sharded training/inference phases.

> All-gather has no arithmetic reduction, so NVLS mainly helps by performing multicast replication. The speedup depends on topology and message size, but it's smaller than the performance gains for NVLS with all-reduce and reduce-scatter.

NCCL can offload collective operations such as all-reduce to SHARP-enabled Infini-Band fabrics by using the NCCL RDMA SHARP plugin with SHARP firmware on the switches and a SHARP Aggregation Manager running on a management server alongside the Subnet Manager. Additionally, each host must load the GPUDirect RDMA kernel module. Once the fabric and hosts are configured and the NCCL RDMA SHARP plugin is selected, NCCL can offload eligible collectives to SHARP. SHARP's performance impact can be substantial. In some cases, NVIDIA reports (*https://oreil.ly/Ml4AI*) 2× to 5× speedups for all-reduce on large-scale AI systems using SHARP.

The gains from SHARP are more pronounced at scale with many GPUs and compute nodes in which the network is usually the bottleneck. On a smaller cluster, say two to four GPU compute nodes, you might not notice as much of a performance improvement. But on 32 nodes, SHARP can reduce collective latency significantly by cutting down the number of overall communication steps.

> SHARP is not enabled by default. It must be configured with a plugin selection or policy. For InfiniBand SHARP, you can enable it using `NCCL_COLLNET_ENABLE=1` for the CollNet path, for instance. This assumes the SHARP plugin and fabric prerequisites are satisfied. To enable NVLS on supported NVSwitch systems, use `NCCL_NVLS_ENABLE=1` when you need to control NVLS availability explicitly. You can also disable SHARP using `NCCL_SHARP_DIS ABLE=1`. This is used primarily as an A/B or troubleshooting override. However, it's recommended to keep SHARE enabled to improve all-reduce latency at scale.

Using SHARP doesn't typically require code changes. One can verify if SHARP is in use by looking at the NCCL logs (`NCCL_DEBUG=INFO`). The logs will mention SHARP if it's being used. There are also diagnostic tools (`ibv_devinfo` etc.) to check if a device supports SHARP.

In summary, SHARP moves reduction computation into the network. This further demonstrates how modern system design blurs the boundaries between computing and communication. For the performance engineer, if your cluster is running on a high-end InfiniBand network, it's worth checking that SHARP is enabled and utilized. It can provide a "turbo button" to provide faster scaling and improved efficiency for massive all-reduce operations. SHARP complements NCCL's GPU-centric optimizations with network-centric optimizations.

It's worth noting that as of this writing, SHARP is primarily an InfiniBand technology. While NVIDIA's Spectrum-X Ethernet platform improves all-reduce performance with congestion control and adaptive routing, as of this writing, it still does not expose switch-resident reduction engines similar to SHARP with InfiniBand. Public material highlights end-to-end telemetry and congestion control for improved NCCL performance across large domains; it does not expose switch-resident reduction engines analogous to SHARP.

SHARP can sometimes incur extra memory overhead on the switches. And since there's a finite amount of buffer for performing reductions on the switch, very large collectives with many MB or GB messages might fall back to regular methods if they exceed hardware limits.

It's recommended to continuously monitor the NCCL logs and set up an alert if it starts falling back to non-SHARP aggregations due to memory pressure over time.

Persistent NCCL User Buffers and Zero-Copy Registration

NCCL supports user buffer registration, which lets collectives operate directly on your tensor buffers without requiring internal staging. This reduces copies and internal channel pressure.

Persistent NCCL user-buffer registration can unlock the best SHARP/NVLS paths when its prerequisites are met. Zero-copy registration can accelerate collectives and reduce SM/channel usage—freeing these resources for higher-value computations.

You can register and deregister persistent NCCL user buffers using explicit `ncclComm Register()` and `ncclCommDeregister()`. If any rank in a communication uses registered buffers, all rank must use them. Furthermore, for some algorithms the offset from the buffer head must match across the ranks.

NVIDIA's NIXL and Disaggregated Inference

While NCCL excels at many-to-many group communication patterns often used during model training, modern AI inference at scale has introduced new communication needs. NVIDIA's NIXL (*https://oreil.ly/anMvQ*) is an open source, high-throughput, low-latency, point-to-point communication library released in early 2025.

NIXL was designed specifically to accelerate large-scale LLM distributed and disaggregated inference. We'll cover how disaggregated inference separates different stages of inference into separate workers. Disaggregating inference uses NIXL for fast data exchange between these stages across GPUs with minimal latency and overhead.

> Disaggregated inference and NIXL are best practices for serving giant models efficiently across a cluster of nodes.

NIXL is a core component of NVIDIA's open source Dynamo (*https://oreil.ly/9bhjx*) inference engine. NIXL streamlines one-to-one and one-to-few data transfers such as moving a key-value (KV) cache (shared by the disaggregated stages) with minimal latency and overhead. It complements NCCL, which is mainly used for many-to-many collectives.

NIXL has a consistent asynchronous API for moving data across GPUs, CPUs, SSDs, and shared network storage. It always picks the fastest path for the placement of each cache chunk of data being moved. This hierarchy is shown in Figure 4-5 in the context of NVIDIA Dynamo's KV Cache Manager (*https://oreil.ly/nsxdl*), which uses NIXL to choose the fastest path available for each KV cache transfer.

When scaling LLM inference, it's important to efficiently transfer large data caches (e.g., transformer's attention KV cache) between peers in a cluster of GPUs, CPUs, compute nodes, and racks. For example, with NIXL, an inference engine can offload a large (e.g., 100 GB) KV cache from a GPU to a peer using NVLink/InfiniBand with minimal overhead. This frees up the GPU to handle new requests. This is critical when serving LLMs with large context windows.

NIXL leverages GPUDirect RDMA to move data directly between GPUs across nodes, entirely bypassing host memory. In practice, the RDMA-capable NIC (or

DPU) performs the transfer directly between GPU memories. This is why latency is so low. The CPU is not involved in the data path.

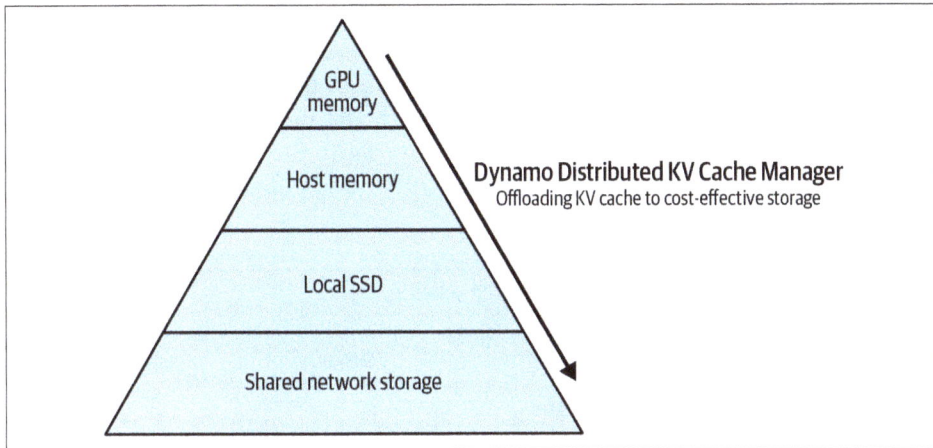

Figure 4-5. NVIDIA Dynamo Distributed KV Cache Manager offloads less frequently accessed KV cache to more economical memory hierarchies (source: https://oreil.ly/nsxdl)

NCCL is still used for synchronized collective operations, but NIXL is focused on efficient one-to-one or one-to-many data transfer scenarios common in LLM inference systems. NVIDIA Dynamo uses NIXL extensively for its disaggregated inference stages of prefill and decode, as we'll cover next.

NCCL remains the standard for many-to-many collective operations common in large-scale training such as all-reduce. NIXL, however, targets one-to-one or one-to-few data transfers that are common in large-scale inference such as moving KV cache data.

NIXL's use in NVIDIA's Dynamo inference framework demonstrates (*https://oreil.ly/nsxdl*) NIXL's throughput boost in multinode LLM serving scenarios. NIXL complements—not replaces—NCCL for high-performance inference pipelines.

Separate Prefill and Decode Inference Stages

We will dive deeper into the performance details of a highly tuned inference system in a later chapter, but it's important to understand a bit of context before going further with NIXL. The inference path of a transformer-based model is actually split into two different stages: prefill and decode.

The first stage, prefill, is often compute bound as it uses many matrix multiplications to build the KV cache from the incoming request data (aka *prompt*). The second stage, decode, is often memory-throughput bound, as it needs to gather the model weights from GPU HBM memory to calculate the next set of tokens (aka *completion* or *response*).

This prefill/decode split is implemented in common inference engines vLLM, SGLang, and NVIDIA's Dynamo and TensorRT-LLM. The *prefill* (prompt ingestion) creates the KV cache, and the *decode* (generation) uses this cache. NIXL specifically accelerates the transfer of the KV cache between nodes in this workflow. Figure 4-6 compares the traditional "monolithic" serving model to the "disaggregated" serving model in which two stages run on different GPU-based compute nodes to increase scale and maximize throughput.

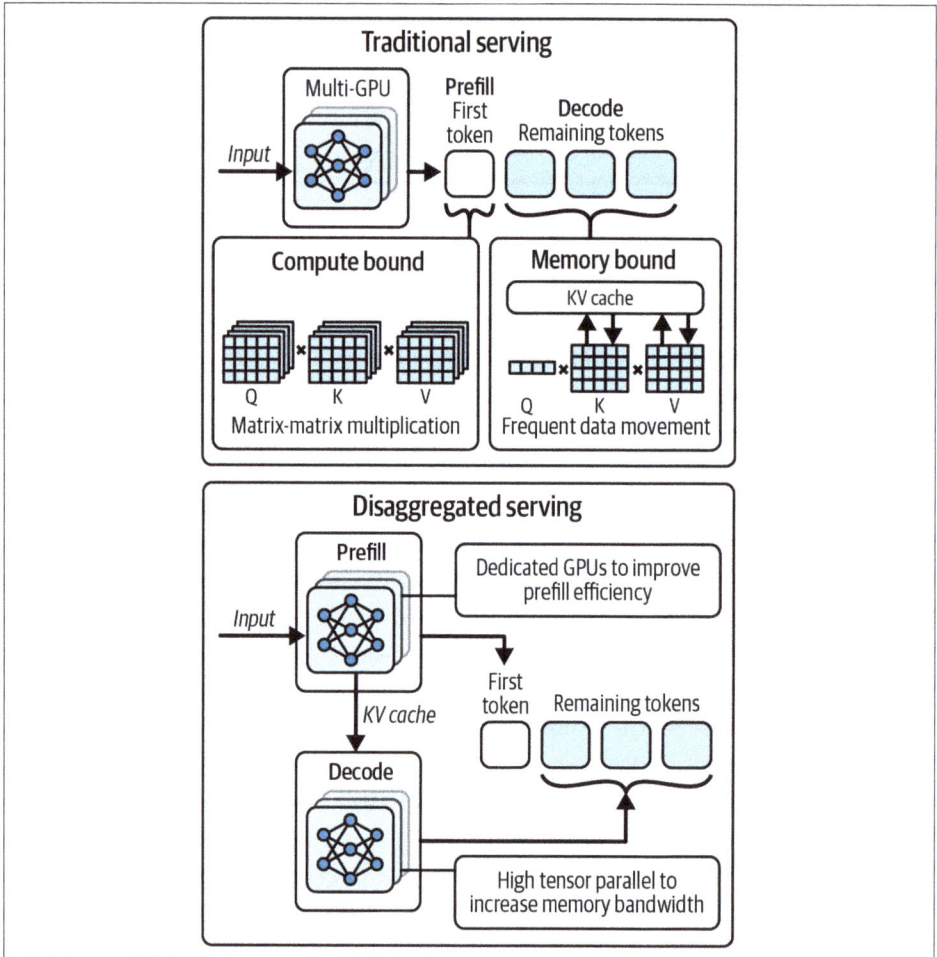

Figure 4-6. Disaggregated serving separates prefill and decode stages onto different GPU clusters (source: https://oreil.ly/nsxdl)

Here, the traditional setup is shown on the top, in which each GPU node handles both the prefill (compute-bound) and decode (memory-bound, I/O-bound) phases. On the bottom, the disaggregated serving configuration places the prefill workers in the GPU cluster and the decode workers in another GPU cluster.

A GPU in the prefill cluster generates the KV cache for the input sequence and uses NIXL to transfer it to a GPU in the decode cluster. This specialization produces higher overall throughput and advanced scaling configurations.

In such cases, the KV cache, which can run into tens of gigabytes in a long prompt, must move seamlessly from one processing unit to another in near-real time. This way, the text generation happens at speeds that are unnoticeable to end users.

Traditional methods that pass the data through CPU memory or even storage fall short in meeting the required pace and low-latency experience. NVIDIA created NIXL to tackle this exact scenario. NIXL allows multinode inference to scale without being bottlenecked by interconnect latency.

What we really want is a high-bandwidth GPU-to-GPU direct transfer between components. And we want this communication to overlap with computation. This way, the destination GPUs can start computing the next token while they're receiving the KV cache for the next set of input tokens from the source GPUs.

NIXL provides a direct channel for transferring data from one GPU to another or a small group of GPUs across compute nodes and even across racks. The system looks at the available pathways and always selects the one that gets the data there the quickest.

This intelligent routing is analogous to NCCL's path selection but optimized for inference patterns, including one-to-one, large-message transfers. For example, in a GB200/GB300 NVL72 rack, NIXL leverages the NVSwitch network first, whereas across NVL72 racks, it will automatically switch to InfiniBand or Ethernet RDMA, depending on what is supported.

In short, NIXL automatically picks the fastest lane, whether it's NVLink/NVLink-C2C on the same board, NVSwitch across a rack domain, InfiniBand/RoCE between racks, or even direct NVMe storage access.

Intelligent Interconnect Routing for KV Cache Transfers

Traditionally, one might transfer this data from GPU to GPU through a CPU, but this would be too slow, as we've already discussed. Another option to improve performance is to require that the source and destination GPUs are on the same compute node, but this limits our scaling flexibility. NIXL was created to address this issue. It was designed for direct GPU-to-GPU transfers of large payloads like the KV cache across GPUs, compute nodes, and racks, if necessary.

NIXL operates at high bandwidth and overlaps communication with computation as much as possible. This allows the destination GPUs to start generating the next set of tokens while they are receiving the KV cache from the source GPU.

Additionally, NIXL is interconnect-agnostic. It will use NVLink if GPUs are in the same compute node, NVSwitch if in the same compute node, InfiniBand or Ethernet with RDMA across nodes, or even PCIe or NVMe if needed. Similar to NCCL, NIXL will always select the fastest interconnects to route the data transfer. It also supports transferring to and from different memory tiers in a unified way across GPU HBM, CPU DRAM, and even to NVMe SSD!

NIXL Asynchronous API with Callbacks

From a developer's perspective, NIXL offers a straightforward API. You post a transfer request with a pointer to the data and a destination—either GPUs, CPUs, or storage targets like Amazon S3. NIXL will transfer that data as fast as possible.

For instance, a NIXL transfer request could send a KV cache segment to another GPU, a CPU host memory buffer, or even an object storage service. And it can do this all within the same API, as shown in Figure 4-7.

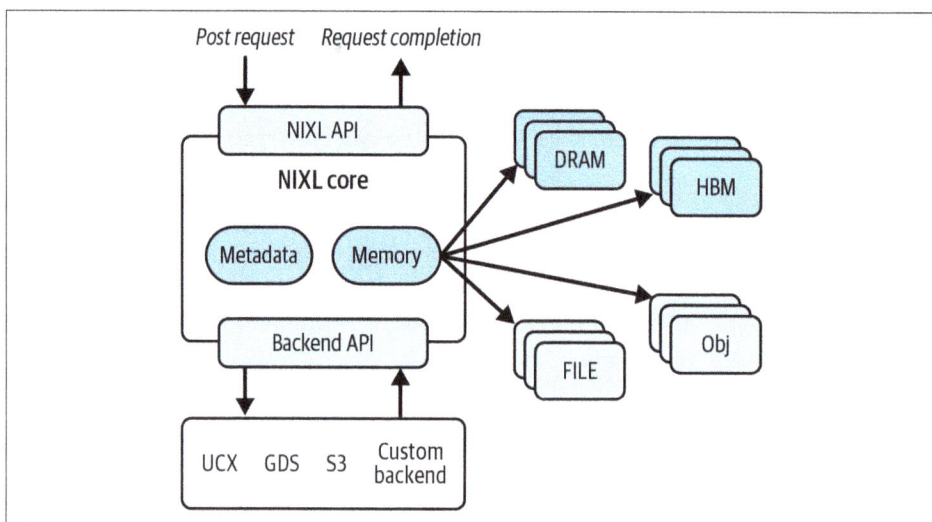

Figure 4-7. NIXL architecture (adapted from NVIDIA's Dynamo architecture overview (https://oreil.ly/nsxdl))

This modular design means that NIXL can adopt future transports as well. For example, it can incorporate upcoming protocols or faster storage-class memory without changing the user-facing API. Under the hood, NIXL coordinates the data movement using whatever backend is appropriate.

NIXL efficiently moves data between different tiers such as GPU HBM, CPU memory (DRAM), file storage (NVMe SSD), and object storage. It provides a single, unified API that automatically selects the fastest transport (e.g., GPU → GPU over NVLink, GPU → NVMe SSD with GDS, or NVSwitch fabric.) This way, you always get near line-rate performance when offloading KV cache segments.

Under the hood, NIXL hides all of this complexity. You register memory with `regis terMem`, obtain transfer descriptors with `trim`, prepare a nonblocking request with `prepXfer`, and submit it with `postXfer`. NIXL chooses whether to perform a direct PCIe or NVLink copy, an RDMA transfer, or a storage path such as GPUDirect Storage.

The NIXL library is nonblocking and returns a request handle that you poll with `checkXfer` to detect completion. This pattern overlaps communication and computation with minimal CPU overhead. The NIXL nonblocking API allows downstream kernels to consume incoming data without blocking on the transfer itself. For example, the destination GPU can begin consuming received KV cache chunks as soon as they arrive—even while the remaining chunks are still in flight.

A `nixlAgent` is NIXL's core transfer object. It encapsulates the endpoint configuration, memory registrations, and backend selection. It also manages metadata, connection information, and asynchronous transfer requests to and from other agents.

You need two agents for a transfer because each `nixlAgent` instance represents one endpoint in the transfer. The source agent (`agentSrc`) encapsulates the context, memory registrations, and backends for the origin of the data. The destination agent (`agentDst`) does the same for the receiver side.

With one agent per endpoint, `agentSrc` and `agentDst`, NIXL negotiates the optimal path between these endpoints and manages their independent resources and request lifecycles. These NIXL agents are shown in the following code to transfer data between a source and destination GPU:

```cpp
// NIXL 0.5.x style example: nonblocking VRAM->VRAM transfer between two agents
#include <nixl.h>
#include <nixl_types.h>

#include <cuda_runtime.h>
#include <iostream>
#include <thread>
#include <vector>
#include <cassert>
#include <cstdint>

int main() {
    // 1) Configure agents. Prefer UCX for GPU<->GPU,
    // allow GDS if you later target storage.
    nixl_agent_config cfg{};
```

```cpp
cfg.backends = {"UCX"};  // {"UCX","GDS"} if you also plan storage transfers
cfg.thread_safe = true;  // thread-safe mode added in early 0.2.x

// 2) Create source and destination agents
nixlAgent agentSrc("srcAgent", cfg);
nixlAgent agentDst("dstAgent", cfg);

// 3) Allocate simple test buffers on the same GPU for illustration
int deviceId = 0;
cudaSetDevice(deviceId);
const size_t bytes = 1 << 20; // 1 MiB

void* d_src = nullptr;
void* d_dst = nullptr;
cudaMalloc(&d_src, bytes);
cudaMalloc(&d_dst, bytes);

// 4) Build registration descriptors for VRAM
//     Each descriptor uses an address, length, and associated device
nixl_desc_t srcDesc{};
srcDesc.addr    = reinterpret_cast<uintptr_t>(d_src);
srcDesc.len     = bytes;
srcDesc.devId   = deviceId;
srcDesc.seg     = VRAM_SEG;

nixl_desc_t dstDesc{};
dstDesc.addr    = reinterpret_cast<uintptr_t>(d_dst);
dstDesc.len     = bytes;
dstDesc.devId   = deviceId;
dstDesc.seg     = VRAM_SEG;

std::vector<nixl_desc_t> srcList{srcDesc};
std::vector<nixl_desc_t> dstList{dstDesc};

// 5) Register memory with each agent and trim to xfer descriptors
auto srcRegs = agentSrc.registerMem(srcList);
auto dstRegs = agentDst.registerMem(dstList);

auto srcXfer = srcRegs.trim();  // metadata-free descriptors used for xfer
auto dstXfer = dstRegs.trim();

// 6) Prepare a WRITE from srcAgent->dstAgent, then post it (nonblocking)
nixlReqH reqHandle = nullptr;

// prepare + post
if (agentSrc.prepXfer(NIXL_WRITE, srcXfer, dstXfer, "dstAgent", reqHandle)
  != NIXL_SUCCESS) {
    std::cerr << "prepXfer failed\n";
    return 1;
}
if (agentSrc.postXfer(NIXL_WRITE, srcXfer, dstXfer, "dstAgent", reqHandle)
  != NIXL_SUCCESS) {
```

```
            std::cerr << "postXfer failed\n";
            return 1;
    }

    std::cout << "Transfer posted - doing other work...\n";

    // 7) Poll for completion (replaces deprecated getNotifs/poll map)
    nixl_status_t st;
    do {
        st = agentSrc.checkXfer(reqHandle);
        if (st == NIXL_INPROGRESS) std::this_thread::yield();
    } while (st == NIXL_INPROGRESS);

    if (st != NIXL_SUCCESS) {
        std::cerr << "Transfer completed with error: " << st << "\n";
        agentSrc.releaseReqH(reqHandle);
        agentSrc.deregisterMem(srcRegs);
        agentDst.deregisterMem(dstRegs);
        cudaFree(d_src);
        cudaFree(d_dst);
        return 1;
    }

    std::cout << "Transfer completed!\n";

    // 8) Cleanup
    agentSrc.releaseReqH(reqHandle);
    agentSrc.deregisterMem(srcRegs);
    agentDst.deregisterMem(dstRegs);

    cudaFree(d_src);
    cudaFree(d_dst);
    return 0;
}
```

Here, the NIXL agents are initialized with names and a configuration. Memory is registered with `registerMem` and trimmed to transfer descriptors with `trim`. A non-blocking write from `srcAgent` to `dstAgent` is prepared with `prepXfer` and submitted with `postXfer`. The program continues doing other work while the transfer is in flight. Completion is detected by polling the request handle with `checkXfer` while yielding the thread if the request is in progress. After success, the handle is released with `releaseReqH` and the registrations are deregistered.

Internally, NIXL uses Unified Communication X (UCX) (*https://oreil.ly/webTn*), an HPC library that provides a unified API over various interconnects that NIXL leverages for low-level transport, including InfiniBand, TCP, shared memory, etc. NIXL also uses GPUDirect RDMA and InfiniBand GPUDirect Async (IBGDA) (*https://oreil.ly/6guAh*) to allow the GPU to initiate transfers without CPU involvement. This is an important optimization, as in older systems, the CPU might need to kick off the transfer—even if the data path is purely RDMA. IBGDA offloads that initiation to the GPU/NIC, which further reduces latency.

Another interesting feature of NIXL is that it avoids unnecessary copies such as staging buffers. For example, if data is in pageable CPU memory, it would choose to pin the data to prevent it from being paged out. But if the data is in GPU memory, it would just send the data directly. In other words, NIXL tries to avoid staging buffers that copy to an intermediate host buffer before transferring the data to the destination.

KV Cache Offloading with NIXL

The design motivation for NIXL is closely related to best practices for handling large memory for LLM inference. If GPUs don't have enough memory to hold the entire KV cache for a long sequence or multiturn conversation, NIXL allows the inference server (e.g., NVIDIA Dynamo) to offload the KV cache to CPU memory—or even NVMe SSD—and bring it back as needed.

NIXL, in conjunction with the KV Cache Manager in Dynamo, for instance, can manage this transfer hierarchy efficiently. Consider NVIDIA's Grace Hopper and Grace Blackwell Superchips with a huge amount of unified CPU and GPU memory shared over the fast NVLink interconnect (see Figure 4-8).

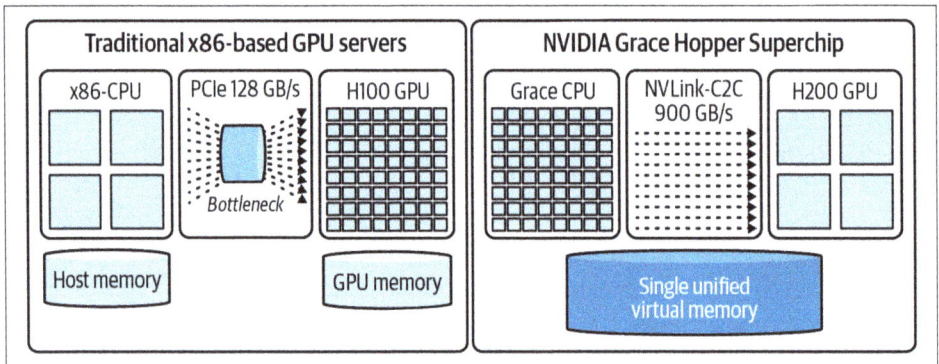

Figure 4-8. *ARM-based Grace Hopper Superchip architecture leverages the 900 GB/s NVLink-C2C and overcomes traditional PCIe bottlenecks (source: https://oreil.ly/zf6rF)*

The inference server can quickly offload a large KV cache to the large CPU memory to free up the limited GPU HBM. This yields a huge boost in inference performance. Specifically, a PCIe-based x86 + H100 system can improve time-to-first-token (TTFT) latency by as much as 14× for long input sequences compared to recomputing the cache. This speedup (*https://oreil.ly/zf6rF*) is shown in Figure 4-9.

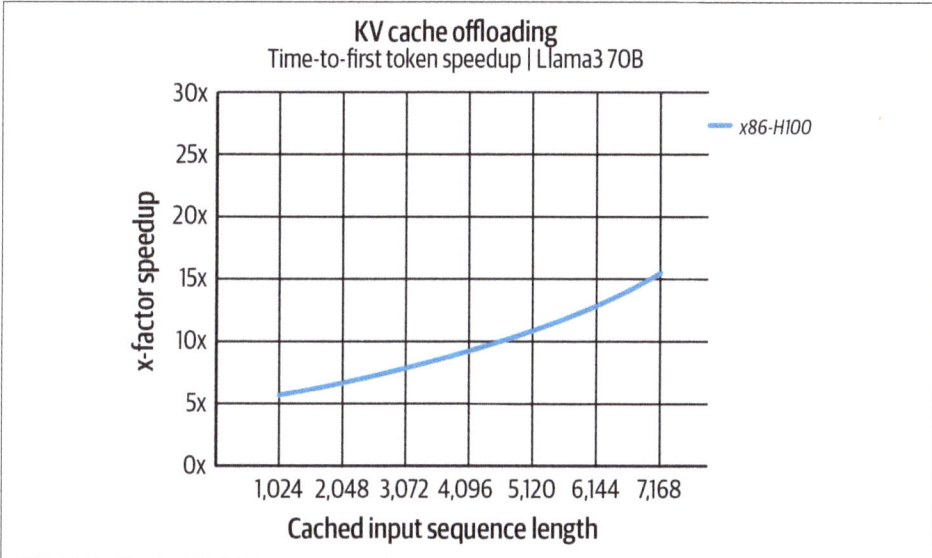

Figure 4-9. Measured 14× TTFT speedup with KV cache offloading for an x86-based NVIDIA H100 GPU system on large input sequence lengths compared to recalculating it from scratch (source: https://oreil.ly/zf6rF)

Furthermore, with its 900 GB/s NVLink-C2C interconnect, the ARM-based Grace Hopper Superchip delivers 2× faster TTFT latency compared (*https://oreil.ly/AAkvr*) to the non-superchip, x86-based H100 version described previously. This speedup is shown in Figure 4-10.

These are impressive gains enabled by codesigning NIXL software with NVIDIA superchip hardware. And NIXL, designed exactly with those numbers in mind, makes offloading the KV cache a viable option by keeping transfer costs low. KV cache offloading is a key part of large-scale inference deployments, as we'll see in an upcoming chapter—especially for massive LLMs where memory capacity is a limiting factor.

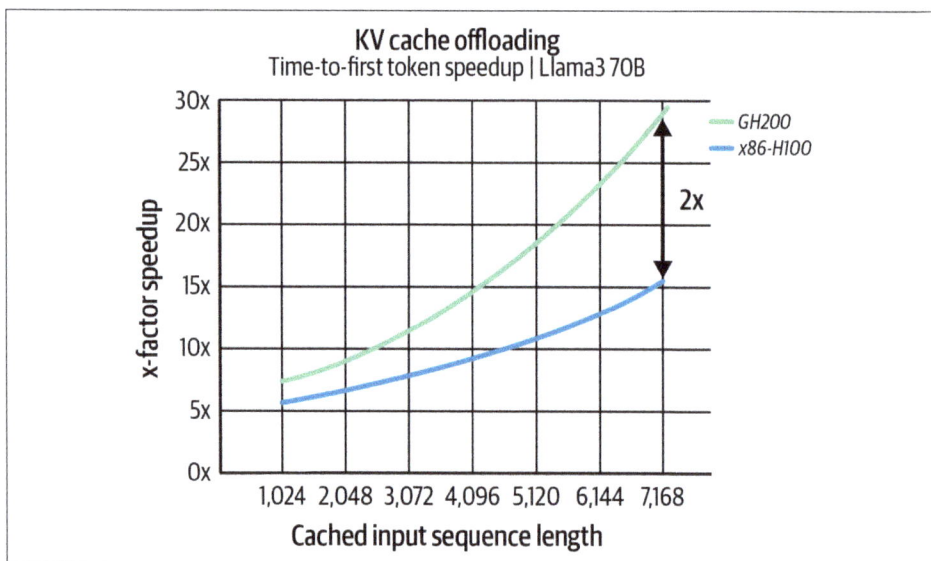

Figure 4-10. 2× speedup in TTFT for the ARM-based Grace Hopper Superchip compared to the x86-based H100 GPU system due to KV cache offloading with the 900 GB/s NVLink-C2C interconnect (source: https://oreil.ly/zf6rF)

As models get bigger and workloads get more complex, having a library like NIXL to efficiently move large blobs of data asynchronously is critical. For performance engineers, if your use case involves moving large amounts of data between stages (e.g., pipeline parallelism) and other components (e.g., GPUs or storage) in a system, consider whether NCCL is sufficient or whether a specialized solution like NIXL is an option to optimize that flow of data.

NIXL and High-Performance Inference Systems Like NVIDIA Dynamo

The impact of NIXL on performance is huge for distributed inference systems like NVIDIA Dynamo, also released in early 2025. According to NVIDIA's internal testing (*https://oreil.ly/sxdPg*), the open source NVIDIA Dynamo framework used NIXL to achieve up to 30× higher inference throughput on a ~680B-parameter LLM when using a 72-GPU Blackwell NVL72 rack.

What was once a major latency barrier—shifting many gigabytes of context data between nodes—is now a relatively quick, asynchronous operation under NIXL. We will cover NVIDIA Dynamo, TensorRT, vLLM, and respective model inference optimizations in depth in a later chapter.

NCCL Versus NIXL

It's important to note that NIXL is not a replacement for NCCL but a complement. NCCL still handles synchronized collectives for GPUs working on a single task/stage in parallel, such as an all-reduce split across multiple GPUs. NIXL, on the other hand, performs asynchronous data transfers between tasks/stages—or between distinct components (e.g., GPUs, CPUs, storage) in a distributed system. Table 4-5 shows a comparison of NCCL versus NIXL.

Table 4-5. Comparison of NCCL and NIXL

Aspect	NCCL (collective communication)	NIXL (point-to-point communication)
Primary use case	Many-to-many collectives (e.g., all-reduce, all-gather) for tightly coupled GPU groups in training.	One-to-one or one-to-few transfers (e.g., sending large tensors or caches) for distributed inference or pipelining.
Communication pattern	Synchronized collective operations—all participants must reach the call (barrier semantics).	Asynchronous send/receive—one initiator, one or multiple targets (supports one-way data movement).
Overlap with compute	Can overlap to some extent (e.g., overlap backward compute with all-reduce in DDP) using separate CUDA streams.	Designed for maximal overlap—transfers run fully in parallel with compute, with polling notification to detect completion.
Topology awareness	Yes—auto-detects topology, uses rings/trees and NVLink/NVSwitch optimally for collectives.	Yes—interconnect-agnostic; automatically uses NVLink, NVSwitch, PCIe, InfiniBand/RDMA, or GDS, depending on source-dest locations.
Data scope	Typically small-to-medium tensors (e.g., gradients) that need aggregation across all GPUs.	Optimized for large data blobs (e.g., hundreds of MBs or more, like LLM KV cache or model shards) that need fast point-to-point transit.
Integration	Integrated in training frameworks (PyTorch DDP, Horovod, etc., call NCCL under the hood).	Provided as an open source library used by NVIDIA Dynamo. It is developed in the Dynamo project. The developer calls the NIXL API to send/receive as needed in the inference server or custom code.
Example	All-reduce of 100 MB of gradients across 8 GPUs in parallel.	Send a 1 GB KV cache from GPU 0 to GPU 1 (or to CPU memory or an NVMe SSD) during an inference pipeline.

While NCCL does support peer-to-peer `send()`/`recv()` operations, it's best suited for collective operations in synchronous training environments. NIXL, on the other hand, addresses the needs of asynchronous, point-to-point data transfers common in large-scale inference and pipeline parallelism. For instance, NVIDIA's Dynamo inference server, discussed in a later chapter, uses NIXL to orchestrate KV cache movement across inference components, including GPUs, CPUs, and SSDs.

In summary, NCCL is designed to maximize collective throughput across multiple GPUs both within a single host and across nodes. It automatically selects hardware topology-aware ring and tree communication algorithms that fully saturate the given PCIe, NVLink, InfiniBand, and Ethernet links. NCCL is typically associated with ultrascale model training workloads. NIXL builds on NCCL's high-performance principles and orchestrates asynchronous, hardware-agnostic point-to-point transfers across GPUs, CPUs, and storage devices. NIXL was designed for large-scale distributed inference workloads, including super fast KV cache data transfers.

Key Takeaways

With careful engineering—and using the techniques described in this chapter—you can often reach performance at or near the physical "speed of light" hardware limits. Here are some key lessons to remember when tuning your network layer:

Topology matters
> The interconnects between nodes (internode, InfiniBand) and within nodes (intranode, NVLink/NVSwitch) influence the optimal communication strategy. Consider hierarchical approaches for multinode and multi-GPU configurations. Always ensure that you're using the fastest interconnect available—and not accidentally sending data over slow paths due to a misconfiguration or unexpected default value! In practice, check NCCL's behavior and utilize features like SHARP for large-scale, in-network aggregations/reductions if available.

Tune the environment and system
> Sometimes a single environment variable or OS setting can boost throughput. For instance, one can increase NIC buffers, enable/disable NCCL features and logging, and pin CPUs correctly. Performing system optimizations at the OS and driver levels (e.g., IRQ affinity) can help remove bottlenecks, as described in Chapter 3.

Utilize the latest hardware innovations
> New hardware like NVIDIA Grace Hopper and Grace Blackwell Superchips provide massive CPU memory and fast CPU-GPU interconnects. Use them for things like hosting large datasets, splitting your data, partitioning your model, and offloading large KV caches to the CPU. In-network computing like SHARP can accelerate collective operations by 2×–5×—especially at scale. Stay informed on these new compute and networking hardware innovations because they will change the optimal configuration with each new generation.

You want to saturate your GPUs to the point where they're computing 100% of the time while simultaneously communicating in the background. You also want to saturate your network links with useful data. And you want to keep your disks streaming data at full throttle. All of this should happen together in perfect harmony.

Achieving all of this requires iterative tuning and validation, as well as some trade-offs like more memory usage and more code complexity. But this kind of tuning pays off with faster model training and inference—as well as better overall utilization of expensive infrastructure.

Conclusion

The evolution of high-performance, distributed, and multi-GPU communication and storage systems represents the foundation for tuning large, complex AI systems. By utilizing specialized libraries such as NCCL for collective operations, NIXL for efficient inference data transfers, and RDMA for ultra-low-latency communication, AI systems can significantly reduce bottlenecks and increase performance.

The integration of smart networking hardware like NVSwitch and SHARP-enabled InfiniBand switches translates directly into higher training and inference performance. Likewise, keeping software up-to-date is key, as newer versions of CUDA and PyTorch come with these optimizations built in for the latest GPUs and networking technology (e.g., SHARP). Utilizing NVIDIA Dynamo, vLLM, and similar serving frameworks can help deploy these improvements easily for inference workloads.

Ultimately, this chapter highlights that no single component can provide peak performance alone. It is the careful coordination and codesign of high-speed communication, efficient data handling, and system-wide tuning that leads to scalable and robust AI systems.

For performance engineers, the lesson is that fast data movement is as critical as raw compute power. The fastest GPU in the world provides little benefit if it's constantly waiting for data from a CPU or another GPU.

In the next chapter, we will explore GPU-based storage strategies and optimizations. Complementing networking protocols and libraries like RDMA, NCCL, and NIXL, GDS, and highly efficient input pipelines are part of the holistic approach to keeping the GPUs fed with continuous work.

## CHAPTER 5

GPU-Based Storage I/O Optimizations

Feeding data to the GPUs is as important as the compute itself for AI workloads. Consider a scenario with a 100-trillion-parameter model training on thousands of GPUs. Such a model might process billions of training samples, including tokens, images, audio, video, etc.

This means that an enormous amount of data must be read from storage and fed to the GPUs as quickly as possible. If the storage pipeline is slow, the GPUs will starve and sit idle. This results in low utilization despite the sophisticated communication optimizations that we've discussed.

This chapter addresses storage and input pipeline optimizations. Specifically, it demonstrates how to read data efficiently from disk or remote storage, how to preprocess it, and how to overlap its I/O with GPU compute.

Fast Storage and Data Locality

Large model training jobs usually need to read huge datasets. It's common to have on the order of billions or even trillions of training samples for large language models. This is in the range of terabytes of text data for language models and petabytes of images for vision models.

At ultra scale, your storage system must consistently provide massive throughput to keep up with the thousands and millions of GPUs potentially running for months at a time. Colocating NVMe SSDs within racks—or using NVMe over Fabrics (NVMe-oF) with rack-local switch topologies—minimizes network hops and improves performance consistency.

If your data lives in network-attached storage like an NFS server or cloud object storage (e.g., Amazon S3), you need to ensure that the aggregate read bandwidth from all of your compute nodes is sufficient. Consider a scenario in which each GPU needs 200 MB/s of training data to stay busy based on the model and batch size. If you have 8 GPUs total, that's about 1.6 GB/s aggregate bandwidth needed. Modern high-end GPUs like Blackwell and Rubin demand even more bandwidth to keep them saturated.

An NVIDIA Grace Blackwell GB200/GB300 NVL72 rack with 72 Blackwell GPUs connected in one NVLink domain. If each GPU needs 200 MB/s of training data to stay busy, this can require 14–20 GB/s of aggregate storage throughput to keep all 72 GPUs busy. For these types of ultrascale workloads, your storage solution needs to scale accordingly.

> If your workload streams heavier media or multimodal samples, calibrate using your measured bytes-per-sample and samples-per-second. In such cases, aggregate demand can be much higher.

One solution is to use faster local storage such as NVMe SSDs in the same rack—or NVMe-oF network topology. Another solution is to use a parallel filesystem like Lustre or General Parallel File System (GPFS), etc., to cache the data on local SSDs. Assuming the storage system can keep up, it's important to provision multiple data loading threads to keep the pipe saturated. Watch out for the Python GIL!

Whenever possible, place data as physically close to the compute nodes as possible. "Close" could mean on the same physical node, such as a local NVMe SSD drive, or at least in the same rack with a high-speed interconnect with something like NVMe over Fabric (NVME-oF) or an advanced storage accelerator.

For distributed, multinode model training, a common approach is to shard the dataset across nodes so that each node primarily reads a subset of data from its local disk. For example, if you have 100 TB of data and 10 nodes, you might presplit 10 TB to each node's local storage. Then each node's data loader reads only from its local 10 TB. This avoids saturating the network with redundant reads—especially if the dataset size does not easily fit in RAM.

Frameworks like PyTorch's `DistributedSampler` will coordinate workers such that each process gets a unique slice of data per epoch. This aligns well with the goal of sharding the data over multiple cluster nodes.

Sequential Versus Random Read Patterns

GPUs are extremely fast at crunching data, but they prefer that the data be read in large contiguous chunks for efficiency. Similarly, storage measures much higher throughput for large, sequential reads than for small, random reads. As such, when preparing your datasets or storage layout, try to arrange for sequential access as much as possible.

For instance, when training with images, avoid storing millions of individual image files since this will lead to lots of random seeks all over the disk. Consider, instead, storing them in a few large binary (e.g., Arrow, TFRecord, or Parquet) files, database files, WebDataset tar files, or equivalents. In these cases, each file contains many concatenated samples, which is ideal.

> Combining small files into large shards is even more important with today's faster GPUs, since excessive small random reads will more quickly become a bottleneck. And while most modern parallel filesystems and object stores can handle a degree of small random reads, it's best to verify the performance explicitly.

Reading a chunk of data from the larger files will naturally get many samples in one pass. If using an object store like Amazon S3, it's common to combine smaller objects into larger ones ahead of time for this exact reason.

Also, it's important to tune the read size since reading in 1 MB chunks will yield better throughput than 4 KB chunks due to the lower per-read overhead. Many data loader libraries allow adjusting buffer size and prefetch chunk size. For example, Python's `open()` uses the OS's read-ahead buffer to accelerate sequential scans, but random reads won't benefit much from larger buffers or buffered I/O libraries.

Instead, you should batch your reads into larger contiguous chunks or use a high-level dataset API (e.g., `TFRecordDataset` or PyTorch's `IterableDataset` and `Data Loader` with configurable prefetch sizes). And while many of these frameworks and libraries are internally optimized for large sequential reads, tuning their buffer and prefetch parameters is still important.

If your access pattern still must be random, issue multiple reads in parallel using either threads calling `pread()` or Linux's asynchronous I/O interfaces like `io_uring`. With features like preregistered buffers and polling, `io_uring` allows submitting batches of I/O requests with minimal kernel overhead. It can further improve random read throughput by reducing per-syscall overhead. This helps hide latency and achieve high IOPS.

One should use a filesystem optimized for large, concurrent I/O. XFS is common on Linux NVMe servers. You should mount it with `noatime` to eliminate costly access-time updates on each read. For networked storage services like Amazon EFS, make sure your EFS filesystem is in Max I/O performance mode (*https://oreil.ly/Xz-9d*) for the highest aggregate throughput. If you need consistent bandwidth, you can switch from the default Bursting throughput mode (*https://oreil.ly/GxzAE*) to Provisioned throughput. These settings ensure your I/O layer can keep up with massive, parallel AI workloads.

Tuning NVMe and Filesystem for Throughput

Modern Linux uses a multiqueue block I/O scheduler, `blk-mq`, that spreads I/O across the CPU cores. For fast NVMe SSDs, you might need to tune the queue depths and number of submission queues. Usually the defaults are fine, but if you know that your workload is heavily sequential, you might use the "none" I/O scheduler.

The legacy completely fair queueing (CFQ) scheduler is obsolete. Modern kernels use the `none` or `mq-deadline` multiqueue scheduler by default for NVMe. This setting can be checked using `/sys/block/<device>/queue/scheduler`. The "none" scheduler is standard for low latency workloads. On some storage devices, you might encounter the budget fair queueing (BFQ) scheduler.

> For high-performance NVMe, it's recommended to still use the `none` or `mq-deadline` multiqueue scheduler to maximize through-put. You can verify and set the scheduler using `/sys/block/nvme*/queue/scheduler`. It's almost always configured properly out of the box, but it's worth verifying with a quick check.

Another tuning aspect is read ahead. The kernel will automatically read ahead extra data when it detects sequential reads. You can see the read ahead setting in `/sys/block/<device>/queue/read_ahead_kb`. For example, by default it is likely set to 128 KB. If you are streaming large files, increase this to a few MB. This will improve your throughput by reducing syscall overhead and pipelining reads. This can be done using `blockdev --setra` on the device.

If using NVMe SSD disks, ensure that they are set up on the fastest interface available on your system. And make sure you have enough lanes (e.g., PCIe) so they're not bot-tlenecked. Sometimes, multiple SSDs can be striped using RAID 0, for instance, to fully utilize these devices and maximize throughput—especially if a single disk cannot saturate your GPUs.

The Linux page cache will automatically cache recently read data into RAM from disk. For large datasets, you might exceed the available RAM and thrash the cache. But for moderately large datasets, warm caches can greatly speed up training.

If your data—or a large portion of it—can fit into RAM (including CPU + GPU unified memory on a Grace Blackwell Superchip, for example), you should consider preloading it completely into memory at startup. This effectively creates an ultrafast in-memory cache for the GPU. This can greatly reduce disk I/O during training. However, for massive petabyte-scale datasets, that's usually not feasible. In these cases, streaming the data with optimized I/O is the way to go.

Be sure to use multiple workers in data loading (e.g., PyTorch's `DataLoader(num_workers=N)`). These separate CPU threads/processes will fetch and preprocess data in parallel to feed the many GPUs in your training job. Finding the right number of workers is empirical.

We will dive into PyTorch performance tuning in Chapters 13 and 14, but it's worth noting here that you should enable `pin_memory=True` and use `non_blocking=True` to enable overlapping host-to-device copies. And by setting `persistent_workers=True`, you avoid worker respawn overhead across epochs. It's also useful to tune `pre fetch_factor` per workload. The default `prefetch_factor` is 2 for `num_workers` greater than 0.

Too few workers and the GPU will be idle. Too many workers and their threads will start contending for available CPU cores and I/O bandwidth. Monitor CPU usage and disk throughput. Ideally, you want near 100% utilization of disk throughput and some headroom on CPU.

> For CPUs with a very high core count, such as the 72-core NVIDIA Grace CPU used in the GB200/GB300 Superchips, you can often utilize more data loader workers. Just be mindful of diminishing returns caused by excessive I/O contention.

Using NVIDIA GDS

GDS is a feature that allows GPUs to read data directly from storage devices, or through the network storage stack, without creating extra copies in CPU memory. Normally, when a GPU wants to read data from an NVMe SSD, the data first goes from SSD to CPU memory. Then a CUDA call copies the data from CPU memory to GPU memory.

GDS complements GPUDirect RDMA since GDS accelerates storage-to-GPU DMA, while GPUDirect RDMA accelerates network-to-GPU DMA. Neither eliminates CPU orchestration. Both remove the host memory bounce buffer.

With GDS, the GPU can initiate a direct memory access (DMA) against the SSD or NIC to move the data into its own HBM memory. This bypasses the extra copy through the CPU's path. GDS supports local NVMe devices and remote storage using NVMe-oF.

In practice, GDS creates a direct DMA path that bypasses host memory bounce buffers between storage and GPU memory. This broadens the applicability of GDS to cluster filesystems and even some object storage systems. (Note: the CPU still configures and orchestrates the I/O.)

Enabling GDS requires a modern NVIDIA GPU and a storage stack that supports direct memory access—as well as the correct NVIDIA drivers and CUDA toolkit. Typically, local NVMe SSDs or RAID volumes are used. GDS support depends on the filesystem and RDMA-capable stack. As of this writing, supported stacks include local NVMe and NVMe-oF on XFS/EXT4 with O_DIRECT, NFS over RDMA, and select parallel filesystems such as BeeGFS, WekaFS, VAST, IBM Storage Scale, and others that integrate with nvidia-fs.

The application needs to use the correct APIs. You can use CUDA's cuFile library to read files through GDS. cuFile supports features like automatic buffer alignment and integration with common filesystems.

In practical terms, if you have GDS set up and your read path uses cuFileRead, the data can flow from disk to GPU memory directly. This reduces CPU utilization (allowing CPUs to do other preprocessing) and can improve throughput, especially when the CPU is a bottleneck. cuFileRead integrates directly with the Linux filesystem. You can also use cuFile's asynchronous APIs, such as cuFileReadAsync and cuFileWriteAsync to integrate storage I/O on CUDA streams (discussed in Chapter 11) for overlap and pipelining.

Use O_DIRECT when possible to enable direct DMA and bypass the OS page cache. With modern GDS releases, cuFile can also operate on non-O_DIRECT file descriptors, but misalignment may incur extra copies or reduced performance.

Many storage vendors like WekaIO, DDN, VAST, Cloudian, etc., have released GDS-aware solutions or plugins so their systems can deliver data using RDMA directly into GPU memory. This ecosystem support means GDS can be used by enterprise network-attached storage (NAS) and parallel filesystems out of the box.

Reports from VAST Data (*https://oreil.ly/895IU*) show a 20% boost in read throughput using GDS on certain AI workloads. In their case, using GDS on a single A100 GPU achieved 20% higher read throughput for sequential reads, which pushed significantly closer to the 100 Gb/s link capacity per NIC when applicable. Figure 5-1 shows the architecture with and without GDS.

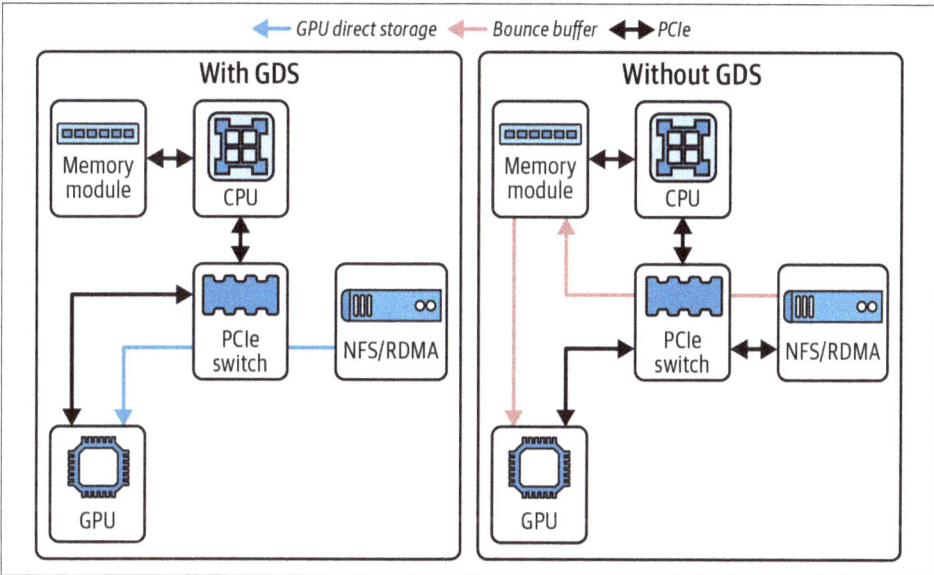

Figure 5-1. VAST Data's network architecture with GDS versus without GDS

Here on the left, we see traditional staged DMA that copies through host memory. On the right is a direct GPU pull using GDS that bypasses host memory copies and reduces CPU utilization. A report by VAST (*https://oreil.ly/895IU*) measured a 20% read-throughput boost on an NVIDIA Ampere A100 GPU and a 30%+ increase on a Hopper H100 GPU due to its higher NIC bandwidth and greater CPU burden.

> Validate on your workload and fabric, as uplifts vary by IO size, queue depth, NIC generation, filesystem implementation, etc.

However, GDS may need tuning, and not all workloads see a huge boost. If your CPU was easily handling the data transfers, GDS might not change throughput much. However, it will lower CPU usage, which frees up the CPU to perform data processing and other tasks. On the other hand, if the CPU is saturated with many memcpy operations, then GDS will help a lot.

One has to make sure that O_DIRECT semantics and alignment are applied correctly when using GDS. Host pinned memory is not used in the storage-to-GPU data path. cuFile registers GPU device buffers, and the nvidia-fs kernel driver orchestrates DMA directly between the storage device or RDMA NIC and GPU memory. It integrates directly with the POSIX file descriptors, so you can use cuFile with regular files—including network filesystems if they support RDMA.

Consider having a tiny training batch size of 1 MB and wanting to feed 1,000 batches each second to the GPUs. This is roughly 1,000 MB/s. Doing that copy with the CPU would easily consume a few cores. With GDS, the GPU would pull that 1,000 MB/s directly from disk and free up the CPU. At higher rates—or with thousands of GPUs—this becomes even more pronounced.

Since training workloads are overwhelmingly read-heavy, most GDS performance gains are evaluated when reading data from storage. However, it's important to have fast checkpoint writes as well. For RDMA-accelerated writes, the filesystem must support RDMA writes for GDS.

WekaFS is a well-known storage provider for ultrascale AI training workloads. They offer a parallel filesystem that ships with GDS-aware plugins for both read and write workloads over RDMA.

Checkpointing GPU State with cuda-checkpoint

You can checkpoint GPU state on Linux using NVIDIA's cuda-checkpoint utility together with a CPU process checkpoint tool such as Checkpoint/Restore in User-space (CRIU). cuda-checkpoint suspends CUDA inside a running process, waits for submitted work to complete, copies device memory to host allocations managed by the driver, and releases GPU resources. This way, a CPU-side checkpointer can snapshot the process.

The suspend path locks CUDA driver entry points, drains outstanding work, copies device memory to host, and releases GPU resources. When estimating suspend time, consider the amount of device memory in use—as well as the host-link bandwidth available during suspend.

Since the driver copies device memory into host allocations during the suspend phase, the effective suspend time is bounded by the memory image size and your platform interconnect. You should profile with Nsight Systems markers around the lock and checkpoint calls to verify actual time spent during the suspend phase.

When you want the process to resume, the driver reacquires the GPUs, maps device memory to their original addresses, restores CUDA objects such as streams and contexts, and then unlocks the driver and process to allow CUDA calls to proceed.

Specifically, the CUDA Driver API exposes cuCheckpointProcessLock, cuCheckpoint ProcessCheckpoint, cuCheckpointProcessRestore, and cuCheckpointProcess Unlock. Restore requires persistence mode enabled (or a call to cuInit) and it can remap to different physical GPUs of the same chip type.

It's important to note that this path is orthogonal to framework-level model checkpoints (e.g., PyTorch checkpoints). CUDA checkpoints are useful for fault tolerance, preemption, and migration of long-running training and inference jobs.

Unlike data ingestion with GDS, the checkpoint path does not DMA directly from GPU memory to storage. Instead, the device memory image is first brought into host memory by the driver during suspend. CRIU then persists that process memory to the checkpoint image. Use this to complement, not replace, your framework's state-dict or sharded checkpoint files.

Measuring GDS with gdsio

NVIDIA provides a tool called gdsio, installed under /usr/local/cuda/gds/tools by default, to benchmark GDS throughput between disk and GPU. This is super useful.

When using GDS, it's not uncommon to see improvements on the order of 10%–20% in throughput or more—especially in CPU-constrained scenarios. Let's take a look at an example and compare a pure CPU-mediated read ("before") versus a direct GDS read ("after") using NVIDIA's gdsio tool (*https://oreil.ly/rALpT*). Here are the CLI command and throughput/latency results:

```
# Before (Storage → CPU Memory only)

# CPU path, host memory, async copies (-x 2)
$ /usr/local/cuda/gds/tools/gdsio \
    -f /mnt/data/large_file \
    -d 0 -w 4 -s 10G -i 1M -I 0 -x 2

Total Throughput: 8.0 GB/s
Average Latency: 1.25 ms
```

The first call shown here uses the CPU path with pinned host memory and async copies (-x 2) in read mode (-I 0) to gather a baseline. The second call below enables the GDS path (-x 0) in read mode (-I 0) for the same configuration. Make sure to use the transfer selector consistently when comparing paths. For `gdsio`, `-x 2` measures CPU-mediated transfers, and `-x 0` measures the GDS path:

```
# After (Storage → GPU Memory using GPUDirect Storage)
#   - same config, GDS path (-x 0)
$ /usr/local/cuda/gds/tools/gdsio \
    -f /mnt/data/large_file \
    -d 0 -w 4 -s 10G -i 1M -I 0 -x 0

Total Throughput: 9.6 GB/s
Average Latency: 1.00 ms
```

We see that using GDS to create a direct data path from disk into GPU memory increases throughput by 20% with a corresponding decrease in average I/O latency, as shown in Table 5-1. It does this while freeing up CPU cycles previously spent moving data through host buffers. This simple benchmark shows how to verify GDS's benefits in your system.

Table 5-1. Throughput and latency before GDS versus after GDS

Path	Throughput	Latency
Storage → CPU (without GDS)	8.0 GB/s	1.25 ms
Storage → GPU (with GDS)	9.6 GB/s (+20%)	1.00 ms (−20%)

In this example, using GDS (Storage → GPU) increased read throughput from 8.0 GB/s to 9.6 GB/s and reduced latency from 1.25 ms to 1.00 ms. This translates to ~20% improvement in both throughput (higher) and latency (lower).

DeepSeek's Fire-Flyer File System

DeepSeek created a custom, open source filesystem called Fire-Flyer File System (3FS) (*https://oreil.ly/haIQx*) from the ground up. It was born out of their observation that AI workloads perform massive numbers of random reads.

These random reads make conventional read data caching ineffective—and even counterproductive—for LLM training and inference workloads. By eliminating caching and employing direct file I/O, 3FS ensures that every request goes straight to the NVMe SSD device and avoids wasteful cache management. This approach is similar to modern HPC filesystems that prioritize direct storage access. As such, 3FS minimizes kernel page-cache involvement and host memory copies during reads.

> 3FS mirrors the trend of codesigning storage specifically for AI. This is similar to NVIDIA's GDS, which is designed to work with high-performance parallel filesystems to achieve similar direct-GPU throughput.

3FS consists of four key components: cluster manager, metadata service, storage service, and client. These are interconnected over an RDMA-capable fabric like InfiniBand or RoCE to minimize CPU involvement and host-side copies. These components and connections are shown in Figure 5-2.

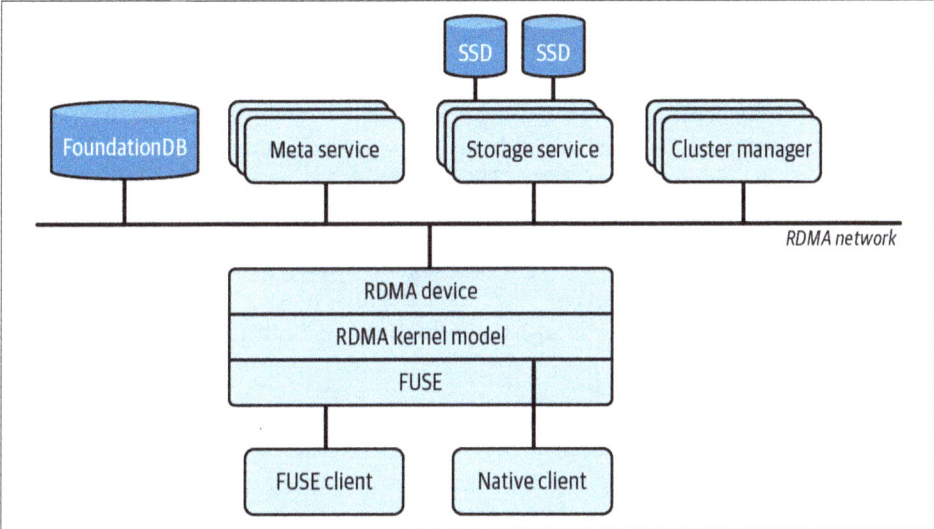

Figure 5-2. Components of DeepSeek's Fire-Flyer File System (3FS) (source: https://oreil.ly/xD3id)

3FS is a Linux-based filesystem, which allows compatibility with existing applications while leveraging RDMA reads for direct GPU-accessible data transfers. Metadata is sharded and replicated across multiple nodes for scale-out performance. Data paths bypass the OS page cache entirely to maintain optimal throughput.

> If a file system is implemented using FUSE in user space, it will not be able to deliver a GDS path because GDS requires kernel-level filesystem integration with O_DIRECT semantics. Only GDS-enabled kernel clients or specifically integrated parallel file systems can provide direct transfers into GPU memory.

To feed data directly into GPU pipelines, DeepSeek integrates RDMA-based transfers in 3FS. If you require a true GDS path, use a GDS-enabled kernel filesystem client such as NVMe, NVMe-oF, BeeGFS, WekaFS, IBM Storage Scale, or VAST. This allows asynchronous, zero-copy data movement directly into GPU device memory with minimal overheads.

3FS complements this chapter's techniques for overlapping I/O with computation by enabling data prefetch and transfer to run concurrently with GPU kernels. 3FS effectively extends the cascading pipeline/wave concept (discussed in Chapter 4) to storage layers.

DeepSeek has publicly reported multi-terabyte-per-second aggregate read throughput for 3FS on large clusters, with results up to 7.3 TB/s in their environment. In another benchmark (*https://oreil.ly/FJovC*), a large 3FS cluster achieved aggregated read throughput on the order of 6.6 TB/s using a 68-node AI-HPC cluster with 10×16 TB NVMe SSDs and dual 100 Gb/s. It did this while concurrently serving background workloads at an additional 1.4 TB/s. This reported 3FS throughput, 6.6 TB/s, far exceeds Ceph's ~1.1 TB/s on similar hardware.

3FS achieves this performance by coordinating I/O across nodes. This level of sustained bandwidth helps prevent the data-staging phase from becoming the bottleneck—and helps keep GPU utilization high across both training and inference workloads.

By creating their own filesystem optimized for random reads and integrating it with RDMA-first data paths, DeepSeek demonstrates how end-to-end, full-stack performance engineering—including storage design—is essential for utilizing the full performance potential of large-scale AI systems.

3FS shows how rethinking the storage layer can remove the last bits of I/O bottlenecks. Building your own filesystem is an advanced technique that requires a lot of upfront investment and ongoing maintenance. Instead, it's more likely that you will start with an existing distributed filesystem or object store. Let's discuss these next.

Distributed, Parallel Filesystems and Object Stores

When training on multiple nodes, a common setup is to use a shared filesystem like an NFS server, or a parallel filesystem like Lustre, GPFS, Ceph, etc. With these systems, all nodes can access the same dataset. While convenient, these filesystems can become a bottleneck if not configured properly.

Though it's simple to set up, a single NFS server can easily become a throughput bottleneck if many nodes are reading at once. If you must use NFS, ensure the server has multiple fast NICs. You should also consider using multiple NFS servers to split up the dataset so that each server handles a partition of data.

For multi-GPU clusters, you should consider NFS only for modest scales such as a few nodes. For larger training clusters, a single NFS server—even a high-end implementation—is likely to become a bottleneck. This is why parallel filesystems and cloud storage caches like Amazon FSx for Lustre are preferred for modern AI training clusters.

For cloud storage caches like Amazon FSx for Lustre, it's important to verify the performance improvement and justify the additional cost of the cache. If you're not seeing the performance that you expect, work directly with the cloud provider to validate your architecture and confirm your configuration settings.

NFS also has tuning parameters like rsize/wsize (read/write request sizes). It's recommended to use the max value (e.g., 1 MB) to improve throughput. Make sure the underlying NFS storage is fast enough using NVMe SSD—and potentially in a RAID 0 configuration. And don't forget to check the NFS client mount options. They should be tuned as well.

You can mount your NFS client with `rsize=1048576,wsize=1048576,noa time,async`, for instance, to use 1 MiB blocks and eliminate access-time updates (`noa time`). You can also add `actimeo=60,lookupcache=pos` to cache file attributes and directory entries for 60 seconds. These simple tweaks can vastly reduce per-request overhead and boost parallel read throughput on large, shared datasets.

Object storage like Amazon S3 is not a typical filesystem, but it is very common in AI workloads. Accessing object storage during training can be slow if done naively. The solution often involves staging data on local NVMe SSD storage—or using a caching layer on top of object storage (e.g., Amazon FSx for Lustre on top of S3). Tools like `s5cmd` and `aws s3 cp` let you download data before training starts.

Make sure you use highly parallel, optimized data-transfer tools such as the AWS S3 C++ SDK and multithreaded utilities like `s5cmd` to get the best performance.

You can also use a streaming library that reads objects from Amazon S3 with range requests and performs caching. If directly reading from Amazon S3, use as large requests as possible—and use multithreaded range `Get` operations.

Parallel filesystems like Lustre and GPFS are designed for high concurrency and throughput. A Lustre setup, for instance, has multiple Object Storage Targets (OSTs) that serve data. By striping files across OSTs, you can multiply your throughput. If you have such a parallel filesystem, ensure your large data files are striped across many OSTs.

Striping files across implies that chunks of the file live on different servers. This allows parallel reads. For instance, you might stripe your Arrow, TFRecord, or Parquet files across 4 OSTs. If each OST gives 500 MB/s, you can achieve a theoretical peak read throughput of 2 GB/s.

Tuning, Replicating, and Compressing Data

To tune these filesystems, make sure to check the documentation. For instance, `lfs setstripe` is used on Lustre to set striping for a large dataset across 4 or 8 OSTs to aggregate OST bandwidth.

Monitor the filesystem's I/O during training, using tools like `lmt` for Lustre—or vendor-specific monitoring tools. You'll be looking to see if individual nodes in the storage cluster are hot. If so, you need to identify why. The cause is most likely a sharding issue in which many more reads/writes are ending up on a smaller number of nodes.

To eliminate network reads entirely, you can, in some cases, choose to replicate the dataset onto each node in the compute cluster. This assumes you have enough storage on each node. This is an admittedly brute-force but relatively common and very effective solution to eliminate network reads entirely. You will see an immediate performance win—at the cost of extra storage.

Another option to improve performance is to store data compressed on the filesystem or object store—and decompress them on the fly. Examples include images (JPEGs) and compressed text (Arrow and Parquet). This can save I/O bandwidth at the cost of some extra CPU or GPU cycles. However, if I/O is the bottleneck and the CPUs and GPUs are idle, this is a reasonable trade-off.

Many data pipelines are already doing this, so you'll just want to verify the compression ratio and make sure you're using it at every step in the pipeline. The key is to find a balance such that the decompression step doesn't become the bottleneck.

Libraries like nvJPEG can decode images on GPU. Modern GPUs add an on-die Decompression Engine supporting formats such as LZ4, Snappy, and Deflate to accelerate moving and unpacking data into GPU memory. If you store compressed batches on disk, Blackwell GPUs can decompress them in-pipeline using the Decompression Engine. This frees SMs to run higher-value tasks such as compute kernels. You should favor these compression formats for I/O bound workloads.

This is another way to offload arithmetic operations from the CPU to the GPU—and possibly overlap data decoding with gradient computations during training, for instance. And because of the high-bandwidth CPU-to-GPU NVLink-C2C interconnect (up to 900 GB/s bidirectional bandwidth), you can prevent CPU-assisted stages from becoming bottlenecks.

Utilizing these clever software and hardware GPU offload features can further shift workloads off the CPU and keep the input data pipeline balanced. The key is still to make sure that the decompression time does not replace I/O as the bottleneck, otherwise it likely isn't worth the extra compression computations.

Monitoring Storage I/O

As with any performance engineering task, measurement is key. Similar to monitoring network communication, it's important to use all of your available tools to monitor your storage pipeline communication.

These tools include Linux `iostat`, `iotop`, `nvme-cli`, `perf`, and `eBPF`. In addition, you can use vendor-specific utilities and dashboards to monitor queues, latencies, read-ahead effects, and cache hit ratios. These will help to show local NVMe device usage and determine if you're saturating network links when reading data from a NAS or object store.

Also consider tools like Nsight Systems to trace I/O wait times and visualize overlap with GPU kernels. Use the Nsight Systems option `--trace=gds`. This will capture `cuFile` API activity and tracing on the timeline. You can also enable GDS `cuFile` static tracepoints using `/etc/cufile.json` to see `cuFile` events in Nsight Systems. Kernel-mode counters for NVMe peer-to-peer DMA paths are not exposed in Nsight Systems and may not be available for all GDS stacks.

Another tool is NVIDIA's Data Center GPU Manager (DCGM), which reports useful GPU I/O statistics. Together, these GPU-specific tools complement host OS tools and give a more complete picture of GPU starvation due to I/O.

In PyTorch, calling `next(data_iterator)` measures the total time your GPU sits idle waiting for the next batch. This time includes any background prefetching and the host → device copy—and not just the Python data-loading logic.

If you want to isolate pure data-loading cost, you can temporarily set `num_workers=0` so there's no prefetch. Then you can time only the iterator pull. You can separately wrap your `.to("cuda")` or pinned-memory staging in its own timer (or use CUDA events) to capture the host → device copy overhead.

Because your bottleneck might be in the Python pipeline *or* in the `memcpy` into GPU memory, you can distinguish them by doing the following and comparing the timings with the overall "GPU idle" time:

DataLoader versus Python cost
> Profile with `num_workers=0` to see how long the Python loop and transforms themselves take. This removes any background thread scheduling.

Host → Device copy cost
> Measure only the device-transfer time by inspecting the "Copy" lanes in Nsight Systems to quantify how long staging data into GPU buffers actually stalls the GPU. You can also wrap `torch.cuda.Event` around your `.to("cuda")` calls.

By comparing these two timings to your overall "GPU idle" time, you'll know whether to speed up your Python pipeline (e.g., add workers, simplify transforms) or optimize the H2D transfer path (e.g., use pinned memory, increase interconnect bandwidth, or switch to GDS).

By monitoring your storage pipeline, you might find, for instance, that your GPUs are spending 30% of their time waiting for data. In this case, the GPU's overall throughput is limited by I/O, so you'll want to implement some of the strategies mentioned here to reduce the I/O stalls and increase compute throughput. After tuning, for instance, maybe your GPUs are waiting only 5% of the time for data. You'd also see overall training steps per second increase proportionally—6× in this case.

Storage and I/O optimization is often about eliminating small inefficiencies that add up; for instance, a 5 ms latency here and a 10 MB too-small buffer there. But at scale, fixing these inefficiencies makes a huge difference. The bottom line is similar to earlier sections: keep the pipeline full. In this case, not just the compute pipeline but the data pipeline as well. Every component from disk to GPU memory should be monitored, profiled, analyzed, and improved to ensure that data is streaming into those GPUs as continuously as possible.

Tuning the Data Pipeline

In addition to raw storage I/O, the preprocessing and data loading pipeline on the CPU (or GPU) is a critical part of overall AI workload performance. A well-tuned data pipeline ensures that GPUs are never idle waiting for new data. Additionally, it's important that the right amount of CPU work is being done in parallel to feed the GPU beast.

Modern deep learning frameworks provide high-level APIs to load and preprocess data. These can—and should—be tuned for performance. We will discuss general strategies and NVIDIA's tools like DALI and NeMo for advanced data pipeline management.

Efficient Data Loading and Preprocessing

The typical data loading process in training involves reading data from storage, decoding or deserializing the data like parsing JSON and decoding JPEGs, applying some transformations like tokenizing text and cropping images, and collating the data into batches. These steps can be CPU-intensive but can also be offloaded to the GPU if they are compute-heavy. To maintain high throughput, you can employ a number of techniques described here:

Use multiple worker processes/threads

As mentioned, frameworks like PyTorch `DataLoader` let you specify `num_work ers`. Each worker runs in parallel to fetch and preprocess data. Usually these are separate processes to avoid Python GIL issues. The main process asynchronously fetches batches from the worker processes using a queue.

Avoid Python bottlenecks

If your data loading logic is in Python, be wary of heavy Python-level processing. If you see pure Python code being used to tokenize individual lines of text in a loop, this is a red flag. In these cases, change to vectorize the operations, if possible. Or use C++/C bindings for improved performance. Many libraries exist for these types of common tasks, including the Hugging Face Tokenizers library and TorchText. While they have Python bindings, they are written in fast Rust/C++ under the hood for speed. At this point, Python is just an easy-to-use interface on top of the C/C++ code.

Overlap CPU-GPU

The idea is to overlap data preparation with GPU processing. In a perfect scenario, while the GPU is processing batch N, the CPU has already loaded and preprocessed batch N+1 and made it available in pinned memory. When the GPU is done processing batch N, it just DMA copies batch N+1 and starts computing immediately. Meanwhile, the CPU moves on to process batch N+2. This pipelining is crucial for performance. Most frameworks do this by default when using multiple workers, but you should monitor to ensure that it's happening. If not, you might see the GPU go idle at the start of every iteration while it waits for more data.

Perform operations in batches by collating tensors

If possible, you want your loader to perform operations in batches instead of per sample. For example, you want to apply transformations to a whole batch of tensors at once using vectorized operations. You do this by collating the batch with a custom `collate_fn()`—or perhaps in the training loop itself on the GPU. This is much better than performing these operations on each row of input data separately. However, some transformations need to be performed per sample, so you sometimes need to understand the workload before you can batch and collate effectively.

Use memory pinning with data loading

Enabling `pin_memory=True` in PyTorch DataLoader makes the host → GPU (H2D) transfer faster and allows truly asynchronous `.to(..., non_block ing=True)` copies when the source is pinned. DMA from pinned memory avoids extra copies and page faults because the data is locked in RAM and ready for direct transfer. This is almost always beneficial when transferring data to the GPU. Make sure you set a high `ulimit -l` (or container `--ulimit memlock`) to avoid allocation failures for large pinned buffers.

Prefetch batches

Some frameworks let you specify a prefetch queue length. This is how many batches it should load ahead. By default, PyTorch's DataLoader uses a conservative value such as `prefetch_factor=2`. In this case, PyTorch prefetches two batches per worker. Under the hood it keeps up to `num_workers * prefetch_factor` batches queued. As such, before blocking, each worker loads two batches of data. If your workload has bursty I/O—or you see workers starving the GPU occasionally—you can increase `prefetch_factor` to 4 or 8, for example. Here is a PyTorch snippet that demonstrates the PyTorch `DataLoader` using both `pin_memory` and `prefetch_factor=4`:

```python
import torch
from torch.utils.data import Dataset, DataLoader

# Create a Dataset and DataLoader that prefetches 4 batches
# per worker into pinned CPU memory.
class Synthetic(Dataset):
    def __init__(self, n, shape): self.n, self.shape = n, shape
    def __len__(self): return self.n
    def __getitem__(self, i):
        # Cheap CPU-side work; replace with real parse/decode
        return torch.ones(self.shape,  dtype=torch.float32)

B, C, H, W = 32, 3, 224, 224
dataset = Synthetic(n=100_000, shape=(B, C, H, W))

loader = DataLoader(
    dataset,
    batch_size=B,
    num_workers=8,
    pin_memory=True,
    persistent_workers=True,
    prefetch_factor=4,
  )

copy_stream = torch.cuda.Stream()
compute_stream = torch.cuda.current_stream()

for batch in loader:
    with torch.cuda.stream(copy_stream):
        batch_gpu = batch.to(device, non_blocking=True)
    # ensure pending H2D completes before compute uses it
    with torch.cuda.stream(compute_stream):
        torch.cuda.current_stream().wait_stream(copy_stream)
        outputs = model(batch_gpu)
```

In this example, each of the 8 worker processes preloads batches of size 4 into pinned memory. Because the host memory is pinned, the asynchronous `.to(device, non_blocking=True)` transfer can use DMA for high-speed data copying.

Consequently, while the GPU processes the current batch (batch N), the DataLoader is already preparing and transferring the next batch (batch N+1) in parallel. This overlap is critical. Without pinned memory, the system would need to pin the memory on the fly for each transfer, which would introduce unwanted latency. In essence, pinned memory ensures that data transfers from CPU to GPU happen more rapidly and concurrently with GPU computation, maximizing overall throughput.

Another option is to enable `persistent_workers=True` so workers stay alive and keep filling the queue across epochs. This is most effective when you loop over the same dataset many times—especially if these iterations (aka *epochs*) are very short. Persistent workers can also help when worker startup incurs significant overhead due to importing modules, opening files, etc. With persistent workers, you avoid the cost of spawning and tearing down processes at each epoch boundary. Your workers stay alive so they can immediately begin prefetching for the next epoch with minimal overhead.

A common pitfall is introducing a hidden bottleneck in your pipeline. This is relatively easy to do by adding debug logging or expensive CPU transforms. Delays may only show up under load. To catch these, first profile the DataLoader in isolation by timing how long it takes to produce 100 batches with all downstream GPU work disabled. Once you've measured that baseline, compare it to your target iteration time and to the total GPU-idle time measured during normal training.

If the DataLoader alone is too slow, optimize your Python pipeline by removing per-element logging, simplifying transforms, or adding more workers. If the gap between isolated loader speed and real-run loader speed is large, you're likely bound by host → device transfers or kernel-launch overhead.

> If you disable GPU kernels to isolate the DataLoader for profiling, you are also reducing CPU-side kernel-launch overhead. As such, your "pure" data-loading throughput will often appear lower than what you'll see in a real training run. This is still a useful technique; just keep this in mind.

Scaling Out Workers as You Scale Out Number of GPUs

As you add more GPUs, you should also expand your data pipeline, or you will starve the devices. In practice this means increasing your DataLoader's worker count or I/O bandwidth so you can feed every GPU. This is required to raise the total batch size so that each iteration moves more samples across your larger number of devices.

Scaling out compute without scaling out the ingestion pipeline resources will shift the bottleneck even further toward the data loading pipeline. In a multinode, data-parallel configuration, each rank reads a distinct shard. Together, the aggregate data loading workload scales with cluster size.

Always measure CPU utilization, as the data input pipeline will become the bottleneck as GPU training accelerates.

To sustain the necessary throughput, you will need parallel, high-bandwidth, and distributed storage backends, as discussed earlier, to support ultrascale data sharding across the many nodes in your cluster. And recall from our discussion earlier on sharding the dataset per node. Specifically, as you add more nodes, make sure that each node's local storage can handle its share of the dataset.

Multimodal Data Processing with NVIDIA DALI

For complex or heavy data preprocessing, NVIDIA provides their Data Loading Library (DALI) (*https://oreil.ly/NrGK3*). DALI accelerates data processing by either moving it to the GPU or using optimized CPU code written in C++. It's especially useful for image and video data where decoding and augmentation can benefit from GPU acceleration.

For example, DALI can decode JPEG images on the GPU and apply augmentations like random crop, resize, and normalization, all on the GPU. This is often faster than on a CPU—assuming the GPU has available cycles. This offloads processing from the CPU and reduces the number of CPU workers needed.

DALI pipelines are defined declaratively as a static graph of operators. You subclass `nvidia.dali.pipeline.Pipeline` and declare your data sources and CPU/GPU ops in `define_graph()`. DALI then handles the execution, prefetching, and threading internally using its own thread pools and queues.

If your workload is input-bound (e.g., model training), integrating DALI might significantly boost throughput. However, one must integrate it into the training loop itself, which adds some complexity and has a bit of a learning curve.

For many common workloads like classification, object detection, and segmentation, NVIDIA DALI provides prebuilt pipelines that decode images and videos on the GPU. This fully utilizes the GPU's media-acceleration hardware.

Consider a data pipeline that reads images and videos, performs augmentations, and trains an object detection model. You might observe CPU usage at 800%, which is eight cores running at 100% utilization. But the GPU is still stalling occasionally.

By using DALI, you might drop CPU utilization to 200%, or just two cores, to perform the file reads while the GPU does the actual image and video decoding. And the GPU can perform the reads concurrently with computations.

In practice, the real speedup depends entirely on where you place DALI in your flow. If you use DALI merely to decompress JPEGs and then immediately hand the raw pixels back to the CPU for augmentations and collation, you will incur extra host-device-host copies that can negate the performance gains of using DALI.

> A better approach to DALI might be to identify GPU-friendly pre-processing operations and fuse them directly into your GPU-based preprocessing computation graph. Most preprocessing can be done using existing CUDA-based libraries like TorchVision and TensorRT—or using custom CUDA kernels. This way, you avoid excessively moving data back and forth between the CPU and GPU. This could produce higher end-to-end performance than using DALI in your pipeline, so it's worth exploring.

As always, benchmark the end-to-end system under realistic conditions. Compare a CPU-only pipeline, a DALI-enabled pipeline, and a fully fused GPU-graph implementation to determine which delivers the best balance of CPU savings and GPU utilization for your model and dataset.

Creating High-Quality LLM Datasets with NVIDIA NeMo Curator

NVIDIA NeMo (*https://oreil.ly/Kx5qz*) is a toolkit for developing and training language models. Within the NeMo toolkit is the NeMo suite of libraries and frameworks, including the open source NeMo Curator (*https://oreil.ly/Geh8o*) framework.

Curator (*https://oreil.ly/BnSst*) helps prepare large multimodal datasets for LLM training. It's helpful when dealing with terabytes of data from different sources. Curator supports data processing steps such as cleansing, tokenizing, and shuffling.

NeMo Curator can distribute the dataset preprocessing across multiple GPUs or nodes. This makes use of multiple accelerators to prepare data faster—an important consideration when assembling multiterabyte training datasets.

In addition, Curator can compress and pack data into a small number of large files—or transform the data into a binary format for easier consumption by machines. It can also create new, synthetic training datasets to augment human datasets, which are relatively limited and becoming more and more scarce.

With Curator doing the heavy preprocessing offline and ahead of the training process, the online training data pipeline becomes much simpler since it's just reading the prepared data and maybe performing some lightweight, "last mile" shuffling, for instance.

NeMo Curator can also enforce data quality filters by deduplicating data and removing problematic content. This is important for both LLM training quality and for performance. Having a well-structured, preprocessed, and cleansed dataset upfront means the training pipeline has a consistent flow of well-structured and evenly sized data (e.g., padded to a fixed length), doesn't have to tokenize text on the fly, and can avoid gnarly string processing.

If you have access to tools such as NeMo Curator, it's wise to leverage them so that your training job is mostly GPU forward and backward passes—and not processing text and reading millions of randomly sized small files. For NeMo-based training, preprocessed datasets are typically stored as memory-mappable *.bin* data files with *.idx* index files. NeMo Curator's `DocumentDataset` then reads and writes sharded JSONL or Parquet. Downstream conversion to *.bin/.idx* is handled when you build the indexed dataset.

> You may want to consider storing *N* copies of the data shuffled in *N* number of different ways to avoid runtime shuffling cost over *N* epochs of training. The obvious trade-off is disk space and memory, but this it's a trade-off worth considering.

In general, prepare your data before training. You should almost never be training with raw text. It might take some time to preprocess the data offline, but it pays off in the long run with faster training runs, quicker iterations, and more predictable scaling.

All the techniques described here are designed to never let the data loading pipeline cause your expensive GPU cluster to sit idle. The highest-performing GPU is useless if the data pipeline cannot supply inputs fast enough. Therefore, a holistic, full-stack optimization approach is required at all layers, including storage, network, CPU, and GPU.

> NeMo's data loading still runs on CPUs. To bypass CPU I/O, you need to integrate it with tools like GDS.

In many cases, optimizing the data pipeline yields more improvement than any algorithmic tweak. A poorly tuned input pipeline could waste 50% of your GPU time, whereas algorithmic optimizations might give only a few percent.

Continuous Profiling and Tuning Workflow

Performance engineering is an iterative process. To ensure that your distributed training or inference application stays efficient as you scale or modify it, you should adopt a continuous profiling and tuning workflow. This means regularly collecting performance data, identifying bottlenecks, applying optimizations, and then measuring again.

Over time, hardware and software updates will change the optimal settings, so you need to continuously profile and tune. To stay ahead of this, performance-focused engineering teams often maintain performance dashboards to track metrics like samples/sec over time.

Consider setting up automated nightly runs that profile your training and inference workloads. This way, you can catch regressions or improvements and trace them to code changes.

Let's look at a typical workflow and set of best practices that can be applied broadly for all profiling and debugging situations—not just specific to the topics described in this chapter:

Establish a baseline
Start with a single GPU or a minimal setup and measure performance such as training throughput measured in samples/sec or inference latency measured in milliseconds (hopefully!). Then scale up to multiple GPUs on a single node, then multiple nodes—each time analyzing how performance is scaling using a high-level metric like overall throughput. Ideally, N GPUs give Nx more throughput for a simple data-parallel workload. If you see much less than this, it's a sign that your system is incurring too much overhead. The next step is to quantify the bottleneck. For instance, 8 GPUs giving only a 5× increase in throughput reveals a system that is only 62.5% efficient. This is not ideal.

Profile the multi-GPU run for bottlenecks
To diagnose the exact cause of the bottleneck, we dive deeper and use a system-profiling tool like Nsight Systems (nsys) on the multi-GPU job as a whole to get an overview of where time is spent. The first step is to look at the GPU utilization timeline. Are the GPUs stalling frequently? If so, what are they waiting for? Also check CPU timelines. Is the main process lagging behind the other worker processes? Are there synchronization points where every thread is waiting? For example, if GPUs are idle during model training in a gradient all-reduce, you know communication is a bottleneck. If they are idle at the start of each iteration, perhaps data loading or a specific kernel is the bottleneck.

Zoom into specific kernels if needed
If you identify that a certain GPU operation (network or compute) is running slower than expected, you can dive deeper into the kernel using Nsight Compute (ncu) on that kernel to check its efficiency. For instance, in our earlier discussion, we looked at a NCCL kernel and saw only 60% SM utilization and high memory-stall counters when communication was traveling over PCIe instead of NVLink. After optimizing the communication to use NVLink, SM utilization rose to 90%

SM busy—and measured fewer memory stalls. This kind of deep dive can confirm whether a kernel is network-bandwidth bound, memory-bandwidth bound, or compute bound. It will be one of these.

Identify the cause

Once you spot a bottleneck, map it to a set of hypothetical causes and validate (or invalidate) them one by one. For example, if the bottleneck is network bound, maybe you're not using RDMA or your message sizes are too small or you need better overlapping, etc. If the GPU is idle waiting for other GPUs, you might have a straggler situation in which one GPU is doing more work than others due to a data imbalance. If your workload is CPU bound, perhaps the data loader is not configured correctly or there is a CPU aggregation operation that is better suited for the GPU, etc. If the bottleneck is memory bound on the GPU, maybe some kernels are transferring too much data between registers and HBM memory, so you might try reducing the batch size or introducing kernel fusion, etc.

Apply fixes or optimizations

After running through your hypotheses and finding the actual cause, it's now time to take action. For network and communication bottleneck fixes, ensure GPUDirect RDMA is enabled, increase `NCCL_NSOCKS_PERTHREAD` if you have multiple NICs and are still network-bandwidth limited, and consider compressing data using techniques like gradient compression, which we cover in a later chapter. If you are crossing NUMA nodes, try a hierarchical approach or configure the NCCL topology to use fewer GPUs per NUMA node, etc.

For intranode topology issues, if your GPUs are spread across PCIe switches, try binding your job to a single NUMA node's GPUs if possible to avoid slow interconnects—or use more topology-aware algorithms. For CPU and data issues, check if the data loader is too slow. In this case, add more worker processes/threads or move some preprocessing to the GPU using DALI, for instance. Or do more offline preprocessing ahead of time. If one GPU is slower, maybe doing extra validation or logging, try reducing the work or moving it off the critical path using asynchronous operations.

If synchronizations are an issue, remove unnecessary `torch.cuda.synchronize()` calls or barriers in your code that might be inadvertently serializing execution (more on this in Chapter 13). If the environment needs tuning, maybe set `NCCL_IGNORE_CPU_AFFINITY=1` if needed. Or pin CPU threads to a different topology configuration, etc. With relatively little effort, one can sometimes turn very poor resource utilization into maximum utilization with just a few small changes (easier said than done, of course, but it's good to stay positive!):

Remeasure after every change

As with any debugging effort, it's important to change only one or two things at a time—and then measure. Otherwise, you won't know which change helped.

When you achieve good scaling on the current configuration, note the good metric values and aim toward maintaining those good values as you scale.

Keep software updated, but always verify
New versions of NCCL or CUDA often bring improvements that can boost performance. For instance, a newer NCCL might automatically do something hierarchically or use a communication/computation overlap mechanism. Or a PyTorch update can reduce DDP overhead or introduce a more efficient distributed optimizer. However, each update can bring instability by shifting the optimal settings. Run your profiling workflow again and make sure you are maintaining those good metric values from your last-known-good system configuration.

Leverage modern hardware features
Let's say you are suddenly given the latest hardware with more unified memory, more memory bandwidth, and faster interconnects. The first step is to understand the new improvements and use them to your advantage. You can now use larger batch sizes of input data and fit larger models into memory. Just be sure to ramp up slowly and monitor resource utilization. If you scale up too aggressively, you will saturate the new and improved resources—and have to restart the profiling and tuning workflow all over again!

Automate monitoring in production
If you regularly run large training and inference workloads, it's always good to have consistent monitoring setup in production to continuously profile GPU utilization, network throughput, and memory throughput over time. That way, if a job or inference request is running slower than expected due to an environment issue, kernel update, or data pipeline regression, you catch it quickly. Kubernetes and other job schedulers integrate well with monitoring tools. Set up alerts if utilization drops below some threshold, for example.

Document and educate
Performance tuning often involves tacit knowledge among the team for things like which environment variables are overridden and which library versions are buggy, etc. Document these findings directly in the code or configuration file so that others, or a future you, are reminded of them every time you open up those files. For instance, note that "in this cluster configuration, we found that setting `NCCL_SOCKET_NTHREADS=2` improved multinode throughput by 10%." Hopefully, this is a standard practice.

By continuously following this workflow, you essentially create a feedback loop: Run → Measure → Tune → Run → Measure → Tune →… This feedback loop ensures that, as you scale to more GPUs and move to better models, you continue to maintain your system's performance and efficiency. It's much easier to maintain good performance than to regain it after performance degrades over a period of time. It's a constant battle to keep so many moving parts performing at the highest levels.

In summary, treat performance just like a feature that needs constant testing and validation. Just like you write tests for code correctness, you should instrument tests for performance. For instance, does doubling GPUs roughly double throughput? If it doesn't, dive in with the profiler and start the profiling and tuning workflow. It's recommended to combine Nsight Systems for a high-level system view, Nsight Compute for low-level GPU kernel profiles, and logging for NCCL and PyTorch. Together, these will give you a comprehensive toolkit to pinpoint issues when they arise.

By the end of this process, you will have a finely tuned AI system. And as you update either code or hardware, iterate again. Performance tuning is never done in a dynamic, fast-moving environment like AI. But it gets easier when you know what to look for. This is exactly why you're reading this book!

Diagnosing Communication- Versus Compute-Bound Workloads

To understand if computation or communication is the limiting factor in a model training workload, for example, you can change the ratio of computation to communication and see how this affects the achieved network throughput measured in GB/s on the NIC. Consider profiling the backward pass of a training job. It currently shows your gradient all-reduce is utilizing only 60 GB/s across a 100 GB/s NIC.

To figure out if the network is clogged or if the GPUs are too slow in this scenario, you can fix the amount of communication and increase/decrease the amount of compute by increasing/decreasing the batch size. This is perfect because increasing the batch size does not affect the amount of data transferred during the backward pass's gradient all-reduce. This is because the number of gradients scales with the number of model parameters—and not the batch size.

With the amount of communication fixed, reduce the batch size by half and see how this affects the achieved network throughput. If it remains at 60 GB/s, then the GPUs could have done more work, but the network isn't letting them do more work. As such, the network is the limiting factor.

However, if the achieved network utilization drops below 60 GB/s to, say, 40 GB/s, the GPUs are starving the network by not finishing computations fast enough to keep the NIC busy. In this case, the network is idle, waiting for more data from the GPUs. As such, compute is the limiting factor and not the network.

You can further validate this hypothesis by reversing the experiment and doubling the batch size. Again, the amount of all-reduce gradient communication stays the same. So if communication is the true limiter, you will see the NIC stay at 60 GB/s as the batch size and compute workload increase. But if compute was the limiter, the percentage of total iteration time spent in all-reduce communication will shrink relative to the growing compute time.

Watching both the absolute GB/s on the NIC and the relative time spent in communication relative to computation for these two experiments will pinpoint exactly which subsystem to tune. More concretely, you can plot the GB/s versus communication percentage as you increase/decrease the batch size. This will show you exactly where the roofline is and determine if the workload is communication bound (network) or compute bound (GPU SMs).

> Use Nsight Systems to get an end-to-end timeline. If you see GPUs idle, waiting on data in the form of long gaps between compute kernels corresponding to NCCL wait, then you're most likely communication bound. If the GPUs are busy but not reaching expected FLOPS, you are likely memory bound or compute bound. Nsight Compute and the PyTorch profiler can help determine the kernel's memory and compute efficiency.

Key Takeaways

Peak performance in distributed AI comes from co-optimizing across the full stack from GPU kernels and network transfers to CPU threads and storage. A weakness in any one of these can bottleneck the whole system. Here are the key lessons to remember when tuning your storage layer:

Scale the input data pipeline along with scaling your compute
  Don't neglect storage and data loading when scaling up GPUs. Ensure that your storage system offers enough bandwidth—and that you are fully utilizing this bandwidth. Increase data loader parallelism inline with the increasing number of GPUs. Otherwise, you will hit a point where adding GPUs gives no speedup because your input pipeline can't keep up.

Use the right tools for the job
  NCCL is designed for scalable collective (all-reduce, etc.) communication often used in model training. NIXL is targeted at high-throughput point-to-point and streaming transfers common in model inference. Use NIXL where token streaming dominates the workload. In contrast, prefer NCCL/NVSHMEM for bulk collective and symmetric-memory patterns. GPUDirect RDMA and GDS remove the host memory bounce buffer for network and storage I/O, respectively, while the CPU still schedules and controls transfers. Always use `DistributedData Parallel` over `DataParallel` for multi-GPU training. These purpose-built libraries and frameworks exist—and are heavily tuned—to squeeze performance out of hardware. Leverage them instead of reinventing the wheel.

Profile end-to-end

It's not always obvious where the bottleneck is. Use profilers like Nsight Systems, Nsight Compute, and PyTorch profiler to see where time is spent. GPUs are either compute bound, communication bound, or I/O bound. Following the profiling examples that we discussed earlier can help guide you to the source of the problem. For instance, you can verify that NCCL kernels are interwoven properly with compute and check GPU idle times in Nsight Systems.

Conclusion

High-performance and distributed storage systems are a foundational component to tuning large, complex AI systems. By integrating advanced storage technologies like NVMe SSD and GDS, you can improve your data loading pipeline performance, reduce your training time, and increase the rate of experimentation and iteration.

Addressing challenges in storage and I/O through techniques like offline preprocessing data pipelines, efficient data caching, and asynchronous communication allows modern AI deployments to sustain high throughput even as model complexity and dataset sizes scale up.

For practitioners, the takeaway is that you don't need to invent custom I/O solutions from scratch. NVIDIA and the open source community provide highly tuned, purpose-built libraries and tools so that you can focus on your model, data, and application logic rather than the low-level plumbing.

For performance engineers, the lesson is that fast data movement is as critical as raw compute power. The fastest GPU in the world provides little benefit if it's constantly waiting for data from storage.

Technologies like GDS and advanced input pipelines are part of the full-stack approach to keep the data flowing smoothly and the GPUs fed with work. By leveraging these and continuously profiling and tuning, you can push a distributed AI system closer to its theoretical peak limits at scale.

In the next chapters, we will build upon this foundation and dive into CUDA and PyTorch optimization strategies as well as some advanced system-tuning topics. The principles learned here will continue to apply at every layer of the stack as we continue to overlap communication/computation, utilize the fastest links possible, and get closer to the theoretical maximum hardware performance. Ultimately, this will all lead to faster time-to-insight, better utilization of resources, and cost savings.

## CHAPTER 6

GPU Architecture, CUDA Programming, and Maximizing Occupancy

In this chapter, we'll start by reviewing the single instruction, multiple-threads (SIMT) execution model and how warps, thread blocks, and grids map your GPU-based algorithms onto streaming multiprocessors (SMs).

We'll review the SIMT execution model on modern NVIDIA GPUs, including how warps, thread blocks, and grids map to SMs. We'll then dive into CUDA programming patterns, discuss the on-chip memory hierarchy (register file, shared/L1, L2, HBM3e), and demonstrate the GPUs asynchronous data transfer capabilities, including the Tensor Memory Accelerator (TMA) and the Tensor Memory (TMEM) that serves as the accumulator for Tensor Core operations.

We'll also introduce roofline analysis to identify compute-bound versus memory-bound kernels. This will provide the fundamentals to push modern GPU systems toward their theoretical peak throughput ceilings.

Understanding GPU Architecture

Unlike CPUs, which optimize for low-latency single-thread performance, GPUs are throughput-optimized processors built to run thousands of threads in parallel. A simple CUDA programming flow between the CPU and GPU is shown in Figure 6-1.

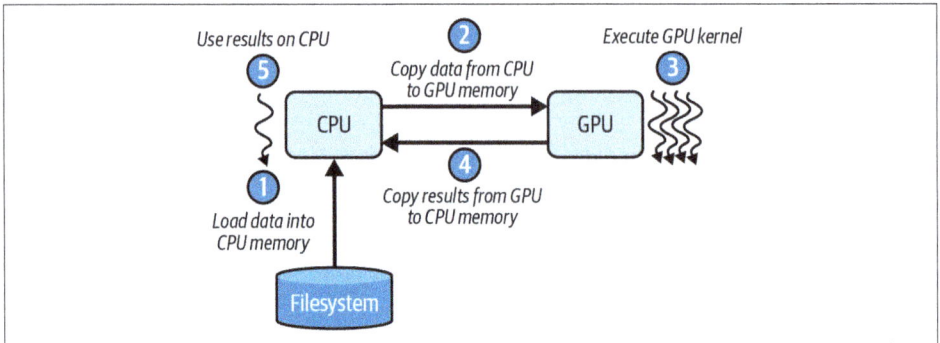

Figure 6-1. Simple CUDA programming flow

Initially, the host loads data into CPU memory. It then copies the data from the CPU to the GPU memory. After calling the GPU kernel with the data in GPU memory, the CPU copies the results back from GPU memory to CPU memory. Now the results live back on the CPU for further processing.

GPUs rely on massive parallelism to hide data-transfer latency such as the CPU-GPU data transfer described in Figure 6-1. Each GPU comprises many SMs, which are roughly analogous to CPU cores but streamlined for parallelism. Each SM can track up to 64 warps (32-thread groups) on Blackwell.

Each GPU includes many SMs—similar to CPU cores but optimized for throughput. On modern GPUs, each SM tracks up to 64 warps (2,048 threads) concurrently. Blackwell GPUs feature 64K 32-bit registers per SM (256 KB total) and a combined 256 KB L1 cache/shared memory per SM. Up to 228 KB (227 KB usable) of that SRAM can be configured as user-managed shared memory per SM. Any single thread block can request up to 227 KB of dynamic shared memory (1 KB is of the 228 KB is reserved by CUDA). These help the SMs support the GPU's high amount of thread-level parallelism.

Within a Blackwell SM, multiple warp schedulers issue instructions to the available pipelines; four independent warp schedulers allow up to four warps to issue instructions to the available pipelines on every cycle. Furthermore, each scheduler supports dual-issue capable of issuing two independent instructions (e.g., one arithmetic and one memory operation) per warp. Note that the dual-issue must come from the same warp—and not across warps.

In the best case, one warp from each scheduler can issue an instruction concurrently each cycle, allowing four warps to execute in parallel per cycle. This further boosts throughput when instruction mixing is utilized, as shown in Figure 6-2.

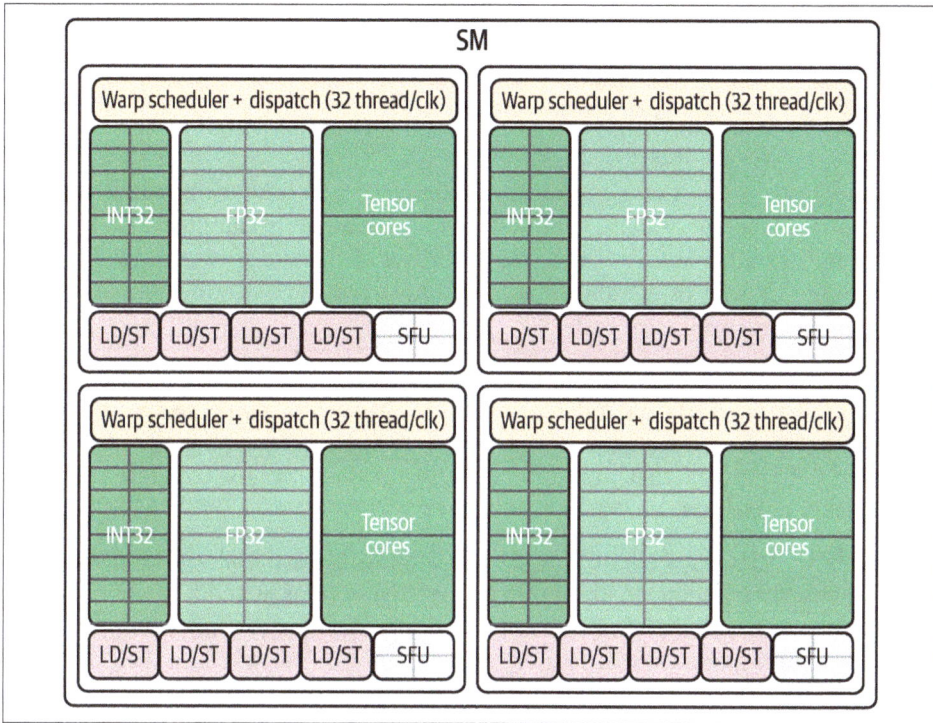

Figure 6-2. Blackwell SMs contain four independent warp schedulers, each capable of issuing one warp instruction per cycle with dual-issue of one math and one memory operation per scheduler

Here, each SM is subdivided into four independent scheduling partitions—each with its own warp scheduler and dispatch logic. You can think of the SM as four "mini-SMs" sharing on-chip resources. This lets the hardware pick ready warps and issue instructions from up to four different warps each clock cycle.

Within each of the four "mini-SM" partitions, the scheduler can issue two instructions per cycle from the same warp: one arithmetic instruction (e.g., INT32, FP32, or Tensor Core) and one memory instruction (a load or store). This is why the scheduler is called *dual-issue*. Table 6-1 summarizes these numbers.

Table 6-1. Key SM scheduler and instruction-issue limits (per clock cycle)

Metric	Value
Number of schedulers	Four
Maximum warps issued	Four (one per scheduler)
Maximum math operations	Four (one per scheduler's arithmetic issue)
Maximum memory operations	Four (one per scheduler's load/store issue)

Note: The numeric values in all metrics tables are illustrative to explain the concepts. For actual benchmark results on different GPU architectures, see the GitHub repository (*https://github.com/cfregly/ai-performance-engineering*).

So in the best case you could dual-issue four math and four memory instructions across four warps every cycle. This would maximize both compute and memory throughput simultaneously. These numbers are a result of the SM's four-way partitioning—as well as its ability to pick one warp per partition and issue two orthogonal instructions each cycle.

The Special Function Unit (SFU) sits alongside the INT32, FP32, and Tensor Core pipelines. They handle transcendental operations (e.g., sine, cosine, reciprocal, square root). However, they are not part of the dual-issue math and memory pair. SFUs use a dedicated SFU pipeline that runs independently of the main INT32/FP32 and load/store (LD/ST) pipelines.

Because SFUs occupy a separate pipeline and can execute in parallel when needed, the SM can continue issuing math and memory instructions without waiting for the slower functions to complete. This separation increases instruction-level parallelism and overall throughput even further for mixed-operation kernels. They keep complex math operations from stalling the core compute and memory pipelines.

Because there are four schedulers—and each can typically issue one warp instruction per cycle—up to four warps can make forward progress each cycle when there is sufficient independent work and issue-pairing. For instance, the memory operations can flow through the SM's combined 16 load/store (LD/ST) pipelines (four LD/ST pipelines per scheduler). These will read or write data to L1/shared memory, L2 cache, or global memory (covered in an upcoming section).

Exact LD/ST pipeline counts and pairings are not guaranteed. Rely on profiling counters to determine whether your kernel is limited by memory issue or compute issue. And consult the NVIDIA documentation for specifics of your architecture. The Blackwell tuning guide (*https://oreil.ly/DRKh5*) is a good place to start.

In short, GPUs excel at data-parallel workloads, including large matrix multiplies, convolutions, and other operations where the same instruction applies to many elements. Developers write kernels directly in CUDA C++ or indirectly through high-level frameworks like PyTorch and domain-specific, Python-based GPU languages like OpenAI's Triton.

Before diving into kernel development and memory-access optimizations, let's review the CUDA thread hierarchy and key terminology that underpins all of these practices.

Threads, Warps, Blocks, and Grids

CUDA structures parallel work into a three-level hierarchy—threads, thread blocks (aka *cooperative thread arrays* [CTAs]), and grids—to balance programmability with massive throughput. At the lowest level, each thread executes your kernel code. You group threads into thread blocks of up to 1,024 threads each on modern GPUs. Thread blocks form a grid when you launch the kernel, as seen in Figure 6-3.

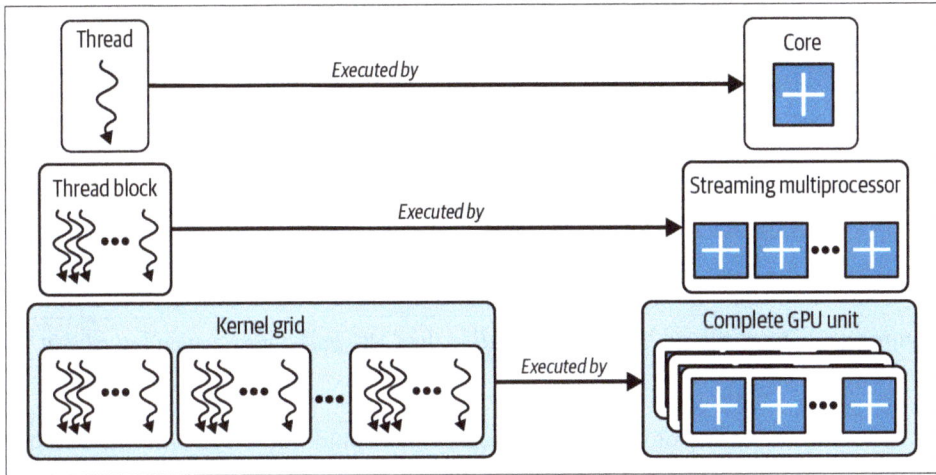

Figure 6-3. *Threads, thread blocks (aka CTAs), and grids*

By sizing your grid appropriately, you can scale to millions of threads without changing your kernel logic. CUDA's runtime (and frameworks like PyTorch) handle scheduling and distribution across all SMs. Figure 6-4 shows another view of the thread hierarchy, including the CPU-based host, which invokes a CUDA kernel running on the GPU device.

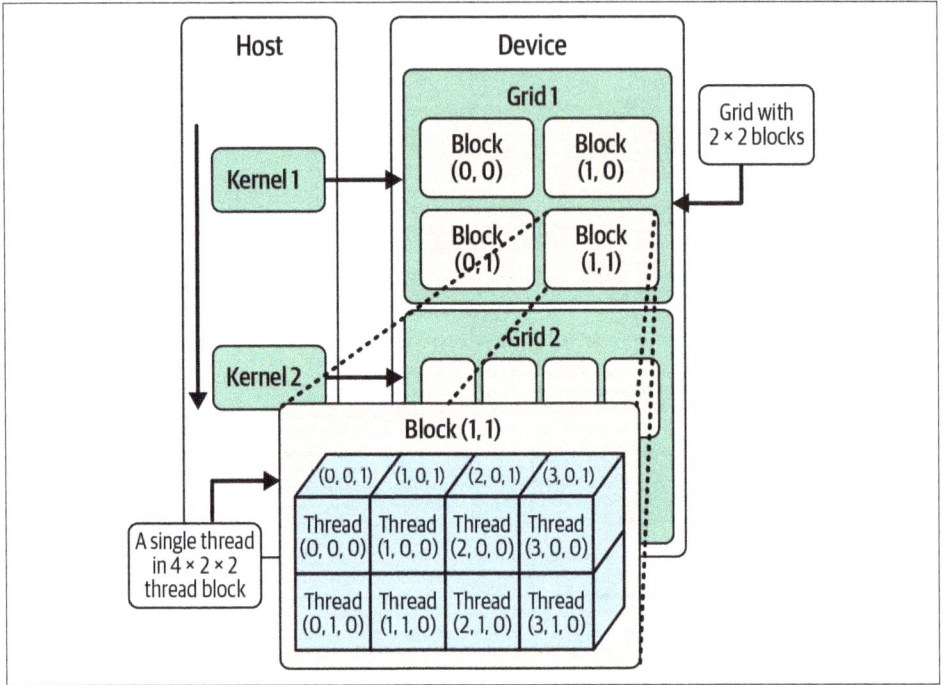

Figure 6-4. View of thread hierarchy, including the CPU-based host, which launches a kernel running on the GPU device

Traditionally, threads from different thread blocks could not work with one another directly. However, modern GPU architectures and CUDA versions support thread block clusters. Threadblock clusters are groups of thread blocks that can communicate with one another across SMs.

Specifically, within a thread block cluster, threads in different thread blocks can access one another's shared memory and use hardware-supported, cluster-scoped barriers. These allow for much larger compute operations, including matrix multiplies, which are very common in today's massive LLM workloads. Thread block clusters share a distributed shared-memory (DSMEM) address space between SMs that participate in the thread block cluster, as shown in Figure 6-5.

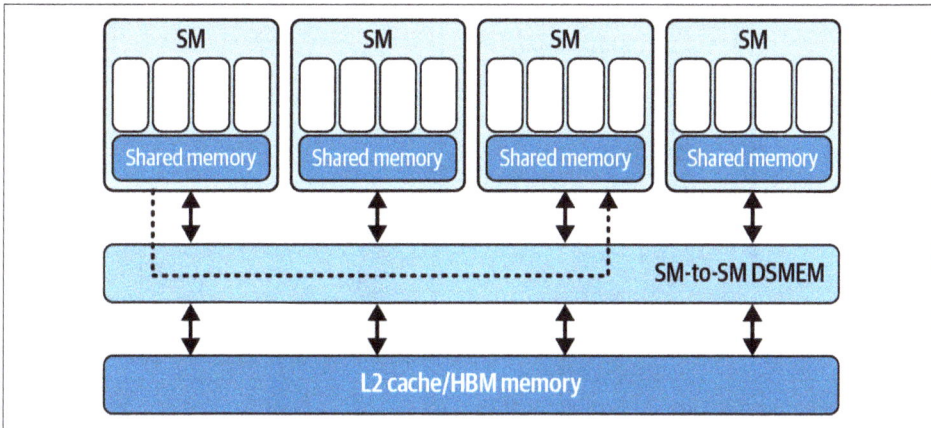

Figure 6-5. Hardware-supported DSMEM used in thread block clusters containing multiple thread blocks

DSMEM is a hardware feature that links the shared-memory banks of all SMs into a thread block cluster over a fast on-chip interconnect. With DSMEM, the SMs share a combined multi-SM distributed shared-memory pool. This unification allows threads in different blocks to read, write, and atomically update one another's shared buffers at on-chip speeds—and without using global memory bandwidth.

> We'll cover advanced topics like thread block clusters and DSMEM in Chapter 10. These are an extremely important addition to modern GPU processing—and very important for an AI systems performance engineer to understand. For this chapter, our focus remains on intrablock shared-memory optimizations.

Within each thread block, threads share data using low-latency on-chip shared memory and synchronize with __syncthreads(). Because each barrier incurs overhead, you should minimize synchronization points, as shown in Figure 6-6.

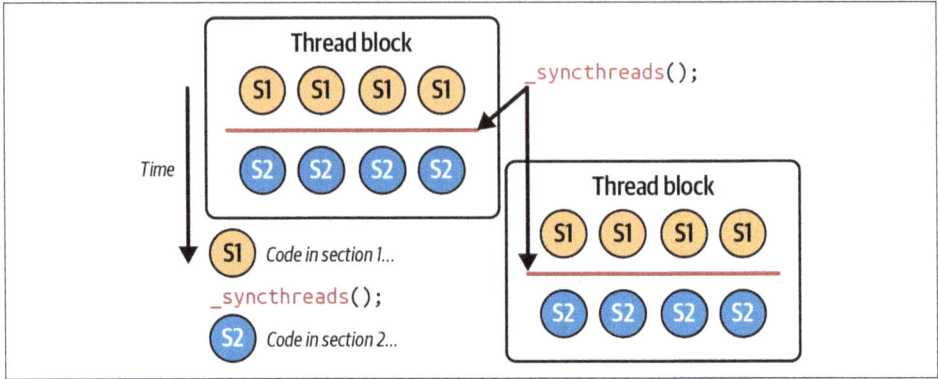

Figure 6-6. Synchronizing all threads within a thread block between two sections of code

The goal is to minimize synchronization points. However, the GPU hardware will attempt to hide long-latency events such as global-memory loads, cache fills, and pipeline stalls by rapidly switching among warps.

Thread blocks are subdivided into warps of 32 threads that execute in lockstep under the SIMT model using a warp scheduler. This is shown in Figure 6-7.

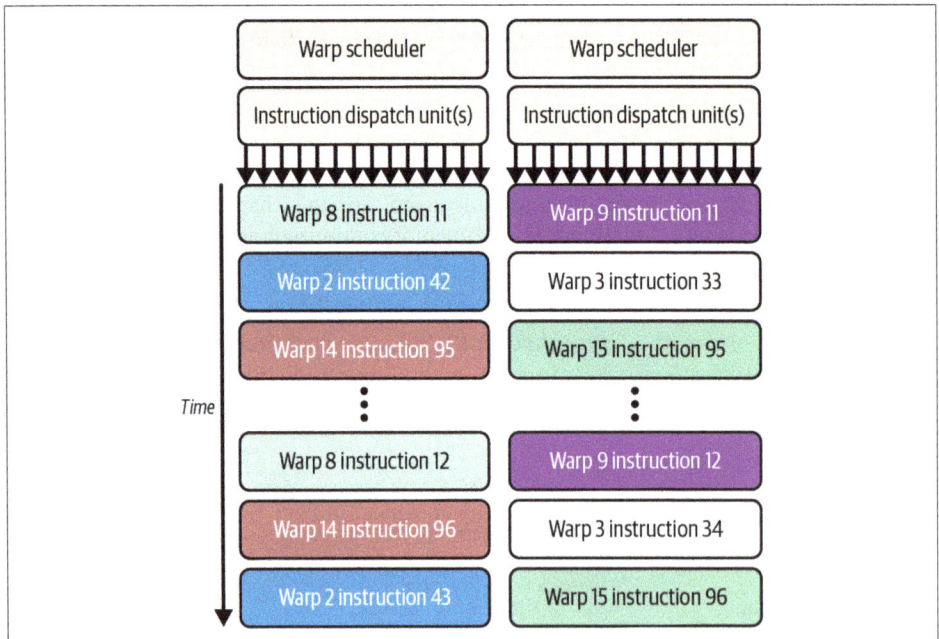

Figure 6-7. Warps (32 threads) advance as a whole with instructions managed by the warp scheduler

Keeping more warps in flight is known as *high occupancy* on the SM. When your CUDA code allows high occupancy, it means that when one warp stalls, another is ready to run. This keeps the GPU's compute units busy.

However, high occupancy must be balanced against per-thread resource limits, such as registers and shared memory. Spilling registers to slower memory can create new stalls. Profiling occupancy alongside register and shared-memory usage helps you choose a block size that maximizes throughput without triggering resource contention.

> We will cover occupancy tuning in Chapter 8, but it's a key concept to understand in the context of SMs, warps, threads, etc.

Thread blocks execute independently and in no guaranteed order. This allows the GPU scheduler to dispatch them across all SMs and fully exploit hardware parallelism. This grid–block–warp hierarchy guarantees that your CUDA kernels will run unmodified on future GPU architectures with more SMs and threads.

Throughput also hinges on warp execution efficiency. Threads in a warp must follow the same control-flow path and perform coalesced memory accesses. If some threads diverge such that one branch takes the `if` path and others take the `else` path, the warp serializes execution, processing each branch path sequentially. This is called *warp divergence*, and it's shown in Figure 6-8.

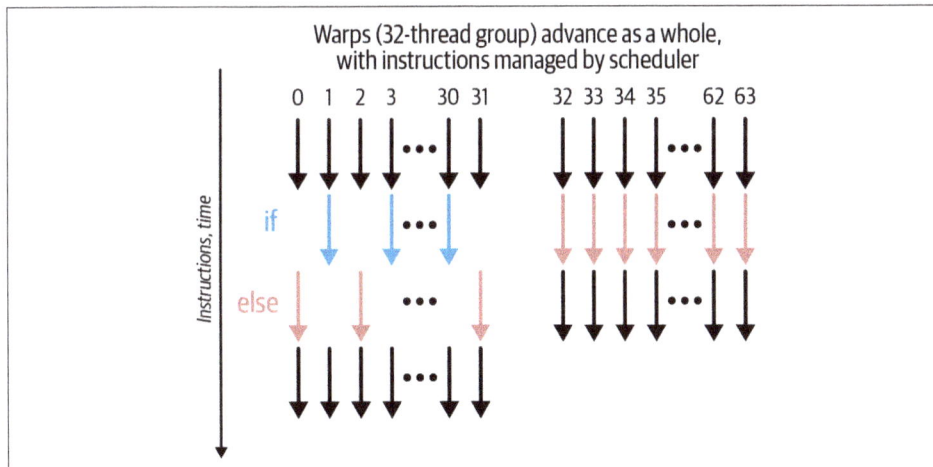

Figure 6-8. SIMT warp divergence (left) versus uniformity (right)

By masking inactive lanes and running extra passes to cover each branch, warp divergence multiplies the overall execution time by the number of branches. We'll dive deeper into warp divergence in Chapter 8—as well as ways to detect, profile, and mitigate it.

> Divergence is an issue only for threads within a single warp. Different warps can follow different branches with no performance penalty.

Choosing Threads-per-Block and Blocks-per-Grid Sizes

A critical aspect of GPU performance is choosing a thread block size that aligns with the hardware's 32-thread warp size. As such, you typically pick thread block sizes that are exact multiples of 32. For example, a 256-thread block (8 warps = 256 ÷ 32) fully occupies each warp, whereas a 33-thread block will require two warp slots and use only 1/32 of the second warp's lanes. This wastes parallelism opportunities since every warp occupies a scheduler slot whether it's actively running 32 threads or just 1 thread.

Additionally, different GPU generations have different hardware limits, including maximum threads per SM and the number of registers per SM. This naturally limits the size of our blocks if we want to maintain good performance. For instance, too large a block might require too many registers, which will cause *register spilling* and decrease the kernel's performance.

A large block might also require too much shared memory, which is finite in GPU hardware. Specifically, Blackwell provides only 228 KB (227 KB usable) per SM of shared memory addressable by all resident thread blocks running on the SM.

These hardware limits affect how many blocks/warps can be active on an SM at once. This is a measurement of occupancy, as we introduced earlier. Smaller blocks might enable higher occupancy if they allow more concurrent warps to run concurrently on the SM.

It's important to understand the relative scale and hardware thread limits for your GPU generation, including number of threads, thread blocks, warps, and SMs. Figure 6-9 shows the relative scale of these resources, including their limits.

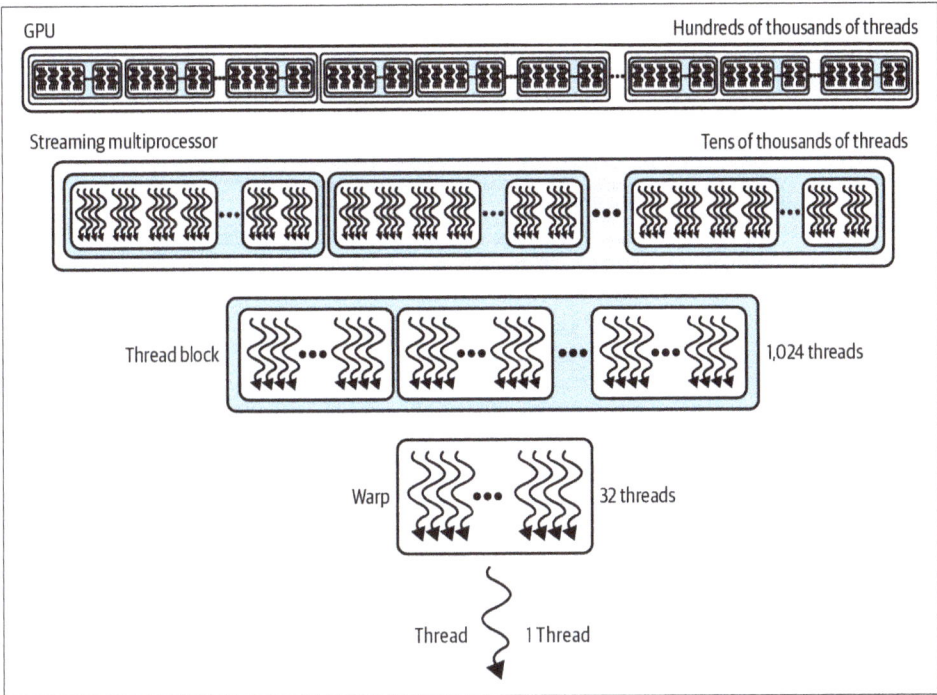

Figure 6-9. Relative scale and hardware limits for threads on a Blackwell GPU

Table 6-2 summarizes these GPU limits for the Blackwell B200 GPU. The rest of the limits are available on NVIDIA's website (*https://oreil.ly/DRKh5*). (Other GPU generations will have different limits, so be sure to check the exact specifications for your system.)

Table 6-2. Thread-level and block-level limits (Blackwell B200)

Resource	Hardware limit	Notes
Warp size	32 threads	The fundamental SIMT execution unit is 32 threads (a warp). Always use a multiple of 32 to avoid waste.
Maximum threads per thread block	1,024 threads	`blockDim.x * blockDim.y * blockDim.z ≤ 1024.`
Maximum warps per thread block	32 warps	(1,024 threads ÷ 32 threads-per-warp) = 32 warps max per block.

We already discussed the warp size limit of 32 threads, which encourages us to choose block dimensions that are multiples of 32 threads to create "full warps" and avoid underutilized warps. Note that each block can have up to 1,024 threads and, correspondingly, a block can contain only 32 warps. These limits affect your occupancy since, once a block is scheduled, each SM can host a limited number of warps and blocks simultaneously.

Additionally, there are per-SM limits, or *SM-resident limits* as they are commonly called, for the different GPU generations. These SM-resident Blackwell limits are summarized in Table 6-3.

Table 6-3. SM-resident resource limits (Blackwell B200)

Resource (per SM)	Hardware limit	Notes
Maximum resident warps per SM	64 warps	Hardware can keep up to 64 warps in flight (64×32 threads = 2,048 threads). Note: This limit has held for many generations and remains true for Blackwell.
Maximum resident threads per SM	2,048 threads	Equals 64 warps $\times$ 32 threads/warp. If each block uses 1,024 threads, then at most 2 such blocks (64 warps) can reside on one SM concurrently. Using smaller blocks (e.g., 256 threads) allows more blocks to reside on the SM (up to 8 blocks $\times$ 256 = 2,048 threads), which can increase occupancy and help hide latency—though too many tiny blocks can add scheduling overhead.
Maximum active blocks per SM	32 blocks	At most, 32 thread blocks can be simultaneously resident on one SM (if blocks are smaller, more can fit up to this limit).

Here, we see that the maximum number of concurrent warps per SM on Blackwell is 64. This hasn't changed for recent GPU generations, so occupancy considerations carry over. Maximum active blocks on an SM is 32, and, correspondingly, maximum resident threads per SM is 2,048 threads. CUDA grids also have maximum dimensions, as shown in Table 6-4.

Table 6-4. CUDA grid limits

Grid dimension	Limit	Notes
Maximum blocks in X, Y, or Z	X: 2,147,483,647 blocks Y: 65,535 blocks Z: 65,535 blocks	A 3D grid can be as large as $2,147,483,647 \times 65,535 \times 65,535$ blocks.
Maximum concurrent grids (kernels)	128 grids	Up to 128 kernels can execute concurrently on one device (i.e., 128 grids resident at once).

While it's good to know the theoretical grid limits, you will typically be bound by the thread/block/per-SM limits shown previously. If you ever need more than 65,535 blocks in one dimension, you can launch a 2D or 3D grid to split your work across multiple kernel launches (multilaunch). We show an example of this in a later section. In practice, it's rare to hit the grid size limit before hitting other resource limits.

CUDA GPU Backward and Forward Compatibility Model

One of CUDA's core strengths is its forward and backward compatibility model. Kernels compiled today will generally run unmodified on future GPU generations—as long as you include PTX in your binary for forward compatibility. If you ship only SASS for a single architecture (e.g., `sm_90` for Hopper or `sm_100` for Blackwell) without PTX, that binary will not forward-run on newer architectures. Family-specific targets such as `sm_100f` or `compute_100f` restrict portability to devices in the same feature family. It's best to ship a fatbin that includes both generic cubin/PTX and family-specific cubins needed (e.g., optimizations, etc.).

You can verify compatibility by forcing PTX JIT compilation at load time by setting `CUDA_FORCE_PTX_JIT=1` to JIT-compile the PTX and cache the result. If your binary lacks PTX, the kernel launch will fail. This forces you to rebuild with PTX support. This compatibility model is fundamental to the large CUDA ecosystem. It lets you target both legacy and cutting-edge hardware from a single codebase.

> To truly maintain both backward and forward compatibility across current and future GPU generations, you should compile with generic targets—or explicitly include the PTX. When you need specific optimizations from newer hardware features, you can use generation-specific targets. When doing this, be sure to provide fallback paths for other architectures.

CUDA Programming Refresher

In CUDA C++, you define parallel work by writing kernels. These are special functions annotated with `__global__` that execute on the GPU device. When you invoke a kernel from the CPU (host) code, you use the `<<< >>>` "chevron" syntax to specify how many threads should run—and how they're organized—using two configuration parameters: `blocksPerGrid` for the number of thread blocks and `threadsPerBlock` for the number of threads within each block.

Here is a simple example that demonstrates the key components of a CUDA kernel and kernel launch. This kernel simply doubles every element in the input array in place so no additional memory is created—just the input array. Behind the scenes, CUDA compiles the `__global__` function into GPU device code that can be executed by thousands or millions of lightweight threads in parallel:

```
//------------------------------------------------------
// Kernel: myKernel running on the device (GPU)
//   - input : device pointer to float array of length N
//   - N   : total number of elements in the input
//------------------------------------------------------
```

```cpp
__global__ void myKernel(float* input, int N) {
    // Compute a unique global thread index
    int idx = blockIdx.x * blockDim.x + threadIdx.x;

    // Only process valid elements
    if (idx < N) {
        input[idx] *= 2.0f;
    }
}

// This code runs on the host (CPU)
int main() {
    // 1) Problem size: one million floats
    const int N = 1'000'000;
    float *h_input = nullptr;
    float *d_input = nullptr;

    // 1) Allocate input float array of size N on host
    cudaMallocHost(&h_input, N * sizeof(float));

    // 2) Initialize host data (for example, all ones)
    for (int i = 0; i < N; ++i) {
        h_input[i] = 1.0f;
    }

    // 3) Allocate device memory for input on the device
    cudaMalloc(&d_input, N * sizeof(float));

    // 4) Copy data from the host to the device
    cudaMemcpy(d_input, h_input, N * sizeof(float),
        cudaMemcpyHostToDevice);

    // 5) Choose kernel launch parameters

    // Number of threads per block (multiple of 32)
    const int threadsPerBlock = 256;

    // Number of blocks per grid (3,907 for N = 1000000)
    const int blocksPerGrid = (N + threadsPerBlock - 1) /
        threadsPerBlock;

    // 6) Launch myKernel across blocksPerGrid blocks
    // Each block has threadsPerBlock number of threads
    // Pass a reference to the d_input device array
    myKernel<<<blocksPerGrid, threadsPerBlock>>>(d_input,
        N);
    // 7) Wait for the kernel to finish running on device
    cudaDeviceSynchronize();

    // 8) When finished, copy the results
    //     (stored in d_input) from the device back to
    //       host (stored in h_input)
```

```
cudaMemcpy(h_input, d_input, N * sizeof(float),
          cudaMemcpyDeviceToHost);

// Cleanup: Free memory on the device and host
cudaFree(d_input);
cudaFreeHost(h_input);

// return 0 for success!
return 0;
```

This code is not fully optimized. We will optimize performance as we continue through the book. But this gives you a simple, complete template to start building your own CUDA kernels.

Here, we are passing kernel input arguments, d_input and N, which are accessible inside the kernel function for processing. The processing is shared, in parallel, across many threads. This is by design.

The full data flow is as follows:

1. Allocate memory on the host (h_input).

2. Copy data from the host (h_input) to device (d_input) using cudaMemcpy with cudaMemcpyHostToDevice.

3. Run the kernel on the device with d_input.

4. Synchronize to ensure the kernel has finished executing on the device.

5. Transfer the results (d_input) from device to host (h_input) using cudaMemcpy with cudaMemcpyDeviceToHost.

6. Clean up memory on the device and host with cudaFree and cudaFreeHost.

You can pass additional, advanced, CUDA-specific parameters to your kernel at launch time with <<< >>>, including shared-memory size (and many others), but the two core launch parameters, blocksPerGrid and threadsPerBlock, are the foundation of any CUDA kernel invocation. In the next section, we will discuss how to best choose these launch parameter values.

And you might be wondering why we have to pass N, the size of the input array. This seems redundant since the kernel should be able to inspect the size of the array. However, this is the core difference between a GPU CUDA kernel function and a typical CPU function: a CUDA kernel function is designed to work inside of a single thread, alongside thousands of other threads, on a partition of the input data. As such, N defines the size of the partition that this particular kernel will process.

Combined with the built-in kernel variables `blockDim` (1 in this case since we're passing a one-dimensional input array), `blockIdx`, and `threadIdx`, the kernel calculates the specific `idx` into the input array. This unique `idx` lets the kernel process every element of the input array cleanly and uniquely, in parallel, across many threads running across many different SMs simultaneously.

Note the bounds check `if (idx < N)`. This is needed to avoid out-of-range access (bounds check) since `N` may not be an exact multiple of the block size. For instance, consider a scenario in which the input array is size 63, so `N = 63`. The warp scheduler will likely assign two warps (32 threads each) to process the 63 elements in the input array.

The first warp will run 32 instances of the kernel simultaneously to process elements 0–31 and never exceed `N = 63`. That's straightforward. The second warp, running in parallel with the first warp, will expect to process elements 32–64. However, it will stop when it reaches `N = 63`.

Without the `if (idx < N)` bounds check, the second warp will try to process `idx = 64`, and it will throw an illegal memory access error (e.g., `cudaErrorIllegalAddress`). The bounds check ensures that every thread either works on a valid input element or exits immediately if its `idx` is out of range.

CUDA kernels execute asynchronously on the device without per-thread exceptions; instead, any illegal operation (out-of-bounds access, misaligned access, etc.) sets a global fault flag for the entire launch. The host driver only checks that flag when you next call a synchronization or another CUDA API function, so errors surface lazily (e.g., as `cudaErrorIllegalAddress` or a generic launch failure).

This design keeps the GPU's pipelines and interconnects fully occupied but requires you to explicitly synchronize and poll for errors on the host—usually with `cudaGetLastError()` and `cudaDeviceSynchronize()` immediately after kernel launches. This way, you catch faults as soon as they occur.

You will see a bounds check in a lot of CUDA kernels. If you don't see it, you should understand why it's not there. It's likely there in some fashion—or the CUDA kernel developer can somehow guarantee the illegal memory access error will never happen.

And finally, we get to the actual kernel logic. After computing its unique index `idx` into the input array, this kernel (running separately on thousands of threads in parallel across many SMs) multiplies the value at index `idx` in the input array by 2. It then updates the value (in place) in the input array. In this specific kernel, no additional memory is needed except the temporary `idx` variable of type `int`.

Configuring Launch Parameters: Blocks per Grid and Threads per Block

As discussed earlier, using a block size that's a multiple of the warp size (32) is critical. A `threadsPerBlock` size of 256 (eight warps) is a common starting point to balance occupancy and resource usage. This will help us avoid partially filled warps during kernel execution, hide latency, and balance SMs and other hardware resources:

Multiple of 32 threads
   Choosing a block size that is a multiple of 32 threads helps to avoid empty warp slots. Otherwise those underfilled warps occupy scarce scheduler resources—without contributing useful work.

Latency hiding
   Hundreds of threads per SM are needed to hide DRAM and instruction-latency stalls. If you launch, say, eight blocks of 256 threads on an SM with 2,048 threads of capacity, you can keep the pipeline busy without oversubscribing.

Occupancy
   With 256 `threadsPerBlock`, for example, you need only eight warps per block. This tends to give good occupancy without running out of registers or shared memory per block.

> For modern GPUs like Blackwell, consider 256–512 threads per block to maximize occupancy while respecting register and shared-memory limits.

Resource-balanced
   256 is small enough that you rarely exceed the 1,024-thread-per-block limit. And it's large enough that you're not leaving too many warps idle when threads in other warps stall.

   Starting with `threadsPerBlock=256`, you can tune up or down (128, 512, etc.) based on your kernel's register and shared-memory requirements—as well as occupancy characteristics.

For `blocksPerGrid`, you can base this on the number of N input elements and the value of `threadsPerBlock`. For instance, the `blocksPerGrid` is commonly set to (N + `threadsPerBlock` - 1) / `threadsPerBlock` to round up so that you cover all elements if N is not an exact multiple of `threadsPerBlock`. This is a common choice that guarantees every input element is covered by a thread. Here is the code that shows the calculation:

```
//---------------------------------------------------------
// Kernel: myKernel running on the device (GPU)
//    - input : device pointer to float array of length N
//    - N    : total number of elements in the input
//---------------------------------------------------------
__global__ void myKernel(float* input, int N) {
    // Compute a unique global thread index
    int idx = blockIdx.x * blockDim.x + threadIdx.x;

    // Only process valid elements
    if (idx < N) {
        input[idx] *= 2.0f;
    }
}

// This code runs on the host (CPU)
int main() {
    // 1) Problem size: one million floats
    const int N = 1'000'000;

    float* h_input = nullptr;
    cudaMallocHost(&h_input, N * sizeof(float));

    // Initialize host data (for example, all ones)
    for (int i = 0; i < N; ++i) {
        h_input[i] = 1.0f;
    }

    // Allocate device memory for input on the device (d_)
    float* d_input = nullptr;
    cudaMalloc(&d_input, N * sizeof(float));

    // Copy data from the host to the device using cudaMemcpyHostToDevice
    cudaMemcpy(d_input, h_input, N * sizeof(float),
      cudaMemcpyHostToDevice);

    // 2) Tune launch parameters
    const int threadsPerBlock = 256; // multiple of 32
    const int blocksPerGrid = (N + threadsPerBlock - 1) /
      threadsPerBlock; // 3,907, in this case

    // Launch myKernel across blocksPerGrid number of blocks
    // Each block has threadsPerBlock number of threads
    // Pass a reference to the d_input device array
    myKernel<<<blocksPerGrid, threadsPerBlock>>>(d_input, N);
    // Wait for the kernel to finish running on the device
    cudaDeviceSynchronize();

    // When finished, copy results (stored in d_input) from device to host
    // (stored in h_input) using cudaMemcpyDeviceToHost
    cudaMemcpy(h_input, d_input, N * sizeof(float), cudaMemcpyDeviceToHost);
```

```
    // Cleanup: Free memory on the device and host
    cudaFree(d_input);
    cudaFreeHost(h_input);

    return 0; // return 0 for success!
```

This is the same kernel as previously but calculates the `blocksPerGrid` and `threadsPerBlock` dynamically based on the size of N. Note the familiar `if (idx < N)` bounds check. This ensures that any "extra" threads in the final block that fall outside of N will simply do nothing—and not cause an illegal memory address error. Next, let's explore multidimensional inputs like 2D images and 3D volumes.

2D and 3D Kernel Inputs

When your input data naturally lives in two dimensions (e.g., images), you can launch a 2D grid of 2D blocks. For example, here's a kernel that processes a two-dimensional $1{,}024 \times 1{,}024$ matrix using a 16×16 dimensional thread block for a total of 256 threads:

```
// 2d_kernel.cu

#include <cuda_runtime.h>
#include <iostream>

//-------------------------------------------------------
// Kernel: my2DKernel running on the device (GPU)
//    - input  : device pointer to float array of size width×height
//    - width  : number of columns
//    - height : number of rows
//-------------------------------------------------------
__global__ void my2DKernel(float* input, int width, int height) {
    // Compute 2D thread coordinates
    int x = blockIdx.x * blockDim.x + threadIdx.x;
    int y = blockIdx.y * blockDim.y + threadIdx.y;

    // Only process valid pixels
    if (x < width && y < height) {
        int idx = y * width + x;
        input[idx] *= 2.0f;
    }
}

int main() {
    // Image dimensions
    const int width  = 1024;
    const int height = 1024;
    const int N      = width * height;

    // 1) Allocate and initialize host image
    float* h_image = nullptr;
    cudaMallocHost(&h_image, N * sizeof(float));
```

```
for (int i = 0; i < N; ++i) {
    h_image[i] = 1.0f;  // e.g., initialize all pixels to 1.0f
}

// 2) Allocate device image and copy data to device
cudaStream_t s; cudaStreamCreateWithFlags(&s, cudaStreamNonBlocking);
float* d_image = nullptr;
cudaMallocAsync(&d_image, N * sizeof(float), s);
cudaMemcpyAsync(d_image, h_image, N * sizeof(float),
                cudaMemcpyHostToDevice, s);

// 3) Configure and launch the 2D kernel
dim3 threadsPerBlock2D(16, 16); // 256 threads per block
dim3 blocksPerGrid2D((width + threadsPerBlock2D.x - 1)
                     / threadsPerBlock2D.x,
                     (height + threadsPerBlock2D.y - 1)
                     / threadsPerBlock2D.y);

// 4) Launch the kernel
my2DKernel<<<blocksPerGrid2D, threadsPerBlock2D,
            0, s>>>(d_image, width, height);

cudaMemcpyAsync(h_image, d_image, N * sizeof(float),
                cudaMemcpyDeviceToHost, s);
cudaStreamSynchronize(s);

cudaFreeAsync(d_image, s);
cudaStreamDestroy(s);
```

Here, again, is the full kernel (device) and invocation (host) code. This same pattern generalizes to 3D by using dim3(x, y, z) for both blocksPerGrid and threadsPer Block, letting you map volumetric data directly onto the GPU's thread hierarchy.

> For the most part, this book uses 1D or 2D (tiled) values for blocks PerGrid and threadsPerBlock. In the 1D case, you can define blocksPerGrid and threadsPerBlock as simple constants instead of dim3.

Asynchronous Memory Allocation and Memory Pools

Standard cudaMalloc/cudaFree calls, as shown in the previous examples, are synchronous and relatively expensive. They require a full device synchronization (relatively slow) and involve OS-level calls like mmap/ioctl to manage GPU memory.

This OS-level interaction incurs kernel-space context switches and driver overhead, which makes them relatively slow compared to purely device-side operations. As such, it's recommended to use the asynchronous versions, cudaMallocAsync and cudaFreeAsync, for more efficient memory allocations on the GPU.

By default, the CUDA runtime maintains a global pool of GPU memory. When you free memory asynchronously, it goes back into the pool for potential reuse in subsequent allocations. `cudaMallocAsync` and `cudaFreeAsync` use the CUDA memory pool under the hood.

A memory pool recycles freed memory buffers and avoids repeated OS calls to allocate new memory. This helps to reduce memory fragmentation over time by reusing previously freed blocks instead of creating new ones for each iteration in a long-running training loop, for instance. Memory pools are enabled by default in many high-performance libraries and runtimes such as PyTorch.

In fact, PyTorch uses a custom memory caching allocator, configured with `PYTORCH_ALLOC_CONF` (formerly `PYTORCH_CUDA_ALLOC_CONF`). The PyTorch memory caching allocator is similar in spirit to CUDA's memory pool: it reuses GPU memory and avoids the cost of calling the synchronous `cudaMalloc` operation for every new PyTorch tensor created during each iteration of a long-running training loop, for instance.

In CUDA applications that perform frequent, fine-grained allocations, it's far more efficient to use the asynchronous pool-based routines—`cudaMallocAsync` and `cuda FreeAsync`—rather than the traditional synchronous `cudaMalloc/cudaFree`, which incur full-device synchronization and even OS-level calls. To use stream-ordered allocation, create a non-blocking stream:

```
cudaStream_t stream1;
cudaStreamCreateWithFlags(&stream1, cudaStreamNonBlocking);
```

> Using explicit CUDA streams is a best practice for overlapping transfers, kernels, and memory operations. Think of each stream as an isolated channel that enforces ordering among its own operations. Also, it's recommended to create nonblocking streams with `cudaStreamCreateWithFlags(..., cudaStreamNonBlocking)` to avoid legacy default-stream barriers. We'll explore multistream overlap techniques and best practices in more detail in Chapter 11.

Then, whenever you need a buffer of N floats, you allocate and free it on that stream using `cudaMallocAsync` and `cudaFreeAsync`, as shown here:

```
float* d_buf = nullptr;
cudaMallocAsync(&d_buf, N * sizeof(float), stream1);

// ... launch kernels into stream1 that use d_buf ...
myKernel<<<blocksPerGrid, threadsPerBlock, 0, stream1>>>(d_buf, N);

// Free is deferred until all work in stream1 completes—
cudaFreeAsync(d_buf, stream1);
```

These APIs allocate from a per-device memory pool but respect the ordering of the stream you pass, so frees are deferred until that stream's work completes. And because `cudaFreeAsync` waits for only `stream1` to finish, there is no expensive global `cudaDeviceSynchronize` and no implicit synchronization with other streams. The result is much lower allocation overhead when your code issues thousands—or millions—of allocate/free cycles, reducing fragmentation and smoothing out latency spikes. Overall, this pattern reduces global synchronization and fragmentation relative to traditional `cudaMalloc` and `cudaFree`.

You can further tune the behavior of stream-ordered allocations from the device's memory pool—for example, by setting `cudaMemPoolAttrReleaseThreshold` to hint how much reserved memory the pool should retain before attempting to release it. You can also use `cudaMemPoolTrimTo` to proactively return memory. These will help balance total GPU memory footprint against fragmentation.

For simple, one-time buffers, a blocking `cudaMalloc` and `cudaFree` may suffice. In more complex, long-running loops where you repeatedly allocate and free memory, however, switching to `cudaMallocAsync` and `cudaFreeAsync` on dedicated streams and leveraging their pools will yield more consistent performance and higher throughput.

Switching to `cudaMallocAsync` and `cudaFreeAsync` on dedicated streams and leveraging their pools will yield more consistent performance and higher throughput. You can further tune pool behavior with `cudaMemPoolSetAttribute` (for example, adjusting `cudaMemPoolAttrReleaseThreshold`) to *tune release thresholds and strike the right trade-off between a minimal memory footprint and low fragmentation.*

Understanding GPU Memory Hierarchy

So far, we've been discussing memory allocations broadly at a high level and typically from global memory. These allocations come from a stream's memory pool—including the default stream 0 memory pool.

In reality, however, the GPU provides a multilevel memory hierarchy and helps balance capacity and speed. The hierarchy includes registers, shared memory, caches, global memory, and a specialized TMEM on Blackwell GPUs and beyond. TMEM, discussed in more detail in a bit, is a dedicated ~256 KB per-SM on-chip memory used by Blackwell's 5th-generation Tensor Core instructions (`tcgen05.*`). It isn't directly pointer-addressable from CUDA C++. Instead, data movement is orchestrated by TMA hardware (global memory ↔ SMEM) and tcgen05 Tensor Core data-movement instructions (SMEM ↔ TMEM implicitly using tensor descriptors.

Global memory (HBM or DRAM) is large, off-chip, and relatively slow. Registers are tiny, on-chip, and extremely fast. L1 cache, L2 cache, and shared memory are somewhere in between. The benefit of caching and shared memory is that they hide the relatively long latency of accessing the large off-chip memory stores. A high-level view of the GPU memory hierarchy (including the CPU) is shown in Figure 6-10.

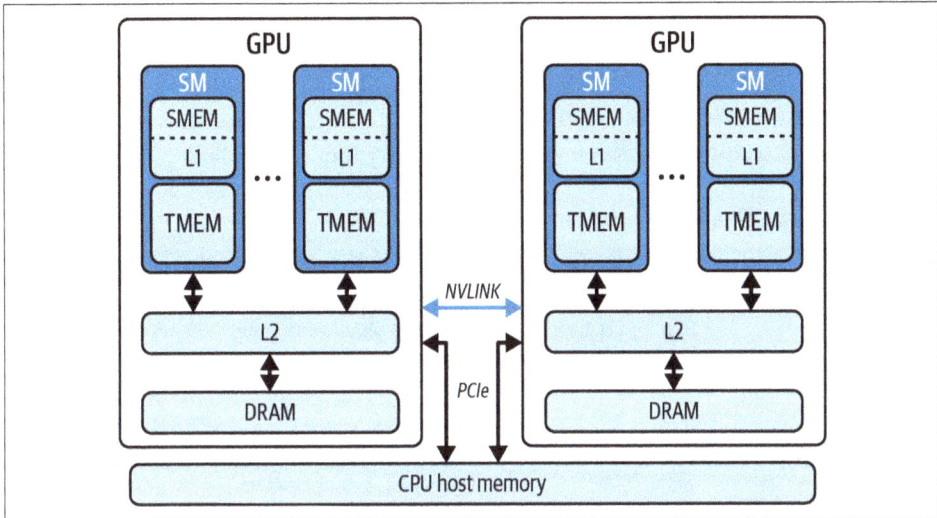

Figure 6-10. GPU memory hierarchy, including the CPU

TMEM is a dedicated 256 KB per-SM buffer that transparently communicates with the Tensor Cores at tens of terabytes per second of bandwidth. This reduces the Tensor Core's reliance on global memory. Figure 6-11 shows TMEM servicing the Tensor Cores—along with SMEM—to compute a C = A × B matrix multiply.

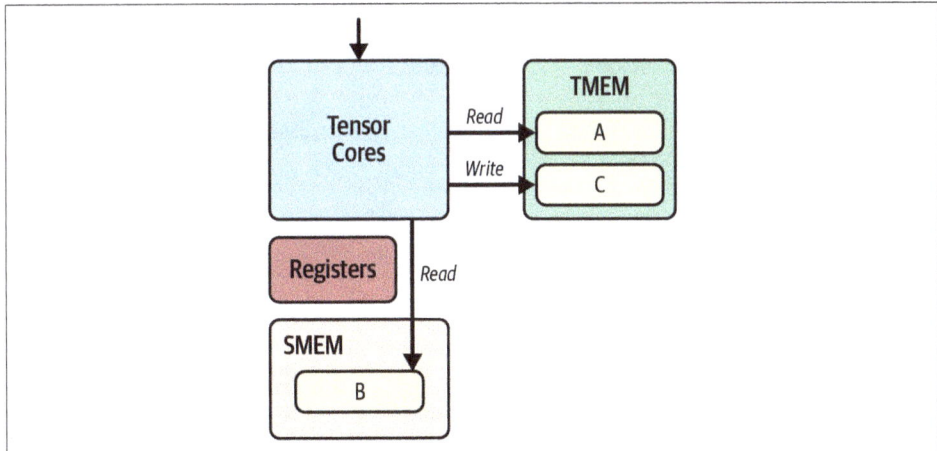

Figure 6-11. TMEM and SMEM servicing the Tensor Cores for C = A × B matrix multiply

Here, operand B is sourced from SMEM. Operand A is in TMEM (although it may be in SMEM, as well). The accumulator is in TMEM, as well. Tiles flow from global memory to SMEM through L2 cache using TMA (e.g., `cuda::memcpy_async`). Operands move between SMEM and TMEM implicitly through Tensor Core instructions such as unified matrix-multiply-accumulate (UMMA) and `tcgen05.mma`.

Table 6-5 shows the different levels of memory and their characteristics for the Blackwell GPU. A description of each level of the memory hierarchy follows.

Table 6-5. Blackwell memory hierarchy and characteristics

Level	Scope	Capacity	Latency	Bandwidth (approx.)
Registers	Per thread (on SM)	64 K 32-bit registers per SM (max 255 per thread)	near-register latency (register reads/writes are single-cycle and essentially free)	Tens of TB/s per SM (register-file ports)
Shared memory and L1 cache	Per SM	228 KB (227 KB usable) shared + remainder as L1/data cache	~20–30 cycles (L1/shared benchmarks)	TB/s per SM (bank-conflict-free)
TMEM	Per SM	256 KB SRAM per SM dedicated to Tensor Cores	~10 cycles (dedicated SRAM on the SM)	TB/s-scale communication with Tensor Cores
Constant memory cache	Per SM	~8 KB cache for 64 KB `__constant__` space	~1 cycle (warp-broadcast) As fast as a register when cached and all threads in a warp access the same address due to the constant cache and broadcast behavior. Divergent or missed cases serialize or incur higher latency	TB/s-scale (broadcast throughput)
L2 cache	GPU-wide (all SMs)	126 MB total	~200 cycles	Multi TB/s aggregate
Local memory	Per thread (spills to DRAM)	Near-unlimited (backed by global memory)	100s → 1,000 cycles (DRAM-like)	~8 TB/s (HBM3e)
Global memory (HBM or DRAM)	Device-wide (off-chip DRAM)	Up to 180 GB per Blackwell B200 GPU (up to ~288 GB per Blackwell B300 GPU)	100s → 1,000 cycles (global-memory latency)	~8 TB/s total

Here, you can see why maximizing data reuse in registers, shared memory, and L1/L2 cache—and minimizing reliance on global memory and local memory (backed by global memory)—is essential for high-throughput GPU kernels. Next is a bit more detail about each of these levels of the hierarchy:

Registers

On Blackwell, every thread begins its journey at the register file, a tiny on-SM SRAM array that holds each thread's local variables with essentially zero added latency. Each SM houses 64 K 32-bit registers (256 KB total), but the hardware exposes at most 255 registers per thread.

Because reads and writes complete in a single cycle and contend with almost nothing else, register bandwidth can reach tens of terabytes per second per SM. However, if your kernel needs more registers—either through many thread-local variables or compiler temporaries—the overflow spills into local memory, mapped to off-chip DRAM, and incurs hundreds to over a thousand cycles of latency. This local memory is shown in Figure 6-12.

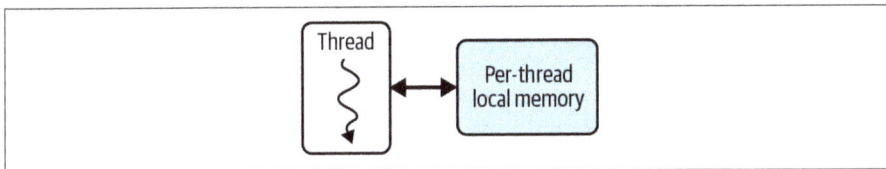

Figure 6-12. Local memory per thread

Shared memory and L1 data cache

One step up is a unified L1/data cache and shared-memory block. This is 256 KB of on-SM SRAM per SM that you can dynamically split between user-managed shared memory (up to 228 KB per block) using `cudaFuncSetAttribute()` with `cudaFuncAttributePreferredSharedMemoryCarveout` to select the memory carveout on architectures like Blackwell with unified L1/Texture/Shared Memory. The maximum dynamic shared memory per block is 227 KB (CUDA reserves 1KB per block), and the total allocatable shared memory per SM is also bounded by this limit.

Accesses here cost roughly 20–30 cycles, but if you design your thread blocks to avoid bank conflicts, you can achieve terabytes-per-second throughput. Thread-block shared memory is shown in Figure 6-13.

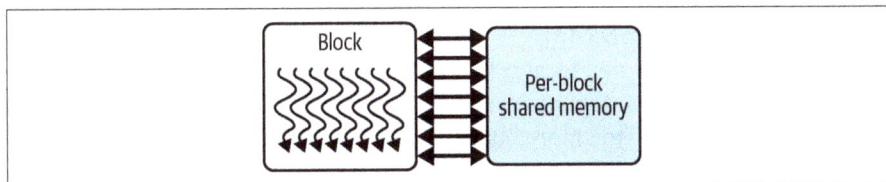

Figure 6-13. Thread-block shared memory

TMEM

TMEM is a dedicated on-chip memory per SM (256 KB on Blackwell) used by Tensor Core–specific operations and instructions including unified matrix-multiply-accumulate and tcgen05, discussed in Chapter 10. It is not a normal pointer addressable space in CUDA C++. Instead, transfers are orchestrated with the Tensor Memory Accelerator (TMA) using descriptors. This frees the developer from having to manually manage data flow with the Tensor Cores. Some arithmetic operands, for instance, reside in shared memory, while the accumulator resides in TMEM. TMA is then responsible for moving the data between global memory, shared memory, and TMEM memory to perform the computations.

Constant memory cache

For tiny, read-only tables, Blackwell provides a per-SM constant memory cache of about 8 KB fronting the 64 KB __constant__ space. When all 32 threads in a warp load the same address, this cache broadcasts the value in a single cycle.

Divergent reads serialize across lanes. It's perfect for sharing small lookup tables for rotary positional encodings, Attention with Linear Biases (ALiBi) slopes, LayerNorm γ/β vectors, and embedding quantization scales. These are shared across every thread without global-memory traffic.

L2 cache

Beyond on-chip SRAM sits the L2 cache, a 126 MB GPU-wide buffer that glues all SMs to off-chip HBM3e. With latencies near 200 cycles and aggregate bandwidth in the tens of terabytes per second, L2 absorbs spillover from L1.

With the L2, data is fetched by one thread block and reused by other thread blocks without revisiting DRAM. To maximize L2's benefits, structure your global loads into 128-byte, coalesced transactions that map cleanly to cache lines. We'll show how to do this in a bit.

Structure your global loads into 128-byte aligned, coalesced segments that map cleanly to cache lines. This avoids split transactions and maximizes use of the L2 and DRAM bandwidth.

Global memory (HBM or DRAM)

The global memory tier, local spill space and HBM, live off-chip. Any spilled registers or oversized automatic arrays reside in local memory, paying full DRAM latency (hundreds to more than 1,000 cycles) despite HBM3e's ~8 TB/s bandwidth.

For Blackwell, the HBM3e tier provides up to 180 GB of device-wide storage at ~8 TB/s total. However, its high latency makes it the slowest link in the chain. Per-device global memory is shown in Figure 6-14.

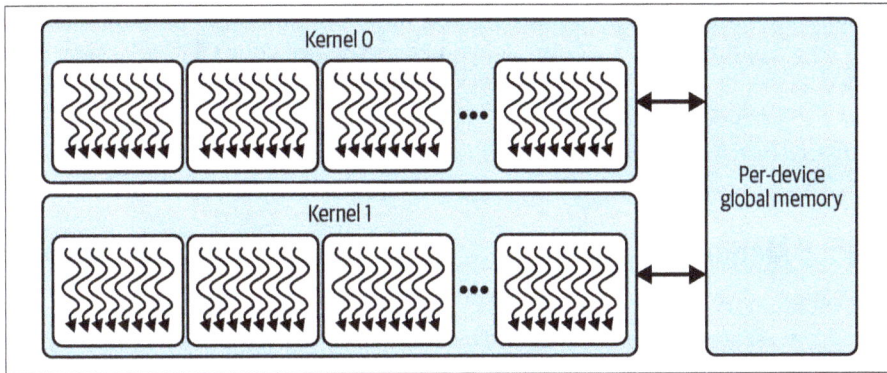

Figure 6-14. Per-device global memory, or HBM

Using tools like Nsight Compute to track spills and cache hit rates, you can keep your kernels operating as close as possible to the on-chip peaks of this memory hierarchy. These tools can help you orchestrate data effectively through registers, shared/L1, constant cache, and L2 cache. Modern GPUs like Blackwell allow kernel developers to exploit the memory hierarchy by using L2 caches and unified L1/shared memory to buffer and coalesce accesses to HBM, as we'll soon see.

> The Blackwell B200 presents as a single GPU built with a unified, global address space. However, it's made up of two reticle-limited dies connected by a 10 TB/s chip-to-chip interconnect. Each die is connected to four HBM3e stacks for a total of eight HBM3e stacks. From a developer's perspective, however, HBM memory access is uniform across this combined address space, but it's worth understanding the low-level details of this architecture.

The point of coherency (PoC) for the different levels in the memory hierarchy depends on your needs and the level at which the threads are communicating. It typically happens at the following levels: thread, thread-block (aka *CTA*), thread block cluster (aka *CTA cluster*), device, or system, as shown in Figure 6-15.

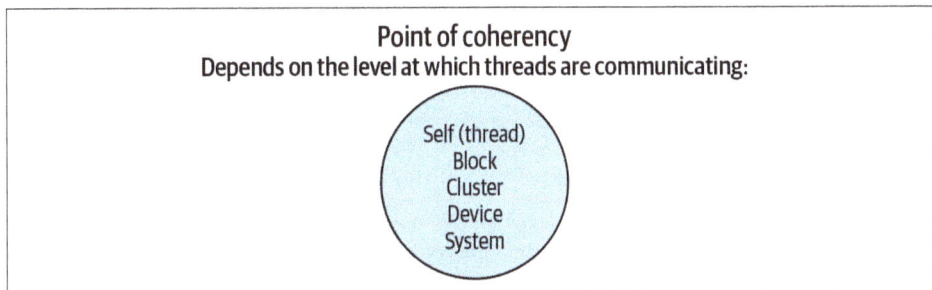

Figure 6-15. Point-of-memory coherency for your GPU threads

In summary, it's important to understand the GPU's memory hierarchy and target each level appropriately. By doing so, you can structure your CUDA kernels to maximize data locality, hide memory-access latency, increase occupancy, and fully leverage Blackwell's massive parallel compute capabilities, as we'll explore in a bit. First, let's discuss NVIDIA's unified memory, which is important to understand given the unified CPU-GPU superchip designs of Grace Hopper and Grace Blackwell.

Unified Memory

Unified Memory (also known as CUDA Managed Memory) gives you a single, coherent address space that spans both CPU and GPU, so you no longer have to juggle separate host and device buffers or issue explicit `cudaMemcpy` calls. Under the hood, the CUDA runtime backs every `cudaMallocManaged()` allocation with pages that can migrate on-demand over whatever interconnect links your CPU and GPU, as shown in Figure 6-16.

While accessing Unified Memory is super developer-friendly, it can cause unwanted on-demand page migrations between the CPU and the GPU. This will introduce hidden latency and execution stalls. For example, if a GPU thread accesses data that currently resides in CPU memory, the GPU will page-fault and wait while that data is transferred over the NVLink-C2C interconnect. Unified Memory performance depends greatly on the underlying hardware.

On traditional PCIe or early NVLink systems, those migrations travel at relatively low bandwidth—often making on-fault transfers slower than a manual `cudaMemcpy`. But on Grace Hopper and Grace Blackwell Superchips, the NVLink-C2C fabric delivers up to ~900 GB/s between the CPU's HBM and the GPU's HBM3e. As such, page-fault–driven migrations come far closer to device-native speed—although they still carry nonzero latency.

That said, any unexpected page-fault during a kernel launch will stall the GPU while the runtime moves the needed page into place. To avoid those "surprise" stalls, you can prefetch memory in advance with `cudaMemPrefetchAsync()`, as shown in Figure 6-17.

This hints to the driver to move the specified range onto the target GPU (or CPU) before you launch your kernel, turning costly first-touch migrations into overlappable, asynchronous transfers. You can also give memory advice, as shown in this code:

```
cudaMemAdvise(ptr, size, cudaMemAdviseSetPreferredLocation, gpuId);
cudaMemAdvise(ptr, size, cudaMemAdviseSetReadMostly, gpuId);
```

Here, you can use `PreferredLocation` to tell the driver where you'll mostly use the data, and `ReadMostly` when it's largely read-only, as shown in Figure 6-18.

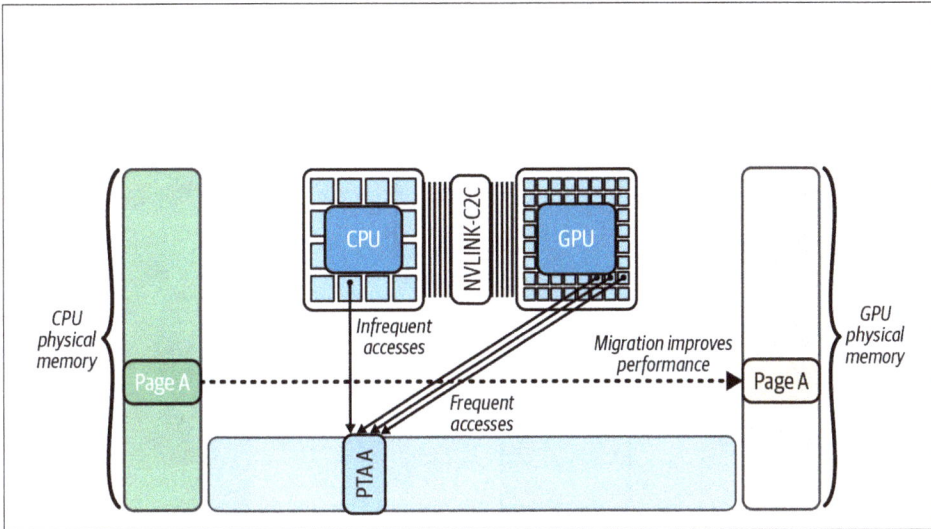

Figure 6-16. Automatic page migrations with CPU-GPU Unified Memory

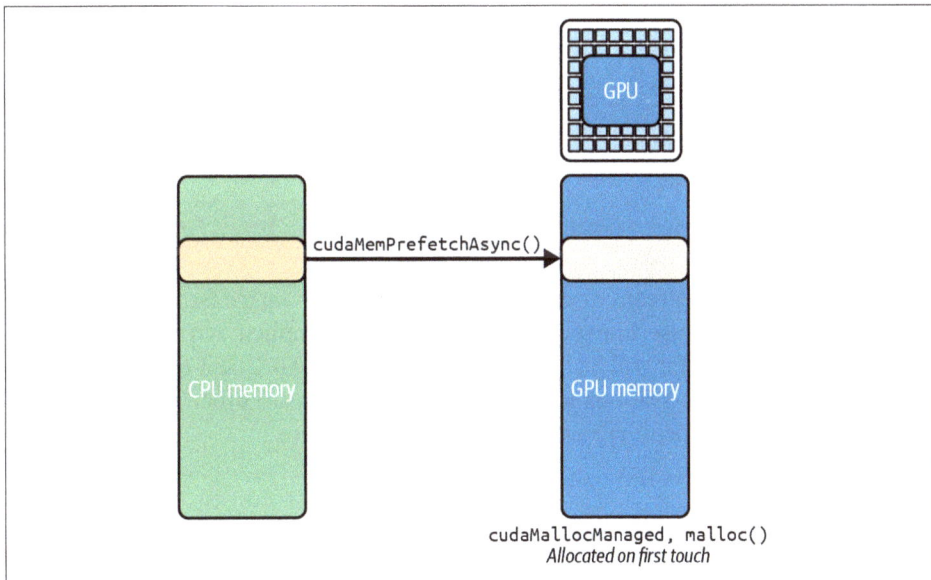

Figure 6-17. Streaming data from CPU to GPU over NVLink-C2C with `cudaMemPrefetchAsync()`

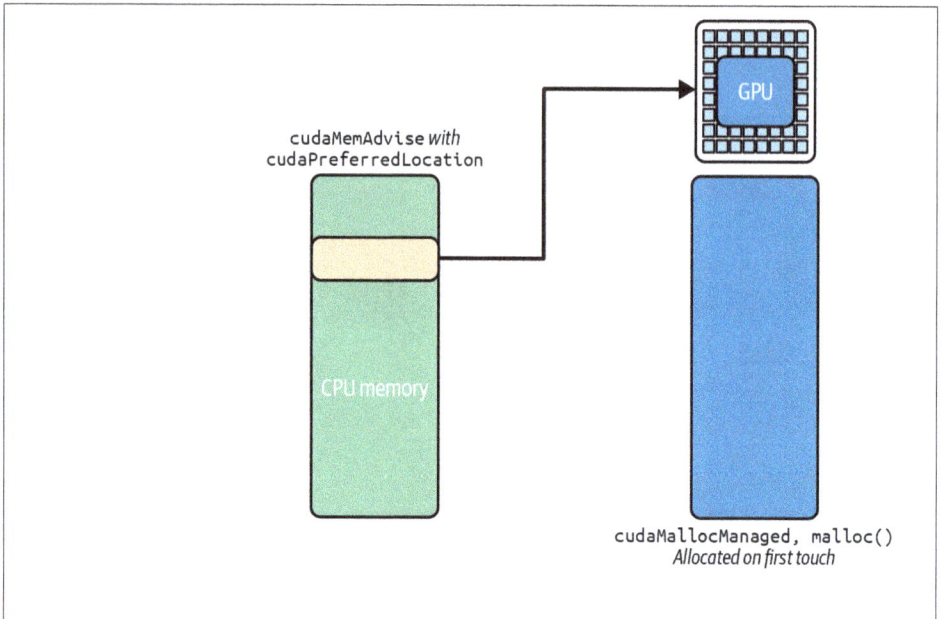

Figure 6-18. Specifying "preferred location" to tell the CUDA driver how the data is mostly used (e.g., ReadMostly for largely read-only workloads)

You can also call the following to let a second GPU map those pages without triggering migrations at launch:

```
cudaMemAdvise(ptr, size, cudaMemAdviseSetAccessedBy,
    otherGpuId);
```

By default, any CUDA stream or device kernel can trigger a page fault on a managed allocation. This can cause unexpected migrations and implicit synchronizations. If you know a certain buffer will be used only in one stream/GPU at a time, attaching it to that stream allows migrations to overlap with operations in other streams. Calling the following ties that memory range to the specified stream:

```
cudaStreamAttachMemAsync(stream, ptr, 0,
    cudaMemAttachSingle);
```

In this case, only operations in that stream will fault and migrate its pages. This prevents other streams from accidentally stalling on it. As such, attaching a range to a particular stream defers its migrations so they overlap with only that stream's work. This avoids cross-stream synchronization.

In multi-GPU systems without NVLink-C2C, you can also use `cudaMemcpyPeerAsync()` or a prefetch to a specific device to pin data in the nearest NUMA-local GPU memory, preventing slow remote accesses.

In short, explicitly prefetching managed memory and providing memory advice can eliminate most of the "surprise" stalls from Unified Memory. Instead of the GPU pausing to fetch data on demand, the data is already where it needs to be when the kernel runs.

With techniques like proactive prefetching, targeted memory advice, and stream attachment, Unified Memory can deliver performance very close to manual `cuda Memcpy` while preserving the simplicity of a unified address space.

Maintaining High Occupancy and GPU Utilization

GPUs sustain performance by running many warps concurrently so that when one warp stalls waiting for data, another warp can run. This ability to rapidly switch between warps allows a GPU to hide memory latency. As we described earlier, the fraction of an SM's capacity actually occupied by active warps is called *occupancy*.

If occupancy is low (just a few active warps), an SM may sit idle while one warp is waiting on memory. This leads to poor SM utilization. On Blackwell, achieving high occupancy is a bit easier given its large register file (64K registers per SM), which can support many warps without spilling.

As you saw earlier, each thread in a warp can use up to 255 registers. Make sure to use your profiling tools to check achieved occupancy—and adjust your kernel's block size and register usage accordingly.

Conversely, high occupancy (many active warps per SM) will keep the GPU compute units busy since, while one warp waits on memory access, others will swap in to the SM and execute. This masks the long memory access delays. This is often referred to as *hiding latency*.

Let's show an example that improves occupancy and ultimately GPU utilization, throughput, and overall kernel performance. This is one of the most fundamental rules of CUDA performance optimization: launch enough parallel work to fully occupy the GPU.

If your achieved occupancy (the fraction of hardware thread slots in use) is well below the GPU's limit and performance is poor, the first remedy is to increase parallelism—use more blocks or threads so that occupancy approaches the 80%–100% range on modern GPUs.

Conversely, if occupancy is already moderate to high but the kernel is bottlenecked by memory throughput, pushing it to 100% may not help. You generally need just enough warps to hide latency, and beyond that the bottleneck might lie elsewhere (e.g., memory bandwidth).

To illustrate the impact of occupancy, consider a very simple operation: adding two vectors of length N (computing C = A + B). We'll examine two kernel implementations: addSequential and addParallel. addSequential uses a single thread (or a single warp) to add all N elements in a loop. addParallel uses many threads so that the additions are done concurrently across the array.

In the sequential version, one GPU thread handles the entire workload serially, as shown here:

```
#include <cuda_runtime.h>

const int N = 1'000'000;

// Single thread does all N additions
__global__ void addSequential(const float* A,
                              const float* B,
                                    float* C,
                              int N)
{
    if (blockIdx.x == 0 && threadIdx.x == 0) {
        for (int i = 0; i < N; ++i) {
            C[i] = A[i] + B[i];
        }
    }
}

int main()
{
    // Allocate and initialize host
    float* h_A = nullptr;
    float* h_B = nullptr;
    float* h_C = nullptr;
    cudaMallocHost(&h_A, N * sizeof(float));
    cudaMallocHost(&h_B, N * sizeof(float));
    cudaMallocHost(&h_C, N * sizeof(float));

    for (int i = 0; i < N; ++i) {
        h_A[i] = float(i);
        h_B[i] = float(i * 2);
    }
```

```
// Allocate device
float *d_A, *d_B, *d_C;
cudaMalloc(&d_A, N * sizeof(float));
cudaMalloc(&d_B, N * sizeof(float));
cudaMalloc(&d_C, N * sizeof(float));

// Copy inputs to device
cudaMemcpy(d_A, h_A, N * sizeof(float), cudaMemcpyHostToDevice);
cudaMemcpy(d_B, h_B, N * sizeof(float), cudaMemcpyHostToDevice);

// Launch: one thread
// Note: This kernel assumes <<<1,1>>>
// (one block, one thread).
// Do not change the launch config when running this example.
addSequential<<<1,1>>>(d_A, d_B, d_C, N);

// Ensure completion before exit
cudaDeviceSynchronize();

// Copy d_C => h_C (back to host)
cudaMemcpy(h_C, d_C, N * sizeof(float), cudaMemcpyDeviceToHost);

// Cleanup
cudaFree(d_A);
cudaFree(d_B);
cudaFree(d_C);
cudaFreeHost(h_A);
cudaFreeHost(h_B);
cudaFreeHost(h_C);

return 0;
}
```

In this single-threaded version, the GPU's vast resources are mostly idle. Only one warp, or even one thread within the warp, is doing work while all others sit idle. The result is very poor occupancy and, ultimately, low performance.

One must be also careful to avoid indirectly executing inefficient GPU code in high-level libraries and frameworks like PyTorch. For instance, the naive PyTorch code that follows mistakenly performs elementwise operations using a Python for-loop that issues N separate add operations on the GPU one after another:

```
import torch

N = 1_000_000
A = torch.arange(N, dtype=torch.float32, device='cuda')
B = 2 * A
C = torch.empty_like(A)

# Ensure all previous work is done
torch.cuda.synchronize()
```

```
# Naive, Sequential GPU operations - DO NOT DO THIS
with torch.inference_mode(): # avoids unnecessary autograd graph construction
    # This launches N tiny GPU operations serially
    for i in range(N):
        C[i] = A[i] + B[i]

torch.cuda.synchronize()
```

This code effectively uses the GPU like a scalar, nonparallel processor. It achieves very low occupancy similar to the previous native `addSequential` CUDA C++ code.

Let's optimize the CUDA kernel and PyTorch code to implement a parallel version of the vector add operation. Figure 6-19 shows how a vectorized add operation works.

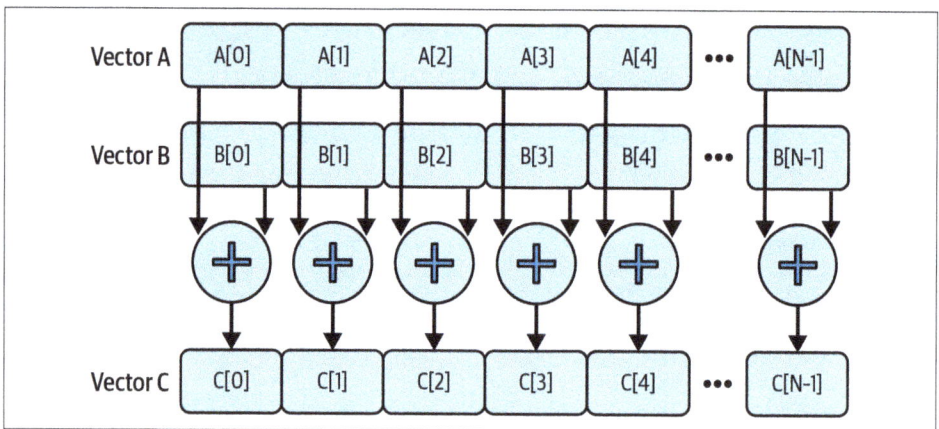

Figure 6-19. Vectorized addition happening in parallel across elements in the vectors

In the following CUDA C++ code, we launch enough threads to cover all elements (`<<< (N+255)/256, 256 >>>`) so that 256 threads per block process N elements in parallel across however many blocks are needed:

```
#include <cuda_runtime.h>

const int N = 1'000'000;

// One thread per element
__global__ void addParallel(const float* __restrict__ A,
                             const float* __restrict__ B,
                                   float* __restrict__ C,
                             int N)
{
    int idx = blockIdx.x * blockDim.x + threadIdx.x;
    if (idx < N) {
        C[idx] = A[idx] + B[idx];
    }
}
```

```cpp
int main()
{
  // Allocate and initialize host (pinned for faster DMA)
  float* h_A = nullptr;
  float* h_B = nullptr;
  float* h_C = nullptr;
  cudaMallocHost(&h_A, N * sizeof(float));
  cudaMallocHost(&h_B, N * sizeof(float));
  cudaMallocHost(&h_C, N * sizeof(float));
  for (int i = 0; i *lt; N; ++i) { h_A[i] = float(i); h_B[i] = float(2*i); }

  // Create a non-blocking stream and allocate device buffers
  cudaStream_t s; cudaStreamCreateWithFlags(&s, cudaStreamNonBlocking);
  float *d_A = nullptr, *d_B = nullptr, *d_C = nullptr;
  cudaMallocAsync(&d_A, N * sizeof(float), s);
  cudaMallocAsync(&d_B, N * sizeof(float), s);
  cudaMallocAsync(&d_C, N * sizeof(float), s);

  // Async HtoD copies on the same stream
  cudaMemcpyAsync(d_A, h_A, N*sizeof(float), cudaMemcpyHostToDevice, s);
  cudaMemcpyAsync(d_B, h_B, N*sizeof(float), cudaMemcpyHostToDevice, s);

  // Launch (same stream)
  int threads = 256;
  int blocks  = (N + threads - 1) / threads;
  addParallel<<<blocks, threads, 0, s>>>(d_A, d_B, d_C, N);

  // Async DtoH copy and stream sync
  cudaMemcpyAsync(h_C, d_C, N*sizeof(float), cudaMemcpyDeviceToHost, s);
  cudaStreamSynchronize(s);

  // Cleanup (stream-ordered free)
  cudaFreeAsync(d_A, s); cudaFreeAsync(d_B, s); cudaFreeAsync(d_C, s);
  cudaStreamDestroy(s);
  cudaFreeHost(h_A); cudaFreeHost(h_B); cudaFreeHost(h_C);
  return 0;
}
```

With a sufficiently large N, the difference in GPU utilization is significant. Now let's optimize the PyTorch code, which launches a single vectorized kernel (A + B) that engages many threads on the GPU concurrently like the previous optimized addParallel CUDA C++ example. Here is the parallel version of the PyTorch code:

```python
# add_parallel.py
import torch

N = 1_000_000
A = torch.arange(N, dtype=torch.float32, device='cuda')
B = 2 * A

torch.cuda.synchronize()
```

```
# Proper parallel approach using vectorized operation
# Launches a single GPU kernel that adds all elements in parallel
C = A + B

torch.cuda.synchronize()
```

> In practice, high-level frameworks like PyTorch will do the right thing when you use vectorized tensor operations. Just be aware that introducing Python-level loops around GPU operations will serialize work and negatively impact performance. Avoid them if possible. Unless you are writing something novel, there is almost always an optimized PyTorch-native implementation available—including code emitted by the PyTorch compiler.

To quantify the performance impact of using a parallel versus sequential implementation, we can use Nsight Systems and Nsight Compute to measure the total kernel execution time, GPU utilization, occupancy, and warp execution efficiency metrics for the two approaches. Here are the Nsight Systems (nsys) and Nsight Compute (ncu) commands:

```
# Sequential add
nsys profile \
  --stats=true \
  -t cuda,nvtx \
  -o sequential_nsys_report \
  ./add_sequential.py

ncu \
 --section SpeedOfLight \
 --metrics
     sm__warps_active.avg.pct_of_peak_sustained_active,gpu__time_duration.avg \
 --target-processes all \
 --print-summary per-gpu \
 -o sequential_ncu_report \
 ./add_sequential.py

# Parallel add
nsys profile \
  --stats=true \
  -t cuda,nvtx \
  -o parallel_nsys_report \
  ./add_parallel.py

ncu \
 --section SpeedOfLight \
 --metrics sm__warps_active.avg.pct_of_peak_sustained_active \
 --target-processes all \
 --print-summary per-gpu \
```

```
    -o parallel_ncu_report \
    ./add_parallel.py
```

We use nsys to uncover where the time is spent and whether the GPU is starved or blocked. Then we use ncu to explain why the kernel is performing the way it is—perhaps due to poor occupancy, etc.

If you run only nsys, you may miss fine-grained kernel inefficiencies. And if run you only ncu, you won't know if your kernels are being fed data fast enough, for example. Table 6-6 shows the unified results.

Table 6-6. Comparing a sequential versus parallel CUDA kernel

Metric	add_sequential	add_parallel
Kernel execution time (ms)	48.21	2.17
GPU utilization	1.5%	95%
Achieved occupancy	1.3%	38.7%
Warp execution efficiency	3.1%	100%

> Other profiling tools may label these metrics differently. For example, Nsight Systems reports overall "GPU Utilization," while Nsight Compute provides a per-kernel "SM Active %" metric—but both reflect how fully the GPU's SMs were occupied by active warps.

As expected, moving from a single-thread, single-warp implementation to a fully parallel, multiwarp implementation improves occupancy from 1.3% to ~38.7% on average. This reduces the runtime by about 22× from 48.21 ms down to 2.17 ms.

In the sequential case, only one warp, and just one thread, is doing work on a single SM. This is why we see a low 1.5% GPU utilization, whereas in the parallel case, many SMs are running multiple active warps. This increases warp execution efficiency from 3.1% to 100% since all 32 threads in a warp are doing useful work during each instruction. This improves GPU utilization from 1.5% to 95%.

This example shows why sufficient parallelism is critical on GPUs. No matter how fast each thread is, you need lots of threads to leverage the GPU's throughput potential.

Remember that the GPU is a throughput-optimized processor that interacts with CPUs to launch the CUDA kernel—as well as the memory subsystem to load data from caches, shared memory, and global memory. As such, GPU performance greatly benefits from hiding these latencies.

When written properly, kernels will instruct the GPU to interleave memory loads and computations (e.g., additions) from different warps in parallel. This helps to hide memory latency across the warps.

The parallel kernel running within multiple warps, in particular, benefits from warp-level latency hiding. While one warp is waiting for a memory load, another warp can be executing the add computation, while yet another could be fetching the next data, etc. We'll explore many techniques to hide memory latency in the upcoming chapters.

In the sequential kernel, there are no other warps to run while one is waiting, so the hardware pipelines often sit idle. The timeline is one long series of operations with idle gaps during memory waits. In the parallel version, those gaps are filled by other warps' work, so the GPU is busy continuously. The comparison is shown in Figure 6-20.

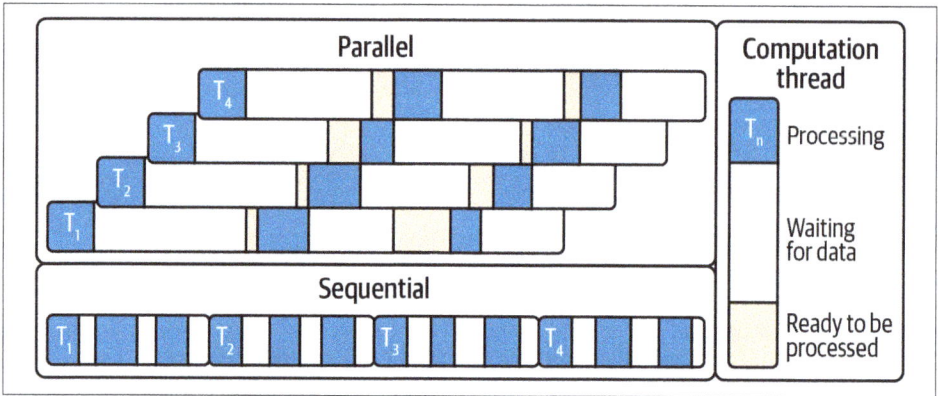

Figure 6-20. Parallel versus sequential timeline comparison

Here, the sequential timeline is one long series of operations with idle gaps during memory waits. In the parallel version, those gaps are filled by other warps' work, so the GPU is busy continuously.

The key takeaway is to first ensure enough parallel work to fully occupy the GPU. High occupancy—enough warps to cover latency—maximizes throughput and minimizes idle stalls—in our example, parallelizing boosted GPU utilization to ~95%.

Once sufficient threads are launched, the next step is optimizing how efficiently each warp executes, through instruction-level parallelism and other per-thread improvements. But note: even at 100% occupancy, performance can still suffer if the workload is memory bound—that is, limited by slow memory access rather than compute.

A well-known example of a memory bound workload is the "decode" phase of an LLM. During decode, the LLM needs to move a large amount of data (model weights or parameters) from global HBM memory into the GPU registers and shared memory.

Since modern LLMs contain hundreds of billions of parameters (multiplied by, let's say, 8 bits per parameter, or 1 byte), the models can be many hundreds of gigabytes in size. Moving this much data in and out of the GPU can easily saturate the memory bandwidth.

> GPU FLOPS are outpacing memory bandwidth. For instance, Blackwell's HBM3e delivers ~8 TB/s, but compute capability and model sizes are growing even faster. As such, optimizing memory movement is absolutely critical to avoid memory-bound bottlenecks in modern AI workloads.

Tuning Occupancy with Launch Bounds

In some cases, simply using more threads isn't enough—especially if each thread uses a lot of resources such as registers and shared memory. We can guide the compiler to optimize for occupancy by using CUDA's __launch_bounds__ kernel annotation.

This annotation lets us specify two parameters for a kernel at compile time: a maximum number of threads per block we will launch and minimum number of thread blocks we want to keep resident on each SM. These hints influence the compiler's register allocation and inlining decisions. An example is shown here:

```
__global__ __launch_bounds__(256, 16)
void myKernel(...) { /* ... */ }
```

Here, __launch_bounds__(256, 16) promises that the CUDA kernel will never be launched with more than 256 threads in a block. It also requests that the compiler allocate enough registers and inline functions so that at least 16 blocks of 256 threads, or 4,096 threads (16 blocks × 256 threads per block), can be resident on the SM simultaneously.

> Remember that we can have only 1,024 threads per block and at most 2,048 resident threads per SM on modern GPUs (e.g., Blackwell).

In practice, since current NVIDIA GPUs limit each SM to 2,048 total threads and each block to 1,024 threads, the compiler will reduce your request to the hardware maximum—in this case, 2,048 threads (8 blocks × 256 threads per block) per SM. And it will emit a warning since the 4,096 request (16 blocks × 256 threads per block) exceeds the SM's capacity.

> The warning will be something like "ptxas warning: Value of threads per SM...is out of range. .minnctapersm will be ignored."

In practice, using __launch_bounds__ often causes the compiler to cap per-thread register usage (and to sometimes restrict unrolling or inlining) to avoid spilling and to allow higher occupancy. We are essentially trading a bit of per-thread performance and not using every last register or unrolling to the max. This is in exchange for more consistent warp throughput by keeping more warps in flight.

Increasing occupancy must be balanced against per-thread resources. You want to avoid register spilling (which occurs if you force too many threads such that they run out of registers and spill to local memory, causing slow memory accesses).

You can also determine an optimal launch configuration at runtime using the CUDA Occupancy API. For example, cudaOccupancyMaxPotentialBlockSize() will calculate the block size that produces the highest occupancy for a given kernel, considering its register and shared memory usage. Essentially, cudaOccupancyMaxPotentialBlock Size can autotune your block size for optimal occupancy, as shown here:

```
int minGridSize = 0, bestBlockSize = 0;

// If your kernel uses dynamic shared memory (extern __shared__),
// set this correctly:
size_t dynSmemBytes = /* bytes per block (e.g., tiles * sizeof(T)) */ 0;

cudaOccupancyMaxPotentialBlockSize(
  &minGridSize, &bestBlockSize,
  myKernel,
  dynSmemBytes,      // must match your kernel's dynamic shared memory use
  /* blockSizeLimit = */ 0);

// Compute a grid that covers N, but don't go below the min grid
// that saturates occupancy
int gridSize = std::max(minGridSize, (N + bestBlockSize - 1) / bestBlockSize);

myKernel<<<gridSize, bestBlockSize, dynSmemBytes>>>(...);
```

This API computes how many threads per block would likely optimize occupancy given the kernel's resource usage. We can then use bestBlockSize (and the suggested grid size) for our kernel launch. It's important to note that minGridSize is the minimum grid size that saturates occupancy for this kernel on this device. It is not necessarily the right grid size to cover an input of length N. Compute gridSize = max(minGridSize, ceil_div(N, bestBlockSize)), and pass the kernel's actual dynamic shared-memory bytes if it uses extern __shared__.

Validate Occupancy API suggestions by timing kernels at ±1–2 candidate block sizes. Register pressure and L2 behavior on modern GPUs can actually make a slightly sub-maximal occupancy configuration faster in practice.

When applied, the compiler's heuristics are usually good, but __launch_bounds__ and occupancy calculators give you explicit control when needed. Use them when you *know* your kernel can trade some per-thread resource usage for more active warps. This helps prevent underoccupying SMs due to heavy threads.

The trade-off between registers and occupancy is important. Using fewer registers per thread—or capping them using launch bounds—allows more warps to be resident, which improves latency hiding. However, using too few registers can force the compiler to spill data to local memory, hurting performance. Finding the sweet spot often requires experimentation. Nsight Compute's "Registers Per Thread" and "Occupancy" metrics can guide you here.

Debugging Functional Correctness with NVIDIA Compute Sanitizer

Since CUDA applications can spawn thousands of threads per kernel, traditional debugging may fail to catch subtle memory bugs and race conditions. NVIDIA Compute Sanitizer (*https://oreil.ly/qzhW5*), a functional-correctness suite included with the CUDA Toolkit, addresses these challenges by instrumenting code at runtime to find errors early in development. This reduces debugging interactions—and improves overall code reliability.

Sanitizer is invoked using the compute-sanitizer CLI and supports NVIDIA Tools Extension (NVTX) annotations for finer-grained analysis. NVTX should be used extensively for both correctness and performance analysis. To use the CLI, you can specify options with --option value and include flags like --error-exitcode to fail on errors. You can also apply filters to sanitize only specific kernels, such as using --kernel-name and --kernel-name-exclude. You can enable NVTX with --nvtx yes to help narrow the scope of your analysis and minimize false positives in memory-leak reports, for instance:

```
compute-sanitizer [--tool toolname] [options] <application> [app_args]
```

It's recommended to integrate Compute Sanitizer into your continuous integration (CI) pipelines with `--error-exitcode` to catch correctness regressions using kernel filters and NVTX region annotations.

Compute Sanitizer consists of four primary tools: memcheck, racecheck, initcheck, and synccheck. These help detect out-of-bounds memory accesses, data races, uninitialized memory reads, and synchronization issues in your CUDA code:

Memcheck

The memcheck tool precisely detects and attributes out-of-bounds or misaligned accesses in global, local, and shared memory; reports GPU hardware exceptions; and can identify device-side memory leaks. It supports additional checks such as `--check-device-heap` for heap allocations using command-line switches.

Racecheck

Racecheck reports shared-memory data hazards, including Write-After-Write, Write-After-Read, and Read-After-Write, which can lead to nondeterministic behavior. Racecheck helps developers verify correct thread-to-thread communication within warps and thread blocks.

Initcheck

Initcheck flags any access to uninitialized device global memory. This can be due to missing host-to-device copies or skipped device-side writes. This tool helps avoid subtle bugs that arise from stale or garbage data.

Synccheck

Synccheck detects invalid uses of synchronization primitives such as mismatched barriers. It identifies thread-ordering hazards that can cause deadlocks and inconsistent state across threads.

In short, NVIDIA Compute Sanitizer provides a set of tools for uncovering and resolving memory, race, initialization, and synchronization bugs in CUDA applications. These tools, when integrated with CI systems, can help developers find correctness issues early. This way, they can ship reliable, high-performance code with confidence.

Roofline Model: Compute-Bound or Memory-Bound Workloads

A roofline model is a useful visualization that charts two hardware-imposed performance ceilings: one horizontal line at the processor's peak floating-point rate and one diagonal line set by the peak memory bandwidth. Together, these form a "roofline" envelope that reveals whether a given kernel is limited by computation (compute bound) or data movement (memory bound).

Where these lines intersect is called the *ridge point*. This corresponds to the "arithmetic intensity" threshold at which a kernel transitions from being memory bound (left of the ridge) to compute bound (right of the ridge). Arithmetic intensity is measured as the number of FLOPS performed per byte transferred between off-chip global memory and the GPU.

Let's consider a simple example to illustrate why arithmetic intensity matters. Suppose a kernel loads two 32-bit floats (8 bytes total), adds them (1 FLOP), and writes back one 32-bit float result (4 bytes). In this case, the algorithm carries out 1 FLOP for 12 bytes of memory traffic, yielding an arithmetic intensity of 0.083 FLOPs/byte (1 FLOP/12 bytes ≈ 0.083 FLOPs per byte).

Compare this to a GPU's ridge point of 10 FLOPs per byte (10 FLOPs = ~80 TFLOPs ÷ 8 TB/s). This float-add kernel's ridge point of 0.083 is orders of magnitude to the left (memory-bound side) of the roofline. This is more than 100× below that threshold, so it cannot keep the arithmetic logic units (ALUs) busy. This kernel is in the memory-bound regime, where performance is dominated by memory stalls rather than compute. Figure 6-21 shows a representative of the roofline model for Blackwell, including peak compute performance (horizontal line at ~80 FLOPs/sec) and peak memory bandwidth (diagonal line corresponding to 8 TB/s).

Here, we see that the ridge point for the Blackwell GPU is the sustained FLOPs/sec divided by the sustained HBM bandwidth. Here, it's the intersection point shown at 10 FLOPs/byte. Our example kernel's arithmetic intensity is to the left along the slanted, memory-bandwidth diagonal at 0.083 FLOPs/byte. As such, this kernel lies on the slanted, memory-bandwidth ceiling of the roofline. This confirms that it is memory bound.

To make this kernel less memory bound (and thus more compute bound), you can increase its arithmetic intensity by doing more work per byte of data. This will move the kernel to the right, which pushes performance up toward the compute roofline.

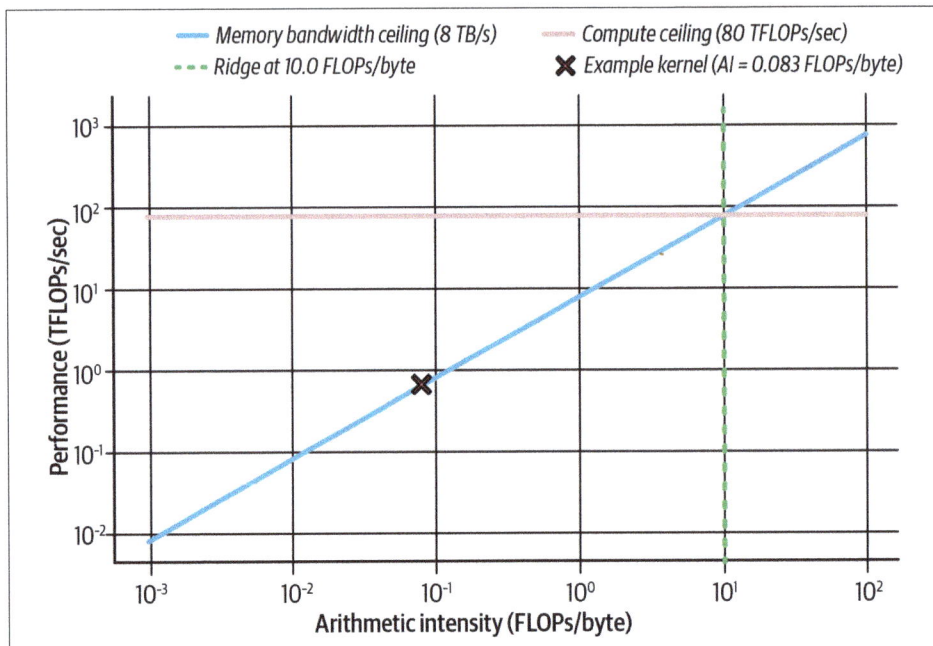

Figure 6-21. Roofline model for a Blackwell-class GPU (~80 TFLOPs/sec FP32, ~8 TB/s HBM3e) showing our kernel's point and the ~10 FLOPs/byte arithmetic intensity ridge

One simple way to make the kernel less memory bound is to use lower-precision data. For instance, if you used 16-bit floats (FP16) instead of 32-bit (FP32), you'd halve the bytes transferred per operation and instantly double the FLOPs/byte intensity.

Modern GPUs also support dedicated 8-bit floating point (FP8) Tensor Cores. Blackwell also introduced native support for 4-bit floating point (FP4) Tensor Cores for certain AI workloads. These further reduce the bytes per operation and increase the FLOPs/byte intensity even more.

For example, Blackwell supports FP8 Tensor Cores (1 byte per value), which doubles throughput and halves memory use relative to FP16. It also supports FP4 (half a byte per value) for some workloads like model inference.

A single 128-byte memory transaction can carry 32 FP32, 64 FP16, 128 FP8, or 256 FP4 values. Blackwell introduces hardware decompression to accelerate compressed model weights. For instance, models can be stored compressed in HBM, even beyond FP4 compression, and the hardware can decompress the weights on the fly. This effectively increases the usable memory bandwidth further when reading those weights.

As such, Blackwell has an architecture advantage for memory-bound workloads like transformer-based token generation. Weights are stored in a compressed 4-bit or 2-bit scheme and decompressed by hardware at load time and cast to FP16/FP32 for higher-precision aggregations and computations. This shows how lower precision can reduce the amount of data transferred, increase arithmetic intensity for your kernel, and improve overall memory throughput for your workload.

For memory-bound workloads, the goal is to push the kernel's operational point to the right on the roofline to increase its arithmetic intensity and move closer to becoming compute bound. By moving closer to the compute-bound regime, your kernel can better exploit the GPU's full floating-point horsepower.

> Transformer-based models (e.g., LLMs) can be both compute bound and memory bound in different phases. For example, attention layers (prefill phase) are typically compute bound, while matrix multiplications (decode phase) are often memory bound. We will discuss this more in Chapters 15–18 when we dive deep into inference.

When a kernel is memory bound, Nsight Compute will report very high DRAM bandwidth utilization alongside low achieved compute metrics such as low ALU utilization. This indicates that warps spend most of their time stalled on memory accesses.

To drill into what's happening, it's best to use Nsight Compute for per-kernel counters, including latencies, cache hit rates, and warp issue stalls. In addition, modern versions of Nsight Compute have range replay (with instruction-level source metrics), improved source correlation navigation, and a launch-stack size metric. These features help diagnose dependency stalls, register pressure, and launch configuration effects more quickly.

You can then use Nsight Systems for a holistic timeline view showing GPU idle gaps, overlap with CPU work, and PCIe/NVLink transfers. Together they give you both the *why* (which stalls and which resources) and the *when* (how those stalls fit into your application's overall execution.)

The key is to iteratively profile and identify memory hotspots using metrics from both Nsight Compute and Nsight Systems. You should add NVTX ranges around suspect code, zoom in on timeline behavior, and use the feedback to optimize.

For instance, you can use NVTX to label regions as "memory copy" or "kernel execution" and see them in the Nsight Systems timeline. This is incredibly useful to confirm overlapping host-device transfers with compute, as discussed earlier.

For instance, to verify the overlap, you can mark the start/end of both the data transfer and kernel calls with NVTX markers. Nsight Systems will show these NVTX ranges on a timeline, making it easy to see overlap. With asynchronous memory copies (cudaMemcpyAsync), the data transfer overlaps with kernel execution on the GPU (see Figure 6-22), comparing a synchronous and asynchronous memory transfer.

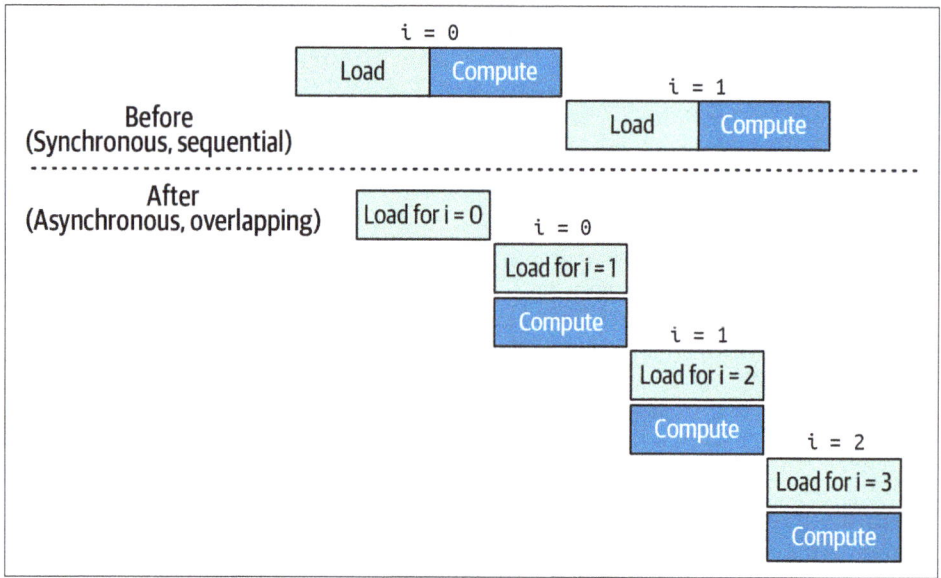

Figure 6-22. Synchronous (sequential) and asynchronous (overlapping) data transfers with kernel computations

If you expect overlap but see the copies and kernels running sequentially versus parallel, then it's something like an unwanted default-stream synchronization. Otherwise, a missing pinned-memory buffer is likely preventing true overlap.

> Without using pinned (page-locked) memory, the cudaMemcpy Async transfer cannot overlap with kernel execution. This is a common performance issue.

When you suspect a kernel is starved for data, start by running it under Nsight Compute and Nsight Systems. In Nsight Compute you'll see the global load efficiency metric drop. This signals that your DRAM requests aren't being satisfied quickly enough. At the same time, the Nsight Systems timeline will reveal idle stretches between kernel launches as the GPU waits on data transfers.

Once you've applied the memory-hierarchy optimizations from this chapter, those idle gaps will all but disappear, and Nsight Compute will show memory pipe utilization percentage climbing toward its peak. You'll also see a corresponding jump in end-to-end kernel throughput.

> Always measure after each change. Profiling tools will confirm if an optimization actually reduces memory stalls or not.

Key Takeaways

In this chapter, you learned how to choose launch parameters that optimize occupancy, manage GPU memory asynchronously, and apply roofline analysis to distinguish compute-bound from memory-bound kernels. Here are some key takeaways worth reviewing:

SIMT execution model
 GPUs execute threads in warps (32 threads) under the single-instruction, multiple thread (SIMT) model, with each warp issuing instructions in lockstep. High occupancy—keeping many warps in flight—hides memory and pipeline latency.

Thread hierarchy: threads → locks → grids
 Threads are grouped into thread blocks (up to 1,024 threads), and thread blocks form a grid to scale across millions of threads without code changes. Synchronization (`__syncthreads()` or cooperative groups) enables data reuse in shared memory but incurs overhead, so minimize barriers.

Occupancy versus resource limits
 Choose block sizes as multiples of 32 to avoid underfilled warps and maximize scheduler utilization. Be mindful of per-SM limits. For Blackwell, the maximum registers per thread is 255, maximum per-SM shared memory is 228 KB, maximum resident warps is 64, and maximum resident thread blocks is 32.

CUDA kernel-launch parameters
 Start with `threadsPerBlock = 256` (8 warps) for a balance of occupancy and resource use; compute `blocksPerGrid = (N + threadsPerBlock - 1) / threadsPerBlock` to cover all elements. Tune these values based on profiling feedback (register/register spilling, shared-memory usage, achieved occupancy).

Asynchronous memory management
 Prefer `cudaMallocAsync`/`cudaFreeAsync` on dedicated streams and leverage CUDA memory pools to avoid global synchronizations and OS-level overhead. PyTorch's caching allocator follows a similar pattern (*https://oreil.ly/KyJ2V*) for efficient tensor allocations and avoids costly `cudaMalloc()` and `cudaFree()` invocations.

GPU memory hierarchy

Registers → L1/shared → L2 → global (HBM3e) → host: each level trades capacity for latency/bandwidth. Maximize data reuse in registers and shared/L1 cache.

Unified Memory considerations

CUDA Managed Memory (Unified Memory) simplifies programming but can incur implicit page migrations; use `cudaMemPrefetchAsync` and memory advice to avoid surprise stalls.

Roofline model analysis

Arithmetic intensity (FLOPS per byte) determines whether a kernel is memory bound or compute bound. Use lower precision (FP16/FP8/FP4 and hardware decompression) to boost FLOPS/byte ratio and push kernels toward the compute roofline. Profile with Nsight Compute (per-kernel metrics) and Nsight Systems (timeline) to identify and eliminate memory stalls. Using TMEM with Blackwell unified matrix-multiply-accumulate (UMMA) can shift kernels from memory-bound to compute-bound when combined with FP8 and FP4. We'll cover UMMA in more detail in Chapter 10.

Conclusion

This chapter has laid the groundwork for high-performance CUDA development by demystifying the GPU's SIMT model, thread hierarchy, and multilevel memory system. Remember that occupancy, the ratio of active warps to the theoretical GPU maximum, is important for latency hiding.

However, maximizing occupancy does not guarantee best performance in every case. GPUs can often achieve very high throughput at moderate or even low occupancy if threads have sufficient instruction-level parallelism (ILP)—or if other resources are the bottleneck.

While higher occupancy helps to hide latency, there are scenarios in which reducing the number of active threads will free up registers for other threads. This allows more computations per thread—and ultimately boosts throughput. Always benchmark different occupancy levels to find the optimal setting for your workload and hardware.

With these fundamentals and profiling techniques in hand, you're now ready to dive into targeted optimizations such as avoiding warp divergency, exploiting the GPU memory hierarchy, and asynchronously prefetching memory. We'll also dive into the TMA, which handles bulk memory transfers and frees up the GPU to focus on useful work and increase computational goodput.

## CHAPTER 7

Profiling and Tuning GPU Memory Access Patterns

As AI models grow in size and complexity, a GPU's memory system often becomes the bottleneck that stands between theoretical compute capability and real-world performance. As you saw in Chapter 6, modern NVIDIA GPUs combine thousands of simple, throughput-optimized cores with specialized Tensor Cores. They also include high-bandwidth memory (HBM), coherent CPU-GPU unified memory address space (e.g., Grace Blackwell Superchip), on-chip shared memory, caches, and specialized direct memory access (DMA) engines like the Tensor Memory Accelerator (TMA).

In this chapter, you'll see various CUDA C++ and PyTorch optimization techniques to align data structures for efficient memory access, eliminate redundant data loads, and overlap data transfers with computation using hardware.

Through concrete before-and-after examples of matrix multiplies, tensor operations, and more, you'll see how small changes in memory access patterns, tiling strategies, and asynchronous data transfers can reduce wasted bandwidth, boost arithmetic efficiency, and transform kernels from memory bound to compute bound.

By the end of this chapter, you'll know how to write CUDA kernels that can better utilize the GPU's memory hierarchy and hardware-optimized data transfer engines.

Coalesced Versus Uncoalesced Global Memory Access

The memory access pattern of your code can greatly impact performance. Global memory accesses are fastest when threads in a warp access contiguous memory addresses that the hardware can combine into fewer, larger transactions. If threads access scattered or misaligned addresses, the device cannot coalesce requests into the minimal number of cache line transactions, which on modern GPUs are 128-byte lines composed of four 32-byte sectors. This results in many more memory transactions retrieving unused data, which quickly eats up memory bandwidth.

On a Blackwell GPU, per-device HBM3e bandwidth is up to 8 TB/s. Within the Grace Blackwell GB200 and GB300 (two GPU superchips), this increases 16 TB/s across both GPUs. Using uncoalesced memory accesses will leave most of this bandwidth unused due to excess memory transactions and stalls.

In the uncoalesced case, each thread in a warp loads from scattered addresses. This results in many separate memory transactions. Even if threads in a warp access consecutive addresses, if the first address isn't 128-byte aligned, the warp's request will span two 128-byte cache lines.

For example, if a warp's first thread starts at an address that isn't 128-byte aligned, the warp's memory request will cross a cache-line boundary, often resulting in two 128-byte transactions instead of one. In that case the warp may fetch an extra sector beyond the optimal four sectors, for a total of five sectors across the two lines. This is a waste of bandwidth. Whether a misaligned, contiguous 128-byte warp load touches 5× 32 B sectors or 8× 32 B sectors depends on the start offset. Aligned accesses keep it to 4× 32 B sectors.

In the coalesced case, however, threads load from consecutive addresses combined into a single wide transaction. Figure 7-1 compares coalesced and uncoalesced memory access.

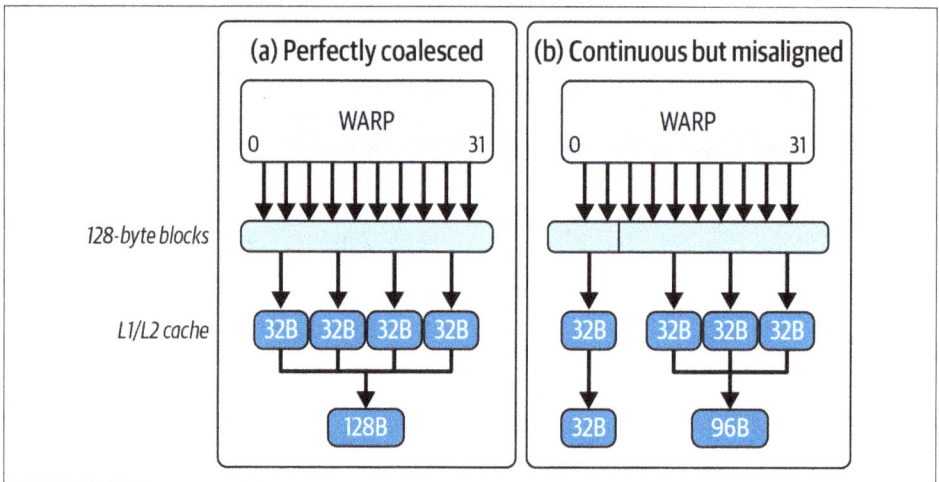

Figure 7-1. Comparing coalesced versus uncoalesced memory access pattern

In kernel code, this problem typically appears as *strided* or irregular indexing such that each thread reaches into different cache lines. When a kernel's threads fetch data with strided or irregular indices, the GPU issues many small, uncoalesced global-memory transactions rather than a handful of full-width loads.

In Nsight Compute, the Memory Workload Analysis section will show lower Global Memory Load Efficiency, higher DRAM sector read counts, and average sectors per request above 4.0 when uncoalesced patterns are present. This is because more sectors are being fetched than a properly coalesced memory access pattern, and it indicates that you're wasting bandwidth by fetching mostly unused bytes. And DRAM throughput percentage will remain well below peak. This confirms that your warp is spending cycles stalled on memory rather than driving the ALUs.

To break out of this memory-bound regime, you can reorganize your data so that each warp's 32 threads load contiguous elements. Either index the array with `input[idx]` where `idx = blockIdx.x * blockDim.x + threadIdx.x` or switch to a structure-of-arrays (SoA) layout so that thread i always touches element i. The difference between an array of structures (AoS) and an SoA is shown in Figure 7-2. Specifically, AoS allows adjacent threads to step through strided fields, while SoA aligns thread i with contiguous element i in memory.

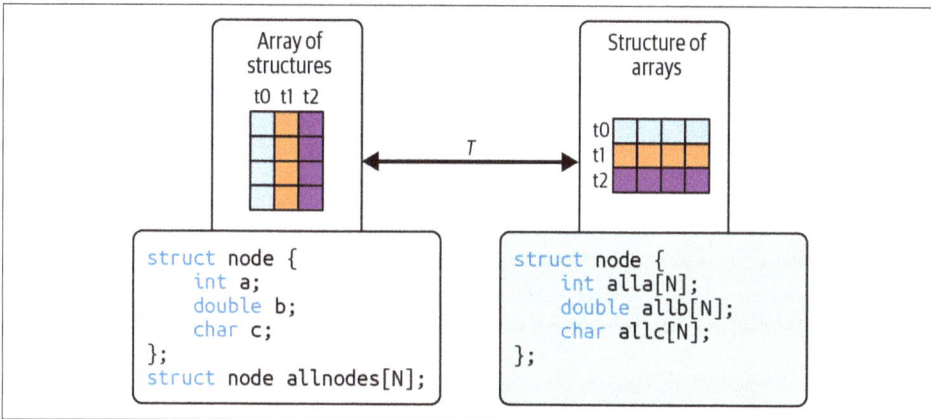

Figure 7-2. Array of structures (AoS) strided access versus structure of arrays (SoA) contiguous access

Once you make the change, the hardware will automatically combine the warp's global memory loads into fewer, wider transactions with more usable (less wasted) data being returned. The Nsight Compute counters will immediately show improvement.

Let's demonstrate this with an example. The following before-and-after code demonstrates how restructuring global memory accesses from a strided pattern to a contiguous pattern produces a significant performance gain.

Before example (C++): uncoalesced strided access. In this example, each thread copies from an input array with a stride of 2, causing misaligned memory accesses:

```cpp
#include <cuda_runtime.h>
#include <iostream>

__global__ void uncoalescedCopy(const float* __restrict__ in,
float* __restrict__ out,
int N, int stride) {
    // n = 1048576, stride = 2
    int idx = blockIdx.x * blockDim.x + threadIdx.x;
    if (idx < N) {
        // Loads from in[] with a stride, causing
        // multiple memory segments to be fetched
        out[idx] = in[idx * stride];
    }
}

int main() {
    const int N = 1 << 20;
    const int stride = 2;

    float* h_in = nullptr;
    float* h_out = nullptr;
    cudaMallocHost(&h_in, N * stride * sizeof(float));
    cudaMallocHost(&h_out, N * sizeof(float));

    for (int i = 0; i < N * stride; ++i) {
        h_in[i] = static_cast<float>(i);
    }

    float *d_in, *d_out;
    cudaMalloc(&d_in,  N * stride * sizeof(float));
    cudaMalloc(&d_out, N * sizeof(float));
    cudaMemcpy(d_in, h_in, N * stride * sizeof(float),
      cudaMemcpyHostToDevice);

    // Number of threads per block (multiple of 32)
    const int threadsPerBlock = 256;

    // Number of blocks per grid
    const int blocksPerGrid = (N + threadsPerBlock - 1) /
      threadsPerBlock;

    uncoalescedCopy<<<blocksPerGrid,
      threadsPerBlock>>>(d_in, d_out, N, stride);
    cudaDeviceSynchronize();

    cudaFree(d_in);
    cudaFree(d_out);
    cudaFreeHost(h_in);
    cudaFreeHost(h_out);
```

```
    return 0;
}
```

The CUDA C++ kernel issues global memory loads at addresses separated by a stride > 1, which is, by definition, noncontiguous. This causes each warp to generate multiple small transactions instead of a single wide transaction.

Before example (PyTorch). In PyTorch, an analogous situation can be created using a strided index for a gather operation:

```python
import torch

def uncoalesced_copy(input_tensor, stride):
    # Flatten to 1D so we know exactly
    #    which dimension we're indexing
    flat_tensor = input_tensor.contiguous().view(-1)

    # Generate indices with a fixed stride to gather
    assert flat_tensor.numel() % stride == 0,"stride must divide tensor length"
    idx = torch.arange(0, flat_tensor.numel(), stride,
        device=flat_tensor.device, dtype=torch.long)
    # index_select uses a gather kernel that issues uncoalesced loads
    return torch.index_select(flat_tensor, 0, idx)

# Usage
n, stride = 1 << 20, 2
inp = torch.arange(n * stride, device='cuda',
                    dtype=torch.float32)
out = uncoalesced_copy(inp, stride)
```

This PyTorch snippet uses `torch.index_select` with a strided index pattern, which causes the underlying GPU gather kernel to perform uncoalesced loads. Specifically, a warp of 32 threads will access addresses that are `stride * 4 bytes` apart.

This does not allow a single wide transaction and instead generates 32 separate loads. Each thread loads a value from `inp` that is far apart in memory from the value loaded by the next thread, which prevents coalescing. Figure 7-3 shows the coalesced versus strided access pattern—as well as random access.

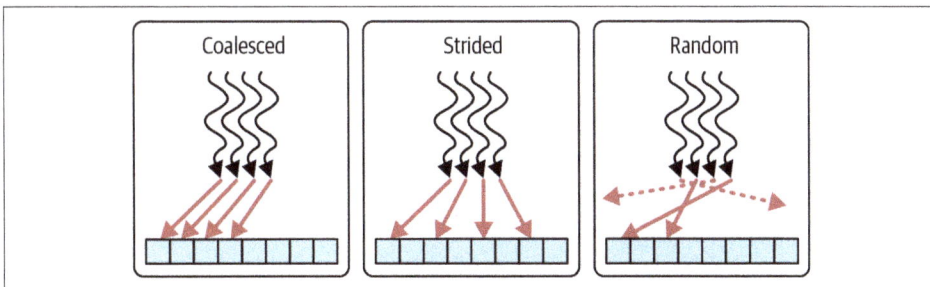

Figure 7-3. Coalesced, strided, and random memory access patterns

After running the C++ and PyTorch codes on a GPU, we measure performance metrics. In the uncoalesced version, each warp's memory request is broken into 8 separate 32-byte sectors on average. Since each 128-byte cache line fetch is split into 4 separate 32-byte sectors (more on this number 4 in a bit), the access pattern spans two lines per warp to retrieve the 8 separate 32-byte sectors.

In the unoptimized version, each warp's uncoalesced loads break a single logical request into up to eight separate 32-byte sectors, ballooning transaction counts and starving the memory pipeline. As a result, Nsight Compute reports only about 25% of sustained peak dynamic random-access memory (DRAM) throughput.

Now, let's optimize this by coalescing the memory accesses and making threads read contiguous elements so each warp issues fewer, larger transactions.

After example (C++): coalesced access. By simply removing the stride (or setting it to 1), each thread copies a contiguous element. This alignment of thread accesses allows the hardware to coalesce memory requests into full 128-byte transactions:

```cpp
#include <cuda_runtime.h>
#include <iostream>

__global__ void coalescedCopy(const float* __restrict__ in,
                              float* __restrict__ out,
                              int n) {
    int idx = blockIdx.x * blockDim.x + threadIdx.x;
    if (idx < n) {
        // Contiguous load
        // Threads copy neighboring elements
        out[idx] = in[idx];
    }
}

int main() {
    const int n = 1 << 20;
    const size_t bytes = n * sizeof(float);

    // 1) Allocate pinned host memory
    float *h_in = nullptr, *h_out = nullptr;
    cudaMallocHost(&h_in,  bytes);  // page-locked host alloc
    cudaMallocHost(&h_out, bytes);

    // 2) Initialize input
    for (int i = 0; i < n; ++i) {
        h_in[i] = static_cast<float>(i);
    }

    // 3) Allocate device memory
    float *d_in = nullptr, *d_out = nullptr;
    cudaMalloc(&d_in,  bytes);
    cudaMalloc(&d_out, bytes);
```

```
// 4) Copy to device
cudaMemcpy(d_in, h_in, bytes,
  cudaMemcpyHostToDevice);

// 5) Launch kernel
dim3 block(256);
dim3 grid((n + block.x - 1) / block.x);
coalescedCopy<<<grid, block>>>(d_in, d_out, n);
cudaDeviceSynchronize();

// 6) Copy back to host
cudaMemcpy(h_out, d_out, bytes,
  cudaMemcpyDeviceToHost);

// 7) Clean up
cudaFree(d_in);
cudaFree(d_out);
cudaFreeHost(h_in);
cudaFreeHost(h_out);

return 0;
}
```

We leave out the coalesced PyTorch implementation for brevity since it's already built into PyTorch. A coalesced version in PyTorch would simply do something like out = inp.clone(). This copies contiguous elements efficiently. In fact, clone() on a contiguous tensor uses a vectorized memory copy under the hood, analogous to our coalesced kernel.

You can also use torch.compile with the default TorchInductor backend to reduce redundant copies and to fuse adjacent operations when safe. clone() is already a device-to-device copy, so it's typically not fused into a separate custom kernel. Enable autotuning (e.g., mode="max-autotune") to help TorchInductor pick coalesced and vectorized schedules when shapes are stable. We'll cover the PyTorch compiler in depth in Chapters 13 and 14.

With coalesced access, or no stride, each warp's threads access adjacent addresses. In this case, the hardware coalesces each warp's loads into the minimum number of 128-byte transactions—often one 128-byte transaction per warp when the first address is 128-byte aligned, or two if the access straddles a boundary. Table 7-1 shows the dramatic improvements resulting from this optimization.

Table 7-1. Coalesced versus uncoalesced memory access performance

Metric	Before (uncoalesced)	After (coalesced)
DRAM throughput (% of peak)	25%	90% (3.6×)
Global Memory Load Efficiency	23%	99%
Average sectors per request	8.0	4.0 (optimal)
SM Active %	62%	99%
Kernel execution time (ms)	4.8 ms	1.3 ms (3.7×)

> Note: The numeric values in all metrics tables are illustrative to explain the concepts. For actual benchmark results on different GPU architectures, see the GitHub repository (*https://github.com/cfregly/ai-performance-engineering*).

After fixing the data layout and coalescing global memory accesses, DRAM throughput rises from 25% to 90% of peak, about 3.6× higher. Kernel execution time improves by about 3.7×, from 4.8 ms to 1.3 ms, as fewer stalls free the SMs to make forward progress.

Global Memory Load Efficiency rises from 23% to 99%, meaning nearly every fetched byte is useful. At the same time, Average Sectors per Request falls to about 4.0.

> A value near 4.0 means the warp's loads are fully coalesced. With the first address 128-byte aligned, all 32 threads map to one 128-byte line. This line has four 32-byte sectors, so the metric reports an average of 4.0 sectors per request.

In the worst case with strided or scattered access, the value can approach 32 because activity is reported in 32-byte sectors at L2. Values above 4.0 indicate uncoalesced or misaligned access. In an unoptimized version, uncoalesced loads can break a single logical access into many sectors per request, approaching the worst case.

Here we are at about 4.0 sectors per request, which indicates that requests map cleanly to 128-byte lines with no unused sectors. With fewer memory stalls, SM Active percent improves from 62% to 99%.

In summary, by aligning each warp's threads on successive addresses, the GPU's memory controller can service each warp with a few large transactions instead of dozens of tiny ones. This boosts the Global Memory Load Efficiency (fraction of each transaction that returns useful data) to near 100% and raises SM Active % by keeping warps busy instead of idle.

And with that, you've seen how coalescing reshapes your thread-to-address mapping so an entire warp's loads line up on the GPU's 128-byte segments. However, even a fully coalesced warp still issues 32 individual 4-byte reads under the hood, one per thread, forcing the hardware to stitch them back together into each 128-byte transaction.

To eliminate that last layer of inefficiency, we turn to vectorized memory access: having each thread fetch a wider, aligned chunk (e.g., a 16-byte float4) in a single instruction so that a coalesced warp issues exactly four 128-byte transactions, not 32. Let's dive into how to pack your per-thread loads into CUDA's built-in vector types.

Vectorized Memory Access

While memory coalescing is a runtime hardware optimization on NVIDIA GPUs, vectorized memory access is a compile-time strategy in which each load or store instruction explicitly fetches multiple contiguous elements (e.g., float4, or 16 bytes) per thread. This reduces instruction count and eliminates stitching overhead.

Efficient global-memory access on Blackwell relies on matching your loads to the GPU's native 128-byte transaction size. When each thread reads only a 4-byte float, a 32-thread warp still has to stitch together 32 4-byte requests to fill one 128-byte line.

In ideal coalesced cases, a warp that reads 32 4-byte words aligned to a 128-byte boundary maps to exactly four 32-byte sectors. Nsight Compute captures this waste in the average sectors per request metric, which can climb well above 4.0 when your accesses are misaligned, strided, or scattered. As such, you'll see Global Memory Load Efficiency drop as bandwidth goes underutilized.

The fix is to bundle each thread's work into a larger, naturally aligned vector that maps cleanly onto those 128-byte transactions. CUDA's built-in float4 type does exactly that: it packs four 4-byte floats into a 16-byte struct guaranteed by the compiler to be 16-byte aligned. For illustration purposes, it looks something like the following code:

```
// Example of a custom float4 for illustration purposes.
// Note: it's recommended to use the built-in CUDA float4 type.
// Note: if N is not divisible by 4, handle the last N % 4 elements
// (e.g., a short scalar cleanup) or assert divisibility in host code. The
// input and output pointers must be 16-byte aligned for float4 loads/stores.
struct my_float4 {
    float x;  // 4 bytes
    float y;  // 4 bytes
    float z;  // 4 bytes
    float w;  // 4 bytes
};
```

When all 32 threads in a warp issue a `float4` load, they together fetch 32×16 bytes = 512 bytes of contiguous data, which the Blackwell memory controller then splits into exactly four 128-byte transactions (512 bytes ÷ 128 bytes per transaction = 4 transactions). This preserves the ideal 4.0 sectors per 128-byte transaction (discussed earlier re: coalesced memory access) because the warp requests 512 bytes, and the hardware services the request with four aligned 128-byte transactions for a total of 16 sectors, each fully utilized.

Compared to an unaligned or strided case that can inflate sector counts, vectorized `float4` loads reduce per-thread load instructions by 4×. This helps maintain the ideal 4.0 sectors per request when alignment is satisfied.

> High-level GPU compilers like the PyTorch compiler can often generate vectorized memory operations when alignment and contiguity requirements are met. You can encourage this behavior by using per-thread tiles that match vector widths. As such, frameworks can usually achieve a similar reduction in memory transactions under the hood. However, it's still beneficial to align data properly from the start.

As a result of this vectorized memory access optimization, global memory load efficiency increases toward 100%. Sectors per transaction remain at 4.0 when each 128-byte transaction is fully utilized, while the warp issues multiple aligned transactions to serve a wider request.

Vectorized loads reduce the number of memory instructions per byte moved and often increase effective bandwidth. To benefit from vectorized loads, data pointers must be aligned to the vector width. The CUDA runtime and driver allocation functions, such as `cudaMalloc` return device pointers aligned to at least 256 bytes.

The base alignment is sufficient for 16-byte and 32-byte vector alignment at the allocation boundary. Adding an element offset can break alignment if the offset is not a multiple of the vector width. The following cast asserts the intended type to the compiler and assumes the pointer is already correctly aligned:

```
auto ptr4 = reinterpret_cast<const float4*>(ptr);
```

Make sure the pointer value is a multiple of 16 bytes (4 `float`s) before casting. This is because `cudaMalloc()` returns at least 256-byte alignment. Adding an element offset can break alignment if the offset is not a multiple of 4 `float`s. Correct alignment is a precondition for vectorized loads.

With a base address aligned to 32 bytes, each thread reads 32 bytes per iteration, typically compiling into two 16-byte vector load instructions per thread (Hopper) or one 32-byte load instruction (Blackwell). A 32-thread warp therefore requests 1,024 bytes. Each 128-byte cache line comprises four 32-byte sectors. As such, the warp generates eight aligned 128-byte transactions for a total of 32 sectors when accesses are aligned properly. This way, each access falls on a natural boundary and avoids split transactions.

It's worth noting that CUDA, as of this writing, does not provide a built-in 8-float aggregate CUDA vector type (e.g., eight combined float32s) in its <vector_types.h>. You can define your own struct of 8 float values, then load it as two float4 values per thread. You would use 32-byte alignment on the type with alignas(32). This way, the pointer value is a multiple of 32 bytes. Global memory vector instructions on modern GPUs typically load 16 bytes per thread (Hopper) or 32 bytes per thread (Blackwell). In the case of Hopper's 16 bytes per thread, an 8-float aggregate load will compile into two 16-byte loads per thread to include all 32 bytes. Blackwell, on the other hand, would compile into a single 32-byte load per thread when using proper 32-byte aligned data.

With 32-byte per-thread loads (e.g., 8 floats × 4 bytes per float), a warp moves 1,024 bytes (1,024 bytes = 32 threads per warp × 32 bytes per thread). This typically maps to 8 × 128-byte lines since each line consists of four 32-byte sectors. With 16-byte per-thread loads (e.g., four float4s), a warp moves 512 bytes (512 bytes = 32 threads per warp × 16 bytes per thread) or 4 × 128-byte lines. When the base pointer and per-thread stride are naturally aligned, the hardware coalescer combines lane accesses into full lines and avoids split sectors. This type of mechanical sympathy is crucial to achieving peak throughput. Therefore, for 256-bit loads on Blackwell, you should enforce 32-byte alignment to maintain peak performance.

Let's see an example of scalar versus vectorized memory access in a simple vector copy kernel.

Before example (C++): scalar copy. Each thread copies one float:

```
#include <cuda_runtime.h>

__global__ void copyScalar(
const float* __restrict__ in,
float* __restrict__ out, int N) {
    int idx = blockIdx.x * blockDim.x + threadIdx.x;
    if (idx < N) {
        // Scalar load: 4-byte copy per thread
        out[idx] = in[idx];
    }
}

int main() {
    const int N = 1 << 20;

    float* h_in = nullptr;
    float* h_out = nullptr;
    cudaMallocHost(&h_in, N * sizeof(float));
```

```
    cudaMallocHost(&h_out, N * sizeof(float));

    for (int i = 0; i < N; ++i) h_in[i] = float(i);

    float *d_in, *d_out;
    cudaMalloc(&d_in, N * sizeof(float));
    cudaMalloc(&d_out, N * sizeof(float));
    cudaMemcpy(d_in, h_in, N * sizeof(float), cudaMemcpyHostToDevice);

    dim3 block(256), grid((N + 255) / 256);
    copyScalar<<<grid, block>>>(d_in, d_out, N);
    cudaDeviceSynchronize();

    cudaFree(d_in); cudaFree(d_out);
    cudaFreeHost(h_in);
    cudaFreeHost(h_out);
    return 0;
}
```

Before example (PyTorch). A scalar elementwise copy in PyTorch could be done with a Python loop for illustration:

```python
import torch

def copy_scalar(inp: torch.Tensor) -> torch.Tensor:
    out = torch.empty_like(inp)
    flat_in = inp.view(-1)
    flat_out = out.view(-1)
    for i in range(flat_in.numel()):
        # Each iteration issues a 4-byte load on the GPU
        # This is extremely slow. DO NOT DO THIS!
        # Use vectorized operations to avoid Python loops
        # on GPU tensors as shown in optimized version
        flat_out[i] = flat_in[i]
    return out

# Usage
N = 1 << 20
inp = torch.arange(N, device='cuda', dtype=torch.float32)
out = copy_scalar(inp)
```

With scalar 4-byte loads, a warp often issues one 128-byte transaction for 128 bytes when aligned. Otherwise, it uses two transactions if the access straddles a 128-byte boundary. Using `float4` (16 bytes per thread) means each warp issues 4× more data per memory instruction—512 bytes per warp—split into four 128-byte transactions. This allows the transfer to complete in fewer instructions. Next, let's optimize by using vector loads.

After example (C++): vectorized copy. Each thread copies a `float4` (16 bytes):

```cpp
#include <cuda_runtime.h>

// 16-byte (128-bit) vector copy: one float4 per thread
static_assert(alignof(float4) == 16, "float4 alignment must be 16 bytes");
__global__ void copyVector16B(const float4* __restrict__ in,
                              float4* __restrict__ out,
                              int N4)  // number of float4 elements
{
    int idx = blockIdx.x * blockDim.x + threadIdx.x;
    if (idx < N4) {
        // Per-thread 16B load+store.
        // On sm_90, NVCC emits ld.global.v4.f32 / st.global.v4.f32.
        // for 16-byte vector loads and stores
        // On sm_90 (Hopper) (Blackwell), NVCC emits
        // ld.global.v8.f32 and st.global.v8.f32 for 32-byte aligned data
        out[idx] = in[idx];
    }
}

int main() {
    const int N  = 1 << 20;   // total number of floats
    const int N4 = N / 4;     // total number of float4s (16B chunks)

    float4 *d_in = nullptr, *d_out = nullptr;
    cudaMalloc(&d_in,  N4 * sizeof(float4));   // >=256B aligned
    cudaMalloc(&d_out, N4 * sizeof(float4));

    dim3 block(256);
    dim3 grid((N4 + block.x - 1) / block.x);
    copyVector16B<<<grid, block>>>(d_in, d_out, N4);
    cudaDeviceSynchronize();

    cudaFree(d_in);
    cudaFree(d_out);
    return 0;
}
```

Here we use CUDA's built-in `float4` type from `<cuda_runtime.h>`. We launch N/4 threads to maintain 16-byte alignment and issue true vector loads/stores, and each thread copies one `float4` (16 bytes). This means each thread handles four `float`s, and each warp handles 128 floats total in four transactions. `cudaMalloc` returns pointers aligned to at least 256 bytes which satisfies the `float4` (16-byte) requirement and helps with 32-byte aligned vectors when you use 32-byte alignment for the data's starting address. It's important to note that misaligned casts can forfeit vectorization. Following is an example that takes advantage of Blackwell's support for 32-byte vectorized loads:

```
// --- Blackwell-only variant: 32-byte per-thread vector copy
// (PTX: ld.global.v8.f32)
// Requires 32B alignment.
#include <cuda_runtime.h>

// Proof of 32-byte alignment
static_assert(alignof(float8) == 32, "float8 alignment must be 32 bytes");
struct alignas(32) float8 { float v[8]; };

__global__ void copyVector32B(const float8* __restrict__ in,
                              float8* __restrict__ out, int N8) {
    int idx = blockIdx.x * blockDim.x + threadIdx.x;
    if (idx < N8) {
        // Per-thread 32B load+store
        // NVCC emits ld.global.v8.f32/st.global.v8.f32 on sm_100
        out[idx] = in[idx];
    }
}

int main() {
    const int N = 1 << 20;
    const int N8 = N / 8;

    float8 *d_in, *d_out;
    // cudaMalloc returns pointers aligned to ≥256 bytes
    // This will allow the compiler to emit
    // optimized ld.global.v8.f32 and st.global.v8.f32 instructions
    cudaMalloc(&d_in,  N8 * sizeof(float8));
    cudaMalloc(&d_out, N8 * sizeof(float8));

    dim3 block(256), grid((N8 + block.x - 1) / block.x);
    copyVector32B<<<grid, block>>>(d_in, d_out, N8);
    cudaDeviceSynchronize();

    cudaFree(d_in); cudaFree(d_out);
    return 0;
}
```

After example (PyTorch). We can simulate vectorized copy by using a tensor view and clone:

```
import torch

def copy_vectorized(inp: torch.Tensor) -> torch.Tensor:
    # Reshape into groups of 4 floats for bulk copy
    vec = inp.view(-1, 4)
    # clone() on a contiguous CUDA tensor performs a device-to-device copy
    # using optimized runtime paths such as cudaMemcpyAsync().

    out_vec = vec.clone()
    return out_vec.view(-1)

# Usage
```

```
N = 1 << 20
inp = torch.arange(N, device='cuda', dtype=torch.float32)
out = copy_vectorized(inp)
```

Calling `clone()` on the reshaped tensor causes PyTorch to perform contiguous copies. This is in contrast to copying element by element. By using `float4` vector loads, each thread moves 16 bytes per instruction, which is optimized for Hopper. (Blackwell supports 32-byte vector loads per thread.) A warp issues 512 bytes for that load, typically split into four 128-byte transactions when aligned. The benefit comes from fewer instructions per byte moved, better sector utilization, and proper alignment to maximize memory throughput on modern GPUs. This shows far better utilization of memory bandwidth, as shown in Table 7-2.

Blackwell doubles the number of bytes for vector loads/stores per thread relative to Hopper. With CUDA 13, Blackwell can perform 32-byte vector loads and stores instead of 16 bytes on Hopper. This requires that the compiler can prove 32-byte alignment. Otherwise, it may split the per-thread load/store into two 16-byte instructions. This will increase the number of instructions required to load/store the same amount of data which will negatively impact performance.

By using properly aligned `float4` vector loads, each thread moves 16 bytes per instruction. This shows far better utilization of memory bandwidth, as shown in the results in Table 7-2.

Table 7-2. Nsight Compute metrics for scalar versus vectorizing memory access

Metric	Before (scalar)	After (vectorized)
Global Memory Load Efficiency	28%	97%
Average sectors per request	31.8	4.0
DRAM throughput (% of peak)	25%	90% (3.6×)
Kernel execution time	4.2 ms	1.2 ms (3.5× improvement)

These metrics confirm the improvement. Global Memory Load Efficiency jumped from 28% to 97% (~3.5×), and percentage of peak DRAM throughput increased from 25% to 90% (~3.6×), trimming the overall kernel runtime by ~3.5×.

This optimization trimmed the kernel execution runtime by roughly 3.5× from 4.2 ms down to 1.2 ms. Global Memory Load Efficiency jumps from 28% (scalar) to 97% (vectorized), meaning that almost every fetched 128-byte transaction is now used.

The average sectors per request drops toward the 4.0 sector-per-line ideal value. This indicates that each 128-byte line is fully utilized. Each warp-wide `float4` instruction issues four aligned 128-byte transactions to move 512 bytes. As such, every transaction is fully utilized.

The reduction in memory requests and the replacement of four scalar loads with one vector load increase global memory load efficiency from 28% to 97% and raise sustained DRAM throughput from about 25% to about 90% of peak. In this case, warps are doing far fewer memory operations and get more data with each operation, so they spend much less time waiting on memory and more time executing useful work. The end result is a significantly faster kernel.

> Vectorization reduces instruction count. Coalescing and alignment improve the number of sectors per request.

Let's quickly compare coalesced global memory access from the previous section to vectorized memory access discussed here. Coalescing makes sure threads in a warp all hit one big contiguous block. Vectorizing makes sure each thread fetches a wide chunk that exactly maps onto those big blocks. The differences are summarized in Table 7-3.

Table 7-3. Comparing coalesced memory access (previous section) and vectorized memory access

Aspect	Coalesced warp load (interthread)	Vectorizing (intrathread)
Granularity	Threads ↔ contiguous memory addresses	Per thread ↔ vector loads
Typical fix	Contiguous indexing (stride = 1)	Use `float4`, a custom 32-byte struct with explicit 32-byte alignment, or a 32-byte-aligned vector type (e.g., Blackwell and CUDA 13+)
Transactions/warp	32 threads × 4 bytes → 128 bytes, equal to 4 32-byte sectors if aligned (4 sectors)	32 threads × 16 bytes → 512 bytes, equal to 4 128-byte transactions, which correspond to 16 32-byte sectors (16 sectors)
Instruction count change	Same number of loads	1 vector load instead of 4 scalars
Benefit	Fewer scattered sectors	Perfectly sized, fewer sectors

By combining both strategies, you ensure that warps hit contiguous blocks such that each thread fetches a wide, aligned vector. This helps you push your kernel's memory bandwidth utilization to its peak and unlock the full power of your GPU.

It's worth noting that, prior to Blackwell and CUDA 13, global memory vector loads were limited to 16 bytes (128 bits) per thread. However, Blackwell and CUDA 13 added 32-byte (256-bit) load/store instructions and data types for specific vector types with 32-byte alignment.

When available, prefer these wider 32-byte types and instructions for user-defined 8-float aggregates. This will reduce the number of instructions needed to load and store wider 32-byte aligned data.

Custom 8-float aggregates will still compile into two 16-byte loads unless you explicitly use the 32-byte-aligned types that map to a single 32-byte instruction.

> Even though a Blackwell thread can load a full 32-byte vector type, the memory coalescer can still only service requests in 128-byte chunks, or four 32-byte sectors. On Blackwell, a 32-thread warp moving 32 B per thread transfers 1024 B (8×128 B lines). Hopper's 16 B/thread variant moves 512 B (4×128 B). Note that the transaction count scales with bytes moved. Both are fully efficient when properly aligned: 16-byte (Hopper) or 32-byte (Blackwell and beyond).

Tiling and Data Reuse Using Shared Memory

A common performance pitfall is repeatedly reading the same data from global memory. *Tiling* is a technique to avoid this by loading chunks of data into faster on-chip shared memory—and reusing those chunks across many threads.

For example, a naive matrix multiplication of size $N \times N$ might load each element of matrix A from HBM N times, once for each row of B it multiplies with. This results in N–1 redundant loads per element. And on Blackwell, which can easily execute tens of teraFLOPS (TFLOPS), redundant loads can waste memory bandwidth, which could otherwise be feeding more math operations to the GPU SMs.

Tiling eliminates this waste by having each thread block pull a small submatrix (a *tile*) of A and B into shared memory exactly once. It then reuses the cached values across all threads for multiple multiply-accumulate operations. In our next example, we'll use a 32×32 tile, which is a common choice that fits well in shared memory.

Threads within a block can cooperatively load the tile into shared memory, then call __syncthreads() to synchronize the data. Then the threads perform parallel matrix-multiply computations using the data in shared memory. This amortizes the global memory access cost over many threads and computations. It's worth noting that these tile loads are also arranged to be coalesced. Specifically, each warp loads a full 128-byte segment from global memory into shared memory—consistent with the coalescing example from earlier.

By reading each element from DRAM only once (into shared memory) and reusing it for many calculations, we reduce global memory traffic. Let's illustrate this with an $N \times N$ matrix multiplication example. First, consider a naive implementation.

Before example (CUDA C++): naive matrix multiply. Each thread computes one element of the result matrix C, reading entire rows of A and columns of B from global memory for each output:

```cpp
#include <cuda_runtime.h>
#include <iostream>

__global__ void naiveMatMul(const float* A, const float* B, float* C, int N) {
    int row = blockIdx.y * blockDim.y + threadIdx.y;
    int col = blockIdx.x * blockDim.x + threadIdx.x;
    if (row < N && col < N) {
        float sum = 0.0f;
        for (int k = 0; k < N; ++k) {
            // Each thread loads A[row, k] and B[k, col]
            // from global memory for every k.
            // This is very memory heavy.
            sum += A[row * N + k] * B[k * N + col];
        }
        C[row * N + col] = sum;
    }
}

int main() {
    const int N = 1024;
    size_t bytes = N * N * sizeof(float);

    float* h_A = nullptr;
    float* h_B = nullptr;
    float* h_C = nullptr;
    cudaMallocHost(&h_A, N*N * sizeof(float));
    cudaMallocHost(&h_B, N*N * sizeof(float));
    cudaMallocHost(&h_C, N*N * sizeof(float));

    for (int i = 0; i < N*N; ++i) { h_A[i] = 1.0f; h_B[i] = 1.0f; }

    float *d_A, *d_B, *d_C;
    cudaMalloc(&d_A, bytes);
    cudaMalloc(&d_B, bytes);
    cudaMalloc(&d_C, bytes);
    cudaMemcpy(d_A, h_A, bytes, cudaMemcpyHostToDevice);
    cudaMemcpy(d_B, h_B, bytes, cudaMemcpyHostToDevice);

    dim3 block(32, 32);
    dim3 grid((N + 31) / 32, (N + 31) / 32);
    naiveMatMul<<<grid, block>>>(d_A, d_B, d_C, N);
    cudaDeviceSynchronize();

    cudaFree(d_A);
    cudaFree(d_B);
    cudaFree(d_C);
    cudaFreeHost(h_A);
    cudaFreeHost(h_B);
```

```
        cudaFreeHost(h_C);
        return 0;
}
```

This CUDA C++ kernel issues global memory loads for every multiplication inside the inner loop. Each thread reads A[row, k] and B[k, col] from DRAM for every k, causing massive redundant traffic. The result is a heavily memory-bound kernel with low SM utilization and frequent stalls waiting on global memory. Here is the PyTorch version of the naive matrix multiplication:

```
import torch

def naive_matmul(A, B):
    N = A.size(0)
    C = torch.zeros((N, N), device='cuda')
    for i in range(N):
        for j in range(N):
            # Each dot product loads A[i,:] B[:,j] from global memory repeatedly
            C[i, j] = (A[i, :] * B[:, j]).sum()
    return C

# Usage
N = 1024
A = torch.ones((N, N), device='cuda', dtype=torch.float32)
B = torch.ones((N, N), device='cuda', dtype=torch.float32)
C = naive_matmul(A, B)
```

This PyTorch implementation uses nested Python loops. While the innermost operations are offloaded to GPU as elementwise multiply and sum operations, it still triggers repeated global memory loads under the hood for each dot product. This mimics the memory-bound behavior of the naive CUDA kernel since the GPU spends most cycles waiting on memory rather than computing multiplications.

This PyTorch code is extremely slow on purpose to illustrate the extreme case of performing redundant global memory access loads inside of a loop. In practice, frameworks like PyTorch use optimized kernels for this type of operation.

Now, let's apply tiling to improve this. We divide the matrices into 32 × 32 tiles. 32 × 32 is a convenient tile size since it aligns with a warp size of 32, it fits well in shared memory, and it maps to a full warp of 32 threads reading each row. This allows each warp to collaboratively load and process one single row (per tile) at a time.

As such, each thread block loads one 32 × 32 tile of A and one 32 × 32 tile of B into shared memory, performs the 32 × 32 matrix multiplies, and accumulates the results. This way, each element of A and B is loaded from HBM only once per tile instead of 32 times in the naive version. The optimized version using shared memory to cache tiles for matrix multiplies is shown here:

```
#include <cuda_runtime.h>
#include <iostream>
#define TILE_SIZE 32

__global__ void tiledMatMul(const float* A, const float* B, float* C, int N) {
    __shared__ float sA[TILE_SIZE][TILE_SIZE];
    __shared__ float sB[TILE_SIZE][TILE_SIZE];

    int row = blockIdx.y * TILE_SIZE + threadIdx.y;
    int col = blockIdx.x * TILE_SIZE + threadIdx.x;
    float sum = 0.0f;

    // compute partial results using the tile
    // in shared memory
    for (int t = 0; t < N; t += TILE_SIZE) {
        // Cooperative load of a tile of A and B into shared memory
        // Load tile A with boundary check
        if (row < N && (t + threadIdx.x) < N) {
            sA[threadIdx.y][threadIdx.x] = A[row * N + t + threadIdx.x];
        } else {
            sA[threadIdx.y][threadIdx.x] = 0.0f;
        }

        // Load tile B with boundary check
        if ((t + threadIdx.y) < N && col < N) {
            sB[threadIdx.y][threadIdx.x] = B[(t + threadIdx.y) * N + col];
        } else {
            sB[threadIdx.y][threadIdx.x] = 0.0f;
        }

        // We will optimize this later to use a
        // thread-block-scoped cooperative-groups barrier
        __syncthreads();

        // Compute using the tile loaded in shared memory
        for (int k = 0; k < TILE_SIZE; ++k) {
            sum += sA[threadIdx.y][k] * sB[k][threadIdx.x];
        }
        // We will optimize this later to use a
        // thread-block-scoped cooperative-groups barrier
        __syncthreads();
    }

    if (row < N && col < N) {
        C[row * N + col] = sum;
    }
}

int main() {
    const int N = 1024;
    size_t bytes = N * N * sizeof(float);
```

```
float* h_A = nullptr;
float* h_B = nullptr;
float* h_C = nullptr;
cudaMallocHost(&h_A, N*N * sizeof(float));
cudaMallocHost(&h_B, N*N * sizeof(float));
cudaMallocHost(&h_C, N*N * sizeof(float));

for (int i = 0; i < N*N; ++i) { h_A[i] = 1.0f; h_B[i] = 1.0f; }

float *d_A, *d_B, *d_C;
cudaMalloc(&d_A, bytes);
cudaMalloc(&d_B, bytes);
cudaMalloc(&d_C, bytes);
cudaMemcpy(d_A, h_A, bytes, cudaMemcpyHostToDevice);
cudaMemcpy(d_B, h_B, bytes, cudaMemcpyHostToDevice);

dim3 block(TILE_SIZE, TILE_SIZE);
dim3 grid((N + TILE_SIZE - 1) / TILE_SIZE, (N + TILE_SIZE - 1) / TILE_SIZE);
tiledMatMul<<<grid, block>>>(d_A, d_B, d_C, N);

// synchronize the kernel with the device
// for timing accuracy
cudaDeviceSynchronize();

cudaFree(d_A);
cudaFree(d_B);
cudaFree(d_C);
cudaFreeHost(h_A);
cudaFreeHost(h_B);
cudaFreeHost(h_C);

return 0;
}
```

In this tiled kernel, each block cooperatively loads a 32 × 32 tile of A (into sA) and a 32 × 32 tile of B (into sB) from global memory. These loads happen in the first two lines inside the loop and are followed by __syncthreads() to ensure the tile is fully loaded before use.

Then the block performs 32 × 32 multiply-accumulate operations using the shared memory tiles. This inner loop, running over k in steps of 32, reuses each loaded value 32×, yielding a 32× reduction in global memory reads for those elements.

After finishing all tile iterations, each thread writes its result to C. The result is a dramatic 8× reduction in global memory accesses per thread, as you'll see in a bit.

These examples are focused on memory access patterns and are using FP32 CUDA cores—not the reduced-precision Tensor Cores. Chapter 9 demonstrates the use of reduced-precision computations (e.g., 16-bit, 8-bit, 4-bit) to improve performance even further.

This PyTorch version manually tiles the matrices and invokes `torch.mm` on each tile. PyTorch's `torch.mm` leverages NVIDIA's cuBLAS and CUTLASS, which implement shared memory tiling and reuse internally at the C++ level. Here is the PyTorch version of the tiled matrix multiply:

```python
import torch

def tiled_matmul(A, B, tile_size=32):
    N = A.size(0)
    C = torch.zeros((N, N), device='cuda')
    for i in range(0, N, tile_size):
        for j in range(0, N, tile_size):
            C_block = torch.zeros((tile_size, tile_size), device='cuda')
            for k in range(0, N, tile_size):
                A_block = A[i:i+tile_size, k:k+tile_size]
                B_block = B[k:k+tile_size, j:j+tile_size]
                # torch.mm uses an optimized kernel (likely tiling internally)
                C_block += torch.mm(A_block, B_block)
            C[i:i+tile_size, j:j+tile_size] = C_block
    return C

# Usage
N = 1024
A = torch.ones((N, N), device='cuda', dtype=torch.float32)
B = torch.ones((N, N), device='cuda', dtype=torch.float32)
C = tiled_matmul(A, B)
```

> With a 32 × 32 tile, threads in a warp will contend for the same shared-memory bank when they all access the same column. In practice, you can avoid this by padding the tile to 33 columns—or using techniques like swizzling—so that each access falls in a different bank. We will apply this optimization in the next section. For now, let's focus on tiling as an optimization on its own.

The performance impact of tiling is significant. By structuring the computation in tiles and reusing data in shared memory, we reduce DRAM traffic and raise arithmetic intensity because each byte retrieved from memory is used for many more floating-point operations. Along with fewer global memory transactions, we also observe higher achieved occupancy. Table 7-4 compares key metrics before and after applying shared memory tiling.

Table 7-4. Performance improvement with shared memory tiling

Metric	Before (naive kernel)	After (tiled kernel)	Notes
DRAM throughput (% of peak)	90%	25% (3.6× less)	Naive uses more bandwidth, but it's wasteful. The tile implementation is lower because it's more efficient after tiling due to fewer redundant loads.
Achieved occupancy (%)	42%	89%	More resident warps make forward progress with fewer stalls.
Floating-point throughput (GFLOPS)	15 GFLOPS	170 GFLOPS	Small matrix size limits the absolute value. Reuse increases sustained compute. (The absolute GFLOPS numbers are low because the matrix size ($N = 1,024$) is small and the kernel is memory limited.)
Global memory load sectors	9800	1200	Each element is fetched once per tile instead of 32 times (once per thread). Total number of 32-byte sector reads issued by the kernel. The decrease reflects the elimination of redundant loads thanks to shared-memory tiling.
Shared memory throughput (% of peak)	52%	99%	Tiled kernel access pattern avoids memory-bank conflicts on sA and sB.

Staging 32 × 32 tiles in shared memory makes sure that each element is fetched once from DRAM and reused across all threads in a block. DRAM throughput falls from 90% to 25%, a reduction of about 3.6×, which is expected when redundant traffic is removed.

The drop in DRAM throughput is desirable because the kernel now performs more work per byte moved. Arithmetic intensity increases, and sustained floating-point throughput rises from 15 GFLOPS to 170 GFLOPS, a gain of nearly 11×.

> The optimized 170 GFLOPS is far below Blackwell's theoretical FP32 peak near 80 TFLOPS. This is expected for small tiles and frequent memory access. The important result is the 11× improvement after removing the memory bottleneck. Larger problems or more compute work per byte would move performance closer to peak.

This shift in arithmetic intensity moves the kernel from memory bound toward compute bound, which is ideal because performance becomes limited by abundant floating-point throughput rather than comparatively scarce chip bandwidth. Global memory load sectors drop substantially from 9,800 down to 1,200 because each element is fetched once into shared memory and reused across threads. This eliminates redundant loads. The tiled kernel also accesses sA and sB in a way that avoids shared-memory bank conflicts, which is why shared memory throughput approaches 100%.

Overall, we shifted this kernel from memory bound to compute bound, which was the goal. We successfully relieved memory pressure, freed up the memory bus for other useful work, and achieved higher compute throughput.

We also see a large increase in achieved occupancy percentage from 42% to 89%. This metric nearly doubles because the tiled kernel keeps allowing more resident warps to make progress with fewer stalls. As such, the SMs remain busy more consistently.

By introducing shared memory tiling, we increased per-thread work without increasing per-thread resource usage beyond available registers and shared memory. This helped our kernel achieve higher occupancy and utilization, which is important on GPUs like Blackwell, which offer a very large register file (65,536 32-bit registers per SM) that threads can exploit up to the 255-register per-thread limit without spilling.

> Recall that each thread can use up to 255 registers. Our tiling kernel implementation stays within this limit, avoids register spilling, and preserves high performance.

We can compare the arithmetic intensity of the naive and tiled kernels by examining their sustained FLOP rates and average DRAM bandwidth. The naive version ran at 15 GFLOPS while moving 10 GB/s of data on average, or 1.5 FLOPS per byte. The tiled implementation, by contrast, sustained 170 GFLOPS while moving 21 GB/s on average, or 8 FLOPS/byte.

It might be tempting to increase the tile size further to 64×64 or 128×128 in order to reduce memory traffic even more and increase data reuse. Just remember that larger tiles consume more on-chip resources, including both registers and shared memory. This leaves less capacity for additional thread blocks on each SM.

For instance, Blackwell GPUs provide up to 228 KB of allocatable shared memory per SM. This can easily accommodate a 64×64 tile of 4-byte floats in which each A and B tile requires 16 KB (16,384 bytes = 64×64 floats $\times$ 4 bytes per float). However, in addition to shared-memory usage, you need to budget for the additional registers per thread.

Each Blackwell SM provides up to 64K registers (32-bit each) in total with a per-thread maximum of 255 registers. When you launch a 32×32 thread block (1,024 threads) to compute a 64×64 tile, each thread handles a 2×2 subtile, which produces 4 outputs.

For a 64×64 tile size, you need the following: four accumulator registers (one per output), two registers for A-tile elements (reused across two outputs), two registers for B-tile elements (same reuse), and ~4 registers for loop counters, thread indices, and address arithmetic. In total, this is ~12 registers per thread.

12 registers per thread × 1,024 threads per block = 12,288 registers needed per thread block. And since each Blackwell SM has 65,536 32-bit registers (maximum 255 registers per thread), in theory, up to 5 blocks' worth of registers can fit (≈61,440 registers). However, the SM can support only 2,048 concurrent threads (64 warps). So, in practice, occupancy is limited by the smaller limits of registers, shared memory, warps, and threads. For this configuration, two blocks per SM will saturate the 2,048-thread limit.

> If your kernel uses additional registers for double-buffering registers, vectorized loads, etc., you can recalculate the occupancy with `cudaOccupancyMaxPotentialBlockSize` or Nsight Compute's occupancy report.

For a 64 × 64 tile size, 22 registers per thread are needed for a total of 22,528 registers for a 32 × 32 thread block (1,024 threads). In this case, you can only fit up to two thread blocks per Blackwell SM. This translates to a maximum occupancy of only 2,048 threads—hitting the SM's thread limit with only two blocks (out of the 16 maximum concurrent blocks per SM).

A reduction in concurrent thread blocks caused by using a larger tile size will lower occupancy and hurt performance if you exceed the hardware's limits. In practice, your tile dimensions must fit within the GPU's shared-memory and register budgets to maintain high occupancy and throughput.

For a Blackwell GPU with ~228 KB of allocatable shared memory per SM, a 64 × 64 tile (~16 KB per input matrix tile) might still fit, but doubling the tile dimensions squares the reuse factor while quadrupling shared memory usage. There are diminishing returns and possible trade-offs.

It is recommended to experiment with different tile dimensions to balance on-chip reuse against resource limits. A 32 × 32 tile is a solid starting point on modern NVIDIA GPUs, but depending on your shared-memory and register usage, you may find that a slightly smaller or larger tile delivers better throughput.

> Libraries like CUTLASS also include profilers that automate this exploration, letting you find the optimal tile size for your kernel and hardware.

In short, we transformed a naive, global-memory-only matrix multiplication into a tiled implementation that uses shared memory. This enabled cooperative data reuse, reduced the number of DRAM transactions, and boosted arithmetic intensity. Both the CUDA C++ and PyTorch implementations benefited from this tiling technique.

It's worth noting that the tiling techniques we applied manually are exactly what high-performance GPU libraries do under the hood. NVIDIA's CUTLASS library, for instance, provides templated components to implement general matrix multiplies (GEMMs) with multiple layers of tiling. These CUTLASS components load fragments of matrices into registers and shared memory—and then compute partial results much like our previous 32×32 tile example.

In fact, NVIDIA's optimized cuBLAS and cuDNN libraries use similar blocking strategies at the thread, warp, and block levels to achieve near-peak throughput. NVIDIA even announced a Python-first API in early 2025 called cuTile that lets programmers describe these tile shapes in a more convenient Pythonic way. In fact, NVIDIA has developed a Tile-based intermediate representation (IR) called TileIR to support cuTile and facilitate automatic compilation and tuning.

Other high-performance libraries encapsulate these tiling patterns as well. For instance, NVIDIA's CUTLASS C++ and Python libraries expose templated tile iterators and profilers. And PyTorch-based compilers like TorchInductor (using the OpenAI Triton library) generate tiled kernels automatically when shapes and alignment permit. These libraries lower the barrier to using these tiling optimizations—and reduce the amount of boilerplate code.

The key idea is that reusing data in registers/shared memory as much as possible before going back to DRAM is fundamental, and libraries encapsulate this. So whenever possible, leverage these highly optimized libraries (or refer to them) for performant tiling patterns.

For instance, if you use `torch.mm` in PyTorch or `cublasSgemm` in your code, under the covers it's doing exactly this kind of tiling and memory coalescing. This is why our PyTorch example saw the same benefits automatically.

In practice, you would use high-performance libraries like cuBLAS and PyTorch's `torch.matmul`, which already implement tiling and other optimizations in C++. In production code, directly using `torch.mm` or `torch.matmul` would produce the same benefits—and possibly more, thanks to highly tuned kernels.

> While you can definitely reuse existing tiling libraries and frameworks, understanding how they work, as we've done here, is invaluable for when you need to diagnose performance issues and possibly write your own custom kernels for specialized situations that these libraries and frameworks don't cover. Just don't forget to give back to the community as they've given you a lot!

As mentioned earlier in this section, when using a 32×32 tile, the threads in a warp will contend for the same shared-memory bank when they access the same column. Let's explain this issue—as well as some optimizations—in the next section.

Avoid Shared-Memory Bank Conflicts

On modern NVIDIA GPUs, including Blackwell, shared memory has 32 banks with a 4-byte bank width (i.e., addresses map mod 32). As such, a warp that strides by 128 B (32 floats × 4 B) maps all threads to the same bank. If multiple threads in a warp access the same bank, a *bank conflict* occurs. This forces the memory accesses to serialize, which negates the speed advantage of shared memory.

In code, bank conflicts often occur when threads access a shared-memory array with a stride that causes them to fall into the same bank. Figure 7-4 shows two examples of conflict-free memory bank accesses.

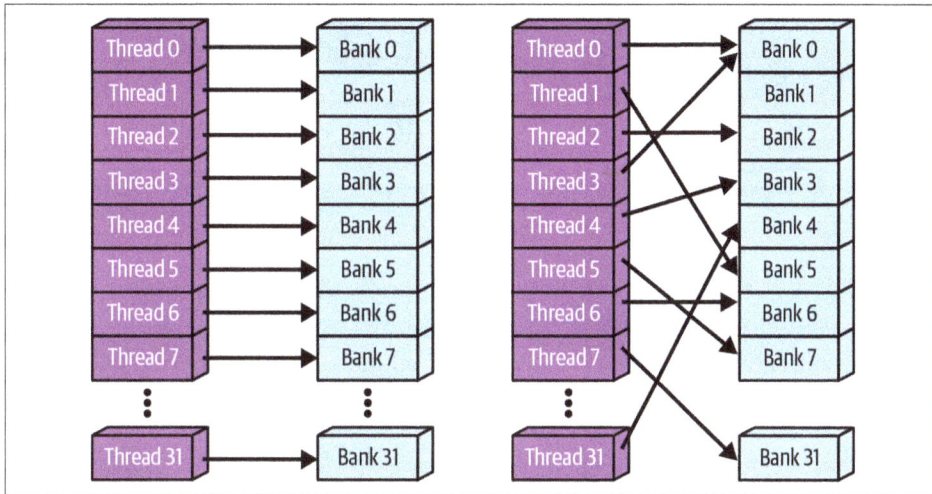

Figure 7-4. No bank conflicts

Here, there are no two threads accessing the same memory bank concurrently. This is ideal. Figure 7-5 shows examples of both a 2-way and 16-way bank conflict.

Here, multiple threads are accessing the same memory bank, which will cause conflicts and impact performance. A classic example of a bank conflict is a naive matrix transpose that uses a 32 × 32 shared memory tile. If 32 threads each read tile[i][threadIdx.x] such that the same column index (threadIdx.x) is read across different rows (i), all 32 threads in the warp will each access memory addresses that lie in the same shared-memory bank, causing a 32-way bank conflict.

Specifically, during a matrix transpose, you are reading down the same column of a row-major tile by holding the column index constant (threadIdx.x) and varying the row index (i) across threads. And because each row is 128 bytes apart in memory (32 columns × 4 bytes per column = 128 bytes), the accessed memory addresses will differ by exact multiples of 128 bytes.

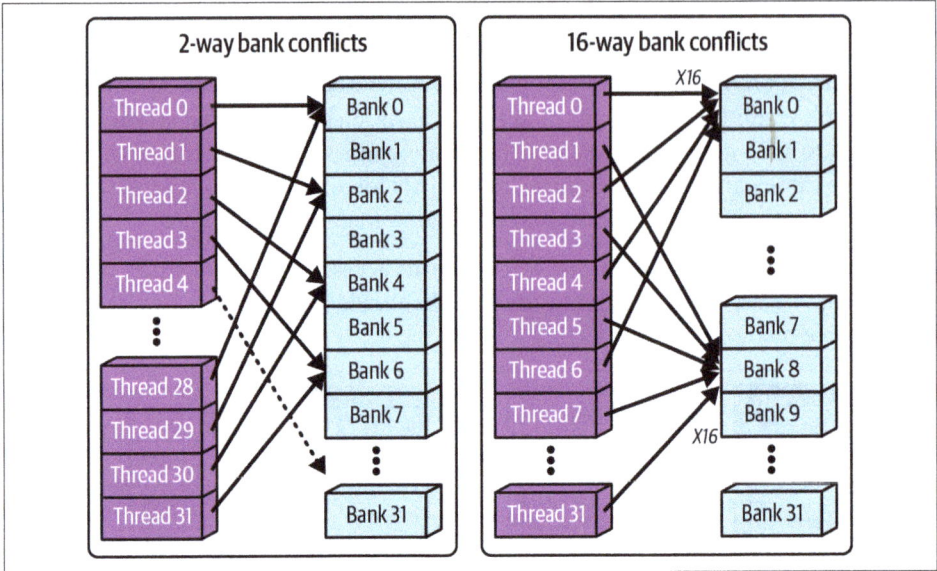

Figure 7-5. 2-way and 16-way bank conflicts

Remember that the address-to-bank mapping repeats every 128 bytes because there are 32 banks with a 4-byte bank width (per access). Therefore, accessing memory addresses offset by 128 bytes will always land back in bank 0—hence, the full 32-way bank conflict.

> There is one exception worth noting: If all 32 threads in a warp access the exact same address in the same memory bank, the hardware will broadcast the value to all threads in a single cycle. This avoids the bank conflict. Any other scenario in which two or more different memory addresses are accessing the same bank will cause a bank conflict and serialize the memory accesses.

Another common pitfall is using a stride equal to the number of memory banks, 32 in this case. For instance, if you stride your index by exactly 32 floats, each 4 bytes, then every thread's address ends up differing by multiples of 128 bytes. In this case, all threads map to bank 0, as shown in this code:

```
// Allocate a shared buffer big enough for several warps (warpCount)
__shared__ float arr[32 * warpCount];

// Each thread reads from arr[threadIdx.x * 32]
float x = arr[threadIdx.x * 32];
```

Here, threadIdx.x * 32 in floats becomes (threadIdx.x * 32 * 4) bytes. Because 32 * 4 = 128, every thread's memory-load address is threadIdx.x * 128 bytes.

And `threadIdx.x * 128 mod 128 = 0` for all threads. They all hit bank 0 simultane-ously, creating a 32-way bank conflict.

When this happens, the hardware must serialize what should have been 32 parallel reads into a sequence of single-bank accesses. In Nsight Compute (Shared Memory section), you will see an increased bank conflict count and lower shared-memory effi-ciency. At the same time, the shared-memory throughput is a fraction of its expected bandwidth. In Nsight Systems, you'll see warps are waiting on long bank-conflict stalls rather than doing useful work.

Bank conflicts force what should be parallel on-chip shared-memory accesses to replay one by one, wiping out any speedup you expected from buffering and often yielding disappointing, lower-than-anticipated performance. If your kernel isn't accelerating as it should, bank conflicts are a likely culprit.

> Always choose your stride and data layout so that threads in the same warp hit different banks and avoid that serializing bottleneck.

The solution is to adjust data layouts in shared memory to avoid conflicts. A com-mon technique is *padding* shared arrays so that each row, or each memory-access pat-tern, maps to different banks. For instance, if you have a 32 × 32 shared tile, you can declare it as [32][33] by adding one extra padding column so that each row now occupies 33 floats. This extra 1-element offset means that when thread k of a warp accesses `tile[i][k]`, successive rows start at addresses that shift across shared-memory banks. This keeps all threads from hitting the same bank, as shown in Figure 7-6.

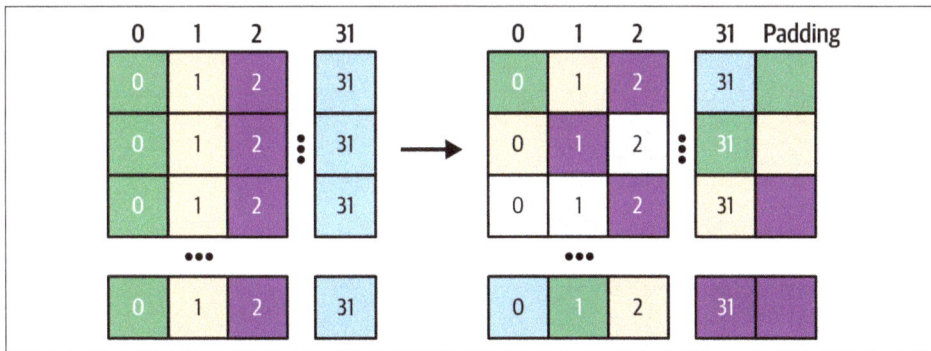

Figure 7-6. Avoiding bank conflicts with padding

By changing the stride to 33, no two threads in a warp will contend for the same bank when accessing a given column. This eliminates what would have been a 32-way bank conflict.

The padding adds a negligible overhead, ~3% more memory for a 32-wide tile, but it completely eliminates the conflicts, which greatly improves performance. And remember that Blackwell has > 200 KB shared memory per SM. A 3% memory overhead is only 1 KB for a 32 × 32 tile. This is worth the performance increase.

Let's show an example of removing shared-memory bank conflicts for a simple transpose kernel. In this example, each thread accesses shared memory addresses that fall into the same shared-memory bank as other threads. This causes the memory access to serialize, prevents parallelism, and shows slow performance. Here is the native implementation of the transpose kernel that incurs bank conflicts.

Before example (C++): naive transpose with bank conflicts:

```cpp
#include <cuda_runtime.h>
#define TILE_DIM 32

__global__ void transposeNaive(const float *idata, float *odata, int width) {
    __shared__ float tile[TILE_DIM][TILE_DIM];
    int x = blockIdx.x * TILE_DIM + threadIdx.x;
    int y = blockIdx.y * TILE_DIM + threadIdx.y;

    // threads in a warp write a row
    tile[threadIdx.y][threadIdx.x] = idata[y * width + x];
    __syncthreads();

    // Read from shared memory with transposed indices
    // This is a classic case of all threads in a warp
    // hitting the same bank causing a bank conflict
    // Read transposed from shared memory and write out
    odata[x * width + y] = tile[threadIdx.x][threadIdx.y];
}

int main() {
    const int N = 1024;
    size_t size = N * N * sizeof(float);
    float *h_idata = (float*)malloc(size);
    float *h_odata = (float*)malloc(size);
    // Initialize input h_idata...
    float *d_idata, *d_odata;
    cudaMalloc(&d_idata, size);
    cudaMalloc(&d_odata, size);
    cudaMemcpy(d_idata, h_idata, size, cudaMemcpyHostToDevice);

    dim3 block(TILE_DIM, TILE_DIM);
    dim3 grid(N / TILE_DIM, N / TILE_DIM);
    transposeNaive<<<grid, block>>>(d_idata, d_odata, N);
    cudaDeviceSynchronize();
```

```
        cudaFree(d_idata);
        cudaFree(d_odata);
        free(h_idata);
        free(h_odata);
        return 0;
}
```

In this kernel, the `tile` write into shared memory is row-major (`tile[ty][tx]`) and therefore coalesced such that each warp writes a full row of 32 floats to shared memory in a contiguous manner. (Note: Writing the tile to shared memory with column-major `tile[tx][ty]` would make the warp stride by 128 bytes and trigger a 32-way bank conflict.) In contrast, the `tile` read is transposed since each thread reads a value where `threadIdx.y` is the row index and `threadIdx.x` is the column index.

As such, for a given warp, fixed `threadIdx.y` across threads 0–31, all threads access `tile[constant_row][varying_col]`, meaning the same row index is used across different columns. This means all 32 addresses are in the same row of the `tile` array, which occupies a single memory bank segment and causes a 32-way bank conflict. As a result, those reads are serialized by a factor of 32.

Remember that Blackwell's shared memory has 32 banks. This number exactly matches the number of threads in a warp, 32. So if all threads index into the same bank, as happens when you fix the row and vary the column, you will always get a full 32-way conflict. This one-to-one correspondence means any misaligned access pattern at warp granularity will force every thread to serialize through the same bank—regardless of the GPU's architectural advancements.

In this case, 32 threads attempt to read from 32 different addresses, all in bank 0. This results in heavy serialization of memory accesses and poor performance. Let's apply padding to remove the conflicts.

After example (C++): padded transpose (avoiding bank conflicts). Here, we add a small padding, an extra unused column, so that each row of shared memory starts at a different bank modulo. This way, the bank-index collisions are eliminated by the offset:

```
#include <cuda_runtime.h>
#define TILE_DIM 32
#define PAD 1  // padding columns to avoid bank conflicts

__global__ void transposePadded(const float *idata, float *odata, int width) {
    // Each row is TILE_DIM+1 elements to shift bank mapping
    __shared__ float tile[TILE_DIM][TILE_DIM + PAD];
    int x = blockIdx.x * TILE_DIM + threadIdx.x;
    int y = blockIdx.y * TILE_DIM + threadIdx.y;

    tile[threadIdx.y][threadIdx.x] = idata[y * width + x];
```

```
// We will optimize this later to use a thread-block-scoped
// cooperative-groups barrier
__syncthreads();

odata[x * width + y] = tile[threadIdx.x][threadIdx.y];
}
```

(The host code and setup are the same as in the naive version and omitted for brevity.)

> PyTorch itself doesn't expose any high-level APIs for shared-memory padding, so you would have to implement those manually in CUDA kernels and load them with `torch.utils.cpp_exten sion`). However, in practice, PyTorch relies on optimized libraries like cuDNN and cuBLAS, which implement techniques under the hood to avoid bank conflicts and maximize throughput.

Padding each shared-memory row with an extra element makes each row 33 floats long. Padding by 1 changes the indexing math so that `tile[row][col]` addresses differ in the lower 5 bits for each thread, rather than all threads sharing the same 5-bit bank index. This ensures each thread index maps to a different bank.

In the padded kernel, when a warp reads `tile[threadIdx.y][threadIdx.x]`, the addresses for threads 0–31 span multiple banks rather than all hitting bank 0. Now that each thread in the warp accesses distinct banks on reads, bank conflicts are eliminated entirely, as shown in Table 7-5.

Table 7-5. Effect of eliminating shared-memory bank conflicts

Metric	Before (no padding)	After (padding)
Shared-memory load bank conflicts	4.8 million	0
Shared-memory utilization (percentage of peak)	52%	100%
Warp stall fraction (memory)	38%	0.5%
Kernel execution time (ms)	4 ms	1.3 ms (3× improvement)

The Nsight Compute metrics in Table 7-5 confirm the impact: shared-memory load bank conflicts dropped to 0. Shared memory throughput, according to Nsight Compute, rose from 52% to 100% after eliminating conflicts. The warp stall fraction, the percentage of cycles warps spend stalled on shared-memory reads, dropped from ~38% to near 0%.

Here, we have successfully eliminated bank conflicts and unlocked the full performance of the on-chip shared memory. This change improved the kernel's execution time by about 3× from 4 ms to 1.3 ms since shared-memory accesses went from serialized to fully parallel.

This restores full parallelism for the shared-memory accesses. The cost of padding, 1 extra float per 32, is trivial (~3% memory overhead) compared to the performance gain.

An effective alternative to padding is *swizzling*. Swizzling is a compile-time index transformation that "scrambles" the linear index used for shared memory so that sequential threads map to different banks. For example, one can XOR the index with a bit mask or use a modulo offset to achieve a conflict-free pattern.

Swizzling avoids the slight memory overhead of padding while still ensuring perfect bank parallelism. Padding is simpler to implement, but swizzling can achieve the same goal with zero memory overhead—and it's fun to say!

NVIDIA's CUTLASS library and other high-performance CUDA-based libraries use index swizzling in their tile iterators to ensure threads map to separate banks, avoid bank conflicts, and optimize shared-memory usage.

In summary, when using shared memory, it's important that threads in a warp access different memory banks in parallel rather than queueing up on the same bank. Techniques like padding and swizzling improve shared-memory load/store efficiency, yielding higher throughput and better performance whenever shared memory is used.

Next, let's explore a technique to avoid shared memory altogether and communicate directly between threads.

Warp Shuffle Intrinsics: Avoid Shared Memory and Explicit Synchronization

The preceding avoiding-bank-conflicts technique assumes that we use shared memory for communication between threads. But what if we could avoid shared memory altogether—and its bank conflict issues?

NVIDIA GPUs support warp-synchronous primitives that allow threads in the same warp to exchange data through registers instead of shared memory. In fact, these primitives work only within a single warp such that threads exchange data with their 31 siblings. So no memory banks are involved for this intrawarp communication—and therefore no bank conflicts are possible.

The most common are the __shfl_sync intrinsics (shuffle). __shfl_sync lets you broadcast a value from one thread to all other threads in a warp. You can also perform warp-level reductions without ever writing to shared memory. And remember that these intrinsics let threads exchange values through registers (instead of shared memory), which completely eliminates shared-memory bank conflicts.

> Modern GPUs will automatically broadcast a single shared-memory value if all threads access the exact same memory address (*https://oreil.ly/KNTOo*). This will avoid a bank conflict in this special, single-address case. Warp shuffles, on the other hand, use broadcasting to avoid bank issues for the more general, arbitrary, multivalue pattern of data access.

Imagine you need to sum the 32 per-thread partial results within a single warp. The naive shared-memory approach would have each thread write its value into a shared array, call a synchronization barrier, and then read and accumulate all 32 entries. This risks bank conflicts and adds additional synchronization overhead.

With __shfl_sync, you can do a tree-style reduction entirely in registers. For example, let's use a convenience variant called __shfl_down_sync to perform a butterfly-style reduction such that each thread reads the value held by another thread that is offset a number of lanes away, as shown here:

```
unsigned mask = __activemask();
float val = threadVal;  // each thread's partial sum

// Perform butterfly reduction: exchange values with increasingly distant lanes
for (int offset = 16; offset > 0; offset >>= 1) {
    float other = __shfl_down_sync(mask, val, offset);
    val += other;
}

// After the loop, lane 0 holds the warp's total sum
```

Here, each __shfl_down_sync directly reads another lane's register, halving the active threads each step, until lane 0 accumulates the full sum. Because all communication stays in registers, there's no shared-memory traffic and thus zero bank conflicts or extra synchronizations.

In short, __shfl_sync and its variants perform operations entirely within the warp's execution lanes. This avoids bank conflicts because no shared memory is used. And it's often faster since it uses registers and cuts down on the number of shared-memory instructions.

Many high-performance warp-level reductions bypass shared memory entirely by using shuffle intrinsics, which exchange values directly through registers in just a few instructions and incur no bank conflicts. CUDA's Cooperative Groups API builds on these primitives. This API provides calls like thread_group.shuffle() to simplify intrawarp communication. Helper intrinsics like __reduce_sync() ultimately compile down to these shuffle patterns for intra-warp data exchange on modern NVIDIA GPUs.

Shuffles work within a single warp only. For interwarp exchange on modern GPU architectures, also consider thread-block-wide reductions using cooperative groups or thread-block-cluster-level communication when supported. We will discuss these concepts in Chapter 10.

Remember, however, that shuffles are limited to the 32 threads within a single warp. Whenever you need to pass data across warps, you must still fall back on shared or global memory with proper synchronization.

In Chapter 10, we'll explore interwarp patterns like cooperative group (CG) synchronization primitives, multiwarp shuffle methods, and thread block clusters (CTA clusters). All of these ultimately use the same hardware intrinsics under the hood. Mastering both intrawarp and interwarp techniques is essential because memory-related bottlenecks remain one of the most common causes of GPU performance issues.

Read-Only Data Caches

When all threads read the same values or a thread rereads data that does not change, failing to use the GPU's caching mechanisms can bottleneck performance. For example, consider a large lookup table such as an embedding vector in a natural language processing (NLP) model that is read-only during inference. Many threads might need to access this vector in parallel. A naive implementation might fetch from global memory each time, even though the data is immutable and could be cached on-chip.

Note that the read-only cache we refer to here is different from the 64 KB constant memory cache discussed previously in the GPU memory hierarchy section. It's a large cache for immutable data. The constant memory cache, on the other hand, is too small for big arrays. Modern architectures rely on the larger L1/read-only cache for these types of embedding-vector lookups—rather than trying to squeeze this data into the small 64 KB constant memory cache.

On modern GPUs, global memory loads are automatically cached in L2 and often L1. You can use `const __restrict__` qualified pointers to define your function arguments as non-coherent and read-mostly (versus read-only). For read-only data, the compiler may route loads through this read-only path when it can prove immutability, nonaliasing, and safety. This lets the compiler/hardware route unchanging data through the read-only L1 cache, which has lower latency—especially for broadcast accesses—and doesn't evict other cached data.

In modern CUDA, you usually don't need to call __ldg() explicitly. If a pointer is const __restrict__, the compiler may use the read-only data cache for global memory loads when it can provide safety. The older __ldg() intrinsic is still available for explicit control, but it's generally not needed with modern compilers.

A common performance pitfall is forgetting to tell the compiler that a buffer is truly read-only, which means it won't use the read-only (non-coherent) data path and won't route those loads through the specialized read-only cache. Instead, every access becomes a plain global memory load, resulting in redundant DRAM traffic and spurious cache misses.

When you profile such a kernel, you'll spot the same addresses fetched repeatedly from off-chip memory, see no __ldg() operations in the instruction stream, observe a surprisingly low L2 hit rate for that array, and measure elevated DRAM throughput reminiscent of an uncached workload.

The solution is to leverage the read-only path by marking data as const __restrict__ , or by explicitly using the __ldg() intrinsic to load it. This tells the hardware that the data will not be modified, allowing it to be cached in the specialized read-only cache, which sits alongside L1 and has lower latency for broadcast loads.

When a warp issues a constant-cache load (__constant__ or uniform __ldg() in older GPUs), the hardware can service all 32 lanes with a single transaction if they hit the same address. By broadcasting that value to every thread, it uses only one cycle instead of doing 32 separate loads. This warp-wide broadcast reduces both latency and memory bandwidth usage for uniform data like lookup tables, coefficients, etc. This lets you fetch a shared constant, for free essentially, once per warp rather than 32 times per warp (1 per thread).

As an example of caching benefits using the standard read-only cache, suppose we have a kernel that, for each thread, looks up a value from a table of size T = 1,024 and writes it to an output. This simulates an embedding-lookup pattern and is shown here in both CUDA C++ and PyTorch:

```
#include <cuda_runtime.h>
#define T 1024

__global__ void naiveLookup(const float* table, float* out, int N) {
    int idx = blockIdx.x * blockDim.x + threadIdx.x;
    if (idx < N) {
        // __ldg not used here, each access goes to
        // global memory without using read-only cache
        int t = idx % T;
        out[idx] = table[t];
    }
}
```

```
int main() {
    const int N = 1 << 20;

    float* h_table = nullptr;
    float* h_out = nullptr;
    cudaMallocHost(&h_table, T * sizeof(float));
    cudaMallocHost(&h_out, N * sizeof(float));

    for (int i = 0; i < T; ++i) h_table[i] = float(i);

    float *d_table, *d_out;
    cudaMalloc(&d_table, T * sizeof(float));
    cudaMalloc(&d_out, N * sizeof(float));
    cudaMemcpy(d_table, h_table, T * sizeof(float),
        cudaMemcpyHostToDevice);

    dim3 block(256), grid((N + 255) / 256);
    naiveLookup<<<grid, block>>>(d_table, d_out, N);
    cudaDeviceSynchronize();
    cudaMemcpy(h_out, d_out, N * sizeof(float), cudaMemcpyDeviceToHost);
    cudaFree(d_table);
    cudaFree(d_out);
    cudaFreeHost(h_table);
    cudaFreeHost(h_out);

    return 0;
}
```

Here is a rough PyTorch equivalent to the naive version shown in CUDA C++:

```python
import torch

def vectorized_lookup(table, N):
    flat = table.view(-1)
    T = flat.size(0)

    # build indices [0,1,2,...,N-1] % T all on GPU
    idx = torch.arange(N, device=flat.device) % T

    # one gather kernel does all N loads in parallel
    return flat.index_select(0, idx)


# Usage
T = 1024
N = 1 << 20
table = torch.arange(T, dtype=torch.float32,
                     device='cuda')
out = vectorized_lookup(table, N)
```

In these naive versions, each lookup likely hits in L2 after the first use (since L2 will cache it), but there is no use of the specialized read-only cache. The hardware may still treat it as normal global data, which could evict other useful data or not take full advantage of broadcast caching if multiple threads read the same table[t] in a warp.

Now we optimize the kernel by marking the table as const __restrict__. This will hint to the hardware that it should use the read-only cache path, which is shown here:

```
#include <cuda_runtime.h>
#define T 1024

__global__ void lookup(const float* __restrict__ table,
        float* out, int N) {
    int idx = blockIdx.x * blockDim.x + threadIdx.x;
    if (idx < N) {
        int t = idx % T;
        // Compiler can turn this into a load from the
        // read-only cache for faster loads
        out[idx] = table[t];
    }
}


int main() {
    const int N = 1 << 20;

    float* h_table = nullptr;
    float* h_out = nullptr;
    cudaMallocHost(&h_table, T * sizeof(float));
    cudaMallocHost(&h_out, N * sizeof(float));

    for (int i = 0; i < T; ++i) h_table[i] = float(i);

    float *d_table, *d_out;
    cudaMalloc(&d_table, T * sizeof(float));
    cudaMalloc(&d_out, N * sizeof(float));
    cudaMemcpy(d_table, h_table, T * sizeof(float), cudaMemcpyHostToDevice);

    dim3 block(256), grid((N + 255) / 256);
    lookup<<<grid, block>>>(d_table, d_out, N);
    cudaDeviceSynchronize();
    cudaMemcpy(h_out, d_out, N * sizeof(float), cudaMemcpyDeviceToHost);
    cudaFree(d_table);
    cudaFree(d_out);
    cudaFreeHost(h_table);
    cudaFreeHost(h_out);

    return 0;
}
```

In a PyTorch setting, you could implement the same trick by writing a small CUDA extension with `torch.utils.cpp_extension` that declares your embedding table pointer as `const __restrict__`. You could also use the PyTorch compiler to optimize this code. We'll cover the PyTorch compiler in depth in Chapters 13 and 14.

In short, marking the table `const __restrict__` tells the compiler that these values are immutable and not aliased, which permits the use of the read-only data path when safe to do so. This increases cache hit rate and reduces off-chip traffic. Table 7-6 shows Nsight Compute measurements before and after this change.

Table 7-6. Benefit of read-only cache

Metric	Before (no `__restrict__`)	After (`__restrict__` used)
Global Memory Load Efficiency	52%	97%
DRAM throughput (GB/s)	600 GB/s	200 GB/s
L2 read throughput (GB/s)	1,500 GB/s	1,800 GB/s
SM Active %	45%	93%
Kernel execution time (ms)	2.5 ms	1.0 ms

After adding `const __restrict__`, the kernel time improves by about 2.5×, from 2.5 milliseconds to 1.0 millisecond, because warps spend less time stalled on DRAM. SM Active % rises from 45% to 93%, indicating that nearly every cycle has active work rather than idle memory waits.

DRAM throughput falls from 600 GB/s to 200 GB/s, while L2 read throughput increases from 1,500 GB/s to 1,800 GB/s as more requests are satisfied in cache. Global Memory Load Efficiency increases from 52% to 97%, confirming that most fetched cache lines carry useful data.

Nsight Systems presents a timeline view of overall GPU activity, while Nsight Compute reports per-kernel metrics such as SM Active %. Use Nsight Compute when you need quantitative per-kernel analysis.

Because more traffic is served by on-chip caches rather than traveling to DRAM, the compute units remain fed and arithmetic intensity increases. This balance is what moves a kernel from the memory-bound regime toward the compute-bound regime. Texture objects and surface objects are also available for read-only and read/write access patterns with strong two-dimensional or three-dimensional locality. By binding an array to a `cudaTextureObject_t` and using `tex1Dfetch` or `tex2D` fetches, the hardware can exploit spatial locality with high cache hit rates and features such as wrapping and interpolation. Surface objects allow writes on similar access patterns.

While texture reference and surface reference APIs are deprecated, texture object and surface object APIs remain supported and are appropriate for access patterns with two- or three-dimensional locality. However, for most AI workloads involving 1D data, using the read-only data cache with constant memory is much simpler and preferred.

In summary, mark read-only data as `const __restrict__` to tap into the low-latency read-only cache, cutting DRAM traffic and lifting SM activity. Consider texture or surface memory whenever your access pattern has 2D/3D locality that a regular cache might not handle optimally. Together, these techniques collapse memory stalls, boost cache utilization, and unlock substantial performance gains for memory-bound kernels.

Asynchronous Memory Prefetching and Tensor Memory Accelerator

In earlier sections, we saw how coalescing dozens of 4-byte loads into a single 128-byte transaction significantly improved global-load efficiency and cut wasted sectors per request. Yet even a perfectly coalesced load still stalls a warp for the full DRAM round trip.

On Blackwell, for instance, a full DRAM round-trip is on the order of hundreds of cycles before any computation can begin. To hide that latency, we need to overlap data transfer with compute. This overlap is what hides most of the DRAM latency.

CUDA's Pipeline API together with the Tensor Memory Accelerator (TMA) hardware engine take this idea to the thread-block level. Instead of having each warp use the SM's load and store (LD/ST) units to fetch data from global memory, you can invoke the TMA engine to asynchronously fetch an entire tile from global memory into shared memory, as shown in Figure 7-7.

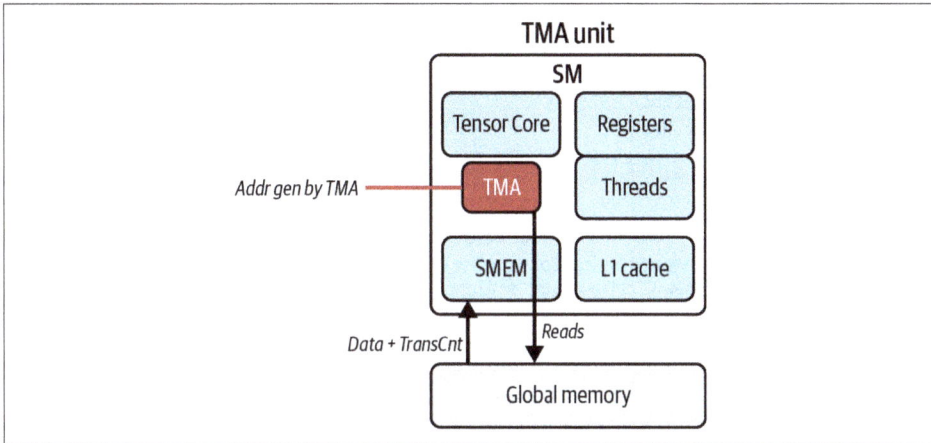

Figure 7-7. TMA asynchronously fetching data from global HBM into shared memory

To start the TMA transfer, you can call `cuda::memcpy_async()`. On modern GPU architectures, `cuda::memcpy_async()` together with `cuda::pipeline` exposes the hardware engines for asynchronous global to shared transfers. This includes the TMA when available. This will use TMA's on-chip DMA engine to perform the asynchronous bulk data transfer. This is implemented in CUDA as follows:

```
cuda::memcpy_async(sharedBuf,
                   globalPtr + offset,
                   cuda::aligned_size_t<16>(bytes),
                   pipe);
pipe.producer_commit();
```

And while TMA handles the bulk copy, including coalescing, strided transfers, and even multidimensional transfers, the kernel computes the previous tile. This is called *double buffering*, or *ping-ponging*.

By implementing double buffering with TMA, the SM's load/store units are now free to do real work because TMA's DMA engine moves data for us in the background. In effect, data movement becomes asynchronous such that while TMA streams in the next tile of data, the SM's warps compute on the previous tile. This overlap is what hides the 800-cycle DRAM latency.

Specifically, TMA is capable of 1D–5D bulk copies and arbitrary strides between global and shared memory without blocking the SM instruction pipeline. By offloading these transfers from the SM to TMA, your kernel issues far fewer LD/ST instructions, eliminates extra synchronization, and lets the warp schedulers spend almost every cycle on useful computation instead of waiting on memory.

Here is a code snippet showing how to initiate an asynchronous copy from global to shared memory using the CUDA C++ Pipeline API and the TMA hardware engine:

```
#include <cuda/pipeline>
#include <cuda_runtime.h>
#include <cstdint>
#include <cassert>

#define TILE_SIZE 1024  // example tile size
// User-provided compute function operating on a shared-memory tile
__device__ void processTile(const float* tile);

__global__ void kernelWithTMA(const float* __restrict__ global_ptr,
                              int nTiles) {
    // Two ping-pong buffers in shared memory
    // On Blackwell (CUDA 13+), prefer 32B alignment for 256-bit vectors
    // (v8.f32 / double4).
    __shared__ __align__(VEC_BYTES) float tile0[TILE_SIZE];
    __shared__ __align__(VEC_BYTES) float tile1[TILE_SIZE];

float* tiles[2] = { tile0, tile1 };

    // Alignment / size guards for vectorized copies
    // --- choose vector width -------------------------------------------
    #ifndef VEC_BYTES
      // Prefer 32B vectors on CUDA 13+/Blackwell.
      // Define -DUSE_256B_VEC to force.
      #if defined(USE_256B_VEC) || (defined(CUDA_VERSION)&&CUDA_VERSION >= 13000)
        #define VEC_BYTES 32     // 256-bit: v8.f32, double4
      #else
        #define VEC_BYTES 16     // 128-bit: v4.f32, float4
      #endif
    #endif
    constexpr int VEC_ELEMS = VEC_BYTES / sizeof(float); // 4 (128b) or 8 (256b)
    constexpr int WARP      = 32;

    // Alignment / size guards for vectorized copies/compute
    static_assert((TILE_SIZE % (WARP * VEC_ELEMS)) == 0,
                  "TILE_SIZE must be a multiple of WARP_SIZE * VEC_ELEMS");
    // Also guarantee the tile byte count
    //  is a multiple of the vector width
    static_assert(((TILE_SIZE * sizeof(float)) % VEC_BYTES) == 0,
                  "Tile byte size must be a multiple of VEC_BYTES");

    // On Blackwell (CUDA 13+), prefer 32B alignment
    // for 256-bit vectors (v8.f32 / double4).

    assert((reinterpret_cast<std::uintptr_t>(global_ptr) % VEC_BYTES) == 0);

    size_t bytes = TILE_SIZE * sizeof(float);
    // Block-scoped pipeline for TMA
    __shared__ cuda::pipeline_shared_state<
```

```
    cuda::thread_scope_block, 2> state;

auto pipe =
    cuda::make_pipeline(cuda::this_thread_block(),
        &state);

// Prime pipeline with the first async copy into tile0
pipe.producer_acquire();
cuda::memcpy_async(tiles[0],
                   global_ptr + 0 * TILE_SIZE,
                   cuda::aligned_size_t<32>{bytes},
                   pipe);
pipe.producer_commit();

// Loop over the remaining tiles
for (int t = 1; t < nTiles; ++t) {
    // Wait for the previous copy to finish, then compute on it
    pipe.consumer_wait();
    processTile(tiles[(t - 1) & 1]);
    pipe.consumer_release();

    // Enqueue the next async copy into the alternate buffer
    pipe.producer_acquire();
    cuda::memcpy_async(tiles[t & 1],
                       global_ptr + t * TILE_SIZE,
                       cuda::aligned_size_t<32>{bytes},,
                       pipe);
    pipe.producer_commit();
}

// Final wait and compute on the last tile
pipe.consumer_wait();
processTile(tiles[(nTiles - 1) & 1]);
pipe.consumer_release();
}
```

Immediately after kernel launch, each block allocates two shared-memory tiles (tile0, tile1) and constructs a block-scoped pipeline so all threads in the thread block coordinate their asynchronous DMA, as shown here:

```
__shared__ cuda::pipeline_shared_state<
    cuda::thread_scope_block, 2> state;

auto pipe =
    cuda::make_pipeline(cuda::this_thread_block(),
        &state);
```

To prime the pipeline, we submit an asynchronous copy using the TMA, which coalesces even strided or multidimensional transfers and streams bytes from global memory into tiles[0] in the background, as seen here:

```
pipe.producer_acquire();
cuda::memcpy_async(tiles[0],
                   global_ptr + 0 * TILE_SIZE,
                   cuda::aligned_size_t<32>{bytes},
                   pipe);
pipe.producer_commit();
```

Before using that data, we do the following to ensure we block just long enough for the TMA to finish the copy:

```
pipe.consumer_wait();
processTile(tiles[0]);
pipe.consumer_release();
```

Inside the main loop, we alternate buffers using `pipe.consumer_wait(); + process Tile()` on the previous tile, `pipe.consumer_release()`, `pipe.producer_acquire() + new cuda::memcpy_async()` into the other tile, and `pipe.producer_commit()`. Then we repeat!

By ping-ponging between `tile0` and `tile1`, each new `memcpy_async` overlaps `processTile` on the previous buffer. The load and store units on the SM experience lower pressure with more instruction issue slots available for computation. At the same time, the TMA moves data in parallel. This eliminates redundant global memory loads, reduces synchronization overhead, and keeps warps busy rather than stalled on memory.

Asynchronous prefetching from global memory to shared memory hides latency behind compute. Threads preload upcoming data into shared memory while they compute on data that was previously loaded.

This pattern is especially effective in memory-bound loops and tensor computations. On modern GPUs, the TMA can stream the next tile for a matrix multiply while the current tile is being processed.

> TMA is the preferred path for tiled bulk copies when moving 2D and N-dimensional tiles between global memory and SMEM/TMEM. Prefer `cuda::memcpy_async` with `cuda::pipeline` at block scope; on Hopper/Blackwell the implementation will leverage TMA (`cp.async.bulk.*` family) when alignment and direction permit (e.g., global memory ↔ shared memory).

We trade many scattered global reads for one coalesced global copy plus many fast shared-memory loads. This is favorable given the gap between DRAM and on-chip SRAM. Table 7-7 summarizes Nsight Compute metrics before and after a TMA-based double-buffering implementation.

Table 7-7. Comparing naive kernel (no prefetch) to TMA-accelerated double buffering

Metric	Before (no prefetch)	After (async prefetch)
Global Memory Load Efficiency	23%	99%
Average sectors per request	6.4	4.0
DRAM throughput (% of peak)	25%	90%
SM Active %	62%	100%
Kernel execution time	18 ms	7 ms

Here, we see SM Active % approaches 100%, which shows that the SMs have active warps for nearly all cycles. Global Memory Load Efficiency increases from 23% to 99%, meaning nearly every fetched byte is useful.

Average sectors per request falls from 6.4 to about 4.0, which indicates that requests map cleanly to 128-byte lines at the cache. DRAM throughput rises from 25% to 90% of peak, and overall time improves from 18 milliseconds to 7 milliseconds, about 2.6× faster. These results confirm that offloading bulk copies to the TMA and ping-ponging shared memory buffers keep the GPU busy and hide most of the DRAM latency behind useful work.

NVIDIA's CUDA `pipeline` API plus TMA is a textbook example of hardware-software codesign. The Pipeline API specifically exposes TMA's capabilities—and the TMA hardware supports exactly the asynchronous, coalesced, multidimensional copies that `cuda::memcpy_async` needs.

The API and the TMA DMA engine were developed hand in hand so you can express high-level pipeline operations that map closely to the hardware transfer capabilities. This allows the efficient overlap of memory movement with compute to boost performance.

> For almost all cases, you should write your CUDA kernels with the highest-level and most-recent APIs available for global-to-shared tiling. This includes the CUDA Pipeline API (`cuda::mem cpy_async`). These APIs and libraries are constantly improving and will transparently leverage the latest hardware features like TMA for bulk, strided, and 2D/3D transfers. In addition, they enable advanced performance optimization features like multicast with thread block clusters. When using these APIs, you get all of this "for free"-without requiring code changes.

In summary, when memory access limits your kernel's performance, offload and overlap data movement by combining careful tiling, double buffering, and TMA-driven asynchronous prefetching. By staging tiles in shared memory and using `cuda::memcpy_async` alongside `pipe.producer_commit` and `pipe.consumer_wait`, you hand off coalesced, multidimensional DMA transfers to the TMA, offloading the global to shared memory transfer.

Using TMA to offload memory transfers helps to relieve pressure on the SM's load/store units to help keep the computation pipeline full. As such, the SM focuses on compute, while shared memory traffic uses the on-chip TMA path. On Blackwell's massive-bandwidth HBM3e fabric, these techniques are essential to hide DRAM latency, sustain peak throughput, and turn memory-bound kernels into near-compute-bound workhorses.

Key Takeaways

Optimizing memory access patterns on GPUs—through coalescing, data reuse, and asynchronous transfers—can shift a kernel from being memory bound to approaching the hardware's peak capabilities. Small code changes to better align with GPU architecture (such as proper thread grouping, using shared memory, avoiding bank conflicts) can yield massive performance gains. Here are the key takeaways from this chapter:

Global-memory coalescing
> Coalescing is achieved when each warp's accesses fall within as few 128-byte cache lines as possible. Arrange your data and thread indexes so that each warp's threads read consecutive 4-byte words, letting the hardware fuse them into a few 128-byte transactions. Coalesced memory loads maximize effective DRAM bandwidth, or Global Memory Load Efficiency, and minimize average sectors per request down to the optimal 4.0 value. When using modern versions of Nsight Compute, you can also use `sm__sass_data_bytes_mem_*` counters and `gpu__dram_throughput .avg.pct_of_peak_sustained_elapsed` to profile and optimize memory coalescing.

Vectorized loads/stores
> Use built-in vector types such as `float4` for 16-byte vectors. On Blackwell with CUDA 13+, prefer 32-byte per-thread vectors when 32-byte alignment is provable. This includes `double4` or a custom struct `alignas(32) { float v[8]; }`. This reduces instructions per byte and keeps sectors/request at the ideal 4.0 when properly aligned. This way, each thread moves as many elements as possible in one instruction. The number of 128-byte transactions per warp scales with the total bytes requested. Be mindful of alignment: ensure your arrays are allocated with at least 16-byte alignment for `float4`, which `cudaMalloc` does by default using 256-byte alignment, typically. Misaligned vector accesses will forfeit these benefits.

Bank-conflict avoidance

Pad your shared-memory arrays (e.g., make rows 33 floats wide for 32-thread warps) so that no two threads hit the same bank in the same cycle. Removing bank conflicts restores full shared-memory throughput. Try swizzling for a slightly more memory-efficient implementation than padding.

Shared-memory tiling and data reuse

Stage working sets in on-chip shared memory (e.g., tiling a matrix in 32 × 32 blocks) so each element is fetched once from DRAM but used many times on the SM. This raises arithmetic intensity and shifts kernels toward being compute bound.

Read-only data cache

Mark small, static lookup tables or coefficients as const __restrict__ so the compiler can route loads through the read-only data path when applicable. Uniform broadcasts are lower-latency than DRAM, avoid redundant transactions, and can be served from on-chip cache.

Overlap host–GPU copies with streams

Allocate your host buffers as page-locked ("pinned") memory, and use cuda MemcpyAsync on multiple streams to overlap H2D/D2H transfers with kernel execution. Pinned memory enables asynchronous DMA transfers, and multiple streams allow copies to overlap with kernel execution to hide PCIe or NVLink transfer latency. Prefer cudaMemcpyAsync with explicit streams and events to overlap H2D/D2H and kernels. Remember that pageable (non-pinned) memory will disable DMA overlap. You should verify whether pageable or pinned memory is used, as observed transfer rates will vary widely depending on this configuration.

Asynchronous prefetch with TMA + Pipeline API

Use the C++ libcu++ barrier and pipeline APIs (cuda::barrier and cuda::pipe line) with cuda::memcpy_async to drive TMA (cp.async.bulk.tensor) for global memory → shared memory bulk copies when alignment and scope requirements are met. This offloads coalesced, strided (even multidimensional) copies into shared memory and overlaps them with computation with double buffering. This will reduce pressure on the SM's LD/ST units and let the SM focus on compute.

It's important to note that the libcu++ pipeline APIs and TMA continue to evolve. Prefer the staged forms (e.g., producer_acquire(), producer_commit(), consumer_wait(), consumer_release()) for two-stage ping-pong buffers. Use a block-scoped pipeline (e.g., cuda::thread_scope_block) or block-scoped barrier (e.g., cuda::barrier<cuda::thread_scope_block>) unless you specifically need cluster-scoped or grid-scoped copies.

Profile to guide you

Rely on Nsight Compute metrics like Global Memory Load Efficiency, average sectors per request, shared-memory bank conflicts, SM Active %, warp stall reasons, etc. Also, review Nsight Systems timelines to visualize overlaps and stalls, pinpoint bottlenecks, and verify each optimization.

Conclusion

With your memory-access pipeline now firing on all cylinders with coalesced global memory loads, conflict-free tiling, vectorized fetches, read-only caching, and TMA-driven prefetching, you've removed the biggest data-movement bottlenecks and freed the SMs to run at full speed.

Throughout this chapter we've relied on Nsight Compute and Nsight Systems to expose exactly where warps were starving for data. We also used them to confirm, step by step, that each optimization really did reduce stalls, collapse wasted transactions, and boost sustained bandwidth. Those tools remain your north star whenever you tune a new kernel.

In the next chapter, we'll cover some fundamental latency-hiding techniques in CUDA and GPU programming. These techniques include tuning occupancy, increasing warp efficiency, avoiding warp divergence, and exposing instruction-level parallelism.

## CHAPTER 8

Occupancy Tuning, Warp Efficiency, and Instruction-Level Parallelism

Modern GPU-accelerated workloads are pushing hardware to its limits. Multi-die GPUs like Blackwell connect multiple reticle-limited dies with a 10 TB/s NV-HBI link and increase L2 to 126 MB. These hardware design choices materially change memory-vs-compute tradeoffs and occupancy sweet spots. This makes profiling and optimization even more critical than ever. Building on the fundamentals of memory optimizations, we now turn to advanced latency-hiding techniques and throughput enhancements designed to fully leverage the full power of modern GPUs.

We will focus on identifying performance bottlenecks and then applying a systematic set of optimization strategies to eliminate them one by one. Key themes in this chapter include tuning occupancy, optimizing warp efficiency, and increasing instruction-level parallelism.

By the end of the chapter, you will be able to identify root causes of GPU underutilization—as well as apply the right combination of optimizations. We will also prepare you for more advanced techniques like kernel fusion and pipelining with primitives like CUDA Graphs and CUDA streams, which we cover in subsequent chapters.

While our focus is higher-level languages like CUDA C++ and AI frameworks like PyTorch, the principles of profiling and tuning apply at all levels of the stack right down to the hardware. As such, understanding low-level hardware performance remains critical for diagnosing bottlenecks that higher-level abstractions make difficult to fully resolve.

Profiling and Diagnosing GPU Bottlenecks

Before optimizing, we must first identify the bottlenecks in our code to determine which hardware or software resource is limiting our performance. Modern NVIDIA GPUs are complex, and a slowdown could come from many sources, including memory bandwidth, memory latency, instruction throughput, synchronization overheads, insufficient parallelism, host-device transfer delays, and more.

NVIDIA's profiling ecosystem includes Nsight Systems (command-line interface nsys) and Nsight Compute (command-line interface ncu). Nsight Systems captures a system-level timeline of CPU threads, GPU kernels, and memory transfers. It can also capture Python backtraces and Python sampling.

Combined with PyTorch profiler and various visualization tools, Nsight Systems and Nsight Compute can help you diagnose kernel performance bottlenecks, analyze roofline plots, and measure the effectiveness of your iterative optimization efforts.

Nsight Systems Timeline View

The Nsight Systems timeline view helps pinpoint concurrency issues, transfer overhead, and idle periods. For example, run the following code to produce a detailed timeline showing kernel launch overlaps, CPU preparation gaps, data transfer timings, and NVTX-marked ranges:

```
nsys profile \
    --trace=... \
    --capture-range=... \
    --force-overwrite=true \
    <application>
```

In addition, the Nsight Systems GUI lets you interactively inspect the timeline. It visualizes CPU threads, GPU kernels, and even user-defined NVTX ranges with zoom and pan features for detailed analysis (see Figure 8-1).

Remember that NVTX annotations are essential for complex applications. Use NVTX ranges in your code to mark regions of interest. You can then use Nsight Systems to capture range profiles. And while the CUDA profiler Start and Stop API is supported for capture control, NVTX ranges are the recommended mechanism for framework workflows. For instance, you can use NVTX range push/pop, available using torch.cuda.nvtx in PyTorch, to label phases such as "forward pass" and "backprop." This makes the Nsight Systems timeline far more interpretable since the profiler can capture the performance-critical iterations and clearly delineate key computation segments.

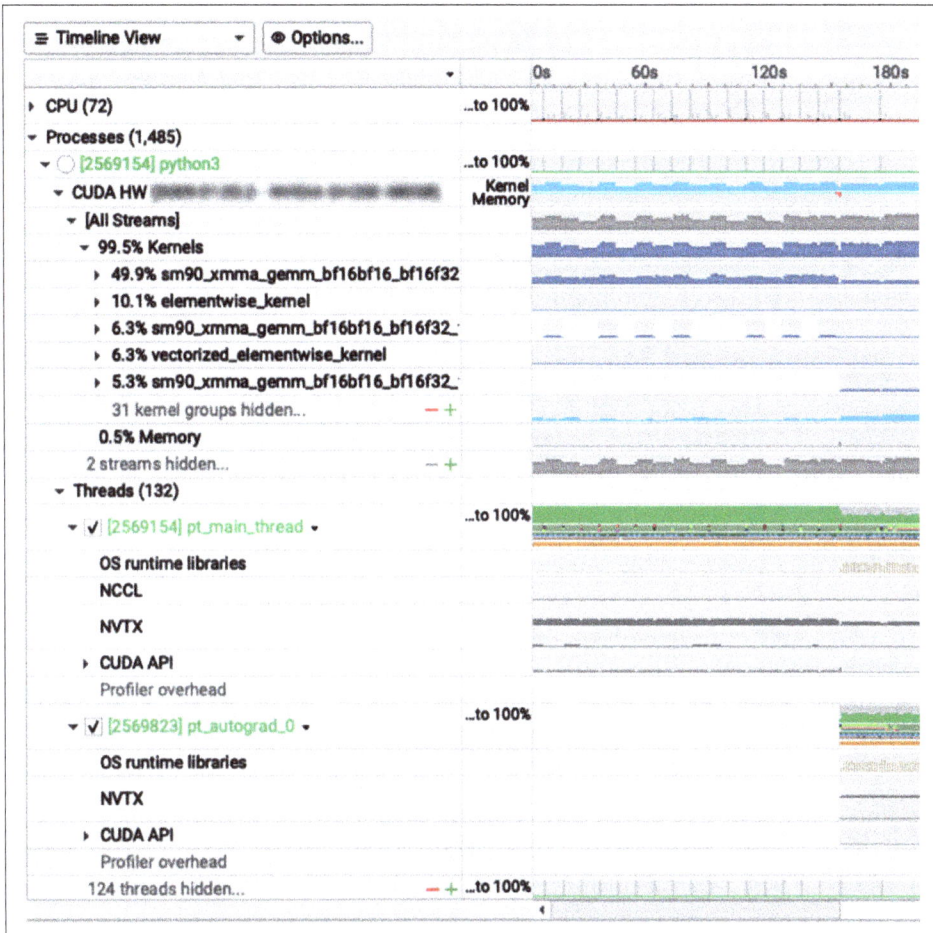

Figure 8-1. Nsight Systems interactive UI (source: https://oreil.ly/YEiWS)

Profiling and Tuning the Data Pipeline

As mentioned earlier, Nsight Systems provides a high-level view of the entire pipeline, including the data loading and processing steps. For instance, if you see the GPU idle while the CPU is busy preparing data or running augmentation, common in training loops, the bottleneck might not be the GPU kernel but the data pipeline itself.

For scenarios in which the bottleneck is the data pipeline on a realistic and representative dataset, you can tune the number of data loader threads, overlap CPU preprocessing with GPU compute using double buffering, or move more preprocessing onto the GPU.

Always ensure that what you perceive as a "GPU performance issue" is not actually caused by something upstream or downstream of the kernel execution like data loading.

With a clear picture from profiling, we can now proceed to address specific bottlenecks. The next sections cover the core optimization techniques in detail. We'll start with occupancy tuning since a sufficient supply of warps is fundamental to hiding latency and maximizing throughput.

Nsight Compute and Roofline Analysis

Nsight Compute (ncu), on the other hand, is a profiler that collects in-depth metrics for individual kernels. For instance, it tracks achieved occupancy, issued warp instructions per cycle, memory throughput (GB/s), utilization of execution units, and many others. Together, these paint a complete picture of your system's performance profile.

These metrics are organized into sections such as memory, compute, and throughput, etc. Nsight Compute's automated analysis rules will flag inefficiencies such as low-memory utilization and divergent branches—and even provide optimization hints. These built-in rules are updated continuously for new GPU architectures. They can quickly highlight if you are memory bound, latency bound, etc., based on metrics like FLOPS per byte ratios, stall reasons, etc.

Nsight Compute includes a Roofline analysis section as well as automated guidance. This can plot your kernel's achieved FLOPS against hardware rooflines—and even highlight if you are near the memory bandwidth or compute limits.

Remember that the memory-versus-compute distinction is quantified using the Roofline model, which plots kernel performance against hardware ceilings for memory bandwidth and compute throughput. Nsight Compute now directly provides Roofline analysis, showing each kernel's achieved GFLOPS relative to peak and its arithmetic intensity (FLOPS per byte). A kernel falling below the memory roof indicates memory-bound behavior, while one near the compute roof is ALU bound. Use the Roofline section in Nsight Compute to obtain arithmetic intensity (FLOPs/byte) and FLOPs by precision directly. Compare this to the hardware's theoretical peak FLOPS per byte, you can see how far below the roofline the kernel is operating. An example Roofline chart is shown in Figure 8-2.

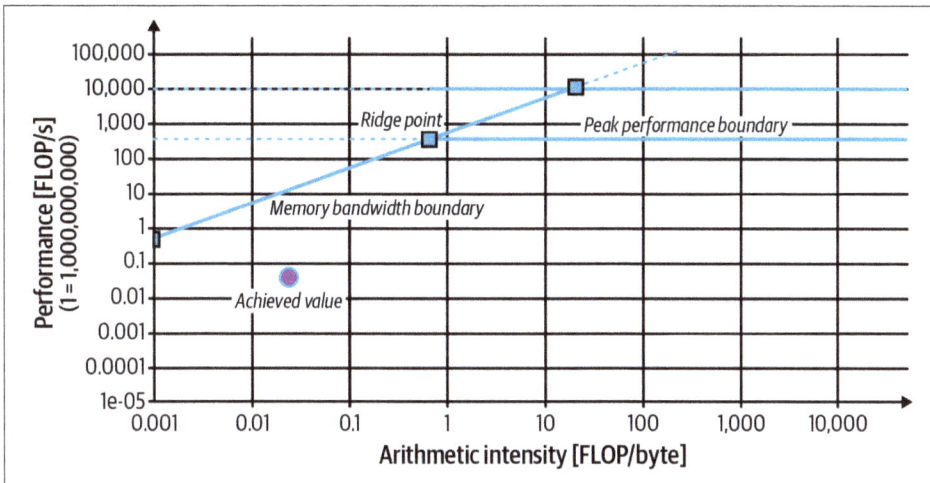

Figure 8-2. Roofline chart shown in the Nsight Compute UI (https://oreil.ly/wUbIz)

It's often effective to first use Nsight Systems to find hot kernels or bottleneck operations on the timeline. Then, you can zoom into each of these kernels with Nsight
Compute to perform a more fine-grained analysis and diagnosis. This two-step workflow, moving from a system-wide view to a kernel-level deep dive is a common
approach to handling complex GPU performance debugging and tuning.

PyTorch Profiler and Visualization Tools

When using high-level frameworks like PyTorch, the `torch.profiler` API (*https://
oreil.ly/GlT7l*) can collect similar performance metrics during model training/infer-
ence. The PyTorch profiler uses the Kineto library to actually perform the data collection under the hood.

Kineto (*https://oreil.ly/Rwwwh*) integrates with CUDA's Performance Tools Interface
(CUPTI (*https://oreil.ly/oO6Ti*)) backend to capture operator-wise execution times,
GPU kernel launches, memory copies, and hardware counter metrics. It also integrates with Linux `perf` to record CPU events. Kineto merges all of this information
into a coherence, time-ordered trace, which can be visualized using the PyTorch profiler UI, Nsight Systems GUI, or just a Chrome browser (e.g., Chrome tracing format). An example Chrome tracing visualization is shown in Figure 8-3.

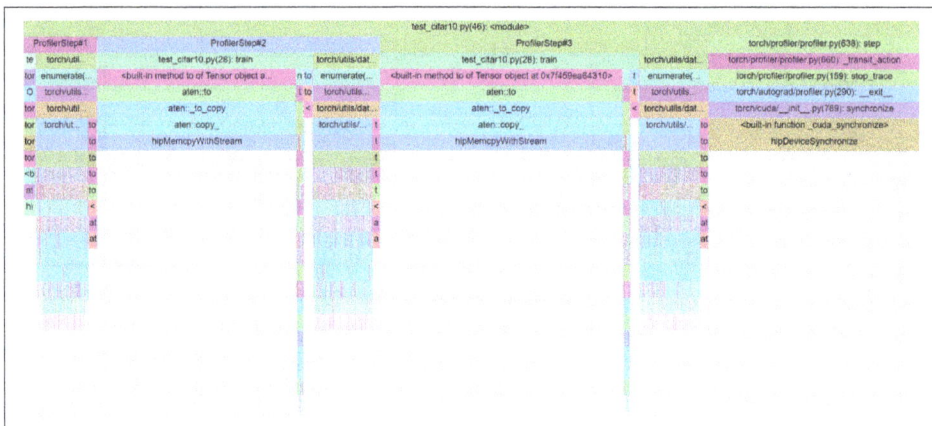

Figure 8-3. Chrome tracing visualization generated by the PyTorch profiler

PyTorch profiler allows you to identify bottleneck operations in your model code directly. For example, you can profile a training loop with `torch.profiler.pro file(..., with_flops=True, profile_memory=True)` to record memory usage and to estimate FLOPs for supported operators such as matrix multiplication. (Note: These are formula-based estimates at the operator level rather than per-kernel hardware counters.) Such integration makes it easier to bridge the gap between PyTorch model code and low-level CUDA performance analysis.

Modern versions of Nsight Systems can collect Python backtrace sampling and also provide a PyTorch-focused mode, which supports Python call-stack sampling and a PyTorch domain for more correlated tracing." This helps correlate framework activity with the system timeline. Nsight Compute correlates to CUDA C or C++ source and PTX or SASS. You can compile device code with `-lineinfo` to enable source line mapping. To correlate model code with kernels, use NVTX ranges from Python using `torch.cuda.nvtx`. In addition, modern versions of Nsight Compute provide a source view, which includes instruction mix—as well as a throughput breakdown that helps pinpoint the source code lines impacted by stalls and throughput limitations.

> The lack of capturing Python information traditionally discouraged PyTorch developers from using Nsight Systems/Compute. However, if you are using PyTorch/Python, it's worth revisiting these tools to provide a more holistic and correlated analysis with the rest of the system.

This section outlines a workflow for diagnosing GPU bottlenecks, including how to interpret key profiler metrics and what they imply about the bottleneck type. We will focus on Nsight Compute for deep-dive kernel analysis, including warp stalls and memory throughput—and Nsight Systems for high-level application profiling, including concurrency and CPU-GPU overlap.

Profiler-Guided Analysis

The key is to use all of these insights to guide your next steps since different bottle-necks require different optimizations. For instance, you can take advantage of Nsight Compute's guided analysis rules, which might flag "Memory Bound: L2 transactions per FLOP high" or "Compute Bound: issue stall reasons indicate pipe contention."

These rules are updated for each architecture, including Blackwell. They can quickly confirm whether a bottleneck is in memory throughput, instruction dispatch, latency hiding, etc. This can direct you to the most relevant metrics and improve your bottle-neck time-to-resolution.

> Nsight Systems and Nsight Compute are constantly updated to the latest GPU architectures to assist performance engineers in diag-nosing and fixing performance issues when migrating workloads to newer GPU generations.

Analyzing Warp Stall Reasons with Nsight Compute

As discussed in Chapter 6, NVIDIA GPUs execute warps, or groups of 32 threads, in SIMT fashion. If warps are frequently pausing instead of issuing instructions, the profiler categorizes the reasons why.

One of the most insightful views in Nsight Compute is the Warp State Statistics breakdown for a kernel. This is sometimes called the *warp stall reasons*. By examining these stall reasons, you can often pinpoint the limiting factor.

There are a few different types of warp stalls: memory-related, execution dependency, execution contention, and others like texture-cache-related stalls. Let's take a look at each of these.

Memory-Related Stalls

If a kernel is waiting on global memory loads, Nsight Compute reports a high per-centage of "Stall: Long Scoreboard" cycles. The scoreboard tracks each warp's out-standing memory requests, so *Long Scoreboard* indicates warps frequently waiting on the high latency of global DRAM loads, as shown in Figure 8-4.

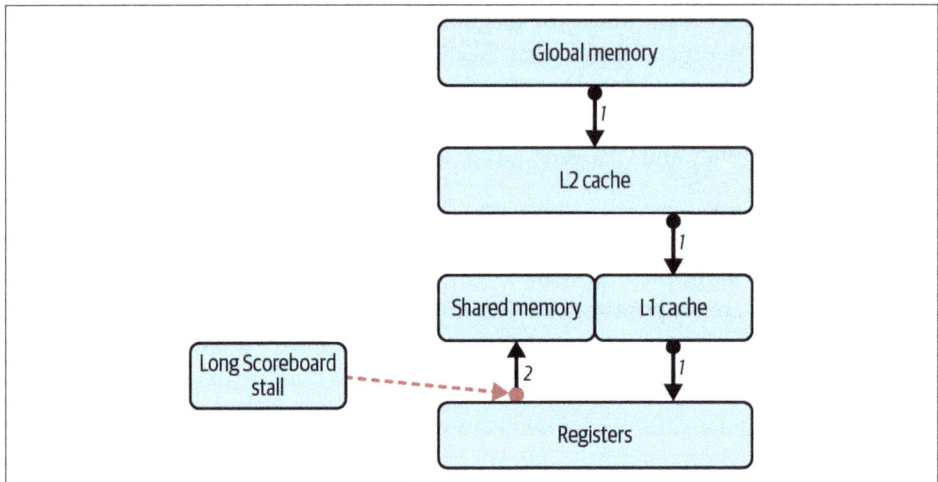

Figure 8-4. Long Scoreboard stall caused by waiting on high-latency global memory accesses (e.g., waiting for data fetched from device memory into registers, or for spilled local memory to be written to/from device memory)

Similarly, a *Short Scoreboard* stall is caused by waiting on memory transfers between shared memory and the registers. This is shown in Figure 8-5.

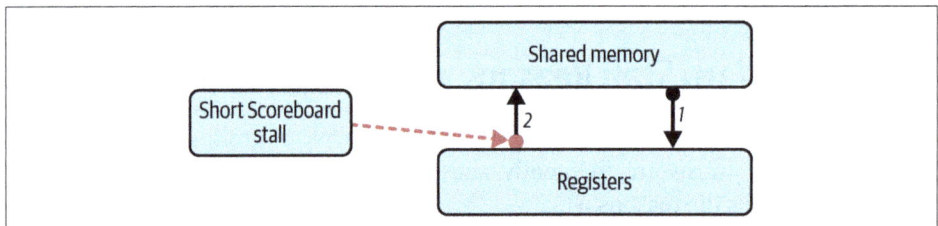

Figure 8-5. Short Scoreboard stall caused by high-latency data transfers between shared memory and the registers

Similarly, metrics labeled "Stall: Memory Throttle" mean the load/store pipelines are saturated so that no additional memory requests can be issued because the hardware's memory queues are full. "Stall: Not Selected" means that although warps are eligible to issue, they must wait for free memory transaction slots before they can proceed. Whenever these memory-related stall reasons dominate your stall profile, it is a clear sign the kernel is memory bound.

> Use Nsight Compute's source code view to highlight code impacted by scoreboard dependencies and other hardware limitations (e.g., special function unit throughput, etc.).

Execution-Dependency Stalls

A high fraction of "Stall: Exec Dependency" means that warps are often waiting on the results of previous instructions. For instance, one instruction depends on the output of a prior instruction that has not yet completed. This is usually a sign of insufficient instruction-level parallelism within each thread—or an ALU latency bottleneck.

In a simple sequence of dependent arithmetic operations, later instructions must wait for earlier ones to finish. This causes the warp to go idle. If Exec Dependency stalls dominate, the kernel is likely latency bound waiting on compute. In other words, each thread's instruction pipeline isn't busy enough due to sequential dependencies.

Execution Unit Contention

If you see significant "Stall: Compute Unit Busy"—or simply very high active utilization of the FP32 CUDA cores or Tensor Cores—the kernel is likely compute bound. In this case, the math units (FP32/FP64 ALUs, Tensor Cores, etc.) are saturated. Specifically, warps are ready to execute more instructions, but the execution units can't service them any faster. This often manifests as near-peak "ALU pipe busy" metrics and can correlate with high power usage. A related stall reason on some GPUs is "Stall: Math Pipe Throttle," which means that warps are waiting because the math pipelines are fully occupied on every cycle.

Other Stall Reasons

While the previous stall reasons are the most common culprits, there are many other less common stall categories, including instruction fetch stalls, texture unit stalls, synchronization stalls, etc. For instance, "Stall: Memory Dependency" is similar to Long Scoreboard in which an operation is waiting on a prior memory operation.

"Stall: Texture Throttle" indicates a bottleneck in the texture caching subsystem. "No Eligible" or "Idle" indicates the warp scheduler had no warps ready to issue at a given cycle. This is often due to a prior synchronization—or simply not enough warps launched.

In practice, you don't need to memorize every stall reason. Instead, look at the largest portions of the stall breakdown. If memory-related stalls dominate, it's memory bound. If execution dependency dominates, it's latency bound on ALU.

If there are almost no stalls and near 100% pipeline active, it's likely compute bound. If warps are often "not selected" or idle, it could indicate insufficient parallel work or an occupancy issue. By examining the warp stall breakdown for your kernel, you can narrow down the bottleneck category.

Nsight Compute provides these stall metrics per kernel launch. Make sure to profile representative workloads. A tiny test kernel might not exhibit the same stall profile as your real application. Always collect data from realistic runs before drawing conclusions.

Table 8-1 shows a list of common warp stall reasons, their typical interpretation, and possible optimization approaches.

Table 8-1. Common warp stall reasons and optimization hints

Warp stall reason	Meaning/cause	Potential optimizations
Execution dependency	Warp is stalled on a prior, dependent instruction. This often indicates insufficient instruction-level parallelism (ILP) within the thread.	Increase ILP (do independent work in the same thread). Unroll loops or reorder instructions so that long-latency operations (like multiplies or complex math) have other work to overlap with. If ILP is maxed and still stalling, rely on more warps (occupancy) to hide the latency.
Memory dependency (Long Scoreboard stall)	The warp is waiting on memory loads ("long-latency") to complete before it can proceed. No other work in the warp can proceed until data arrives.	Hide memory latency by having more warps ready to run, or higher occupancy, so that other warps can run while this warp waits. Or use asynchronous memory prefetch to copy data to shared memory, then continue computing. This will overlap memory operations with computation. To minimize latency, make sure that memory accesses are efficient, use proper coalescing, and exploit proper cache hierarchies. On modern GPUs, you should use the Tensor Memory Accelerator (TMA) for bulk multidimensional copies so memory movement overlaps compute with low thread overhead.
Synchronization (barrier)	Warp is waiting at a `__sync threads()` or other synchronization, idle until all threads reach the barrier. Often indicates either frequent synchronization or load imbalance (some warps arrive earlier and wait).	Reduce unnecessary synchronization. Reexamine the algorithm for ways to combine phases or use fine-grained sync. Ensure work is evenly distributed so warps reach barriers at roughly the same time. In some cases, use newer sync primitives (e.g., warp-level sync or cluster sync) to limit scope of synchronization.
Instruction fetch/ issue	Warp is stalled waiting to fetch the next instruction (could be an instruction cache miss or pipeline issue) or not issued because the required execution pipe was busy. This can happen with very large kernels or under certain pipeline contention scenarios.	If instruction cache misses are an issue, consider reducing kernel size (split kernel or avoid excessive unrolling that blows up code size). If pipeline issue (one type of instruction saturating a functional unit), try to mix instruction types or again use ILP to utilize different pipelines.

Warp stall reason	Meaning/cause	Potential optimizations
Not selected (scheduler)	The warp is ready but was not selected to issue in that cycle (scheduler picked another warp). This typically means there were other warps available and this one simply waited its turn. It is not a dependency stall. It usually indicates that other ready warps were chosen to issue that cycle, which is expected at healthy occupancy.	Usually not a problem—it means the GPU had other work to do and chose a different warp for that cycle. If you see a high percentage of "Not Selected," it implies high occupancy is doing its job (hiding latency). No action needed unless it indicates an imbalance (one warp hogging the scheduler; in rare cases, you might use scheduler hints or yield).

By interpreting these stall reasons, you can decide which optimization to pursue. For example, high memory stall time means you should try to hide latency with more warps, better memory access patterns, or asynchronous prefetch.

Seeing high execution dependency stalls suggests that you should increase ILP or rearrange code. Frequent barrier stalls mean you should likely rework synchronization. This profiling step guides you to the most effective optimizations rather than blindly tuning everything.

Inspecting Achieved Occupancy and GPU Utilization

Another key metric reported by profilers is *achieved occupancy*, or the average fraction of hardware thread slots, warps, that were occupied on each SM during execution. For example, if a GPU supports 64 warps per streaming multiprocessor (SM) and achieved occupancy is 30%, then on average 19 warps were active per SM.

Low achieved occupancy often signals underutilization since you can't hide enough latency with only a few active warps. On the other hand, if you're running at near-maximum occupancy, but still not seeing the expected performance benefits, other bottlenecks are likely the cause. These include memory bandwidth limitations, inefficient instruction streams, and suboptimal memory-access patterns.

In these nonideal cases, simply adding more threads won't help. Instead, you should investigate to improve memory coalescing, increase arithmetic intensity, and optimize warp-level efficiency. We'll cover these techniques in the upcoming sections.

Nsight Compute also reports occupancy limiters, including which resource is constraining the theoretical occupancy. For example, "Limited by max registers per thread" means your kernel's register usage is preventing more warps from being scheduled per SM.

However, "Limited by shared memory per block" means the kernel's shared memory allocation per block is the bottleneck for occupancy. And "Limited by thread count" means the launch configuration itself, grid, or block size didn't request enough threads to fill the GPU.

Each of these limiters hints at different fixes, which we will discuss in more detail in the next section. For instance, if registers are the limiter, you might reduce register usage or use __launch_bounds__ to allow more blocks. If shared memory is the limiter, you can try to use smaller tiles and less shared memory per block.

Beyond a certain point, increasing occupancy may not produce a speedup. Very low occupancy (e.g., 10%–20%) will hurt performance due to poor latency hiding. On the other hand, pushing occupancy to 100% isn't always beneficial if other factors like memory bandwidth and instruction dependencies become the bottleneck.

As such, you should examine hardware utilization beyond just occupancy. Nsight Compute reports metrics such as achieved memory bandwidth in GB/s, achieved FLOPS in TFLOPS, instructions per cycle (IPC), issue-slot utilization, and other resource utilization statistics. These numbers will show how close your kernel is to the GPU's physical hardware limits.

For example, if your kernel's ALU utilization is low while its memory throughput is at 95% of peak, you are almost certainly memory-bandwidth bound. Conversely, if ALU utilization is near its maximum but memory throughput remains modest, the kernel is compute bound. In this case, you'll gain speed only by increasing arithmetic throughput—typically by switching to lower-precision types (FP16, FP8, or FP4) and moving work onto the faster Tensor Cores of the GPUs.

If both ALU utilization and memory throughput are low, your kernel may be experiencing long-latency operations, synchronization overhead, or simply insufficient parallel work. This could indicate low *instruction-level parallelism* (discussed in an upcoming section)—or that you haven't launched enough threads to fully utilize the GPU.

You can frame this analysis using the Roofline model, which plots a kernel's FLOPS against its arithmetic intensity (FLOPS per byte of memory accessed). The roofline defines a *compute roof* (the maximum FLOPS the GPU can sustain) and a *memory roof* (the maximum memory bandwidth).

If your kernel's FLOP/byte ratio falls below the hardware's compute-to-memory ratio, you are memory bound because you cannot supply data fast enough. If the ratio is high but actual FLOPS remains far below peak, the kernel may be latency bound or lacking sufficient ILP to saturate the compute units.

> With each new GPU generation, memory bandwidth increases modestly, but compute capacity grows much faster. As such, kernels tend to become more memory bound over time.

In practice, always compare two key figures: your kernel's memory throughput versus the hardware's peak memory bandwidth—as well as your kernel's compute throughput versus the hardware's peak FLOPS. Those comparisons will tell you whether your next optimization should focus on memory access, compute work, or parallelism. Let's look at each of these next.

Kernel Memory Throughput Versus Peak HBM Memory Bandwidth

Nsight Compute reports how many GB/s your kernel achieves. If your kernel is showing near-peak memory bandwidth utilization, performing more computations won't help. You would have to increase arithmetic intensity by reducing memory traffic per operation.

You can increase arithmetic intensity by using reduced precision with Tensor Cores, hiding more latency with concurrency, and using kernel fusion, which we'll cover in a bit. These techniques help reduce global memory traffic by decreasing the size of intermediate data that is being transferred.

For instance, if a kernel hits ~80% or more of the GPU's memory bandwidth, it's likely memory bound since there is little headroom left.

However, note that Blackwell GPUs have a relatively large 126 MB L2 cache. And their dual-die design uses a high-bandwidth 10 TB/s interconnect, NVIDIA High-Bandwidth Interface (NV-HBI), so the two GPU dies behave as one for memory access. As such, many kernels that were previously memory bound on older GPUs might better utilize the cache with newer GPU generations.

You can use Nsight Compute's memory chart to see how much traffic goes to L2 versus DRAM. A high L2 hit rate could alleviate global memory bottlenecks, which means the kernel might actually be compute-limited despite performing heavy memory accesses. The on-chip cache is servicing a lot of the memory accesses.

> On Blackwell, you can control L2 data persistence to keep critical working sets resident.

Kernel Compute Throughput Versus Peak GPU FLOPS

Low achieved FLOPS can be caused by low occupancy or instruction-level stalls. For example, if only 30% of warps are active on average—or if pipelines are often idle due to memory waits—the kernel will sit far below the compute roof.

You can use Nsight Compute's Occupancy section and Source Counters to pinpoint these issues. Ensure the kernel launches enough threads to fill the GPU, up to the per-SM resident warps limit for your device (e.g., 64 resident warps per SM.)

> Only warps within the same SM must share resources—and they can hide one another's latency. Warps on different SMs have no interaction. As such, achieved occupancy is measured per SM. We'll cover occupancy in a bit.

Additionally, examine instruction issue efficiency and throughput metrics. Blackwell scales to many SMs per device, so underutilization at the kernel level can translate to large aggregate losses. (Note: The dual-die packaging does not, by itself, increase the per-SM issue rate.)

If the achieved FLOPS are moderate to high but memory throughput is low, the kernel might be mostly compute-focused but limited by instruction dependencies. You can confirm by checking the "Exec Dependency" stalls metric in Nsight Compute—and any other stall reasons.

If compute throughput is near peak, then you are truly compute bound. In this case, you have already optimized the kernel's memory access patterns—or you are already using lower-precision Tensor Cores to reach such high FLOPS.

Prolonged near-peak compute utilization can sometimes invoke power management compute limiters on modern GPUs to keep them healthy. Be sure to take this into account when you're profiling, benchmarking, and tuning. The easiest way to see if you're being power-limited is to use the following to monitor the enforced power limit alongside any "HW Slowdown" flags in real time:

```
nvidia-smi \
  --query-gpu=\
  power.draw,clocks.current.sm,clocks.current.memory,\
  clocks_event_reasons.active \
  --format=csv -l 1
```

This command prints a new line every 1 second with current power draw, graphics/memory clocks, and throttle reasons. With this information you can pinpoint when the GPU hits its power cap and downclocks.

You can also use NVIDIA's Management Library (NVML) API, which provides programmatic access to the CUDA C++ nvmlDeviceGetPowerUsage() and nvmlDeviceGetEnforcedPowerLimit() APIs—as well as the equivalent NVML Python APIs (*https://oreil.ly/72x6m*). These are ideal for custom scripts or integration with monitoring systems.

In short, use a combination of occupancy, warp stall reasons, memory throughput, and compute throughput metrics together to diagnose the bottleneck. Make sure you see high occupancy, high warp efficiency, and a balanced usage of execution units, including Tensor Cores.

Iteratively Profiling and Determining the Kernel Bottleneck

GPUs can stall for four fundamentally different reasons: underutilization, latency bound, memory bound, and compute bound. These regimes are related, but it's important to understand each of them independently in order to choose the right optimizations to pursue. Often, fixing one bottleneck will reveal another.

Underutilization happens when you simply haven't launched enough threads or work. In this case, both FLOPS and memory bandwidth stay low and the execution timeline has idle gaps. Once you increase parallelism, you will find your warps are now stalling and waiting on memory loads.

Once you more fully utilize your GPU, you can now distinguish between latency bound and memory bound. A latency-bound kernel issues far fewer bytes/sec than the hardware can deliver because individual memory loads are stalling the warps. The fix is to increase memory-compute overlap by increasing occupancy, using more ILP, prefetching, and pipelining.

A memory-bound kernel, in contrast, is saturating DRAM bandwidth, but your ALUs are sitting idle, not because of stalls but because there's simply no more data you can fetch per second due to the memory pipe saturation. In this case, you must raise arithmetic intensity with tiling, fusing, exploiting caches (L1/texture), or reducing precision to reduce memory traffic.

If neither of those fixes produces more speed, you've moved into compute-bound territory in which the GPU's arithmetic pipes (e.g., ALUs and Tensor Cores) are the limiting factor. Here you can increase per-thread ILP by overlapping independent instructions with unrolling and software pipelining. On modern GPUs, unified cores cannot execute an INT32 and an FP32 instruction in the same clock. In other words, mixed INT32 and FP32 workloads do not execute both types from the same core in the same cycle. As such, the achievable issue rate depends on your instruction mix.

As you optimize, you'll often find yourself working through these regimes as follows: underutilized → latency bound → memory bound → compute bound. After each fix, you will likely hit a new bottleneck and apply the corresponding strategy. When optimizing GPU code, you should follow a structured approach as described here.

First, you should profile. Next, you can identify the bottleneck. You can use Nsight Compute for kernel-level metrics (e.g., warp stalls, achieved occupancy, memory versus compute utilization) and Nsight Systems for application-level timelines (e.g., concurrency, idle gaps).

Once you identify the bottlenecks, you can determine if the kernel is memory bound, compute bound, latency bound, or simply underutilizing the GPU. The GPU is underutilized when it is not issuing enough work. Table 8-2 summarizes these four regimes, including common profiling indicators and remedies.

Table 8-2. Memory bound versus latency bound versus compute bound versus underutilizing the GPU

Limiting factor	Description	Profiler indicators	Remedies
Memory bound	You're moving as much data as you can—close to peak DRAM bandwidth—but you don't have enough work per byte to fully utilize the ALUs.	High memory-bandwidth utilization is near peak, low FLOPS.	Increase arithmetic intensity (e.g., tiling, fusion) and improve coalescing and caching.
Compute bound	You've hidden memory latency and are no longer saturating memory bandwidth. Now the ALUs (e.g., CUDA cores and Tensor Cores) are the bottleneck.	High FLOPS are approaching GPU peak, low memory utilization.	Exploit more ILP (e.g., dual-issue, loop unroll), use specialized units (e.g., FP16/FP8/FP4/Tensor Cores), reduce dependencies, fuse work, leverage lower precision or sparsity.
Latency bound	You're not sustaining enough concurrent work to hide individual load/store latencies, so warps stall waiting on data.	Low achieved bandwidth well below peak, high "stall-on-scoreboard" or "not selected" percentages.	Raise occupancy, add ILP (e.g., unroll, multiple accumulators), intra-kernel pipelining, and software prefetch.
Underutilizing the GPU	You're not fully occupying SMs or launching enough work—both memory and compute resources remain idle.	Low occupancy and low achieved bandwidth, low FLOPS, timeline shows gaps or sparse kernel activity.	Increase problem size or batch work, launch more threads/blocks, fuse tasks, use persistent kernels (Chapter 10) or streams (Chapter 11).

A memory-bound kernel is one where performance is limited by memory throughput—specifically, if the GPU's global memory is unable to feed data to the compute units fast enough. In this case, your kernel's achieved FLOPS will sit near the roofline set by memory bandwidth. This happens if you have plenty of threads but can't move data any faster. As such, you're up against the memory-bandwidth ceiling.

Conversely, a compute-bound kernel saturates the GPU's arithmetic units (ALU FP32 CUDA cores or reduced-precision Tensor Cores). This is noticeable if the kernel is approaching the peak FLOPS roofline for the cores. Profiling metrics like achieved occupancy, memory utilization, and execution dependency stalls can help confirm this classification.

When a kernel is latency bound, on the other hand, each thread spends a large fraction of its time waiting on individual memory loads instead of doing useful work. In practical terms, this means that when a warp issues a global-memory load to fetch A[idx], for instance, all 32 threads in that warp will stall until that fetch completes. If the code immediately issues another dependent load or computation, the warp simply sits idle for hundreds of cycles on each load.

The GPU's warp scheduler may switch to other warps when it is latency bound, but if every warp is structured the same way (e.g., one load → wait → compute → write), there is rarely any other work to fill in those idle cycles. As such, the kernel never has enough independent operations in flight to hide the latency of a long-latency DRAM access.

To break out of the latency-bound situation, you need to give the GPU multiple operations to overlap. One approach is to increase occupancy by launching more threads and warps. This way, when one warp stalls on its load, another warp is ready to run.

Equally important, though, is increasing each warp's ILP. We'll cover ILP in more detail later in this chapter. At a high level, if each thread issues two or more independent loads back-to-back by loading A[idx] and B[idx] before doing any arithmetic, the GPU can start overlapping those loads in hardware.

In this case, while the first load waits for DRAM, load two (and three and four, etc.) can already be in flight. As soon as any of these loads return, the dependent arithmetic can execute. This will further overlap with the remaining pending loads.

You can also increase ILP by unrolling a small loop so that multiple values are fetched before any computation. More on this later.

By increasing ILP, each thread and warp always has enough work in flight so that the DRAM latency is masked by other outstanding operations. The net effect is to transform a latency-bound kernel into one that keeps the SM's pipelines busy. This will increase throughput and overall kernel performance.

When the GPU is underutilized, you're not launching enough work to keep SMs and memory pipelines busy, so many resources remain idle. In this case, it will help to increase the amount of work by increasing the batch size or launching more threads.

Optimizing the Kernel

In practice, performance tuning should follow a clear, step-by-step workflow. First, identify which regime your kernel occupies: memory bound, latency bound, compute bound, or underutilized. Next, apply the corresponding optimizations.

If your kernel is memory bound, concentrate on reducing and hiding memory traffic. You can do this by improving coalescing, raising occupancy, increasing ILP, and introducing data reuse through caching or tiling.

When the kernel is latency bound, meaning individual load or instruction latencies dominate, make sure there is enough independent work in flight. You can do this by issuing multiple nondependent loads/operations per thread or increasing overall occupancy so the scheduler always has ready warps to run.

If the kernel is compute-bound (i.e., the ALUs or Tensor Cores are saturated while memory is idle), shifting to lower-precision arithmetic (FP16/FP8/FP4), offloading work onto Tensor Cores, or fusing more operations together can raise arithmetic throughput. Finally, if the GPU appears underutilized with low occupancy and frequent idle cycles, simply launching more threads or blocks (so that all SMs have work) is often enough to get the hardware busy before applying deeper optimizations.

Here is a list of high-level optimization techniques that help you treat GPU performance tuning as a scientific process. We'll dive into these over the next few chapters, but they should each include identifying the limiting factor, applying the appropriate optimization, and measuring the outcome:

Convert memory-bound workloads to compute bound

> If memory bound (low arithmetic intensity), increase data reuse and work per launch as follows: apply tiling to use fast shared memory and reduce redundant accesses, fuse kernels to avoid unnecessary memory round trips, ensure memory accesses are optimized (coalesced, avoiding bank conflicts as per Chapter 6), and consider using compression or lower precision to move less data.

Further optimize compute-bound workloads

> If compute bound (e.g., high utilization of ALUs but not hitting peak due to dependencies), increase effective instruction throughput as follows: use ILP techniques (e.g., unroll loops, multiple accumulators to overlap independent ops), check for branch divergence (see Chapter 6) and try to reorganize work to reduce it since divergence wastes ALU cycles, and move to Tensor Cores and lower precision to raise the compute ceiling. If the kernel is at compute roof, see if reducing precision (FP32 $\rightarrow$ FP16 $\rightarrow$ FP8 $\rightarrow$ FP4) can give further speedups.

Increase parallelism for latency-bound workloads

> If latency bound (e.g., frequent warp stalls and not enough parallelism to hide latency), increase concurrency at various levels as follows: launch more threads/blocks if possible until latency is hidden, ensure registers/shared memory are not overly limiting occupancy (e.g., occupancy tuning and balancing resource usage), overlap memory and compute within each thread/warp using async copies (e.g., intra-kernel pipelining), and use multiple streams to overlap independent tasks or overlap copies with compute (e.g., inter-kernel concurrency described in Chapter 11). If launch overhead is an issue (e.g., many tiny kernels), consider merging them with cooperative groups or simply combining their code (e.g., kernel fusion).

Increase GPU utilization

If the GPU is underutilized (e.g., low SM Active, low occupancy), ensure you launch enough work to use all SMs. Specifically, make sure your kernel is launching with a grid size large enough to fully utilize the GPU. A common mistake is launching as many threads as elements but forgetting that each thread does only a little bit of work. Sometimes you need multiple passes or more threads per element.

Reduce synchronizations and host-side (CPU) stalls

You should remove any unnecessary cudaDeviceSynchronize() or host-side waits that stall the GPU. If the workload is inherently small, consider batching it with other work or running multiple instances concurrently (e.g., CUDA streams). You can also use CUDA Graphs (see Chapter 12) to predefine and efficiently launch an execution graph of many small kernels.

Leverage specialized hardware and reduced/mixed precision

Blackwell Tensor Cores expose fifth-generation MMA instructions in PTX as `tcgen05.mma` and associated loads/stores (e.g., `tcgen05.ld` and `tcgen05.st`). Tensor Cores accelerate microscaling formats including MXFP8, MXFP4 (OCP MX formats), and NVIDIA's NVFP4 format. They also support block-scaled matmuls (K-grouped) that libraries select automatically when scale metadata is present. TMEM and TMA underpin these high-throughput data paths. We'll discuss these techniques in more detail later in this chapter and in Chapter 9.

Verify and iterate

After each optimization, reprofile. Confirm the targeted stall or metric improved (e.g., memory stalls reduced after tiling, achieved occupancy went up after tuning block size, "SM Throughput %" increased after using CUDA streams, etc.). Also watch total runtime improvement. Sometimes one bottleneck masks another; you might fix memory bandwidth only to become compute bound next (which is fine—then address that if needed).

Maintain correctness and acceptable accuracy

When using lower-precision or new parallel strategies, test with assertions or comparisons to reference results. Ensure the speedup doesn't come at the cost of accuracy unless that's acceptable for the application. Typically, techniques like FP16 or even FP8 are carefully validated to have negligible accuracy impact on AI models.

Tuning Occupancy

Remember from Chapter 6 that occupancy is the ratio of active warps on the SM to the maximum number of warps that could be active on the SM. Low occupancy (< 50%) means that, on average, half of the possible warps were active. This might indicate that your kernel is limited by resources such as registers or shared memory per thread block—rather than just available parallelism.

Occupancy is the measure of how many threads, or warps, are active on an SM relative to the hardware's maximum capacity. Higher occupancy, or more warps in flight, allows the GPU to better hide latency. This is because when one warp stalls waiting on a memory load, for instance, the scheduler can quickly switch to run another warp.

More warps per SM generally means the GPU's pipelines stay busier, and fewer cycles are wasted waiting on memory. *Occupancy tuning* is the practice of adjusting your kernel launch parameters and resource usage (e.g., registers and shared memory) to maximize useful parallelism on each SM, as shown in Figure 8-6.

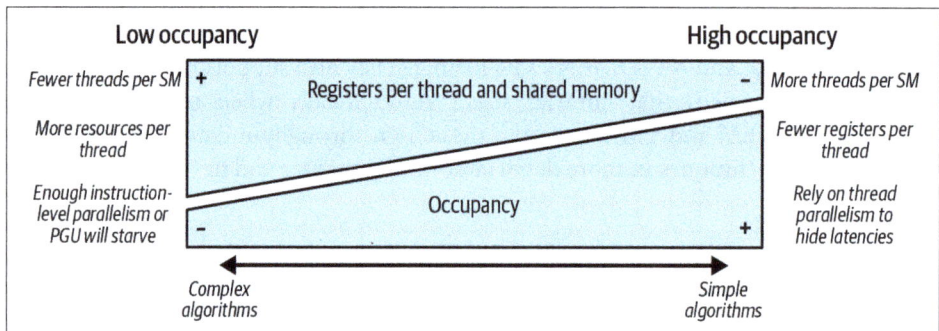

Figure 8-6. Tuning occupancy by balancing resource usage (e.g., registers per thread and shared memory) with parallelism (e.g., number of threads and warps)

Remember that the goal of occupancy tuning is to keep enough warps active to fully utilize the SM's pipelines and hide long-latency operations. In an ideal case, you would achieve 100% occupancy, filling all available warp slots. For instance, there are 64 warp slots, or 2,048 threads, available in each Blackwell B200 (compute capability 10.0) SM.

This per-SM limit of 64 warps has remained the same for modern datacenter GPU architectures like Ampere, Hopper, and Blackwell—even as the overall GPU core counts have increased. The hardware-performance improvements come from more SMs, larger caches, multidie, etc. You can use Nsight Compute's Occupancy analysis to confirm the exact limits on your target device. Interestingly, the NVIDIA RTX PRO 6000 and Spark DGX (GB10 superchip) support a higher compute capability (12.x), but only allow 48 warps (1,536 threads) per SM.

Many real-world kernels still perform well at lower occupancy—especially if their memory or arithmetic latencies are already small. Or if they leverage high-throughput units like Tensor Cores that keep the pipelines busy without needing as many active warps.

For instance, a compute-bound kernel might achieve peak performance with only 50% occupancy because each warp is doing lots of work without waiting. In contrast, a memory-bound kernel often benefits from high occupancy since some warps can run on the SM since other warps are stalled waiting for memory transfers.

Find the Right Occupancy for Your Workload

In practice, effective occupancy tuning often produces diminishing returns after a certain point. If a kernel is severely memory bound, for instance, going from 10% to 50% achieved occupancy might give a huge boost because now you have enough warps to cover latency.

But going from 50% to 100% might give only a small further gain since other factors start to dominate, such as cache misses, memory bandwidth saturation, etc. Profiling helps determine the optimal occupancy. For example, you can evaluate profile metrics such as *eligible warps per cycle* and *active warps per scheduler*. These give insight into how many warps are ready to issue versus how many the hardware could handle.

Eligible warps per cycle reports the average number of warps that are in a "ready-to-run" state each cycle and have no outstanding data or dependency stalls. Active warps per scheduler, often equal to the number of schedulers on the SM, is the maximum number of warps that could issue an instruction per cycle.

If eligible warps per cycle is lower than active warps per scheduler, the GPU often runs out of ready warps. In this case, when one warp stalls on memory or a long-latency instruction, there isn't another ready warp to switch to. This indicates you need more concurrency in the form of higher occupancy or ILP to hide the latency.

In contrast, if eligible warps per cycle meets or exceeds the scheduler limit but your kernel still runs slowly, it means you have enough warps ready, but they cannot issue because of other stalls such as memory-bandwidth saturation or execution dependencies. In this case, it's best to focus on hiding memory latency through better coalescing and asynchronous copies—or increasing ILP by unrolling independent work. This is a better approach than simply adding more threads.

And if you raise occupancy and see the "Stall: Not Selected" or idle percentages drop, and memory pipes are busy more often, you've successfully improved occupancy. If occupancy is high but Long Scoreboard is still dominant, you might need other techniques like improving memory access patterns or overlapping computation.

In practice, once you reach a moderate occupancy (e.g., 60%–70%), the returns will start to diminish. As such, it's often more effective to pursue better memory locality, higher ILP, and the use of on-chip memory like shared memory and registers to cache data.

While maximizing occupancy ensures that many warps are available to run, those warps might still be idle if waiting on memory or if executing divergent code. Therefore, after achieving a reasonable occupancy (e.g., 50%–70%), focus on warp efficiency and latency-hiding rather than obsessing over 100% occupancy.

> Occupancy is a means to an end (hiding latency), not the end goal itself. Once you have enough warps to keep the GPU busy, other optimizations will give better returns.

Techniques for Occupancy Tuning

There are a few straightforward steps to improve occupancy when profiling suggests that it's the limiting factor: increase parallelism by launching more threads, adjust the block size, reduce per-thread resource usage, and use __launch_bounds__ or the occupancy API. Let's discuss each of these here:

Increase parallelism (launch more threads)
> The simplest way to improve occupancy is to launch more work if your current kernel launch isn't already using all SMs. For instance, if you launch only 20 warps per SM and the GPU can support 64, increasing your grid size or threads per block can raise occupancy (assuming enough data to process).

> Be sure to utilize all SMs by launching at least as many blocks as SMs—and often many more since blocks execute in parallel on each SM. If your GPU shows low "SM Active Cycles" because not all SMs have work, scale up the workload or batch size. However, simply using more threads isn't enough—especially if each thread uses a lot of resources such as registers and shared memory.

Adjust block size

Sometimes the number of threads per block, or thread-block size, can limit occupancy. Very large thread blocks (e.g., 1,024 threads) might use so many registers or so much shared memory that only one block can fit on an SM at a time. This results in low occupancy. In contrast, using moderately sized blocks (e.g., 128–256 threads) allows multiple blocks to reside concurrently on one SM, which increases the total number of possible active warps.

The optimal block size can vary by kernel. The key is to balance block size against resource usage. Smaller blocks use fewer resources individually and therefore allow more blocks in parallel.

You can use the built-in Nsight Compute Occupancy Calculator and the CUDA Occupancy API to experiment with different launch configurations to help find a sweet spot that maximizes occupancy without incurring other overheads.

The Occupancy Calculator suggests configurations for maximum theoretical occupancy. However, the best performance in practice might come from an occupancy that is slightly less than this theoretical maximum.

> Always validate the Occupancy Calculator's suggested `best`
> `BlockSize` with actual timing experiments, as sometimes a
> configuration with a bit lower occupancy produces higher
> throughput due to less register spilling or better memory
> coalescing.

Reduce per-thread register and shared-memory usage

Each thread consumes registers—and likely shared memory. If a kernel uses too many registers or shared memory per thread, the compiler must reduce how many threads or warps can be active on an SM. Otherwise, it will exceed the SM's total register file or shared-memory allocation.

To address register usage, you can refactor your code to use fewer live variables, and therefore fewer registers, to free up register capacity. This allows more warps to be resident simultaneously. Similarly, you can pass `-maxrregcount=<N>` to the compiler to cap the number of registers allocated per thread.

When you cap the number of registers per thread, the compiler is forced to fit each thread into fewer registers. This allows the hardware to schedule additional warps on the SM—and therefore raises occupancy.

Of course, if you cap registers too aggressively, the compiler will spill excess variables into local memory, which will hurt performance. As such, you should find the smallest register limit that maximizes occupancy without excessive spilling.

Similarly, if each block uses a large amount of shared memory such as a large tile, shared memory will limit how many blocks fit on an SM. By optimizing the shared memory footprint, storing only what's needed, and using on-chip caches when possible, you can free up capacity for additional blocks. Essentially, you can increase occupancy by using leaner resources per thread/block.

Be mindful, however, that reducing registers or shared memory might degrade single-thread performance if taken too far. It's a trade-off. The profiler's Occupancy limiter readout will tell you if registers or shared memory are the bottleneck. This will help guide your optimization efforts.

For instance, on Blackwell, you may see "Limited by max registers per thread" if you aggressively unroll loops. In this case, consider using fewer unrolled iterations or splitting the work. This is because Blackwell has a 255 register-per-thread limit. The Occupancy report helps quantify these trade-offs.

Use `__launch_bounds__`

In some scenarios, you might deliberately limit occupancy or guide the compiler to optimize for a specific occupancy. CUDA allows you to set launch bounds in the kernel code using the `__launch_bounds__` annotation. This gives a hint to the compiler of the kernel's intended usage pattern and launch configuration.

If you profile and find that performance peaks at an occupancy around 50% rather than 100%, it often means that each thread is using a lot of registers or shared memory. This will further limit occupancy. In such cases, you can guide the compiler using `__launch_bounds__`.

For example, you can use `__launch_bounds__` to limit the threads-per-block and specify a minimum blocks-per-SM to allow more warps to reside on the SM. Essentially, you're telling the compiler to trade some per-thread register/shared-memory resource usage for a higher warp count.

This will improve throughput when your kernel is latency bound because more warps will hide memory latency and dependency stalls. This is opposed to a purely compute-bound kernel, which wouldn't see the same gain from this type of optimization.

Use the CUDA Occupancy API

In addition to the `__launch_bounds__` annotation, CUDA's Occupancy API functions (e.g., `cudaOccupancyMaxPotentialBlockSize()` and `cudaOccupancyMaxActiveBlocksPerMultiprocessor()`) let you determine, at runtime, the block size that produces the highest occupancy given your kernel's actual register and shared-memory demands.

These functions provide recommended values for threads per block and the number of blocks per SM. This way, you don't have to guess which configuration is most efficient. In practice, you might use the Occupancy API to find a candidate block size and then fine-tune it with a `__launch_bounds__` hint to lock in a specific occupancy level.

Another approach is to use CUDA Graphs to launch predefined workloads efficiently once you've determined the optimal configuration. While not directly changing occupancy, CUDA Graphs can reduce per-launch overhead, which is beneficial for occupancy when you increase the number of blocks. We'll cover CUDA Graphs in Chapter 12 and PyTorch's use of CUDA Graphs in Chapters 13 and 14, but it's worth mentioning them in this context.

In short, it's recommended to use a multiphased approach by profiling your system to discover the ideal occupancy range—and then using compiler and runtime hints to achieve the ideal occupancy. The goal is to size your thread blocks efficiently to keep enough warps in flight without over allocating scarce on-chip resources like registers and shared memory. Next, let's take a closer look at tuning occupancy with `__launch_bounds__`, the Occupancy API, and PyTorch.

Compiler Hints to Optimize Occupancy

We can guide the compiler to optimize for occupancy by using CUDA's `__launch_bounds__` kernel annotation. This annotation lets us specify two parameters for a kernel: the maximum number of threads per block that we want to launch (e.g., 256) and the minimum number of thread blocks we want to keep resident on each SM (e.g., 4), as shown here:

```
__global__ __launch_bounds__(256, 8)
void myKernel(...) { /* ... */ }
```

Here, we promise never to launch `myKernel` with more than 256 threads per block. And we request that the GPU tries to keep at least 8 blocks active per SM. These hints influence the compiler's register allocation and inlining decisions.

Specifically, `__launch_bounds__` will limit each thread's register usage such that up to 256 threads can fit in one block—and at least 8 blocks can be active per SM. This is a total of 2,048 threads active per SM (8 blocks × 256 threads per block = 2,048 threads). This fills the thread slots for devices like the B200 with a 2,048-thread per-SM limit (e.g., Blackwell). In practice, `__launch_bounds__` can cause the compiler to cap per-thread register usage and restrict unrolling/inlining. This avoids spilling and allows higher occupancy. As such, we are effectively trading a bit of per-thread performance (e.g., not using every last register or unrolling to the max) in exchange for steadier warp throughput by keeping more warps in flight.

Increased occupancy must be balanced with increased per-thread resources. You want to avoid register spilling by forcing too many threads. This causes slow memory access because they run out of registers and spill to local memory (backed by global HBM.) Finding the sweet spot often requires experimentation. Nsight Compute's "Registers per Thread" and "Occupancy" metrics can guide you here.

Determine Optimal Launch Configuration with the Occupancy API

You can determine an optimal launch configuration at runtime using the CUDA Occupancy API (*https://oreil.ly/ocpdq*), including cudaOccupancyMaxActiveBlocks PerMultiprocessor() and cudaOccupancyMaxPotentialBlockSize(). For instance, cudaOccupancyMaxPotentialBlockSize() will calculate the block size that produces the optimal occupancy for a given kernel, considering its register and shared memory usage as shown here:

```
int minGridSize = 0, bestBlockSize = 0;

cudaOccupancyMaxPotentialBlockSize(
    &minGridSize, &bestBlockSize,
    myKernel,
    /* dynamicSmemBytes = */ 0,
    /* blockSizeLimit = */ 0 );

// bestBlockSize contains number of threads per block that maximizes occupancy
myKernel<<<minGridSize, bestBlockSize>>>(...);
```

This API computes how many threads per block would likely maximize occupancy given the kernel's resource usage. We can then use the suggested bestBlockSize and minGridSize for our kernel launch.

In practice, the compiler's heuristics are usually pretty good. But using __launch_bounds__ and the occupancy API can give you explicit control when needed. Use them when you know your kernel can trade some per-thread resource usage for more active warps. This helps prevent underoccupying SMs due to heavy threads.

Tuning Occupancy with PyTorch

For PyTorch users writing high-level code, you don't usually manage occupancy directly—PyTorch's CUDA kernels and libraries handle launch parameters under the hood. Operations like matrix multiplies, convolutions, etc., are already tuned to use the GPU effectively.

However, understanding occupancy can still be valuable. If you write custom CUDA kernels as PyTorch extensions, the same principles apply: launch enough threads/

blocks to utilize the GPU, choose reasonable block sizes, and avoid using excessive registers or shared memory per thread if it limits occupancy.

Even at the Python level, there are a few things to be mindful of. If you are using PyTorch and notice that your GPU is underutilized (e.g., in a profiling trace you see only a small fraction of SMs active), it could be because of very small tensor operations that don't launch many threads.

Extremely small workloads might not scale well to a large GPU. In such cases, try batching or combining operations so that each launch does more work. PyTorch's graph compiler can fuse certain operations using `torch.compile`. This increases the work per kernel launch—and therefore improves occupancy and efficiency.

Under the hood, `torch.compile` generates fused GPU kernels. It does this by merging many small operations into one larger kernel. Whenever possible, leverage the PyTorch compiler, as it can achieve the efficiency of a manually written CUDA kernel in some cases. Prefer `torch.compile(mode="max-autotune")` for long-running training/inference on stable shapes, or `mode="reduce-overhead"` for small-batch, graph-friendly loops. Both enable CUDA Graphs when profitable. You can also use `mode="max-autotune-no-cudagraphs"` if graphs are undesirable. We dive deep into the PyTorch compiler and its different mode options in Chapters 13 and 14.

It's also worth noting that PyTorch's built-in kernels often use best practices internally. For example, reduction operations and elementwise operations in PyTorch are implemented with launch configurators that pick an optimal block size and number of blocks based on the device and tensor size.

If you ever dig into PyTorch's C++ CUDA code, you'll see logic to cap block sizes and to launch multiple blocks per SM for certain algorithms. This is essentially automated occupancy tuning. To reduce optimizer overhead, enable fused implementations where available. For instance, use `torch.optim.AdamW(..., fused=True)` and pair with automatic mixed-precision (AMP).

The takeaway for PyTorch users is to prefer high-level libraries and operations that are already optimized. This is in preference to writing custom kernels. If you do need custom kernels, apply the same occupancy principles that we discussed.

Now that we see how to keep the GPU busy with enough threads, we next turn to making each warp more efficient. High occupancy means little if each warp is wasting cycles. This leads us to our discussion on warp-level efficiency optimizations, including warp divergence and intrawarp thread cooperation.

Improving Warp Execution Efficiency (Warp Divergence)

Even with plenty of warps available, thanks to good occupancy, each warp's internal efficiency matters. Warp execution efficiency measures the fraction of warp lanes that are active on average. Warp-level inefficiencies arise when threads within a warp do not all do the same work, called *warp divergence*. Another cause is if the threads are waiting on data loads.

Specifically, a low warp execution efficiency value typically shows a high divergent branch count, low predicate efficiency, and possibly a high number of memory-related stalls. This means that the warp threads are idle due to branching divergence caused by if/else statements in the kernel or by data-dependencies.

In this case, you should try to restructure your code to avoid the inefficiencies. To improve warp execution efficiency, you should try to improve memory coalescing, minimize thread divergence, and use warp-level intrinsics for optimal intrawarp (thread-level) communication.

These techniques often produce modest speedups (say, 5%–30%) compared to higher-level algorithmic changes, but they can be crucial in highly optimized code where every cycle counts. They also complement other optimizations in that, after you've optimized occupancy and improved memory access, you can still squeeze out extra performance by ensuring each warp executes as efficiently as possible.

Causes of Warp Divergence

As mentioned in Chapter 7, warp divergence, or branch divergence, occurs when threads in the same warp take different control-flow paths. For example, consider an if/else inside a kernel where some threads in a warp execute the if clause and others execute the else.

In SIMT execution, the warp must execute both paths serially: first, all threads that take the if branch execute while the others in that warp are masked off (idle). Then the threads that took else execute while the first group idles, as shown in Figure 8-7.

During the divergent sections, effectively only half, or some fraction, of the warp is doing useful work. This reduces overall throughput. In the case of a 50/50 split between if and else, the warp's active utilization drops to 50% for that portion of code. If the split is 1 thread versus 31 threads, then 31/32 threads will be idle in one of the subbranches.

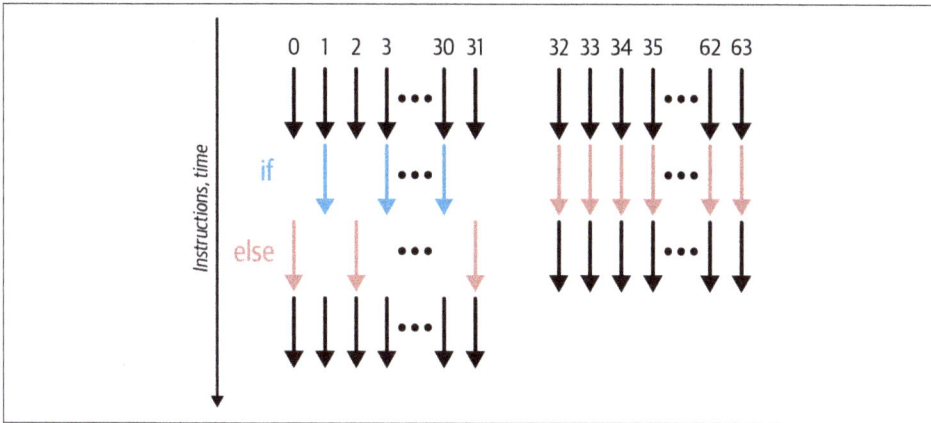

Figure 8-7. Divergent versus nondivergent warp execution

If your kernel contains multiple divergence points or if each divergent branch carries heavier work, removing those branches can compound these gains. In the ideal case (e.g., a 50/50 split branch), removing that divergent branch can nearly double throughput up to ~2× speedup. Eliminating multiple heavy divergence paths can compound these gains.

The overall effect is that warp divergence causes some GPU cores to sit idle. This increases the total instruction count since each branch path is executed serially by different subsets of threads. Therefore, minimizing intrawarp divergence is a key to warp-level efficiency.

Techniques to Avoid Warp Divergence

There are various best practices to minimize warp divergence, including restructuring conditions and separating branches into multiple kernels.

Warp divergence only affects threads within a warp. Threads in different warps do not cause each other to stall.

Additionally, you can use warp-unanimous branches, warp-vote intrinsics, and predication. Let's discuss each of these:

Restructure conditions

Wherever possible, organize your computations so that threads in the same warp follow the same execution path. This might involve moving a divergent condition to a higher level outside of the inner loops—or into a separate kernel launch. You could also sort or group your data so that each warp handles more homogeneous cases.

For instance, if you have an array of values and you want to process negative values differently from nonnegative ones, a naive approach might put an `if(x<0)` inside the kernel that diverges per element. A smarter approach is to partition the data such that one kernel handles all negatives and another kernel handles nonnegatives. By aligning data with warps, you reduce the chance that a single warp has to split its execution.

Separate into multiple kernels

Another approach is to separate the work into multiple kernel launches such that one kernel handles the `if` case and another handles the `else` case. You can use a prefix sum or compaction to distribute threads to the different kernels. This avoids divergence at the cost of launching more kernels and adding logic to distribute data between the kernels. This might be worth it if divergence is a big issue and the divergent sections are large enough in instruction count.

Rewrite conditions to be warp-unanimous

In some cases, you can rewrite a condition to be *warp-unanimous*. This means that either all 32 threads in a warp satisfy the condition or none do. A common trick is to use the warp index in the condition statement. For instance, you first compute a warp ID as `int warpId = threadIdx.x / 32;`. Then half of your warps do task A and the other half do task B. For this, you write: `if (warpId % 2 == 0) { /* Task A */ } else { /* Task B */ }`.

In this case, all threads in a given warp either go into task A or task B together, and there's no warp divergence since one warp executes one branch while another warp executes the other branch. But within a single warp, all threads agree on the branch to execute.

The slight overhead is that every warp still evaluates the branch condition, but since they all agree on it, each warp executes only one of the branches. This technique essentially trades some flexibility—since you're constraining how work is divided—to gain warp coherence.

Use warp-unanimous branches when you can divide work into coarse increments of 32 threads.

Utilize warp-vote parallel algorithms

Warp intrinsics (`__ballot_sync`, `__any_sync`, `__all_sync`), cooperative-groups' `warp.ballot/any/all`, and device-side vote masks (`%WarpVote`) let a warp collectively decide, or vote, which lanes need "special" work. The warp then dynamically delegates, repartitions, and compacts that work into one (or a few) lane(s) instead of diverging all 32 threads. This avoids per-lane branch divergence but introduces some potential load-imbalance trade-offs that you should profile for impact. We will cover warp intrinsics in more detail in a bit.

Predicate short lanes

The CUDA compiler will sometimes *predicate* short conditional code. Predication means that the compiler converts an `if` into a boolean mask for each thread—and executes both paths for all threads. However, it only commits the results appropriate to each thread's path.

Predication avoids divergent branching at the cost of doing extra work per thread. This is beneficial when the branches are very short and divergence is high. As a programmer, you can encourage predication by writing branch-free constructs, including the `?:` ternary operator or bitwise logic tricks for simple conditions. For instance, consider this naive implementation, which uses an if/else statement:

```
if (x > 0)
    y = f(x);
else
    y = g(x);
```

Instead, you could write the following, which computes both `f(x)` and `g(x)` for all threads but multiplies each result by `cond` to select the result that matches the condition:

```
float cond = x > 0 ? 1.0f : 0.0f;
y = cond * f(x) + (1.0f - cond) * g(x);
```

Here, there's no branch, thus no divergence, but we did extra work for each thread since both functions still run, including the one that wasn't needed for a given case. As such, predication is worthwhile only if the extra work is cheaper than the cost of divergence would be.

In practice, you should profile the effects of these optimizations. Specifically, if using predication, check metrics like "predicated-off threads" and overall instruction count. Profilers like Nsight Compute will show if predication is reducing warp stalls—or if it's performing unnecessary work that reduces goodput.

Typically, predication is good for very short, simple branches with just a few instructions each—especially if many warps would diverge due to the given conditions. So if the branch involves a lot of work—or only a handful of threads diverge—predication could actually be worse. Use this technique carefully—and only for small conditional workloads.

> CUDA compilers will often apply simple predication automatically for you, but it's still worth profiling for performance-critical kernels.

In short, minimizing warp divergence requires careful algorithm and data organization. Whenever possible, restructure your problem so that each warp follows a uniform execution path. This might mean splitting the kernel to handle different cases in separate launches, rearranging the data so that each warp processes similar items, or pulling divergent conditions out of inner loops.

When divergence is unavoidable (e.g., tree or graph workloads with inherently varying per-thread work), keep the divergent sections as short and infrequent as possible so that warps reconverge quickly. You can also leverage warp-level intrinsics like `__any_sync`, `__ballot_sync`, and other voting primitives to have threads agree on conditions together. You can also try to compact work into fewer lanes rather than branch all 32.

Profiling and Detecting Warp Divergence

Nsight Compute's Source Counters and Warp State stats will pinpoint issues like divergent warps. You can detect these by looking for high Branch Divergence metric values or poorly coalesced loads that will show many replay or L2 cache miss events.

Nsight Compute can also flag inefficiencies, including shared-memory bank conflicts and Tensor Core pipeline stalls. For example, if your kernel shows a high percentage of `memory_throttle` stalls, it might indicate that there is not enough memory-level parallelism for the GPUs, deep instruction pipelines. You can try increasing the number of independent memory accesses in flight—or use asynchronous copy instructions like `cp.async` and the CUDA Pipeline API (covered in Chapters 9 and 10)—to hide latency.

A profiler will show symptoms of warp divergence in the form of low *warp execution efficiency*. This measures the average percentage of threads in a warp that are active. A warp execution efficiency of 30% means, on average, only 30% of the threads are doing useful work at any time. The rest were inactive due to divergence.

When you profile a kernel with divergent branches, the profiler will flag a high percentage of *predicated-off* instructions. These are instructions that are fetched and issued but do no work because their lane mask is disabled. You'll also see an inflated "dynamic instruction" count compared to the data you actually processed. Together, those two numbers tell you that every warp is walking down all sides of your conditionals in turn and serially.

For instance, one subset of threads, or *lanes*, executes path A while the rest of the threads sit idle. Subsequently, the idle threads become active threads and execute path B. The result is a doubling of your instruction traffic and a serious reduction in your warp's effective throughput, or goodput, since each inactive set of threads still fetches and issues instructions—even though they're masked out.

This is somewhat easy to spot in source code, as any per-thread conditional, whether it's a threshold check, a sparse-data loop, or a data-dependent filter, will trigger this serialized, repeated execution. To reclaim performance, you must eliminate or flatten those divergent branches.

You can make the condition uniform across the warp, pull it out of tight loops, or replace it with arithmetic or lookup-table techniques so that all 32 threads execute the same instruction stream and perform useful work. Let's look at an example to make things clearer.

If you see low warp execution efficiency, inspect your kernel's branches. It may be beneficial to refactor conditional logic into separate kernels or use warp-level primitives (e.g., ballot sync) to handle divergence more efficiently, as we'll cover next.

Using Predication to Minimize Divergence

Let's show an example using predication to profile and eliminate warp divergence and branches. Consider a kernel that thresholds an array using if (x[i] > 0) y[i] = x[i]; else y[i] = 0;.

If half the values are positive and half are not, then most warps will have some threads take the if branch and some take the else branch. The warp will first execute the if branch instructions for the threads when the condition is true. It will simply mask out the other threads. It then runs again and executes the else branch for the remaining threads. So this took two sets of instructions to accomplish one logical set of operations. This decreases efficiency by 50%.

Before example (CUDA C++). In this example, if some threads in a warp satisfy X[i] > threshold and others do not, the warp will diverge. This is a clear example of a kernel that will cause warp branch divergence:

```
// threshold_naive.cu
__global__ void threshold_naive(const float* X, float* Y,
                                float threshold, int N) {
    int i = blockIdx.x * blockDim.x + threadIdx.x;
    if (i < N) {
        if (X[i] > threshold) {
            Y[i] = X[i];      // branch 1
        } else {
            Y[i] = 0.0f;      // branch 2
        }
    }
}
```

This results in executing the warp twice, one after another in serial. One execution will run with the assignment Y[i]=X[i] for one subset of threads, and the other execution will run with Y[i]=0 for the other subset of threads. The warp execution efficiency will be low—approximately 50% if half of the threads take each path.

After example (CUDA C++). Here is a divergence-reduced approach using predication. In this version, we use the ternary operator, which the compiler is likely to translate into a predicated move instruction (SEL/MOV based on condition) rather than an actual branch:

```
// threshold_predicated.cu
__global__ void threshold_predicated(const float* X, float* Y,
                                     float threshold, int N) {
    int i = blockIdx.x * blockDim.x + threadIdx.x;
    if (i < N) {
        float x = X[i];
        // Use a conditional move or multiplication by boolean
        float val = (x > threshold) ? x : 0.0f;
        Y[i] = val;
    }
}
```

In this case, all threads execute the same instruction sequence of computing val, then storing it. This avoids warp divergence because the control flow is uniform across the warp. But threads for which the condition is false will just set val=0. The result is that warp execution efficiency stays high since all threads follow one path.

> In simple cases, the CUDA NVCC compiler likely generated a predicated move for the ternary operator, as expected. In PTX/assembly, you would see the PTX @p predicate syntax to guard the write without splitting into separate warp paths.

After example (PyTorch). In PyTorch, the threshold operation can be done with vectorized operations as follows:

```python
# threshold_op.py
import torch

X = torch.randn(N, device='cuda')
Y = torch.maximum(X, torch.zeros_like(X))  # equivalent to Y = X > 0 ? X : 0
torch.cuda.synchronize()
```

The `torch.maximum` with 0 will execute on the GPU without branching since it uses elementwise max, which is implemented in a vectorized manner. Libraries like PyTorch ensure these elementwise ops are divergence-free at the warp level by using predication or bitwise tricks under the hood:

```python
# jit_threshold_op.py
import torch

# In PyTorch, we can compile and fuse this operation
# for even higher throughput
@torch.compile()
def threshold_op(X):
    return torch.maximum(X, torch.zeros_like(X))

X = torch.randn(N, device='cuda')
Y = threshold_op(X)
torch.cuda.synchronize()
```

> As you will see in Chapters 13 and 14, `torch.compile` uses Torch-Inductor to fuse many pointwise operations into kernels, which better match the performance of the manual CUDA C++ example. However, `torch.compile` does not guarantee optimal occupancy or ILP, so you may still need to profile and tune performance further.

Under the hood, these types of elementwise functions compile down to single-instruction, multiple data (SIMD)-style predication or bitwise select operations on GPUs. This ensures that every thread in a warp follows the same instruction stream and avoids the serialization penalties of divergent control flow.

Overall, reducing warp divergence improves the warp's efficiency and yields substantial speedups in which divergence was a major issue. Table 8-3 shows the results of reducing warp divergence by replacing branches with predicated operations.

Table 8-3. Profiling results of removing warp divergence

Metric	Before	After
Kernel execution time	30 ms	15 ms (−50%)
Dynamic instruction count	600 M instructions	300 M instructions (−50%)
Average warp branch-resolving stall latency	200 cycles	100 cycles (−50%)
Warp execution efficiency	50%	99%
Predicated-off threads (%)	50%	0%

> Note: The numeric values in all metrics tables are illustrative to explain the concepts. For actual benchmark results on different GPU architectures, see the GitHub repository (*https://github.com/cfregly/ai-performance-engineering*).

By replacing the two-path branches with a single predicated max() operation, we saw dramatic improvements across all key Nsight Compute metrics. The kernel execution time measured by gpu__time_elapsed.avg dropped from 30 ms to 15 ms, effectively doubling throughput.

Warp execution efficiency climbed to nearly 100% since all threads in each warp stayed active with useful work. And the profiler further reports a 0% predicated-off ratio, indicating that no lanes were ever masked off under the predicated max() approach. This confirms that nearly all reconvergence overhead has been eliminated.

At the same time, the dynamic instruction count (smsp__inst_executed.sum) dropped by 50% from 600 million to 300 million instructions, since each warp no longer spent cycles executing both sides of the branch serially. The average warp branch-resolving stall latency (smsp__average_warp_latency_issue_stal led_branch_resolving) also halved, from 200 cycles down to 100 cycles.

> If your kernel contains multiple divergence points or if each divergent branch carries heavier work, removing those branches can compound these gains—potentially yielding more than a 2× speedup per branch eliminated.

Note that predication isn't free. Some threads still compute values (e.g., val = x) and their results are never used. If each branch carries substantial work, computing both sides for every thread can actually cost more than a mild divergence.

In simple cases like our threshold example, predication wins, but you should always benchmark. Try both branch-based and predicated versions under Nsight Compute's warp execution efficiency metric. If efficiency is low and each branch is light, predication will likely help.

If a branch is heavy, allowing some divergence—or using a separate kernel—may be the better path. Ultimately, minimizing divergence is crucial for SIMT performance, so structure your algorithms to keep warps on a single path when possible, and isolate any remaining divergent logic into its own kernel or warp-sized region.

> CUDA compilers will often apply simple predication automatically for you, but it's still worth hand-tuning and profiling for performance-critical kernels.

Efficient Intrawarp Communication with Warp Intrinsics

When threads within a warp must share data to compute a reduction/aggregation, for instance, you can use warp shuffle intrinsics, including __shfl_sync and __shfl_down_sync (introduced in Chapter 6) to exchange values directly through registers. This is in contrast to staging them in shared memory and calling __syncthreads(), which negatively impacts performance.

Unlike the shared memory approach that generates extra L1/L2 traffic and requires a full-block barrier, shuffles move data only between registers and implicitly synchronize the 32 lanes in a warp at each instruction. This adds only a few clock cycles of latency.

For a full discussion, including performance comparisons, code examples, and how to implement warp-level reductions or prefix sums, see Chapter 6. If your cooperation spans multiple warps, you must still use block-level or grid-level synchronization (e.g., __syncthreads()) or use cooperative groups (covered in Chapter 10.) But for purely intrawarp communication, shuffles are almost always the fastest choice.

In short, if your algorithm requires threads in the same warp to share intermediate results or coordinate on a computation, reach for __shfl_sync and related warp-level options. Only use block-level shared memory and __syncthreads() if the cooperation truly spans multiple warps.

PyTorch Considerations for Warp-Level Efficiency

At the pure Python level, PyTorch doesn't expose warp intrinsics or allow you to directly control warp-level execution. However, as an end user of PyTorch, you indirectly benefit from these optimizations because many of PyTorch's internal CUDA kernels use warp-level tricks.

For instance, the implementation of torch.sum(x, dim=0), which sums across a dimension of a tensor, will often use warp-level reductions when the dimension being reduced is small (e.g., within 32 elements). In such cases, each warp of threads cooperates using shuffle instructions to produce a partial sum without diverging or using shared memory. This logic is implemented inside the library so that you don't have to implement it yourself.

If you write a custom CUDA kernel as a PyTorch extension, you can—and should—use these warp-level optimizations in your device code when possible. For instance, if your operation requires summing values within a warp or exchanging data between threads, prefer using intrinsics like __shfl_sync over naive shared memory approaches to increase speed and reduce overhead. Also be mindful of warp divergence in any custom CUDA code.

And if you find yourself using if statements per element, you can instead express the condition as a tensor-level operation using torch.where, for instance, on the whole tensor. This allows the library to handle the condition more efficiently—likely in a vectorized and warp-coherent way.

PyTorch's JIT compiler and graph executor, discussed in Chapter 10, can fuse elementwise operations. This increases warp efficiency and arithmetic intensity by doing more work per kernel—and more work per byte of memory moved.

When multiple operations are fused into one kernel, a warp processes more work in a single pass. While kernel fusion can't magically eliminate divergence inherent in the algorithm, it does mean that each warp does more useful work. As such, any divergence overhead is amortized over more computations.

For example, if you have a rectified linear unit (ReLU) operation followed by an abs() operation, a fused kernel could handle both in one pass. So even if there's a branch, it's handling the two operations together per warp.

As a CUDA programmer, you should avoid intrawarp divergence and use warp intrinsics for any collective operations within a warp. This ensures all 32 threads in the warp stay busy doing useful work in parallel.

As a PyTorch user, be aware that the library is already doing this for you under the hood. Your role is to write your computations in a way that allows these optimizations to be utilized. For instance, use built-in tensor operations (optimized with CUDA C++) instead of writing explicit Python loops with per-element conditionals. If you are using custom CUDA extensions, apply the same best practices we've discussed.

Each warp's 32 lanes working in unison is the ideal. By minimizing divergence and using fast intrinsics for any needed communication, you ensure warp execution efficiency. These techniques often yield a modest, but meaningful, speedup—perhaps a 1.1× to 1.3× improvement. This can be significant in a tight kernel.

These optimizations also set the stage for instruction-level parallelism, which allows each thread to do more useful work. Let's cover this next.

Exposing Instruction-Level Parallelism

As we saw in the occupancy discussion, running many warps concurrently lets the SM's scheduler switch away from any warp that stalls on a long-latency operation such as a global-memory load. In addition to launching enough threads, we can also exploit ILP within each warp so that a single warp does not need to wait for one instruction to complete before issuing the next.

You can rearrange or unroll your code so that each thread issues multiple independent operations (e.g., memory loads and arithmetic instructions) before consuming their results. This way, the GPU keeps its execution units busy while earlier instructions are still pending.

Leveraging ILP allows a single warp to issue certain independent instructions back-to-back, which improves latency hiding. For instance, a thread might load data and then perform unrelated arithmetic while waiting for that load to complete. Figure 8-8 shows an example of multiple instructions overlapping during each cycle.

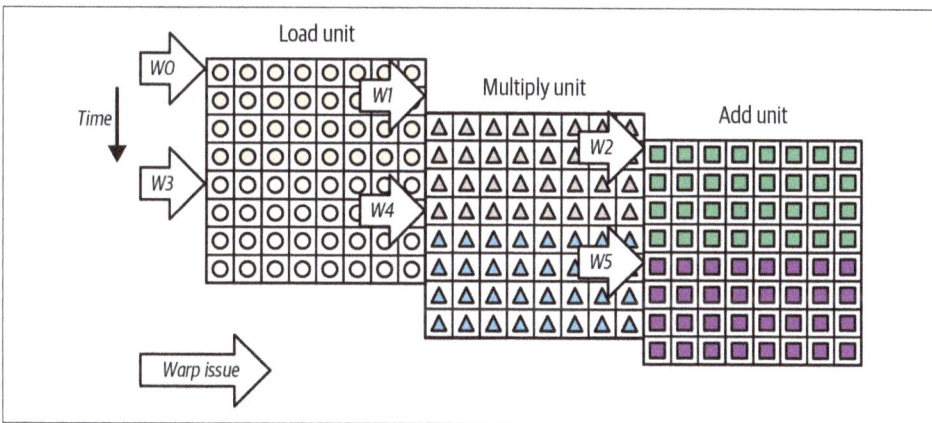

Figure 8-8. Overlapping with ILP

By unrolling your loop body, you turn what was once "load → multiply → store" each iteration into a sequence that loads and multiplies multiple elements before looping back. For example, instead of:

```
for (int i = 0; i < N; ++i) {

    float ai = a[i];      // load
    float bi = b[i];      // load
    sum += ai * bi;       // multiply after both loads complete
}
```

You can unroll such that each loop iteration issues two independent multiply operations instead of one, as shown in the next code block. This gives the hardware an opportunity to execute the second multiply while the first multiply is still in progress—or while it's waiting for its operands to load from memory.

This properly overlaps and hides latency. The result is a higher instructions-per-cycle (IPC) and better latency hiding as shown below by computing the two multiplies, `ai0*bi0` and `ai1*bi1`, in parallel:

```
for (int i = 0; i + 1 < N; i += 2) {
    float ai0 = a[i];        // load a[i]
    float bi0 = b[i];        // load b[i]
    float ai1 = a[i + 1];    // load a[i+1]
    float bi1 = b[i + 1];    // load b[i+1]
    sum += ai0 * bi0 + ai1 * bi1;
}
```

Here, we're loading pairs of values (`a[i]`, `b[i]` and `a[i+1]`, `b[i+1]`) before doing any multiplies. Unrolling exposes two independent multiply instructions per loop iteration. This way, the GPU can overlap those arithmetic operations and hide the latency of each operand load.

ILP does not directly change arithmetic intensity (FLOPS per byte). However, it raises overall throughput (FLOPS) by overlapping compute with memory or compute-to-compute dependencies. We explicitly unroll to increase independent work per thread and help dual-issue. In other words, ILP boosts throughput by time-multiplexing independent work—not by doing extra work.

A common misconception is that increasing ILP will perform more operations. However, it doesn't—it just keeps the GPU's multiple functional units busy. ILP helps only if your program has idle issue slots due to latency. If your kernel is already fully utilizing the execution units on every cycle (e.g., a tight compute-bound loop with no stalls), increasing ILP won't actually increase performance.

To encourage the compiler to increase, or expose, ILP, you can use `#pragma unroll` on short loops or tune `-maxrregcount` to allow the compiler to allocate more registers for holding intermediate values. This explicitly acknowledges that you want the compiler to increase register usage and potentially reduce occupancy.

In this way, ILP complements occupancy. High occupancy ensures there are many warps to switch to when one stalls, and ILP makes sure that a single warp can issue as many independent instructions as possible to fill the pipeline and hide latency. This is much like superscalar and out-of-order execution in CPUs, except it's directed explicitly by the compiler's scheduling of your CUDA code.

Warp Scheduling and Dual Issue Instructions

Each SM contains multiple warp schedulers. For example, Blackwell SMs have four warp schedulers. Each scheduler can issue up to two independent instructions per cycle, as shown in Figure 8-9.

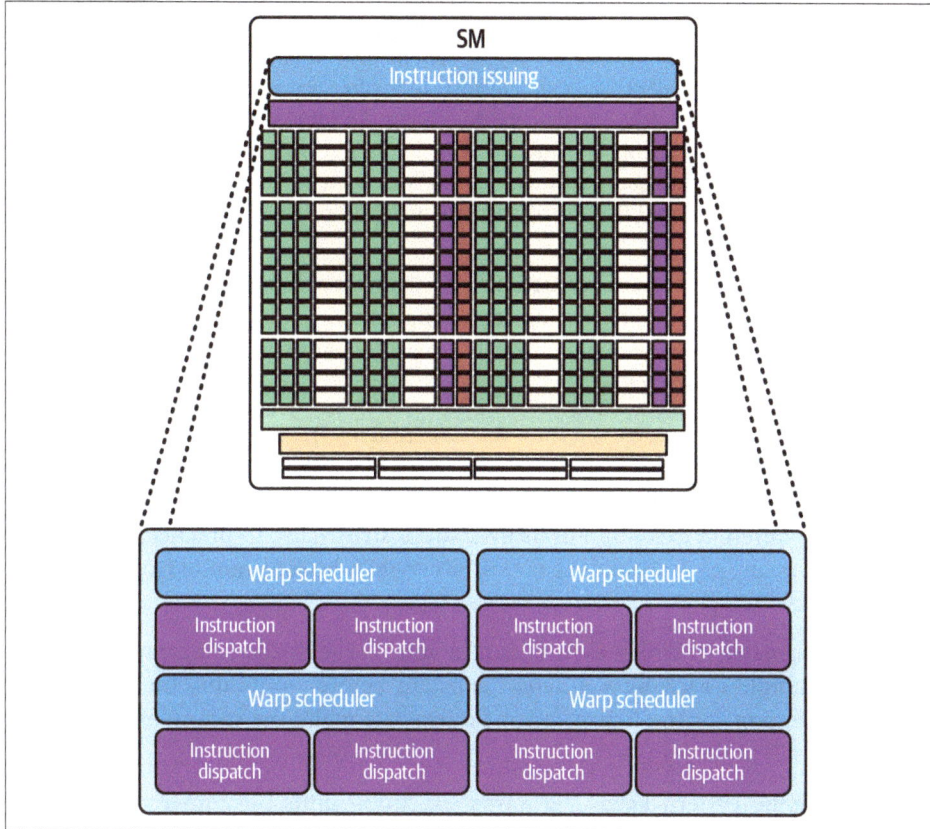

Figure 8-9. Each warp scheduler can dispatch up to two instructions per cycle called "dual issue"

In practice, this means that a single warp can overlap multiple independent operations across successive cycles—and sometimes even in the same cycle if they target different pipelines such as one math, one memory, or one special-function unit (SFU) pipeline. This means that multiple instructions can be in flight and progressing through the pipeline simultaneously. This overlap is the ILP that we discussed earlier.

On Blackwell, the FP32 and INT32 pipelines have been merged into a single set of unified CUDA cores. As such, they can only execute either FP32 or INT32 instructions in a given cycle—not both at once. Each core must pick one data type each cycle. As a result, any ILP that depended on dual-issuing an INT and an FP in the same cycle will no longer work since Blackwell must choose one or the other per cycle on each core. As such, mixed INT32 and FP32 instruction streams no longer benefit from dual issue on a single core. Mixed streams should instead exploit warp/SM concurrency —and not rely on per-core dual issue. As such, you should prefer dual issue with two independent math and memory instructions (or two independent math instructions such as FP32 and FP16) in flight using ILP. This will increase instruction-issue efficiency.

ILP does not require that two instructions physically fire in the same cycle. Instead, it makes sure that while one instruction (e.g., long-latency global memory load) is still pending, the warp can immediately issue another independent instruction (e.g., arithmetic operation) on the next cycle.

As a result of this overlap, by the time the data returns from memory, the arithmetic work has already made progress. This effectively hides the load's latency. On Blackwell, multiple instructions can be in flight per warp due to pipelining, and the schedulers issue to different execution units over successive cycles. In practice, ILP appears as a steady stream of independent issues rather than a fixed number of concurrent instructions per warp.

Consider a scenario in which each thread in your kernel loads two array elements— and then multiplies each by a different constant before combining the results. The multiply operation for the first element can execute while the second element's load operation is still underway.

This overlapping pattern keeps the warps' execution units busy instead of waiting. This raises overall throughput without changing how many loads and multiplies occur per element. Here is a concrete example of increasing ILP:

```
// Launch configuration: e.g., 256 threads per block, enough blocks to cover N
__global__ void independentOps(const float *a, const float *b,
                               float *out, int N) {
    int i = blockIdx.x * blockDim.x + threadIdx.x;
    if (i < N) {
        float x = a[i];
        float y = b[i];
        // Two independent operations (no dependency between u and v):
        float u = x * x;
        float v = y * y;
        // Dependent operation that uses both results:
        float sum = u + v;
        out[i] = sqrtf(sum);
```

```
      }
   }
```

In this kernel, each thread loads two values x and y from different arrays and computes two results u and v. The calculations of u = x*x and v = y*y are independent of each other since neither uses the result of the other.

Structuring the code this way, instead of sum = x*x + y*y, gives the compiler an opportunity to arrange the instruction sequence to expose ILP and increase performance. Specifically, it can issue the instruction for u = x*x, then in the next cycle issue v = y*y before u has finished.

While the first multiplication is running—or waiting for a pipeline slot—the second one can run in parallel in another arithmetic unit. By the time it needs to do sum = u + v, likely both multiplications have been completed. The warp thus had multiple instructions in flight, which helps to hide the latency of those two multiply operations.

In contrast, consider the code here in which v's computation was placed after using u. In this scenario, we'd create an unnecessary dependency chain that limits ILP:

```
float u = x * x;
float temp = u + 1.0f;    // some dependent use of u
float v = y * y;
...
```

The kernel computes u = x * x and immediately uses that result to form temp = u + 1.0f. Only *after* computing temp do you issue v = y * y, which does not depend on u or temp. Therefore, its placement after temp forces the GPU to wait until the u + 1.0f instruction finishes before it can issue the multiply for v.

In effect, you create a serial dependency chain: first x * x → u, then u + 1.0f → temp, and only then y * y → v. During the time the hardware is executing (or waiting for) the u + 1.0f operation, it cannot begin y * y even though v is mathematically independent. This ordering artificially limits instruction-level parallelism because one independent multiply must park itself behind a dependent instruction.

By contrast, consider the following reordered and optimized code:

```
// Optimized ordering with better ILP:

float u = x * x;     // Independent multiply on x
float v = y * y;     // Independent multiply on y (issues immediately after u)
float temp = u + 1.0f; // Only now use u
// ... use v or temp as needed ...
```

Here, we reordered the code such that both x * x and y * y occur back-to-back (i.e., float u = x * x; float v = y * y; float temp = u + 1.0f;). In this case, the GPU can issue the two independent multiplies in successive cycles without waiting for the u + 1.0f add to finish.

This means that while the result of x * x may still be lingering in a "pending" pipeline slot, the hardware can already start executing y * y. Only once both of those multiplies have calculated their results does the GPU perform temp = u + 1.0f.

In other words, you now have two multiplies in flight at once. This fills the execution units and hides latency. This improved ILP, issuing v = y * y as soon as possible, makes sure that the multiply on y overlaps with both the multiply on x and the later add—instead of being forced to wait. Consequently, the warp spends fewer cycles idle, which translates directly into higher throughput.

GPUs rely on the compiler, and sometimes the programmer's hints, to schedule independent instructions. On modern CUDA compilers, simple patterns like the preceding are usually detected and scheduled optimally. But you can encourage ILP by structuring your code appropriately or using pragma compiler directives.

This example is simple, but it demonstrates the idea that you should not serialize independent work within a thread if you can help it. If a thread needs to load two arrays and do math on both, doing them in parallel, or interleaving them, is better than doing one after the other in a serial manner.

ILP and Occupancy

On modern GPUs, the maximum resident warps per SM is 64 warps, or 2,048 threads (2,048 threads = 32 threads per warp × 64 warps). The warp schedulers can issue multiple instructions per cycle when dependencies permit. The INT32 and FP32 cores are unified and operate as either FP32 or INT32 in a given clock rather than both at once. The register file per SM is 256 KB, which is 64K 32-bit registers. This large register file is important for sustaining ILP without spilling, as we'll see in a bit.

If you write a kernel with little to no ILP such that each thread issues exactly one operation at a time, you typically need on the order of 1,536 active threads (~48 warps, or 75% occupancy) to saturate the SM's execution units (these are not hard limits but rather approximations).

By contrast, exposing even a modest amount of ILP can significantly lower the number of threads required. Table 8-4 summarizes how ILP reduces the threads/occupancy needed to saturate a Blackwell SM at different ILP values.

Table 8-4. How ILP reduces the threads/occupancy needed to saturate a Blackwell SM

ILP (independent ops/thread)	Threads/SM for ~100% utilization	Occupancy (% of 2,048 threads)
1 (no ILP)	~1,536 threads (48 warps)	75%
2	~1,024 threads (32 warps)	50%
3	~768 threads (24 warps)	37.5%
4	~512 threads (16 warps)	25%

Here, two-way ILP, in which each thread issues two independent operations back-to-back, often achieves full throughput with roughly 1,024 active threads (≈32 warps, or 50% occupancy). This is because each warp keeps two operations in flight whenever one is still pending.

Three-way ILP, on the other hand, can saturate with about 768 threads (≈24 warps, or 37.5% occupancy). A four-way ILP may need only 512 threads (≈16 warps, or 25% occupancy) to fill the pipelines. This is because each warp itself does the work of four independent operations.

> More in-flight operations per thread lets each warp keep the math pipelines busy—even at lower thread counts.

Clearly, increasing ILP lets you achieve peak compute throughput with fewer warps. This is especially valuable when your workload cannot launch huge numbers of threads—or when you want to free up on-chip resources for other tasks.

It's important to note that there is a practical limit on how much ILP you can expose. Even though Blackwell SMs can keep many instructions in flight per warp, each warp can hold only a finite number of pending instructions.

On top of that, the compiler must schedule independent instructions without exceeding the available registers or overwhelming the GPU's instruction decode bandwidth. The decode bandwidth is the maximum number of instructions per cycle that the instruction-fetch and decode hardware can push to execution units. Once you hit those limits, adding more independent operations produces diminishing returns.

Once you have enough independent work to keep the issue slots and memory system busy, there is little practical benefit in increasing ILP further. Pushing to five-way or six-way ILP produces little gain and can even hurt performance due to the extra register pressure and instruction overhead.

On Blackwell, the ideal ILP configuration is often between two and four independent operations per thread. At this point, its schedulers and caches are typically saturated. However, the exact point is kernel and workload dependent. Use Nsight Compute issue and stall metrics to decide where to stop.

Loop Unrolling, Interleaving, and Compiler Hinting

To exploit ILP in your own kernels, look for opportunities in which each thread issues multiple independent arithmetic or memory instructions before any one result is needed. Common patterns include the following:

Unrolling small loops

Unrolling loops allows each thread to perform N accumulations (e.g., 2× or 4×) with separate accumulator registers. For example, consider the following loop:

```
float sum = 0.0f;
for (int k = 0; k < 4; ++k) {
    float a = A[idx * 4 + k];
    sum += a * w[k];  // dependent on load a
}
```

You can rewrite this to take advantage of ILP, as shown next. This transformation creates four independent load-multiply pairs—one per a0..a3—that can be issued in rapid succession:

```
float a0 = A[idx * 4 + 0];
float a1 = A[idx * 4 + 1];
float a2 = A[idx * 4 + 2];
float a3 = A[idx * 4 + 3];
float sum0 = a0 * w[0];
float sum1 = a1 * w[1];
float sum2 = a2 * w[2];
float sum3 = a3 * w[3];
float sum = sum0 + sum1 + sum2 + sum3;
```

Here, all four loads are issued first. As each load completes, its corresponding multiply can execute and overlap subsequent loads with computations to hide the latency of the memory load. In other words, the GPU interleaves these operations such that while one pair is waiting on memory, another pair can be multiplying. This increases ILP and hides latency.

Interleaving independent operations

You can interleave operations that use different data elements, as shown here:

```
float x = A[idx];
float y = B[idx];
// If you wrote float u = x * c; then float v = y * d;,
// the multiplies are independent.
```

```
float u = x * c;  // can start as soon as x is ready
float v = y * d;  // can start as soon as y is ready, overlapping with u
```

Here, you keep the execution units busy on every cycle by not letting one dependent instruction block the next independent instruction, etc. In this interleaved code, u = x*c and v = y*d are independent instructions and can be executed concurrently. The compiler will schedule them back-to-back such that one multiply can proceed while the other multiply is still completing. This is ILP in action.

Using compiler hints

Compiler hints such as `#pragma unroll` on small loops can help the compiler explicitly create multiple arithmetic chains. If needed, you can adjust `-maxrregcount` to allow the compiler to use more registers per thread for the unrolled variables. By allowing more resources per thread, you are increasing ILP at the cost of fewer threads. This naturally trades off some occupancy for higher ILP.

In short, to hide latency and maximize throughput on Blackwell's deep pipelines, you should combine high occupancy (e.g., enough warps/threads to hide stalls) with high ILP (e.g., multiple independent instructions per thread). Here, you make sure that even when one instruction is waiting (e.g., memory load or long-latency arithmetic), the warp can issue other instructions immediately. This will significantly increase the kernel's achieved FLOPS.

> On large unrolls, watch instruction-fetch and issue stalls in Nsight Compute. Excessive unrolling can bloat code size—or saturate decode and dispatch—without further throughput gains.

Profiling and Mitigating Register Pressure

However, be mindful of register pressure since ILP typically requires more registers to hold multiple independent values and results. If you unroll too much—or add too many parallel computations—you might increase register usage to the point that occupancy falls significantly. As always, finding the right balance is key.

The CUDA compiler does a good job of unrolling loops automatically. But if you push ILP too far by manually unrolling too many iterations using `#pragma unroll`, for instance, you may notice that occupancy drops.

In this case, Nsight Compute will show "Limited by Registers" within its Occupancy analysis. This is usually a clear signal that you've gone too far. If you see this, you should dial back the unrolling, reduce the number of independent accumulator variables, or relax your launch bounds.

Specifically, you can reduce the required `MinBlocksPerSM` or increase `MaxThreadsPer Block` so that each block can use more registers without spilling. In other words, allow a bit lower occupancy to avoid severe spilling. This way the register pressure eases and occupancy is recovered.

From a profiling perspective, if ILP is helping, you should see the "Stall: Exec Dependency" percentage drop since warps are spending less time waiting on prior instructions. And you should see higher instructions per cycle.

Nsight Compute reports an *Issue Efficiency* or *IPC* metric. This should rise as ILP increases. For example, you should see the issue efficiency or instructions-per-cycle metric rise as you increase ILP. For example, if you see the IPC metric increase from 1.0 to 1.8 per warp scheduler when you unroll, this indicates that the warp is now issuing close to two instructions per cycle on average instead of just one. However, the actual values depend on the instruction mix and the architecture scheduling constraints.

You might also see that you can achieve good performance at lower occupancy than before. The ideal scenario is that you have enough ILP to keep each warp busy—and enough warps to keep the SM busy. Between those two, you're covering latency both within and across warps.

At this point, we've tackled warp-level parallelism and instruction-level parallelism. These are two ways to keep the GPU's computational units busy. Next, we turn to measuring and improving arithmetic intensity. This is about maximizing the useful work done per memory access.

Key Takeaways

In this chapter, you saw how to uncover and eliminate GPU kernel bottlenecks by moving work from slow global memory into faster on-chip resources and compute units. By following a cycle of profiling, diagnosing, optimizing, and reprofiling, you can transform kernels from underutilized or memory-bound into compute-saturated, high-throughput routines. These techniques will help utilize the full power of your GPUs:

Profiling with Nsight and `torch.profiler`
    Start with Nsight Systems to visualize end-to-end timelines and reveal CPU-GPU gaps, kernel overlaps, and NVTX spans. Then drill into individual kernels with Nsight Compute's stall metrics, roofline analysis, and occupancy reports. In PyTorch code, you can insert profiler instrumentation (using the `torch.pro filer` API, built on the Kineto library) to map Python-level operations directly to GPU activities. Remember that the PyTorch profiler's `with_flops` estimates are formula-based on a limited set of operators. It does not read GPU hardware counters. For hardware counters, use Nsight Compute on the kernels of interest.

Tuning occupancy to hide latency

Adequate warps per SM are essential to cover memory and instruction latencies. You can reduce per-thread register/shared-memory usage through code refactoring or compiler hints. You should also choose block sizes (e.g., 128–256 threads) that fit the SM resources. Doing these will increase your kernel's achieved occupancy to an optimal range—around 50%–75%—and stop underutilization (e.g., ~32-48 warps on Blackwell).

Minimizing warp divergence for SIMT efficiency

Because warps execute in lockstep, any branch divergence means masked lanes sit idle. Restructure kernels so that all threads in a warp follow the same path. Use predicated operations like ternary math and `torch.maximum`—or employ warp-vote intrinsics to compact active lanes. This will boost warp execution efficiency and reduce serialized execution.

Recognizing performance regimes

Every kernel falls into one of four buckets: underutilized, latency bound, memory bound, or compute bound. This is based on FLOPS, bandwidth usage, and stall reasons. Understanding which regime applies will help direct the exact optimization strategy. For instance, a high Long Scoreboard stall means the workload is latency bound.

Exposing ILP

By unrolling loops, breaking dependency chains, and prefetching data, you expose instruction-level parallelism so that each thread can issue multiple independent operations per cycle. This lets two- or four-way ILP reduce the warps needed to fill an SM in half—reducing execution-dependency stalls, raising IPC, and decreasing the "Stall: Exec Dependency" metric. Always profile different ILP depths alongside thread counts to find your kernel's sweet spot.

Iterative optimization and validation

After each change, including occupancy tweaks, ILP restructuring, tiling, or precision scaling, you should reprofile to confirm reduced memory stalls, fewer execution dependencies, and higher achieved occupancy or FLOPS. Always compare results to a FP32 baseline using asserts or numeric checks to guard against unacceptable accuracy regressions when lowering precision.

Conclusion

You saw how effectively tuning GPU performance requires an iterative workflow. First, measure with profilers. Then identify your primary bottlenecks (compute, memory, interconnects, etc.). Last, apply the right optimizations and repeat.

While each new GPU architecture brings improvements in compute and memory bandwidth, they also add complexity. You must constantly stay on top of these innovations in order to sustain peak performance.

We covered how to tune occupancy, avoid warp divergence, and increase ILP. You also saw how to use profilers to correlate CPU, kernel, and NVLink traffic across GPUs. Then we went into Nsight Compute for per-kernel details.

In the next chapters, we'll extend this foundation by focusing on kernel-level efficiency to increase arithmetic intensity. To do this you will fully utilize the GPUs hardware-optimized resources such as Tensor Cores for compute, TMEM to service the Tensor Cores, and TMA for data transfers. TMA remains the preferred method for bulk copies from global to shared on modern GPUs that support it. Let's continue pushing toward the hardware's peak performance limits!

## CHAPTER 9

Increasing CUDA Kernel Efficiency and Arithmetic Intensity

Even if you fully hide latency with massive parallelism and high ILP, a kernel's performance may still be limited by how much useful work it does per memory access. *Arithmetic intensity*, also called *operational intensity*, measures how many floating-point operations are performed per byte of data transferred from memory, or FLOPS per byte.

Newer GPU generations are advancing compute throughput well beyond memory bandwidth. This widening gap means that increasing arithmetic intensity is even more critical than ever. Higher arithmetic intensity indicates a kernel does more computation for each byte fetched, which is essential for fully utilizing the GPU's computational capabilities.

Arithmetic intensity is a key metric in the Roofline performance model. The Roofline model is a useful visual tool that plots kernel performance (FLOPs/sec) against arithmetic intensity (FLOPs/byte). It shows hardware ceilings (roofs) for memory bandwidth and compute throughput, allowing us to see if a kernel is memory bound, performance limited by memory transfers, or compute bound, performance limited by ALU throughput.

In practice, you can generate roofline charts using tools like Nsight Compute, which includes a Roofline analysis view. Using these tools, you can verify if your kernel is initially memory bound or compute bound—then continue to profile and verify improvements as you make optimizations.

The goal is to push the kernel toward the compute-bound regime and leverage the GPUs increasing computational power. A Roofline performance model can properly guide your optimizations toward that goal.

As shown in a previous chapter, a roofline chart uses one horizontal line to represent the hardware's peak compute throughput (the roof)—and a diagonal line from the origin represents the peak achievable throughput limited by memory bandwidth. A kernel's arithmetic intensity determines where it falls on the x-axis, and its performance can be compared against these ceilings, as shown in Figure 9-1.

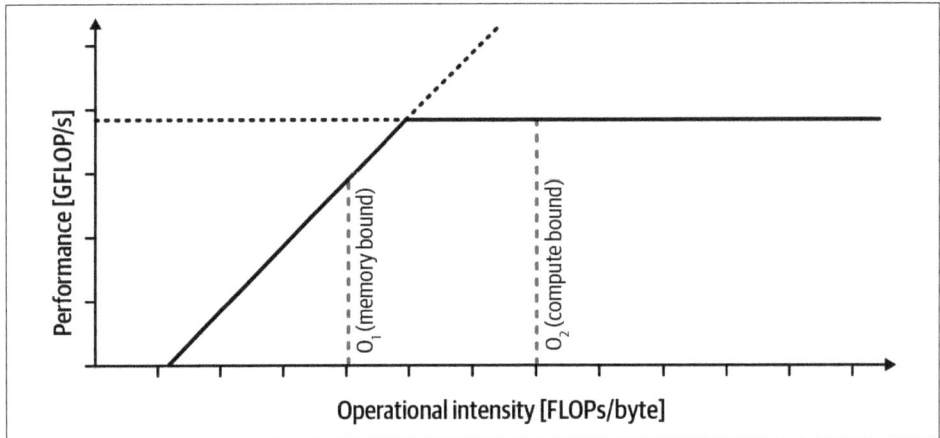

Figure 9-1. Example Roofline model (GFLOP/s versus arithmetic intensity in FLOPs/byte

A kernel with low arithmetic intensity, or few math operations per byte of data moved, will be memory bound. In this case, the kernel's speed is capped by the hardware's memory bandwidth, because the GPU spends most of its time waiting for data rather than crunching numbers.

Conversely, a kernel with very high arithmetic intensity, or many FLOPs per byte moved, will be compute bound because it is utilizing the ALUs and Tensor Cores near their peak capabilities. In this case, the kernel's memory bandwidth usage is a secondary concern.

The goal is always to increase arithmetic intensity where possible by doing more computational work for each byte of data transferred to and from global memory (FLOPs per byte). You can increase arithmetic intensity using techniques like loop tiling to reuse data, using on-chip L1/shared memory for reuse, and fusing multiple kernels into one so that intermediate results don't get written to global memory.

> Modern compiler frameworks such as PyTorch's TorchInductor automatically do some of these optimizations to keep computations on the GPU, reduce off-chip memory traffic, and increase effective arithmetic intensity. However, as a developer, you may still need to manually combine these techniques or write custom CUDA kernels to ensure that data is reused optimally before being evicted from caches, for instance.

You can also use lower-precision data types (FP16, FP8, FP4) to reduce the amount of memory transfers—and utilize Tensor Cores to increase FLOPs per second. Together, these will increase the FLOPs per byte ratio and increase arithmetic intensity. Next, let's discuss some of these techniques.

Keep in mind that not every workload can easily increase its arithmetic intensity. It's constrained by algorithm characteristics. However, you should look for any opportunity to improve the algorithm, reuse data, fuse operations, and increase batch sizes to raise arithmetic intensity without changing the algorithm's result (e.g., accuracy).

Multilevel Microtiling and Software Prefetching

As discussed in Chapter 7, tiling (aka *chunking* or *blocking*) and data reuse are an effective way to raise arithmetic intensity. In that chapter, we showed how loading a small submatrix (tile) of A and B into shared memory lets each byte fetched from global memory be used for many multiply-accumulate operations at static random-access memory (SRAM) speed.

Whenever you restructure code so that each element is loaded once and used tens or hundreds of times, like in the case of tiling, you multiply your FLOPs per byte ratio by the reuse factor. For instance, in a typical matrix multiply, a 32×32 tile of A and B produces 1,024 (1,024 = 32 × 32) independent multiplies for each element in shared memory. As such, the arithmetic intensity rises compared to fetching each element directly from DRAM for every operation.

Beyond simple shared-memory tiling, you can further increase intensity and expose more ILP with multilevel tiling. With multilevel tiling, after staging a tile into shared memory, you have each thread load microtiles into registers using vectorized types such as `float4` and `<half2>`. This way, repeated operations happen entirely in registers. An example of multilevel tiling is shown in Figure 9-2.

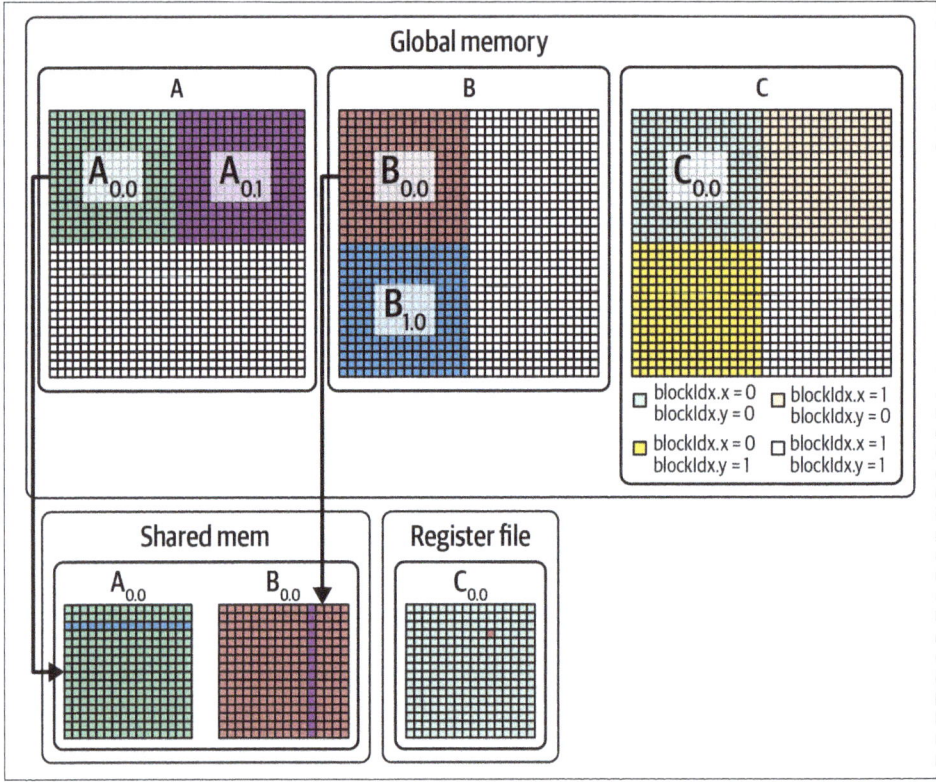

Figure 9-2. Multilevel tiling between global memory (DRAM), shared memory (SMEM), and registers

This intra-SM reuse (register → SMEM → DRAM) reduces the working set at every level—and minimizes off-chip traffic. As always, be sure to coalesce global reads when filling shared memory and pad/swizzle shared data to avoid memory-bank conflicts, as we covered in Chapter 7.

On modern GPUs, these inner-loop tiling steps are often covered by using MMA fragment APIs. The hardware moves data between shared memory and Tensor Memory (TMEM) implicitly using Tensor Core instructions. TMEM usage is managed by the compiler and libraries. On modern GPUs, `tcgen05` instructions implicitly stage data between shared memory and TMEM. They use a distinct TMEM address space. However, developers can still manually move tiles into shared memory with `cp.async` or TMA when implementing certain algorithms and need explicit control.

A closely related technique is software prefetching, which is often implemented as double buffering. For instance, instead of waiting until the current tile's computations finish, you can issue asynchronous loads for the next tile into shared memory. This will overlap DRAM → shared-memory (SMEM) transfers with ongoing arithmetic. Careful prefetching can significantly reduce stall time and improve throughput. The idea is to overlap data transfer with computation so the ALUs never starve waiting for data.

When using unified memory with a CPU-GPU superchip like Grace Blackwell, you can use `cudaMemPrefetchAsync()` to hint that a tile will be needed soon. This hints at the runtime to migrate pages over NVLink-C2C. However, prefetch is just a hint and not a guarantee. You still want to make sure you are overlapping transfers and synchronizing appropriately to avoid page fault stalls. Overlapping data movement with compute in this way ensures the ALUs remain fed whenever a new tile is needed. This further hides memory latency—and boosts achieved FLOPS.

> Unified memory eases development but may not produce the best performance. Expert users often prefer explicit `cudaMemcpy` or pinned memory allocations to fully avoid page migration overheads.

In short, the more times that each byte from DRAM is reused at the on-chip levels (registers or shared memory), the higher your arithmetic intensity. And higher arithmetic intensity moves the kernel closer into the compute-bound regime.

Tiling with Thread Block Clusters

On modern GPUs, you can extend the tiling-reuse idea using CUDA thread-block clusters from Cooperative Groups (discussed in Chapter 10). These allow multiple thread blocks to share data using distributed shared memory (DSMEM), as shown in Figure 9-3.

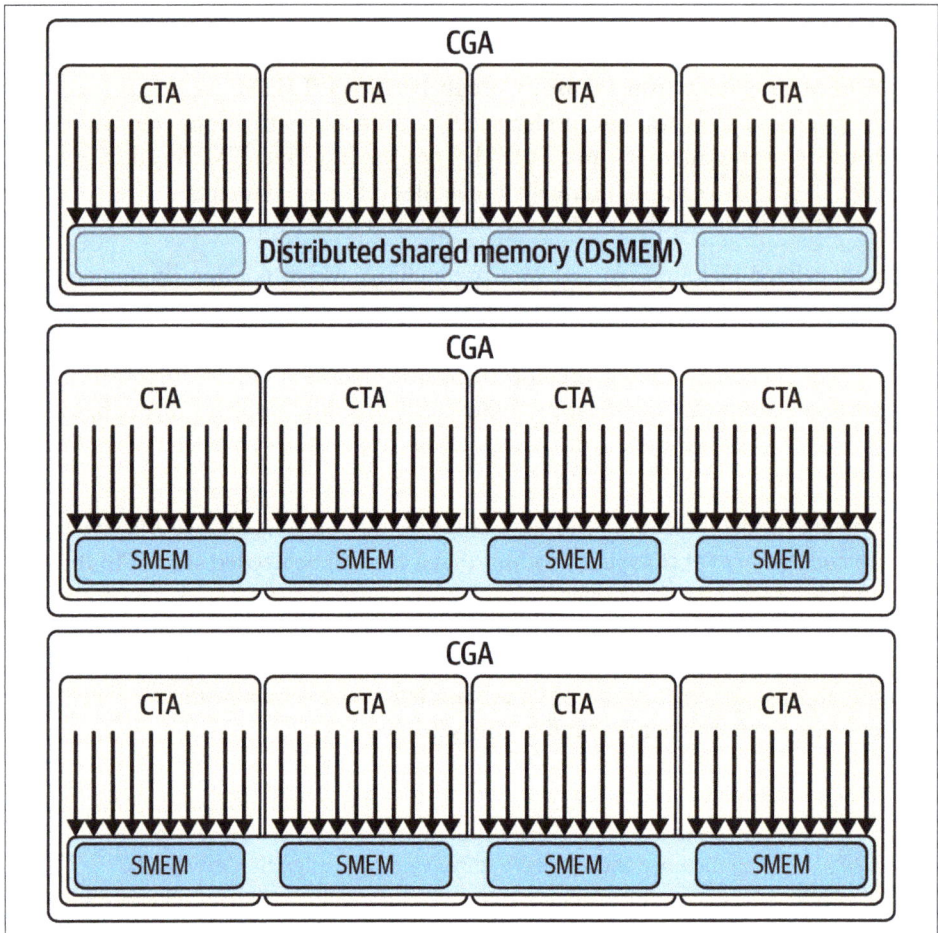

Figure 9-3. DSMEM shared by CTAs (thread blocks) within a CGA

We cover CGAs and thread block clusters in detail in the next chapter, but they're worth mentioning here, as they can directly increase arithmetic intensity. For example, a cluster of four thread blocks can cooperatively load one tile using the Tensor Memory Accelerator (TMA) multicast feature, as shown in Figure 9-4, which uses four CTAs to demonstrate this mechanism.

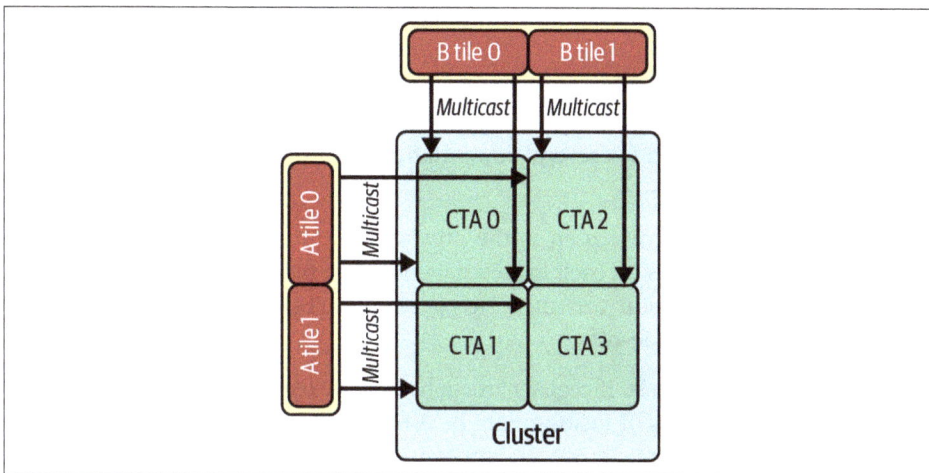

Figure 9-4. For these four (2 × 2) thread block clusters, each tile of A and B is loaded into four CTAs (thread blocks) simultaneously using multicast (source: https://oreil.ly/ EEO_O)

Each tile is partitioned across the four thread blocks so that global memory traffic for that tile is amortized over the cluster. The tiles are fetched only once and reused by all four thread blocks.

Thread block clusters can reduce global memory traffic by up to 4× in a 2 × 2 cluster when four CTAs reuse the same data using multicast. Also, thread block clusters increase arithmetic intensity per GPU by lowering the denominator, or number of bytes moved from global memory. A specialized form of these called *thread block pairs* will be discussed in a bit—in the context of tiling with Tensor Cores.

> Blackwell supports thread block clusters up to 16 thread blocks when you opt into a nonportable cluster size beyond the default portable limit of 8 CTAs. To enable this, set the `cudaFunc AttributeNonPortableClusterSizeAllowed` attribute on the kernel. Larger clusters can raise reuse but may reduce occupancy, so profile before enabling 16. This can support even larger multi-SM tiles, which maximizes data reuse (16×) and increases arithmetic intensity by a similar factor.

Kernel Fusion

Another way to increase arithmetic intensity is to fuse multiple operations—or loop iterations—into one operation. By fusing together multiple kernels, the data loaded from memory can be used for several computations and iterations before being written back.

Similarly, loop unrolling, discussed in the previous section, allows a single thread to perform more calculations on each loaded data element, but at the cost of more register usage. Too much fusion can increase per-thread register pressure and reduce occupancy, so there's a trade-off.

Always profile fused kernels. If register usage becomes excessive and starts spilling to local memory, the benefits of fusion might be offset by the additional memory traffic. If you find the right balance, however, you can improve the FLOPS per byte moved, and this is beneficial if memory bandwidth is a limiting factor.

Modern deep learning frameworks can automatically fuse and unroll through their just-in-time compilers and graph optimizers. For instance, PyTorch's `torch.compile`, and specifically TorchInductor, can automatically fuse sequences of elementwise operations. We cover the PyTorch compiler in Chapters 13 and 14.

> *Elementwise operations*, also called *pointwise operations*, apply a simple computation independently to each element of a tensor.

Fusing these elementwise operations eliminates unnecessary memory traffic by keeping intermediate values on-chip. This increases the amount of work done per byte fetched from global memory—raising the arithmetic intensity.

For instance, the naive implementation launches two kernels. The first kernel reads x and writes y to global memory. The second reads y and writes z:

```
y = sin(x);
z = sqrt(y);
```

Here, each element is touched twice: once after `sin(x)` and once after `sqrt(y)`. As such, each kernel's arithmetic intensity is very low, since it performs just one expensive math function (a multicycle ALU instruction) per element—per load/store operation. In contrast, the fused kernel performs this same set of operations in a single pass:

```
z[i] = sqrt(sin(x[i]));
```

Each x[i] is loaded once, then both sin and sqrt are applied in registers, and only the final z[i] is written to memory. Because the intermediate y never goes out to global memory, the effective FLOPS per byte jump sharply, moving the operation closer to the compute roof.

> As a rule of thumb, if data will be read more than once by threads in the same thread block, it's often worth staging the data into shared memory to eliminate redundant global loads. This will help lift your kernel out of the memory-bound regime and into the compute-bound regime to better utilize the ample GPU FLOPS.

Fusion reduces global memory traffic and increases arithmetic intensity since each element now undergoes two math operations for each read and write memory operation. In our example, we doubled the FLOPS per element (sin + sqrt) while roughly halving the memory traffic since there is no intermediate write. This produces a significantly higher arithmetic intensity, or FLOPS/byte.

To drive this point home, let's demonstrate arithmetic intensity with a concrete example. Suppose we want to L2-normalize each length-hidden row of a 2D tensor x (shape [batch, hidden]). For each row b, compute a single norm, norm_b = sqrt(Σ_i x[b,i]*x[b,i] + ε), and then write y[b,i] = x[b,i] / norm_b for all i.

A naive implementation would square in one kernel, reduce each row to a scalar in a second kernel, and divide in a third kernel. This would require multiple kernel launches with intermediate writes to HBM.

Let's assume that each of the 4 kernels requires 1 FLOP of compute. As such, the arithmetic intensity of each of the 4 kernels is 1 FLOP per 12 bytes (2 float reads, 1 float write), or 0.083 FLOPS/byte.

Instead, we can fuse the 4 kernels into a single kernel and increase the arithmetic intensity. The manually fused kernel code is shown here:

```
__global__ void fusedL2Norm(const float* __restrict__ x,
                            float* __restrict__ y,
                            int hidden) {
  extern __shared__ float sdata[];      // reduction buffer
  const int batch    = blockIdx.x;      // one block per batch row
  const int tid      = threadIdx.x;
  const float* batch_ptr = x + size_t(batch) * hidden;

  // 1) Accumulate sum of squares into shared memory
  float local = 0.f;
  for (int i = tid; i < hidden; i += blockDim.x) {
    float v = batch_ptr[i];
    local   = fmaf(v, v, local);        // v*v + local
  }
  sdata[tid] = local;
```

```
__syncthreads();

// 2) Parallel reduction to sdata[0]
for (int offset = blockDim.x >> 1; offset > 0; offset >>= 1) {
  if (tid < offset) sdata[tid] += sdata[tid + offset];
  __syncthreads();
}

// 3) Normalize (guard tiny norms)
float norm = sqrtf(sdata[0]);
float inv = rsqrtf(sdata[0]); // prefer inverse

float* out_batch = y + size_t(batch) * hidden;
for (int i = tid; i < hidden; i += blockDim.x) {
  // multiply by inverse (rsqrt) vs. divide by sqrt
  out_batch[i] = batch_ptr[i] * inv;
}
}
```

In this fused kernel, each thread walks its slice of x[b,*] twice—once to accumulate a local sum of squares and once to write the normalized outputs—so global traffic is ~12 bytes per element (two reads + one write). Per element the kernel does ~1 multiply + 1 add during the reduction and 1 multiply during the normalize.

The sqrt and rsqrt are amortized over the whole row. For roofline placement, a conservative arithmetic intensity is ≈3 FLOPs / 12 bytes ≈ 0.25 FLOPs/byte (plus the tiny 1/(hidden * 12) contribution from the per-row sqrt). This lets us hide sqrt and rsqrt latency by giving each thread multiple elements to increase ILP.

Additionally, as shown in the previous code, we compute the inverse sqrt (rsqrtf) and multiply instead of dividing. This is a common micro-optimization—especially for hot inner loops. The idea is to replace a slow division instruction stream for a high-throughput multiply instruction stream. We are also trading a sqrtf with a cheaper rsqrtf approximation. These are micro-optimizations because overall, this pipeline is memory-bound and not compute-bound—but it's interesting to highlight. There is yet another optimization not shown here. It involves doing one rsqrtf/sqrtf in a single thread within the thread block and broadcasting the scalar result to the other threads using shared memory. This has more impact on improving performance. Please see the book's GitHub repo (*https://github.com/cfregly/ai-performance-engineering*) for more details on this optimization.

Compared to a naive three-kernel pipeline (square → reduce → divide) with intermediate writes to HBM, the fused version removes at least one global write/read round trip and one launch barrier. As such, its intensity and runtime are much better in practice—even though the per-element FLOP/byte is only ~0.25. This is due to latency savings and cache locality improvements.

In practice, this single fused kernel executes faster than a series of separate kernels due to higher arithmetic intensity (FLOPS/byte), better cache locality, and reduced launch overhead by collapsing three separate kernels into one.

Fusing not only increases arithmetic intensity and pushes the kernel more toward the compute-bound side of the roofline, but it also saves memory bandwidth. In the naive, multikernel version, we have to write intermediate results to global memory and read them back in the next kernel. In the fused version, the intermediate results (e.g., `ai*ai`) never have to leave the thread's registers.

In the code example, the addition can use those registers directly to calculate the sum. The `sqrt` can then use the sum—all without requiring additional global memory traffic. Only the final result is written back to global memory.

As such, the fused kernel achieves perhaps 4 FLOPS for 12 bytes of data movement from/to global memory, whereas the naive, unfused approach achieves 4 FLOPS for 36 bytes loaded and stored after accounting for the intermediate memory movement. This means less DRAM traffic and lower latency.

This simple example shows how fusion increases our kernel's arithmetic intensity and overall performance. Let's look at another way to increase arithmetic intensity by utilizing our GPUs' Tensor Core hardware units.

> State-of-the-art GPU kernels achieve higher arithmetic intensity using vertical fusion, which combines sequential operations on the same data—as well as horizontal fusion, which combines parallel operations across data. Libraries like NVIDIA's CUTLASS or OpenAI's Triton (integrated into PyTorch's compiler backend, TorchInductor) can help you implement these different types of fused kernels very efficiently using Tensor Cores, TMEM, TMA, etc.

Structured Sparsity

On modern GPUs, 2:4 structured sparsity is accelerated in hardware by Sparse Tensor Cores and cuSPARSELt. 2:4 means that exactly two out of every four consecutive weights are nonzero. Creating this type of sparsity is sometimes called *pruning*.

By pruning half of the weights into a 2:4 pattern, each memory load now delivers twice as many nonzero values that actually participate in multiplication. In other words, you are no longer fetching weights that turn out to be zero. As such, you are not wasting a matrix multiply operation on something that you know is zero, as shown in Figure 9-5.

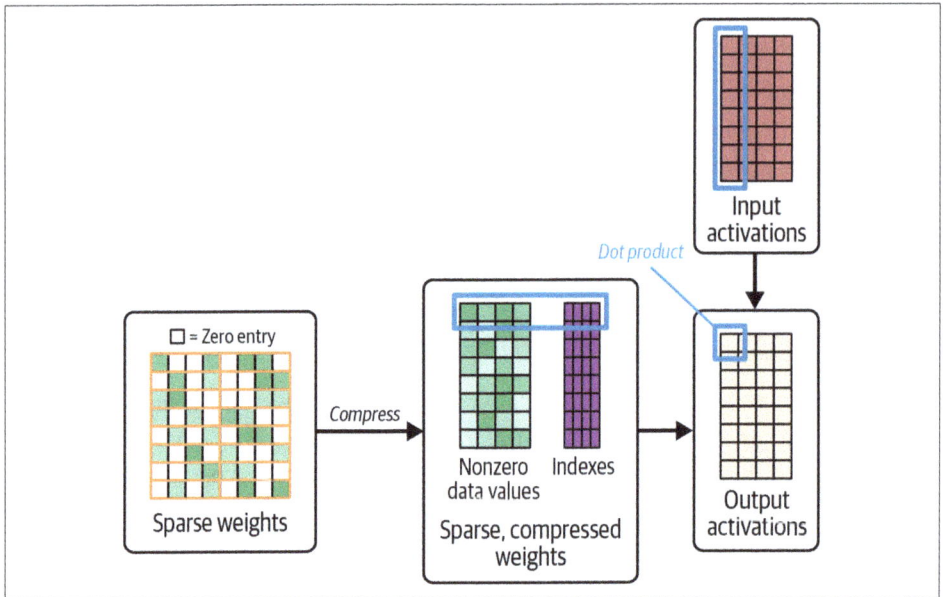

Figure 9-5. 2:4 structured sparsity

Structured sparsity is applied after a model is trained. The model is pruned and optimized for inference. Pruning and format conversion are done in software stacks such as cuSPARSELt and framework tooling. Note that the Transformer Engine accelerates supported sparse executions but does not enforce sparsity during conversion.

Pruning and format conversion are handled in software—typically through cuSPARSELt and framework tooling. In PyTorch, use `to_sparse_semi_structured()` to convert trained dense modules into 2:4 sparse format before deploying sparse GEMMs on Sparse Tensor Cores.

Once your model is converted, it will invoke optimized sparse GEMM kernels running on the Sparse Tensor Cores instead of standard kernels. Sparse Tensor Cores can approach up to a 2× speedup over their dense counterparts for many inference workloads—especially when submitting large batches of inputs, as these amortize kernel launch overhead.

> Batching is a very common and practical way to increase arithmetic intensity. Instead of processing one item at a time—with all of the associated memory I/O, etc.—you process multiple items in one pass so that memory access (e.g., loading weights, etc.) is amortized over multiple computations.

This gives the sparse-accelerated matrix multiplies enough parallel work to hide any overhead from handling indices or compressed representations. In smaller batches, this overhead can dominate and limit how much speedup you observe.

2:4 sparsity will produce maximum benefit when using large matrix multiplies, which are common in transformer-based models like LLMs. This is because the hardware can fully utilize the dedicated Sparse Tensor Cores. These Sparse Tensor Cores operate on half-width data directly in hardware. This skips zeros and performs twice the work on the nonzero elements in the same cycle budget.

Because compute capacity on Blackwell has grown faster than HBM bandwidth, structured sparsity is a great way to stay compute bound. Even on a Grace Blackwell system in which NVLink-C2C lets the GPU stream data from CPU memory at very high throughput, you still want to maximize FLOPS per byte on every loaded tile.

By pruning 50% of weights in a 2:4 pattern, for instance, you ensure that half of your memory traffic is never needed. This immediately reduces global-memory reads and raises effective arithmetic intensity by almost 2×.

NVIDIA GPUs implement this 2:4 structured sparsity in hardware such that every 16-element chunk can zero out 8 elements. This is the pattern used to double Tensor Core throughput for sparse matrices. As of this writing, no other arbitrary sparsity pattern gains this special acceleration in hardware.

> The speedups from sparsity assume that the model's accuracy is maintained. In practice, it's important to fine-tune or carefully calibrate after pruning. This way, you can minimize accuracy loss.

Before applying sparsity, it is important to first implement the fundamental optimizations covered previously: coalesce all global loads, reuse data using tiling, and fuse pointwise operations to eliminate extra memory round trips. Once these basics are in place and verified, structured sparsity can provide another speedup for inference.

> Structured sparsity typically applies to inference workloads. During training, gradients do not benefit from 2:4 sparsity. In addition, maintaining sparsity in gradient updates is complex. As such, it's recommended to use it for deployment scenarios in which you've prepruned and calibrated the model. NVIDIA's 2:4 sparse Tensor Core feature is primarily used for inference. Training support is limited and model-dependent and framework-dependent. Verify support in your software stack before relying on it.

Recomputation Versus Memory Trade-Off

Also, instead of storing or loading precomputed values (e.g., x^2), consider recomputing them on demand if memory bandwidth is the bottleneck. For instance, repeatedly computing x*x in registers is often faster than loading a previously computed x^2 from global memory. Continuous recomputation of cheap expressions can increase arithmetic intensity and is a useful technique whenever memory is scarce.

Many LLM inference engines use this technique to save memory. Instead of storing large activation tensors in HBM and reading them back later, they can recompute certain layers and activations on the fly. This is similar to *activation checkpointing* in a model training context.

Recomputation improves effective FLOPS/byte and can fit large models into a smaller amount of memory. In addition, recomputation frees up memory for larger batch sizes and trades a few extra FLOPS for a significant decrease in memory traffic.

PyTorch and Arithmetic Intensity

In PyTorch, many of these ideas are automatically applied. As mentioned, PyTorch compiler (discussed in Chapters 13 and 14) can automatically fuse chains of element-wise operations—and even some reductions. It uses execution-graph-level optimizations to keep data on the GPU and reuse it as much as possible.

Because it uses optimized libraries like cuDNN and cuBLAS under the hood, PyTorch will perform tiling and use shared memory for you when performing matrix operations with `torch.matmul`. In addition, PyTorch's `scaled_dot_product_attention` (SPDA) may dispatch to FlashAttention, memory-efficient, or cuDNN backends depending on tensor shapes and `dtypes`. To control the backend selection, use `torch.nn.attention.sdpa_kernel(SDPBackend.FLASH_ATTENTION)`, for instance. As a performance-minded developer, you should be aware of these optimizations and how to verify when they're being used.

It's important to note that while PyTorch can recognize and compile most operations, some nonstandard operations or custom CUDA operations might not get fused. In these cases, manual optimization may still be required, such as fusion, tiling, etc.

> If you're writing PyTorch code, prefer fused operations and optimized library calls that perform multiple computations rather than long sequences of individual kernel launches. In practice, this means using high-level operations like `torch.nn.functional` activations or `torch.matmul` instead of writing many small element-wise kernels in Python. These libraries call efficient kernels for these types of high-level operations. And the compiler knows how to fuse them efficiently with surrounding operations.

PyTorch's nested tensors (*https://oreil.ly/ecX61*), or ragged tensors, let you represent batches of variable-length inputs without padding. Each nested tensor packs the variable-length sequences into a single, efficient underlying buffer. `NestedTensor` exposes the normal tensor interface, but it eliminates unnecessary zero-padding. As such, global-memory loads become more efficient because each byte that is fetched is useful in the computation.

Nested tensors are useful for LLMs with varying-length sequences. When using nested tensors, operations like attention and batch-matrix multiplies will retrieve only the essential data from memory. This moves your kernel closer to the compute-bound regime on the Roofline model and helps to reduce memory-bound stalls. The result is higher sustained throughput—especially on memory-sensitive workloads.

> In practice, nested tensors require careful validation for operator coverage and performance characteristics. Support is workload dependent, and speedups are shape dependent. You can verify end-to-end benefits with representative sequence length distributions and attention patterns. Profile both memory traffic and kernel time.

In short, PyTorch exposes various mechanisms to increase your kernel's arithmetic intensity. It's important to understand these options and decide what works best for your workload. Another effective method to increase arithmetic intensity on modern GPUs is by using the reduced-precision Tensor Cores. Let's cover these mechanisms next.

Mixed Precision and Utilizing Tensor Cores

Modern NVIDIA GPUs implement reduced-precision computations like TF32, FP16, FP8, FP4, and INT8 in Tensor Cores. Each SM in Blackwell has a 256 KB on-chip TMEM dedicated to Tensor Core data. It also has a specialized TMA unit that asynchronously copies tiles between global memory and shared memory. Tensor Core instructions (e.g., `tcgen05.mma`) then move operands and accumulators between shared memory and TMEM implicitly. This design feeds the Tensor Cores at high throughput and minimizes stalls. Blackwell's TMEM-based accumulators help to reduce register pressure relative to previous GPU generations which accumulated directly in registers.

When used correctly, these features can transform a once memory-bound, tensor-heavy kernel into a fully compute-bound one by raising arithmetic intensity (FLOPS per byte) by 2×, 4×, or even 8×. You can verify the impact by monitoring the Roofline chart and Stall Stats in Nsight Compute.

Nsight Compute's *Speed of Light* analysis shows memory-bound stall reasons such as "Memory Throttle" and cache misses. These will drop significantly when using Tensor Cores with lower precision formats. And Nsight Compute integrates a Roofline chart to cross-check if arithmetic intensity increased to push your kernel toward the compute roof.

As you move from FP32 to lower-precision Tensor Core kernels such as TF32, FP16, FP8, or FP4, Nsight Compute's Warp Stall metrics typically show a reduction in memory-related stall as well as a relative increase in dependency or pipeline stalls. This indicates an increase in arithmetic intensity and a shift from memory-bound toward compute-bound execution.

Feeding Tensor Cores with TMEM and TMA

At the heart of high-throughput tensor computation is TMEM, a 256 KB SRAM buffer per SM. At a high level, programmers do not explicitly allocate or manage TMEM, however. TMEM is handled by the hardware or libraries when you use Tensor Core operations. TMEM is shown in Figure 9-6.

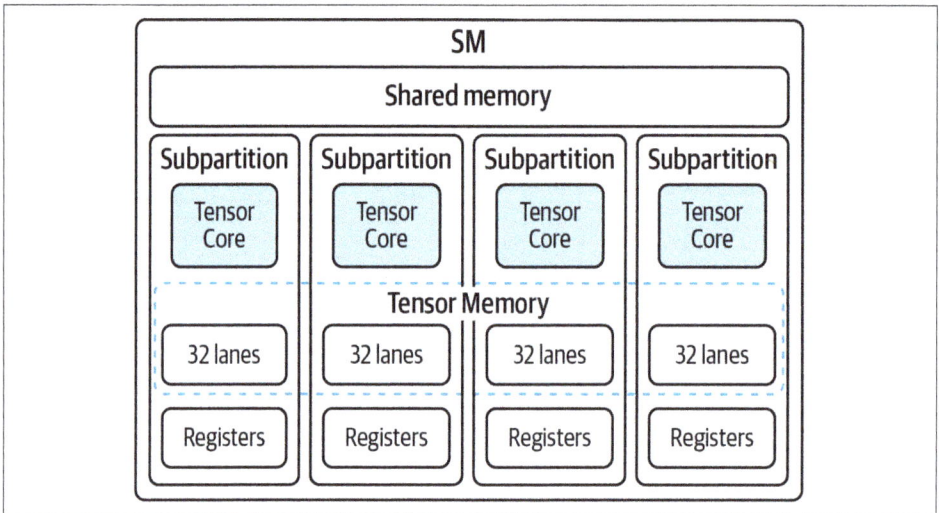

Figure 9-6. TMEM supports the Tensor Cores by accumulating partial results (instead of registers)

Under the hood, Blackwell uses `tcgen05.mma` instructions that operate with TMEM for operand and accumulator storage. CUTLASS and library kernels manage the required allocation and usage through the kernel configuration and Parallel Thread Execution (PTX) assembly. As such, the Transformer Engine uses TMEM for partial results. This reduces the MMA dependencies on registers.

High-level APIs like CUTLASS handle all of this complexity for you automatically. Use CUTLASS and other high-level libraries when possible as CUTLASS uses the `tcgen05.*` PTX instructions, which implement the Tensor Core matrix operations and memory load/store interfaces. Whenever you launch a Tensor Core MMA operation using CUDA MMA intrinsics or a CUTLASS GEMM, the implementation manages operand movement through shared memory and TMEM. TMA streams tiles between global memory and shared memory, and Tensor Core instructions move operands between shared memory and TMEM implicitly.

> Nsight Compute includes a built-in roofline and speed-of-light analysis to confirm whether your kernel shifted from memory bound to compute bound after adopting low-precision Tensor Core paths.

Tensor Core instructions then move operands between shared memory and TMEM as part of the MMA pipeline. This happens behind the scenes and without explicit user code. This way, the data is staged where the Tensor Cores need it. To perform this data transfer from global memory into shared memory, use TMA or `cuda::mem cpy_async` with a pipeline from the CUDA Pipeline API (`<cuda/pipeline>`.) In code, implementing a simple two-stage pipeline with `cuda::memcpy_async` and the CUDA Pipeline API looks like the following:

```
# two_stage_pipeline.cu

#include <cuda/pipeline>
#include <cooperative_groups.h>
namespace cg = cooperative_groups;

extern "C" __global__
void stage_ab_tiles(const float* __restrict__ globalA,
                    const float* __restrict__ globalB,
                    float* __restrict__ outC,
                    int tile_elems,
                    int num_tiles) {
    // Alignment / size guards for vectorized copies (runtime parameter)
    assert((tile_elems % (32 * 4)) == 0 &&
           "tile_elems must be multiple of 128 for float4 vectorization");
    // If you cannot guarantee 16B alignment or sizes, handle
    // the tail/ragged edges with a fallback 4B loop.
    extern __shared__ float smem[];
    auto block = cg::this_thread_block();

    // Shared buffers for double buffering of A and B
    float* A0 = smem + 0 * tile_elems;
    float* A1 = smem + 1 * tile_elems;
    float* B0 = smem + 2 * tile_elems;
    float* B1 = smem + 3 * tile_elems;
```

```
constexpr auto scope = cuda::thread_scope_block;
constexpr int stages = 2;
__shared__ cuda::pipeline_shared_state<scope, stages> pstate;
auto pipe = cuda::make_pipeline(block, &pstate);

// Prime the pipeline with tile 0
pipe.producer_acquire();
cuda::memcpy_async(block, A0, globalA + 0 * tile_elems,
                   cuda::aligned_size_t<32>{tile_elems * sizeof(float)}, pipe);
cuda::memcpy_async(block, B0, globalB + 0 * tile_elems,
                   cuda::aligned_size_t<32>{tile_elems * sizeof(float)}, pipe);
pipe.producer_commit();

for (int t = 1; t < num_tiles; ++t) {
  // Stage the next A and B tiles
  pipe.producer_acquire();
  cuda::memcpy_async(block, (t & 1) ? A1 : A0,
                     globalA + t * tile_elems,
                     cuda::aligned_size_t<32>{tile_elems*sizeof(float)}, pipe);
  cuda::memcpy_async(block, (t & 1) ? B1 : B0,
                     globalB + t * tile_elems,
                     cuda::aligned_size_t<32>{tile_elems*sizeof(float)}, pipe);
  pipe.producer_commit();

  // Consume the previously staged tiles
  pipe.consumer_wait();
  float* prevA = (t & 1) ? A0 : A1;
  float* prevB = (t & 1) ? B0 : B1;
  // Perform compute using prevA and prevB
  pipe.consumer_release();
}

// Consume the final staged tiles
pipe.consumer_wait();
int last = (num_tiles - 1) & 1;
float* lastA = last ? A1 : A0;
float* lastB = last ? B1 : B0;
// Perform compute using lastA and lastB
pipe.consumer_release();
}
```

When launching this kernel, set the dynamic shared memory size to 4 x tile_elems x sizeof(float) to allocate A0, A1, B0, and B1 in shared memory. This double buffering pattern ensures that as soon as one tile is resident in shared memory, Tensor Cores can begin processing it. Meanwhile cuda::memcpy_async fetches the next tile into shared memory in parallel. Because TMEM provides an on-chip data buffer for Tensor Core instructions and shared memory provides the staging space, you can stage and reuse FP16, FP8, or FP4 tiles entirely on chip. The result is fewer stalls when the pipeline is tuned and the tiles and copies are sized appropriately. cuda::memcpy_async can overlap transfers from HBM to shared memory and keep the kernel busy. This helps hide memory latency behind computation.

TF32 and Automatic Mixed Precision (PyTorch)

While Tensor Cores were originally designed for FP16, they also support TF32, which sits between FP32 and FP16. TF32 uses an 8-bit exponent like FP32 and a 10-bit mantissa like FP16. TF32 executes on Tensor Cores at substantially higher through-put than FP32 on CUDA cores while preserving FP32's exponent range. In PyTorch, enabling TF32 is as simple as setting the following in your PyTorch code:

```
import torch
torch.set_float32_matmul_precision('high') # {'highest'|'high'|'medium'}
```

Once these flags are set, high-level operations such as `torch.matmul` and `torch.nn.Linear` automatically execute as TF32 Tensor Core kernels rather than in FP32 on standard CUDA cores.

Beyond TF32, PyTorch's automatic mixed precision (AMP) can choose the optimal precision (FP16 or BF16) for each operation and accumulate the results in FP32 for stability. BF16 helps avoid FP16's overflow issues. By default, CUDA `autocast` uses float-16. Simply pass `dtype=torch.bfloat16` to opt into BF16 on GPUs that support it. For instance, you can wrap your model code in a context manager, as shown here:

```
with torch.amp.autocast("cuda", dtype=torch.bfloat16):
    output = model(input)
```

Under the hood, TorchInductor (covered in Chapters 13 and 14) fuses these precision conversions automatically to ensure the following: large GEMM operations run on Tensor Cores in FP16 or TF32, accumulation remains in FP32 for numeric stability, small "sensitive" kernels like layer normalization and softmax run in FP32, and `GradScaler` prevents underflow during training with FP16. Note that BF16 has FP32 exponent range. As such, `GradScaler` typically isn't needed when training with BF16.

In PyTorch, these mixed-precision decisions are integrated into the compiler so you get optimal `dtype` selection (e.g., FP16/FP8 for compute, FP32 for accumulations) without requiring manual intervention. This is shown in Figure 9-7 as a mixed-precision matrix multiply-accumulate (MMA).

This automatic mixed-precision pipeline maximizes arithmetic intensity with minimal code changes. The fused Tensor Core kernels minimize round trips to HBM by staging and reusing data in shared memory (e.g., operands) and TMEM (e.g., accumulators).

| FP16 storage/input | Full-precision product | Sum with FP32 accumulator | Convert to FP32 result |

More products

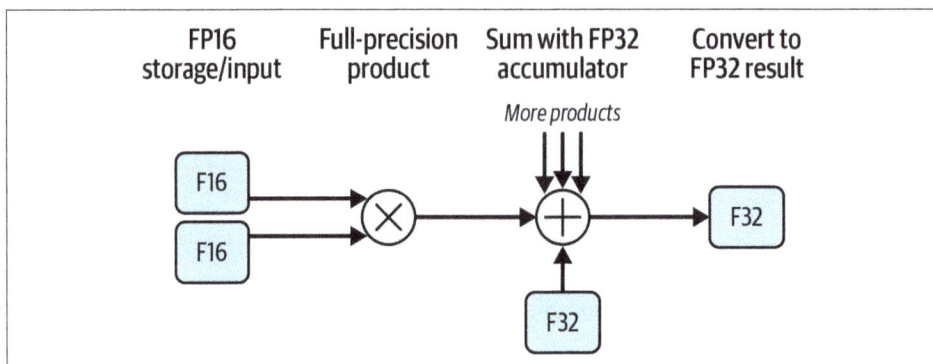

Figure 9-7. *Mixed-precision and matrix multiply-accumulate (MMA)*

When using structured sparsity, described earlier, or extreme low-precision (FP8/FP4), be sure to maintain a large enough batch size or tile granularity so that TMEM and Tensor Cores remain fully utilized. Small batches incur overhead, including format conversions, sparse index handling, irregular memory patterns, etc. This can reduce achieved speedups.

For example, when using FP8 or 2:4 sparsity, a batch size of 1 may see little benefit because the fixed overhead isn't amortized. In contrast, a batch size of 128 or 256 will fully utilize the TMEM pipeline and produce near-peak throughput.

BF16/FP16, FP8, and FP4 Reduced Precision

BF16/FP16 (half-precision) has been supported for many GPU generations, but Tensor Cores on modern GPUs can often sustain greater than 90% of the BF16/FP16 peak throughput, around 4× the FP32 peak throughput. This is because at each cycle, the hardware issues many BF16/FP16 FMA operations in parallel.

FP16 training uses a narrower 5-bit exponent than FP32, so very small gradient values can underflow to zero unless you apply loss scaling. Loss scaling preserves numerical stability during backpropagation. This scaling can either be static or dynamic.

In contrast, BF16 matches FP32's 8-bit exponent range and natively avoids underflow. There, it rarely (if ever) requires loss scaling. This simplifies mixed-precision workflows and often improves training accuracy on modern GPUs.

> BF16 is typically preferred for training on modern GPUs as it can maintain accuracy comparable to FP32 without the complexity of loss scaling that FP16 demands.

To push throughput even higher, you can use FP8. By reducing 16-bit weights by 50% down to 8 bits, you cut memory traffic in half—and double the number of weights loaded per HBM transaction. In practice, FP8 `matmuls` with FP32 or TF32 accumulation achieve 2–3× the BF16/FP16 TFLOPS—assuming that the model's slight loss in accuracy due to quantization errors remains acceptable.

To address accuracy concerns at very low precision, the Transformer Engine supports FP8 as well as NVIDIA's 4-bit NVFP4 format with micro-scaling. NVFP4 applies two-level scaling, combining per-microblock scaling and a higher-level scale so that models can retain accuracy while using 4-bit storage for weights. In addition, Blackwell B200's NVFP4's aggressive microscaling quantization provides 10 petaFLOPS (dense), while FP32 peak is about 80 teraFLOPS (dense). This is a speedup of approximately two orders of magnitude higher theoretical throughput per weight. And Blackwell's B300 (Ultra) boasts 50% higher NVFP4 compute capacity than B200 at 15 petaFLOPS (dense).

If your model tolerates the precision drop after calibration, NVFP4 kernels can deliver substantially higher throughput than FP32 on supported hardware, but accuracy must be validated per model.

And since the precision is so low, the 256 KB TMEM per SM can hold large FP4 tiles (e.g., 256 × 256), which further increases on-chip reuse and improves performance. Note that all low-precision → accumulation conversions happen automatically. The kernel reads FP4 inputs from HBM, the Tensor Cores perform FP4 × FP4 multiplies, and the MMA API accumulates the results into BF16/FP16 or FP32 accumulators.

Each drop in precision doubles or quadruples the number of operations per byte and therefore increases arithmetic intensity. When TMEM/TMA overlap memory and compute, these low-precision formats turn formerly memory-bound kernels into entirely compute-bound ones. This fully utilizes the multi-PFLOPS-per-GPU Tensor Core engines in modern GPUs.

INT8 Reduced Precision and DP4A Instructions for Inference

LLM inference use cases can typically tolerate reduced-precision INT8 quantization supported by modern GPUs using DP4A (SIMD dot-product) instructions on regular CUDA cores and integer matrix-multiply/accumulate (MMA) instructions on Tensor Cores. At the instruction level, DP4A performs four INT8 multiply-accumulate (MAC) operations per instruction compared to one FP32 fused multiply-add (FMA) per instruction.

Because weight traffic for INT8 is only one byte per element instead of four bytes for FP32, memory traffic for weights drops by 75%. INT8 inference workloads can significantly outperform FP32 due to higher peak INT8 Tensor Core throughput and reduced memory traffic. This is because each GPU can process approximately 4×

more data per second from memory when using INT8 weights. This is made possible by TMEM and TMA keeping data and compute perfectly overlapped—and feeding the Tensor Cores as efficiently as possible.

Transformer Engine and TMEM in Depth

Modern NVIDIA GPUs include a Transformer Engine that combines Tensor Core hardware support for low-precision formats with a software runtime for scaling and casting. Kernels in cuBLASLt, cuDNN, CUTLASS, or OpenAI's Triton perform cp.async instructions or TMA transfers into shared memory. The Tensor Core instructions then move operands between shared memory and TMEM implicitly.

Remember that TMEM is the 256 KB per-SM SRAM buffer that the Transformer Engine and Tensor Cores use to store results (instead of registers). In practice, you never explicitly allocate TMEM. It's all handled by the hardware. For instance, when invoking Tensor Core's MMA operations, the hardware handles all of the memory allocations and data transfers.

With the MMA instructions, each warp directly drives the Tensor Cores to perform high-throughput mixed-precision MMA operations. These operations manage fragment loads, register mappings, and mixed-precision MMA operations.

> As of this writing, PyTorch's INT8 quantization support is provided through TorchAO (*https://oreil.ly/lGuUY*) and vendor backends. Quantized modules run using dedicated INT8 kernels. Using cuBLASLt or CUTLASS for low-level INT8 GEMM can ensure Tensor Core utilization.

Any time you launch a Tensor-Core-based kernel or a GEMM library function (e.g., CUTLASS), the implementation manages operand movement through shared memory and TMEM automatically. This keeps the Tensor Cores full of tiles that are ready to be processed. (Note that the application code does not allocate TMEM directly.)

The Transformer Engine workflow is straightforward. First, your kernel issues a MMA call or launches a CUTLASS GEMM. Next, the Transformer Engine's firmware arranges for TMA (or cuda::memcpy_async) to copy weights and activations from HBM into shared memory (SMEM). Tensor Core instructions (e.g., tcgen05.mma) then move operands between SMEM and TMEM implicitly during the MMA pipeline. Ideally, the weights are in FP8 or FP4, and the activations are cast to FP8/FP4 when possible—otherwise, the activations can be left in FP16/FP32 format.

Tensor Core MMA operations execute at low precision, such as FP8 × FP8 with higher-precision accumulation or FP16 × FP16 with FP32 accumulation. Partial sums accumulate in TMEM with higher precision (e.g., BF16, FP16, FP32) and are kernel dependent. The accumulator state resides in TMEM. This state is accessed using tcgen05 load and store interfaces. The hardware manages these moves transparently.

If you build a custom tile loop, you can overlap data movement with Tensor Core compute. You can do this using cuda::memcpy_async and the CUDA Pipeline API, as shown in the code here:

```cpp
#include <cuda/pipeline>
#include <cooperative_groups.h>
namespace cg = cooperative_groups;

extern "C" __global__
void double_buffer_a(const float* __restrict__ globalA,
                     int tile_elems,
                     int numTiles) {
  __shared__ float tileA0[TILE][TILE];
  __shared__ float tileA1[TILE][TILE];

  auto block = cg::this_thread_block();

  constexpr auto scope = cuda::thread_scope_block;
  constexpr int stages = 2;
  __shared__ cuda::pipeline_shared_state<scope, stages> pstate;
  auto pipe = cuda::make_pipeline(block, &pstate);

  // Prime pipeline with tile 0
  pipe.producer_acquire();
  cuda::memcpy_async(block,
                     &tileA0[0][0],
                     globalA + 0 * tile_elems,
                     cuda::aligned_size_t<32>{tile_elems * sizeof(float)}
                     pipe);
  pipe.producer_commit();

  for (int t = 1; t < numTiles; ++t) {
    // Stage next tile into the alternate buffer
    pipe.producer_acquire();
    float* nxtA = (t & 1) ? &tileA1[0][0] : &tileA0[0][0];
    cuda::memcpy_async(block,
                       nxtA,
                       globalA + t * tile_elems,
                       cuda::aligned_size_t<32>{tile_elems * sizeof(float)}
                       pipe);
    pipe.producer_commit();

    // Consume the previously staged tile
    pipe.consumer_wait();
    float* curA = ((t - 1) & 1) ? &tileA1[0][0] : &tileA0[0][0];
    pipe.consumer_release();
  }

  // Consume the final staged tile
```

```
    pipe.consumer_wait();
    float* lastA = ((numTiles - 1) & 1) ? &tileA1[0][0] : &tileA0[0][0];
    // Use lastA with your compute
    pipe.consumer_release();
}
```

Because TMEM is a dedicated on-chip buffer used by Tensor Core instructions, data is kept close to the compute units. While Tensor Cores process the current tile, `cuda::memcpy_async` streams the next tile from HBM into shared memory.

This overlap helps hide memory latency and can keep Tensor Cores busy when the pipeline is tuned. This collaboration between the Transformer Engine, TMEM, and TMA can substantially raise arithmetic intensity and approach speed-of-light efficiency in optimized cases.

> While load and store operations are synchronous with respect to the calling warp, the overlap of compute and data movement should come from the CUDA Pipeline API. Used with pipeline primitives like wait/release, `cuda::memcpy_async` maps to the Tensor Memory Accelerator (TMA) and should always be preferred for bulk tensor transfers. Reserve `cp.async` for niche cases that TMA cannot express. However, these are rare. You should also make sure that copies complete before using the data.

Using CUTLASS for Optimal Arithmetic Intensity and Tensor Core Performance

One of the easiest ways to leverage these optimizations yourself is to use NVIDIA's CUTLASS library. With CUTLASS, you write a single templated call, and it will automatically apply many advanced optimizations.

Some optimizations that CUTLASS applies are shared-memory tiling, asynchronous memory transfers, and double buffering with the help of TMEM's 256 KB per-SM buffer. This way, your Tensor Cores run at near-peak throughput without any manual kernel tuning.

> CUTLASS also implements warp specialization, which is a high-performance GPU optimization technique that we'll discuss in the next chapter.

For example, suppose you want to compute a GEMM, C = A * B, with half-precision inputs and a half-precision output accumulating in FP16 or FP32 as appropriate. Instead of writing a hand-tuned MMA loop, you can simply include CUTLASS and instantiate a template, as shown in the following code:

```
#include <cutlass/numeric_types.h>
#include <cutlass/gemm/device/gemm.h>

using Gemm = cutlass::gemm::device::Gemm<
  cutlass::half_t,  // A (FP16)
  cutlass::layout::RowMajor,
  cutlass::half_t,  // B (FP16)
  cutlass::layout::ColumnMajor,
  cutlass::half_t,  // C / output (FP16)
  cutlass::layout::RowMajor,
  float, // accumulator (FP32 accumulate)
  cutlass::arch::OpClassTensorOp,
  cutlass::arch::Sm100 // e.g., Blackwell B200
>;

// ... (allocate device pointers A_d, B_d, C_d,
// set up dimensions M,N,K, and strides lda, ldb, ldc) ...

Gemm gemm_op;
cutlass::Status status = gemm_op(
    { M, N, K },            // GEMM shape
    float(1.0f)             // alpha
    A_d, lda,               // A pointer + leading dimension
    B_d, ldb,               // B pointer + leading dimension
    float(0.0f),            // beta
    C_d, ldc                // C pointer + leading dimension
);
```

When you compile and run this code, CUTLASS does several key things automatically. First, CUTLASS selects tiles to balance register pressure, shared memory capacity, and Tensor Core utilization. On modern GPUs, TMEM exists alongside shared memory and L1. CUTLASS stages tiles in shared memory and uses Tensor Core instructions that interact with TMEM to store accumulator data. The tile shapes are chosen empirically and per-kernel. For instance, it may select tile sizes such as 128×128 or 256×128. These would fit into TMEM's 256 KB per-SM buffer and would remain on-chip throughout the Tensor Core computation.

Depending on the precision, a 256×512 tile would max out the 256 KB per-SM TMEM budget since 256×512 elements $\times$ 2 bytes per element = 256 KiB. And 256×256 elements $\times$ 4 bytes per element = 256 KB. Larger tiles improve per-tile throughput but reduce the number of concurrent tiles per SM. This can lead to underutilization on smaller GEMMs. In contrast, very small tiles sacrifice arithmetic intensity for parallelism.

CUTLASS then emits asynchronous memory copies (cp.async or TMA) that stream each tile from DRAM into shared memory. The cp.async instruction stages data from global memory into shared memory without using per-thread registers (or optionally L1 cache), as shown in Figure 9-8. The caching behavior is controlled using cp.async modifiers or by using TMA for bulk tensor transfers.

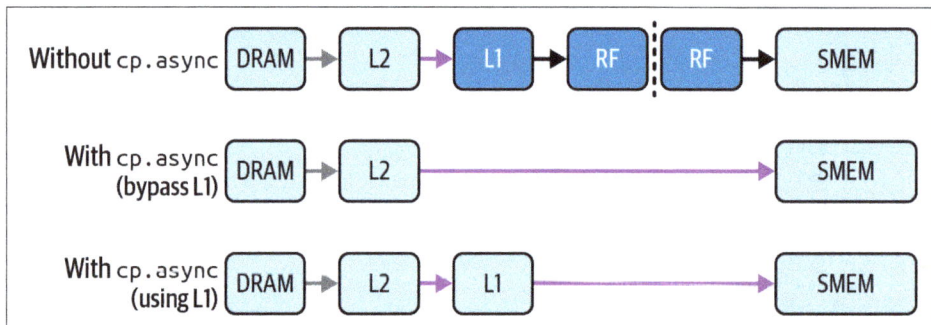

Figure 9-8. Using the asynchronous memory copy instruction (cp.async) to load data from global memory into shared memory without involving the register file and optionally the L1 cache

CUTLASS stages tiles from global DRAM into SMEM using cp.async or TMA (cp.async.bulk.tensor). Tensor Core tcgen05.mma instructions then read operands from SMEM and accumulate the results implicitly into TMEM. This creates a software-managed staging area in shared memory, which is used for double-buffering. This way, while the Tensor Cores are processing the current tile, TMA is already fetching the next tile into shared memory.

Using the CUDA Pipeline API and warp-specialized compute stages (discussed in the next chapter), CUTLASS keeps all of the Tensor Core pipelines busy. It accumulates partial sums in the precision that you specify (for example, FP32 when inputs are FP16 or FP8) to ensure numerical fidelity—and then writes the results from TMEM out to shared or global memory in a coalesced fashion.

> CUTLASS also leverages thread block clusters when beneficial by tiling across multiple SMs for even larger effective tiles. We'll cover thread block clusters in the next chapter.

Because all of this complexity is hidden, CUTLASS gives you a drop-in, high-performance GEMM kernel that matches a hand-tuned MMA kernel—often within a few percent of overall Tensor Core utilization and performance compared to the hand-written version, as shown in Table 9-1.

Table 9-1. Hand-tuned MMA versus CUTLASS kernel performance and resource usage

Metric	Hand-tuned MMA kernel	CUTLASS GEMM
Tensor Core utilization	98%	98%
Registers per thread	~52	~60 (slightly higher)
Shared memory per thread block (CTA)	~2 KB	~4 KB
Development effort	High	Low (simple template configuration)

> Note: The numeric values in all metrics tables are illustrative to explain the concepts. For actual benchmark results on different GPU architectures, see the GitHub repository (*https://github.com/cfregly/ai-performance-engineering*).

Here, both use FP16 inputs with FP32 accumulation. And both aim to maximize Tensor Core utilization. As the table shows, CUTLASS matches or exceeds hand-tuned MMA performance within about 2%. And although CUTLASS used a few more registers and doubled the shared memory in this case, it stayed well within the hardware limits. The slight increases do not impact occupancy.

> The small differences in register and shared memory usage are due to CUTLASS generalizing the kernel for flexibility. While this can be optimized away with hand-tuning, the extra complexity is likely not worth the effort in most cases—and the performance of CUTLASS remains virtually identical to the hand-tuned option.

It requires only a few lines of template code instead of weeks of low-level tuning. In addition, CUTLASS templates already support FP4, FP8, FP16, and TF32 operand types. And they can fuse common postprocessing operations like bias-add and activation into the same kernel.

> And remember that CUTLASS templates transparently use thread block pairs, multi-SM tiling, and TMA multicast with distributed shared memory (DSMEM) to maximize data reuse, as mentioned earlier—and covered in more detail in the next chapter.

This is in contrast to writing a custom MMA kernel, which requires manually selecting tile sizes, writing asynchronous copy loops, managing double buffers, implementing warp specialization pipelines, and thread block cluster tiles. All of this is done for you automatically with CUTLASS.

Optimized libraries such as cuBLAS are built on CUTLASS. And high-level libraries like PyTorch call these optimized libraries for many kernels. In our earlier fused-attention example, we showed that TorchInductor dispatched a CUTLASS fused-attention kernel that used exactly the same double-buffered TMEM pipeline. This results in 98% Tensor Core utilization and near-zero memory stalls.

As more operators in PyTorch and other higher-level libraries adopt CUTLASS under the hood, you can utilize these same optimizations without writing any CUDA C++ code yourself.

There may still be scenarios in which you need to write a manual MMA kernel—for instance, when you need a highly specialized data layout or a unique fusion pattern that CUTLASS does not yet support.

In these cases, you would need to implement this complexity yourself. You would first need to choose a tile size that fits within TMEM (e.g., 128 × 128 FP16), then use `<cuda/pipeline>` to perform asynchronous memory copy (`cp.async`) instructions for each tile.

You would then need to implement warp-specialized MMA loops and double-buffer TMEM to hide DRAM latency. Last, you would interleave any custom postprocessing steps like softmax and elementwise nonlinearities—all within the same loop, if possible.

However, for almost every standard GEMM or fused-attention use case, CUTLASS and the libraries built on it are the recommended approach.

Its template-based design, GPU-specific tuning, and built-in support for TMEM and TMA pipelines typically achieve high Tensor Core utilization on supported shapes. This allows you to achieve 96%–98% Tensor Core utilization, in some cases, with minimal developer effort.

By depending on CUTLASS's automatic optimizations, you can spend your time on model architecture, numeric precision strategies, and end-to-end performance. CUTLASS gives you the confidence that your low-level tensor operations will run at near-peak arithmetic intensity optimized for your specific GPU hardware.

NVIDIA continually updates libraries like CUTLASS and cuBLAS to utilize the latest hardware features like FP8, FP4, thread block cluster pairs, TMEM, etc. Using these libraries keeps you from needing to rewrite new kernels for every new GPU generation. Always check for a new version of CUTLASS when switching to a new GPU architecture.

Inline PTX and SASS Tuning for Microoptimizations

For those willing to venture beyond C++ and into low-level microoptimizations, CUDA allows inline Parallel Thread Execution (PTX) code and SASS (NVIDIA's assembly language) to bring out the last bits of performance that may be left on the table.

This is truly advanced territory, as the CUDA compiler is already quite good at optimization. But in some extreme cases, you can hand-schedule assembly instructions—or use special-purpose instructions—to gain a small percentage of performance gain in very specific situations.

With PTX and Streaming Assembler (SASS), you can also enable features not yet exposed in the higher-level CUDA language. Modern GPUs don't typically introduce radical new assembly instructions, but they do offer opportunities for custom tuning. For instance, you can tweak the GPU caching strategy, modify the coordination of CPU-GPU unified memory access, and implement other fine-grained micro-optimizations.

> PTX ("pee-tex") is a low-level parallel-thread execution virtual machine and exposes the GPU as a parallel computing device. It provides the programming model and instruction for NVIDIA GPUs. A high-level compiler (e.g., CUDA C++) generates PTX instructions, which are translated into native target-architecture instructions. SASS is the low-level assembly language that actually executes natively on NVIDIA GPU hardware.

As an example, consider a piece of code in which you know that a specific instruction sequence would be optimal, but the compiler isn't generating the specific sequence. Common scenarios include using a GPU instruction that has no direct CUDA intrinsic, applying memory load modifiers (cache hints) on specific accesses, inserting memory fences or barriers at precise points, or manually reordering instructions to avoid pipeline stalls.

Another use is to read special registers or states such as SM ID, warp lane ID, etc., which might not have a high-level API. Inline PTX lets you embed assembly right in your CUDA C++ code using `asm()` statements. You can mix C++ and PTX by specifying inputs and outputs to the assembly code. The compiler will then incorporate your PTX instructions into the final SASS.

Let's look at a simple example that uses an inline PTX directive to prefetch a global memory address into L2 cache. Here, we are using kernel-side prefetching using the PTX instruction `cp.async.bulk.prefetch.global`:

```
__global__ void PrefetchExample(const float *in, float *out) {
    // ... assume idx is our thread's data index
    int idx = blockIdx.x * blockDim.x + threadIdx.x;
    // Manually prefetch the next cache line (128B) of in[] into L2:
    // Prefetch 128B from global to L2.
    // Address must be 16B-aligned
    // and size is a 16B multiple.
    asm volatile("cp.async.bulk.prefetch.L2.global [%0], %1;"
                 :: "l"(in + idx + 32), "n"(128));
    float x = in[idx];
    // (do some work here before using in[idx+32] to give time for prefetch)
    out[idx] = x;
}
```

In this snippet, the inline PTX `cp.async.bulk.prefetch.L2.global [%0]` uses the address operand we provide (`in + idx + 32` bytes, i.e., 32 floats ahead) and issues a prefetch to L2. We mark it `volatile` to ensure the compiler doesn't optimize it away.

These PTX instructions will be injected into the machine code. Using inline assembly like this will give us very fine-grained control. For instance, we could prefetch to L2 or L1 (by using `.L1`) or choose the distance (32 floats ahead, in this case).

It's essentially what `__prefetch_async` likely compiles down to. More generally, we can use inline PTX to control the caching behavior of normal loads. For example, we might write `asm("ld.global.cg.f32 %0, [%1];" : "=f"(val) : "l"(ptr))` to load a float with the `.cg` ("cache global") modifier.

On some architectures, this means we want to cache the data in L2 but bypass the L1 cache. If we knew a certain access was thrashing L1 and we preferred to use only L2, this could help. Normally, the compiler's choice might default to caching in L1 (`.ca`), but we can use PTX to override the compiler's decision.

> For L2 prefetch on modern architectures, use `cp.async.bulk.pre fetch.tensor.L2` where available. This is preferred over using undocumented built-ins. Regardless, it's useful to know that this capability exists.

Another area in which inline PTX is helpful is instruction scheduling. By default, the compiler will issue instructions in the order that it deems optimal. But you might spot a case in which you want to intermix operations more effectively.

For instance, say you have two independent memory loads and then two uses of those results. The compiler might issue load1, then use1, then load2, then use2. But maybe the better instruction schedule is to perform load1 and load2 (back-to-back) and then use both results. This could overlap the memory latencies.

By writing inline PTX for the loads, you can enforce them early, then do the computations. This is a form of manually increasing ILP, discussed earlier. In practice, the compiler will already do a good job here since modern compilers try to fill load latency with other independent instructions. But inline PTX and SASS assembly can give you certainty.

On modern CPU-GPU superchips that share CPU and GPU memory, such fine-grained control might be useful if you're managing a workload in which the GPU polls a memory location updated by the CPU. Here, you could use appropriate memory fences such as `membar.sys` or `__threadfence_system()` together with the desired cache operators on loads and stores to ensure coherence at the intended scope. This is something that high-level CUDA might not expose directly.

> PTX is generally forward compatible; however, SASS assembly will change per GPU architecture generation.

You can also use inline PTX to leverage special registers. For instance, although there's no C++ intrinsic for SM ID (the SM that a thread block is running on), you can do `asm("mov.u32 %0, %smid;" : "=r"(smid))` to get the SM ID. This flexibility is useful for debugging and work partitioning.

Some developers have used `%smid` in persistent kernels to have only one block per SM do certain work, for instance. This effectively performs manual SM partitioning, which is beyond what the CUDA C++ API offers.

If your code is already well optimized at the algorithmic level, gains from inline PTX/ SASS tend to be just incremental and on the order of a few percent in most cases. For instance, in a memory-bound kernel you can carefully unroll and schedule instructions to reduce load-to-use latency bubbles and see maybe a 5%–10% speedup by using two independent load streams with PTX. In this case, the compiler may be more conservative.

In a compute-bound scenario, you might use inline assembly to use a faster math instruction instead of a more precise instruction. CUDA provides fast math intrinsics for this, including `__sinf()`.

Before the C++ intrinsics were available, developers writing matrix multiply kernels would sometimes embed PTX instructions to use Tensor Cores. Today, we have higher-level intrinsics for this purpose. But, in short, assembly lets you tap hardware features as soon as you know about them—without waiting for CUDA to support them.

Nsight Compute can help inform assembly tuning. By inspecting the "SASS through-put" metrics and the "Warp Stall Reasons," you might identify a lot of stalls due to memory dependencies. You could attempt to reorder the loads as mentioned earlier.

After your change, you'd hope to see less "Stall Memory Dependency"—and perhaps higher instruction issue rate for more instructions executed per cycle. Note that assembly tweaking is labor-intensive—and can reduce code portability.

It's usually only worth it for very hot inner loops in which you've exhausted higher-level optimizations. Also, any change in GPU generation might require retuning and verifying that your assumptions still hold, including memory latencies, cache behavior, etc.

To illustrate the potential microoptimizations, consider a scenario in which a kernel was already quite optimized but had one remaining bottleneck: a tight loop doing integer index calculations and memory loads.

You can use inline PTX to compute the byte address in one instruction with `mad.wide.u32 (base + index * stride)`. Next, issue the load as `ld.global.cg` to bypass L1 for this streaming access pattern. The result is that the loop uses fewer instructions and avoids L1 evictions. In this case, we squeeze about a 7% speedup in that kernel from 1.07 ms down to 1.0 ms. Table 9-2 summarizes a hypothetical before-and-after for optimized CUDA C++ versus hand-written PTX with manual scheduling and cache hints.

Table 9-2. Optimized CUDA C++ versus hand-written PTX with manual scheduling and cache hints

Version	Warp stall (memory)	Issue IPC	Kernel time	Speedup
Optimized C++ (compiler schedule)	35% of cycles	1.5	1.07 ms	1.0× base
Hand-tuned PTX (manual scheduling and hints)	20% of cycles	1.6	1.00 ms	1.07×

Here we see that after tuning, our kernel's memory stalls decreased by overlapping loads, and cache hints reduced some latency. Additionally, we increased ILP and the instructions per cycle (IPC). This gave a 7% net improvement in overall kernel execution time.

These numbers are in line with what to expect from manual assembly on an already-optimized kernel. In some cases, the gains might be larger if the compiler made a poor choice, for instance—and you can implement the fix. Otherwise, the gain is essentially zero if the compiler already chose the optimal implementation. It's also possible to hurt performance with incorrect assembly ordering, so one must experiment and profile each change.

Inline PTX and SASS assembly can be viewed as the last resort optimization tool. It provides ultimate control at the cost of complexity. It's recommended to use this last resource when you need a hardware feature or instruction that isn't accessible in CUDA C++—or when you have pinpointed a small piece of code where the compiler's scheduling can be improved upon. Examples include custom memory access patterns (cache hints, prefetches), fine-grained synchronization or fences, and utilizing new instructions before they are officially supported.

When applying inline assembly, it's especially important to verify the impact with profiling. You want to see reductions in stall reasons or instruction count as intended. Also, you should keep such code isolated and well-documented. It will likely need updates for new GPU architectures—especially if you use SASS assembly, which is not always forward-compatible.

> While PTX is more stable than SASS, some hardware changes may still require you to update the inline PTX for performance reasons.

Inline PTX/SASS tuning is for expert-level tweaking to shave off extra latency or enforce a specific scheduling. It can produce modest speedups and enable certain custom behaviors, but it should come after exhausting all other high-level optimizations. For instance, you may want to handcraft the assembly for critical loops that run millions of times. At the very least, it's an effective way to learn exactly how the hardware executes your code.

In short, use inline PTX/SASS sparingly and profile diligently. The gains are real but usually incremental. The maintenance cost is much higher. For most use cases, relying on CUDA's built-in optimizations—or highly tuned libraries like CUB and Thrust—is likely good enough. But it's good to know that, if needed, you can drop to assembly and gain full control over the GPU.

DeepSeek's Use of Inline PTX for Memory Allocation Optimization

A well-known example of custom PTX is from DeepSeek's DeepEP expert parallelism library. This library used a bespoke PTX instruction, `ld.global.nc.l1::no_allocate.l2::256b`, to optimize global memory access by bypassing L1 cache allocations, preserving critical data, and leveraging 256-byte L2 cache chunks. This is ideal for streaming large datasets directly into the L2 cache without disrupting frequent-access memory operations in the L1 cache.

This instruction is not part of NVIDIA's official PTX ISA specification but was discovered "out-of-doc" by DeepSeek engineers to fine-tune cache behavior on their US-export-constrained H800 variant of the Hopper GPU.

Let's break down the `ld.global.nc.l1::no_allocate.l2::256b` PTX instruction. The `ld.global.nc` prefix issues a noncoherent (nc) global memory load (`ld.global`), while the modifiers `l1::no_allocate` and `l2::256b` instruct the hardware to avoid allocating the data in the L1 cache (`l1::no_allocate`). Instead, it fetches 256 bytes at a time into L2 (`l2::256b`).

By bypassing L1, loads can stream large blocks of data directly into L2 without evicting frequently used L1-resident data. This is critical when you have hot working sets that need to stay in L1 for low-latency memory access.

In practice, streaming workloads such as expert-parallel all-to-all communication kernels benefit from this approach because they often read large contiguous buffers exactly once per dispatch. If these loads went through L1, they could evict earlier cache lines that are still actively in use by the SMs.

By fetching in 256-byte aligned chunks directly into L2, the instruction reduces unnecessary L1 traffic. This helps maintain high throughput for both memory-bound communication and compute operations.

However, using PTX in this way carries some risks because `ld.global.nc.l1::no_allo cate.l2::256b` is not guaranteed to remain stable across GPU generations. As such, code that relies on it may break or produce incorrect results on future architectures.

DeepSeek's DeepEP setup even includes a build-time flag, `DISABLE_AGGRES SIVE_PTX_INSTRS=1`, to disable these aggressive instructions if compatibility issues arise. While DeepEP's bespoke PTX hack can produce significant speedup, inline PTX/SASS should be used with caution and tested thoroughly whenever updating to a new GPU architecture.

Key Takeaways

You saw how to uncover and eliminate GPU kernel bottlenecks by moving work from slow global memory into faster on-chip resources and compute units. By following a cycle of profiling, diagnosing, optimizing, and reprofiling, you can transform kernels from underutilized or memory-bound into compute-saturated, high-throughput routines. These techniques will help utilize the full power of your GPUs:

Increase arithmetic intensity with tiling and fusion
To elevate FLOPS per byte transferred, stage data into shared memory and registers using multilevel tiling. Load a 32×32 submatrix into SMEM, for instance, so that each element is reused across many FMAs. Combine consecutive kernels by fusing elementwise operations so intermediate results stay on-chip. Utilize software prefetching through asynchronous memory loading with the CUDA Pipeline API's `cuda::memcpy_async` to overlap data movement with computation. This will hide DRAM latencies.

Leverage mixed precision, Tensor Cores, and Transformer Engine

Dropping from FP32 to TF32/BF16/FP16/FP8/FP4 cuts weight traffic by 2× to 8×. This boosts arithmetic intensity accordingly. In PyTorch, you can use `torch.set_float32_matmul_precision('high')` and `torch.cuda.amp` to enable mixed precision. On modern GPUs, the TMEM and TMA engines stream tiles to Tensor Cores. Modern GPUs also provide a Transformer Engine to utilize these lower precisions specifically for AI workloads. This can further increase throughput.

Utilize CUTLASS for high-performance GEMM and fused kernels

Rather than hand-coding MMA loops, instantiate CUTLASS GEMM templates to automatically manage double buffering, TMEM staging, and Tensor Core pipelines. This will produce a kernel that performs within a few percent of a hand-tuned kernel. High-level frameworks like cuBLAS and TorchInductor already rely on CUTLASS. Customizations are needed only when you require nonstandard layouts or unique fusion patterns.

PyTorch-specific best practices

Favor built-in tensor operations such as `torch.matmul`, fused attention, and nested tensors since PyTorch typically inherits Tensor Core and other hardware optimizations from CUDA over time. And if you write custom kernel extensions for PyTorch, carry over the same strategies: minimize register usage, align data for coalesced memory loads, and target Tensor Cores. This makes sure your kernels are at parity with native kernels.

By following the systematic workflow of profiling, diagnosing, and applying targeted optimizations, from occupancy tuning and warp-level refinements to ILP and high arithmetic intensity with tiling, fusion, and Tensor Cores, you can transform a memory-bound GPU kernel into a compute-bound one. This can provide large speedups, and in strongly memory bound workloads, sometimes order-of-magnitude gains.

Conclusion

In this chapter, you learned about optimization techniques related to advanced memory and compute hardware features such as TMA, TMEM, Transformer Engine, and Tensor Cores. The same principles scale from single GPUs to multi-GPU clusters. First, use a system-level profiler (e.g., NVIDIA Nsight Systems) to correlate CPU activity, GPU kernels, and NVLink/NVSwitch traffic across multiple GPUs. Then use Nsight Compute for deep dive into per-kernel details.

By systematically profiling, eliminating the dominant stalls, and mastering advanced hardware features, you can turn a memory-bound workload into a compute-bound workload—often producing large speedups, including order-of-magnitude improvements on strongly memory-bound paths.

And even with ultrascale, multi-GPU systems like NVIDIA's GB200/GB300 NVL72 with its high NVLink/NVSwitch bandwidth, per-GPU arithmetic intensity optimizations are still the key to removing most bottlenecks. Kernels that do too little work per byte will require too much memory movement, saturate the interconnects, and max out memory bandwidth.

This interconnect and memory bandwidth saturation will happen well before our kernels can fully utilize the compute capabilities of the many interconnected GPUs (e.g., 72 in the case of NVL72). As such, increasing kernel arithmetic intensity is the key to scaling efficiently for multi-GPU training and inference workloads.

In the next chapter, we'll continue diving deep into techniques like persistent kernels, megakernels, warp specialization, cooperative groups, and thread block clusters. These ideas are the basis of most modern LLM runtime optimizations, so it's important to understand their implementation—and how to apply them in your own low-level system optimization efforts.

Intra-Kernel Pipelining, Warp Specialization, and Cooperative Thread Block Clusters

In the previous chapters, we covered fundamental optimizations such as tuning memory access, maximizing parallelism, overlapping computation and data transfer, boosting occupancy, and minimizing warp stalls. These helped hide latency and eliminate bottlenecks. Modern GPUs, however, offer advanced hardware features and execution models that let us take the fundamental optimization techniques even further.

In this chapter, we introduce some more advanced CUDA techniques such as warp-specialized pipelines, cooperative groups with grid-level and cluster-level synchronization, persistent kernels that loop over dynamic work queues, and thread block clusters (aka *cooperative thread array cluster* [CTA]) that use distributed shared memory (DSMEM or DSM) and Tensor Memory Accelerator (TMA) multicast. At a high level, a thread block cluster is a group of thread blocks that are guaranteed to run concurrently. They can read, write, and perform atomics to each other's shared memory using DSMEM.

These methods let us overlap memory accesses and compute operations without host intervention. We can also share data on-chip across thread blocks—and keep every SM fully utilized.

By understanding these modern GPU execution models, you'll be ready to progress to the next chapter where we extend these optimizations even further by exploring inter-kernel pipelines with CUDA streams. The next chapter builds inter-kernel pipelines on the foundation of intra-kernel optimizations discussed throughout this chapter.

Intra-Kernel Pipelining Techniques

Intra-kernel pipelining refers to a set of techniques that overlap memory operations and computations within a single kernel execution. (In the next chapter, we'll explore inter-kernel pipelining, which overlaps work across multiple kernels running in different streams.)

The core idea is to structure a kernel into concurrent stages such that while one piece of data is being loaded or stored, previously loaded data is being processed. These stages operate in parallel over different tiles or data chunks. This improves throughput and efficiently hides latency.

Traditionally, GPUs rely on warp-level multithreading to hide latency. While one warp stalls on a memory load, other warps proceed with computation. This is the foundation of single instruction, multiple threads (SIMT) latency hiding in the execution model.

Intra-kernel pipelining pushes this further by overlapping memory and compute within the same warp or kernel. It uses fine-grained coordination to stagger memory loads and compute—sometimes within a single warp.

Intra-kernel pipelining with the CUDA Pipeline API overlaps asynchronous memory transfers and computation without any `__syncthreads()`. The two common approaches to intra-kernel pipelining are double buffering and warp specialization.

In the double-buffered (two stages) pipeline approach, all threads cooperate uniformly. In the warp-specialized pipeline approach, warps are specialized into distinct roles like memory loader, compute, and memory storer. The choice depends on your workload and performance requirements. Table 10-1 summarizes these two `<cuda/pipeline>` variants.

Table 10-1. Two approaches for intra-kernel pipelining on modern GPUs using the CUDA Pipeline API

API variant	Best for	Main use
Double-buffered pipeline	Loop-based tiling and double buffering	Overlapping loads and compute in the same warp or block
Warp-specialized pipeline (e.g., three-stage memory loader, compute, memory storer)	Persistent kernels with multiple distinct warp roles (3 in our case)	Assigning warps to separate roles/stages such as memory load, compute, and memory store

Cooperative Tiling and Double-Buffering with the CUDA Pipeline API

You can implement the traditional double-buffered tiling pattern using the C++ Pipeline API by instantiating a two-stage pipeline to overlap memory loads and computations. Specifically, you can declare a two-stage `cuda::pipeline_shared_state <cuda::thread_scope_block, 2>` object, which is scoped to a specific thread block using cooperative groups (discussed in a bit). This is essentially a producer-consumer pattern, as shown in Figure 10-1.

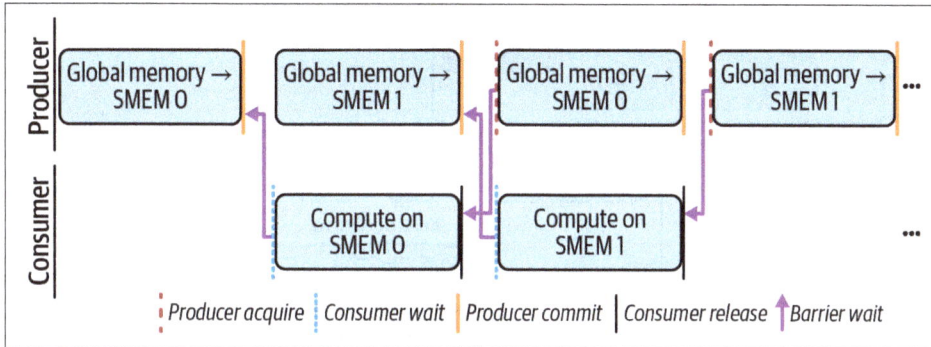

Figure 10-1. Two-stage producer-consumer pattern with the CUDA Pipeline API

The key CUDA Pipeline API calls are shown next. They are followed by an implementation of a double-buffered, cooperative tiling kernel using this API to demonstrate modern CUDA techniques that align with hardware features:

`pipe.producer_acquire()`
Reserves the next pipeline stage for writing

`pipe.producer_commit()`
Signals that the previously issued asynchronous operations for this stage are ready for consumption

`pipe.consumer_wait()`
Waits until the previously committed operations for this stage complete to avoid race conditions in loops

`pipe.consumer_release()`
Releases the current stage so it can be reused

The two stages in the pipeline overlap global-memory loads with computations. In the first, Stage 0, one warp in the thread block issues an asynchronous prefetch for the next tile into shared memory. The prefetch issues cooperative `cuda::mem cpy_async` copies that lower to per thread `cp.async` into shared memory.

While Stage 0 is producing (loading) the data in one warp, the remaining warps in the thread block are consuming (computing) the loaded data in the second stage, 1. This simple producer-consumer implementation hides DRAM latency with ongoing computations, as shown in Figure 10-2.

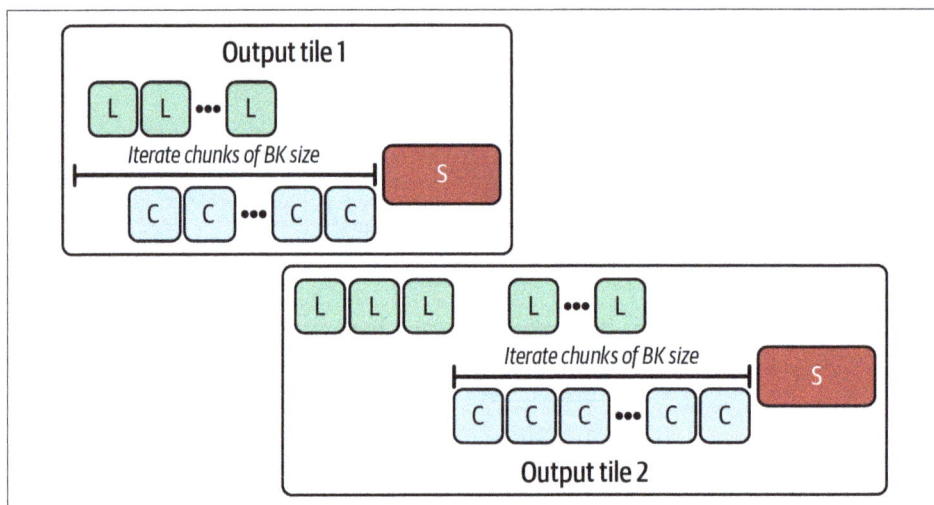

Figure 10-2. Hiding global DRAM load (L) latency with (C) compute using a producer–consumer pipeline

This pattern can raise SM utilization and reduce kernel time, but whether you are compute bound or memory bound depends on the operation, tile sizes, and overlap efficiency. Even highly optimized attention kernels like FlashAttention-3 report around 75% percent of peak FP16 FLOPs due to practical limits in overlap and data movement.

This is a two-stage, double-buffering example using the CUDA C++ Pipeline API. This API enables the fine-grained producer-consumer synchronization code used here:

```
#include <cuda/pipeline>
#include <cooperative_groups.h>
#include <algorithm>
namespace cg = cooperative_groups;

#ifndef TILE_SIZE
#define TILE_SIZE 32
#endif
#ifndef STAGES
#define STAGES 2              // 2 = double buffer, 3 = triple buffer, etc.
#endif

__device__ float computeTile(const float* __restrict__ A_sub,
                             const float* __restrict__ B_sub,
                             int tx, int ty) {
```

```
        float s = 0.0f;
        #pragma unroll
        for (int k = 0; k < TILE_SIZE; ++k) {
            s += A_sub[ty * TILE_SIZE + k] * B_sub[k * TILE_SIZE + tx];
        }
        return s;
}

extern "C" __global__
void gemm_tiled_pipeline(const float* __restrict__ A_global, // [M x K]
                         const float* __restrict__ B_global, // [K x N]
                         float* __restrict__ C_global,       // [M x N]
                         int M, int N, int K) {
    cg::thread_block cta = cg::this_thread_block();

    // Shared memory layout: A[STAGES] then B[STAGES]
    extern __shared__ float shared_mem[];
    float* A_buf[STAGES];
    float* B_buf[STAGES];
    {
        float* p = shared_mem;
        for (int s = 0; s < STAGES; ++s) {
            A_buf[s] = p;
            p += TILE_SIZE * TILE_SIZE;
        }

        for (int s = 0; s < STAGES; ++s) {
            B_buf[s] = p;
            p += TILE_SIZE * TILE_SIZE;
        }
    }

    __shared__ cuda::pipeline_shared_state<cuda::thread_scope_block, STAGES> state;
    auto pipe = cuda::make_pipeline(cta, &state);

    int tx = threadIdx.x, ty = threadIdx.y;
    int block_row = blockIdx.y * TILE_SIZE;
    int block_col = blockIdx.x * TILE_SIZE;

    float accum = 0.0f;
    int numTiles = (K + TILE_SIZE - 1) / TILE_SIZE;

    // Prologue: load first STAGES tiles (or fewer if short)
    for (int s = 0; s < std::min(STAGES, numTiles); ++s) {
        int aRow = block_row + ty;
        int aCol = s * TILE_SIZE + tx;
        int bRow = s * TILE_SIZE + ty;
        int bCol = block_col + tx;

        pipe.producer_acquire();
        if (aRow < M && aCol < K) {
            cuda::memcpy_async(cta, A_buf[s] + ty*TILE_SIZE + tx,
                               &A_global[aRow*K + aCol],
                               cuda::aligned_size_t<32>(sizeof(float)), pipe);
        } else {
            A_buf[s][ty*TILE_SIZE + tx] = 0.0f;
        }
```

```
        if (bRow < K && bCol < N) {
            cuda::memcpy_async(cta, B_buf[s] + ty*TILE_SIZE + tx,
                               &B_global[bRow*N + bCol],
                               cuda::aligned_size_t<32>(sizeof(float)), pipe);
        } else {
            B_buf[s][ty*TILE_SIZE + tx] = 0.0f;
        }
        pipe.producer_commit();
    }

    // Steady state
    for (int tile = 0; tile < numTiles; ++tile) {
        int s = tile % STAGES;

        // Block-scope wait
        pipe.consumer_wait();

        accum += computeTile(A_buf[s], B_buf[s], tx, ty);
        pipe.consumer_release();

        // Prefetch next tile into the same slot s (ring buffer)
        int nextTile = tile + STAGES;
        if (nextTile < numTiles) {
            int aRow = block_row + ty;
            int aCol = nextTile * TILE_SIZE + tx;
            int bRow = nextTile * TILE_SIZE + ty;
            int bCol = block_col + tx;

            pipe.producer_acquire();
            if (aRow < M && aCol < K) {
                cuda::memcpy_async(cta, A_buf[s] + ty*TILE_SIZE + tx,
                                   &A_global[aRow*K + aCol],
                                   cuda::aligned_size_t<32>{sizeof(float)}, pipe);
            } else {
                A_buf[s][ty*TILE_SIZE + tx] = 0.0f;
            }
            if (bRow < K && bCol < N) {
                cuda::memcpy_async(cta, B_buf[s] + ty*TILE_SIZE + tx,
                                   &B_global[bRow*N + bCol],
                                   cuda::aligned_size_t<32>{sizeof(float)}, pipe);
            } else {
                B_buf[s][ty*TILE_SIZE + tx] = 0.0f;
            }
            pipe.producer_commit();
        }
    }

    // Epilogue: final store (guard tails)
    int cRow = block_row + ty;
    int cCol = block_col + tx;
    if (cRow < M && cCol < N) {
        C_global[cRow * N + cCol] = accum;
    }
}
```

The code first retrieves a handle to the current thread block using cooperative groups (CG), discussed in a bit. It then immediately instantiates a two-stage `cuda::pipeline` object bound to that block. By creating the pipeline before any asynchronous operations, the pipelines' internal barriers and internal synchronization mechanisms are in place prior to performing data movement.

The kernel then allocates one contiguous shared-memory region for both A and B tiles by defining an `extern __shared__ float shared_mem[]`. It divides this buffer into four subregions, two for A and two for B, using pointer arithmetic (`float* A_buf[2]` and `float* B_buf[2]`). This allows true double-buffering without extra dynamic allocations.

Before entering the main loop, the kernel asynchronously prefetches the first STAGES tiles using asynchronous copies bound to the following pipeline: `pro ducer_acquire()` → `memcpy_async()` → `producer_commit()`. Consumer warps use `consumer_wait()` and `consumer_release()` so the compute starts exactly when the prefetched tile is ready.

This initial barrier replaces a future need for `__syncthreads()` and ensures the pipeline's stage 0 and stage 1 buffers are correctly populated for the first iteration of the producer-consumer sequence.

Within each iteration, the kernel reserves the next buffer to load subsequent tiles by calling `pipe.producer_acquire()`. It then launches two `cuda::memcpy_async` operations—one for the A tile and one for the B tile. Each load is bound to the pipeline object with `cuda::memcpy_async(..., pipe)`, which issues asynchronous copies from global memory into shared memory.

These asynchronous copies can overlap well with compute when accesses are coalesced and tiled correctly. This way, the pipeline stays fed with data to perform maximum useful work. Immediately after queuing the `memcpy_async` calls, the kernel signals completion with `pipe.producer_commit()`. This commit records the copy's arrival and allows consumer warps to wait on that specific stage without blocking the entire thread block.

Concurrently, other warps in the block invoke `pipe.consumer_wait()`. This stalls only the threads dependent on the stage indexed by `s = tile % STAGES`. Progress continues when that stage is committed by the producer. Once the wait completes, each thread calls the device function `computeTile(...)` to perform its `TILE_SIZE x TILE_SIZE` dot-product computation. The results are incrementally accumulated in registers.

After finishing the computation on the current buffer, the warps invoke `pipe.con sumer_release()` to free that stage for reuse in subsequent iterations. This fine-grained release prevents block-wide stalls and maximizes overlap between compute and memory transfer phases.

At the end of each iteration, the ring buffer advances by stage index. The next prefetch uses `nextTile = tile + STAGES` and writes into the same slot `s` modulo `STAGES`.

These producer and consumer stages are repeated for all K-dimension tiles. After processing the final tile, each thread's accumulator contains the full `TILE_SIZE` x `TILE_SIZE` dot-product result. This result is then written back to the appropriate element of `C_global`.

When using double buffering, it's recommended to make sure that each asynchronous copy (`memcpy_async`) is followed by the appropriate `producer_commit()` and `consumer_wait()` calls for synchronization. This guarantees that the compute kernels will use the data only after it's properly loaded. Modern CUDA compilers will often perform these optimizations automatically for simple loops.

> It's recommended to validate that the pipeline is executing as expected using Nsight Compute's asynchronous copy metrics. In particular, pay attention to warp occupancy and shared-memory bank conflicts. The goal is to increase SM Active percent and reduce stall cycles. Full hiding of DRAM latency depends on occupancy, access patterns, and shared-memory bank behavior.

This simple double-buffered scheme is roughly 2× faster than naive tiling, as described in Table 10-2's performance comparison between the naive tiling implementation and the optimized, double-buffered, pipeline implementation.

Table 10-2. Performance comparison between the naive tiling and double-buffered kernel using the CUDA Pipeline API

Metric	Naive tiling	Two-stage, double-buffered pipeline (`double_buffered_pipeline`)
Kernel execution time	41.3 ms	20.5 ms (~2× faster versus naive)
SM Active %	68%	92% (+24% versus naive)

> Note: The numeric values in all metrics tables are illustrative to explain the concepts. For actual benchmark results on different GPU architectures, see the GitHub repository (*https://github.com/cfregly/ai-performance-engineering*).

In this experiment, the `gemm_tiled_pipeline` kernel using the CUDA C++ Pipeline API achieves a 2× speedup over the naive tiling version. By using the fine-grained `pipe.producer_commit()` and `pipe.consumer_wait()` primitives, the pipeline remains filled, and SM Active % jumps 24% from 68% to 92%.

Warp Specialization and the Producer-Consumer Model

Warp specialization extends double buffering by assigning operations to warps that use different hardware, such as data movement (e.g., TMA) and compute (e.g., Tensor Cores). This is in contrast to reusing the same warps for both loading data and computing, as shown in Figure 10-3.

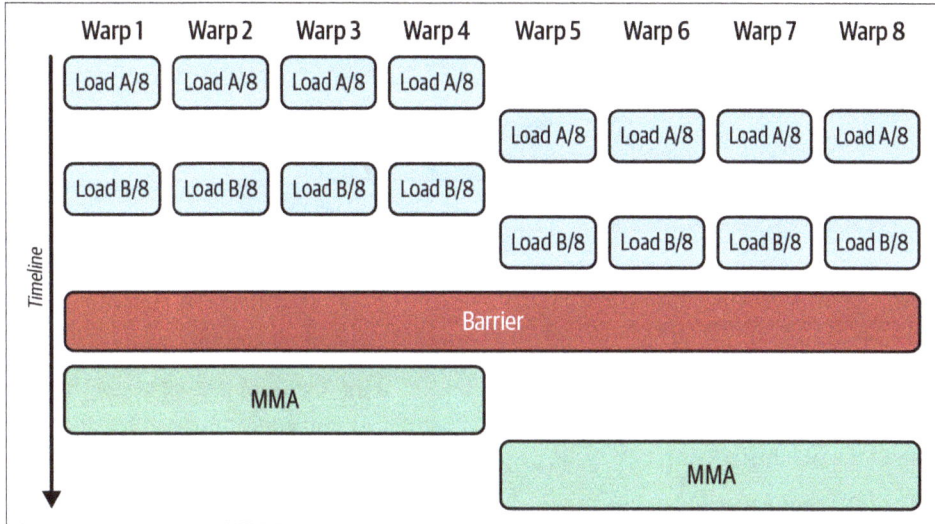

Figure 10-3. Nonwarp specialized kernel with each warp performing a mix of both data loading and compute (source: https://oreil.ly/WZDbM)

This type of specialization allows each set of warps to have their own instruction sequences. As such, instructions are issued and executed continuously without being interrupted by other types of operations. Specifically, warp specialization lets you assign one set of "producer" or "memory" warps to prefetch tiles asynchronously using `cuda::memcpy_async`. Then all other "consumer" or "compute" warps perform the computations, as shown in Figure 10-4.

Here, four warps are assigned the producer role, while the remaining eight warps are assigned the consumer role. Like most producer-consumer patterns, you can assign a different number of warps for the producer and consumer.

Because each warp has its own scheduler, the GPU can issue a load instruction, a math instruction, and a write instruction—all in the same cycle from different warps using different warp schedulers. So an SM with multiple schedulers can issue a memory instruction from Warp 0, a math instruction from Warp 1, and so on, in one cycle.

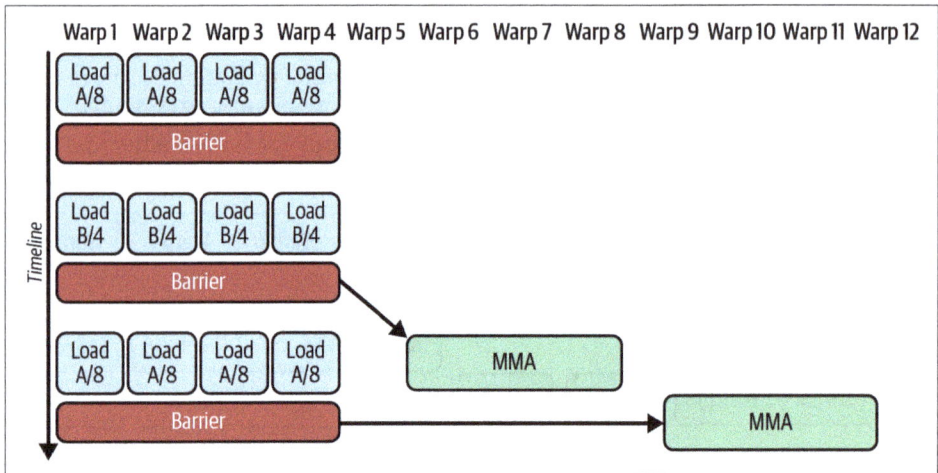

Figure 10-4. Warp-specialized kernel with one set of warps for loading data and all other warps for computations (source: https://oreil.ly/WZDbM)

This effectively creates a thread-block-level multi-issue scenario across warps. This is not possible with single-warp double buffering because a single warp's scheduler can issue only one instruction per cycle.

An interesting pattern for warp specialization is using three different types of warps, such as "loader," "compute," and "storer" warps. The loader warp pushes tiles into the pipeline's queue. The compute warp runs the compute kernel on each tile. And the storer warp writes out the results, as shown in Figure 10-5.

This warp-specialized pipeline squeezes out the idle cycles that a single-warp, double-buffered, sequential load-and-compute loop cannot address. Warp specialization's efficient overlap of data transfer and computation increases GPU utilization—especially for long-running loops and persistent kernels. In these cases, the overhead of role coordination and data handoff is amortized over many iterations.

A paper on warp scheduling (*https://oreil.ly/uhqP1*) demonstrated that warp specialization can achieve nearly perfect overlap of memory and compute. In this case, the GPU kernel had distinct memory and compute phases such that memory and compute took turns being the bottleneck. By applying warp specialization, their workload transformed into a state in which both the SM's memory subsystem and compute units were simultaneously busy almost the entire time.

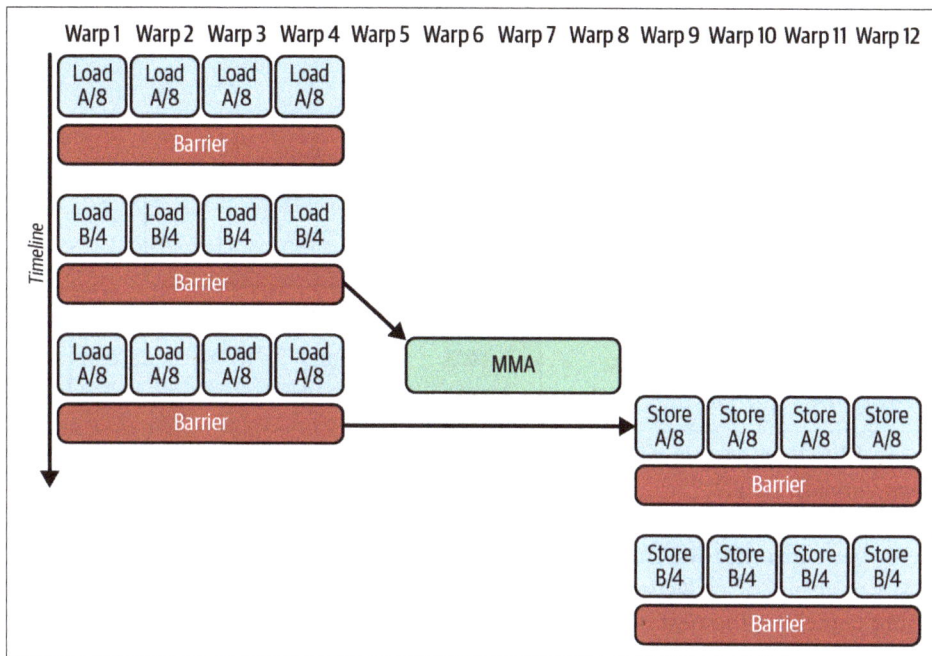

Figure 10-5. Three-role warp-specialized pipeline configuration with one set of warps for loading data, another set for compute, and another set for data storing (source: https:// oreil.ly/xs7YN (https://oreil.ly/JlpQE))

The profiling showed that before using warp specialization, their L2 bandwidth utilization and Tensor Core utilization were out of phase. After warp specialization, L2 bandwidth and Tensor Core utilization became in-phase. This resulted in much higher effective throughput and showed that warp specialization can squeeze out the last bits of idle time—even for a well-tuned asynchronous pipeline that might be left on the table.

Another warp specialization pattern is a modification of the three-role warp-specialized pipeline. It assigns a set of warps to the memory loader as before, but then uses two sets of consumer warps that "ping-pong" between the roles of compute and memory-storer. This three-role warp-specialization architecture is exposed in CUT-LASS as gemm_tma_warpspecialized_pingpong (*https://oreil.ly/xs7YN*) and shown in Figure 10-6.

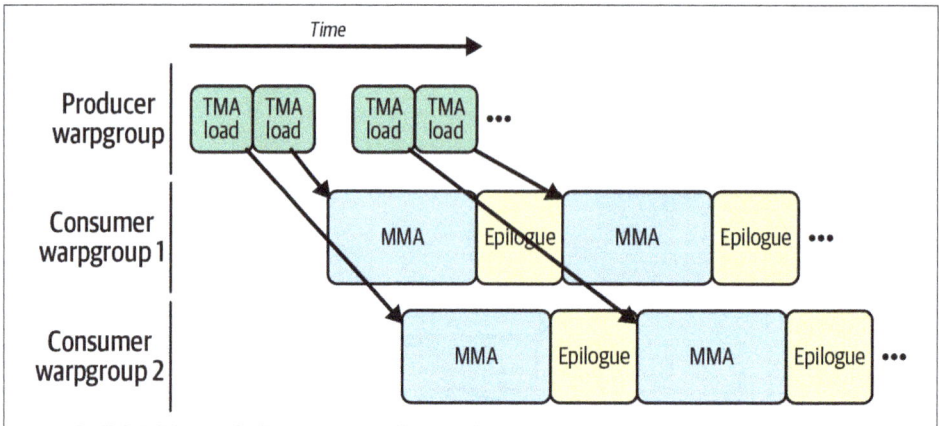

Figure 10-6. Ping-pong architecture with three-role warp-specialized kernel (source: https://oreil.ly/xs7YN)

Here, the consumer MMAs are overlapping and include a small amount of post-MMA wrap-up, or *epilogue,* processing. This per-MMA epilogue cleanup is required before launching the next MMA. Specifically, the epilogue can include accumulating, scaling, writing back to global memory, or shuffling results to another warp. Additionally, the epilogue can perform housekeeping like advancing tile pointers, updating loop counters, and signaling that this tile is done so the next TMA load or MMA can kick off.

> While not shown here, there is also an equivalent prologue processing step that happens before the MMA operation. In this case, the prologue phase would fill the pipeline with a few TMA requests to move data into registers before the MMA consumers can start doing useful work on the Tensor Cores.

In practice, warp specialization is extremely effective at squeezing out the last bits of performance. In fact, FlashAttention v3 attributes its speedups partially to warp-specialized pipelines that overlap GEMM and softmax computations—along with data transfers—to keep all hardware units busy. This helps achieve near-peak FLOPS for attention computations due to aggressive overlap of compute and TMA-driven data movement.

In addition, the PyTorch compiler (covered in Chapters 13 and 14) generates kernels that use warp specialization to schedule separate warps for loading and computing data. It also uses low-cost barriers to synchronize the warps, similar to the CUDA Pipeline API implementation detailed in the next section. The PyTorch compiler system also integrates with CUTLASS's ping-pong GEMM. Both `torch.compile` and Triton may generate warp specialized kernels for supported operations. However, they apply warp specialization selectively based on heuristics and do not enable warp specialization for every operator.

> Use warp specialization for imbalanced or latency-hiding scenarios—especially when a single warp's compute is not enough to hide memory-load latency. However, if a kernel is small—or extremely memory bound—sticking to a simpler double-buffering scheme may produce similar benefits without the extra code complexity.

Using CUDA Pipeline API for Warp Specialization

Warp specialization builds on the CUDA Pipeline API by allowing specialized warps to communicate using fine-grained producer and consumer primitives. These calls avoid full block barriers while composing naturally with asynchronous copies such as `cuda::memcpy_async`.

The key advantage of using the CUDA Pipeline API's producer and consumer calls (e.g., `pipe.producer_acquire()`, `pipe.producer_commit()`, `pipe.consumer_wait()`, and `pipe.consumer_release()`) is that they synchronize only the specific warps or stages that actually need to hand off data. This is in contrast to forcing every thread in a block to wait.

A block-wide barrier would stall every warp—even those that are not involved with the producer-consumer pipeline. All execution in that block must pause until every thread reaches the barrier, as shown in Figure 10-7. For the unified block-scoped pipeline shown there (`cuda::make_pipeline(cta, &pipe_state)`), the producer and consumer calls (`pipe.producer_acquire()`, `pipe.producer_commit()`, `pipe.consumer_wait()`, and `pipe.consumer_release()`) are collective across the participating CTA threads and must execute in a consistent order.

By comparison, the Pipeline API maintains per-stage state internally while still requiring ordered collective participation at each acquire/commit/wait/release point in this unified example. Warp specialization remains valid because only role-specific warps perform role-specific work between the collective calls (e.g., loader-staged copy work, compute, and store) with explicit handoff synchronization points. If you want different warps to call different pipeline primitives directly, you need to use a partitioned pipeline with explicit producer/consumer roles instead of a unified CTA pipeline.

You can implement warp specialization with the CUDA Pipeline API in a three-role pattern. A loader warp produces inputs for a compute warp, the compute warp consumes those inputs and produces results, and a storer warp consumes those results and writes them out. The pipeline object is block scoped, and it tracks the stage order internally.

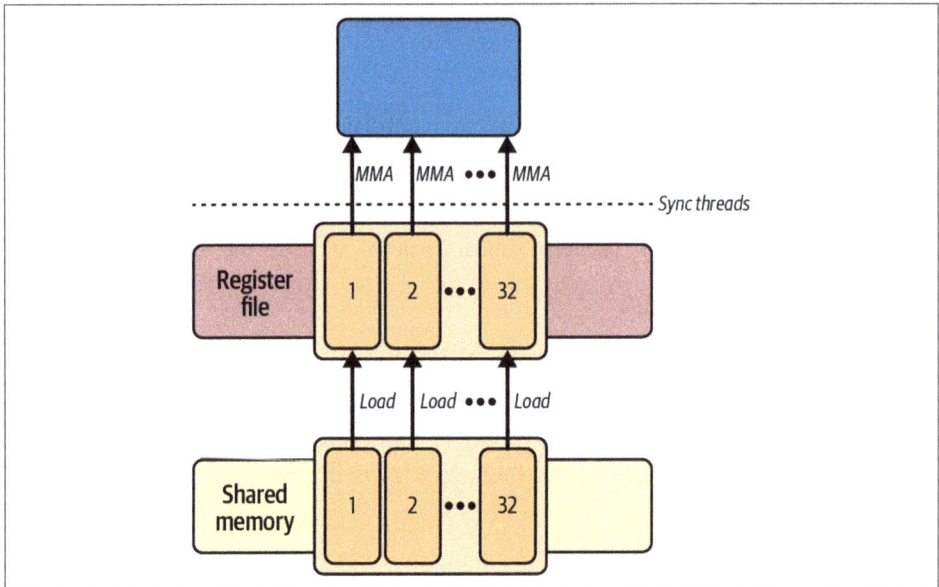

Figure 10-7. Block-wide barrier prevents threads from proceeding until they synchronize and load the new data

Here is an example of a warp-specialized, three-role kernel that computes tiles of data using a loader warp (`warp_id 0`), compute warp (`warp_id 1`), and storer warp (`warp_id 2`):

```
// warp specialized roles using the CUDA Pipeline API

#include <cuda/pipeline>
#include <cooperative_groups.h>
namespace cg = cooperative_groups;

// smem_bytes = 3×TILE_SIZE^2×sizeof(float) (three roles, single-pipeline)
// 3 tiles * 112 * 112 * 4 byte per float =
// 150,528 bytes < 227,328 bytes (~227 KB)
// per-block dynamic SMEM limit on Blackwell
// Choose TILE_* so total shared memory per block is ≤ the device's
// reported per-block shared memory limit.
// Query cudaDevAttrMaxSharedMemoryPerBlockOption and set
// cudaFuncAttributeMaxDynamicSharedMemorySize accordingly.
#define TILE_SIZE 112

// Example tile compute: C = A x B for one TILE_SIZE by TILE_SIZE tile
__device__ void compute_full_tile(const float* __restrict__ A_tile,
                                   const float* __restrict__ B_tile,
                                   float* __restrict__ C_tile,
                                   int lane_id) {
    for (int idx = lane_id; idx < TILE_SIZE * TILE_SIZE; idx += warpSize) {
        int row = idx / TILE_SIZE;
        int col = idx % TILE_SIZE;
```

```
        float acc = 0.0f;
        #pragma unroll
        for (int k = 0; k < TILE_SIZE; ++k) {
            acc += A_tile[row * TILE_SIZE + k] * B_tile[k * TILE_SIZE + col];
        }
        C_tile[idx] = acc;
    }
}

extern "C"
__global__ void warp_specialized_pipeline_kernel(
        const float* __restrict__ A_global,
        const float* __restrict__ B_global,
        float* __restrict__ C_global,
        int numTiles) {
    thread_block cta = this_thread_block();

    // three square tiles in dynamic shared memory: A, B, and C
    extern __shared__ float shared_mem[];
    float* A_tile = shared_mem;
    float* B_tile = A_tile + TILE_SIZE * TILE_SIZE;
    float* C_tile = B_tile + TILE_SIZE * TILE_SIZE;

    // three stage pipeline shared by the block
    __shared__ cuda::pipeline_shared_state<cuda::thread_scope_block, 3>
        pipe_state;
    auto pipe = cuda::make_pipeline(cta, &pipe_state);

    int warp_id  = threadIdx.x >> 5;
    int lane_id  = threadIdx.x & 31;
    int warps_per_block = blockDim.x >> 5;

    // grid wide warp indexing for persistent tiling
    int totalWarps = gridDim.x * warps_per_block;
    int global_warp = warp_id + blockIdx.x * warps_per_block;

    for (int tile = global_warp; tile < numTiles; tile += totalWarps) {
        size_t offset = static_cast<size_t>(tile) * TILE_SIZE * TILE_SIZE;

        if (warp_id == 0) {
            // loader produces A_tile and B_tile
            pipe.producer_acquire();

            auto bytes = TILE_SIZE * TILE_SIZE * sizeof(float);
            cuda::memcpy_async(cta, A_tile, A_global + offset,
                               cuda::aligned_size_t<32>{bytes}, pipe);
            cuda::memcpy_async(cta, B_tile, B_global + offset,
                               cuda::aligned_size_t<32>{bytes}, pipe);
            pipe.producer_commit();
        }

        extern "C"
        __global__ void warp_specialized_pipeline_kernel(
                const float* __restrict__ A_global,
            const float* __restrict__ B_global,
            float* __restrict__ C_global,
            int numTiles) {
```

```
thread_block cta = this_thread_block();

// three square tiles in dynamic shared memory: A, B, and C
extern __shared__ float shared_mem[];
float* A_tile = shared_mem;
float* B_tile = A_tile + TILE_SIZE * TILE_SIZE;
float* C_tile = B_tile + TILE_SIZE * TILE_SIZE;

int warp_id = threadIdx.x >> 5;
int lane_id = threadIdx.x & 31;
const int bytes = TILE_SIZE * TILE_SIZE * sizeof(float);

// three stage pipeline shared by the block
__shared__ cuda::pipeline_shared_state<cuda::thread_scope_block, 3>
pipe_state;
auto pipe = cuda::make_pipeline(cta, &pipe_state);

// Block-strided tile ownership: one tile per block iteration.
for (int tile = blockIdx.x; tile < numTiles; tile += gridDim.x) {
    size_t offset = static_cast<size_t>(tile) * TILE_SIZE * TILE_SIZE;

    // Block-scoped pipeline collectives execute
    // before role-specific branches.
    pipe.producer_acquire();
    cuda::memcpy_async(cta, A_tile, A_global + offset,
                       cuda::aligned_size_t<16>{bytes}, pipe);
    cuda::memcpy_async(cta, B_tile, B_global + offset,
                       cuda::aligned_size_t<16>{bytes}, pipe);
    pipe.producer_commit();

    pipe.consumer_wait();
    cta.sync();

    if (warp_id == 1) {
        compute_full_tile(A_tile, B_tile, C_tile, lane_id);
    }
    cta.sync();

    if (warp_id == 2) {
        for (int idx = lane_id; idx < TILE_SIZE * TILE_SIZE;
          idx += warpSize) {
            C_global[offset + idx] = C_tile[idx];
        }
    }
    cta.sync();
    pipe.consumer_release();
    cta.sync();
}
}
```

Here each warp works in a distinct role for compute and store, while the unified block-scoped pipeline collectives execute uniformly before role-specific branches. Each iteration calls `producer_acquire()`, performs cooperative staged copy under pipeline collectives (e.g., `cuda::memcpy_async` where that path is selected), then calls `producer_commit()`. After `consumer_wait()`, `cta.sync()` enforces handoff order:

load -> compute -> store. Another `cta.sync()` plus `consumer_release()` recycles the stage.

Important correctness rule for this unified example: `producer_acquire()`, `pro ducer_commit()`, `consumer_wait()`, and `consumer_release()` must occur in a consistent collective sequence across the participating CTA threads. Do not place those collectives inside divergent warp-role branches unless you intentionally switch to a partitioned pipeline API with explicit producer/consumer roles. If warp 0 loads, warp 1 computes, and warp 2 stores, keep the unified pipeline collectives outside the branches and use `cta.sync()` between role phases.

> This kernel runs as a persistent kernel across many tiles to amortize launch overhead. More on persistent kernels in a bit.

In short, using the CUDA Pipeline API together with cooperative groups allows fine-grained, SM-wide producer-consumer handoffs with minimal CTA barriers at explicit handoff points. Table 10-3 compares three implementations: a naive tiled kernel, a two-stage double-buffered GEMM using `double_buffered_pipeline`, and our warp-specialized pipeline kernel `warp_specialized_pipeline`.

Table 10-3. Comparison of three implementations: a naive tiled kernel, a two-stage double-buffered GEMM, and a warp-specialized pipeline kernel

Metric	Naive tiling	Two-stage, double-buffered pipeline (`double_buffered_pipeline`)	Warp-specialized pipeline (`warp_specialized_pipeline`)
Kernel execution time	41.3 ms	20.5 ms (2.01× faster versus naive)	18.4 ms (10.2% speedup versus two-stage)
Warp execution efficiency	68%	92% (+24% versus naive)	96% (+4% versus two-stage)
Shared memory stall latency/ warp sync stalls	High	Low	Minimal
L2 throughput	80 GB/s	155 GB/s (+94% versus naive)	165 GB/s (+6.45% versus two-stage)
Throughput scalability	Scales up to only 2–3 warps per SM	Scales well up to ~6 warps per SM	Scales nearly linearly to the SM's warps (e.g., 64 warps)
DRAM bytes read versus SM cycles	Poor overlap	Great overlap	Excellent overlap
Instruction count	1.7 B	1.05 B (−38% versus naive)	~1.00 B (−5% versus two-stage)

Here, the double-buffered pipeline finishes GEMM in 20.5 ms, whereas the warp-specialized version completes in just 18.4 ms. The warp-specialized kernel keeps pipeline collectives legal by issuing them before branch divergence. It then uses explicit handoff points between loader, compute, and storer work. In the previous two-stage, double-buffered kernel, every thread participates in the consumer phase. As such, `consumer_wait()` effectively stalls the entire thread block.

This finer-grained, per-warp synchronization eliminates the implicit full-block wait and allows all three warps (loader, compute, and storer) to overlap continuously. As a result, average SM utilization rises from roughly 92% in the double-buffered design to about 96% in the warp-specialized version—and warp-stall cycles drop to near-zero.

From a scalability standpoint, Nsight Compute shows that the naive tiling kernel saturates after just two to three active warps per SM. This is because each tile load must complete before any computation can start.

The two-stage, double-buffered kernel improves on this by overlapping loads and compute. This implementation scales up to 6 warps per SM before shared-memory or register limits become an issue.

In contrast, the `warp_specialized_pipeline` scales almost linearly as long as you can assign additional warps for load, compute, and store. On Blackwell, for instance, you can keep up to the architectural limit of 64 resident warps per SM. (Actual residency depends on registers, shared memory, and block size.)

As Table 10-3 shows, both the double-buffered and warp-specialized approaches substantially outperform the naive tiled kernel. The `double_buffer_pipeline` halves the runtime by overlapping tile loads and computation, while the `warp_special ized_pipeline` adds another 10.2% speedup by avoiding unnecessary block-wide producer/consumer participation and by keeping the role handoff explicit at CTA synchronization points.

Instruction counts drop from 1.7 billion in the naive version to 1.05 billion in the two-stage pipeline, a 38% reduction, and further to ~1.00 billion in the warp-specialized kernel for an additional 4.76% reduction.

L2 load throughput climbs from 80 GB/s in naive tiling to 155 GB/s in the two-stage approach (+94%) and then to 165 GB/s in the warp-specialized kernel (+6.45% versus two-stage). This is because this warp-specialized kernel dedicates one warp to loading each tile into shared memory once—and then multicasts that single copy to all compute lanes. This eliminates any remaining redundant L2 reads. As such, after tiling and double-buffering, nearly all redundancy is already removed from the pipeline.

In practice, the two-stage double-buffered pipeline is ideal for uniformly tiled GEMM workloads. Its simpler producer/consumer model hides most of the DRAM latency under compute. Meanwhile, the warp-specialized approach is optimized for irregular or deeper pipelines such as fused attention kernels. This is because each warp can continuously perform its assigned role—loading, computing, or storing—without ever forcing the rest of the block to stall.

PyTorch, CUDA Pipeline API, and Warp Specialization

PyTorch's public API doesn't expose `cuda::pipeline` directly, but when you invoke `torch.compile`, the compiler generates kernels (implemented in OpenAI's Triton language) that use optimizations that implement functionality equivalent to `<cuda/pipeline>` primitives and warp-specialized producers/consumers.

So while you won't see `cuda::pipeline` calls explicitly generated, you will see the underlying instructions and barriers. These optimizations help to improve occupancy and increase data-transfer/computation overlap. In other words, you get the same low-latency, high-throughput behavior of a handwritten `<cuda/pipeline>` implementation without writing any CUDA code yourself.

PyTorch's fused attention kernels, produced by TorchInductor, use warp specialization with producer and consumer groups. For instance, consider three separate GPU kernels in PyTorch shown here:

```
scores = torch.matmul(queries, keys.transpose(-2, -1))
probabilities = F.softmax(scores, dim=-1)
context = torch.matmul(probabilities, values)
```

You can simply rewrite this with one line in PyTorch as shown here:

```
context = torch.nn.functional.scaled_dot_product_attention(queries,
    keys, values)
```

Under the hood, the loader warps fetch tiles into shared memory. the compute warps process the tiles, and the store warps write results back. This eliminates expensive round trips to global memory between `matmul` and `softmax` stages.

Overall, `torch.compile` is ideal for performance-sensitive and irregular workloads. Modern GPUs like Blackwell have abundant SM resources and high memory bandwidth. As such, techniques like warp specialization minimize idle cycles and allow near-linear scaling across warps—at least until the SMs—or memory bandwidth—are fully saturated.

Even highly optimized kernels like FlashAttention-3 (*https://oreil.ly/dRBM3*) reach only about ~75% of peak FP16 FLOPS using warp-specialized overlap. This shows that you don't need to achieve 100% compute utilization to achieve a significant optimization milestone.

By decoupling load, compute, and store into independent stages, the pipeline model maximizes throughput and resource utilization, making it the preferred approach for long-running kernels, including such processes as transformer attention, fused operator pipelines, and custom task schedulers. These kernels use the fine-grained inter-warp communication, deep pipelining, and linear warp scaling to provide high performance.

Persistent Kernels and Megakernels

Persistent kernels, also called *persistent threads*, invert the usual one-kernel-per-task approach. Instead of launching many small kernels in which each incurs significant overhead, you can launch a single, long-running kernel whose threads continually pull work from a shared producer-consumer queue in global or shared memory.

When persistent threads loop, they handle data chunks as they arrive—often using memory copies or host signals—without exiting the kernel. This avoids repeated kernel launch overhead entirely. For instance, a persistent kernel might use one thread block's Warp 0 to copy data from global memory (or CPU host memory) to shared memory. In the meantime, Warp 1 computes the previous batch. This is a form of software pipelining on GPU.

For instance, consider having 1,000 tiny, independent tasks. Traditionally, one might launch 1,000 separate kernels. Each kernel occupies only a few SMs for a brief moment before exiting.

In practice, the GPU would repeatedly ramp up for each tiny kernel and ramp down afterward. This would leave most SMs idle between launches—and would fail to utilize the hardware fully.

With a persistent kernel, you instead launch one large grid designed to keep the GPU busy for the entire workload. On a GPU with 132 SMs, for instance, this might mean launching one block per SM with 256 threads per block. That's 33,792 threads in total. Each thread then executes code that looks roughly like the following:

```
__device__ int g_index;  // global counter for next task; initialize to 0 on host

__global__ void persistentKernel(Task* tasks, int totalTasks) {
    // Every thread loops, atomically grabbing next task index until none remain
    while (true) {
        int idx = atomicAdd(&g_index, 1);
        if (idx >= totalTasks) break;
        processTask(tasks[idx]);
    }
}
```

Before launching this kernel, the host would set `g_index = 0` in device memory. It would then invoke the kernel as shown here:

```
cudaMemset(&g_index, 0, sizeof(int));

// one block per SM on a 132 SM GPU
int blocks        = 132;
int threadsPerBlock = 256;

persistentKernel<<<blocks, threadsPerBlock>>>(d_tasks,
    totalTasks);

cudaDeviceSynchronize();
```

Now, instead of paying launch overhead for every single task, you pay only once to launch the `persistentKernel`. Assuming the launch takes roughly 0.02 ms and each of the 1,000 tasks runs in 0.1 ms, the kernels would run back to back for approximately 100 ms of total work.

By comparison, running 1,000 tiny kernels back to back, each taking 0.02 ms to launch, would add 20 ms in overhead to the execution time—separate from the 100 ms of total runtime for all 1,000 tasks. In short, consolidating small tasks into a persistent loop can cut tens of milliseconds of launch overhead.

Using persistent kernels, the GPU stays highly utilized—with nearly all SMs actively working on tasks concurrently—because tens of thousands of threads are available to process the ~1,000 tasks. In contrast, launching 1,000 tiny kernels sequentially leaves much of the GPU underutilized at any given time. In our example this equates to only ~35% of the GPU's capacity being used on average.

In this persistent kernel scenario, each SM is running one block of 256 threads (out of 2,048 total threads max), so every SM is doing work. As such, nearly 100% of SMs are active even though each SM's own occupancy is relatively low at 12% (256 ÷ 2048 threads.)

Using persistent kernels in this manner, the GPU can maintain high measured SM Active percent, subject to register and shared memory usage. Remember to always verify with Nsight Compute.

On modern GPUs, persistent kernels are particularly effective because their larger shared-memory capacity and expanded register file allow each thread to hold more intermediate state on-chip. Threads can use TMA to prefetch tensor tiles for upcoming tasks while other warps compute. So while some threads are processing one task, other threads use TMA to prefetch data for upcoming tasks—without burdening the SM's compute pipelines with memory transfer instructions.

Common Workloads for Persistent Kernels

Persistent kernels shine when you have many small or unevenly sized tasks that would incur high launch overhead if handled separately. They allow dynamic load balancing. This allows faster threads to continue looping and grab more work. Using persistent kernels, no SM ever goes idle prematurely.

This pattern is common in irregular workloads such as graph traversals, custom batched transformations, and per-token operations common in LLM inference. In these cases, each task's time can vary significantly.

There are downsides to persistent kernels, however. First, you must explicitly manage your task queue and synchronization using atomics. This can introduce contention if many threads attempt to increment the same counter simultaneously.

Debugging a single, giant persistent loop is more complex than debugging multiple small kernels. This is because a single divergent thread or an unexpected branch can cause the entire kernel to hang. Furthermore, one persistent kernel can monopolize the GPU indefinitely. So if other workloads need to run concurrently, you must carefully assign streams or partition resources.

In short, persistent kernels can increase overall throughput substantially (e.g., 2–3×) compared to naive kernels by turning the GPU into a dynamic "worker-thread" pool that continuously fetches and processes tasks. On modern GPU hardware, this approach eliminates launch overhead, maximizes SM occupancy, and—when combined with cooperative groups or thread block clusters (described in a bit)—keeps data on-chip throughout multistage pipelines.

More and more frameworks and libraries are using persistent kernels and megakernels to avoid wasted capacity and improve performance of latency-sensitive workloads like inference. The key is to eliminate repeated launches and use device-side task queues on the GPU to keep the SMs fully occupied and performing useful work.

> As of this writing, PyTorch does not automatically fuse an entire multistage workload into one kernel due to scheduling complexity. As such, achieving the full benefits of persistent kernels and megakernels requires custom CUDA code or specialized compilers. Nevertheless, for multiphase algorithms, refactoring into persistent megakernels can produce significant performance gains—as long as you properly handle synchronizations and avoid deadlocks.

Megakernels for Inference

Additionally, a modern approach to persistent kernels originating from large-scale inference is called a *megakernel* (*https://oreil.ly/697m8*). A megakernel fuses entire sequences of operations across layers—and even across GPUs—into a single large kernel. As shown in Figure 10-8, persistent megakernels have shown (*https://oreil.ly/2aZiF*) to reduce latency by 1.2× to 6.7× versus traditional per-layer launches by eliminating repeated kernel launch overhead.

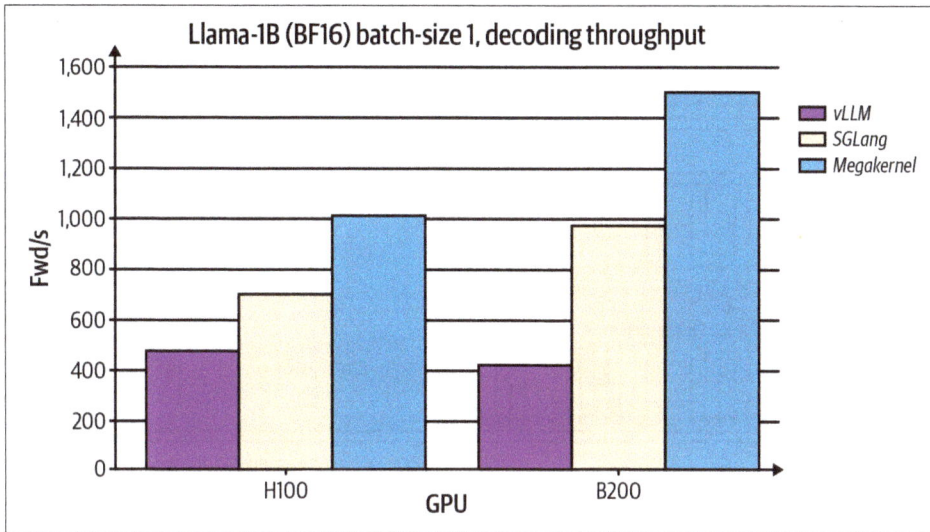

Figure 10-8. Decode throughput improvement with megakernels relative to vLLM and SGLang (source: https://oreil.ly/2aZiF)

Persistent Kernels and Warp Specialization

Warp specialization is typically used with persistent kernels in which threads perform many iterations over a relatively long period of time. This allows for deeper pipelines, better overlap, and efficient utilization of long-lived resources. For shorter-running kernels, the added code complexity of persistent kernels and warp specialization might not pay off.

And a limitation of persistent-kernel scheduling is finding enough SMs for the persistent kernel to utilize. If too many SMs are occupied by another kernel, there might not be enough resources for the persistent kernel to launch. This makes it challenging when trying to schedule and load-balance work across SMs.

To facilitate persistent kernels (and therefore warp specialization), modern GPUs support *thread block clusters*—also called *cooperative thread array (CTA) clusters* since a thread block is also called a cooperative thread array. We will discuss thread block (CTA) clusters in an upcoming section, but, in short, they let you combine thread blocks into "clusters" that occupy multiple nearby SMs on the GPU.

Cooperative Groups

Cooperative groups let you define and synchronize groups of threads at arbitrary granularities. For example, you can create groups with individual threads, warps, tiles, blocks, and clusters, as shown in Figure 10-9.

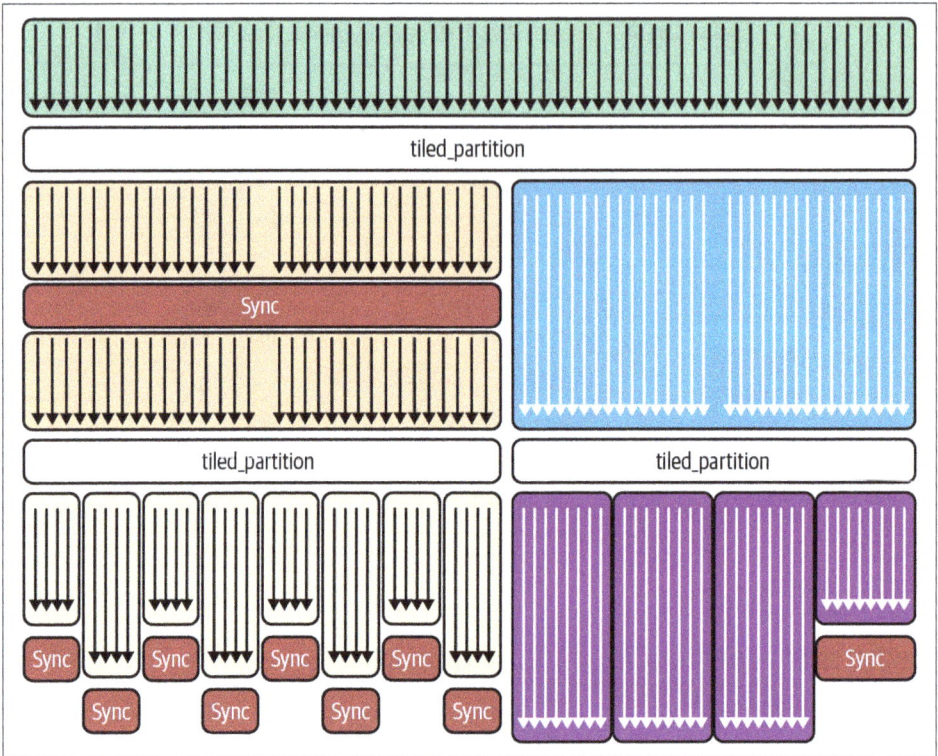

Figure 10-9. Synchronizing across different granularities of threads using cooperative groups

Cooperative groups provide safe, reusable collectives like sync, broadcast, and reduce. This is in contrast to using ad hoc synchronization barriers. Normally, threads can only synchronize within their own block using __syncthreads()—and there is no built-in global barrier for the entire grid, for example.

Cooperative groups give you fine-grained synchronization inside the kernel. The API is ideal for coordinating multistage pipelines across warps, blocks, and clusters. To use the Cooperative Groups API with your kernels, you simply include <coopera tive_groups.h>, obtain group objects, then synchronize and coordinate across these groups.

The API includes calls like cg::this_thread_block(), cg::tiled_partition(), and cg::this_cluster(). You then call group.sync()—or similar collectives—to coordinate the threads in these groups.

To launch a kernel in cooperative mode, you use cudaLaunchCooperativeKernel(). In cooperative mode, CUDA ensures the grid you launch can be resident concurrently—otherwise, the launch fails. As such, it's recommended to always size the cooperative grid using `cudaOccupancyMaxActiveBlocksPerMultiprocessor` and clamp grid size to avoid launch failure. Inside the kernel, you can then call the following to implement an all-thread-block barrier:

```
cooperative_groups::this_grid().sync(); // or grid.sync()
```

In this case, no thread in any block can proceed past that point until every thread in every block has reached it. This barrier allows you to split a kernel into sequential phases without ending the launch or returning control to the host.

For instance, consider the softmax algorithm, common in LLMs, that has two stages: a reduction across the entire array to compute an aggregate sum, and then a subsequent per-element computation that uses the aggregate sum. Traditionally, you would launch one kernel to do the reduction, copy the result back to host memory or global memory, launch a second kernel to consume the result from host or global memory, then calculate the softmax. This requires a lot of relatively slow memory movement.

With cooperative groups, you can perform both stages in one kernel such that each block computes its partial sum, one block aggregates those partial sums into a final result, all blocks call `grid.sync()` to wait until aggregation is complete, then all threads proceed to the second stage. Each thread would then read the aggregate sum from a register or shared memory—rather than from global memory.

CUDA guarantees that every block in a cooperative launch is resident on the GPU at the same time. If you request more blocks than can fit concurrently, the launch simply fails.

Because cooperative kernels must be launched with a grid size that the GPU can run concurrently, `grid.sync()` will not hang waiting for nonexistent blocks. In other words, the CUDA runtime guarantees that all thread blocks are active and will reach the `grid.sync()` barrier. If the kernel launch were too large to run at once, it would simply fail to launch. As such, it's important to check the return status of `cudaLaunchCooperativeKernel()`.

For instance, if a GPU has 132 SMs and your kernel uses enough resources that each SM can run four blocks, the grid must be no larger than 528 blocks to succeed. If you exceed that limit, the cooperative launch will simply fail. Use `cudaOccupancyMaxActiveBlocksPerMultiprocessor` to size the grid for a cooperative kernel and check the `cudaLaunchCooperativeKernel` return status before assuming progress has been made.

Prior to Blackwell, developers often used `cudaLaunchCooperativeKernel` together with global-memory atomics or flags to coordinate multiple blocks that did not share on-chip memory. This approach worked but forced intermediate results to be moved to global memory. This incurred extra HBM traffic.

On Blackwell, thread block clusters and DSMEM provide a far more efficient alternative. A thread block cluster can share data in on-chip SRAM—and synchronize without global memory round trips. We will cover thread block clusters and DSMEM later in this chapter.

You should use cooperative kernels when you need a true, all-thread-block barrier within a single kernel launch. Also, they're useful when you want to keep intermediate results in fast memory (e.g., registers or shared memory) rather than repeatedly writing to and reading from global memory. It's recommended that you constrain your grid size to the GPU's maximum concurrent block capacity—or choose larger blocks—to reduce overall block count and a failed kernel launch.

The downsides of cooperative kernels are that your grid size is limited by capacity. This may force you to use fewer, larger blocks—or rely on thread block clusters (later in this chapter).

Even though all blocks run concurrently, a cooperative barrier still requires every thread in every block to call `grid.sync()`. If any single thread skips—or never reaches—the `grid.sync()` call (e.g., because of a divergent `if` statement), then every other thread that did call `grid.sync()` will wait forever. This results in a deadlock.

In short, cooperative group kernels let you treat the entire GPU as a single collaborative resource, with `grid.sync()` acting as a global barrier. This is ideal for multistage algorithms requiring global synchronization and data sharing. Just remember that `grid.sync()` is a relatively heavyweight synchronization with higher overhead than block-scoped or cluster-scoped barriers. This is because it must coordinate across all thread blocks running on multiple SMs. As such, you should use `grid.sync()` sparingly and, at the very least, make sure that your kernel does a significant amount of work between heavyweight synchronization calls.

> For cases where you need only limited cross-block coordination, using global-memory atomics or per-block flags can be safer and simpler than relying on a full-grid barrier. However, they are less efficient than using thread block clusters and DSMEM, as we'll discuss in a bit.

Cooperative Grid Synchronization and Persistent Kernels

If your workload occasionally needs cross-thread-block barriers inside a persistent loop to aggregate partial results, you can combine persistent kernels with cooperative groups by calling `grid.sync()`. This will provide a grid-wide barrier to avoid ending the kernel and having to relaunch it. In this way, a multistage pipeline of reductions and other global steps remains entirely on-device.

For instance, consider a workload that performs two different computations repeatedly across 1,000 iterations such that each computation requires a global barrier because of cross-block data dependencies. A naive implementation might launch two separate kernels per iteration, resulting in 2,000 kernel launches. In a single stream, the second kernel waits for the first automatically—no explicit host-side sync—but you still pay launch overhead. Instead, you can fuse everything into one cooperative, persistent kernel, as shown here:

```
#include <cuda_runtime.h>
#include <cooperative_groups.h>
namespace cg = cooperative_groups;

__device__ inline float someComputationA(float x) { return x * 2.0f; }
__device__ inline float someComputationB(float a, float b) { return a + b; }

__global__ void combinedKernel(float* __restrict__ dataA,
                               float* __restrict__ dataB,
                               int N,
                               int iterations) {
    cg::grid_group grid = cg::this_grid();                 // whole-grid group
    const int tid = blockIdx.x * blockDim.x + threadIdx.x; // thread's linear id
    const int stride = gridDim.x * blockDim.x;             // total grid threads

    for (int it = 0; it < iterations; ++it) {
        // Stage 1: update all elements of A using a grid-stride loop
        for (int i = tid; i < N; i += stride) {
            dataA[i] = someComputationA(dataA[i]);
        }

        grid.sync();  // global barrier; also provides memory visibility

        // Stage 2: use finished A to update B (again grid-stride)
        for (int i = tid; i < N; i += stride) {
            const float mid = dataA[i];
            dataB[i] = someComputationB(mid, dataB[i]);
        }

        grid.sync();  // barrier before next iteration
    }
}
```

On the host side, you would simply invoke this combined cooperative and persistent kernel, as shown here:

```
// ... allocate/copy dA, dB, set N, iterations, choose blockSize
cudaDeviceProp prop{};
cudaGetDeviceProperties(&prop, 0);
if (!prop.cooperativeLaunch) {
    // Fallback: run two kernels per iteration instead of grid.sync()
    // (see alternative below)
}
```

```
// Compute the maximum grid size allowed for a cooperative kernel
int maxBlocksPerSm = 0;
const int blockSize = 256;
cudaOccupancyMaxActiveBlocksPerMultiprocessor(&maxBlocksPerSm,
                                              combinedKernel,
                                              blockSize, 0);
const int maxCoopGrid = maxBlocksPerSm * prop.multiProcessorCount;

// Choose grid size, but clamp to cooperative limit
int gridSize = (N + blockSize - 1) / blockSize;
if (gridSize > maxCoopGrid) gridSize = maxCoopGrid;

// Launch cooperatively
void* args[] = { &dA, &dB, &N, &iterations };
cudaLaunchCooperativeKernel((void*)combinedKernel, gridSize, blockSize, args);
cudaDeviceSynchronize();
```

This single kernel replaces what would otherwise be 2 × 1,000 = 2,000 kernel launches and avoids repeated launch overhead. Inside the loop, `grid.sync()` ensures correct ordering (every block finishes Stage 1 before any block begins Stage 2—and before the next iteration) without any host-side synchronization.

Per-thread and per-block data can remain in registers/shared memory across `grid.sync()`. For cross-block data exchange, use global memory (or thread block clusters and distributed shared memory, as we'll cover in a bit). Meanwhile, because the work is looped on the GPU, there is no launch overhead after the first invocation.

Cooperative kernels require device support (`cooperativeLaunch`) and must be launched with `cudaLaunchCooperativeKernel`. All blocks in the grid must be resident concurrently. Size and clamp the grid using the CUDA Occupancy APIs so all CTAs can co-reside. Otherwise the launch will fail. An example is when `((N + threads - 1) ÷ threads)` exceeds the cooperative capacity.

> Use the CUDA Occupancy APIs to size cooperative grids.

Modern GPUs can run on the order of a few thousand thread blocks concurrently (assuming each uses a modest amount of resources, including registers and shared memory), so there is considerable headroom. However, you should still verify block size and resource consumption before proceeding with this implementation.

In this kernel example, the kernel never returns control to the host between iterations. As such, it behaves like a persistent kernel for the outer loop but enforces global synchronization points in the inner stages.

This combined pattern is especially powerful for multistep algorithms in LLM inference in which each layer may require a reduction or normalization (Stage 1) followed by a per-element transformation (Stage 2). By capturing everything in a cooperative persistent kernel, you eliminate all inter-kernel round trips and maximize on-chip data locality.

When to Combine Persistent Kernels and Cooperative Groups

A common best practice is to launch a persistent kernel with one thread block per SM if resources allow. This way, each SM has a resident thread block that iteratively processes tasks from a work queue. This maximizes occupancy and keeps SMs from becoming idle. The thread blocks would then use `grid.sync()` to coordinate between their phases. However, when deciding between cooperative and persistent strategies—and whether to combine them—ask the following questions:

Do you have multiple sequential phases that need global synchronization?
> If yes, use cooperative kernels (or cooperative persistent kernels) so you can call `grid.sync()` between phases.

Do you have many small or irregular tasks that suffer from launch overhead?
> If yes, use persistent kernels so your threads loop over a shared queue without returning to the host.

Can you afford to reserve the entire grid (or a thread block cluster) exclusively for this workload?
> If yes, a cooperative persistent kernel may yield the best performance.

Do you need to share SMs with other work?
> If yes, consider using thread block clusters (next section) so the persistent or cooperative kernel does not serve other workloads.

In short, when you use a single kernel that both loops persistently over tasks and includes `grid.sync()` calls to synchronize all thread blocks between stages, you eliminate the pauses and extra memory transfers that normally occur between separate kernel launches.

With modern GPUs, this means data stays in shared memory or registers throughout the entire computation. This is in contrast to writing the data back to global memory after each phase. As a result, the GPU stays busy doing useful work almost all the time—achieving performance close to its peak hardware limits.

One important caveat: cooperative kernels reserve all SMs in the grid, so no other kernels can run concurrently on those SMs. If you need to coschedule other work such as asynchronous data prefetch on a separate stream or lower-priority inference kernels, you may need to partition the GPU into thread block clusters, covered in the next section.

Thread Block Clusters and Distributed Shared Memory

A *cooperative group* is a software-level abstraction that provides an API that lets you carve up kernel threads into arbitrary collectives for synchronization and data movement. This includes warps, tiles, thread blocks—even entire grids or multidevice grids.

In contrast, a thread block cluster (or cooperative thread array [CTA] cluster), is a hardware-level hierarchy. It grants a subset of SMs to your cooperative grid—and leaves the remainder free for other kernels to use. This mitigates the risk of one kernel monopolizing the GPU. The GPU guarantees the thread blocks will be coscheduled on the same GPU processing cluster (GPC), as shown in Figure 10-10.

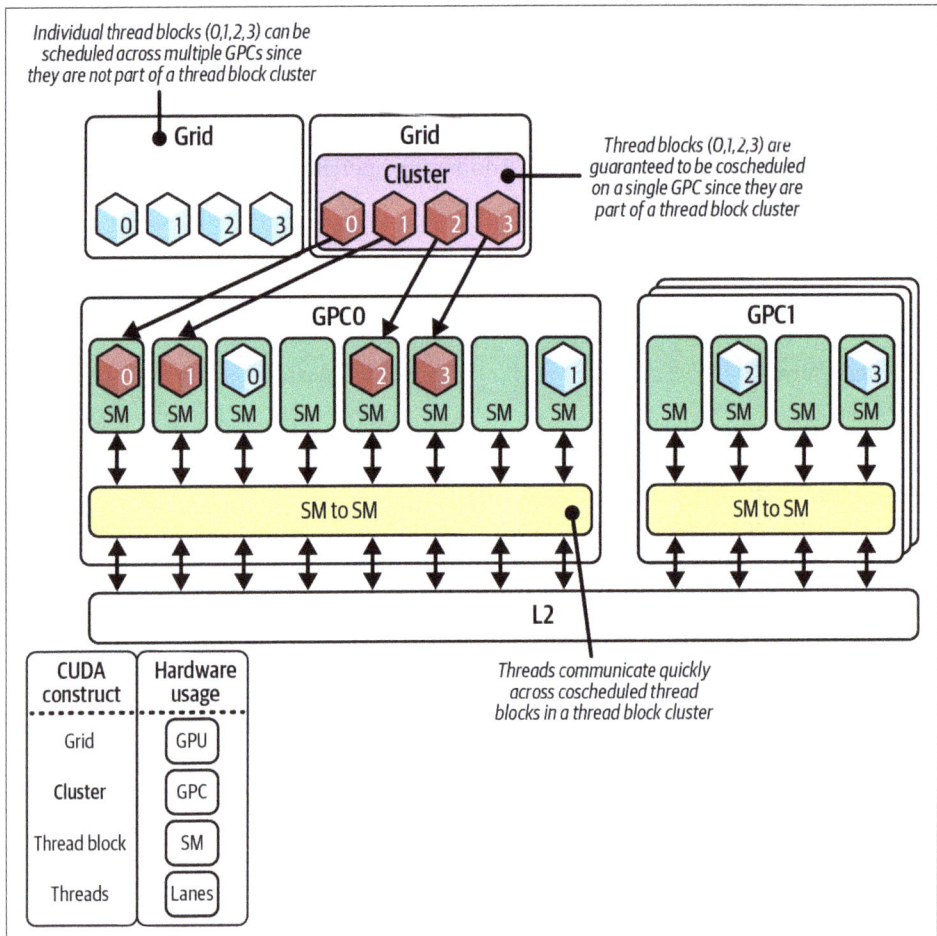

Figure 10-10. Multiple thread block clusters are guaranteed to be coscheduled on the same GPC or GPC partition

A GPC is a collection of nearby SMs. The GPU schedules thread blocks onto GPCs similar to how it schedules threads of a thread block onto the same SM.

> There are actually multiple GPC "partitions" on multidie modules like the NVIDIA Blackwell B200/300 and GB200/300—one GPC partition per die. Since Blackwell is a two-die GPU, it has two GPC partitions. Remember that Blackwell's two GPU dies are linked with NV-HBI and present as a single CUDA device with full cache coherence across dies. The L2 caches are coherent across dies, as well. As such, the dies form a combined logical GPC so the architecture handles the separate GPC partitions for you.

The GPU provides distributed shared memory (DSMEM), discussed in the next section, for the thread block cluster to use across those blocks. It also supports a cluster-level barrier using the Cluster Group API (`cluster.sync()`).

This cluster-level barrier lets you synchronize only a subset of thread blocks without blocking the entire GPU. Thread block clusters let you launch a cooperative kernel that subdivides the grid into smaller groups of blocks, as shown in Figure 10-11.

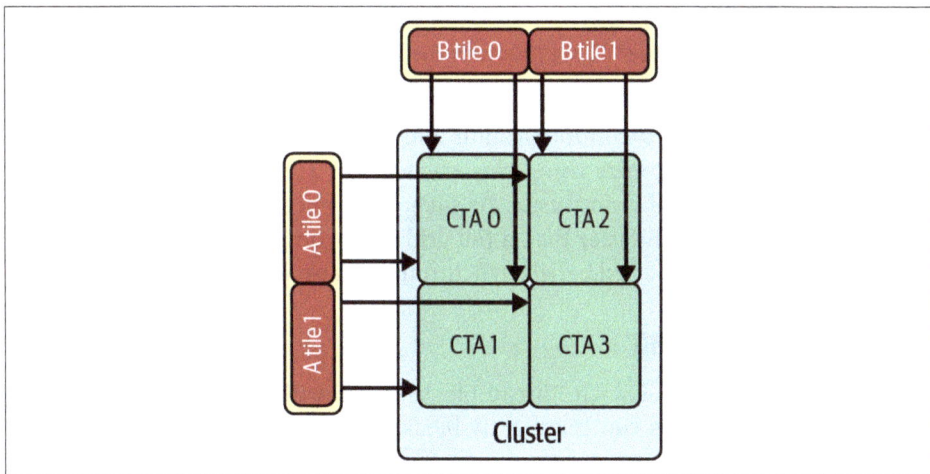

Figure 10-11. For these four (2 × 2) thread clusters, each tile of A and B is loaded into two thread blocks simultaneously (source: https://oreil.ly/kEZsv)

Within each group, calling `cluster.sync()` provides a local barrier. This lets blocks inside a cluster share data through dedicated on-chip resources without monopolizing every SM. On modern GPUs, you can use DSMEM, which allows thread block clusters to share a contiguous region of on-chip SRAM. This enables low-latency communication between blocks in the same cluster with native hardware support.

Thread block clusters group a subset of thread blocks and call `cluster.sync()` within each cluster to synchronize "locally" within just those thread blocks. While threads within a thread block could traditionally cooperate using shared memory, on modern GPUs, they can now collaborate with each other using thread block clusters and DSMEM.

Said differently, without thread block clusters, only threads within the same thread block could share data in shared memory. Different thread blocks would have to coordinate using global memory and global barriers (e.g., a `grid.sync()`), which stalls all threads and limits scalability.

And, furthermore, threads in different thread blocks previously could not efficiently share state and synchronize except using either global memory or `grid.sync()` for coarse-grained, grid-wide synchronization, as described in the previous section. Unfortunately, both global memory and `grid.sync()` are relatively slow and, as such, can become bottlenecks.

Thread block clusters are supported natively by the GPU hardware, including *cluster launch control*. Cluster launch control is a hardware-level mechanism that launches and schedules persistent thread block clusters. Specifically, it allows a persistent kernel (and its thread block cluster) to maintain a balanced load of work—even when some of the SMs are occupied. This provides the basis for an efficient warp specialization implementation.

Using hardware-supported communication and synchronization constructs, thread block clusters can synchronize using cluster-wide barriers in the form of low-level PTX instructions and CUDA intrinsics. As such, blocks in a cluster can perform barrier synchronization much faster than a full grid synchronization using `grid.sync()` due to the hardware-supported barrier synchronization between the thread blocks.

Thread Block Swizzling

In a straightforward grid launch, thread blocks process tiles in strict row-major or column-major order. This can cause early blocks to evict data that later blocks will need—resulting in poor reuse and extra memory traffic. Instead, you want tiles A and B within a single wave, which can be read out of L2 cache.

To work around this inefficiency, you can use thread block swizzling. Similar to using swizzling to optimize memory access and avoid shared-memory bank conflicts, you can use thread block swizzling to avoid assigning tiles in the inefficient row-major and column-major order, as shown in Figure 10-12.

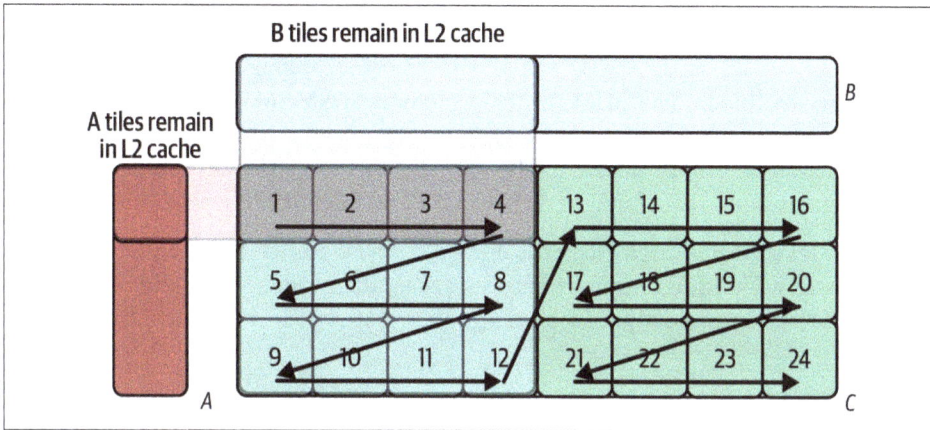

Figure 10-12. Thread block swizzling to read tiles A and B in a single wave out of L2 cache

Thread block swizzling lets tiles of both A and B matrices, needed by the same wave, stay in L2 for maximum reuse. When applied to persistent and tiled GEMM workloads, this type of swizzling can produce double-digit performance gains by reducing memory misses and bandwidth pressure. Thread-block swizzling is a simple yet powerful pattern-reordering technique that aligns kernel launch order with cache locality.

With hardware support for thread block clusters, a relatively large number of SMs, and improved pipeline scheduling, modern GPUs can host large persistent kernels with a sophisticated warp specialization pipeline to optimize kernel performance.

In short, thread block clusters build on the cooperative groups model by allowing a subset of blocks to synchronize and share state without locking out the entire GPU. This lets you build multistage, fine-grained pipelines inside one launch without locking out the rest of the device. This leaves the remaining SMs free to perform independent work.

Within thread block clusters, there are two key mechanisms to share state between thread blocks: DSMEM and scratch memory. Let's describe these next.

Distributed Shared Memory

Distributed shared memory (DSMEM) extends the concept of __shared__ memory beyond a single thread block to span an entire thread block cluster. In a traditional kernel, each thread block has its own private __shared__ region and is inaccessible to other thread blocks.

With DSMEM, however, multiple blocks in the same cluster can read/write into a shared memory space that logically combines all of their local __shared__ regions. In effect, the cluster's shared memory is stitched together into one distributed on-chip buffer.

By keeping interblock data inside on-chip memory, DSMEM significantly increases effective arithmetic intensity since blocks can exchange intermediate results or perform reductions without round-tripping to global memory. This is especially valuable when a dataset is too large for a single block's shared memory.

Instead of falling back to global loads and stores, you launch a thread block cluster whose blocks each work on a portion of the data, then synchronize and share using DSMEM. All communication happens at SM-to-SM speed, which avoids expensive HBM traffic.

In short, DSMEM is a faster, more structured alternative to using global memory for block-to-block communication. But its scope is limited to the blocks in the same cluster. DSMEM is ideal for persistent kernels that require frequent, low-latency interblock coordination, attention mechanisms, or other multistage algorithms in LLMs in which every block must exchange intermediate state before proceeding—as well as any workload that benefits from keeping interim results on-chip rather than writing back to and reloading from global memory.

> The portable (*https://oreil.ly/M29T9*) maximum cluster size is 8 blocks. Some GPUs support larger non-portable cluster sizes (e.g., up to 16 CTAs) when explicitly enabled with the `cudaFuncAttribute NonPortableClusterSizeAllowed` attribute. This increases your DSMEM footprint at the cost of occupying more SMs in the cluster.

Scratch Memory

Scratch memory is the low-level hardware infrastructure that underpins DSMEM and thread block cluster synchronization, whereas DSMEM is the shared data buffer that is implicitly visible to your CUDA code, scratch memory is a separate on-chip SRAM region used by the GPU to track coordination metadata such as barrier state, group progress, and access flags for DSMEM.

You do not access scratch memory directly from your kernels. Instead, the GPU manages it automatically. When you launch a thread block cluster, the hardware allocates a portion of scratch memory to maintain cluster-wide barrier counters (`cluster.sync()` state), track which blocks have arrived at DSMEM operations or synchronization points, and coordinate safe access to the distributed `shared` regions across SMs.

Because scratch memory is optimized for these metadata operations, it enables cluster-level barriers and DSMEM accesses to complete very quickly. If the metadata size exceeds available scratch SRAM for very large clusters or complex synchronization patterns, the GPU transparently spills some state into local memory, which is backed by L1/L2 caches. This spill ensures correctness while still preserving as much on-chip efficiency as possible.

In short, DSMEM is the abstraction you use to share data between blocks and scratch memory in the behind-the-scenes facility that makes those DSMEM operations fast and scalable. Together, they allow a thread block cluster to behave like a single logical unit that breaks the traditional barrier between thread blocks. This improves performance for workloads that need tightly coordinated parallelism across multiple thread blocks.

Launching a Thread Block Cluster

Let's illustrate how to use thread block clusters in practice. First, we need to launch a kernel with a cluster dimension that we haven't used before.

In CUDA, this is done with an extended launch API that allows specifying the cluster size. For example, if we want clusters of two blocks, also called a *thread block pair*, or *CTA pair*, we can configure a special launch attribute, as shown here:

```
// Host code: launch a kernel with thread block clusters of size 2
cudaLaunchConfig_t config{};
config.gridDim = dim3(128, 1, 1);
config.blockDim = dim3(256, 1, 1);
config.dynamicSmemBytes = 0;

cudaLaunchAttribute attr{};
attr.id = cudaLaunchAttributeClusterDimension;
attr.val.clusterDim.x = 2;
attr.val.clusterDim.y = 1;
attr.val.clusterDim.z = 1;

config.attrs = &attr;
config.numAttrs = 1;

// Allow non-portable cluster sizes if you intend to use > 8 later
cudaFuncSetAttribute(MyClusterKernel,
                     cudaFuncAttributeNonPortableClusterSizeAllowed,
                     1);

cudaLaunchKernelEx(&config, MyClusterKernel, args, nullptr);
```

In this host code, we use `cudaLaunchKernelEx` to launch `MyClusterKernel` with clusters of 2 thread blocks (so 64 clusters total since 128 blocks ÷ 2 per cluster). The `clusterDim` is set to 2, meaning each cluster will contain 2 thread blocks. This replaces the traditional `<<<gridDim, blockDim>>>` syntax for cases where we want cluster-cooperative kernels. Under the hood, the CUDA runtime ensures those paired blocks are scheduled such that they can communicate with DSMEM.

Remember that each thread block cluster needs to physically fit into the SMs and resources that you specify. The portable maximum cluster dimension is 8 thread blocks. To launch 16 on supported Blackwell parts, you must enable the non-portable attribute and size blocks so the cluster stays resident on the SMs. Keep this in mind when sizing your thread block clusters.

Coordinating Thread Block Clusters with Cooperative Groups API

To coordinate work across multiple thread blocks in a cluster, you first obtain a handle to that group of blocks using `cooperative_groups::this_cluster()`. This cluster handle lets you perform hardware-accelerated cluster-wide barriers—and directly access another block's shared memory.

This all happens without leaving the kernel or resorting to global-memory flags. Here is an example kernel that sums a local value from each thread block into thread block 0's shared memory:

```
#include <cuda_runtime.h>
#include <cooperative_groups.h>
namespace cg = cooperative_groups;

__global__ void MyClusterKernel(/* args */) {
    // 1. Form a cluster group for all thread blocks in this thread block cluster
    cg::cluster_group cluster = cg::this_cluster();

    // 2. Allocate the same extern shared buffer in each block
    extern __shared__ int shared_buffer[];

    // 3. Each block learns its rank and the total cluster size
    int clusterRank = cluster.block_rank();
    int clusterSize = cluster.num_blocks();

    // 4. Initialize this block's portion of shared memory (a simple local sum)
    int localSum = threadIdx.x;
    shared_buffer[threadIdx.x] = localSum;

    // 5. Barrier across all blocks in the cluster; no block proceeds until
    //    every block reaches this point and has written its shared_buffer.
    cluster.sync();

    // 6. Map a pointer to block 0's shared_buffer so block can write into it
    // Pointers returned by cluster.map_shared_rank
    // refer to the remote CTA's shared memory
    // and support remote atomics
    // and memory operations within
    // the cluster
    // Pair updates with cluster.sync at well defined point
    int* remote_buffer = cluster.map_shared_rank(shared_buffer, 0);
```

```
if (clusterRank != 0) {
    // 7. Nonzero blocks atomically add their local shared_buffer[0] into
    //    rank 0's buffer. This atomicAdd is routed on-chip over DSMEM
    //    (not through DRAM.)
    atomicAdd(&remote_buffer[0], shared_buffer[0]);
}

// 8. Another cluster-wide barrier ensures all atomic adds have completed
cluster.sync();

// 9. Finally, block 0 (rank 0, thread 0) can read the combined result
if (clusterRank == 0 && threadIdx.x == 0) {
    printf("Combined sum in cluster[0]: %d\n", shared_buffer[0]);
}
}
```

Here, we obtain a cluster handle by calling cg::this_cluster(). This returns a cluster_group object that represents exactly those blocks launched together as one thread block cluster. The runtime guarantees that every thread block in this cluster group is resident simultaneously—otherwise, the launch will fail.

A uniform shared memory allocation is implicitly provided. Each block in the cluster must declare the same size for extern __shared__ int shared_buffer[]. The DSMEM hardware will then logically combine each block's shared memory into one virtual address space. And because all blocks reserve the same shared_buffer size, a pointer to the buffer of thread block 0, or rank 0, will coordinate properly across SMs.

> When using thread block clusters, make sure to organize each thread block's DSMEM accesses just like global-memory coalescing. In other words, have each warp read or write contiguous, 32-byte-aligned sectors. That way, the hardware can route cluster-wide DSMEM transfers without bank conflicts or unexpected serialization. In practice, lay out your tile data so that the warp i in thread block j always touches a unique, aligned range. This will avoid memory bank contention and keep DSMEM data transfers performing at full speed.

In the previous example code, we also see that cluster.sync() is used as a cluster-wide barrier across thread blocks in the cluster. Unlike __syncthreads(), which only synchronizes threads within a single block, cluster.sync() synchronizes all threads in every block of this cluster.

This barrier is implemented in hardware and generally has lower latency than a grid-level synchronization, because it coordinates only the blocks in the cluster. This means you can synchronize blocks frequently with minimal impact—as long as they are within a cluster.

And there is no risk of deadlock caused by missing blocks since CUDA enforces that the grid launches properly and fits on the GPU. As such, there is no scenario in which some blocks reach the barrier and then hang forever waiting for "missing" blocks that never started. All blocks are already present, so the barrier completes cleanly once every block calls it.

In the previous code block, you see that cross-block shared memory access happens using `map_shared_rank()`. After the first barrier, every block's `shared_buffer[]` is initialized. To get a pointer into block 0's shared memory, the other blocks call `int* remote_buffer = cluster.map_shared_rank(shared_buffer, 0)`, which specifies the thread block id (0) in the cluster.

The GPU hardware automatically translates that pointer so any load or store goes over the on-chip DSMEM network rather than out to global DRAM. As such, any write operation into `remote_buffer`—either an atomic or regular write—will update block 0's shared memory directly on-chip. It's worth highlighting that the performance characteristics of remote DSMEM accesses differ from local shared memory. Remote loads and stores benefit from coalesced, aligned 32-byte segments.

For instance, in the previous code block, when blocks 1...n need to add their local values into block ID 0's shared buffer, they call `atomicAdd(&remote_buffer[0], shared_buffer[0])`. And because `remote_buffer` was obtained with `cluster.map_shared_rank()`, the `atomicAdd` goes directly into block 0's SMEM over the on-chip DSMEM network. In other words, there is no round trip to DRAM or L2 cache. Every write happens at on-chip speeds.

In the previous code example, you see that once all blocks have performed their `atomicAdd`, a second `cluster.sync()` ensures that block 0 sees the complete sum in its own `shared_buffer[0]` before proceeding.

In short, `cooperative_groups::this_cluster()` plus `cluster.sync()` and `cluster.map_shared_rank()` give you a simple, efficient way to synchronize and share data across multiple thread blocks in a thread block cluster. All of these operations occur on-chip, avoid global-memory round trips, and enable fine-grained cooperation among blocks. This combination of thread block clusters and DSMEM provides much higher performance than any global-memory fallback or manual atomic-flag approach.

Thread Block Pair

With modern NVIDIA, GPUs let you coschedule exactly two thread blocks in a cluster, or a thread block pair (aka *CTA pair*), across SMs within a single GPC. By grouping thread blocks in a cluster (e.g., a 2-block cluster, as shown in Figure 10-13), kernels that share data can use TMA to move tiles into each block's shared memory.

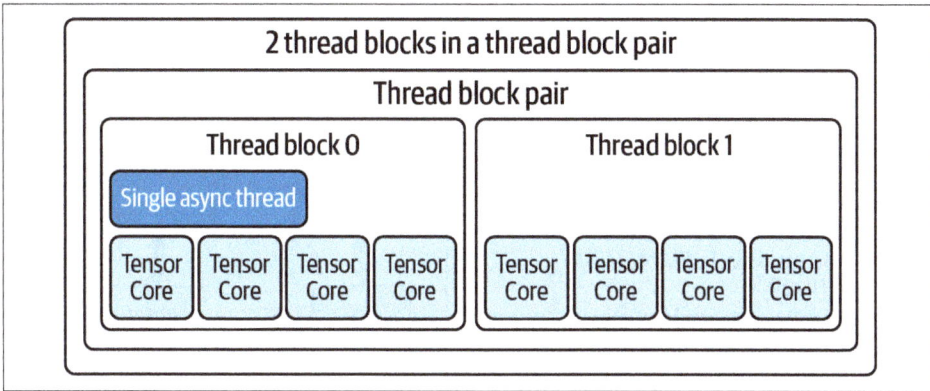

Figure 10-13. Thread block pair combines two thread blocks

A single thread block might lack the registers or shared-memory capacity to process a very large tile (for example, a 256 × 256 matrix subtile) by itself. By pairing two thread blocks on nearby SMs within a GPC and using DSMEM, those two blocks can split the work on one large tile yet share data through a unified shared-memory region, as shown in Figure 10-14.

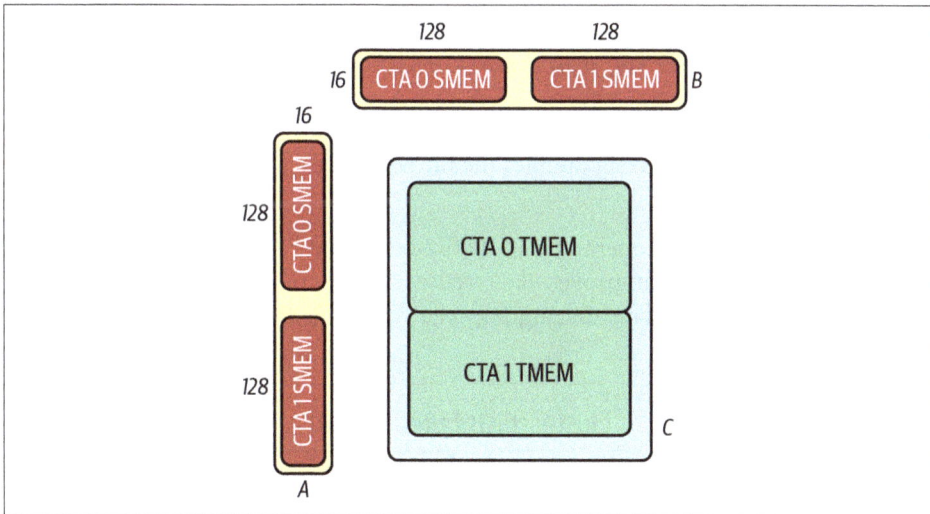

*Figure 10-14. Thread block pair (aka CTA pair) loading tiles as operands for an A * B matrix multiply (source: https://oreil.ly/kEZsv)*

Here, each thread block in the pair can load a fraction of the operand tile (e.g., 128 × 16) into its on-chip SMEM for the matrix multiply. In addition, each thread block holds part of the accumulator (e.g., 128 × 256) in Tensor Memory (TMEM). This allows the two thread blocks in the CTA pair to collaborate on a single tile, as shown in Figure 10-15.

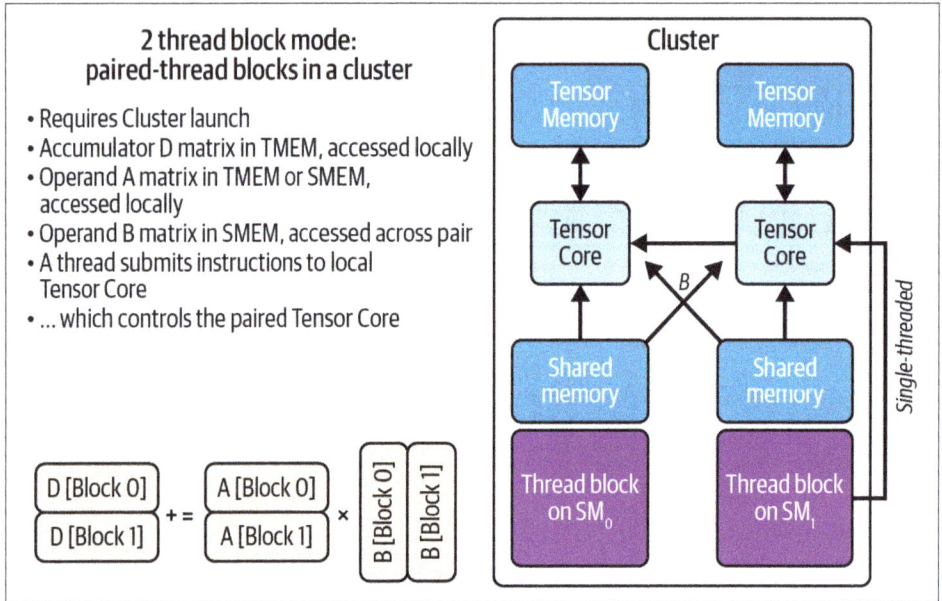

2 thread block mode: paired-thread blocks in a cluster

- Requires Cluster launch
- Accumulator D matrix in TMEM, accessed locally
- Operand A matrix in TMEM or SMEM, accessed locally
- Operand B matrix in SMEM, accessed across pair
- A thread submits instructions to local Tensor Core
- … which controls the paired Tensor Core

Figure 10-15. Thread block pair with Tensor Cores and TMEM

Thread block pairs allow larger matrix multiplies that span two physical SMs. Using a pair of thread blocks effectively doubles the tile size since each SM handles half of the tile's data.

The SM hardware shares operand data between the SMs using DSMEM. DSMEM reduces duplicate loads, improves data reuse, and increases arithmetic intensity. Figure 10-16 shows this data sharing between SMs in a thread block cluster using DSMEM.

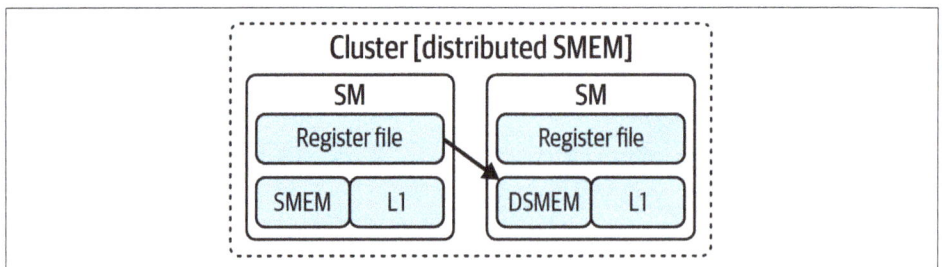

Figure 10-16. Sharing data between SMs in a thread block cluster using DSMEM

CUDA provides enhanced multicast barrier and synchronization primitives for these multi-SM operations. The pair synchronizes with each other using the lightweight `cluster.sync()` call. This way, when one SM finishes using a tile, the adjacent SM in the CTA pair can consume it.

Each tile is fed into the pair of thread blocks without redundant global-memory transactions. This better occupies otherwise idle registers, shared-memory banks, and Tensor Cores. And a thread block pair achieves higher Tensor Core utilization by doubling the threads and shared memory available for one tile.

Any boost in performance will happen transparently. From a programmer's perspective, you simply launch a cluster of two blocks and treat it as one large thread block split across two thread blocks. In CUTLASS, for instance, this is exposed as a 2-SM UMMA (Unified MMA) GEMM operation that uses DSMEM and cluster barriers for inter-CTA data sharing. You simply request two SMs for a single GEMM tile, and CUTLASS handles the cluster launch, DSMEM setup, and interthread block synchronization automatically.

If you request a tile size that a single thread block can't handle (say, 128×128 for FP16 Tensor Core operations), CUTLASS will automatically allocate two thread blocks as a pair. The SMs split the work and rely on DSMEM + `cluster.sync()` under the hood to share the tile. This way, you can do pairwise overlapping of UMMA operations with DSMEM.

In short, thread block pairs and DSMEM provide parallelism in the form of multi-SM cooperation. They provide fast, on-chip data sharing and synchronization across thread blocks. This eliminates many scenarios that previously required global-memory handoffs or additional kernel launches. This benefits many multithread block algorithms and simplifies their implementation.

Reducing Global Memory Traffic with Thread Block Clusters

From a performance perspective, DSMEM can significantly cut down redundant global-memory traffic and enable higher effective bandwidth. For instance, in a tiled GEMM where multiple thread blocks within a cluster share chunks of the A or B matrix, one block can load a tile from global memory and multicast the tile to other blocks in the cluster using the TMA.

The TMA engine supports a multicast copy mode that feeds directly into DSMEM when thread blocks belong to the same cluster. A single TMA transfer from global memory can place data into each participating block's shared memory simultaneously. This avoids redundant DRAM fetches.

With TMA multicast, the GPU ensures that L2-cached data is broadcast into the shared memory of each cluster member (thread block) in one pass. As a result, you avoid repeated global-memory loads of the same tile. This improves bandwidth utilization and shrinks DRAM traffic—especially when many blocks need the same input, as shown in Figure 10-17.

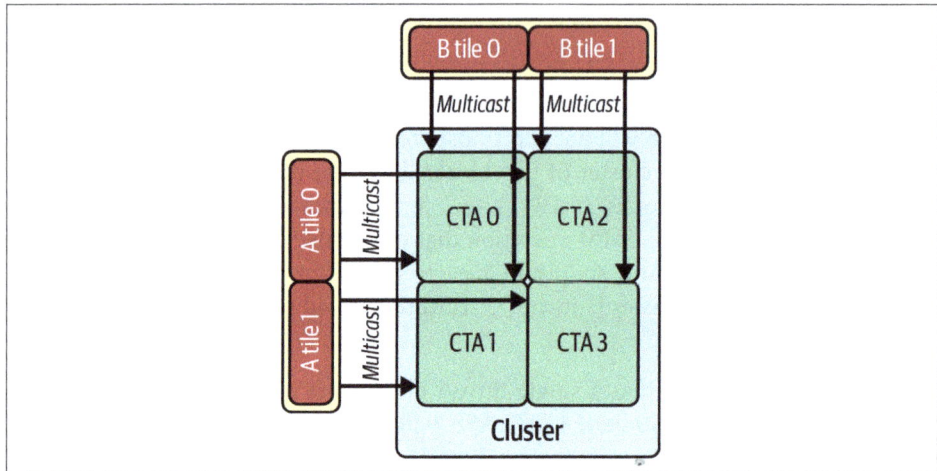

Figure 10-17. For these four (2 × 2) thread clusters, each tile is loaded once and multicast into the shared memory of all CTAs in each cluster (source: https://oreil.ly/kEZsv)

Here, the TMA engine performs a single multicast from global memory into DSMEM, broadcasting the tile to every thread block's SMEM in the cluster and eliminating redundant DRAM reads. TMA multicast is configured through a tensor-map descriptor and issued as `cp.async.bulk.tensor` targeting `shared::cluster`. Fortunately, higher-level libraries like CUTLASS/cuTe and Triton generate these multicast operations, tensor-map descriptors, and bulk tensor copies for you. Specifically, these libraries can issue the relevant PTX (*https://oreil.ly/uFO4C*) instructions including `cp.async.bulk.tensor` with a tensor-map operand. They can issue PTX instructions that target `shared::cluster` for multicast. In these cases, the hardware delivers the tile to each thread block's SMEM.

Another common use case is multiblock reductions or scans. Instead of having each block write out its partial sum or scan result to global memory and then launching a separate kernel to combine them, thread blocks in a thread block cluster can write their partial results into DSMEM.

Within that same cluster, you can perform a fast on-chip reduction or prefix-sum across these partial results using shared memory and a cluster-level barrier, `cluster.sync()`. Only the final result needs to go to global memory. This greatly reduces global memory reads and writes.

By combining thread block clusters, DSMEM, and TMA multicast, you can build multistage, fine-grained pipelines that keep most data exchanges on-chip. Whether you are sharing tiles for GEMM, accumulating partial sums for a reduction, or performing a multiblock scan, these mechanisms let you minimize HBM round trips and maximize arithmetic intensity.

> A block scoped `cuda::pipeline` does not synchronize other blocks; cluster wide distribution uses TMA multicast or DSMEM with `cluster.sync`.

Consider two thread blocks, CTA 0 and CTA 1, that both need the same tile of matrix A. Without DSMEM, each CTA issues its own global-memory load, which wastes DRAM bandwidth by fetching the identical data twice.

With DSMEM, however, CTA 0 loads the tile once into its shared memory and then multicasts it over the on-chip DSMEM network so that CTA 1 can read it directly from shared memory. If more than two CTAs form a cluster, the same tile will be shared across all thread blocks in the cluster, but this still requires only one global HBM load. Table 10-4 shows a comparison using a cluster of two thread blocks versus two independent thread blocks.

Table 10-4. Performance impact of DSMEM on a two-block workload

Metric	Two independent CTAs (no DSMEM)	CTA pair with DSMEM (cluster of 2)
Global load transactions	2× (each thread block loads tile)	1× (tile loaded once)
L2 cache hit rate	50%	85%
Inter-CTA data reuse	N/A (no reuse)	Significant (tile reused by CTA 1)
Effective DRAM BW per CTA	300 GB/s	50% less 150 GB/s
Kernel time (relative)	1.0×	0.6× (40% speedup)

Here, we see a 40% speedup in kernel execution when using a thread block pair (aka *CTA pair*) with DSMEM. This is consistent with the bandwidth savings as well. The DRAM bandwidth per thread block drops by 50% from 300 GB/s to 150 GB/s since each tile is fetched only once. The L2 hit rate jumps from 50% to 85% since the TMA hardware is performing a multicast copy on-chip—and therefore avoiding multiple loads from global memory.

In short, by multicasting shared data, thread block clusters allow multiple blocks to reuse data at on-chip speeds. This leads to substantial speedups for memory-bound workloads.

It's important to note that both DSMEM and L2 operate in parallel. This provides two "lanes" for interblock data sharing. This dual-path design combines DSMEM's ultra-fast cluster-wide communication with L2's broader caching coverage. In other words, DSMEM access is bypassing the L2 cache for cluster-local addresses. Instead, DSMEM uses the dedicated SM-to-SM network, as shown in Figure 10-18.

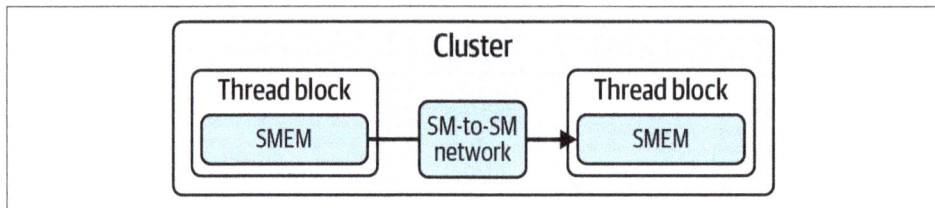

Figure 10-18. DSMEM uses an SM-to-SM thread block cluster-local network between two thread block clusters for its data exchange

Remote DSMEM accesses are routed using the thread block cluster interconnect and are distinct from global-memory traffic. For example, when a thread block pulls a tile using DSMEM, it uses low-latency shared-memory transfers. This ensures that inter-thread block data sharing in a thread block cluster is as fast as on-chip shared memory.

If a tile is not present in DSMEM, it must be fetched from global memory (following the normal cache hierarchy that may hit in L2, for example). This way, if a tile has already been evicted from DSMEM, for instance, the thread block can still retrieve the tile data from the L2 cache instead of going all the way back to global DRAM.

As a result, memory stalls are rare, occupancy remains high, and overall execution runs significantly faster than the unoptimized, two-independent-thread-blocks, non-DSMEM implementation.

Designing Efficient Algorithms with Thread Block Clusters

Thread block clusters enable new strategies for parallelizing workloads that previously required global memory communication or multiple kernel launches. For example, imagine a large matrix multiplication in which the output tile is too large to be handled by a single thread block due to shared memory limits.

In the past, you might split the work across two thread blocks, but then each block would have to exchange partial results with global memory, which is relatively slow and inefficient. Otherwise, you'd have to launch a separate reduction kernel to combine the outputs of the two thread blocks.

With thread block clusters and DSMEM, those two blocks can form a cluster and directly share a joint region of on-chip shared memory to seamlessly combine their results using hardware-supported primitives. The DSMEM hardware allows an SM to perform loads/stores/atomics to another SM's shared memory through a fast network.

It's important to carefully design algorithms to use thread block clusters effectively. Synchronization overhead is low, but it is still nonzero. Performing very fine-grained data sharing might not pay off.

Thread block cluster barriers work like warp-level intrinsics (e.g., `__shfl_sync()`), introduced in Chapter 7, in that every participant must arrive at the synchronization point together. When you call `cluster.sync()`, all thread blocks in the cluster must reach that line before any block can continue.

If one block finishes its work early, it simply waits. If a block never reaches the barrier, because its threads took a different branch, for instance, the entire cluster will deadlock.

In other words, just as warp intrinsics demand that all threads in a warp execute the same instruction path to avoid divergence, thread block clusters demand that all blocks follow the same control flow up to each `cluster.sync()` call.

Because of this lockstep requirement, fine-grained data sharing between blocks must be balanced against the overhead and risk of deadlock. Synchronization itself is inexpensive when done correctly, but if even one block bypasses or delays reaching a `cluster.sync()`, performance may be impacted—or, even worse, the kernel might hang.

You should structure code such that every block arrives at each barrier in unison— just as every thread in a warp must arrive at the barrier with warp-level intrinsics. This is essential to take full advantage of the thread block clusters' low-latency, on-chip communication without falling into deadlocks.

Typically, thread block clusters perform the best when each block has a sizable amount of work that can run independently until a synchronization or data exchange point is needed. Once the synchronization happens and the data is transferred on-chip, the thread blocks can continue processing.

Thread block clusters are especially effective for block-sparse matrix operations— common in sparse attention, model pruning, and compression in LLMs. In these cases, the blocks process different nonzero regions and share their boundary data.

Thread block clusters are also useful for multiphase reductions such as the softmax and normalization steps in transformer layers. These require a final combine step using the partial results of each thread block in the thread block cluster.

More generally, large GEMMs benefit from thread block clusters when they exceed the resources of a single block. GEMMs, of course, are central to the transformer attention and multilayer perceptron (MLP) layers and embedding lookups common in modern LLMs.

Larger cluster sizes can reduce overall occupancy, however. For instance, a cluster of 16 blocks might monopolize 16 SMs for one task. This could leave fewer SMs for other tasks needed by that kernel launch. It's recommended to start with small clusters, two- or four-thread block clusters, unless a bigger cluster is needed for special cases. As always, you should profile with your specific workload to confirm that sharing on-chip resources across thread block clusters outweighs the potential loss of parallelism.

When using cluster launches, verify active blocks and cluster residency with Nsight Compute launch statistics and the standard occupancy APIs, such as `cudaOccupancyMaxActiveBlocksPer Multiprocessor`. For nonportable cluster sizes, set `cudaFuncAttri buteNonPortableClusterSizeAllowed` (or pass `cudaLaunchAttrib uteNonPortableClusterSizeAllowed` using `cudaLaunchKernelEx` attributes). Otherwise the launch may fail or measure low occupancy.

Warp Specialization with Thread Block Clusters

Let's now revisit warp specialization using a thread block cluster with the CUDA Pipeline API. We use a thread-block scoped pipeline as the cluster leader to stage the copies and perform cluster-wide barriers with DSMEM. This way, every block in the cluster consumes the same input tiles without reloading them from global memory.

Roles are assigned per warp inside each block. The leader block's loader warp performs the cooperative copies into its shared memory once per tile. After a cluster-wide barrier publishes those tiles, every block uses a compute warp to read the leader's tiles through DSMEM and compute a disjoint band of rows. A storer warp in each block writes that band back to global memory. The block-scoped pipeline is used only by the leader for the asynchronous copies. Other blocks do not wait on that pipeline. Here is the code:

```
// Warp specialization across a thread-block cluster
// using DSMEM and a block-scoped pipeline

#include <cuda/pipeline>
#include <cooperative_groups.h>
#include <algorithm>
namespace cg = cooperative_groups;

#define TILE_SIZE 128
#define TILE_ELEMS (TILE_SIZE * TILE_SIZE)

// Compute a band of rows of the TILE_SIZE×TILE_SIZE product from DSMEM sources.
// Each lane processes rows [row_begin, row_end) in a 32-way striped loop.
__device__ void compute_rows_from_ds(const float* __restrict__ A_src,
```

```
                          const float* __restrict__ B_src,
                          float* __restrict__ C_dst,
                          int row_begin, int row_end,
                          int lane_id) {
    for (int row = row_begin + lane_id; row < row_end; row += warpSize) {
        for (int col = 0; col < TILE_SIZE; ++col) {
            float acc = 0.0f;
            #pragma unroll
            for (int k = 0; k < TILE_SIZE; ++k) {
                acc += A_src[row * TILE_SIZE + k] * B_src[k * TILE_SIZE + col];
            }
            C_dst[row * TILE_SIZE + col] = acc;
        }
    }
}

extern "C"
__global__ void warp_specialized_cluster_pipeline(
    const float* __restrict__ A_global,
    const float* __restrict__ B_global,
    float* __restrict__ C_global,
    int numTiles) {
    thread_block cta = this_thread_block();
    cluster_group  cluster = this_cluster();

    extern __shared__ float shared_mem[];
    float* A_tile_local = shared_mem;
    float* B_tile_local = A_tile_local + TILE_ELEMS;
    float* C_tile_local = B_tile_local + TILE_ELEMS;

    // Block-scoped pipeline used only by the cluster leader
    // to stage asynchronous copies
    __shared__
    cuda::pipeline_shared_state<cuda::thread_scope_block, 2> pipe_state;
    auto pipe = cuda::make_pipeline(cta, &pipe_state);

    const int lane_id = threadIdx.x & 31;
    const int warp_id = threadIdx.x >> 5;

    auto warp = tiled_partition<32>(cta);

    const int cluster_rank      = cluster.block_rank();
    const dim3 cluster_dims      = cluster.dim_blocks();
    const int  blocks_in_cluster = cluster_dims.x * cluster_dims.y *
                                   cluster_dims.z;

    // 1D cluster arrangement along x;
    // each iteration processes one tile per cluster
    auto loader = cooperative_groups::tiled_partition<32>(cta);
    for (int tile = blockIdx.x / cluster_dims.x; tile < numTiles;
         tile += gridDim.x / cluster_dims.x) {
        const size_t offset = static_cast<size_t>(tile) * TILE_ELEMS;
```

```
// Leader block stages A and B once for the entire cluster.
// For block-scoped pipeline collectives, entire leader CTA participates.
if (cluster_rank == 0) {
    pipe.producer_acquire();
    if (warp_id == 0) {
        cuda::memcpy_async(warp, A_tile_local, A_global + offset,
                           TILE_ELEMS * sizeof(float), pipe);
        cuda::memcpy_async(warp, B_tile_local, B_global + offset,
                           TILE_ELEMS * sizeof(float), pipe);
    }
    pipe.producer_commit();
    // Make loads visible to leader CTA before publishing cluster-wide.
    cuda::pipeline_consumer_wait_prior<1>(pipe);
}

// Publish the leader's tiles to every block via DSMEM
cluster.sync();

const float* A_src = cluster.map_shared_rank(A_tile_local, 0);
const float* B_src = cluster.map_shared_rank(B_tile_local, 0);

// Divide rows among blocks in the cluster
const int rows_per_block = (TILE_SIZE + blocks_in_cluster - 1)
                           / blocks_in_cluster;
const int row_begin = std::min(cluster_rank * rows_per_block, TILE_SIZE);
const int row_end   = std::min(row_begin + rows_per_block, TILE_SIZE);

// Compute warp produces block's band of rows into local shared memory
if (warp_id == 1) {
    pipe.producer_acquire();
    compute_rows_from_ds(A_src, B_src, C_tile_local, row_begin, row_end,
                         lane_id);
    pipe.producer_commit(); // publish C_tile_local
}

// Storer warp writes this block's rows back to global memory
if (warp_id == 2) {
    pipe.consumer_wait(); // observe C_tile_local
    for (int row = row_begin + lane_id; row < row_end; row += warpSize) {
        for (int col = 0; col < TILE_SIZE; ++col) {
            C_global[offset + row * TILE_SIZE + col] =
                C_tile_local[row * TILE_SIZE + col];
        }
    }
    pipe.consumer_release();
}

// All blocks finish this tile before the leader reuses its buffers
cluster.sync();
}
```

```
    // dynamic shared memory size: 3 * TILE_ELEMS * sizeof(float)
}
```

Here, the leader performs one pair of cooperative copies of each tile into its shared memory using a block-scoped pipeline. The cluster-wide barrier makes the data visible to all cluster members through DSMEM.

This "copy once, share through DSMEM" pattern shares the leader's tiles using DSMEM and `map_shared_rank` following a cluster barrier. It does not perform a TMA multicast as we covered previously with tensor-map descriptors, `cp.async.bulk.tensor`, and `shared::cluster`. This is an important distinction to understand as, without the `cluster.sync()` in the DSMEM pattern, followers can read stale leader SMEM data. As such, `cluster.sync()` is required before `map_shared_rank()`.

> The following should help you choose TMA multicast versus DSMEM sharing: If tile reuse per block is high (e.g., each block touches the same tile many times) or the cluster size (C) is large (8-16 CTAs), TMA multicast usually wins since this pattern writes once, then reads locally many times. If SMEM is tight (e.g., large tiles) or cluster size (C) is small (2-4 CTAs) and each follower touches the tile once, DSMEM sharing is usually the better option since it uses a smaller footprint.

Every block computes a distinct band of rows directly from the leader's shared memory by using `map_shared_rank` and writes its results to global memory. This removes duplicate global loads across the cluster and keeps the overlap advantages of a pipeline at the points where it matters.

The leader block's loader warp calls `producer_commit()` to publish its local stage to that block. Other blocks do not wait on the leader's pipeline. Instead, they observe the leader's tiles after the cluster wide barrier and then read from distributed shared memory.

This allows tile loading, computing, and storing to interleave across multiple thread blocks, which drives the SMs to even higher utilization. Table 10-5 compares the single-block warp-specialized kernel with the thread-block-clustered (multiblock) warp-specialized kernel presented in this section.

Table 10-5. Comparison of naive tiling, two-stage double buffering, warp-specialized, and thread block cluster pipeline kernels

Metric	Naive tiling	Two-stage, double-buffered (`double_buffer_pipeline`)	Warp-specialized (`warp_special ized_pipeline`)	Thread block cluster pipeline (`warp_special ized_cluster_ pipeline`)
Kernel execution time	41.3 ms	20.5 ms (+2.01× faster versus naive)	18.4 ms (+10.2% speedup versus two-stage)	17.2 ms (+6.5% speedup versus warp-specialized)
Warp execution efficiency	68%	92% (+24% versus naive)	96% (+4% versus two-stage)	97% (+1% versus warp-specialized)
Warp state stall % (for shared memory and barrier waits)	High	Low	Minimal	Minimal (further reduced)
L2 throughput	80 GB/s	155 GB/s (+94% versus naive)	165 GB/s (+6.45% versus two stage)	170 GB/s (+3% versus warp-specialized)
Throughput scalability	Scales up to 2–3 warps/SM	Scales to ~6 warps/SM	Scales nearly linearly to SM warp limit (64 resident warps per SM on Blackwell)	Scales fully across thread blocks until they are constrained by SM warp limit of 64 resident warps per SM on Blackwell
DRAM read throughput versus kernel duration	Poor overlap	Great overlap	Excellent overlap	Excellent overlap (even under thread block handoff)
Instruction count	1.7 B	1.05 B (−38% versus naive)	~1.00 B (−4.76% versus two-stage)	~0.98 B (−2% versus warp-specialized)

Here, we see that the thread block cluster implementation further improves on warp-specialized by distributing loader, compute, and storer roles across multiple thread blocks in one cooperative launch. This increases overall SM utilization and reduces both execution time and redundant memory traffic.

Specifically, the thread block cluster pipeline kernel implementation (`warp_special ized_cluster_pipeline`) squeezes out another ~1.2 ms (6.5%) over the single-thread-block, warp-specialized kernel. This is because the thread block cluster version interleaves tile loads, computes, and stores across all thread blocks.

SM utilization reaches ~97%, since any idle SM in one thread block can be kept busy by another thread block performing a different pipeline stage. L2 load throughput peaks around 170 GB/s, thanks to better shared-memory reuse and fewer redundant loads. As such, the cluster can avoid duplicate global reads. With DSMEM, the leader block loads a tile once and other blocks read it using `map_shared_rank()` after `cluster.sync()` is called. With TMA multicast, a single tensor copy from global can be broadcast directly into each block's shared memory.

Instruction count drops to ~0.98 B because thread-block-wide pipelining further reduces wasted cycles on redundant global reads. Throughput scalability is also maintained since, as long as you have enough thread blocks and warps, the pipeline can keep them all saturated up to the warps-per-SM hardware limit of your GPU, or 64 warps per SM on Blackwell.

Note that both the single thread block and thread block cluster versions of warp specialization will eventually hit that same "warps-per-SM" ceiling, but they differ in how those warps are fed data and synchronized. This difference translates into a measurable performance advantage for the thread block cluster implementation, as we saw in Table 10-5.

Specifically, in the single thread block, warp-specialized kernel, each thread block allocates exactly three warps: one to load a tile-sized chunk of A and B into shared memory, one to compute on that chunk, and one to store the results back to global memory. Once those three warps complete their roles, the thread block moves on to its next tile, and the cycle repeats.

Even if every SM has three active warps for load, compute, and store, you are not saturating the warp limit of the SM. Modern GPUs allow up to 64 concurrent warps per SM, and actual residency is limited by registers, shared memory, and blocks per SM.

At similar total live warp counts, a single-block warp specialized design and a cooperative grid can show comparable occupancy, but the memory behavior differs. In a single-block design, each block fetches its own copy of any input tile that it touches. When multiple blocks reuse the same tile at about the same time, the device performs duplicate reads that consume L2 capacity and HBM bandwidth.

A thread block cluster changes that pattern. Blocks in the cluster can share data through distributed shared memory and can receive one multicast of a global tile into the shared memory of all blocks in the cluster. Use a block-scoped pipeline in the leader block together with cluster synchronization and `map_shared_rank`, or configure for multicast when broadcast from global memory is preferred. This removes duplicate loads within the cluster and reduces pressure on L2 and HBM.

A `cuda::pipeline` is scoped to the creating block. A `producer_commit()` in one block does not release `consumer_wait()` in other blocks. To coordinate across blocks in a cluster, first publish data (e.g., into the leader's shared memory), then use `clus ter.sync()`. Followers then access the leader's shared memory with `map_shared_rank()`. Optional TMA multicast can broadcast from global memory directly into each block's shared memory.

At this point, every block observes the leader's tiles through DSMEM (or TMA multicast) and proceeds. The block-scoped pipeline does not explicitly synchronize other blocks. cluster.sync() and DSMEM semantics provide the cluster-wide visibility.

When designed to use TMA multicast and DSMEM efficiently, the thread block cluster pipeline will fetch each tile exactly once and multicast it into every thread block's shared memory. This is in contrast to redundantly reloading the data from each thread block. As such, although every SM still cannot exceed its 64-warp limit, the global thread block cluster coordination ensures that those warps spend far less time on duplicate loads and far more time on actual computation.

Moreover, in the single thread block version, each block loads its next tile as soon as it finishes computing the current one. If one thread block completes its computation slightly earlier than another, it immediately issues its own load for the next tile—even if that tile is already being loaded by another block. This results in redundant memory traffic.

However, with the thread block cluster pipeline version, if a compute warp on SM 0 finishes early, it does not fetch its next tile immediately. Instead, it stalls at con sumer_wait() until the global loader—possibly running on SM 7—finishes bringing that tile into shared memory for all thread blocks. In other words, the compute warp waits for the cluster's single, shared load rather than issuing its own redundant copy.

By pausing until the tile is guaranteed available, each SM participating in a thread block cluster avoids spinning idle or performing duplicate loads. This alignment across thread block clusters smooths out variations in load times and keeps every SM's compute warps busy with data loaded only once per cluster. This improves overall throughput.

Consider a problem so large and a grid so full of work that every SM already has loader, compute, and storer warps active under the single-block approach. In that case the raw warp counts and per-SM occupancy can look similar between the two kernels. The cluster version helps when multiple blocks reuse the same input tiles by eliminating duplicate global reads within a cluster and by using cluster-wide synchronization to align stages.

This often produces a modest throughput improvement on reuse-heavy workloads, but the gain depends on tile reuse, alignment, and resource limits. Both designs remain bounded by the same architectural limits, such as resident warps, registers, and shared memory.

All of the kernels here use the CUDA pipeline for producer and consumer handoffs without calling a block-wide __syncthreads. The naive tiled kernel does not overlap memory and compute. The two-stage double-buffered pipeline overlaps copies with compute and can significantly reduce time to solution on memory-bound cases.

The warp-specialized pipeline dedicates separate warps to load, compute, and store to avoid implicit full-block waits. The thread block cluster variant shares tiles across blocks in a cluster through distributed shared memory or multicast so that a tile is fetched once per cluster rather than once per block. These patterns improve utilization and reduce redundant memory traffic.

Key Takeaways

The following are key takeaways from this chapter, which is focused on extracting peak performance on modern GPUs. These will keep kernels from idling on DRAM, warp schedulers, and global barriers:

Hide latency with pipeline depth

Use two-stage (`cuda::pipeline_shared_state<cuda::thread_scope_block, 2>`) tiling to overlap asynchronous loads with compute and add another stage (`cuda::pipeline_shared_state<cuda::thread_scope_block, 3>`) when compute outweighs memory (e.g., modern GPUs like Blackwell.) This will help to eliminate idle warps.

Balance workloads with warp specialization

Assign separate warps to loading, computing, and storing when compute phases dominate, ensuring near-peak warp efficiency on modern GPU hardware.

Remove launch overhead with persistent kernels

Run a single long-lived kernel over a device-side work queue and use `grid.sync()` for multiphase algorithms. This will reduce host-device round trips and overall launch costs.

Enable on-chip sharing with thread block clusters and DSMEM

Group thread blocks (CTAs) into clusters so they share a contiguous on-chip buffer. For a cluster-wide broadcast, use `cp.async.bulk.tensor` with a TMA multicast descriptor. Use TMA multicast to broadcast tiles once to every thread block. This will boost L2 hit rates and trim DRAM bandwidth.

Pay special attention to barrier semantics

Both `cluster.sync()` and `grid.sync()` require every participating thread block to reach the same synchronization point. Mismatched control flow—or an excessive cluster size—may lead to deadlock or launch failure.

Profile before tuning

Use Nsight Compute to identify whether your kernel is memory bound or compute bound. If memory bound, start with a two-stage pipeline. If compute bound, consider warp specialization or thread block clustering.

Verify compiler-generated pipelines before hand-tuning

> Profile and inspect the framework's generated code from compilers like PyTorch's compiler and NVCC. If the compiled code uses an asynchronous pipeline using `cuda::memcpy_async`, `producer_commit()`, and `consumer_wait()`, manual tuning likely won't produce much of a speedup.

Conclusion

The techniques discussed in this chapter help to systematically hide latency and remove redundant loads. This keeps the GPU at near-peak utilization for the duration of the kernel's execution.

Warp-specialized pipelines overlap load, compute, and store operations. Cooperative-group barriers (`grid.sync()` and `cluster.sync()`) help coordinate multiphase work without host round trips. And persistent kernels loop over a device-side queue to eliminate launch overhead.

As always, you should start by profiling. If global-memory stalls dominate, a two-stage asynchronous-copy pipeline like double buffer usually suffices. If compute warps still stall, switch to a multistage warp-specialized pipeline such that loader, compute, and storer warps can operate with minimal contention. The only contention would be at the memory subsystem.

> Remember that concurrency is beneficial up to the point of hardware (e.g., memory bandwidth) saturation. Beyond that, parallel tasks contend for throughput.

For multiphase reductions or irregular tasks, replace multiple launches with a single persistent kernel plus `grid.sync()` to preserve occupancy. And when thread blocks need the same data (e.g., multiheaded attention), you can form a thread block cluster so that DSMEM and TMA load each tile only once—and multicast the data to the other thread blocks—without repeatedly accessing global memory. These techniques will move performance closer to the GPU's peak theoretical limits.

As you continue through the next chapters, it's important to remember these principles because they apply to many more optimizations. Specifically, you should overlap work at the warp and thread block levels, synchronize directly on-device (versus on the host), and share data on chip. These are essential mechanisms for tuning ultra-high-performance GPU workloads.

In the next chapter, we keep these intra-kernel building blocks—`cuda::pipeline` double-buffering, warp-specialized roles, and thread-block clusters—and show how to drive them through CUDA streams. The goal is to hide latency between kernels

---

and between host $\leftrightarrow$ device communication and not just inside a single kernel. Concretely, we will reuse the kernels from this chapter and run them in multistream pipelines with `cudaMemcpyAsync`, `cudaMallocAsync`/`cudaFreeAsync`, and event-based synchronization. This will help push the entire system toward achieving peak performance across many GPUs in your AI system.

## CHAPTER 11

Inter-Kernel Pipelining, Synchronization, and CUDA Stream-Ordered Memory Allocations

So far, we have focused on the intra-kernel tools—`cuda::pipeline` double-buffering, warp specialization (loader/compute/storer warps), persistent kernels, and thread-block clusters with DSMEM/TMA—to keep the SMs busy for a single kernel. In this chapter we keep those kernels and show how to pipeline across kernels and batches with CUDA streams, events, and the stream-ordered memory allocator. In short, Chapter 10 focused on hiding latency within a kernel. This chapter shows how to hide latency between kernels and between the GPU and the host.

This kind of inter-kernel concurrency is essential for keeping all of the GPU's engines busy in real-world workloads. To achieve peak GPU utilization with modern GPUs, we need to keep the GPU's compute engines and direct memory access (DMA) engines busy and running in parallel.

CUDA streams provide the foundation for this inter-kernel concurrency. By combining asynchronous memory operations, fine-grained synchronization, and CUDA Graphs (briefly introduced in this chapter and covered in more detail in the next chapter), you can construct highly efficient pipelines that avoid host-side stalls.

Overlapping Kernel Execution with CUDA Streams

A CUDA stream is a sequence of operations—kernel launches, memory copies, and memory allocations—that execute in the order they are issued. Consider launching 5 kernels from the CPU onto the GPU using 2 streams, as shown in Figure 11-1.

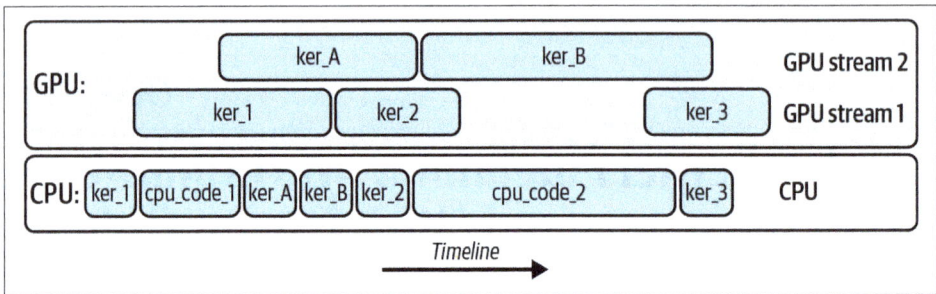

Figure 11-1. Launching five kernels from the CPU onto the two streams running on the GPU

Here, we see `ker_A` and `ker_B` are running on stream 2, while `ker_1`, `ker_2`, and `ker_3` are running on stream 1. All kernels may overlap with one another—and across CUDA streams—as long as hardware resources permit.

The CPU is able to continue performing work (`cpu_code_1` and `cpu_code_2`) while the streams perform the kernel operations asynchronously. The code to launch these five kernels on the two CUDA streams is shown here:

```cpp
#include <cstdio>
#include <cuda_runtime.h>

__global__ void ker_A() { /* ... do some work ... */ }
__global__ void ker_B() { /* ... do some work ... */ }

__global__ void ker_1() { /* ... do some work ... */ }
__global__ void ker_2() { /* ... do some work ... */ }
__global__ void ker_3() { /* ... do some work ... */ }

int main() {
    // 1) Create two CUDA streams
    cudaStream_t stream1, stream2;
    cudaStreamCreateWithFlags(&stream1, cudaStreamNonBlocking);
    cudaStreamCreateWithFlags(&stream2, cudaStreamNonBlocking);

    // 2) Define your grid/block sizes
    dim3 grid(128);
    dim3 block(256);

    // 3) Launch ker_1 on stream1
    ker_1<<<grid, block, 0, stream1>>>();

    // 4) CPU code 1 runs immediately (asynchronously wrt GPU)
    printf("CPU code 1 executing\n");

    // ... do some host-side work here ...
    cpu_code_1();
```

```
// 5) Launch ker_A on stream2
ker_A<<<grid, block, 0, stream2>>>();

// 6) Launch ker_B on stream1
ker_B<<<grid, block, 0, stream1>>>();

// 7) Launch ker_2 on stream2
ker_2<<<grid, block, 0, stream2>>>();

// 8) CPU code 2 runs immediately
printf("CPU code 2 executing\n");

// ... do some other host-side work here ...
cpu_code_2();

// 9) Launch ker_3 on stream1
ker_3<<<grid, block, 0, stream1>>>();

// 10) Wait for work on each stream to finish
cudaStreamSynchronize(stream1);
cudaStreamSynchronize(stream2);

// 11) Clean up
cudaStreamDestroy(stream1);
cudaStreamDestroy(stream2);

    return 0;
}
```

ker_1 is enqueued on stream1, then control returns immediately to the CPU. cpu_code_1() runs on the host while ker_1 executes on the GPU. Meanwhile, we enqueue ker_A on stream2 and ker_B on stream1. We then enqueue ker_2 on stream2, interleave cpu_code_2, and enqueue ker_3 on stream1. Finally, we synchronize on each stream to wait for all of the work to complete and then destroy the streams to clean up the resources.

This example highlights five different kernel executions overlapping across two different streams. Increasing the complexity a bit, and building upon Chapter 10, following is the same warp specialization pipeline example but using CUDA streams:

```
// Run the warp-specialized kernel in multiple CUDA streams.

#include <cuda_runtime.h>
#include <cuda/pipeline>
#include <cooperative_groups.h>
namespace cg = cooperative_groups;

#define TILE_SIZE 128
#define TILE_ELEMS (TILE_SIZE * TILE_SIZE)

// re-using from Chapter 10
```

```
__global__ void warp_specialized_pipeline(const float* __restrict__ A_global,
                                           const float* __restrict__ B_global,
                                           float*       __restrict__ C_global,
                                           int numTiles);

int main() {
    const int NUM_STREAMS = 2;              // keep it small; tune as needed
    const int batches     = 8;              // in-flight batches
    const size_t elems    = TILE_ELEMS;     // elements per batch
    const size_t bytes    = elems * sizeof(float);

    // Create streams that do NOT synchronize with the legacy default stream
    cudaStream_t s[NUM_STREAMS];
    for (int i = 0; i < NUM_STREAMS; ++i)
        cudaStreamCreateWithFlags(&s[i], cudaStreamNonBlocking);

    // Allocate pinned host buffers so H2D/D2H can truly overlap
    float *hA = nullptr, *hB = nullptr, *hC = nullptr;
    cudaMallocHost(&hA, batches * bytes);
    cudaMallocHost(&hB, batches * bytes);
    cudaMallocHost(&hC, batches * bytes);

    // ... initialize hA/hB ...

    for (int b = 0; b < batches; ++b) {
        const int sid = b % NUM_STREAMS;

        float *dA = nullptr, *dB = nullptr, *dC = nullptr;
        cudaMallocAsync(&dA, bytes, s[sid]);
        cudaMallocAsync(&dB, bytes, s[sid]);
        cudaMallocAsync(&dC, bytes, s[sid]);

        cudaMemcpyAsync(dA, hA + b * elems, bytes,
                        cudaMemcpyHostToDevice, s[sid]);
        cudaMemcpyAsync(dB, hB + b * elems, bytes,
                        cudaMemcpyHostToDevice, s[sid]);

        const dim3 block(96);     // three warps: loader(0), compute(1), storer(2)
        const dim3 grid(1);
        const size_t shmem = 3 * elems * sizeof(float); // [A|B|C] per tile

        // Reuse the Chapter 10 kernel exactly as-is
        warp_specialized_pipeline<<<grid, block, shmem, s[sid]>>>(dA, dB, dC,
                                                        /*numTiles=*/1);

        cudaMemcpyAsync(hC+b*elems, dC, bytes, cudaMemcpyDeviceToHost, s[sid]);

        cudaFreeAsync(dA, s[sid]);
        cudaFreeAsync(dB, s[sid]);
        cudaFreeAsync(dC, s[sid]);
    }
```

```
for (int i = 0; i < NUM_STREAMS; ++i) {
    cudaStreamSynchronize(s[i]);
    cudaStreamDestroy(s[i]);
}

cudaFreeHost(hA); cudaFreeHost(hB); cudaFreeHost(hC);
return 0;
}
```

Here, we are re-using the warp-specialized pipeline and showing how streams add a second layer of overlap such that while stream 1 computes on batch n, stream 2 is performing DMA-loads on batch b+1. At the same time, it can copy back batch b−1. The kernel's internal `cuda::pipeline` overlap remains unchanged.

We'll continue to build out the complexity later in the chapter by layering in thread block clusters, but let's first dive into how streams help to overlap compute with data transfers. This will help solidify the fundamentals of CUDA streams and their role in GPU-based performance engineering.

Using Streams to Overlap Compute with Data Transfers

For instance, you can enqueue each kernel launch and memory copy into its own stream. This allows the SMs to execute kernels while the two dedicated DMA engines (one for Host → Device transfers and one for Device → Host transfers) move data concurrently.

Since the SM compute pipeline runs independently of the two DMA engines, you can fully overlap the kernel's computation with the two data transfers using CUDA streams. However, if the compute is fully maxed out by a kernel using all SM throughput—or a copy pipeline is saturating the memory bandwidth with excessive, additional overlapping—it will not improve performance.

When compute and memory throughput are saturated, you'll start seeing two concurrent operations each running at 50%, for instance, since they are both contending for the same resource. You can profile GPU utilization to identify these saturation thresholds.

For example, consider an AI model training or inference workload that breaks work into batches. Here, you would launch a kernel on batch 0 in stream 0 at the same time that stream 1 invokes `cudaMemcpyAsync()` to copy batch 1 from the host to device, as shown in Figure 11-2.

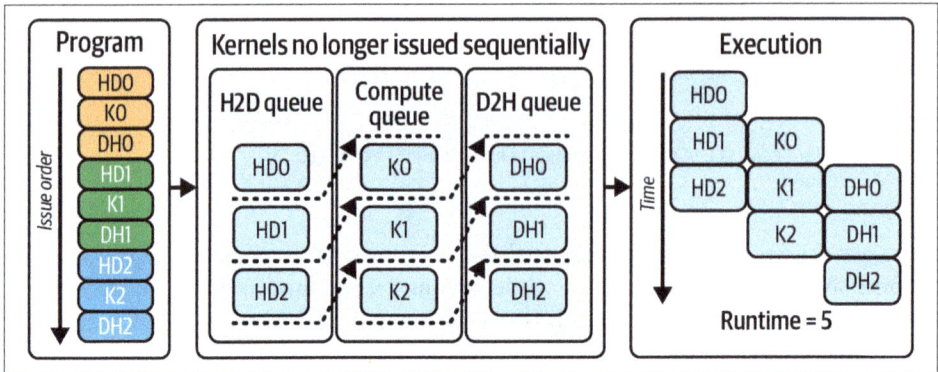

Figure 11-2. Timeline of three-way overlap

On modern GPUs with at least two copy engines (`deviceProp.asyncEngine Count()`), you can extend this to a three-way overlap such that stream 0 runs the kernel for batch 0, stream 1 copies batch 1 host to device, and stream 2 writes the results of the previous batch back to the host. This extends to additional streams. This pattern hides data-transfer latency behind computation, and vice versa, keeping all of the GPU's engines busy and minimizing idle time.

In practice, your kernel must meet several requirements to achieve this concurrent behavior. First, any host pointer used in an asynchronous transfer must be page-locked, or pinned. If you call `cudaMemcpyAsync()` on pageable memory, the runtime performs a host-side staging copy into pinned memory that blocks the calling host thread and the enqueuing stream until staging completes.

This prevents that transfer from being asynchronous. While this blocks the calling host thread, the GPU can still overlap compute and copies in other streams. But that specific transfer will not overlap correctly. To achieve fully asynchronous transfers in your stream, you must use pinned host memory.

> By setting `pin_memory=True` with PyTorch's DataLoader, you are page locking your host buffers so that data can be transferred using DMA directly into GPU memory. This allows the copy to overlap with computation and return control to the host immediately. DMA engines can overlap transfers with compute. Pageable memory forces a hidden staging copy and defeats overlap for that transfer.

Second, you should use the asynchronous allocation and deallocation routines, `cuda MallocAsync()` and `cudaFreeAsync()`, instead of the synchronous and blocking `cuda Malloc()` or `cudaFree()` calls. Frameworks like PyTorch provide the option to use

CUDA's asynchronous, stream-ordered memory allocator. The idea is to not stall all active streams when you allocate memory. This would be very bad for performance.

The asynchronous stream-ordered allocator allows each stream to request or return device memory without waiting on other streams. Using the asynchronous allocator ensures memory operations in one stream don't stall operations in other streams. This will avoid unnecessary global synchronization. Let's explore the stream-ordered memory allocator in the next section.

PyTorch's default CUDA caching allocator is stream-aware and, in normal operation (e.g., servicing allocations from its cache), it avoids device-wide synchronization. Only when it has to request more memory from the OS using cudaMalloc would a synchronization occur. In practice this means most tensor allocations and frees don't block other streams. Enabling the cudaMallocAsync backend can further reduce fragmentation and improve reuse in many workloads, as you'll see next.

Stream-Ordered Memory Allocator

In PyTorch, you can enable CUDA's stream-ordered allocator by setting the environment variable PYTORCH_ALLOC_CONF=backend:cudaMallocAsync before launching your PyTorch script. If this variable is set, PyTorch tensor memory allocation (cudaMallocAsync()) and free (cudaFreeAsync()) operations are enqueued in separate CUDA streams in the order in which they are invoked. When this environment variant is not set, PyTorch uses its own caching allocator.

If you use the legacy cudaMalloc(...), remember that it's a blocking, device-wide operation that synchronizes the device before returning. This can stall work in other streams since every allocation forces the entire GPU to stall until the memory is reserved. This pauses all streams, limits parallelism, and destroys your workload's performance.

In contrast, using the stream-ordered allocator with cudaMallocAsync(...) simply records the allocation request in the same CUDA stream that will use it—whether the stream is performing a kernel or memory operation. It will not block the other streams. This way, memory management never serializes streams that are feeding those kernels.

> CUDA's stream-ordered allocator, used in PyTorch, avoids global device locks and reduces allocation overhead.

In practice, stream 0 might be executing an attention kernel on batch N, stream 1 copies batch N+1 from host to device, and stream 2 enqueues a `cudaMalloc Async(...)` for batch N+2. Because `cudaMallocAsync(...)` simply appends its work into stream 2's queue, streams 0 and 1 continue without interruption.

With the stream-aware allocator, GPU memory for each mini-batch is allocated without blocking other streams. This is important for LLM pipelines that allocate per-batch scratch space. The asynchronous allocator prevents stalls—even under heavy memory churn.

> Using the stream-ordered memory allocator is particularly important if your pipeline allocates a scratch buffer for each mini-batch—common in LLM training and inference. For instance, each mini-batch in an LLM pipeline needs its own temporary workspace to hold attention keys/values or intermediate activation buffers. In this case, you often call an allocator to reserve that "scratch buffer" on the GPU.

Allocations are satisfied from a per-device memory pool. You can tune the pool's release threshold using `cudaMemPoolSetAttribute()` to trade off returning memory to the OS versus reusing it for performance. A higher threshold means the pool will keep memory allocated longer. This will reduce the number of times the memory is returned back to the OS. This leads to fewer OS calls and better performance by avoiding repetitive memory allocations and de-allocations.

The following example shows how to implement stream-based overlap using the stream-ordered memory allocator with `cudaMallocAsync` and `cudaFreeAsync` and demonstrates the use of `cudaMemPoolSetAttribute()`. This highlights how memory allocation, data transfer, and kernel execution can be fully pipelined using CUDA streams:

```
// initialize the async memory allocator
cudaMemPool_t pool;
int device = -1;
cudaGetDevice(&device); // Current device
cudaDeviceGetDefaultMemPool(&pool, device);

// Desired number of bytes to keep in pool before
// releasing back to the OS (tune as needed)
uint64_t threshold =/* e.g., prop.totalGlobalMem / 2 */; // bytes

cudaMemPoolSetAttribute(pool,
  cudaMemPoolAttrReleaseThreshold, &threshold);

cudaStream_t stream1, stream2;
cudaStreamCreateWithFlags(&stream1, cudaStreamNonBlocking);
cudaStreamCreateWithFlags(&stream2, cudaStreamNonBlocking);
```

```
// Allocate memory using stream-ordered async allocation
void *d_data1, *d_result1;
void *d_data2, *d_result2;

size_t dataSizeBytes = N * sizeof(float);

// Use cudaMallocAsync as a best practice in modern multi-stream apps
cudaMallocAsync(&d_data1, dataSizeBytes, stream1);
cudaMallocAsync(&d_result1, dataSizeBytes, stream1);
cudaMallocAsync(&d_data2, dataSizeBytes, stream2);
cudaMallocAsync(&d_result2, dataSizeBytes, stream2);

// Asynchronously copy first chunk and launch its kernel in stream1
cudaMemcpyAsync(d_data1, h_data1, dataSizeBytes,
  cudaMemcpyHostToDevice, stream1);
computeKernel<<<gridDim, blockDim, 0,
  stream1>>>((float*)d_data1, (float*)d_result1);
cudaMemcpyAsync(h_result1, d_result1, dataSizeBytes,
  cudaMemcpyDeviceToHost, stream1);

// In parallel, do the same on stream2
cudaMemcpyAsync(d_data2, h_data2, dataSizeBytes,
                cudaMemcpyHostToDevice, stream2);
computeKernel<<<gridDim, blockDim, 0,
  stream2>>>((float*)d_data2, (float*)d_result2);
cudaMemcpyAsync(h_result2, d_result2, dataSizeBytes,
   cudaMemcpyDeviceToHost, stream2);

// Wait for both streams to finish
cudaStreamSynchronize(stream1);
cudaStreamSynchronize(stream2);

// Cleanup
cudaFreeAsync(d_data1, stream1);
cudaFreeAsync(d_result1, stream1);
cudaFreeAsync(d_data2, stream2);
cudaFreeAsync(d_result2, stream2);

cudaStreamDestroy(stream1);
cudaStreamDestroy(stream2);
```

Here, we create two CUDA streams (stream1 and stream2) and allocate device memory using cudaMallocAsync, ensuring that each stream has its own stream-ordered memory buffers. We then issue work for two independent data chunks.

On stream1, we perform an asynchronous copy from host to device (H2D), launch a compute kernel, and then asynchronously copy the results back from device to host (D2H). Simultaneously, we do the same for a second chunk of data on stream2.

Because these operations are issued on separate streams, the GPU device overlaps work between them. `stream1` executes the kernel concurrently with the H2D copy on `stream2`. Once the `stream1` kernel completes, it can copy the data back to the host (D2H) overlapping with `stream2`'s kernel execution.

Here, the memory allocations overlap with kernel computations thanks to CUDA streams and stream-ordered memory allocations. The staggered scheduling shown in this example reduces idle time and maximizes throughput. Without stream-ordered allocation, you'd either have to allocate all the memory upfront—increasing memory footprint—or incur heavy synchronization penalties.

With `cudaMallocAsync`, memory management is seamlessly integrated into CUDA streams. This allows per-stream allocations and deallocations without triggering a global device synchronization.

In addition, the stream-ordered allocator lets you issue fine-grained memory requests for variable-length buffers—such as token caches or intermediate activations. You can then immediately launch kernels that depend on those buffers. This happens all within the same stream.

> In practice, achieving peak throughput requires carefully tuning data-chunk sizes and staying within your GPU's concurrency limits. Modern GPU devices provide multiple copy engines and can overlap host-to-device (H2D) and device-to-host (D2H) transfers. Query `deviceProp.asyncEngineCount` to determine how many copy engines your device supports to plan overlap accordingly.

Modern GPUs have a hard limit for the number of concurrent kernels that can run across all SMs on a device (up to the 128 resident-grid limit.) As discussed in Chapter 5, the modern GPU limit is 128 concurrently executing kernels per device. Once you exceed the limit of active kernels, additional kernel launches will queue until a slot frees up on one of the SMs.

And remember that kernels that share an SM will only execute together if their combined registers, shared memory, and thread block requirements fit within the SM's resource limits. Balancing chunk (tile) sizes, launch order, and per-kernel resource usage is essential.

If chunks are too small, you will underutilize the copy engines and SM resources. If chunks are too large or too many kernels are enqueued simultaneously, you will exceed kernel slots or exhaust per-SM resources. This will lead to stalls.

In short, when tuned correctly, however, CUDA streams, combined with the stream-ordered memory allocator (`cudaMallocAsync`), will ensure that data transfers, kernel execution, and memory management will overlap seamlessly. This keeps the multiple DMA engines and SMs busy without unnecessary queuing.

Using CUDA Streams and Stream-Ordered Memory Allocator with LLMs

The nonblocking behavior of CUDA streams combined with the stream-ordered memory allocator is crucial for LLM training and inference workloads. These workloads overlap computation and data movement across multiple streams to increase GPU utilization and reduce end-to-end latency.

In addition, LLMs utilize on-the-fly "scratch memory" allocations, which are facilitated by the stream-ordered memory allocator discussed in the previous section. For instance, when running a transformer layer, you often need extra shared memory or device memory, called *scratch memory*, to store the results of a matrix multiply before feeding it into the softmax operation.

Because different mini-batches in LLM workloads can vary in length (token count), you will want to use the stream-ordered memory allocator to provide a fresh scratch buffer on the GPU specifically for each input batch. This way, you have exactly enough space allocated for that batch's intermediate computations—and not a single byte more.

If you use the old, blocking allocation API (cudaMalloc(...) and cudaFree(...)) to allocate these scratch buffers on the fly, every single allocation or deallocation would synchronize with the entire GPU since calling cudaMalloc(...) forces a global device synchronization. As such, no overlap is possible until all pending kernels and copies finish.

Global device synchronizations are absolutely disastrous for performance. Avoid using blocking calls like cudaMalloc() and cudaFree() in your CUDA streams. Prefer events and stream waits. And definitely avoid synchronizing on the default stream 0 with cudaStreamSynchronize(0)!

In a pipeline where one stream is busy running an attention kernel for batch *N* and another stream is preparing batch N+1 for the attention kernel, calling a blocking cudaMalloc(...) on the second stream will stall all streams. Until the allocator finishes, every SM is effectively paused. This can wipe out any overlap you hoped to achieve between data transfers, computation, and memory management.

The solution is to use the stream-ordered allocator with cudaMallocAsync() and cudaFreeAsync(). These APIs enqueue the work of allocating and freeing regions of device memory at the stream level. As such, they synchronize only at the stream level—and not the device level.

For instance, consider a stream that needs a scratch buffer of 16 MB for attention on a batch of input data. It would invoke `cudaMallocAsync(&scratchPtr, scratch Bytes, stream1)`, which records this allocation request in its operation queue but does not force any other stream to wait, as shown in Figure 11-3.

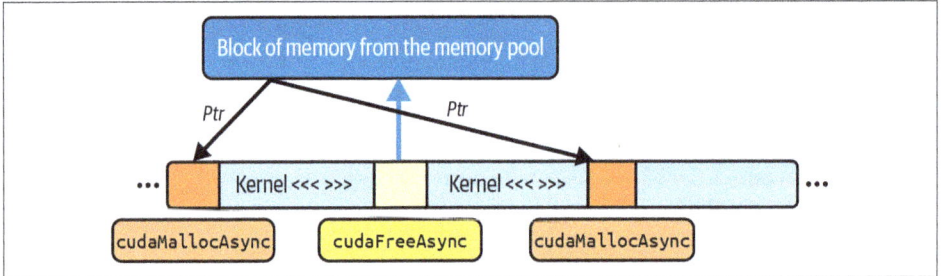

Figure 11-3. Stream-ordered memory allocation

The other streams continue launching kernels, copying data, or doing whatever they were doing—even while stream 1's allocation is in flight. And once the CUDA runtime has reserved the memory behind the scenes, stream 1 can make progress again and launch the attention kernel into that newly allocated region—all without halting any other streams.

> Unlike legacy `cudaMalloc`, `cudaMallocAsync` does not stall other streams. Each allocation is synchronized only within its own stream.

In the context of LLM training and inference, this is particularly valuable because variable-length sequences often produce scratch-buffer size fluctuations. If batch N has 512 tokens per sequence and batch N+1 has 1,024 tokens, your attention module will need more space for batch N+1 than batch N, so reusing batch N's allocation is not sufficient. With `cudaMallocAsync()`, you can enqueue a single, nonblocking allocation for the larger buffer without dragging all other streams to a stop.

Additionally, a typical LLM's autoregressive token-by-token generation (aka *decoding*) phase uses a growing key/value cache. Each generated token requires appending new KV pairs to a per-sequence buffer. As the buffer grows, you need to reallocate or extend the scratch region. `cudaMallocAsync(...)` lets you do this in the same stream that runs the attention kernel. Meanwhile, upstream data-loading and downstream result-copying operations continue making progress in parallel, running in their own streams.

Another use of CUDA streams in an LLM context is layerwise pipelining in large LLMs. Suppose that you divide a large, transformer-based LLM model into two halves that run on different CUDA streams—stream 0 runs layers 0–5 and stream 1 runs layers 6–11. Between these halves, you need intermediate buffers for activations.

Each time stream 0 finishes its work on a mini-batch, it might call `cudaMalloc Async(...)` to grab a new buffer for the next batch's activations. Because that call does not synchronize the device, stream 1 can continue computing layers 6–11 on the previous batch's results while stream 0 allocates memory for the next batch's inputs.

By contrast, if you had used the legacy `cudaMalloc(...)` inside that pipeline, every time you allocated a new scratch region for the next mini-batch or an expanded KV cache, the entire GPU would pause until the allocation completed. That would break any chance of overlapping computation and data movement across streams.

To summarize, in an LLM context, you frequently need temporary buffers for attention, layer normalization, softmax, KV cache, or intermediate activations. These are collectively referred to as a *scratch buffer*.

Using `cudaMallocAsync(...)` and `cudaFreeAsync(...)` to manage these scratch buffers within separate streams ensures that memory management never forces a global, cross-stream stall. Instead, the allocation enqueues into the same stream as your kernel or copy operation.

This allows all other streams to continue running and keeps your attention kernels, data transfers, and any host-side work overlapping as much as possible. This maximizes GPU utilization in large-scale, real-time LLM workloads.

Legacy Default Stream

When you do not explicitly create or specify a stream, the operations go into the legacy default stream, often called *stream 0*. By default, stream 0 has two important behaviors that are worth highlighting:

Implicit synchronization with itself
> Any two operations enqueued into stream 0 execute strictly one after the other. You cannot overlap two kernels or a copy and a kernel in stream 0, because stream 0 serializes all of its own commands.

Implicit synchronization with other streams
> In the legacy default stream model, any operation launched into stream 0 will wait for all previously enqueued work in every other stream to finish before it begins. Conversely, any operation launched into a nondefault stream will also block until all prior work in stream 0 has completed. In effect, stream 0 acts as a global "barrier" across the entire GPU. Even if you issue commands into different streams, once you submit something into stream 0, it forces every other stream

to stall until stream 0 is caught up, and vice versa. This is very bad for performance and should be avoided when possible.

Because of these implicit dependencies, putting all work into stream 0 prevents any form of concurrency. For instance, kernels and copy engines cannot overlap. As such, your GPU spends cycles idle waiting for the default-stream barrier to clear.

To unlock true parallelism, you should avoid using stream 0 for anything but operations that truly need to serialize with every other stream, which is relatively rare.

Modern Per-Thread Default Stream

To mitigate the "global barrier" behavior of the legacy default stream, CUDA introduced per-thread default streams, sometimes abbreviated PTDS (as opposed to the posttraumatic stress disorder (PTSD) that the legacy stream has given us throughout the years).

Under per-thread default stream semantics, each CPU thread's default stream is independent. In other words, when per-thread default streams are enabled, each host thread has its own implicit "stream 0."

Operations enqueued into thread A's default stream do not wait for work in thread B's default stream. They run concurrently whenever hardware resources allow. Likewise, operations in thread B's default stream do not wait for thread A's default stream, and so on.

PTDS is widely used in multithreaded CUDA applications to avoid the "host-wide barrier" issue. To enable PTDS, you can compile your code using nvcc --default-stream per-thread or set the CUDA_API_PER_THREAD_DEFAULT_STREAM=1 environment variable (before including any CUDA headers).

> Once PTDS is active, each host CPU thread's default stream behaves like a user-created stream that does not implicitly synchronize with other threads' default streams. If you mix PTDS with the legacy default stream in the same process, PTDS streams still synchronize with the legacy default stream.

With PTDS, any kernel launch, copy, or allocation without an explicit stream parameter goes into a thread-local queue. Only commands within the same host thread's default stream serialize, and they never impose an implicit global barrier on streams belonging to other threads.

In short, by enabling per-thread default streams, the legacy default-stream synchronization barrier is removed. Each host thread's default stream never waits on other threads' streams. This allows full overlap of multiple kernel launches across threads.

And if you issue kernel launches (or memory copies) from different CPU threads without specifying an explicit stream, the operations will overlap on the GPU whenever resources permit. This is shown in Figure 11-4.

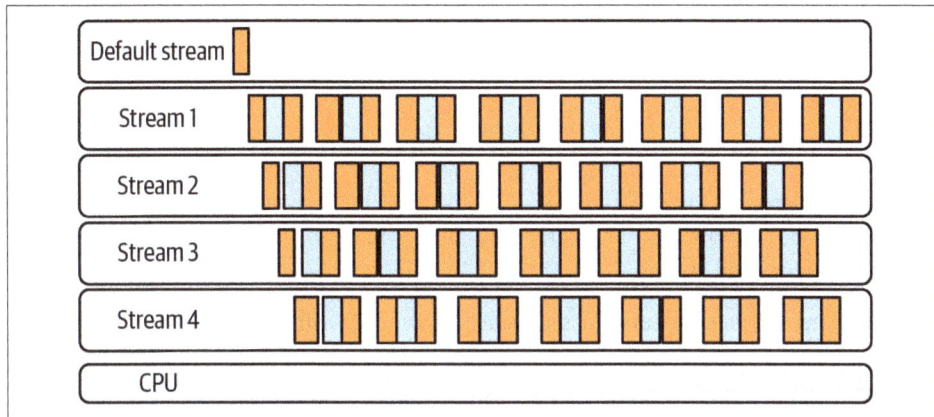

Figure 11-4. Timeline showing multiple GPU kernels running concurrently across separate CUDA streams issued from different threads on their respective default streams with PTDS enabled

Default Versus Explicit (Nondefault) Streams

Relying on default-stream behavior will eventually cause problems. It always does. Any work enqueued into the legacy default stream (stream 0) implicitly waits for—and blocks—every other stream, and vice versa.

In performance-critical code, it's best to create and use your own nondefault, explicit, and named streams so that nothing accidentally goes into stream 0. If you accidentally use one kernel on stream 0—or copy data into it—you can stall every other active stream. Many libraries, such as cuBLAS, Thrust, etc., accept an explicit stream parameter. It's recommended that you always create explicit streams and use those.

> In PyTorch, operations are scheduled on nondefault streams under the hood to avoid unintended synchronization. For example, PyTorch's internal calls to cuDNN, cuBLAS, etc., use their own streams to avoid blocking the default stream 0. Also, PyTorch's distributed backend launches NCCL communication operations on separate CUDA streams rather than the default stream. This lets it overlap gradient communication with compute, for instance. In addition, NCCL's communication operations often run in a high-priority stream, as we'll cover in a bit.

By managing your own streams—or using per-thread defaults—you retain control over concurrency. Here is an example of creating explicit, nondefault streams in CUDA C++ (we will show how to use streams in PyTorch in Chapters 13 and 14):

```
cudaStream_t streamA, streamB;
cudaStreamCreateWithFlags(&streamA, cudaStreamNonBlocking);
cudaStreamCreateWithFlags(&streamB, cudaStreamNonBlocking);

myKernel<<<grid, block, 0, streamA>>>(...);                    // streamA
cudaMemcpyAsync(dest, src, size, cudaMemcpyHostToDevice, streamB); // streamB
```

Here, `streamA` and `streamB` can overlap freely. Under the legacy default-stream model (PTDS disabled), however, any later call into stream 0 forces both `streamA` and `streamB` to wait until stream 0 is empty.

Similarly, any work enqueued in `streamA` or `streamB` will block if stream 0 still has pending tasks. To avoid these hidden global barriers, keep stream 0 idle and use it only for one-time operations for initial setup, final cleanup, etc.

In short, enable per-thread default streams so that each CPU thread's default stream no longer synchronizes with any other thread's default stream. Then create and use explicit streams (like `streamA` and `streamB`) for all performance-critical kernels and copies.

By doing both, nothing you enqueue into your explicit streams can accidentally collide with work in another explicit stream, another thread's default stream, or the legacy default stream 0. This ensures safe, predictable overlap without implicit synchronization. Creating streams with `cudaStreamNonBlocking` ensures that they do not synchronize with the legacy default stream. This is required to avoid hidden barriers.

Best Practices for Default Stream Usage

Because default streams can be problematic for performance, let's highlight the synchronization characteristics of each type of stream—legacy default, per-thread default, and explicit (nondefault):

Legacy default stream (`cudaStreamLegacy`)
    This blocks and is blocked by every other stream. Do not issue work here if you need any form of concurrency.

Per-thread default stream (`cudaStreamPerThread`)
    Each host thread's default stream is private. It still serializes its own commands but does not wait on or block any other thread's default stream or explicit streams.

Explicit streams (created with `cudaStreamCreateWithFlags()`)
Explicit streams are independent queues that only synchronize when you explicitly insert dependencies using `cudaStreamWaitEvent()`, for instance.

Here are some best practices to help guide your use of default and explicit (nondefault) streams:

Never launch performance-critical kernels into stream 0 (legacy default) unless you intend to serialize all GPU work
Even one stray kernel or copy into stream 0 will stall every other active stream. Older CUDA APIs, for example, might implicitly use stream 0. For example, when calling CUDA driver APIs without an explicit stream, you will likely use the legacy stream. This is another reason to migrate to newer APIs or always specify streams.

Enable per-thread default streams
Use PTDS if your application uses multiple CPU threads that each enqueue GPU work. This avoids hidden host-side barriers between those threads' default streams. On modern systems, you can also use `cudaStreamCreateWith Flags(&stream, cudaStreamNonBlocking)` to create a stream that does not synchronize with stream 0.

Create and manage explicit, nondefault streams
Explicit streams are a best practice since they allow overlapping kernels and memory copies. Always pass a nondefault `cudaStream_t` to `<<<...>>>()`, `cuda MemcpyAsync()`, or `cudaMallocAsync()`. This guarantees that no implicit default-stream synchronization will interfere with your pipelined workflow.

Use `cudaStreamWaitEvent()` to coordinate fine-grained dependencies instead of `cudaStreamSynchronize()`
You should use stream events rather than `cudaStreamSynchronize()` on the default stream. Call `cudaStreamSynchronize()` only at well-defined global points (e.g., the end of a model-training epoch) to avoid stalling unrelated streams.

Be explicit about your stream flags
If you enable PTDS, set the device flags before any CUDA call. Otherwise, you remain in the legacy default-stream mode. Any mention of stream 0 will create a global barrier.

Put simply, the legacy default stream (stream 0) always acts as a global barrier. Any work you enqueue there waits for, and forces, every other stream to finish, and every other stream will wait if stream 0 has pending work.

To avoid these invisible stalls, don't put performance-critical kernels or copies into stream 0. Instead, create your own named streams using `cudaStreamCreateWith Flags` and launch everything into those streams so they run independently.

If your program has multiple CPU threads—each issuing their own GPU work—you should also enable per-thread default streams. With PTDS turned on, each thread's "default" stream no longer synchronizes with other threads' defaults—or with stream 0.

This way, even code that doesn't explicitly create new streams won't accidentally block any other threads' work. In all cases, whenever you want two operations to overlap (e.g., a copy and a kernel), you should give them their own explicit, nondefault streams. Then you'll avoid the hidden global synchronization rules of stream 0 and let the GPU run with maximum parallelism.

Fine-Grained Synchronization with Events and Callbacks

Even when multiple streams and DMA engines overlap, there are times when one stream's operation must wait for another. Consider a pair of producer-consumer streams. The producer stream 0 is loading and preparing data for the consumer stream 1 to process.

In this case, it is tempting to synchronize these streams on the host side and block the CPU with a full `cudaDeviceSynchronize()`. However, this will block the CPU until all streams and all operations on the GPU complete. This is very bad for performance. You can also use `cudaStreamSynchronize()`, as shown in Figure 11-5, but this will block until all operations in the stream's queue complete.

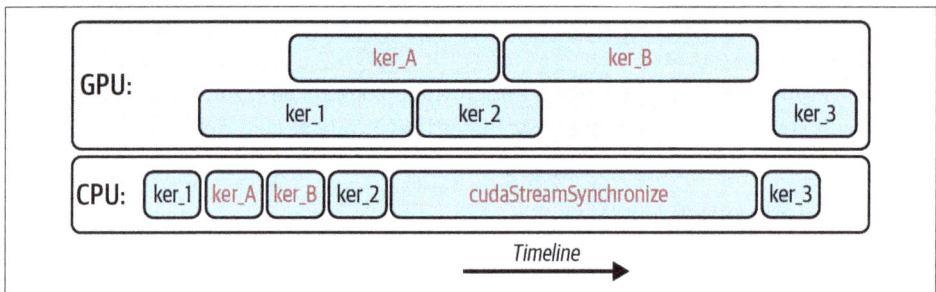

Figure 11-5. Using `cudaStreamSynchronize()` *will block the CPU until all operations in the stream have synchronized*

Instead, you can use CUDA events to provide a much finer-grained synchronization mechanism for streams. With CUDA events, you record a `cudaEvent_t` in the stream that produces data and then have the consumer stream wait for that event.

For instance, you would launch a producer kernel on stream 0 and call cudaEvent Record(doneEvent, stream0) when the data is ready to be consumed. In stream 1, you would then call cudaStreamWaitEvent(stream1, doneEvent, 0) before launching the consumer kernel. In this way, only stream 1 is stalled waiting for the event to be recorded—the host thread and all other streams will continue executing, as shown in Figure 11-6.

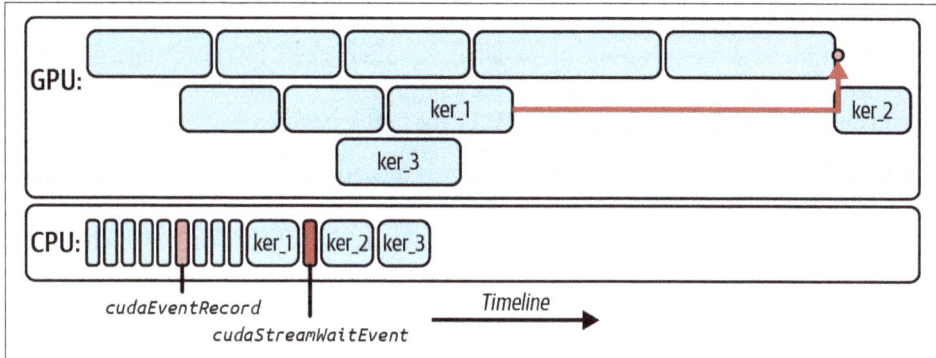

Figure 11-6. Using CUDA events to synchronize in a fine-grained manner

In addition to using CUDA events for interstream coordination, you can also use them to communicate between the GPU device and the CPU host. To do this, you would register a host callback with cudaLaunchHostFunc() from the host.

Suppose you need to recycle a custom memory pool back on the host as soon as a GPU kernel finishes in stream 0. In this case, you would register a callback from the host with cudaLaunchHostFunc() and specify the event that you are interested in. You would then launch the kernel on stream 0.

When the kernel is complete, it will record the event, and the host will run the callback function and update the memory pool on the CPU. All of this happens without a polling loop or a full cudaDeviceSynchronize().

The CUDA runtime executes the callback function on a host thread once the GPU work is completed. This keeps the CPU free until the precise moment that you need it—and avoids wasting host cycles and blocking unrelated GPU work.

You should not call any device-side GPU APIs from within the host callback launched with cudaLaunchHostFunc(). If you call cudaMemcpy(), for instance, from inside the callback, it can deadlock because the callback runs on a host thread managed by the CUDA runtime. Calling CUDA APIs from within it can deadlock because the device may be waiting for the callback to finish.

The callback should be limited to CPU-side tasks such as freeing or recycling host memory. This suggestion prevents deadlocks in the circular case in which a callback tries to launch new work on the GPU at the same time that the GPU is waiting for the callback to complete.

Using CUDA Events for Cross-Stream Synchronization

With multiple streams running in parallel, we often need to coordinate and synchronize between them. CUDA events are the primary mechanism for cross-stream synchronization without stalling the CPU or the entire device.

An event is like a marker that a stream records at a specific point. Other streams, or even the host, can wait on that marker and know when a certain event has happened (e.g., a kernel has finished). Unlike a full `cudaDeviceSynchronize()`, which blocks until all streams finish, events allow fine-grained ordering between streams.

Streams can be used to make sure that each transformer layer's data is present before computing. They can also improve pipeline parallelism by ensuring GPU 0 has finished producing a tensor before GPU 1 consumes it. And all of this happens without idling other independent work.

For example, consider a set of four streams (`Streams A-D`) that pipeline operations and depend on one another in some cases. We can enforce these dependencies using CUDA events (see Figure 11-7).

To ensure stream B doesn't start processing until stream A produces the data, we can record an event in stream A and make stream B wait for that before continuing. Similarly, stream D can wait on stream B as shown here. By chaining events in this manner, we maintain correct ordering between streams while still running different batches concurrently.

This event-based synchronization is heavily used in deep learning frameworks to overlap gradient computations with all-reduce communications. The compute stream records an event when gradients are ready, and a communication stream waits on that event to start an NCCL operation, thereby overlapping communication with remaining computation.

In short, CUDA events are lightweight and optimized for device signaling. A stream records an event when it reaches a specific point in its command queue. And other streams can efficiently poll/wait for it. They let us orchestrate complex dependency graphs across streams without forcing global waits. And they provide the necessary control to implement pipelined execution in multistream LLM workloads.

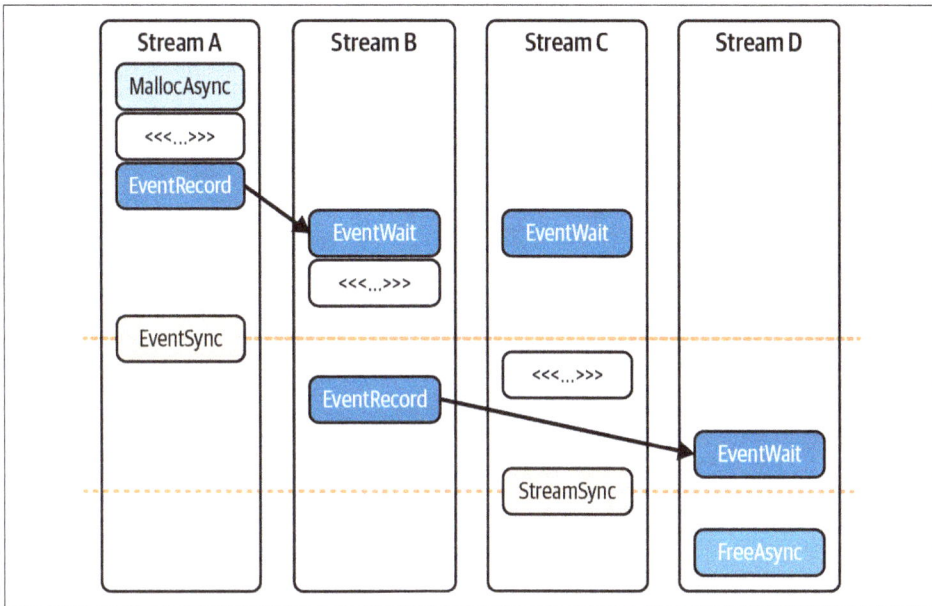

Figure 11-7. Synchronizing CUDA streams with events (adapted from NVIDIA's stream-ordered memory allocator overview (https://oreil.ly/MynOA))

> NVIDIA continues to improve event-time granularity and reduce event-recording overhead. As such, events are a good choice for profiling since they record event timestamps in the GPU timeline and can measure execution time, etc.

Pipelining with Warp Specialization (Intra-Kernel) and CUDA Streams (Inter-Kernel)

Chapter 10 demonstrated how to use warp specialization and the CUDA Pipeline API to hide memory latency within a single kernel. In that section, we launched a single, persistent, and warp-specialized kernel in which each thread block is split into three different types of warps: loader, compute, and storer warps. These warps shared a contiguous chunk of shared memory and a two-stage (double-buffered) CUDA Pipeline (`<cuda::pipeline>`) object to coordinate their work.

Let's keep that same warp-specialized device kernel and now drive multiple batches through it using separate CUDA streams. The result is a two-level pipeline as follows:

Intra-kernel overlap (within each block)
   The loader ↔ compute ↔ storer run concurrently using separate pipelines.

Inter-kernel overlap (across batches)

While stream 0 computes on batch *t*, stream 1 DMA-loads batch t+1, and stream 2 returns results of batch t−1. This uses nonblocking streams, pinned host memory, and the stream-ordered allocator so allocations/copies don't serialize other work.

If multiple blocks need the same tile, the thread block cluster + DSMEM path described in Chapter 10 removes redundant global loads across blocks. However, cooperative/cluster launches serialize with other cooperative kernels. The stream pattern used here targets the host ↔ device overlap and works with a noncooperative kernel.

If your bottleneck is on-device tile reuse, use thread block clusters. If the bottleneck is host ↔ device communication and batching, use CUDA streams. We'll show how to combine these in a bit, but this is a good starting point for initial decision making.

The next kernel uses three warps per block (0 = loader, 1 = compute, 2 = storer) and two pipelines to ping-pong stages. Therefore, it requires 6 * TILE_SIZE * sizeof(float) dynamic shared memory ([A0|B0|C0|A1|B1|C1]). It's worth noting that we are switching to use two independent block-scoped pipelines, each with depth 2. One is for the loader → compute (pipe_lc) handoff, and another is for compute → storer (pipe_cs).

In addition, we are using double-buffered shared memory so the kernel can be loading tile i+1 while computing tile *i* and storing tile i−1. That's why you see two cuda::pipeline objects and "[A|B|C] × 2 stages" in shared memory in the code that follows. The two pipelines are an intra-kernel choice to deepen overlap inside each kernel. (Note: you can use streams with either kernel style.) Here is the code:

```
#include <cooperative_groups.h>    // thread_block, etc.
#include <cuda/pipeline>           // CUDA Pipeline API
namespace cg = cooperative_groups;

// shmem bytes = 2(stages)×3(buffers)×TILE_SIZE×sizeof(float)=6×TILE_SIZE×4
//             = 6 * 1024 * 4 = 24,576 B (24 KB) << 227 KB SMEM
// We keep this at 1024 (versus going higher) as a safe starting point
// (good occupancy balance)
#define TILE_SIZE 1024  // one tile = 1,024 floats per buffer (1-Dimension)

    // Alignment / size guards for vectorized copies
    static_assert((TILE_SIZE % (32 * 4)) == 0,
                  "TILE_SIZE must be multiple of 128 for float4 vectorization");
    // If you cannot guarantee 16B alignment or sizes, handle
    //   the tail/ragged edges with a fallback 4B loop.

// Three warps per block: 0 loads, 1 computes, 2 stores.
// Two block-scoped pipelines (each depth=2) implement ping-pong across tiles.
```

```
__global__ void warp_specialized_two_pipelines(
    const float* __restrict__ A_global,
    const float* __restrict__ B_global,
    float*       __restrict__ C_global,
    int          numTiles)
{
    thread_block cta = this_thread_block();

    // Stage s∈{0,1}: [A_s | B_s | C_s], each length TILE_SIZE
    extern __shared__ float shared_mem[];

    // loader -> compute pipeline (2 in-flight stages)
    using pipe_state = cuda::pipeline_shared_state<cuda::thread_scope_block, 2>;
    __shared__
    alignas(pipe_state) unsigned char state_lc_storage[sizeof(pipe_state)];
    __shared__
    alignas(pipe_state) unsigned char state_cs_storage[sizeof(pipe_state)];
    auto* state_lc = reinterpret_cast<pipe_state*>(state_lc_storage);
    auto* state_cs = reinterpret_cast<pipe_state*>(state_cs_storage);
    if (threadIdx.x == 0) {
        new (state_lc) pipe_state();
        new (state_cs) pipe_state();
    }
    cta.sync();
    auto pipe_lc = cuda::make_pipeline(cta, state_lc);

    // compute -> storer pipeline (2 in-flight stages)
    auto pipe_cs = cuda::make_pipeline(cta, state_cs);

    const int warp_id = threadIdx.x >> 5;            // 0,1,2
    const int lane_id = threadIdx.x & 31;
    auto warp = tiled_partition<32>(cta);

    // Prime first tile handled by this block
    const int first = blockIdx.x;
    if (first > numTiles) {
        const int stage0 = first & 1;
        float* A0 = shared_mem + stage0 * 3 * TILE_SIZE;
        float* B0 = A0 + TILE_SIZE;

        pipe_lc.producer_acquire();
        #pragma unroll
        for (int chunk = 0; chunk < TILE_SIZE; chunk += 32 * 4) {
            if (warp_id == 0) {
                cuda::memcpy_async(
                    warp,
                    reinterpret_cast<float4*>(A0 + chunk) + lane_id,
                    reinterpret_cast<const float4*>(A_global + size_t(first) *
                      TILE_SIZE + chunk) + lane_id,
                    sizeof(float4),
                    pipe_lc);
                cuda::memcpy_async(
                    warp,
                    reinterpret_cast<float4*>(B0 + chunk) + lane_id,
                    reinterpret_cast<const float4*>(B_global + size_t(first) *
                      TILE_SIZE + chunk) + lane_id,
                    sizeof(float4),
```

```
                              pipe_lc);
            }
        }
        pipe_lc.producer_commit();
}

// Block-scoped collectives remain CTA-uniform
pipe_lc.consumer_wait();
cta.sync();

// Compute consumes loader output and signals storer.
if (warp_id == 1) {
    #pragma unroll
    for (int chunk = 0; chunk < TILE_SIZE; chunk += 32) {
        C_buf[chunk+lane_id] = A_buf[chunk+lane_id]
                                    + B_buf[chunk+lane_id];
    }
}
cta.sync();
pipe_lc.consumer_release();

pipe_cs.producer_acquire();
pipe_cs.producer_commit();
pipe_cs.consumer_wait();
cta.sync();

// Storer waits on compute and writes back.
if (warp_id == 2) {
    #pragma unroll
    for (int chunk = 0; chunk < TILE_SIZE; chunk += 32) {
        C_global[offset + chunk + lane_id] = C_buf[chunk + lane_id];
    }
}
cta.sync();
pipe_cs.consumer_release();

// Loader prefetches next tile after the current stage is released.
const int next = tile + gridDim.x;
if (next < numTiles) {
    const int next_stage = next & 1;
    float* A_next = shared_mem + next_stage * 3 * TILE_SIZE;
    float* B_next = A_next + TILE_SIZE;
    pipe_lc.producer_acquire();
    if (warp_id == 0) {
        #pragma unroll
        for (int chunk = 0; chunk < TILE_SIZE; chunk += 32 * 4) {
            cuda::memcpy_async(
                warp,
                reinterpret_cast<float4*>(A_next + chunk) + lane_id,
                reinterpret_cast<const float4*>(A_global +
                    size_t(next) * TILE_SIZE + chunk) + lane_id,
                    sizeof(float4), pipe_lc);
            cuda::memcpy_async(
                warp,
                reinterpret_cast<float4*>(B_next + chunk) + lane_id,
                reinterpret_cast<const float4*>(B_global +
                    size_t(next) * TILE_SIZE + chunk) + lane_id,
```

```
                        sizeof(float4), pipe_lc);
            }
        }
        pipe_lc.producer_commit();
    }

    // Launch requirements: blockDim.x = 96 (3 warps), gridDim as needed,
    // dynamic shared memory = 6 * TILE_SIZE * sizeof(float).
}
```

Here, we are including some performance highlights worth noting. First, we are requiring 16-byte alignment of A0, B0, A_global + base, and B_global + base. If a path isn't 16-byte aligned, we fall back to the 4-byte loop for the misaligned prologue/epilogue.

16-bytes per lane (float4/int4) aligns with modern GPU best practice to reach 128-byte coalesced accesses at the warp level. This helps to reduce pipeline overhead.

Next, we are assuming the TILE_SIZE is a multiple of 128 (32 lanes × 4 floats). If not, handle the tail with a scalar loop. In addition, use cooperative staged copy under pipeline collectives such as a cuda::memcpy_async + float4 path where selected, or equivalent coalesced cooperative copy loops. This preserves asynchronous pipeline semantics and lowers per-tile copy overhead.

And here is the host driver, which cycles batches across nonblocking streams and uses pinned host memory and the stream-ordered allocator (cudaMallocAsync ÷ cudaFreeAsync). It launches the warp_specialized_two_pipelines in the previous kernel:

```
#include <cstdio>
#include <cuda_runtime.h>

#define TILE_SIZE    1024
#define NUM_STREAMS 2
#define BATCHES     8

// Device kernel
__global__ void warp_specialized_two_pipelines(
    const float* __restrict__ A_global,
    const float* __restrict__ B_global,
    float*       __restrict__ C_global,
    int          numTiles);

int main() {
    // Create nonblocking streams (do NOT use legacy default stream)
    cudaStream_t s[NUM_STREAMS];
    for (int i = 0; i < NUM_STREAMS; ++i)
```

```
        cudaStreamCreateWithFlags(&s[i], cudaStreamNonBlocking);

    // Pinned host buffers so cudaMemcpyAsync truly overlaps
    float *hA = nullptr, *hB = nullptr, *hC = nullptr;
    const size_t bytesPerBatch = TILE_SIZE * sizeof(float);
    cudaMallocHost(&hA, BATCHES * bytesPerBatch);
    cudaMallocHost(&hB, BATCHES * bytesPerBatch);
    cudaMallocHost(&hC, BATCHES * bytesPerBatch);

    // Initialize inputs
    for (int b = 0; b < BATCHES; ++b) {
        for (int i = 0; i < TILE_SIZE; ++i) {
            hA[b * TILE_SIZE + i] = float(i);
            hB[b * TILE_SIZE + i] = 1.0f;
        }
    }

    // Enqueue batches in a round-robin across streams
    for (int b = 0; b < BATCHES; ++b) {
        cudaStream_t st = s[b % NUM_STREAMS];

        float *dA = nullptr, *dB = nullptr, *dC = nullptr;
        cudaMallocAsync(&dA, bytesPerBatch, st);   // stream-ordered allocator
        cudaMallocAsync(&dB, bytesPerBatch, st);
        cudaMallocAsync(&dC, bytesPerBatch, st);

        cudaMemcpyAsync(dA, hA + size_t(b) * TILE_SIZE, bytesPerBatch,
                        cudaMemcpyHostToDevice, st);
        cudaMemcpyAsync(dB, hB + size_t(b) * TILE_SIZE, bytesPerBatch,
                        cudaMemcpyHostToDevice, st);

        const dim3 block(96);           // 3 warps: loader/compute/storer
        const dim3 grid(1);
        const size_t shmem = 6 * TILE_SIZE * sizeof(float); //[A0|B0|C0|A1|B1|C1]

        // Each batch is one tile in this 1-D example
        warp_specialized_two_pipelines<<<grid, block, shmem, st>>>(
            dA, dB, dC, /*numTiles=*/1);

        cudaMemcpyAsync(hC + size_t(b) * TILE_SIZE, dC, bytesPerBatch,
                        cudaMemcpyDeviceToHost, st);

        cudaFreeAsync(dA, st);          // stream-ordered free
        cudaFreeAsync(dB, st);
        cudaFreeAsync(dC, st);
    }

    // Clean up
    for (int i = 0; i < NUM_STREAMS; ++i) {
        cudaStreamSynchronize(s[i]);
        cudaStreamDestroy(s[i]);
    }
```

```
        cudaFreeHost(hA); cudaFreeHost(hB); cudaFreeHost(hC);
        return 0;
    }
```

Here, each stream carries its own sequence: allocate → H2D → kernel → D2H → free. Because allocations and copies are enqueued in stream order and the host buffers are pinned, the GPU's copy engines can overlap H2D/D2H with the SM compute from another stream. This is the inter-kernel layer that complements the intra-kernel overlap created by warp specialization and introduced in Chapter 10.

Specifically, this example shows shared memory holding two sets of three buffers of length TILE_SIZE each so that one set can be used while the next tile is prepared. A <cuda::pipeline> with two stages provides double buffering across tiles and enforces the correct ordering so the loader, compute, and storer warps can overlap on different tiles. The kernel primes the first tile before the loop and then prefetches tile i plus gridDim.x while computing tile i.

In isolation, this warp-specialized kernel hides memory latency by overlapping three roles within each tile. However, a single warp-specialized kernel can process only one batch of tiles at a time.

To keep the GPU busy with multiple batches—and overlap H2D transfers, kernel computation, and D2H transfers across those batches, we launch multiple instances of this same warp-specialized kernel in separate CUDA streams. This will use the stream-ordered allocator for each batch.

This second layer of pipelining, inter-kernel concurrency, lets us wave successive mini-batches through the GPU. This way, while one batch's kernel is computing in stream 0, another batch's data is still arriving in stream 1. And, concurrently, a previous batch's results might be streaming back to the host in stream 2.

In practice, we pick a small number of streams, two or three, and cycle through them. Each stream allocates its own device buffers using cudaMallocAsync, copies input data asynchronously with cudaMemcpyAsync, launches the warp-specialized kernel to process those buffers, copies the results back to the host asynchronously, and then frees the buffers with cudaFreeAsync.

Because each of these operations is enqueued in a specific stream, they can all overlap with equivalent operations in other streams. On modern GPUs with multiple copy engines and stream-ordered allocators, this pattern can substantially increase utilization by saturating every part of the chip simultaneously. The actual overlap is bounded by copy-engine counts (query cudaDeviceProp::asyncEngineCount), bandwidth, and kernel occupancy.

As soon as the loader warp in one kernel is waiting on a global-memory fetch, the H2D copy for the next batch is in flight on the copy engine. As soon as the storer warp in a previous batch is writing back to global memory, the allocator in another stream can grab memory for the next batch without forcing a global sync.

In essence, the warp-specialization example from Chapter 10 taught us how to make one kernel hide its memory latency by overlapping load/compute/store inside a thread block. The multistream example in this chapter builds on that by showing how to feed many of those kernels—each processing a different batch—into the GPU simultaneously by overlapping host ↔ device transfers, compute, and device ↔ host transfers across the entire pipeline.

Modern GPUs have multiple copy engines and perform asynchronous memory allocations. Together with Tensor Cores, they work in parallel to create a two-level pipelining strategy with intra-kernel warp specialization and inter-kernel streams. These mechanisms allow our kernels to approach peak hardware utilization for LLM workloads.

Warp Specialization with Thread Block Clusters and CUDA Streams

We will now put everything together from this chapter—and previous chapters—to drive multiple in-flight mini-batches through multiple streams, each of which launches a cooperative thread-block-clustered, warp-specialized kernel. This represents the pinnacle of CUDA performance optimizations on the latest GPU hardware.

> While we cover this topic for comprehensiveness, it's important to note that, due to the complexity, this combination of techniques is rarely seen outside of very specialized research projects and ultra-latency-sensitive inference engines. It's still worth covering, however, as it combines many of the concepts that we learned so far into one code example.

Chapter 10 showed warp specialization inside a single thread block as well as combining warp specialization with thread-block clusters using DSMEM. This way, one leader thread block loads a tile once—and every block in the thread block cluster computes from that shared on-chip copy. This removes duplicate global loads.

This example reuses that exact pattern in which the leader uses a block-scoped pipeline to stage the copies. All blocks are read using `cluster.map_shared_rank`, so it inherits the data-reuse win.

In the previous warp-specialized example with CUDA streams, each thread block was responsible for all three pipeline stages—loader, compute, and storer—within its own shared-memory region. Now, let's extend that earlier implementation to use a thread block cluster pipeline. This way, the loader, compute, and storer warps are distributed across the thread block cluster. This is in contrast to the previous implementation, which is confined to a single thread block.

The code for the thread block cluster plus warp specialization example with CUDA streams follows. In this example, we pick NUM_STREAMS = 2 so that the host can queue two independent launches in separate CUDA streams. We reuse the same warp_speci alized_cluster_pipeline implementation from Chapter 10's section on warp specialization with thread block clusters and add CUDA streams:

```
// Warp specialization across a thread block cluster using DSMEM
// and a block scoped pipeline, launched from multiple CUDA streams

#include <cuda_runtime.h>
#include <cuda/pipeline>
#include <cooperative_groups.h>
#include <algorithm>
namespace cg = cooperative_groups;

#define TILE_SIZE    128    // 3×TILE_ELEMS×4 bytes=196,608 bytes < 227 KB SMEM
#define TILE_ELEMS   (TILE_SIZE * TILE_SIZE)
#define NUM_STREAMS 2
#define CLUSTER_BLOCKS 4   // blocks per cluster along x (tune to device)

// ---- Device helpers ----

__device__ void compute_rows_from_ds(const float* __restrict__ A_src,
                                     const float* __restrict__ B_src,
                                     float*       __restrict__ C_dst,
                                     int row_begin, int row_end, int lane_id)
{
    for (int row = row_begin + lane_id; row < row_end; row += warpSize) {
        for (int col = 0; col < TILE_SIZE; ++col) {
            float acc = 0.0f;
            #pragma unroll
            for (int k = 0; k < TILE_SIZE; ++k) {
                acc += A_src[row * TILE_SIZE + k] * B_src[k * TILE_SIZE + col];
            }
            C_dst[row * TILE_SIZE + col] = acc;
        }
    }
}

// Clustered, warp-specialized kernel (leader loads once, others consume DSMEM)
extern "C"
__global__ void warp_specialized_cluster_pipeline(
    const float* __restrict__ A_global,
    const float* __restrict__ B_global,
    float*       __restrict__ C_global,
    int numTiles)
{
    thread_block cta     = this_thread_block();
```

```
cluster_group cluster = this_cluster();

extern __shared__ float smem[];
float* A_tile_local = smem;
float* B_tile_local = A_tile_local + TILE_ELEMS;
float* C_tile_local = B_tile_local + TILE_ELEMS;

// Leader uses a block-scoped pipeline to stage A/B exactly once per tile
using pipe_state_t = cuda::pipeline_shared_state<cuda::thread_scope_block,1>;
__shared__
alignas(pipe_state_t) unsigned char pipe_storage[sizeof(pipe_state_t)];
auto* pipe_state = reinterpret_cast<pipe_state_t*>(pipe_storage);
if (threadIdx.x == 0) { new (pipe_state) pipe_state_t(); }
cta.sync();
auto pipe = cuda::make_pipeline(cta, pipe_state);

const int lane_id = threadIdx.x & 31;
const int warp_id = threadIdx.x >> 5;
auto warp = tiled_partition<32>(cta);

const int cluster_rank      = cluster.block_rank();
const dim3 cluster_dims     = cluster.dim_blocks();
const int blocks_in_cluster = cluster_dims.x*cluster_dims.y*cluster_dims.z;

// Each iteration handles one tile per cluster (1-D cluster along x)
for (int tile = blockIdx.x / cluster_dims.x; tile < numTiles;
     tile += gridDim.x / cluster_dims.x) {
  const size_t offset = static_cast<size_t>(tile) * TILE_ELEMS;

  // Leader block stages A and B once for the entire cluster.
  // Block-scoped pipeline collectives stay CTA-uniform.
  if (cluster_rank == 0) {
     pipe.producer_acquire();
     if (warp_id == 0) {
        cuda::memcpy_async(warp, A_tile_local, A_global + offset,
                           TILE_ELEMS * sizeof(float), pipe);
        cuda::memcpy_async(warp, B_tile_local, B_global + offset,
                           TILE_ELEMS * sizeof(float), pipe);
     }
     pipe.producer_commit();
     // Make visible inside leader before publishing
     pipe.consumer_wait();
     pipe.consumer_release();
  }

  // Publish to all blocks in the cluster
  cluster.sync();

  const float* A_src = cluster.map_shared_rank(A_tile_local, 0);
  const float* B_src = cluster.map_shared_rank(B_tile_local, 0);

  // Divide rows among blocks in the cluster
```

```
            const int rows_per_block = (TILE_SIZE + blocks_in_cluster - 1)
                                       / blocks_in_cluster;
            const int row_begin = std::min(cluster_rank * rows_per_block, TILE_SIZE);
            const int row_end   = std::min(row_begin + rows_per_block, TILE_SIZE);

            // Compute warp produces this block's band into local SMEM
            if (warp_id == 1) {
                compute_rows_from_ds(A_src, B_src, C_tile_local,
                                     row_begin, row_end, lane_id);
            }

            // Ensure the storer sees computed rows
            cta.sync();

            // Storer warp writes band back to global
            if (warp_id == 2) {
                for (int row = row_begin + lane_id; row < row_end; row += warpSize){
                    for (int col = 0; col < TILE_SIZE; ++col) {
                        C_global[offset + row * TILE_SIZE + col] =
                            C_tile_local[row * TILE_SIZE + col];
                    }
                }
            }

            // Done with this tile; allow leader to reuse buffers
            cluster.sync();
        }
        // Dynamic shared memory size: 3 * TILE_ELEMS * sizeof(float)
}

// ---- Host driver: stream-staged batches + clustered kernel launch ----

void launch_warp_specialized_cluster_pipeline_multistream(
    const float* h_A,        // Host input A: length = numBatches * batchLength
    const float* h_B,        // Host input B: length = numBatches * batchLength
    float*       h_C,        // Host output C: length = numBatches * batchLength
    int          batchLength,// elems per batch; must be multiple of TILE_ELEMS
    int          numBatches)
{
    // Basic validation
    if (batchLength % TILE_ELEMS != 0) {
        fprintf(stderr, "batchLength must be a multiple of TILE_ELEMS (%d)\n",
                TILE_ELEMS);
        return;
    }
    const int numTiles = batchLength / TILE_ELEMS;

    // Nonblocking streams avoid legacy default-stream barriers
    cudaStream_t streams[NUM_STREAMS];
    for (int i = 0; i < NUM_STREAMS; ++i)
        cudaStreamCreateWithFlags(&streams[i], cudaStreamNonBlocking);
```

```
// Size and launch geometry
int device = 0;
cudaGetDevice(&device);
cudaDeviceProp prop{};
cudaGetDeviceProperties(&prop, device);

// grid.x must be a multiple of CLUSTER_BLOCKS
const int blocksPerGrid = prop.multiProcessorCount * CLUSTER_BLOCKS;
const dim3 blockDim(96);  // 3 warps: loader/compute/storer
const size_t shmemBytes = 3ull * TILE_ELEMS * sizeof(float);

// Cluster attributes
cudaLaunchAttribute attr[2]{};
attr[0].id = cudaLaunchAttributeClusterDimension;
attr[0].val.clusterDim = dim3(CLUSTER_BLOCKS, 1, 1);
attr[1].id = cudaLaunchAttributeNonPortableClusterSizeAllowed;
attr[1].val.nonPortableClusterSizeAllowed = 1;

// Enqueue batches round-robin across streams
for (int b = 0; b < numBatches; ++b) {
    cudaStream_t st = streams[b % NUM_STREAMS];

    float *dA = nullptr, *dB = nullptr, *dC = nullptr;
    const size_t bytes = static_cast<size_t>(batchLength) * sizeof(float);

    // Stream-ordered allocator avoids global sync
    cudaMallocAsync(&dA, bytes, st);
    cudaMallocAsync(&dB, bytes, st);
    cudaMallocAsync(&dC, bytes, st);

    // H2D (host pointers should be pinned for true overlap)
    cudaMemcpyAsync(dA, h_A + static_cast<size_t>(b) * batchLength, bytes,
                    cudaMemcpyHostToDevice, st);
    cudaMemcpyAsync(dB, h_B + static_cast<size_t>(b) * batchLength, bytes,
                    cudaMemcpyHostToDevice, st);

    // Clustered launch config
    void* args[] = { &dA, &dB, &dC, (void*)&numTiles };
    cudaLaunchConfig_t cfg{};
    cfg.gridDim  = dim3(blocksPerGrid);
    cfg.blockDim = blockDim;
    cfg.dynamicSmemBytes = shmemBytes;
    cfg.stream = st;
    cfg.attrs = attr;
    cfg.numAttrs = 2;

    // Launch the clustered kernel (cooperative/cluster launch)
    cudaKernel_t k;
    cudaGetKernel(&k, warp_specialized_cluster_pipeline);
    void* fptr = reinterpret_cast<void*>(k);
    cudaLaunchKernelExC(&cfg, fptr, args);
```

```
            // D2H and cleanup
            cudaMemcpyAsync(h_C + static_cast<size_t>(b) * batchLength, dC, bytes,
                            cudaMemcpyDeviceToHost, st);
            cudaFreeAsync(dA, st);
            cudaFreeAsync(dB, st);
            cudaFreeAsync(dC, st);
        }

        for (int i = 0; i < NUM_STREAMS; ++i) {
            cudaStreamSynchronize(streams[i]);
            cudaStreamDestroy(streams[i]);
        }
    }
```

This example uses a cluster launch configured with cudaLaunchKer
nelExC. Cooperative launches (including cluster launches) require
enough resources to keep their blocks resident per the launch constraints. This often limits concurrency, but cooperative kernels may
still be interleaved with other work when resources permit. Concurrency is not guaranteed as it's topology- and launch-dependent.
(Note: data transfers and kernels in other streams can still overlap
subject to resource limits and launch constraints.)

As in Chapter 10, we launch the kernel with a cluster dimension so that blocks join a
cluster_group and can access each other's distributed shared memory. The leader
block stages its copies through a block-scoped cuda::thread_scope_block, while all
blocks read the leader's tiles using cluster.map_shared_rank.

Using cluster scope and distributed shared memory, the load stage runs once per
cluster in the leader, while compute and store run concurrently across the cluster's
blocks. As before, each warp's warp_id determines its role, and warps loop persistently over all tiles, fetching, computing, and storing in a synchronized rotation.

By adding CUDA streams and launching independent copies of this kernel in separate CUDA streams (NUM_STREAMS = 2), we keep the GPU busy on multiple batches
of input data. In each stream, we perform the following steps:

1. Allocate per-batch device buffers for each thread block to use with cudaMalloc
   Async.

2. Stage inputs from host to device with cudaMemcpyAsync.

3. Launch the clustered warp-specialized kernel using cudaLaunchKernelExC.

4. Copy the outputs back to the host with cudaMemcpyAsync.

5. Free device buffers with cudaFreeAsync.

Because each stream enqueues its own cooperative launch along with its asynchronous copies and frees, the host can keep several mini-batches in flight even though only one cooperative kernel runs at a time. Remember that the GPU serializes cooperative kernel launches because each cooperative kernel pins every thread block simultaneously (this limitation will be reemphasized after the code example).

Using multiple streams (NUM_STREAMS = 2) still lets us overlap host-side allocations and copies with the previous kernel's execution. For instance, while stream 0's thread block cluster works on tile n, stream 1 can asynchronously allocate buffers (cudaMalloc Async) and copy tile n+1 into device memory, and stream 2 could be writing tile n–1's results back to the host.

> The cooperative kernel must occupy every thread-block slot (CTA) that it needs on the GPU. This prevents any other cooperative launch from running simultaneously because all those CTA resources are already in use.

In practice, stream 0 issues its cooperative launch and begins executing, while stream 1 can immediately enqueue its own launch. But the second launch remains pending until stream 0's kernel finishes.

However, as soon as stream 0 completes, stream 1's launch starts instantly. This is because its inputs were already staged by cudaMemcpyAsync—and its buffers were already allocated by cudaMallocAsync.

We create two layers of pipelining that span multiple thread blocks by combining thread block clusters. Specifically, we combine inter-kernel CUDA streams with intra-kernel warp specialization. This is implemented as a block-scoped pipeline inside the leader CTA with cluster-wide synchronization and DSMEM sharing. This two-layer pipeline pushes the hardware to its peak.

In the first layer, the thread block cluster pipeline lets loader, compute, and storer warps cooperate across all thread blocks. Thread block clusters can use TMA multicast to replicate a global memory tile transfer into the shared memory of each block within the cluster. Multicast is local to the thread block cluster. In essence, the thread block cluster fetches each tile exactly once. In the second layer, multiple streams hide host-side allocations, copies, and kernel launches behind one another.

In short, these combined techniques make sure that memory latency is hidden at both the grid level and the host-to-device level. This drives hardware utilization close to peak on modern GPUs—and maximizes throughput for LLM workloads.

In many scenarios, memory-hierarchy bottlenecks like DRAM bandwidth and model-parallel communication like NCCL all-reduce will dominate the workload. So once your kernel is close to saturating the HBM bandwidth and your streams already hide CPU → GPU latency, the additional few percent of SM utilization that you'd get by adding warp specialization on top of that—and then adding thread block clusters on top of that—rarely justifies the steep engineering cost. In practice, most real-world LLM training and inference workloads benefit sufficiently from simpler designs presented earlier, such as double-buffered kernels or two-stage pipelines with CUDA streams.

Multi-GPU Compute and Data Transfer Overlap with CUDA Streams

When training or serving LLMs across multiple GPUs, CUDA streams let you overlap local compute, peer-to-peer transfers, collective communication, data preparation, and memory management so that no device idles. For instance, suppose you split a transformer model across two GPUs such that GPU 0 handles layers 0–3 and GPU B handles layers 4–7. On GPU A, you might write:

```
// Stream 0 on GPU A: compute layers 0-3
myTransformerLayers0to3<<<gridA, blockA, 0, stream0_A>>>(
    inputActivationsA, outputActivationsA);
cudaEvent_t eventA, eventFromA;
cudaEventCreateWithFlags(eventA,
    cudaEventDisableTiming); // lowers overhead for sync-only events
cudaEventCreateWithFlags(eventFromA,
    cudaEventDisableTiming);  // lowers overhead for sync-only events
cudaEventRecord(eventA, stream0_A);
```

Meanwhile, on the CPU, you have already decoded or prepared the next microbatch (N+1) and issued a `cudaMemcpyAsync` into a pinned host buffer. This way, by the time GPU A's stream 0 finishes the forward pass for batch *N*, the CPU-to-GPU copy for batch N+1 can begin immediately without waiting.

At the same time, you call `cudaStreamWaitEvent(stream1_A, eventA, 0)` to ensure that `stream1_A` waits until `outputActivationsA` is ready before launching the direct NVLink/PCIe copy into GPU B's memory, as shown here:

```
// Stream 1 on GPU A: wait for layer computation, then copy to GPU B
cudaStreamWaitEvent(stream1_A, eventA, 0);
cudaMemcpyPeerAsync(
    destActivationsB, /*dstGPU=*/1,
    outputActivationsA, /*srcGPU=*/0,
    bytes, stream1_A);
```

As soon as you record `eventA`, GPU A's `stream0` can immediately launch the next forward kernel for batch N+1, using `cudaMemcpyAsync` to copy its inputs from the pinned host buffer into device memory without blocking. On GPU B, you record a matching event when the copy begins or ends:

```
// Stream 1 on GPU A: after peer copy starts,
// record eventFromA
cudaEventRecord(eventFromA, stream1_A);
```

Then on GPU B, you wait for data to arrive and run layers 4–7, as shown here:

```
// Stream 1 on GPU B: wait for data arrival, then run layers 4-7
cudaStreamWaitEvent(stream1_B, eventFromA, 0);
myTransformerLayers4to7<<<gridB, blockB, 0, stream1_B>>>(
    destActivationsB, nextActivationsB);
```

This explicit event-and-wait pattern guarantees that GPU B's layers 4–7 compute only begins after the peer copy has completed. Meanwhile, GPU B's `stream0_B` can simultaneously prefetch weights or perform other preparatory work.

The P2P transfer used here runs on GPU A's DMA copy engine and doesn't use any of GPU A's SMs. This way, GPU A's compute stream can immediately proceed to batch N+1 without having to manage the data transfer.

The result is a three-way overlap: GPU A's SMs can immediately start batch N+1 in `stream0_A`, GPU A's peer DMA engine can shuttle batch N activations to GPU B in `stream1_A`, and GPU B's SMs can run batch N in `stream0_B` or begin batch N in its `stream1_B`. By partitioning work into separate streams and using pinned memory on the host, we hide P2P and H2D latency behind ongoing computation and data preparation.

When it's time to synchronize gradients or broadcast parameters across many GPUs, NCCL handles the communication at scale using low-occupancy device kernels that drive GPUDirect P2P or RDMA over NVLink, PCIe, or InfiniBand. Under the hood, NCCL breaks the tensors into multiple contiguous chunks.

This design shows that each GPU can have multiple streams, including a compute stream for its primary work, a receive stream for incoming data, and a communication stream for reductions. Using dedicated streams per role—and giving communication streams higher priority—allows for optimal overlap. In fact, frameworks like PyTorch typically run NCCL collectives on these dedicated streams with higher priority for network transfers.

PyTorch and NCCL both use dedicated, high-priority streams to interleave communication with compute-intensive operations. This way, they don't get delayed behind large compute kernels.

NCCL will choose a ring or tree algorithm based on NVLink or PCIe topology. Consider a four-GPU ring, as shown in Figure 11-8, with four chunks (1–4).

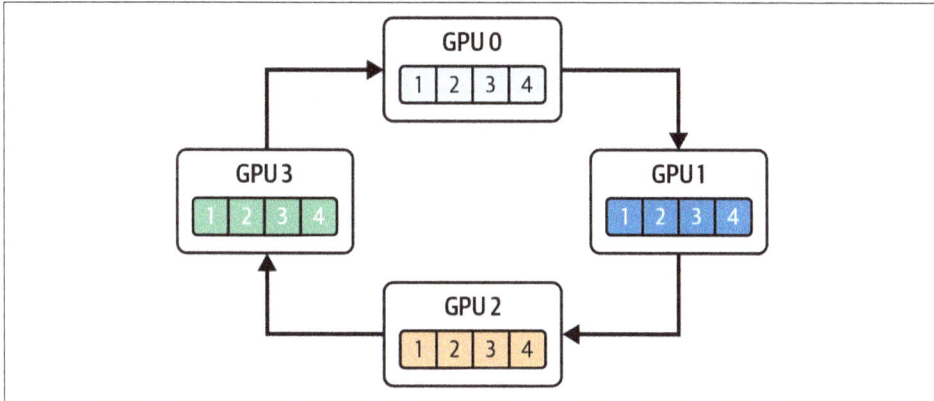

Figure 11-8. Chunked all-reduce with four GPUs in a ring

In this ring all-reduce, each GPU sends chunk *i* to its neighbor (k → k+1) while receiving chunk i−1 from its other neighbor (k−1 → k), using device kernels to move and reduce chunks over NVLink or PCIe.

By pipelining these chunked sends and receives, NCCL keeps NVLink fully saturated. While chunk *i* traverses from GPU 0 → GPU 1, chunk i−1 moves GPU 1 → GPU 2, and so on. This minimizes idle gaps. In code, you would see something like the following:

```
// In a high-priority communication stream on each GPU:
cudaEventRecord(eventK, computeStream);
cudaStreamWaitEvent(commStream, eventK, 0);
ncclAllReduce( // this is asynchronous
    gradBuffer, gradBuffer, numElements,
    ncclFloat, ncclSum, comm, commStream);
```

Because NCCL uses only a few SM thread blocks, it orchestrates the chunked send/recv + reduce across NVLink or NVSwitch in a low-occupancy manner on the SMs. Meanwhile, your main compute stream running a backward pass for layer k+1, for instance, can continue running. When the all-reduce completes, the event is recorded as shown here:

```
cudaEventRecord(eventAllReduceDone, commStream); // signals collective completion
cudaStreamWaitEvent(computeStream, eventAllReduceDone, 0);
// Now apply optimizer updates on computeStream...
```

Remember that NCCL collectives like all-reduce are asynchronous. They return control immediately. By recording an event after the call and waiting on it in the compute stream, you ensure that the compute stream doesn't resume until the reduction is actually completed.

NCCL's kernels have been purposely optimized to achieve maximum bandwidth at low occupancy using a small amount of SM resources per GPU. In practice, NCCL can saturate NVLink or PCIe bandwidth with a small number of thread blocks per GPU, thanks to low-occupancy kernels tuned for the interconnect. In addition, you can offload some of these collective aggregation operations to NVIDIA SHARP if your network hardware supports it. This will free up even more SM resources to perform more useful computational work.

NIXL provides a unified, high-throughput API for point-to-point and disaggregated transfers across NVLink, RDMA, and storage backends, so you typically use NIXL APIs instead of calling `cudaMemcpyPeerAsync` yourself. NIXL moves data quickly and asynchronously across different tiers of memory and interconnects. When you invoke a NIXL operation with `nixlCommStream`, the data is chunked and pipelined over the network using the fastest transport mechanism available, such as GPUDirect RDMA or NVLink.

And like NCCL, NIXL can use dedicated high-priority streams for chunked peer-to-peer and collective data transfers. This can reduce queuing delays so their copy commands hit the GPU's DMA engines soon after they are issued—likely preempting lower-priority work.

Marking these transfer streams as high priority doesn't mean they consume SM resources upfront. It simply guarantees that when the copy commands are ready, they'll be issued ahead of other low-priority operations.

In practice, the copy engines then take advantage of whatever DRAM-to-DRAM bandwidth isn't already being used by your compute kernels. As such, they effectively use only idle memory-fabric bandwidth to move data across the interconnects.

This design maximizes overlap such that while one stream drives `cudaMemcpyPeerAsync` transfers or NCCL reduction kernels on the copy engine, another stream's SM kernels can continue processing forward/backward work. And a third stream can perform asynchronous allocations or event waits. This keeps all of the hardware units busy and without contention.

Peer-to-peer transfers launched using `cudaMemcpyPeerAsync` run entirely on the GPU's copy engines, so they consume only DRAM-to-DRAM bandwidth and no SM cycles. Collective operations such as all-reduce, on the other hand, are implemented as device kernels that use a small number of SMs while driving interconnect bandwidth toward the peak.

At the same time, temporary buffers for activations or mixed-precision gradients are allocated and freed asynchronously to avoid global stalls. For example, inside each GPU's compute stream, you would call the following code:

```
cudaMallocAsync(&tempBuffer, tempBytes, computeStream);
// ...use tempBuffer in kernels...
cudaFreeAsync(tempBuffer, computeStream);
```

Because the stream-ordered memory allocator records these operations without forcing a device-wide synchronization, CUDA does not pause the other streams such as P2P, NCCL, and NIXL streams when allocating or freeing memory. This makes sure that buffer management never interrupts the overlapped compute and communication pipeline.

> This is exactly the stream-ordered memory allocator that we discussed earlier—but now applied to multiple GPUs. Using this will help prevent memory management from bottlenecking your distributed workloads.

After you enqueue the forward pass, backward pass, P2P copies, NCCL all-reduce, memory free, and event-wait operations for a single iteration, you can capture an execution chain (e.g., training or inference iteration) into a single CUDA Graph.

Specifically, when you call cudaStreamBeginCapture, every operation you enqueue into the stream (e.g., kernel launches, computations, communications, data transfers, events, etc.) are inserted as nodes in the graph. This can include ncclAllReduce(), cudaMemcpyAsync, cudaMemcpyPeerAsync, cudaMallocAsync, cudaFreeAsync, cuda EventRecord, cudaStreamWaitEvent—as well as their dependencies. You end the capture with cudaStreamEndCapture(stream, &graph). The code looks something like this:

```
cudaStreamBeginCapture(streamA, cudaStreamCaptureModeGlobal);

computeGradientsLayer1<<<... , 0, streamA>>>(...);
ncclAllReduce(..., comm, streamB);
computeGradientsLayer2<<<... , 0, streamA>>>(...);
ncclAllReduce(..., comm, streamB);
cudaStreamEndCapture(streamA, &graph);
```

When capturing work submitted to multiple streams, use cudaStreamCaptureMode Global so operations enqueued on any participating stream in the same thread are recorded into the same capture session—and cross-stream dependencies are preserved. Otherwise, only the operations enqueued on the stream passed to cudaStream BeginCapture are captured.

You can then instantiate and launch the graph with cudaGraphLaunch(). This will replay the entire DAG with near-zero CPU overhead. By capturing the whole multi-GPU iteration once, you eliminate per-operation enqueue and launch overhead.

Moreover, CUDA Graphs support conditional nodes (e.g., gradient clipping), so infrequent branches stay inside the graph's logic. We'll cover CUDA Graphs in more detail in the next chapter, but it's important to understand their relationship to CUDA streams, including `cudaStreamBeginCapture` and `cudaStreamEndCapture`.

> Modern frameworks like PyTorch hide much of this complexity. For example, PyTorch's `DistributedDataParallel` automatically schedules data transfers, compute, and communications in separate streams. It also uses CUDA Graphs to reduce per-iteration overhead. While it can use CUDA Graphs to reduce overhead, you must explicitly enable this by using capture-safe code and APIs because it's not automatically enabled.

While you don't need to explicitly use these CUDA stream begin and end APIs to build a CUDA Graph, they are convenient when you want to capture the graph at the same time you are enqueuing operations into your stream (we'll cover CUDA Graphs in more detail in the next chapter).

CUDA streams enable finely tuned pipelines in multi-GPU systems by overlapping work across CPUs, DMA engines, and SMs. On the CPU side, `cudaMemcpyAsync` into pinned host buffers stages data for the next batch while the GPU executes the current workload, ensuring that inputs for batch N+1 are ready before batch N completes. At the same time, peer-to-peer transfers between GPUs (using `cudaMemcpyPeerAsync`) can be scheduled on dedicated streams, synchronized with `cudaStreamWaitEvent` to hand off activations or gradients without stalling ongoing compute.

As mentioned, collective communication libraries like NCCL or NIXL are low-occupancy communication kernels that use separate streams. This way, while one GPU is reducing gradients or broadcasting parameters, other streams on that same GPU can continue executing local compute kernels (e.g., forward or backward passes for subsequent layers). In addition, using `cudaMallocAsync` and `cudaFreeAsync` in stream order prevents global synchronization for temporary buffers, letting allocation and deallocation proceed concurrently with compute and communication.

Capturing the entire iteration (e.g., CPU staging, P2P transfers, compute kernels, NCCL calls, allocations, frees, and events/waits) into a CUDA Graph can further reduce CPU overhead. Once the graph is instantiated, invoking `cudaGraphLaunch()` replays the recorded DAG in one go. This eliminates per-call enqueue overhead and preserves all dependencies automatically.

Together, these techniques ensure that each GPU's SM pipelines, copy engines, and interconnect links remain busy. While one stream runs matrix-multiply kernels, another performs peer-to-peer copies, a third executes collective communication, and the CPU stages data for the next microbatch.

In short, you can use CUDA streams to orchestrate work across multiple layers and overlap computation, memory operations, and data transfers. This approach drives every hardware unit to its limits by hiding peer-to-peer and collective communication latencies behind active compute. Overall, CUDA streams maximize throughput, utilization, and efficiency for many AI workloads, including LLM training and inference.

Programmatic Dependent Launch

Another type of inter-kernel pipelining and communication is called *Programmatic Dependent Launch* (PDL). PDL lets a kernel trigger another kernel's execution directly on the device using the same CUDA stream—and without involving the CPU. For instance, Kernel A, the primary kernel, can trigger Kernel B, the secondary kernel, which is waiting on a signal from Kernel A.

This trigger can happen even before Kernel A finishes execution. To do this, it uses `cudaTriggerProgrammaticLaunchCompletion()`, as shown in Figure 11-9. Here, Kernel B is waiting on Kernel A with a call to `cudaGridDependencySynchronize()`.

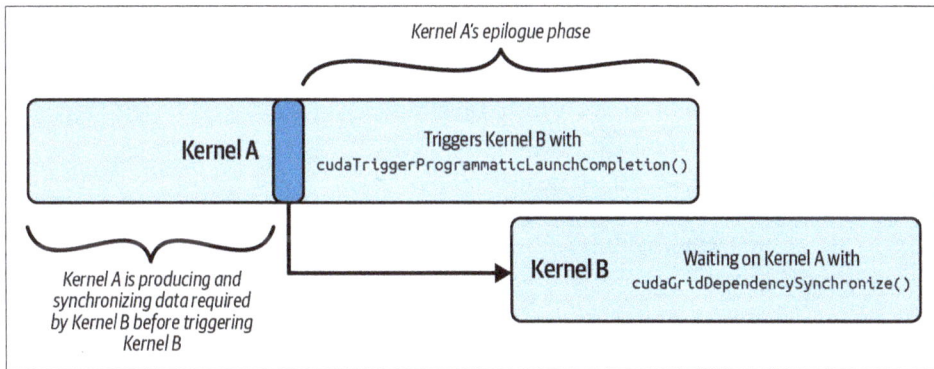

Figure 11-9. Using PDL to launch Kernel B from Kernel A—partially overlapping Kernel B's execution with Kernel A's epilogue (in the same CUDA stream)

Using the constructs provided by PDL, Kernel A can signal Kernel B to execute during Kernel A's *epilogue* (e.g., wrap-up) phase. This way, Kernel A can execute alongside Kernel B for a bit of time. It's important to note that Kernel A should not trigger Kernel B to execute until Kernel A has produced and synchronized all data (e.g., L2/shared memory/global memory) needed by Kernel B.

> The data dependencies of the dependent kernel should be visible in L2, shared memory, global memory, etc., before it continues processing.

The code here shows Kernel A using `cudaTriggerProgrammaticLaunchComple
tion()` to signal to Kernel B that its main work has completed. This also notifies Ker-
nel B that all necessary global-memory flushes have occurred—and that it's safe to
continue:

```
#include <cuda_runtime.h>
#include <cuda_runtime_api.h>

// Kernel A must trigger the PDL flag when it's
//    safe to launch Kernel B
__global__ void kernel_A(int *d_ptr) {
    // Perform work that produces data used by
    //    Kernel B

    // Signals that Kernel A's global-memory
    //    flushes are complete
    // This enables dependent Kernel B's launch

    cudaTriggerProgrammaticLaunchCompletion();

    // ... any further work that can overlap with  ...
    ...
}

// Kernel B must wait for Kernel A to write its memory
//    to global memory and become visible to Kernel B
__global__ void kernel_B(int *d_ptr) {

    // Wait on Kernel A to complete.
    // This ensures the Kernel B waits for the
    //    memory flush before accessing shared data
    cudaGridDependencySynchronize();

    // ... dependent work on d_ptr ...
    ...
}

int main() {
    // 1) Allocate device buffer
    int *d_ptr = nullptr;
    // Allocate an int (example)
    cudaMalloc((void**)&d_ptr, sizeof(int));

    // 2) Create a nonblocking stream for maximum overlap
    cudaStream_t stream;
    cudaStreamCreateWithFlags(&stream,
        cudaStreamNonBlocking);  // Nonblocking

    // 3) Define grid/block sizes
    dim3 gridDim(128), blockDim(256);

    // 4) Launch Kernel A asynchronously
```

```
kernel_A<<<gridDim, blockDim, 0,
    stream>>>(d_ptr);    // Async launch

// 5) Configure PDL for Kernel B
cudaLaunchConfig_t launch_cfg{};
launch_cfg.gridDim          = gridDim;
launch_cfg.blockDim         = blockDim;
launch_cfg.dynamicSmemBytes = 0;
launch_cfg.stream           = stream;

// Sets the PDL flag so cudaLaunchKernelExC overlaps
//   with Kernel A's epilogue
static cudaLaunchAttribute attrs[1];
attrs[0].id  = cudaLaunchAttributeProgrammaticStreamSerialization;
attrs[0].val.programmaticStreamSerializationAllowed =
    1;
launch_cfg.attrs    = attrs;
launch_cfg.numAttrs = 1;

// 6) Pack the pointer argument
void* kernelArgs[] = { &d_ptr };

// 7) Launch Kernel B kernel early using PDL
// Lookup device pointer for secondary_kernel
cudaKernel_t kB;
cudaGetKernel(&kB, kernel_B);
void* funcPtr_kernel_B = reinterpret_cast<void*>(kB);
cudaLaunchKernelExC(&launch_cfg, funcPtr_kernel_B, kernelArgs);

// 8) Wait until all work in the stream completes
cudaStreamSynchronize(stream);

// 9) Cleanup
cudaStreamDestroy(stream);
cudaFree(d_ptr);

return 0;
}
```

Here, Kernel B is waiting on cudaGridDependencySynchronize() until it receives this programmatic-launch completion signal from Kernel A. Once the handoff occurs, the two kernels can overlap their execution. By pairing the trigger in Kernel A, the synchronize in Kernel B, and the launch attribute on the host, this code achieves as much overlap as possible between kernels A and B.

As seen in this example, you need to create a cudaLaunchConfig_t and use special attributes with the cudaLaunchKernelExC() CUDA call when using PDL. Specifically, on the host side, PDL is enabled by configuring a cudaLaunchConfig_t for Kernel B's launch with the cudaLaunchAttributeProgrammaticStreamSerialization attribute enabled to allow early, overlapped dispatch.

Calling `cudaLaunchKernelExC()` with `cudaLaunchAttributeProgrammaticStream Serialization` tells the CUDA runtime that it's safe to enqueue Kernel B—even if Kernel A isn't fully complete. `cudaLaunchKernelExC()` is then used to perform the actual launch with these extended attributes, which relies on the trigger mechanism to perform the handoff.

Combining PDL and Thread Block Clusters with Warp Specialization

Let's bring together three orthogonal techniques—PDL, warp-specialized pipelining, and thread block clusters—into one execution model.

PDL provides the mechanism for one kernel to signal completion of its prologue and trigger a dependent kernel to execute. It will then ramp down while the dependent kernel ramps up and executes.

Warp specialization subdivides each thread block into producer and consumer warps. Specifically, the producer warp asynchronously transfers tiles using TMA, while the compute warp executes matrix-multiply-accumulate (MMA) operations.

And thread block clusters guarantee that multiple thread blocks run on nearby groups of SMs. This facilitates multi-SM cooperation and shared-memory multicast for large-scale workloads.

Together, this combination of inter-kernel and intra-kernel techniques hides DRAM latency, reduces kernel-boundary overheads, and maximizes Tensor Core utilization. They create a pipeline with the following characteristics:

Intra-kernel pipelining
> Warp specialization makes sure that within each thread block, data transfers (producer warps) and compute (consumer warps) are fully overlapped using a multistage pipeline.

Inter-kernel overlap
> PDL allows the prologue of a dependent GEMM kernel, potentially operating on the next layer in a neural network, to begin as soon as the primary kernel finishes prefetching data (weights)—without waiting for the full thread block to tear down.

Interblock cooperation
> Thread block clusters enable groups of thread blocks to coordinate prefetch (e.g., multicast) and perform dynamic load balancing across SMs. This way, both producer and consumer tasks are evenly distributed cluster-wide.

For example, you can overlap the movement of model weights (data transfer) with GEMMs (compute) inside the same kernel so that one tile is being computed while the next tile is in flight. A warp-specialized, multistage software pipeline (stages 0…N) can coordinate these roles using PDL and *mbarrier* primitives, as shown in Figure 11-10.

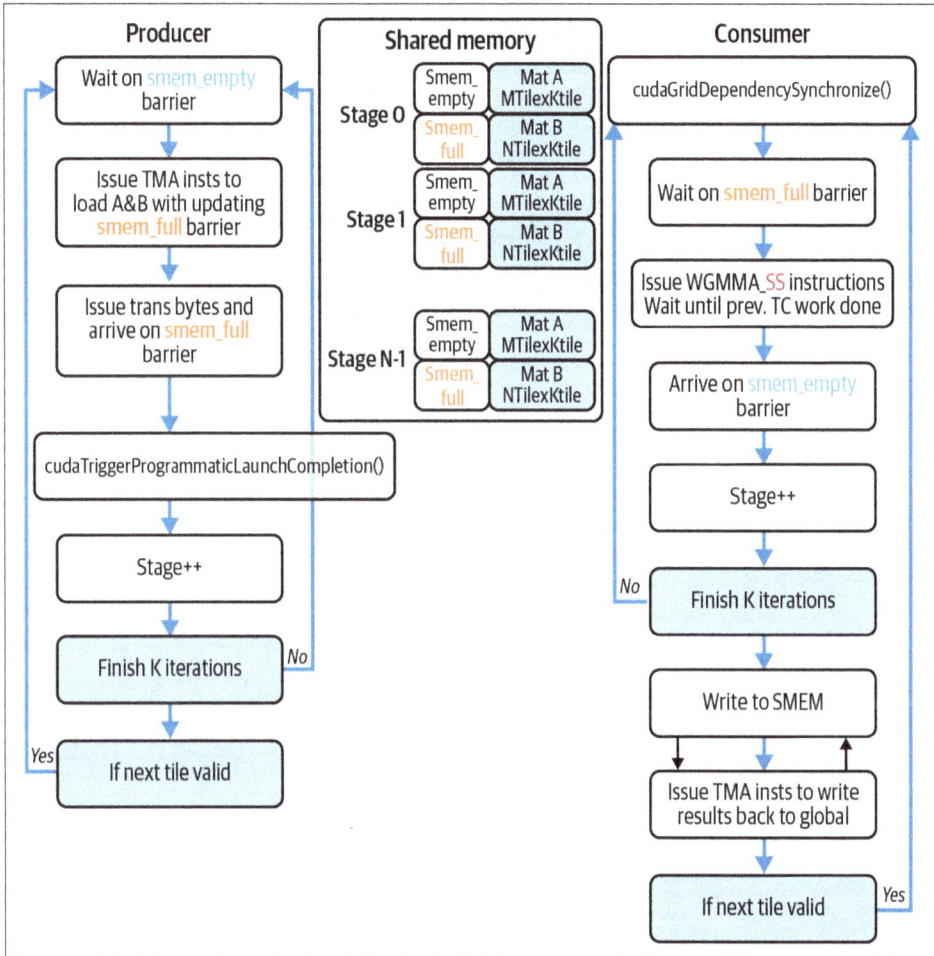

Figure 11-10. Warp-specialized, multistage pipeline with PDL and thread block clusters and TMA multicast for a high-performance, inter-kernel and intra-kernel GEMM implementation

Here is a CUDA C++ example that shows how to combine PDL, thread block clusters, and warp specialization with a simple TMA-style async copy + compute pipeline. Specifically, the primary kernel, `primary_gemm`, uses `cudaTriggerProgrammatic LaunchCompletion()` to signal to the secondary kernel that all memory flushes have completed and the data is ready to be consumed. As such, it's now safe for the

secondary kernel, `secondary_gemm`, to continue from cudaGridDependencySynchron
ize(), as shown here:

```
#include <cstdio>
#include <cuda_runtime.h>
// Cooperative Groups for clusters/barriers
#include <cooperative_groups.h>
// C++ barrier for TMA-like sync
#include <cuda/barrier>
// Async copy API
#include <cuda/pipeline>

namespace cg = cooperative_groups;

// Tile size for our toy GEMM
constexpr int TILE_M = 128;
constexpr int TILE_K = 128;
constexpr int TILE_N = 128;

// A very simple "producer/consumer" pipeline within each CTA
__global__ __cluster_dims__(2,1,1)    // Compile-time cluster of 2 CTAs
void primary_gemm(const float* __restrict__ A,
                  const float* __restrict__ B,
                        float* __restrict__ C,
                  int M, int N, int K)
{
    // Identify thread-block cluster & within-block group
    cg::thread_block_cluster cluster = cg::this_thread_block_cluster();
    cg::thread_block        cta     = cg::this_thread_block();
    int tid = threadIdx.x + threadIdx.y * blockDim.x;
    int warpId = tid / warpSize;
    const int numProducerWarps = 1;

    // Shared-memory tile buffers
    __shared__ float tileA[TILE_M * TILE_K];
    __shared__ float tileB[TILE_K * TILE_N];

    __shared__
    cuda::pipeline_shared_state<cuda::thread_scope_block, 1> pipe_state;
    auto pipe = cuda::make_pipeline(cta, &pipe_state);
    auto warp = tiled_partition<32>(cta);
    pipe.producer_acquire();
    if (warpId < numProducerWarps) {
        // Producer warps issue copies,
        // but pipeline collectives are CTA-uniform.
        cuda::memcpy_async(warp, tileA, A, TILE_M * TILE_K * sizeof(float), pipe);
        cuda::memcpy_async(warp, tileB, B, TILE_K * TILE_N * sizeof(float), pipe);
    }
    pipe.producer_commit();
    cta.sync();
    pipe.consumer_wait();
```

```
    // ... perform "compute" on the tile ...
    // (e.g., a few fused multiply-adds)
    do_compute();

    // Inter-CTA cluster-scope sync for load balancing
    cluster.sync();

    // Signal to dependent kernel that prologue is done
    cudaTriggerProgrammaticLaunchCompletion();

    // ... perform remaining epilogue work ...
    // ...
}

__global__ __cluster_dims__(2,1,1)
void secondary_gemm(const float* __restrict__ A,
                    const float* __restrict__ B,
                          float* __restrict__ C,
                    int M, int N, int K)
{
    // Wait for primary's PDL signal before starting
    cudaGridDependencySynchronize();

    // Similar warp-specialized pipeline as above...
    //   (Omitted for brevity. Duplicate of primary logic,
    //    but reading from different offsets to compute
    //    next GEMM tile.)
}

// cudaLaunchKernelExC, cudaGetKernel
#include <cuda_runtime_api.h>
// cudaLaunchConfig_t
#include <cuda/launch_config.h>

int main()
{
    // Problem dimensions (must be multiples of TILE_)
    int M = TILE_M, N = TILE_N, K = TILE_K;

    // Allocate and initialize matrices A, B, C on device
    float *d_A, *d_B, *d_C;
    cudaMalloc(&d_A, M*K*sizeof(float));
    cudaMalloc(&d_B, K*N*sizeof(float));
    cudaMalloc(&d_C, M*N*sizeof(float));
    // (Initialize d_A, d_B via cudaMemcpy or kernels...)

    // Create a nonblocking stream for overlap
    cudaStream_t stream;
    cudaStreamCreateWithFlags(&stream,
        cudaStreamNonBlocking);

    // Launch primary GEMM
```

```
    dim3 gridDim(M/TILE_M, N/TILE_N), blockDim(256);
    primary_gemm<<<gridDim, blockDim, 0, stream>>>(d_A,
d_B, d_C, M, N, K);

    // Configure PDL attributes for secondary launch
    cudaLaunchConfig_t launch_cfg = {};
    launch_cfg.gridDim           = gridDim;
    launch_cfg.blockDim          = blockDim;
    launch_cfg.dynamicSmemBytes = 0;
    launch_cfg.stream            = stream;
    static cudaLaunchAttribute attrs[1];
    attrs[0].id = cudaLaunchAttributeProgrammaticStreamSerialization;
    attrs[0].val.programmaticStreamSerializationAllowed = 1;
    launch_cfg.attrs     = attrs;
    launch_cfg.numAttrs = 1;

    // Prepare arguments and get function pointer
    //    for secondary_gemm
    void* kernelArgs[] = {&d_A, &d_B, &d_C, &M, &N, &K};

    cudaKernel_t k;
    cudaGetKernel(&k, secondary_gemm);
    void* funcPtr = reinterpret_cast<void*>(k);

    // Early enqueue of secondary GEMM via PDL
    cudaLaunchKernelExC(&launch_cfg, funcPtr, kernelArgs);

    // Wait for everything to finish
    cudaStreamSynchronize(stream);

    // Cleanup
    cudaFree(d_A);
    cudaFree(d_B);
    cudaFree(d_C);
    cudaStreamDestroy(stream);
    return 0;
}
```

One subtle but important legal rule is that in the unified block-scoped pipeline examples in this chapter, the participating CTA threads execute `producer_acquire/commit` and `consumer_wait`/release in a consistent order. You can still keep warp specialization by letting only selected warps issue staged copy work between those collectives.

For memory visibility and cross-role handoff, combine the unified pipeline sequence with explicit `cta.sync()` points where ownership changes. If you want different warps to call different pipeline primitives directly, use a partitioned pipeline API with explicit producer/consumer roles rather than branching a unified pipeline sequence.

On the host, you launch the primary kernel (`primary_gemm`) into a nonblocking stream and create a `cudaLaunchConfig_t` with the `ProgrammaticStreamSerialization` attribute. You use this to call `cudaLaunchKernelExC` for the secondary kernel (`secondary_gemm`).

Inside `primary_gemm`, a call to `cudaTriggerProgrammaticLaunchCompletion()` marks the completion of the memory flush and allows the dependent kernel's processing to begin—even before the primary has fully torn down.

The dependent kernel then calls `cudaGridDependencySynchronize()`. This waits for the signal and the necessary memory flush from the primary kernel so that it can start executing in parallel with the primary kernel's epilogue.

Within each thread block, we use warp specialization to overlap data movement and computation. By splitting each block into a single "producer" warp and multiple "consumer" warps, the producer issues cooperative staged copy work under pipeline collectives. This can use TMA multicast-capable paths to broadcast a single DMA transfer to all thread blocks in the cluster, as shown in Figure 11-11.

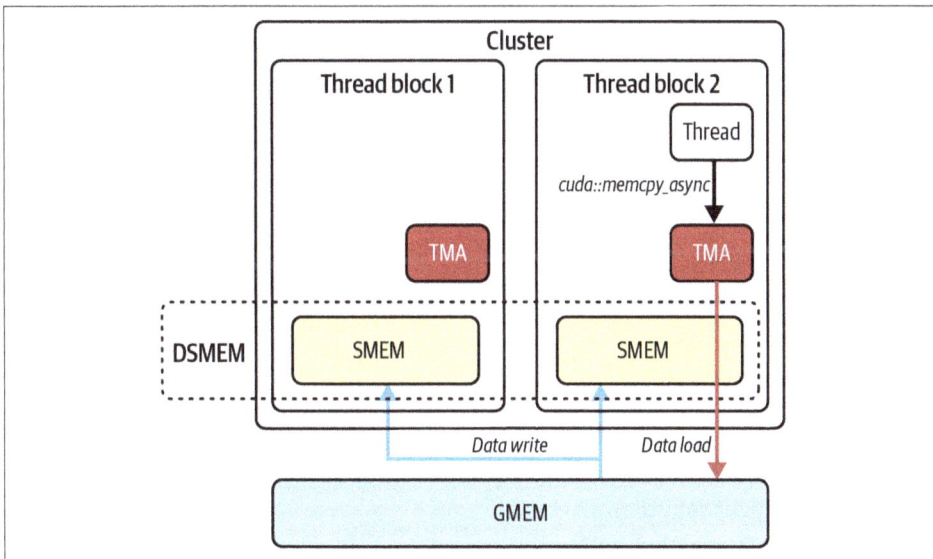

Figure 11-11. TMA multicast: a leader CTA issues `cp.async.bulk.tensor` *into DSMEM (cluster shared memory); the follower CTAs consume tiles using* `cluster.map_shared_rank`; *cooperative-staged copies (under pipeline collectives) can drive this path including* `cuda::memcpy_async`*-based implementations*

While the producer warp is loading data with TMA multicast, the consumers spin on a C++ block-scope barrier (`cuda::barrier<cuda::thread_scope_block>`) before executing their matrix-multiply steps (`do_compute()`). This lets each tile's load and its fused-multiply-add (FMA) operations interleave in a fine-grained, multistage software pipeline that hides global-memory latency inside the kernel.

To coordinate work across SMs, we annotate both kernels with `__cluster_dims__(2,1,1)`. This groups pairs of thread blocks on nearby SMs. A call to `cluster.sync()` (the cooperative-group's wrapper over PTX's `mbarrier` instructions) serves as a cluster-wide barrier and shared-memory fence. This way, all of the thread blocks in the cluster see the same TMA-loaded data and can dynamically rebalance remaining tiles. This interblock cooperation prevents idle SMs and increases the benefit of the warp-specialized pipeline.

> Production kernels typically use the Tensor Memory Accelerator (TMA) `cp.async.bulk.tensor` for 2D tiles and multicast across a thread block cluster when multiple thread blocks need the same tile.
>
> Consider using descriptor-based TMA reduce operations (e.g., `cp.reduce.async.bulk(.tensor)`) for on-the-fly reductions during tiled copies on Blackwell. Prefer descriptor-based loads/stores plus TMA reduce operations when fusing small reductions into the data-movement pipeline. This will reduce register pressure and improver overlap.

Let's wrap up by revisiting the three characteristics of this high-performance GEMM pipeline:

Intra-kernel pipelining
  Achieved within each thread block using warp specialization to subdivide work so that producer warps issue cooperative staged copy tiles under pipeline collectives (e.g., `cuda::memcpy_async`) while consumer warps spin on a block-scope barrier. This lets data transfer and compute operations fully overlap.

Inter-kernel pipelining
  Uses PDL, which lets the next GEMM kernel's processing begin (using the `cudaTriggerProgrammaticLaunchCompletion()` → `cudaGridDependencySynchronize()` mechanism) before the primary kernel is completely torn down. This masks kernel-launch overhead.

Interblock cooperation
  By annotating kernels with `__cluster_dims__`, this code creates thread block pairs that are coscheduled on nearby SMs. Along with calling `cluster.sync()` (the mbarrier-based cluster barrier), these thread blocks share TMA-multicast data and dynamically load balance work across the grid.

In short, by layering warp-level pipelining with TMA, cluster-level synchronization and multicast, and inter-kernel overlap using PDL, you form a highly overlapping pipeline that hides DRAM latency, masks kernel-launch overheads, and maximizes Tensor Core utilization. The result is a high-performance GEMM in every stage: within warp copies, cross-thread-block barriers, and during kernel handoffs. These operate together to keep the hardware busy and avoid stalls.

Key Takeaways

This chapter covered some advanced topics related to CUDA streams, stream-ordered memory allocators, event-based synchronization, inter-kernel pipelining, thread block clusters, and PDLs. These help to create highly efficient pipelines for inference and training workloads. The following are some key takeaways:

Explicit versus default streams

Avoid the legacy default stream (stream 0), which serializes all work and acts as a global barrier. Instead, create explicit non-blocking streams (`cudaStreamCreate WithFlags(..., cudaStreamNonBlocking)`) so kernels and copies can run concurrently without hidden synchronizations.

Stream-ordered memory allocator

Use `cudaMallocAsync` and `cudaFreeAsync` to allocate/free device memory within a specific stream. This nonblocking allocator records requests in the stream's queue, avoids global device synchronizations, and enables allocation overlap with in-flight kernels and copies.

Overlapping H2D, compute, and D2H

By enqueuing asynchronous host-to-device (`cudaMemcpyAsync`), kernel launches, and device-to-host copies on different streams, you can achieve three-way overlap. While one stream runs a kernel, another can copy the next batch H2D, and a third can copy results D2H. This hides latency and reduces idle periods.

CUDA events for fine-grained synchronization

Use `cudaEventRecord` and `cudaStreamWaitEvent` to coordinate producer-consumer dependencies across streams without stalling the entire GPU or CPU. Events enable a consumer stream to wait precisely until a producer stream finishes a copy or kernel, preserving maximum concurrency.

Inter-kernel pipelining

Combine warp-specialized (multirole), two-stage (double-buffered) pipeline within a kernel with multistream launches. Launching multiple instances of a warp-specialized kernel (loader → compute → storer) in separate streams feeds successive mini-batches into the GPU. This combines intra-kernel memory/compute overlap with inter-kernel concurrency.

Thread block clusters with streams

Extending intra-kernel warp-specialized pipelines to a grid-wide thread block cluster (cooperative launch) allows loader/compute/storer warps across blocks. Launching these cooperative kernels in multiple streams lets host-side allocations and copies for subsequent batches occur while a cooperative kernel is executing.

In-kernel signaling and overlap with PDL

Kernel A calls `cudaTriggerProgrammaticLaunchCompletion()` once its data writes are flushed, and Kernel B uses `cudaGridDependencySynchronize()` to wait on that signal. This allows Kernel B's prologue to begin and overlap with A's epilogue—without CPU intervention.

Host-side PDL setup

The host configures Kernel B's launch via `cudaLaunchKernelExC()` with a `cuda LaunchConfig_t` that sets `cudaLaunchAttributeProgrammaticStreamSerializa tion`. This allows the driver to enqueue B early and maximize inter-kernel overlap. PDL uses `cudaTriggerProgrammaticLaunchCompletion` in the primary kernel, `cudaGridDependencySynchronize` in the dependent kernel, and the `cudaLaunchAt tributeProgrammaticStreamSerialization` launch attribute on the host.

Conclusion

In conclusion, inter-kernel concurrency with CUDA streams has evolved from a manual optimization to an automatic feature used by modern AI frameworks and GPU runtimes. By understanding the core principles such as streams, resource occupancy, and synchronization points, developers can maximize GPU utilization.

Inter-kernel concurrency is critical for maximizing GPU utilization in modern workloads by overlapping kernel execution and data transfers both within a single GPU and across multiple GPUs. As hardware continues to add more parallelism—and software abstracts more of the scheduling complexity—understanding how to maximize concurrency is a critical part of getting the most from your high-performance AI system hardware.

This chapter demonstrated how to orchestrate kernels, memory operations, and allocations across multiple CUDA streams to keep all GPU hardware units actively running. These hardware units include compute pipelines, DMA engines, and interconnects. CUDA streams serve as the foundational mechanism to enqueue kernels, memory operations, and allocations in independent queues, allowing the GPU's compute engines and DMA engines to run simultaneously.

By avoiding the default stream's hidden barriers, leveraging the stream-ordered allocator, employing events for precise synchronization, and combining intra-kernel warp specialization with inter-kernel multistream pipelines (extending to thread block clusters from Chapter 10), you can achieve near-peak utilization even for complex LLM workloads.

In multi-GPU contexts, overlapping peer-to-peer transfers, collective communications, and computations across distinct streams further minimize idle time. We looked back at Chapter 10 by showing how to capture these stream workflows using CUDA Graphs to reduce CPU overhead for repeated iterations.

In the next chapter, we will dive even deeper and build upon these principles by introducing dynamic kernel orchestration and meta-scheduling with dynamic parallelism and CUDA Graphs. We'll coordinate entire pipelines of kernels and data movements—at runtime—to adapt to changing workloads. This dynamic resource balancing and device-side orchestration will push us to the next level of performance optimizations for large-scale AI systems.

## CHAPTER 12

Dynamic Scheduling, CUDA Graphs, and Device-Initiated Kernel Orchestration

So far, we have unlocked compute and memory throughput at the individual kernel level. Now it's time to orchestrate these kernels so the GPU never goes idle.

In this chapter, we move from scheduling on the host to scheduling on the device itself. We'll explore dynamic work queues driven by fast L2-cache atomics, collapse repeated kernel launches, and use CUDA Graphs for batching fixed pipelines and minimizing CPU handshakes.

Then we'll push orchestration even further, with device-side graph launches and dynamic parallelism. These let the GPU decide what to run next without needing to call back to the CPU.

Finally, we'll dive into a multi-GPU environment by overlapping peer-to-peer copies, NCCL collectives, CUDA-aware MPI, and NVSHMEM one-sided puts/gets. This way, clusters of GPUs behave like one giant, shared-memory coprocessor. For instance, NVIDIA's DGX GB200 NVL72 system connects 36 Grace CPUs and 72 Blackwell GPUs into a single NVLink domain with unified addressing and up to 30 TB of combined CPU and GPU unified memory within that domain. It enables remote HBM access across the NVLink fabric inside the 72-GPU domain. Larger NVLink network topologies can extend beyond a single rack.

Along the way, we'll tie each technique back to roofline analysis, helping you choose the right tool—streams, graphs, atomics, or dynamic kernels—to increase your kernel's operational intensity. This will help improve your workload's overall performance.

By the end of this chapter, you will have an understanding of dynamic, device-side, and graph-based kernel orchestration techniques that keep every SM fed across multi-GPU clusters.

Dynamic Scheduling with Atomic Work Queues

Uneven work assignments between threads can leave some SMs idle while others are still busy. This wastes compute resources and reduces overall throughput.

Imbalance often occurs when different threads or blocks process variable amounts of work due to input-dependent loops or conditional workloads. Some blocks complete quickly, leaving their SMs idle, while other SMs continue with longer-running blocks. On modern GPUs with hundreds of SMs, idle periods can leave many SMs idle if work is not evenly distributed. This can significantly hurt performance.

By the time the longest-running work finishes, a portion of the GPU has been idle. This reduces the achieved occupancy since many cycles ran with no active warps. Remember that you can use Nsight Systems to profile and show these idle gaps clearly on the GPU timeline.

You can also compare active SM cycles to total elapsed SM cycles to gauge underutilization. Nsight Compute provides this as a single metric, which represents the fraction of time that at least one warp was active. A low active-to-elapsed ratio indicates that many cycles ran with no active warps. In other words, the GPU was often idle.

In addition to Nsight Systems, you can use Nsight Compute to inspect achieved occupancy (the average fraction of active warps per SM relative to the hardware maximum) or the SM Active cycles percentage (the fraction of time at least one warp was active) to quantify this underutilization.

> To correlate timeline gaps with specific code sections, insert NVTX range markers around significant GPU work.

Next, we'll discuss how to implement atomic queues to allocate work dynamically inside a kernel. These are important to balance arbitrary workloads across all SMs to avoid idle threads. Before we do that, we need to introduce atomic counters.

Atomic Counters

Atomic counters are the foundation for atomic queues, which allow dynamic work allocation.

On modern GPUs, global atomics are serviced and serialized in the on-device L2 cache. This reduces latency versus DRAM round trips when the target line is resident. Atomic counters still incur latency and serialize under contention. But uncontended `atomicAdd` operations happen extremely quickly by remaining on-chip. An example of two threads incrementing an atomic is shown in Figure 12-1.

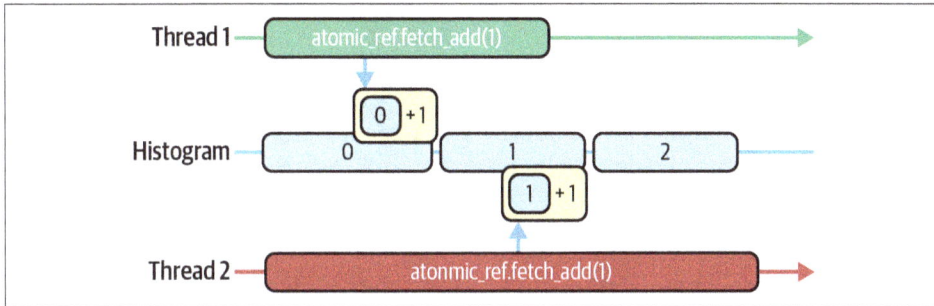

Figure 12-1. Superfast, on-chip atomic-memory add operations across multiple threads in the context of a histogram computation

However, `atomicAdd` does not come for free. It still has latency and, under contention, can serialize threads waiting on the same memory address. As such, the L2 needs to serialize the updates as well. This creates a hotspot, which needs to be optimized. Nsight Compute can help you quantify the cost.

In the Memory Workload Analysis section of Nsight Compute, you'll find `atomic_transactions` and `atomic_transactions_per_request`. The atomic transactions counter represents the total number of L2-cache atomic transactions, including any replays caused by contention. The atomic transactions per request metric, or contention ratio, represents the average number of L2 transactions generated by each `atomicAdd` instruction.

When every `atomicAdd` fires exactly one L2 transaction, your `atomic_transactions_per_request` hovers around 1.0, which means it's paying the bare minimum. If this ratio climbs above 1.0, it signals that the threads are stalling and retrying atomic updates instead of doing useful work. Each retry indicates contention.

The optimization here is to amortize your atomics by grabbing work in batches. So instead of each thread, or warp, performing an `atomicAdd`, you batch a group of tasks per atomic. Here is the before and after with a batch size of 32:

```
// Before batching
int idx = atomicAdd(&queue_head, 1);
if (idx < N) process(data[idx]);

// After batching
const int batchSize = 32;
int start = atomicAdd(&queue_head, batchSize);
for (int i = start; i < start + batchSize && i < N; ++i) {
    process(data[i]);
}
```

Now a single atomic update awards a warp (or thread block) a whole slice of work— 32 items in this example—before touching the counter again. You still pay one L2 transaction per batch, but you do 32× as much useful work in between.

In practice, only one thread per warp performs this `atomicAdd` to fetch the next batch start index. The thread then broadcasts it to the rest of the warp (e.g., using `__shfl_sync`). The entire warp then processes those 32 items in parallel. This produces one atomic operation per warp instead of per thread, drastically reducing contention.

In Nsight Compute you'll see `atomic_transactions` plummet and your transactions-per-request collapse back toward 1.0. This proves that you've traded costly contention for sustained computation.

With modern GPUs in which L2-cache atomics are exceptionally fast, even a modest batch size of 8 or 16 can eliminate most contention due to the high L2 bandwidth. That said, always verify that you haven't simply shifted the bottleneck elsewhere.

To verify that this optimization hasn't negatively affected other performance metrics, use Nsight Compute's Warp Stall Reasons and Register Pressure reports to make sure your fused loop isn't now limited by register spills or shared-memory bank conflicts.

If atomics are still hot after these optimizations, consider alternative designs like per-block counters or hierarchical reduction of work distribution.

In short, by batching work per atomic operation, you keep the GPU's many warps busy doing real computation. This is in contrast to queuing up at a single counter that can't keep up.

Atomic Queues

Let's now use a global atomic counter to coordinate a dynamic work queue. The goal is to use the atomic counter and `atomicAdd` to balance arbitrary workloads across all SMs so that no thread, or warp, sits idle. An example of this dynamic work queue is shown in Figure 12-2.

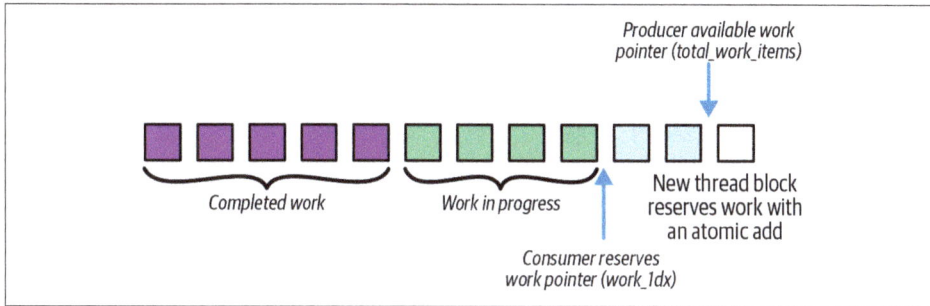

Figure 12-2. Using atomic counter and `atomicAdd` as a dynamic work queue to balance workloads across SMs and warps

In the next code example (`computeKernel`), each thread computes a different number of iterations based on `idx % 256`. Threads with a small value for `idx % 256` do very little work, while threads with a large value for `idx % 256` will do a lot of work. As a result of this imbalance, threads finish at different times, and some SMs go idle waiting for the longest threads to complete. Here is the code that uses a static, uneven workload per thread:

```
// uneven_static.cu
#include <cuda_runtime.h>
#include <cmath>

__global__ void computeKernel(const float* input, float* output, int N) {
    int idx = blockIdx.x * blockDim.x + threadIdx.x;
    if (idx < N) {
        // Each thread does a variable amount of work based on idx
        int work = idx % 256;
        float result = 0.0f;
        for (int i = 0; i < work; ++i) {
            result += sinf(input[idx]) * cosf(input[idx]);
        }
        output[idx] = result;
    }
}

int main() {
    const int N = 1<<20;

    float* h_in = nullptr;
```

```
    float* h_out = nullptr;
    cudaMallocHost(&h_in, N * sizeof(float));
    cudaMallocHost(&h_out, N * sizeof(float));

    for (int i = 0; i < N; ++i) h_in[i] = float(i) / N;

    float *d_in, *d_out;
    cudaMalloc(&d_in, N * sizeof(float));
    cudaMalloc(&d_out, N * sizeof(float));
    cudaMemcpy(d_in, h_in, N * sizeof(float), cudaMemcpyHostToDevice);

    dim3 block(256), grid((N + 255) / 256);
    computeKernel<<<grid, block>>>(d_in, d_out, N);
    cudaDeviceSynchronize();

    cudaMemcpy(h_out, d_out, N * sizeof(float), cudaMemcpyDeviceToHost);

    cudaFree(d_in);
    cudaFree(d_out);
    cudaFreeHost(h_in);
    cudaFreeHost(h_out);

    return 0;
}
```

There isn't a high-level PyTorch API for dynamic GPU-side work distribution, so we would need to implement it with a custom CUDA kernel. We leave that out for brevity.

In the optimized dynamic task dispatch version shown next, a single global counter (in device memory) is used as a warp-level work queue. We turn the counter into a persistent warp-level work queue using batched atomics. This way, the warps that finish early immediately fetch another batch instead of idling:

```
// uneven_dynamic.cu

#include <cuda_runtime.h>

__device__ unsigned int globalIndex = 0;

// Warp-batched dynamic queue: 1 atomic per active warp
__global__ void computeKernelDynamicBatch(const float* input,
                                          float* output,
                                          int N) {
    // lane id in [0,31]
    int lane = threadIdx.x & (warpSize - 1);

    while (true) {
        // Elect an active leader each iteration (handles divergence safely)
```

```
    unsigned mask = __activemask();
    int leader = __ffs(mask) - 1;

    // Warp leader atomically grabs a contiguous batch for the whole warp
    unsigned int base = 0;
    if (lane == leader) {
      base = atomicAdd(&globalIndex, warpSize);
    }

    // Broadcast starting index to all active lanes in the warp
    base = __shfl_sync(mask, base, leader);

    unsigned int idx = base + lane;
    if (idx >= (unsigned)N) break;  // dynamic termination

    // Hoist invariants out of the variable trip-count loop
    // Note: You can also use __sincosf on Blackwell
    float s = sinf(input[idx]);
    float c = cosf(input[idx]);
    int   work = idx % 256;

    float result = 0.0f;
    #pragma unroll 1
    for (int i = 0; i < work; ++i) {
      result += s * c;
    }
    output[idx] = result;
    // loop continues until counter >= N
  }
}

int main() {
    const int N = 1 << 20;
    float *d_in, *d_out;
    cudaMalloc(&d_in,  N * sizeof(float));
    cudaMalloc(&d_out, N * sizeof(float));
    // Host buffers (pinned) for a realistic data path
    float *h_in = nullptr, *h_out = nullptr;
    cudaMallocHost(&h_in,  N * sizeof(float));
    cudaMallocHost(&h_out, N * sizeof(float));
    for (int i = 0; i < N; ++i) {
        h_in[i] = static_cast<float>(i % 1000);
    }

    // Copy inputs to device
    cudaMemcpy(d_in, h_in, N * sizeof(float),
        cudaMemcpyHostToDevice);

    // Reset global counter
    unsigned int zero = 0;
    // If you call this kernel repeatedly (e.g., in a loop),
    // reset 'globalIndex' to 0 before each launch.
```

```
cudaMemcpyToSymbol(globalIndex, &zero,
    sizeof(unsigned int));

// Launch with 256 threads per block
dim3 block(256), grid((N + 255) / 256);
cudaStream_t stream;

cudaStreamCreateWithFlags(&stream, cudaStreamNonBlocking);

computeKernelDynamicBatch<<<grid, block, 0, stream>>>(d_in, d_out, N);

cudaStreamSynchronize(stream);
cudaStreamDestroy(stream);
cudaDeviceSynchronize();

// Copy results back and clean up
cudaMemcpy(h_out, d_out, N * sizeof(float),
        cudaMemcpyDeviceToHost);

cudaFree(d_in);
cudaFree(d_out);
cudaFreeHost(h_in);
cudaFreeHost(h_out);

return 0;
}
```

Each warp atomically claims the next batch of tasks of size warpSize (32 threads) from the global queue and processes them in a loop. This makes sure that no SM ever goes idle. This code performs dynamic work distribution implemented with a single global atomic work queue.

Here, each warp repeatedly pulls the next batch base index from that global counter. The first thread (if (lane==0)) of each warp, called the warp leader, performs an atomic add to get the starting index of this contiguous block using base=atomic Add(&globalIndex, warpSize). It then broadcasts this base to the rest of its warp using __shfl_sync(__activemask(), base, 0), as described earlier in the chapter.

In other words, instead of each thread being tied to a fixed element index, every warp now grabs a contiguous block of tasks from a shared counter. It then computes using idx = base + lane.

All threads in that warp execute the same sin/cos loop for their dynamically fetched indices. As such, work is no longer preassigned per thread. Instead, work is pulled and balanced at runtime using the global atomic queue.

Remember that the if (idx >= N) bounds check will cause the warp to exit when there's no more work to do. This prevents out-of-bounds memory accesses. Otherwise, each thread in the warp executes the exact same sin/cos loop as in the static version.

In a simple microbenchmark with N = 1 << 20 and work = idx % 256, the statically assigned kernel took about 200 ms, whereas the dynamic-queue version ran in roughly 100 ms. This 2× speedup is a result of eliminating SM idle time and reducing atomic contention. Nsight Compute defines active SM cycles as the fraction of elapsed cycles with at least one active warp.

The speedup will vary depending on the work imbalance, but dynamic work distribution is an optimization worth exploring any time your profiling shows warp-idle stalls, low achieved occupancy, or visible timeline gaps from uneven per-task runtimes. In these scenarios, especially with moderate imbalance, you can often get a 10%–20% speedup.

> In extreme-imbalance cases, you can get this 2× speedup simply by replacing static indexing with an atomic-driven work queue. For mild imbalance, the overhead of the atomic and shuffle may offset gains.

In short, dynamic work distribution ensures near-uniform SM utilization since every warp keeps fetching and processing new tasks until the counter exceeds N. This is in contrast to many warps finishing long before the slowest ones and leaving hardware resources unused.

CUDA Graphs

When your pipeline consists of multiple kernels, copies, stream-event records, and callbacks, launching them one by one on the host every iteration still incurs CPU overhead. CUDA Graphs let you capture that entire workflow once and replay it repeatedly with essentially zero CPU overhead. Figure 12-3 compares kernel launches without (top) and with (bottom) CUDA Graphs.

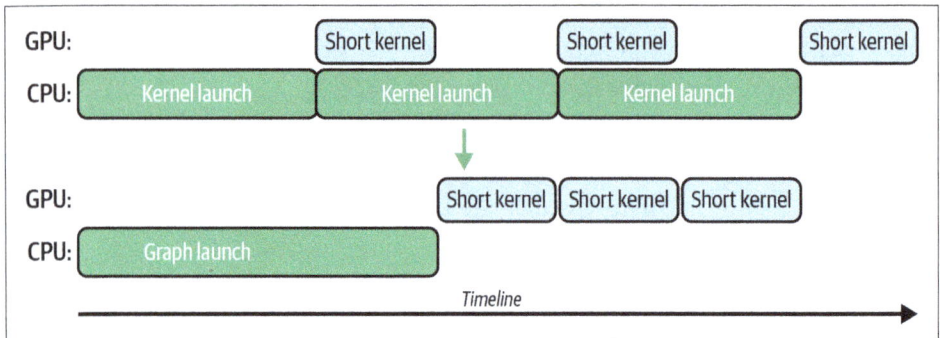

Figure 12-3. Kernel-launch timeline without (top) and with (bottom) CUDA Graphs

Why use CUDA Graphs? First, they cut down launch overhead. Multiple small kernels or copies can be launched with essentially one CPU call. Second, they enable better scheduling on the GPU. The work is submitted as a batch, so the CUDA driver can potentially reduce some internal latency between operations.

Also, with CUDA Graphs, dependencies are known upfront, so there's less need for the CPU to synchronize in between. In the context of memory transfers, a CUDA Graph ensures that asynchronous copies and kernel executions are linked as dependencies correctly without any manual synchronization. It doesn't inherently overlap copies and kernels more so than normal streams would, but a CUDA Graph streamlines their execution.

PyTorch, Inference Engines, and CUDA Graphs

AI frameworks like PyTorch leverage CUDA Graphs under the hood for static portions of deep learning models. Specifically, PyTorch supports a `torch.cuda.Graph` context for capturing a sequence of operations. In addition, PyTorch continues to optimize its internals to use CUDA Graphs for predictable portions of code.

High-performance inference engines like vLLM and NVIDIA's TensorRT-LLM can also leverage CUDA Graphs by capturing a model's execution into a set of predefined graphs for different sequence-length ranges and input-batch sizes. When graph capture is enabled, these systems often bucket or pad inputs to match supported graph batch sizes so that captured graphs can be replayed with fixed shapes. This can significantly reduce latency for large-scale, production inference workloads.

For example, you would capture one CUDA Graph per batch size during startup or model-load time. Then, at runtime, you would launch the precaptured graph that matches the incoming request's batch size.

> PyTorch compiler `mode='reduce-overhead'` may wrap eligible segments in CUDA Graphs to reduce launch overhead, subject to capture requirements such as static tensor addresses and CUDA-only regions. It does not guarantee graphing of all code paths. And it may increase memory use due to pooled buffers. Always profile to confirm benefits on your model.

Memory Pools for CUDA Graphs

One important consideration is memory management with CUDA Graphs. Memory operations inside a CUDA Graph obey the same rules as in CUDA streams. If you allocate GPU memory inside the capture, that allocation becomes part of the graph execution.

You generally want to avoid allocating GPU memory inside your graph and preallocating memory outside of the graph. Many frameworks, such as PyTorch, use static memory pools with CUDA Graphs, as shown in Figure 12-4. The use of static memory pools keeps memory allocations from becoming part of the captured graph sequence.

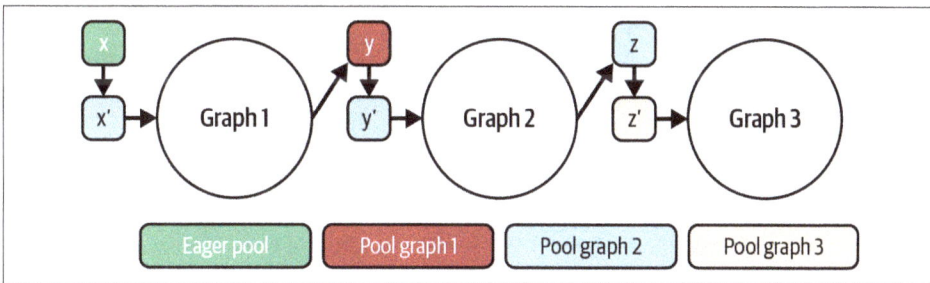

Figure 12-4. PyTorch uses static memory pools for CUDA Graphs

While CUDA Graphs won't make an individual memory copy or kernel execution faster, they can automatically overlap independent data transfers and computations within the graph—similar to CUDA streams. This eliminates the per-iteration CPU scheduling and is made possible since the dependency graph is known upfront.

Capturing a CUDA Graph with a CUDA Stream

To capture a graph, you call `cudaStreamBeginCapture()` on a stream, enqueue all your memory transfers (`cudaMemcpyAsync()`), kernel launches, events (`cudaEvent Record()`), and callbacks (`cudaLaunchHostFunc()`), then call `cudaStreamEndCap ture()` to create a CUDA Graph definition (`cudaGraph_t`).

The CUDA driver can then launch the CUDA Graph with `cudaGraphLaunch()` every iteration. Because the CUDA driver knows the entire dependency graph in advance, it replays the prebuilt stream sequence directly on the GPU. This incurs minimal launch overhead.

> `cudaGraphExecUpdate`, discussed in the next section, allows limited changes to a captured graph for scenarios where sizes, dimensions, or pointers change between iterations. This is useful if the size of the inputs varies since you can just update the graph's node parameters instead of recapturing a whole new graph for each new input size.

Even if only some of your pipeline is repetitive, CUDA Graphs can capture that portion. For example, if you always perform a Host → Device copy, followed by two kernels, followed by a Device → Host copy, you can capture just that subgraph and replay it with a single function call.

To replay the CUDA Graph, you supply the stream handles, and the GPU executes the sequence of operations without additional CPU instructions. This ties directly to inter-kernel concurrency because CUDA Graphs let you maintain complex overlapping behavior by mixing asynchronous copies, fine-grained event barriers, and kernels—while removing the CPU as a bottleneck entirely.

Typically, you do a replay dry run to ensure correctness. You would instantiate the graph by creating a `cudaGraphExec_t` executable graph and then launch it with a single graph-replay invocation. When you launch the captured graph, the runtime will execute all the operations in the correct order on the GPU.

To show the usage of CUDA Graphs, consider a simple sequence of kernels. Here we show a code snippet for capturing and launching a CUDA Graph in both C++ and PyTorch:

```
cudaStream_t stream;
cudaStreamCreateWithFlags(&stream, cudaStreamNonBlocking);
cudaGraph_t graph;
cudaGraphExec_t instance;

cudaStreamBeginCapture(stream, cudaStreamCaptureModeGlobal);

// Enqueue operations on 'stream' as usual
```

```
kernelA<<<grid, block, 0, stream>>>(d_X);
kernelB<<<grid, block, 0, stream>>>(d_Y);
kernelC<<<grid, block, 0, stream>>>(d_Z);

cudaStreamEndCapture(stream, &graph);
cudaGraphInstantiate(&instance, graph, nullptr, nullptr, 0);

// Now 'instance' can be launched in a loop
for (int iter = 0; iter < 100; ++iter) {
    cudaGraphLaunch(instance, stream);
    // No per-kernel sync needed; graph ensures dependencies
}
cudaStreamSynchronize(stream);

// (Destroy graph and instance when done)
cudaGraphExecDestroy(instance);
cudaGraphDestroy(graph);
```

In this pseudocode, we begin capturing on a CUDA stream, launch three kernels (A, B, and C) in sequence on that stream, and end capture to obtain a graph. Then we instantiate the graph.

Now we can replay the entire sequence A → B → C by calling cudaGraph Launch (instance, stream) as many times as we want. We only pay for the cost of a single launch per iteration instead of three separate launches. And the GPU executes kernels A, B, and C in the same sequence they were recorded, or back-to-back in this case. We will synchronize after the loop to ensure that all iterations are complete.

As mentioned earlier, high-level AI frameworks like PyTorch support CUDA Graphs. PyTorch provides Python developers with near-native CUDA performance without requiring deep knowledge of CUDA C++. Here, we show PyTorch's torch.cuda.Graph context manager to capture and replay operations:

```python
import torch, time

X = torch.randn(1<<20, device='cuda')

# Define operations for reference
def opA(x): return x * 1.1
def opB(x): return x + 2.0
def opC(x): return x.sqrt()

# Persistent buffers for pointer stability
static_x = torch.empty_like(X)
static_y = torch.empty_like(X)
static_z = torch.empty_like(X)
static_w = torch.empty_like(X)

# Warm up once to initialize CUDA kernels and caches
_ = opC(opB(opA(X)))
torch.cuda.synchronize()
```

```
# Seed the static input before capture
static_x.copy_(X)

# Capture the graph
g = torch.cuda.CUDAGraph()
stream = torch.cuda.Stream()
torch.cuda.synchronize()
with torch.cuda.graph(g, stream=stream):
    # Record A then B then C using out parameters to avoid allocations
    torch.mul(static_x, 1.1, out=static_y)
    torch.add(static_y, 2.0, out=static_z)
    torch.sqrt(static_z, out=static_w)

# Replay the captured graph 100 times
for i in range(100):
    # If inputs change, copy new values into static_x before replay
    # static_x.copy_(new_X)
    g.replay()
```

In production you should allocate persistent input and output buffers so captured kernels see fixed memory addresses. For example, create `static_y = torch.empty_like(X)` before capture, and then inside the graph write `static_y.copy_(opA(X))`. This avoids allocations during capture and satisfies the stability rules of CUDA Graph pointers. PyTorch CUDA Graphs requires that replay uses the same memory addresses for captured tensors.

In this PyTorch example, we define operations `opA`, `opB`, and `opC`. In practice, these could be neural network layers or any GPU operation. We run one warm-up pass `opC(opB(opA(X)))` to ensure that all kernels, memory allocations, and library contexts (e.g., cuBLAS/cuDNN) are initialized upfront. This is needed because a CUDA Graphs capture won't record these lazy setup steps.

> Skipping the warm-up pass may cause your graph capture to fail or introduce unexpected stalls when lazy initializations occur.

We first warm up the GPU by running the sequence once to initialize all kernels and libraries. Then we capture the forward (A), transform (B), and backward (C) operations into a single `torch.cuda.CUDAGraph` by enclosing them in the `with torch.cuda.graph(g, stream=stream):` Python context manager block on a fresh CUDA stream. After capture, calling `g.replay()` 100 times launches the entire A → B → C pipeline with one host call per iteration. The results are summarized in Table 12-1.

Table 12-1. Impact of CUDA Graphs on iteration overheads

Metric	Before CUDA Graphs	After CUDA Graphs
CPU launch calls per 100 iterations	300 separate kernel launches	100 graph replays (1 per iteration)
Host synchronization calls	300 `cudaDeviceSynchronize` calls	0
Average GPU idle between kernels	~3 µs gaps per iteration	0 µs (continuous back-to-back execution)
End-to-end iteration latency	~1.00 ms	~0.75 ms (25% faster)

> Note: The numeric values in all metrics tables are illustrative to explain the concepts. For actual benchmark results on different GPU architectures, see the GitHub repository (*https://github.com/cfregly/ai-performance-engineering*).

Here we see that CUDA Graphs eliminate per-iteration CPU scheduling and host-device handshakes. This is because the GPU work for each iteration is batched into a single `g.replay()` call instead of three separate kernel launches. As a result, iterations execute 25% faster since the CPU simply issues lightweight replay commands and stays fully asynchronous to the GPU.

There are some common pitfalls when using CUDA Graphs, and it's important to handle them appropriately. For example, if your workload size changes, a captured graph might not be valid. This would require a recapture or a call to `cudaGraphExec Update`, which we cover in the next section.

Certain CUDA API calls—like allocating memory and host-device synchronization primitives—should generally not be included in a graph capture. While modern versions of CUDA Graphs support limited memory management operations inside a captured graph, it's recommended to perform all memory allocations before the capture. You must also ensure that the data used in the graph remains at the same memory addresses.

> The requirement for memory to remain at the same memory address during graph execution is a primary reason why frameworks like PyTorch use static memory pools with CUDA Graphs. For example, PyTorch provides the `torch.cuda.graph_pool_han dle()` API to create a dedicated memory pool for pointer-stable CUDA graph capture. Using a separate allocator pool ensures that tensor addresses remain fixed across captures and replays. This satisfies the pointer stability requirement. Between iterations, update inputs by copying into static tensors. Don't reallocate the tensors on every iteration.

You should also avoid including any host-side callbacks or unsupported operations inside a CUDA Graphs capture. This includes things like `print()`, random number generator (RNG) calls, nested captures, and new memory allocations. This is because the graph must record a pure, deterministic sequence of GPU work.

In addition, all tensors used in the capture must already be allocated at fixed addresses with fixed shapes. Resizing or calling `cudaMalloc` during capture will break the graph.

Dynamic Graph Update

Once you've recorded a CUDA Graph, you don't need to throw it away just because some launch parameters change. Instead of recapturing, you call the graph-update API to update grid/block dimensions, pointer addresses, or kernel parameters directly in the existing graph. The graph-update API includes `cudaGraphExecUpdate` and the lower-level `cudaGraphExecKernelNodeSetParams`.

`cudaGraphExecUpdate` lets you swap a kernel node with a new one of the same shape. For example, you can swap in a different fused kernel implementation—as long as it's the same shape. The CUDA runtime will validate your tweaks and let you replay the modified graph immediately. This avoids the cost of a full capture.

As of this writing, you cannot add or remove nodes arbitrarily. The runtime will return an error if an update violates what the existing graph can handle. In this case, you must capture a new graph.

For example, consider our three-kernel A → B → C graph from earlier, using your maximum batch size. During each inference loop, you simply update Kernel B's launch dimensions to match the current batch, then replay the same graph. This reduces overhead for semistatic workloads in which the overall pipeline is fixed but a few parameters may vary.

In practice, a typical workflow is three steps. First, capture a template graph using the maximum expected sizes (e.g., the largest batch). For example, you might capture your graph with a maximum batch size of 128. Later, if a request comes in with batch 64, you call `cudaGraphExecUpdate` to adjust the launch parameters to 64—and perhaps update the memory pointers to a smaller buffer.

Using `cudaGraphExecUpdate` keeps you from having to rebuild the graph when kernel parameters, grid/block dimensions, or memory addresses change. And it takes only a few microseconds, so you preserve the fast sub-100 μs launch overhead of a CUDA Graph replay. In addition, you maintain the flexibility of adjusting key parameters at runtime. Note that incompatible changes will return an error status and require recapture.

If you do need to change the graph's structure to specify a different number of kernels, for instance, you can fall back to a recapture-then-update workflow. In this case, you wrap one iteration of your code with `cudaStreamBeginCapture` and `cudaStreamEndCapture` to build the new graph. Then use the lighter-weight `cudaGraphExecUpdate` for minor tweaks on subsequent runs.

In effect, dynamic graph updates let you create "parameterized" or conditional execution paths entirely on the GPU. Whenever you have a high-frequency loop of GPU work but only a few changing parameters, like batch size, you can capture once, update quickly, and enjoy both minimal CPU overhead and the adaptability that your use case requires.

Device-Initiated CUDA Graph Launch

Now that you understand how to launch and adapt a captured pipeline from the CPU with low overhead, the next step is to remove the CPU from the launch decision entirely. With device-initiated CUDA Graph launches, a running GPU kernel can trigger a prerecorded graph directly on the device and avoid the host entirely.

To enable device-side launch, first capture the graph as usual on the host. Then instantiate it with `cudaGraphInstantiate` and pass `cudaGraphInstantiateFlag DeviceLaunch`. After instantiation, upload the executable with `cudaGraphUpload` on a host stream before any device-side launch.

You then upload the graph to GPU memory using `cudaGraphUpload`. This must be done before the GPU can launch the graph. (Attempting a device launch without uploading the graph will cause an error.)

In practice, this embeds a "graph launch" node, or calls the device-side graph API, inside your persistent or dynamic kernel. When the time comes, the GPU will kick off the entire graph on a stream that it owns, as shown in Figure 12-5.

Device-initiated graph launches keep data-driven workflows completely on the GPU. Your kernel is responsible for computing the decision conditions, not the CPU. As such, it can spawn the next graph directly, eliminate CPU round trips, and further reduce latency.

Because the graph is already resident on the GPU and no CPU-GPU handshake is needed, device-initiated launches remove host scheduling from the critical path and can reduce end-to-end latency in host-bound loops. In practice, device-initiated CUDA graph launches have shown roughly 2× lower launch latency compared to equivalent host-side graph launches. And the overhead stays flat even as the graph grows in size or complexity.

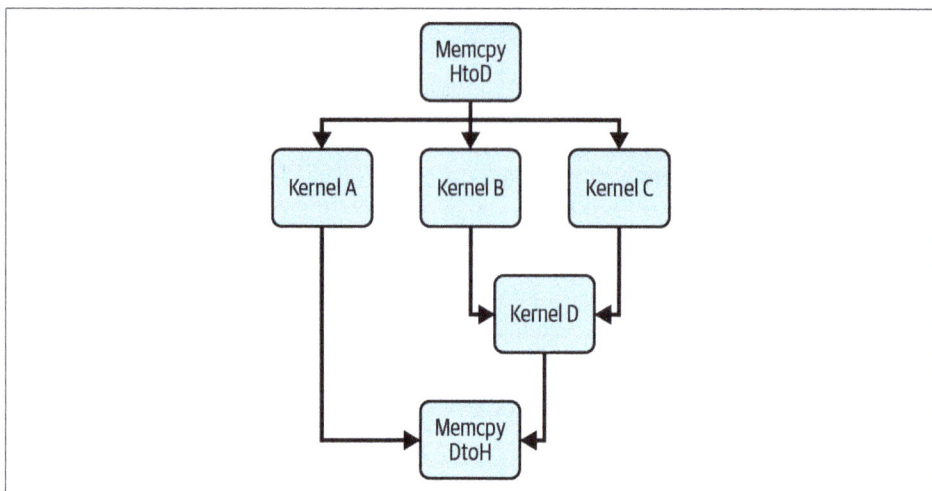

Figure 12-5. Sequence of operations (nodes for kernels and data transfers) and their dependencies (edges) launched by a CUDA Graph

Device-launch graph latency is not impacted by how many nodes or parallel branches are in the graph. This is in contrast to host-launch graph latency, which would increase with a larger graph due to CPU scheduling overhead.

In addition, device launches scale well with graph width. As more parallel nodes are added, host-side launching would suffer from additional synchronization costs, but the device launch latency remains nearly flat.

Debugging device-launched graphs can be tricky, but tools like Nsight Systems will show the child graphs on the GPU timeline as separate streams of work. It's recommended to use NVTX markers in the parent kernel before and after cuda Graph Launch calls to mark where device launches occur. This can help verify that the graphs run as expected in relation to the parent thread.

Inside your device code, you launch the graph with the simple API, cuda Graph Launch(graphExec, stream). The runtime uses special, reserved cudaStream_t values to distinguish between the following supported launch modes: "fire-and-forget" (cudaStreamGraphFireAndForget), "tail" (cudaStreamGraphTailLaunch), and "sibling" (cudaStreamGraphFireAndForgetAsSibling). These modes will automatically enforce the correct ordering in the CUDA stream without any host intervention.

In a fire-and-forget launch, the child graph begins executing immediately and concurrently with the launching parent kernel. The parent kernel doesn't wait for the child to finish—much like launching an independent thread of work. Fire-and-forget launches are useful for spawning asynchronous tasks from within a kernel.

A graph can have up to 120 total fire-and-forget graphs during the course of its execution.

By contrast, a device-initiated graph tail launch defers execution of the graph until the launching kernel reaches a synchronization point or completes. This effectively queues the graph to run after the current kernel as a continuation, as shown in Figure 12-6.

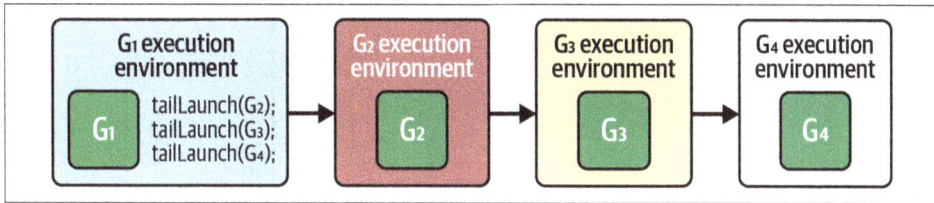

Figure 12-6. Tail launches enqueued by a given graph will execute one at a time, in order of when they were enqueued

Tail launches are especially powerful when implementing GPU-resident work schedulers. A persistent "scheduler" kernel can tail-launch a graph, then relaunch itself once that graph finishes. This technique effectively creates a loop on the GPU without requiring host re-invocation. To relaunch itself, the kernel calls `cudaGetCurrent GraphExec()` to get a handle to its own executing graph. It then launches the graph using `cudaGraphLaunch(..., cudaStreamGraphTailLaunch)` to enqueue itself again.

Additionally, tail graphs can perform additional tail launches. In this case, the new tail launches will execute before the previous graph's tail launch, as shown in Figure 12-7.

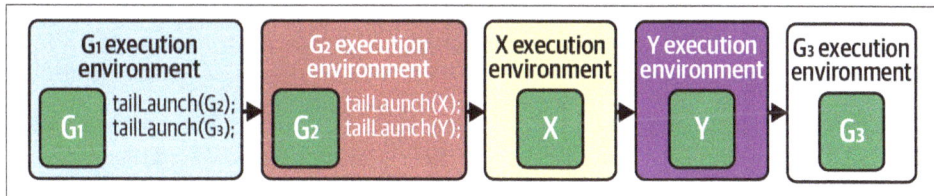

Figure 12-7. Tail launches enqueued from multiple graphs

You can have up to 255 pending tail launches enqueued in a CUDA Graph. However, when it comes to a self-tail-launch (e.g., a graph enqueues itself for relaunch), you can have only one pending self-tail-launch at a time.

A sibling launch is a variation of fire-and-forget in which the launched graph executes as a peer to the parent graph—instead of as a child. Additionally, the sibling runs in the parent's stream environment. This means it runs immediately and independently but without delaying any tail launches of the parent graph, as shown in Figure 12-8.

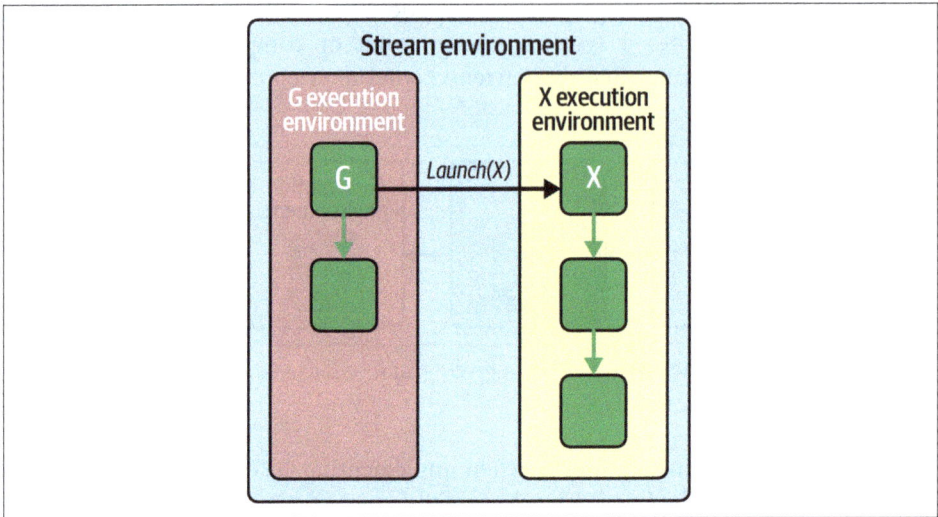

Figure 12-8. Sibling graph launch in the parent's stream environment

For this mode, you can use `cudaGraphLaunch(graphExec, cudaStreamGraphFireAnd ForgetAsSibling)` to launch in "sibling mode." This submits the graph as a sibling of the current graph's execution environment.

When using device-initiated CUDA Graphs, you need to carefully manage dependencies. For instance, if the launched kernel must consume results from the graph, a tail launch is appropriate because the parent kernel will pause until the graph's work is done. In contrast, if the launched graph is more of a side task, the fire-and-forget mode allows the parent kernel to proceed without waiting.

In practice, device-initiated CUDA Graphs open up new patterns. For example, imagine a GPU compression pipeline where a kernel must choose between different compression algorithms based on data content. Rather than ending the kernel and telling the CPU to launch the chosen compression kernel, the GPU kernel can directly launch a prerecorded graph corresponding to, say, "LZ compression" or "Huffman compression."

In this compression example, the GPU never idles waiting for the CPU to decide. Let's take a look at another useful pattern that combines atomic queues/counters and device-initiated, tail-launched CUDA Graphs for LLM inference scheduling inside of a persistent kernel.

Atomic Queues and Device-Initiated CUDA Graphs for In-Kernel Persistent Scheduling

We can combine our atomic-counter work queue from earlier with device-initiated graph tail launches. Consider an LLM inference loop use case, which uses a CUDA Graph to perform a decode by capturing a graph that includes the transformer-block's forward pass (attention + feed-forward).

A lightweight, persistent scheduler kernel can use `atomicAdd(&queueHead,1)` to claim the next work item. It then tail-launches the precaptured decode CUDA Graph to compute the output and immediately loops back for the next item in the queue.

When each CUDA Graph completes, the in-kernel scheduler loop grabs the next index using `atomicAdd(&queueHead,1)` and tail-launches another decode graph. This effectively creates a fully GPU-resident scheduler that both decides and executes tasks without touching the CPU.

By chaining these tail launches, each token is processed start-to-finish on the device with virtually zero CPU overhead. And since the CPU never reenters the critical path, SMs remain fully utilized, per-token latency drops, and you can adapt to different sequence lengths and batch sizes on the fly. To do this, you simply update graph parameters or switch between prerecorded graphs.

Conditional Graph Nodes

In a traditional CUDA Graph, every node and its dependencies are fixed at capture time, forcing any decision-making logic back to the host. Conditional graph nodes break this rigidity by deferring branch decisions to the GPU itself—based on a small "condition handle" associated with the node.

As the graph executes, the GPU evaluates that handle and selectively runs one of its body subgraphs (or loops through it) without ever returning control to the CPU. Specifically, conditional graph nodes let you embed the control flow (IF, IF/ELSE, WHILE, SWITCH) directly into CUDA Graphs to run on the GPU device. Conditional graph nodes eliminate host round trips and can provide significant performance gains on modern GPUs.

In essence, conditional graph nodes let you control graph execution based on values computed in device kernels—all without involving the CPU. This capability allows complex branching workflows to be implemented as a single, repeatable graph launch. CUDA Graphs support multiple types of conditional nodes, as shown in Figure 12-9:

IF

Executes its single-body graph exactly once when the condition is nonzero.

IF/ELSE

By specifying two body graphs, one is chosen when the condition is true, the other when false.

WHILE

Repeatedly executes its body graph as long as the condition remains nonzero, checking again after each iteration.

SWITCH

Holds N body graphs and executes the ith one when the condition equals i; if the condition $\geq N$, it skips execution altogether.

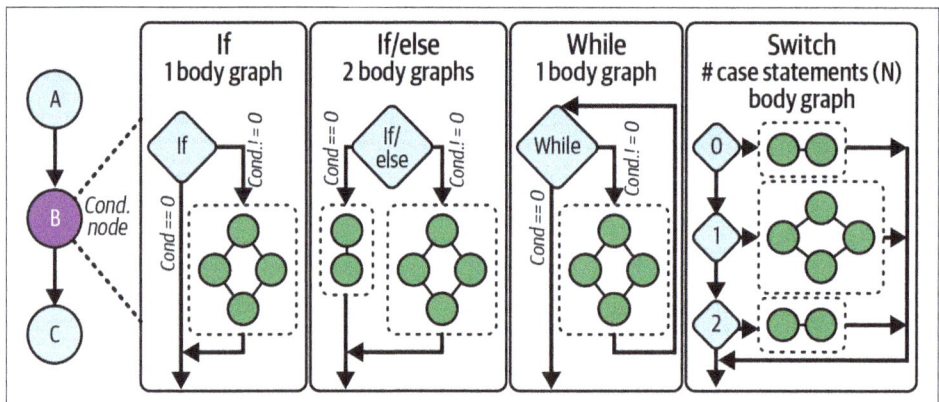

Figure 12-9. Types of conditional graph nodes

Next is an example showing how to create and populate an IF conditional node. Note the use of cudaGraphSetConditional to write the flag that controls the IF node. In this case, the condition checks if the sum is greater than a given threshold. This way, if the data meets the given criteria (flag = 1u), it runs the next subgraph. Otherwise, if the condition is not met, the conditional node does not run the subgraph:

```
#include <cuda_runtime.h>
#include <cstdio>

// Device kernel that computes and sets the condition handle
__global__ void setHandle(cudaGraphConditionalHandle handle,
                          int *data, size_t N) {
```

```cpp
    // Example threshold
    constexpr int threshold    = 123456;

    // Test whether the sum of data exceeds a threshold
    //     using a custom reduce_sum() function
    //     (recommended to implement this with
    //     CUB's DeviceReduce::Sum routine.)
    unsigned int flag =
        (reduce_sum(data, N) > threshold) ? 1u : 0u;

    cudaGraphSetConditional(handle, flag);
}

// A simple body kernel that runs only if flag != 0
__global__ void bodyKernel() {
    printf("Conditional body executed on GPU!\n");
}

int main() {
    cudaStream_t stream;
    cudaStreamCreateWithFlags(&stream,
        cudaStreamNonBlocking);

    // 1) Create the graph
    cudaGraph_t graph;
    cudaGraphCreate(&graph, 0);

    // 2) Create a condition handle associated with graph
    cudaGraphConditionalHandle condHandle;
    cudaGraphConditionalHandleCreate(&condHandle, graph);

    // 3) Add the upstream kernel node to set the handle
    cudaGraphNode_t setNode;
    cudaKernelNodeParams setParams = {};
    setParams.func          = (void*)setHandle;
    setParams.gridDim       = dim3(1);
    setParams.blockDim      = dim3(32);

    // 4) Allocate input data
    constexpr size_t N            = 1 << 20;
    int*          d_data          = nullptr;
    cudaMalloc(&d_data, N * sizeof(int));

    void* setArgs[] = { &condHandle, &d_data, &N };
    setParams.kernelParams  = setArgs;
    cudaGraphAddKernelNode(&setNode, graph, nullptr, 0,
        &setParams);

    // 5) Add the IF conditional node
    cudaGraphNode_t condNode;
    cudaConditionalNodeParams ifParams = {};
    ifParams.handle = condHandle;
```

```
ifParams.type    = cudaGraphCondTypeIf;
// One-node body graph, in this case
ifParams.size    = 1;
cudaGraphAddConditionalNode(&condNode,
                            graph,
                            &setNode,
                            1,
                            &ifParams);

// 6) Populate the body graph: one kernel that prints a message
cudaGraph_t bodyGraph = ifParams.phGraphOut[0];
cudaGraphNode_t bodyNode;
cudaKernelNodeParams bodyParams = {};
bodyParams.func        = (void*)bodyKernel;
bodyParams.gridDim     = dim3(1);
bodyParams.blockDim    = dim3(32);
cudaGraphAddKernelNode(&bodyNode, bodyGraph, nullptr,
    0, &bodyParams);

// 7) Instantiate, upload, and launch the graph on the device
cudaGraphExec_t graphExec;
cudaGraphInstantiate(&graphExec, graph, nullptr, nullptr,
cudaGraphInstantiateFlagDeviceLaunch);
cudaGraphUpload(graphExec, stream);
cudaGraphLaunch(graphExec, stream);


// 8) Wait for completion and clean up
cudaStreamSynchronize(stream);
cudaGraphExecDestroy(graphExec);
cudaGraphDestroy(graph);
cudaStreamDestroy(stream);

cudaFree(d_data);

return 0;
}
```

Here, we create a new CUDA Graph with cudaGraphCreate, which will hold all subsequent nodes. We then create a condition handle using cudaGraphConditional HandleCreate. (This associates a small integer value to the graph that can be set on the device.)

An upstream kernel, setHandle, is then added. This kernel runs on one thread to avoid race conditions. It then calls cudaGraphSetConditional to write the flag that controls the IF node.

The IF conditional node is added with cudaGraphAddConditionalNode—specifying cudaGraphCondTypeIf and size=1. This defines how many conditional branches or iterations we plan to support.

Here, we allocate one empty subgraph (body) to be executed if the conditional flag returns nonzero. The body graph is retrieved from `ifParams.phGraphOut[0]` and populates it by adding `bodyKernel`, which simply prints a message when executed.

After graph construction, call `cudaGraphInstantiate` to produce an executable graph object. To launch a graph from device code, you must instantiate it with the `cudaGraphInstantiateFlagDeviceLaunch` flag and upload it with `cudaGraphUpload` before any device-side launch.

Launching with `cudaGraphLaunch` on a CUDA stream triggers execution of the upstream set-handle kernel, the conditional check, and then, if the flag was set, the body kernel. And all of this happens directly on the GPU, as shown in Figure 12-10.

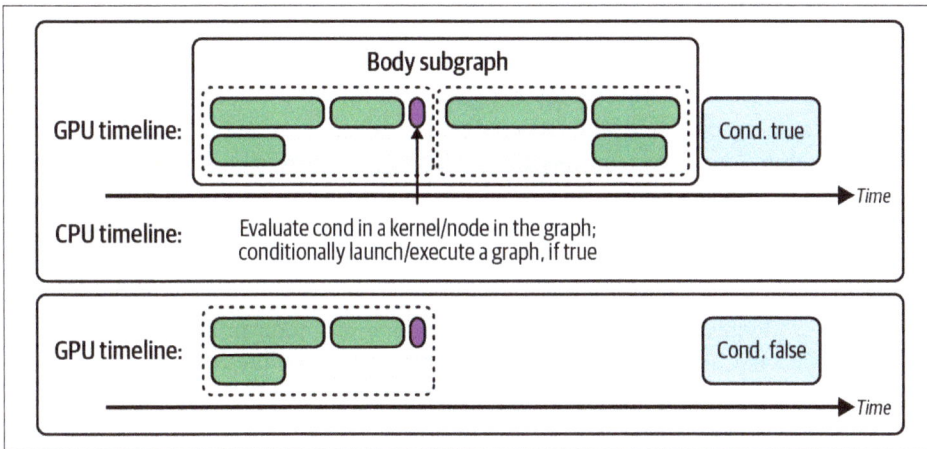

Figure 12-10. Additional processing (body subgraph) if condition is met

We then synchronize the stream with `cudaStreamSynchronize` to wait for completion. Finally, we clean up by destroying the instantiated graph, the graph itself, and the stream.

To minimize race conditions, it's important to always set the condition in a single thread (e.g., `if (threadIdx.x == 0)`). And make sure that the preceding kernels flush memory to make the value visible before the conditional node executes.

Conditional nodes can be nested as well. For instance, a WHILE node's body can contain an IF node, as shown in Figure 12-11. This allows multilevel decision logic without requiring CPU hops.

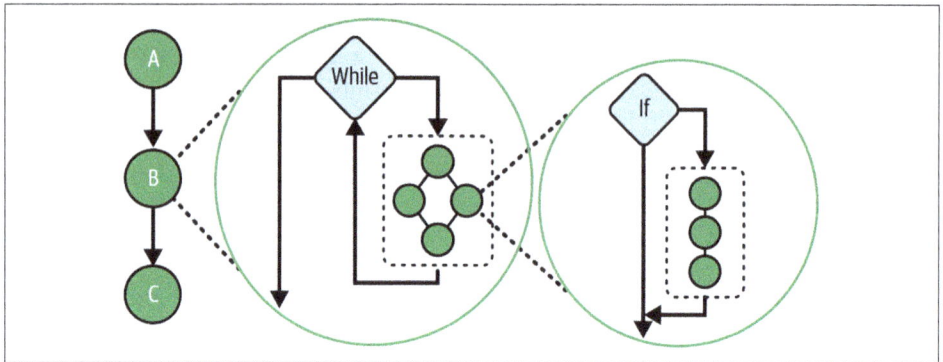

Figure 12-11. Nested conditional graph nodes

In short, you should use conditional graph nodes to keep decisions on the GPU, reduce CPU overhead, and express complex control flow directly in your CUDA Graph. Because graph creation costs can be amortized over many iterations, representing dynamic workflows entirely on-device can produce significant performance improvements.

> As of this writing, PyTorch's CUDA Graphs API does not provide a way to create conditional CUDA graph nodes directly with the Python. Support for conditional graph execution in frameworks and tools is evolving. As of this writing, this feature requires custom C++ integrations if you need to implement if/while/switch nodes with PyTorch.

Dynamic Parallelism

Previously, we saw how the device-initiated CUDA Graph launches capture and replay fixed sequences of operations with minimal CPU involvement. But that model expects that your entire execution flow is known ahead of time, which isn't always possible. Many workloads change shape at runtime based on input data, intermediate results, or problem complexity. That's where Dynamic parallelism (DP) comes in.

DP gives your GPU kernels the power to spawn new work for themselves instead of waiting on the CPU. Whereas CUDA Graphs require you to know your entire pipeline in advance, DP lets a running "parent" kernel examine its own outputs and decide on the fly how many "child" kernels to launch next. This is a game-changer for truly irregular problems—hierarchical reductions, adaptive mesh refinement, and graph traversals—where the number of subsequent tasks becomes clear only as you process your data.

Imagine an inference pipeline that occasionally needs a special "plugin" model evaluation for certain inputs. In a CPU-driven flow, you'd run Kernel A, copy its results back to the host, decide whether to launch Kernel B, and then issue that launch—leaving the GPU idle during the round trip. With DP, Kernel A inspects its outputs and, if the condition holds, launches Kernel B directly on the device. The entire decision-and-dispatch happens inside one GPU-resident workload, collapsing the idle gap and keeping SMs busy.

In the context of an LLM, most tokens follow the standard transformer path, but some require an auxiliary attention block. A DP-enabled transformer kernel can detect those special tokens at runtime and tail-launch the extra attention kernel only for those positions—no host intervention, no wasted cycles. NVIDIA's libraries already exploit DP for similar patterns in adaptive algorithms: new subtasks emerge dynamically as data flows through the computation.

You'll know DP is right for you when your profiler timeline shows a back-to-back pattern like Kernel A → GPU idle gap → Kernel B. Here, the idle time corresponds to the CPU preparing the next launch. Replacing that gap with a device-side launch keeps every SM occupied and slashes the latency between dependent stages.

Of course, the performance benefits of DP don't come for free. Each child launch uses GPU scheduling resources and requires additional stack space. To avoid "stack overflow" errors, you may need to bump the runtime stack size with cudaDeviceSetLimit(cudaLimitStackSize, newSize). CUDA will warn you if you hit its default limit.

On a related note, CUDA has a maximum limit on how many child-kernel launches can be pending. By default, CUDA allows 2,048 outstanding device launches at one time. However, this is configurable.

If a parent kernel needs to spawn more than 2,048 child kernels because it's using a large loop to launch thousands of tiny kernels, you can raise this limit using the API cudaDeviceSetLimit(cudaLimitDevRuntimePendingLaunchCount, newLimit). Otherwise, exceeding the default 2,048 limit will cause a runtime error. In practice, the default value is usually enough for most uses. But it's an important consideration for extreme cases.

> When spawning many child kernels on the GPU, be sure to monitor device memory usage since each pending child-kernel launch reserves resources and may exceed the hard limits of your GPU hardware.

Because DP adds some instruction-level overhead, it's best reserved for cases where static orchestration like persistent kernels, streams, or CUDA Graphs would otherwise leave the GPU idling while the CPU decides the next step. In other words, when your workload is truly a fixed sequence of operations, you're often better off capturing it as a CUDA Graph and replaying it device-side.

When your work emerges dynamically from the data itself, DP lets you keep both scheduling and execution entirely on the GPU. This will deliver better scaling and lower end-to-end latency for nested, data-dependent, or unpredictable parallelism.

> Because DP incurs per-launch overhead and consumes pending-launch slots, use DP when new parallelism emerges from the data at runtime and can't be expressed as a pre-recorded CUDA Graph. In contrast, favor device-launched CUDA Graphs when the control flow is expression-level and repeated since CUDA Graphs amortize the costs.

Let's compare two implementations of a simple parent-child workflow. The host-driven version shown next launches a parent kernel, waits for it to finish, then issues two child kernels from the CPU. This leaves the GPU idle during those decision gaps:

```
// dp_host_launched.cu
#include <cuda_runtime.h>

__global__ void childKernel(float* data, int N) {
    int idx = blockIdx.x * blockDim.x + threadIdx.x;
    if (idx < N) {
        data[idx] = data[idx] * data[idx];
    }
}

__global__ void parentKernel(float* data, int N) {
    // Parent does setup work. Here, CPU decides on child launches.
    if (threadIdx.x == 0 && blockIdx.x == 0) {
        // maybe mark regions or compute flags here
    }
}

int main() {
    const int N = 1 << 20;
    float* d_data;
    cudaMalloc(&d_data, N * sizeof(float));
    // ... initialize d_data ...

    // 1) Launch parent and wait
    cudaStream_t s; cudaStreamCreateWithFlags(&s, cudaStreamNonBlocking);

    parentKernel<<<1,1,0,s>>>(d_data, N);

    cudaStreamSynchronize(s);

    // 2) CPU splits work in half and launches children
    int half = N / 2;
```

```
childKernel<<<(half+255)/256,256>>>(d_data,     half);
childKernel<<<(half+255)/256,256>>>(d_data+half, half);
cudaStreamSynchronize(s);
cudaStreamDestroy(s);

cudaFree(d_data);
return 0;
}
```

In the host-driven version, the GPU runs `parentKernel` and then idles while the CPU prepares and launches each `childKernel` in turn. Note the explicit `cudaDevice Synchronize()` calls after the parent and between children. These calls lead to idle gaps that should be eliminated, as shown in Figure 12-12.

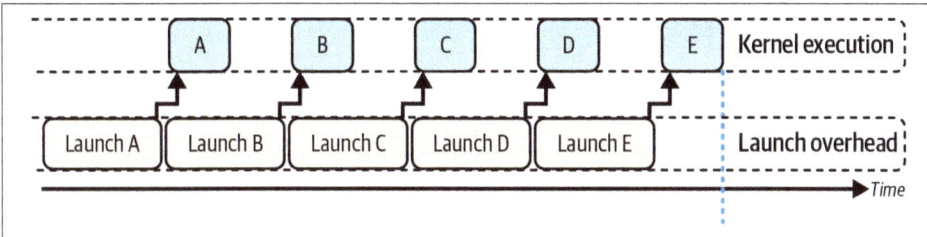

Figure 12-12. Idle gaps caused by child-kernel launches

In contrast, the device-launched DP version lets the parent-kernel spawn its children on the device. This approach requires no host synchronization between the parent and child kernel launches. This way, the parent's child-kernel launches implicitly queue the children and synchronize only at the end, as shown in the code here:

```
// dp_device_launched.cu
// Dynamic parallelism requires relocatable device code enabled with -rdc=true.

#include <cuda_runtime.h>

__global__ void childKernel(float* data, int n) {
    int idx = blockIdx.x * blockDim.x + threadIdx.x;
    if (idx < n) {
        data[idx] = data[idx] * data[idx];
    }
}

__global__ void parentKernel(float* data, int n) {
    // Launch children from a single thread to avoid duplicate launches.
    if (blockIdx.x == 0 && threadIdx.x == 0) {
        const int threadsPerBlock = 256;
        const int firstHalfCount  = n / 2;
        const int secondHalfCount = n - firstHalfCount;

        const int blocksFirst  = (firstHalfCount  + threadsPerBlock - 1)
                                  / threadsPerBlock;
```

```
            const int blocksSecond = (secondHalfCount + threadsPerBlock - 1)
                                      / threadsPerBlock;

            // Device launched child kernels.
            // No device side cudaDeviceSynchronize is needed.
            childKernel<<<blocksFirst,  threadsPerBlock>>>(data,
                                                     firstHalfCount);
            childKernel<<<blocksSecond, threadsPerBlock>>>(data + firstHalfCount,
                                                     secondHalfCount);
            // Parent kernel will not finish until both children finish.
        }
    }

    int main() {
        const int N = 1024 * 1024;    // 1M elements, avoids bit shifting for clarity
        float* d_data = nullptr;

        cudaMalloc(&d_data, N * sizeof(float));
        // Initialize to zero as a concrete, valid initialization.
        cudaMemset(d_data, 0, N * sizeof(float));

        // Launch parent on the default stream.
        parentKernel<<<1, 1>>>(d_data, N);

        // Wait for completion without cudaDeviceSynchronize. Sync stream instead.
        cudaStreamSynchronize(0);

        cudaFree(d_data);
        return 0;
    }
```

Here, the `parentKernel` issues both child launches directly on the GPU. The host
submits only one kernel and then waits once. When the parent kernel completes, the
device runtime makes sure that all launched child kernels are complete before moving on.

Note that this dynamic parallelism version avoids any use of `cuda`
`DeviceSynchronize()`. It relies on the implicit rule that a parent
kernel does not complete until all its device-launched children
complete, and the host simply waits on the stream.

With the device-side DP approach, there are no idle gaps for CPU decision making.
As such, it collapses the latency between dependent stages and keeps SMs busy end to
end. This increases GPU utilization at the slight cost of a small amount of per-launch
overhead incurred on the device, as you see in Figure 12-13's timeline.

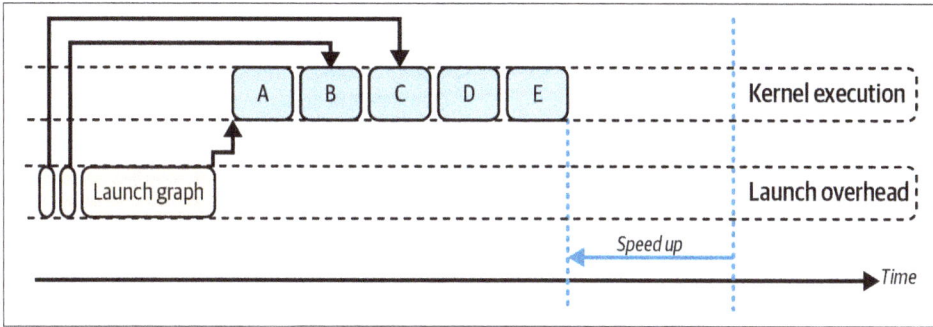

Figure 12-13. No gaps with device-side launch and dynamic parallelism

In our simple two-child example, the host-driven version issues three separate launches (1 parent + 2 children). In this case, the GPU idles while the CPU decides when to launch each child kernel.

This is in contrast to the device-driven DP version that performs just one host-side launch for the parent kernel. The parent kernel then spawns both children on the GPU without further host intervention. Table 12-2 compares performance for the host-driven and device-driven DP child launches.

Table 12-2. Host-driven versus GPU-driven nested child-kernel-launches performance comparison (2 children)

Metric	Before (host launch)	After (device launch)
Total host launches	3	1
Average launch overhead per call	~20 µs	~25 µs
GPU idle cycles (during sequence)	~40%	~5%
Overall execution time	1.00 ms	0.75 ms

Here, we see that by moving the child dispatch into the GPU, DP eliminates roughly 35% of the idle time and reduces total runtime by about 25%. The slight rise in per-launch cost (20 µs → 25 µs) reflects the GPU's on-device scheduling overhead. However, this overhead is negligible compared to the savings from removing multiple CPU-GPU handshakes.

An additional benefit of GPU-driven launches is improved data locality since intermediate results never have to be copied back to the CPU between stages. In our example, the data computed by the parent kernel is immediately usable by the child kernels without leaving GPU memory. This avoids extra memory transfers and preserves cache data. No CPU intervention also means fewer chances for cache eviction or DRAM refetch of data that would have been reused on the GPU.

In short, DP transforms a stop-start host-driven workflow into a seamless GPU-resident pipeline, sustaining high SM utilization and minimizing host-GPU coordination. And remember that dynamic parallelism, like other advanced techniques, should be tested for impact.

While DP eliminates CPU interaction, a device-initiated kernel launch still has roughly the same order of overhead as a host launch. As such, not all algorithms will see gains. In fact, some algorithms may even run slower with DP—especially if the work from the launched kernel is too small to amortize the overhead. In other words, device-side launch overhead might negate DP's benefits for some small kernels.

> Always profile the before and after making a change. Tools like Nsight Compute can profile child kernels launched using DP to help quantify their cost and make sure the benefits of a GPU-resident pipeline truly outweigh the extra overhead and improve throughput.

Having covered single-GPU orchestration, we next turn to multi-GPU and multinode scenarios, where interconnect bandwidths and collective operations extend our roofline considerations to the cluster level.

Orchestrate Across Multiple GPUs and Cluster Nodes (NVSHMEM)

When you scale from one GPU to many, the core goal remains the same: keep every device busy by hiding data movement behind useful work. Once the host has dispatched a task to each GPU, whether through separate CPU threads, asynchronous launches, or a multi-GPU graph, the GPUs take over. While one stream on each device drives computation, a second stream can shuttle data peer-to-peer over NVLink or PCIe without ever involving host memory.

This means that, at scale, you must overlap peer-to-peer transfers with computation. It's important to note that even with NVLink, the bandwidth and latency are not equal to on-device HBM. This communication must therefore be hidden with overlap.

In practice, as the cluster size grows, overlapping work with data transfer is absolutely essential to scaling the environment linearly. For straightforward hand-offs, you can use GPUDirect Peer Access to move large blocks of memory in the background, as shown here:

```
cudaMemcpyPeerAsync(dest_ptr, dest_gpu, src_ptr, src_gpu, size, comm_stream);
```

When you need collective communication such as gradient all-reduces in PyTorch Distributed Data Parallel (DDP), you launch NCCL's nonblocking routines on a separate stream using NCCL's asynchronous collective calls. NCCL then arranges your tensors into rings or trees that saturate every NVLink and NVSwitch path—all while your compute kernels continue running on their own streams.

If your MPI library is CUDA-aware and recognizes GPU device pointers, it will automatically use GPUDirect RDMA to send data over InfiniBand using calls like the one here:

```
MPI_Send(device_buf, count, MPI_FLOAT, peer_rank, ...);
```

This CUDA-awareness in MPI (and NCCL) means GPU data moves directly across the network using GPUDirect RDMA over InfiniBand without staging through host memory. (Note that within a node, peer copies run over NVLink or PCIe using GPU-Direct Peer-to-Peer.)

Using these primitives and avoiding the CPU helps decrease data transfer latency and achieve near-wire-speed for GPU-to-GPU transfers. As a result, internode data transfer and communication can properly overlap with GPU computations.

Fine-Grained GPU-to-GPU Memory Sharing with NVSHMEM

For workloads needing ultratight, event-driven coordination, such as dynamic task queues and fine-grained event notifications, NVIDIA's NVIDIA SHMEM (NVSHMEM) library is an excellent option. It treats each GPU as a processing element (PE) in a partitioned global address space (PGAS).

With PGAS, a GPU can directly write into another GPU's memory from device code, bypassing the CPU. Latency depends on the interconnect, with NVLink generally lower than PCIe or network transports. Here is the classic send-and-signal pattern using NVSHMEM:

```cpp
#include <cstdio>
#include <cuda_runtime.h>
#include <nvshmem.h>
#include <nvshmemx.h>

// Device symbols for the symmetric buffers
__device__ int   *remote_flag;
__device__ float *remote_data;

//-----------------------------------------------------------------------
// GPU 0: send data then signal GPU 1
//-----------------------------------------------------------------------
__global__ void sender_kernel(float *local_data, int dest_pe) {
    int idx = blockIdx.x * blockDim.x + threadIdx.x;
    float value = local_data[idx];

    // 1) Put the payload into remote_data[1] on dest_pe
    nvshmem_float_p(remote_data + 1, value, dest_pe);
    // 2) Wait for the RMA to complete before setting the flag
    nvshmem_quiet();
```

```
    // 3) Signal completion by setting remote_flag[0] = 1 on dest_pe
    nvshmem_int_p(remote_flag + 0, 1, dest_pe);
}


//----------------------------------------------------------------------------
// GPU 1: wait for flag then consume payload
//----------------------------------------------------------------------------
__global__ void receiver_kernel(float *recv_buffer) {
    // 1) Spin until remote_flag[0] == 1
    nvshmem_int_wait_until(remote_flag + 0,
        NVSHMEM_CMP_EQ, 1);
    // 2) Once flag is set, the payload at remote_data[1] is valid
    float val = remote_data[1];
    recv_buffer[0] = val * 2.0f;
}


//----------------------------------------------------------------------------
// Host-side setup and teardown
//----------------------------------------------------------------------------
int main(int argc, char **argv) {
    // 1) Initialize the NVSHMEM runtime
    nvshmem_init();

    // 2) Determine this PE's rank and bind to the matching GPU
    int mype = nvshmem_my_pe();
    cudaSetDevice(mype);

    // 3) Allocate symmetric buffers on each PE
    //     - Two ints for the flag
    //     - Two floats for the data payload
    int   *flag_buf = (int*)   nvshmem_malloc(2 * sizeof(int));
    float *data_buf = (float*) nvshmem_malloc(2 * sizeof(float));

    // 4) Zero out flags on PE 0 and synchronize
    nvshmem_barrier_all();
    if (mype == 0) {
        int zeros[2] = {0, 0};
        cudaMemcpy(flag_buf, zeros, 2 * sizeof(int),
                   cudaMemcpyHostToDevice);
    }
    nvshmem_barrier_all();

    // 5) Register the device pointers for use in kernels
    cudaMemcpyToSymbol(remote_flag, &flag_buf, sizeof(int*));
    cudaMemcpyToSymbol(remote_data, &data_buf, sizeof(float*));

    // 6) Launch either the sender or receiver kernel
    dim3 grid(1), block(128);
    if (mype == 0) {
        // Example input buffer for the sender
        float *local_data;
        cudaMalloc(&local_data, 128 * sizeof(float));
```

```
        // ... initialize local_data as needed ...
        sender_kernel<<<grid, block>>>(local_data, 1);
        cudaFree(local_data);
    } else {
        float *recv_buffer;
        cudaMalloc(&recv_buffer, sizeof(float));
        receiver_kernel<<<grid, block>>>(recv_buffer);
        cudaFree(recv_buffer);
    }

    // 7) Wait for all GPU work to finish
    cudaDeviceSynchronize();

    // 8) Clean up NVSHMEM resources
    nvshmem_free(flag_buf);
    nvshmem_free(data_buf);
    nvshmem_finalize();

    return 0;
}
```

Here, the one-sided remote memory operations happen entirely on-device. GPU/PE 0 writes its result straight into GPU/PE 1's memory and flips a flag there. Specifically, GPU/PE 0 issues a `nvshmem_float_p` to write payload data directly into GPU/PE 1's memory, calls `nvshmem_quiet()` to ensure completion, then uses `nvshmem_int_p` to flip a flag.

Meanwhile, GPU/PE 1's kernel spins on `nvshmem_int_wait_until()` and, as soon as the flag is set, reads the payload. This requires no CPU intervention or extra copies— just hardware-accelerated, GPU-to-GPU transfers over NVLink.

Since NVSHMEM communication uses GPU-initiated, one-sided operations over NVLink or PCIe, it eliminates host staging. As such, NVSHMEM communication can achieve near-peak wire speed. This is because NVSHMEM one-sided operations bypass the CPU as well as the software overhead of kernel launches. Essentially, NVSHMEM turns formerly multistep communications into a single hardware transaction.

Of course, with great power comes great responsibility. Because NVSHMEM is essentially GPU-level shared-memory programming, you must carefully manage synchronization and avoid races. Additionally, overusing global barriers can also stall all GPUs on the slowest peer.

In practice, avoid over-synchronizing. Use NVSHMEM's fine-grained signals or point-to-point synchronization when possible. This is in contrast to always calling `nvshmem_barrier_all()`.

Modern implementations of NVSHMEM provide efficiency improvements for these synchronization routines. However, they are still a synchronization point that can become a bottleneck if misused. NVSHMEM provides fine-grained primitives such as nvshmem_wait_until for waiting on device variables and signal (*https://oreil.ly/o3reh*) operations like nvshmem_signal_fetch, nvshmem_signal_wait_until, or the nvshmemx_signal_op variants for point-to-point synchronization when only a subset of devices needs to coordinate. The low-level details showing NVSHMEM sharing data and synchronizing with signals between a sender and a receiver GPU are shown in Figure 12-14.

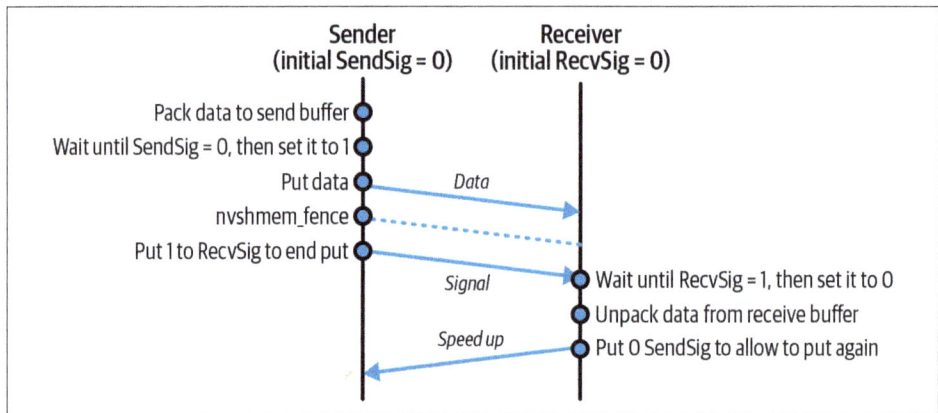

Figure 12-14. NVSHMEM one-sided communication example

NVSHMEM shines when workloads are irregular or data-dependent, such as graph algorithms, dynamic load balancing, and discrete-event simulations. In these cases, static graphs and collectives are not sufficient.

Kernels that use NVSHMEM can be captured inside CUDA Graphs like any other kernel. The NVSHMEM device operations occur inside those kernels and are not separate graph nodes. However, NVSHMEM's true strength is in letting kernels adapt and coordinate on the fly, without a fixed communication script used by a graph.

In short, NVSHMEM transforms a cluster of GPUs into a shared-memory domain, enabling device-only kernel launches, data transfers, and synchronization at latencies and throughputs that far outpace any CPU-mediated approach.

Imagine a two-stage transformer inference pipeline (attention + multilayer perceptron) that does the following: GPU 0 computes attention, then NVSHMEM puts its activations to GPU 1 and signals. GPU 1, running a persistent kernel, sees the flag and begins the MLP stage.

Because GPU 0 immediately moves on to batch 2 while GPU 1 is still on batch 1, after a few iterations both devices are working in perfect tandem. Each handoff is hidden behind active compute warps. This drives near-100% utilization without incurring host stalls.

When you need flexible load balancing, NVSHMEM's atomic operations let each PE grab work dynamically. A PE is an OS process that is part of a parallel NVSHMEM application.

The code here shows each GPU pulling the next index from a global counter, processing the chunk, then looping. This enables true work-stealing entirely on the device—without host coordination:

```
__global__ void work_steal_kernel(/*...*/, int *queue_head, Task *tasks) {
    while (true) {
        // Atomically claim the next task index
        int idx = nvshmem_int_atomic_inc(queue_head);
        if (idx >= N_tasks) break;
        // Process tasks[idx]...
    }
}
```

For scenarios that require the lowest possible jitter, such as a tight multi-GPU collective or synchronous model-parallel step, you can launch one cooperative kernel using NVSHMEM and spanning all GPUs by using nvshmemx_collective_launch() to start the sender and received kernels on GPU 0 and GPU 1 simultaneously. This allows the to coordinate using NVSHMEM without any host intervention. Then, you can use NVSHMEM's device-side barriers, as shown here:

```
__global__ void synchronized_step_kernel(/*...*/) {
    nvshmem_barrier_all();
    // All GPUs proceed in lockstep here
    // ...
}
```

Here, every PE enters nvshmem_barrier_all() together and then continues simultaneously. This guarantees perfectly aligned execution across the cluster.

> All kernels that use NVSHMEM's device-level synchronization or collectives must be launched with nvshmemx_collective_launch(). This ensures that the kernel runs concurrently on all PEs (GPUs) in the job.

Capturing Multi-GPU Collectives with NCCL and CUDA Graphs

When you need bulk collective operations such as broadcasts, reductions, and all-to-all transfers, NVIDIA's NCCL library is the go-to on multi-GPU systems. Traditionally, each GPU launches an ncclAllReduce or similar collective from the host. It then waits (synchronizes) before proceeding to the next compute phase. This sequential host orchestration adds overhead and idle time between the forward and backward passes.

However, NCCL calls can also be recorded into CUDA Graphs just like kernels. This lets you "bake in" your forward kernels, the all-reduce, and your backward kernels into a single graph that you replay each iteration:

```
cudaStreamBeginCapture(captureStream,
    cudaStreamCaptureModeGlobal);

forwardKernel<<<...>>>(...);

ncclAllReduce(sendBuf, recvBuf, count, ncclFloat,
    ncclSum, comm, captureStream);

backwardKernel<<<...>>>(...);

cudaStreamEndCapture(captureStream, &graph);

// Instantiate and upload before launching
cudaGraphExec_t graphExec;
cudaGraphInstantiate(&graphExec, graph, ...);
cudaGraphUpload(graphExec, captureStream);

// Each training step:
cudaGraphLaunch(graphExec, captureStream);
```

Notice the use of the same capture stream for all operations—including NCCL. Using a graph, NCCL calls become graph nodes just like kernels. Because each process is replaying an identical graph, NCCL's internal logic finds peers and executes the all-reduce without additional host coordination. This graph-captured all-reduce is especially powerful on large clusters, as it eliminates per-iteration launch jitter and keeps all GPUs busy overlapping compute and network operations.

Because each GPU launches the same graph, including its collective node, NCCL internally rendezvous across ranks without extra host intervention. The host's per-iteration work drops to a single cudaGraphLaunch, which reduces CPU overhead and launch jitter.

On top of reduced CPU load, capturing your all-reduce inside a graph allows true overlap of communication and computation across multiple GPUs and compute nodes. Suppose you split gradient computation into two passes, layers 1 through $L/2$ and layers $(L/2 + 1)$ through L, and map them to separate streams, as shown here:

```
// Pseudocode in capture:
computeGradientsLayer1<<<...>>>(..., streamA);
ncclAllReduce(..., comm, streamB);      // in streamB, overlaps with streamA
computeGradientsLayer2<<<...>>>(..., streamA);
ncclAllReduce(..., comm, streamB);
```

Since these nodes are captured with their unique stream assignments and dependencies, the CUDA driver can overlap NCCL's network transfers on streamB with independent work on `streamA`. This bucketed-all-reduce pattern consistently hides communication latency behind computation, improving multi-GPU scaling.

> NCCL collectives are graph capture–compatible when all ranks capture and replay the same sequence with the same communicator. However, all ranks must capture and replay the same NCCL sequence with the same communicator. Mismatched communicators across graph replays will risk deadlock (at best, relatively easy to debug) or incorrect results (at worst, silent failure, and difficult to debug). Also, it's recommended to capture preliminary warmup collectives, run them ahead of time to initialize communicators, and reuse the instantiated graph to achieve minimal steady-state latency.

In practice, this bucketed all-reduce approach is standard in large-model training. By overlapping chunks of gradient reduction with computation of the next layers, you hide nearly all network time. An example of a bucketed all-reduce with DDP running in separate processes (process 1 and process 2) is shown in Figure 12-15.

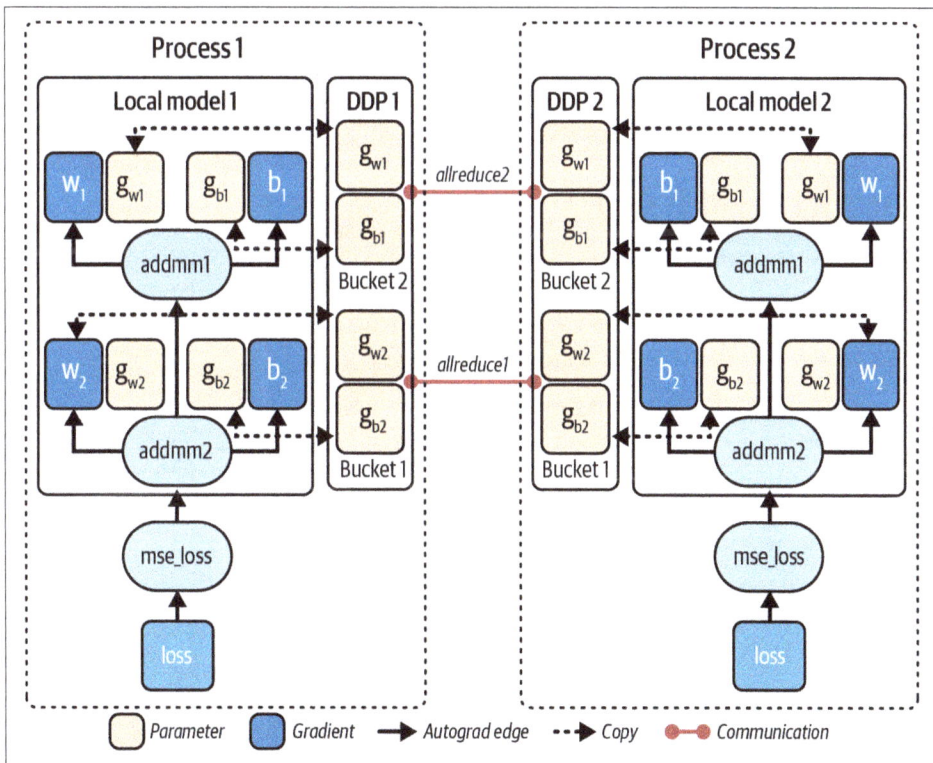

Figure 12-15. Overlapping all-reduce with computation

Modern libraries like PyTorch DDP implement variants of this approach automatically. But capturing a CUDA Graph can further reduce CPU overhead and provide more deterministic performance.

Keep in mind a few considerations for using CUDA Graphs in multi-GPU environments. First, all participating GPUs must record and replay collectives in the identical sequence to avoid deadlock—much like MPI's collective rules in which all ranks must enter the collective in the same order.

Next, while CUDA Graphs pin and reuse GPU buffers, make sure allocations for your gradients and communication buffers are done before capture. Also, as discussed earlier, if you need to modify parameters in your graph, such as batch size, you can use `cudaGraphExecUpdate` to patch those parameters without a full recapture.

In practice, capturing NCCL plus compute in a graph can cut per-step CPU time and speed up large-model training across many GPUs. At a massive scale, with hundreds of thousands of GPUs, these savings compound—creating tighter synchronization and higher utilization across the whole cluster.

> NCCL and CUDA Graphs give us an efficient way to schedule collective communication alongside computation. However, not all multi-GPU communication is collective—sometimes we need more fine-grained or asynchronous sharing of data between GPUs. This is exactly where NVSHMEM, described earlier, can help.

Pattern for N-GPU Scaling

Whether you're using simple peer copies, NCCL rings, or NVSHMEM one-sided atomics, the pattern of scaling to many GPUs is always the same. The system should dispatch kernels once, pipeline and overlap your data transfers with compute, and scale linearly—especially with the host CPU off the critical path.

For example, 4 GPUs should ideally behave like a single GPU that is 4× faster—assuming you can keep all the GPUs fed with data in parallel (see Figure 12-16) and the host out of the loop. If you can do this, you should achieve near-linear speedups by properly overlapping communication computation. Without overlap, scaling will plateau once the communication time equals the computation time.

As you increase GPUs, you need to use more aggressive pipelining of data transfers and computations—and use less CPU-side orchestration and synchronization. As such, you should offload more orchestration to the devices using asynchronous copies, NCCL collectives in graphs, and NVSHMEM's PGAS primitives. This shifts even more responsibility to software.

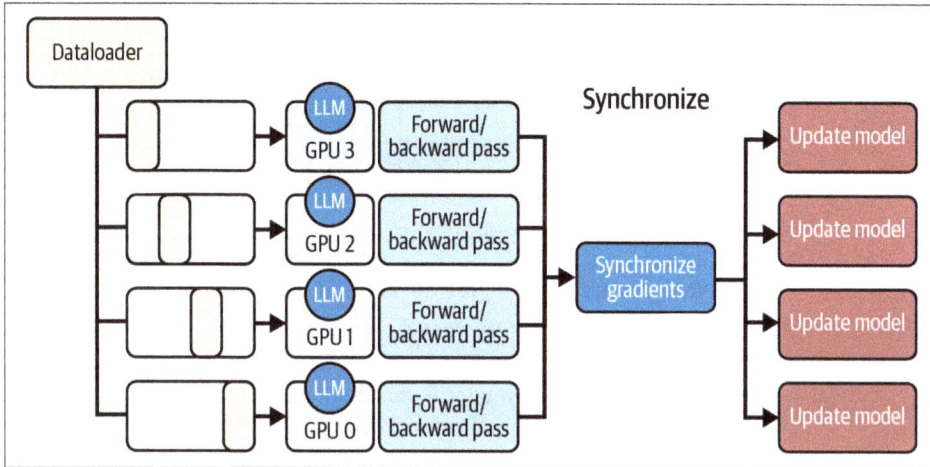

Figure 12-16. Each GPU computes in parallel while exchanging data concurrently—no idle GPUs and no stalled data transfers

Applying these techniques, you can eliminate the CPU bottleneck, saturate the fast interconnects, max out the compute FLOPS, and build truly low-latency multi-GPU pipelines. Next, let's revisit roofline models in the context of dynamic and device-side scheduling and orchestration.

Roofline-Guided Scheduling and Orchestration Decisions

Over the last couple of chapters, we have collected a solid set of orchestration techniques, including CUDA streams, kernel fusion, persistent kernels, CUDA Graphs, dynamic parallelism, and more. The roofline model helps decide which tool will likely give the biggest win for your situation.

At its heart, roofline boils down to operational arithmetic intensity, or the ratio of FLOPS performed to bytes moved. It consists of two hardware "ceilings": memory roof (sloped) showing the peak throughput if you're limited by bandwidth, and compute roof (flat) marking the peak arithmetic rate when you're ALU-bound, as shown in Figure 12-17.

If your kernel lies near the memory roof (e.g., low FLOPS/byte) and is therefore memory bound, the best optimizations are those that hide or overlap memory transfers with computation. That means you should use asynchronous copies with CUDA streams—or even run multiple memory-bound kernels concurrently. This way, you can better saturate different parts of the memory system.

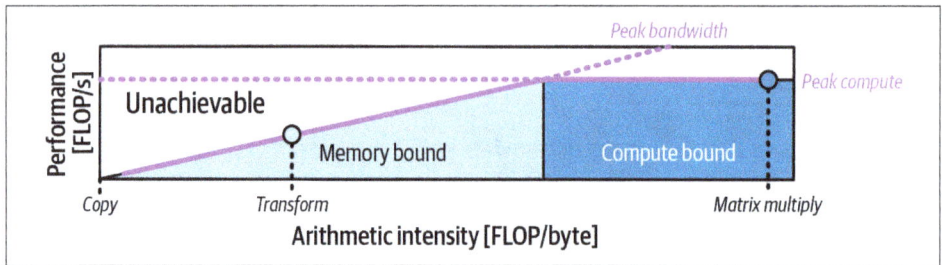

Figure 12-17. Arithmetic intensity with two hardware ceilings: memory bound (e.g., data transform operation) and compute bound (e.g., matrix multiply)

Kernel fusion helps only modestly for memory-bound workloads. It can shave off a number of intermediate global-memory round trips. But the real gains come from masking latency and packing more loads/stores in flight.

In contrast, a high-intensity kernel sitting under the compute roof needs to keep its ALUs busy. Here kernel fusion shines by combining separate add+scale (our fused example from earlier) into one pass to increase FLOPS per byte, shift the point rightwards on the roofline plot, and push the kernel toward a higher percentage of peak FLOP/s.

Likewise, persistent kernels, thread block clusters, and device-initiated CUDA Graphs don't change your intensity number, but they reduce idle gaps caused by repeated launches. This pushes your kernel's performance closer to the flat compute ceiling.

Many real workloads fall in between. They are neither strongly memory bound nor compute bound. In those cases, concurrency is your friend. By launching several modest-intensity kernels in parallel, whether using streams, concurrent graphs, or multiple persistent kernels, you are combining them such that the aggregate-throughput point sits higher on both axes. This better utilizes the device's resources.

Thorough roofline analysis requires disciplined measurement. Use Nsight Compute to count FLOPS and bytes transferred, plot your kernel's point, and see how far it lies below each roofline.

If the workload is memory bound, reach for streams, overlap, and maybe reduce precision (FP16, FP8, FP4) to reduce the denominator in the arithmetic intensity equation (e.g., the number of bytes transferred.)

And if your kernel is compute bound but not hitting peak FLOPS due to launch overhead or idle periods, focus on reducing launch overhead. As we've learned, you can do this by fusing operations into one kernel, using persistent kernels, capturing CUDA Graphs, or performing device-side launches. This will keep the ALUs fed.

If your kernel sits well under both roofs and is neither fully memory nor compute bound, then try to increase concurrency. Run multiple kernels and streams in parallel. This will better utilize all of your system resources.

With this quantitative guidance, you can pick the right orchestration strategy for your kernel rather than trying every trick all at once. Just remember to validate that each optimization moves you closer to the hardware's true potential. Always measure after applying an optimization.

The roofline model guides expectations, but real performance measurements, including compute throughput, achieved occupancy, memory throughput, etc., will tell the full story. A roofline analysis combined with iterative and continuous profiling will verify that your chosen optimization strategies are actually effective.

Key Takeaways

Achieving peak GPU performance hinges on weaving together computation and data movement with minimal overhead. Efficient orchestration streamlines complex workloads across CPU and GPU, ensuring neither side stalls the other. Here are some key takeaways from this chapter:

Dynamic scheduling with L2-cache atomic queues
> L2-cache atomics on modern GPUs are exceptionally fast. Use fast L2-cache atomics with batched increments to balance irregular workloads on-GPU. This batched-work allocation reduces contention and keeps warps busy by eliminating warp idle gaps. It can significantly boost throughput up to ~2× in extreme imbalance cases but typically between 10% and 30%. Even a modest batch size of 8 or 16 can eliminate most contention due to the high L2 bandwidth.

CUDA Graphs for fixed pipelines
> Record a sequence of GPU operations once and then replay it with a single host call each iteration. This reduces per-iteration CPU scheduling overhead, often a 20%–30% latency reduction (more at a larger scale). Make sure you're achieving maximum overlap of dependent operations on the GPU.

Low-overhead launch with CUDA Graphs
> Capture a sequence of asynchronous copies, kernel launches, event records, and allocations in a CUDA Graph (`cudaStreamBeginCapture`/`cudaStreamEndCap ture`). Replaying the graph with `cudaGraphLaunch` eliminates per-call CPU enqueue overhead while preserving all interstream dependencies, further reducing runtime bottlenecks.

Device-side orchestration

Launch work from the GPU itself by tail-launching a prerecorded CUDA Graph or using dynamic parallelism to spawn child kernels. This eliminates CPU scheduling gaps entirely and allows the GPU to remain busy end to end with no host intervention.

Multi-GPU overlap

Always overlap communication with computation. Use separate streams to pipeline GPU peer-to-peer transfers (`cudaMemcpyPeerAsync`), NCCL collectives, CUDA-aware MPI (RDMA), or NVSHMEM one-sided operations. This hides communication latency behind useful work and can approach linear scaling across many GPUs under favorable compute-to-communication ratios and adequate overlap—and even across cluster nodes—when overlap is sufficient.

Roofline-guided choices

Let the roofline chart drive your strategy. If your kernel is memory bound, focus on overlap and reducing data movement with asynchronous memcopies and mixed precision like FP8/FP4. If it's compute bound but underachieving due to overhead, use launch-reduction techniques like kernel fusion, persistent kernels, and CUDA Graphs to approach the compute ceiling. For kernels in-between, increase concurrency by running multiple operations in parallel to utilize all hardware units. Always verify with profiling that the chosen optimization moves the needle.

By weaving these techniques together—dynamic dispatch, cooperative kernels, graph capture/replay, and GPU-native memory sharing—you create pipelines that saturate every part of the GPU cluster for ultrascale AI workloads.

Conclusion

In this chapter, we moved beyond single-kernel optimizations and explored end-to-end orchestration techniques. We covered how to launch work entirely on the device with dynamic parallelism, capture complex workflows in CUDA Graphs, and coordinate many GPUs using NCCL and NVSHMEM. Each technique shares the same goal: keep every engine fueled with work, hide latency, and collapse host–device gaps so that your hardware runs flat-out.

NVIDIA's modern GPU platforms blur the line between CPU and GPU more than ever. The Grace Blackwell and Vera Rubin Superchips, for example, connect the CPU with multiple GPUs using coherent NVLink with enormous bandwidth.

But even as hardware reduces CPU-GPU barriers, the responsibility still falls on software to fully exploit this high-performance hardware. The approaches in this chapter, whether with CUDA in C++ or higher-level library APIs, are how we take advantage of these advancements.

In the next chapter, we'll see how PyTorch integrates many of these ideas, including streams, graphs, asynchronous operations, and optimized kernels, so you can achieve this performance in just a few lines of Python. Let's dive into the PyTorch ecosystem and understand why it's so popular for implementing high-performance AI workloads.

## CHAPTER 13

Profiling, Tuning, and Scaling PyTorch

AI training and inference pipelines can suffer from performance bottlenecks at every layer, including Python interpreter overhead, CPU host-side data-loading stalls, CUDA kernel underutilization, and GPU device-memory contention. To optimize effectively, you need to profile at multiple levels of the stack using multiple tools that cover the entire system.

This chapter focuses on profiling, debugging, and system-level tuning of PyTorch workloads running on modern NVIDIA GPUs. We will explore how to identify and fix bottlenecks using PyTorch's built-in profiler, NVIDIA's Nsight tools, and CPU profiling with Linux `perf`—as well as PyTorch memory profiling and memory allocator tuning. We'll also discuss how PyTorch uses CUDA streams for concurrency and CUDA Graphs to reduce kernel launch overhead.

Next, we'll show how to optimize data pipelines and scale out to multiple GPUs with PyTorch Distributed Data Parallel (DDP), Fully Sharded Data Parallel (FSDP), and other model parallelism strategies. We'll then demonstrate how to profile multi-GPU and multinode environments, including Holistic Trace Analysis (HTA) and Perfetto.

Throughout the chapter, we emphasize performance trade-offs and quantitative examples that focus on kernel execution times, hardware utilization metrics, memory footprint, data loading efficiency, and overall cost-efficiency of scaling. By the end of this chapter, you should have an understanding of how to implement an effective, holistic approach to profiling and tuning PyTorch workloads across the entire stack.

NVTX Markers and Profiling Tools

To capture a holistic view of performance, it's important to profile at multiple levels and use tools that cover the entire system. There exists a set of common tools and best practices used by practitioners and performance engineers to perform holistic profiling across all the layers in the system stack.

Before we get to the tools, it's important to highlight the NVIDIA Tools Extension (NVTX) and NVTX markers. These markers denote time ranges in a profiler's timeline view and allow different profilers to correlate events across the same phases.

For example, an NVTX range for `"forward"` will appear in both PyTorch profiler traces and Nsight Systems' timelines. This makes cross-tool analysis much easier at different layers of the stack. NVTX markers are supported by most modern AI frameworks and libraries, including PyTorch and anything related to the CUDA ecosystem.

NVTX markers are injected into code using either CUDA C++, PyTorch, or any C++ or Python library that supports NVIDIA GPUs (e.g., OpenAI Triton, PyCUDA, CuPy, cuTile, cuTe, CUTLASS, etc.). Most libraries already inject NVTX markers on your behalf for critical regions of code, such as `"train_step"`, `"forward"`, `"backward"`, `"optimizer_step"`, etc. But you can also inject them yourself using `torch.pro filer.record_function()` and `torch.cuda.nvtx.range_push()` in PyTorch, for instance.

Now that we've described how to annotate interesting sections of your code using NVTX markers, let's discuss the tools that can ingest, align, and visualize these markers. Common profiling tools are summarized in Table 13-1 along with their scope, key features, and typical use cases. This table can help you choose the right tool for each stage of your optimization journey.

Table 13-1. Summary of profiling and visualization tools

Tool	Scope	Features	Typical use case
PyTorch profiler (Kineto)	In-PyTorch op-level profiling (CPU/GPU)	NVTX marker support, shape recording, memory stats, trace export, identification of compile graph breaks	Fine-grained breakdown of model code; identify slow ops, GPU kernel launch overhead, or imbalance between forward/backward times.
Nsight Systems (nsys)	System-wide timeline (CPU, GPU, OS, I/O)	Unified timeline of CPU threads and GPU streams, NVTX integration, multiprocess support	End-to-end view of training/inference pipeline; detect data loader stalls, CPU-GPU overlap issues, or inter-GPU synchronization delays.
Nsight Compute (ncu)	GPU kernel analysis (per kernel)	Per-kernel hardware metrics, source correlation, roofline analysis, occupancy. and throughput reports	Deep dive into kernel efficiency after identifying hot kernels; determine if a kernel is memory bound or compute bound, and why.

Tool	Scope	Features	Typical use case
PyTorch memory profiler	GPU memory usage by operation	Memory snapshot timeline, per-op peak memory, `torch.cuda.memory_stats()` and `torch.cuda.mem_get_info()` integration	Diagnose fragmentation or unexpectedly high memory usage. See which ops allocate the most memory and when, to optimize memory footprint.
Linux `perf`	CPU profiling and system events	Sampling of CPU cycles/instructions/cache, flame graphs, off-CPU (sleep) analysis	Identify Python overhead (interpreter time, GIL contention), CPU-side data loading bottlenecks, or host OS scheduling issues.
Holistic Trace Analysis	Distributed training trace visualization	Browser-based Kineto trace explorer, multiworker trace aggregation; incorporates Perfetto backend	Analyze multi-GPU/multinode execution holistically. Find imbalances or idle times, verify overlap of communication with computation.
Chrome trace/ Perfetto	Offline trace viewing (web-based)	Web UIs for standard trace formats, advanced filtering (Perfetto SQL engine), easy trace sharing	Inspect traces without specialized software. It's useful for performance dashboards or remote collaboration on profiling data.
TorchEval (metrics)	Model metrics and performance logging	Standardized metrics API (throughput, accuracy, etc.), easy integration	Log and monitor model throughput/latency alongside accuracy during training and evaluation to correlate performance with model quality.
ExecuTorch	Deployment runtime for mobile, embedded, and edge devices with lightweight profiling hooks and export tooling	Model exporting, profiling, debugging, memory analysis, visualization	Use it to run PyTorch models and collect runtime metrics on constrained platforms, such as mobile, embedded, and edge devices, including Meta glasses, etc.

Here is a detailed description of each profiling tool in Table 13-1:

PyTorch profiler (Kineto)

Within PyTorch, the `torch.profiler`, based on the Kineto (*https://oreil.ly/Rwwwh*) open source project, provides operator-level breakdowns of CPU and CUDA/GPU runtimes. In addition, it can record input shapes and take memory snapshots using simple Python context managers. The PyTorch profiler can capture detailed timeline traces and hardware counters across training and inference workloads using NVTX ranges to align the events. It provides end-to-end observability from Python code down to the CUDA kernels—and even provides performance tips for common issues like data-loading stalls and inefficient CUDA code.

Nsight Systems (`nsys`*)*

For system-wide correlation, including CPU threads, GPU kernels, OS events, I/O, and interconnect traffic, NVIDIA Nsight Systems produces a unified timeline view. Its GUI and CLI reports can merge NVTX zones, Python call stacks, and CUDA streams across multiprocess and multinode runs. This makes it easy to spot where I/O and synchronization stalls might be impacting compute performance.

Nsight Compute (`ncu`*)*

Complementing Nsight Systems is NVIDIA Nsight Compute for per-kernel analysis. Nsight Compute collects detailed hardware metrics such as occupancy, memory bandwidth, and SM utilization. It can even generate roofline charts mapped to source code. Nsight Compute helps answer why a particular kernel is slow (e.g., memory bound, low occupancy) after other higher-level tools identify which kernels are the hotspots.

PyTorch memory profiler

PyTorch also includes a memory profiler, which you can enable with `pro file_memory=True` in `torch.profiler`. The PyTorch memory profiler breaks down peak and cumulative GPU memory allocations per operation. This reveals memory usage hotspots that might otherwise go unnoticed.

Linux `perf`

On the host side, Linux's `perf` tool can sample CPU hardware counters, including cycles, instructions, and cache misses—and unwind full C/C++ and Python call graphs. Starting with `perf sched`, you can see when CPU threads sit idle due to I/O or thread scheduling/synchronizing. This uncovers bottlenecks in data preprocessing loops, Python's GIL, or synchronization that can starve the GPU.

Holistic Trace Analysis

Meta's open source Holistic Trace Analysis (HTA) tool ingests PyTorch profiler traces to help diagnose multi-GPU bottlenecks. With HTA, one can visualize distributed training timelines with NVTX ranges alongside CUDA kernel traces. By drilling into memory allocation patterns over time, you can identify periods of idle GPU—including when GPUs are waiting on each other.

TensorBoard's PyTorch trace visualization plugin is deprecated. Instead, use Perfetto for timeline viewing and Meta's HTA for distributed trace analysis.

Chrome trace and Perfetto viewer

For web-based exploration of large PyTorch profiler trace files, you can use Chrome tracing (e.g., `chrome://tracing` in the browser) and Perfetto (*https://oreil.ly/r03TA*) UIs. These will load the JSON traces and let you interactively explore timeline views and flame charts. They even let you perform fine-grained filtering and SQL queries on the trace data—down to the submillisecond level for event tracing and correlation. Chrome traces and the Perfetto UI are ideal for sharing profile results between members of your organization for cross-team analysis. (Note: Chrome's legacy trace viewer is deprecated, so you should prefer the Perfetto web UI and SQL engine for viewing and analyzing traces.)

TorchEval (PyTorch's metrics library)

Another project, TorchEval (*https://oreil.ly/yluDV*), lets you log and monitor model throughput, latency, and quality metrics alongside training and evaluation metrics—all within a unified interface. TorchEval is PyTorch's official metrics library and provides a simple API for end-to-end performance and quality metrics. This library makes it easy to plug into training loops and integrate across distributed environments.

ExecuTorch

For embedded, mobile, and edge devices, the ExecuTorch (*https://oreil.ly/DUUR7*) project allows profiling, visualizing, and debugging PyTorch models in lightweight runtime environments like Meta glasses (*https://oreil.ly/wxUyA*). ExecuTorch has a small, dynamic memory footprint and supports Linux, iOS, Android, and embedded systems. Hugging Face supports ExecuTorch through its Optimum ExecuTorch (*https://oreil.ly/JyyxZ*) project, which makes this environment easy to integrate if you're already using the Hugging Face ecosystem, like Hugging Face Transformers (*https://oreil.ly/OMCWt*).

Next, let's dive into an example of using these profilers to identify performance bottlenecks. We'll then apply targeted optimizations and verify the performance improvements.

Profiling PyTorch to Identify Bottlenecks

Let's profile an example mixture-of-experts (MoE) transformer model to see these tools in action. MoEs are LLMs with multiple expert layers—each expert is a feedforward network. Routing tokens to experts is managed by an expert gating system. We will run a single training iteration, capture detailed performance traces, and analyze the output to guide our optimizations.

Using PyTorch Profiler

First, we set up the model and input. We use Hugging Face Transformers to load the model and tokenizer, move the model to GPU, and prepare a small batch of inputs, as shown here:

```python
# train.py

# Set up model and data
model_name = "..."

tokenizer = AutoTokenizer.from_pretrained(model_name)
device = torch.device("cuda")
model = AutoModelForCausalLM.from_pretrained(model_name).to(device)
optimizer = torch.optim.AdamW(model.parameters(), lr=1e-4, fused=True)

batch_size = 4
input_texts = ["MoEs are great."] * batch_size
enc = tokenizer(input_texts, return_tensors="pt", padding=True, truncation=True)
input_ids = enc.input_ids.to(device)
attention_mask = enc.attention_mask.to(device)
labels = input_ids.clone()   # For LM training, labels are the inputs
                             # (next-token prediction)
```

To avoid capturing one-time setup costs, we run a few warm-up iterations before profiling. This will prepare the model for analyzing and benchmarking by compiling JIT kernels, filling caches, etc. This way, our measured iteration is representative of steady-state performance. Here is the code to prepare the model:

```python
# Warm-up (not profiled)
for _ in range(5):
    with torch.autocast(device_type="cuda", dtype=torch.bfloat16):
        outputs = model(input_ids, attention_mask=attention_mask, labels=labels)
    loss = outputs.loss
    loss.backward()
    optimizer.step()
    optimizer.zero_grad(set_to_none=True)
```

Now we profile one training iteration using PyTorch's profiler and NVTX. We wrap the iteration in `torch.profiler.profile()` and mark high-level regions with `record_function` and NVTX ranges, including "forward", "backward", and "optimizer_step", as shown here:

```python
from torch import profiler

with profiler.profile(
    activities=[profiler.ProfilerActivity.CPU,
                profiler.ProfilerActivity.CUDA],
    record_shapes=True,   # record tensor shapes
    profile_memory=True,  # track GPU memory usage per op
    with_stack=True,      # enable stack tracing
```

```
    with_flops=True        # capture FLOPs counters
) as prof:
    with profiler.record_function("train_step"):
        # Forward pass
        torch.cuda.nvtx.range_push("forward")
        with torch.autocast(device_type="cuda", dtype=torch.bfloat16):
            outputs = model(input_ids, attention_mask=attention_mask,
                            labels=labels)
        loss = outputs.loss

        # end of forward
        torch.cuda.nvtx.range_pop()

        # Backward pass and optimization
        torch.cuda.nvtx.range_push("backward")
        loss.backward()
        torch.cuda.nvtx.range_push("optimizer_step")
        optimizer.step()

        # end of optimizer_step
        torch.cuda.nvtx.range_pop()
        optimizer.zero_grad()

        # end of backward
        torch.cuda.nvtx.range_pop()
```

In this code, the PyTorch profiler is recording all CPU and GPU activities during the
train_step. We use record_function("train_step") to define a top-level region.
We also insert NVTX markers for the subphases ("forward", "backward", "opti
mizer_step"). These markers will appear in profiler timelines to delineate phases of
the iteration.

The profiler can also highlight compiled versus noncompiled regions of the model.
We'll cover the PyTorch Compiler, graph breaks, and mechanisms to mitigate graph
breaks later in this chapter—as well as the next chapter.

For instance, when using torch.compile, the trace will show events like Compiled
Function and indicate any graph breaks (see Figure 13-1). This helps pinpoint where
the model fell back to eager execution, which will guide further optimizations.

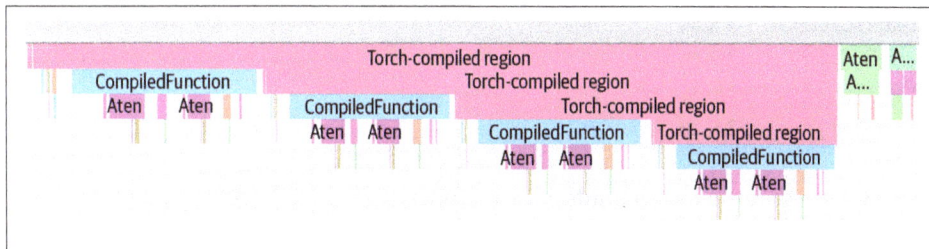

*Figure 13-1. Compiled (left and middle, pink) versus noncompiled (right, green) regions
(source: https://oreil.ly/Z_fJG)*

After execution, we can examine the operation-level results by calling `prof.key_aver ages().table()` to print a concise table of the top operators by runtime. In the next code block, we request the top 10 operations sorted by their self CUDA time, which is the time spent in each operation's own CUDA kernels excluding child operations spawned by the kernel. The top 10 operations by CUDA execution time are summarized in Table 13-2:

```
with profiler.profile(
    activities=[ProfilerActivity.CPU,
                ProfilerActivity.CUDA],
    record_shapes=True,
    profile_memory=True,
) as prof:
    train_step(...)

...

print(
    prof.key_averages()
        .table(
            sort_by="self_cuda_time_total",
            row_limit=10,
            fields=["self_cuda_time_total",
                    "calls"]
        )
)
```

Table 13-2. Profiler's top 10 operations by CUDA execution time over one training iteration

Operation	Self CUDA total	Calls
aten::matmul	43.00 ms	128
aten::linear	35.50 ms	64
dispatch	18.70 ms	2
combine	12.10 ms	2
aten::layer_norm	10.20 ms	16
aten::softmax	5.70 ms	4
aten::scatter	4.10 ms	16
aten::gather	3.60 ms	16
aten::to	2.90 ms	8
aten::add_	2.20 ms	64

Here, we see that the matrix multiplication operations (`aten::matmul`, and its use in `aten::linear`) dominate the CUDA time and consume the majority of the iteration. These operations correspond to the expert feed-forward network (FFN) GEMMs. Specifically, there are 128 calls to `matmul` per iteration. This makes sense since we have 64 experts—and each expert does a `matmul` in both the forward and backward passes.

In Table 13-2, we see the next largest costs are from the `dispatch` and `combine` operations. These are custom C++/CUDA kernels that redistribute tokens to experts—and then gather the outputs of the expert. The `dispatch` operation runs twice—once in the forward pass and once in the backward pass—for a total of 18.7 ms. The `combine` ran twice for 12.1 ms total. Together, these two operations account for another 30.8 ms of GPU time. The remaining time is spread across other smaller ops like layer norms, activations, etc.

The key takeaway from this profiling example is that the expert FFN `matmul` is the top bottleneck, followed by the dispatch and combine kernels. Together, these dominate a training iteration's runtime. To improve performance further, we should target those operations either by optimizing them directly or by reducing the number of times they're called.

System Profiling with Nsight Systems and NVTX Timelines

The NVTX markers that we inserted make it straightforward to analyze the timeline with Nsight Systems. To aggregate metrics per phase, we can profile the code using `nsys` with an NVTX-based summary, as shown in the CLI command here:

```
nsys profile \
    --output=profile \
    --stats=true \
    -t cuda,nvtx \
    python train.py
```

Here, the `-t cuda,nvtx` option instructs Nsight Systems to trace both CUDA API calls and NVTX ranges. After profiling, we can open the `profile.nsys-rep` file (`--output=profile`) in the Nsight Systems GUI or use the CLI to print the NVTX summary to the terminal. We can then use the CLI to generate the NVTX GPU Projection Summary using one of the following commands on the `profile.nsys-rep` file, as shown here to validate ranges against projected GPU work with Nsight Systems:

```
nsys stats --report=nvtx_gpu_proj_sum \
    profile.nsys-rep

# or

nsys recipe nvtx_gpu_proj_sum \
    profile.nsys-rep
```

You can use one of these commands in your continuous build and integration pipelines to monitor and detect any performance regressions. The results of this CLI command are summarized in Table 13-3.

Table 13-3. NVTX GPU projection summary for one `train_step` iteration using Nsight Systems

NVTX range	GPU time (ms)	Self GPU time (ms)	Child GPU time (ms)	Instances (calls)
train_step	138.0	0.0	138.0	1
forward	60.5	60.5	0.0	130
backward	58.3	58.3	0.0	130
optimizer_step	19.2	19.2	0.0	1

Here, we see the `train_step` range includes the forward, backward, and optimizer subranges. This NVTX GPU Projection Summary confirms that the total GPU time under `train_step` is 138 ms. This time matches the sum of the `forward`, `backward`, and `optimizer_step` times from the PyTorch profiler output in Table 13-2. This shows consistency between tools.

And although Table 13-3 shows a single `optimizer_step` call, its NVTX range actually brackets all 64 `aten::add_` CUDA kernel launches (one `add_` per expert as shown in Table 13-2) under the single `optimizer_step` marker.

Note that Nsight Systems groups the 64 `aten::add_` calls (e.g., 64-way expert parallelism strategy) into a single `optimizer_step` marker because it uses the CUDA Profiling Tools Interface (CUPTI) (*https://oreil.ly/oO6Ti*) to capture NVTX push/pop events on the host. It then "projects" asynchronous GPU kernel execution times onto these CPU-defined intervals. As such, it sums the durations of every kernel with GPU start/end timestamps that fall between the corresponding push and pop calls. This produces one cumulative GPU time that exactly matches the total of the individual `aten::add_` kernels.

> Because NVTX markers have very low overhead when no profiler is attached, this projection mechanism is ideal because it adds negligible overhead while still providing end-to-end correlation of GPU work with high-level code regions.

The forward and backward ranges each have self GPU time equal to their total time since we didn't choose to nest deeper ranges inside of them. As such, child GPU time is 0 ms. However, `train_step` has nearly all of its time as child GPU time since it's just a wrapper around the nested phases.

The NVTX GPU projection summary also shows that, in each iteration, we observed 130 GPU activities inside `train_step`. These include kernel launches and other device operations such as memory copies, so they are not strictly one-to-one with kernels.

As you can see in Table 13-3, the 130 GPU kernel calls happen for both the backward and forward passes as well. This one-to-one correspondence between operations and NVTX instances means that our instrumentation captures every important operation.

> The NVTX summary we show in Table 13-3 is a convenient text overview. For visual analysis, the timeline GUI can show overlapping kernel execution, CPU thread states, and even CUDA API overhead events. In practice, you want to verify that host-side data loading and preprocessing are overlapping with GPU compute in the visual timeline. Any large gaps, or "bubbles," indicate a problem. Small gaps for synchronization are expected and appropriate.

On a multi-GPU run, the Nsight Systems or HTA timeline view can reveal if NVLink or InfiniBand/Ethernet is being utilized effectively—or if a node is starved for work while waiting for communication or network delays. This would hint at suboptimal synchronization or load imbalance.

It's important to trace GPU communication events, including NCCL all-reduce calls and NVLink/NVSwitch activity using Nsight Systems and HTA to provide traces. These help verify that the GPUs stay busy in massive GPU domains such as an NVL72-based system.

Careful profiling makes sure the system is using proper inter-GPU synchronization and balancing the workload in these large NVLink clusters. Let's now zoom in on one of the most expensive kernels in the system: the matrix multiply, or matmul.

Kernel Roofline Analysis for General Matrix Multiply (GEMM)

To dive deeper and analyze the expert matmul, we invoke the CLI profiler Nsight Compute (ncu) to target specific GEMM kernels by name. We'll collect roofline-related metrics to determine if it's compute bound or memory bound, as shown here:

```
ncu \
  --target-processes all \
  --kernel-name-regex "matmul" \
  --metrics \
    gpu__time_duration.avg, \
    gpu__dram_throughput.avg.pct_of_peak_sustained_elapsed, \
    lts__throughput.avg.pct_of_peak_sustained_elapsed, \
    sm__sass_thread_inst_executed_op_fp32_pred_on.sum, \
    sm__warps_active.avg.pct_of_peak_sustained_active \
  --csv full \
  -o matmul_roofline_report \
  python train.py
```

Here, we are collecting hardware counters for any kernel whose name matches "matmul". Specifically, we collect a few key metrics, including GPU DRAM bandwidth and

L2 bandwidth as a percent of peak (gpu__dram_throughput.avg.pct_of_peak_sustained_elapsed, lts__throughput.avg.pct_of_peak_sustained_elapsed), FP32 instruction count as a compute proxy (sm__sass_thread_inst_executed_op_fp32_pred_on.sum), kernel time (gpu__time_duration.avg), and achieved occupancy (sm__warps_active.avg.pct_of_peak_sustained_active).

> Metric identifiers can vary slightly across Nsight Compute releases. If a metric is not found, use the UI to locate the current name and substitute accordingly. Here, we are profiling SM and DRAM % of peak sustained and achieved occupancy.

After applying the optimizations discussed until now, like reducing precision, fusing kernels, and increasing arithmetic intensity, we can rerun the ncu command to verify that our optimizations made a positive impact. Table 13-4 shows the comparison before and after applying these optimizations to improve arithmetic intensity.

Table 13-4. Roofline analysis for the expert matmul kernel before and after arithmetic intensity optimizations

Kernel configuration	% of peak FLOPS (SM compute throughput)	% of peak memory BW (memory throughput)	Achieved SM occupancy	Characteristic
Baseline	50%	70%	60%	Memory bound (stalling on memory transfers)
Optimized	85%	40%	80%	Compute bound (near hardware roofline)

Here we see, in the baseline run, the primary GEMM kernel achieves only about 50% of peak compute FLOPS, 70% of peak memory bandwidth, and a moderate 60% SM occupancy (average active warps per SM). This occupancy is not enough to fully hide memory latency.

> There is no universal occupancy target. Many high-performance kernels achieve full latency hiding at 25–50% achieved occupancy. Use Nsight Compute's occupancy metrics together with stall-reason breakdowns and eligible warps per active cycle to judge whether more occupancy would reduce stalls for the kernel. If the kernel can't schedule enough warps to cover the stall periods, this will lead to idle cycles since memory requests aren't being serviced quickly enough.

The baseline metrics indicate a kernel that is memory bound since its execution is stalled by memory transfers. The result is a substantial amount of unused compute capacity, which further reinforces that this workload is not currently compute bound. The goal is to make this kernel more compute bound to take advantage of the large number of FLOPS available with this GPU.

In the optimized version (e.g., fusing kernels, increasing arithmetic intensity, and reducing memory movement), the peak FLOPS increases to 85%, peak memory bandwidth drops to 40%, and occupancy increases to 80%. We effectively shifted the kernel from memory bound to compute bound—much closer to the hardware's roofline limits, as shown in Figure 13-2.

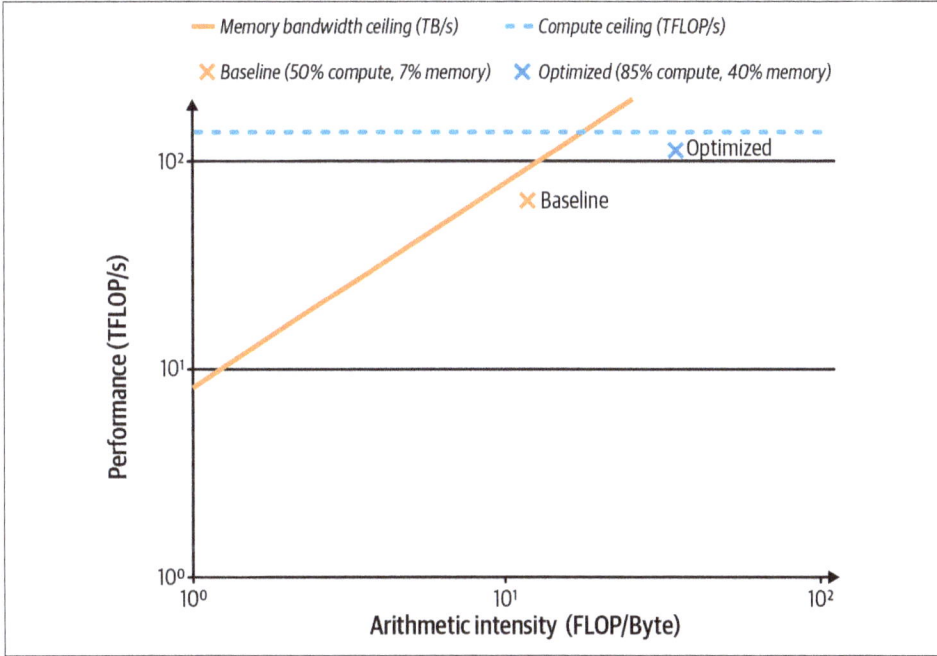

Figure 13-2. Roofline chart before and after increasing arithmetic intensity of this kernel

Up to this point, our profiling has focused on GPU performance. It's also important to not waste time on the CPU or performing I/O. In the next section, we continue our profiling journey on the host side.

CPU and GPU Profiling with Linux perf

To get a more holistic view of where time is being spent across both the host and device, we can use Linux `perf` to analyze CPU cycles, cache misses, branch misses, etc. We can then use these insights to drive a series of optimizations, apply them one by one, and measure the improvements.

First, let's run a lightweight `perf stat` to gather CPU-side statistics during the MoE training run on a node with an ARM-based Grace CPU paired with a Blackwell GPU. Here is the CLI command followed by example output:

```
perf stat -e \
  cycles,instructions,cache-misses,branch-misses \
  python train.py

  Performance counter stats for 'python train.py':

# 0.600 CPUs utilized
1,200.345 msec task-clock
# Approximately 2.0 GHz
2,400,567,890      cycles
# 1.58 insn per cycle
3,800,123,456          instructions
# 0.32% of all cache refs
12,345,678         cache-misses
# 0.12% of all branches
4,567,890          branch-misses

  1.234567890 seconds time elapsed
```

This report from `perf stat` shows the CPU utilization, cycles, instructions per cycle (IPC), and cache/branch misses. In our run, the task clock shows ~1.2 seconds with only ~60% (0.600) of a single CPU core used over the measured interval. This is expected, as the GPU is doing most of the heavy lifting. The low cache-miss and branch-miss rates hint that memory access patterns and branch prediction were relatively efficient on the CPU side for this workload.

However, the instructions per cycle (IPC) measurement of just 1.58 shows that the CPU is issuing well below the eight instructions per cycle theoretical maximum IPC for a single Grace CPU core (ARM Neoverse V2). This indicates potential inefficiencies such as memory latency, I/O stalls, or host-compute issues in this specific workload.

We can explore further using `perf record` and `perf report` to pinpoint which Python and C++ functions dominate the CPU execution time during training. These CLI commands are shown here:

```
perf record -F 2000 -g --call-graph dwarf -o perf.data \
    python train.py
```

Here, we use `perf record` to collect samples at 2000 Hz (`-F 2000`) and capture full C/C++ and Python call stacks by specifying `-g --call-graph dwarf`. DWARF (*https://dwarfstd.org*) stands for Debugging With Attributed Record Formats, and it's a standard debugging data format embedded in compiled binary files (e.g., ELF files). The DWARF output trace is saved to `perf.data` (`-o perf.data`). We then use `perf report` to generate a summary report of the hottest call stacks and their sample percentages:

```
perf report --stdio -n -g -i perf.data

# Samples  Command   Shared Object        Symbol
# ........  ........  ..................  ................................
    45.0%   python    python               py::forward <...> /src/train.py
    20.5%   python    python               aten::matmul
    10.2%   python    python               dataloader_iter_next
     8.7%   python    libnccl.so           ncclAllReduce
     5.3%   python    libc.so.6            read
    ...     ...       ...                  ...
```

Here, we see that the Python interpreter's forward function, the Python side of our training loop, accounts for 45.0% of CPU samples. PyTorch's C++ aten::matmul operation accounts for 20.5%, the DataLoader's iterator next function for 10.2%, an NCCL all-reduce call for 8.7%, and I/O reads for 5.3%.

These percentages tell us where to invest our optimization effort. Based on this profile, we address each bottleneck with a specific mitigation plan to improve performance of our system:

Excess Python overhead (45% in py::forward*)*
Use PyTorch's JIT compiler using torch.compile (discussed in the next section) to eliminate interpreter overhead and fuse Python-side operations into optimized CUDA code.

Large matmul *hotspot (20.5% in* aten::matmul*)*
Either use the PyTorch Compiler to optimize this code or move this critical matrix multiply into a custom CUDA C++ kernel (e.g., fused kernel) to bypass Python and use the optimized CUDA code directly.

Data loading stalls (10.2% in dataloader_iter_next*)*
Increase PyTorch's DataLoader num_workers. A common guideline is one worker per CPU, but you can experiment with more to find the right level of I/O parallelization. Just make sure you don't oversubscribe the CPU cores. You should also enable persistent_workers=True so that worker processes stay alive across epochs and avoid startup overhead for each epoch. Fuse or parallelize multiple torch.utils.data.DataPipe. This can reduce Python overhead in complex data pipelines.

Gradient synchronization overhead (8.7% in ncclAllReduce*)*
Optimize multi-GPU communication. For instance, tune DDP gradient bucket size (bucket_cap_mb) empirically. A larger bucket can reduce per-collective overhead, but it also becomes ready later in the backward computation. Depending on model/layer timing, this may improve or hurt overlap with backward computation. Tune for your specific workload. You can also consider gradient compression

techniques or NVIDIA's NCCL compression for 8-bit gradients to reduce bandwidth usage. These may incur a slight cost to accuracy.

Host I/O bottleneck (5.3% in `read syscalls`*)*

Use pinned memory (`pin_memory=True`) and nonblocking GPU copies (`.to(device, non_blocking=True)`) in the DataLoader to overlap CPU-to-GPU data transfers. Also, you can batch file reads or bundle many small files into an optimized dataset format like Arrow, WebDataset (tar shards), TFRecord, or Parquet chunks that facilitate large sequential reads. It's best to prefer contiguous shard formats over per-sample files. Prefer pinned host buffers when using a larger prefetch depth (e.g., `prefetch_factor=4` or `8`). Combined with `persis tent_workers=True`, your system will keep loader threads busy since compute-communication are overlapping efficiently. This will eliminate per-file overhead when reading many small files in large corpora.

These approaches, combined with large OS read-ahead and NVMe SSDs, will boost I/O throughput. Also, newer filesystems and storage libraries like NVIDIA Magnum IO can help pipeline data efficiently to the GPU.

After formulating this plan, you should systematically apply each optimization and measure the effect. Remember to implement and test these optimizations one by one to verify that each actually improves performance. This helps avoid situations in which multiple changes interact in unexpected ways. By isolating each change, you know which adjustments have a positive effect and which do not.

On systems with the NVIDIA Performance Monitoring Unit (PMU) (*https://oreil.ly/ xd6wu*) drivers present, you can use `perf` to sample NVIDIA chip interconnect and fabric counters alongside CPU counters, including NVLink-C2C devices exposed under /sys/bus/event_source/devices as `nvidia_nvlink_c2c*`, for instance. Verify availability with `perf list` and by checking the `nvidia_pmu` entries under `sysfs`.

> Linux `perf` for NVIDIA PMUs is limited to device-level link and fabric events such as NVLink-C2C on Grace-Blackwell. SM pipeline, warp stall, and memory throughput counters remain CUPTI and Nsight tools only. These PMUs do not expose SM-level kernel metrics. For SM utilization, occupancy, and memory throughput, use Nsight Compute or a CUPTI-based profiler. Make sure to set `NVreg_RestrictProfilingToAdminUsers=0` to allow non-root profiling of SM-level hardware counters.

Once the PMU devices are present, you can collect CPU and NVIDIA events together. Use symbolic event names reported by `perf list`:

```
perf list | grep -i nvidia
```

```
perf stat -a \
  -e nvidia_nvlink_c2c0_pmu_0/cycles/ \
  -e cycles,cache-misses \
  python train.py
```

Here, the cycles event on the NVLink-C2C PMU lets you correlate GPU interconnect activity with host CPU behavior. The following is example output from the preceding `perf stat` command, which shows the NVLink C2C PMU recorded activity during the run while the CPU incurred cycles and cache misses:

```
Performance counter stats for 'python train_deepseek_v3.py':

    3,567,890,123  nvidia_nvlink_c2c0_pmu_0/cycles
       45,678,901  cycles
        7,890,123  cache-misses

    2.345678901 seconds time elapsed
```

Our initial profiling revealed that GPU compute (e.g., expert matrix multiplies) and GPU communication (e.g., dispatch and combine operations) are the primary bottlenecks based on the PyTorch profiler and Nsight tools. However, CPU, data loading, and GPU collective communication operations also impact performance as `perf` demonstrates by showing which CPU threads and interconnect PMUs are active during the slow regions.

> To dig into additional link and fabric request counters, pick additional NVIDIA PMU events that appear on your system from `perf list` and add them to the `perf stat` command, as shown previously.

In short, by combining high-level CPU throughput metrics and call graph hotspots from `perf` with device metrics and timelines from Nsight Systems and Nsight Compute, you can build a holistic performance story across host and device. Start by addressing the largest CPU-side bottlenecks and data stalls. Next, optimize GPU communication and tune the GPU kernels.

PyTorch Compiler (torch.compile)

One of the quickest wins in PyTorch is to use the PyTorch compiler with `torch.compile()`. The compiler stack includes TorchDynamo, AOT Autograd, and TorchInductor, which capture graphs, fuse ops, and generate high-performance code for the target backend (e.g., NVIDIA GPUs).

The PyTorch Compiler can eliminate a lot of Python interpreter overhead and GPU kernel launch latency by fusing together many small operations into larger kernels.

After doing our baseline profiling, we enabled `torch.compile` on the model to see if we could get an easy speedup. Next, let's describe this process—and the results.

Using the PyTorch Compiler

Using the PyTorch compiler with the default settings is straightforward and requires no code changes besides wrapping the model as shown here: `model = torch.com pile(model)`. Under the hood, TorchDynamo traces the Python code, AOT Autograd captures the backward pass, and TorchInductor, which leverages OpenAI's Triton for GPU kernel code generation (as discussed in the next chapter), produces efficient fused kernels automatically.

The compiler observes our model's forward pass and identifies many opportunities to fuse consecutive operations, such as elementwise activations, layer norms, etc. It generates fused kernels for those operations—and also for parts of the backward pass. The result is significantly fewer kernel launches and less CPU overhead per iteration.

The compile step does introduce some overhead on the order of seconds—or even minutes for very large models—but this cost is amortized over long training jobs or repeated inference runs. Fortunately, TorchInductor caches compiled kernels so that subsequent runs don't pay the compile cost again. The PyTorch community is also continuously working to improve compile/startup performance by allowing you to save and reuse compiled artifacts across runs. Use `torch.compiler.save_ cache_artifacts()` and `torch.compiler .load_cache_artifacts()` to persist TorchInductor outputs across runs or nodes. This reduces startup on long-running training or serving.

One example is the PyTorch Mega-Cache feature. This is an end-to-end compile cache that lets you save compiled kernels to disk and reload them in future runs. With PyTorch Mega-Cache, you can compile once (e.g., offline) and reuse the optimized kernels across multiple training sessions. This helps to reduce startup time. You'll still benefit from TorchInductor's kernel optimizations like warp specialization, but you'll avoid recompiling the graph each time.

> You can even use this compile cache on other compute nodes. If you do this, make sure CUDA, PyTorch, and Triton versions are compatible across the nodes.

It's worth noting that PyTorch's Compiler applies sophisticated optimization techniques internally. For example, we mentioned warp specialization in Chapter 10. TorchInductor's autotuner generates multiple kernel variants across tile sizes, memory access patterns, etc. It will apply techniques like memory-warp versus compute-warp specialization behind the scenes. It will then choose the fastest variant for your hardware automatically.

TorchInductor supports prologue and epilogue fusion around GEMM kernels. For example, bias-add comes before the `matmul`. And, after the `matmul`, the epilogue consists of elementwise operations such as activation, dropout, and residual.

By merging these kernel prologue and epilogue operations into a single optimized kernel, TorchInductor reduces memory traffic, minimizes kernel-launch overhead, and increases occupancy. You can verify this with the profiler, which will show higher SM utilization.

This optimization complexity remains entirely transparent to the developer since PyTorch presents a clean, tensor-centric interface without exposing CUDA-level warp details. So while you won't see "memory warp" or "compute warp" flags in the PyTorch API, just know that these techniques are being used under the hood. Once the code is compiled, you will notice the benefits of warp specialization in profiler metrics, including higher occupancy, fewer memory latency stalls, and increased SM utilization.

To illustrate the benefit of a compiled mode, let's compare PyTorch's eager mode versus compiled execution on an MoE model. We'll time a single training iteration of the model in regular eager mode and then again with the `"max-autotune"` compiled mode. The code is shown here, followed by the example output:

```python
import torch
from transformers import AutoModelForCausalLM, AutoTokenizer

# ---- Setup Model ----
device = 'cuda'
model_name = "..."
tokenizer = AutoTokenizer.from_pretrained(model_name)
model = AutoModelForCausalLM.from_pretrained(model_name).to(device)
optimizer = torch.optim.AdamW(model.parameters(), lr=1e-4, fused=True)

# ---- Create a dummy batch of token IDs ----
batch_size = 4
input_texts = ["MoE's are awesome!"] * batch_size
enc = tokenizer(input_texts, return_tensors="pt", padding=True, truncation=True)
input_ids = enc.input_ids.to(device)
attention_mask = enc.attention_mask.to(device)
labels = input_ids.clone()  # for causal LM, labels = input_ids

# ---- Make runs deterministic ----
torch.backends.cudnn.benchmark = False
torch.backends.cudnn.deterministic = True

# --- Eager timing ---
torch.cuda.synchronize()
start = torch.cuda.Event(enable_timing=True)
```

```python
end = torch.cuda.Event(enable_timing=True)

for _ in range(iters_warmup):
    out = model(input_ids, attention_mask=attention_mask, labels=labels)
    loss = out.loss if hasattr(out, "loss") else out
    loss.backward()
    optimizer.step()
    optimizer.zero_grad(set_to_none=True)

torch.cuda.synchronize()
start.record()
for _ in range(iters_meas):
    out = model(input_ids, attention_mask=attention_mask, labels=labels)
    loss = out.loss if hasattr(out, "loss") else out
    loss.backward()
    optimizer.step()
    optimizer.zero_grad(set_to_none=True)
end.record()
torch.cuda.synchronize()
print(f"Eager mode step time: {start.elapsed_time(end)/iters_meas:.3f} ms")

# --- Compile the model (choose one mode)
# enables graph trees
compiled_model = torch.compile(model, mode="reduce-overhead")
# Alternatives:
# more tuning, longer compile
# compiled_model = torch.compile(model, mode="max-autotune")
# balanced
# compiled_model = torch.compile(model, mode="default")

# Warm-up compiled
for _ in range(iters_warmup):
    out = compiled_model(input_ids, attention_mask=attention_mask, labels=labels)
    loss = out.loss if hasattr(out, "loss") else out
    loss.backward()
    optimizer.step()
    optimizer.zero_grad(set_to_none=True)

torch.cuda.synchronize()
start.record()
for _ in range(iters_meas):
    out = compiled_model(input_ids, attention_mask=attention_mask, labels=labels)
    loss = out.loss if hasattr(out, "loss") else out
    loss.backward()
    optimizer.step()
    optimizer.zero_grad(set_to_none=True)
end.record()
torch.cuda.synchronize()
print(f"Compiled mode step time: {start.elapsed_time(end)/iters_meas:.3f} ms")
```

In this case, PyTorch eager mode takes roughly 248 ms per iteration. After warming up and letting the compiler perform its optimizations, the compiled mode runs in about 173 ms. Our compiled version, using `"max-autotune"`, runs ~30% faster than eager execution. Actual speedup varies with model structure, batch size, and dynamic shapes. Dense models dominated by a single large GEMM may only see <10% speedup.

These savings come primarily from combining many small GPU kernels. Small GPU kernels are common in an MoE architecture for token dispatch/combine and per-token activation patterns. By fusing these small operations into fewer, larger kernels, we keep intermediate data in faster on-chip memory—such as registers and shared memory—rather than repeatedly moving data to and from global device memory (HBM).

> For highly dynamic token routing used by MoE architectures, pre-fer default or `max-autotune-no-cudagraphs`. Then switch to `max-autotune` once input shapes stabilize—or when you use CUDA Graph Trees with limited discrete shapes.

In this case, many of the small operations, like dispatch/combine, activation functions, etc., are fused away by TorchInductor. If you examine the trace of the compiled run, you'll see far fewer GPU kernels on the timeline. Instead, there will be fewer, but slightly longer-running, kernels that correspond to merged operations performing multiple steps at once.

Over many iterations, the benefit is even more pronounced as the one-time compilation overhead is amortized. Profiling the compiled model's execution shows far fewer GPU kernel launches, as many operations that were separate in eager mode are now fused together.

It's worth noting that if a dense model is dominated by one massive GEMM due to a large linear layer, for example, it may see only modest gains (e.g., < 10%) from `torch.compile`. This is because the model is likely using Tensor Cores efficiently—and because there is little opportunity for kernel fusion and Python overhead removal.

However, sparse architectures like MoE, with hundreds of medium-sized `matmul` operations, will see big wins since compilation reduces Python overhead, lowers kernel launch latency, and fuses multiple steps into optimized kernels. As such, the PyTorch compiler leads to significantly larger performance gains for MoEs compared to dense models.

In addition to automatic operator fusion, you can integrate user-defined custom kernels directly into the `torch.compile` workflow. This approach combines the best of both worlds since it uses compiler-managed graph-level optimizations for general patterns while giving you full control when needed.

For instance, you can write a specialized Triton or CUDA kernel for a performance-critical operation and register it as a custom operator. When the model is traced and compiled, TorchInductor will treat it as a single fused operation within the larger execution graph. The result is a combination of custom hand-tuned code embedded in a fully optimized, compiler-managed execution graph.

TorchInductor's flexibility lets your custom kernel benefit from the compiler optimizing the surrounding operations (e.g., fusion with adjacent layers, etc.). In practice, this means you can use your own high-performance kernel without losing PyTorch compiler's ability to optimize the rest of the model.

In short, by using PyTorch compile, including its `"max-autotune"` mode within our training loop, you can get decent speedups on modern GPUs with relatively low effort. This can be verified holistically using `torch.profiler`, Linux `perf`, Nsight Systems, Nsight Compute, and other helpful profilers.

Compiling Versus Writing Custom Kernels

With a compiler backend like TorchInductor, many operations will be fused into efficient kernels automatically. As we saw, simply using `torch.compile` gives a decent-sized boost with minimal effort. However, there may be times when the automatically generated code is not as optimal as a custom-crafted kernel—or when an operation isn't captured by the compiler at all. This raises the question: when should you rely on the compiler's fusion versus writing a custom CUDA kernel yourself?

For most cases, using high-level `torch.compile` with graph capture—and TorchInductor under the hood—is preferred. This is much less effort than writing custom CUDA kernels—and often produces good enough performance improvement without specialized coding.

TorchInductor already applies many advanced optimizations internally, such as fusion of elementwise operations, merging of layer operations, layout optimization, etc. Writing fused kernels by hand would be time-consuming and brittle, whereas the compiler can do these automatically in most cases.

If your model uses a novel operation or pattern that the compiler doesn't handle well, you may need to write a custom kernel and integrate (*https://oreil.ly/Wt25P*) a custom operator with PyTorch. In the next chapter, you'll see how to do this in more detail.

In short, use `torch.compile` as the first resort for performance tuning since it's easy, sufficient, and relatively "free." Creating custom kernels is the next level of optimization and is used when built-in automation isn't enough. Only after that should you consider writing custom kernels for the remaining hotspots to fuse certain unsupported optimizer operations or specialized attention patterns. However, even for specialized attention patterns, PyTorch provides the FlexAttention API (`prefill`) and

FlexDecoding API (`decode`), which are the preferred ways to implement custom attention kernels in PyTorch for training and inference, as we'll see in an upcoming section.

Compilation Modes and Trade-Offs in Speed, Memory, and Compile Time

PyTorch provides several modes for `torch.compile` that tune the compiler's aggressiveness and capabilities for different scenarios. You can explicitly select a mode using `torch.compile(model, mode="...")`. The choices are `"default"`, `"reduce-overhead"`, `"max-autotune"`, and `"max-autotune-no-cudagraphs"`. Each mode provides a combination of options regarding CUDA Graphs, autotuning, and optimization level. The modes are summarized in Table 13-5.

Table 13-5. Summary of compilation modes and their key characteristics

Mode	Description	Compile time	Extra memory	Notable features
`default`	Balanced optimizations (good speed without long compile or extra mem); includes minor autotuning; may use CUDA Graphs for stable segments	Low–Medium	No	General fusion, basic autotuning
`reduce-overhead`	Reduces per-iteration overhead (good for small batches); ideal for inference or small batches; automatically skips CUDA Graphs if it detects dynamic shapes to preserve correctness	Medium	Yes (workspace caching)	Uses CUDA Graphs (if possible) to eliminate launch overhead
`max-autotune`	Maximizes runtime performance (best for long runs); longer compile time; best for aggressive tuning for a large amount of SMs and GPU memory	High (slow compile)	Maybe (if graphs are used)	Aggressive Triton autotuning; enables CUDA Graphs on GPU
`max-autotune-no-cudagraphs`	Does everything `max-autotune` does but without CUDA Graph capture. Best for dynamic shapes or for debugging issues masked by CUDA Graphs	High	No	Same as `max-autotune` but disables graphs for flexibility

Here's a detailed description of the modes in Table 13-5:

`default`

This is the default mode if no mode is explicitly specified. This mode provides a balance of reasonably fast compiled code without excessive compile time or memory usage. It will do standard optimizations and use the default TorchInductor backend. This mode is often best for large models where compile time needs to be moderate—or when memory is tight. This mode includes minor autotuning and may use CUDA Graphs for stable segments. But it tries to balance speed and compile-time cost.

reduce-overhead

This mode focuses on minimizing Python and runtime overhead. This is especially useful for small models—or models that perform a short number of executions per iteration. In these cases, even a little bit of overhead hurts performance. This mode leverages CUDA Graphs aggressively to eliminate per-iteration launch overhead. It may also allocate some extra memory for persistent use, such as workspace memory that is reused. This avoids frequent CUDA malloc and free calls. For example, it might cache a large working tensor instead of allocating it each iteration. This mode will automatically skip CUDA Graphs and fall back to eager if it detects dynamic shapes. It does this to preserve correctness.

This mode can speed up inference and training in low-latency scenarios—at the cost of some additional memory. Note that CUDA Graphs require that the graph's memory addresses stay constant, so this mode can be used only when input sizes do not change and certain operations, such as dynamic-shape operations, are not present. Otherwise, graphs would break or be recompiled. The compiler will automatically fall back if it can't apply a CUDA Graph in a given segment.

max-autotune

This mode generates the fastest possible code without regard for compile time. It will run extensive autotuning of kernels by trying many tiling configurations for matrix multiplications, for instance, and utilize any known performance optimizations in TorchInductor. On modern GPUs, `max-autotune` also enables CUDA Graphs by default for stable execution.

The compilation process in this mode can be significantly longer—on the order of minutes for a large model. It's intended for scenarios in which you compile once and run the model many times, such as running long training jobs or deploying a model that will handle a lot of requests over time. In exchange for long upfront compile times, you often get the best runtime performance. For instance, after automatic tuning, your `matmuls` might run with an optimal block size for your specific GPU and tensor shapes. This gives this mode an edge over default heuristics.

max-autotune-no-cudagraphs

As the name suggests, this mode is the same as `max-autotune` but with CUDA Graph capture disabled. This is important for cases in which CUDA Graphs interfere with desired runtime behaviors that are not compatible with CUDA Graphs. For instance, since CUDA Graphs require static shapes and memory addresses, you can't use varying input shapes or rely on allocating new memory for each iteration.

Also, when measuring performance, using CUDA Graphs can mask the overhead of launching kernels, which might not be desired in some benchmarks. So this mode allows maximal kernel optimization without CUDA Graphs. This will help maintain flexibility and allow you to debug any issues that CUDA Graphs might introduce (or mask), such as shape-dependent control flow or occasional allocator readdressing during graph capture. Use this mode when input sizes vary each iteration—or for debugging issues that might be masked by the use of CUDA Graphs.

For most use cases, the default mode is a good start. It's meant to give sizable speed-ups with minimal hassle. If you find that your model still isn't fast enough and you can tolerate longer compilation, try `reduce-overhead` and `max-autotune` for potentially better fused kernels—especially if your model is dominated by large `matmul` operations that can be autotuned. `max-autotune` can sometimes regress latency on some models. Be sure to profile the different modes for your specific workload and hardware.

On the other hand, if you are optimizing a very small model or a portion of code where Python overhead is the bottleneck, such as a tight training loop with lots of small tensor operations, using `reduce-overhead` can produce the best gains by removing virtually all kernel-launch runtime overhead using CUDA Graph capture. Just be mindful of the constraints of `reduce-overhead`. It works best when the workload per iteration is consistent and fits the graph-capture requirements, including no dynamic shape changes, no new memory allocations, etc.

The `max-autotune-no-cudagraphs` mode is more of a specialized option. It's useful if you want maximum kernel optimization but either cannot use graphs due to varying input sizes or want to measure raw kernel performance without graph amortization.

In all cases, it's wise to profile and measure after changing the PyTorch compiler mode. The different modes exist because one size doesn't fit all in performance engineering. Furthermore, you should monitor memory usage when choosing a mode. Modes that use CUDA Graphs will allocate large, static buffers that increase memory footprint.

For extremely memory-constrained cases, you might prefer this no-graphs mode to avoid the extra memory overhead of CUDA Graphs. Next, let's discuss how to inspect what the compiler is doing, including whether it created one graph or many—or whether it used CUDA Graphs, etc.

Regional Compilation

For models with many identical blocks, such as Transformers and MoEs, you can use regional compilation to decrease cold-start execution time. Additionally, it's useful to reduce recompilation churn—all without sacrificing the power of kernel fusion.

Specifically, regional compilation reduces compile time by compiling the repeated block (e.g., a Transformer block) once and reusing that code across all occurrences.

PyTorch supports regional compilation with `torch.compiler.nested_com` `pile_region()`. This API marks a block as a nested compile region. This region is compiled the first time and then reused for subsequent runs.

In addition, regional compilation preserves correctness. If the compiler detects new input conditions (`shape`, `dtype`, `device`, `stride`, `globals`), it will transparently recompile the region.

Regional compilation benefits inference engines and short jobs in which startup latency matters—or when graph invalidations occur frequently. The performance of code compiled regionally is similar to the throughput of code compiled in full.

Profiling and Debugging Compiler Performance Issues

When using `torch.compile`, it's useful to know how to debug cases in which the compiler is unable to optimize part of your model—for instance, if certain operations are not being fused and you suspect a "graph break" is causing fallback to eager execution. PyTorch provides tools to inspect these situations.

> Modern PyTorch versions implement partial support for dynamic shapes using shape guards. These can eliminate some unnecessary graph breaks. However, truly dynamic workloads may still require falling back to eager execution (or use `max-autotune-no-cudagraphs`) to ensure correctness.

`torch._dynamo.explain(model)` prints a report of any graph breaks (e.g., parts of the model not captured by TorchDynamo), the reason the graph break occurred, and which parts of the model were not captured by TorchDynamo. It will also list the operations or data-dependent control flows that were not captured by TorchDynamo and needed to be executed in the slower Python eager mode.

A common cause of graph breaks is unsupported operations in the model. The Dynamo `explain()` output will make suggestions on how to get more details and help diagnose the issue. Taking advantage of these hints can help pinpoint the exact operation or control flow that caused the break.

Another useful technique is to set the environment variable `TORCH_LOGS="+dynamo"` or `TORCH_LOGS="+dynamo,+inductor"` before running your script. The + prefix enables verbose (`DEBUG`-level) logging for components like TorchDynamo and TorchInductor in the `torch.compile` pipeline. The verbose logs include details about graph breaks, fallbacks to eager mode, and compilation phases. If a model is unexpectedly slow with `torch.compile`, these logs can help identify when and where the execution is exiting the compiled graph.

If the model has truly dynamic shapes or dynamic control flow that can't be resolved at compile time, you might need to guide the compiler. For example, you can break the model into sections that are compilable and leave the truly dynamic parts to run in Python.

To profile and benchmark the kernels generated by TorchInductor, you can specify the `TORCHINDUCTOR_UNIQUE_KERNEL_NAMES=1` and `TORCHINDUCTOR_BENCHMARK_KER NEL=1` environment variables. When these are set, Inductor will generate benchmark harness code for the generated kernel modules. The logs generated by this harness code can help pinpoint unexpected graph breaks and performance issues.

You can also mark part of the code as `torch._dynamo.mark_dynamic(tensor, dim)` to let the compiler know to expect dynamic shapes. This can eliminate unnecessary graph breaks due to shape mismatches. We'll cover these techniques in more detail in the next chapter's deep dive into the PyTorch compiler.

In short, when `torch.compile` doesn't produce the expected speedup, you can use `torch._dynamo.explain()`—along with compiler logging—to identify which operations or code regions caused the fallback. From there, you will need to apply a workaround such as replacing an operation, reshaping a tensor differently, accepting less dynamic behavior, or simply disabling compilation for that specific part of the model. The result is that you keep the performance benefits for the majority of the model while still handling edge cases.

PyTorch Optimized Attention Mechanisms

Transformer models spend significant time in their attention mechanisms. You can apply several PyTorch attention-optimization techniques to make sure it's not a bottleneck. Here is a quick summary of a few of these techniques and when to use them:

Scaled dot-product attention (SDPA)
   PyTorch's high-level API `torch.nn.functional.scaled_dot_product_atten tion`, or SDPA, automatically uses the fastest available attention kernel for the given hardware (e.g., FlashAttention). Use this for a no-hassle speedup when your model's attention pattern and dtype are supported by the selected backend (Flash, memory-efficient, or math). If it's not supported, it will fall back to the standard attention implementation.

FlexAttention
   A compiler-based approach for custom sparsity patterns in attention. FlexAttention can be substantially faster for specific sparse attention patterns (e.g., block-sparse or sliding-window attention) by generating optimized kernels for these patterns, as shown in Figure 13-3. Use FlexAttention for special cases that `scaled_dot_product_attention` does not support.

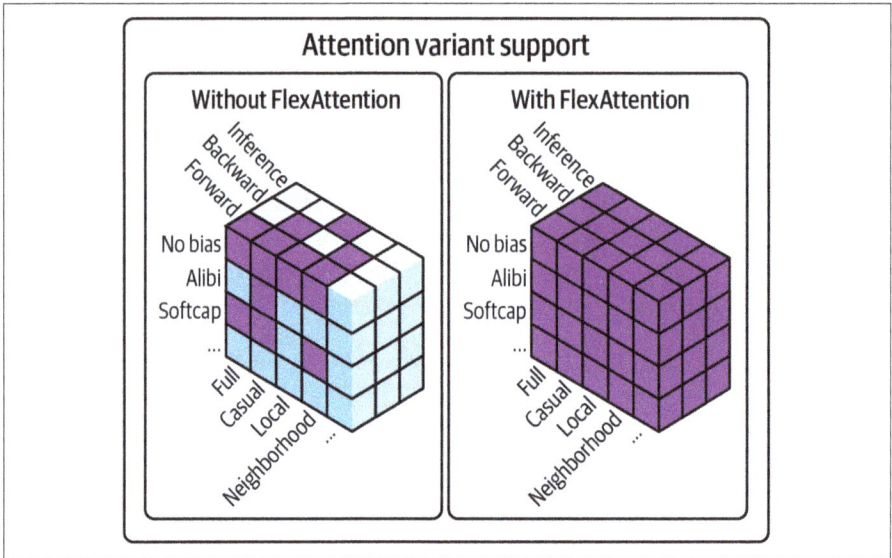

Figure 13-3. FlexAttention provides support for custom attention variants

FlexDecoding

This is a counterpart to FlexAttention that optimizes the decoding or text generation phases. FlexDecoding integrates with `torch.compile` and dynamic cache
layouts. It uses compile-time optimizations for the decoder side of sequence generation, including KV caching efficiently across time steps. FlexDecoding can
speed up autoregressive generation by reducing redundant compute during
decoding. FlexDecoding is intended for LLM inference workloads, including
those with long-generation sequences. It does not change training-time attention
semantics.

Context parallel

Context Parallel shards attention along the sequence-length dimension across
participating devices or ranks to scale context length. Use the `context_paral`
`lel()` API to scope replacement of `scaled_dot_product_attention` with
context-parallel-aware kernels. The mechanism splits query-key-value (QKV) by
sequence across ranks and synchronizes during attention, rather than parallelizing attention across threads within a single GPU.

PyTorch Architecture Optimization (torchao), Quantization, Sparsity, and Pruning

PyTorch Architecture Optimization (torchao) brings together quantization, sparsity, pruning, and related numerical-debugging tools into a single namespace. Its quantization subpackage (`torchao.quantization`) provides common FX-graph-mode workflows, including post-training quantization (PTQ), quantization-aware training (QAT), and `QConfigMapping` APIs to convert and optimize models for INT8, FP8, and emerging formats.

Beyond quantization, `torchao` supports pruning (`torchao.pruning`) and sparsity techniques like 2:4 and block sparsity (`torchao.sparsity`). These provide significant speedups with minimal loss in accuracy.

`torch.compile()` integrates with the `torchao` framework for quantization. Under the hood, TorchDynamo captures each submodule's computation as an optimized graph, then TorchInductor emits hardware-aware kernels that leverage `torchao`. This produces consistent, end-to-end performance improvements for both model training and inference. Meanwhile, it preserves precise control over numerical formats and memory layouts. This makes it a great library for production-level performance optimizations such as quantization.

Concurrency with CUDA Streams

As covered in an earlier chapter, CUDA streams enable concurrency and overlap of operations on the GPU. By default, PyTorch schedules all operations on the device's default stream, stream 0, sequentially. However, many tasks are independent, and, if resources permit, a GPU can perform them in parallel using multiple streams. For example, GPUs can overlap data transfers with compute—or run separate neural network branches concurrently—by using separate, nondefault streams.

> Remember that modern GPUs have multiple DMA copy engines. Using separate streams for H2D copies can achieve truly parallel data transfers without blocking compute. This hardware support makes stream concurrency even more effective.

In PyTorch, you create a stream with `torch.cuda .Stream()`. You can then launch work on this stream using the Python context manager, with `torch.cuda .stream(stream)`, or by explicitly assigning operations to that stream. PyTorch will issue operations (e.g., memory transfers, CUDA kernels, etc.) into the specified stream in a FIFO order—just as it does on the default stream.

Overlapping Communication and Computation

A common use of CUDA streams is to overlap host-to-device (H2D) data loading with GPU computation. This helps mask the data transfer latency incurred when using an external device such as a GPU—relative to the CPU running on the host.

For instance, one stream can copy the next batch of input data from CPU to GPU memory while the default stream is busy training on the current batch. By the time the default stream is ready for the next batch, the data transfer is already done, and the GPU can process this next batch. This effectively hides the I/O latency. Here is an example of using two streams, the `compute_stream` (default) and the `transfer_stream` (nondefault), to overlap data transfer and compute in PyTorch:

```python
# Set up streams
device = 'cuda'

# for H2D data transfers
transfer_stream = torch.cuda.Stream(device=device)

# for compute
compute_stream  = torch.cuda.default_stream(device=device)

# Create an iterator so we can preload "next" batches
dataloader_iter = iter(dataloader)

# Preload the very first batch onto GPU
first_batch = next(dataloader_iter, None)
if first_batch:
    with torch.cuda.stream(transfer_stream):
        next_inputs, next_labels = (
            first_batch[0].to(device, non_blocking=True),
            first_batch[1].to(device, non_blocking=True),
        )

for _ in range(len(dataloader)):
    # 1) Wait for transfer of `next` batch to finish, then swap into compute var
    # Multiple copy engines allow H2D/peer copy concurrency.
    # Verify parallelism in Nsight Systems (Copy engines lanes)
    # And tracing/profiling tools (HTA, etc.)
    compute_stream.wait_stream(transfer_stream)
    inputs, labels = next_inputs, next_labels

    # 2) Kick off transfer of the *following* batch on the transfer_stream
    batch = next(dataloader_iter, None)
    if batch:
        with torch.cuda.stream(transfer_stream):
            next_inputs, next_labels = (
                batch[0].to(device, non_blocking=True),
                batch[1].to(device, non_blocking=True),
            )
```

```
# 3) Run forward/backward on compute_stream
with torch.cuda.stream(compute_stream):
    outputs = model(inputs)
    loss    = loss_fn(outputs, labels)
    loss.backward()
    optimizer.step()
    optimizer.zero_grad(set_to_none=True)
```

This example uses two CUDA streams: a dedicated transfer stream for asynchronous host-to-device copies and the default compute stream for model work. This hides H2D latency and matches PyTorch's recommended pattern (*https://oreil.ly/W0o0e*) for overlapping communication and computation.

Specifically, while the model is processing a batch on the default stream, the next batch's data transfer is already underway on the `transfer_stream`. Synchronizing with `compute_stream.wait_stream(transfer_stream)` before consuming the preloaded batch enforces correct ordering without a full device-wide barrier. And the `.to(device, non_blocking=True)` calls make sure that the copy uses asynchronous DMA-based copies that don't block the calling CPU thread.

Using `next(dataloader_iter, None)` gives explicit control over when transfers are enqueued versus when the kernel operations run. This makes sure one batch of data is moving on the transfer stream while another batch is executing on the compute stream, as shown in Figure 13-4.

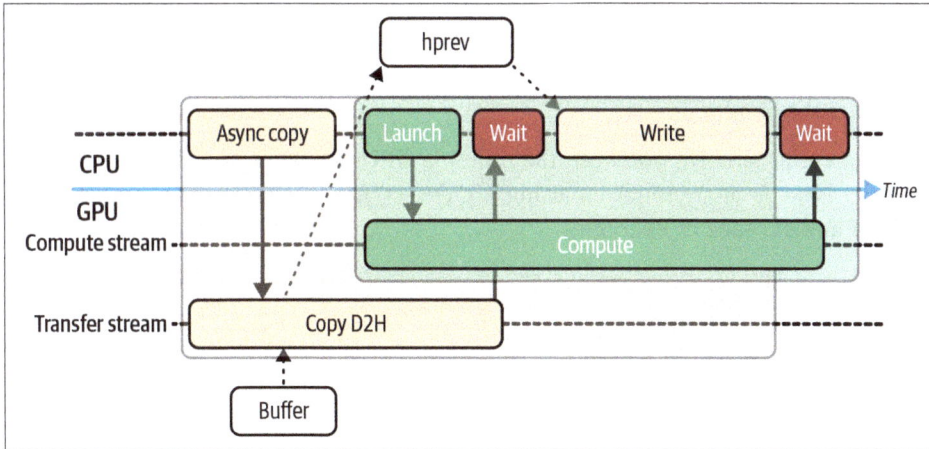

Figure 13-4. Overlapping compute and data transfer with dedicated compute and transfer streams

Additionally, by pulling from `dataloader_iter` ahead of time and storing in `next_inputs next_labels`, this code separates batch loading (running on the CPU in `transfer_stream`) from batch processing (running on the GPU in `compute_stream`).

This split means you always have one batch in flight for each stream. This decouples data loading from compute and maximizes overlap.

> Always profile with Nsight Systems or the PyTorch profiler when adding streams. Look at GPU utilization, and, if done correctly, you'll see near 100% utilization with transfer and compute overlapping. If utilization drops—or you see data transfers and compute happening sequentially—double-check for any implicit synchronizations such as CUDA tensor print()—or extra CUDA synchronizations in your code.

Stream Synchronization with Events

When using multiple streams, it's sometimes necessary to coordinate between them to make sure that one stream's work is done before another stream uses its results, for instance. A lightweight way to synchronize specific points is using CUDA events, as discussed in Chapter 11.

With CUDA events, you can record an event on one stream and make another stream wait for that event. This avoids the heavyweight full synchronization of `torch.cuda.synchronize()` and, instead, synchronizes only the necessary streams needed to process an individual event.

In fact, even in a multi-GPU context, events can be used to synchronize work across devices. In this case, one GPU records an event on its device stream while another GPU waits for the event on its device stream. This is how NCCL handles dependencies under the hood.

By using events smartly, you keep the multiple GPUs working in parallel as much as possible. Next is an example of using CUDA events to synchronize two streams, `stream1` and `stream2` in PyTorch:

```
# Disable timing on the event since we're using it purely for synchronization.
event = torch.cuda.Event(enable_timing=False)

# In first stream:
with torch.cuda.stream(stream1):
    kernel_launch(...)
    event.record()             # record event at end of work in stream1

# In another stream or on host:
stream2.wait_event(event)    # make stream2 wait until event is signaled

with torch.cuda.stream(stream2):
    other_kernel_launch(...)
```

In this code, we record an event at the end of some work on `stream1`. Later, before launching work on `stream2`, we call `stream2.wait_event(event)`. This inserts a dependency such that `stream2` will not execute its next kernel until the event is signaled by `stream1` reaching that point. Events are useful for scheduling lightweight dependencies between streams, as they avoid heavy, global synchronizations that will stall all stream execution.

Let's revisit the PyTorch data loader/overlap example in the previous section and rewrite it to synchronize with CUDA events. We are using the same pair of streams from earlier (`transfer_stream` and `compute_stream`), but we're adding a `transfer_done` CUDA event to synchronize at a fine-grained, event-specific level:

```python
import torch

device = 'cuda'

# for H2D copies
transfer_stream = torch.cuda.Stream(device=device)

# for compute
compute_stream  = torch.cuda.default_stream(device=device)
# sync-only event (low overhead)
transfer_done = torch.cuda.Event(enable_timing=False)

# Iterator so we can preload ahead
dataloader_iter = iter(dataloader)

# ---- Preload first batch ----
first_batch = next(dataloader_iter, None)
if first_batch:
    with torch.cuda.stream(transfer_stream):
        next_inputs, next_labels = (
            first_batch[0].to(device, non_blocking=True),
            first_batch[1].to(device, non_blocking=True),
        )
        # mark when H2D is done
        transfer_done.record(stream=transfer_stream)

for _ in range(len(dataloader)):
    # ---- Sync: wait for the transfer to complete ----
    compute_stream.wait_event(transfer_done)
    inputs, labels = next_inputs, next_labels

    # ---- Kick off next transfer ----
    batch = next(dataloader_iter, None)
    if batch:
        with torch.cuda.stream(transfer_stream):
            next_inputs, next_labels = (
                batch[0].to(device, non_blocking=True),
                batch[1].to(device, non_blocking=True),
            )
            transfer_done.record(stream=transfer_stream)
```

```
# ---- Compute on the compute stream ----
with torch.cuda.stream(compute_stream):
    outputs = model(inputs)
    loss    = loss_fn(outputs, labels)
    loss.backward()
    optimizer.step()
    optimizer.zero_grad(set_to_none=True)
```

This is the same overlap pattern as the previous section, but it uses a CUDA event for the transfer → compute synchronization. This is in contrast to the `wait_stream()` mechanism used in the other example.

This code still uses `next(dataloader_iter)` to preload batches ahead of time (same as the example in the previous section). This way, data transfer and compute are always overlapping.

However, in this example, the `transfer_done` event is recorded with `transfer_done.record(stream=transfer_stream)` on the `transfer_stream` right after the asynchronous copy is enqueued. This timestamps the event.

The `compute_stream.wait_event(transfer_done)` then stalls the `compute_stream` until the copy is complete and the `transfer_done` event is triggered. It then consumes the prefetched batch and performs its compute operations on the `compute_stream`.

Besides data loading, CUDA streams are useful in a lot of different contexts. Let's discuss how they're used in MoE models.

Using CUDA Streams with MoE Models

In practice, transformer-model layers are sequentially dependent, so you can't arbitrarily run layers in parallel. However, in an MoE architecture, different experts can run concurrently on separate CUDA streams since their computations are independent.

Each expert processes a distinct segment of the input. At the join point, the expert outputs are aggregated. It's essential that each expert writes only to its assigned slice of the output tensor. If two experts accidentally write to overlapping memory regions, this will introduce a race condition, which can corrupt the results—or trigger synchronization issues caused by the nondeterministic order of writes from the experts.

To avoid such issues, you should make sure to use proper stream-level synchronization (e.g., stream events) and verify that memory is cleanly partitioned across expert kernels. By enforcing this separation between expert execution and output aggregation, you will maintain correctness without sacrificing parallelism.

NVIDIA's Compute Sanitizer (*https://oreil.ly/u_7gc*) can detect concurrency and synchronization issues in CUDA code, including race conditions and deadlocks. Also, you can set `CUDA_LAUNCH_BLOCK ING=1` to force synchronous kernel execution. This will surface ordering and dependency bugs by making kernel execution deterministic. This will reveal if outputs are being consumed before they're fully produced.

In our example, each expert could, in theory, run on its own stream—or even its own GPU if the framework is extended to multiple GPUs. In this case, synchronization—ideally using stream events—is needed when gathering the results.

Pipeline parallelism, or pipelining microbatches through different model stages on different devices, and serving multiple inference requests are two scenarios that naturally benefit from multiple streams. In a pipeline parallel workflow, for instance, each stage of the model has its own stream that processes a different microbatch concurrently. Meanwhile, it's also communicating with neighboring stages.

In multirequest inference serving, each request's model execution can be launched in its own stream. With sufficient hardware resources, this can increase throughput by overlapping inference computations—at the cost of some per-request latency due to resource-sharing overhead.

In short, CUDA streams help to squeeze extra performance out of your hardware by overlapping work across multiple kernels, stages, or requests. They require careful synchronization to avoid race conditions. But, when used correctly, they can hide latency and keep a GPU more fully utilized.

It's recommended to continuously profile your code when introducing concurrency. And keep in mind that sequential execution at 100% utilization may actually perform better than parallel execution that introduces resource contention. Often, though, streams let you utilize parts of the GPU that would otherwise sit idle. Finding the right balance is important.

Always make sure you are launching on the intended stream. Accidentally using the default stream, for example, can reintroduce unnecessary serialization. This is easy to mess up, so it's worth repeating again.

Reducing Kernel Launch Overhead with CUDA Graphs

We've seen in earlier chapters that CUDA Graphs eliminate per-iteration launch overhead, reduce CPU launch overhead, and eliminate tiny idle gaps between kernels. And removing even the smallest idle gaps leads to higher effective utilization—and more consistent iteration times. Now let's show how to use them in PyTorch.

Capturing a CUDA Graph and Preallocating Memory

PyTorch provides a `torch.cuda.CUDAGraph` API to capture and replay CUDA Graphs. The general usage pattern is to first warm up the model by running a few iterations normally to initialize all necessary data and allocations. Next, you create a `CUDAGraph` object and a dedicated, nondefault CUDA stream to isolate the capture.

> When using `"reduce-overhead"` or `"max-autotune"`, the compiler will automatically capture CUDA Graphs for you if the model is stable. In this case, you don't even need to write this boilerplate since it's done for you automatically if you're using the PyTorch compiler with these modes. And if your model has varying shapes each iteration, consider the `"max-autotune-no-cudagraphs"` mode to avoid graph capture, as CUDA Graphs currently require static shapes.

You then perform a full pass of the model's execution to record the sequence of operations using the capture stream specified in the `torch.cuda.graph()` context. Once the operations are captured in the CUDA Graph, you can `replay()` the graph on new inputs as needed (e.g., model training or inference.)

Before capturing a CUDA Graph, all static memory used during capture must be preallocated—and preferably at its maximum size. These buffers include inputs, outputs, and intermediate tensors. If any new memory allocation happens during capture, the graph will fail with an error such as "operation not permitted when stream is capturing."

To reduce fragmentation and maximize contiguous memory space for these fixed buffers, you can invoke `torch.cuda.empty_cache()` immediately before entering the capture block. This will clear unused cached memory and give the allocator the best chance to lay out your prereserved buffers without interruption.

> Frequent use of `torch.cuda.empty_cache()` can disrupt allocator efficiency and incur longer-term performance costs. Treat this call as a one-time safety mechanism when capturing a graph—and not a regular maintenance tool.

Remember that PyTorch's caching allocator supports CUDA's asynchronous allocator (`cudaMallocAsync`) to reuse fixed memory addresses. However, this does not bypass CUDA Graphs' requirement to not create new allocations within the graph.

You still need to allocate fixed-size buffers upfront to avoid a runtime error if you try to allocate new memory inside the graph. Make sure all tensors reach their maximum required size during the warm-up prior to graph capture. We'll cover more about this in the upcoming graph replay section.

You need to use a dedicated, nondefault stream for graph capture to avoid interference with any operations that should not be included in the CUDA Graph. Here is a code snippet demonstrating how to capture a CUDA Graph in PyTorch with a dedicated `capture_stream`:

```
g = torch.cuda.CUDAGraph()
capture_stream = torch.cuda.Stream()

# Prepare static inputs and outputs
static_input = torch.randn(batch_shape, device='cuda')
static_output = torch.empty(output_shape, device='cuda')

# Warm-up step on capture_stream to allocate buffers without recording
with torch.cuda.stream(capture_stream):
    tmp = model(static_input)
    static_output.copy_(tmp)

# ensure warm-up is complete
capture_stream.synchronize()

# Begin graph capture
with torch.cuda.graph(g, stream=capture_stream):
    tmp = model(static_input)
    static_output.copy_(tmp)

# ensure capture is complete before using the graph
capture_stream.synchronize()
```

In this code, we first allocate `static_input` and `static_output` on the GPU with fixed shapes. We run one warm-up iteration on `capture_stream` to ensure that any memory needed inside `model(static_input)` is allocated—and to perform any one-time setup.

> By preallocating the output buffer and using `static_out put.copy_(tmp)` in both warm-up and capture phases, the code writes its results into a fixed memory region. This makes the captured CUDA Graph correct, replayable, and reproducible without unexpected tensor allocations.

We then synchronize the `capture_stream` to make sure that the warm-up step is fully complete before beginning the actual graph capture. Next, we enter the `torch.cuda.graph(...)` context on the same stream and rerun the model forward pass.

During the capture phase, no kernels are actually launched. Instead, the operations are just recorded into the CUDA Graph object g. After exiting the capture block, we need to synchronize once more to make sure the recording is finalized.

When capturing a CUDA Graph, strict isolation is essential. Operations on the capture stream must not be affected by activity on any other streams. Even a seemingly unrelated kernel launch on another thread can invalidate the capture. This could lead to runtime errors like "operation not permitted when stream is capturing."

This error happens if you accidentally perform CUDA operations on other streams while the capture is in progress. In this case, it invalidates the graph context and triggers this error. This can also happen if you launch a kernel on the capture stream that performs dynamic memory allocation, like tensor creation or calling `torch.empty` during capture.

> Always call `capture_stream.synchronize()` both before starting the graph capture and after exiting it. This ensures that all operations are correctly recorded and that the graph is ready for safe replay. The previous code example follows this best practice.

After capturing the graph, it can be replayed on any stream, including the default stream—and regardless of which stream was used for capture. If you trigger any CUDA operations that depend on the graph completing fully, you must synchronize before running the operations, as shown next. Otherwise, because the graph runs asynchronously when replayed, the CUDA operations that depend on the graph results may run before the graph completes execution:

```
# replay the graph which writes to static_output
g.replay()

# synchronize on the stream that is replaying the graph
torch.cuda.current_stream().synchronize()

# Now it's safe to read or post-process the output
print(static_output)
...
```

Without this explicit synchronization, your program could proceed and incorrectly assume that the graph has finished executing and written its results to static_out put. If no synchronization is in place, the code may read stale or partially written data because the graph may not have finished writing to static_output. This scenario will cause nondeterministic behaviors, corrupted reads, subtle race conditions, and deadlocks.

Replaying the Graph

To replay the graph with new data, you copy the new inputs into the preallocated input tensors, static_input, and call g.replay(). The GPU will execute the entire captured sequence of operations using the current contents of those tensors as input. The graph will place the results in the preallocated output tensor (static_output), as shown here:

```
# load new data into pre-allocated input tensor
static_input.copy_(new_batch)

# execute the captured graph
g.replay()

# retrieve the output (clone if you plan to modify it)
result = static_output.clone()
```

Here, we load new_batch data into the memory space of static_input and then call g.replay(). The graph runs the exact captured operations using the current static_input data and writes the outputs into static_output. We can then use or clone static_output as needed.

It's recommended to validate that the graph's output matches a normal execution for a few test inputs to make sure the capture was successful. Also, remember that you cannot directly print or call .item() on static_output without syncing. If needed, do result = static_output.cpu().numpy() after replay and outside of any asynchronous regions for debugging.

Since the graph reuses the same input, output, and internal memory allocations each time, it will overwrite the same output tensor on each iteration. So if you need to preserve the output beyond a single iteration, you need to clone() the buffer, as shown in the previous code. This is why we need to make sure that the allocations in the warm-up/capture step cover the maximum sizes needed. Remember that the graph cannot handle additional memory allocations on the fly.

It's worth noting that after using a CUDA Graph, certain PyTorch operations will not be reflected until you recapture the graph. For instance, if you change model weights on the fly and outside of the graph, these updates won't apply because the graph has its own copy of operations. As such, graphs work best in steady-state loops in which operations are repeated on each iteration.

Also, when using `cudaMallocAsync` to preallocate memory for a CUDA Graph, it will reuse the same memory addresses during replay that it preallocated during graph capture—or during warm-up if the graph is loaded from disk, for instance. This way, subsequent graph replays do not require additional memory.

By default, every instance of a CUDA Graph uses its own private memory pool. This way, you're guaranteed that each graph preallocates its own memory buffers and does not compete with other instances of the graph. In other words, two identical graphs will not compete for memory if they're replayed concurrently since they each use their own memory pool and buffer space.

You can choose to share a memory pool between graph instances by passing `torch.cuda.graph(pool=...)`. However, this is useful only in very special cases when you want to purposely orchestrate related graphs to reuse the preallocated memory buffers for performance reasons. For example, consider simultaneously running multiple inference graph variants—each using a different batch size (e.g., 1, 2, 4, 8, etc.). In this case, you can reduce overall memory usage by having the shape-specialized variants reuse a single, large memory allocation for PagedAttention, which uses a varying-size tensor called `block_tables`.

This approach is described in a FireworksAI blog post (*https://oreil.ly/FeMsO*). Here, they compile a different CUDA Graph variant for each batch size. And, instead of creating a separate memory pool for each graph, they share a single shared memory pool across all graph variants. By compiling graphs in decreasing order of batch size, memory from the shared pool is reused from the largest variant (e.g., 8, in this case). Smaller batch-size graph variants are serviced by the larger allocated buffers from a previous iteration. This way, multiple graph variants are supported without using excessive GPU memory.

> This is an obscure and clever implementation choice that requires careful coordination of the memory segments. However, it does reduce the total GPU memory usage when running multiple shape-specialized graphs simultaneously. This is great for deployment scenarios in which minimizing overall memory usage is critical.

Best Practices for CUDA Graphs

CUDA Graphs are a powerful way to reach peak steady-state throughput in both training and inference. They are especially useful for large deployments in which CPU overhead and kernel-launch variability are hurting performance. On modern GPUs, which execute thousands of operations extremely quickly, graphs become essential to keep the GPU devices busy and minimize per-kernel launch overhead.

It's worth noting that PyTorch's `torch.compile` uses CUDA Graphs under the hood in many cases—unless explicitly disabled. CUDA Graphs are used to minimize kernel launch overhead for compiled models. Here are a few important things to remember when using CUDA Graphs:

Avoid allocating memory during graph capture

> Remember that you can't dynamically allocate GPU memory inside the graph capture. Any tensor that's needed should be allocated beforehand during the warm-up step, as shown previously. If your graph needs temporary buffers, use PyTorch's graph-aware caching allocator using the `cudaMallocAsync` CUDA backend. This way, each replay reuses the same buffer addresses. Make sure these temporary tensors are created during the warm-up phase (before graph capture) using their maximum potential size. This will preallocate all the needed memory upfront.

Keep the graph structure fixed

> A captured graph cannot change the sequence of operations, tensor shapes, or memory sizes. If your workload has occasional shape variations, one strategy is to capture multiple graphs (e.g., one for each input size you expect) and then select the appropriate graph at runtime. Alternatively, you can disable graphs for those iterations (PyTorch's compiler has a mode `max-autotune-no-cudagraphs` for such cases).

> CUDA supports a low-level Graph Management API (*https://oreil.ly/FXkzK*), including `cudaGraphExecUpdate()`, described in an earlier chapter, which allows minor modifications to a captured graph. However, as of this writing, PyTorch does not expose this. Within PyTorch currently, it's best to treat graphs as immutable.

Capture as much as possible

> Include as much of the training loop as you can in the graph—ideally an entire iteration (forward pass, backward pass, optimizer step, and any all-reduce communications). The more you capture, the more CPU overhead and launch latency you eliminate.

Also, consider capturing multiple iterations in one graph if memory allows (including loop unrolling, etc.). Although this makes the graph bigger, it can often improve throughput by enabling even more optimizations across iterations. This comes at the cost of flexibility, but it's worth exploring and profiling.

When capturing large graphs in multi-GPU setups, use CUDA stream priorities if supported. For instance, you can set NCCL calls to a lower-priority stream if you want the compute kernels to run at a higher priority and not be delayed. Graph capture will record these priorities as well.

> NVIDIA's MLPerf submissions (and internal benchmarks) often capture the entire training step into one graph per iteration. This includes the forward pass, backward pass, optimizer, and all-reduce communication steps. This eliminates nearly all runtime overhead (launch jitter, etc.), at the expense of memory and flexibility.

Plan for memory reuse

After a graph is captured, you can't free or reallocate any tensors used by that graph—or change any of their sizes. It's best to reserve a bit more capacity than needed by capturing with the maximum batch size that you expect. This way, a slightly larger input won't break the graph later during replay.

For example, if your maximum batch size is 64 but you occasionally run with 96, consider capturing with batch size 96 just to be safe. It's usually better to capture the worst-case scenario, run smaller batches, and waste a bit of memory—rather than risking a graph failure.

> Remember to account for the sizes of the optimizer states (e.g., the Adam optimizer intermediate buffers) since they're part of model-training graphs. These are somewhat easy to forget!

When used appropriately, CUDA Graphs can provide significant speedups for large model training and inference workloads. With compute optimizations in place, let's turn to memory optimizations in PyTorch.

CUDA Graph Trees (PyTorch Compiler Internal)

We've covered the PyTorch compiler in a previous section, but in the context of CUDA Graphs, it's worth mentioning PyTorch's CUDA Graph Trees (*https://oreil.ly/iQNJ2*). These are used by `torch.compile`, and specifically `mode="reduce-overhead"`, to compile and cache separate static graphs for each input shape.

Once a static graph is recorded, its tensor dimensions must remain fixed. Any new input shape will trigger a fresh recording and cache entry. To maximize cache hits and reduce graph captures, it's recommended to keep your input shapes as consistent as possible across iterations. Fewer distinct shapes mean more reuse of the recorded graphs and less overhead.

It's worth noting that you don't typically invoke the CUDA Graph Trees API directly. This is handled for you by `torch.compile` when specifying `mode="reduce-overhead"`.

Since CUDA Graphs require static addresses and steady control flow, full-graph capture is difficult for LLM inference, which supports variable input sizes, batch sizes and number of steps (e.g., sampling, KV cache growth, host-side decisions, etc.)

For model training, CUDA Graph Trees allow multiple captured subgraphs to share a single memory pool across forward and backward captures. CUDA Graph Trees are also useful for inference since they allow dynamic subgraph selection depending on the input shape and batch size. This is commonly called "piecewise capture." PyTorch leverages CUDA Graph Trees to maintain per-shape piecewise captures and manage shared pools.

> The piecewise capture pattern provided by CUDA Graph Trees is the mechanism used by the vLLM inference engine to support different graphs for different input shape and batch-size combinations. We cover vLLM and inference-engine optimizations in more detail starting in Chapter 15.

Profiling and Tuning Memory in PyTorch

Large models can be limited by GPU memory capacity and memory bandwidth. Additionally, inefficient memory use such as memory fragmentation can hurt performance even if HBM capacity is sufficient. You can address memory issues on several fronts, including memory-allocator tuning, activation checkpointing, memory offloading, and input-pipeline optimization.

Also, PyTorch has a memory profiler that's built into `torch.profiler` by enabling `profile_memory=True`, as shown earlier. You can use this to find out which operations allocate a lot of memory—and try to address those operations first, as shown in the visualization in Figure 13-5 generated by the PyTorch memory visualizer tool (*https://oreil.ly/tX6gA*).

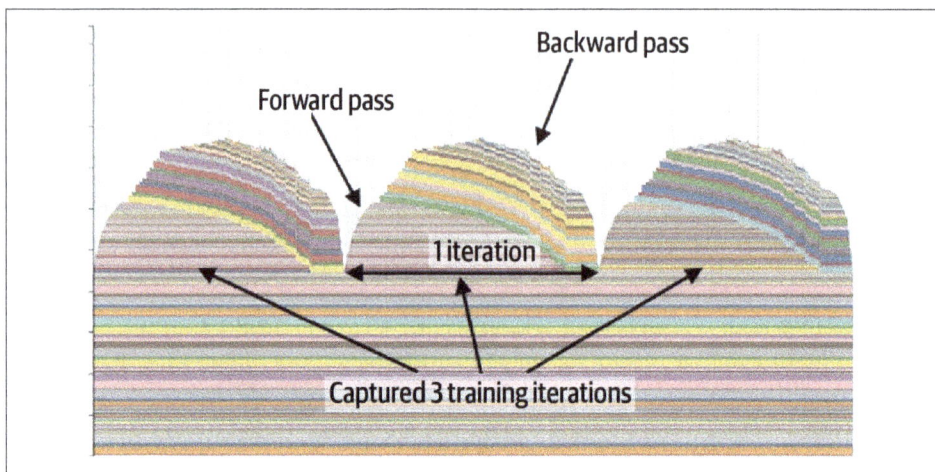

Figure 13-5. PyTorch memory profile visualization for three iterations of a forward and backward pass

Also, NVIDIA's Nsight System's CUDA Memory Inspector can help visualize how memory fragmentation happens over time. Utilizing these can guide your memory-allocator tuning efforts, as we'll explore next.

Tuning the CUDA Memory Allocator

PyTorch uses a caching memory allocator for CUDA memory. By default, it adapts to allocation patterns by splitting and recycling GPU memory blocks on demand. However, certain workload patterns that use variable-sized memory allocations can lead to memory fragmentation.

Memory fragmentation happens when GPU memory gets split into many noncontiguous free chunks over time. This makes it difficult to allocate a large tensor even if enough total memory remains free. In MoE models, this is especially problematic because the number of tokens routed to each expert can change with every batch. As such, each expert's output activation tensor may be a different size on every iteration.

Variable-sized memory allocations leave behind uneven, fragmented memory blocks. These fragment memory blocks accumulate across training or inference runs.

To avoid this, you should allocate a fixed-size expert output buffer upfront and size it to the maximum possible number of tokens any expert may process in your batch. Then you can reuse this buffer on every iteration.

By keeping the buffer dimensions constant, the GPU memory allocator won't fragment memory over time. Each expert writes into its slice of the preallocated buffer rather than triggering new allocations. This method stabilizes memory usage, improves reuse efficiency, and avoids fragmentation-related failures or slowdowns.

You can adjust PyTorch's allocator configuration using an environment variable to tune its behavior. Here is an example:

```
export PYTORCH_ALLOC_CONF=\
max_split_size_mb:256,\
roundup_power2_divisions:[256:1,512:2,1024:4,>:8],\
backend:cudaMallocAsync
```

Next is a description of each specified configuration parameter in the code:

max_split_size_mb:256

> This parameter instructs the allocator to keep large free blocks intact (up to 256 MB) rather than continually splitting them into tiny pieces. This helps reduce fragmentation. By default, PyTorch splits large allocations less aggressively. Setting max_split_size_mb explicitly allows large contiguous free blocks to be available for large neural network layers in modern LLMs.

roundup_power2_divisions:[N:M,...]

> This parameter controls how PyTorch's CUDA caching allocator groups requests for tensor sizes into fixed buckets. It divides each "power-of-two" range into N equal subbuckets—for example, if a request falls between 512 MB and 1,024 MB. With 512:2 specified in the code, the range between 512 and 1,024 MB is divided into :2 buckets and rounded up to one of [512MB, 768 MB, 1 GB]. For example, in the 512 to 1,024 MB range with '512:2', a 600 MB request rounds up to 768 MB. Check allocator logs to confirm actual bucketing in your environment. This strategy reduces memory fragmentation, standardizes allocation sizes, and increases cache reuse since similar requests hit the same bucket.

backend:cudaMallocAsync

> Specifying this will enable NVIDIA's CUDA asynchronous allocator as the underlying memory-allocation mechanism. This can help avoid synchronizations on memory free events—and can improve performance in multithreaded contexts like multiworker data loading.

By customizing a memory allocator configuration, you can maintain a steadier, more predictable memory usage pattern. You can monitor memory fragmentation with torch.cuda.memory_stats() over long runs to make sure your memory footprint stays stable and doesn't explode in size.

You can also use torch.cuda.mem_get_info() at runtime to get free versus total memory. This tracks fragmentation indirectly since, if free memory drops while the number of allocated tensors stays constant, fragmentation is increasing.

Activation Checkpointing for Memory Savings

For extremely large models, activation checkpointing, also called gradient checkpointing by some practitioners, is essential to manage memory. With a large LLM, it's sometimes not possible to store all intermediate activations for backpropagation without running out of memory.

With activation checkpointing, instead of storing intermediate activations during the forward pass (to be used on the backward pass), you can recompute them on the fly during the backward pass only when needed. PyTorch provides `torch.utils.check point` to automate this. You simply wrap your model layer—or sequence of layers—and their `forward` activations won't be stored.

You can apply checkpointing at the granularity of each transformer block and each expert Feedforward Neural Network (FFN) layer in your mode. This way, after computing each block's forward output, you don't need to keep those intermediate activations in memory. Instead, during the backward pass, PyTorch will rerun that block's forward pass to regenerate the activations for gradient computation.

It's worth noting that you don't have to checkpoint everything. You can just focus on the largest layers. A common strategy is checkpointing only the transformer blocks, which hold a massive number of activations, but not checkpointing the smaller layers like layer norms and embedding layers. This produces the most memory savings with minimal recompute overhead.

> When using FSDP, you can also enable automated checkpointing, which will recursively apply checkpointing to multiple layers for you.

This trade increases compute for reduced memory usage. Fortunately, modern GPUs provide abundant FLOPS relative to the amount of HBM memory, so this technique is a natural fit for the latest generations of hardware. As such, the GPU has extra compute headroom to afford these extra recomputations.

This trade-off often proves worthwhile. Without activation checkpointing, you would need to reduce your input batch size—or the number of experts—to fit into limited GPU memory. With checkpointing, however, you can comfortably fit the model into memory and preserve the larger batch size.

And while activation checkpointing slows training down a bit, it allows you to train larger model variants—and use larger input batch sizes—that would otherwise not fit into memory. Essentially, you exchange some of the GPU's ample compute FLOPS to overcome its limited HBM capacity.

Offloading Parameters to CPU and NVMe

In addition to checkpointing, you can offload some of the models' parameters that don't need to be actively stored on the GPU. For instance, an MoE model has some less frequently accessed expert layers that could be offloaded to CPU memory—and transfer them to the GPU only when needed.

It's important to overlap transfers with computations such that while one layer is running on GPU, it's asynchronously prefetching the next layer's weights from CPU or SSD. In practice, frameworks like DeepSpeed's ZeRO-Infinity (*https://oreil.ly/_DOQe*) (for training) and ZeRO-Inference (*https://oreil.ly/JHkVh*) (for inference) can automate this prefetching. They stream model weights layer-by-layer from CPU or NVMe to GPU, minimizing peak GPU memory usage while overlapping data transfers with computation.

You can pin these components on the host and use asynchronous, nonblocking DMA calls like `.to(device)` and `cudaMemcpyAsync` to transfer them into the GPU while other computations are running. This will hide the extra transfer latency incurred by copying from the CPU.

NVIDIA's Unified Memory is also an option—especially for superchip systems like Grace Blackwell GB200/GB300 with high-speed interconnects like NVLink-C2C between the CPU and GPU. In these cases, Unified Memory allows rarely used GPU memory pages to be evicted to the CPU's system memory.

The OS may even swap them to NVMe/SSD if needed for capacity. NVMe should be used as a last resort through normal OS swapping, not as a primary target of Unified Memory.

However, unified memory can introduce unpredictability due to memory paging, etc. As such, explicitly managing the offloading is often preferable to maintain full control and predictable performance.

Recent advancements like GPUDirect Storage allow GPUs to directly read from NVMe drives. This means that, in some cases, your model parameters could be paged directly from NVMe on the fly without any CPU involvement. This is useful for both training and inference serving when using massive models.

For larger models on the order of trillions of parameters, you can offload components to NVMe storage and swap them into GPU memory just-in-time. The key is to overlap the data transfers with computations so they don't stall the training loop.

SuperOffload: Optimized CPU-GPU Superchip Offload

SuperOffload (*https://oreil.ly/uupE1*) is an offload system designed specifically to take advantage of CPU-GPU superchip hardware efficiencies. Superchips (e.g., Grace Hopper, Grace Blackwell, Vera Rubin, etc.) provide high-bandwidth NVLink-C2C interconnects between the CPU and GPU. Combined with a shared, coherent memory address space, a superchip-optimized offload strategy can produce huge speedups and utilization gains compared to traditional offload techniques.

There are a few key innovations that SuperOffload demonstrates including speculation-then-validation (STV), heterogeneous optimization computations, superchip-aware data type conversions, and memory copies. Let's discuss each of these next.

Compared to traditional offloading, which waits for gradient reduction and global checks before updating parameters, STV overlaps these steps by performing speculative optimizer updates on the CPU while backpropagation is running on the GPU. It then validates the results afterward. This effectively reduces synchronization stalls and improves overall GPU utilization.

SuperOffload uses heterogeneous optimizer computations to partition optimizer work between the CPU and GPU. For instance, it assigns compute-heavy tensors updates to the GPU while CPU cores handle lighter state updates such as momentum buffers used by the Adam optimizer. This keeps both devices busy, reduces idle cycles, and increases overall chip utilization.

Because NVLink-C2C provides high bandwidth between the CPU and GPU, SuperOffload can change the precision and placement strategy for tensor type casts and data transfers. By shifting type conversions and copies toward the GPU, SuperOffload takes advantage of the fast, coherent interconnects to minimize CPU-GPU transfer latency.

In addition, SuperOffload uses a CPU-optimized variant of the Adam optimizer called GraceAdam, which is designed for Grace's ARM Scalable Vector Extension (SVE) architecture (*https://oreil.ly/ojyYy*). SVE is a long-vector architecture used by the ARM A64 instruction set. Specifically, it has 32 vector registers and 16 predicate registers that, in combination with SuperOffload, help to improve throughput and energy efficiency for offloaded parameter updates.

FSDP Automatic Checkpointing and Offloading

PyTorch's FSDP is a distributed parallelism strategy that shards model parameters, gradients, and activations across GPUs during model training. This reduces memory overhead during training—and lets you train larger models than you could without sharding. Technically, FSDP implements the ZeRO (*https://oreil.ly/x0i7v*) Stage-3 strategy to shard model states across GPUs, as shown in Figure 13-6.

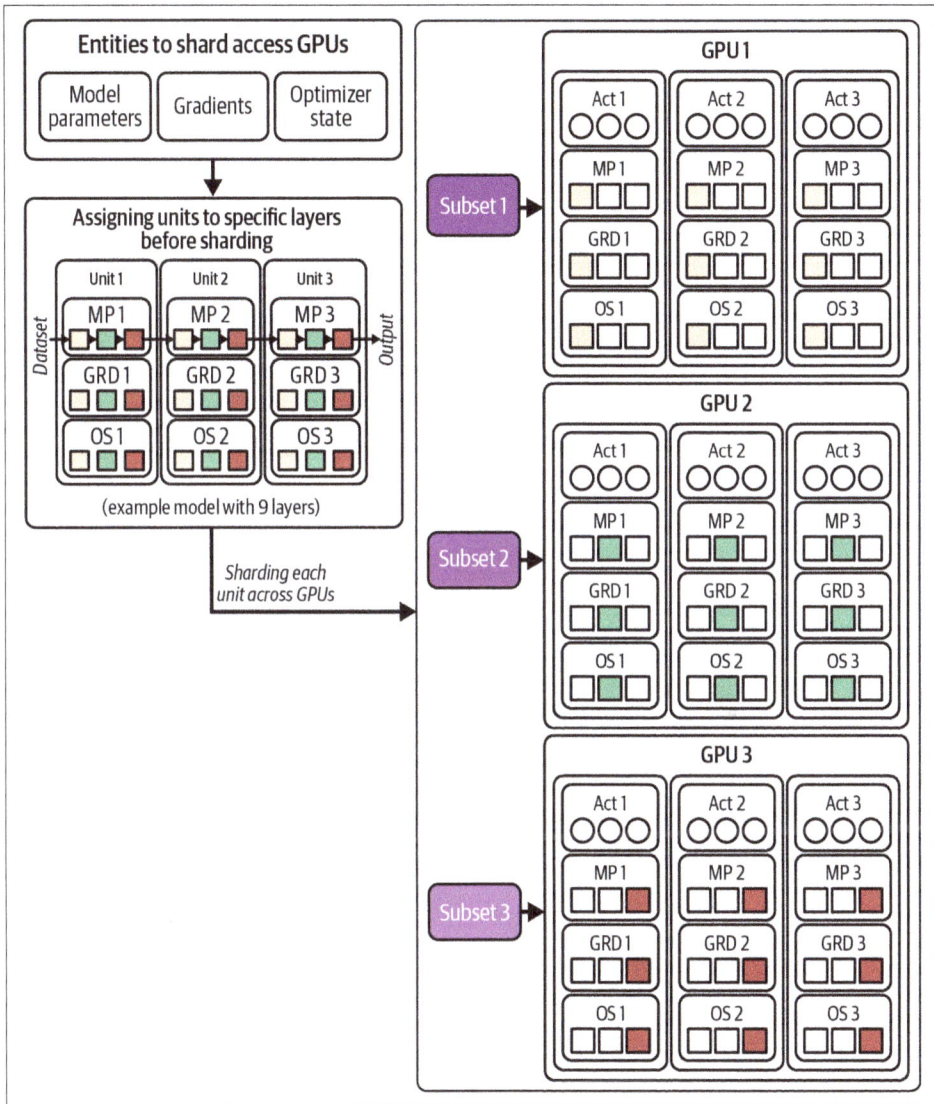

Figure 13-6. FSDP shards model parameters, gradients, and optimizer states across the GPUs (ZeRO Stage-3)

FSDP can automatically apply activation checkpointing and offload parameters/ gradients under the hood. Simply wrap the model with FSDP(), then specify the `activation_checkpointing_policy` and `CPUOffload` parameters as shown here:

```
import torch
import torch.nn as nn
import torch.distributed as dist
from torch.distributed.fsdp import (
```

```
        FullyShardedDataParallel as FSDP,
        CPUOffload, ShardingStrategy, BackwardPrefetch, MixedPrecision
)
from torch.distributed.fsdp.wrap import transformer_auto_wrap_policy

# Initialize distributed
dist.init_process_group("nccl")
torch.cuda.set_device(dist.get_rank() % torch.cuda.device_count())

# Build your model
class MyModel(nn.Module):
    def __init__(self):
        super().__init__()
        self.layers = nn.Sequential(
            nn.Linear(4096, 4096),
            nn.ReLU(),
            nn.Linear(4096, 4096),
        )

    def forward(self, x):
        return self.layers(x)

model = MyModel().cuda()

# Auto-wrap transformer blocks if needed
auto_wrap_policy = transformer_auto_wrap_policy(
    model,
    min_num_params=1e8,
)

# Wrap with FSDP + checkpointing + CPU offload
fsdp_model = FSDP(
    model,
    auto_wrap_policy=auto_wrap_policy,
    sharding_strategy=ShardingStrategy.FULL_SHARD,
    use_orig_params=True,
    cpu_offload=CPUOffload(offload_params=True, pin_memory=True),
    mixed_precision=MixedPrecision(
        param_dtype=torch.bfloat16,
        reduce_dtype=torch.bfloat16,
        buffer_dtype=torch.bfloat16
    ),
    backward_prefetch=BackwardPrefetch.BACKWARD_PRE,
    activation_checkpointing_policy={
        nn.TransformerEncoderLayer,
        nn.TransformerDecoderLayer,
        nn.MultiheadAttention
    }
)

# Setup optimizer
optimizer = torch.optim.AdamW(fsdp_model.parameters(), weight_decay=0.01)

...
```

Here we use `transformer_auto_wrap_policy` so that FSDP will automatically shard parameters, gradients, and optimizer states according to your transformer block

structure. We also enable offloading to the CPU with `CPUOffload(offload_par`
`ams=True)`. This will transparently move both parameters and gradients to the CPU
when they're not needed on the GPU. This will reduce peak GPU memory usage.

> By setting `use_orig_params=True`, each FSDP unit handles its
> parameters without flattening. This allows better overlap and sim-
> pler state-dictionary handling—improving memory management
> and optimizer compatibility.

Setting `activation_checkpointing_policy` tells FSDP to recompute, or rematerial-
ize, activations in those specific core transformer submodules. This will trade extra
compute for significantly lower peak memory. This achieves the same large memory
savings as manual `checkpoint()` wrappers and custom offload scripts but without the
additional boilerplate code. FSDP even handles uneven per-GPU batch sizes, which is
useful for MoE workloads.

FSDP also supports a hybrid sharding strategy using `ShardingStrategy`
`.HYBRID_SHARD`. This strategy shards each node's parameters, gradients, and optimizer states across the GPUs on that node while replicating those same shards onto
other nodes. In essence, hybrid sharing provides higher throughput than `FULL_SHARD`,
but at the cost of more per-node memory.

Use `HYBRID_SHARD` when your interconnect is decent but not blisteringly fast. This
shards parameters, grads, and optimizer states within each node—and replicates
those shards across nodes. This reduces cross-node traffic at the cost of slightly
higher per-node memory than full sharding.

Hybrid sharding lets you manage the memory versus communication trade-off. For
instance, you can use more per-node memory than `FULL_SHARD` (ZeRO 3) because
you hold a full local shard on each node. This reduces internode communication and
often provides higher end-to-end throughput. `FULL_SHARD` is best when you have a
very fast multinode fabric and want the smallest per-GPU memory footprint.

When your network is slow—or you have only a handful of GPUs—you can use `Shar`
`dingStrategy.SHARD_GRAD_OP` (ZeRO Stage-2) to shard only the gradients and opti-
mizer state across all GPUs. This strategy keeps a full copy of the parameters on every
GPU.

Combining FSDP with Tensor Parallel and Pipeline Parallel

If the model is so large that a single layer won't fit into a single GPU's memory, you
will need to combine FSDP with other parallelism strategies like tensor parallel (TP)
to spread the large model layer across multiple GPUs.

You can also use FSDP across both GPUs and compute nodes by using TP within a node to split huge layers across the multiple GPUs and pipeline parallel (PP) to chain those TP-split layers together across nodes. FSDP allows these types of flexible combinations.

In short, FSDP can reduce memory usage with far less coding effort. After applying checkpointing and offloading, you fit the model into memory and enable larger batch sizes. This will help improve GPU utilization.

Pluggable Memory Allocators and Cross-GPU Data Transfers

You can configure PyTorch to use a specialized memory allocator for critical GPU communication operations like NCCL gradient all-reduce. By plugging in custom allocators with `torch.cuda.MemPool`, you let NCCL allocate buffers in a way that leverages dedicated hardware engines such as NVLink copy engines, InfiniBand offloads, or NVIDIA SHARP. These help improve overlap between communication and computation. For example, PyTorch supports using NCCL's memory allocator for fast, zero-copy reductions on NVSwitch setups, as shown here:

```python
import torch
import torch.distributed as dist
from torch.cuda.memory import MemPool
from torch.distributed.distributed_c10d import _get_default_group

# Initialize NCCL distributed backend
dist.init_process_group(backend="nccl")
torch.cuda.set_device(
    dist.get_rank() % torch.cuda.device_count()
)

# Get the NCCL backend object for this device
default_pg = _get_default_group()
backend = default_pg._get_backend(
    torch.device(f"cuda:{torch.cuda.current_device()}")
)

# The backend exposes ncclMemAlloc using mem_allocator
nccl_allocator = backend.mem_allocator

# Create a dedicated memory pool using this allocator
nccl_pool = MemPool(nccl_allocator)

# Register the pool so NCCL uses it for collective gradient buffers
backend.register_mem_pool(nccl_pool)

# Use the pool explicitly for NCCL operations
with torch.cuda.use_mem_pool(nccl_pool):
    tensor = torch.randn(10_000_000, device="cuda")
    dist.all_reduce(tensor)
```

By binding NCCL's native allocator (`backend.mem_allocator`) into a `torch.cuda`
`.memory.MemPool` and using `backend.register_mem_pool(...)`, PyTorch places
gradient-reduction buffers directly in memory regions optimized for optimal routing
through NVLink, InfiniBand, and NVIDIA SHARP-enabled hardware. This way, all-
reduce operations benefit from hardware acceleration by reducing SM contention
during large data reductions. This results in improved throughput for large, multi-
GPU workloads.

> Using SHARP, discussed in Chapter 4, requires a compatible net-
> work fabric (e.g., HDR InfiniBand with SHARP support). If avail-
> able, enabling NCCL's in-network aggregation with SHARP can
> greatly lower all-reduce latency for large clusters. This is definitely
> something to consider when scaling to a large number of nodes.

By using NCCL's native allocator with `backend.mem_allocator` and wrapping it in
PyTorch's `MemPool`, the gradient all-reduce buffers are allocated in memory regions
optimized for GPUDirect RDMA and in-network SHARP offload. This will align
buffers on large page boundaries and can help place data transfers onto dedicated
DMA engines—reducing SM involvement and freeing up compute capacity to perform more useful computational work.

As a result, NCCL collective operations like tensor-parallel reductions benefit from
both hardware acceleration and lower SM contention. This significantly improves
multi-GPU synchronization throughput, which reduces contention between overlapping compute and communication kernels on SMs and copy engines—especially for
tensor-parallel workloads.

These kinds of optimizations become more important as you push bandwidth limits.
For example, Blackwell's NVLink 5 provides up to 1.8 TB/s of bidirectional bandwidth per GPU (about 900 GB/s in each direction) in theory. Using dedicated copy
engines, network hardware (SHARP), and optimized memory allocators can help
approach peak network throughput and free up the SMs to achieve peak FLOPS at
the same time.

With `torch.cuda.MemPool`, you can also create your own memory allocator by registering a custom library (shared object, or `.so`). In addition, you can mix different
CUDA memory allocators in the same PyTorch application, as shown here:

```
import torch  # PyTorch main namespace
import os     # for path operations (used here for .so extensions)
from torch.cuda.memory import CUDAPluggableAllocator

# 1. Create a CUDAPluggableAllocator and MemPool

# Build a pluggable allocator that calls into your NCCL library:
#   - allocator_path: path to your .so
```

```python
#   - "ncclMemAlloc": symbol for allocation
#   - "ncclMemFree":  symbol for deallocation
# .allocator() returns a callable that matches the CUB/CUDA allocator API
allocator = CUDAPluggableAllocator(
    "./nccl_allocator.so",
    "ncclMemAlloc",
    "ncclMemFree"
).allocator()

# Wrap that allocator in a MemPool for efficient sub-allocations
pool = torch.cuda.memory.MemPool(allocator)

# 2. Start recording events (set a high cap for long runs)
torch.cuda.memory._record_memory_history(max_entries=100000)

# 3. Allocate tensors with different allocators

# tensor0 uses the *default* cudaMalloc allocator
# - Shape: (1024, 1024), you can change to your desired size
tensor0 = torch.randn(1024, 1024, device="cuda")

# tensor1 uses *your* NCCL-backed allocator using MemPool
with torch.cuda.use_mem_pool(pool):
    # Inside this context, all cuda allocations go through `pool`
    tensor1 = torch.randn(1024, 1024, device="cuda")

# Exiting the context restores the default allocator
# tensor2 again uses the *default* cudaMalloc allocator
tensor2 = torch.randn(1024, 1024, device="cuda")

# 4. Inspect memory pool stats

# Pool-specific snapshot with list of segments/blocks in use
pool_state = pool.snapshot()
print(f"Pool segments count: {len(pool_state)}")

# 5. Dump the snapshot and optionally load in the PyTorch
# memory viewer tool (https://oreil.ly/tX6gA)
torch.cuda.memory._dump_snapshot('memory_snapshot.pkl')

# Global allocator stats (allocated/reserved, peak, counts)
global_stats = torch.cuda.memory_stats()
print("Peak allocated bytes:", global_stats["allocated_bytes.all.peak"])

# 6. Stop recording
torch.cuda.memory._record_memory_history(enabled=None)

# 7. Reset peak counters for a fresh measurement
torch.cuda.reset_peak_memory_stats()
```

Here, the `CUDAPluggableAllocator` loads your custom `.so` and binds to the two symbols you specify. `MemPool` wraps the low-level CUDA memory allocator in a cache for memory allocations and memory frees for better performance.

`torch.cuda.use_mem_pool(pool)` swaps in your pool for all subsequent memory allocations inside the Python context manager (e.g., `with`) block. Exiting the context manager block restores the previous allocator.

Enabling Peer-to-Peer DMA and UCX

When using pipeline parallel in a multi-GPU system, you typically want to move activations directly from one GPU to the next GPU using the fastest peer-to-peer (P2P) connection possible—and avoid round-trips and host CPU resources. PyTorch will probe and enable peer access automatically when tensors are moved across devices in a process. However, if you want to confirm manually, you can use `torch.cuda.can_device_access_peer(i, j)` to confirm PSP DMA between GPU `i` and GPU `j`. For custom C++ operations, you can enable peers explicitly with CUDA driver APIs.

Enabling P2P DMA provides efficient direct transfers without involving the GPU's SM or CPU memory. Once enabled, cross-GPU `copy_()` and `.to()` will use the faster peer-memory path without additional code overhead, as shown here:

```
dst.copy_(src, non_blocking=True)
# or
src.to(device="cuda:1", non_blocking=True)
```

These methods use `cudaMemcpyPeerAsync` when P2P access is enabled on your topology. For P2P transfers to work correctly, your hardware topology must support it. The GB200/GB300 NVL72 rack uses P2P-capable NVLink and NVSwitch internally, so it's already set up for the P2P DMA out of the box.

So far, we've discussed only multi-GPU configurations in the context of P2P data transfers. However, when using multinode GPU topologies, you need to fall back to NCCL, which communicates over the network. Sometimes this will happen over GPUDirect RDMA. But using UCX (Unified Communication X) with NCCL can improve performance. On GB200 and GB300 NVL72 topologies, NVLink and NVSwitch provide the P2P path inside the rack. Across racks, you will need to traverse the network fabric with UCX-enabled NCCL transports.

To route cross-node transfers through UCX, install the NCCL-UCX plugin and set `NCCL_PLUGIN_P2P=ucx`. Many environments also require `NCCL_NET=UCX` and appropriate `UCX_TLS` transport selections configured for your fabric. This enables hardware offloads and improves pipelining on InfiniBand fabrics between NVL72 racks.

The following is an example configuration for the NCCL-UCX plugin:

```
export NCCL_NET=UCX
export NCCL_PLUGIN_P2P=ucx
# UCX transports vary by fabric.
# These are safe defaults to start with:
export UCX_TLS=rc,self,gdr_copy,cuda_copy
```

If your application needs to scale across multiple nodes or racks training terabyte-scale models, inference massive LLMs across many tenants, or manage data-intensive pipelines, UCX is essential. And using NCCL with UCX provides high-throughput, low-latency, cross-node communication that supports both hardware offloads (RDMA) and intelligent topology awareness. UCX is a core part of production-level AI infrastructure, and it's essential when scaling beyond a single NVLink domain.

In short, direct P2P DMA communication and UCX achieve better overlap with compute compared to an equivalent send/recv call using NCCL. This is a relatively low-level optimization, but if you have the right topology with dedicated high-speed interconnects such as NVLink/NVSwitch, this can improve system performance greatly.

PyTorch Symmetric Memory

Symmetric memory is a programming model that exposes a partitioned global address space across GPUs so that kernels can do one-sided puts and gets. This lets them invoke ultra-low-latency, cross-GPU, direct-access collectives without CPU handshakes or interventions. Essentially, symmetric memory allocates buffers that are directly addressable from any GPU in the group—without requiring explicit peer-to-peer copies.

When using symmetric memory, you can perform all-to-all operations like MoE token shuffles completely on-device. Since no CPU is involved, the entire all-to-all can be captured by a CUDA Graph. Without symmetric memory, an all-to-all triggers a host synchronization that leads to device-to-host (D2H) gaps in the timeline. This will create an unwanted break in the CUDA Graph.

You can allocate symmetric tensors, perform a rendezvous across a process group to obtain remote access handles, and then call direct-access collectives (e.g., `all_to_all_v`, `one_shot_all_reduce`). Additionally, you can launch kernels that perform one-sided reads/writes using the remote access handles. Combined with OpenAI Triton and NVSHMEM (`triton.nvshmem.put()/get()`), symmetric memory is a powerful communication mechanism for custom, in-kernel data transfers.

You should use symmetric memory in PyTorch for fine-grained, latency-sensitive, on-device exchanges like MoE all-to-all token shuffles without host CPU intervention. This will eliminate device-to-host (D2H) timeline gaps and enable better CUDA Graph capture.

Optimizing the Data Input Pipeline

With the model's memory and compute covered, let's turn to the data input pipeline. A common cause of inefficiency is GPUs sitting idle waiting for data. PyTorch's Data-Loader supports spawning multiple worker threads or processes to load and preprocess data (e.g., text tokenization) in parallel while training a model. Make sure to specify pin_memory=True so that the host CPU memory-to-GPU device transfers use page-locked (pinned) memory.

If you don't pin memory, you may see high CPU utilization in the data-loader process and low GPU utilization in the training process. This is doubly bad. These nonideal utilizations are observable with tools like htop and Nsight Systems. You'll see CPU threads busy performing data loading while the GPU sits idle.

This indicates that data loading isn't keeping up for every iteration. You can address this by increasing the value of the DataLoader's num_workers parameter until the data queue has enough batches ready. A common heuristic is 4 workers per GPU for CPU-bound data pipelines, but the optimal number can vary based on your workload.

To find the optimal number, you can do a quick sweep (e.g., 4, 8, 16, 32) to find the point where adding more workers no longer helps. Keep an eye on CPU saturation. If all cores are at 100%, more workers won't help.

Remember that NVLink C2C superchip systems like Grace Hopper, Grace Blackwell, and Vera Rubin provide a large, coherent, high-bandwidth CPU–GPU memory address space. In these environments, page-locked pin_memory=True is often less critical because transfers already use a high-bandwidth coherent path.

Pinned memory may still be required to maximize overlap for pageable host-to-device copies in non-coherent paths. While unified memory and coherent mappings may reduce the need for pinning on NVLink-C2C systems, it's important to measure performance of your workload.

Even with CPU-GPU superchip architectures, it's still recommended to combine pin_memory=True (or large pages) with non_blocking=True and persistent_work ers=True when the loader thread is CPU-bound. Using persistent_workers=True avoids process respawns across epochs. This is helpful with tokenization-heavy workloads such as LLM training and inference. Use Nsight Systems to profile and verify actual overlap. Before removing pinning, be sure to enable large pages on the host and confirm that H2D traffic overlaps compute.

The CPU and GPU share a coherent memory space, so transfers already use a high-speed path without explicit pinning. In contrast, on standard (nonsuperchip) CPU + GPU systems without such hardware coherence, enabling `pin_memory=True` will page-lock the host memory and provide a noticeable increase in data transfer throughput.

> If you don't pin memory, but rather rely on the unified CPU-GPU memory of superchip systems like Grace Blackwell and Vera Rubin, be sure to enable large pages and verify with Nsight Systems that transfers are actually overlapped. This is because unified CPU-GPU memory on NVLink-C2C superchips changes the pinning trade-offs.

Another technique to improve data-loading responsiveness is increasing the Data-Loader's `prefetch_factor`. This controls how many batches each worker preloads ahead of time and is calculated as `prefetch_factor * num_workers` (*https://oreil.ly/wT1Mh*). This means that while your model is busy processing the current batch, workers are already loading and caching subsequent batches.

Prefetching keeps the data pipeline full and avoids idle GPU time. You should adjust `prefetch_factor` alongside `num_workers` based on your dataset and hardware capabilities. Verify with profiling to avoid overfetching and causing unnecessary memory utilization.

You can also precompute tokenized datasets and store the tokenized dataset on disk to avoid heavy processing in the data-loader loop. Tools like Hugging Face's `Dataset.cache()` and WebDataset allow you to preprocess the files once and reuse them. Also, consider using mixed precision and compression for your datasets to reduce I/O bandwidth needs.

There's also PyTorch's native TorchData with DataPipes. This provides good composability and integrates with the PyTorch scheduler to overlap with training computations.

Another useful tool is NVIDIA Data Loading Library (DALI). DALI can perform CPU or GPU preprocessing in parallel with training. It's especially useful for image/video data (e.g., decoding and augmentations) and can feed data through a CUDA pipeline directly to your training code. It's a useful tool for on-the-fly data transformations that benefit from being offloaded to the GPU.

The goal in all cases is to overlap data loading with GPU compute as much as possible. By profiling with Nsight Systems, you can confirm that the data loader is working in parallel with the GPU. The Nsight Systems' timeline should show one CPU thread constantly loading/preprocessing the next batch while many GPU streams perform the training steps. Also, verify that there are no gaps in which the GPU is waiting for data. This makes sure that your GPU SMs remain busy nearly 100% of the time doing useful training work.

Assuming memory constraints are addressed with activation checkpointing and offloading, you can increase the input batch size per GPU. By using a larger batch, you can increase arithmetic intensity, improve GPU utilization, and reduce the relative overhead of communications in multi-GPU training since there are fewer steps per epoch.

However, too large of a batch size can affect convergence by pushing the optimizer toward a sharp minima, which reduces generalization. When increasing the batch size significantly, make sure to monitor your GPU memory usage. Remember that gradient accumulation increases the effective batch size (`batch_size * accumulation_steps`). PyTorch's TorchEval metrics (*https://oreil.ly/yluDV*) can help determine if a larger batch size is hurting validation loss or not.

You can potentially minimize the instability effect of a large batch size by adjusting hyperparameters accordingly. For instance, you can change the learning rate, apply a linear learning-rate scaling with a warm-up period, or use a large-batch optimizer like LAMB.

In short, if memory allows—and the other memory optimizations from previous sections have already been implemented and verified—increasing the batch size can increase arithmetic intensity and better utilize the GPU.

> As you optimize the system, you should periodically revisit and retune hyperparameters like batch size, learning rate, etc. The initially chosen values might not be optimal after making changes in batch size, etc.

Scaling with PyTorch Distributed

Scaling and profiling PyTorch with multiple GPUs and compute nodes typically uses PyTorch's distributed libraries like PyTorch DDP and FSDP. The good news is that PyTorch's compiler can work with these parallelism approaches, but there are some nuances, as described next.

DDP with torch.compile

When using `DistributedDataParallel`, which synchronizes gradients between GPUs using the all-reduce collective, PyTorch automatically creates graph breaks at the synchronization points. In practice, DDP divides gradients into buckets and overlaps communication with computation. PyTorch's design is to compile each bucket's backward computation as a separate graph so that, between those graphs, it can perform the all-reduce.

In the `torch._dynamo.explain(model, ...)` output, you will see graph breaks related to all-reduce and `torch.distributed` operations. This is expected since each bucket's work is compiled—and the all-reduce happens in between subgraphs. This way, the communication overlap is preserved, which is critical for performance.

If you use DDP with the compiler, make sure your DDP bucket size is reasonable. By default, DDP buckets are 25 MB. If you choose to override this default and use one giant bucket for all gradients, then one giant graph is created with one big all-reduce at the end. This leads to fewer, larger graph segments with minimal opportunity to interleave communication and computation.

It's tempting to use a single bucket so the entire backward pass happens in a single graph for maximum kernel fusion, for example. However, you will lose overlap opportunities. It's recommended to profile the system and find the right balance for your workload and hardware environment.

> When using DDP with `torch.compile`, you'll see intentional graph breaks at communication points. These are normal and required to let networking happen. TorchDynamo's `explain()` output will show messages about all-reduce and scatter causing a break—this is expected.

FSDP with torch.compile

PyTorch's FSDP parallelism strategy shards model parameters, gradients, and optimizer states across GPUs. It performs an all-gather collective during the forward pass and a reduce-scatter during the backward pass. This allows larger models to fit into GPU memory relative to using DDP.

With `torch.compile`, FSDP can be even more efficient, but it requires careful wrapping to maximize compute-communication overlap. It's recommended that you wrap each transformer block—and not just a single low-level layer—in its own FSDP module using `use_orig_params=True`. This way, TorchDynamo inserts a graph break at each shard boundary when communication is needed.

Each block's forward and backward computation then executes as a single compiled graph with the all-gather (forward) and reduce-scatter (backward) communication happening between those graphs. This mirrors DDP's bucketed approach, which compiles each communication chunk separately. This allows appropriate overlap between compute and communication steps.

This is in contrast to wrapping the full model in a single FSDP instance, which is tempting. If you do this, TorchDynamo will produce fewer, larger graphs. This results in fewer communication points, fewer communication-compute overlap opportunities, and limited inter-graph fusion across both the forward and backward phases.

By wrapping your model with FSDP at a transformer-block granularity, you facilitate maximum overlap in your training pipelines. This is because each block's compute-intensive logic is compiled and fused. And this compute is overlapped with the communication needed to link the blocks together.

PyTorch provides a `transformer_auto_wrap_policy` callable in `torch.distributed` `.fsdp.wrap` to make it straightforward to apply FSDP to every `TransformerBlock` in your model without manual nesting. With block-level sharding, only one block's full weights are materialized in memory at a time. The all-gather and reduce-scatter collectives are interleaved and hidden behind each block's computation. Here is an end-to-end example using PyTorch that defines an autowrap policy, wraps a sample transformer block, and runs an example of the forward and backward steps:

```
import torch
import torch.nn as nn
import torch.distributed as dist
from torch.distributed.fsdp import FullyShardedDataParallel as FSDP,
    CPUOffload, ShardingStrategy, BackwardPrefetch, MixedPrecision
from torch.distributed.fsdp.wrap import transformer_auto_wrap_policy
from torch.distributed.algorithms._checkpoint.checkpoint_wrapper
    import apply_activation_checkpointing, checkpoint_wrapper

# Prefer BF16 for Blackwell/Hopper-class GPUs; allow TF32 matmul for speed
# where numerically safe.
# enables TF32 use for FP32 matmuls when allowed
torch.set_float32_matmul_precision('high') # {'highest'|'high'|'medium'}

# Compile the model with a mode that reduces Python/launch overhead and
# enables CUDA Graphs
compiled_model = torch.compile(model, mode="reduce-overhead")

# Auto-wrap transformer blocks; adjust set below to match model's block classes
auto_wrap_policy = torch.partial(
    transformer_auto_wrap_policy,
    transformer_layer_cls={
        nn.TransformerEncoderLayer,
        nn.TransformerDecoderLayer,
        nn.MultiheadAttention,
```

```
    },
    min_num_params=int(1e8),
)

# Optional activation checkpointing for target modules
def _ckpt_check_fn(m: nn.Module) -> bool:
    return isinstance(m, (nn.TransformerEncoderLayer,
                          nn.TransformerDecoderLayer,
                          nn.MultiheadAttention))

apply_activation_checkpointing(
    compiled_model,
    checkpoint_wrapper_fn=checkpoint_wrapper,
    check_fn=_ckpt_check_fn,
)

# FSDP wrapper with correct argument types; MixedPrecision explicitly specified
fsdp_model = FSDP(
    compiled_model,
    auto_wrap_policy=auto_wrap_policy,
    sharding_strategy=ShardingStrategy.HYBRID_SHARD,
    cpu_offload=CPUOffload(offload_params=True),
    use_orig_params=True,
    mixed_precision=MixedPrecision(param_dtype=torch.bfloat16,
                                   reduce_dtype=torch.bfloat16,
                                   buffer_dtype=torch.bfloat16),
    backward_prefetch=BackwardPrefetch.BACKWARD_PRE,
)

# Example input
batch = torch.randn(8, 128, dtype=torch.float32, device='cuda')
labels = torch.empty(8, 128, dtype=torch.long, device='cuda').random_(0, 100)

optimizer = torch.optim.AdamW(fsdp_model.parameters(), lr=1e-4, fused=True)

# Forward + backward
outputs = fsdp_model(batch)
loss    = nn.CrossEntropyLoss()(outputs.view(-1, outputs.size(-1)),
                                labels.view(-1))
loss.backward()
optimizer.step()
optimizer.zero_grad(set_to_none=True)
```

Here, `transformer_layer_cls` is set to your block class so that each block is independently sharded. Wrapping at block granularity means each forward pass will invoke all-gather for only the current block, and then it will drop its shards. As such, only one block's parameters and optimizer states are fully materialized at a time, reducing peak memory footprint by up to the block-size fraction of total parameters.

Additionally, as each block's computation runs, the next block's weights can be pre-fetched or moved asynchronously. This hides communication latency behind block computations.

Note that the training loop does not change. The `auto_wrap_policy` abstracts away manual nesting, so you need to specify your block class only once and let FSDP handle the rest—including per-block communication—under the hood.

In short, wrapping FSDP at the transformer-block level provides better performance and memory efficiency. Each compiled block uses less peak memory due to its fused, optimized kernels. Communication is overlapped appropriately with computation. And FSDP's sharding and on-demand, layer-wise all-gather collectives mean that only one block's weights exist fully in memory at a time—and only when they're needed during each forward and backward pass.

> Remember that TorchDynamo's `explain()` output will show graph breaks at each FSDP boundary. These breaks are expected and reflect correct overlap behavior.

Tensor and Pipeline Parallelism with torch.compile

Tensor parallel and pipeline parallel are orthogonal to `torch.compile`. As long as the cross-GPU communication operations are recognized by TorchDynamo as collective calls, Dynamo will either trace them or break them accordingly.

The PyTorch compiler is mostly focused on optimizing the compute within each segment. It doesn't (currently) fuse communication operations or change their schedule—except for the natural overlapping, as described earlier. Specifically, Torch-Inductor chooses cublasLt/cuDNN/Triton kernels for compute but leaves NCCL collectives (and their ordering) to the distributed strategy. When using any distributed training strategy, you should always test with and without `torch.compile` to ensure you get expected results. Always validate overlap with profiler traces when enabling compilation.

It's recommended to use `torch.compile` to optimize compute within each layer or bucket—and trust the distributed strategy (DDP, FSDP, TP, PP, etc.) to handle the between-GPU communication as usual. Keep an eye on any all-reduce-related warnings in TorchDynamo's `explain()` output, but just remember that PyTorch's design tries to ensure overlap is preserved. As such, you shouldn't need to make too many changes as `torch.compile`'s support for distributed training is relatively mature.

TorchTitan, AsyncTP, AutoParallel, and SimpleFSDP

TorchTitan (*https://github.com/pytorch/torchtitan*) is a popular PyTorch-based set of reference implementations for large-scale model training. It provides a set of scalable recipes that compose multiple distributed training strategies including FSDP, tensor parallel, and asynchronous tensor parallel (AsyncTP).

Specifically, AsyncTP uses dual streams and an SM-wave aware schedule to stagger TP collectives and overlap late-arriving TP all-gathers with the next wave's matmuls. This overlap helps to hide communication and scheduling gaps that occur in traditional TP. Teams are seeing speedups (*https://oreil.ly/qHNok*) in both forward-pass and end-to-end speedups when using these types of asynchronous parallelism strategies. Make sure to use asynchronous parallelism only where you can validate numerics and scaling.

You can enable AsyncTP through `torch.compile`. This will make matmuls eligible to be lowered into fused all-gathers and reduce-scatters. AsyncTP composes well with `torch.compile` so that the fused compute kernels run in lock-step with the scheduled communication.

AutoParallel (*https://oreil.ly/cNoyd*) is another PyTorch initiative that automatically plans and applies different combinations of FSDP, Tensor Parallel, and Pipeline Parallel to a model graph.

AutoParallel builds on the operator-strategy system for DTensor (*https://oreil.ly/tdmy0*), PyTorch's native PyTorch sharding primitive that underpins PyTorch's composable tensor and pipeline parallel approaches. DTensor is used heavily in the TorchTitan reference implementations.

Using a heuristic-based selection mechanism, AutoParallel applies sharding and partitioning using different parallelism plans that consider the specific memory and communication costs for the given workload.

You should use AutoParallel for large models and complex clusters to help reduce manual parallelization tuning—and it composes well with TorchTitan.

SimpleFSDP reimplements FSDP in a `torch.compile`-friendly way using DTensor and techniques like selective activation checkpointing. The compiler helps trace and optimize compute and communication overlap using TorchInductor to bucket and reorder intermediate representation (IR) nodes.

In TorchTitan experiments, SimpleFSDP (*https://oreil.ly/rQCAP*) reduced memory usage by up to ~28%. And when composed with other distributed techniques, it improved training throughput by up to ~69% versus the traditional FSDP2 eager path.

TorchTitan, AsyncTP, AutoParallel, and SimpleFSDP are well-maintained projects that are worth following. They represent practical PyTorch reference implementations and include many optimizations from PyTorch experts across the industry.

Multi-GPU Profiling with HTA

As you scale to millions of GPUs, wrangling millions of separate traces and profiles can become unwieldy. Meta's HTA helps to merge and visualize multiworker traces. HTA, open sourced by Meta AI, ingests the JSON traces produced by `torch.pro filer` from each GPU/rank and presents a unified timeline.

With HTA, you can, for example, see all 8 GPUs' traces aligned by time. NVTX markers from each rank are aligned and visible. This way, you might notice that rank 0 enters the "backward" pass at time T, but rank 1 only enters at T+1—perhaps because rank 1 was waiting for rank 0 in an all-reduce. Or you might see that rank 0 has a gap during which ranks 1–7 are busy in computations—perhaps indicating a load imbalance if rank 0 finishes early and is sitting idle.

HTA also provides a report of GPU idle times—and even offers suggestions for improving efficiency through overlap. For distributed training, HTA is super useful for pinpointing stragglers and synchronization issues.

In the past, people tried to use TensorBoard's trace viewer by manually combining traces. But, as of 2025, the PyTorch TensorBoard profiler plugin for trace visualization is deprecated. Instead, use Perfetto's Trace Viewer for timelines and Meta's Holistic Trace Analysis (HTA) for multinode aggregation.

Using HTA typically involves generating traces from each rank using mechanisms like `torch.profiler.schedule` to record traces for a few iterations on each GPU and then saving the results in a shared location. After loading these traces into the HTA tool, you can see a timeline of each thread, operation overlaps, and even memory usage per rank.

You can use HTA to confirm that your all-reduce optimizations are working, for instance. In this case, the traces before optimization show a clear sequential pattern such that the backward pass computation finishes, then a gap occurs while waiting for the all-reduce to complete, then another computation begins. After increasing bucket size and overlapping, HTA should show a smaller gap since most of the communication now happens concurrently with the remaining backward-pass computations.

In short, HTA is designed for PyTorch multi-GPU profiling. It's recommended to use HTA for deep analysis of training loop behavior in a distributed PyTorch environment across multiple GPUs and compute nodes.

Continuous Integration and Performance Benchmarking

After applying all your optimizations, it's critical to sustain them and continuously check for performance regressions. As code and configurations evolve (e.g., new PyTorch releases, new model features, code refactorings, etc.), it's easy for performance to regress if not tracked.

You should set up a simple performance regression continuous integration (CI) using TorchBench (*https://oreil.ly/T_1U2*) and GitHub Actions to automatically catch slow-downs. TorchBench is an open source suite of PyTorch model benchmarks. TorchBench also includes popular models and benchmarks that run with `torch.compile` to also track compiler performance.

You can also extend TorchBench with your own model—or a smaller proxy model. For instance, you can fork TorchBench locally, add your model, and run TorchBench as part of your build and CI workflows. This way, you have a first-class performance-regression job that continuously runs—either on a schedule or with every code commit.

The performance-regression job loads your model—or potentially a smaller but representative variant of your model—runs a few iterations, and measures throughput, for instance, in tokens/sec or samples/sec. The CI job compares this against a stored baseline number and fails the CI build if throughput drops below a certain threshold. Here is a GitHub Action snippet that defines a TorchBench-based performance-regression job:

```
- name: Run MoE benchmark
  run: |
    torchbench run --model moe --iters 10 --batch-size 4 --json results.json

- name: Compare throughput
  run: |
    python scripts/compare_perf.py baseline.json results.json
```

The first step runs our MoE benchmark for 10 iterations and batch size 4. This short run is enough to gauge performance in CI. However, for final numbers, you'll want to measure longer runs. We keep it short to fit CI time limits.

Here, the output is a JSON file, `--json results.json`. The second step runs a small script to compare the new results with a baseline JSON stored on the main branch, for example. If the new commit was, say, ≥ 5% slower, we would flag it as a regression and fail the CI build.

Make sure that the CI runners have consistent hardware—or use cloud-based reserved and dedicated instances for reproducible results. Performance numbers can vary widely across different types of GPUs and on different cloud providers.

You should also write correctness unit tests to make sure that optimized custom kernels produce the same results as PyTorch's equivalent operations. In particular, test edge cases and random seeds.

A custom kernel might pass basic tests but fail on extreme inputs with very large values that can cause overflow if not handled properly. Use PyTorch's `torch.allclose` with strict tolerances for numerical accuracy checks on your optimizations. This way, you catch any correctness issues early.

It's also useful to log memory usage and data loading times as part of the CI workflow. For example, you should capture `torch.cuda.max_memory_allocated()` during the run—as well as timing the actual data loading. Remember that performance optimizations are multidimensional. A change that speeds up computations by 20% but increases memory usage by 200% might produce a net negative improvement in practice.

And remember that software is not perfect. Even PyTorch updates can inadvertently change the performance profile of your workload. For example, a newer version of PyTorch might alter kernel-fusion patterns or scheduling heuristics.

If this type of update causes a 5% slowdown in your model, you want to catch this early, adjust your code, and report it upstream as a PyTorch issue. While this is more common for custom or less used LLMs that are not included in PyTorch's regular performance tests, it's something to keep an eye on.

The PyTorch team is usually very responsive to performance regressions. They often push fixes in nightly builds once alerted. By catching regressions early, you can even contribute a fix yourself—or at least provide an informative report.

In short, it's not enough to optimize once. You need to protect the effectiveness of your optimizations as the system evolves, new performance optimizations are applied, and new features are added. By integrating performance testing into your CI, any code change that hurts performance will be immediately visible and addressed. This will give you the confidence that your performance gains aren't going to silently erode with the next code refactor.

It's recommended to incorporate some tolerance to variance by running multiple iterations before failing the build. Performance can fluctuate slightly due to external noise. For instance, you can require a 5% regression sustained over 3 runs before failing the build. PyTorch's own continuous performance-regression system (discussed in the next section) uses statistical smoothing to avoid false alarms.

Beyond your own CI, it's useful to keep an eye on PyTorch's performance *heads-up display* (HUD) (*https://oreil.ly/GXWkH*). This is a public dashboard that tracks the performance of common models using PyTorch's CI system, as we'll discuss next.

PyTorch HUD Performance Dashboard

While optimizing, it's useful to have visibility into performance changes over time in the broader framework. PyTorch's open source performance HUD provides real-time feedback from nightly benchmark runs. This web UI shows build statuses, test results, and performance metrics for the PyTorch repository across multiple hardware backends, including NVIDIA GPUs, AMD GPUs, and CPUs—as well as many common models.

PyTorch engineers, and anyone in the community, can rely on the HUD to detect regressions. If a new commit causes any model's tokens/sec to drop significantly, the HUD marks it in red as an early warning. This prompts a deeper investigation into the changes that caused the regression.

Typically the threshold for HUD is around a 5% regression. Minor noise fluctuations are normal, but anything beyond that threshold will trigger an investigation. HUD also includes trend lines. So if you see a gradual performance decay over weeks due to many small commits, for example, this will also be flagged for investigation.

By navigating to the Benchmarks → vLLM (*https://oreil.ly/JxLKJ*) section of the HUD, you can see benchmark results for various language models. The dashboard tracks metrics over time, such as compilation time, memory usage, throughput (tokens per second), and FLOPS utilization for each model and hardware type, as shown in Figure 13-7.

For example, you might see that, after a certain date, throughput dropped while memory usage increased. This indicates a potential increase in memory fragmentation—or that a less efficient kernel was picked. HUD helps correlate these types of changes directly with GitHub commits.

It's useful to monitor HUD to gauge if upstream PyTorch changes might affect your model. If your model is not included directly in the HUD, a model with a similar architecture may serve as a proxy. Also, HUD is open source, so you can mimic it yourself for your own model, hardware, and environment.

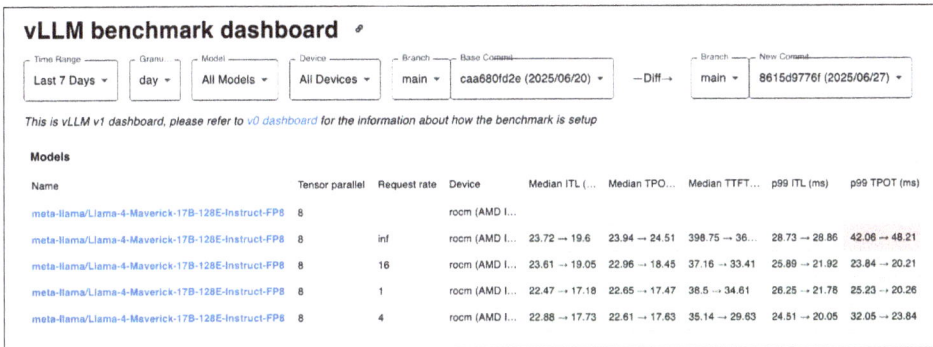

Figure 13-7. PyTorch HUD dashboard (source: https://oreil.ly/JxLKJ)

Each data point on the chart is generated by comparing a performance benchmark between a base commit and the latest commit on PyTorch's `main` branch. The dashboard allows selecting the time range (e.g., last 7 days, 30 days) and granularity (hourly, daily, weekly) to zoom in or out to show trends over time.

The HUD's implementation is open source in the `pytorch/test-infra` repository (*https://oreil.ly/4nDs3*). It uses a combination of Python scripts and Grafana dashboards. You can run a mini-HUD internally by collecting your model's performance data over time and visualizing it. Even a simple spreadsheet or Grafana instance can mimic this type of visualization. The key is to track the same metrics consistently.

It's fairly straightforward to add or modify dashboards, contribute new YAML configs, and update benchmark scripts in the CI. In principle, if you want to track your custom model in the HUD, you could add a benchmark for it and have it run in PyTorch's CI. This way, any PyTorch change that affects your model's performance will show up in the chart.

> It's highly recommended to set up a continuous benchmarking and performance-regression system like `pytorch/test-infra` for your own models to catch regressions early for your specific workload.

Performance Benchmarks and MLPerf Logging

Beyond ad hoc benchmarks and CI, industry-standard benchmarks like MLPerf (*https://oreil.ly/ZU2hI*) provide valuable feedback and encourage good practices. MLPerf Training and Inference benchmarks push state-of-the-art performance with rigorous logging to make sure the results are trustworthy and hold up to apples-to-apples comparisons. Even if you're not entering the competition, the MLPerf logging methodology is useful for your own system's performance analysis.

MLPerf logging standardizes the output of key events and metrics during a training run. Each log entry is a JSON object printed with a prefix like ::::MLL. Entries include key-value pairs along with metadata. In PyTorch, you can use the open source MLPerf Logging library on GitHub to format your output to MLPerf standards.

In an MLPerf training run, the log includes entries for initialization start time, training start time, each epoch's time, end of training time, final accuracy, etc. Everything is timestamped to the millisecond and labeled properly.

The MLPerf compliance scripts parse these logs to verify the run obeyed the rules. For instance, there should be no hyperparameter changes after the start; you must use the proper number of epochs, etc.

The log will also include calculated throughput—and whether the run achieved a target accuracy within the allowed time. This ensures fairness since you can't claim a throughput number without also meeting the accuracy requirement.

> In your own training, you should always pair performance measurements with accuracy checks. This way, you don't optimize the model into an unstable condition.

Some MLPerf logs, especially in research submissions, include a breakdown of each epoch and iteration timing. This level of detail isn't required for the competition, but it's very useful internally. For instance, you can log how much of each iteration was spent in the forward pass, backward pass, and communication such as all-reduce. You can also log averages of these timings across all nodes in a multinode cluster to pinpoint distributed bottlenecks.

Here is a small example snippet of an MLPerf JSON log. This is followed by example Table 13-6, which is derived from these logs and includes the percentage of each component relative to the overall step time:

```
{
    "step_time_ms": 24.0,
    "forward_ms": 10.5,
    "backward_ms": 9.0,
    "allreduce_ms": 4.0,
    "other_ms": 0.5
}
```

Table 13-6. Example MLPerf Logging breakdown of time per training iteration

Step component	Time per iteration (ms)	Percentage of step
Forward pass	10.5 ms	43.8%
Backward pass	9.0 ms	37.5%
All-reduce (grad sync)	4.0 ms	16.7%
Other overhead	0.5 ms	2.1%
Total step time	**24.0 ms**	**100%**

In this example 24 ms training step, the computation (forward and backward) takes 19.5 ms (10.5 ms + 9.0 ms), or 81.3% (43.8% + 37.5%) of the step time. The communication (gradient all-reduce) takes 4.0 ms (16.7%), and other overhead (e.g., data loading) takes 0.5 ms (2.1%) of the step time.

Such a breakdown is extremely useful, as it tells us that roughly one-sixth of the time is spent in gradient synchronization. If we wanted to speed up training further, we could focus on overlapping or reducing the all-reduce time.

For instance, we could try activation compression or try to better overlap communication with computation using techniques like asynchronous all-reduce or pipeline parallelism to reduce the 4 ms spent in all-reduce. If "other overhead" were large enough, we would target data loading, which we'd address differently.

MLPerf optimizations for all-reduce include techniques like delayed all-reduce (called *slack*) or overlapping multiple smaller all-reduces with computation. These are advanced tricks beyond the scope of this discussion, but the point is that this type of breakdown directs you to exactly where you need to optimize.

While MLPerf Logging is specific to competition rules, the general practice of structured logging, performance metrics, and timing breakdowns can be applied to your own training and inference simulations. For example, you can instrument your training loop to log a JSON line each epoch with additional metrics like throughput, latency, GPU utilization (from `nvidia-smi`), etc.

Over a long training run, these logs become a treasure trove for post-training analysis. You can plot how performance changed from day 1 to day 7 of training to determine if the job slowed down due to memory fragmentation. Or you can see how different phases scale, including data loading, compute, etc.

By logging metrics and not just the final accuracy, you make your results reproducible and debuggable. If someone retrains your model later and it's slower, the logs will help pinpoint the problem. Maybe the data input layer is slower. Or maybe they're using a different hardware config. This practice goes hand-in-hand with CI, which encourages a log, monitor, and compare methodology.

By instrumenting your pipelines to emit JSON logs of various timing components, you can track improvements as you implement your optimizations. This also makes it easier to communicate bottlenecks—and performance-tuning results—with the team in a standardized way.

> Since MLPerf includes benchmarks for massive models across multiple GPUs and multiple compute nodes, you can study MLPerf submissions to get insight into best practices for popular LLMs and cluster configurations. Many of the optimizations we discuss in this book are used by the winning MLPerf submissions. This is an excellent source for ongoing performance tips and tricks—as well as optimal cluster topologies at a large scale.

Key Takeaways

PyTorch's relative simplicity and high level of abstraction can sometimes lead to a false sense of performance safety. As such, it's surprisingly easy to introduce subtle performance bugs during development. Here is a summary of common PyTorch performance pitfalls—and how to address them:

Maintain a profile-first approach
> At ultrascale, bottlenecks can hide at any layer—Python overhead, PyTorch framework scheduling, CPU data-loading stalls, GPU kernel inefficiencies, memory issues, etc. Relying on intuition alone often misses the true hotspots. Use a holistic profiling strategy with multiple tools (as we did in this chapter) to capture performance at every level. Modern profilers have low-overhead modes that can be used in production to catch regressions. Combining these with hardware metrics like GPU SM utilization from `nvidia-smi`, you can identify the bottlenecks with confidence and prioritize optimizations correctly—rather than optimizing in the wrong place.

Prefer compile mode versus eager mode
> In eager mode, every tiny operation is launched as its own kernel. This incurs Python dispatch and GPU launch overhead each time. Instead, use PyTorch's JIT compilation with `torch.compile`. With essentially a one-line change (`model = torch.compile(model)`), PyTorch can capture the model graph and generate fused, optimized code.

Use the highest optimization compiler mode that your workload allows
> For long-running jobs, `max-autotune` often wins on steady-state speed, but `reduce-overhead` can be better for small batches or dynamic shapes. Validate modes on your workload. CUDA Graphs in `max-autotune` can mask launch overhead and are incompatible with frequently changing shapes.

Save compiled artifacts to reuse

If startup time is a concern, it's best to cache the compiled artifacts for reuse later. To do this, you can use `torch.compiler.save_cache_artifacts()` and `load_cache_artifacts()`. For long-running jobs on multinode fleets, it's recommended to persist compiler artifacts as a "mega-cache" in a shared path (e.g., `TORCHINDUCTOR_CACHE_DIR` environment variable) mounted at identical locations across nodes. This will help avoid cold starts when new nodes are started.

Avoid synchronization gotchas

PyTorch is designed for usability, which means it's easy to inadvertently write code that forces synchronization between CPU and GPU. For example, calling `tensor.item()` on a CUDA tensor to retrieve a Python value will synchronize the GPU. Use `torch.cuda.Stream.wait_stream()` with stream events instead of forcing synchronizations when coordinating between streams. Similarly, transferring data from GPU to CPU without using `non_blocking=True` will cause a synchronization. Use asynchronous transfers and let the profilers guide you to any hidden synchronizations.

Avoid Python-side profiling with `time.time()`, *as this will implicitly synchronize*

Timing GPU code blocks with `time.time()` as this includes a synchronization. It's better to use `torch.cuda.Event(enable_timing=True)` for timing GPU code without extraneous synchronizations.

Utilize the Tensor Cores

It's surprisingly easy, and not ideal, to fall back to full FP32—and not use the Tensor Cores—without realizing it. To ensure you are using the Tensor Cores, wrap the forward pass and loss computation in `torch.autocast` and choose a lower-precision `dtype` so that GEMMs can use the Tensor Cores. (Note that `autocast` does not change the storage `dtype` of model weights unless you explicitly cast the model. Instead, it selects compute `dtype`s for eligible operations and leaves numerically sensitive operations in `float32`.)

Use TF32 over FP32 to activate the Tensor Cores

For `FP32` workloads that can tolerate TF32 precision, use `torch.set_float32_matmul_precision()` with either `"high"` or `"medium"` to enable TF32. This setting maps to `torch.backends.cuda.matmul.fp32_precision` under the hood on CUDA devices. On modern GPUs, TF32 uses Tensor Cores, which is ideal. Be sure to verify that your kernel uses Tensor Cores with Nsight Compute's SpeedOfLight view or the `sm__inst_executed_pipe_tensor` metric. (Note: using `"highest"` will enforce true `FP32` and disable TF32, so be careful. This can be useful for debugging but is discouraged if your goal is to improve performance.)

Verify the Tensor Cores are actually being used

To verify that kernels are using the Tensor Cores and the intended `dtype`, you should use your profilers. In PyTorch, inspect operator timing with `torch.profiler`, then use Nsight Compute to confirm Tensor pipeline activity. The SpeedOfLight and Compute Workload Analysis sections in Nsight Compute will report Tensor pipeline utilization and a kernel-execution timeline using performance monitor (PM) sampling.

Prefer BF16 over FP16 when possible

Prefer `dtype=torch.bfloat16` on modern GPUs because `BF16` keeps the `FP32` exponent range and normally does not require gradient scaling. If you must train in FP16, enable `torch.cuda.amp.GradScaler` and verify no overflow/underflow in logs. BF16 generally avoids scaling on modern GPU Tensor Cores.

Fuse small operations

Many model computations involve long sequences of small elementwise or matrix operations. These small operations each incur extra memory reads/writes and launch overhead. Use `torch.profiler` to spot many small (e.g., < 1 ms) operations in a row. If you see a pattern like linear → gelu → dropout, consider replacing it with a fused module or relying on `torch.compile` to fuse it. And, for any operations that it misses, consider writing custom fused kernels. Each custom fusion can save a few percent. Together, these small "last mile" gains will add up.

Reduce memory fragmentation

If your training job or inference pipeline runs for days/weeks/months, memory fragmentation can become an issue—especially since tensor sizes vary from iteration to iteration in most LLM applications. Consider using memory pooling libraries like PyTorch's caching allocator that can allocate all large tensors upfront. The fewer distinct allocation sizes you have, the better. So reuse and stick to constant shapes when possible. Proactively manage memory by tuning the CUDA allocator with environment variables (e.g., `max_split_size_mb`). And avoid breaking large chunks into many small pieces, preallocate frequently used buffers at a fixed maximum size, and reuse buffers to keep allocation sizes consistent. These practices will keep memory usage stable over time and prevent fragmentation-related slowdowns and crashes.

Use activation checkpointing

By default, PyTorch saves all activations needed for the backward pass, which consumes enormous memory for large models. Consider using activation checkpointing to trade compute for memory. `torch.utils.checkpoint` makes it easy to apply by wrapping segments of your forward pass so their activations aren't saved. They'll just be recomputed in the backward pass. This will reduce memory usage at the cost of extra compute. However, this is usually worthwhile since

GPU memory is at more of a premium than compute for modern GPUs. This is almost mandatory for models above tens of billions of parameters on modern GPU hardware. Also remember that you can mix precision. For instance, you might keep a few critical activations in higher precision to preserve accuracy and recompute others in lower precision to save memory and time.

Offload memory to CPU or NVMe storage

Model parameters, gradients, optimizer states, and activations all compete for limited GPU VRAM. Even with large HBM, a multi-hundred-billion-parameter model will exceed it—even at reduced precision. Leverage the system's memory hierarchy and offload less frequently used data to CPU RAM or NVMe disk—and bring them back in only when needed. These data transfers can be streamed and overlapped with computations using asynchronous copies. Monitor interconnect throughput when you do this to make sure you're not saturating the link.

Reduce input pipeline stalls

Even a perfectly optimized training loop can be bottlenecked if the input pipeline can't feed data fast enough. This typically manifests as bubbles of idle GPU time waiting for the next batch. This is often obvious in profiling since most tools show gaps before iterations—or CPU threads busy in data loading code while the GPU sits idle. Maximize data throughput using a sufficient number of DataLoader workers and `prefetch_factor` size.

It's important to utilize all CPU cores for data loading and preparation. Use `pin_memory=True` and nonblocking transfers for faster H2D copies. Preprocess your dataset (e.g., tokenization) offline so the data loader does minimal work. Also, you can increase the DataLoader `prefetch_factor`. It's recommended to continuously fetch additional batches slightly ahead of their usage.

Profile and possibly offload CPU-side data transformations

Since Python data transformations (e.g., tokenization) can be surprisingly slow, make sure these host-side transformations are vectorized. Consider using optimized C++ libraries when available. And potentially offload complex transformations to the GPU using libraries like NVIDIA DALI.

Optimize multi-GPU and multinode communication

Distributed training often hits a ceiling due to communication overhead if not managed properly. Use optimized PyTorch distributed implementations like DDP, which overlaps communication with computation by default. Tune the gradient `bucket_cap_mb` empirically. Larger buckets can reduce per-message overhead, but they also tend to delay when the first reduction can begin. Smaller buckets can start earlier, but incurs the overhead of a larger number of collectives.

Monitor network bandwidth

If it's maxed out, you can explore activation compression techniques to reduce bandwidth usage. Be sure to overlap the all-reduce collective with backward computation so you can hide the communication time. For multinode, consider the topology and place processes that frequently communicate on the same node or switch to reduce latency.

Avoid "bit rot" over time

It's easy for performance to regress due to ongoing code changes, framework updates, and new application features. For instance, a minor refactoring might introduce an unexpected synchronization, or a PyTorch upgrade might change an operation's implementation. Treat performance as a first-class metric and set up continuous integration tests, dashboards, and alerts to monitor performance. Every code commit (or daily/weekly run) should include a quick performance benchmark to catch performance regressions.

Update your baselines whenever hardware changes

If you move from the B200 to the GB300, for example, make sure to reestablish your performance baseline and thresholds. New hardware will handle certain patterns better or worse. Recalibrate and adjust your alerts accordingly.

Use tools like TorchBench or custom timing scripts in automated workflows

Keep an eye on external signals from PyTorch's nightly performance benchmarks (reported in the public HUD regressions dashboard)—especially for models similar to yours. If a general regression happens in PyTorch, you'll know before upgrading. Whenever a slowdown is detected, investigate immediately, identify the root cause (e.g., your code or an upstream change), mitigate it (e.g., revert or adapt the code), and report it upstream (e.g., PyTorch, Triton, NVIDIA, etc.) so the respective community can address the issue and benefit from the fix. Also, maintain correctness tests for your optimizations so you don't silently break accuracy. By making performance-regression testing part of your workflow, your speedup will last the test of time.

Conclusion

It's important to combine microlevel profiling (e.g., per-operator and per-kernel) with macrolevel benchmarking (e.g., end-to-end throughput and latency). This way, you have a comprehensive view of system performance. It's as important to optimize individual kernels as it is to tune your complete, end-to-end training and inference pipeline—and keep it tuned over time. This holistic approach is critical as hardware evolves.

The fundamentals in this chapter will help you adapt to new platforms. Always profile, identify bottlenecks, and apply the appropriate optimizations at each level of the stack. By systematically applying compiler and memory optimizations, you can significantly boost your workload's performance closer to the hardware limits—while still maintaining acceptable accuracy.

As we showed, careful profiling will identify the true bottlenecks. And targeted optimizations can produce large speedups in training and inference performance. It's also important to set up automation to protect these gains against performance regressions over time.

This end-to-end optimization journey required effort at every level of the stack. The end result is an optimized, efficient, and regression-resistant system that produces maximum performance from modern GPU hardware, scales to multinode cluster and rack-level topologies, and adapts to future advancements in hardware, software, and algorithms.

## CHAPTER 14

PyTorch Compiler, OpenAI Triton, and XLA Backends

In Chapter 13, we discussed multiple ways to optimize and tune PyTorch-based training and inference workloads. We touched on the PyTorch compiler and how it automates kernel fusion and other kernel-level techniques to improve performance with very little changes to your code.

In this chapter, we dive deeper into the dynamic PyTorch compilation stack, including components like TorchDynamo, Ahead-of-Time Autograd (AOT Autograd), and PrimTorch Intermediate Representation (IR) (aka *Prims* or *Prims IR*)—as well as compiler backends like TorchInductor, Accelerated Linear Algebra (XLA), and OpenAI's Triton ecosystem. The PyTorch compiler stack is shown in Figure 14-1.

We also cover tools for debugging the compilation pipeline as well as libraries for scaling PyTorch across multi-GPU and multinode clusters. We will then explore how torch.compile works under the hood and how to handle dynamic shapes and variable sequence lengths efficiently.

We will also examine the PyTorch compiler's integration with the OpenAI Triton ecosystem. Our goal is to accelerate and scale our PyTorch models and applications without sacrificing the flexible, eager-execution development experience of PyTorch.

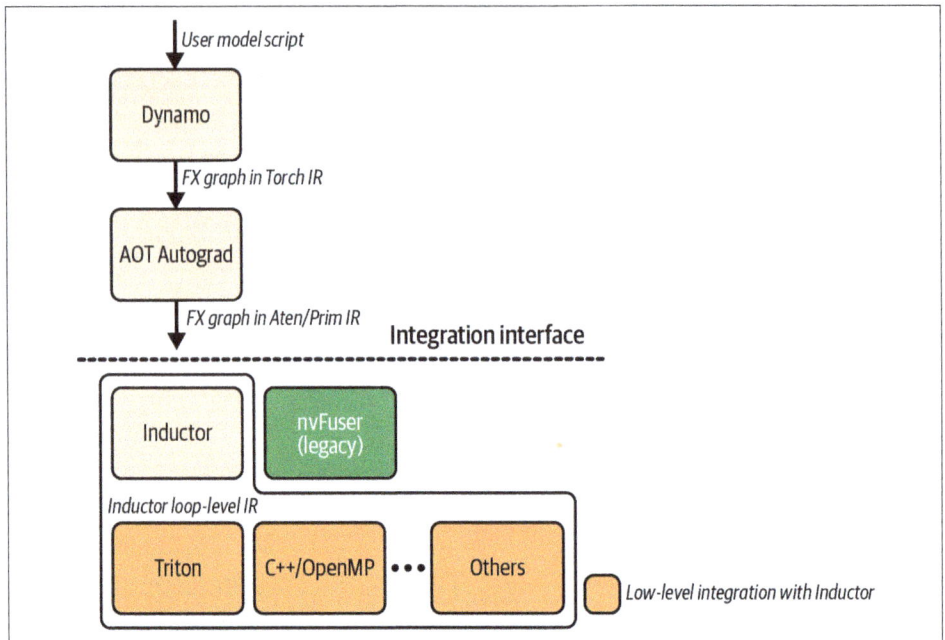

Figure 14-1. Overview of PyTorch compiler stack

PyTorch Compiler Deep Dive

As described in Chapter 13, PyTorch's `torch.compile` will compile your PyTorch code (and models) to produce significant speedups. In most cases, you can do this in just a single line of code, as shown next. We'll talk about the different options as we go along:

```
compiled_model = torch.compile(model,
  mode="max-autotune",
# ...
)
```

This section breaks down the PyTorch compilation pipeline steps, including Torch-Dynamo's graph capture, AOT Autograd's combined forward/backward graph optimization, PrimTorch IR, and TorchInductor's code generation. This pipeline is responsible for producing optimized kernels for the target GPU hardware and is shown in Figure 14-2.

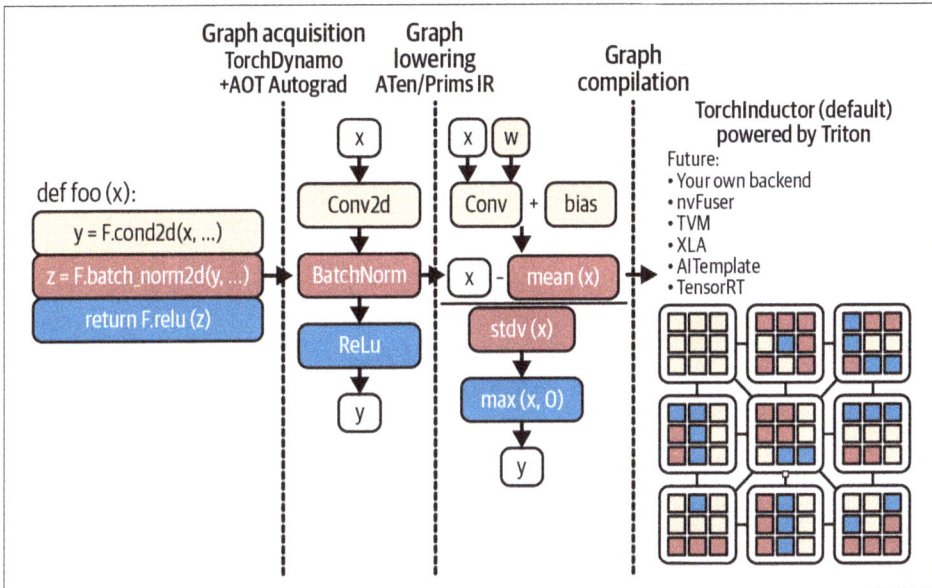

Figure 14-2. PyTorch compiler pipeline (adapted from the PyTorch 2.x overview (https://oreil.ly/55JDn))

TorchDynamo for Bytecode Capture and Graph Extraction

TorchDynamo, or just Dynamo, is the first stage of `torch.compile`. It hooks into Python's frame-evaluation mechanism to intercept model execution at the bytecode level.

Dynamo hooks into CPython's frame evaluation to identify tensor-producing bytecode regions and constructs an execution graph for those regions. It then executes the compiled graph using the chosen backend. Unsupported code is left to run eagerly.

This interception and rewriting mechanism is what lets TorchDynamo capture sequences of PyTorch operations into a graph representation that can be optimized by the next steps, AOT Autograd and PrimTorch IR, covered in the next sections.

TorchDynamo leverages the CPython Frame Evaluation API (PEP 523 (*https://oreil.ly/8Bglo*)) to capture the operations safely—and with minimal overhead. Normally, the Python interpreter executes each operation one by one. With Dynamo enabled, however, the interpreter redirects its execution to Dynamo, which aggregates the tensor operations into a graph before executing them. This enables whole-graph optimizations like kernel fusion, which reduces per-operation Python and host-side overhead.

Instead of launching a new GPU kernel for each operation and paying per-operation Python overhead, the compiled graph can fuse many operations into one or a few kernels. This reduces dispatch overhead and improves memory access patterns.

In Chapter 13, we saw how Python overhead and many small operations can bottleneck models. We also saw that TorchDynamo addresses this issue by batching small operations into larger units when possible—assuming the chain of operations is graph-friendly and doesn't cause too many graph breaks.

When TorchDynamo is enabled by `torch.compile`, it inspects each Python opcode. Whenever it encounters a PyTorch tensor operation such as arithmetic or a neural network layer, it doesn't execute it immediately. Instead, Dynamo appends the operation as a node in an FX graph and defers execution to the compiled backend for captured regions. TorchDynamo continues this process until it hits some code it can't handle. At this point, a graph break occurs (more on this in a bit), and the unsupported operations run in regular, noncompiled eager mode.

TorchDynamo tries to compile as large a portion of your program as possible into a single graph, but it will fall back to Python eager execution when it can't proceed due to unsupported constructs such as complex control flow or non-PyTorch library calls. It does this to ensure correctness.

After a block of unsupported operations has passed, Dynamo will resume capturing subsequent operations into a new graph after that point. This mix of compiled and noncompiled execution gives you the best of both worlds: you keep PyTorch's flexibility where needed but compile everything else for speed.

> You want to avoid graph breaks whenever possible, as they interrupt whole-graph optimizations and limit the performance benefits of the compiler.

You can use `torch.compiler.set_stance("fail_on_recompile")` to force Dynamo to raise an error to catch unsafe recompilations. It will log the reason for recompile and help you debug the graph break. This gives you full visibility into why your graph is splitting. The code is shown here:

```
// fail on graph breaks, recompiles
torch.compiler.set_stance("fail_on_recompile")
compiled_model = torch.compile(model,
  mode="max-autotune",
  ...
)
```

This way, you can refactor the code paths that are causing the break—or mark them as expected graph boundaries with `torch._dynamo.allow_in_graph()`, as you'll see in a bit. Once your graph is clean, you can switch back to `torch.com` `piler.set_stance("eager_on_recompile")`. Remember, setting this back will cause TorchDynamo to silently fall back to eager mode if a subsequent graph break occurs.

The output of TorchDynamo's capture is called an *FX Graph* of your code. FX is an intermediate representation (IR) in which each node is a call to a PyTorch `aten` (*https://oreil.ly/dB_5I*) operator or built-in Python function. For example, consider a simple Python function, as shown here:

```
def f(x, y):
    z = x.sin() + y
    return z.sum()
```

Here, TorchDynamo will produce an FX Graph roughly equivalent to the following pseudocode:

```
graph():  # pseudo-code for FX IR
    %x : Tensor = Placeholder[target=x]
    %y : Tensor = Placeholder[target=y]
    %sin : Tensor = torch.sin(%x)
    %add : Tensor = torch.add(%sin, %y)
    %sum : Tensor = torch.sum(%add)
    return %sum
```

The FX Graph nodes correspond to `Placeholder` inputs and calls to primitive ATen operations like `aten::sin`, `aten::add`, `aten::sum`, clearly representing the computation graph structure. Once constructed, this FX Graph is handed off to AOT Autograd for combined forward-pass and backward-pass tracing.

AOT Autograd's generated forward and backward combined trace is then sent to a backend compiler such as TorchInductor or XLA to perform kernel fusion and generate optimized device code. TorchDynamo itself remains framework-agnostic and focuses on accurate, low-overhead graph capture. TorchDynamo delegates all heavy optimizations to downstream compiler stages.

TorchDynamo inserts guards on Python values—such as tensor shapes, dtypes, and even global variables—that affect the graph trace. These guards ensure that if something changes that was assumed to be constant (e.g., tensor shape or dtype), the compiled graph is invalidated and recompiled if needed. This allows robust handling of dynamic shapes and model modifications—at the cost of additional recompilations when assumptions are violated.

> It's recommended to monitor the number of graph recompilations when using the PyTorch compiler.

Using the default `dynamic=None`, the compiler will specialize using the observed shapes. When it encounters dynamic shapes, it will recompile a more dynamic kernel. It may recompile again if it later detects additional sources of dynamism.

In practice, this means you'll see one extra compilation on the first varying-shape input—and only one extra compile. If you already know which input dimensions will vary, you can use `torch._dynamo.mark_dynamic(tensor, dim)` before running your model. This will preempt the initial compile.

You can further tune the compiler's "stance" with `torch.compiler.set_stance()` to change how and when TorchDynamo falls back to eager or recompiles. A stance governs the compiler's tolerance or strictness in the face of errors or fallbacks. This gives you more control of the trade-off between developer feedback and uninterrupted execution. The following are the stances as of this writing:

default
> The compiler tries to compile what it can, silently falling back to eager execution when unsupported code is encountered. This is the standard, default setting, which causes normal compilation behavior and fallbacks.

fail_on_recompile
> If a graph break or unsupported operation is encountered, the compiler raises an error. This is useful during development when you want to catch unexpected breaks or uncompiled paths.

eager_on_recompile
> When a recompile is necessary, run the code in eager mode. If compiled code is already cached (and valid for the input), it should still be used.

force_eager
> Use eager mode and ignore all `torch.compile` directives.

By capturing whole sequences of operations, TorchDynamo can perform whole-graph optimizations like kernel fusion to reduce launch overhead and minimize memory movement. It also eliminates Python-layer overhead for those fused operations. Figure 14-3 compares eager versus compiled modes, including the compiler cache.

Instead of executing each small operation and kernel launch separately, the compiler can fuse many operations into a single kernel. This reduces CPU-GPU synchronization points and improves memory locality. Otherwise, the GPU would be bottlenecked with lots of fine-grained operations, heavy synchronization, and excessive global memory accesses.

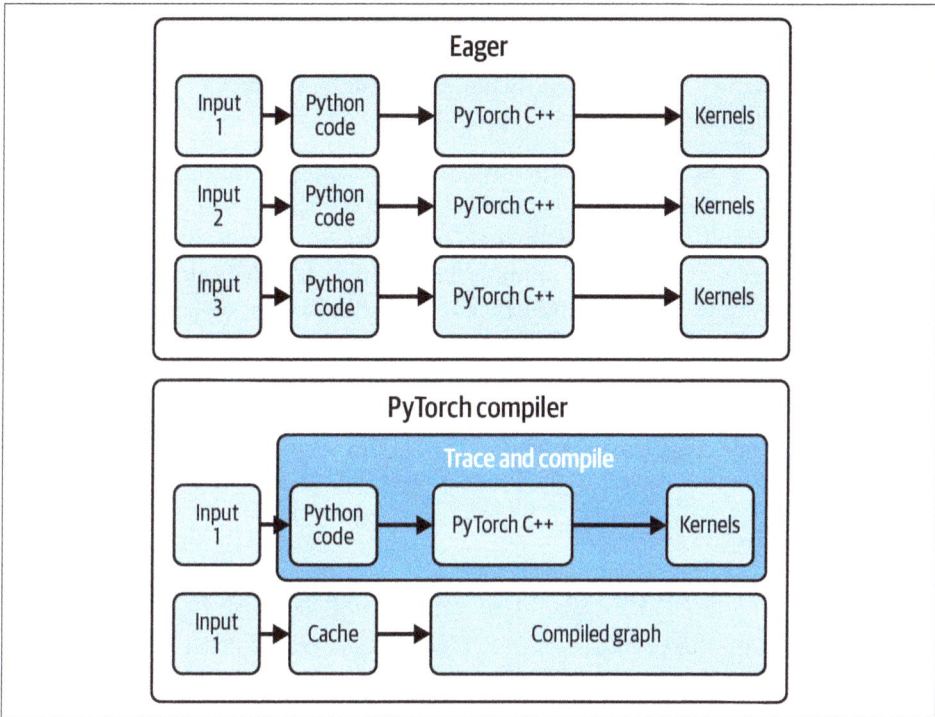

Figure 14-3. PyTorch eager versus compiled modes

TorchDynamo continues capturing until a graph break is needed. A graph break can be triggered by unsupported Python constructs (like certain control flows, e.g., an `if` statement using a Python bool instead of tensor operations) or by unsupported operations. When a graph break occurs, the current graph segment ends, and Dynamo falls back to eager mode for the code that can't be captured. After that, TorchDynamo will start a new graph trace once it returns to traceable code.

You can successfully implement compiler-graph-friendly conditionals in PyTorch by expressing the logic as pure PyTorch tensor operations, including `torch.where()` with a mask. Here is an example that replaces a non-graph-friendly Python `if` statement with a pure-tensor operation masking approach:

```python
# Compute a boolean mask from a data-dependent tensor condition
# mask shape (batch_size,1) broadcastable to x's
mask = x.sum(dim=1, keepdim=True) > 0

# Use torch.where to select element-wise between two tensor expressions
# picks f(x) where mask is True, otherwise g(x)
out = torch.where(mask, f(x), g(x))
```

This avoids a Python `if x.sum() > 0:` statement, which causes a graph break. It does this by staying entirely within PyTorch's graph-friendly tensor operations. In this case, TorchDynamo captures the whole sequence, including the mask and `torch.where()` without breaking the graph.

With each new release, PyTorch expands which operations can be captured without causing a graph break. For instance, high-level conditional primitives like `torch.cond` can capture certain if/else logic in graphs. Specifically, both branches are traced and compiled. `torch.cond` requires a boolean scalar predicate. Both branches must return the same structure and `dtypes`. And shapes must be consistent at runtime. Data-dependent branches will often lead to graph breaks.

> It's recommended to minimize graph breaks by refactoring your code using tensor operations like `torch.where()` to maximize the continuous regions that TorchDynamo can capture.

AOT Autograd Fusion for Forward and Backward Passes

Once TorchDynamo has captured an FX Graph for as much of the forward pass as possible, the next compiler phase is AOT Autograd. AOT Autograd runs the Dynamo-captured forward graph through PyTorch's autograd engine in "functional" mode to record the backward operations. This is how the static backward graph is produced (this is in contrast to relying on PyTorch's default autograd engine to execute the backward-pass operations one by one).

In essence, AOT Autograd generates a joint forward-backward graph that can then be optimized and fused as a whole. And it guarantees the same forward and backward results as eager mode.

AOT Autograd works by tracing the forward graph through the autograd engine to capture the gradient computations. It effectively runs the forward graph with `torch.autograd.forward_ad` (or a similar technique) to record which operations are needed for the backward computations. The result is a combined forward and backward graph. The combined graph can then be optimized using common-subexpression elimination, etc. Later, it's compiled by a backend like TorchInductor or XLA.

By planning both the forward and backward ahead of time, the PyTorch compiler can holistically fuse across the boundary of the forward and backward passes together. This results in ahead-of-time fusion of operations that span the two phases. For example, it can fuse an elementwise operation in the forward pass with the corresponding elementwise gradient computation in the backward pass, if possible, into one kernel.

The compiler can also eliminate overhead by reusing intermediate results between forward and backward computations when safe to do so. This can improve performance greatly for model training workloads in which backward operations can dominate the overall runtime.

Without AOT Autograd, PyTorch would need to execute each backward operation separately using the default PyTorch autograd engine—independently of the forward pass. With AOT Autograd, the graph of execution is optimized holistically.

The resulting joint graph produced by AOT Autograd is guaranteed to compute the same results (this is why graph breaks are needed when the graph can't guarantee correctness). This joint graph can be further optimized because the whole sequence of operations, forward and backward, is known.

By fusing operations and memory usage across the forward and backward passes, we reduce memory accesses and kernel-launch overhead. PyTorch's compiled mode automatically uses AOT Autograd under the hood when you call `torch.compile` for operations and workloads that involve gradients, such as model training.

In short, AOT Autograd is used by `torch.compile` to compute gradients ahead of time during model training. It handles most autograd operations seamlessly and guarantees the same results as eager mode. It reuses buffers across the forward and backward passes to reduce peak memory usage. And while this phase is mostly invisible to the end user, it's a key component to enabling large speedups in modern AI model training workloads.

PrimTorch IR (Prims) Simplified Operator Set

Before handing the graph over to a low-level code generator, PyTorch performs an intermediate representation (IR) transformation known as PrimTorch IR (Prims) in some documentation and source code. PrimTorch IR is an IR that reduces the variety of operations in the graph down to a smaller core set of "primitive" operations, hence the name *PrimTorch*.

For context, PyTorch has thousands (> 2,000) of operations in its full API. PrimTorch IR reduces this to a much smaller set of primitives on which the compiler can focus. In practice, PrimTorch IR defines around 250 primitive operations, such as basic arithmetic, reductions, copy, reshape, etc.

Many complex or high-level PyTorch `aten` operations can be decomposed into these primitives with PrimTorch IR. For instance, an "in-place" PyTorch operation like `x.add_(y)` is lowered into a functional `add` followed by an explicit `copy` back into x's storage, as shown here:

```
%z    = aten::add(x, y)
%copy = aten::copy_(x, %z)    # writes z's data into x
```

Here, the IR contains a separate `aten::copy_` node instead of a special in-place mutation. This makes all tensor updates explicit and simplifies downstream compiler kernels by treating mutations as ordinary copy operations.

Specifically, by converting in-place mutations into functional operations plus distinct copy nodes, the compiler no longer has to reason about aliasing or hidden side effects. As a result, fusion passes and memory-planning algorithms can operate on a purely functional dataflow. This allows more aggressive kernel fusion and predictable, high-performance code generation.

PrimTorch IR also helps with things like eliminating aliasing and mutation in the graph. It tries to convert operations into a form that does not perform in-place updates when possible since these can complicate optimization. The output of the PrimTorch IR pass is an FX Graph that contains only `aten` IR and PrimTorch IR operations (*https://oreil.ly/BvHzg*). The FX Graph is then ready for lowering by the backend.

By doing this IR standardization, PrimTorch IR provides a stable, simplified interface for compiler backends to target. Instead of having to implement thousands of PyTorch operations, a backend like TorchInductor only needs to support the 250 primitives—other higher-level operations are derived from the primitives. This greatly reduces complexity.

And since most high-level operations (e.g., 2,000+ PyTorch ops) can be decomposed into the existing primitives, the set of PrimTorch IR primitives evolves relatively slowly—even as PyTorch adds new operations to adapt to new algorithms, models, and techniques.

> The stable PrimTorch IR interface means that to support a new accelerator, for example, developers need only implement the 250 primitives rather than thousands of ATen operations.

To summarize the pipeline so far: TorchDynamo captures a graph, AOT Autograd adds a backward pass and forms a joint forward-backward graph, and then PrimTorch IR canonicalizes the operations to a leaner, more primitive set. At this point, we have a fairly standard, device-agnostic representation of the whole computation—including the forward and backward passes—in terms of core operations. Now let's turn to the actual code-generation stage performed by the compiler backend.

TorchInductor Backend Code Generation

The final stage of the `torch.compile` stack is the compiler backend. TorchInductor, or Inductor, is PyTorch's default compiler backend. Inductor takes the optimized, joined forward and backward FX Graph consisting of `aten` (*https://oreil.ly/BvHzg*) + PrimTorch IR operations (*https://oreil.ly/BvHzg*) and generates high-performance code for the target hardware, including NVIDIA GPUs, AMD GPUs, CPUs, and others.

> XLA is an alternate backend targeting non-CUDA hardware. It's mainly used for Google Cloud TPUs through the OpenXLA project. But it can support other accelerators that adopt XLA IR. For example, Meta's in-house inference ASIC, Meta Training & Inference Accelerator (MTIA (*https://oreil.ly/vs-pg*)), uses XLA. Additionally, AWS's custom Inferentia and Trainium acclerator chips run PyTorch with an XLA compiler in its open source AWS Neuron SDK (*https://github.com/aws-neuron/aws-neuron-sdk*). NVIDIA GPUs typically use TorchInductor, however.

TorchInductor works by *lowering* the graph to a loop-level, define-by-run IR that it compiles to efficient code. Internally, Inductor represents operations as loops over multidimensional data. It automatically groups nodes from the FX Graph into fused loop blocks when possible. Each group becomes a kernel during code generation.

Inductor also supports symbolic shapes, which allow dynamic dimensions. The IR is somewhat higher-level than raw CUDA, as it represents things like elementwise computations as loops over tensor indices. The IR is user-inspectable, which helps debugging and even extending.

TorchInductor's IR can also be used for ahead-of-time compilation flows with `torch.export()` and AOTInductor. AOTInductor compiles artifacts produced by `torch.export` for AOT use cases such as packaging and deployment. This allows saving and reusing the compiled code across runs. Export is highlighted in the context of `torch.compile()` in Figure 14-4.

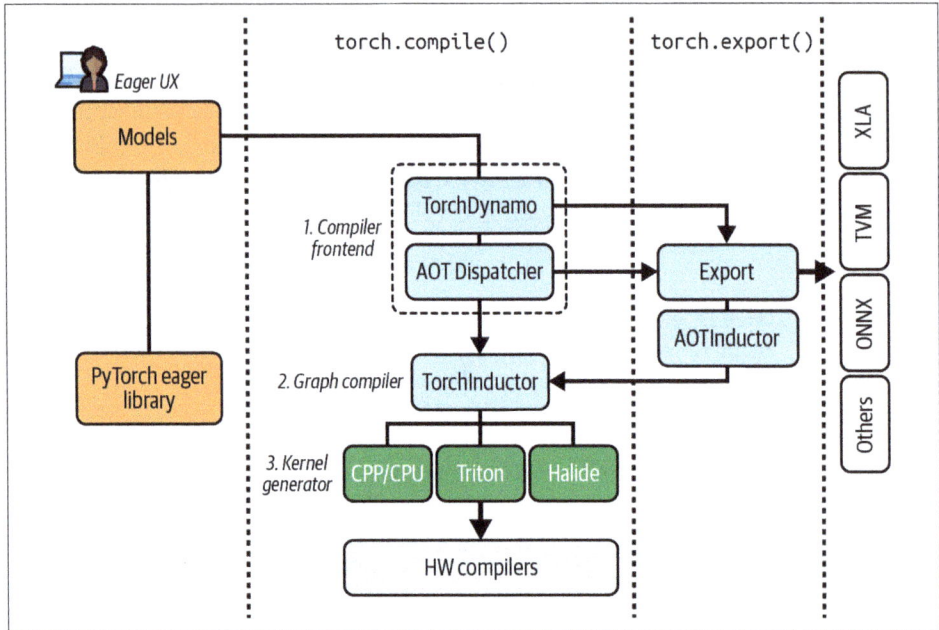

Figure 14-4. PyTorch compile and export (TorchDynamo → AOT Autograd → PrimTorch IR → TorchInductor → Triton/LLVM NVPTX); export via `torch.export`/AOTInductor; CUDA Graphs are used when shapes are static

For NVIDIA GPU backends, TorchInductor uses OpenAI's Triton JIT compiler to generate the actual GPU kernels. Triton is a CUDA-like domain-specific language (DSL) written in Python. Triton also includes a compiler for its DSL (we'll cover Triton more in a bit).

TorchInductor translates its loop-level IR into Triton code and then uses the Triton compiler to convert the Triton code into NVIDIA PTX directly using LLVM. Remember that PTX is NVIDIA's low-level instruction set architecture (ISA) for its NVIDIA GPUs.

> Importantly, Triton lowers to NVIDIA PTX using LLVM NVPTX. It does not invoke NVCC for kernel compilation. This approach lets TorchInductor produce custom kernels on the fly that are tailored to your specific model or algorithm.

The loop-level IR is implemented in Python, which makes it easy to inspect and extend. For example, suppose a graph has an operation z = x.permute(1,0) + x[2,:]. Inductor might represent this operation with the following IR:

```
def inner_fn(index: List[sympy.Expr]):
    i1, i0 = index  # index variables for dims
    tmp0 = ops.load("x", i1 + i0*size1)    # x[i1, i0]
    tmp1 = ops.load("x", 2*size1 + i0)     # x[2, i0]
    return ops.add(tmp0, tmp1)             # elementwise add

torchinductor.ir.Pointwise(
    device=torch.device("cuda"), dtype=torch.float32,
    inner_fn=inner_fn, ranges=[size0, size1]
)
```

Here, `size0` and `size1` are the dimensions of the input, x. And `inner_fn` describes how to compute one element of the output. The `Pointwise` node represents a loop nest over those ranges that applies `inner_fn` elementwise to produce the output.

This is a define-by-run style IR. By running this IR, it's executing Python that iterates and calls `ops.load` + `ops.add`. Inductor then generates the corresponding NVIDIA PTX code using the Triton JIT compiler and LLVM.

> Use `torch.library.wrap_triton` with `triton_op` to register a Triton kernel as a first-class PyTorch op with autograd and fake-tensor support. This means you can write a Triton kernel and have TorchInductor optimize it as part of your model graph.

Autotuning with TorchInductor

TorchInductor includes an autotuner built on Triton's autotuning capabilities, which we'll describe in an upcoming section. The autotuner finds the best launch configuration for each generated GPU kernel. The autotuned configuration is cached per kernel so that subsequent runs don't need to redo the tuning step.

The first time you compile code with the TorchInductor backend, it will spend extra time benchmarking different kernel variants using different block sizes, tile sizes, etc. Inductor picks the fastest variant and uses this going forward. Kernel autotuning increases initial compile-time latency, but the resulting kernels are highly optimized for runtime.

> If you recall from the last chapter, this aggressive autotuning is described as the `max-autotune` compiler mode. This is the most time-consuming compiler mode—and this is what's happening under the hood.

Beyond kernel fusion and autotuning, TorchInductor applies many low-level optimizations. These include index simplification to reduce complex index arithmetic in loops, common-subexpression elimination within the generated code, and efficient memory planning to reuse buffers and reduce allocations.

TorchInductor also uses CUDA Graphs to capture sequences of kernels at runtime for faster graph replay with minimal CPU overhead. By default, Inductor will try to wrap its generated kernels into a CUDA Graph to reduce launch overhead on each iteration. This is especially beneficial for inference—or when running any code or model with many kernels.

> The `reduce-overhead` and `max-autotune` compiler modes, described in Chapter 13, trigger the use of CUDA Graphs. However, CUDA Graphs require static shapes, so they are not used when dynamic-shape compilation is enabled. Said differently, if dynamic shapes are enabled with `dynamic=True`, TorchInductor will not use CUDA Graphs. Also, you can use `max-autotune-no-cudagraphs` when you need autotuning without CUDA Graph capture.
>
> In general, start with the default mode and use `max-autotune` to provide additional speedup for large/critical workloads as the expense of significant compile time. You may not see much benefit for smaller models.

The end result of TorchInductor is highly optimized, device-specific code for your workload. In many cases, Inductor achieves performance close to, or even exceeding, hand-tuned libraries. For instance, Inductor can fuse an entire sequence of elementwise operations, including activations and pointwise transformations, into a single kernel. It can even fuse certain patterns of matrix multiplication followed by elementwise operations like bias-add + activation into one launch. This is relatively difficult to do by hand—and requires ongoing maintenance.

The PyTorch compiler uses heuristics and backends that may route certain operations (e.g., large GEMMs) to high-performance libraries such as cuBLAS/cuBLASLt or CUTLASS. It can even emit Triton kernels for fusable patterns. In practice, TorchInductor selects and caches whichever path performs best—or is known to be optimal for the given shapes.

For transformer models, TorchInductor will fuse the layernorm and residual connection elementwise operations around a large GEMM—while still using cuBLAS for the actual GEMM computation itself. Or, for models with irregular memory access, Inductor's custom Triton kernel can outperform an existing library's kernel by doing just the work that's needed—and not benefit from a general-purpose library like cuBLAS or CUTLASS.

On modern GPUs, PyTorch's compiler can work with NVIDIA's Transformer Engine (TE) for certain transformer blocks and layers. However, PyTorch does not automatically substitute NVIDIA TE kernels when you call `torch.compile`. TE is a separate library that you must use explicitly via its modules or fused ops. But when you call TE APIs, `torch.compile` can compile and fuse around them. This complements the generated Triton kernels to provide maximum performance.

> Make sure to install NVIDIA Transformer Engine only if you plan to call TE modules directly in your model—for example, `trans former_engine.pytorch.layers`. `torch.compile` will not automatically swap TE kernels into a plain PyTorch model.

In essence, TorchInductor does the heavy lifting of turning code and models into high-performance GPU kernels. With each PyTorch release, hardware coverage is expanding and new optimized techniques are emerging. For example, PyTorch provides FlexAttention, a new attention operator that TorchInductor can compile into fused kernels approaching FlashAttention performance. Specifically, FlexAttention's fused kernels have been measured to reach up to ~85–90% (*https://oreil.ly/BHIWu*) of modern FlashAttention performance in both forward and backward passes, while allowing more flexibility including block-sparsity and custom masks. To enable the fast paths, set the following `torch.backend.cuda` attributes to `True`:

```
# Ensure SDPA fast paths are enabled
torch.backends.cuda.enable_flash_sdp(True)
torch.backends.cuda.enable_math_sdp(True)
torch.backends.cuda.enable_mem_efficient_sdp(True)
```

When using `torch.nn.attention.flex_attention`, make sure your inputs meet the fast-path constraints. This way, TorchInductor can emit the fused Triton kernels.

TorchInductor and Triton support automated warp specialization on modern GPUs. The compiler will enable it selectively when it's deemed beneficial. Warp specialization can be tuned using Triton meta-parameters such as `num_consumer_groups` and `num_buffers_warp_spec`. These optimizations further improve GEMM throughput. Triton's automatic warp specialization supports TMA and tensor descriptor APIs on modern GPU targets including Blackwell (e.g., `tcgen05`).

> It's recommended to use descriptor-based tiled loads/stores to map to TMA and reduce register pressure. This method is preferred over manual `tl.load` loops.

In short, many models run significantly faster with `torch.compile`, though the exact gains depend on your models' characteristics. The first time you run `torch.compile`, you pay a compile and autotune cost, but subsequent runs use the cached graph and kernels for lightning-fast execution.

Dynamic Shapes and Variable Sequence Lengths

A major challenge with LLM training and inference is the variable-sized sequence inputs. In traditional compilers and accelerators, varying shapes often cause recompilation or otherwise require padding inputs to a fixed, common size. This section discusses how dynamic shape tracing works in `torch.compile` to handle variable-length sequences.

Fortunately, the PyTorch compiler stack is designed to handle dynamic shapes gracefully. Specifically, it allows models to accept different input sizes without recompiling every time by using the SymPy library (*https://www.sympy.org*) to represent unknown dimensions symbolically, as we'll cover in a bit.

The PyTorch compiler will automatically mark dimensions as dynamic if it observes changes in their size. TorchInductor starts with static assumptions and then generalizes on recompile if it detects shape variability. You typically see one extra compile for the first new shape. By setting the `dynamic=True` flag upfront, you will force the compiler to consider all dimensions as dynamic from the start. However, remember that setting `dynamic=True` will disable CUDA Graphs. Prefer marking the code with only known varying dimensions using `torch._dynamo.mark_dynamic()`.

TorchDynamo and TorchInductor insert a guard-like `sequence_length <= 256` (or whatever range you specify) during tracing on dynamic dimensions to generate code that works for a variety and range of sizes. For instance, if an output size is `x.size(0) + y.size(0)`, Inductor can represent that as a symbolic expression and ensure the generated code works for any values that satisfy the guard conditions.

When Dynamo encounters a new shape for `sequence_length`, it sets a new guard such as `sequence_length <= 1024` and compiles the kernels under this new assumption—treating the dimension as dynamic from that point on. Later, if a longer sequence is seen that violates the guard, the compiler will recompile a new version of the graph that handles the larger range. Over time, it builds up a cache of compiled kernels for each different shape range.

You can also manually mark expected dynamic dimensions on a tensor with `torch._dynamo.mark_dynamic(tensor, dim)` to preempt a recompile. You can also use `torch.compiler.set_stance()`, which lets you adjust how recompilations are handled. For instance, you can use an eager-on-recompile stance to fall back to eager mode after a certain number of recompiles. We'll discuss best practices for avoiding recompiles in a bit.

TorchInductor attempts to generalize shapes after the first recompilation instead of repeatedly specializing on each new shape. For instance, it will emit conditional code inside the generated kernel using an `if` statement so that one kernel works for a range of `sequence_lengths` without erroring out. This reduces the need for separate compilation for every single size.

> Certain operations with data-dependent output ranks—or extremely complex indexing—may still trigger shape specialization. In these cases, the compiler will insert more guards—and if those are frequently violated, you might see frequent recompilations with `mark_dynamic()` or `set_stance()`.

For context, a simple but inefficient way to handle variable-length sequences without supporting dynamic shapes is to pad all input sequences to the max length in the batch. This way, you can use one static computation for all inputs. While padding simplifies the implementation, it is inefficient when input lengths vary widely since a lot of compute is wasted on the meaningless padding tokens.

Padding can hurt GPU utilization if the maximum length is much bigger than the average length of all the inputs. With dynamic shape-compilation, however, we can let the compiler generate code that only iterates up to the actual sequence length of each input. Dynamic shapes let you avoid excessive padding for variable lengths.

Let's look at a typical text-based generative AI scenario in which sequence lengths continue to grow as the generation progresses. Compiling with dynamic shapes can consistently outperform eager execution—even as sequence length increases.

In contrast, if one were to pad everything to a power-of-two length to use static shapes, it would introduce a lot of wasted computation and increase compile time due to larger tensor sizes. In other words, using dynamic shapes provides better compile-time performance and runtime performance and easier usage since you don't have to manually pad the inputs.

> It's recommended to bucket inputs by size in order to limit the number of distinct shapes. This will enable dynamic shapes for the remaining variability. This hybrid approach avoids excessive recompilations while still reducing padding waste.

With dynamic shapes, you can compile once and use the same compiled model on inputs of different shapes. If the variations are within the supported range, one compiled model can handle multiple configurations.

Internally, TorchInductor uses the SymPy library (*https://www.sympy.org*) to represent dynamic dimensions symbolically. It will propagate these symbols through the

IR so that an expression like `z.size(0) = x.size(0) + y.size(0)` can be handled symbolically. Inductor will reduce conditions to guard expressions.

If a guard fails because the dimension fell outside an expected range—or a data-dependent condition changed, Inductor will trigger a recompile. In essence, TorchInductor attempts to compile a general kernel for a range of sizes instead of a single fixed size.

Dynamic shape has significantly improved in recent releases. However, certain operations may force shape specialization if the compiler can't handle them symbolically. In this case, the compiler might insert more guards, which, if violated often, could lead to frequent recompilations and negate the benefits of compiling.

Data-dependent control flow still triggers specialization. Use dynamic shapes for varying sequence lengths but not for truly data-dependent branches.

It's worth noting that as of this writing, CUDA Graph replay requires static shapes (and fixed memory addresses). And only limited parameter updates are supported on instantiated graphs. Memory addresses and kernel-launch topology must remain compatible with capture. As such, enabling dynamic shapes will typically disable graph capture for those regions. This prevents the compiler from gaining the performance benefits of CUDA Graphs, including reduced kernel-launch overhead.

> If you specify the `reduce-overhead` compiler mode but also set `dynamic=True`, the CUDA Graph optimization from `reduce-overhead` won't apply since you are specifying that the shapes can vary. Enabling dynamic shapes will change guards and memory planning, which will disable graph capture. In practice, use `mode="reduce-overhead"` only with stable shapes to get CUDA Graphs. For variable sequence lengths, prefer `mode="default"` or `mode="max-autotune-no-cudagraphs"` and bucket/pad within ±10–20% to limit recompiles.

It's recommended to profile your system to see if dynamic shapes are worth using for your use case. In certain cases, it might be better to pad to a fixed size, use static shapes with CUDA Graphs, and achieve higher throughput by not having to recompile for each unique length. In other cases, dynamic shapes will be better.

You should profile different approaches to find what works best for you. When you do this, be sure to monitor memory usage. Code that supports dynamic shapes will incur a slightly higher memory footprint due to the additional guards and generalized code needed for the maximum range.

A rule of thumb is that if your sequence lengths vary by only 10%–20%, you will likely benefit from fixed-length padding.

In short, dynamic shape support means you don't have to disable `torch.compile` for variable-length inputs common in LLM models. By supporting dynamic shapes, the PyTorch compiler can perform kernel fusion and other optimizations across different input sizes.

Disabling the PyTorch Compiler and Reverting Back to Eager Mode

If you want to completely disable `torch.compile` without changing your code—useful for A/B testing performance and isolating issues—you can use the `@torch.com piler.disable` decorator to disable compilation for that function. For region-scoped control, use `torch.compiler.set_stance()` as a context manager. This will force the code to run in eager mode. For example, you might want to disable compilation for complex data loading or one-time initialization logic to keep the compiled graph focused on computations. This is also useful around code that does not work well with tracing, as we'll cover in a bit.

Or, you can simply change to use the eager backend as follows: `torch.compile(model, backend="eager")`. This will revert your code to run in eager mode. This lets you easily debug and compare correctness/performance results between compiled and eager modes.

`torch.compiler.disable()` and `torch.compiler.set_stance()` are a valuable escape hatches when certain operations don't work with PyTorch compile—or you simply don't want them in the graph for performance reasons. Speaking of performance, let's explore ways to improve the performance of our compiled graphs and code using the PyTorch compiler logs.

Performance Hints and Debugging Generated Code

Another extremely useful logging option to enable is `TORCH_LOGS="perf_hints"`. These logs will show you missed performance-optimization opportunities. For example, if a certain pattern could not be fused—or if a CUDA Graph could not be used—it will log a hint like "*PerfHint: CUDA Graph not used because input is mutated*" or "*PerfHint: fell back to eager for random op*," etc. These hints guide you on what might be limiting the performance of your code or model.

For deeper performance debugging and tuning, you likely want to see the exact code that TorchInductor generates. There are a couple of ways to inspect the code. First, you can set `TORCH_LOGS="output_code"` to print the generated code for each compiled graph. This will show the raw source code for the generated kernels. You can even modify the source code and further optimize, if needed.

You can also enable TorchInductor's debug mode by setting `TORCH_COMPILE_DEBUG=1`. When you run your program with debug mode enabled, Inductor will create a debug directory (e.g., `/tmp/torchinductor_<pid>/...`) that contains the FX Graph (`.fx`), Inductor artifacts such as `outputcode.py`, *fx_graph_runnable.py*, IR dumps, and generated Triton sources.

When reading the generated `.triton` code, you may notice Triton-specific constructs —or even raw PTX in advanced cases. If you also inspect the compiled PTX in the debug artifacts, you may see `mma.sync` instructions where `tl.dot` is lowered to Tensor Core operations. These logs, tools, and artifacts are incredibly useful for performance tuning because they let you see exactly what the compiler is doing. Understanding these can help you verify that the compiler is applying optimizations like kernel fusion, warp specialization, or double buffering. If you spot an inefficiency, you can manually create a custom Triton kernel for your specific use case.

> If you're feeling benevolent, you can even contribute your custom kernel back to the PyTorch and Triton ecosystems since it's likely that somebody else can benefit from your optimization.

Debugging Numerical Correctness and Accuracy

While very rare, it's possible that `torch.compile` produces a result that is numerically different compared to eager mode. If you suspect a bug in the compiler, there are a few strategies to verify and collect data before notifying the community and creating a GitHub issue.

First, you can use PyTorch's minifier tools to create reproducible scripts. PyTorch has a TorchDynamo minifier tool (*https://oreil.ly/KjHAO*) and TorchInductor minifier tool (*https://oreil.ly/UAsTQ*), which will try to reduce your program to the smallest version that still reproduces the error. It's very helpful to create a small, reproducible script for the PyTorch team to use if needed. You would attach this file to your GitHub issue if it gets to this point.

Additionally, you can configure TorchDynamo to debug numerical accuracy at each layer of the compiler stack. To help determine where a numerical discrepancy is introduced, you can set the following environment variables during compilation to compare eager mode to the different compiler stages and isolate if the issue is in TorchDynamo, AOT Autograd, or TorchInductor:

```
# Dump the outputs after each compilation stage
TORCHDYNAMO_REPRO_AFTER="aot"
TORCHDYNAMO_REPRO_LEVEL=4
```

These settings will cause TorchDynamo to dump the graph after each stage—and run each graph in eager mode for comparison. This can help pinpoint which stage introduced the error.

Specifically, setting `TORCHDYNAMO_REPRO_AFTER="aot"` tells TorchDynamo to dump the FX Graph and trigger the logic to generate a script to reproduce the error after the AOT Autograd stage. This is in contrast to generating the reproduction script after the initial Dynamo capture.

Using `TORCHDYNAMO_REPRO_LEVEL=4`, TorchDynamo will run each dumped graph in eager mode and compare its outputs to the compiled version. This halts and saves a minimal reproduction script if any numeric mismatch is detected.

> The PyTorch compiler team loves fixing correctness bugs, so if you do find a true error, report the issue on GitHub. Make sure to include the minified reproducible set of artifacts by setting `TORCHDYNAMO_REPRO_AFTER="aot"` and `TORCHDYNAMO_REPRO_LEVEL=4`.

If using random numbers (seeds) or sequences, you should make sure they are being generated consistently. By default, TorchInductor might not produce the exact same random seed or sequence as with eager mode. One reason is that fused or reordered kernels may not generate numbers in the same, expected order as eager mode.

If needed, you can set `torch._inductor.config.fallback_random=True` to force TorchInductor to generate random numbers exactly like it would with eager mode. This will incur a slight performance hit, but it may be required for numerical correctness when using the PyTorch compiler.

Numerical differences can also stem from floating-point precision. For example, if you use PyTorch automatic mixed precision (AMP) or BF16, the order of operations in a fused kernel might introduce slight numerical differences versus eager's unfused sequence.

While such differences rarely affect convergence, they can in some cases. If you suspect precision-related instability, try disabling `torch.compile` and run the model in full FP32 to isolate the issue. You can also use `torch.set_float32_matmul_preci sion('highest')` to control TF32 usage and the accuracy-performance trade-off for full FP32 `matmuls` and maximum numerical accuracy.

It's also important to understand that small discrepancies may arise from using mixed precision (e.g., FP16/BF16). You can enforce deterministic behavior by setting `torch.use_deterministic_algorithms(True)`. This causes PyTorch to throw an error if a nondeterministic operation is used. While `torch.compile` does reduce some sources of nondeterminism by design, it's still good practice to enable this flag during debugging.

Keep in mind, however, that not all operations have deterministic implementations. For example, the default `torch.matmul()` operation that relies on cuBLAS does not have a deterministic implementation.

Specifically, the cuBLAS implementation relies on parallel optimizations like split-K, which can reduce operations in varying orders. This results in floating-point results that aren't bitwise reproducible across runs.

As such, enabling this setting may cause your code to fail unless there is a fallback alternative available. To enforce full determinism for cuBLAS-dependent operations like `torch.matmul()`, you need to call `torch.use_deterministic_algorithms(True)` and set the `CUBLAS_WORKSPACE_CONFIG` to a fixed size, as shown here:

```
# Set this before starting the Python/PyTorch process
export CUBLAS_WORKSPACE_CONFIG=:4096:8    # or :16:8

# Use this with the PyTorch process
torch.use_deterministic_algorithms(True)
```

Here, the first value (e.g., 4096 or 16) selects the size of the cuBLAS workspace buffer in bytes rounded to an internal bucket. The second value (e.g., 8) selects how many such buffers are reserved. Set either :4096:8 or :16:8 as documented to enforce deterministic algorithms.

To force cuBLAS to use deterministic algorithms under `torch.use_deterministic_algorithms(True)`, set `CUBLAS_WORKSPACE_CONFIG` to a supported value like :4096:8 or :16:8, as documented. If you enforce determinism without setting this, PyTorch will raise at runtime for operations that would otherwise select nondeterministic cuBLAS algorithms.

Always test determinism on your actual hardware and model configuration to confirm reproducibility.

Also, for critical workloads, you might temporarily disable certain compiler optimizations by setting flags like `torch._inductor.config.triton.cudagraphs=False` to better isolate the cause of a discrepancy. This disables CUDA Graph capture for TorchInductor-generated Triton kernels.

Debugging PyTorch compiler optimizations requires a slightly different mindset since you're looking at the meta-level execution steps through logs and graph visualizations—in addition to the low-level generated code. Tools like `torch._dynamo.explain()` give a high-level overview of how your code is converted into graphs, graph breaks, and subgraphs, while the various `TORCH_LOGS` options let you peek into the decisions that the compiler makes—as well as the exact code that it generates.

In short, with these combined tools and debugging mechanisms, you can iteratively eliminate graph breaks and make sure your model and code are fully captured and optimized. The payoff is worth it, as a well-compiled model can significantly outperform its eager-execution counterpart—especially for large LLM architectures in which every bit of performance improvement will add up.

Explaining and Minimizing Graph Breaks

When using `torch.compile`, diagnosing performance and correctness requires specialized tools. In this section, we'll show you how to use various tools and best practices to debug and pinpoint excessive graph breaks. These include `torch._dynamo.explain()`, environment variables to log compiler decisions, and best practices for debugging both the captured graphs and the kernels that they generate.

Graph Breaks and TorchDynamo explain()

A graph break occurs when TorchDynamo cannot continue capturing a continuous sequence of operations into a single graph. When this happens, it falls back to eager execution for this part of the code.

Graph breaks are the enemy of performance. Each break means an optimized graph is cut short—and more Python overhead is introduced. If you compile a model and see only modest speedups, it may be caused by frequent graph breaks that are preventing large, fused graphs. Ideally, we want as few breaks as possible—ideally one large graph for the whole model or whole training step.

Complex graphs that involve collective communications (e.g., all-gather, reduce-scatter, etc.) often require graph breaks. Figure 14-5 shows the graph breaks in PyTorch's FSDP strategy due to collective communication.

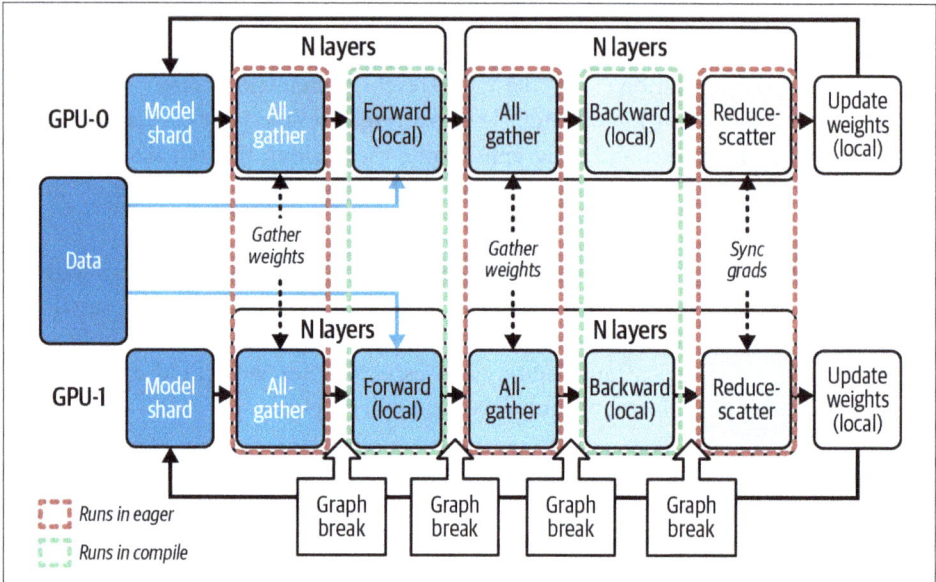

Figure 14-5. Graph breaks in PyTorch FSDP caused by communication layers (source: https://oreil.ly/TJW42)

PyTorch provides `torch._dynamo.explain()` to help analyze and debug graph breaks. When invoking this debugging function with your model and example inputs, it will run the model within TorchDynamo and return a report of how many graphs were generated, where the breaks occurred, and why they happened, as shown here, followed by the detailed graph-break analysis and explanation:

```python
import torch._dynamo as dynamo

def toy_example(a, b):
    x = a / (torch.abs(a) + 1)
    print("woo")          # a print statement in the model
    if b.sum() < 0:       # dynamic control flow depending on data
        b = -b
    return x * b

explanation = dynamo.explain(toy_example)(torch.randn(10), torch.randn(10))
print(explanation)

Graph Count: 3
Graph Break Count: 2
Op Count: 5

Break Reasons:

  Break Reason 1:
    Reason: builtin: print [...ConstantVariable] False
    User Stack:
```

```
      <frame at toy_example: line 3, in toy_example>

  Break Reason 2:
    Reason: generic_jump TensorVariable()
    User Stack:
      <frame at toy_example: line 5, in toy_example>

Ops per Graph:
  ...
```

Here, the explanation shows that TorchDynamo splits the code into three graph segments across two graph breaks. Note the "User Stack" portions of the output that point to the specific line of code where the issue happens. This is very useful for pinpointing the code causing the graph break.

The first break is caused by the print("woo") near line 3. Because print() has a "side effect" of writing text to stdio, it isn't capturable. As such, Dynamo breaks the graph into two graphs: before and after the print().

The second graph break is caused by the dynamic control flow logic if b.sum() < 0: near line 5, which Dynamo couldn't handle in a single graph because of the data-dependent dynamic control flow logic used in this specific scenario—and mentioned as a limitation in a previous section.

Using dynamo.explain() on your model—with representative inputs—is one of the first things to do if you're not getting the performance you expect from the PyTorch compiler. It gives you a quick overview of how many graphs were made—and why it couldn't make just one large graph.

Once you understand the causes, you can refactor the code to address the graph breaks one by one. In the preceding example, you can remove the print() or wrap it in a guard such as if not torch._dynamo.is_compiling() to avoid executing during tracing, as shown here:

```python
import torch

def model(a, b):
    x = a / (torch.abs(a) + 1)

    # avoid during compiling/tracing
    if not torch._dynamo.is_compiling():
        print("do not print during tracing/compiling")

    if b.sum() < 0:
        b = -b
    return x * b

explanation = dynamo.explain(model)(torch.randn(10),
  torch.randn(10))
print(explanation)
```

As mentioned earlier, if your model truly needs data-dependent branches, you can wrap them in `torch.cond()`. This will capture both the "true" and "false" branches as graph subroutines, as shown here:

```python
import torch

def model_cond(a: torch.Tensor, b: torch.Tensor) -> torch.Tensor:
    # Compute x as before
    x = a / (torch.abs(a) + 1)

    # Retain the compile-time check as a
    #    Python-level guard
    # Avoid side-effects during tracing/compilation
    if not torch._dynamo.is_compiling():
        print("do not print during tracing/compiling")

    # Handle the data-dependent sign flip on b
    b = torch.cond(
        b.sum() < 0,  # predicate (0-dim bool tensor)
        lambda b: -b, # true_fn: flip sign
        lambda b: b.clone(), # false_fn: leave unchanged (clone() avoids aliasing)
        (b,)              # operands tuple
    )

    return x * b

# Generate and print the Dynamo explanation just like before
explanation = dynamo.explain(model_cond)(torch.randn(10), torch.randn(10))
print(explanation)
```

Here, the predicate `b.sum() < 0` must be either a Python `bool` or a one-element `torch.bool` tensor. The `true_fn` and `false_fn` are callables taking the same operands (here, just `(b,)`) and returning tensors of the same shape and dtype.

This code keeps the Dynamo compile-time check (`dynamo.is_compiling()`) as a Python `if` since it's not data-dependent at runtime and we want to avoid side-effects (e.g., `print`) during tracing.

Note that `torch.cond()` currently only accepts a tensor predicate, requires both branches to have the same inputs and return a single tensor of identical shape and dtype, and does not allow in-place mutations or arbitrary side-effects.

In contrast, you can use a pure-tensor masking approach with `torch.where()`, as described earlier. This will impose no such restrictions and avoids graph breaks, making it the simpler, more reliable choice when you don't need the full expressivity of `torch.cond()`. This code is shown here:

```python
import torch
import torch._dynamo as dynamo
```

```
def model_where(a: torch.Tensor, b: torch.Tensor) -> torch.Tensor:
    # Compute x as before
    x = a / (torch.abs(a) + 1)

    # Preserve compile-time guard to avoid side-effects during tracing
    if not torch._dynamo.is_compiling():
    print("do not print during tracing/compiling")

    # Data-dependent branch expressed using torch.where
    b = torch.where(
        b.sum() < 0,    # predicate: a 0-dim bool tensor
        -b,             # true branch: flip sign
        b               # false branch: unchanged
    )

    return x * b

# Display the Dynamo explanation just as before
explanation = dynamo.explain(model_where)(torch.randn(10), torch.randn(10))
print(explanation)
```

Here, torch.where(condition, input, other) returns a tensor selecting elements from input where condition is True and from other where condition is False. Because b.sum() < 0 produces a 0-dimensional Boolean tensor, it can be broadcast across all elements of b. This allows a single, vectorized sign flip instead of an elementwise Python if.

Using torch.where() can avoid graph breaks in compiled and traced pipelines. This allows TorchDynamo to optimize operations inline.

It's also helpful to use torch.compiler.set_stance("fail_on_recompile") to force an error and refuse to run if the code is not cleanly capturable into a full graph. This is useful during development since it lets you catch graph breaks upfront at compile time instead of silently falling back to slower PyTorch eager execution.

torch.compiler.set_stance("fail_on_recompile") is also useful to add in your CI build to catch any graph breaks introduced later in the development process. Having robust and continuous performance-regression tests is extremely important throughout the life of a project.

Minimize Graph Recompilations

Besides graph breaks, you should also monitor the number of recompilations. Torch-Dynamo might be compiling the graph many times if its guards keep invalidating input tensor shapes, etc. If a tensor's shape changes at runtime, the guard fails and triggers a recompile. If you see more recompiles than expected, investigate which guard (shape, dtype, etc.) is causing it—and address the issue.

Typically, you'll notice recompilations happening because iterations will continue to be slow—even after the initial warm-up/compile iterations. Fortunately, you can have PyTorch log each guard evaluation and any trigger recompilation using `TORCH_LOGS="graph_breaks,recompiles,guards"`.

If you observe frequent guard failures, it often means a Python-side constant, such as a random number seed, timestamp, or loop-varying value, is changing on every iteration—and continuously invalidating the guard and triggering a recompile. In this case, you'll need to ensure those values are either made static or handled with the dynamic-shape APIs presented earlier (e.g., `torch._dynamo.mark_dynamic`). This will help avoid needless and excessive recompiles.

There are a few common mechanisms to minimize graph recompilations depending on the situation. First, for the constant scenario just mentioned, you can pass the constant into the code block as a tensor to prevent the compiler from guarding on the value and repeatedly failing.

Next, as mentioned earlier, you can mark dynamic dimensions that you know will change using `torch._dynamo.mark_dynamic(tensor, dim)` to preempt a recompile. Another option is to use `torch.compiler.set_stance("eager_on_recompile")` to avoid repeated recompiles by falling back to eager mode after N number of recompiles. This effectively caps the limit of recompilations.

Another option is to explicitly mark that part of the graph as safe using `torch._dynamo.allow_in_graph`. Let's dive into this technique a bit more in the next section.

Mark Functions and Code Blocks as Safe with allow_in_graph

When TorchDynamo doesn't know how to handle a function or code block because it's using unsupported operations, for example, you can decorate the function or wrap the code with `torch._dynamo.allow_in_graph`—as either a Python decorator or context manager—to tell Dynamo that it has no side effects. When you do this, Dynamo will then include the code in the trace using a more lenient analysis and acceptance policy. `allow_in_graph` bypasses some Dynamo safety checks. As such, prefer fixing the root cause of graph breaks first.

This is an advanced feature and should be used carefully. You are essentially promising that the function is pure, always returns the same output tensor for the same input tensor, depends only on its tensor inputs, and has no side effects. If used incorrectly, you may silently get the wrong results. However, when used correctly, it can be a performance lifesaver if a specific function or code block is causing a graph break even though it's safe to be traced.

In general, you should use `allow_in_graph` sparingly. It's a tool for power users to override Dynamo's conservative nature—but only when you're absolutely sure that the function does not have side effects or hidden state that could impact the code's correctness.

Tips for Handling Graph Breaks

Graph breaks limit the compiler's ability to perform large optimizations such as fusing many kernels into a smaller number of efficient kernels. This forces PyTorch to fall back to slower eager execution for certain parts of the graph.

It's critical to understand what triggers graph breaks—and how to prevent them. Here are some common causes of graph breaks and tips on how to minimize them:

Avoid in-place operations and unexpected mutations
TorchDynamo can handle some mutations using a mechanism called *functionalization*, which converts in-place operations to out-of-place for tracing. But certain in-place operations might still cause a graph break. If you see a break reason about mutation, such as "mutation on data" or "modifying a global," try to rewrite that part to avoid in-place operations. Often, you can simply rewrite in-place `x.relu_()` to out-of-place `x = x.relu()` to avoid a graph break if being in-place was causing the issue.

Prefer PyTorch data structures, collections, and tensor operations over equivalent Python implementations
Appending to a Python list of tensors inside a function will confuse TorchDynamo since it doesn't trace growing lists very well. Try to preallocate tensors or use tensor operations like `torch.stack()` instead of building Python (non-PyTorch) lists dynamically. Calls to many Python libraries, including I/O operations, `print`, `logging`, and `math.*` functions will most likely cause a graph break. It's recommended to remove these from the performance-critical code paths.

It's always recommended to use the PyTorch equivalent of Python data structures, collections, and tensor operations whenever possible. These are heavily optimized for PyTorch compilation, GPU processing, and distributed data transfers, which are common in PyTorch-based AI applications and models.

Avoid data-dependent control flow, if possible

If you have `if tensor.sum() > 0:` style logic, TorchDynamo cannot easily trace through this because the condition is unknown at compile time. It would need to choose one branch or the other based on the first run, guard on that condition, and enforce this guard for subsequent invocations. Since this is incorrect, Dynamo will create a graph break.

PyTorch supports a high-level operation called `torch.cond()` to capture certain dynamic flows in graphs. This can encapsulate `if/else` statements such that both branches are compiled. However, it requires the condition to be a tensor and typically works best for things like parameter-dependent switches rather than arbitrary Python logic.

Apart from this, most data-dependent control flow still breaks graphs. Continue to prefer tensor operations (`torch.where()`, masks, etc.) when possible. If neither `torch.cond()` nor refactoring is feasible, you may have to accept the graph break and its performance impact.

Understand performance characteristics of overlapping and synchronizing subgraphs with PyTorch DDP

PyTorch's DDP works with TorchDynamo by explicitly breaking graphs at synchronization points, including the all-reduce buckets. You might see breaks in the explain output related to `allreduce` or `torch.distributed` ops. This is expected, as PyTorch may compile each gradient bucket's reduction separately so that it can remove overlap communication with backward computation.

You can't avoid graph breaks at DDP communication boundaries if you want to preserve compute-communication overlap. PyTorch's compiler and DDP intentionally insert breaks at each all-reduce bucket so that gradient synchronization happens between subgraphs. This lets one bucket's communication overlap with the backward computation of the next bucket.

While this does prevent a single monolithic graph, it preserves performance. TorchDynamo + DDP runs with similar performance to eager-mode DDP. And it can even outperform eager DDP at scale. So, although you can't eliminate these communication graph breaks, they are necessary to achieve correct and efficient distributed training with the proper overlap.

Wrap graph submodules with PyTorch FSDP

PyTorch supports FSDP in compiled mode by using `use_original_par ams=True`. A best practice is to wrap submodules, like each transformer block, into their own FSDP submodule. Dynamo will then create explicit graph breaks at each FSDP submodule boundary. This allows each shard's communication to overlap with computation, similar to the bucketization strategy described for DDP.

Compiled FSDP fuses forward and backward passes and reuses buffers across model shards using AOT Autograd and Inductor's memory planner. As such, only the active parameter slices and minimal intermediate memory buffers are resident on each GPU. This reduces peak memory usage compared to DDP or eager mode.

The memory savings comes from avoiding redundant gradient storage, reusing intermediate allocations, and overlapping communication with computation across shards. And these allow larger models to fit into each GPU. If you don't wrap submodules individually, FSDP falls back to treating all parameters as one big bucket. This still works, but it limits memory benefits and overlap potential. As such, combining `torch.compile` with per-module FSDP wrappers is recommended for maximum speed and memory efficiency—especially on large-scale training jobs.

> Debugging can be very complex if issues arise—and even more complex in a larger cluster/configuration. Always test on a smaller configuration when using FSDP with `torch.compile`.

Monitor performance tradeoffs when using custom and third-party CUDA C++ and Triton operations

If you rely on a custom or third-party CUDA extension that PyTorch doesn't know about, Dynamo will create a graph break because it can't reason about what that operation does—or whether it's safe. If it's performance-critical, consider rewriting the custom operation in Python using Triton.

PyTorch supports `torch.library.triton_op()` API that lets you integrate Triton kernels as custom operations into PyTorch seamlessly. This lets the compiler peek inside the Triton code to perform optimizations. Before diving into Triton, let's quickly summarize how to debug various compiler phases, graph breaks, and compiler performance.

> Many popular third-party libraries now provide either a Triton implementation or Dynamo/FX wrappers for their operations. Check if these exist before writing your own.

Debugging Compiler Phases, Graph Breaks, and Performance

You can log and debug different types of compiler events at runtime by setting various environment variables such as `TORCH_LOGS`, `TORCH_COMPILE_DEBUG`, and `TORCH DYNAMO_REPRO_*`. These include graph breaks, recompiles, guards, and other compiler decisions. An example of setting `TORCH_LOGS` is shown next (see Table 14-1 for common values):

```
# "graph_breaks", "dynamo", "aot_graphs", "inductor",
# "graph_outputs", "graph_code", "dynamic", "perf_hints",
# "output_code", "recompiles", "guards", etc.
TORCH_LOGS="graph_breaks" python train.py
```

This will cause PyTorch to print out whenever a graph break occurs. To summarize the different logging options, you can set `TORCH_LOGS` to the following to debug `torch.compile`, including the different phases (TorchDynamo, AOT Autograd, and TorchInductor), graphs, graph breaks, generated code, performance, recompiles, and guards—as well as compiler decisions and performance, as shown in Table 14-1.

Table 14-1. Logging options for `torch.compile`

TORCH_LOGS value	Description
graph_breaks	Logs graph break events
dynamo	Verbose logging from TorchDynamo
aot_graphs	Verbose logging from AOT Autograd
inductor	Verbose logging from TorchInductor
graph_outputs	Shows the compiled FX graphs
graph_code	Dumps the Python code for each FX graph that TorchDynamo produces
dynamic	Traces decisions around dynamic shapes and when dimensions are marked as dynamic
perf_hints	Shows you the missed performance-optimization opportunities
output_code	Prints the generated code for each compiled graph
recompiles	Logs recompilation triggers
guards	Logs guards and guard evaluations

These settings can be useful if you suspect an issue in how the subgraphs were segmented—and which shapes were compiled. With these settings, you will get a lot of internal debugging information without changing your code.

> Be prepared for very verbose output. It's recommended to start with just `"graph_breaks"` when debugging just graph breaks, for example.

Under the hood, setting `TORCH_LOGS` is analogous to using the `torch._logging.set_logs()` API. However, setting `TORCH_LOGS` is sometimes easier to configure externally as an environment variable.

And remember that you can also set `TORCH_COMPILE_DEBUG=1` to enable TorchInductor's debug mode. This will log the FX Graph, the TorchInductor IR, the generated Triton code, and an HTML report with visualizations if Graphviz is installed.

You can also set `TORCHDYNAMO_REPRO_AFTER` and `TORCHDYNAMO_REPRO_LEVEL` to force TorchDynamo to dump its graph after each stage. It will also perform a runtime comparison against a noncompiled, eager-mode version of the code.

It's also possible to trace through compilations logs using a tool called `tlparse` (*https://github.com/pytorch/tlparse*). Trace logs are useful for debugging compilation events (e.g., recompilations) as well as generating bug reports.

To enable trace logs, specify the *trace-log* directory using the `TORCH_TRACE` environment variable. Then run `tlparse` on the *trace-log* directory to produce a tree representation of stack frames as shown here:

```
- /workspace/networks/layers/transformer.py:634 in forward
  .../torch/nn/modules/module.py in _wrapped_call_impl
  .../torch/nn/modules/module.py in _call_impl
  - [2/2] [2/3] ../torch/_dynamo/convert_frame.py in __call__
  - /workspace/networks/layers/transformer.py:753 in forward
    - [8/2] [8/3] .../torch/_dynamo/convert_frame.py in __call__
...
```

In addition, you can use the Perfetto UI to display a trace timeline visualization. And since tracing incurs minimal overhead, it's even possible to enable `TORCH_TRACE` in production.

Let's now dive deeper into OpenAI's Triton language and compiler used by TorchInductor. We'll write some basic and advanced Triton kernels and then register them with PyTorch.

Writing Custom Kernels with OpenAI Triton

Up until now, we've only briefly mentioned OpenAI's open source Triton language and compiler. Now it's time to dive deeper since TorchInductor uses Triton as its backend code-generation implementation—and because Triton is growing in popularity with backing from large companies like OpenAI.

As mentioned, Inductor uses Triton to generate optimized GPU kernels under the hood. By examining, understanding, and customizing these kernels, you can further improve performance beyond what TorchInductor could produce. Learning Triton is critical to performance optimizations in a PyTorch and NVIDIA GPU environment.

At a high level, OpenAI Triton is an open source, Python-native domain-specific language (DSL) for writing GPU kernels in familiar Python. Triton also includes a JIT compiler that converts Triton code into NVIDIA PTX code directly. In other words, Triton lets you create high-performance custom GPU operations in Python—without writing CUDA C++ by hand. Triton remains tightly integrated with PyTorch, making it the go-to choice for custom GPU kernels in this ecosystem.

Writing a GPU kernel in Triton is much more familiar and simpler than CUDA C++. This is especially true for researchers who prefer to stay in Python, iterate quickly, and not worry about complex C++ templates or detailed memory management. They simply don't need to use C++ in an era when GPU-performance-focused compilers like PyTorch and Triton exist.

> NVIDIA has recognized this trend. In 2025, they announced Python-centric CUDA libraries (e.g., cuTile, CuTe Python DSL, CUTLASS Python DSL, and cuPyNumeric `numpy` replacement). These are essentially competing libraries to Triton. Integration with `torch.compile` continues to evolve, and as of this writing, TorchInductor still uses Triton as its primary GPU code generation path.

While PyTorch's `torch.compile` automates a lot of kernel generation, custom Triton kernels can squeeze out the last drops of performance—especially for operations outside of TorchInductor's current scope like complex sparse patterns and novel layer types. It's sometimes possible to beat the performance of TorchInductor's generated code—especially if you have domain-specific knowledge. However, this is very advanced and will require ongoing maintenance and potential rewrites for new hardware support.

Let's now start with a quick Triton programming primer. Then we'll dive into some interesting Triton topics, including accessing shared-memory, registering a Triton kernel with PyTorch, autotuning kernel-launch parameters, and profiling. Then we'll progress to cover advanced Triton topics such as warp specialization and software pipelining (e.g., double buffering).

Triton Programming Model

Triton uses a single-program, multiple-data (SPMD) model, as opposed to CUDA's SIMT model. This is significant because Triton intentionally abstracts away the low-level details of CUDA instructions and threads.

Triton kernels (aka *programs*) operate at a higher level by running instances of the program on separate thread blocks (aka *cooperative thread arrays*, or CTAs) as the fundamental unit of compute. This is in contrast to CUDA kernels, which run on individual threads in a thread block.

> The community tends to use Triton *kernel* and Triton *program* interchangeably—typically preferring Triton *kernel*, so this book uses Triton *kernel* for the most part.

You write a Triton kernel with the Triton Python DSL. Then the Triton JIT compiler compiles the kernel into GPU code that runs many parallel instances of this kernel. Each program instance maps to a CUDA thread block.

Triton kernels (aka *programs*) are defined by decorating a Python function with @triton.jit. Within the kernel, you use special primitives from the triton.lan guage module, commonly aliased as tl, to work with memory pointers, perform vectorized loads/stores, and compute per-program indices using tl.program_id and block offset arithmetic.

Triton's SPMD model means you typically work with vectorized operations such as adding two tl.arange vectors. The Triton compiler maps vectorized SPMD code across the threads in a CUDA block. There is no guaranteed one-element-to-one-thread mapping.

You don't explicitly need to manage individual threads or warps with Triton since its compiler does this for you. Here is a simple Triton kernel that adds two vectors of equal size, n_elements, in this case:

```python
import triton
import triton.language as tl

BLOCK_SIZE = 1024

@triton.jit
def vector_add_kernel(x_ptr,y_ptr,out_ptr,n_elements,BLOCK_SIZE: tl.constexpr):
    pid = tl.program_id(axis=0)              # unique program ID for each block
    block_start = pid * BLOCK_SIZE
    # each program handles BLOCK_SIZE elements
    offsets = block_start + tl.arange(0, BLOCK_SIZE)
    # Create a mask to guard against out-of-bounds
    # (if n is not divisible by BLOCK_SIZE)
    mask = offsets < n_elements
    x = tl.load(x_ptr + offsets, mask=mask)        # masked load
    y = tl.load(y_ptr + offsets, mask=mask)
    result = x + y
    tl.store(out_ptr + offsets, result, mask=mask) # masked store
```

Here, you see that Triton abstracts away threads and warps. Note that BLOCK_SIZE is a compile-time constant that defines how many elements each program instance processes. The number of threads per CUDA block is controlled by the kernel's configuration using num_warps and is not equal to BLOCK_SIZE.

Specifically, in the preceding code, tl.arange(0, BLOCK_SIZE) returns a vector of indices of size BLOCK_SIZE ([0, 1, ..., BLOCK_SIZE-1]). We add pid * BLOCK_SIZE, or block_start, to the vector of indices in order to derive the actual indices, x_ptr + offsets and y_ptr + offsets, into each vector for this instance of the kernel running on a thread block.

Assuming we launch enough Triton kernel instances to cover the total number of elements, n_elements, in each of the vectors, this kernel will add together every element of the two vectors, x_ptr and y_ptr, and store the result in out_ptr. In essence, Triton lets you write kernel logic in a tensorized manner.

Here, for example, we operate on a whole block of indices (**offsets**) at once. The Triton compiler takes care of splitting this work among actual GPU threads and makes sure that memory accesses (tl.load and tl.store) are coalesced when possible.

To launch instances of this Triton kernel, pass a grid function that computes the number of program instances from meta['BLOCK_SIZE']:

```python
import triton

def grid(meta):
    return (triton.cdiv(n_elements, meta['BLOCK_SIZE']),)

vector_add_kernel[grid](x_ptr, y_ptr, out_ptr, n_elements, BLOCK_SIZE=1024)
```

Here, the code uses a mask to avoid out-of-bounds memory access when n_elements isn't a multiple of BLOCK_SIZE. This is similar to earlier chapters on CUDA in which we used if (idx < N) within our kernel to avoid out-of-bounds index errors.

> The use of a mask in loads/stores is a clever and convenient way to handle boundary conditions without requiring explicit checks or if/else branches.

Under the hood, Triton converts this program to NVIDIA PTX such that each program uses a single CUDA thread block. Each program maps to a CUDA thread block. tl.arange produces per-lane indices within the program, and the compiler maps this vectorized index space across the thread in the block. You can also manage multidimensional indices for matrix operations in a straightforward way. Triton will automatically handle vectorizing your arithmetic and memory operations for you.

In short, Triton gives you the productivity of Python with the performance of optimized CUDA C++ kernels. It also lets you drop down into low-level optimizations to manipulate and utilize the full memory hierarchy (e.g., shared-memory tiling, etc.), as we demonstrate in the next section.

Accessing Shared Memory in Triton

Efficient Triton kernels take advantage of the L2 cache and software-managed shared memory on each SM. When using shared memory, each thread block loads a tile from both matrix A and B into shared memory. This is in contrast to each thread repeatedly loading the same values from global memory.

The kernel then reuses those tiles for multiple computations. This better utilizes the on-chip memory caches and reduces the amount of data traveling between global HBM and the registers.

Triton does not expose an explicit shared-memory allocator. Instead, it stages tiles in on-chip shared memory using tensor descriptors (`tl.make_tensor_descriptor(...)`) and an asynchronous pipeline using the intended shapes and strides. This way, you can issue loads and stores through those descriptors inside a pipelined `tl.range(..., num_stages=...)`. This loop lowers to `cp.async`, TMA, and barriers.

Registering Custom Kernels with PyTorch

After writing a Triton kernel, you can register it as a custom operation in PyTorch using `torch.library.triton_op`. This makes the Triton kernel visible to `torch.compile` without treating it as an opaque, black-box operation that could fall back to eager execution mode. This way, the compiler knows about the Triton kernel, includes it during graph capture, and optimizes it along with the rest of the graph. This allows additional optimizations such as fusion.

Registering the Triton kernel helps avoid graph breaks when using custom Triton kernels/programs with the PyTorch compiler. Here is an example of registering and calling the Triton kernel `vector_add_kernel` from PyTorch:

```python
import torch
import triton
import triton.language as tl
from torch.library import triton_op, wrap_triton
from torch import Tensor

# Triton compute kernel
@triton.jit
def vector_add_kernel(
    x_ptr, y_ptr, out_ptr, n_elements,
    BLOCK_SIZE: tl.constexpr
):
```

```
        pid = tl.program_id(0)
        start = pid * BLOCK_SIZE
        offsets = start + tl.arange(0, BLOCK_SIZE)
        mask = offsets < n_elements
        x = tl.load(x_ptr + offsets, mask=mask)
        y = tl.load(y_ptr + offsets, mask=mask)
        tl.store(out_ptr + offsets, x + y, mask=mask)

# Register as a Triton-backed PyTorch op
@triton_op("my_triton_lib::vector_add", mutates_args=())
def vector_add(x: Tensor, y: Tensor) -> Tensor:
    assert x.device.type == "cuda" and y.device.type == "cuda"
    n = x.numel()
    out = torch.empty_like(x)
    # Compute grid size
    def grid_fn(meta):
        return (triton.cdiv(n, meta["BLOCK_SIZE"]),)
    # Wrap and launch the Triton kernel
    wrap_triton(vector_add_kernel)[grid_fn](x, y, out, n, BLOCK_SIZE=1024)
    return out

# Usage
a = torch.randn(10_000, device="cuda")
b = torch.randn(10_000, device="cuda")
c = torch.ops.my_triton_lib.vector_add(a, b)
```

Here, triton_op("my_triton_lib::vector_add", mutates_args=()) registers the operator name and mutation metadata (empty) with PyTorch. Then wrap_triton (vector_add_kernel) wraps the raw Triton kernel into a callable that the compiler can inline and optimize within the torch.compile graph. The compiler will then fuse, reorder, and inline this kernel within the rest of the torch.compile graph.

Registering forward-only operations is straightforward. However, to leverage PyTorch's automatic differentiation for full training support, you typically need to implement and register a custom backward computation. Otherwise, you need to compose it from existing differentiable primitives.

For training support, register an autograd formula using vector_add.register_auto grad(backward, setup_context=setup_context). If you prefer, you can wrap the logic in a torch.autograd.Function and register both the forward and backward arguments. However, register_autograd is the recommended path for torch.com pile composability.

If OpenAI Triton doesn't support something that you need—or doesn't provide the performance that you expected—you can rewrite the kernel using CUDA C++ with a library like CUTLASS for efficiency. We would then register the CUDA C++ extension with PyTorch in a similar manner, including registering the autograd gradient computation for the backward pass.

Tuning Kernel-Launch Parameters

Triton programs typically use 4 warps, or 128 threads, per block for many kernels. However, with modern GPU hardware's larger shared memory and register file sizes per SM, you can typically push `num_warps` higher to 8 or 16 warps per block. For instance, you can increase `num_warps` to 8 when `BLOCK_SIZE >= 2048` and to 16 when `BLOCK_SIZE >= 4096`.

The number of warps is dependent on whether your kernel can make use of the parallelism without causing excessive contention. The optimal setting depends on the kernel's arithmetic intensity and memory access pattern.

Consider launching a kernel as follows: `my_kernel[grid](..., num_warps=8)`. In this case, we are specifying 8 warps (256 threads) per Triton kernel. This configuration is typically effective for compute-heavy kernels. However, memory-bound kernels might still top out around 4 warps due to memory throughput limits.

For memory-bound kernels, using more warps per thread block can help hide memory latency by doing more in parallel. But too many warps per thread block can cause contention or cache thrashing.

New GPU generations are gaining more SMs and wider memory buses. This lets us increase the number of warps per block from the default 4 warps to 8 or 16 warps. This helps to increase occupancy, cover more memory-access latency, and saturate the available memory and compute.

Manually exploring combinations of `BLOCK_SIZE` and `num_warps` for each kernel can be tedious. As such, it's usually best to use Triton's built-in autotuner. This will benchmark and automatically pick the optimal `BLOCK_SIZE`, `num_warps`, tile size, and other parameters for you. Let's explore the autotuner in the next section.

Autotuning Triton Kernels

GPU kernel performance is highly sensitive to compile-time parameters such as tile dimensions, warp counts, loop unrolling stages, and the use of on-chip resources like registers and shared memory. Triton's built-in autotuner automates the search for these optimal settings by letting you decorate a `triton.jit` kernel with `@triton.autotune`. You can pass in a list of `triton.Config` objects that describe the different candidate combinations of BLOCK_SIZE, num_warps, num_stages, tile size, and other kernel meta-parameters.

During the first kernel invocation, the Triton JIT-compiles and benchmarks each configuration combination. Be sure to use a representative input workload on this initial invocation, as Triton will cache the fastest configuration for that input using a key derived from its characteristics, such as input size/shape.

All subsequent calls that have these same input characteristics will automatically reuse the cached (fastest) configuration. This way, you only pay the autotuning cost once for each input size/shape—and immediately start benefiting from the optimal configuration in later kernel invocations.

If Triton detects a new input shape, it will perform another autotune process by iterating through the triton.Config objects using the new input characteristics. It will again choose the best configuration for this input and cache it for subsequent kernel invocations.

To avoid suboptimal tuning results, it's recommended that you warm up the autotuner with realistic and representative inputs that closely match your production workload. This way, Triton populates the cache with an optimal configuration that closely reflects your production inputs.

> You can override the optimal settings for specific input shapes and workloads by supplying a custom key_fn to @triton.auto tune(key_fn=...) that maps the input metadata (e.g., tensor shapes) to a custom cache key. This is an advanced technique that gives you more control of the cache configurations for different types of input workloads.

When choosing possible kernel configurations, it's worth remembering that larger tiles and more warps will increase arithmetic intensity at the expense of consuming additional registers and shared memory per thread block. In other words, by increasing the compute-to-memory ratio, you limit occupancy since fewer thread blocks can execute on each SM due to the increased resource needs.

Conversely, using smaller tiles and fewer warps will reduce per-thread work and data reuse but allow more blocks and warps to be active on each SM concurrently. This improves occupancy at the expense of lower arithmetic intensity.

In short, the optimal trade-off depends on both your input-matrix dimensions and your GPU's specific resource limits. Manually tuning is time-consuming and error-prone. Triton's autotuner handles this complexity automatically using a data-driven approach on realistic workloads to determine the optimal configuration that a manual search might miss. Using higher num_warps (e.g., 8–16) and multistage pipelining will often saturate `tcgen05.*` paths on Blackwell. It's recommended to use autotuning as much as possible.

Advanced Triton Kernel Implementations

To solidify these concepts, next are some self-contained Triton kernel examples for warp specialization and asynchronous double buffering of data transfers/computations. These illustrate how you can implement Triton to transform high-level Python code into highly optimized GPU kernels.

Warp Specialization with Triton

TorchInductor can target Triton's warp specialization support for many of its generated GPU kernels (*https://oreil.ly/xBYHI*). It will try to split each thread block's warps into "producer" (memory) and "consumer" (compute) roles by emitting `tl.range()` loops with `warp_specialize=True`, similar to the example shown here:

```
// warp_specialize=True is supported on modern GPUs
// Use it together with num_stages > 1
// to enable producer/consumer warp partitioning
// and overlap
for k in tl.range(0, K_tiles, _warn_unused=False, warp_specialize=True):
    # loop body
    ...
```

The memory warp prefetches the next tile while another warp computes the current tile. This will overlap memory latency with computation to produce higher throughput. Warp specialization works hand-in-hand with descriptor-based TMA copies. You can also use this in your own custom Triton kernels by passing `warp_special ize=True` to `tl.range()`, as shown in the code.

You can also drive warp specialization through Triton autotune configs by setting `num_consumer_groups>0` (e.g., 2) and `num_buffers_warp_spec` (e.g., 3) in `triton .Config` as shown in the following code snippet. This will keep the producers and consumers busy with work. If provided, TorchInductor will use these values under the hood:

```
triton.Config(
    { 'BLOCK_M': 128, 'BLOCK_N': 128, 'BLOCK_K': 64,
      'num_warps': 8, 'num_stages': 2,
      'num_consumer_groups': 2, '
    num_buffers_warp_spec': 3 }
)
```

This specialization approach is especially effective for long-running loops that iterate over a large *K* dimension in a GEMM. This dedicated approach keeps both the memory subsystem and the ALUs busy at all times and maximizes hardware utilization.

Tiled and Persistent GEMM Kernel (Triton)

This Triton kernel computes a matrix multiplication (C = A * B) efficiently since each kernel launch does all the work by looping over the K dimension internally, instead of launching multiple kernels for each K chunk. This way, we pay the launch overhead only once, and warps stay busy until every tile is done. The following example tiles over K inside one launch but does not reuse the same thread block across multiple output tiles:

```python
@triton.jit
def tiled_gemm_kernel(
    A_ptr, B_ptr, C_ptr,
    M, N, K,
    stride_am, stride_ak,
    stride_bk, stride_bn,
    stride_cm, stride_cn,
    BLOCK_M: tl.constexpr, BLOCK_N: tl.constexpr, BLOCK_K: tl.constexpr,
):
    """
    Tiled GEMM with Triton tensor descriptors + autotuning.

    This is the BASIC PRODUCTION example showing:
    1. Tensor descriptors (maps to TMA on Blackwell)
    2. Autotuning across block sizes
    3. Standard 2D grid decomposition
    """
    pid_m = tl.program_id(0)
    pid_n = tl.program_id(1)

    m0 = pid_m * BLOCK_M
    n0 = pid_n * BLOCK_N

    offs_m = m0 + tl.arange(0, BLOCK_M)
    offs_n = n0 + tl.arange(0, BLOCK_N)
    offs_k = tl.arange(0, BLOCK_K)

    # On Blackwell, descriptor .load/.store map to TMA
    # tl.dot lowers to UMMA (tcgen05) with accumulators in TMEM.
    A_desc = tl.make_tensor_descriptor(
        A_ptr,
        shape=[M, K],
        strides=[stride_am, stride_ak],
        block_shape=[BLOCK_M, BLOCK_K],
    )
    B_desc = tl.make_tensor_descriptor(
        B_ptr,
        shape=[K, N],
        strides=[stride_bk, stride_bn],
        block_shape=[BLOCK_K, BLOCK_N],
    )
```

```
acc = tl.zeros((BLOCK_M, BLOCK_N), dtype=tl.float32)

K_tiles = (K + BLOCK_K - 1) // BLOCK_K
if K_tiles == 0:
    c_ptrs = C_ptr + (offs_m[:, None] * stride_cm
                      + offs_n[None, :] * stride_cn)
    c_mask = (offs_m[:, None] < M) & (offs_n[None, :] < N)
    tl.store(c_ptrs, acc, mask=c_mask)
    return

k0 = 0
if (m0 + BLOCK_M <= M) and (k0 + BLOCK_K <= K):
    a_cur = A_desc.load([m0, k0])
else:
    col_ids = k0 + offs_k
    row_offsets = offs_m[:, None] + tl.zeros((BLOCK_M, BLOCK_K),
                                             dtype=offs_m.dtype)
    col_offsets = col_ids[None, :] + tl.zeros((BLOCK_M, BLOCK_K),
                                              dtype=col_ids.dtype)
    a_cur = tl.load(
        A_desc,
        offsets=(row_offsets, col_offsets),
        boundary_check=(0, 1),
        padding_option="zero",
    )

if (n0 + BLOCK_N <= N) and (k0 + BLOCK_K <= K):
    b_cur = B_desc.load([k0, n0])
else:
    row_ids = k0 + offs_k
    row_offsets = row_ids[:, None] + tl.zeros((BLOCK_K, BLOCK_N),
                                              dtype=row_ids.dtype)
    col_offsets = offs_n[None, :] + tl.zeros((BLOCK_K, BLOCK_N),
                                             dtype=offs_n.dtype)
    b_cur = tl.load(
        B_desc,
        offsets=(row_offsets, col_offsets),
        boundary_check=(0, 1),
        padding_option="zero",
    )

for kt in tl.range(0, K_tiles, num_stages=2):
    k0 = kt * BLOCK_K
    acc += tl.dot(a_cur, b_cur)

    next_k = k0 + BLOCK_K
    if next_k < K:
        if (m0 + BLOCK_M <= M) and (next_k + BLOCK_K <= K):
            a_cur = A_desc.load([m0, next_k])
        else:
            col_ids = next_k + offs_k
            row_offsets = offs_m[:, None] + tl.zeros((BLOCK_M, BLOCK_K),
```

```
                                     dtype=offs_m.dtype)
        col_offsets = col_ids[None, :] + tl.zeros((BLOCK_M, BLOCK_K),
                                          dtype=col_ids.dtype)
        a_cur = tl.load(
            A_desc,
            offsets=(row_offsets, col_offsets),
            boundary_check=(0, 1),
            padding_option="zero",
        )

        if (n0 + BLOCK_N <= N) and (next_k + BLOCK_K <= K):
            b_cur = B_desc.load([next_k, n0])
        else:
            row_ids = next_k + offs_k
            row_offsets = row_ids[:, None] + tl.zeros((BLOCK_K, BLOCK_N),
                                              dtype=row_ids.dtype)
            col_offsets = offs_n[None, :] + tl.zeros((BLOCK_K, BLOCK_N),
                                              dtype=offs_n.dtype)
            b_cur = tl.load(
                B_desc,
                offsets=(row_offsets, col_offsets),
                boundary_check=(0, 1),
                padding_option="zero",
            )

    # Store results with masking
    c_ptrs = C_ptr + (offs_m[:, None] * stride_cm + offs_n[None, :] * stride_cn)
    c_mask = (offs_m[:, None] < M) & (offs_n[None, :] < N)
    tl.store(c_ptrs, acc, mask=c_mask)

def persistent_matmul(A: torch.Tensor, B: torch.Tensor) -> torch.Tensor:
    M, K = A.shape
    K2, N = B.shape
    assert K == K2
    C = torch.empty((M, N), device=A.device, dtype=torch.float32)

    MT = triton.cdiv(M, 128)
    NT = triton.cdiv(N, 128)
    grid = lambda META: (min(65536, MT * NT),)  # bound launch overhead

    matmul_kernel_persistent[grid](
        A, B, C, M, N, K,
        A.stride(0), A.stride(1),
        B.stride(0), B.stride(1),
        C.stride(0), C.stride(1),
    )
    return C
```

Here, the kernel launches a 2-D grid over the M×N tiles and performs the full K-loop inside a single kernel launch. This reduces launch overhead and can increase utilization when K is large, but comes at the cost of holding resources longer in a single kernel. Each program (thread block) loads tiles of A and B into shared memory and computes a partial dot product of the tiles with `tl.dot`. Triton accumulates the results in FP32. And, on Blackwell, Triton lowers the `tl.dot` to `tcgen05` and UMMA to engage the Tensor Cores. The Tensor Cores then accumulate results in specialized TMEM rather than general registers.

> It's best to express shared-memory–backed tile movement in Triton using tensor descriptors. For instance, `desc=tl.make_tensor_descriptor(...)`. On modern GPUs, these tensor-descriptor calls map to TMA-based hardware operations using asynchronous, coalesced transfers.

Triton will unroll/vectorize these loops and computations for efficiency. In addition, when `dtypes` and tile shapes are supported (e.g., FP16/BF16, or TF32 for FP32), Triton lowers `tl.dot` to Tensor Core instructions. Here is a simple Python wrapper that launches this Triton kernel:

```python
def tiled_matmul(A: torch.Tensor, B: torch.Tensor) -> torch.Tensor:
    """
    Tiled matrix multiplication using autotuned Triton kernel.

    The kernel will automatically select the best block size configuration
    for the given matrix dimensions (M, N, K).
    """
    M, K = A.shape
    K2, N = B.shape
    assert K == K2, f"Inner dimensions must match: {K} != {K2}"
    C = torch.empty((M, N), device=A.device, dtype=torch.float32)

    # Grid is computed based on max block size from autotuning configs
    # Triton's autotuner will pick the optimal block size at runtime
    MAX_BLOCK_M = 128  # From largest config
    MAX_BLOCK_N = 128
    grid = (triton.cdiv(M, MAX_BLOCK_M), triton.cdiv(N, MAX_BLOCK_N))

    # Launch with autotuning - Triton will select best config
    tiled_gemm_kernel[grid](
        A, B, C, M, N, K,
        A.stride(0), A.stride(1),
        B.stride(0), B.stride(1),
        C.stride(0), C.stride(1),
    )
    return C
```

Here, we see that by doing the entire K-loop inside one kernel launch, we avoid launching multiple kernels per output tile. On modern GPUs, this approach can increase utilization when K is large—at the cost of holding resources for longer in a single kernel.

You can combine this tiled approach with a persistent kernel. This would reuse the same thread block across multiple output tiles. The persistent kernel would use a 1-D grid and stride the tile index by `tl.num_programs(0)` as shown in this code block:

```
@triton.jit
def matmul_kernel_persistent(
    A_ptr, B_ptr, C_ptr,
    M, N, K,
    stride_am, stride_ak,
    stride_bk, stride_bn,
    stride_cm, stride_cn,
    # compile-time constants
    BLOCK_M: tl.constexpr, BLOCK_N: tl.constexpr, BLOCK_K: tl.constexpr,
    NUM_STAGES: tl.constexpr,
):
    """
    Persistent thread GEMM with Triton tensor descriptors + autotuning.

    Key Blackwell Optimizations:
      1) Tensor descriptors -> TMA hardware acceleration
      2) Autotuning across multiple block-size configurations
      3) Persistent threads to amortize launch overhead
      4) TMEM accumulation (accumulators live in ~256 KB/SM TMEM on Blackwell)

    This is the PRODUCTION-READY version combining these best practices.
    """

    # 1-D persistent launch: each program processes multiple tiles
    pid  = tl.program_id(0)
    nprog = tl.num_programs(0)

    MT = tl.cdiv(M, BLOCK_M)
    NT = tl.cdiv(N, BLOCK_N)
    TILE_COUNT = MT * NT

    # --- Tensor descriptors (map to TMA on NVIDIA). Descriptor rules:
    #     leading strides must be multiples of 16 BYTES;
    #     last dimension contiguous.
    A_desc = tl.make_tensor_descriptor(
        A_ptr, shape=[M, K], strides=[stride_am, stride_ak],
        block_shape=[BLOCK_M, BLOCK_K],
    )
    B_desc = tl.make_tensor_descriptor(
        B_ptr, shape=[K, N], strides=[stride_bk, stride_bn],
        block_shape=[BLOCK_K, BLOCK_N],
    )

    # Persistent stride over all output tiles handled by this program.
    tile_idx = pid
    while tile_idx < TILE_COUNT:
        pid_m = tile_idx // NT
```

```
pid_n = tile_idx %  NT

m0 = pid_m * BLOCK_M
n0 = pid_n * BLOCK_N

offs_m = m0 + tl.arange(0, BLOCK_M)
offs_n = n0 + tl.arange(0, BLOCK_N)
offs_k = tl.arange(0, BLOCK_K)

# FP32 accumulator (on Blackwell, accumulators live in TMEM,
# not registers)
acc = tl.zeros((BLOCK_M, BLOCK_N), dtype=tl.float32)

# ---- K loop (double-buffered ring-of-two using descriptors -> TMA) ----
K_tiles = (K + BLOCK_K - 1) // BLOCK_K
if K_tiles == 0:
    # Masked store of zeros when K == 0
    c_ptrs = C_ptr + (offs_m[:, None] * stride_cm + offs_n[None, :]
                      * stride_cn)
    c_mask = (offs_m[:, None] < M) & (offs_n[None, :] < N)
    tl.store(c_ptrs, acc, mask=c_mask)
    tile_idx += nprog
    continue

# Prefetch first CURRENT tiles
k0 = 0
if (m0 + BLOCK_M <= M) and (k0 + BLOCK_K <= K):
    a_cur = A_desc.load([m0, k0])
else:
    row_offsets = offs_m[:, None] + tl.zeros((BLOCK_M, BLOCK_K),
                                             dtype=offs_m.dtype)
    col_offsets = (k0 + offs_k)[None, :] + tl.zeros((BLOCK_M, BLOCK_K),
                                                    dtype=offs_k.dtype)
    a_cur = tl.load(A_desc, offsets=(row_offsets, col_offsets),
                    boundary_check=(0, 1), padding_option="zero")

if (n0 + BLOCK_N <= N) and (k0 + BLOCK_K <= K):
    b_cur = B_desc.load([k0, n0])
else:
    row_offsets = (k0 + offs_k)[:, None] + tl.zeros((BLOCK_K, BLOCK_N),
                                                    dtype=offs_k.dtype)
    col_offsets = offs_n[None, :] + tl.zeros((BLOCK_K, BLOCK_N),
                                             dtype=offs_n.dtype)
    b_cur = tl.load(B_desc, offsets=(row_offsets, col_offsets),
                    boundary_check=(0, 1), padding_option="zero")

# Pipeline: prefetch-NEXT -> compute-CURRENT -> swap
for kt in tl.range(0, K_tiles, num_stages=NUM_STAGES,
                   warp_specialize=True):
    next_k = (kt + 1) * BLOCK_K

    if kt + 1 < K_tiles:
```

```
if (m0 + BLOCK_M <= M) and (next_k + BLOCK_K <= K):
    a_next = A_desc.load([m0, next_k])
else:
    row_offsets = offs_m[:, None] + tl.zeros((BLOCK_M, BLOCK_K),
                                              dtype=offs_m.dtype)
    col_offsets = (next_k + offs_k)[None, :]
                    + tl.zeros((BLOCK_M, BLOCK_K),
                    dtype=offs_k.dtype)
    a_next = tl.load(A_desc, offsets=(row_offsets, col_offsets),
                        boundary_check=(0, 1),
                        padding_option="zero")

if (n0 + BLOCK_N <= N) and (next_k + BLOCK_K <= K):
    b_next = B_desc.load([next_k, n0])
else:
    row_offsets = (next_k + offs_k)[:, None]
                    + tl.zeros((BLOCK_K, BLOCK_N),
                    dtype=offs_k.dtype)
    col_offsets = offs_n[None, :] + tl.zeros((BLOCK_K, BLOCK_N),
                                              dtype=offs_n.dtype)
    b_next = tl.load(B_desc, offsets=(row_offsets, col_offsets),
                        boundary_check=(0, 1),
                        padding_option="zero")

# Compute on CURRENT tiles (UMMA on Blackwell; accumulators in TMEM)
acc += tl.dot(a_cur, b_cur)

# Swap in the prefetched NEXT tiles
if kt + 1 < K_tiles:
    a_cur = a_next
    b_cur = b_next

# ---- Store C with masking --------------------------------------
c_ptrs = C_ptr + (offs_m[:, None] * stride_cm
                + offs_n[None, :] * stride_cn)
c_mask = (offs_m[:, None] < M) & (offs_n[None, :] < N)
tl.store(c_ptrs, acc, mask=c_mask)

# Advance to the next tile handled by this program (persistent stepping)
tile_idx += nprog
```

This persistent approach aligns well with modern GPUs, which have relatively large register files, shared memory, and L2 cache. These can accommodate larger tile sizes (BLOCK_K). This means more of the K-loop can be unrolled per iteration.

A persistent kernel like this will usually outperform a sequence of smaller matmul kernels—especially when K is very large (e.g., > 1,024). The trade-off is that one SM is occupied longer. But if the kernel can fully utilize the SM, this is often ideal.

In the preceding code, you can experiment with increasing BLOCK_K on modern GPUs since they have increased on-chip memory and can handle more data per tile.

However, beyond a certain point, register pressure may increase and lead to register spilling. As such, it's always important to profile and find the right balance for your workload and hardware.

Software Pipelining and Double Buffering with Triton

This example shows how to implement double buffering with Triton. Double buffering, a two-stage form of software pipelining, overlaps memory loads and computations in a single loop.

On modern NVIDIA GPUs, asynchronous global-to-shared copies allow multiple inflight stages of prefetch to overlap memory transfers with compute. This makes double buffering (and triple buffering, etc.) a valuable and important performance optimization technique.

Triton implements pipelining through a `num_stages` meta-parameter used by Triton loop iterators. This parameter is passed to the `tl.range()` loop iterators. When you pass `num_stages>1`, the iterators automatically pipeline the loop by issuing asynchronous copy operations for up to `num_stages` iterations in flight.

This will overlap memory loads with computations across those staged iterations. This process continues until all tiles are processed. Here is an implementation of tile-based double buffering (`num_stages=2`) in Triton:

```python
@triton.jit
def pipelined_matmul(
    A_ptr, B_ptr, C_ptr,
    M, N, K,
    stride_am, stride_ak,
    stride_bk, stride_bn,
    stride_cm, stride_cn,
    # compile-time constants:
    BLOCK_M: tl.constexpr, BLOCK_N: tl.constexpr, BLOCK_K: tl.constexpr,
    NUM_STAGES: tl.constexpr,
):
    # Program (CTA) ids for the MxN tiling
    pid_m = tl.program_id(0)
    pid_n = tl.program_id(1)
    m0 = pid_m * BLOCK_M
    n0 = pid_n * BLOCK_N

    offs_m = m0 + tl.arange(0, BLOCK_M)
    offs_n = n0 + tl.arange(0, BLOCK_N)
    offs_k = tl.arange(0, BLOCK_K)

    # --------------- Descriptor creation (maps to TMA on Blackwell) ----------
    # Requirements for descriptor/TMA on NVIDIA GPUs:
    #  - leading strides are multiples of 16 BYTES
    #  - last dimension contiguous
```

```
#  - block_shape matches the tile you intend to move
A_desc = tl.make_tensor_descriptor(
    A_ptr,
    shape=[M, K],
    strides=[stride_am, stride_ak],
    block_shape=[BLOCK_M, BLOCK_K],
)
B_desc = tl.make_tensor_descriptor(
    B_ptr,
    shape=[K, N],
    strides=[stride_bk, stride_bn],
    block_shape=[BLOCK_K, BLOCK_N],
)

# Accumulator in FP32; on Blackwell this resides in TMEM, not registers.
acc = tl.zeros((BLOCK_M, BLOCK_N), dtype=tl.float32)

# Number of K tiles
K_tiles = (K + BLOCK_K - 1) // BLOCK_K
if K_tiles == 0:
    # Nothing to do, store zeros (masked)
    c_ptrs = C_ptr + (offs_m[:, None]
                    * stride_cm + offs_n[None, :] * stride_cn)
    c_mask = (offs_m[:, None] < M) & (offs_n[None, :] < N)
    tl.store(c_ptrs, acc, mask=c_mask)
    return

# --------- Prefetch the first "current" tiles (fast path if fully in-bounds)
k0 = 0
if (m0 + BLOCK_M <= M) and (k0 + BLOCK_K <= K):
    a_cur = A_desc.load([m0, k0])
else:
    # Boundary: compute row/col offsets and use boundary-checked load
    row_offsets = offs_m[:, None] + tl.zeros((BLOCK_M, BLOCK_K),
                                        dtype=offs_m.dtype)
    col_offsets = (k0 + offs_k)[None, :] + tl.zeros((BLOCK_M, BLOCK_K),
                                        dtype=offs_k.dtype)
    a_cur = tl.load(A_desc, offsets=(row_offsets, col_offsets),
                boundary_check=(0, 1), padding_option="zero")

if (n0 + BLOCK_N <= N) and (k0 + BLOCK_K <= K):
    b_cur = B_desc.load([k0, n0])
else:
    row_offsets = (k0 + offs_k)[:, None] + tl.zeros((BLOCK_K, BLOCK_N),
                                        dtype=offs_k.dtype)
    col_offsets = offs_n[None, :] + tl.zeros((BLOCK_K, BLOCK_N),
                                        dtype=offs_n.dtype)
    b_cur = tl.load(B_desc, offsets=(row_offsets, col_offsets),
                boundary_check=(0, 1), padding_option="zero")

# ------------- K loop with software pipelining and TMA prefetch -----------
# Put prefetch as early as possible in loop body; keep separate "current"
```

```
# tile so loads for the next iteration can overlap with the dot-product of
# current tile. Use warp_specialize to partition producer/consumer warps.
for kt in tl.range(0, K_tiles, num_stages=NUM_STAGES, warp_specialize=True):
    next_k = (kt + 1) * BLOCK_K

    # Prefetch NEXT tiles early (TMA), if there is a next tile
    if kt + 1 < K_tiles:
        if (m0 + BLOCK_M <= M) and (next_k + BLOCK_K <= K):
            a_next = A_desc.load([m0, next_k])
        else:
            row_offsets = offs_m[:, None] + tl.zeros((BLOCK_M, BLOCK_K),
                                                     dtype=offs_m.dtype)
            col_offsets = (next_k + offs_k)[None, :]
                        + tl.zeros((BLOCK_M, BLOCK_K), dtype=offs_k.dtype)
            a_next = tl.load(A_desc, offsets=(row_offsets, col_offsets),
                             boundary_check=(0, 1), padding_option="zero")

        if (n0 + BLOCK_N <= N) and (next_k + BLOCK_K <= K):
            b_next = B_desc.load([next_k, n0])
        else:
            row_offsets = (next_k + offs_k)[:, None]
                        + tl.zeros((BLOCK_K, BLOCK_N), dtype=offs_k.dtype)
            col_offsets = offs_n[None, :] + tl.zeros((BLOCK_K, BLOCK_N),
                                                     dtype=offs_n.dtype)
            b_next = tl.load(B_desc, offsets=(row_offsets, col_offsets),
                             boundary_check=(0, 1), padding_option="zero")

    # Compute on the CURRENT tiles (UMMA; accumulators in TMEM on Blackwell)
    acc += tl.dot(a_cur, b_cur)

    # Swap in prefetched NEXT tiles
    if kt + 1 < K_tiles:
        a_cur = a_next
        b_cur = b_next

# ------------------------------- Store C --------------------------------
c_ptrs = C_ptr + (offs_m[:, None] * stride_cm + offs_n[None, :] * stride_cn)
c_mask = (offs_m[:, None] < M) & (offs_n[None, :] < N)
tl.store(c_ptrs, acc, mask=c_mask)
```

Triton's compiler sees num_stages, generates asynchronous loads/stores with TMA and TMEM using Triton tensor descriptors, and automatically manages the synchronization. The use of TMA tensor descriptors and TMEM reduces register pressure and simplifies expressing multidimensional transfers. The preceding loop performs prefetch-next → compute-current → swap. This preserves overlap with num_stages>1 and avoids silent overlap collapse when you overwrite the current tile too early. Specifically, while one tile is being loaded into shared memory, the previous tile's computation is being performed.

You can also use warp specialization, in which Triton partitions producer and consumer warps to overlap global-to-shared copies with compute. This is automatically enabled when heuristics select it.

It's important to keep the pipeline's overlap intact. When you set `num_stages > 1`, make sure the tile you are currently computing stays live across loop iterations. You don't want to overwrite or drop its reference until the math that consumes it is finished.

Consider a 2-stage ring buffer in which you compute the `current` buffer while asynchronously fetching the `next` buffer. You then swap the `current` and `next` buffers. In this scenario, you need to wait and consume the "current" buffer before releasing it. At the same time, you need to use commit/wait to guard the "next" buffer (tile) until the swap.

If the current tile doesn't survive across iterations (e.g., you overwrite its buffer or let the reference die), the compiler is free to reorder, sink, or hoist the "next" iteration's copies past the "current" uses. This will cause your load/compute overlap to quietly disappear.

And If you manage shared-memory block pointers/TMA yourself, make sure to use the explicit handshake: enqueue async copies → `tl.commit()` → (later) `tl.wait()` → consume the tile → advance pointers. If you call `tl.wait()` right before you read the tile—and only release/swap after consumption—you will preserve true overlap.

> On modern GPUs, Triton backs descriptor loads and stores with the Tensor Memory Accelerator (TMA). When you pipeline a loop (`num_stages > 1`), prefetch the next tile early and keep a separate variable for the current tile. Don't overwrite or drop the "current" reference until the operation that consumes it is finished. Otherwise, the compiler may legally reorder the next iteration's copies past current uses and your overlap will collapse. The simplest pattern is `prefetch-next` → `compute-current` → `swap`.

In short, software pipelining improves memory bandwidth utilization and hides latency. And if memory bandwidth isn't the bottleneck, you can increase `num_stages` to 3 (e.g., triple buffering) to prefetch two tiles in flight and further improve performance at the cost of more shared memory usage for the additional buffers. However, on hardware with tighter shared-memory budgets—or for compute-heavy kernels—the extra stages might lead to a diminishing return, lower occupancy, and reduced overall performance.

Profiling with Triton Proton Profiler

To deeply profile Triton kernel performance, use Triton's Proton (*https://oreil.ly/ MckBB*) profiler. This is a separate profiling package that integrates with Triton and emits NVTX ranges visible in Nsight Systems timelines. These NVTX ranges instrument code regions, collect timings, and track key metrics. The NVTX markers then appear in Nsight Systems timelines. Use these NVTX regions to jump from Proton summaries into Nsight Compute for more focused kernel-level analysis.

In practice, you wrap critical sections of Triton code using the `with` `proton.scope("name", metadata)` Python context manager. Before running the workload, you activate the profiler with `proton.start("matmul", hook="triton")`.

`metadata` in Proton is any user-provided dictionary of annotations or metrics, such as total FLOPS, memory byte counts, thread block indices, warp-level indices, or the number of recorded slots. These get recorded alongside timing data for richer performance analysis.

After execution, you finalize and fetch the profiling data. The output can be printed as a hierarchical table of timings. Here is an excerpt of a Proton profiling result that compares different `matmul` kernels for multiplying $8{,}192 \times 8{,}192$ matrices:

```
168.314 ms    16331.291   ROOT
├─ 174.920 ms   3928.623   cublas [M=8192,N=8192,K=512]
├─ 165.349 ms   4156.033   matmul_kernel [M=8192,N=8192,K=512]
├─ 159.352 ms   4312.421   matmul_kernel_persistent [M=8192,N=8192,K=512]
└─ 174.671 ms   3934.214   torch [M=8192,N=8192,K=512]
```

In the preceding profiling output, the label K denotes the reduction dimension, or the shared inner size of the matrix multiply (e.g., an M × K matrix multiplied by a K × N matrix). This represents the length of the dot product that drives both compute cost and memory traffic.

In this profile report, we see the Triton persistent kernel outperforms cuBLAS, 159.352 ms versus 174.920 ms. Proton makes it easy to quantify such differences. It also computes derived metrics like effective TFLOPS and memory bandwidth. If you supply additional `metadata` such as the total FLOPS count, Proton will show you if you're nearing the theoretical hardware TFLOPS limit for the precision you are using (e.g., BF16/FP16, FP8, FP4, etc.). For many matrix shapes and precisions, cuBLASLt or CUTLASS paths in PyTorch will match or exceed a custom Triton kernel.

NVIDIA's Nsight Systems and Nsight Compute tools support Triton kernels as well. For instance, Nsight Systems shows kernel-launch names and any NVTX ranges emitted by PyTorch or Proton. These can be used to correlate Proton scopes with Nsight timelines. This way, you can use Proton's output to pinpoint interesting kernels in Nsight Systems and then dive deeper into Nsight Compute for low-level analysis. You would use Nsight Compute to analyze register usage, achieved occupancy, etc. Using these tools together provides a more complete system performance analysis.

PyTorch XLA Backend

While TorchInductor is the PyTorch default backend for GPUs and CPUs, PyTorch XLA is a separate backend-compilation option that targets Google Cloud TPUs and other accelerators. PyTorch XLA allows PyTorch models to run on these accelerators by mapping PyTorch operations into XLA's graph IR and executing them using the target hardware's runtime, as shown in Figure 14-6.

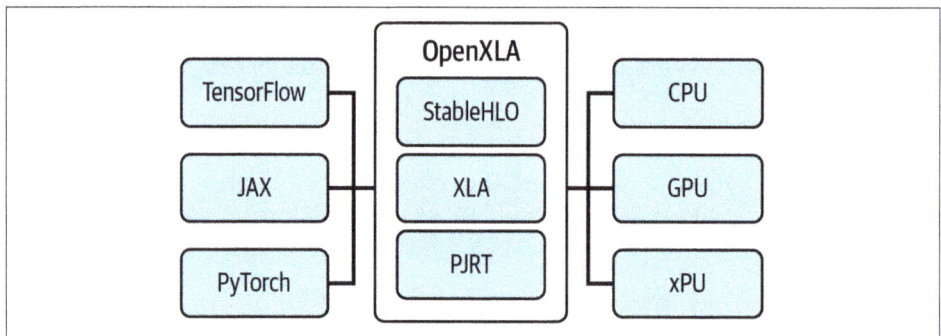

Figure 14-6. OpenXLA, the basis of the PyTorch XLA compiler backend

To activate the XLA backend, you can use `torch.compile(..., backend="open xla")`, which activates PyTorch XLA based on OpenXLA (*https://openxla.org*). This backend string is supported by the PyTorch XLA project and activates OpenXLA-based compilation. Similar to TorchDynamo and TorchInductor, XLA captures the graph of computations. However, it compiles whole programs ahead of time because XLA is designed to generate static graphs.

XLA is optimized for static shapes or bounded dynamic shapes. As such, when using XLA, dynamic shape support is a bit more limited. New shapes trigger whole-program recompilation, which is expensive for latency-sensitive inference. However, OpenXLA caches executables per shape signature, which can improve performance.

> You may need to pad or use fixed-size buckets for your inputs. This is because XLA will recompile for new shapes rather than handling them symbolically.

The XLA compiler will cache each compiled graph per unique input shape and signature. As such, performance will improve after a few warm-up steps similar to Torch-Inductor. The major difference is that XLA will not incrementally compile mid-run. The graph is built statically ahead of time. And if a new shape is encountered, it will trigger a new whole-graph compilation, which is very expensive and impacts latency-sensitive workloads like inference.

In short, if you're running on a hardware device not currently supported by the TorchInductor backend, you can potentially use the XLA backend if the device supports XLA. Many of the same principles apply, such as minimizing graph breaks. You can also use some distributed strategies with XLA, such as data and model parallelism. While XLA isn't commonly used with NVIDIA GPUs, it's a powerful backend for non-NVIDIA hardware (e.g., Google TPUs using OpenXLA or other accelerators that support XLA IR). XLA benefits from many similar compilation techniques discussed in this chapter.

Key Takeaways

We covered quite a lot in this chapter, and we dove super deep into the PyTorch compiler stack and OpenAI's Triton language and compiler. The following are some key takeaways:

Leverage `torch.compile` *for easy speedups*
Choose the compilation `mode` based on your needs (e.g., `"default"` for quicker startup, `"max-autotune"` for maximum performance). Always perform a few warm-up iterations to get past the initial compile. For short-running jobs or small models, the compile overhead might outweigh the speedup, so use it when you have enough work to amortize the one-time cost.

Set performance flags early
Following are the flags you should enable for fast FP32 matmuls and SDPA variants including Flash Attention. Always validate accuracy for your model and keep these enabled for the best performance:

```python
import torch
 # maps to TF32/BF16 fast paths
torch.set_float32_matmul_precision("high")
torch.backends.cuda.matmul.allow_tf32 = True
# affects convs
torch.backends.cudnn.allow_tf32 = True
torch.backends.cuda.enable_flash_sdp(True)
torch.backends.cuda.enable_mem_efficient_sdp(True)
```

Minimize graph breaks
Inspect graph breaks using `torch._dynamo.explain` or `TORCH_LOGS= "graph_ breaks"`. Remove or refactor code that causes breaks (e.g., prints, data-dependent

Python control flow, unsupported ops) to maximize the contiguous regions that can be compiled. Fewer, larger graphs generally mean better performance. If needed, use the new `torch.cond` API for conditional logic or move noncritical Python-side processing out of the model's forward function. The goal is to present the compiler a long, purely tensor-in and tensor-out code path.

Use dynamic shapes carefully

While not necessary, setting `torch.compile(dynamic=True)` upfront forces the compiler to consider all dimensions as dynamic. This way, one compiled model can handle a wide range of input shapes—reducing the need for padding. The compiler will do this dynamically, but setting `dynamic=True` forces the compiler to do this upfront. You can also mark only specific dimensions dynamic with `mark_dynamic()` instead of all dimensions. This way, you localize the flexibility to where it's actually needed. This is great for variable sequence lengths, but make sure to measure the trade-offs. Enabling dynamic-shape support can disable CUDA Graphs and insert additional guards. If your shapes don't vary too widely, a hybrid approach can work best. Specifically, you can bucket inputs by size—up to limit the number of distinct shapes and then enable dynamic shapes for the remaining variability. This hybrid approach avoids excessive recompilations while still reducing padding waste.

Profile for recompilation guards

Use `TORCH_LOGS="graph_breaks,guards,recompiles"` to find which guard is triggering if you see multiple compilations. Common culprits are Python random values, changing tensor ranks, or varying device/dtype. Make those aspects static or mark them as safe with `allow_in_graph` if appropriate.

Avoid recompilations if possible

In a well-tuned training loop, you should see zero recompilations after the initial few iterations. If you do see continued recompiling, investigate immediately, as it usually means something is changing on every iteration. This includes debug print statements with an incrementing counter, etc. Use the `set_stance()` API and guard-logging to catch these. Also make sure that you're not unintentionally mixing devices by sending a CPU tensor on one iteration and then a GPU on the next. This will trigger a recompile.

Tune and monitor memory usage

Compiled mode might use more memory for larger fused kernels and guard buffers. Monitor GPU memory. If you hit memory issues, consider using a smaller `BLOCK_SIZE` in Triton kernels or disabling certain fusions. Also ensure you free any large intermediate results promptly, as they might hang around longer in a compiled graph's lifecycle. If you see out-of-memory errors during compilation, you might need to split your model or use lower `max_autotune` settings. PyTorch supports automatic checkpointing for large graphs to reduce memory pressure, but it's not foolproof. You can also try compiling submodules (e.g., each layer or block) separately instead of compiling the entire model at once to limit memory usage during kernel generation.

Combine the PyTorch compiler with distributed training wisely
When using DDP or FSDP, be aware of intentional graph breaks at communication points. They are expected and optimized by overlapping communication with computation. Wrap submodules in FSDP to get shard-wise compilation and memory savings. Keep an eye on any all-reduce-related warnings in `dynamo.explain`. PyTorch's design tries to minimize performance degradation due to graph breaks. When using FSDP with `torch.compile`, you may see graph breaks for gradient prereduction and postreduction steps. These are expected and handled. Focus on the main forward and backward passes within each shard being compiled.

Use `TORCH_LOGS="perf_hints"` to catch missed optimizations
This will tell you, for example, if CUDA Graphs weren't used due to input mutation—or if an operation fell back to eager mode. These hints can guide you to potential improvements by telling you to avoid certain patterns or wait for future support. Often, a hint will directly suggest the workaround. For instance, the "input is mutated" hint implies that you should avoid in-place operations on the input before compiling.

Debug with small inputs first
When developing custom kernels or testing compiled mode, use small tensor sizes to quickly catch correctness issues. Once it's working, scale up. Use PyTorch's `torch._dynamo.config.verbose` or even `TORCH_LOGS="output_code"` to inspect generated code for small cases. Be aware that performance measured on tiny inputs may not reflect behavior on real sizes. But, for debugging correctness and seeing what kernels are generated, this is a useful technique.

Write custom kernels only for the true bottlenecks
Before embarking on Triton kernel development, profile your model with and without compiling to identify hotspots. Often, TorchInductor already fuses many things. Focus your efforts on areas where Inductor falls short—maybe a custom op or an atypical fusion. Do not prematurely optimize everything. Use the compiler for most—and hand-tune the rest. For example, if TorchInductor fails to fuse a particular sequence of operations that is performance-critical, such as a multistep custom activation, this might justify a separate Triton kernel. Just weigh the maintenance cost since each custom kernel is code, and you may need to update this code when you change hardware—or if PyTorch eventually adds native support. Often, filing an issue or feature request for TorchInductor to support a pattern is worthwhile if it benefits many other users.

Follow Triton best practices

When writing Triton code, ensure memory accesses are coalesced, avoid bank conflicts in shared memory (pad if needed), mask `tl.load()` and `tl.store()` at boundaries, choose block and tile sizes that align with warp sizes (multiples of 32 threads), select tile sizes that fit into the L1/shared carve-out, and tune `num_warps` and `num_stages` settings with `@triton.autotune([... triton.Config(num_warps=..., num_stages=...) ...], key=[...])`.. Use Triton's autotuner to find the best configuration if performance is critical. Start with `num_warps` $\in$ `{4,8}` and `num_stages` $\in$ `{2,3,4}`. Remember to check the Triton documentation (*https://oreil.ly/MY3Uc*) and examples (*https://oreil.ly/xam0Z*) since many common patterns like FlashAttention have already been implemented and optimized by the community. At a minimum, these existing examples are a good starting point for your own implementation.

Cache hint caution

Some forms of PTX loads (e.g., DeepSeek-style non-coherent + L1 no-allocate + 256B L2 prefetch) are undocumented and potentially undefined on certain hardware. This may break across driver versions and hardware generations. Prefer Triton's `eviction_policy=` (e.g., `evict_last`) and `cache_modifier=` knobs to improve portability. Remember to profile when migrating to different CUDA drivers and GPU generations. Avoid introducing conflicting cache hints, as these are extremely difficult to debug.

Keep an eye on new PyTorch releases

PyTorch is rapidly evolving its compiler. Each version brings expanded operator support, better performance, and fewer graph breaks. Upgrading can often give free speedups or fix issues. The same goes for Triton. Staying up-to-date ensures you benefit from the latest work. This is especially important for rapidly evolving GPU hardware.

Conclusion

As complexity increases and the PyTorch ecosystem continues to expand, it's important that you embrace performance profiling and iterative optimizations. You should use Nsight Systems, Nsight Compute, PyTorch profiler, or Triton profiler together to verify that you're getting the GPU utilization and performance that you expect. If not, adjust your performance strategy.

And remember to maintain a holistic view during your iterative approach. When one bottleneck is removed, the next one will emerge. Iterative performance tuning can lead you from GPU kernel occupancy to CPU overhead to tuning the input pipeline. The compiler helps with a big piece of this puzzle, but you likely need to optimize data loading, I/O, and algorithmic choices to achieve optimal performance.

## CHAPTER 15

Multinode Inference, Parallelism, Decoding, and Routing Optimizations

LLMs continue to scale up to a massive number of parameters. In particular, the emergence of mixture-of-experts (MoE) LLMs, models that combine many specialist subnetworks ("experts") with a built-in, expert-gating mechanism, has pushed model parameter sizes into the hundreds of billions or multiple trillions. And while only a fraction of those parameters are active for a given input, running inference on these enormous model sizes requires distributing the workload across multiple GPUs.

This chapter focuses on advanced optimization techniques used to perform efficient, high-performance multinode inference for these massive LLMs using modern NVIDIA GPUs. We will discuss how to architect distributed inference systems that minimize latency and maximize throughput—leveraging both hardware and algorithmic innovations.

We start by discussing disaggregated prefill and decode (PD, disagg PD) architectures that split the inference workload into distinct stages, which can be tuned independently. Next, we explore core inference-focused parallelism strategies like data, tensor, pipeline, expert, and context—and how they can be used in combination to serve large models across many GPUs.

We then cover speculative decoding methods, including techniques like Medusa, EAGLE, and draft-and-verify schemes. These allow multiple tokens to be generated and evaluated during inference instead of the standard single-token generation from traditional autoregressive LLMs. This helps overcome the sequential decoding bottleneck. We also discuss constrained decoding for enforcing output formats (e.g., custom JSON schemas) and dynamic routing strategies for MoE models to improve the system's expert gating and load-balancing efficiency.

Disaggregated Prefill and Decode Architecture

As mentioned previously, the inference workflow for modern LLMs consists of two different phases: prefill and decode. We can implement *disaggregated prefill and decode* to separate the stages. This lets us scale the prefill and decode clusters independently—even on different hardware platforms—and significantly improve performance for large-scale LLM serving, as detailed later in this chapter.

> Cross-vendor or cross-architecture deployments require that the KV cache layout and dtypes match across both sides. In practice, production systems should keep prefill and decode on compatible GPU families. This way, they use the same numeric formats to easily enable KV cache transfer and data reuse.

In the prefill stage, the model processes the entire input prompt—often thousands, tens of thousands, or even millions of tokens—in a single forward pass to produce initial hidden states as calculated by the LLM. It then populates the attention key-value (KV) cache for all tokens in the input prompt. Figure 15-1 shows how disaggregated prefill and decode share the KV cache and overlap KV transfers with computations.

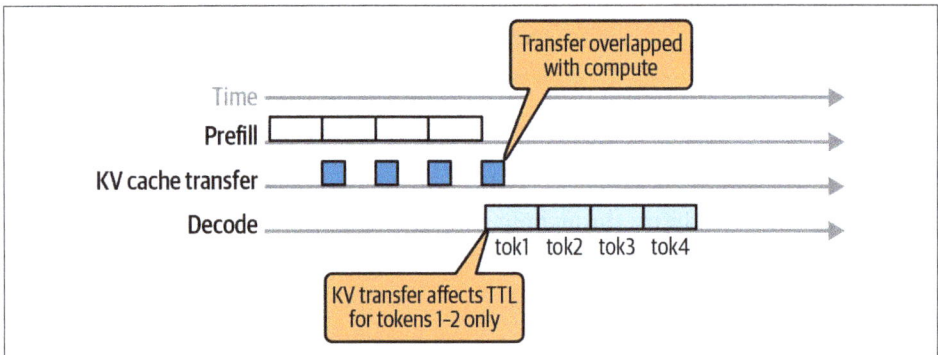

Figure 15-1. Disaggregated prefill and decode sharing the KV cache and overlapping KV transfers with computations

In the decode stage, the model performs an autoregressive generation to predict each new token in the sequence. It does this by consuming the cached attention KV representations of all previously generated tokens.

Speculative decoding accelerates the decode process by pregenerating multiple tokens in a single batch. In parallel, it then verifies that the tokens are correct. This reduces the sequential nature of standard token-by-token autoregressive decoding. We'll cover speculative decoding in a bit.

Prefill-Decode Interference

Traditionally, LLM inference systems colocate these two stages on the same nodes and simply batch all computations together. However, this naive approach leads to what's commonly called *prefill-decode interference*. For instance, a long prompt prefill can occupy the GPU and delay time-sensitive decoding work for other requests—and vice versa.

Colocating prefill and decode on the same nodes forces a single scheduling and resource allocation strategy for these two phases, which have very different characteristics. Prefill consists of large, parallel computations. In contrast, decode requires many small, sequential computations. As a result, systems have to either prioritize one phase's performance over the other or over-provision hardware to meet both demands.

With a *disaggregated prefill and decode* architecture, the prefill and decode phases are assigned to different GPU pools. This eliminates direct interference between the two workloads. The DistServe system (*https://oreil.ly/mgbd9*), by disaggregating prefill and decode, reported up to 7.4× more goodput requests served within both TTFT and TPOT constraints (up to 12.6× tighter latency SLOs).

Scaling Prefill and Worker Nodes Independently

If we can eliminate cross-phase interference, we can reduce resource "dead time" in which decode tasks are stalled behind long prefill computations—and vice versa. This way, GPUs spend more time doing more useful work and less time idling. This increases utilization and useful throughput at a given latency target (aka *goodput*).

We can scale prefill and decode separately by dedicating one set of nodes to handle the prefill and another set of nodes to handle the decode. The two clusters communicate only when transferring the encoded prompt state, or attention KV cache, from the prefill workers to the decode workers, as shown in Figure 15-2.

Here, you see separate GPU workers handling the prefill stage to process the input prompt—along with the decode stage to generate output tokens iteratively. The output of the prefill stage includes the KV cache for the prompt. It is transferred to the decode workers to generate the next tokens.

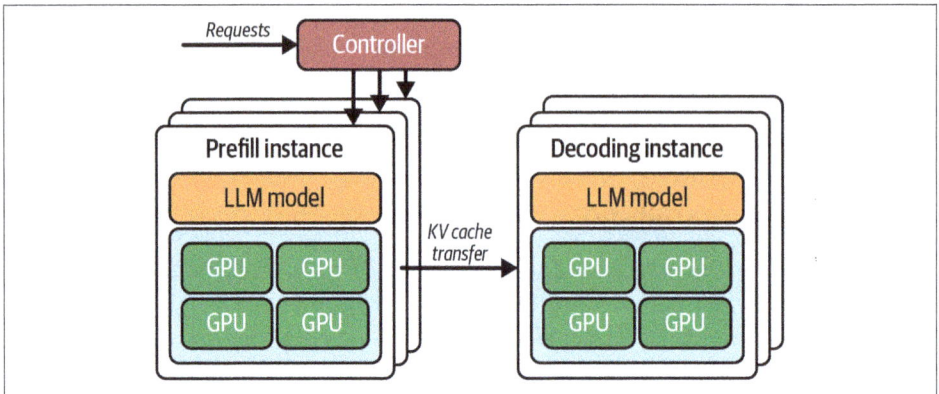

Figure 15-2. Disaggregated inference: Prefill pool (hidden state + KV) → KV handoff using NVLink/NVSwitch (intranode) or GPUDirect RDMA (internode) → Decode pool

By dedicating separate GPU pools, the system keeps both prefill and decode pipelines busy in parallel. In practice, disaggregation has been shown to significantly improve throughput under strict latency constraints. Some studies show that large gains are possible, but results range from moderate improvements to several times higher goodput once the prefill and decode stages are separated. The results greatly depend on the workload and network fabric.

This separation allows each stage to be optimized and scaled independently for throughput or latency. Prefills can be batched aggressively on the prefill GPUs to maximize throughput without burdening the decode performance (e.g., increased decode latency). Also, with separate clusters we can tune parallelism settings, instance counts, and scheduling policies specific to each phase.

Impact on Latency (TTFT) and Throughput (TPOT)

Decode GPUs can run at lower batch sizes—or with specialized scheduling—to minimize *time per output token* (TPOT) for streaming generation. For example, you can use a scheduler that prioritizes urgent decode tasks to avoid queuing delays.

This separation works well because each phase has different performance expectations. *Time to first token* (TTFT) for the prefill stage is optimized for low latency, while the decode stage prioritizes low time per output token (TPOT) and stable streaming latency. End-to-end throughput is largely determined by concurrency and scheduling. In traditional setups, one had to compromise between TTFT and TPOT per-token latency. Disaggregation allows both SLO targets to be met simultaneously.

Monitor NVLink and NIC utilization during KV transfer and all-to-all phases. The goal is to overlap cop and compute using separate streams and events.

The KV handoff incurs minimal additional latency because the communication uses high-bandwidth interconnects for multi-GPU and multinode transfers. These interconnects include NVLink, NVSwitch, InfiniBand, and Ethernet (RoCE on Ethernet) using GPUDirect RDMA. For instance, multinode clusters with ConnectX-8 SuperNICs (800 GbE-class) provides up to 800 Gb/s per port with GPUDirect RDMA. This greatly reduces KV transfer time compared to host-mediated communication paths. Additionally, it's recommended to deploy 1 NIC per GPU to optimize prefill-decode disaggregation and improve MoE all-to-all performance.

KV Cache Data Transfer and NIXL

Disaggregated systems use a connector or scheduler to transfer the prompt's intermediate results (the final hidden state and the KV cache) from the prefill workers to the decode workers once the prompt processing is done. This handoff incurs some communication overhead, but if the cluster's interconnect is high-bandwidth (e.g., NVLink or InfiniBand), this overhead is small compared to the gains from eliminating resource contention.

In practice, NVIDIA's NIXL library minimizes transfer overhead by selecting NVLink/NVSwitch, RDMA, or host-staged paths automatically based on topology and policy. For example, NVIDIA's NIXL library, introduced in Chapter 4, will automatically select the fastest available path to transmit the KV cache. NIXL integrates with frameworks and inference engines, including Dynamo and vLLM. The NIXL-vLLM integration is shown in Figure 15-3.

Specifically, LMCache and NIXL are integrated in vLLM's disaggregated prefilling as the supported path. NIXL is also used by NVIDIA Dynamo and TensorRT-LLM to transport KV cache data using peer-to-peer GPU interconnects and RDMA.

Within a node, NIXL performs device-to-device transfers over NVLink and NVSwitch without host staging. Across nodes, NIXL uses GPUDirect RDMA over InfiniBand or RoCEv2 to avoid host copies. These paths keep KV cache handoff latency low even for multigigabyte payloads.

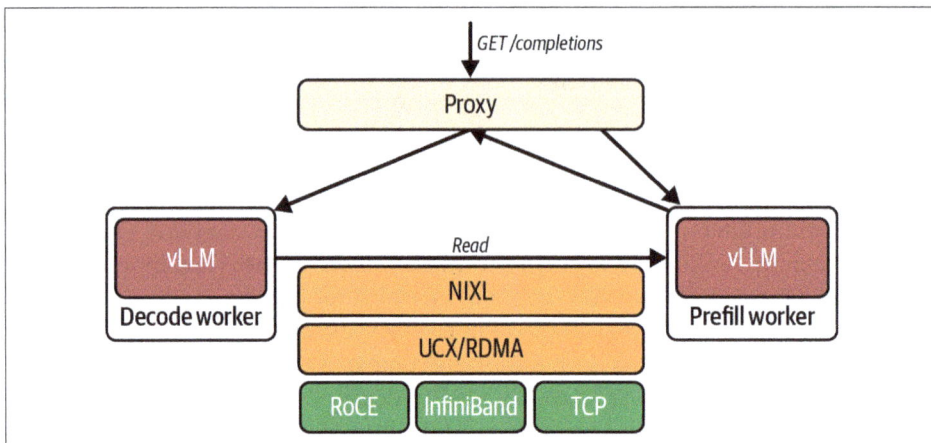

Figure 15-3. KV cache data transfers with NIXL in the vLLM inference engine; Intra-node: NVLink/NVSwitch (device-to-device); Internode: GPUDirect RDMA (InfiniBand/RoCEv2) using ConnectX-class NICs

Placement of prefill and decode workers should follow the fabric. Same node placement keeps KV transfers on NVLink and NVSwitch via CUDA peer access, while cross-node placement should use GPUDirect RDMA over InfiniBand or RoCEv2. NVIDIA Dynamo integrates with NIXL to move KV cache between GPUs, CPU memory, and storage across nodes, and vLLM integrates through LMCache and NIXL for disaggregated prefilling.

> When the fabric or virtualization layer prevents direct peer access, NIXL can fall back to host-staged paths, which are nonoptimal. Always validate end-to-end KV transfer time on your deployment.

Deploying Disaggregated Prefill and Decode with Kubernetes

In an advanced deployment, a cluster orchestration system like Kubernetes can dynamically shift the GPU pool allocations—or scale the pools out separately—based on load and input characteristics. For instance, if many users arrive with superlong prompts and relatively small outputs (e.g., large-document summarization use cases), Kubernetes can temporarily shift the allocation to use more GPUs in the prefill pool. This will decrease the number of GPUs allocated to the decode phase.

In contrast, if many users arrive requesting superlong outputs (e.g., long reasoning chains, "think step-by-step," etc.), more GPUs can be shifted to the decode pool. In both cases, new instances can be scaled out for each worker type.

Figure 15-4 shows a distributed, Kubernetes-based vLLM cluster of separate prefill and decode workers using the open source llm-d project (*https://oreil.ly/65U-M*). vLLM implements disaggregated prefilling by running two instances and handing off KV using LMCache and NIXL, but llm-d extends this with Kubernetes native orchestration for disaggregated serving and KV-aware routing. This diagram shows a component called the *variant autoscaler*, which is responsible for updating the number of replicas for the prefill and decode workers in the pool.

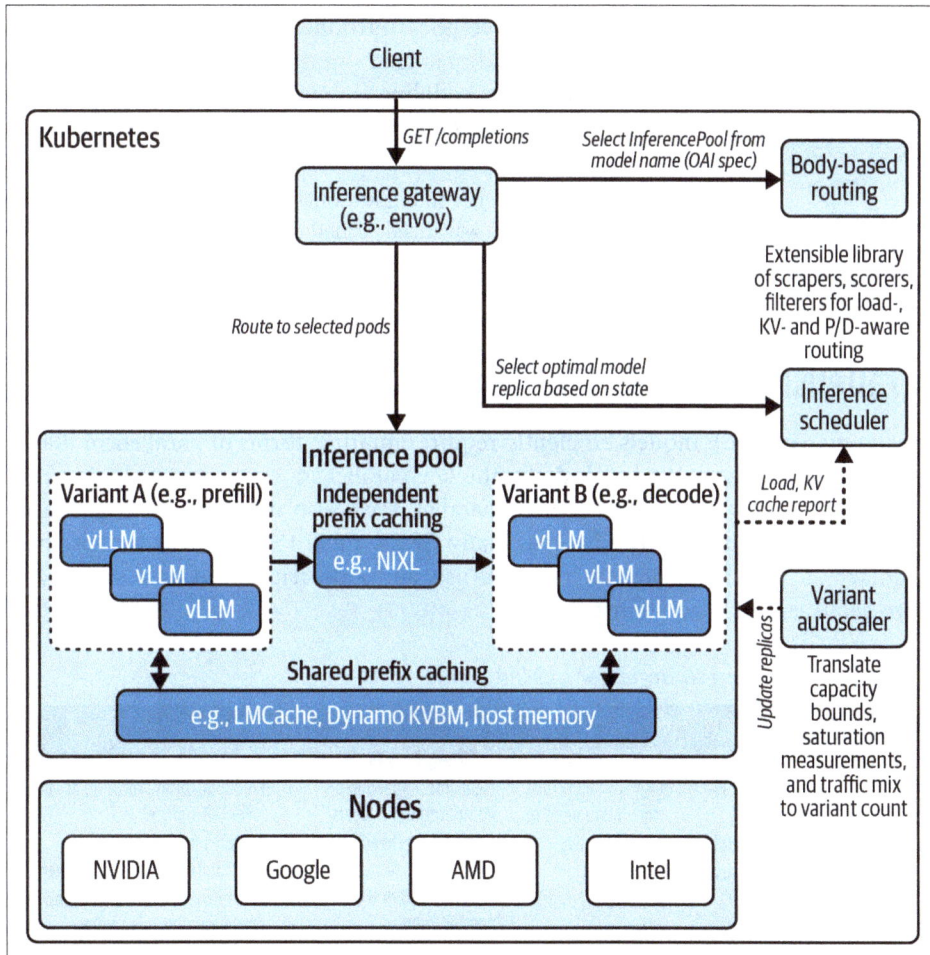

Figure 15-4. Kubernetes-based vLLM cluster of separate prefill and decode workers using the open source llm-d project (https://oreil.ly/65U-M); variant autoscaler tunes prefill/ decode replica counts based on the prompt-response mix; KV moved using LMCache and NIXL

In modern inference deployments, all nodes can perform both prefill and decode functionality since they all share the same runtime and code base (e.g., vLLM, SGLang, NVIDIA Dynamo, etc.). It's up to the cluster orchestrator to assign them a specific role, either prefill or decode, statically upon startup—and dynamically throughout the worker's lifecycle.

Overall, a disaggregated prefill/decode architecture provides a foundation for high-throughput, low-latency LLM serving. It does introduce complexity, however, as intermediate data must be transferred and managed—on the order of a few gigabytes for the KV cache of a long prompt. And scheduling is more involved, but the benefits of utilizing hardware efficiently are significant at ultra scale.

Chapters 17 and 18 dive deeper into additional techniques for disaggregated PD, including advanced scheduling, routing, and deployment optimizations.

Parallelism Strategies for Serving Massive MoE Models

Serving massive MoE models efficiently requires multiple forms of parallelism due to limited GPU memory. We break down the key parallelism strategies, including tensor, pipeline, expert, data, and context parallel. We'll also discuss how they can be combined to distribute an LLM across many GPUs. Table 15-1 provides a high-level summary of these strategies, their typical use, and a description of each strategy in more detail as they relate to inference.

Table 15-1. Parallelism strategies for LLM inference

Parallelism strategy	Partition basis	Use case	Pros	Cons
Tensor parallelism	Within each layer (split neural network weight matrices across GPUs)	Single model is too large or you need to speed up heavy compute within layers across multiple GPUs	Near-linear speedup on compute-bound layers Reduced overhead due to overlapping all-reduce communication with computation	Frequent communication at each layer (all-reduce) Requires high-bandwidth interconnect (NVLink/NVSwitch) Less efficient across nodes and slow networks due to high latencies (Recommended to keep tensor parallel groups within a single node)

Parallelism strategy	Partition basis	Use case	Pros	Cons
Pipeline parallelism	Different layers on different GPUs (the model is sliced by layer sequence)	Extremely deep models that don't fit on one GPU Memory scaling across layers	Allows distribution of model state Uses microbatching to process multiple tokens from different users/requests concurrently Multiple layers can be processed in parallel for long sequences (improves throughput for large batches or long inputs)	Adds pipeline fill/flush latency (bubbles)—not helpful for one-token-at-a-time decoding More complex to implement and higher activation memory footprint (must store intermediate activations between pipeline stages)
Expert parallelism	Different MoE on different GPUs (sparse activation per token)	Massive MoE models with many experts Needed to shard model parameters across GPUs	Enables virtually unlimited model size—total parameters scale with number of GPUs Each GPU computes only a fraction of tokens (sparse compute) High parameter count boosts model capacity/quality	High runtime communication overhead (all-to-all) at each MoE layer Potential load imbalance if gating is uneven Each GPU must have enough work (tokens) per expert to amortize communication
Data parallelism	Replicate the entire model on multiple GPUs, serving different requests on each	Scaling out throughput (more concurrent requests) once model deployment is fixed Multi-instance serving for many users	Nearly linear throughput scaling Simple to implement (no model partitioning needed)	No latency improvement for individual queries (aka *per-query latency*) Multiplies memory usage (each replica uses full memory) Must handle consistency if stateful (e.g., caches) or use stateless model calls
Context parallelism	Partition the input sequence tokens across GPUs at each layer	Ultralong sequences (e.g., 100k+ tokens) to reduce prompt latency and memory per GPU	Achieves near-linear speedup for long context prefill Enables processing contexts that exceed one GPU's memory by splitting KV cache	Requires custom attention algorithms to handle attention across partitions Adds communication per layer for boundary tokens Beneficial for very long contexts (100k+ tokens) due to additional communication overhead

> For intranode TP on Blackwell NVL72, prefer keeping TP groups within a single NVSwitch domain; extend inter-rack only when topology permits to avoid extra hops.

These parallelism strategies define how the model weights and data are split over the GPUs. Figure 15-5 shows how they are split up for the different parallelism strategies—as well as common combinations of strategies.

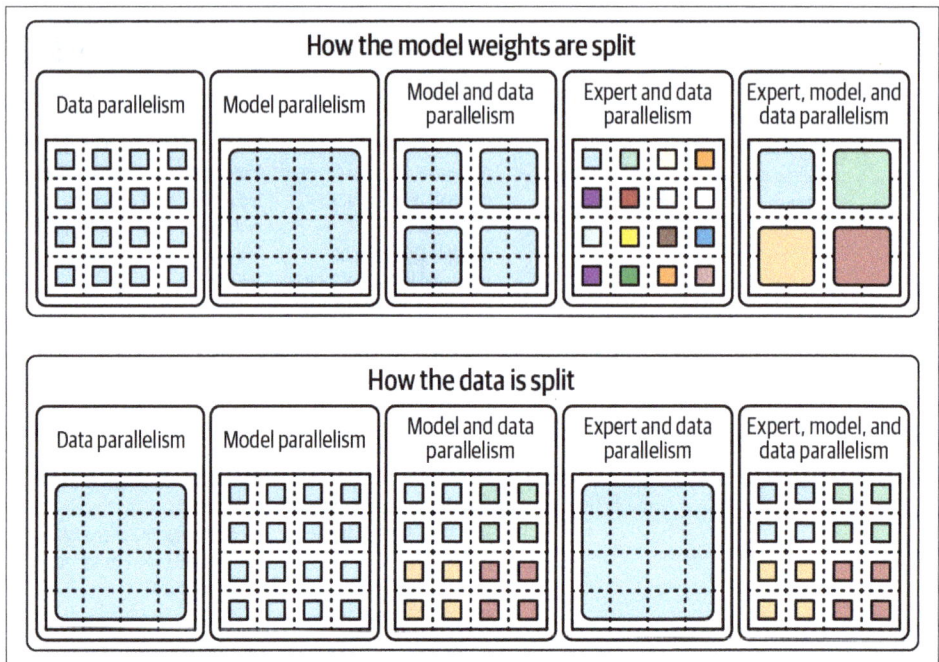

Figure 15-5. Model weights and input data split over the GPUs

Tensor Parallelism

Tensor parallelism (TP) splits the computations within each layer of the neural network across multiple GPUs. For instance, a large matrix multiply in a transformer layer can be partitioned by columns or rows—and computed in parallel on two or more GPUs. These GPUs then exchange their results by performing an all-reduce to aggregate their partial outputs.

TP is commonly used when a model's layers, called *hidden layers*, are too large to fit into a single GPU's memory—or when we want to accelerate a single instance of a model by utilizing multiple GPUs for the same layer in parallel. It keeps all GPUs in lockstep for each layer's computation, which requires extremely high inter-GPU bandwidth to be efficient.

Ideally, TP runs on GPUs that are connected with high-bandwidth NVLink and NVSwitch interconnects. On multi-GPU Blackwell systems that use fifth-generation NVLink (up to 1.8 TB/s aggregate bidirectional GPU-to-GPU bandwidth and advanced network topologies), TP can scale efficiently across a node of 8–16 GPUs— or even up to 72 GPUs in the case of an NVL72 rack. Remember, within the GB200/ GB300 NVL72 racks, NVLink Switch provides about 130 TB/s of aggregate GPU bandwidth within the 72 GPU domain. This is a large amount of intra-rack bandwidth.

TP provides near-linear speedups for compute-bound portions of the model as long as collective communications, such as the all-reduce of activations, are fast relative to computation. In inference, tensor parallelism is mainly applied to the large matrix multiplications of the attention projections and feed-forward multilayer perceptron (MLP) networks.

Since the activations for one token are relatively small, those all-reduce communications are not too costly on NVLink. As such, TP is a common strategy for splitting giant dense models across GPUs without approximating model weights.

We mainly use TP to serve models in which single MoE experts or transformer layers are too large for a single GPU. However, we also use it when we want to reduce latency by parallelizing each layer's computations across multiple GPUs.

One must be mindful that beyond a certain scale, however, TP efficiency drops—especially when using it across nodes or racks running over InfiniBand or Ethernet. In practice, it's best to use TP for intranode communication—or between nodes in an NVLink domain.

Modern multi-GPU racks like NVIDIA's GB200/GB300 NVL72 allow TP to be used at a much larger scale without saturating interconnect bandwidth. NVLink Switch extends the NVLink domain across the rack to 72 GPUs per NVL72. NVLink Switch Systems can scale an all-to-all, fully connected NVLink fabric across up to 8 racks, or 576 GPUs (576 GPUs = 8 racks * 72 GPUs per rack). This enables large-scale parallelism strategies, not just inside a single NVL72 but also across multiple racks. For instance, in an 8-rack topology, you can increase to 576-way tensor parallelism using the 576 GPUs across 8 racks (576 GPUs = 8 racks × 72 GPUs per rack.)

> While it's possible to extend TP across racks, it's recommended to choose your TP group sizes with topology-awareness in mind and within a single NVLink/NVSwitch island whenever possible. This will avoid unnecessary inter-rack switch latency and help to increase overall system efficiency.

Pipeline Parallelism

Pipeline parallelism (PP) partitions the model *layer-wise* across different GPUs. For example, in a 60-layer transformer-based model, GPU 0 might hold layers 1–20, GPU 1 holds layers 21–40, and GPU 2 holds layers 41–60.

When processing a sequence of tokens, the data flows through the GPUs in sequence such that GPU 0 computes layers 1–20, then passes its intermediate activations to GPU 1 for layers 21–40, and so on. This allows models that are too deep to fit on one accelerator to be distributed.

In inference, PP can improve throughput by partitioning the model across multiple batches—similar to an assembly line. During the *prefill* phase, which processes a long sequence of input tokens, PP achieves high GPU utilization by streaming different portions of the sequence into the layers in staggered fashion.

In contrast, during the *decode* phase, generating one token at a time, pure PP offers less benefit since each new token must still pass through the pipeline stages sequentially. This creates pipeline bubbles, or idle periods, in which earlier stages wait for later ones to finish for each and every token.

To reduce pipeline bubbles, implementations use microbatching, which allows the pipeline to process multiple tokens from different requests concurrently. Still, pipeline parallelism primarily helps with memory scaling by enabling very large models to split layers among GPUs. It also helps throughput—especially when handling large batch sizes or long inputs.

PP tends to increase end-to-end latency for a single item due to transfer overhead between pipeline stages. As such, PP is usually chosen for model capacity reasons—rather than latency reasons. This is because it can fit the model into memory. The slight latency hit is acceptable when no single GPU can hold the whole model.

Additionally, PP is often used in combination with other parallelism strategies like TP to balance memory and speed. When serving large MoE models, one might use pipeline parallelism across 2–4 GPUs to split the deep layer stack—while relying on TP to handle the wide, intralayer compute.

> PP splits the model across layers, and TP splits the model within layers. TP is mainly used for models with layers or experts that are too wide for a single GPU, while PP is primarily used for models that are too deep to fit into a single GPU. Note that TP and PP can be combined, which we'll see in a bit.

Expert Parallelism

Expert parallelism (EP) is specific to MoE architectures. In an MoE layer, there are many expert networks, or feed-forward sublayers. For each input token, only one or a few experts are activated. This naturally lends itself to distributing different experts on different GPUs.

For instance, if an MoE layer has 16 experts and we have 4 GPUs, each GPU could host 4 experts. During inference, when a token arrives at that MoE layer, its internal gating network will choose the top two experts, for instance, for that token. The token's data is then sent to whichever GPUs own those two experts for processing. Then the results are combined back to generate the next token, as shown in Figure 15-6.

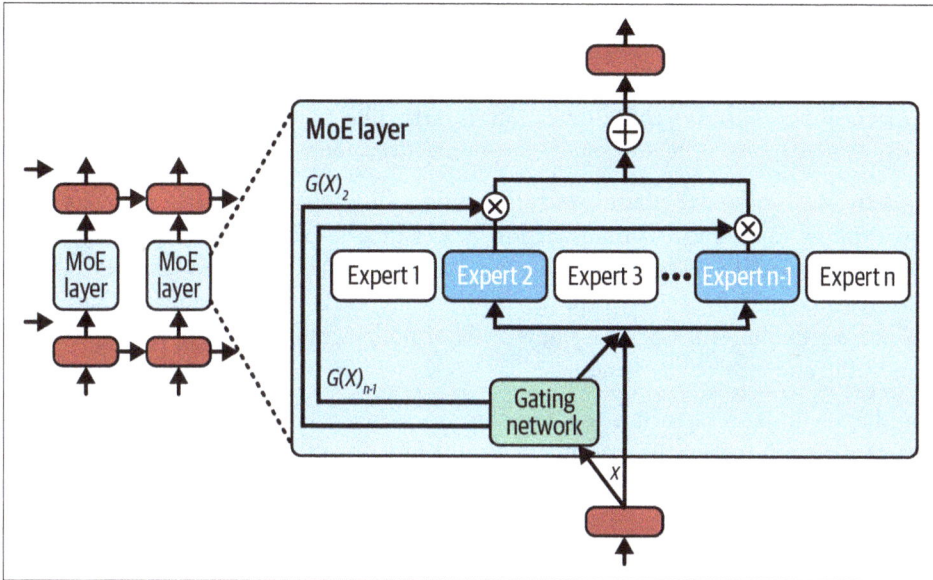

Figure 15-6. Mixture-of-experts (MoE) communication (source: https://oreil.ly/pzn5t)

Implementing this requires an all-to-all communication pattern such that tokens (technically, their activation vectors) are dynamically shuffled between GPUs so that each token lands on the GPU of its assigned expert. After each expert computes its output for its assigned tokens, another all-to-all is performed to return the token outputs back to their original order.

This dynamic routing introduces a communication-heavy step at each MoE layer. This can become a performance bottleneck if not carefully optimized—especially as the number of experts/GPUs increases. The upside is that expert parallelism allows the total model capacity to scale almost linearly with the number of GPUs.

Consider an MoE with 100 experts distributed across 100 GPUs. If each token activates only two experts, the compute per token is similar to a smaller dense model. As such, expert parallelism is what allows some massive MoE models to be served at all since the model weights are sharded across many GPUs—and each GPU handles only a fraction of the tokens at any given layer.

> At scale, and with a properly balanced set of experts in an MoE model, all of the experts will likely be active simultaneously. So, while an individual token activates only a small number of experts, in aggregate across all tokens across all end users, all experts will be active, consuming and contending for all GPU resources concurrently.

Efficient expert parallel inference requires careful load balancing—as well as high-bandwidth interconnects, such as NVLink/NVSwitch for intra-rack communication and InfiniBand/RDMA for internode communication. Modern MoE inference frameworks use fast collective communication libraries like NCCL. It often helps to group multiple experts per GPU to reduce communication steps.

Modern MoE inference often uses top-2 gating, in which each token is assigned to two experts. To reduce communication, you can group commonly paired experts onto the same GPU or compute node. For instance, if tokens use two experts, placing those two frequently paired experts on the same GPU or node means that many token assignments will stay on a single GPU or node, which will localize communication traffic and reduce overhead.

Another technique is to use top-1 gating, in which each token goes to only one expert. This will reduce the communication volume relative to top-2 gating described previously, which doubles the number of expert outputs. While top-1 gating is faster, it can lead to a lower model quality and uneven load.

> Google's GLaM (*https://oreil.ly/sKTeL*) introduced load-balancing losses (and gating noise) to achieve balanced expert usage during MoE model training. Building on this, researchers are exploring truly adaptive, inference-time gating that uses real-time load metrics to reroute tokens when an expert is overloaded. These improve utilization without degrading quality.
>
> However, in most production serving environments, top-2 gating with a modest capacity factor—and occasional load-based expert swapping or replication—remains the most common compromise technique to balance both quality and performance.

Many MoE LLMs use at least top-2 gating for better quality, good speed, and balanced load. Additionally, it's important to place experts strategically—or even use backup expert replicas to avoid overloading experts.

When experts become overloaded, or hot, they can become throughput bottlenecks if the gating network is disproportionately routing tokens to them. The *straggler effect*, as it's called, requires that all expert computations be complete before they can progress. As such, an overloaded expert that receives more work (tokens) than other experts will stall the inference pipeline. This will leave some experts, and their GPUs, idle while the other experts catch up.

To prevent this, high-performance MoE serving systems expose a capacity factor parameter, typically set at 1.2–1.5× the average token load, which caps how many tokens each expert can process per batch. Tokens beyond that are routed to a second-choice overflow expert—or queued for a second pass. This complements any load-balancing loss or gating noise used during training to encourage the MoE to assign tokens to experts uniformly.

Some full-featured inference servers can also replicate hot experts onto multiple GPUs to split the load if necessary. This comes at a cost of additional GPU memory. We will see an example of load imbalance a bit later.

The combination of inference-time spillover (capacity factor), training-time penalties (load-balancing loss and gating noise), and hot-expert replicas should smooth out the token-expert load distribution when capacity is reached—maximizing overall MoE inference throughput.

Data Parallelism

In inference, *data parallelism* (DP) refers to replicating the entire model on multiple GPUs and assigning different incoming requests—or shards of a request batch—to each GPU. Unlike data parallelism in training, which keeps models in sync with gradient averaging, data parallelism in inference runs independent forward passes on each replica. This is the simplest way to scale out throughput.

For instance, with DP, if one GPU can handle 10 requests per second, using 8 GPUs with 8 replicas ideally gives 80 requests per second of throughput—assuming the requests are independent. In practice, using data parallelism for inference requires spinning up multiple model-serving engines and load-balancing requests among them.

When using DP, each GPU, or group of GPUs, handles a subset of queries from start to finish. The advantage is linear scaling of throughput and no inter-GPU communication during inference since each replica runs in isolation. The disadvantages are significant, however.

DP multiplies the memory requirement since each replica needs a full copy of model weights and cache. As such, serving a model with eight replicas uses 8× the GPU memory—and roughly 8× the hardware cost—compared to hosting the model on a single GPU.

In practice, data parallelism is often combined with request batching and multistream execution on each GPU to maximize utilization. Each replica should ideally be stateless—or use synchronized caches to avoid consistency issues.

It's important to note that DP does not reduce latency for any single request. It does, however, improve throughput since there are more replicas available to handle requests—assuming the memory and compute resources are available and relatively free of contention.

Because GPU memory is relatively scarce and expensive, DP is usually worthwhile for inference only when your throughput needs are very high—or if you can combine DP with other parallelism approaches, such as TP and PP.

For inference, DP is often used in combination with other parallelism approaches, such as TP and PP, due to the additional memory and cost requirements of DP. For example, if a model must be spread across eight GPUs due to memory limitations, it should use DP with TP, PP, or EP—or even all of them together—to create four-dimensional (4D) parallelism (add in context parallelism (CP), and you're using 5D parallelism!).

Specifically, you can use DP with TP to deploy two large, 8-GPU model replicas using two DP groups of eight GPUs. This will double the throughput and shard each of the large model replicas across eight GPUs within its layers using TP.

In a massive inference cluster, you can dedicate a large number of GPUs and nodes to serve multiple copies of the large model to handle high request volumes. DP is particularly useful when throughput needs to scale beyond what a single model instance can provide. In practice, production systems often run many DP replicas of the large model to meet traffic demands.

Modern inference servers treat each replica as a separate model instance behind a load balancer. This requires careful request routing, but it's relatively straightforward compared to other complex model-sharding methods.

Context (Sequence) Parallelism

Context parallelism (CP) is more of a specialized strategy that partitions a single sequence of tokens across multiple GPUs. This technique benefits extremely long context inputs on the order of tens of thousands and millions of tokens. These would otherwise be too slow or memory-heavy or simply not fit on a single GPU.

The idea behind CP is to split the sequence into chunks and have different GPUs handle different parts of the sequence in parallel at each layer. The GPUs exchange only the necessary information at the boundary between chunks of the sequence.

CP handles contexts larger than a single GPU's memory by splitting the KV cache across GPUs. It also reduces prompt-processing latency roughly in proportion to the number of GPUs used. As such, CP can achieve near-linear speedup for very long context prefill runs by using multiple GPUs to perform the prefill for a long context in parallel.

The challenge with CP is that transformers have global self-attention such that every token attends to every earlier token. Naively splitting the sequence would require lots of information exchange between GPUs to compute attention across the partition boundary.

CP methods use clever schemes like ring parallelism and blocked attention to reduce the quadratic self-attention communication time complexity—and limit each GPU to attending mostly within its partition of the context as well as a small amount of chunk-boundary data.

In effect, each GPU handles a subset of positions in the input sequence for each layer. They pass intermediate results around in a pipelined fashion—often arranged in a ring. CP is analogous to pipeline parallelism but along the sequence-length dimension instead of the layer dimension.

Context parallelism excels at prefill for very long inputs by slicing a document into segments, allocating segments across multiple GPUs, and processing each segment concurrently. This reduces prompt-processing time roughly in half for every doubling of GPUs—with only a bit of overhead for cross-segment attention at the boundaries.

In short, while CP doesn't speed up the sequential, token-by-token decode phase, it can shorten TTFT for extremely long prompts. It does this by distributing the attention KV cache across devices such that each GPU stores only its segment's cache. CP also lets you handle contexts larger than what a single GPU can fit into memory.

> Context parallelism requires an attention implementation that communicates across partitions. This adds extra per-layer communication. As such, for short prompts, CP often adds outsized overhead. But for very long inputs and strict TTFT goals, CP can reduce prefill latency and memory per GPU. Measure both prefill speed and accuracy for your maximum context.

Hybrid Parallelism

In practice, serving massive MoE LLMs uses a combination of the previous parallelism strategies. Today's LLM models are so large and complex that no single parallelization method is sufficient. Figure 15-7 shows a hybrid parallel configuration using four GPUs.

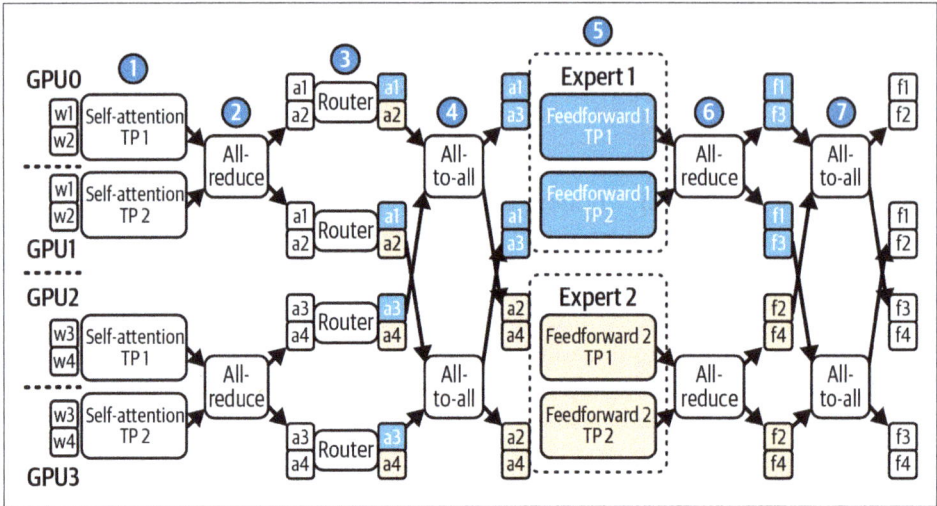

Figure 15-7. High-level diagram of a 4 × 2 × EP hybrid parallel combination (source: https://oreil.ly/q1AEf)

Here, we are using four pipeline stages (one per GPU) and two-way tensor parallelism. The tokens are routed across two experts using expert parallelism. This is called a *4 × 2 EP hybrid parallel strategy*.

Let's go even larger and create logic groups of GPUs. For example, consider a cluster of 64 GPUs. We can group the GPUs into 16 groups of 4 GPUs each. Using an MoE with 60 layers and 64 experts, we can use 4-way pipeline parallelism with 15 layers per stage. This splits the depth of the model. Then, within each stage (15 layers), we can use 2-way TP to split the heavy matrix multiplies within each layer. This splits the width of the model.

For the MoE layers, you can use EP to spread 16 experts per group using top-2 gating. This will send tokens to, at most, two GPUs in the group. Finally, data parallelism can deploy two such 64-GPU replicas to double your system's throughput.

This is just one configuration. In practice, you'll need to experiment with different combinations of parallelism strategies. Your profiling tools will help you find the right balance. Specifically, you can use Nsight Systems for end-to-end traces and Nsight Compute for kernel-specific GPU metrics.

Remember to always verify interconnect traffic, Tensor Core utilization, and other performance-enhancing mechanisms before and after making each change.

The guiding principle is to use TP up to the point of diminishing returns—usually within a node or in a tightly coupled unit like an NVL72 chassis. You would then use pipeline parallelism minimally—just enough to fit the model in memory. Then, you want to maximize EP to distribute MoE parameters across experts and GPUs. Finally, you add data parallel replicas to improve throughput as you scale to more and more end users and concurrent inference requests (CP can be optionally layered on top if extremely long inputs are expected).

We also want to align parallelization with our hardware topology. For instance, if using an NVL72 system, all 72 GPUs are fully connected using NVLink and NVSwitch. In this case, you can form TP and EP groups within the 72 GPU NVLink domain. However, TP groups that approach the full domain will often see diminishing returns from the all-reduce latency. As such, many production systems keep TP groups smaller and topology aware—even inside NVL72.

In contrast, a smaller cluster of two 8-GPU nodes connected with InfiniBand has full NVLink connectivity only within each node—with cross-node traffic traveling along the InfiniBand fabric. In such environments, it's best to keep TP local to each 8-GPU node—and avoid internode parallelism if possible to avoid the higher latency and lower bandwidth of internode communications.

In the next sections, we discuss higher-level optimizations that can be combined with these parallelism strategies to achieve even faster inference on multinode clusters. As we shall see, a well-designed serving system will combine many of these high-level and low-level techniques.

Speculative Decoding and Parallel Token Generation Techniques

One of the fundamental performance challenges in LLM inference is the sequential nature of decoding. Remember that after the initial prompt is processed during prefill, the model typically generates one token at a time. Each token's computation depends on the result of the previous token, so this is difficult to parallelize as it's inherently a serial process, which introduces a latency bottleneck—even with the latest, fastest GPUs. Generating hundreds of tokens sequentially can take on the order of seconds for massive models on modern GPU hardware.

In this section, we discuss several techniques to accelerate the decode stage. Some of these techniques involve generating multiple tokens per inference step, while others reduce the number of sequential inference steps altogether.

Speculative decoding traditionally pairs a small, fast "draft" model that proposes several tokens in one batch with a larger "target" model that then validates each candidate. This trades a second inference pass for parallel generation to achieve higher, multitoken throughput. However, running two separate models adds deployment complexity and can still stall inference when the verification pass becomes a bottleneck.

Medusa simplifies this by attaching multiple lightweight decoding heads directly to a single LLM. At each step, these heads use a tree-based attention mechanism to concurrently generate and verify several token candidates within a single forward pass.

This unified design of Medusa avoids cross-model token transfers and achieves large speedups without sacrificing the quality of the token generation. By consolidating draft-and-verify into a single-model pass, Medusa is an improvement over conventional two-model speculative decoding techniques. Let's take a closer look at some of these techniques.

Two-Model, Draft-Based Speculative Decoding and EAGLE

Speculative decoding is a technique that trades extra work on a small model to save time on the expensive large model. The idea is to run a lightweight "draft" LLM alongside the main LLM. The draft model is faster and generates a batch of k tokens speculatively beyond the current context.

The big model, called the *target* model, then validates the draft tokens by predicting next-token probabilities for the entire k-token sequence in a single batch sent to the GPU. By handling all k tokens at once, the target model increases arithmetic intensity by performing more computations per byte of data transferred. This results in efficient and fast verification of the draft sequence tokens.

If the target model's output agrees with the draft model's k proposed tokens, then we have effectively generated k tokens in the same time that a large model would have generated a single token. If the large model's verification diverges from the draft model's prediction at any token in the sequence of k tokens generated by the draft model, the speculative tokens beyond that point are discarded. At least one generated token will be kept in each step because the verification procedure always accepts the first token from either the draft or the target model.

Once the target model's corrected token is used and decoding continues, a new speculative decoding cycle can start from that point. Figure 15-8 shows a small draft model predicting multiple tokens ahead. Then the target (big) model verifies these tokens one by one.

Over time, speculative decoding reduces the overall number of one-by-one, sequential invocations needed by the large model. In theory, it provides a theoretical k× speedup, where k is the number of tokens generated by the draft model. In practice, with overhead and occasional speculative-token rejections, the gain is more like a 2× speedup.

```
┌──────────────────────────────────────────┐  ┌──────────────────────────────────────────┐
│  ┌──────┐   ┌──────┐   ┌──────┐  ┌──────┐  │  │  ✓┌──────┐  ✓┌──────┐  ✓┌──────┐ ✗┌──────┐ │
│  │ upon │   │  a   │   │ time │  │ there│  │  │   │ upon │   │  a   │   │ time │  │ there│ │
│  └──────┘   └──────┘   └──────┘  └──────┘  │  │   └──────┘   └──────┘   └──────┘  └──────┘ │
│  ┌──────┐   ┌──────┐   ┌──────┐  ┌──────┐  │  │  ┌──────────────────────────────────────┐ │
│  │Draft │   │Draft │   │Draft │  │Draft │  │  │  │           Target model               │ │
│  │model │   │model │   │model │  │model │  │  │  └──────────────────────────────────────┘ │
│  └──────┘   └──────┘   └──────┘  └──────┘  │  │                                            │
│  ┌──────┐   ┌──────┐   ┌──────┐  ┌──────┐  │  │  ┌──────┐  ┌──────┐  ┌──────┐  ┌──────┐    │
│  │ Once │   │ upon │   │  a   │  │ time │  │  │  │ upon │  │ upon │  │  a   │  │ time │    │
│  └──────┘   └──────┘   └──────┘  └──────┘  │  │  └──────┘  └──────┘  └──────┘  └──────┘    │
│        Step 1: autoregressive generation   │  │       Step 2: parallel verification        │
└──────────────────────────────────────────┘  └──────────────────────────────────────────┘
```

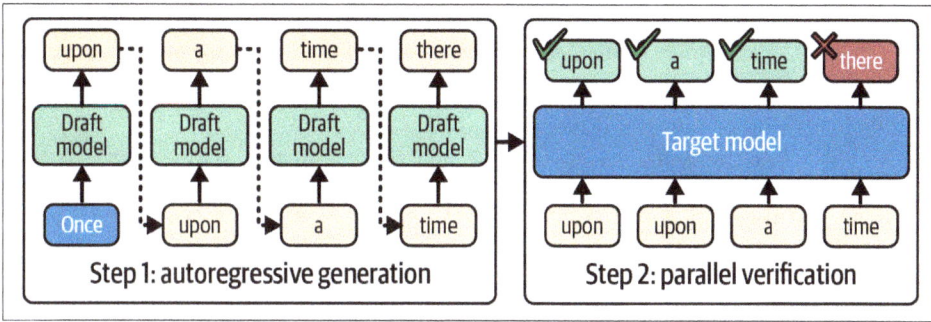

Figure 15-8. Speculative decoding with a draft (small) for decoding and a target (large) model for multitoken verification

The draft model must be chosen to have reasonably high fidelity to the large model's distribution. This means that the draft model's predictions should have high overlap with the large model's likely outputs. If the draft frequently guesses wrong, speculative decoding provides little benefit and wastes compute. If it often predicts tokens that the larger target model would not, many speculative tokens will be rejected. This will waste compute time.

The draft model must also be much faster than the large model—typically by a factor of 4× or more—for speculative decoding to provide a practical performance improvement. A common strategy is to use a distilled version of the main model—or a smaller model fine-tuned on the same data so that its outputs correlate well.

> The draft model must use the same tokenizer and vocabulary as the large model. This is sometimes overlooked, and it will lead to poor results.

The draft model generates tokens using the same prompt and perhaps a higher temperature to increase the chance of matching one of the large model's probable continuations. Meanwhile, the target model skips ahead and processes all of the draft tokens in one single batch.

Under the standard speculative decoding acceptance procedure, the target model's output distribution is preserved. As such, the final samples match the large model's distribution when sampling settings are aligned. If the draft diverges, the target model's verification rejects those tokens and correctness is maintained. The only difference is that up to k number of target-model calls are avoided when the small model guesses correctly for these speculative tokens.

Speculative decoding can be implemented in a variety of ways. Most modern LLM inference engines like vLLM, SGLang, and TensorRT-LLM have built-in support to

coordinate draft and target model generation. Empirically, speedups around 1.5–2.5×
are common, and higher gains are possible with careful batching and draft model
design.

> In PyTorch, the operation `torch.nn.functional. scaled_ dot_`
> `product_attention` auto-selects the optimal backend (FlashAtten-
> tion or a cuDNN kernel) based on device generation, shapes, mask,
> and dtype. You can pin a backend using `torch.nn.atten`
> `tion.sdpa_kernel()` with an explicit `SDPABackend` type. It's impor-
> tant to verify that the fused backend is active when benchmarking
> LLM decoding, for instance.

For instance, the Extrapolation Algorithm for Greater LLM Efficiency (EAGLE) algorithm (*https://oreil.ly/vCQCb*) rethinks speculative decoding by operating at the feature level rather than the token level. EAGLE uses a one-step extrapolation of the
large model's own intermediate representation to predict the next token's features.
This resolves uncertainty and achieves higher acceptance rates.

EAGLE reported up to about 3.5× speedup over vanilla decoding for a 4-token draft
while preserving the large model's output distribution. EAGLE approaches the theoretical limit of its draft depth in favorable environments. And it shows that, with
innovative techniques, speculative decoding can reduce decoding time even further—
and preserve output quality at the same time.

EAGLE-2 (*https://oreil.ly/hBhtq*) extends EAGLE by introducing a context-aware
dynamic *draft tree* of possibilities. While EAGLE achieved up to 3.5× speedup versus
vanilla decoding in some evaluations, EAGLE-2's approach reported speedups of
about 20%–40% faster (*https://oreil.ly/_NiU9*) than EAGLE depending on the task
and model. With EAGLE-2, the draft model generates a branching set of token
sequences, which further increases parallelism in the verification step. This is shown
in Figure 15-9.

EAGLE-3 (*https://oreil.ly/0DDYf*) continues to improve on earlier versions, EAGLE-1
and EAGLE-2, by preferring direct token prediction and fusing multi-layer features.
EAGLE-3 reports (*https://oreil.ly/07WZ0*) up to 1.4× improvements over EAGLE-2 in
certain tasks—and up to 6.5× speedups over non-optimized baseline variants. In
EAGLE-1 and EAGLE-2, the draft model predicts internal feature vectors which are
then decoded to tokens. These earlier EAGLE methods worked by guessing internal
features, essentially—and then mapping them to tokens.

EAGLE-3 skips the feature-level prediction step and predicts the draft tokens more
directly. However, it still uses internal features but fused into multiple layer representations (lower, middle, upper) to guide the draft predictions. This is in contrast to using

just the top layer. This makes EAGLE-3 more streamlined and less constrained—allowing better scaling.

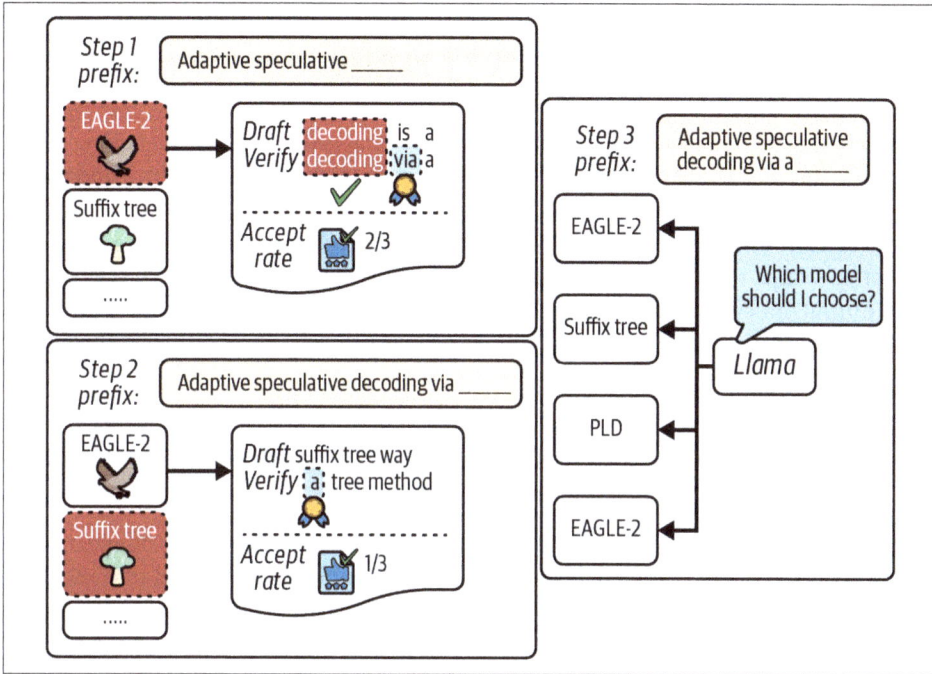

Figure 15-9. Speculative decoding with EAGLE-2 (source: https://oreil.ly/uG07b)

Another technique is *dynamic depth decoding* (*https://oreil.ly/9sHn6*), which can adaptively skip layers that minimize the impact on output quality. Other techniques that reduce computations include skipping every Nth transformer layer, using lower precision (e.g., FFP8 and NVFP4) for the draft model, and using a smaller hidden size temporarily for the draft stage.

> Some research prototypes offer modes that skip portions of the network or reduce precision during decoding to trade accuracy for speed. As of this writing, these are not universally available in production models, so always validate quality and speed on your target tasks before enabling any such mode.

Future LLMs might include an optimized "fast-generation" mode. For example, a model might have alternate lightweight layers or a configuration for reduced-precision decoding. This built-in optimization would allow the model to skip computations.

Single-Model Self-Speculative Decoding

Another approach to speculative decoding is to avoid using an external draft model altogether and use the larger target model to both draft and verify its own outputs by selectively skipping some computations. One such method is self-speculative decoding, also called the draft-and-verify scheme.

With self-speculative decoding, the large target model generates k tokens using a fast, approximate pass. For instance, it can choose to run only half of its layers—and possibly in reduced precision—for each new token. It would skip every other layer. This produces draft output much like the smaller draft model would. And it can approach similar speedups when acceptance rates and draft depth are favorable. This produces draft output much like the smaller draft model would—and achieves a similar 2× speedup as well.

Then, in a second stage of self-speculative decoding, the target model performs a full forward pass to verify those k tokens in one go. If they all match, then we save executing half the layers for those tokens. If not, we simply fall back to the traditional speculative approach by accepting tokens up to the mismatch and proceeding normally.

Because it's the same model doing both draft and verification in self-speculative decoding, no separate model needs to be trained, maintained, or loaded into memory at runtime. The challenge is finding a good way to reduce the amount of compute needed in the draft stage (dropping layers, reducing precision, etc.) without hurting accuracy too much.

A related technique is *consistent decoding*, in which you train one LLM to both generate and validate multiple tokens. This single-model approach (*https://oreil.ly/X60jM*) produces ~3× speedups without a separate draft model. This shows a trend of baking speculative decoding into the model's own weights.

These methods represent very active areas of research. And they are particularly exciting and promising because they let the model accelerate itself using its inherent internal redundancy. And since the optimizations are local to the model, the inference engine's implementation can be simplified.

Multitoken Decoding with Medusa's Multiple Heads

Speculative decoding still ultimately generates tokens one by one using the draft model—it's just faster because the draft model is smaller. However, the Medusa framework takes a more radical approach. It modifies the model architecture itself to predict multiple new tokens in parallel for each decoding step.

Unlike two-model speculative decoding, which still generates tokens one by one (albeit faster), Medusa's architecture truly generates multiple tokens per iteration from a single model. As such, Medusa's multiheaded approach has reported about

2.2–3.6× speedups in published experiments (*https://oreil.ly/vejse*) across both Medusa-1 and Medusa-2.

However, Medusa requires custom model training since it modifies the transformer-based LLM with additional decoder heads that branch off at certain layers—hence, the name *Medusa*. This lets the model propose several next tokens simultaneously.

The multiple token candidates generated by the different Medusa heads are structured like a tree. For instance, Medusa can generate a binary tree of depth 2 in one pass to produce up to 4 tokens. It can then verify the sequence of multiple tokens in parallel, as shown in Figure 15-10.

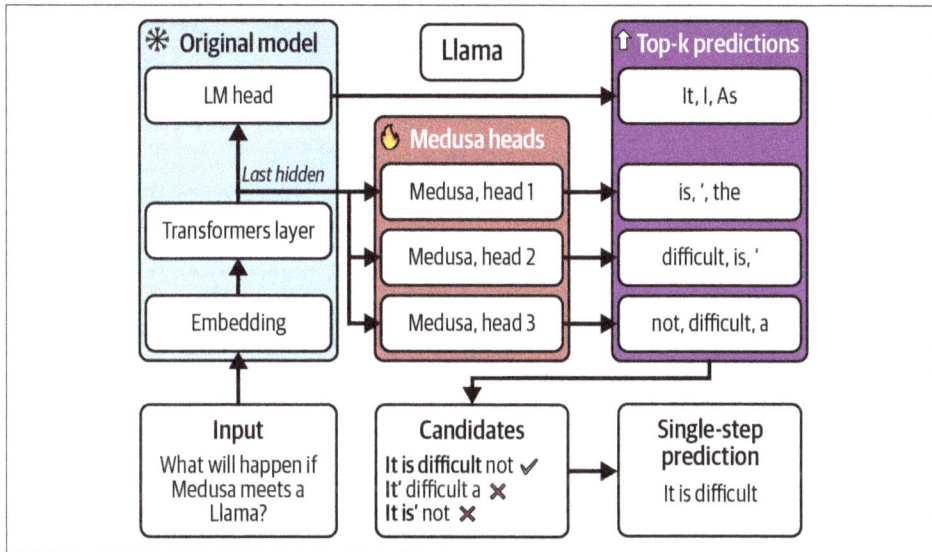

Figure 15-10. Multitoken decoding with Medusa (source: https://oreil.ly/MJMOQ)

Internally, Medusa uses a specialized, tree-based attention pattern to improve consistency among the parallel token predictions. The model learns to extend and verify the multiple-token sequences concurrently. With Medusa, the LLM essentially learns to "think ahead" by a few tokens—and output them all at once.

During inference, Medusa can reduce the number of sequential decoding iterations by the factor of the parallel predictions. For instance, if Medusa predicts 4 tokens in one pass, it can reduce the required number of forward passes by up to 4× for depth-2 binary tree outputs.

In practice, however, Medusa typically achieves about a 2–3× speedup due to the overhead of occasionally having to backtrack when a prediction branch fails validation and needs a partial redo. This is similar to the overhead of speculative decoding verification and rejection. For example, if a Medusa LLM generates 4 tokens per iteration, a reply of 100 tokens would take only 25 iterations of the model instead of 100.

Medusa requires modifying and retraining the model to add these extra heads. In addition, Medusa models are slightly larger in size given the additional head parameters. This increases development complexity and training cost a bit. However, once trained, Medusa models can significantly reduce inference times.

If trained for your use case, a Medusa-enabled LLM can provide excellent low-latency performance. However, this technique requires modifying and fine-tuning the model architecture to add the additional heads.

Interleaving Decode Steps from Multiple Requests

Another parallel decoding technique is to interleave decode steps from multiple concurrent requests across multiple end users. This parallelism is more of an inference-engine capability than an algorithmic trick or model architecture modification. But it helps keep the GPUs busy by batching at the token level—and across end-user requests.

Frameworks like vLLM implement this in the form of request routing, continuous batching, and token scheduling. The idea is to keep the GPUs busy by filling in the gaps between sequential steps. Specifically, if a GPU is stalled due to a sequence waiting on I/O or a data dependency, the scheduler can run another sequence's next token prediction on that same GPU in the meantime.

> Combining an inference engine's advanced routing, batching, and scheduling capabilities with CUDA streams. Then verify with Nsight Systems that token-step kernels overlap with NIC/NVLink transfers rather than serializing on a single stream. Then you can achieve massive parallelism at the application, system, and hardware levels.

It's important to note that interleaving decode steps doesn't speed up a single sequence's latency. In fact, it can even add a tiny bit of overhead per token due to the additional context switching. However, it can greatly improve overall throughput and GPU utilization when serving many users concurrently. This will reduce the average end-user request latency under heavy load.

Combining Decoding Techniques and Evaluating Complexity

It's worth noting that these decoding optimizations can be combined. For instance, one could use speculative decoding with a Medusa-enabled target model in which the big target model verifies multiple tokens at a time predicted by a small model.

These techniques also come at the cost of additional complexity. Either you have to maintain an extra model, alter the main model, or manage more elaborate control logic. In production, you should evaluate this complexity against the performance gains. For interactive applications, reducing response time by even a few milliseconds is worth the complexity—especially at scale.

In short, advanced decoding techniques like speculative decoding—with or without a draft model—and Medusa-style multitoken prediction can reduce overall inference times of modern autoregressive LLMs that traditionally generate one token at a time. By generating more tokens at a time, increasing overall arithmetic intensity, and pushing the decoding step toward the compute-bound regime, you can take advantage of the GPU's extreme compute capabilities.

> The decoding-optimization landscape is continuously evolving and growing in complexity; the trend is clear: make LLM decoding more parallel and efficient.

Constrained Decoding Performance Implications

A separate but important aspect of the LLM decoding process is generating text under certain constraints. For instance, the model can force the output to match a predefined format (JSON), use a particular grammar, or disallow certain sequences for safety. As such, constrained decoding, often called *structured outputs*, is often required for production use cases.

OpenAI's function-calling API, for example, relies on well-structured output formats to determine which function to call—as well as the functions' inputs and outputs. These constraints are designed to match the function's API signature and are simply nonnegotiable at the application level.

Constrained decoding alters the model's token-selection process so that, at each step, only valid tokens are allowed. This might be as simple as supplying a list of allowed tokens—or as sophisticated as embedding a formal grammar and using a state machine to filter out invalid tokens.

The drawback of constrained decoding is that extra latency is needed to enforce these constraints. Naive implementations can add milliseconds per token, but optimized, grammar-masked engines can significantly reduce the cost. (The exact overhead depends on the runtime, grammar structure, and implementation path.) Backtracking happens inside the LLM's generation loop. As such, debugging, profiling, and tuning constrained decoding can be difficult without fine-grained telemetry in the model itself.

Another performance consideration is cache efficiency. Pruning the full probability distribution at every decode step can blow caches and reduce throughput even further. This is particularly noticeable when the allowed token set is heavily limited.

To mitigate these costs, many frameworks compile a JSON grammar and precompute valid tokens for each state. This allows the inference engine to mask out invalid softmax outputs at runtime. This approach reduces backtracking, improves caching, and raises acceptance rates.

For moderate constraints such as simple JSON schemas, modern engines that use compiled grammars and overlap mask computation with GPU execution can push overhead into the low single-digit percent range at scale, but complex grammars or small batches can still incur double-digit overhead. Always measure TTFT and tokens per second under your exact schema.

These techniques have been implemented in popular libraries and inference engines, including Hugging Face Transformers, NVIDIA NeMo, and vLLM. For instance, NVIDIA's TensorRT-LLM and Hugging Face Transformers both allow user-defined vocabulary masks to enforce constraints with negligible speed penalty. Specifically, TensorRT-LLM exposes guided decoding with JSON schema and context-free grammar (CFG) support through the XGrammar backend (*https://oreil.ly/cis8-*). And vLLM and Transformers provide structured output APIs.

> When using TensorRT-LLM's guided decoding, XGrammar supplies JSON-schema and CFG support on-GPU. XGrammar compiles constraints and avoids large Python-side token-mask overhead. However, be aware that certain configurations may fall back to slower backends and cause excessive first-request stalls. As such, it's important to keep grammars compact to preserve cache locality and token-mask bandwidth.

Another popular strategy is to push constrained decoding into the kernel itself. In this case, it would inject token masks during the final softmax step to achieve similar performance gains.

When implemented efficiently, constrained decoding can often run as fast as unconstrained decoding—especially if the constraint ruleset is not too large or too restrictive. If the decoding constraints are too restrictive, decoding effectively becomes a search through a small token space. This leads to more backtracking and slower token generation.

When possible, avoid large or overly restrictive constraints, such as grammars, formats, and vocabularies. One option is to let the LLM decode as normal and simply postprocess or filter the outputs. However, this is not always a performant or viable option. Profile the different options and choose what's best for your use case.

Dynamic Routing Strategies for MoE Inference

Serving MoE models efficiently requires careful partitioning of experts across GPUs using expert parallelism. In addition, you need an intelligent and dynamic mechanism, or gating network, to dynamically route tokens to these experts at runtime.

During MoE inference, each token's forward pass must be routed by the gating network to one or more expert GPUs. The system needs to handle this communication in a balanced way to keep the GPUs busy—and avoid overloaded GPUs, or hotspots. Let's examine how to address these in a high-scale, multinode inference environment.

Expert Communication Optimization

During the all-to-all exchange of token activations across experts, an MoE shuffles a batch of tokens between the GPUs. Each GPU receives only the tokens it needs for the experts that it hosts, as shown in Figure 15-11. This happens for every layer in the MoE and is a costly operation, which can potentially dominate inference time if not handled efficiently.

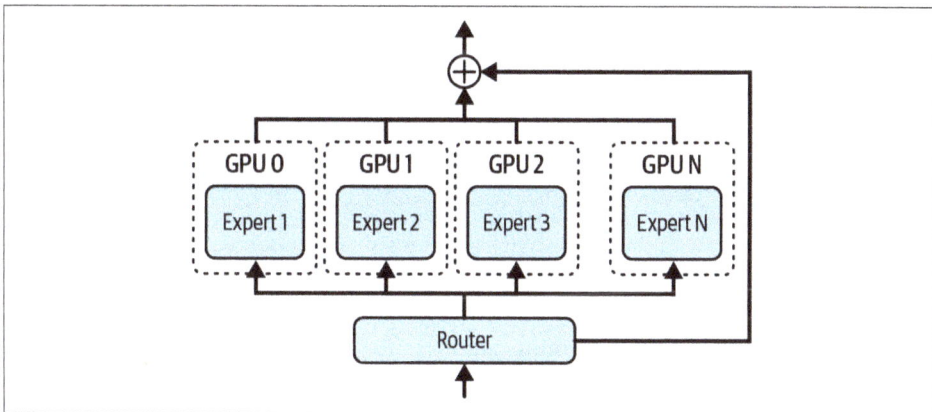

Figure 15-11. Each GPU receives only the tokens it needs for the expert(s) that it hosts

One strategy to reduce communication overhead is to use a hierarchical routing strategy for our GPU cluster by first routing tokens between GPUs within the same node using NVSwitch/NVLink (fast) and routing across nodes only for any remaining tokens that need nonlocal experts. This two-stage all-to-all can reduce the volume of internode traffic.

Additionally, you can use asynchronous communication by overlapping the communication with computation. High-performance MoE inference servers use double-buffer communications so that while one batch of tokens is being sent around, the previous batch's expert computations occur in parallel. This pipelining hides much of the communication latency.

> It's possible to achieve near-optimal all-to-all completion times when the internode fabric is kept fully utilized while intranode shuffles run in the background. Be sure to measure link utilization on both the internode NIC and intranode NVLink paths.

A naive implementation of expert routing that uses a single global all-to-all barrier can leave GPUs waiting on synchronization overhead. This wastes bandwidth if not all links are utilized optimally.

Techniques such as a *butterfly schedule* (aka *shifted all-to-all schedule*) can break the communication into phased rounds. This way, every NVLink/NIC is busy with partial exchanges—as opposed to one big synchronization. This staggered approach improves link utilization and reduces idle time.

All-to-all exchanges may use the built-in `ncclAllToAll` collective or grouped send and receive calls. Throughput often improves when the exchange is chunked and pipelined or when a hierarchical schedule such as butterfly is used across nodes. Validate and choose the algorithm that matches your topology.

> Keep first-stage all-to-all intra-rack (NVLink) and spill inter-rack only for residual tokens. Profile link utilization to confirm NICs are saturated while NVLink shuffles run in the background. Also, when internode links are the bottleneck, it's recommended to double-buffer MoE all-to-all communication with expert computation. You can use chunked/pipelined exchanges and butterfly/shifted schedules to avoid global barrier slowdowns and outperform float global collectives.

Another solution to reduce communication traffic is called *expert collocation*. The idea is to collocate certain experts together on the same GPU or node to avoid unnecessary communication. Consider two experts, experts 5 and 7, that are often activated for the same token by the token router. Placing experts 5 and 7 on the same GPU can eliminate an extra all-to-all hop. Profiling tools and gating-frequency analysis can help identify such pairings for your workload.

And yet another solution is to compress the communication between experts, including expert-exchange activations. For instance, you can cast to FP8 or NVFP4 on Tensor Cores with the NVIDIA Transformer Engine before performing an all-to-all communication. This will reduce NIC load which amortizes the compression computation. This trades a tiny bit of numerical precision for faster activation transfers between GPUs. The overhead to cast and pack/unpack is usually small relative to network and memory transfer costs.

In short, optimizing MoE communication involves analyzing the hardware and network topology to optimize the placement of experts onto GPUs. For your deployments, it's important to configure the cluster's interconnects for efficient all-to-all communication. For instance, use the NVLink Switch mesh in an NVL72 rack to get the full bandwidth communication between up to 72 GPUs in a single domain. Naive all-to-all choices can dominate layer time and achieve very low SM efficiency. Prioritize expert traffic and overlap where possible, and make sure to profile and verify when making different interconnect and communication-algorithm choices.

> For MoEs, configure your cluster to optimize for all-to-all communication. This means selecting the appropriate NCCL all-to-all algorithm or grouped send and receive implementation for your topology, then confirming GPUDirect RDMA is enabled for the internode paths. Also, make sure your InfiniBand links are properly bonded such that multiple physical links (ports) are configured as a single logical channel. Their bandwidth should be combined—and failover should be seamless. In other words, make sure your network topology is tuned for MoEs. This includes both the hardware and software layers in the stack.

Load Balancing, Capacity Factor, and Expert Replication

It's recommended that each expert and GPU get an equal share of the work to avoid "hotspots." Otherwise, if the MoE's gating network directs a disproportionate number of tokens to a particular expert, those GPUs will become overloaded. This will increase latency and reduce overall system throughput.

Consider a single expert GPU that becomes a hotspot with utilization hitting 99% while the other expert GPUs are averaging around 60% utilization. This can bottleneck an entire training or inference cluster if not properly handled.

During model training, hotspots can be addressed by adding a load-balancing loss term that penalizes the gate if it overuses some experts and underuses others. The result is that the trained MoE model tends to distribute tokens fairly evenly across the experts.

At inference time, however, specific input prompts or topics might still cause imbalance by concentrating on a subset of "hot" experts. One strategy to avoid inference hot spots is to use a *capacity factor* that triggers an overflow mechanism.

By specifying a capacity factor, the model can be configured such that each expert can process only a maximum number of tokens (e.g., 32 tokens) at a given time. If an expert receives more than this capacity of tokens, the extra tokens can either be forwarded to a fallback expert with the next highest routing score or the tokens will be serialized and processed in a second pass. Figure 15-12 compares a capacity factor of 1.0 versus 1.5.

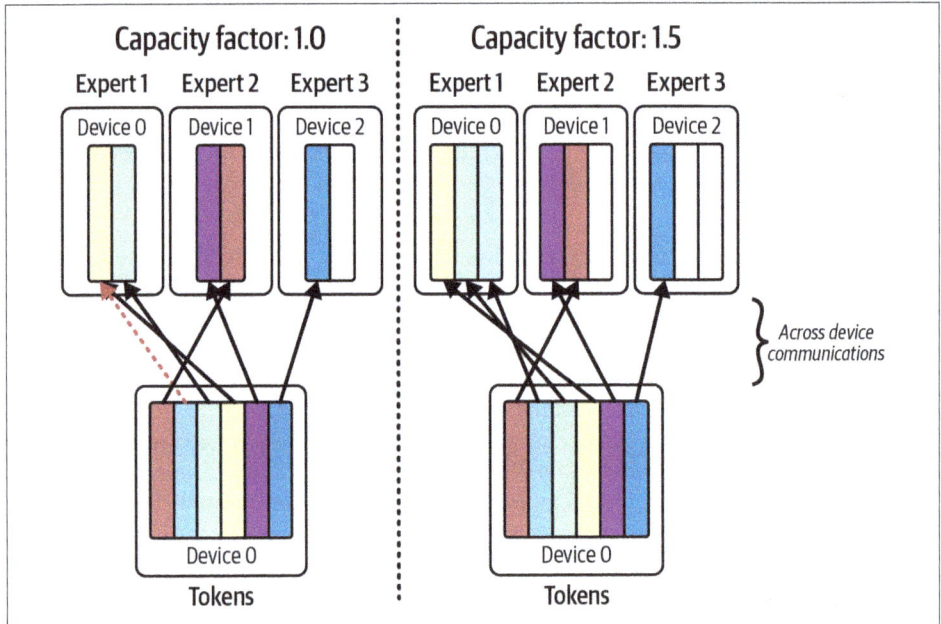

Figure 15-12. Comparing expert capacity factors of 1.0 versus 1.5

In practice, a capacity factor of 1.2 (20% overflow allowance) with top-2 gating is common. This means that each expert will take up to 120% of its average load. After that, it will send excess tokens to the next expert. This will effectively smooth out the load across experts in the system.

Another strategy to avoid hotspots is expert replication. If one expert is consistently a hotspot, the system can clone that expert onto another GPU. This way, the gating function can send some fraction of tokens to the expert clone running on the other GPU.

The replicas are a pure application-level optimization implemented by the inference engine. The model itself is not aware of the replicas. Because replicas are registered as separate experts with their own indices—and often on different GPUs—the engine can route tokens across both the original experts and their clones according to their relative routing scores.

Replicating experts will increase the memory—and cost—of each replicated expert. But since only a few experts tend to be overloaded, replicating a small number of hot experts is a targeted fix—and won't double the cost by replicating a full model and all of its experts.

Also, replication requires careful handling to keep the replicas synchronized if the model is updated. It's important that all replica experts remain identical (e.g., same weights) since the gating router knows about only a single expert and does not actually know about the replicas.

Typically, replicas are loaded from the same checkpoint as the original model—and not updated independently. This prevents divergence between the original expert and its replica.

Adaptive Expert Routing and Real-Time Monitoring

Unlike traditional MoE expert gating, which is fixed after training, adaptive routing can adjust the gate's decisions in real time during inference to react to current conditions and expert load. For instance, if the system detects that one expert GPU is lagging behind, it could instruct the gating function to divert some tokens to another expert. The other expert might have a slightly lower routing score, but it receives the request because it has available capacity.

You should implement continuous monitoring of per-expert utilization and response latency metrics. Modern MoE systems integrate with telemetry frameworks such that each expert emits utilization metrics to Prometheus/Grafana. This way, the system can dynamically adjust the capacity factor or gating algorithm on the fly.

Most LLM expert gating functions only consider routing scores determined at training time. However, a truly adaptive system needs to be handled by the inference engine and performed dynamically at inference time.

To implement adaptive routing, the inference engine needs to wrap the model's forward pass in custom logic. For example, it can intercept the gating softmax and reallocate some tokens to different experts based on current load metrics.

Inference engines rely on real-time metrics like per-GPU utilization and per-expert token counts to continuously measure expert load. If the system sees one expert's GPU at 99% utilization while other experts' GPUs are at 60%, the system could temporarily lower its load by routing some tokens to its expert replica—or to a different expert with a slightly lower expert-preference score.

Figure 15-13 shows an adaptive MoE routing strategy that uses a biased gating score approach. While this approach was originally used in a training context, a simpler approach applies to inference. In this case, it would use a modified expert-bias algorithm to divert tokens to alternate experts when the primary experts are heavily loaded.

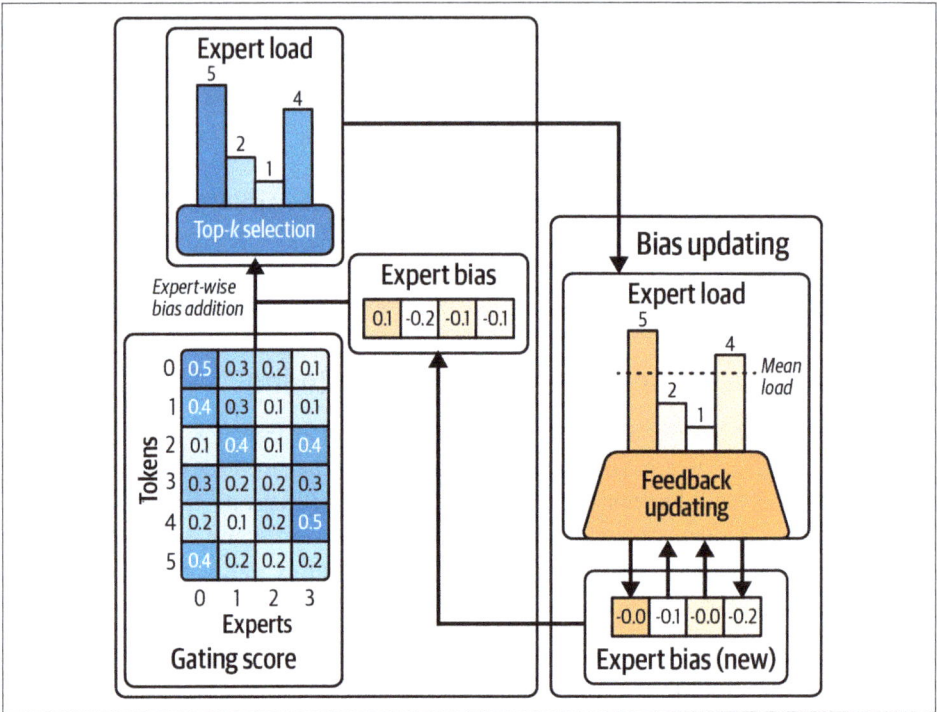

Figure 15-13. Adaptive MoE routing in action

This approach can reduce unnecessary communication and balance the load more uniformly. However, it does incur some additional cost in the form of extra monitoring, decision making, complexity, configuration management, and logging. The benefits may or may not outweigh the cost. Every scenario and workload is unique, but it's definitely something worth exploring.

When profiling with tools like Nsight Systems, you want to monitor the timeline traces of the expert GPUs' all-to-all communications. If one GPU's segment in the timeline is much longer, for instance, it is likely processing more tokens.

Your inference system can use these insights to adjust the expert gating probabilities and dynamically reassign experts to different GPUs. It can also spawn additional expert replica instances, etc. This helps to rebalance the load by adjusting the expert gating algorithm, modifying expert placement, or creating/removing expert replicas.

Dynamically spawning new expert replicas at inference time is nontrivial. This approach requires pre-provisioned capacity or rapid model loading for those experts. This is an advanced optimization technique."

Grouping certain experts differently across GPUs can lead to more uniform token routing and increased overall throughput due to better parallelism. This is because the GPUs can finish each layer's work more synchronously. If persistent imbalance is detected, modern MoE schedulers can dispatch additional expert replicas on the fly by adjusting the capacity factor. This can mitigate a hotspot caused by uneven gating.

Remember to log any dynamic changes that the system makes. It's also recommended to set up alerts for when a particular expert's utilization goes above a threshold, such as 80% utilization.

Dynamic routing strategies target two core objectives: reduce routing overhead and evenly distribute work across expert GPUs. Achieving low overhead depends on utilizing high-bandwidth interconnects, overlapping data transfers with computation, and minimizing redundant data movement with co-location and intelligent scheduling.

Load balancing is achieved using simple top-1 or top-2 gating or more advanced capacity-aware gates. It can also be achieved using dynamic replication and expert reassignment. Using a combination of these techniques is common to keep the GPUs busy with maximum computations and minimal communication delays.

As long as routing overhead is minimized and the load is balanced, adaptive MoE inference systems can achieve near-linear throughput scaling as you increase the number of experts. For example, doubling GPUs can nearly double your inference throughput.

In short, these adaptive export routing and load-balancing optimizations can be integrated with the parallelism and decoding techniques covered earlier. This way, you can tune your MoE inference system for high performance at ultrascale. Continuous profiling and adaptive algorithms can keep your GPUs busy with computations and avoid idling on communication delays.

Advanced inference engines can dynamically bypass certain expert computations, turn off underutilized experts, or use caching to skip experts for certain tokens. This further reduces latency. These techniques build on the concepts described in this chapter.

Key Takeaways

Serving massive LLMs to billions of end users requires optimizations at every stage of the inference pipeline. The following are some key takeaways from this chapter:

Disaggregate to optimize both latency and throughput
Splitting the prompt prefill and decode stages onto separate GPU pools eliminates interference. This lets you achieve low time-to-first-token and high tokens-per-second simultaneously, instead of trading one for the other. It's a foundational technique for large-scale LLM serving.

Use hybrid parallelism for massive models
No single parallelism strategy is sufficient for multi-trillion-parameter models. Combine tensor, pipeline, expert, and data parallelism as needed. For example, shard layers across GPUs (TP/PP) to fit the model in memory, use expert parallelism for MoE layers to scale model capacity, and add data-parallel replicas to meet throughput demands. The optimal mix is hardware-dependent. Always profile and tune your configuration for your workload.

Mitigate sequential decoding bottlenecks
Advanced decoding methods can greatly accelerate generation. Two-model speculative decoding with a fast draft model often delivers about a 2–3× speedup when acceptance rates are tuned for the task. EAGLE-2 reports up to 3.5× speedup (20%–40% more than EAGLE-1) on some tasks while preserving the target distribution. Medusa implementations report up to 3.6× speedup over nonspeculative decoding when trained and validated for the target workload. These techniques increase token-level parallelism and arithmetic intensity while preserving the large model's output distribution under standard verification. Overall, the result is faster responses without retraining the main model's output. This shows that speculative decoding is a quality-preserving technique.

Maintain output quality and format with constraints
In production, you often need the LLM to follow strict formats or avoid certain tokens. Constrained-decoding techniques let you enforce rules—like JSON schemas and banned words—during generation. They add some overhead per token, but with compiled grammars and optimized mask paths, constrained decoding can often run within a low single-digit percent of normal decoding at scale, though complex grammars or small batches may incur higher overhead. Always test the performance impact of your constraints. Avoid extremely strict rules, if possible. They can slow down generation by causing excessive backtracking.

Balance MoE workloads to scale effectively
Mixture-of-experts models offer almost linear scaling of model size versus GPU/expert count—but only if you handle routing efficiently. Use high-bandwidth interconnects and hierarchical all-to-all communication to reduce network

bottlenecks. Ensure each expert gets a similar amount of work by applying capacity limits and top-2 gating to avoid straggler experts. Replicate any consistently hot experts to split their load. A well-tuned MoE inference system can approach near-linear throughput scaling as you add GPUs.

Leverage hardware-software codesign
Modern GPU hardware is built to support these parallel and distributed inference methods. Use software that takes full advantage of the hardware and topology, including inference engines like vLLM, SGLang, and NVIDIA Dynamo. These can orchestrate multi-GPU and multinode inference with minimal overhead. Align your strategy with your hardware's strengths by keeping intranode communication on NVSwitch, using InfiniBand only when necessary, and overlapping communications with computations. This alignment is key to achieving the best latency and cost-efficiency.

Understand complexity versus return on investment (ROI)
Each optimization adds system complexity. Techniques like speculative decoding and adaptive MoE routing can significantly improve performance, but they require extra models or intricate logic. Always weigh the cost. For interactive applications, a 2–3× latency improvement is usually worth it. For simpler use cases, a straightforward approach might suffice. Start with the biggest bottlenecks, such as eliminating prefill/decode interference. Then incrementally add complexity if needed. Monitor and profile to determine which optimizations give the best return on investment.

Conclusion

By bringing together disaggregated prefill/decode pipelines, multitoken speculative decoding, dynamic expert routing, and adaptive orchestration, it's possible to serve LLMs in real time with minimal resource contention and ultra-low latency.

Modern inference-serving platforms like vLLM, SGLang, and NVIDIA Dynamo embrace many of these optimizations. They efficiently allocate cluster resources, coordinate the KV cache across nodes, implement speculative and constrained decoding, schedule prefill/decode tasks, and much more.

The key is an end-to-end, adaptable architecture that matches algorithmic innovations with high-performance hardware capabilities. Over the next few chapters, we'll dive deeper into model inference performance optimizations, including dynamic, adaptive, and multinode serving strategies.

We'll cover everything from application-level prefix caching, latency-aware request routing, and reinforcement-learning (RL)-based cluster tuning to systems-level adaptive memory allocation, precision switching, and congestion-aware resource scheduling.

## CHAPTER 16

Profiling, Debugging, and Tuning Inference at Scale

Operating a large LLM inference cluster requires monitoring and debugging tools that make sure everything is running as expected. They also help you quickly identify bottlenecks when performance strays from its target.

In this chapter, we demonstrate how to monitor and debug these complex systems using tools such as NVIDIA Nsight Systems for profiling and Prometheus/Grafana for cluster-wide telemetry. We also show how to collect and interpret key metrics like GPU utilization, memory pressure, tail latency percentiles, cache hit rates, per-token timing, and more. These help guide our inference engine performance optimizations.

Next, we discuss operational performance tuning, including production-proven methods to optimize GPU utilization, reduce inference latency, and increase throughput in large clusters. This includes techniques for overlapping computation and communication, scheduling and batching requests, and using high-speed interconnects like NVLink, NVSwitch, and InfiniBand effectively.

We'll also compare techniques for real-time quantization for inference, including methods to compress models to 8-bit and 4-bit precision using implementations like Generalized Post-Training Quantization (GPTQ) and Activation-Aware Weight Quantization (AWQ). Along the way, we'll discuss the trade-offs between weight-only quantization versus quantizing both weights and activations. We provide practical guidance on applying quantization in serving pipelines to reduce memory usage and increase throughput—all while preserving model accuracy.

Finally, we consider application-level optimizations that complement low-level performance tuning. These include strategies like prompt compression, prefix caching, deduplication, query routing (e.g., fallback models), and partial-output streaming.

Profiling, Debugging, and Tuning Inference Performance

There are a lot of moving parts in modern LLM inference engines—especially with disaggregated prefill and decode. The lifecycle of a typical request involves many components, as shown in Figure 16-1.

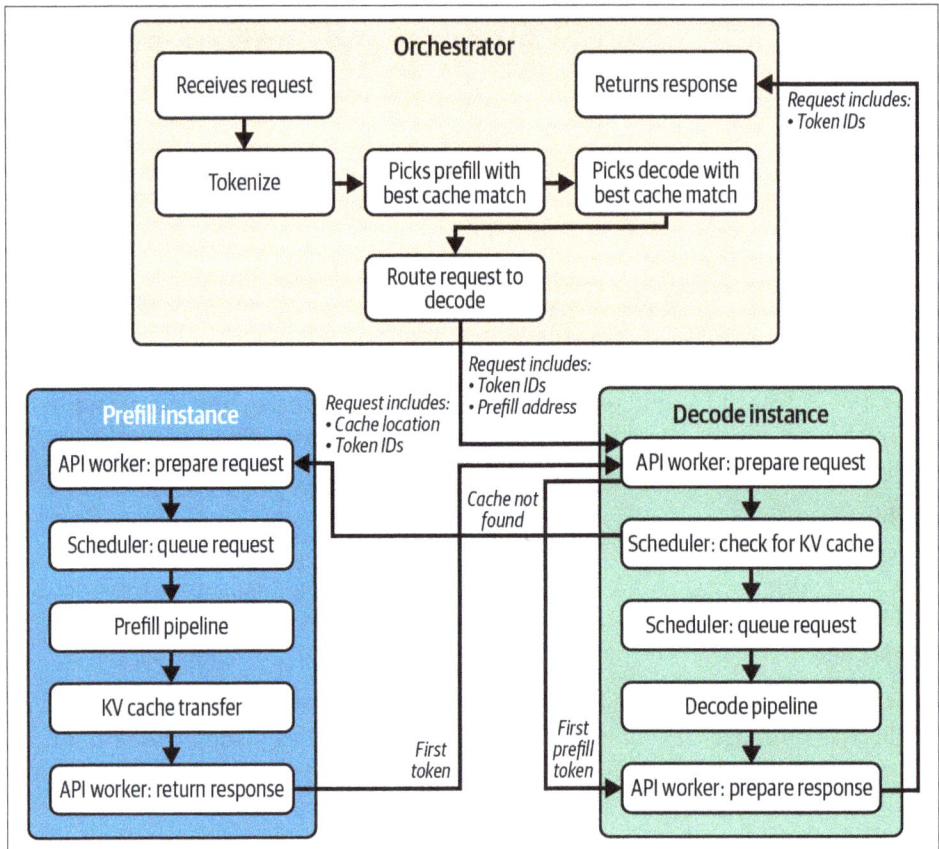

Figure 16-1. Lifecycle of a typical request in a disaggregated prefill and decode LLM inference system

Given such complexity, the workflow for tuning inference performance is very iterative. It requires careful tuning and continuous verification.

First, you should observe metrics and identify the current bottleneck, including a GPU not fully utilized or higher-than-expected latency. Next, form a hypothesis for improvement, such as "increase the batch size" or "increase communication-computation overlap for operation X." Then, implement a fix and test the hypothesis.

Then, you should ideally test the fix in a staging environment with a representative workload using profiling tools to validate that the change behaves as expected. For instance, you can verify that an operation is demonstrating proper memory and compute overlap.

Last, you should deploy the fix into production and monitor Grafana and the logs to validate that the fix improved throughput and latency on a real workload. Repeat this workflow as new bottlenecks appear.

This observe-hypothesize-tune loop should be continuous. Modern deployments often automate these steps. For instance, you can use scheduled load tests—and subsequent anomaly detection on key metrics—to trigger a tuning workflow.

> It's recommended to perform canary rollouts when deploying optimizations to production, including updated inference runtimes and model variants. By deploying the optimization to a small subset of traffic running on a small number of servers, you can validate the optimizations before full production deployment to all end users. This incremental approach helps reduce the "blast radius" of unexpected side effects by catching them early without impacting all users.

Consider a scenario in which host-side CPU utilization is spiking to 100% due to excessive tokenization or inference data preprocessing. This will limit how many concurrent streams the inference engine can handle. One fix might be to move the preprocessing to the GPU using a GPU-accelerated tokenizer library or a custom GPU kernel written in CUDA or OpenAI's Triton language.

After deploying the new library or kernel, you should monitor CPU utilization before and after. If you see the CPU utilization decrease and overall throughput increase, then the system is no longer bottlenecked by the CPU-based input preprocessing.

You should also pay attention to cache hit rates for any type of cache, including prefix cache, prompt-embedding cache, and KV cache. You should have metrics for "cache hits" versus "cache misses." A high cache-hit rate means that the system is reusing data effectively. In contrast, if you see a high cache-miss rate, then you likely want to tune the cache size, eviction policy, or caching strategy to maximize cache hits.

vLLM's LMCache component (*https://lmcache.ai*) allows adjusting the GPU versus CPU cache ratio. If misses are high due to GPU memory limits, you can enable its paged cache offload capability so that the CPU can help out. Always make sure your cache eviction policy (Least Recently Used [LRU], Least Frequently Used [LFU], etc.) aligns with the access patterns.

Another scenario is using a KV cache to reuse data for identical input-sequence prefixes among batched requests to avoid recomputing the KV for the prefix. In this case, you want to measure how often requests share a prefix. This leads to a *prefix merge* event and increments the prefix cache hit metrics in vLLM including `vllm:gpu_prefix_cache_queries` and `vllm:gpu_prefix_cache_hits`. These let you compute the hit rate as hits per queries, for example.

Measuring prefix-merge rates helps you correlate with actual cache-hit rates to gauge the real benefit of your caching layer. This way, you can adjust batching and scheduling policies to maximize shared prefixes—and predict end-to-end throughput and latency improvements under different workloads.

You can run synthetically generated data on the inference engine to test prompts with many repeated prefixes. Hopefully, you will see a reduction in prefill compute due to the prefix merging.

Modern LLM inference engines like vLLM and SGLang expose prefix-merge metrics natively. But if prefix-merging is not a first-class metric exported by your inference engine, you should instrument a custom counter for "prefix deduplicated tokens" to monitor its effectiveness.

> If you see that prefix merging is not performing as expected, you should check if the prefix-matching logic is failing. Start the debugging process by checking if there are tokenizer differences. This is the likely cause of most prefix-matching issues.

In addition to performance, monitoring helps with capacity planning. By tracking how utilization and latency behave as load increases, you can project at what point the system will hit a particular limit, such as p95 (95th percentile) latency starting to rise exponentially. In this case, the dynamic batch size might be increasing to a point of diminishing return.

> If you are using a tiered caching strategy, including an NVMe-based KV cache extension, make sure to monitor the I/O latency of the device. High I/O latency will significantly decrease cache performance.

When per-GPU concurrency reaches its limit and further batch-size increases no longer increase throughput, you may want to scale out by adding more GPUs, deploying additional model replicas, or increasing the number of experts to distribute work across more compute units.

You should also consider model compression—or switching to lower precision (FP8/FP4)—to get more effective throughput per GPU before scaling out. However, once hardware is saturated (e.g., SMs at 100% and memory bandwidth near peak utilization), adding more GPUs or using tensor/pipeline parallelism is likely the only path to higher throughput.

And remember to always weigh the cost of new hardware against the efficiency gains. There are times when upgrading to newer GPUs with more memory and FLOPS will be more cost-effective than scaling out a fleet of older GPUs.

Increasing the expert count can raise your throughput ceiling—but only if you also improve expert routing and scheduling to manage the extra all-to-all communication. Otherwise, naive scaling may simply shift the bottleneck to the network. Next, let's discuss monitoring and how to verify that our optimization efforts are actually paying off.

Monitoring System Metrics and Counters

Unlike traditional microservice invocations, which are relatively uniform and predictable in their execution time, LLM requests are nonuniform and can vary wildly in terms of latency. This difference is shown in Figure 16-2.

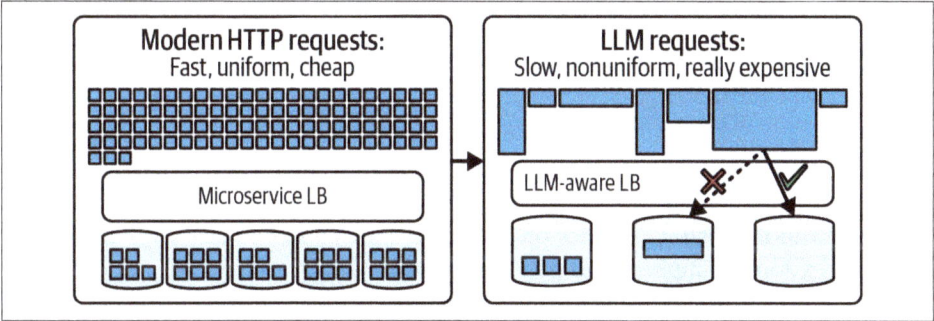

Figure 16-2. Difference between traditional microservice invocations and LLM invocations

For ongoing monitoring in production, it's common to use Prometheus to collect metrics from each GPU compute node—as well as Grafana dashboards to visualize them. Key GPU metrics to track include GPU utilization (percent of time the SMs are busy), GPU memory usage, copy engine utilization, PCIe and NVLink throughput, and GPU temperature and power (e.g., throttling). Note: Low-level counters such as L1 and L2 activity, occupancy, and instruction throughput can be collected with Nsight Compute or CUPTI rather than DCGM and Prometheus.

> The cudaMemPool metrics and asynchronous allocator statistics are helpful when monitoring memory fragmentation. These should be integrated into your monitoring, as this will greatly facilitate debugging system performance issues in production.

It's also important to monitor interconnect utilization, including NVLink, NVSwitch bandwidth, and NIC throughput. This way, you will catch communication bottlenecks in multi-GPU and multinode cluster configurations.

NVIDIA's Data Center GPU Manager (DCGM) exposes many GPU metrics, which Prometheus can scrape and collect. For instance, DCGM provides `DCGM_FI_DEV_GPU_UTIL` for SM utilization %, `DCGM_FI_DEV_MEM_COPY_UTIL` for memory copy engine utilization, and `DCGM_FI_DEV_FB_USED` for framebuffer memory used, among others.

DCGM exposes NVLink error counters and can expose throughput counters on some platforms and driver versions. For sustained link utilization, also use `nvidia-smi nvlink` and Nsight tools. You should integrate these metrics into your dashboards and set up alerts to help identify when the network is saturated with cross-GPU and cross-node communication traffic. DCGM tracks Xid counters, as well as critical GPU errors.

> While DCGM exposes NVLink counters, as of this writing, `dcgm-exporter` does not expose per-link bandwidth on all platforms by default. So if you need link-level throughput, you may need to query DCGM directly or extend the exporter.

It's also recommended to collect high-level application metrics like queries/requests per second, average latency and p95/p99 latency, number of active contexts, and throughput in tokens/sec. Metrics on KV cache utilization and size (overall and per node) are extremely important to monitor as well.

You can set up Prometheus node exporters to gather all of these metrics from each node, collect the data in one place, and even set up alerts for critical thresholds. Grafana can then plot these metrics for real-time dashboards to share with your team. Figure 16-3 shows how the metrics are collected from each GPU in a Kubernetes cluster and exported to Prometheus to be visualized with Grafana, for example.

This way, when you deploy a new optimization to increase batching, for instance, Grafana will immediately show if GPU utilization on each GPU increases. You can also monitor to make sure p95/p99 latencies stay within the target.

Counters are extremely useful to measure as well—especially with dynamic and adaptive systems. For instance, if your inference engine dynamically adapts the batch size to current conditions, you may want to increment a "batch size change" counter.

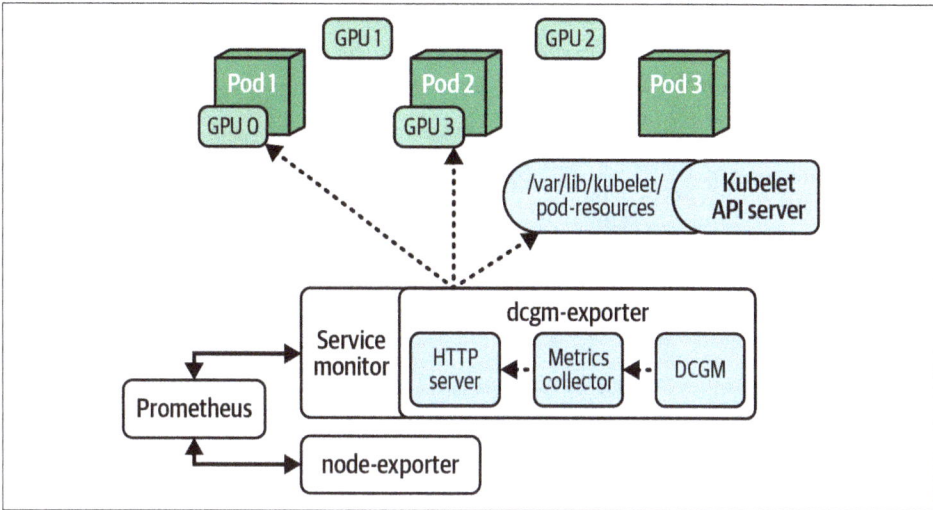

Figure 16-3. DCGM collects metrics from the Kubernetes GPU nodes and sends them to Prometheus

The other option is to log the change in a logfile, but this would require a slow, text-based search/aggregation to analyze the logfile offline using Apache Spark, for instance. You would then need to manually correlate the result of the logfile analysis with the Prometheus metrics.

By incrementing a simple counter for interesting application-level events (including errors), the data is pushed to Prometheus and instantly viewable in the Grafana dashboard alongside all of the other metrics in real time. In addition, consider using structured logging and distributed tracing for critical events.

Modern application performance management (APM) tools—as well as OpenTelemetry—can ingest these logs/traces and correlate them with metrics. This provides a consistent timeline view of events across the entire system. Having insight into this timeline will help speed up the time it takes to debug performance issues.

If you continuously monitor these metrics, you gain insight into where to tune next. For instance, if GPU utilization is below expected, you can check if GPU memory is maxed out or not. If it's not fully utilized, you can try to increase the batch size or maximum number of concurrent requests. Make sure to keep an eye on latency service-level objectives (SLOs), however. You don't want to exceed these.

> Modern inference servers expose a "maximum latency" setting for dynamic batching. Tune this to meet your SLOs. Increasing it raises the batch size (throughput). Increasing it too much will hurt p99 latency. Continuously adjust this in light of your latency targets.

In contrast, if GPU memory is near maximum, the inference engine might start swapping out inactive KV cache data to host CPU memory or NVMe storage. This will reduce GPU utilization, as the GPUs need to wait for the additional data transfers from slow CPU memory or disk.

> If you see a spike in GPU memory copy-engine utilization—or abnormal NVLink utilization that aligns with low SM utilization—your inference engine is likely swapping KV cache data in and out of GPU memory. This will bottleneck your system due to excessive data transfer latency.

If you are swapping, you can adjust the inference engines' paging parameters to reduce thrashing, apply FP8 or FP4 quantization, increase GPU memory allocation for cache, and potentially change the swapping strategy. This should bring copy utilization down and compute utilization up—exactly what you want to see.

Grafana is also used for latency tracking. You can plot the distribution of end-to-end request latency—often measuring both prefill latency and per-token latency as well. If the p99 latency spikes at certain times, you should correlate it with GPU metrics and other logs.

For instance, a p99 latency spike might correlate with a period when GPU utilization drops. Perhaps the latency spike correlates with a traffic surge that triggered a larger dynamic batch size. This could lead to higher latency for that period of time. To verify, you can overlay RPS (requests per second) on the latency graph in the Grafana dashboard to see if the two charts correlate.

If the spike was expected due to a dynamic increase in batch size per our hypothesis, make sure it isn't exceeding your service-level agreement (SLA). If it is, you can try decreasing the maximum request-batch queue delay or reducing the maximum batch size to put a limit on the latency.

Logs are invaluable when diagnosing issues as well. You should instrument the code to log key events such as when a batch is formed, when a communication starts/ends, etc. It's best to use the DEBUG level so that you can enable/disable it as needed—and not impact request-response latency.

When you enable debug logging, you'll see a step-by-step timeline in text format. In one debugging session, it's likely that you'll use both the logging timeline and Prometheus/Grafana metrics together. For instance, you can see how often an all-to-all communication takes longer than 5 ms.

With the combination of log-based timeline and metrics, you can see outliers such as network issues that may have slowed down one iteration in the all-to-all communication exchange. If this continues to happen, you can raise the expert capacity factor so that any excess tokens automatically spill over to a secondary expert replica—ideally hosted on a GPU with a more stable network path. This will balance the load and minimize the latency.

In practice, setting the capacity factor to 1.2–1.5 is common, as this allows 20%–50% extra tokens to be reassigned when a primary expert is overloaded. This can significantly smooth out tail latency in MoE inference. Spilling over to a second expert is better than queuing requests behind a slightly stalled expert on a GPU with a degraded interconnect. This will reduce sensitivity to outliers if your network continues to experience issues for whatever reason.

Profiling with Nsight Systems and Nsight Compute

When developing and tuning your inference code, you can use Nsight Systems to capture traces of the workload across both the CPU and GPU. Nsight Systems provides a timeline view that shows CPU threads, GPU kernels, CUDA events, NCCL communications, and more using microsecond resolution.

By instrumenting your code with NVTX annotations, we can label regions like "Prefill stage," "Decode step," or "All-to-all communication" on the timeline for clarity. The following code shows NVTX range markers around example prefill and decode steps using the NVTX v3 C API with explicit push and pop ranges:

```cpp
// Example C++ snippet with NVTX annotations using the C API.

#include <nvtx3/nvToolsExt.h>    // or <nvToolsExt.h>
#include "my_model.hpp"          // Your model's C++ interface
#include <vector>

// Small helpers to keep callsites tidy.
#define NVTX_PUSH(name, argb)                                        \
  do {                                                               \
    nvtxEventAttributes_t a{};                                       \
    a.version = NVTX_VERSION;                                        \
    a.size = NVTX_EVENT_ATTRIB_STRUCT_SIZE;                          \
    a.colorType = NVTX_COLOR_ARGB;                                   \
    a.color = (unsigned int)(argb);                                  \
    a.messageType = NVTX_MESSAGE_TYPE_ASCII;                         \
    a.message.ascii = (name);                                        \
    nvtxRangePushEx(&a);                                             \
  } while (0)

#define NVTX_POP() do { nvtxRangePop(); } while (0)

struct Token { int id; };

void run_inference(
    const std::vector<Token>& prompt_tokens,
```

```
      Model& model,
      int num_generate_steps) {
  // Prefill
  NVTX_PUSH("Prefill", 0xFF4F86F7);
  model.encode(prompt_tokens);
  NVTX_POP();

  // Decode one token at a time
  for (int t = 0; t < num_generate_steps; ++t) {
    NVTX_PUSH("Decode", 0xFFFF8C00);
    Token next_token = model.decode_next();
    // ... (sampling / streaming to client)
    NVTX_POP();
  }
}
```

Here, we mark regions explicitly with nvtxRangePushEx/nvtxRangePop. We push a
"Prefill" range immediately before model.encode(...) and pop it right after.
Inside the decode loop, we push "Decode" at the top of each iteration and pop it after
model.decode_next(). The small NVTX_PUSH/NVTX_POP helpers also attach color (hex
values) and text. This helps to reduce mismatch in timeline visualizations—while
keeping call sites concise. The explicit push/pop pairings are clearly visible in the
code, which makes them easy to audit.

The colored block annotations will appear in the Nsight Systems GPU activity timeline labeled "Prefill" and "Decode". This makes it easy to see how long each phase
takes—and how the phases overlap with communication operations. This helps to
identify issues such as GPU idle gaps and unexpected synchronizations.

> Note that we use the NVTX C API (nvToolsExt) directly rather
> than PyTorch's record_function(). This lets us annotate hot paths
> in a pure C++ runtime and keeps the markers consistent when
> work is launched from Python or other languages.

By tightening the scope to the smallest region necessary around
model.encode(prompt_tokens), the profiling marker covers exactly the prefill work
and no other code. This improves trace clarity and performance diagnostics.

You should use per-stream ranges when enqueuing work on multiple CUDA streams
(e.g., dedicated "transfer" stream for H2D/D2H copies and "compute" stream for kernels). To do this, you can wrap the host code for each stream with distinct NVTX
ranges.

For instance, you can name streams using nvtxNameCudaStreamA(transfer_stream,
"transfer_stream") and nvtxNameCudaStreamA(compute_stream, "compute_
stream"), for instance. You would then use nvtxRangePushA("transfer_stream")

and nvtxRangePop() around memory copies/transfers and nvtxRangePushA("com pute_stream") and nvtxRangePop() around kernel launches.

Using NVTX-named streams makes overlap (or lack thereof) obvious in the Nsight Systems timeline. Here is some code that demonstrates how these all fit together:

```
// One-time after creating the streams
nvtxNameCudaStreamA(transfer_stream, "transfer_stream");
nvtxNameCudaStreamA(compute_stream,  "compute_stream");

// Around H2D/D2H copies (transfer stream)
nvtxRangePushA("transfer_stream");
cudaMemcpyAsync(h_logits, d_logits, bytes, cudaMemcpyDeviceToHost,
                transfer_stream);
nvtxRangePop();

// Around kernel enqueues (compute stream)
nvtxRangePushA("compute_stream");
my_kernel<<<grid, block, 0, compute_stream>>>(...);
nvtxRangePop();
```

Here, we name the streams and wrap the enqueue sites in per-stream ranges so the Nsight timeline stays readable. It's important to note that the NVTX ranges annotate the host-thread timeline. The GPU lanes show kernels/memcpys by stream. Naming the streams helps tie the host ranges to the right GPU lanes during analysis.

Nsight Compute lets us profile individual kernels to pinpoint inefficiencies. We can use the Nsight Compute's section-based profiling feature to focus on specific parts of the kernel, such as memory transactions.

Another super useful tool that isn't well known is Nsight Compute's CUDA Program Counter (PC) Sampling feature (*https://oreil.ly/Ze2Jj*). This samples program counters and identifies hotspots without requiring full, heavyweight instrumentation, as shown in Figure 16-4.

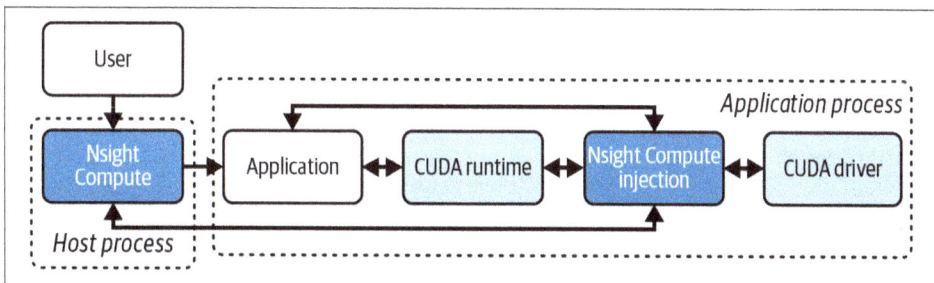

Figure 16-4. Nsight Compute's CUDA Program Counter (PC) sampling feature helps identify hotspots in a low-overhead manner (source: https://oreil.ly/DyKWR)

Specifically, we can use this to profile live inference servers and pinpoint exactly which kernel instructions are taking the most time. And we can do this in a low-overhead manner. Now that we've covered profiling with Nsight Systems and Nsight Compute, let's discuss some common troubleshooting recipes for inference.

> In production investigations on live services, prefer Program Counter Sampling first to localize hotspots with minimal overhead. Only switch to full tracing if the sample points to a specific kernel or phase.

Inference Troubleshooting Recipes

In production environments, it's impractical to run heavy profilers continuously. As such, you need to rely on lightweight, metric-based monitoring such as GPU SM utilization, KV cache warnings, tail-latency percentiles, cache-hit rates, and OOM alerts to detect anomalies and guide targeted fixes. When a metric crosses a specific threshold, you can form a hypothesis about its root cause, such as a small batch size, insufficient KV cache, routing hotspot, unbalanced sharding, memory overcommitment, etc.

Then you apply a fix such as tuning batch sizes, raising memory-utilization limits (if possible), adjusting router thresholds, or enabling CPU offload. Once the fix is pushed, you should verify the impact and confirm that the metrics have settled below their thresholds. Table 16-1 shows some key metrics, symptoms, probable causes, and recommended fixes for common production issues.

Table 16-1. Common troubleshooting symptoms, causes, and recommended actions

Metric/symptom	Probable cause	Recommended action
SM utilization < 50%	Small batches or lack of fused kernels	Increase batch size, enable fused kernels (FlashAttention or the cuDNN-fused `scaled_dot_product_attention` (SDPA) backend in PyTorch), or add custom fused kernels (e.g., using Triton); then profile with `nsys --trace=cuda`.
KV cache preemption warnings	Insufficient KV cache space (vLLM)	Increase GPU memory utilization threshold, reduce max number of batched tokens, consider PagedAttention for dynamic KV allocation.
High tail latency (p95 > 200 ms)	Decode-node hotspot or head-of-line blocking	Inspect router logs for routing patterns. Tune prefetch threshold. Enable speculative decoding paths.
Cache-hit rate < 60% under load	Unbalanced shard placement or missing prefix cache	Validate the prefix caching connector configuration (e.g., LMCache's NIXL for vLLM and NVIDIA Dynamo's NIXL connector), and increase prefix-cache TTL or replica count if needed.
Unexpected OOM on multitenant GPU	Overcommitted GPU memory	Lower per-instance GPU memory utilization, enable CPU/NVMe offload, pin processes to CPU sockets to reduce cross-socket traffic.
Irregular performance outliers	Mismatched clocks or thermal throttling	Make sure all clocks are synchronized, and monitor for thermal and power throttling.

Note: The numeric values in all metrics tables are illustrative to explain the concepts. For actual benchmark results on different GPU architectures, see the GitHub repository (*https://github.com/cfregly/ai-performance-engineering*).

You may also find some of this information buried in logfiles. Cloud providers like AWS support regular expression (RegEx) filters on logfiles to extract numeric values from loglines and export them directly as metrics. AWS CloudWatch, for instance, supports this useful feature. There are example log lines in the next code block that are useful to monitor.

Here is a sample vLLM log snippet that indicates KV cache preemption due to not enough KV cache space. As such, a KV recomputation was triggered, which uses more GPU compute resources and increases latency:

```
WARNING 2025-05-03 14:22:07 scheduler.py:1057 Sequence group 0 is preempted by
PreemptionMode.RECOMPUTE because not enough KV cache space.
total_cumulative_preemption_cnt=1
```

Next is a sample NVIDIA Dynamo routing log. Here, the first line shows a 90% prefix-cache hit on the local decode worker, which kept the prefill running locally. The next line shows a local cache miss. The router then dispatches the prefill to the remote GPU-node-03 worker node:

```
[Router] 2025-05-03T14:23:11Z INFO KVRouter: prefix-cache hit (90%) for
model=DeepSeek-R1; routing to local vLLM worker
[Router] 2025-05-03T14:23:12Z INFO KVRouter: cache miss; dispatching remote
prefill to GPU-node-03
```

Full-Stack Inference Optimizations

High-performance LLM inference demands coordinated optimizations across every layer of the stack. This includes everything from model architecture and kernel implementations to runtime engines, system orchestration, and deployment infrastructure.

Model-level techniques like pruning, distillation, sparsity, MoE routing, efficient attention (e.g., FlashAttention), and quantization-aware training can reduce compute and memory requirements. At the kernel level, fused operations, custom attention engines (e.g., FlashInfer), Tensor Core utilization, block tiling, and asynchronous memory transfers will help maximize GPU throughput.

Runtime strategies like dynamic batching, paged KV caches, CUDA Graphs, and overlap of computation and communication will keep GPUs saturated under variable loads. System orchestration layers can use prefill/decode disaggregation, intelligent routing, multitenancy isolation, and autoscaling (with warm spares) to balance latency and improve cost efficiency.

Many production systems use Kubernetes-based orchestration to run separate prefill versus decode deployments. They use ingress controllers to route requests based on load or user priority. And they keep warm standby GPU pods ready to spin up when traffic spikes.

Finally, you should explore deployment patterns like geo-distributed edge serving, smart API gateway batching, CI/CD for model variants, and real-time profiling. This will provide peak reliability and adaptability in production. Table 16-2 describes some common optimization approaches for each layer in the stack.

Table 16-2. Common optimization approaches for each layer in the stack

Stack layer	Key techniques
Model	Pruning and knowledge distillation to shrink model size with minimal accuracy loss Sparsity (MoE) to skip computations Efficient attention (FlashAttention) to reduce memory footprint and intermediate buffers Quantization-aware training in FP16/BF16 or INT4/FP8 for robustness at low precision
Kernel	Fused operator kernels (e.g., Linear + GELU + LayerNorm) to reduce launch overhead and memory traffic Custom attention kernels (FlashInfer) for block-sparse KV- and JIT-compiled kernels Tensor Core and specialized instruction utilization (cp.async, TMA) for matrix ops
Runtime	Dynamic batching with latency controls as implemented in vLLM, SGLang, and NVIDIA Dynamo (e.g., continuous batching) to consolidate requests Paged KV cache management to flexibly allocate memory and merge batches (vLLM's PagedAttention) CUDA Graphs and buffer pooling to reduce per-inference overhead Use multiple CUDA streams (one stream for data transfer and another stream for compute) to overlap computation and communication. Use event-based synchronization—and only when needed.
System orchestration	Prefill–decode disaggregation for head-of-line blocking elimination Intelligent routing and cache affinity to balance load and cache hits Multitenancy isolation and per-user quotas to prevent noisy neighbors Autoscaling with warm spare instances to hide model load times and accept a slight cost increase for significantly better latency during traffic spikes
Deployment and infrastructure	Geo-distributed and edge deployment to reduce network RTT Smart API gateways with request-level batching across server pools CI/CD pipelines for rolling out new quantized or kernel-optimized model variants in canary mode High-bandwidth interconnects (NVLink/NVSwitch and InfiniBand) and NUMA affinity between GPUs and CPUs for optimal memory access
QoS and scaling	SLA-aware dynamic batching and tail-latency controls GPU isolation with MIG or stream priorities to enforce QoS Real-time profiling dashboards for TTFT, TPOT, utilization, and memory bandwidth utilization Dynamic parallelism switching (TP, PP, DP) based on workload characteristics

When optimizing, it's important to consider cross-layer synergies. For instance, quantization (model) reduces memory footprint, enabling larger batch sizes (runtime) without OOM errors, which in turn allows orchestration components to merge more requests per GPU cycle.

You should also have a profiling-driven focus. Continuous profiling should guide which layer to optimize next. For instance, after fusion and quantization, if the CPU becomes the bottleneck for preprocessing and postprocessing, invest in faster tokenizers or offload some tasks to the GPU.

There are always trade-offs to consider when applying optimizations. Techniques like layer-level CPU offload and advanced decoding methods add complexity. For example, speculative decoding adds a draft model, and Medusa adds multihead parallel decoding. These are typically reserved for extreme cases such as ultralong contexts or erratic latency variances. Lighter-weight methods, including sparsity, batching, and disaggregation, deliver the bulk of benefits in production.

It's recommended to adopt a full-stack optimization approach by aligning model architecture, kernel design, runtime behavior, system orchestration, and deployment strategies. This means keeping your software stack up to date, including CUDA, cuDNN, NCCL, etc. Newer versions often include the latest optimizations and bug fixes.

> For benchmark reproducibility on a fixed host image, keep a tested compatibility matrix for native extension stacks instead of mixing arbitrary versions. This matters most for combinations such as PyTorch, serving engines, and custom/native extensions. Before long sweeps, run a small import smoke test.

A full-stack approach reduces the likelihood that each stack layer becomes a bottleneck. This way, teams can systematically eliminate bottlenecks, achieve consistent low latency, and maximize hardware utilization for large-scale LLM inference.

Debugging Correctness Issues

Monitoring can also help to catch anomalies caused by bugs. For instance, if memory usage keeps climbing over time, it may be caused by a memory leak in your CUDA kernel. It's recommended to use Compute Sanitizer (`compute-sanitizer`) during testing to catch device memory errors, race conditions, and out-of-bounds accesses. An example is shown here:

```
compute-sanitizer --tool memcheck your_binary
```

If one GPU shows much lower utilization than others, it might have dropped out of the NCCL communication group due to a silent NCCL failure or uncaught error. You can check for NCCL error codes in logs by looking for `WARN NCCL_COMM_FAILURE`. It provides very verbose error logs.

Enable NCCL debugging by setting the environment variable, `NCCL_DEBUG=WARN`. This will help surface errors that would otherwise be silent. Be warned, however, that NCCL logs are very verbose!

Use the NCCL test suite to debug all-reduce and all-to-all performance and correctness issues. You can also use `ncclCommGetAsyncError` with `ncclCommAbort` to detect and handle asynchronous communication errors. Consider enabling NCCL's `IB GID` tracing and using NVSwitch system telemetry to detect issues at the interconnect level as well.

You should set up alerts in Prometheus's alert manager to detect unusual patterns like "GPU utilization < 10% for at least 60 seconds," "memory usage above W% threshold," "NVLink error rate > X," "PCIe replays above Y threshold," "temperature above Z degrees," etc.

In practice, you might configure Prometheus Alertmanager rules, as shown in Table 16-3. This way, you can proactively investigate issues.

Table 16-3. Example set of common Prometheus alerts for GPU-based systems

Metric	Condition	Severity	Notes
GPU utilization	< 10% for > 60 s	Idle	Underutilization
GPU utilization	> 90%	Bottleneck	Possible saturation
Memory usage	> 80%	Warning	Approaching OOM
Memory usage	> 95%	Critical	High risk of out-of-memory errors
Temperature	> 85 °C	Warning	Approaching thermal throttling
Temperature	> 95 °C	Critical	Risk of shutdown or hardware damage
NVLink replay/recovery errors	≥ 1	Critical	Indicates link retry or recovery
NVLink CRC errors	> 100 errors/sec	Critical	High CRC failure rate on link
PCIe replay errors	≥ 1	Critical	Packet retries on PCIe bus
Uncorrectable ECC errors	≥ 1	Critical	Data corruption requiring reset

You also want to set up hardware error counters and alerts as well. For example, if ECC errors or NVLink retries are reported, alert immediately, as these can quickly degrade performance or cause drop-outs. Dropouts happen when a GPU—or its interconnect—silently disconnects. For instance, an NVLink might drop—or the GPU might "drop off the bus" after a fatal error.

Use DCGM for per-link NVLink throughput and totals including `DCGM_FI_DEV_NVLINK_TX_BANDWIDTH_L*`, `DCGM_FI_DEV_NVLINK_RX_BANDWIDTH_L*`, and `*_TOTAL`. Fall back to `nvidia-smi nvlink`, Nsight Systems/Compute, or NVSwitch counters if needed.

Consider a NCCL failure case. You might get an alert that shows one node's GPUs are near 0% utilization, while others are at 90%. You can start debugging the issue by checking the node logs and finding which node is generating the NCCL errors.

This type of active monitoring and alerting lets you catch these issues more quickly, find the failed node, and start restoring it back to normal. In this case, you might want to reinitialize the NCCL communicators or perform a full node reboot (just make sure the node rejoins the NCCL group after restart/reboot).

You could catch these issues even quicker by incrementing a "NCCL Error" counter for NCCL errors. In addition, your inference server can log the NCCL errors, which will automatically be scraped by Fluentd or AWS CloudWatch and convert them into counters.

Then you can overlay the error counter chart on top of the per-node GPU utilization chart in Grafana. This will correlate the NCCL errors with a drop in GPU utilization so that you can identify and remediate the failed node much quicker.

> Application-level counters are extremely useful in production—especially when combined with system metrics.

And optimizations should not be considered successful until they are verified with actual metrics that demonstrate increased throughput, reduced latency, improved utilization, etc. A rigorous measurement-driven approach to system performance tuning is essential given the complexity of modern AI inference systems.

In short, you should combine application-level counters, automatically scraped log counters from Fluentd or AWS CloudWatch, and low-level system metrics. This type of full-stack telemetry provides the visibility needed to operate—and optimize—a multinode LLM inference system running at peak performance on production workloads. You should treat metrics, counters, and logs as the ground truth of your system's behavior.

> Our intuitions and gut feelings can often lead us down the wrong debugging path. But metrics don't lie. Instrument your code properly upfront—and trust the metrics when things go wrong.

Dynamic Batching, Scheduling, and Routing

Even after the model has been partitioned and parallelized optimally across the cluster, there are still more opportunities for application-level optimizations in a multi-node inference cluster deployment. In this section, we focus on techniques to maximize GPU utilization, minimize latency, and boost throughput by dynamically batching requests and using optimized scheduling and routing strategies.

Dynamic Batching

One of the most powerful performance techniques in an inference serving system is batching. By combining multiple incoming inputs into a single batch for the model to process together, batching improves throughput by amortizing fixed costs—like kernel launches and memory loads—over multiple inputs. It does this at the expense of individual-request latency, however. Some individual requests may need to wait for a period of time (e.g., 2 ms) to join a batch and be processed.

Dynamic batching is a specialization of request batching that assembles batches of incoming inference requests of dynamic sizes on the fly. It can be configured to buffer requests for a period of time or until a given batch size is reached. All modern LLM inference engines support dynamic batching, including vLLM, SGLang, and NVIDIA Dynamo.

Dynamic batching is in contrast to *static batching*, which locks in a fixed batch size (or pads all sequences to the longest one) and then waits for every request in that batch to finish before returning results. This can incur unbounded queuing delay for early arrivals—and leave GPU cycles wasted on padding.

With dynamic batching, the system accumulates incoming requests and dispatches "whatever has arrived" once either a target batch size is met or a short timeout (e.g., 2 ms) elapses. This bounds maximum latency to the timeout value that you specify.

With its on-the-fly sizing, dynamic batching lets you amortize kernel-launch overheads across multiple sequences—while avoiding the worst-case delays of static batching. This improves both GPU utilization and predictable latency under variable load. Figure 16-5 shows the difference between static batching and dynamic batching.

Dynamic batching lets the system automatically grow or shrink batch sizes based on actual request-arrival patterns and latency targets (e.g., max delay). The key is to batch intelligently in a way that increases overall throughput while maintaining latency within acceptable bounds. Modern inference engines implement microbatching, which accumulates requests for only a few milliseconds before dispatching the batch to the GPU. Typically, a delay of 2–10 ms is used, but this should be tuned to meet latency SLOs.

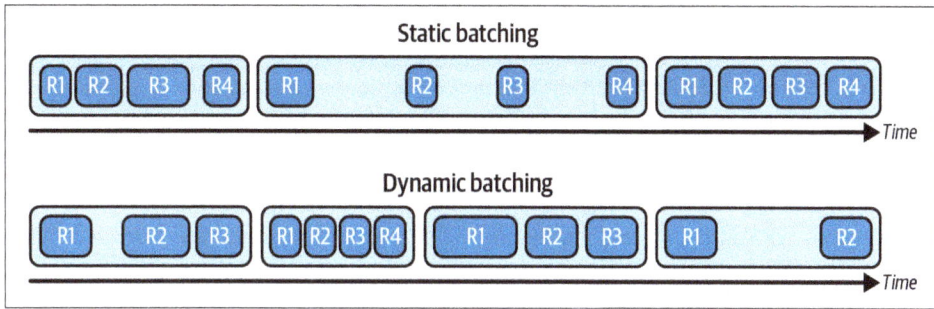

Figure 16-5. Difference between static and dynamic batching

For example, you can configure a batch delay of 2 ms to determine how long the server waits for additional requests before dispatching a batch. If three requests arrive within that interval, the batcher immediately groups and sends them to the GPU. Any further requests that arrive after the 2 ms timer expires will be collected into the next batch. This timeout-driven trigger bounds per-request queuing latency (never exceeding 2 ms) while improving throughput by grouping multiple sequences together.

These microbatches reduce the delay added and allow the GPU to work on multiple requests at once—instead of one at a time. Large LLM models are memory-bandwidth-bound at small batch sizes, so increasing the batch size will improve arithmetic intensity—and overall hardware utilization.

In practice, LLM serving systems pick a balanced batch size that gives good throughput without incurring much latency. Under high load, dynamic batching can improve both throughput and latency because it prevents the GPU from sitting idle between requests. In fact, if the arrival rate of requests is high, batching can reduce overall queue wait times since more work is processed in the same amount of time. This benefits end-to-end latency and tail latency for high-load traffic patterns.

Dynamic batching will, at low RPS (requests per second), add a small delay as it waits for other requests to join the batch. This will slightly increase latency at low RPS. However, at moderate to high RPS, the delay is amortized and becomes negligible compared to the queuing delay that would occur if we ran everything one by one. As such, batching lowers overall latency, including tail latency.

> You should validate the improvement by plotting latency percentiles against load using tools like Grafana. With batching, you'll often see overall p50 latency stay flat—or even drop—as throughput increases. This will happen up until an inflection point. Make note of this inflection point and stay under this value.

It is important to configure batching with respect to latency SLOs. For instance, if you promise a p99 latency of 2 seconds for a request of a certain length, you can't afford to delay one request by 500 ms waiting in a batch queue. By default, your dynamic batch delay should be initially set well below the p99 latency requirement (on the order of 1–2 ms) to avoid excessive batch delays.

Using an adaptive batching delay, the batch delay value can dynamically drop to near 0 ms at low RPS and increase higher to 5–10 ms at peak load when needed. This adaptive approach is used by vLLM and others to maintain SLO compliance across different traffic patterns.

Batching primarily benefits high-traffic scenarios. If traffic is low, the system will just run single requests, and the latency will be very low. At high load, however, the system can apply aggressive batching to achieve high throughput and will provide better overall latency since it avoids queue buildup and amortizes the latency across many requests.

Continuous Batching

Continuous batching, also known as *in-flight batching* or *iteration-level scheduling*, maintains high GPU utilization by refilling batches on every token-generation iteration rather than waiting for complete sequences to finish. It evicts completed requests and immediately pulls in new ones based entirely on GPU readiness. This technique is particularly important for low-latency use cases such as chat assistants.

In contrast to timeout-driven approaches like dynamic batching, the event-driven continuous batching strategy eliminates idle compute slots and the padding overhead of these other approaches. By never relying on a fixed "max-delay" timer, continuous batching allows new requests to join an ongoing batch mid-generation—and without blocking on the longest sequence, as shown in Figure 16-6.

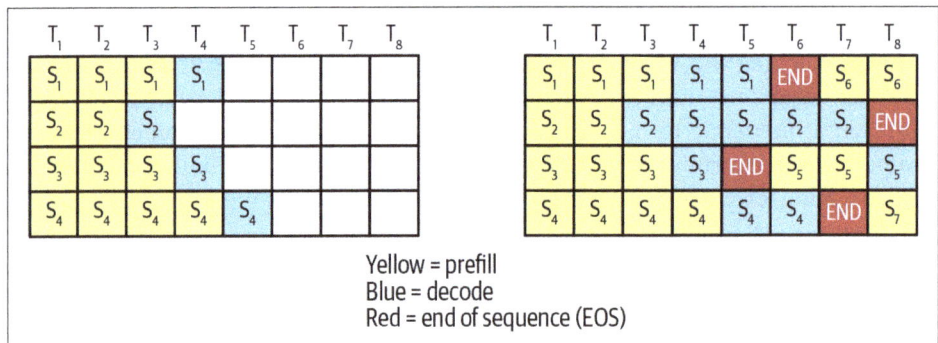

Figure 16-6. Continuous batching allows new sequences (requests) to join a batch mid-generation

Here, continuous batching minimizes wasted slots in the inference compute pipeline. It eliminates the idle time caused by waiting for the longest response to finish for each batch. Instead of waiting for all sequences in a batch to finish (which is inefficient due to variable output lengths and leads to GPU underutilization), continuous batching replaces completed sequences with new ones at each iteration. This approach allows new requests to fill GPU slots immediately—resulting in higher throughput, reduced latency, and more efficient GPU utilization.

Batching 4–8 requests can often double or triple the throughput over 1–2 request batches on large models. This is because the GPU's math units and memory pipelines are better utilized. And the additional latency per request is on the order of only a few milliseconds—making this strategy ideal for low-latency use cases. Table 16-4 summarizes the different batching strategies discussed so far, including a naive static batching strategy.

Table 16-4. Comparing static, dynamic, and continuous batching

Aspect	Static batching	Dynamic batching	Continuous batching
Trigger	Fixed batch size or sequence length	Batch-size target or timeout	Token-generation completion event
Latency bound	Unbounded; wait for full batch	Bounded by `max_batch_delay_ms`	Minimal; evicts and refills mid-batch
Padding overhead	High overhead: pad to longest sequence	Moderate overhead: pad within each batch	Low: slots refilled without waiting for padding
GPU idle mitigation	Poor: especially under variable-sized loads	Better: but can cause idle GPU if the timer fires on a small batch	Excellent: keeps GPU saturated at every iteration
Implementation	Simple	Moderate: requires timers and queue management	Complex: requires per-token coordination and state tracking

Continuous Scheduling

Another dimension of request scheduling involves concurrent model execution. The vLLM community calls this *continuous scheduling*. The idea is that if the model is small—or if the batch size is limited by latency targets—a single model instance might not fully saturate the GPUs.

Continuous scheduling treats the GPU like an OS scheduler treats a CPU. It launches independent small kernels on separate CUDA streams. This lets the hardware warp scheduler interleave warps across tasks without explicit context switching.

For example, if our inference engine is not fully saturating the GPUs, it can run multiple model inference streams concurrently on the same GPU. This way, while one instance is waiting on a data transfer or a non-GPU operation, another instance can execute.

Specifically, during the decode phase, generating one token at a time can often leave the GPU underutilized—especially if performed on a single sequence of text. This is because the workload is relatively small and requires a large amount of memory movement relative to the amount of compute.

To address this inefficiency, the inference engine can interleave multiple decode tasks from across different user requests. For example, if 10 users are decoding different sequences at the same time, you can't simply batch them into one large matrix multiply. This is because each sequence may be a different length. This would prevent the GPU from performing efficient matrix operations without requiring a large amount of padding.

Instead, the continuous scheduler can launch 10 small decode kernels for each sequence's next token in rapid succession on separate CUDA streams. This allows true concurrency across sequences by utilizing the GPU's fine-grained warp scheduler. As such, the kernels interleave execution across SMs. This prevents idle cycles by approximating a round-robin processing pattern.

By enqueuing each decode task on its own stream, the GPU can overlap memory transfers and computation across sequences. This reduces per-token latency and improves overall throughput.

The GPU switches between the kernels at the warp level. And when one decode kernel stalls due to inefficient control flow on the CPU or a network I/O wait, other active kernels can immediately proceed. This keeps the GPUs fully utilized.

Continuous scheduling achieves high utilization even at token-level granularity by maintaining a queue of ready-to-run token tasks. The end result is similar to batching. The GPU is always working on token generation, but it doesn't require combining them into one giant matrix multiply. It just means that we don't let the GPU sit idle between token computations. This type of token-level granularity scheduling is essential to maximizing throughput across millions of users.

At fixed intervals or whenever the GPU frees up, a continuous scheduler gathers all pending next-token requests into a configurable-sized batch and then dispatches the batch as a single GPU call. This helps balance throughput and latency.

> If you are designing a custom scheduler, consider the hybrid approach: use a short timer and a maximum batch size for token scheduling.

State-of-the-art systems like vLLM and SGLang merge dynamic batching with continuous scheduling. Their custom continuous scheduler is built around the idea of squeezing out "bubbles" of GPU time.

vLLM's PagedAttention is a specific example of this hybrid approach. PagedAttention breaks the attention key-value (KV) cache into slices, or pages, and dynamically groups the page-specific compute across active sequences. This sustains near-100% GPU utilization under heavy load by interleaving large prefill GEMMs with rapid, small decode kernels.

vLLM efficiently uses block-level KV cache structures to track each request's state separately. This fine-grained bookkeeping provides fast streaming responses and optimal hardware utilization by continuously packing and multiplexing workloads in real time.

Another example is SGLang's RadixAttention, which uses tree-based KV cache grouping. This achieves similar near-100% GPU utilization and introduces lazy eviction for unused cache pages. We'll cover vLLM's PagedAttention and SGLang's RadixAttention in more detail in a bit. Both approaches are open source, so you can review their scheduling implementations directly in code.

Stall-Free Scheduling (Chunked Prefill)

When prompts are extremely long, you can split them into chunks and interleave the prefill and decode work. This is called *stall-free scheduling* or *chunked prefill*.

Consider a 20K token prompt. By splitting the prompt into 5K token chunks, you reduce the maximum stall per iteration and bound the per-iteration work to a fixed number of tokens. This provides predictable per-iteration latency. The cost of chunked prefill for different chunk sizes is shown in Table 16-5.

Table 16-5. Cost for a 20 K token prompt using chunked prefill of different chunk sizes

Chunk size	Number of chunks	Attention ops per chunk	Total MLP tokens
20K	1	$20K \times (20K + 1) \div 2 = 200M$	$1 \times 20K = 20K$
10K	2	$50M + 150M = 200M$	$2 \times 10K = 20K$
5K	4	$12.5M + 37.5M + 62.5M + 87.5M = 200M$	$4 \times 5K = 20K$

Here, the per-chunk attention cost grows with the full context due to KV caching. Each new chunk computes attention for its own tokens against all prior tokens from previous chunks.

In self-attention, the number of QK dot products for a sequence of length N is triangular, approximately $N(N + 1) \div 2$. This is the number of $Q \times K$ dot product operations per layer per head. This cost is quadratic in N ($O(N^2)$). So for $N = 20,000$, this is about 200 million operations. Chunking does not reduce this total. Chunking only changes when work becomes available to the decoder. The benefit of chunked prefill is latency smoothing and improved overlap, not fewer total attention dot-product operations.

Prefill self-attention performs $N(N + 1) \div 2$ Q × K dot products per layer per head. This cost is quadratic in N, $O(N^2)$. Note that chunking and pipelined prefill change only overlap and latency; they do not change the total amount of attention work. The only ways to reduce the total attention cost are to reduce the effective context or to use local or sparse attention. For example, you can reduce the cost to $O(NW)$ with a fixed attention window W.

In short, the chunked prefill technique schedules prompt prefill processing and token generation in a tightly interleaved way. It unifies the high efficiency of large-batch prefill compute with the responsiveness of streaming decode. This can lower tail latency while maintaining high throughput on many workloads.

Latency-Aware Scheduling and Dynamic Routing

Latency-aware scheduling can analyze incoming requests, create dynamic batches, and route the batches to minimize latency. Consider six prompts arriving into a two-GPU inference system at the same time. The prompt lengths are 6K, 2K, 6K, 2K, 2K, and 2K in that order. Let's compare a naive first-in-first-out (FIFO) scheduler with a latency-aware scheduler.

First, the FIFO scheduler creates two batches based on arrival order. Batch 1 is [6K, 2K, 6K] and is sent to GPU 1. Batch 2 is [2K, 2K, 2K] and is sent to GPU 2. The results are summarized in Table 16-6.

Table 16-6. FIFO versus latency-aware scheduling for a sequence of incoming prompts of length [6K, 2K, 6K, 2K, 2K, 2K]

GPU	Prompt batch	Self-attention QK ops $T(N) = N(N + 1) \div 2$	Tokens N
GPU 1	6K, 2K, 6K	$T(6K) + T(2K) + T(6K) = 18{,}003{,}000 + 2{,}001{,}000 + 18{,}003{,}000 = 38{,}007{,}000$	14K
GPU 2	2K, 2K, 2K	$3 \times T(2K) = 3 \times 2{,}001{,}000 = 6{,}003{,}000$	6K

Here you see that the FIFO strategy sends the first three prompts [6K, 2K, 6K] to GPU 1 for approximately 38,007,000 self-attention Q × K dot products and 14,000 tokens of MLP, while GPU 2 sees approximately 6,003,000 self-attention Q × K computations and 6,000 tokens of MLP. The critical path is determined by GPU 1 at approximately 38,007,000 self-attention Q × K dot products.

In contrast, the latency-aware scheduler analyzes the expected latency of the six requests and rearranges them into two batches of [2K, 2K, 6K]. In this strategy, the self-attention cost per GPU is 22,005,000 dot products with 10,000 tokens of MLP, as shown in Table 16-7.

Table 16-7. Latency-aware scheduling for prompts of length [6K, 2K, 6K, 2K, 2K, 2K] in that order

GPU	Prompt batch	Self-attention QK ops T(N) = N(N + 1) ÷ 2	Tokens N
GPU 1	2K, 2K, 6K	T(2K) + T(2K) + T(6K) = 2,001,000 + 2,001,000 + 18,003,000 = 22,005,000	10K
GPU 2	2K, 2K, 6K	T(2K) + T(2K) + T(6K) = 2,001,000 + 2,001,000 + 18,003,000 = 22,005,000	10K

This reduces the critical path self-attention by about 42% from 38,007,000 to 22,005,000. As such, the latency-aware scheduler can significantly reduce TTFT. Because the latency-aware scheduler is aware of prompt lengths, the triangular $N(N + 1) ÷ 2$ cost in self-attention, and the O(N) cost in MLP, it can balance compute weight and minimize overall latency. For instance, in this example, the latency-aware scheduler moves the 2K token requests earlier. This allows these lighter requests to finish prefill sooner and begin decode without waiting for the heavier 6K token prefill to complete.

> These counts assume a variable-length fused attention kernel that computes only over valid tokens—for example, FlashAttention or PyTorch scaled dot product attention (SDPA) with the cuDNN backend. If your kernel pads to the maximum sequence length in a batch, the attention arithmetic cost approaches the batch size multiplied by T tokens of the longest sequence in that batch. In this case, the difference between FIFO and latency-aware strategies will shrink.

In short, a naive FIFO scheduler can overload one of the GPUs if the arrival order is not globally ideal within the batch. A latency-aware scheduler can analyze incoming requests and rearrange them into more balanced batches to minimize latency.

> Some inference serving frameworks have incorporated reinforcement learning to adjust scheduling policies online. This builds on the latency-aware strategies described here by automatically tuning for changing traffic patterns.

Systems-Level Optimizations

Systems-level optimization techniques include overlapping communication with computation, maximizing GPU utilization, managing power and thermal concerns, handling errors, and optimizing memory access. Overall, we're making sure that our GPU hardware is doing useful work, or goodput, nearly 100% of the time. We also discuss the trade-offs between throughput and latency and how to find a balance appropriate for production SLOs.

Overlapping Communication and Computation

As we've seen repeatedly throughout this book, overlapping communication with computation is critical for inference performance with large models distributed across many GPUs. The massively high bandwidth of systems like the GB200/GB300 NVL72 (up to ~130 TB/s of aggregate GPU-to-GPU NVLink bandwidth within a rack) means that overlap is even more effective because data transfers are fast enough that computation is less likely to be starved. However, even with the NVL72, it's critical to use multiple CUDA streams and nonblocking collectives. This will allow you to perform communication-compute overlap to hide latency and keep all 72 GPUs busy—even at these speeds.

> In practice, you want to enable NCCL's GPUDirect RDMA support—and use NCCL's group calls to overlap multiple small all-reduce operations. Also, consider using SHARP (available on InfiniBand with suitable switches) to offload reduction operations to the network fabric. This optimization can improve throughput on some fabrics and topologies. In some tests, it has shown roughly 10%–20% throughput improvements for large all-to-all communications.

Consider an inference step that requires transferring data between GPUs (e.g., all-to-all for MoE)—or even just sending the prompt data from CPU to GPU and the response from the GPU to the CPU to return to the end user. In all of these scenarios, we want to perform these transfers asynchronously while the GPU is doing other work, whenever possible.

One basic example is using separate CUDA streams to overlap compute and data transfer. For example, launch `cudaMemcpyAsync` on a dedicated transfer stream (with pinned host memory) while compute kernels run on the default stream.

> Remember to use page-locked host buffers for transfers over PCIe or NICs. This way, the CUDA driver can DMA directly and overlap with compute.

You would then synchronize with a CUDA event only when the data is needed. This prevents the GPU from idling on I/O. This way, data transfers will use nonblocking CUDA calls (e.g., pinned memory) and CUDA streams so that the GPU doesn't stall waiting on these operations. On modern GPUs with full duplex NVLink bandwidth, such overlap can largely hide communication latency. However, you should verify this with profiling on your specific workload.

Data transfers in this context can include sending new prompt embeddings from the CPU to the GPU—or moving the last token's logits from the GPU to the CPU. For instance, right after a GPU computes the logits for a batch of new tokens, we can kick off an asynchronous copy of those logits to the CPU for postprocessing (e.g., sampling)—or for sending back to the client as a streaming response—and immediately launch the next compute kernel for another batch of tokens that are still on the GPU.

In multinode scenarios, a communication collective like all-to-all can overlap by dividing work into chunks. A technique used in some MoE runtimes is to split the batch of tokens into two halves, and, while the first half's tokens are being processed by experts, it can start sending the second half's tokens.

By the time the experts finish with the first half, the second half's data has arrived at the destination GPUs—and they can proceed without waiting. This requires careful scheduling of the NCCL calls relative to compute kernels.

For example, you can implement this overlap using CUDA events to signal when half the batch is done. At this point, you can launch the NCCL all-to-all for that portion of the data—while the next portion finishes computing. You can use CUDA Graphs to capture these asynchronous patterns and reduce launch overhead. The result is improved GPU utilization because the GPUs spend less time sitting idle waiting for communications.

Another area of overlap is between the CPU and GPU. For instance, while the GPU is busy generating the next token, the CPU can concurrently prepare the next input or perform result handling for previously generated tokens. A highly optimized inference engine will overlap any CPU-side preprocessing (e.g., input-text tokenization) in parallel with GPU computations from other requests. For example, the engine can prepare the next batch while overlapping with GPU computations of the current batch.

This sounds obvious, but it requires a multithreaded architecture such that one thread handles networking and queuing, while another thread launches GPU operations. And yet another thread might handle response postprocessing, etc. The Python or C++ inference loop should never block the GPU from starting new work due to waiting on an operation that could otherwise be done concurrently.

In pipeline parallel scenarios, the system should overlap communications (between pipeline stages) with computations inside of each stage. For instance, GPU 0, after finishing its part for token t, can start sending activations to GPU 1 at the same time as it begins processing token t+1 for another sequence.

Modern interconnects and frameworks allow compute kernels and data transfers to overlap as long as they use different resources. You should use multiple CUDA streams in an inference pipeline such that each pipeline stage has an independent stream. This way, the sending/receiving of activations can happen in parallel with other streams that are performing computations for different microbatches. The effect is that pipeline bubbles are reduced.

On the networking side, technologies like NVIDIA GPUDirect RDMA allow network adapters like InfiniBand NICs to read and write GPU memory directly without involving the CPU—and without staging through host memory. By utilizing GPU-Direct for cross-node transfers of KV cache or expert activations, the inference engine reduces latency and CPU overhead.

GPUDirect RDMA removes staging through host memory and allows the NIC DMA engines to access GPU memory directly. The CPU posts work requests, but the data path bypasses the CPU. This frees CPU cores for other tasks.

Consider a practical example using InfiniBand for all-to-all communication in an MoE layer across two NVL72 racks. If you do this synchronously by first performing the all-to-all and then computing, the GPU utilization can remain low without over-lap. By overlapping batches of the all-to-all communication with compute, however, you can significantly increase GPU utilization.

Overlapping all-to-all communication in an MoE layer involves splitting the token batch in half and beginning the second half's exchange while the first half's experts are still computing. This hides communication latency by interleaving it with compute.

Essentially, each GPU begins computing its local experts' outputs for the tokens it already has—while simultaneously receiving the remaining tokens from the other node. By the time it finishes the first batch, the second batch has arrived and can be computed immediately.

This kind of optimization is fairly low level and involves CUDA event synchroniza-tion between NCCL groups and CUDA streams, but it produces worthwhile through-put improvements and smoother latencies. In practice, you first launch the NCCL all-to-all as part of a NCCL group without waiting for completion. Then you immediately launch the next compute kernel. Make sure to check for completion using CUDA events.

We can also overlap I/O with compute for streaming outputs. For instance, as soon as a few tokens are generated, we send them over the socket to the end user—while the model is already working on the next tokens. This hides the network latency (e.g., sending the response back to the end user) behind computation (e.g., subsequent tokens). As such, the end user sees a steady stream without pauses.

This pattern of nonblocking streaming to clients is adopted in all modern LLM infer-ence engines. They use separate threads for sending token updates to clients using SSE/WebSockets.

If you are implementing streaming outputs yourself, make sure to use thread-safe queues or locks to hand off generated tokens to the networking thread. You don't want to introduce synchronization issues in this handoff. These can be very difficult to identify and debug.

If we didn't overlap, we would generate a small number of tokens and then have the GPUs sit idle while we send the tokens back to the end user. Instead, our network send is handled by an async thread that takes the output from the response buffer and streams it back to the user. This allows the main inference thread (e.g., CUDA stream) to immediately continue generating more tokens. This effectively pipelines token generation (compute) with output transmission (I/O).

In short, overlapping communication and computation requires thinking in terms of pipelines and using asynchronous operations whenever possible. Modern GPUs and networking hardware provide the primitives to implement this, including CUDA streams, nonblocking collectives, and RDMA. CUDA device-side primitives such as `cuda::memcpy_async` used with `cuda::barrier` (from the CUDA pipeline header) help overlap global to shared memory movement with compute inside a kernel. (Note: Host-to-device and device-to-host transfers still require explicit CUDA streams and pinned host memory to overlap with compute.) Efficient LLM inference systems take full advantage of these features.

In short, always overlap communication with computation whenever possible. Otherwise, scaling to many GPUs—even with NVLink/NVSwitch—will fall short of peak hardware performance. These optimizations are mostly invisible to the end user since there's no change in model outputs. However, these are essential to squeeze out every bit of performance from the inference cluster and keep users coming back to your application.

Maximizing GPU Utilization and Throughput Versus Latency Trade-Offs

The ultimate goal of performance tuning is to keep GPUs as busy as possible doing useful work, such as matrix multiplies—while minimizing any idle and underutilized GPU resources. Many of the techniques described previously, including batching, parallelism, and overlap, are designed to achieve near-100% GPU utilization.

GPU utilization percentage—and specifically useful utilization, or goodput—is an important performance metric to monitor continuously. And while you want to push for 100% useful utilization, you need to make sure you are not violating your SLOs, such as latency. At some point, you may reach a point of diminishing returns.

Consider an inference server that is currently showing 60% GPU utilization with a naive implementation. Investigating, you find that the decode stage is a bottleneck because it's waiting for a single thread to handle all sequences sequentially. Let's introduce concurrent decoding using multiple streams. By interleaving decodes, as described earlier, we raise GPU utilization to 95% and double the throughput. This confirms that concurrent decoding is working.

We can try to reach 100% by putting more requests into a massive batch, but this will slow down individual queries. It's often helpful to plot a throughput-versus-latency curve by testing various batch sizes. In this chart, there's usually a sharp "knee" where throughput gains start costing too much latency.

To find the sweet spot in the throughput-latency curve, first turn on full concurrency and overlap as much as possible so you know the hardware can stay busy. Then gradually increase the batch size until you hit maximum resource utilization. At this point, measure single-query latency and scale back just enough (e.g., from 16 to 8) to meet your response-time targets.

It's recommended to monitor your p95 and p99 tail latencies along with p50 median latency. This is because small jitters and uneven batch fills can produce long-tail outliers noticeable at p95/p99. In a large cluster serving many requests, even a 0.1% outlier can occur frequently. Thus, p99—or even p99.9—might be more important than p50 for measuring user experience. In addition, long-tail latency often forces over-provisioning to meet aggressive SLOs. As such, reducing tail latency has direct cost benefits.

> A good rule of thumb is to cap your batch size slightly below the one that gives peak throughput. Teams typically target 90% of maximum peak throughput, called the *headroom buffer*. This is because running at full speed can cause unpredictable latency spikes. For instance, if increasing the batch size to 16 requests starts to add a small amount of latency to a few requests, you should reduce the batch limit to 8. This will provide more consistent latency and reduce throughput only slightly.

Some inference systems can dynamically adjust the batch size on the fly based on these metrics. We'll cover this technique—and many more adaptive inference strategies—in Chapters 17–19.

It's important to remember that running GPUs at a constant 100% can cause throttling by hitting power and thermal limits. Sometimes running at 90% with efficient kernels can outperform 100% with throttling. Next, let's discuss GPU power and thermal constraints—characteristics that CPU-based application developers and systems engineers often don't consider.

Power and Thermal Constraints

Another dimension to consider is power and thermal constraints. Continuously running GPUs at 100% will cause thermal throttling if cooling is insufficient. Modern GPU systems are liquid-cooled to reduce thermal throttling and sustain performance. If you're running older, air-cooled systems, watch out for downclocks.

You can monitor downclocks with `nvidia-smi` or DCGM when GPU utilization is high. Specifically, DCGM exposes XID throttling reasons through `DCGM_FI_DEV_CLOCK_THROTTLE_REASONS`. And `nvidia-smi` will show a "Pwr Throttle" flag when a GPU is being power-throttled.

You may also hit power limits on the board—especially with boost clocks. Modern GPUs draw significantly more power under boost, so you should monitor if GPUs downclock due to hitting a power limit. If this happens, you will experience less-than-ideal GPU performance. Always monitor the `DCGM_FI_DEV_POWER_USAGE` metric from DCGM and alert anytime this exceeds the normal range.

> If your GPUs consistently hit power limits, consider enabling Dynamic Boost mode—or underclocking slightly—to avoid thermal throttling that can spike latency.

To work around these constraints in software, you can slightly ease off utilization by adding a tiny interbatch delay. You can also limit concurrency. Modern GPUs also support clock capping. So rather than adding delay, you could cap the GPU clocks marginally using `nvidia-smi -lgc` or similar to prevent hitting thermal limits. This will only slightly reduce throughput—and provide more consistent performance.

From a hardware perspective, you can try to improve cooling or raise the power limit if cooling is already adequate. To increase the power cap, use `nvidia-smi -pl` or tune your GPU boost settings.

These are all reminders that pushing real-world systems to their limits can cause unexpected side effects that greatly impact performance. It's recommended to include a "boost-off" flag in your inference engine to apply the software workarounds on the fly when the system detects performance degradation due to throttling caused by power or thermal constraints. This will run your system in a slightly underutilized and cooler state until full stability and performance are restored.

Error Handling

While not typically associated with performance, it's important to handle errors efficiently. A fully utilized inference system has less headroom to handle excessive error spikes—especially since error handling is likely not the most optimal code path in your system.

In failure scenarios, failing fast is the key since, if a request will error, it's best to return the error immediately rather than waste GPU time with a slow failure. Be sure to implement proper exceptions and timeouts around inference calls to catch hangs or crashes.

Additionally, it's recommended to implement backpressure. This means that if errors spike, you can start rejecting new requests—or reduce batch sizes—to give the system some headroom to recover.

At scale, it's recommended to build in some headroom, adding some extra replicas that sit mostly idle. These can act as a buffer for spikes in errors or other unexpected situations. While autoscaling is likely the first option you think of to reduce cost, just remember that autoscaling takes time to provision the new resources.

While idle capacity costs money, the cost of lost customers or SLA violations is often higher. At least 10%–15% of buffer capacity is recommended during steady state. For more critical services that cannot incur downtime, it's recommended to provision 100% buffer capacity—or a full cluster replica.

There is simply no substitute for prewarmed, idle nodes that can handle the extra load immediately on demand. The cost of losing end users is likely higher than the cost of keeping a few replicas idle and ready to handle any additional, unexpected load.

Memory

Optimizing resource utilization extends to memory as well. While GPU memory and memory bandwidth are growing somewhat incrementally, model sizes and context lengths are growing exponentially. As such, memory remains a precious resource to optimize—and will remain precious in the near future.

As such, you want to utilize GPU memory and memory bandwidth effectively. Memory is typically filled by the model weights and KV cache. During inference, it's best to keep the model weights in GPU HBM at all times. If you page memory in and out of CPU DRAM or NVMe storage, you will incur extra page faults and transfer latency.

This additional transfer latency is true even for modern CPU-GPU superchips like Grace Blackwell and Vera Rubin. As such, high-performance LLM inference engines explicitly manage memory rather than relying on on-demand paging.

Compression is an effective technique to reduce memory usage in your inference system. Specifically for the KV cache, which is generated by the prefill stage for every query that comes into the system.

Since the size of the KV cache scales with the number of queries and the size of the inputs, you should consider KV cache compression and quantization. KV cache compression/quantization means storing reduced-precision keys and values if the model can tolerate the precision loss. And, while not ideal, KV cache offloading is an option for rarely used KV cache data.

KV Cache Offloading and Memory Pool Allocation

By offloading (paging out) rarely used KV cache entries to CPU memory or disk, inference engines make room for more active data. This is similar to handling virtual memory.

For instance, vLLM's PagedAttention offloads to CPU memory and NVMe storage using a managed memory pool for the KV cache. Similarly, SGLang's RadixAttention uses a tree-structured cache that can lazily evict least-used prefixes. NVIDIA Dynamo has a similar mechanism for KV cache offloading and memory management.

And without a good KV cache allocator, you can have excessive memory fragmentation (e.g., ~20%–30%) when requests of varying lengths flow through the system. This will limit how many requests you can handle before experiencing an OOM error. Remember to use allocators with large pool sizes, as discussed in an earlier chapter.

Adopting a proper memory-paging strategy will reduce fragmentation down to a tolerable few percent. This means you can pack more contexts into the GPU and keep utilization high without crashing the system.

With proper KV cache memory management, modern inference engines serve many more concurrent users without running out of GPU memory. They do this by managing their own KV cache memory pools and offloading data to CPU and NVMe storage. As such, they achieve near-full memory utilization with minimal fragmentation.

The trade-off is a bit of extra data transfer latency if the contexts become active again and need to be paged in. This overhead is typically small, however, compared to the total request latency.

Memory utilization and compute utilization go hand in hand. If memory is poorly managed, you will waste memory, and you can't fully utilize the GPU with more concurrent tasks. By keeping as much relevant data on the GPU as possible, the system can service a massive number of concurrent requests.

Poor memory management can cause repeated OOM crashes under peak load. This will take GPUs out of the pool and cause cascading latency issues. Avoid OOMs using proper memory management. This will maximize utilization and maintain cluster stability.

In short, efficient memory management can improve effective throughput, reduce memory fragmentation, avoid unexpected OOM errors, and allow more concurrent in-flight requests—especially for high-throughput scenarios.

Quantization Approaches for Real-Time Inference

One of the most effective ways to increase inference performance is to reduce precision. This will instantly decrease memory usage and memory bandwidth utilization—and increase compute speed.

Quantization represents the model's weights—and sometimes the activations—with fewer bits. Modern NVIDIA GPUs support low-precision arithmetic natively using reduced-precision Tensor Cores for FP16, FP8, and FP4 formats, among others.

In this section, we discuss quantization techniques specifically for inference. This includes weight-only quantization methods like GPTQ (*https://oreil.ly/LBvIn*), AWQ (*https://oreil.ly/qLuI7*), SpQR, and other structured-sparsity-aware methods (*https://oreil.ly/olabX*)—as well as full precision reduction for weight and activation quantization. Specifically, GPTQ and AWQ have proven very effective in practice.

For many large models, 4-bit weight-only quantization with GPTQ can retain 99%+ of the accuracy of the FP16 model. And it provides ~2× inference speedups and a ~4× smaller model footprint. AWQ further improves accuracy on 3-4–bit quantization. These techniques are integrated into many AI frameworks, including Hugging Face Transformers, PyTorch, vLLM, and many others. They support loading GPTQ and AWQ quantized models directly.

> Quantization gains are workload-dependent. Do not assume that every reduced-precision path is faster. The realized benefit depends on hardware, kernel coverage, model architecture, sequence-length distribution, and batch-concurrency mix. Always validate each quantization path on your exact serving profile before promoting it to production.

Next, let's cover the trade-offs in accuracy and performance using reduced-precision formats. We'll also cover how to integrate quantization effectively and safely into a serving workflow.

Reducing Precision from FP16 to FP8 and FP4

Initially, LLM inference saw major gains by moving from FP32 to reduced-precision formats like TF32, FP16, or BF16. NVIDIA Tensor Cores, for instance, perform 2× the throughput when using FP16 versus FP32. It does this by fusing half-precision multiply-add operations into the specialized Tensor Core hardware pipelines that double the math performance—and without noticeable accuracy loss.

FP8 reduces precision even lower to 8-bit floating point. This reduces the memory footprint by half compared to FP16/BF16. And it doubles Tensor-Core math throughput again because the GPUs execute twice as many 8-bit multiply-adds per cycle versus 16-bit operations.

And while you can gain a moderate speedup in PyTorch by simply enabling TF32 math with `torch.set_float32_matmul_precision("high")`, you want to fully utilize the 8-bit and 4-bit precision support provided by NVIDIA's Transformer Engine (TE). The TE provides FP8 and FP4 kernels as a library (*https://oreil.ly/-DsQN*), which allows existing code to use these reduced precisions with minimal changes.

NVIDIA's TE automatically manages per-tensor scaling factors at these reduced precisions. At inference time, your inference server can load a model in FP16 but use FP8 matrix multiplies.

The TE applies scaling to each tensor to maintain numerical stability using a scaling factor that is typically chosen one of two ways: a fixed, ahead-of-time calibration step using representative data during training, called *static calibration*—or a dynamically computed value that tracks the tensor's maximum absolute value, called *amax-based dynamic scaling*. Figure 16-7 shows the TE's using range analysis, scaling factor, and target format for the precision conversion.

For more compression, the FP4 format reduces model weight storage and traffic better than FP8 does. Accounting for scaling metadata and packing, the effective reduction is commonly around 1.8× compared with FP8 and about 3.5× compared with FP16. However, because FP4's dynamic range is very limited, reliable inference at FP4 requires per-channel scaling—or other calibration such as NVIDIA's per-block *microscaling* supported in the GPU's TE. These techniques are needed to make FP4 usable for large networks by minimizing accuracy loss.

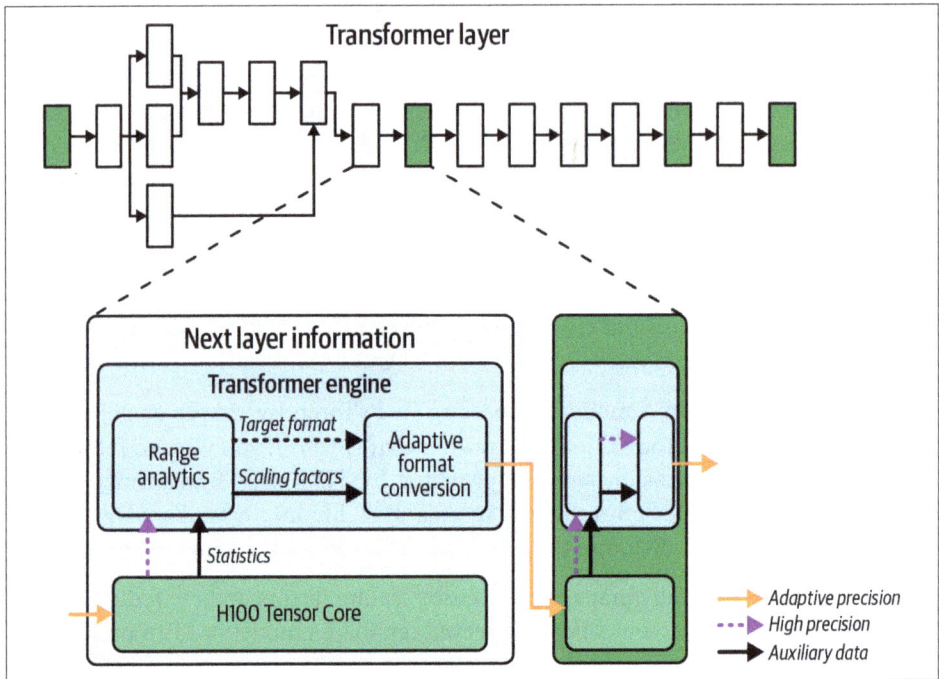

Figure 16-7. NVIDIA Transformer Engine (TE) using range analysis, scaling factor, and target format for the precision conversion on a transformer layer

Weight-Only Quantization (GPTQ, AWQ)

Weight-only quantization in modern LLM serving stacks typically compresses weights to 4-bit integers using methods like GPTQ or AWQ while keeping activations in higher precision such as FP8, FP16, or INT8. This reduces the weight memory footprint by roughly four times versus FP16 and halves or better the weight bandwidth, usually with minimal accuracy loss when properly calibrated.

NVIDIA's FP4 implementation (officially called *NVFP4* but referred to as just *FP4* in this text) uses block-wise microscaling in hardware. The NVIDIA TE provides the hardware support for NVFP4 microscaling at block granularity.

> Use per-tensor or per-channel scaling depending on the kernel. It's recommended to explore per-tensor scaling for activations and per-channel scaling for weights. For instance, when using FP8 E4M3 for KV cache quantization, it's common to use per-tensor scaling.

Per-block microscaling means that instead of using a single scaling factor for an entire tensor, it maintains a separate scale for each fixed-size block, typically 32 elements, within the tensor. These separate scales adapt to local value distributions to preserve range and reduce quantization errors compared to single-scale quantization.

> Always quantize with the calibration data that reflects your inference workload. A one-time calibration on a subset of your training data may not capture runtime usage patterns.

In practice, GPTQ (post-training quantization) and AWQ are commonly used for 4-bit weights on LLMs—often with negligible accuracy loss. Open source tools from Hugging Face and others can apply these techniques automatically.

The MoE expert structure makes weight quantization even more appealing since we can fit even more experts in memory using reduced-precision weights. As such, we can swap fewer experts to/from CPU memory. Additionally, we can use larger models with more active experts—and more expert replicas—if needed.

Post-training quantization (PTQ) tools like GPTQ apply an approximate second-order algorithm to quantize weights, layer-by-layer, down to 3–4 bits in a few GPU hours with almost no accuracy degradation. Newer GPTQ variants further refine this algorithm with asymmetric calibration and parallel computation. This reduces quantization error and extends efficient low-bit support to even larger models.

AWQ identifies a small fraction of "salient" weight channels. Salient channels produce large activation magnitudes that have a disproportionately large effect on model output.

AWQ preserves these channels using channel-specific scaling before casting all weights into 4-bit precision (e.g., INT4). NVIDIA's TE knows how to use the channel-specific scaling factors on the preserved channels to maintain model fidelity.

> Most AI frameworks like PyTorch and inference engines like vLLM and TensorRT-LLM natively support loading GPTQ-quantized and AWQ-quantized model checkpoints.

Activation Quantization

Quantizing activations along with weights can improve performance by using reduced precision for GEMM inputs—and potentially accumulators—using lower-precision values. This will reduce memory traffic for both attention-based KV cache and intermediate activations in MLP layers.

However, activation distributions can vary greatly with varying inputs. As such, activation quantization can sometimes be challenging without proper fine-tuning or calibration. A middle ground is INT8 activation with calibration. This comes from NVIDIA's INT8 mode, which uses per-tensor calibration and is used in TensorRT to choose scaling factors from activation histograms generated from a representative set of calibration data.

SmoothQuant, a training/calibration-free PTQ method for 8-bit activation quantization, can be used to shift some of the quantization error from activations to weights using a simple row/column scaling algorithm. This lets us use INT8 for both weights and activations with minimal fine-tuning—leading to full INT8 inference with low (e.g., < 1%) accuracy loss.

> Using SmoothQuant activation quantization before applying GPTQ/AWQ on weights has been shown to preserve accuracy better at low precision.

Post-Training Quantization Workflow

The quantization techniques described previously are applied post-training—as opposed to quantization-aware training, which is done during model training (aka *model pretraining*). The typical workflow is to train or fine-tune the model in FP16/FP32 and then run a post-training calibration script such as GPTQ or AWQ on a representative dataset to determine quantization parameters. Then you load the quantized model weights into the inference engine for serving.

If needed, you can also run a small fine-tuning job to recover any lost accuracy; however, this is typically not needed with the GPTQ and AWQ techniques. If you need full QAT, you can just run a few epochs of training with "fake quant" operations in the model graph to mimic low-precision math during evaluation. This will help you gauge expected accuracy at this precision.

> In practice, quantization-aware fine-tuning for LLMs is computationally expensive and not always feasible. However, smaller calibration datasets of 1,000 prompts, for instance, can be used with techniques like percentile clipping or LMS (loss-aware quantization) to fine-tune the quantization scales without full retraining.

It's worth noting that you should be extra careful to balance the trade-off between compression and model robustness. Quantization can amplify certain errors. For instance, if a model was barely at the threshold of some factual knowledge, quantization might push it to make an error.

Always validate on downstream tasks since PTQ makes assumptions that might miss subtle distribution shifts. As such, you should do extensive A/B testing of responses when using reduced-precision quantized models to make sure your evaluations show no regressions in quality or safety. If you see regressions, you should leave the model in higher precision—or try performing a light fine-tune in quantized form to restore performance.

Combining Weight and Activation Quantization

Activation quantization to 4-bit remains challenging. Combining low-precision weight quantization with higher-precision activation quantization often produces the best trade-off between memory savings, compute efficiency, and accuracy. As such, many production systems use weight-only 4-bit (e.g., GPTQ/AWQ) quantization combined with 8-bit activation quantization.

Specifically, in one W4A8 (8-bit activation) variant, the runtime unpacks INT4 weights, dequantizes to FP8 using learning or calibration scales, and executes the matrix multiply on FP8 Tensor Cores. This hybrid path is provided by inference engines like TensorRT-LLM and achieves near-lossless accuracy when properly calibrated. This preserves the full dynamic range of activations while reducing weight storage by 4× compared to FP16.

In contrast, the traditional INT4 and INT8 W4A8 scheme pairs 4-bit integer (INT4) weights with 8-bit integer (INT8) activations and runs the computations on INT8 Tensor Cores. This approach relies on histogram-based calibration to map activation ranges into INT8 without quality loss.

Although the INT4/INT8 kernels can deliver slightly higher raw throughput with modern integer Tensor Core pipelines, they require careful activation calibration and don't have as much dynamic range as FP8.

A hybrid INT4 and FP8 approach combines the best of both worlds. In the hybrid approach, 4-bit integer (INT4) weights are unpacked and reinterpreted as FP8 inputs. The computation is then executed on FP8 Tensor Cores. This INT4 and FP8 hybrid W4A8 variant delivers near-lossless accuracy, massive memory-bandwidth reductions, and excellent throughput on modern GPUs.

For modern GPUs, two distinct low-precision paths are common in production. First, NVFP4 workflows use FP4 blocks with microscaling managed by the Transformer Engine or TensorRT. Second, W4A8 workflows use INT4 weights with FP8 or INT8 activations executed using fused dequantization in TensorRT-LLM. Choose the path based on your model calibration and accuracy targets.

In summary, quantization is one of the best ways to reduce inference cost. By cutting model size 2× or more, you effectively double the throughput per GPU. The techniques mentioned previously, including GPTQ, AWQ, and SmoothQuant, help you achieve these gains with minimal accuracy loss (e.g., often < 1% decrease).

> It's recommended that you start with 8-bit weights and then evaluate 4-bit weight-only quantization for additional gains. Then you can move to W4A8 only if you need maximum optimization and can spend time on calibration.

The next step is to eliminate any conversion overhead. By fusing quantize-dequantize operations directly into the compute kernels, you preserve the gains from using quantization.

Fusing Quantization-Dequantization Steps into the Execution Graph

Modern inference engines use the TE to perform weight-packing and provide high-efficiency mixed-precision math computations without the explicit calibration overhead of using INT8. These inference engines typically implement CUDA/Triton kernels to manually fuse "quant-dequant" steps into the execution graph when needed.

These quant-dequant steps should be fused into the graph whenever separate Quantize/Dequantize kernels would introduce too many extra launches and negate the latency and bandwidth benefits of reduced-precision math. This is especially useful for inference backends that lack native fused INT8 support.

Fusing quant-dequant into the main compute kernels is especially valuable for high-throughput inference pipelines to restore performance by removing bottlenecks caused by the conversion. Next, let's explore various application-level optimizations supported by modern AI inference serving engines.

Application-Level Optimizations

Beyond the core model and system optimizations, there are several higher-level techniques that can significantly improve the performance and user experience of an LLM service. These methods operate at the application or inference-serving layer and improve how prompts are constructed and cached, how conversation history is preserved, how requests are routed to different models, etc.

These optimizations don't involve modifying model weights or deploying new hardware. They are algorithmic and system-level improvements at the application layer. They can produce significant gains in efficiency and usability for "free" essentially, as they incur very little cost.

In this section, we discuss a few such optimizations, including prompt compression, prefix caching and deduplication, fallback model routing, and streaming outputs. These strategies improve performance by reducing input size, avoiding redundant computations, providing graceful handling of different request types, and improving perceived latency for end users.

Prompt Compression

Users often send very long prompts or conversation histories to an LLM. However, not all of this context may be necessary for producing an adequate response. Prompt compression refers to a set of techniques that shorten or simplify the input prompt without losing relevant information.

Some system prompts or system-injected instructions are quite verbose ("You are ChatGPT, a friendly assistant designed to help users…"). Large system prompts will occupy a lot of space in the input context—and for every request.

Prompt compression reduces the amount of work that the model needs to do. It directly translates to cost savings because a shorter input means fewer GPU computations.

> Remember that the attention mechanism within a transformer-based LLM model is $O(n^2)$ time complexity, where n is the size of the input measured in number of tokens.

One simple form of prompt compression is removing redundant or irrelevant text. Consider a user prompt that contains a large chunk of text that is not relevant to answering their query. This can include a copy-pasted article in which the question relates to only one paragraph of the text. In this case, an upstream component could summarize or extract the relevant parts before feeding it to the LLM.

Another form of prompt compression is dialogue summarization or truncation. For long chat histories, for instance, early parts of the conversation might no longer be relevant. The system can intelligently trim the conversation by summarizing older parts into a condensed form.

> Many production chatbots like ChatGPT do prompt compression automatically to stay within their context-length limits—and to speed up overall processing. This is a must-have for long-running conversations.

To do this, you can run a small LLM—or a traditional rule-based system—to summarize the oldest parts of the conversation into a brief summary. Often the policy is something like: when the conversation exceeds 75% of the maximum context length, summarize the oldest 25% of messages. This summary would then be prepended to the more recent parts of the conversation. And this becomes the new prompt going forward.

When implementing prompt compression, make sure that no critical facts are lost. One approach is to have the model compress the prompt (e.g., generate a summary) and then verify the compressed prompt by asking the model questions about it. This way, your algorithm checks if key information was retained in the compressed version of the prompt.

This prevents excessive latency on very long chats and keeps the model focused on the most recent parts of the conversation. By truncating earlier turns, you reduce the effective prompt length N, which reduces prefill self-attention work from $N(N + 1) \div 2$ (roughly $O(N^2)$) to a smaller triangular cost for the shorter window. So while the cost approaches quadratic in the window size, the smaller N makes a significant difference for very long conversations.

A good summary can improve the response by filtering out irrelevant details. However, a bad summary can omit important parts of the input that the user really cares about. Summarizing is best when the system is confident—or if the conversation is clearly digressing.

Prompt Cleansing

Another technique is prompt cleansing. This is used to improve input formatting and tokenization. It helps reduce the amount of unnecessary whitespace or markup sent to the model. Tokenizers process every character, including spaces and newlines; the less unnecessary tokens we send, the better.

While tokenizers like OpenAI's tiktoken (*https://oreil.ly/4NdWc*) are very efficient with whitespace, large prompts with lots of markdown and HTML can bloat the token count. Simple preprocessing like removing HTML tags and converting fancy quotes to plain text can avoid odd tokenizations and reduce the number of tokens.

For instance, we can potentially reduce the amount of inference engine computations by not sending blank lines and repeated punctuation marks that don't impact the meaning of the input. This might save only a few tokens here and there, but it adds up across thousands of requests—especially for long input prompts.

In some cases, we can compress prompts by using references instead of the full content. For instance, if a user's prompt includes a long piece of text that our system has seen before—perhaps because they are referring to a document that we have previously stored—we could replace it with a reference like "file0".

The model could then be fine-tuned to retrieve the actual content for that reference—or we can handle it using a retrieval system. This crosses into retrieval-augmented generation (RAG) territory, which we won't cover any further here, but the key point is that we don't always need to feed the raw content through the model if there are alternative ways.

> Some inference engines support setting a system prompt once per session rather than sending it each time. This is a better solution than recompressing the system prompt for each request.

We'll discuss how to improve the efficiency of a large system prompt with prefix caching in the next section. But, for now, let's use prompt compression to create a shorter and functionally equivalent set of instructions. For instance, the model can be trained to use special tokens or metadata to represent a long system prompt. This way, it doesn't have to always process the long natural language version.

Consider a 200-token system prompt full of text-based rules that can be replaced with 10 special tokens that trigger the same text-based rules expressed in 200 tokens of natural language. This requires that the model be trained to parse the metadata, derive the rules, and follow them.

There's ongoing research into "config" tokens that tell the model to load a certain pre-configured set of instructions for a given config token. Think of this like assigning a unique ID for a given prompt prefix (e.g., system prompt). It's common to fine-tune a model to recognize tokens like <POLICY_A> as a stand-in replacement for a long, 500-word policy, for example.

> The Hugging Face Transformers library (*https://oreil.ly/s7Ebu*) implements the popular CTRL (*https://oreil.ly/QNBuk*) approach. This is a good place to start working with config tokens for prompt trimming.

Using special tokens and metadata to replace long system prompts is more of a training consideration. But it can provide a massive inference speedup if it reduces the size of the prompt and decreases prefill overhead. At scale, this directly translates to less compute needed per query—and more cost savings.

Prefix Caching

Often multiple requests to an LLM share a common *prefix* in their input, as many queries might start with the same system prompt. Instead of recomputing the model's output for the same prefix each time, you can compute it once and reuse the same KV cache for subsequent requests.

This technique is known as *prefix caching*, sometimes called prefix memoization. With prefix caching, the transformer's state, including the keys and values in the attention layers, is stored and reused when a request with the same prefix appears again.

> Prefix caching can substantially reduce repeated-prefill work by reusing cached prefix computations. Shared prefix work is done once, and each request then incurs the cost of computing its own uncached suffix.

vLLM implements prefix caching (`enable_prefix_caching=True`) to avoid recomputation. It first identifies if an incoming prompt's first N number of tokens match a prefix that's already in the cache from a previous request—or earlier in the same session. If so, vLLM avoids an expensive attention recomputation for those N tokens—and just copies data from the cached KV into the new context. Make sure you have prefix caching enabled—and with a sufficient memory allocation.

An inference engine like vLLM can automatically group incoming queries into microbatches to achieve high GPU utilization, amortize overheads across many requests, and keep latency low using continuous batching, for instance. Make sure that if you're not using an inference engine like vLLM directly, you look for ways to use prefix-sharing in your stack.

Prefix caching can speed up workloads with repeated prefixes. Consider a scenario in which we want to ask 10 separate questions from a long document. Each would include the document in the prompt followed by one question, such as, "[Long document text] Question 1: ...", "[Long document text] Question 2: ...", etc.

The document text is the same across all 10 prompts. Normally, the model would need to reprocess the KV entries for the whole document for each question. This would lead to 10× redundant work as the model will re-encode the long document 10 times. With prefix caching, it encodes it once, and each subsequent question incurs the compute only for the smaller question suffix.

Specifically, with prefix caching, the first query would compute the transformer states for the document portion, and for subsequent queries, the model can jump straight to processing the "Question 1: ...", "Question 2: ..." parts since the document's content matches a prefix found in the KV cache.

With prefix caching, your inference engine can produce near-linear speedups. For instance, if you ask 10 separate questions on one document, these will be processed roughly 10× faster with prefix caching than without because the long document's attention is calculated only once instead of 10 separate times.

Another application of prefix caching is chat sessions since the conversation history is a common prefix for each new "turn" in a "multiturn" chat session. When the end user sends a new message, the earlier messages form a prefix that keeps growing.

Optimized inference systems keep the KV cache from the last turn and compute KV only for the new user message. This is what most chat models like ChatGPT are doing if you don't reset the conversation in between turns.

> The benefits of prefix caching are most noticeable in interactive settings—especially if users follow up quickly in the same context/session. In this case, the second answer will come much faster than the first since the prefix (conversation history) is already cached.

In addition to supporting state in their ChatGPT consumer product, OpenAI supports stateful conversations in their API as well, which uses a form of prefix caching—among many other optimizations—behind the scenes. For stateless API invocations, prefix caching can achieve a similar effect if the client passes the conversation history. In this case, the server can retrieve the precomputed hidden state from the prefix cache—up to the last turn. It will then continue from there with the new user message.

To implement this yourself, you can hash the conversation histories. This will give you a consistent key to look up in the cache. However, you will have to manage memory carefully, as storing entire KV caches for many conversations can use GPU memory very quickly. vLLM's paging helps by paging inactive caches to CPU memory—or disk—and paging them back into GPU memory on a cache hit.

You can also deduplicate portions of a prompt across multiple requests—or even within a single request. Here, deduplication refers to combining identical subprompts to compute their transformer states just once. For instance, if two users send the exact same prompt prefix at nearly the same time, the system could merge the two prompts and process them only once.

This can also happen within a single request if the input has repeated sequences. This is more common in training, which uses techniques like memoized decoding to deduplicate repetitive text. In inference, it's rare to get long, repeated input sequences in the same request, but it is possible.

> If your workload has many repeat queries on the same prefixes, you should allocate more memory to the cache to maximize hits. Conversely, if prefixes are rarely reused, you should use a smaller cache —or even disable prefix caching entirely. Always measure prefix hit rates in production and tune accordingly.

The prefix cache is typically implemented as a token-sequence *trie* (pronounced "try"). A trie, often called a *prefix tree*, is a tree-based data structure in which each edge represents a single token and each node encodes the sequence of tokens from the root to that point.

In a token-sequence trie, every observed prompt prefix is stored as its own path of tokens. This enables fast lookups of shared prefixes. When a new request arrives, the inference engine traverses the trie—token by token—from the root until it can no longer match the next token. The sequence of matching tokens lands at the node that completes the longest-cached prefix, as shown in Figure 16-8 for an example system prompt, "You are ChatGPT, a friendly assistant designed to help users..."

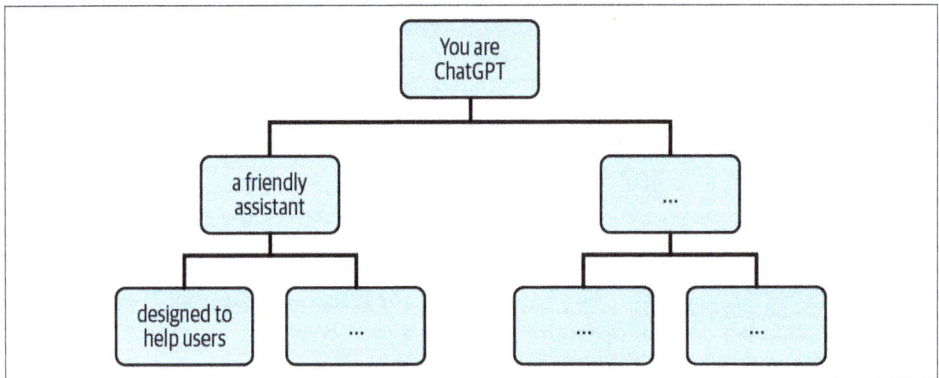

Figure 16-8. Prefix cache implemented as a trie data structure

At this point, the system reuses the shared KV cache data (clones the pointers) and resumes decoding but only for the remaining tokens in the sequence. This avoids redundant self-attention computations for the already-cached prefix since the attention scores for this prefix have already been computed.

SGLang's RadixAttention uses a compressed trie, or radix tree, over entire token sequences. This type of prefix cache collapses token sequences into single edges in the tree to save space. Each node in the tree points to a KV-cache tensor stored as a contiguous GPU page that holds the prefix's KV cache.

The RadixTree data structure is space efficient and provides rapid prefix searches, efficient insertions, and LRU-style eviction. Here is pseudocode that shows a KV cache lookup using a radix tree during token generation:

```
# Simplified RadixAttention KV cache example
# radix_attention_example.py

radix: RadixTree = RadixTree()  # holds edge labels + node.cache pointers

def generate_with_radix(prompt_tokens: List[int]):
    # 1) Find longest cached prefix
```

```
node, prefix_len = radix.longest_prefix(prompt_tokens)
# shallow-clone the KV cache for that prefix
model_state = ModelState.from_cache(node.cache)  # refcount bump

# 2) Process remaining prompt suffix
for token in prompt_tokens[prefix_len:]:
    model_state = model.forward(token, state=model_state)

# 3) As we go, insert or split edges in the radix tree
    matched = prompt_tokens[:prefix_len + 1]
    # insert returns the node for this full prefix
    node = radix.insert(matched, cache=model_state.kv_cache)

    prefix_len += 1

# 4) Now generate new tokens autoregressively
output_tokens = []
while not model_state.is_finished():
    token, model_state = model.generate_next(model_state)
    output_tokens.append(token)

    # cache each generated prefix as well
    matched = prompt_tokens + output_tokens
    node = radix.insert(matched, cache=model_state.kv_cache)

return output_tokens
```

When generation begins, the engine calls `radix.longest_prefix(prompt_tokens)` to walk multitoken edges down the radix tree until it reaches the deepest node matching the prompt's longest cached prefix. It then does a lightweight clone of that node's KV cache page using `ModelState.from_cache(node.cache)`. This seeds `model_state` without recomputing any self-attention for the cached prefix.

Next, it processes only the unseen suffix of the prompt—token by token—and updates the radix tree on the fly. For each new token, it calls `radix.insert(...)`, splits edges, or creates new ones as needed. It then stores the intermediate `model_state.kv_cache` at each new node.

Once the entire prompt has been consumed, the loop switches to the autoregressive decoding phase, which generates new tokens with `model.generate_next(model_state)`. Similarly, this inserts each generated prefix into the radix tree. This approach minimizes redundant computations, uses space-efficient storage of KV pages, and performs fast prefix lookups—all while supporting incremental cache updates.

SGLang's KV cache design automatically captures all common reuse patterns, including multiturn chats, few-shot examples, and branching logic. At the same time, it makes sure that shared prefixes are fetched as large, coalesced memory chunks for efficient GPU access.

Knowing when to invalidate the cache is always a challenge. If the cache memory is needed for other things, you may need to evict some prefixes. Caching systems support different policies, such as "least recently used" (LRU), in which the least recently used prefix gets evicted first. SGLang's RadixAttention, for instance, will lazily evict the least recently used radix-tree leaf when GPU memory is scarce, as shown in Figure 16-9.

This is a prefix cache tree structure—and LRU eviction policy—used by SGLang for multiple incoming requests. This example is based on an awesome SGLang blog post (*https://oreil.ly/7LBoC*) from LMSys.

Here, there are two chat sessions and multiple queries across those chat sessions. The label of each is a sequence of tokens (e.g., substring). Green nodes represent new nodes in the tree. Blue nodes are cached nodes that are currently being accessed. Red nodes have been evicted. Here is the breakdown of each step:

1. The initial empty radix tree is empty.

2. The server processes the incoming prompt "Hello!" and responds with the LLM-generated "Hi!" With this simple response, many tokens are added to the tree as a single edge. This edge is linked to a new node in green. Specifically, the system prompt, "You are a helpful assistant"; the user message, "Hello!"; and the LLM response, "Hi!" are consolidated.

3. The server receives a new prompt. This is the first turn of the multiturn conversation. The server successfully looks up the prompt prefix in the tree and reuses its KV cache data. A new turn is added to the tree as a new green node.

4. A new chat session begins, and node b from step 3 is split into two separate nodes. This lets the two chat sessions share the system prompt.

5. The second chat session from step 4 continues. Memory is limited, however, so node c from step 4 must be evicted, and it's shown in red. A new turn is appended after node d in step 4.

6. The server receives a new prompt (query). After processing, the server inserts the prompt into the tree. This requires the root node to split because this new prompt does not share any prefix with existing prompts/nodes.

7. The server receives a batch with more prompts (queries). These prompts share prefixes with the prompt from step 6. As such, the system splits node e from step 6 and shares the prefix.

8. The server receives a new message from the conversation in step 3 (the first chat session). In this case, it evicts all nodes from the second chat session in step 5 (e.g., nodes g and h). This is because they are the least recently used (LRU) at that moment.

9. The server receives a message requesting more answers for the query in node j from step 8. Due to memory limitations, the system is required to evict nodes i, k, and l from step 8.

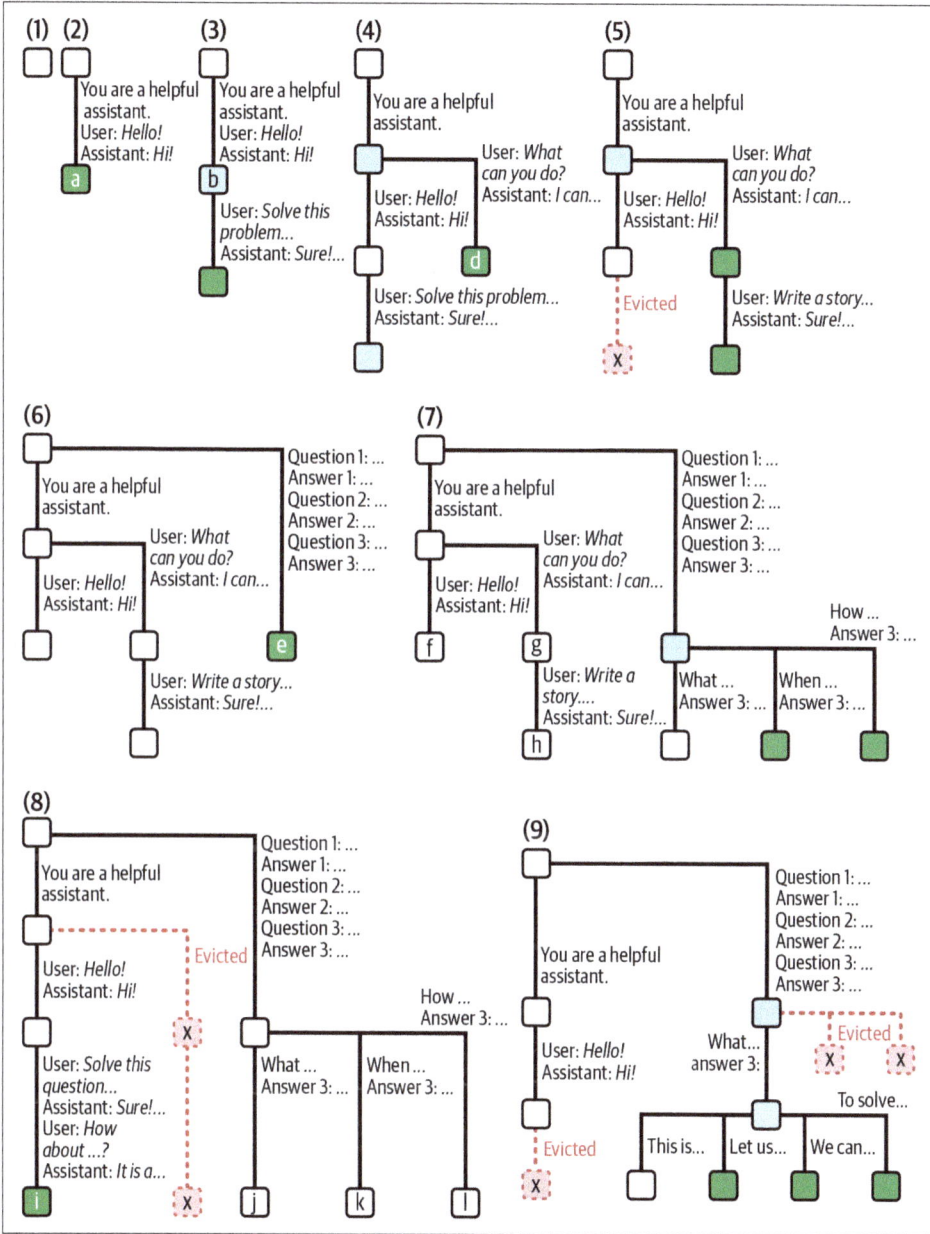

Figure 16-9. SGLang RadixAttention prefix-cache tree with LRU eviction across multiple incoming requests (adapted from SGLang blog post from LMSys (https://oreil.ly/7LBoC))

This example demonstrates how prefixes are shared between multiple requests. In addition, it shows how an LRU cache-eviction policy works in the context of prefix caching. Next, let's turn to using a cascading model deployment pattern to better utilize GPU resources.

Model Cascading and Tiered Model Deployment

Not all queries require the power (and cost) of the largest, state-of-the-art models. Some user requests are simple enough to be answered by a much smaller, faster, and cheaper model. Choosing the right model is called *model cascading* or *fallback model routing*.

To implement model cascading, you can use tiered model deployment. This is an approach that maintains multiple models of different sizes and abilities. For each incoming request, we dynamically choose which model to use based on query complexity, required precision, or current system load.

Consider a question-answer (QA) inference deployment with both a large 700-billion-parameter state-of-the-art model and a smaller 70-billion-parameter model that is faster and cheaper to host since it requires fewer GPU resources. If a user asks a very straightforward and factual question (as determined by a classifier or heuristic), the 70-billion-parameter model might handle it well.

For straightforward questions, you can route the query to the smaller model, which will respond in 50 ms instead of 500 ms with the 700-billion-parameter model. If the small model's answer is deemed unsatisfactory due to low confidence (determined by the logits returned in the response), the system can route the question to the bigger model.

This two-stage approach can reduce overall average latency and compute usage—although individual requests may experience longer latencies if they're routed to both models due to lack of confidence in the small model's initial response. It's widely believed that many commercial AI services, such as ChatGPT, use this approach of routing simpler queries to smaller, faster models to reduce cost and latency.

In practice, routing, say, 60% of queries to a 10× smaller model can cut your inference compute costs significantly—potentially a 5× overall cost reduction if designed and tuned properly. This is because the expensive model is used only when needed.

> Maintaining multiple models and a routing system is an engineering overhead, as you need to monitor not just one model's performance but also the second model, the interplay between the two models, and the routing system. Pursue this only if your traffic volume and cost structure make it worthwhile.

Implementing model cascading requires a query classifier or heuristic mechanism to assist the model-routing decision. And this is a relatively difficult problem to solve correctly, as the mechanism often requires continuous adaptation, comprehensive heuristics, and constant router tuning. As such, many organizations still rely on heuristic and rule-based routers using offline analysis to update the decision criteria.

One approach is to consider this a speculative problem, similar to speculative decoding described earlier. You can first run the smaller model in a draft mode and have it generate the answer with its confidence score. If confidence is high, just return the response. If not, call the bigger model.

Make sure that if the big model is needed, the additional latency of the small model doesn't make the user wait too long. In practice, you might run the small and large models in parallel when you suspect that the question is hard. This overlaps the small model's latency with the large model. This seems wasteful and counterintuitive, but it can be beneficial for some latency-sensitive use cases to keep latency low—at the expense of additional compute.

Another approach is to train a separate classifier for well-known user queries ahead of time. For instance, you can classify complexity and ask, "Does this question require the big model's extensive knowledge or reasoning?" If not, use the small model.

It's important to note that this classifier will itself need periodic retraining as user queries evolve over time. Also, it introduces another component that can degrade and fail—and therefore needs to be monitored. Make sure this model is lightweight, fast, and robust—otherwise it becomes a new bottleneck in your inference system.

It's common to use a simple heuristic initially. For instance, if the user's query is short and factual, such as "What's the weather today?" or "Who is president of X?", you can just use the smaller model. For longer prompts (e.g., > 50 tokens) or more creative queries that contain words like *explain*, *analyze*, or *elaborate*, you can just send it to the big LLM directly and bypass the smaller model.

You should log and tag every request with which model handled it (e.g., "small" versus "large")—and whether it fell back. This lets you break down latency, accuracy, and fallback counts by model.

This tagging data also lets you monitor the dispatchers' decisions. By counting the number of times when the small model's answer was rejected, you can identify patterns that may lead to retraining the smaller model or improving the routers' heuristics.

Conversely, if the small model handles many queries well, you can use this information to raise its confidence threshold. This will increase the small model's usage, reduce response latency, and improve the end user experience.

You can also route based on capacity. If the big model cluster is at maximum load, rather than queue requests and increase latency, we might temporarily route less critical requests to a smaller model, which might not be as good but still gives some answer quickly. This is a form of graceful degradation under heavy load. The user might notice a quality dip, but it's better than timing out or waiting excessively.

Many AI services do this intentionally. For example, during peak loads, free-tier users might silently get routed to a smaller model to free up the larger model for premium-tier (paid) users. This is a realistic trade-off when resources are constrained.

> We will cover more advanced dynamic and adaptive inference server capabilities in Chapters 17–19. These features depend heavily on the current system load, including available GPU memory, memory bandwidth utilization, KV cache utilization, etc.

Another form of model cascading is based on the content itself. For instance, if a user asks something that the LLM refuses to answer due to safety, some inference systems will fall back to a special model fine-tuned specifically to handle unsafe prompts—or even to a retrieval system.

This is more about content policy than performance, but it's still an important consideration for your model-routing logic. And often the fallback model is much smaller, so this actually ends up being a performance win since it handles the unsafe request quickly—and frees up the main model to handle the safe queries.

From a deployment perspective, multimodel setups require careful scaling since each model needs enough instances to handle its portion of traffic. Sometimes one model might become a bottleneck if many simple queries come in, for instance, and the small LLM is saturated while the big model sits idle.

You can autoscale and run more or fewer instances of the small model during certain times of day—or even dynamically shift GPUs from the large model pool to the small model pool as needed using container orchestration.

Streaming Responses

To improve the "perceived" performance of your inference system, you should stream the output tokens as they are generated. This is much better than forcing an end user to wait for the full completion to finish before they see a response. This way, users can begin reading and processing information as it arrives. This can make the effective interaction much faster—even if total time is the same.

Humans can read anywhere from 200 to 300 words per minute, which translates to approximately 4–7 tokens per second—or up to 13 tokens per second for faster readers. Maintaining this pace of streaming response is ideal. Given that every performance decision comes down to trade-offs, this is an important metric to consider when making optimization choices, planning capacity, etc.

It's important to monitor your system's token throughput against this human reading rate. For instance, if you find your system is streaming at only 2 tokens/sec due to model latency, that's a sign to optimize further.

Streaming is supported by most modern inference engines, including vLLM, SGLang, and NVIDIA Dynamo. When you enable streaming, the server flushes tokens to the client using WebSockets, Server-Sent Events (SSEs), the HTTP Streaming protocol, etc. And it should do this immediately when the tokens are generated to meet the 4–13 tokens-per-second human-reading metric mentioned earlier.

The model effectively generates one token at a time—except when using speculative or multitoken decoding techniques like EAGLE or Medusa, respectively. As such, the system needs to group those generated tokens into batches of 2–5 tokens, flush the stream, and send the batched tokens back to the end user.

It's important not to accumulate too many tokens in a batch before flushing, or you defeat the purpose of streaming. On the other hand, sending one token per packet may be inefficient due to overhead. Often frameworks flush on every newline or end-of-sentence token.

For example, if an answer is 100 tokens and takes 5 seconds to fully generate, with streaming, the first batch of tokens would arrive after 0.25 seconds if the batches are 5 tokens each (5 tokens ÷ 20 tokens per second = 0.25 seconds). This would be followed by a steady stream of token batches until the response is complete. This way, the user can start reading after just 0.25 seconds.

Without streaming, the user would stare at a blank screen for 5 seconds, then suddenly see the whole answer shown all at once, which is not ideal. This could lead to rage clicking and other forms of user frustration.

From a performance standpoint, streaming imposes a slight overhead due to additional, small network packets being sent instead of one big message. But this overhead is usually negligible compared to the model's computation time—and compared to the improved end-user experience. Using HTTP/2 and persistent connections helps reduce overhead by sending tokens as a continuous stream without needing to reestablish connections.

Be mindful of Nagle's algorithm and delayed acknowledgments. The interaction can add tens of milliseconds of delay and, on some stacks, up to roughly 200 ms in worst-case settings. Use `TCP_NODE LAY` and, where available, quick-ack or reduced delayed-ack timers to minimize token flush latency. These help reduce token-send latency, which is critical for real-time streaming. The downside is more small packets fill the pipe—and bandwidth efficiency is reduced. But keep this in mind when tuning for ultralow latency.

It's important to properly manage flow control such that if the client is slow to consume the stream due to network issues, for instance, you don't want to block the model's generation. Ideally, the inference engine will continue generating the whole response—even if the client falls behind consuming the stream.

The system should use separate threads and CUDA streams to send the data back to the end user. This way, the main token generation loop isn't interrupted by issues while sending the response.

The inference engine maintains a bounded buffer to manage flow control and prevent unbounded memory growth. This can happen if a client stalls or disconnects. It's important to handle these types of edge case scenarios as they are fairly common in production scenarios. In practice, you might allow up to 50–100 tokens to accumulate.

Beyond a certain limit, the inference engine can either pause generation or close the connection completely. This way, if a client drops mid-generation—or simply can't keep up due to a slow connection—the engine can stop producing tokens and free those resources to handle other requests.

Choosing the buffer limit involves balancing memory use and user experience. This is rarely an issue for short responses, but it is somewhat common for very large responses—especially for slower consumer connections.

Another trick to improve flow control is to use token pooling. If the model generates tokens faster than needed for streaming, the system can intentionally add a delay to smooth out the rate of generation. For instance, if the model bursts out 20 tokens in 0.5 seconds because it was a simple part of the response, for instance, sending them all at once can display a big chunk and then pause for the next part.

You may prefer your application's UI to use a steadier typewriter effect. In this case, you can introduce an artificial stream delay like 50 ms between token sends. This doesn't affect actual latency much, and it improves the UX by avoiding janky bursts of tokens.

You can make the token-pooling delay configurable to adapt to different UXs for different types of users (e.g., paid users, free users, etc.). Paid users can stream faster, while free users will be throttled a bit. This can help manage load with limited resources.

Streaming responses also allow end users to start evaluating the intermediate results and take action before the response completes. For instance, if the user sees the first part of the answer and realizes it's not going in the direction they want, they can stop the generation using a Stop or Interrupt button.

This saves unnecessary compute and improves the UX as the end user doesn't have to wait for a bad completion to finish before they provide their feedback. You should monitor—or at least measure—early stops.

Too many explicit stops might indicate an issue with the model's relevance. If you see many users stopping at a certain point, it might indicate the model often goes off-track or is too verbose beyond that length. This could inform you that the model needs additional fine-tuning to make it more concise. Or you can make adjustments to the maximum tokens generated and sent to the end user.

Or the early stops could be caused by a frustrated "rage click" type of user who changes their mind frequently. Either way, it's best to allow the user to interrupt the token-generation process. This lets the inference cluster reclaim the resources to handle other requests.

In short, streaming is a must-have for a responsive LLM service. It doesn't increase raw throughput—if anything, it adds a slight overhead, but it improves the user-perceived speed of the system. Streaming responses should be implemented carefully to not interfere with generation. Different threads and CUDA streams should handle sending responses back to the end user so that the main token generation loop isn't stalled on flakey end-user network connections.

> It's recommended that you continuously profile your end-to-end latency with streaming enabled versus disabled in a test environment. Make sure that token emission is evenly spaced—and that no significant bottlenecks like lock contention or I/O waits are introduced. Tools like Locust (*https://locust.io*) are Python friendly and can simulate clients. This lets you test your low-latency streaming workloads at scale.

Debouncing and Request Coalescing

Many production systems also implement UX features called *debouncing* and *request coalescing*. By debouncing, or pausing, before responding, the system can recognize if a user sends multiple requests in quick succession—either by accident or from rage clicking, as shown in Figure 16-10.

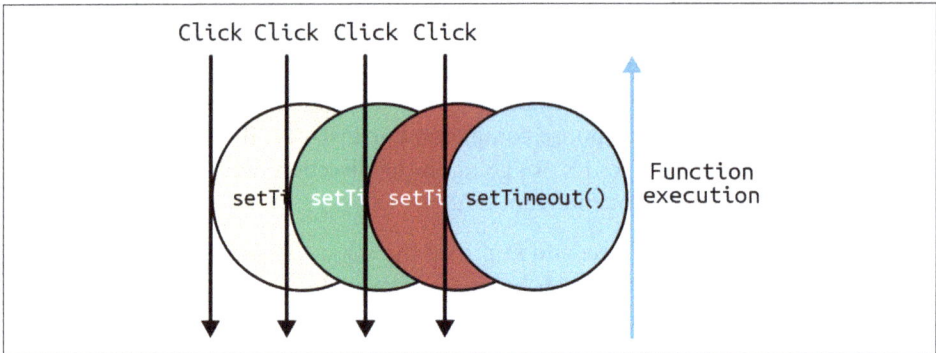

Figure 16-10. Debouncing pauses a bit before performing an action

In this case, the system can either coalesce the multiple queries into one query or drop all but the latest query. These types of application-level guardrails help reduce excessive, repeated, wasteful load on the backend.

For example, if a user double-clicks Submit or sends two very similar queries within a second, the system can drop the duplicate. Rage clickers impatiently resubmit multiple times when they are frustrated—often because of the application's poor response time.

Ironically, debouncing and request coalescing can create more latency, frustrate the "rage" user segment even more, and cause them to click even more! In this case, it's helpful if the UI disables the input while a request is in flight. This can prevent double-clicking at the UI level. But it's also good to have server-side protection in place, as well.

> Modern inference load balancers support a debouncing interval. Use a modest interval (e.g., 2–5 ms), and find a good trade-off between batching efficiency and added latency. And next time you submit something in ChatGPT, notice the debouncing delay. It's a bit annoying now that you know about it, isn't it?!

Token Output Limits and Timeouts

Because response token counts directly influence latency, you can implement output length limits or timeouts. This kind of application-layer constraint can prevent runaway generations in which the model keeps generating beyond a reasonable number of tokens.

Token output limits and timeouts help maintain consistent latencies. They also prevent malicious and accidental prompts from causing extremely long generations that could tie up GPU resources. Many public APIs set strict output limits for exactly this reason. It's both an abuse prevention mechanism as well as a performance safeguard.

Always set server-side timeouts, as well. For example, if a generation exceeds 30 seconds, return a partial result or an apology. Users expect quick failures rather than a hanging response.

> Also monitor if your model tends to ramble. Applying a moderate token limit, perhaps 4,096 tokens for a chat answer, can actually improve quality by keeping the model on track and avoiding long answers.

It's important to choose these limits and timeouts based on user needs. These limits keep latency predictable and also cap the worst-case compute scenario. This helps with capacity planning, etc.

In summary, the combination of input optimizations (e.g., compression and cleansing), caching, smart routing, and UX optimizations (e.g., streaming data) can reduce the workload, reduce the size of the inference cluster, save cost, and improve user satisfaction. These application-level strategies complement the low-level optimizations from earlier sections—rounding out the holistic approach to improving LLM serving performance.

Key Takeaways

The techniques in this chapter show that efficient LLM serving is a holistic engineering effort that combines modern GPU hardware, novel software optimizations, and comprehensive monitoring. Profiling tools identify the bottlenecks. Systematic debugging techniques fix the issues. Here are some key takeaways from this chapter:

Comprehensive profiling
    Perform end-to-end profiling across the inference stack. By measuring latency and resource usage at each stage using profilers, engineers can pinpoint slowdowns and inefficiencies. This data-driven approach guides targeted optimizations to eliminate bottlenecks.

Monitoring and observability
    Implement robust monitoring for deployed inference services. Track key metrics such as latency percentiles, throughput, GPU utilization, and memory usage in real time to detect regressions or resource saturation early. Use logging and tracing to get visibility into per-request processing and identify hotspots or anomalies in a large-scale workload.

Debugging and iterative tuning

By adopting a systematic debugging workflow, you can resolve performance and correctness issues quickly—even across tens of thousands of nodes. This way, when an unexpected spike occurs (e.g., decrease in throughput or increase in latency), you can easily drill down from the high-level symptom to the low-level issue.

Validating optimizations with metrics

Tools such as GPU debuggers, memory leak detectors, and performance-related unit tests help verify that optimizations like quantization and kernel fusion do not introduce silent performance and correctness errors. This iterative tune-and-test cycle is essential for maintaining high performance and reliability with each new optimization released into production.

Efficiency and cost optimization

Focus on improvements that make inference more cost-effective. Every optimization that increases throughput and utilization will directly improve the cost-per-query. By profiling and refining the system, teams can serve more requests with fewer GPUs. This leads to significant savings in infrastructure costs and power efficiency.

Conclusion

Profiling, debugging, and full-stack system tuning are critical for maintaining efficient, reliable, and cost-effective LLM inference at scale. As model sizes grow toward multi-trillion parameters, production clusters are scaling toward hundreds of thousands and even millions of GPUs per deployment. Continued codesign of software and hardware remains essential at this scale. It's no longer enough to rely on just hardware to increase performance—especially as power is becoming a limiting factor. Both the software and hardware need to be codesigned and continuously tuned together—and at every layer in the stack.

An optimized inference infrastructure provides fast response times for end users, predictable and stable system behavior, and low operational costs. Only then can you deliver inference systems that serve the largest and most powerful models in the world.

In the next chapters, we will dive deep to understand and optimize the most compute, memory, and network intensive parts of modern LLM inference systems: calculating (prefilling) the KV cache, sharing it with all workers in cluster, and using it to generate (decode) new tokens.

## CHAPTER 17

Scaling Disaggregated Prefill and Decode for Inference

As mentioned in an earlier chapter, LLM inference can be divided into two distinct phases: the prefill phase and the decode phase. The prefill phase processes the input prompt to produce the model's internal key-value (KV) cache for that prompt, while the decode phase generates output tokens one by one—or a few at a time, in the case of speculative decoding—using those cached values.

These two phases have fundamentally different performance characteristics. The prefill phase is compute bound, involves heavy matrix multiplications over potentially thousands of tokens in parallel, and consumes a significant amount of FLOPS. In contrast, the decode phase is memory I/O bound, reads the large KV cache for each token generation, writes new values, and stresses memory bandwidth. In simpler terms, prefill is a high-throughput, parallel workload, whereas decode is a sequential, latency-sensitive workload.

Early LLM serving systems treated the two phases as one monolithic pipeline on the same hardware. As such, they typically favored the prefill phase by prioritizing throughput using request batching. However, as interactive applications grew, latency metrics like time to first token (TTFT, or prefill latency for all tokens) and time per output token (TPOT, or decode latency per token) became as important as raw throughput. It's difficult for a single GPU-based inference engine to optimize both TTFT and TPOT simultaneously when serving both phases together.

Batching many requests will improve throughput but will worsen TTFT since every request waits for the slowest prefill. It will also impact TPOT since the decode steps will get backlogged behind new-prompt prefills.

Monolithic inference systems must choose between improving (reducing) time to first token at the cost of slower subsequent token generation—or improving (increasing) per-token throughput while subjecting new requests to high initial latency. In extreme cases, one long prompt can completely tie up the GPU, which would block all other prompt prefill work for other users. And then, once decoding begins, the one-token-at-a-time processing would leave the GPU's cores idle between each token generation.

To address these issues, researchers and engineers looked for ways to decouple the two phases. The key insight is that prefill and decode do not actually need to run on the same hardware—or even the same type of hardware.

Disaggregating the prefill and decode phases means assigning them to different resources that are each specialized for the needs of that specific phase. This idea was pioneered by systems in a paper on DistServe (*https://oreil.ly/mgbd9*), which demonstrated that by eliminating interference between the phases, one can meet strict latency requirements for both TTFT and TPOT simultaneously.

DistServe's evaluation showed the potential for serving 7.4× more requests within strict latency service-level objectives (SLOs) compared to a state-of-the-art baseline without prefill/decode disaggregation. As such, industry frameworks began to experiment with separate prefill and decode servers.

The open source vLLM library introduced disaggregated operation in conjunction with LMCache and other components. NVIDIA's Dynamo implements disaggregated prefill and decode with dynamic routing and autoscaling and publicly documents operational details. Many providers and open frameworks implement or evaluate disaggregation. For instance, to meet strict latency SLOs, industry-scale serving systems from OpenAI, Meta, and xAI have reportedly adopted this disaggregated approach. As such, disaggregated prefill and decode is standard practice for LLM inference at scale.

At ultrascale, large inference deployments can involve hundreds of thousands or even millions of GPUs serving billions of requests. In these environments, the cost and performance benefits of disaggregation are massive.

By splitting the workload, you can optimize each phase in isolation and avoid one of them becoming the bottleneck for the other. The remainder of this chapter explores how to design and operate a disaggregated prefill/decode inference system at extreme scale.

In this chapter, we will explore scheduling algorithms to route requests between prefill and decode workers, techniques to maintain quality of service (QoS) under heavy load, and mechanisms that make this separation efficient. We'll explore everything from high-speed interconnects to specialized decoding kernels. We will also discuss heterogeneous hardware strategies that use different GPU types for each phase.

Why Prefill-Decode Disaggregation?

Modern interactive LLM services often target TTFT latency < 200–300 ms for p99 (99% of requests). This is nearly impossible to guarantee without separating the prefill work since a one-size-fits-all approach to LLM serving leaves significant performance on the table.

For context, the MLPerf v5.0's (2025) inference benchmark (*https://oreil.ly/X0yPD*) for Llama2 70B (70 billion parameters) aimed for p99 (99th percentile) SLOs of ~450 ms TTFT and 40 ms TPOT latency. For Llama 3.1 405B (405 billion parameters), the benchmark aimed for ~6 seconds TTFT and 175 ms for TPOT. Specifically, these SLOs reflect p99 TTFT and p99 TPOT targets for Llama 2 Chat 70B and Llama 3.1 405B Instruct.

Consider a scenario in which one user's request has an extremely long prompt on the order of many thousands of tokens—and another user's request has a very short prompt. Without disaggregated prefill and decode, if these requests arrive around the same time, the long prompt's prefill computation will block the GPU for an extended period.

Without disaggregation, the second request with the short prompt needs to wait an unnecessarily long time before even starting their decode. This is called *interference* since the prefill work for one request delays the decode work of another. Interference between prefill and decode is shown in Figure 17-1 in the context of continuous batching.

Under a simple FIFO scheduling strategy, long prompts can amplify tail latency for everyone. In general, long or compute-heavy prefills at the front of the queue will block shorter, lighter requests behind them. This is called *head-of-line blocking*, and it leads to poor utilization, latency outliers, and unhappy end users.

In a flexible disaggregated architecture, it's possible to send a large prompt prefill to the dedicated pool of compute-optimized prefill workers, while a lightweight prompt prefill can be sent to the decode workers directly—bypassing the prefill workers. This type of flexibility allows shorter tokens to not suffer from head-of-line blocking. This maximizes overall throughput and minimizes latency tail effects.

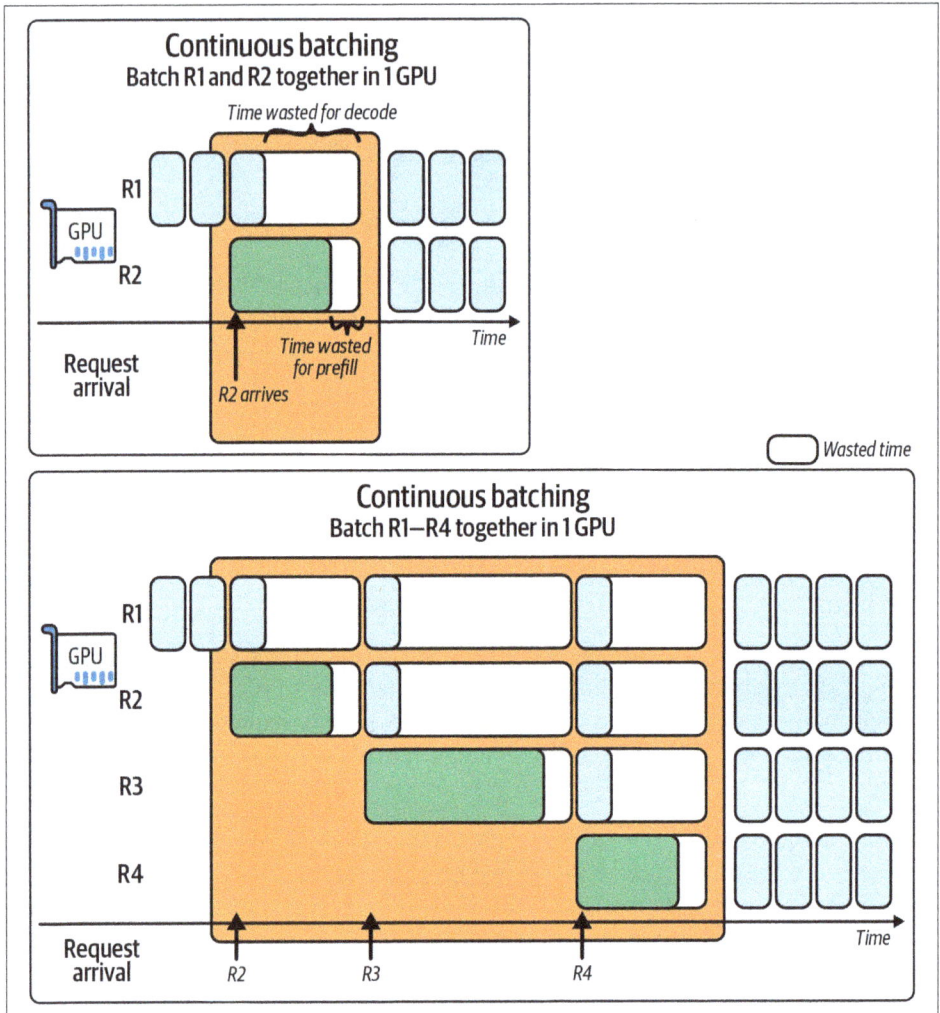

Figure 17-1. Interference caused by colocated prefill and decode running on the same GPU (source: https://oreil.ly/GRkHs)

Advantages of Disaggregation

Disaggregation has two primary advantages: reduced interference and phase-specific optimizations. Let's discuss each of these next.

Reduced interference

With disaggregation, prefill tasks no longer contend with decode tasks on the same device. A busy decode worker, generating many tokens, won't prevent another user's prompt from being processed, and vice versa.

Dedicated resources for each stage mean a long prompt's computation won't block another user's token generation. In practice, this produces more predictable latency. Figure 17-2 shows the comparison between colocated and disaggregated prefill and decode. This experiment is described in more detail in the DistServe paper and subsequent blog post (*https://oreil.ly/GRkHs*) by the authors.

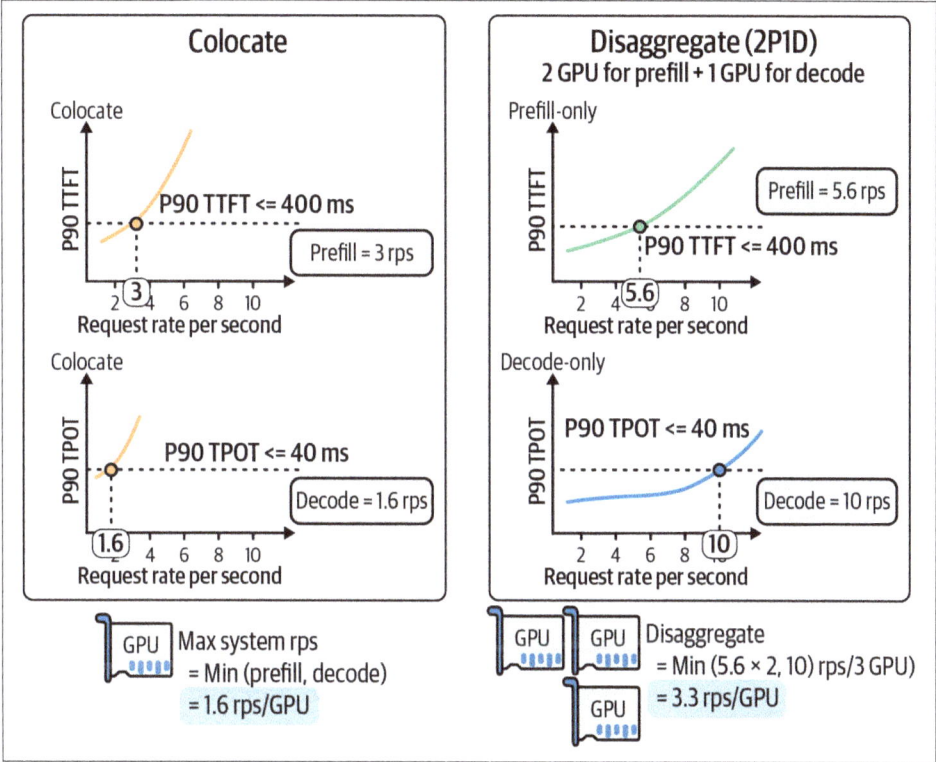

Figure 17-2. Comparison between colocated and disaggregated prefill and decode (source: https://oreil.ly/GRkHs)

Here, the SLO is set to 0.4 seconds for P90 TTFT and 0.04 seconds for P90 TPOT (e.g., horizontal line in Figure 17-2). The colocated system can support only ~3 requests per second (RPS) of goodput within the given TTFT latency bounds. And it can sustain only 1.6 RPS within the given TPOT latency bounds. As such, the goodput of the colocated configuration is only 1.6 RPS since both the TTFT and TPOT latency SLOs need to be met.

After disaggregating the two stages and assigning two prefill workers (two GPUs) and a single decode worker (one GPU), called a *2P1D configuration*, both the prefill and decode workers achieve better overall RPS than the colocated configuration with a single GPU. Specifically, the prefill worker reaches ~5.6 RPS and the decode worker achieves ~10 RPS spread across the three GPUs. As such, the goodput for the 2P1D configuration is 3.3 RPS per GPU.

The 3.3 RPS per GPU is calculated by taking the minimum of the RPS of the prefill workers (5.6 RPS × 2 = 11.2 RPS) and the decode worker (10 RPS). This is 10 RPS total across all three GPUs. As such, we have to divide the RPS by the number of GPUs, or 3 in this case. Under the configured SLOs, this system's goodput result is 10 RPS ÷ 3 GPUs = 3.3 RPS per GPU.

> In this comparison, the decode side improvements primarily impact per-token latency. Meanwhile, prefill isolation primarily improves time to first token. Both SLOs must be satisfied to count as goodput.

This isolation can also improve tail latencies as well. Empirically, systems that disaggregate show tighter latency distributions—and avoid the long tails seen in monolithic systems. By eliminating cross-phase interference, each phase meets its SLO more reliably—and with more predictable consistency.

Now, you should also be asking, "Is the 3× cost worth the 2× improvement?" And you would be right to ask that. Additional tuning is required to make this solution more cost-effective, but it shows the right direction to tighten latency distributions and improve goodput. You need to decide based on your workload. Disaggregation is a popular option to meet goodput RPS needs.

Phase-specific optimizations

Phase-specific optimizations let each phase use the hardware and parallelism that suits it best. The prefill phase, for instance, is compute bound. As such, you'd typically increase tensor parallelism to drive peak FLOPS on a high-FLOPS GPU. Additionally, modern GPUs provide lower precision modes (FP8 and FP4) that can increase throughput for the compute-heavy prefill phase.

> You should prefer FP4 for weights and, where validated, activations, as well. Many stacks use FP4 for weights and FP8 for activations. These reduced precisions help to maximize throughput and minimize HBM footprint—with minimal accuracy loss. These precisions are supported by modern hardware and software stacks, including the NVIDIA Tensor Cores and Transformer Engine.

In contrast, the decode phase is memory-bandwidth-bound and suffers from cross-GPU synchronization overhead. So it's most efficient with little or no tensor parallelism (often TP=1) as it relies more on fused kernels to increase arithmetic intensity—as well as high memory throughput GPUs.

In a monolith you'd have to pick one type of GPU and one parallelism strategy for both phases, which is suboptimal for at least one of the phases. Disaggregation, on the other hand, lets you independently tune each phase for maximum efficiency.

Splitting phases also opens the door to heterogeneous clusters in which different GPU types are assigned to prefill and decode roles for optimal cost-performance. For example, using compute-optimized GPUs for prompt prefill and memory-optimized GPUs for token generation can produce better throughput per dollar than a homogeneous deployment.

> In practice, the latest GPUs typically have both higher FLOPS and more GPU memory. As such, it's tempting—and more common— to just use the latest GPU generation for both prefill and decode. But just know that heterogeneity is a viable option to reduce cost.

We will explore the idea of heterogeneous clusters later in the chapter. We'll show how using high-end GPUs for prompts and cheaper GPUs for generation can lead to significant cost savings at scale.

In summary, disaggregation removes cross-interference and enables specialized treatment of each phase. The expected results include tighter latency distributions since no more long tails are caused by mismatched prompt sizes, improved throughput under latency constraints (goodput), and better overall resource utilization.

> You should use profiling tools (e.g., NVIDIA Nsight Systems) to identify bottlenecks in the prefill and decode phases. These can trace GPU kernels and RDMA transfers across the different worker nodes. This will help validate that decode kernels are fully overlapping communication, etc.

Next, let's discuss how to actually implement a disaggregated serving system, including the system architecture, communication, and scheduling policies that decide how to fully utilize the disaggregated cluster.

Disaggregated Prefill and Decode Cluster Pools

In a disaggregated deployment, we maintain two (or more) pools of workers such that one set of GPUs is dedicated to prefill prompt processing and another set is dedicated to token generation. These workers can be on separate nodes or racks in a data center—or even in separate data centers if the interconnect is fast enough. (Note: keeping prefill and decode within the same data center is the practical design choice to achieve realistic SLOs.)

The worker pools communicate over a network to hand off the model's KV cache produced by the prefill to whichever GPU will perform the decode. A scheduler, or router, coordinates this communication.

Consider a configuration in which the model weights are loaded on two groups of GPU servers. One group, the prefill workers, handles prompts and computes the KV cache. The other group, the decode workers, handles token generation using the KV caches generated from the prefill workers.

The two worker groups typically communicate using a high-speed interconnect (e.g., NVLink/NVSwitch and InfiniBand) and zero-copy GPU-to-GPU transfers with RDMA. In practice, these transfers use GPUDirect RDMA or UCX and can be correlated in Nsight Systems alongside CUDA kernels, NVLink activity, storage metrics, and InfiniBand switch metrics for end-to-end validation.

> For superchip-based NVL fabrics (e.g., Grace-Blackwell, Vera-Rubin, etc.), use NVIDIA Multi-Node NVLink (MNNVL), keep NVLink-first collectives enabled for TP decode, and enable SHARP for AllGather and ReduceScatter collectives when available.

When the system receives a new request, it typically receives it on the decode worker. This is called a *decode-centric design*. This is preferred because the prefill workers are already compute bound with the KV computations.

By having the decode workers handle the client I/O, routing, and session state management, the inference system avoids overloading the prefill workers. Also, centralizing request ingress on the decode nodes simplifies network management, autoscaling, and policy enforcement.

> This is just one style of system architecture for prefill-decode in which the decode worker is the centralized ingress for all requests. This architecture is used in the NVIDIA Dynamo inference system. Another common architecture is to use a dedicated, centralized API router to route the request to either the prefill or decode worker. However, this requires an extra moving part in the system and additional coordination between the router and prefill/decode workers, —as well as additional scaling and latency considerations.

After the decode worker receives the requests, it decides whether to do the prefill itself or "offload" it to the prefill worker pool. If it decides to offload to the prefill worker pool, the decode worker will later receive the KV results back and then continue with decoding and generating the next token.

Next is a snippet from a simplified NVIDIA Dynamo cluster configuration that defines two roles that use NVIDIA's Inference Xfer Library (NIXL) for GPUDirect RDMA-based KV cache transfers to let one GPU write into another GPU's memory directly over the network:

```
roles:
  - name: prefill_worker      # Prefill worker role
    model_path: models/llm-70b
    instance_count: 4         # 4 prefill workers
    gpu_type: B200            # B200 Blackwell compute-bound prefill

  - name: decode_worker       # Decode worker role
    model_path: models/llm-70b
    instance_count: 8         # 8 decode workers
    gpu_type: B300            # B300 Blackwell Ultra high-memory decode
```

> NVIDIA's Rubin CPX accelerator (*https://oreil.ly/Q1_SY*) is another option for prefill workers. Rubin CPX (the CP stands for "context processing") is specifically designed for compute-bound workloads such as prefill. The Rubin CPX marks NVIDIA's departure from "general accelerated computing" GPUs into specialized chips that are optimized for a specific stage (e.g., prefill) within a broader AI workload such as inference.

In this configuration, we have four prefill workers using B200 GPUs (adequate compute for compute-heavy prefills) and eight decode workers using B300 GPUs (high HBM capacity for heavy memory-bound decodes). Mixing B200s and B300s helps to match their FLOPS and HBM capacity characteristics while minimizing cost. Both roles will use NIXL and GPUDirect RDMA to transfer the KV cache blocks. NIXL abstracts transport for GPU-to-GPU data movement over NVLink and RDMA NICs. It also provides connectors for GPUDirect Storage so that KV cache pages can be read from (or written to) different storage tiers.

Under the hood, when this system runs, each decode worker registers a region of its GPU memory so that prefill workers can write directly into it using RDMA. Typically, memory-registration metadata such as NIXL descriptors are exchanged at startup or on first contact. This way, for each remote prefill task, only a small identifier needs to be sent rather than a full memory address structure.

For instance, Dynamo uses etcd (*https://oreil.ly/wAUgO*) for worker discovery and leases. Workers register the necessary memory handles with the router or control plane so that peers can obtain the descriptors when needed. The prefill workers will retrieve them on first use. This way, a prefill request can include just an ID for the target KV buffer, making control messages lightweight.

Furthermore, NVIDIA Dynamo's NIXL implementation provides a high throughput RDMA and storage abstraction for inference data movement and includes plugins for NVLink, UCX-based fabric, and GPUDirect Storage. As such, prefill workers can write KV blocks directly into decode GPU memory.

> In mixed parallelism deployments where prefill and decode use different TP layouts, you need to perform a layout transform on the decode side immediately after the NIXL read. This way, the KV pages match the decode kernel's expected layout. This transform is latency-insignificant compared to network transfer and avoids re-prefill.

This architecture decouples scaling for each phase. If you find that prefill is the throughput bottleneck due to many concurrent long prompts, for instance, you can add more prefill workers to increase prompt processing capacity.

If decode becomes the bottleneck due to many users generating long outputs, for instance, you would scale out decode workers. Because decode and prefill are separated, scaling one doesn't directly interfere with the other.

Systems like NVIDIA Dynamo support dynamic, runtime-configurable disaggregation such that you can add or remove prefill workers on the fly—without stopping the cluster. New prefill workers simply register and start pulling tasks from the queue. If a prefill worker leaves the cluster for whatever reason (crash, restart, autoscale event, network partition, etc.), the decode workers will temporarily do more local prefills to compensate.

NVIDIA Dynamo's distributed runtime uses etcd for worker discovery and leases. Its Planner component can scale workers by revoking leases or launching new workers which are auto-discovered. This dynamic flexibility is crucial at ultrascale when load will often fluctuate. When this happens, you'll want to swap workers between roles as needed.

Prefill workers design

Prefill workers, or *prompt servers*, are the compute nodes dedicated to executing the initial prompt prefill processing phase of requests. This section discusses how prefill nodes are architected to handle the heavy computation efficiently—and how they balance latency versus throughput for KV cache population under load.

Because the prefill workload is computationally intensive, prefill nodes should use GPUs with high FLOPS and be optimized for large matrix multiplications. Each prefill task feeds n input tokens through all model layers.

The prefill workers will use thousands of GPU threads in parallel—and across many GPU nodes, if available. They use familiar parallelism techniques, including tensor parallelism and pipeline parallelism, to reduce TTFT.

Memory management.   Memory-wise, prefill nodes need to load the full model weights and also allocate KV cache for the prompt. This KV cache is then transferred to the decode workers, as we'll see in a bit.

Prefill populates GPU memory with model parameters and the working activations of the model's forward pass with the prompt inputs. Once the KV cache is created, it's immediately sent to the decode workers. The KV cache doesn't persist long in the prefill node's memory.

If a model is extremely large or a prompt is extremely long, prefill may require tensor or parallel splits across GPUs due to memory limitations. Prefill servers should be flexible with their parallelism strategies (data, tensor, pipeline, expert (MoE), and context) to meet latency targets.

Some inference frameworks preallocate a big chunk of GPU memory for prefills to use as working space. This reduces overall memory fragmentation and buffer allocation time.

Optimizing for latency versus throughput.   When tuning a disaggregated prefill cluster, you face a fundamental trade-off between minimizing the TTFT for each individual prompt and maximizing overall requests per second (RPS), or reducing TPOT, under heavy load.

Disaggregated systems handle this trade-off by supporting different scheduling policies for a latency-first approach versus a throughput-first approach. Let's describe each of these approaches next:

Latency-first approach
> To reduce TTFT, prefill nodes should process prompts as soon as they arrive— and with little to no batching. In this mode, you avoid waiting for other requests to fill a batch. As such, every prompt starts execution immediately and finishes as fast as possible—assuming available GPUs in the cluster.
>
> The downside of this latency-first approach is lower GPU utilization since you are using small or no batches. As such, GPUs often sit idle, and your system will serve fewer concurrent requests for a given cluster size. In this case, you can either over-provision your prefill cluster capacity or use a tiny batch size of 1 to guarantee strict latency SLOs for your requests.

Throughput-first approach
> If peak throughput, or RPS, and minimal TPOT are your priorities, you should batch prompts into larger groups to fully load each GPU. By accumulating 8–32

prompts into a single batch, you raise arithmetic intensity and keep the GPU compute units busy. This will increase the overall throughput.

The downside to the throughput-first approach is that each request incurs a batching delay equal to the time it takes to collect the batch. The larger the batch size, the longer the delay.

For extreme throughput inference system configurations, you can choose to assign multiple GPUs per request using either data parallelism or pipeline parallelism.

With data parallelism, the entire model is replicated on each GPU. The batch is split into minibatches across the GPUs. Each GPU performs a forward pass on its subset of data through its complete copy of the model. The output is then aggregated from all the GPUs for the final output.

Data parallelism aggregates memory bandwidth and compute power across all of the GPUs to increase per-batch performance. However, it reduces maximum parallelism to the total # of GPUs ÷ GPUs per request. This reduces your overall concurrent request capacity. This can leave resources idle if the system uses too many GPUs per single request. This will create an imbalance between throughput and concurrency.

Pipeline parallelism divides the model's layers into sequential stages on different GPUs, such as GPU 0 and GPU 1. As soon as GPU 0 finishes its stage for microbatch 0, it forwards activations to GPU 1 and begins stage 1 for microbatch 1. This assembly-line pattern keeps all GPUs busy on different chunks of work.

Pipeline parallelism increases per-batch throughput, but it adds inter-GPU communication overhead and pipeline "bubbles" if the microbatch size or stage splits are not carefully balanced.

Ultimately, each additional GPU that you dedicate will increase throughput but decrease how many requests you can handle at once—given a fixed-size cluster. You can always scale out the GPU cluster, but assuming a fixed cluster size, you should choose your configuration based on whether latency SLOs or throughput SLOs are most important to your use case.

Latency-aware scheduling and batching. Disaggregated systems incorporate the latency-aware scheduling policies mentioned earlier to balance these factors. For instance, they might guarantee single-request execution—and not batch requests—unless load is high enough that combining a small number of requests won't violate the TTFT target.

Many cluster designs include an SLO constraint in the scheduler. For instance, if p90 TTFT must be $\leq X$ ms, the system will choose the largest batch size or parallelism strategy that still meets the SLO for a typical prompt size.

Another strategy is adaptive batching windows. For instance, at low load, it can run requests immediately using a batch size of 1. And at higher loads, the system can allow microbatches of requests arriving within a small time window, such as 2–10 ms. This way, a slight delay can produce a big GPU utilization win—but only when it's needed and tolerable.

Many inference engines favor latency for their prefill workers. Systems often execute prompt tasks as soon as possible and even tolerate some GPU underutilization, because a fast first token significantly improves user experience.

It's common to provision more prefill capacity than needed for an average load. This way, the prefill cluster absorbs bursts of prompts without latency spikes. In the next chapter, we will discuss adaptive mechanisms to rebalance resources on the fly so that neither the prefill nor the decode workers become a bottleneck over time.

Modern orchestrators like Kubernetes can automatically scale each tier. For example, if prefill GPU utilization stays high and decode is low, the orchestrator can trigger an autoscaling event to add prefill pods (or nodes)—and possibly even remove some decode pods/nodes.

This kind of adaptive scaling is often implemented with metrics like prefill queue length to help drive the decisions.

Another option is to implement priority queues such that short prompts are scheduled on a separate fast lane with less batching. Long, batchable prompts go to a throughput-optimized queue. NVIDIA Dynamo supports latency classes in scheduling. You can emulate this by tagging requests and having different batching windows per class.

The key takeaway is that prefill workers prioritize quick turnaround. Disaggregation lets us do this without harming decode performance since decode is running on a different set of workers. We might "waste" some prefill GPU cycles during low-traffic periods, but we maintain low TTFT during peak traffic periods. It's a worthwhile trade-off for interactive services.

Decode workers design

Decode workers, or *generation servers*, are dedicated to the autoregressive decode phase. Once a prompt's KV cache is ready, it is sent to a decode worker, which uses the KV cache to produce the remaining output tokens as quickly as possible to maintain a low TPOT latency.

If a request is initially routed to the decode worker, as in Figure 17-3, it must first decide if the prefill should be done locally or remotely using a disaggregated router. If it decides to prefill remotely, it will push the prefill request into a prefill queue to be picked up by the prefill worker.

The prefill worker continuously pulls from the prefill queue, reads any KV blocks cached in the prefix cache, and computes the prefill operations. It then writes the KV blocks back to the decode worker, which completes the decoding.

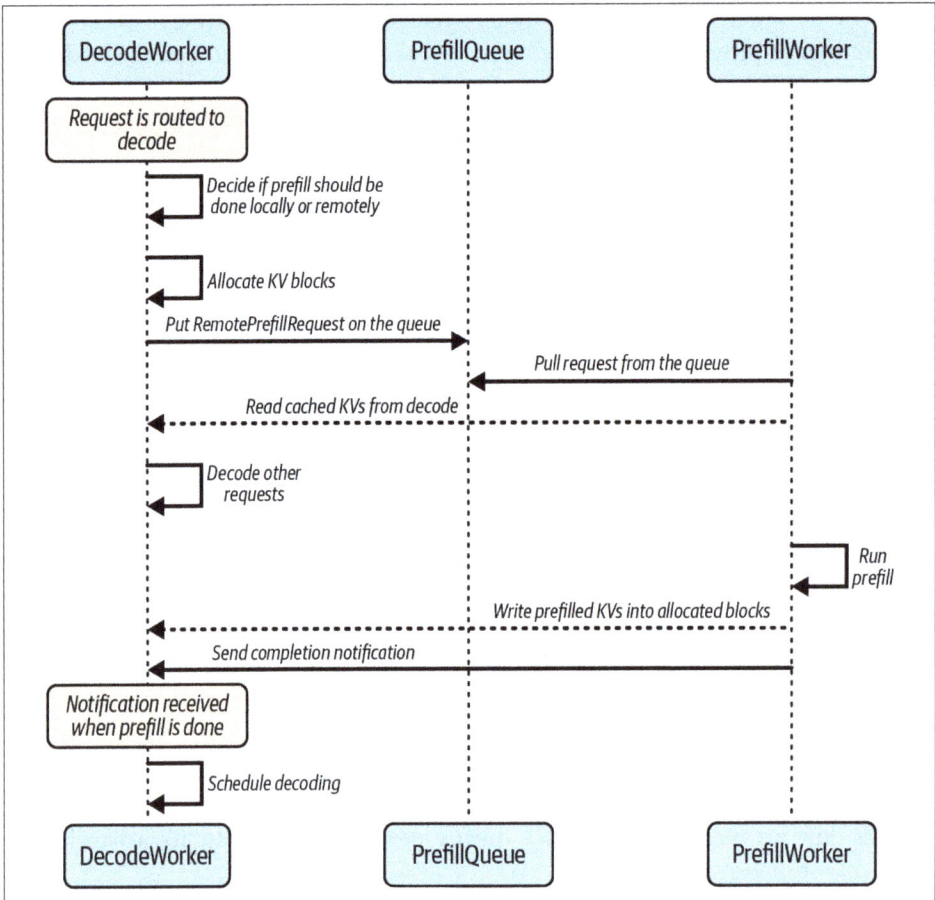

Figure 17-3. Prefill worker design: read prefix cache → compute prefill → write KV cache for decode

The decode worker design is focused on handling many concurrent sequence generations efficiently—as well as managing the memory footprint of the KV cache. In this section, we describe how decode servers achieve high throughput using techniques like continuous batching and clever memory management tricks. These help to reduce TPOT latency and increase scalability—especially for long sequences. Let's start by detailing the KV cache transfer between the two stages.

KV cache transfer between prefill and decode. High-performance disaggregation requires moving KV cache data as efficiently as possible between the prefill and decode workers. By using libraries like NIXL (described in Chapter 4) for direct GPU-to-GPU transfers, we can avoid CPU involvement and utilize nonblocking operations. This way, while one GPU is transferring KV data, it can also service other forward-pass requests without waiting for the transfer to complete.

Consider a user request that arrives at a decode worker. In this case, the decode worker's scheduler allocates the necessary KV blocks and adds a remote prefill request to the prefill queue. This prefill request contains the identifiers for those KV blocks. This interaction is shown in Figure 17-4.

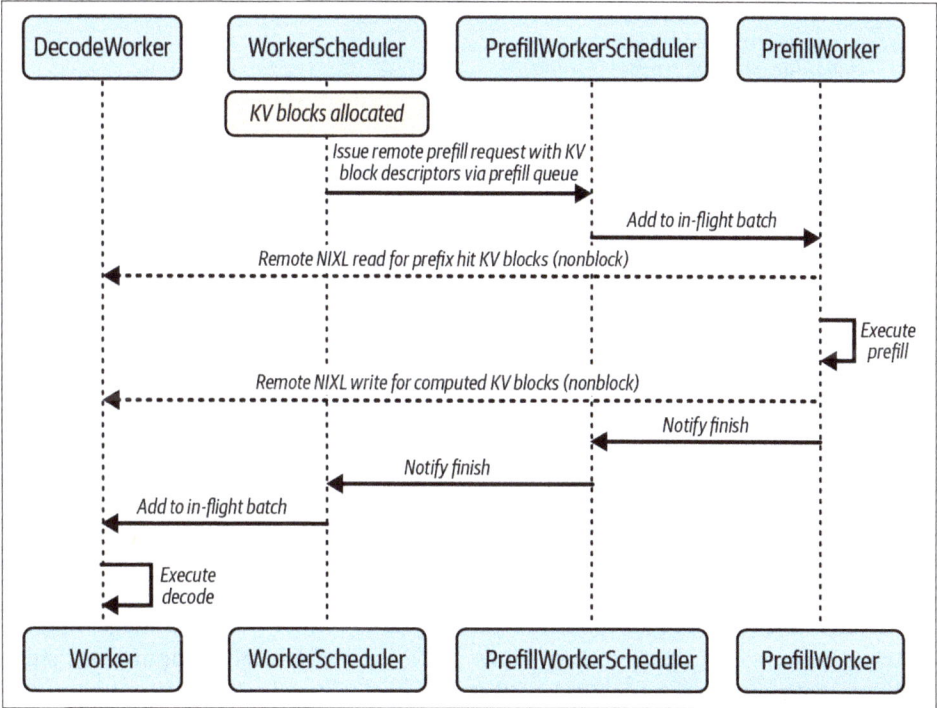

Figure 17-4. Transfer of KV cache data between the prefill and decode workers using NIXL; coalesce multiple PagedAttention blocks into ~128-token payloads before RDMA (note: vLLM defaults to 16 tokens per block on CUDA)

The prefill worker uses NIXL to perform direct remote GPU memory reads and writes over the selected transport. This avoids CPU copies and enables nonblocking progress. As soon as the prefill worker completes the prefill request, the decode worker's scheduler adds a corresponding decode request to its own decode pipeline. This allows compute and data movement to overlap seamlessly. Make sure to use pre-registered peer memory with large pinned window sizes to minimize re-registration churn. You can verify zero-copy transfer overlap with the Nsight Systems timeline.

When validating end-to-end data movement and overlap, it's recommended to profile with Nsight Systems using trace flags. For InfiniBand link telemetry, add --nic-metrics=true for HCA/NIC counters and --ib-switch-metrics-device=<GUIDs> for switch counters. These will capture switch metrics and sample host/device activity. Together, this will produce correlated CUDA kernels, UCX activity, storage metrics, and network behavior. Following is a unified command that enables CUDA/UCX tracing and collects CPU activity, GPU metrics, storage metrics, and InfiniBand switch telemetry:

```
nsys profile --trace=cuda-hw,osrt,nvtx,ucx,gds \
  --trace-fork-before-exec=true \
  --cuda-event-trace=true \
  --cuda-graph-trace=node \
  --cuda-memory-usage=true \
  --sample=cpu \
  --gpu-metrics-device=all \
  --nic-metrics=true \
  --ib-switch-metrics-device=<GUIDs> \
  --storage-metrics --storage-devices=all \
  --gds-metrics=driver \
  -o nsys_reports/prefill_decode \
  <your_launch_here>
```

> It's possible that the prefill and decode engines use different parallelism (e.g., tensor-parallel) layouts. In this case, the system can insert a layout transform kernel on the receiver side—after the NIXL read (and before the data is used) to realign each KV block to the layout expected by the decode worker.

Continuous batching. Decode servers rely heavily on continuous batching, also known as *iteration-level batching*. Unlike the prefill phase, which performs large matrix-matrix computations, the decoding phase performs many small computations since each new token generation is a relatively small vector-matrix computation since the individual token is represented as a vector.

To avoid low GPU utilization for small, per-token workloads, decode workers can batch together multiple input sequences to create larger matrix-matrix computations (e.g., multiple token generations) at each iteration. This increases the arithmetic intensity for each decode task.

For example, suppose 32 different text-generation requests are mid-stream and ready to generate their next token. Instead of computing 32 separate, single-token forward passes, a continuous batching scheduler will combine the requests and perform one forward pass that generates 32 tokens (one per sequence) in parallel.

This way, matrix multiplications see an effective batch size of 32, which keeps the GPU compute units busy. The challenge is that not all sequences request a token at the exact same time. Some may finish early, and others may start late.

Remember that you can batch across different requests and users. Most modern inference servers will automatically group decode steps from different users' requests if the sequences have the same context length at that moment. This effectively performs batched decoding on the fly. Consider such solutions for maximizing decode throughput.

> In vLLM, CUDA Graph capture coverage is controlled by the flag called `--max-seq-len-to-capture`. Capture sizes are typically aligned to the maximum number of sequences. When a sequence exceeds this length, vLLM falls back to eager mode. It's important to note that this flag does not control how many sequences are batched at runtime. The number of concurrent decode slots is controlled by `--max-num-seqs` (upper bound on sequences in an iteration). Set this explicitly for predictable memory use along with `--max-num-batched-tokens`.

Continuous batching addresses the issue of sequences requesting tokens at different times by dynamically updating the batch size at each step. Specifically, at each step, a continuous batching strategy will gather all sequences that are ready for a next token at that moment and batch them into a single decode step.

If new requests finish prefill and become ready while the decode is in progress, they will join the next batch without waiting an arbitrary long idle period. This is in contrast to static batching, which will wait to gather a full batch before decoding.

If a sequence finishes by hitting an end-of-text token or a sequence-length limit, it is removed from subsequent batches immediately. If a sequence is not yet ready—perhaps it's a long prompt still being processed in prefill—it won't be included until it becomes ready.

Effectively, with continuous batching, the batch size on each iteration can fluctuate. However, the server is always trying to maximize the batch size to include whatever sequences are available at that time—up to a limit. This achieves high utilization while minimizing per-token waiting time.

Continuous batching makes sure that decode GPU workers never sit idle. They are always working on available requests. This maximizes their throughput under latency constraints by keeping the GPU busy—even as individual sequences await new tokens.

Similarly, Microsoft's DeepSpeed and NVIDIA's TensorRT-LLM inference engines implement continuous or in-flight batching with paged KV caches to keep GPU utilization high during decoding. Specifically, DeepSpeed combines multiple generation requests, and TensorRT-LLM uses a scheduler to group decoding tasks across streams.

In a disaggregated decode cluster, continuous batching becomes even more powerful. Since decode GPUs handle only generation, they can devote 100% of their cycles to this continuous loop without ever being interrupted by a large, bespoke prompt task. This leads to smoother throughput metrics—especially under load.

Under high load, a decode node might have tens or hundreds of sequences concurrently active. It can batch a large number of them at each iteration. This will maximize hardware utilization.

And under low load, even if only one sequence is active, the decode worker can immediately generate the token. It doesn't have to wait to fill a batch. In this case, the GPU will be underutilized for that moment, but the latency for that single sequence remains low. As such, continuous batching handles both extremes: at high concurrency it's efficient, and at low concurrency it's responsive. This is a good balance of high throughput and low latency.

Grouping variable-length sequences. Handling variable-length sequences in LLM inference requires careful scheduling and batching to avoid wasted computation and memory. Mixing short and long prompts in one batch leads to padding overhead—sometimes up to 50% padding relative to the number of tokens. This wastes scarce GPU and network resources.

When you batch prompts of differing lengths together, every shorter sequence must be padded to match the longest one. This padding introduces "no-op" tokens that still consume GPU cycles, memory bandwidth, and inter-GPU or network transfers. In some cases, padding can account for up to half of all tokens in common generative AI workloads. This significantly reduces inference efficiency.

A straightforward solution is to group requests into buckets based on sequence length. This way, each batch contains sequences of similar sizes. Using static-length buckets like 0–512 tokens, 513–1,024 tokens, etc., fixes the batch boundaries and minimizes padding overhead.

vLLM's decode scheduler maintains a rotating pool of SequenceGroup instances (each prompt is a SequenceGroup). The scheduler advances each group after a fixed token budget per decode iteration. As soon as a SequenceGroup is done processing its chunk, it leaves the pool, and a new SequenceGroup joins the pool. This keeps the pipeline continuously full of work—without relying on static padding buckets or underutilizing GPUs.

These batching and scheduling techniques align well with disaggregated prefill-decode deployments with separate prefill and decode clusters. Using this deployment configuration, the separate decode nodes can use techniques like continuous batching to minimize TPOT variance under strict SLOs. Meanwhile, the dedicated prefill nodes can be tuned independently for maximum input-processing throughput and minimum TPOT.

NVIDIA's Programmatic Dependent Launch (PDL) and device-initiated CUDA Graph Launch (discussed in Chapter 12) are used to reduce per-token launch overhead, overlap work, and eliminate bubbles between decode iterations. These features are generally enabled through the framework rather than manually in application code.

When using device-launched graphs, instantiate with `cudaGraphInstantiateFlagDeviceLaunch` and keep nodes on a single device. Use PDL to overlap dependent kernels at the end of a step (e.g., decode iteration). This further trims per-token launch bubbles.

By combining length-bucketing, continuous batching, disaggregation, PDL, and device-initiated CUDA Graphs, modern inference systems like vLLM, SGLang, and NVIDIA Dynamo can achieve both high throughput and low latency—even for wildly varying prompt lengths. And they do this without impacting resource efficiency or scalability.

> In vLLM, `--max-seq-len-to-capture` controls the maximum sequence length covered by CUDA Graphs. By default, this value is set to 8192. In continuous batching, vLLM may pad to the nearest captured size, so align `--max-num-seqs` and `--max-num-batched-tokens` to minimize padding waste. CUDA Graphs help to minimize repeated CUDA-graph rebuilds for common sequence lengths. It does not directly dictate runtime batching behavior. Runtime batching in vLLM is managed by its decode scheduler's dynamic `SequenceGroup` pool, as described previously. In production, it's recommended to tune `--max-num-seqs` and `--max-num-batched-tokens` alongside `--max-seq-len-to-capture` to bound HBM (KV) usage and reduce padding under continuous batching.

Memory management for the KV cache. Because decoding involves attending to the entire sequence seen so far—including previously decoded tokens—KV cache memory is a critical resource for decode workers. Each sequence stores key and value tensors for each transformer layer—and each past token. Figure 17-5 shows an example KV cache being shared across different requests.

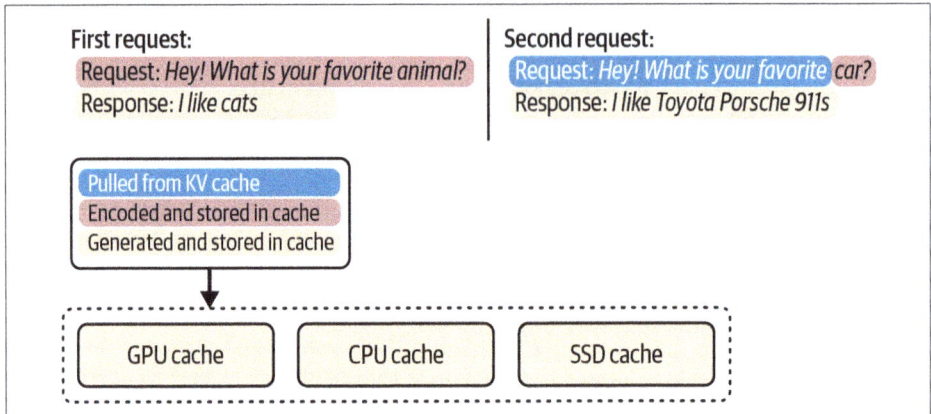

First request:
Request: *Hey! What is your favorite animal?*
Response: *I like cats*

Second request:
Request: *Hey! What is your favorite* car?
Response: *I like Toyota Porsche 911s*

Pulled from KV cache
Encoded and stored in cache
Generated and stored in cache

GPU cache   CPU cache   SSD cache

Figure 17-5. Managing and reusing KV cache data between requests

For large models and long sequences, KV memory grows linearly with tokens and depends on attention layout and dtype. A practical estimate is bytes_per_token = 2 x n_layers x n_kv_heads x head_dim x bytes_per_element. (Note: the 2 x accounts for keys and values per token per layer.)

Consider a Llama-class 13B model with 40 layers, 40 attention heads (head dimension is 128), and FP16. For a 4,096-token context with standard multi-headed attention (MHA), the KV size is ~0.819 MB/token or ~3.36 GB total. With FP8 KV, that becomes ~1.68 GB.

With grouped-query attention (GQA) with 8 query groups (n_kv_heads = 8), the 4,096-token KV is ~0.671 GB at FP16 and ~0.336 GB at FP8. And for multi-query attention (MQA) with 1 kv head, it is ~0.084 GB at FP16.

> Make sure to always compute using the model's actual n_layers, n_kv_heads, head_dim, and KV precision since FP8 and FP4 change the bytes_per_element.

A GPU serving many concurrent sequences can quickly approach its memory limits purely due to KV cache storage—in addition to the model weights. As such, make sure your decode workers use such an optimized memory allocator to prevent GPU memory exhaustion when many long sequences are in flight. The following are strategies that decode workers use to manage KV memory efficiently:

Paged GPU memory allocator

vLLM's PagedAttention mechanism is a prime example—it partitions the KV cache into fixed-size pages and can swap inactive pages to CPU memory. In addition to vLLM, paged KV memory managers are implemented in SGLang and NVIDIA TensorRT-LLM. NVIDIA Dynamo builds on these techniques. These systems also layer external KV tiers using DRAM and NVMe. And they can schedule recomputation versus I/O to balance bandwidth. This is common in projects like LMCache and other similar libraries and runtimes.

High-memory GPUs and custom allocators

Decode servers often use GPUs with large HBM capacity (e.g., Blackwell B200's 180 GB HBM and Blackwell B300's 288 GB HBM) to store the KV cache. Additionally, systems like vLLM and NVIDIA TensorRT-LLM use optimized memory managers that allocate KV memory in fixed-size pages to reduce fragmentation, enable efficient prefix reuse across requests, and manage hundreds of sequences of varying lengths. This efficiently shares memory without causing excessive fragmentation and waste.

KV cache offloading (e.g., paging out)

When GPU memory fills up, the decode workers can offload older KV blocks to CPU RAM or colder storage such as NVMe. For instance, if a sequence generates 1,000 tokens, but not all of them are currently needed right away, some earlier tokens' KV can be moved to host CPU memory.

When they're needed, they can be brought back into GPU memory on demand. Offloading introduces a bit of a latency penalty when the tokens are needed for attention, so you should be careful when using offload. Decode servers often try to prefetch or overlap data transfer so that paging in KV data won't impact generation as much.

Context limits and compression

Some deployments impose a hard limit on the number of decoded tokens, or output sequence length. This is an application-level trade-off that caps the KV cache size and avoids unbounded growth. KV compression can also reduce KV memory required per token. For instance, storing KV at lower precision (FP16, FP8, INT8) can greatly reduce the memory usage.

Another example is using multiquery attention (MQA), in which heads share a KV vector per token. This reduces the KV size proportional to the number of heads. This is a model architecture change that directly lowers the KV footprint. Grouped query attention (GQA) and DeepSeek's Multi-Latent Attention (MLA) also help reduce the size of the KV cache.

Memory hierarchy in disaggregation

Another advantage of the disaggregated design is that the decode cluster's GPU memory is fully dedicated to storing model weights + KV cache. It's also not trying to handle large prompt prefill computations, which, on a monolithic serving system, would consume a lot of extra memory temporarily during prefill.

Each decode GPU typically loads the full model weights—unless using model parallelism—and then uses the remaining memory for KV storage. For instance, if model weights take 70 GB of a GPU's memory and the GPU has 180 GB total, about 122 GB is left for KV.

This directly impacts roughly how many tokens × sequences can be in-flight on that GPU. Disaggregation doesn't eliminate KV memory issues, but by separating roles, you can choose decode node types that optimize for memory capacity and memory bandwidth.

With the cluster configured this way, you need to decide when to offload a prefill to the prefill worker pool—or when to do it locally on the decode worker. Offloading has overhead, including queueing delays, network transfers, etc. As such, it should be used only when it will actually help latency. The decision is made by a routing policy, described next.

Disaggregated Routing and Scheduling Policies

Not every request needs to be offloaded to a prefill worker. In fact, doing so when unnecessary would add overhead and not a lot of benefit. As such, a disaggregated inference system uses a routing policy to conditionally disaggregate and use the remote prefill path only when it is likely to help. Table 17-1 shows a high-level summary of routing strategies, including KV-aware and prefix-aware routing.

Table 17-1. High-level routing strategies, including prefix-aware and KV-aware routing

Routing strategy	Description
Round robin	Routes to each node one by one
Least requests	Routes to the worker with the fewest active requests
Prefix aware	Uses the request's prefix to select a worker
KV aware	Routes to the worker whose KV cache best matches the request

The disaggregated router runs for each new request on the decode worker that initially receives the request. And it makes a quick decision to either prefill locally or prefill remotely on the prefill worker pool.

Routing factors

The decision to offload prefill to the prefill worker pool can be based on several factors related to the request and the system state. Common routing factors include current queue lengths, GPU memory availability, and even specialization since certain GPUs are better for certain models or prompt types.

Advanced routers like vLLM's KV cache-aware router also consider cache locality. They will route a request to a decode worker that already holds some of its prefix in cache. Figure 17-6 shows how an example KV-cache-aware router moves a request through the system based on data received from KV cache events emitted by the workers.

The goal is to route in a way that maximizes cache hits and balances load. Table 17-2 summarizes some key factors that influence the routing decision in a typical disaggregated design.

Table 17-2. Factors influencing the router's decision to offload a prefill

Factor	Description	Effect on routing decision
Prompt length	Number of tokens in the input prompt (after any prefix caching).	Long prompts ⇒ more compute → offload prefill if length exceeds threshold. Short prompts ⇒ do locally.
Prefix cache hit	Extent of prompt already in the decode worker's KV cache (from previous requests).	Large prefix cache hit (most of prompt cached) ⇒ prefill is effectively shorter and more memory bound → do locally. If no cache hits (all new tokens) ⇒ heavy compute → offload likely beneficial.
Prefill queue length	Number of pending tasks in the global prefill queue (how busy the prefill workers are).	If the queue is long (prefill workers lagging) ⇒ avoid offloading new requests (do locally). If the queue is empty or light ⇒ prefill workers have capacity → offload if other conditions are met.
Decode worker load	Current load on the local decode worker (ongoing decode tasks, etc.).	If the decode GPU is busy with many decode streams, offloading helps parallelism (freeing up the GPU from heavy compute). If decode is mostly idle and the prefill queue is backed up, do local prefill to use available capacity.
Latency SLO urgency	Priority or tightness of the request's latency requirement.	Urgent low-latency requirement ⇒ might offload to ensure prompt is computed ASAP (especially if local decode is busy). Relaxed requirements might just run locally to save resources (see "QoS and early rejection policies" on page 794).

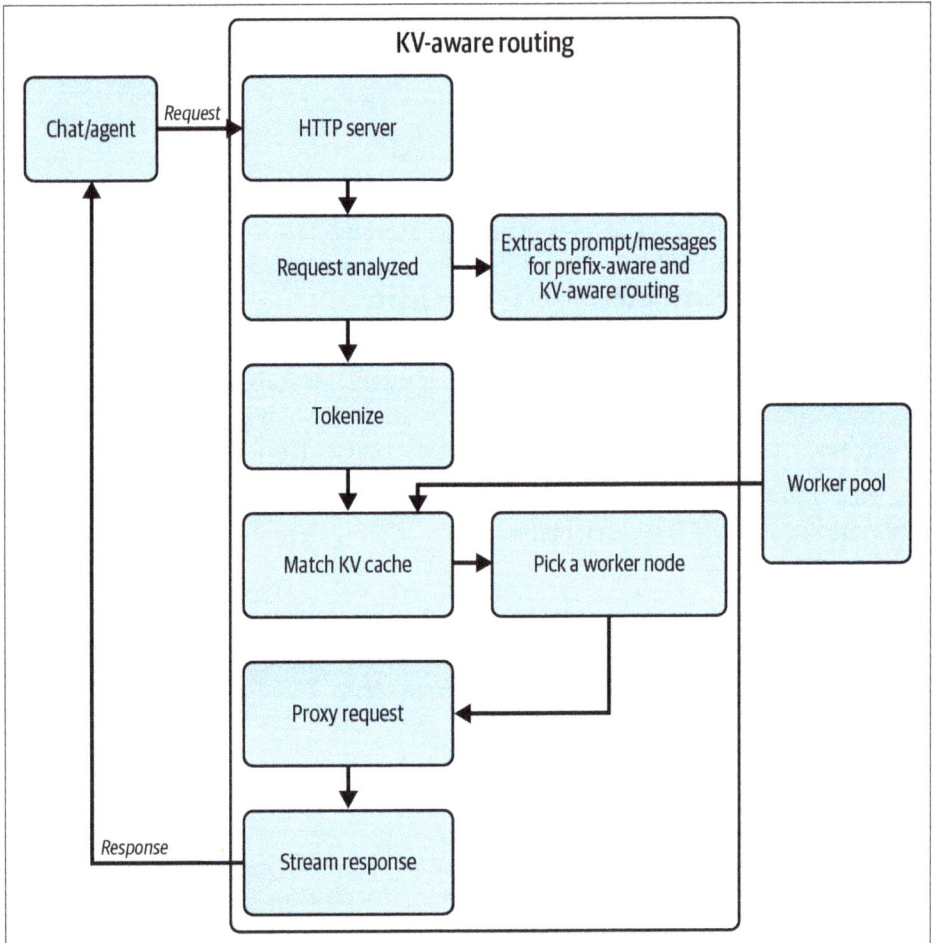

Figure 17-6. KV-cache-aware request routing based on data received from KV cache events emitted by the workers

These factors will prefer to offload only requests that will benefit from the remote execution. These include long and compute-heavy prompts. Meanwhile, short and cache-hitting prompts are handled locally to minimize overhead. The thresholds are tunable. Each factor in Table 17-2 addresses a particular trade-off, as described next:

Prompt length

We don't want to waste time offloading trivial prompts. The overhead of remote execution, even if small, isn't worth it for a five-token prompt, for instance, since the decode GPU can handle that quickly on its own. Offloading is reserved for heavy prompts in which the decode GPU would otherwise be tied up for a long time.

Prefix cache

Modern inference systems often implement a KV cache that can store the KV pairs for previously seen context, such as earlier turns of a conversation or repeated boilerplate system prompts. If a new request's prompt has a long prefix that overlaps with a prompt that has already been processed, the decode worker may already have that prefix's KV data in memory. In that case, it needs to compute only the remainder of the prompt for the cache-miss portion.

If the remaining part is short, the benefit of offloading is reduced. Also, if the entire prompt is already cached due to a complete prefix hit, then no prefill computation is needed at all. The decode can proceed immediately using the cached state. The router takes this into account by effectively considering effective prompt length = (`prompt_length` – `prefix_cached_length`).

A large prefix hit not only reduces compute needed but also means a lot of KV data would have to be transferred to a prefill worker and back, which is pointless. Hence, such requests are kept local and leverage the cache.

Prefill queue length

This essentially measures the load of the prefill worker cluster. If the prefill workers are overwhelmed with many tasks waiting, sending yet another task their way could hurt TTFT more than it helps since the request would just sit in the queue. In those cases, decode workers are instructed to temporarily do more work themselves.

This creates a natural load-shedding mechanism for the prefill cluster since the system gracefully degrades back toward local computation when the dedicated prefill tier is at capacity. When the prefill queue is short again and workers are caught up, offloading resumes for long prompts. This dynamic equilibrium is one reason disaggregation performs well across a variety of conditions.

Decode worker load

While not always explicitly coded as such, the router inherently helps distribute the workload. If a decode worker is already busy decoding many streams, it can still offload new incoming prompts. This is good, as, otherwise, that GPU would have to juggle heavy compute and decoding concurrently—possibly slowing down both.

Conversely, if decode GPUs are free because the system is very lightly loaded, they could handle longer prefills locally. In practice, an idle decode GPU is also likely to have an empty prefill queue since the overall load is low. The conditions already cover this case indirectly. But some implementations might include a direct check on local GPU utilization to decide whether prefill-offload is needed or not.

Latency SLO and priority

In systems with mixed SLAs or priority classes, the routing can be modified to improve QoS. For a high-priority request that must have the fastest TTFT, one might bypass queue checks and immediately offload so that it starts computing immediately—even if the decode GPU is free. In this case, the system can reserve that decode worker for a different high-priority decode task.

Alternatively, if a request is low priority, the system might choose not to use prefill cluster resources at all. Instead, it will just let it happen locally on the decode worker—or even delay it. We revisit priority request handling in "QoS and early rejection policies" on page 794, but just know that the basic router can be extended with these types of considerations.

The specific threshold values and weights used in the routing policy should be determined empirically. For instance, you might find that prompts under 50 tokens are faster to compute locally on a given type of GPU (e.g., Blackwell B200), whereas larger prompts benefit from offload.

As new hardware is released, the thresholds might change since newer GPUs have higher FLOPS and more memory bandwidth. As such, the break-even prompt length for offload might become a bit higher since a single B200 can handle more tokens fully on the decode worker, for instance.

> You should empirically adjust thresholds like `PREFILL_LENGTH_THRESHOLD` when upgrading hardware due to improvements in compute FLOPS and memory bandwidth.

The outcome of effective routing is that the system achieves the best of both worlds. Short prompts are faster TTFT due to running locally—and they incur no extra overhead. Longer prompts get the benefits of parallelism since prefill and decode happen in parallel on different GPUs. Also, the prefill worker pool is utilized only when needed—and it avoids getting flooded when it can't keep up.

This type of conditional strategy was crucial in the DistServe prototype and in modern inference servers like vLLM and Dynamo. This allows them to improve useful throughput under latency constraints (goodput) rather than just raw throughput.

Example dynamic routing policy in code

In practice, the routing policy can be implemented as a simple conditional check. The code here shows a simplified version of this routing logic:

```
# Offload prefill decision running on a decode worker
# (B200/B300 tuned)
def should_offload_prefill(prompt_length: int,
```

```
                    prefix_cached_length: int,
                    prefill_queue_size: int,
                    decode_active_reqs: int,
                    ttft_slo_ms: int = 500) -> bool:
    # Effective prefill after prefix KV hits
    eff_len = max(0, prompt_length - prefix_cached_length)

    # Tunables (kept in config; shown here for clarity)
    PREFILL_LENGTH_THRESHOLD = 256  # see split_policy.prompt_length_threshold
    PREFILL_QUEUE_MAX        = 10   # see autoscale/prefill queue-length guidance
    DECODE_LOAD_THRESHOLD    = 8    # active decode streams

    long_prefill = (eff_len >= PREFILL_LENGTH_THRESHOLD)
    prefill_available = (prefill_queue_size < PREFILL_QUEUE_MAX)

    # Prefer remote when prefill is compute-heavy
    # and the pool has capacity.
    if long_prefill and prefill_available:
        return True

    # If local decode is busy and prefill is moderately long,
    # free decode via offload.
    if decode_active_reqs >= DECODE_LOAD_THRESHOLD and eff_len >= 64:
        return True

    # Otherwise keep prefill local
    # (lower overhead / better cache locality).
    return False
```

In this pseudo-code, PREFILL_LENGTH_THRESHOLD is a system-tuned parameter, such as 50 or 100 tokens, that defines what counts as a "long" prompt. PREFILL_QUEUE_MAX is a threshold beyond which the prefill worker pool is considered saturated, specifically if there are too many outstanding tasks.

The decode worker calls should_offload_prefill() as soon as it receives a new request. If the function returns True, the decode worker will package the prompt into a message and push it onto the global prefill task queue. It then performs other work while waiting for the KV cache result to return.

If should_offload_prefill() returns False, the decode worker immediately performs the prefill computation itself. This way, if prefill workers start lagging behind, new requests will fall back to local computation to avoid queuing delays. It's a form of adaptive routing that balances the load between decode and prefill pools.

Example dynamic routing policy configuration

In a production deployment, the routing policy should be configured through a file or UI rather than hard-coded. For instance, NVIDIA's Dynamo allows specifying complex routing and autoscaling rules in a JSON or YAML config. Here is a simplified example of a Dynamo Planner JSON that encapsulates some of the policy logic:

```
model: ...
split_policy:
  prompt_length_threshold: 256
  prefix_cache_weight: 10.0
  queue_length_weight: 1.5
  decode_load_weight: 0.5
  enable_hotspot_prevention: true
cache:
  reuse_prefix: true
  min_cache_hit_ratio: 0.75
autoscale:
  prefill:
    min_replicas: 4
    max_replicas: 12
    scale_up:   { queue_length: 8,  gpu_utilization: 80 }
    scale_down: { queue_length: 2,  gpu_utilization: 40 }
  decode:
    min_replicas: 8
    max_replicas: 24
    scale_up:   { queue_length: 16, kv_cache_usage: 75 }
    scale_down: { queue_length: 4,  kv_cache_usage: 30 }
qos:
  enable_early_rejection: true
  low_priority_threshold_ms: 500
  reject_on_slo_violation: true
```

Here, the configuration defines a `split_policy` with a `prompt_length_threshold` of 256 tokens. It also specifies weights for factors like cache hit, queue length, decode load, and others. It also configures `autoscale` behavior for both prefill and decode roles, including how to scale up or down based on queue lengths, GPU utilization, and KV cache usage.

In addition, it can apply some QoS rules like early rejection and tune what threshold to consider a request "slow." In practice, Dynamo's router reads this JSON at startup—or fetches it dynamically—to dictate each routing decision for requests spread across the entire cluster.

Capacity-aware routing

As mentioned in the previous section, NVIDIA Dynamo supports dynamic routing policy. An implementation of this dynamic routing capability is Dynamo GPU Planner. The planner uses metrics like TTFT, TPOT, and the estimated cost of KV cache transfer to decide to modify routing—or even reallocate/scale phase-specific GPUs—to reduce bottlenecks and adapt to shifts in the workload. This allows the system to maintain high performance during heavy surges in demand, as shown in Figure 17-7.

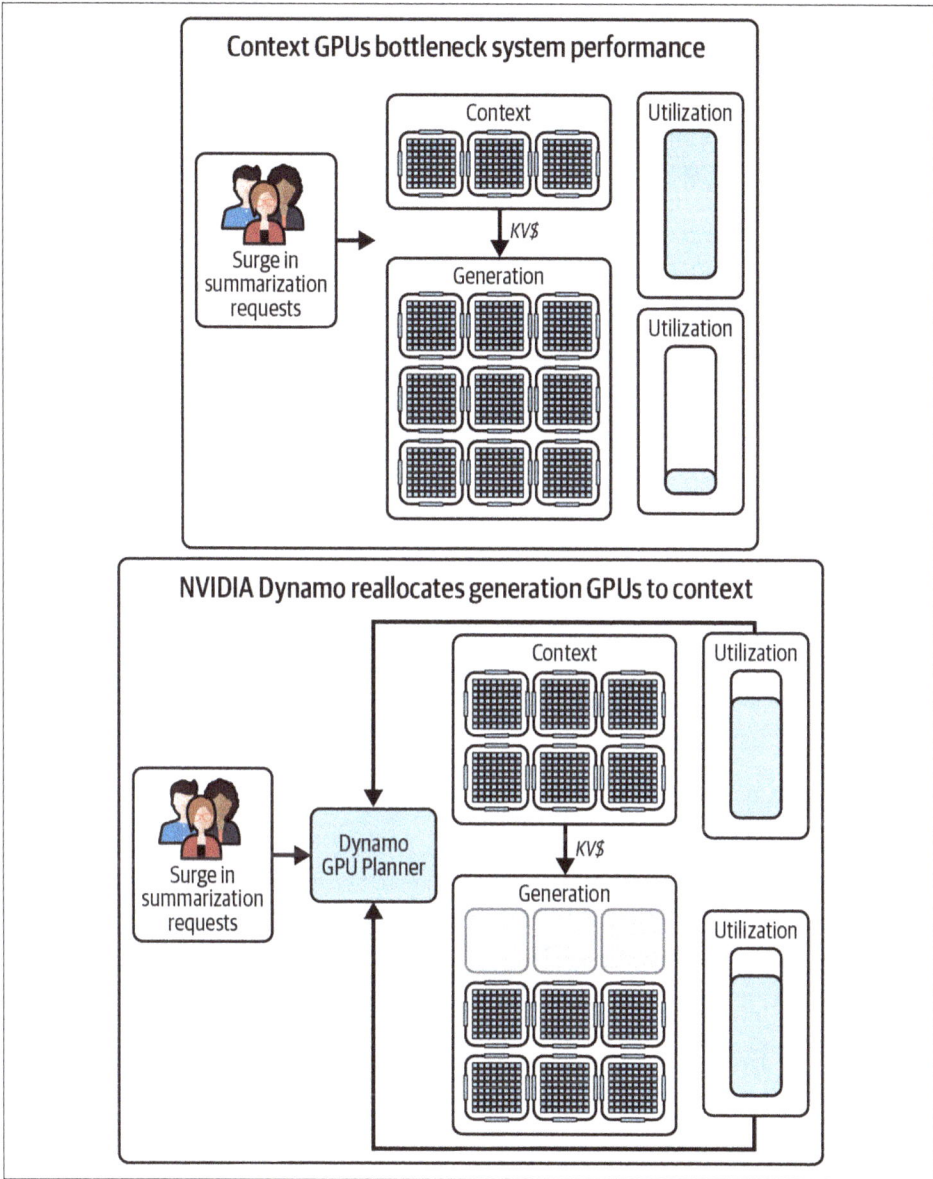

Figure 17-7. NVIDIA's Dynamo GPU Planner decides how to handle incoming requests and allocate GPU workers to prefill and decode based on GPU utilization metrics

Here, Dynamo's Planner chooses to shift more GPUs to the prefill (context) phase because of an influx of large summarization prompts that require a heavy amount of prefill (large inputs) relative to decode (small summary outputs).

In contrast, if there is an influx of reasoning requests, the Planner can choose to reallocate GPUs to the decode phase since reasoning requests generate a lot of output tokens relative to the number of input tokens. In other cases, the Planner might choose to handle the request in a traditional monolithic fashion in which the prefill and decode happen on the same GPU worker node.

In short, a component like NVIDIA's Dynamo Planner can automate this decision process by constantly monitoring real-time metrics and comparing them to application-level SLOs like TTFT and TPOT latencies. Using this information, Dynamo Planner can dynamically determine whether to serve a request with full disaggregation, no disaggregation, or somewhere in between with more or fewer GPU resources allocated to each prefill/decode phase. The resulting adaptive system optimizes resource utilization across prefill and decode workloads—and meets aggressive performance targets.

Latency-aware routing

The inference router can go beyond a simple threshold rule and use a more sophisticated latency score model to pick the best worker for each request. For instance, it might continuously compute a latency cost for each potential worker based on real-time metrics like how busy it is, how much memory is used, whether it has relevant cache, etc. It then sends the request to the worker with the lowest latency cost, for instance.

Let's assume that the worker with the lowest latency cost is the freest and most preferable worker. A simple latency cost function might be as shown here:

```
# Lower cost is preferable
latency_cost = 0.7 * (occupancy_percent)
    + 0.3 * (active_req_count)
```

This particular latency cost function more heavily weighs the occupancy of the GPU. This correlates to how much work the GPU is currently doing. Secondarily, it correlates to how many requests are currently in flight on that engine. A new request would be sent to the engine with the lowest latency cost.

The weights, 0.7 and 0.3 in this example, could be tuned based on empirical data. If KV memory usage is found to be a big predictor of slowdowns due to lots of data to swap or higher memory bandwidth usage, you would want to weigh it more heavily.

A more advanced routing policy might include additional factors. For example, you can incorporate some of the following into your latency cost function:

Exact cache match availability

If a worker already has the needed prefix KV in its cache, a prefix hit, then it can serve the request much faster. In this case, the system can assign a large negative weight to reduce the latency cost and prefer this worker since lower is better in this scenario.

KV occupancy

Higher memory usage means the GPU is busier. In this case, the system assigns a positive weight to increase the latency cost and encourage the router to avoid this worker since lower is more preferable in this scenario.

Active requests

More parallel requests mean potential context-switching overhead, so this adds to the latency cost, which avoids this worker.

Memory bandwidth utilization

If a GPU is currently using a lot of its memory bandwidth by handling many long sequences, for instance, adding more work will just slow things down. This would increase the latency cost and discourage the system from choosing this worker.

Recent KV use

If the exact prefix was used recently on a worker engine—and the cache is "warm"—this will likely improve performance since the KV is still in an L2 cache or currently on its way from a prefill worker. In this case, you might include a small negative weight to reduce the latency cost and prefer this worker since it recently saw the prefix.

Table 17-3 summarizes this type of advanced routing policy configuration. It lists some factors and example costs.

Table 17-3. Routing factors and relative costs

Factor	Interpretation	Impact on latency cost
KV occupancy (%) (`occupancy_percent`)	Higher = more memory pressure	+3
Active requests count (`active_req_count`)	More in flight = potential queuing	+1
KV cache match (`cache_match_flag`)	Engine already has the needed prefix KV	−10 (large negative)
Memory bandwidth % (`mem_bw_percent`)	High = memory bus is busy	+0.5
Recent KV use (`recent_prefix_flag`)	Prefix was used on this engine recently	−1

Let's modify the latency cost calculation with these additional metrics. The router now calculates a composite latency cost, as shown here:

```
# Lower cost is preferable
def latency_cost(occupancy_percent: float,
                 active_reqs: int,
                 cache_match_flag: bool,
                 mem_bw_percent: float,
                 recent_prefix_flag: bool) -> float:
    return (
          3.0 * occupancy_percent
        + 1.0 * active_reqs
        - 10.0 * int(cache_match_flag)
        + 0.5 * mem_bw_percent
        - 1.0 * int(recent_prefix_flag)
    )
```

Prefill and decode clusters might even use slightly different formulas. For prefill, a cache hit (e.g., prefix already computed) might be even more valuable to factor in, whereas for decoding, memory bandwidth or available KV space might dominate the decision.

The router needs telemetry from each worker. This includes metrics like its waiting queue length, KV cache usage, memory utilization, etc., so that the latency cost can be updated continuously.

The outcome is that the system can dynamically route traffic to where it will have the least impact on latency. Under low load, all workers have low scores, and it may not matter which one is chosen, as any worker can handle the request quickly.

Under high load, however, the router effectively load-balances by sending new work to the workers that are most free. This will also take advantage of data locality (cache hits) to reduce work. This reduces both average and tail latencies because work is less likely to pile up behind busy engines when others are free.

Earlier, we saw how factoring in cache hits can cause the router to choose a slightly busier server if it has relevant data cached. This results in faster service for that request. The score function quantitatively captures this trade-off.

NVIDIA Dynamo performs a similar but opposite calculation in which higher is better. Specifically, it computes a remote prefill score, and if the score exceeds a threshold, it will offload to the prefill worker pool. Here is an example YAML snippet that configures the system to use conditional disaggregation if the calculated score is above a configurable remote_prefill_min_score value:

```
disaggregated_router:
  enable: true
  policies:
    - metric: prefill_length    # Prompt length after prefix cache hit
      threshold: 256
```

```
    action: prefer_remote    # if prompt > 256 tokens, offload prefill
    weight: 0.7
  - metric: prefill_queue_depth  # requests queued for prefill workers
    threshold: 10
    action: prefer_local     # if queue > 10, lean toward prefill locally
    weight: 0.3
remote_prefill_min_score: 0.5  # overall threshold decide remote prefill
```

Here, the router computes a score based on prefill_length and prefill_queue_depth. In this case, if the prompt is longer than 256 tokens, it votes to prefill_remote and offload the prefill. This part of the score calculation carries a weight of 0.7, as configured here.

But if the prefill queue is very deep with more than 10 waiting tasks, as configured here, it will vote to prefill_local with a weight of 0.3, as configured here. If the combined score is greater than remote_prefill_min_score, or 0.5 in this case, Dynamo will offload the prefill. Otherwise, it will keep the prefill local and not offload it.

Multipath inference (racing)

Multipath inference, or sending the same request to two different model sizes or two different routes, is used for high reliability. It's essentially racing to the fastest result and is often called *racing*. Google's and Meta's production systems are known to race models to reduce tail latency. It's a costly but effective technique.

> If implementing multipath inference yourself, make sure your requests are idempotent and won't cause issues if both paths execute. And make sure to cancel the slower path promptly to save GPU cycles.

Multibranch, parallel speculative decoding across workers

As discussed in Chapter 15, some advanced inference servers support speculative decoding. Remember that speculative decoding generates multiple token branches in parallel, discarding those that are not the most ideal.

While not a direct part of disaggregation, speculative decoding can be layered on top of the router's decision-making process. For instance, the system could detect an uncertain speculative decoding branch and send multiple speculative requests to different decode workers in parallel. This would generate multiple speculative next-token branches and mask the unpredictability in token-branch generation. This trades extra compute for lower latency for generations with unpredictable branches.

If implemented, the router would coordinate these speculative efforts and then merge results. Resource usage would need to be bound to avoid overwhelming the cluster, but multipath inference is worth noting as a potential optimization for ultra-latency-aware inference, at the expense of additional, potentially wasted compute and memory-bandwidth cluster resources.

In summary, a latency-aware router ensures each request is sent to the optimal place, considering both current load and potential speedups like cache reuse. It acts as the "brain" of a distributed serving system, working in concert with the lower-level scheduling on each GPU. Together with global scaling and KV caching strategies, it forms a comprehensive approach to maximize goodput and minimize latency.

QoS and early rejection policies

QoS policies prioritize or throttle certain requests to meet latency targets. Early rejection, also called *admission control*, can refuse low-priority queries when the system is saturated. This way, it preserves resources and SLOs, such as latency for other requests.

Modern systems do this based on a *queue time threshold*. For example, if a request has sat in queue > X ms, it might be better to reject it or offload it to a lower-tier service rather than let it severely violate the SLO. This kind of QoS guard is increasingly common for mission-critical inference systems.

In ultrascale inference systems, QoS mechanisms are needed to maintain tail latency guarantees under heavy load. Even with an optimized disaggregated cluster configuration, if load exceeds capacity, requests will start queuing and latencies will rise.

Rather than allowing latency SLOs to be violated for all requests, a well-designed system will prefer to shed load gracefully. It can do this by rejecting or deferring some requests, especially lower-priority ones, when it is clear that serving them would break the latency guarantees for others.

This is analogous to how web servers return HTTP 503 (*https://oreil.ly/5Guho*) "overloaded" errors under extreme load. For LLM serving, we might proactively refuse or down-sample requests if we can't guarantee serving them in time. Here are a few components to QoS in the context of prefill/decode disaggregation:

Latency SLO tracking
 The system should be aware of target TTFT and TPOT goals. For instance, the first token must return within 200 ms 99% of the time. Using internal telemetry, each decode worker can estimate the current TTFT for a new request if it were to be accepted right now and based on current queue lengths, etc. It can similarly estimate TPOT if another decode stream is added.

Admission control (early rejection)
 Before a request is fully accepted and assigned, the system can perform a check to see if admitting this request will overload the system or violate SLOs. If yes, it can

reject the request immediately with a "server busy, try later" type of response. This is called *early rejection*. In practice, you can use a global view of system load or simply a single node's heuristic to trigger the early rejection.

OpenAI's public API, for instance, returns an error if the backlog is too high. It does this rather than violate the latency commitment. Some providers dynamically lower the maximum generation length during peak load. This effectively trades off answer quality for latency.

Prioritization

Not all requests are equal. Some requests might be high priority if they come from paying customers or critical services, for instance. Others might be lower if they're from free-tier users or background jobs. The system can incorporate priority into scheduling decisions. For instance, a decode worker's scheduler could serve high-priority decode tasks first. Or the prefill task queue could be ordered by priority. If things get busy, low-priority tasks may wait longer or be fast-failed in favor of high-priority ones.

Graceful degradation

If the system starts to get overloaded, instead of outright rejecting requests, it could degrade service for less important ones. For instance, it might use smaller models for less important requests, truncate their prompts, or cap the number of output tokens. One simple approach is to temporarily reduce the maximum allowed prompt length or output length for lower-tier requests when load is high.

In the context of disaggregation, one interesting form of graceful degradation is to temporarily disable remote prefilling for lower-priority requests when the system is under stress. Since remote prefill uses additional cluster resources to optimize latency, one could decide that low-priority queries should just do local prefill and use only the decode worker resources. This would produce a slower response for these requests, but it frees up the prefill workers for high-priority queries.

For instance, an inference server could tag each request with a priority and have the router ignore the `should_offload_prefill` logic for low-priority requests when prefill workers are busy with high-priority tasks.

Here is an example of an early rejection policy. This could run on each decode worker before processing a request even upstream on an LLM gateway:

```python
# Early rejection based on estimated latency and priority
from dataclasses import dataclass

class QoSController:
    def __init__(self, ttft_slo_ms: int = 500):
        self.ttft_slo_ms = ttft_slo_ms

    def admit_request(self, priority: str) -> bool:
```

```
# The queue length and per-request averages are fed by the metrics system
est_ttft = (get_current_prefill_queue_length()
            * get_avg_prefill_time_per_req()
            + get_current_decode_queue_length()
            * get_avg_decode_time_per_req())

if est_ttft > self.ttft_slo_ms and priority.lower() == "low":
    # reject low priority request to protect SLOs
    return False
return True
```

Here, we estimate TTFT by looking at how many prefill tasks are queued since each will add some delay, as well as how many decode tasks are ahead. Note that decode tasks typically overlap, so this is a rough estimate. If the estimated TTFT exceeds the allowed maximum, the SLO, then for a low-priority request we reject it and return False from the should_offload_prefill function.

For a high-priority request, we still accept it and perhaps sacrifice some other queued work, if necessary. A more sophisticated approach is to preempt a low-priority request that's already queued to make room for the new high-priority one. This is often implemented by maintaining separate queues per priority level.

Diving a bit deeper, in the preceding example, the avg_prefill_time_per_req() and avg_decode_time_per_req() functions compute the values on the fly using an exponential moving average of the observed per-request prefill and decode durations. They're normalized by the number of prompt tokens (prefill) and generated tokens (decode). And for inputs of varying length, the engine extrapolates by multiplying these per-token averages by the actual token count for each request.

The get_current_prefill_queue_length() and get_current_decode_queue_length() functions retrieve the number of pending prefill and decode tasks tracked by the scheduler's internal queues. These values are maintained by the scheduler.

These per-token timing estimates are refreshed in real time using the scheduler loop, which, by default, updates every second from using /metrics endpoint. This captures dynamic workload changes.

Early rejection and prioritization make sure that when the system nears saturation, it fails in a controlled manner rather than collapsing. Users with the most important requests continue to get served within the provided SLO. Meanwhile, less important traffic is shed.

In many production deployments, implementing this requires coordination with the LLM gateway layer. Specifically, the gateway might return a specific error code or return a code indicating server-overload back to the client. The key is that the system keeps itself in a state where it can meet the latency promises for the work it does accept, rather than oversubscribing and missing SLOs for everyone.

Another QoS consideration is adaptive generation limits. If the decode phase threatens to run too long and cause a TPOT SLO violation, the system might cut off the generation early. For instance, if a user requested 1,000 tokens but the system is under pressure, it might only allow 200 tokens to be generated and then stop. This leaves resources for other requests. QoS policies prioritize or throttle certain requests to meet latency targets; early rejection can refuse low-priority queries when the system is saturated to preserve SLA for others.

In short, disaggregation reduces inherent interference, but load spikes can still overwhelm any fixed capacity. QoS mechanisms complement the disaggregation architecture by making sure it delivers on its latency promises. Early rejection will reject or deprioritize some work to protect the latency of the rest of the requests.

When building ultrascale systems, these policies are as important as core performance optimizations. Without them, a flood of requests could ruin all attempts to improve performance by creating huge queues and slowdowns.

Scalability of Disaggregated Prefill and Decode

Another aspect of scalability is how performance holds as more nodes are added. The disaggregated approach, by design, scales relatively linearly in many respects. You can add more prefill nodes to handle more prompt throughput. And you can add more decode nodes to handle more token-generation throughput.

The main challenge is balancing them. Adaptive schedulers become even more important as scale increases. This is because the chance of an imbalance, such as a shifting traffic pattern, is much higher in a large system. A dynamic ratio configuration allows clusters to rebalance the ratio of prefill and decode on the fly.

Another consideration is multimodel serving. Disaggregation allows you to share decode capacity between models if their decoding characteristics are similar. For instance, if model A and model B are hosted on the same cluster, you can dedicate some decode workers to handle both types of models. This is particularly useful when hosting different LoRA (*https://oreil.ly/P1Piz*) adapters that reuse the same base model architecture.

This would give you a super flexible, multitenant, multimodel, prefill-decode-disaggregated inference server system. This is beyond our scope, but just know that disaggregation's modularity gives you this type of flexibility. You can have a common decode pool for multiple models, each with its own prefill frontend.

Finally, let's analyze tail latency in very large systems. As ultrascale inference systems scale out to thousands and millions of GPU nodes, it becomes harder and harder to control tail latency. This is because with more servers, the chance that one fails is much higher.

Disaggregation can help here, too. Isolating prefill tasks on one node and decode tasks on another means a slow node on one side won't drastically impact tasks on the other side.

Techniques like early rejection, two-level scheduling, and KV cache reuse, discussed in this chapter, can help to mitigate stragglers. For instance, caching large parts of a request's context means that one slow operation won't slow down the whole generation as much—because a lot of the computation was already done.

In summary, disaggregated systems are more robust at scale when properly configured and tuned. These systems can maintain consistent latency even as concurrent requests grow into the millions and billions. By removing one interference factor and adding adaptability, the tail latency distribution improves —or, at least, won't degrade as fast with load.

Key Takeaways

The techniques covered in this chapter, from high-speed RDMA transfers of KV cache to dynamic routing algorithms and QoS policies, have proven to be essential components for large-scale production inference workloads. Here are the key takeaways:

Eliminate prefill-decode interference to improve latency
Separating prefill and decode phases removes interference and head-of-line blocking. This yields tighter latency distributions since long prompts won't delay shorter prompts. This also lets each phase meet its latency SLO reliably.

Optimize each phase independently
Prefill (prompt processing) is compute bound and benefits from maximum parallelism and high FLOPS. It prefers high-compute GPUs and techniques like FP8/FP4 reduced precision to minimize TTFT. Decode (token generation) is memory bound and benefits from high-memory bandwidth GPUs and techniques like continuous batching to maximize throughput per token. Disaggregation allows different hardware and parallelism settings for each phase. A fixed, one-size-fits-all configuration does not allow this.

Leverage the KV cache
It's common to use a KV cache to avoid recomputing prompt prefills. A smart router can decide if a new request should be offloaded to a prefill worker or handled directly on the decode worker. The routing policy should consider prompt length, cache hits, and cluster load.

Route intelligently

Modern inference servers like vLLM, SGLang, and NVIDIA Dynamo use a multifactor scoring algorithm to route prefill and decode requests to maximize throughput and maintain adequate latency. Many frameworks also refer to TPOT as *inter-token latency* (ITL) in schedulers and dashboards. It's recommended to track TTFT (p50/p95/p99) and ITL/TPOT (p50/p95/p99) separately for prefill versus decode nodes. This way, performance regressions are easier to debug during upgrades, for instance. For example, they will skip remote prefill if the prefill servers are saturated or if the prompt is short.

Use QoS to maintain SLAs at scale

Apply admission control and prioritization under heavy load. It's best to fast-fail excess or low-priority requests than to let the system's latency explode for everyone. Real-world systems implement early rejection by returning "busy" errors or a degraded response length—to guarantee that 99th-percentile latency stays under a given threshold. Disaggregation and QoS together prevent overload cascades—even in billion-request-per-day scenarios.

Conclusion

Disaggregated prefill and decode is now common in modern high-scale LLM inference. Virtually all major AI providers like Meta, Amazon, NVIDIA, Google, and OpenAI (or "MANGO") have embraced some form of disaggregated architecture in their large-scale LLM deployments.

While most of these companies do not publish their complete production architecture, there are numerous open source implementations (e.g., vLLM, SGLang, NVIDIA's Dynamo) that demonstrate this approach and its benefits. Disaggregated PD produces higher goodput, or useful throughput under latency constraints, and better cost-efficiency than monolithic designs.

In the next chapter, we'll continue combining modern GPU and networking hardware with more advanced scheduling and caching optimizations to serve multi-trillion-parameter model LLMs to billions of users without sacrificing latency or blowing up costs.

## CHAPTER 18

Advanced Prefill-Decode and KV Cache Tuning

This chapter builds upon Chapter 17 and dives deeper into advanced optimizations for the inference prefill and decode phases. We'll build upon the high-level scaling strategies and cover low-level techniques, including single decode "mega kernels," intelligent KV cache tuning and sharing across GPUs, fast GPU-to-GPU transfer of the prompt state, adaptive resource scheduling, and dynamic routing between prefill and decode workers.

We will also highlight hardware and software innovations, which provide new levels of performance and efficiency. By applying these techniques, you can significantly reduce decode latency, improve throughput per GPU, and meet strict latency SLOs at scale.

Optimized Decode Kernels

Until now, we have been focused on high-level system and cluster optimization strategies. Another set of techniques to consider when increasing ultrascale inference is low-level kernel and memory management tuning—especially for the decode phase.

The decode phase is distributed and often memory bound. This has motivated researchers and practitioners to make the decode phase as fast as possible—and tuned for specific hardware. Two notable innovations in this space are FlashMLA (Deep-Seek), ThunderMLA (Stanford), and FlexDecoding (PyTorch). These specifically target the transformer's multihead attention efficiency during decode in variable-sequence scenarios common in LLM workloads. Let's cover each of these next.

FlashMLA (DeepSeek)

Flash Multi-Latent Attention, or FlashMLA, is an optimized decoding kernel introduced by DeepSeek. It specifically focuses on the single-token decode step, which is essentially the forward pass of a transformer layer used to generate the next token. FlashMLA makes decode faster by fusing operations and better using the GPU memory hierarchy.

FlashMLA (decode) is to inference what FlashAttention (prefill) is to training. It reduces memory access overhead and latency. With FlashMLA, you can achieve large latency reductions for the decode phase compared to standard kernels.

FlashMLA increases arithmetic intensity by fusing multiple attention operations into one. This way, it can process multiple heads and multiple time steps in one fused kernel launch. This increases GPU utilization during the decode by keeping the math units busy despite small batch sizes. Figure 18-1 shows the improvement in arithmetic intensity for MLA compared to other attention implementations like grouped-query attention (GQA) and multiquery attention (MQA) on a Hopper H100 GPU. (Note: Blackwell shifts both rooflines upward with higher TFLOPs and HBM bandwidth.)

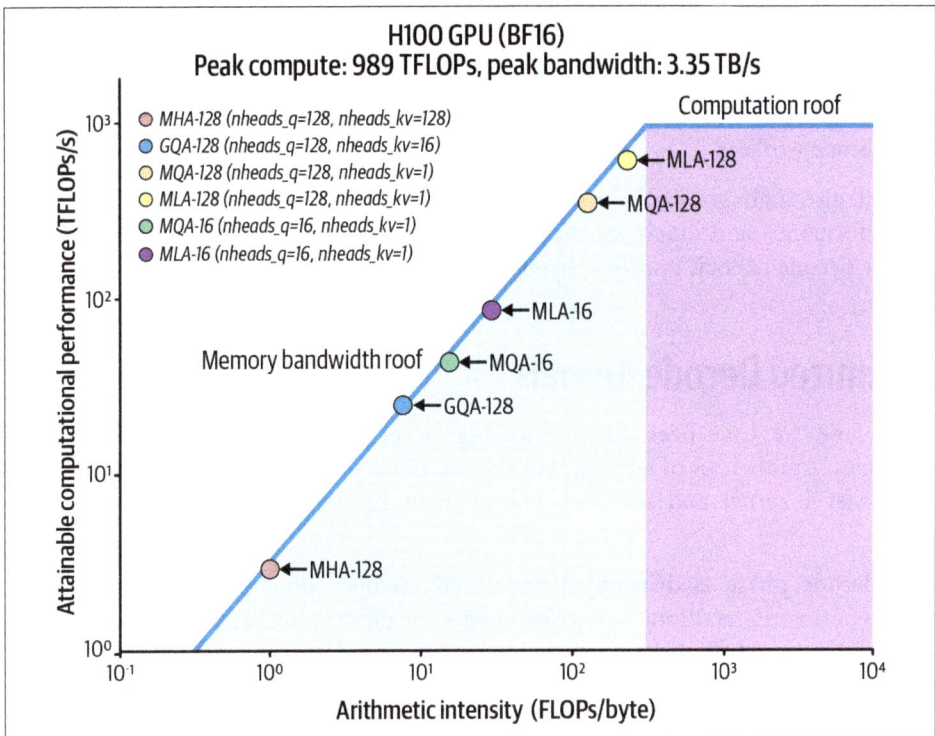

Figure 18-1. MLA approaches the compute-bound regime (measured on the NVIDIA Hopper H100 architecture)

The introduction of FlashMLA was significant because it showed that the decode phase's bottlenecks, memory bandwidth, and kernel-launch overhead can be reduced—even on suboptimal GPU hardware. It reduced the number of separate GPU kernel launches and optimized memory access patterns—squeezing as much performance out of constrained hardware as possible for decoding tasks.

DeepSeek's open sourced FlashMLA implementation is available and seeing adoption. SGLang and vLLM both provide first-class support for DeepSeek models. As such, you should evaluate FlashMLA to increase per-token decode throughput without changing higher-level architecture.

Since DeepSeek's open sourced FlashMLA is integrated into modern inference serving systems, you should explore it as a way to increase the throughput of each decode worker—or reduce latency per token—without any higher-level architectural change.

ThunderMLA (Stanford)

Building on FlashMLA, researchers at Stanford introduced ThunderMLA (*https:// oreil.ly/PZpR3*), a completely fused attention decode "megakernel" that focuses on decoding and scheduling (rather than fusing the full feed-forward block.) This "megakernel" reduces launch overhead and tail effects by combining multiple kernel launches into one—as well as consolidating intermediate memory writes. Thunder-MLA reports 20–35% faster decode (*https://oreil.ly/zEEIE*) throughput compared to FlashMLA across different workloads

The key idea of ThunderMLA is that when decoding sequences of different lengths, using fine-grained scheduling and fused operations can avoid the tail effect in which some sequences finish earlier while others leave the GPU partially idle. ThunderMLA keeps the GPU busy even if some decode streams complete earlier. It does this by dynamically packing and processing the remaining streams using its fused approach.

These benefits are amplified on modern GPUs with larger L2 caches and faster attention primitives. Notably, modern NVIDIA GPUs also provide Transformer Engine support for FP8 and FP4 (and FP6, although we focus mostly on FP8/FP4 formats in this text since FP6 is not widely used in existing AI frameworks and tools). Combined with higher memory bandwidth, the Tensor Cores let kernels like ThunderMLA operate much closer to hardware limits. On modern GPUs, ThunderMLA achieves even lower latency per token due to these architectural advances.

FlexDecoding (PyTorch)

In Chapter 14, we discussed PyTorch's FlexAttention, which lets you JIT-compile fused kernels for arbitrary sparsity patterns in attention, including local windows, block-sparse patterns, etc.—all without writing custom CUDA. Under the hood, TorchInductor + OpenAI's Triton generate a fused kernel that computes only the allowed query-key pairs for that pattern. Triton automatically applies performance optimization techniques like warp specialization and asynchronous copies when beneficial on the given hardware. However, you can also tune `triton.Config` to further customize by configuring `num_consumer_groups` for example.

FlexDecoding is the decoding backend of `torch.nn.attention.flex_attention`. FlexDecoding also lets you manage KV in place and supports masks and biases just like FlexAttention. Specifically, FlexDecoding compiles a specialized kernel for the decode phase (`Q_len=1`) attending over a growing KV cache.

At runtime, the FlexDecoding implementation picks the specialized decode kernel and reuses it across multiple decode steps. This helps to minimize overhead when shapes and dtypes remain compatible—greatly speeding up long-sequence LLM inference.

> Prefer `torch.compile(mode="max-autotune")` for stable, latency-critical decode once recompilations are under control. Keep the capture boundary narrow (per-layer or attention block) to reduce graph invalidations from ragged batching. Prefer Transformer Engine FP8 (MXFP8) for prefill and decode. Consider FP4 (NVFP4) when accuracy permits and performance increases. As of this writing, FP4 support is still maturing and can underperform 8-bit and 16-bit formats in the near-term. Continue to set `torch.set_float32_matmul_precision("high")` to enable TF32 fallback on remaining FP32 ops. FlexAttention's decode backend supports common performance enhancements including grouped-query attention (GQA) and PagedAttention.

A key feature of FlexAttention and FlexDecoding includes support for nested jagged-layout tensors (NJT). These allow ragged batching of variable-length sequences (common in LLM workloads) during decoding. A jagged tensor representation of various sequences is shown in Figure 18-2.

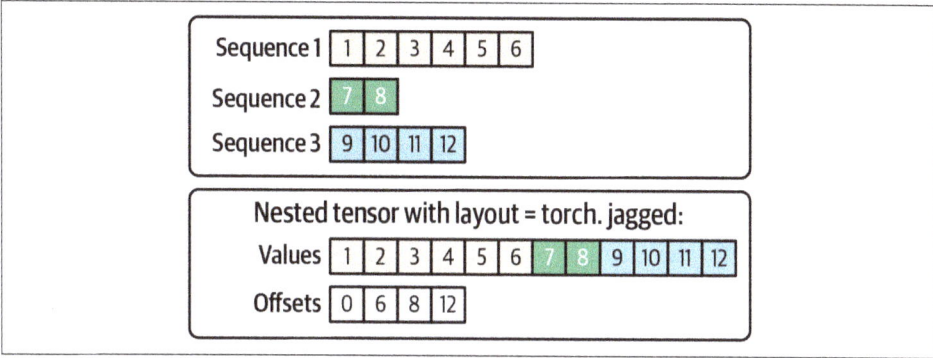

*Figure 18-2. Ragged batch as a nested jagged tensor (offsets); three sequences (top) repre-
sented as a single nested jagged tensor representation with offsets (bottom); prefer
PyTorch NJT for decode-time batching*

Additionally, FlexDecoding supports bias terms and integrates with PagedAttention
by using a block mask conversion interface that maps logical blocks to the physical
cache layout. This scatters logical KV blocks into the physical cache layout—without
creating extra copies, as shown in Figure 18-3.

FlexDecoding leverages captured tensors to vary certain mask or bias values during
each iteration—without requiring a recompile. And it integrates with PagedAttention.
To use a global KV cache such as vLLM LMCache, map the cache's page table to Flex-
Attention's BlockMask. This will translate logical KV pages into physical memory
addresses on the fly.

With FlexDecoding, developers have full Python-level flexibility for custom attention
sparsity patterns. This is particularly useful for MoE model inference. FlexDecoding
allows you to achieve near-optimal performance without requiring you to write any
custom CUDA kernels. Essentially, it allows arbitrary attention patterns to be optimized similarly to dense attention patterns. This becomes even more valuable as new
inference techniques emerge.

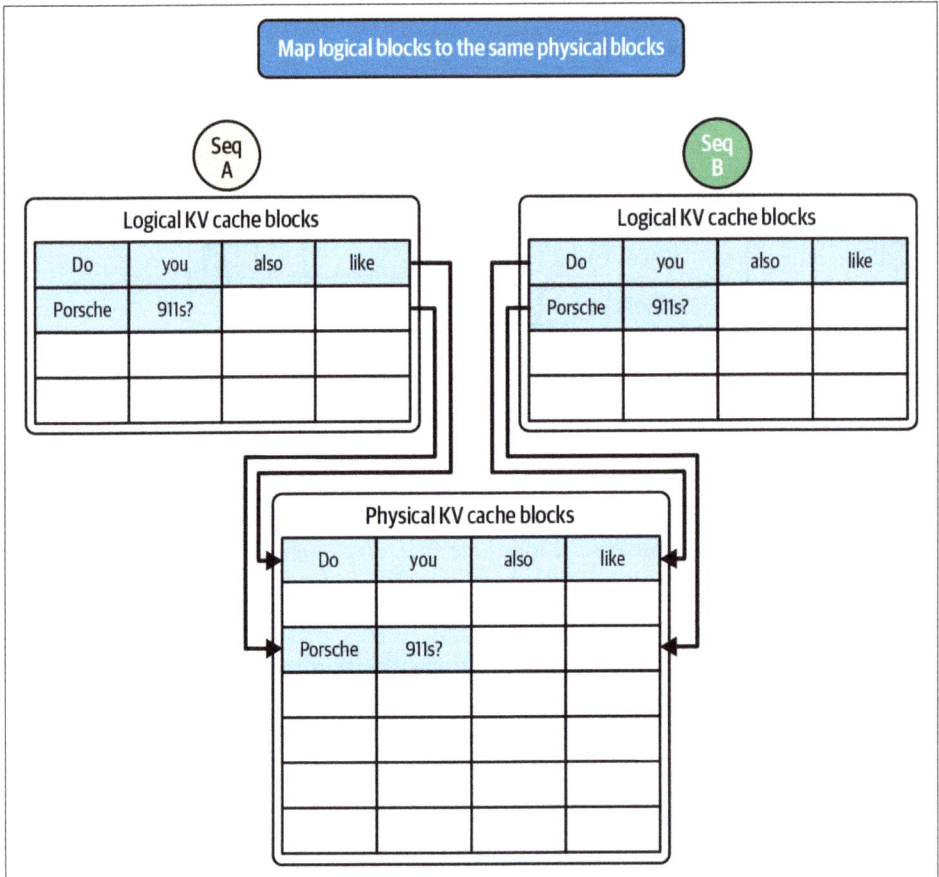

Figure 18-3. PagedAttention scatters logical KV blocks into physical KV blocks for optimal cache reuse between sequences; align block sizes with LMCache page size—larger pages (e.g., 64–128 tokens) reduce RDMA overhead in disaggregated setups

Many of these capabilities, such as fused attention for decoding and support for PyTorch's nested jagged tensors (NJT) batching, are available in the core PyTorch library. This makes custom fusion less necessary for typical patterns.

Prefer the NJT layout when batching ragged sequences common in LLM workloads.

These kernel-level advancements are highly technical and leverage the full power of the GPU, network, and memory. These software optimizations can significantly improve decode performance—even on the same hardware. When designing an ultrascale system, you should incorporate these optimized kernels, if possible. Be sure to verify overlap and kernel efficiency using Nsight Systems with hardware-based CUDA traces. Additionally, use Nsight Compute for specific memory and link metrics.

> Enabling some of these advanced kernels might require installing a custom library or enabling a specialized CUDA kernel—especially for newer techniques. However, these techniques are typically supported by PyTorch and the popular inference engines soon after they are released. Even if you do need to install custom resources, the effort is worthwhile since it will directly translate to lower latency and fewer GPUs in the decode worker pool.

Tuning KV Cache Utilization and Management

Disaggregation requires that you treat the KV cache as a first-class shared resource across the cluster. Since KV caches can now live longer and move between nodes, high-performance inference systems have improved how the KV cache is stored and shared.

In particular, distributed KV cache pools and prefix reuse across requests become powerful techniques. Additionally, it's important to keep an eye on the memory bandwidth improvements with newer GPU and HBM generations. Let's discuss each of these in the context of improving KV cache performance.

Disaggregated KV Cache Pool

Instead of each GPU storing KV only for the requests it's currently serving, a disaggregated KV cache pool decouples KV storage from individual GPUs. Instead, it spreads the data out across the entire cluster's GPU memory.

The pool can also offload to CPU memory, including the unified CPU and GPU memory of the Grace Blackwell and Vera Rubin platforms. It can also offload to persistent storage like NVMe SSDs.

Using a disaggregated KV cache pool, when a prefill computes the KV tensors for a prompt—or when a decode extends the KV tensors—the KV blocks are stored in a distributed manner across many compute nodes. This is shown in Figure 18-4, adapted from work on disaggregated KV pools (*https://oreil.ly/2xtK-*).

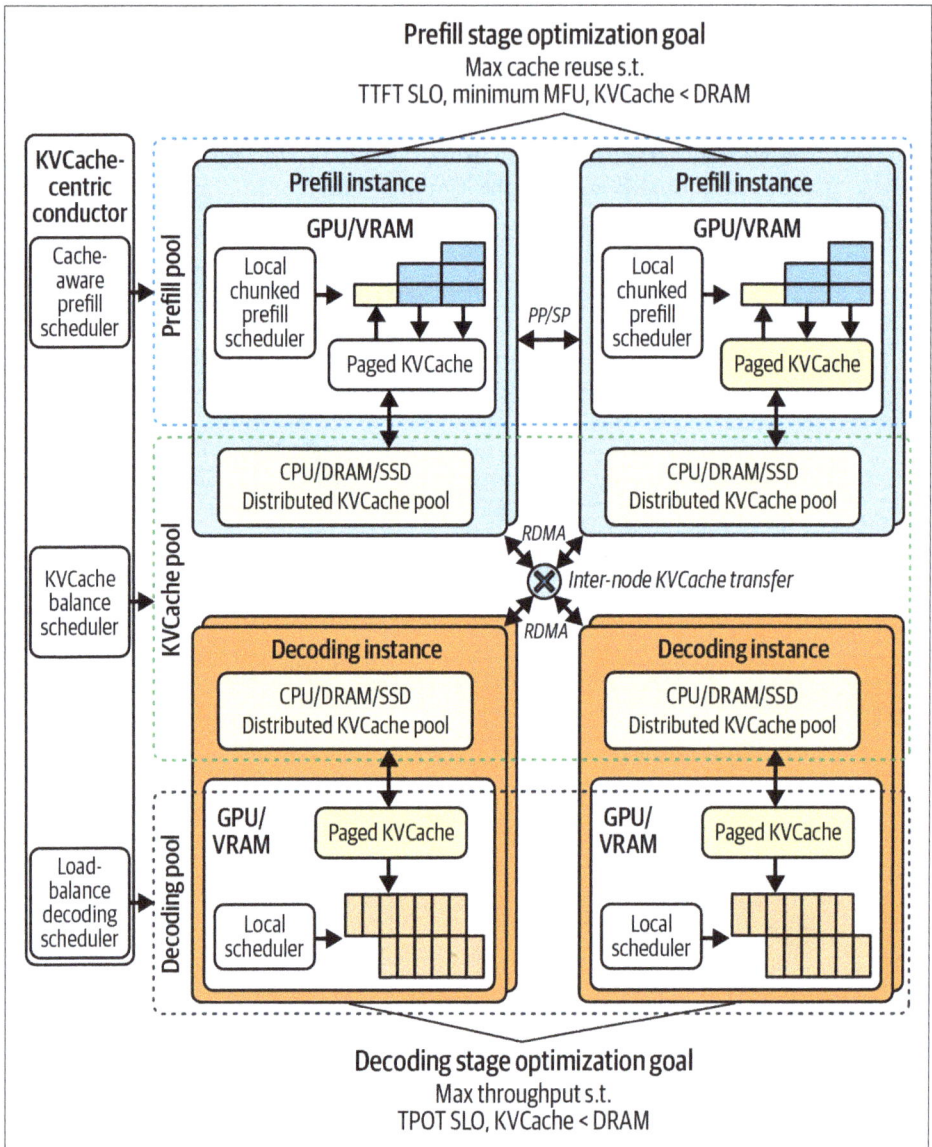

Figure 18-4. Disaggregated (distributed) KV cache pool (source: https://oreil.ly/2xtK-)

Consider a very long 250,000-token context (e.g., a chat session with many turns) using a 70 billion-parameter transformer model with 80 layers and 32 heads in which each head is dimension 128. This generates a huge KV cache footprint per token.

Each token generates a key and value vector of length equal to the model's hidden dimension (num_heads × head_dim). Let's assume this is 4,096 for our model. This results in 8,192 floats per layer. Summing across 80 layers, this creates 655,360 floats of KV data per token. Let's assume 16-bit precision, or 2 bytes per float. This is roughly 1.31 MB needed per token. Scaling this to 250,000 tokens produces about 328 GB—just for the KV data!

> These calculations are based on per-token KV sizes for large models. This shows why FP8 KV caches are widely adopted in engines such as vLLM to reduce footprint and increase batching opportunities.

Assuming we quantize the KV cache down to FP8 and use techniques like selective-layer caching, we can reduce this footprint down to maybe the 100–150 GB range for this 250,000-token prompt. A single GPU will likely not have capacity for all of the tokens' KV along with everything else it needs to hold, such as model weights, etc.—especially as the multiturn conversation continues. As such, the system would need to truncate context—or cause expensive KV recomputation on earlier tokens.

With a disaggregated KV pool, however, older parts of the context's KV can be evicted from the GPU and pushed out to the KV cache pool spread across the cluster—and in CPU DRAM or NVMe storage. The data is then fetched back into GPU memory when it's needed.

A disaggregated KV cache pool implements a multitier memory hierarchy in which GPU device memory holds the active KV cache while the CPU host RAM (or NVMe storage) serves as the overflow backing store. Modern inference engines can choose to offload KV cache to CPU memory or NVMe. This effectively virtualizes GPU memory much like an OS's virtual memory subsystem.

This design allows for ultralong contexts by asynchronously paging KV blocks between GPU memory and the KV cache pool without stalling the compute pipelines—assuming good communication-computation overlap, as discussed throughout this book.

Additionally, by decoupling request state from individual GPUs, the system can use the global KV cache pool to dynamically shard KV data across multiple nodes in the cluster to adaptively balance the load. This simplifies scaling and improves fault isolation in large inference clusters.

And since any decode node can access the global KV pool, then any decode node can participate in decoding any request, if needed due to failover or load balancing. This adds flexibility for the scheduler since it can choose a decode node closest to where the relevant KV cache blocks are located.

If some KV blocks of a prefix are cached in DRAM on server A, it might be faster to schedule the decode on server A since it can quickly pull them into its GPU. This is in contrast to server B, which would have to fetch the KV blocks over the network.

> This describes a classic distributed-systems best practice of choosing a compute node that is closest to the data being computed. This way, the system minimizes expensive data movement.

An efficient KV cache scheduler can look at the distribution of KV blocks in the pool—in addition to the network topology—and assign prefill and decode tasks accordingly. As such, a prefill node can place KV data into a pool implemented as a distributed memory space accessible across the cluster.

With the KV cache in a cluster-side shared-memory space, any decode node can retrieve the data. This avoids having to schedule for direct prefill-to-decode transfers every time.

This adds a bit of extra overhead due to an extra hop to retrieve KV data from the pool, but it allows more flexibility because all decode nodes have access to all KV-cached data. It also means that a decode node that didn't directly receive data from a particular prefill can still access the KV data from the pool, if needed.

If a decode node crashes—or a request needs to move mid-generation for whatever reason—the KV data isn't lost. The data lives in the pool, and another node can pick it up and continue where it left off using the saved KV. This improves fault tolerance.

A global KV cache pool also provides cache persistence across requests. This way, if two requests share some prefix, the KV for that prefix can be computed once and reused across the cluster—even if the requests end up on different decode servers.

In short, a disaggregated KV cache pool trades memory (or colder storage) for compute. By storing a larger KV cache, the system can avoid recomputing KV data in many scenarios. This approach leverages the fact that reusing data—even from DRAM or SSD—is often cheaper than repeatedly recomputing large attention matrix multiplications with quadratic time complexity, $O(N^2)$.

KV Cache Reuse and Prefix Sharing

As mentioned, it's beneficial to reuse cached KV data across requests for prompts that share a common prefix. This scenario arises fairly often in the form of multiturn conversations, shared system prompts, and attached documents.

Instead of recomputing the transformer attention outputs for that prefix for every request, the system can store the KV outputs for the prefix and reuse them directly.

Essentially, this skips the prefill computation for that portion of the input, which saves a lot of time and GPU cycles.

A proper KV-cache-centric scheduler takes into account prefix cache hits by looking at the "prefix cache hit length," or how many tokens of this prompt are already present in the cache pool, when assigning work. In practice, if a new request comes and its first N tokens match some cached prefix in the KV pool, the system can decide to reuse that KV data.

vLLM implements automatic prefix caching using a global hash table of KV "pages" using its PagedAttention mechanism. Here, each unique 16-token block of context has a hash. If a new request needs a prefix that matches a stored block (by hash), it can directly copy those KV tensors instead of recomputing.

If the same context appears again, the system serves it from memory. In essence, it treats the KV of a context as reusable data that can be looked up by content using hashing. Implementations typically maintain a global "prompt tree" to manage these cached contexts and evict them when necessary. This optimizes for the most frequently reused prefixes.

A key to effective KV reuse is identifying identical or overlapping prefixes. Usually, systems focus on exact matches for simplicity such that if the first N tokens match exactly, they reuse that chunk. Combining partial-prefix overlaps is more complex since you need to somehow merge caches, which isn't always straightforward. So typical caching uses exact prefix caching.

There is a trade-off, however. Storing many users' KV caches indefinitely can consume a lot of memory. A system must implement eviction policies like LRU for KV blocks to drop caches that are unlikely to be reused. This frees space for new ones. The scheduler might also decide which caches to keep based on likelihood of reuse. The idea is to maximize cache hits within memory constraints.

If a certain prefill node already holds a portion of the KV needed in its local GPU memory or local DRAM cache, it might be beneficial to route the request to that node to minimize data transfer. This is an example of data-aware scheduling in which it sends the compute to where the data is, rather than always pulling data to wherever compute is available.

This is analogous to locality-aware scheduling in distributed systems. In our earlier routing discussion, we touched on this. If possible, you should route a request to the server that generated its prefix. This maximizes the likelihood of a cache hit.

In the broader context of disaggregation, prefix caching is supported by having a unified view of KV across many requests and possibly storing it in a shareable place like the global pool. This is in contrast to a siloed per-request or per-node approach.

This also helps reduce the overhead of recomputation that disaggregation might otherwise incur if the same prompt goes to different nodes at different times. With a global KV store or coordinated caching, even if a user's requests hit different decode servers, they can benefit from each other's cached work.

Optimized KV Cache Memory Layout

Another area of low-level innovation is optimizing the KV cache memory layouts. The KV cache, which stores keys and values for all past tokens in each sequence, can become huge for many concurrent decode streams since each stream uses memory roughly proportional to `num_layers` $\times 2 \times$ `sequence_length` $\times$ `d_head`.

Techniques like tiered caching are useful since not all KV pairs need to be kept in GPU memory at all times. Older parts of the KV cache can be swapped to CPU—or even compressed.

Since we emphasize keeping decode latency low, most designs keep the active KV cache in GPU memory for quick access. In this case, you can tune how the memory is laid out and accessed.

DeepSeek's FlashMLA pages KV cache and allocates the cache in fixed-size blocks (pages) so that contiguous memory accesses can happen for active sequences. This reduces cache misses and DRAM traffic.

Additionally, some systems implement prefix compression if a prompt's prefix will no longer be attended to because the context window has moved, for instance. In this case, the KV cache manager might drop or compress these KV entries. This is more relevant in long conversations because the context window slides. But it can save memory and bandwidth for extremely long sequences.

> This eviction/compression technique is safe when the model uses a sliding-window or other restricted-attention pattern. However, it should not be applied to layers that retain full attention over the full content window (or retrieval hooks) without careful evaluation.

Another technique called *POD-Attention* (*https://oreil.ly/k6P9M*) similarly reorganizes attention computation to reduce HBM traffic. Specifically, it uses SM-aware thread-block (or cooperative thread array [CTA]) scheduling. This implements *runtime operation binding* to dynamically assign each CTA running on an SM to either perform a prefill or decode task. This is shown in Figure 18-5.

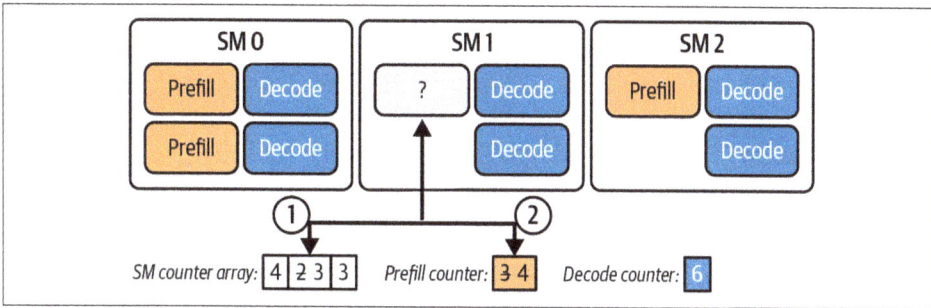

Figure 18-5. SM-aware thread-block (CTA) scheduling to match prefill tasks with decode tasks on SMs to minimize memory movement

So rather than statically launching separate kernels for each phase, a single kernel launches enough CTAs to cover both workloads. At runtime, each CTA inspects which SM it's on and uses per-SM counters to decide which operation (prefill or decode) should be run based on what else is running on that SM.

The SM-aware scheduling logic tries to match prefill with decode operations at runtime. This avoids isolated bursts of memory traffic and smooths out resource demands.

Specifically, POD-Attention colocates prefill and decode work on the same SM so the fused kernel can improve locality and reduce redundant HBM transactions. This minimizes memory movement, maximizes bandwidth utilization, and balances compute-bound and memory-bound workloads on each SM. POD-Attention can improve attention performance by up to about 29% (*https://oreil.ly/rbPZa*) by colocating prefill and decode work on the same SMs with proper SM-aware CTA scheduling to unlock full overlap.

POD-Attention's dynamic binding decouples the hardware's CTA-SM assignment from the software's CTA-role assignment—either prefill or decode. This type of innovation shows a growing focus on hardware and software codesign to minimize memory movement and get the most out of your system's performance.

GPU and CPU-GPU Superchip Improvements

You should also consider memory bandwidth improvements in new hardware. Higher memory bandwidth and larger L2 caches directly benefit the performance of the memory-bound decode phase.

NVIDIA's Grace Blackwell GB200 NVL72 system, a rack-scale platform with 36 Grace CPUs and 72 Blackwell GPUs, allows a single logical decode unit with tens of terabytes of memory for KV cache. This hardware, with its ~30 TB of unified memory, is ideal to keep very large contexts in memory. These contexts can be on the order of millions of tokens.

With such a platform, the unified memory footprint is large. However, for latency-critical decode, you still want the active keys and values to live in GPU HBM. As such, you should use Grace CPU memory (LPDDR5X, not HBM) as a lower-tier cache or for very old tokens. Prefill and key-value offloading remain important when contexts exceed available HBM—even on a system like the NVL72.

In short, disaggregation at a macro level should be paired with microlevel optimizations to fully achieve maximum inference performance. Advanced decode kernels like FlashMLA/ThunderMLA, efficient memory layouts (paged caches, etc.), and the latest GPU architectures will produce efficient and scalable decode.

Fast KV Cache Transfer Between Prefill and Decode

A key requirement of disaggregated inference is quickly and efficiently transferring the KV cache from the prefill worker to a decode worker. If this transfer isn't fast, any time saved by parallelizing prefill and decode could be lost waiting on data movement.

In this section, we discuss the techniques used to minimize transfer overhead. We then describe how systems implement the handoff, using high-speed interconnects and avoiding extra KV copies.

KV Cache Size

Prefill output consists primarily of the KV cache for all prompt tokens. This can be a lot of data. Consider a model with L layers, each with h attention heads of dimension d, and a prompt of N tokens. The KV cache size is roughly $2 \times L \times N \times (h \times d)$, where the factor, 2, is for both keys and values.

The actual size depends on precision (FP16 versus INT8, etc.) and model specifics, but it's large. For instance, a 40-layer model with 16 heads of size 64 and a 1,000-token prompt produces on the order of 40,000 KV vectors. This could be hundreds of MB of data. If the number of tokens is 5,000, it's 5× larger.

Transferring this amount of data over a network can introduce significant latency if done naively. For instance, a naive approach might be to copy the KV to CPU memory on the prefill worker, then send it over TCP—or even write it to disk for the decode process to load. This could be extremely slow, on the order of hundreds of milliseconds for large prompts. The goal is to reduce the transfer time down to only a few milliseconds. This allows prefill and decode to truly overlap in parallel.

Achieving low-latency KV data transfer times typically requires collating small PagedAttention blocks into larger buffers and moving them with GPUDirect RDMA-based paths rather than CPU sockets.

Zero-Copy GPU-to-GPU Transfer

Modern disaggregated systems use zero-copy GPU-to-GPU transfer techniques. In practice, this involves using remote direct memory access (RDMA) over high-speed fabrics. For example, you can use InfiniBand for transfer between racks/nodes—or use NVLink/NVSwitch for direct GPU memory writes within a single node (multi-GPU) platform. These methods send data directly between GPUs without copying through CPU memory.

NVIDIA's high-performance GPU-to-GPU transfer library for inference is called *NVIDIA Inference Xfer Library* (NIXL). NIXL provides a plugin architecture (e.g., NVLink, UCX fabrics, GPUDirect Storage) for zero-copy GPU↔GPU and GPU↔storage data movement.

NIXL streamlines RDMA-style transfers, allowing one GPU to write directly into another GPU's memory over the available high-speed fabric—for example, InfiniBand or NVLink-based connections. In other words, the prefill GPU can directly inject the KV tensors into the decode worker GPU's memory.

RDMA-based protocols bypass the CPU and make full use of the GPU interconnect bandwidth. Systems like NVIDIA Dynamo and the open source vLLM plus LMCache integration rely on NIXL. Specifically, they use NIXL to write KV tensors directly into remote GPU memory over NVLink or RDMA. Modern GPU interconnects provide very high bandwidth, and a 1 GB transfer can complete in a few to tens of milliseconds depending on link type and contention.

In practice, implementations achieve low transfer times by overlapping data transfer with computation. For instance, with RDMA, a decode GPU can continue generating tokens for other sequences while a prefill worker is writing KV data into its memory buffer asynchronously. The prefill can push the data (RDMA write push model), or the decode can pull it (RDMA read), depending on design. Either way, no CPU involvement is needed in the data path.

Common strategies for fast KV transfer include prefill-side push, decode-side pull, shared-memory (CUDA IPC) buffer, connector/queue abstraction, and nonblocking overlap. Let's discuss each of these:

Prefill-side push

> The prefill worker, upon finishing the prompt, initiates an RDMA write of the KV data directly into a reserved buffer on the decode worker's GPU. This can be done nonblockingly; the prefill can start the transfer and then move on to other work while the DMA occurs in the background.

Decode-side pull

Alternatively, the decode worker can RDMA-read directly from the prefill GPU's memory when it's ready to begin decoding. Either push or pull achieves the same end result (no CPU copies). Some implementations might prefer push to offload coordination to the sender; others prefer pull for the receiver to control timing.

Shared-memory (IPC) buffer

If prefill and decode happen to be on the same machine (different GPUs in one server), they might use CUDA interprocess communication to share a memory handle or even a PCIe bar, effectively copying using NVLink or NVSwitch on the same host. This is a local variant of zero-copy transfer without going over the network.

Connector/queue abstraction

vLLM's implementation abstracts the transfer mechanism behind a logical interface (a Pipe or LookupBuffer). The prefill process places the KV into this buffer or signals its availability, and the decode side retrieves it. Under the hood, this can use RDMA or even a high-performance pub-sub message (NATS in Dynamo's case for control signals). The key is to decouple the logical handoff from the transport so different transports (RDMA, shared memory, etc.) can be plugged in.

Nonblocking overlap

As mentioned, optimized systems overlap KV transfer with ongoing decode computations. For example, Dynamo's decode worker continues generating tokens on other requests while a prefill worker is writing KV data into its GPU memory for a new request. This hides much of the transfer latency. As such, you can overlap a ~5 ms KV transfer with decode computation and add virtually zero net latency to the request's first generated token.

With these methods, KV transfers can take on the order of a few milliseconds. This is much less than the hundreds of milliseconds required to actually compute that KV on the prefill worker. As such, the pipeline of prefill → transfer → decode achieves good parallelism since the decode can start almost immediately after prefill completes—without a long stall.

Be careful to avoid fragmentation and overhead when sending KV cache data. For instance, vLLM's PagedAttention stores the KV cache in fixed-size token blocks, commonly 16 tokens per block. The KV blocks are relatively small (although the bytes per block scale with the number of heads, head dimension, number of layers, and dtype.) Naively sending thousands of small KV pages over RDMA would incur excessive overhead since each transfer has fixed latency and protocol overhead. This would lead to poor bandwidth utilization.

Modern LLM engines support multiple page sizes, such as 8, 16, 32, 64, or 128 tokens per block. Larger page sizes can reduce transfer overhead when moving KV over RDMA because sustained link throughput improves with larger collated buffers and fewer work queue elements (WQEs). When possible, collate ≥ 128-token pages per RDMA write. Make sure to overlap the transfer on a dedicated CUDA stream. Prefer nonblocking streams and use event fences. Always profile with tools like Nsight Systems to confirm overlap. LMCache reports ~20 ms → ~8 ms (*https://oreil.ly/l9U-D*) for a 7.5k-token KV after collation on RDMA.

The LMCache extension addresses this inefficiency by collating KV pages into large contiguous buffers before transfer. Essentially, it gathers the small chunks into one big chunk in GPU memory, then sends that large buffer in one transfer.

For instance, if sending a 7,500-token KV cache as 470 small transfers takes 20 ms, collating them into larger blocks (e.g., 128-token pages) reduces transfer time down to 8 ms. This simple batching optimization keeps the network pipe full and reduces per-packet overhead.

Let's show how a system is configured for fast GPU-to-GPU KV transfer. Here is an example config for LMCache's prefill-decode mode using a NIXL transfer channel:

```
# Prefill server config (lmcache-prefiller-config.yaml)
enable_pd: true
transfer_channel: "nixl"
pd_role: "sender"              # this instance sends KV data
pd_proxy_host: "decode-host"   # PD proxy / decode coordinator
pd_proxy_port: 7500            # control-plane port on the proxy/decoder
# size the buffer to the KV you plan to transfer
# FP8/FP4 KV should shrink it significantly
pd_buffer_size: 1073741824     # 1 GiB transfer buffer size
pd_buffer_device: "cuda"       # buffer stays in GPU memory
```

Here, the prefill server is configured as the RDMA sender. It targets the decode host's port 7500 with a 1 GB GPU buffer allocated for KV transfers. The decode server is configured as the receiver on that port with a matching 1 GB GPU buffer, as shown here:

```
# Decode server config (lmcache-decoder-config.yaml)
enable_pd: true
transfer_channel: "nixl"
pd_role: "receiver"            # this instance receives KV
pd_peer_host: "0.0.0.0"        # bind address for NIXL peer
pd_peer_init_port: 7300        # NIXL handshake/control port
pd_peer_alloc_port: 7400       # NIXL allocation/data port
pd_buffer_size: 1073741824     # 1 GiB (match sender unless you plan to shard)
pd_buffer_device: "cuda"       # keep buffer in GPU memory
nixl_backends: [UCX]           # UCX backend is sufficient for disagg
```

This configuration allows the prefill to write the KV cache directly into the decode GPU's memory—up to 1 GB per transfer—with no CPU intervention. Both sides keep the transfer buffer in GPU memory for zero-copy operation.

When sizing the transfer buffer, start at pd_buffer_size = 1 GB. This is roughly a FP16 KV cache estimated at ~4–8k tokens for a model with 70-billion parameters, 80 layers, 32 heads, and 128-dimension heads. Use 2 GB if prompts exceed ~7.5k tokens. You can scale with the dtype and head count: bytes $\approx 2 \times L \times N \times (H \times Dh) \times$ bytes_per_val. Make sure to collate pages before transferring. This will avoid small-IO inefficiency.

> If you quantize the KV cache to FP8 or FP4, the required transfer buffer for a fixed token count decreases since the number of bytes per token decreases accordingly. As such, you can either transfer more tokens per buffer or reduce the buffer size accordingly. A 1-2 GiB buffer works for many deployments, but size it from the KV formula above and round up to a 256 MB boundary. If using FP8 or FP4 KV, you can shrink the buffer proportionally. Always validate against the largest collated page group you'll transfer. Prefer GPUDirect RDMA with collation to ≥ 128-token pages for best link utilization.

In practice, one might launch the decode server with the CLI using the following shell script. This will reduce eager fragmentation and encourage rendezvous on larger buffers:

```
# Example decode worker
# (select device by index or UUID)

UCX_RNDV_THRESH=16384
UCX_MAX_EAGER_RAILS=1
UCX_TLS=cuda_ipc,rc,rdmacm,cuda_copy,cuda_ipc,tcp \
CUDA_VISIBLE_DEVICES=1 \
LMCACHE_CONFIG_FILE=lmcache-decoder-config.yaml \
python run_vllm_decoder.py --port 8200
```

You would similarly start the prefill server on another GPU with its config file. These settings ensure the system uses InfiniBand RDMA across nodes or NVLink peer-to-peer within a node rather than standard TCP sockets for KV transfer.

For single-node, multi-GPU runs, you should enable CUDA IPC. When running across nodes, prefer RDMA. A typical UCX config for LMCache/vLLM workers is to set `UCX_TLS=rc,rdmacm,cuda_copy,cuda_ipc,tcp` and ensure RoCE/IB lossless settings (ECN/PFC) are applied on the fabric. For internode RDMA, consider `UCX_RNDV_THRESH=16384` so that large KV buffers use rendezvous and small KV buffers use eager. Always validate with `ucx_info -f`.

With RDMA and proper buffering in place, the handoff latency can be in the single-digit to tens of milliseconds depending on the interconnect and page size. For example, with a 7,500-token context, LMCache measured about 20 milliseconds with many small transfers and about 8 milliseconds after collating into larger blocks. Specifically, it's recommended to collate 16-token pages into ≥ 128-token slabs before RDMA. This will help reduce per-packet overhead.

In short, disaggregated systems should use fast interconnects and smart data collation to make the prefill → decode transition seamless and fast. Minimizing handoff time is critical because if the handoff is slow, it negates the benefit of parallelizing the phases in the first place.

Use a deterministic hash for KV-chunk routing in multiprocess runs by setting `export PYTHONHASHSEED=0`.

Connector and Data Path Design

Building on the zero-copy optimization, let's see how the prefill and decode nodes coordinate the transfer end to end—beyond just moving the bits. The prefill and decode workers often communicate using a scheduler or router. In practice, this scheduler is often implemented as a centralized component, as used in NVIDIA Dynamo, or a decentralized coordination approach, as used by SGLang.

For instance, NVIDIA Dynamo implements a global scheduling queue in which the decode workers push new prompt tasks into a queue that prefill workers consume. In this design, a decode node enqueues a request for prompt processing, as shown in the "Put RemovePrefillRequest" (step 6) in Figure 18-6.

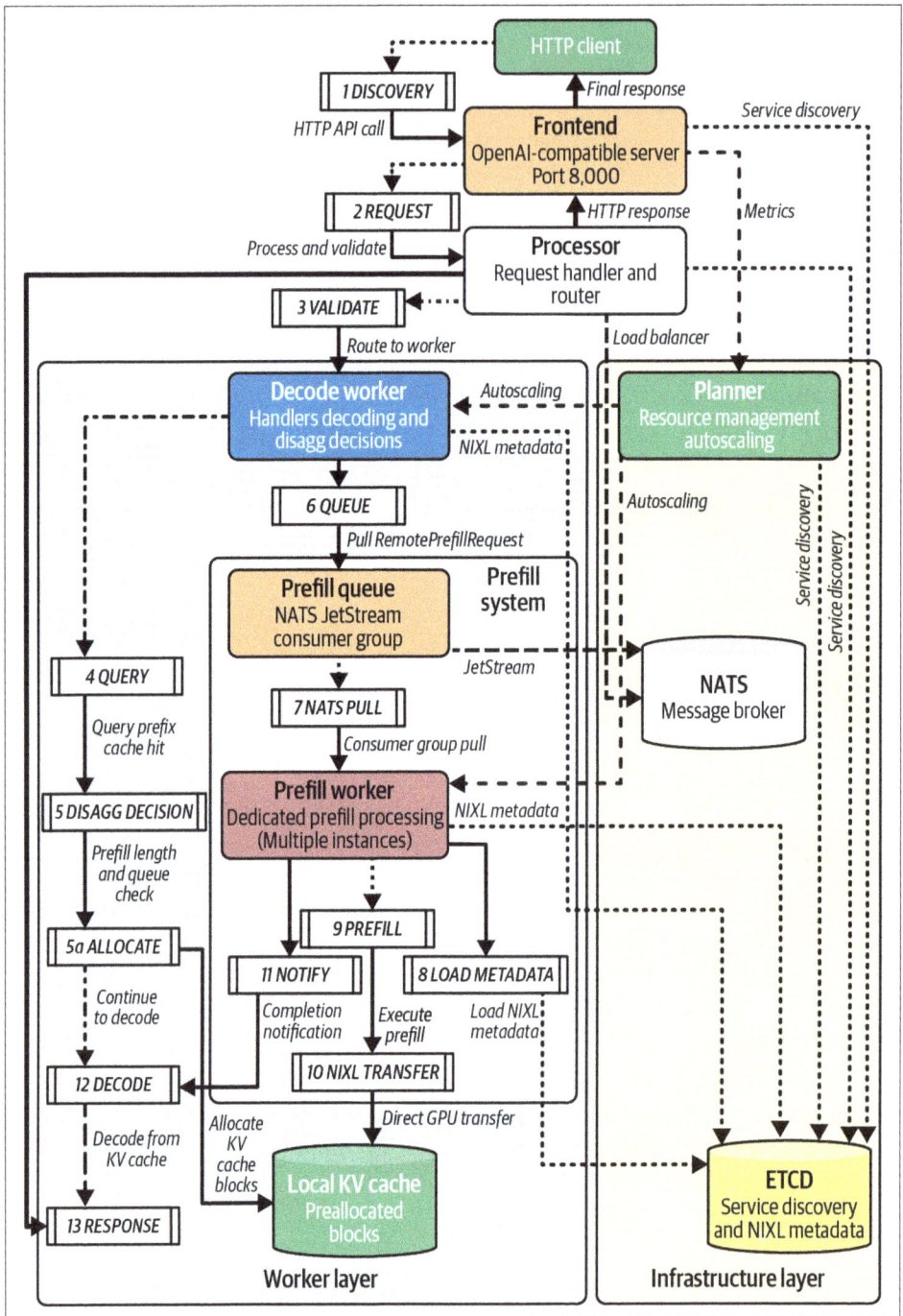

Figure 18-6. Request lifecycle in NVIDIA Dynamo; decode pulls prompts and prefill pushes KV using NIXL (adapted from NVIDIA Dynamo architecture documentation)

A prefill node picks up this request and, when done, knows exactly which decode node to send the results to since the request carries an origin or reply-to ID for the decode node. The KV is then transferred directly to that decode worker's GPU using NIXL RDMA.

In the vLLM + LMCache implementation, a more decentralized approach is used. The decode and prefill processes establish a direct channel using a pipe or buffer for each request's KV. Under the hood, this might use a one-to-one TCP or RDMA connection negotiated at request start. Rather than a global queue, each request sets up its own transfer channel. Both approaches have pros and cons. The global queue is simpler for load balancing and failure handling. Direct channels can minimize queuing.

When deciding which pattern to use, consider your workload and infrastructure constraints. If you need robust multitenant load balancing and easy failover, and you're comfortable with a small queuing delay, the global-queue model is usually the better fit. Conversely, if you have stringent tail-latency requirements, a relatively stable set of decode-prefill pairs, and high-speed interconnects, the per-request direct-channel approach can minimize hop count and jitter.

> In practice, benchmark both designs under your anticipated request mix. Vary the prompt lengths, concurrency levels, and failure scenarios to see which offers the best latency-throughput trade-off for your SLOs.

The key design goal is to make the pipeline nonblocking and high-throughput such that while one request is being decoded, another prompt can start prefilling—meanwhile, another's KV can be in transit. As such, no stage sits idle if there is work to do in another stage. This is the exact reason that disaggregation improves overall throughput at scale—all stages are kept busy in parallel.

> Often, the first generated token's logits from the prefill are often not explicitly transferred because the decode worker can simply recompute the first token's probabilities from the KV directly. Some systems do transfer the first token's output to shave off a few hundred microseconds of extra compute in the decode worker. But other systems keep it simple and just transfer the KV and let the decode worker recompute that final layer.

It's important to make sure that this pipeline is robust to failures. If a decode node fails mid-generation, a global KV cache pool, discussed earlier, can allow another node to pick up where it left off using the saved KV. Similarly, if a prefill node fails mid-prompt, that prompt can be retried elsewhere. The connector design should handle these failures gracefully so that one node's failure doesn't error out the whole request.

Heartbeat checks and timeouts are commonly used by these routers so that if a prefill-to-decode transfer stalls, the request can be reassigned or safely aborted.

Heterogeneous Hardware and Parallelism Strategies for Prefill and Decode

One powerful advantage of disaggregation is the freedom to choose different hardware—and even a different model-parallel configuration—that best suits the needs of the prefill and decode clusters separately. In a unified, monolithic deployment, you typically have only one hardware type and configuration for both phases. With disaggregation, you can mix and match hardware and strategies per phase, as described next.

Compute-Optimized Versus Memory-Optimized Hardware

The prefill phase benefits from GPUs with high compute throughput, lots of TFLOPS, specialized Tensor Cores, and high clock rates. It also benefits from substantial memory bandwidth, but it doesn't necessarily require massive HBM capacity beyond what the prompt's KV cache requires.

The decode phase, on the other hand, benefits from both large memory capacity and memory bandwidth since it handles many tokens' worth of KV. It doesn't need extreme compute power, but the more the better.

This opens up the possibility of using different generations of GPUs for each phase. For example, one design can use the latest high-compute GPUs for the prefill cluster but stick with older-generation or cost-efficient GPUs with sufficient memory bandwidth for the decode cluster.

This way, we avoid wasting the newest GPUs (e.g., the latest Tensor Cores) on a task like decode that doesn't use their full potential. The prefill tasks tend to draw more power by maxing out the GPU math units, whereas the decode tasks use far less power on the same GPU.

Throughput and cost benefits

Splitting the phases among heterogeneous hardware can improve throughput per cost and throughput per watt. In the Splitwise study (*https://oreil.ly/3mzRz*), using phase-specific hardware led to one configuration achieving 1.4× higher throughput at 20% lower cost over a homogeneous baseline.

In another configuration aimed at max performance under a fixed cost/power budget, they achieved 2.35× more throughput for the same cost and power. Specifically, this study used 4× H100 (high-compute) for prefill and 4× A100 (high-memory) for decode. This mixed configuration achieved ~2.35× the RPS of an 8-GPU homogeneous system (either all H100s or all A100s) at the same cost/power.

Alternatively, they found that, to match the baseline throughput, the heterogeneous system could actually use fewer GPUs overall (e.g., five or six instead of eight) by off-loading decode to cheaper GPUs. This highlights the cost-savings opportunity and shows the value of using each type of GPU where it's most effective. Specifically, you can perform compute-bound work on the highest-compute-per-dollar GPUs (e.g., Blackwell or Rubin generation) and assign memory-bound work to more cost-efficient older-generation GPUs with suitable memory bandwidth (e.g., Hopper or Ampere).

The Splitwise evaluation accounted for the overhead of state transfer between hetero-geneous GPUs. This test transferred KV data over an NVSwitch fabric and incurred minimal overhead—even between different generations of GPUs. This indicates that high-bandwidth interconnects like NVSwitch and NVLink can enable prefill/decode disaggregation with negligible impact on performance—even in mixed-GPU setups.

Another system is HexGen-2 (*https://oreil.ly/yFcda*), which is a distributed inference framework that treats the allocation of disaggregated inference on heterogeneous GPUs as an optimization problem. Its scheduler optimizes resource allocation, per-phase parallelism strategy, and communication efficiency together.

In experiments on models like Llama 2 70B, HexGen-2 shows up to a 2× improve-ment in serving throughput (~1.3× on average) as compared to state-of-the-art sys-tems at the same price point. Additionally, it achieves similar throughput to a high-end baseline while using approximately 30% less cost. These improvements came from mixing GPU types and optimizing the work split. This is basically an automated way to do what Splitwise did conceptually.

These results confirm that disaggregation is not just about speed. It's also about effi-ciency and doing more with less. When deploying inference in a cloud environment, this can lead to significant cost savings on the order of millions of dollars in GPU time for a large inference service supporting millions or billions of end users.

For instance, you can fulfill the same traffic with 6 GPUs (prefill + decode mix) instead of 8 top-tier GPUs; you can save roughly 25% on hardware costs for that ser-vice. As such, disaggregation lets you serve more users on the same hardware. This is critical since GPU supply is often limited—especially for the latest GPUs.

Energy efficiency is also important given power constraints in certain parts of the world, including the United States. Splitwise demonstrated better power efficiency by running decode tasks on lower-power GPUs—at a slight decrease in speed.

By assigning prefill and decode tasks onto different hardware types, you can choose where and how to run each phase to increase performance and reduce cost. Disaggre-gation allows this flexibility since phases are independent.

In short, the evaluations from Splitwise, HexGen-2, and related heterogeneous deployment studies show that disaggregation can be leveraged for cost optimization in addition to pure speed. By matching hardware to workload, you can significantly reduce the cost per query and, at the same time, increase performance within a fixed budget.

For large-scale services, this is critical to keep them economically viable. The tradeoffs include a bit more system complexity because you have to manage multiple GPU types. And you will be limited in cluster-configuration flexibility and dynamic reallocation of GPUs across prefill and decode tasks since the GPUs are not matched in capabilities. But, in many cases, using different hardware for each phase may be worth the efficiency gains.

Phase-specific model parallelism

Another form of heterogeneity and per-phase specialization is choosing different model parallelism (e.g., tensor parallel, pipeline parallel, etc.) across GPUs for each phase. This is relevant for very large models sharded across GPUs due to memory constraints.

In a traditional setup, you might run the model with a fixed parallelism strategy and split the model across multiple GPUs using tensor parallelism or pipeline parallelism for both the prefill and decode phases. But the optimal parallelism strategy for prefill may not be the same for decode.

For instance, the prefill phase is a big forward pass through N prompt tokens, and it benefits from a high degree of parallelization. You can use tensor parallelism (TP) across many GPUs to perform the computations faster and reduce TTFT.

The overhead of synchronizing the GPUs is amortized over the large number of tokens that can be processed at once. This reduces the wall-clock time of this stage, which is critical for TTFT.

You might even use pipeline parallelism (PP) to further speed up prefill and increase throughput. This would split the model layers across GPUs and stream the prompt through multiple pipeline stages.

The decode phase, on the other hand, is sequential and latency-sensitive per step. Using too many GPUs for one decode can actually hurt time-per-output-token (TPOT) latency, also called *inter-token latency* (ITL). This is because each token step would require additional multi-GPU communication overhead. As such, the potential for speedup is limited since there's only one token's worth of compute to split at a time (or a few tokens, if using speculative decoding).

Disaggregation makes it possible to mix these approaches and use TP for one phase and PP for another—or use different degrees of each technique. For instance, you can run prefill with TP=8 to span 8 GPUs and minimize prompt latency. You can then run decode with TP=1, or a single GPU, to maximize per-token throughput and minimize step latency. In this way, each phase's throughput and latency can be tuned separately, as shown in Figure 18-7.

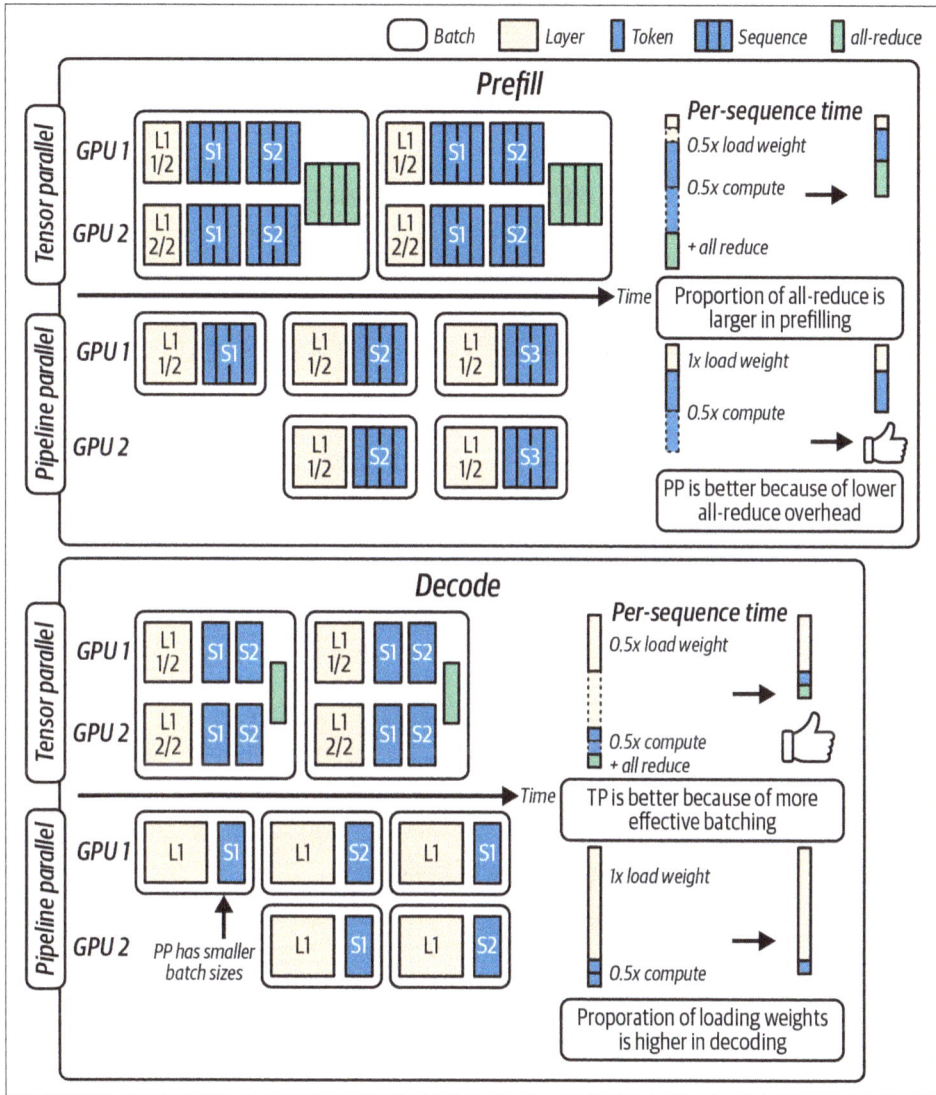

Figure 18-7. Using different parallelism strategies for prefill and decode (source: https:// oreil.ly/1-Ti0)

Here, tensor parallelism's additional all-reduce communication overhead is more prominent during the prefill stage since a large number of tokens are being processed in parallel. As such, we choose pipeline parallelism because it's more efficient for our prefill workload.

Both tensor parallelism and pipeline parallelism can be effective for prefill. The upcoming example uses pipeline parallelism for prefill. However, a large tensor parallel degree can reduce TTFT on certain clusters. The best choice depends on network bandwidth, collective latency, and model shape.

For the decode phase, however, pipeline parallelism can lead to more, albeit smaller, forward passes as the tokens are passed between GPUs. This requires a lot of data movement in and out of the GPUs for just a single token generation. As such, we choose tensor parallelism because it's better suited for our decoding workload.

This introduces a complication, however. Since our model's parallelization scheme differs between the prefill and decode, the format of the KV cache must differ as well. For instance, if the prefill phase uses TP = 1 (since it's using PP) with four GPUs, each of the four GPUs has a full-size KV tensor.

And let's say the decode phase uses TP = 4. In this case, each GPU expects only 1/4 of the KV tensors since the data should be split up along the model's hidden size. To handle this, systems like NVIDIA Dynamo can perform KV transposes, or conversions, during the transfer. Essentially, it converts and rearranges the KV cache from [TP_p parts] into the format needed by [TP_d parts], where TP_p is prefill's parallel degree and TP_d is decode's parallel degree.

Dynamo includes a high-performance kernel to do this transpose on the fly after reading from NIXL—and before writing into the decode worker's memory. This way, the receiving decode gets the KV cache data in the layout that it expects.

The overhead of this transpose can be small compared to the network transfer, however—especially given NVLink throughput, which can handle these data reorganizations quickly. In this case, it's easily justified by the compute savings of using different parallelism strategies optimized for each phase.

Let's explore an example of phase-specific parallelism. Consider a large model where we can apply various parallelism schemes: tensor (TP), pipeline (PP), data (DP), sequence (SP, splitting sequences across GPUs), etc. We might choose separate parallelism configurations. Table 18-1 shows an example parallelism configuration for the prefill phase.

Table 18-1. Prefill parallelism example

Parallelism strategy	Symbol	Value	Description
Tensor parallelism	TP_p	2	Split the model's weight tensors across 2 GPUs to halve prefill latency with manageable communication overhead.
Pipeline parallelism	PP_p	2	Divide the model layers into two pipeline stages, streaming microbatches through each stage for deep models.
Sequence parallelism	SP_p	1	Do not split the input sequence across GPUs (no sequence sharding) unless processing extremely large contexts.
Context parallelism	CP	1	Keep the entire context on a single GPU (no context-level partitioning) when it fits in memory after optimizations.
Data parallelism	DP_p	1 (or 2)	Use one model replica per GPU (or two for doubled throughput on batched prompts by weight replication).

These numbers minimize inter-GPU overhead while still using multiple GPUs to speed up big prompts. Next, let's look at an example parallelism strategy for decode, as shown in Table 18-2.

Table 18-2. Decode parallelism strategy example

Parallelism strategy	Symbol	Value	Description
Tensor parallelism	TP_d	1 (default) ... N (number of GPUs)	Default to TP_d = 1 for simplicity and minimal sync overhead. TP_d = N number of GPUs can improve efficiency for tiny GEMMs on small batches or when a single GPU can't hold the model.
Pipeline parallelism	PP_d	1	Pipeline parallelism adds bubbles for single-token decoding, so PP_d = 1 avoids idle stages.
Sequence parallelism	SP_d	1	Splitting the output sequence across GPUs is uncommon. SP_d = 1 keeps each decode stream local unless handling extremely long outputs.
Data parallelism	DP_d	1	One model replica per GPU per decode stream. Use separate replicas to handle parallel requests rather than replicating for a single stream.

> If the model cannot fit on a single Blackwell B200, for instance, prefer TP_d = 2 or 4 for decode instead of using PP. This will help avoid pipeline bubbles.

Ideally, each decode stream runs on a single GPU and avoids cross-GPU overhead. This is possible only if the model fits into GPU memory. In this case, TP_d = 1, which means it's not using any tensor parallelism during decode. If the model can't fit into memory, you can increase the degree of tensor parallelism (e.g., TP_d = N, where N is the number of GPUs).

Increasing tensor parallelism is also useful if the system is issuing tiny GEMMs to process small batches. This is because distributing small matrix multiplications across devices can hide communication latency behind computation and potentially produce higher overall throughput.

These are illustrative values, but the main point is that disaggregation allows you to configure resources separately on the prompt side to reach a TTFT target. At the same time, you can independently adjust resources on the decode side to hit throughput and latency targets for streaming tokens back to the end user.

This way, the two parallelism strategies do not interfere with each other. In a unified system, if you tried to do this, you'd have to pick one compromise strategy that works suboptimally for both phases.

Different precision for prefill and decode

Some inference engines let you use different precision between prefill and decode. For example, you could perform prefill in a lower precision, such as FP8, INT8, or FP4, to speed it up. At the same time, you could decode in a higher precision if needed for better generation accuracy.

Generally, you have both run in the same precision so that the KV cache computed in the prefill phase is usable in the decode phase. However, you can apply a conversion similar to the parallelism conversion described in the previous section. You would choose to quantize the KV and compress from FP16 to INT8/FP8/FP4 before sending. You would then convert it back on the receiving end, if needed.

For instance, you can choose to send the lower precision over the network to speed up the transfer. Or you could choose to perform the conversion on the sender or receiver based on available FLOPS, etc.

These are advanced ideas. But they highlight that nearly every aspect—hardware type, number of GPUs, and precision—can be independently tuned for each phase in a disaggregated setup.

Hybrid Prefill with GPU-CPU Collaboration

So far, we have assumed that both the prefill and decode phases run on GPUs—and possibly different types of GPUs. However, at extreme scales—or with extremely large models and prompts—it's worth evaluating if CPUs can offload pressure from GPUs.

Modern CPUs are far slower than GPUs for neural network computations, but they come with other advantages like ample RAM, no contention for GPU memory bandwidth, and flexibility to handle tasks that GPUs might not handle as well, like extremely long sequences and nontransformer operations like tokenization, padding, etc.

With a hybrid prefill strategy, part of the prefill computation is done on CPUs. One scenario is CPU offloading for superlong prompts. Consider a prompt with tens of thousands of tokens from a large document attachment. Even a powerful GPU might struggle to process such a large prompt due to memory constraints.

In the case of extremely long prompts, the system could choose to perform the initial layers of the model on a CPU worker with lots of RAM to hold the long sequence. It would then stream intermediate results to a GPU later—or even perform the entire prefill on the CPU if latency isn't an issue. The decode GPU would then receive the huge KV cache from the CPU worker.

> While not common in interactive inference, some batch or offline pipelines, like long-running "Deep Research" jobs, can use CPU preprocessing for very long texts.

A practical use of CPU offloading is processing background or low-priority prefill tasks. For instance, an LLM service might allow very large prompt submissions for offline processing of noninteractive requests. These could be assigned to CPU-only workers that eventually feed into a decode GPU for fast token generation. The latency would be high since CPUs are slower, but since it's an offline job, this might be acceptable. And this configuration frees up GPU resources for more interactive workloads.

Hybrid prefill is more common on CPU-GPU superchips like Grace Blackwell, in which the chip-to-chip interconnect is super fast. And it leverages the fact that CPU memory is massive compared to GPU memory.

Imagine storing a gigantic KV cache in CPU memory with fast access from the GPU. A hybrid prefill would use the CPU's memory to buffer or preprocess input tokens while the GPU focuses on the heavy transformer layers.

A Grace Blackwell Superchip could handle a massive context by letting the CPU manage memory and initial layers and the GPU handle dense attention on chunks of the sequence. The Grace CPU could also be used to spill KV cache data that doesn't fit in HBM into CPU DDR memory. This effectively extends the context length that the GPU can support.

You can slice the transformer across devices by running the first N layers on the GPU in which the bulk of the tokens are handled and the sequence is essentially compressed. You would then offload the next M layers to the CPU, which has lots of memory, before finally bringing the remaining layers back onto the GPU to generate the final outputs.

This layer-partitioning technique adds significant data movement and orchestration complexity—and should be justified only in rare cases, such as ultralong contexts or severe GPU memory limits. Regardless, it shows how you can push hardware boundaries in extreme inference scenarios.

In our disaggregated architecture, involving CPUs would mean introducing a third kind of worker: the CPU prefill worker. The scheduling logic could then choose among three options: GPU prefill worker, CPU prefill worker, or local decode GPU prefill. The decision would depend on factors like prompt length or priority.

For instance, the policy might be: if `prompt_length` > 5,000, route to a CPU prefill worker, knowing it will be slow but at least it won't tie up GPUs and can use large memory. The decode stage would then wait longer for KV. Or possibly, in an extreme case, the decode could also be done on the CPU if truly offline.

Generally, CPU offload would increase TTFT, so it's not used for normal latency-sensitive requests. It's more of an extensibility and safety-net feature. If utilized, the system should monitor how often this path is taken, as frequent CPU offloads might indicate the need for more GPU capacity or model optimization instead.

CPU offload also allows the system to handle edge cases like super long inputs or bursts when GPUs are all busy. It does this by falling back to the slower CPU rather than failing entirely. However, remember that it's best to fail fast if the processing is too slow and exceeds SLO requirements.

From a cost perspective, using CPUs for some work can be more economical since CPU cores are cheaper than GPU hours. Some cloud providers might run a mix of GPU and CPU instances for LLM serving. The CPUs perform input preprocessing—or even small model inferences—before engaging the GPUs.

In short, while core disaggregation logic focuses on distributing work across GPUs, a robust ultrascale inference system can leverage CPUs in creative ways for certain parts of the workload. As hardware evolves and moves toward tightly coupled CPU-GPU superchip designs like Grace Blackwell, the line between using a GPU and CPU will blur.

Efficient scheduling should consider all available compute resources. The guiding principle remains the same, however. Use GPUs for what they do best, including massive parallel compute on moderate sequence lengths. And use CPUs when GPUs might be inefficient, such as for extremely long sequences, memory-heavy tasks, or low-priority tasks.

SLO-Aware Request Management and Fault Tolerance

To hit SLO targets at ultrascale, it's not enough to scale and schedule efficiently. Sometimes you need to also reject or defer work that would violate SLOs under the current load. We touched on this with Mooncake's early rejection.

Early Rejection (Admission Control)

Early rejection, or admission control, was introduced in Chapter 17. In short, it means that if the system predicts that it cannot serve a request within the latency target, it will fail fast by returning an error or responding with "please try later." This prediction can be based on current queue lengths, recent throughput, or even a lightweight ML model that forecasts response time.

Early rejection is in contrast to queuing the request and then missing its SLO deadline. This preserves goodput by making sure requests served by the inference system will meet their guarantees.

In Mooncake (*https://oreil.ly/2xtK-*), the early rejection strategy evaluates incoming requests against the estimated load on both the prefill and decode clusters. For instance, consider a decode cluster that is currently handling a large number of long sequences.

When a new request arrives, and based on its expected output length, the system determines if decode utilization would surpass a safe threshold. Here, the system will immediately reject or defer that request and free up resources on the GPU node, as shown in Figure 18-8.

By doing so, you prevent a situation where the request sits in the queue and then takes so long that it surpasses its latency SLO and slows down all other requests by consuming scarce compute or memory bandwidth resources. This reinforces the fact that it's better to return a quick "too busy" response than to silently accept and then fail the latency guarantee.

This is analogous to how web servers shed load under extreme overload to keep serving the remaining requests with acceptable latency—the dreaded HTTP 503 error. This is better than timing out all requests.

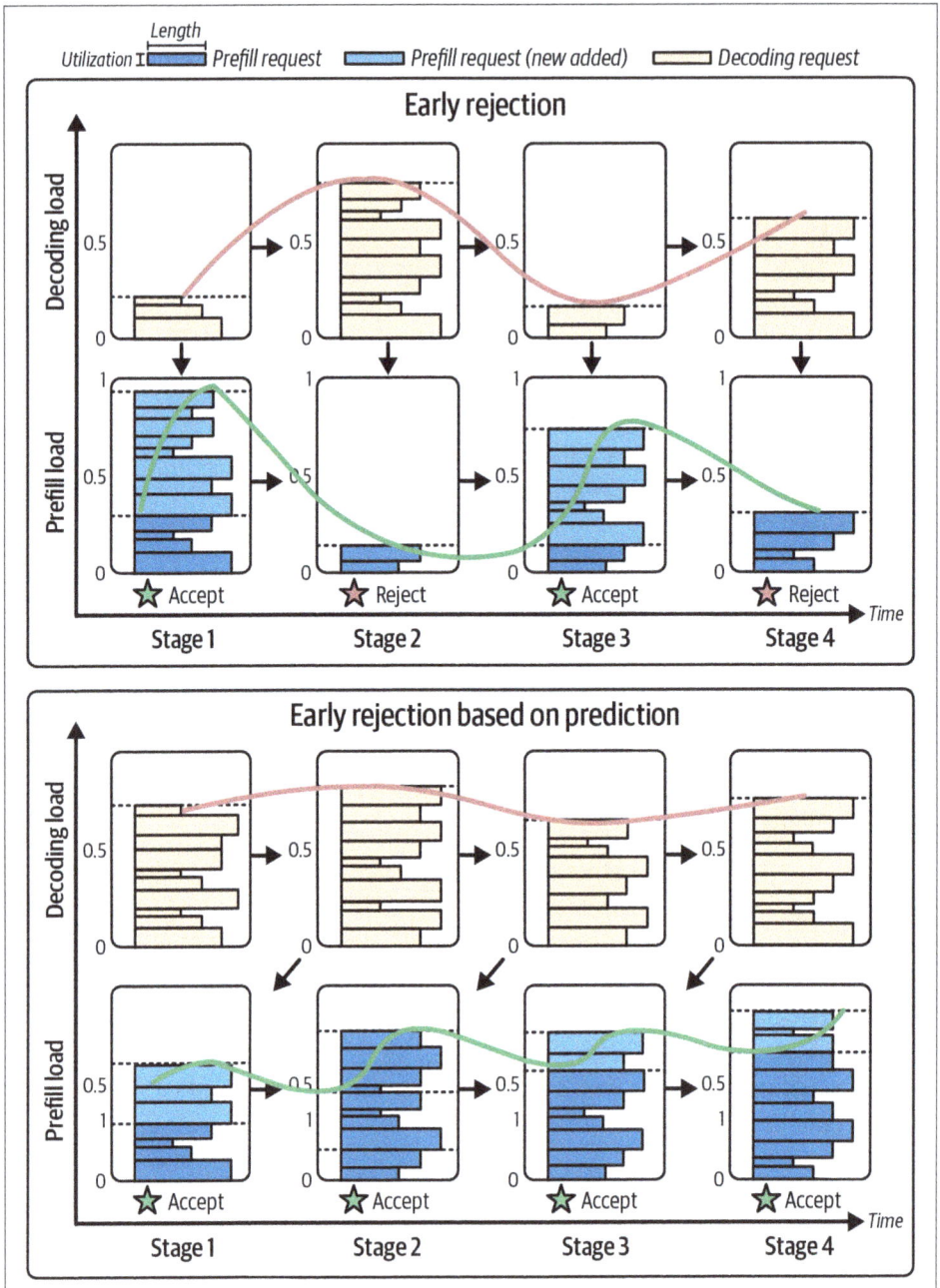

Figure 18-8. Instance load when applying early rejection (source: https://oreil.ly/2xtK-)

In LLM serving, because request sizes and durations vary widely, having a clear admission control step helps maintain performance for accepted requests. A well-behaved admission control keeps the system in a regime where it can meet both TTFT and TPOT targets for the load that it has accepted.

It effectively sets a limit on concurrent work. If doing more would break the SLO, it won't attempt it. This must be combined with scaling policies. For instance, you can scale up rather than reject. However, since scale-up is typically not instantaneous—or you're at max capacity—rejection is the safest and most performant option in the long run.

Quality of Service

Another aspect of SLO-aware management is quality of service (QoS) differentiation. Some requests might include priority levels. For instance, paying customers have higher priority than free-tier customers. Or interactive queries have higher priority than offline batch requests.

A scheduler might prioritize certain requests to always meet SLO—even if others have to wait or be dropped. Disaggregation can aid this by dedicating some portion of prefill and decode workers to high-priority tasks. For instance, you can choose to reserve 10% of cluster capacity exclusively for premium-tier requests and 30% for standard tier.

This tiered approach will guarantee headroom for the paying tiers (premium and standard). It makes sure these requests aren't delayed by lower-priority (free-tier) requests. Here is an example QoS configuration for NVIDIA Dynamo that demonstrates this type of tiered scheduling:

```
# configs/qos.yaml

scheduler:
  # Define QoS classes and their reserved capacity
  qos_classes:
    - name: premium
      reserved_fraction: 0.10   # reserve 10% of prefill/decode workers
      priority: 100
    - name: standard
      reserved_fraction: 0.30   # reserve 30% for standard tier
      priority: 50
    - name: free
      reserved_fraction: 0.60   # share remaining capacity (free tier)
      priority: 10

  # Map incoming requests to QoS classes by label
  request_router:
    routes:
      - match:
          header: "x-customer-tier: premium"
```

```
      qos: premium
  - match:
      header: "x-customer-tier: standard"
    qos: standard
  - match:
      header: "x-customer-tier: free"
    qos: free
  - match:
      # default fallback
    qos: free
```

This tiered approach allows higher-priority requests to be admitted and served with low latency using reserved capacity. Lower-priority requests will be queued—or potentially rejected—if the system is busy processing higher-priority requests.

Latency monitoring and feedback loops are useful for this type of system to continuously monitor TTFT and TPOT p99 and p99.9. If the system sees these metrics approaching SLO limits, it can trigger actions such as scaling or rejecting new load, degrading the requests by limiting the maximum output length, or temporarily reducing the load.

In a disaggregated system, you can observe the prefill queue and decode the queue separately. This helps pinpoint which side is the bottleneck. With this information, the system can adjust accordingly by stopping to accept new prompts if prefill is backed up or limiting long-output reasoning requests if decode is saturated.

You might have experienced "random" errors when using ChatGPT. This can be for a number of reasons, but one of those reasons could be these "circuit breakers" kicking in and shedding load for certain types of requests when the system is under heavy load.

Fault Tolerance

Fault tolerance is another aspect of running a robust inference system. In a disaggregated system, if a decode node fails mid-generation, the KV cache pooling we discussed earlier can enable recovery on another node since the KV was saved in the pool. This way, another decode worker can pick up generating the remaining tokens—perhaps with a slight delay.

If the KV was not saved, the system will have to recalculate the prefill on another node and then continue with the decode. This is why systems like vLLM periodically checkpoint or copy the KV cache to the pool—even if disaggregation isn't strictly needed. This is done to protect against failures.

In addition to framework-level KV snapshots, a Linux process hosting a GPU worker can be suspended and snapshotted with cuda-checkpoint plus Checkpoint/Restore in Userspace (CRIU) as discussed in Chapter 5. This way, the checkpoint can be restored onto another node of the same GPU chip type to minimize work lost on preemption or failure.

> It's possible reduce cold-start latency for inference engines by using cuda-checkpoint to restore prewarmed GPU memory rather than recompiling graphs and reloading weights on every start.

Checkpointing can hurt latency, but at least the request can complete. Prefill node failure is less impactful after it finishes computing and sending the KV data to either a decode worker or the KV cache pool since the KV data is off the failed node. But if the prefill worker fails during a prompt, the prompt task needs to be retried on another prefill node. The architecture should handle these types of failures gracefully so that one node's failure doesn't drop the entire request or cause large cascaded delays.

In short, SLO-aware request management makes sure that even under extreme conditions, the system maintains performance guarantees for the load that it chooses to serve. It does this by intelligently deciding which requests to serve, which to shed, and which to delay. Early rejection is a concrete example that uses load prediction at admission time to prevent overload and maintain high throughput within the SLO constraints.

SLO-aware request management and fault tolerance—combined with all the other strategies we've discussed so far (e.g., scaling, scheduling, and caching)—help maintain strict SLO goals in production.

Disaggregation makes this possible because it provides clear control points. You can observe prefill and decode metrics separately and apply admission controls specifically where they're needed. For instance, stop taking new prompts if the prefill cluster is backed up, or stop allowing long outputs if the decode cluster is at capacity.

The result is a more predictable, stable, and adaptable inference service in which performance doesn't degrade sharply when load exceeds capacity. Instead, it gracefully rejects excess load and rapidly rebalances to handle the changing conditions.

Dynamic Scheduling and Load Balancing

Upfront, you can determine how many resources to dedicate to prefill versus decode. But then you want to dynamically adjust those resource splits as the workload changes.

With a purely static configuration, if the workload mix changes and you require a more prompt-heavy or generation-heavy split, the fixed ratio will become suboptimal. The optimal balance of prefill and decode capacity will shift over time. At one moment, many new requests arrive, and you want a heavy prefill split. Later on, you may have many long, ongoing reasoning generations, and you want a heavy decode split.

Adaptive scheduling and load-balancing mechanisms aim to continuously tune the system so that neither phase becomes a bottleneck. This keeps goodput high under changing conditions.

Modern inference engines like vLLM, SGLang, and NVIDIA Dynamo incorporate load monitoring and dynamic worker assignment into their platforms. In addition, many cloud inference platforms have custom autoscalers and routers that use similar principles.

Adaptive Resource Scheduling and Hotspot Prevention

One issue with disaggregated setups is load imbalance between the prefill and decode clusters. If the ratio of prefill to decode workers is misconfigured for the current load mix, one side might saturate while the other side remains underutilized.

For instance, if there are not enough decode workers relative to prefill, then decode tasks will queue up. This increases TPOT even though prompts are being processed quickly. Conversely, if decode is overprovisioned but prefill is underprovisioned, new requests may wait to start. This leads to high TTFT while many decode GPUs sit idle.

The ideal scenario is when both sides are working near capacity but are not overwhelmed. This way the system keeps both prefill and decode busy but neither has a growing queue.

Static prefill-decode worker allocations are not sufficient in real-world conditions because workloads can vary greatly throughout the day. The mix of input lengths and output lengths can vary significantly from hour to hour in a long-running, large-scale inference system.

For instance, one hour might have a lot of long questions that produce short answers (e.g., summarization). These require more prefill resources and fewer decode resources. The next hour, you might get short questions that produce long answers (e.g., reasoning, web search). These require less prefill but much more decode.

In other words, a static prefill-to-decode ratio that worked for one scenario may not be optimal for another. Thus, the optimal X_p versus Y_d configuration is workload-dependent and will shift over time.

To address this, advanced inference systems can use adaptive scheduling algorithms that can redistribute load or even repurpose instances on the fly. Let's discuss a few of these approaches next.

TetriInfer's two-level scheduler

The research prototype scheduler TetriInfer (*https://oreil.ly/_3KGj*) operates at two granularities. First, at the individual request level, it assigns incoming requests to specific prefill and decode instances based on current load. This is the normal routing that we expect. Second, it monitors resource utilization cluster-wide and predicts where bottlenecks might form. This proactively shifts work to prevent hotspots.

For instance, the scheduler might see that one decode node is getting a bunch of very long sequences queued up. Before it becomes a problem, the scheduler routes some of those sequences to a different decode node that's more available—even if it wouldn't normally route to this decode node. This way, the load is balanced out. Figure 18-9 shows a comparison between existing systems and the TetriInfer work in terms of execution timeline and architecture.

Here, you see that by predicting resource usage through queue lengths, GPU utilization trends, etc., TetriInfer's two-level scheduler smooths out the load across the cluster and prevents any single node from being overloaded.

> The name TetriInfer hints at "packing" requests like Tetris pieces to fill GPU time without interference.

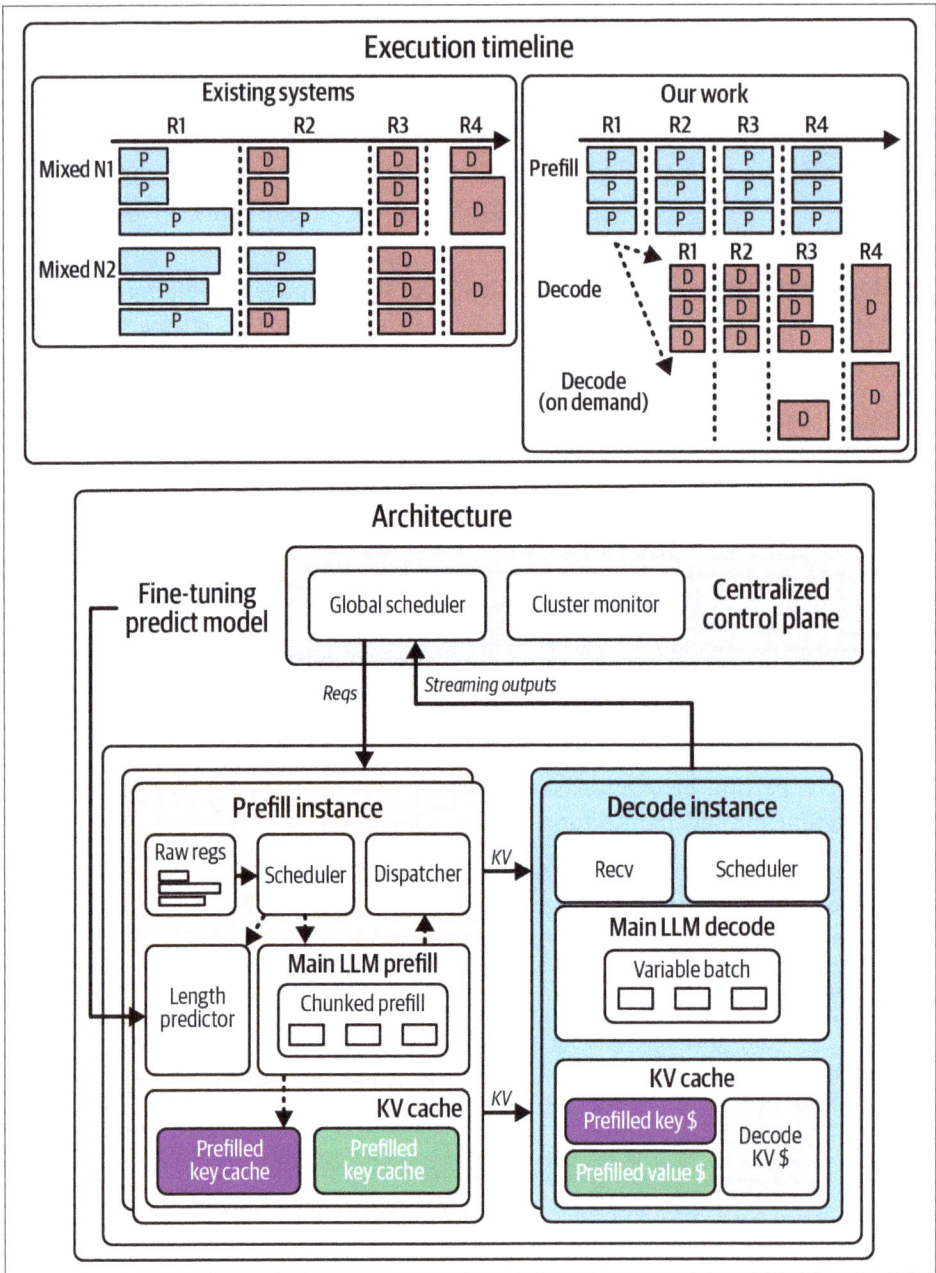

Figure 18-9. Comparison between existing systems and TetriInfer's architecture (source: https://oreil.ly/_3KGj)

Arrow's adaptive instance scaling

Another technique for dynamic resource scheduling is Arrow (*https://oreil.ly/-SUqH*) (not to be confused with the popular Arrow data format). This is an adaptive instance scaling technique that leverages the fact that disaggregated systems often have a lagging response to workload changes. For instance, if the distribution of input versus output changes, the static number of prefill versus decode workers doesn't immediately adjust. This causes a temporary loss of goodput since one side becomes a bottleneck.

Arrow continuously analyzes the workload by measuring input token rate versus output token rate—and the backlog in each worker pool in the cluster. It then dynamically adjusts the allocation of workers, as shown in Figure 18-10.

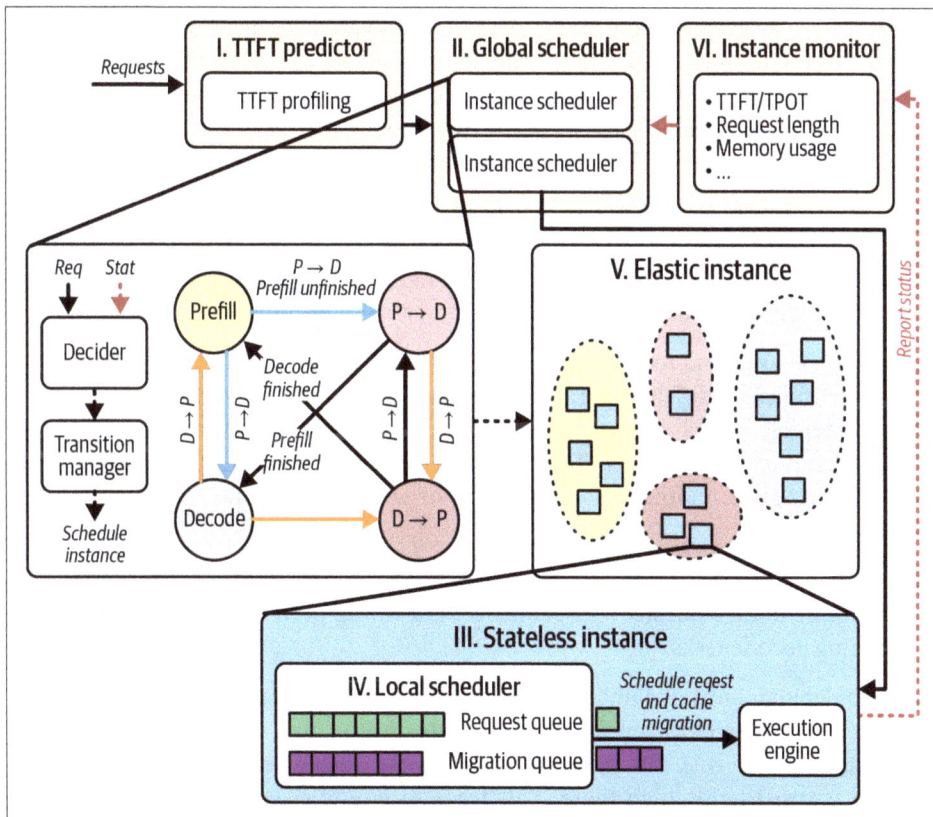

Figure 18-10. Arrow architecture

In a cloud environment, this could mean spinning up additional decode instances when output load increases. You can also scale down decode in favor of more prefill instances if an input-heavy workload is detected.

Arrow's design includes both request scheduling to decide which node handles which requests (similar to other scheduling techniques) and instance scheduling to decide when to launch or shut down instances of either prefill or decode.

Arrow treats the number of prefill and decode workers as a tunable parameter that can be adjusted and scaled in near-real-time. Arrow's design brings an autoscaler logic inside the LLM inference scheduler.

For instance, if a high volume of input-heavy but output-light requests come into the system, prefill nodes could become the bottleneck. In this case, Arrow would detect growing prefill queue times or rising TTFT percentiles and decide to convert some decode workers into prefill workers—or launch extra prefill instances to handle the surge.

Conversely, if a wave of output-heavy requests with very long answers (e.g., reasoning chains) comes in, the decode cluster might start lagging, as indicated by TPOT rising and a long decode queue forming. In this case, Arrow could allocate more GPU workers to the decoding phase—perhaps by temporarily idling some prefill nodes if prompt arrivals have slowed. Otherwise, it could just add new decode nodes.

In a static, on-premises cluster with a fixed number of GPUs, dynamic scaling will involve task reallocation by instructing a few GPUs that were assigned to prefill to switch roles and join the decode pool for a bit of time. This is feasible if each compute node is configured to run as both a prefill worker and a decode worker.

There may be overhead to switching roles since the model may need to load different model partitions for different parallelism strategies or quantization choices, etc. Some designs keep all model weights loaded on every GPU and just feed them different tasks depending on the need. This effectively treats the cluster as a flexible pool where, at any given moment, some fraction of workers are doing prefill and others are doing decode.

This starts to resemble a unified cluster with time-sharing but at a coarse granularity in which one node dedicates some time to performing prefill tasks, then switches to performing decode tasks.

In cloud deployments, dynamic scaling can also mean interfacing with an autoscaler like the Kubernetes Horizontal Pod and Cluster Autoscalers to add or remove pods and nodes for each role. For instance, Arrow could trigger new prefill pods to start if the load is consistently high there. This leads to a fully elastic, disaggregated prefill and decode inference cluster that grows or shrinks each side as needed.

In practice, scaling up new GPU pods can take tens of seconds or more. As such, the system may need to shed load while waiting for capacity. This is how Mooncake handles this situation, as we discuss next.

Mooncake adaptive strategies

Apart from Arrow, the Mooncake system also highlights adaptive strategies. Mooncake introduced a prediction-based admission control called *early rejection*, which is somewhat complementary—managing demand versus managing supply.

Specifically, if the system predicts it doesn't have enough capacity to handle a new request within SLO, it will reject that request rather than accept the request and potentially violate the SLO. This is a form of dynamic *load shedding* rather than scaling, but it aims to prevent overload.

We already covered Mooncake's early rejection approach in the previous section. The point here is that adaptation can happen on the supply side by adding more resources or reallocating them—as well as on the demand side by throttling or rejecting some requests.

The key benefit of dynamic scaling is maintaining high goodput across workload variations. By automatically tuning the prefill-to-decode ratio, the system avoids extended periods of mismatch in which GPUs on one side are idle while the other side is overloaded.

Ideally, both types of nodes are utilized evenly. This improves latency by alleviating bottlenecks as soon as they form—and also raises efficiency since you're not paying for a bunch of idle GPUs of one type while the other type is overloaded. Instead, resources are reallocated or tasks shifted to keep things balanced.

In terms of outcomes, an adaptive system might be able to claim something like, "After applying adaptive scaling, the system maintained > 90% SLO compliance across traffic patterns that a static system could not, and it handled X% more requests during a spike by quickly shifting resources."

Specifically, Arrow's results mention an up to 5.6× higher request serving rate versus a nonadaptive system in a scenario with an extremely shifting workload. Typical improvements were lower but still significant. The exact improvement depends on how dramatic the workload changes are.

All of this shows that disaggregation removes the phase interference issue. And dynamic disaggregation removes the next constraint of phase imbalance caused by a fixed allocation. To implement such adaptivity, the scheduler needs to monitor metrics continuously, including the prefill queue length, decode queue length, and the TTFT/TPOT percentiles. These metrics are often fed into control dashboards using Prometheus and custom controllers in a K8s deployment. Algorithms can then automate the decision making.

Sophisticated inference systems use predictive models like ARIMA (*https://oreil.ly/Qt7Lc*) and other forecasting techniques to foresee surges and predict traffic shifts using time-of-day patterns. If a spike of long outputs is predicted at 9 p.m. due to historically known usage patterns, the scheduler could preemptively allocate more decode capacity just in time. The overall goal is to maintain a high fraction of requests served within SLO—and without manual intervention and reconfiguration.

Dynamic resource scaling

Building on the idea of predictive scheduling, dynamic resource scaling is specifically about changing the distribution of resources between prefill and decode in response to load. For example, Arrow's adaptive instance scheduling adjusts the number of prefill versus decode workers continuously. Here are some ways to balance the load in an inference system:

Elastic instances
> In Kubernetes or similar, you can define an autoscale policy for each deployment. For example, you can specify that you want to maintain average prefill GPU utilization at 70%. If GPU utilization goes higher, the system will add a pod or node to the prefill worker pool. If it goes lower and decode utilization remains high, the system can move one pod from prefill to decode. This could be rule-based or algorithmic, such as solving for the most optimal configuration at each interval to choose new X and Y counts.

Instance "flip" mechanism
> The TetriInfer paper describes an "instance flip" in which some nodes can flip roles if needed. This requires that the model be loaded, sharded, and quantized properly to handle both roles.

Statelessness for elasticity
> Arrow leverages stateless instances. As such, no long-lived session state is stored on the worker. This way, they can be reassigned freely. The KV cache of active requests complicates flipping a decode node to prefill if it's mid-token-generation, so you often have to wait until the decode finishes its task before switching roles.

Stability and oscillation
> Rapidly switching roles can lead to oscillation and thrashing. As such, it's common to enforce some minimum amount of time required for a role to avoid flipping too frequently.

Apart from load balancing, another aspect to consider is multitenancy or mixed workloads. If the cluster serves different models or tasks, you can even repurpose GPUs between them based on demand—and beyond a single model's scope.

Disaggregation's modular configuration allows using idle decode GPUs to run another smaller model's inference tasks. This is an extension that is not yet mainstream as of this writing, but it's conceptually possible as inference engines evolve and become more flexible in their designs.

The bottom line is that an ultrascale inference system requires a feedback loop to continually match resource allocation to the current workload. TetriInfer, Arrow, Mooncake, and others show significant improvements when using such a feedback loop and adapting to load changes. This highlights that while disaggregation removes interference, adaptive disaggregation removes imbalance. Both are needed for the best performance under dynamic conditions.

Key Takeaways

This chapter covered various techniques, such as unified megakernels, efficient memory allocations, fast data transfers, prefill/decode disaggregation, KV cache pools, dynamic scaling, and continuous SLO awareness. Here are some key takeaways:

Accelerate the decode phase
> The decode phase can be greatly accelerated using fused attention kernels including FlashMLA, ThunderMLA, and FlexDecoding. These kernels can improve single-token throughput and GPU utilization.

Treat the KV cache as a first-class citizen
> Share the KV cache across GPUs using disaggregation. Reuse prefixes to avoid redundant computation. These are enabled by global cache pools and hashing.

Strive for near-zero overhead between prefill and decode workers
> Leverage high-speed GPU-to-GPU transfers with GPUDirect RDMA and NIXL. Overlap compute/transfer to achieve near-zero overhead between prefill and decode workers.

Embrace specialized hardware and parallelism for each phase
> Disaggregating prefill and decode allows specialized hardware and parallelism per phase. For example, use high-compute GPUs or multi-GPU nodes for prefill. And use memory-rich GPUs or single GPUs for decode. The goal is to reduce cost and increase throughput.

Use adaptive and dynamic algorithms to optimize the system
> Adaptive scheduling and SLO-aware control (e.g., early rejection and dynamic scaling) are necessary to maintain latency guarantees under varying load—and to fully utilize all GPUs without overload.

Conclusion

Ultrascale LLM inference requires a holistic approach, including both high-level adaptive resource management and low-level kernel and memory optimizations. By combining the techniques presented in this chapter, a highly optimized inference deployment can achieve maximum throughput on modern hardware while meeting strict latency guarantees.

As hardware continues to evolve and GPUs (e.g., increased memory and specialized inference cores) and software frameworks become more sophisticated (e.g., dynamic routing and flexible role assignments), these optimizations will compound and become even more powerful. This will allow inference engines to efficiently handle even larger models, longer contexts, and more users.

## CHAPTER 19

Dynamic and Adaptive Inference Engine Optimizations

Ultralarge language model (LLM) inference on modern hardware requires dynamic runtime adaptation to achieve both high throughput and low latency under varying conditions. A static "one-size-fits-all" approach to model-serving optimizations is no longer sufficient.

Instead, state-of-the-art model serving systems use *adaptive strategies* that adjust parallelism, numerical precision, CUDA-kernel scheduling, and memory usage on the fly. This chapter explores these advanced techniques, including dynamic parallelism switching, precision scaling, real-time cache management, and reinforcement learning (RL)-based tuning.

This chapter provides best practices for ultrascale LLM inference, teaching you how to orchestrate an engine that monitors its own performance and adapts in real time to maximize efficiency.

Adaptive Parallelism Strategies (TP Versus PP Versus Hybrid)

Massive LLMs require model parallelism, such as tensor and pipeline—or a hybrid approach—to spread computation across multiple GPUs. Each approach has benefits and drawbacks. Table 19-1 summarizes the recommended parallelism strategies for specific inference traffic patterns.

Table 19-1. Summary of common inference traffic patterns mapped to the recommended parallelism strategy

Inference traffic p	Recommended parallelism	Rationale
Many short requests (<256 tokens, high RPS)	Data parallel/replica scaling	Minimizes inter-GPU communications; each GPU runs replicas handling independent requests (assuming the model fits into a single GPU's memory)
Few long requests ($\geq$ 8k tokens, low concurrency)	Pipeline parallelism (with microbatches)	Reduces per-request latency by splitting layers across GPUs
Mixed load (short + some long)	Hybrid dynamic (autoswitching)	Runs small chats on single GPUs and pipelines long ones to meet latency SLAs
Extremely large model ($>$ 1 GPU memory)	Tensor + pipeline hybrid	Required to fit the model; balances compute and memory across both dimensions
MoE model inference (sparse expert selection)	Expert parallelism	Distributes individual experts across GPUs; each request invokes only a subset of experts, reducing per-device memory and compute load

The data parallel and replica scaling strategy will replicate the full model on each GPU and load-balance incoming requests across these replicas. This requires no inter-GPU synchronization for individual inferences since each GPU handles separate requests independently.

This maximizes throughput for many small- or medium-sized inputs with minimal communication overhead. However, data parallelism is not an option if the model does not fit into a single GPU's memory.

Tensor parallelism (TP) is a form of model parallelism (as opposed to data parallelism) that splits model matrices (e.g., weights, layers, etc.) across GPUs to speed up matrix multiplies. However, it introduces extra all-reduce communications to keep the GPUs in sync.

Pipeline parallelism (PP) is another form of model parallelism that splits the model as well. But instead of splitting individual model layers and matrices, it assigns whole layers to different GPUs to overcome memory limits—assuming the layers fit into a single GPU. PP incurs additional overhead in the form of sequential stage delays. These are called *pipeline bubbles*, as shown in Figure 19-1.

Expert parallelism, used in mixture-of-experts (MoE) model architectures, assigns each expert subnetwork its own GPU. A lightweight gating network then directs each input request or token to only the top-k active experts identified by the router. In this case, each GPU processes just the subset of experts that it hosts.

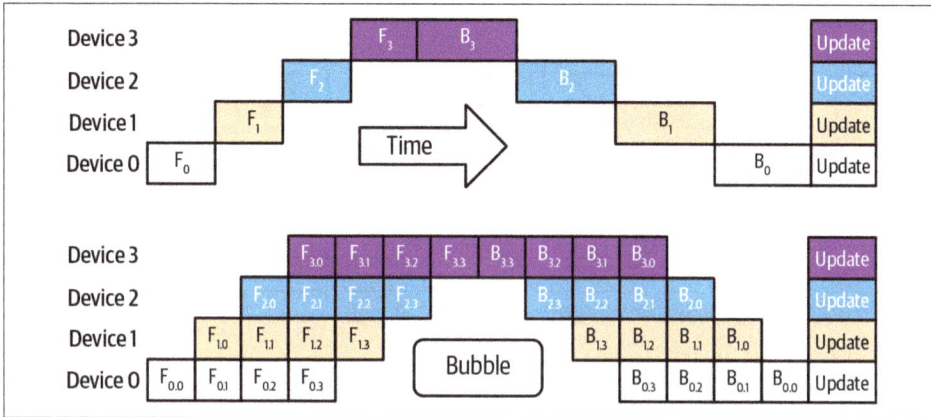

Figure 19-1. Pipeline bubbles caused by PP

By activating only a few experts per input, expert parallelism reduces per-device memory, inference time, and compute costs for models with a large number of experts, often called *wide* expert models. The conditional, router-based expert compute pattern scales efficiently as you add more experts. For instance, DeepSeek-R1 has 256 total experts, but only the top 9 experts (including 1 shared expert) are chosen by the router during inference.

Traditionally, the parallelization strategy—including a hybrid strategy of multiple parallelism techniques combined—is chosen and fixed upfront when the model is loaded. However, to maximize performance under dynamic workloads, modern inference engines can choose different parallelism strategies at runtime based on the characteristics of the input.

High-performance, adaptive inference systems use runtime metrics to choose TP, PP, or a hybrid approach on the fly. Key factors include batch size, sequence length, and memory utilization—as well as response latency and throughput requirements. For instance, very long prompts may be routed to a TP + PP instance since this spreads layers across GPUs to avoid out-of-memory (OOM) errors.

Meanwhile, short latency-sensitive requests would route to a TP-only model instance to avoid pipeline-stage overhead. To support this, your serving engine maintains multiple presharded model instances, each optimized for different workload profiles, and dynamically dispatches incoming queries to the model instance whose parallelism strategy best satisfies the job's SLOs.

You can also use a different number of shards. This is shown in Figure 19-2, which uses two different numbers of TP shards in two different hybrid TP + PP parallelism configurations across eight GPUs.

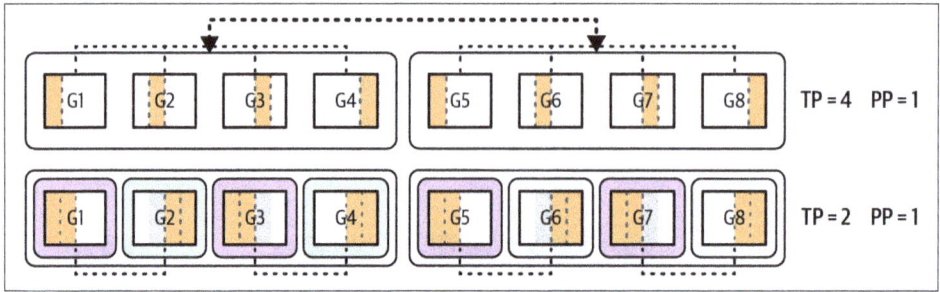

Figure 19-2. Preprovisioning two different hybrid-sharding pools (TP = 4, PP = 1 and TP = 2, PP = 1) for a given model across eight GPUs

Using PP on the fly for long sequence inputs helps to avoid OOM errors caused by the large input sequence. Conversely, for short prompts and latency-sensitive queries, the system can instead route to a tensor-parallel model instance optimized for low latency. In this case, the request avoids the overhead of PP.

Since each request can use a different parallelism strategy, the system needs to maintain multiple instances of the model for the inference scheduler/router to choose. One instance of the model would be optimized for low latency using TP, while another instance is optimized for high throughput and large input sequences using both TP and PP.

Maintaining multiple instances of the model is required because resharding on the fly would wreak havoc on GPU caches. This would also put too much pressure on the memory and network subsystems—especially when resharding massive models.

At runtime, each query is dispatched to the best-fitting model instance (sharding strategy) based on its length and the specified service-level agreements (SLAs). DeepSeek-R1, for instance, is a ~680 billion-parameter sparse mixture-of-experts model that activates only 37 billion parameters per token across the experts.

To support different workload profiles, GPUs can be organized into logical worker pools, each presharded with a specific parallelism strategy—either tensor-parallel or hybrid tensor + pipeline parallel, for instance.

Let's consider an example. If we have an 8× GPU Blackwell B200 server totaling 1,440 GB of HBM memory (1,440 GB = 180 GB per GPU × 8 GPUs), we can serve DeepSeek-R1 with four-way TP across four GPUs—leaving the other four GPUs idle.

If a single query arrives with an extremely long context (e.g., > 1 million tokens), the scheduler can spawn a two-stage pipeline such that stage 1 spans GPUs 0–3 and stage 2 spans GPUs 4–7. This effectively doubles the available GPU memory per stage to ~720 GB (180 GB per GPU × 4 GPUs) of total HBM (720 GB usable HBM). This helps avoid OOM errors when processing large inputs.

Conversely, when dozens of short, latency-sensitive prompts arrive concurrently, the system routes them to the tensor-parallel instance only. By avoiding pipeline bubbles, or idle periods that occur while filling and draining pipeline stages, this configuration delivers the lowest possible per-request latency across all available GPUs.

To implement dynamic parallelism switching, you can implement a decision function that inspects runtime metrics like input sequence length, GPU memory usage, and current load. You would use these metrics to select the best-sharded model instance for each request, as shown here:

```python
def choose_worker_pool(seq_len, gpu_mem_util, concurrent_reqs):
    # For long contexts or high memory pressure,
    # use hybrid pipeline + tensor parallelism
    # (example thresholds shown here)
    if seq_len > 4096 or gpu_mem_util > 0.8:
        return "tp_pp_hybrid"
    # For many simultaneous small requests, stick with tensor parallelism
    if concurrent_reqs > 4:
        return "tensor_parallel"
    # Fallback to tensor-parallel for typical workloads
    return "tensor_parallel"
```

You'd prelaunch multiple model replicas on your GPU cluster—some sharded for TP-only and others for TP + PP—and have a router send each query to the appropriate replica based on the inputs and the decision strategy. This approach ensures that large, memory-intensive jobs get full pipeline support, while short, latency-sensitive calls run on TP-only instances to avoid unnecessary pipeline overhead.

It's recommended to use telemetry from the model and hardware to inform parallelism switching. You can monitor GPU memory utilization, compute utilization, and interconnect (e.g., NVLink/NVSwitch) traffic in real time to make the decision. If you notice idle GPUs because of long pipeline bubbles—and you have extra memory headroom—you can collapse your pipeline into fewer stages so each GPU does more work and stays busy. Conversely, if some stages are hitting memory limits or compute bottlenecks, you can expand into more pipeline stages—or raise your tensor-parallel degree. This will spread the computations and memory footprint across additional GPUs.

The key is to adjust the balance of tensor and pipeline splits dynamically to keep every GPU well utilized. At the same time, you need to stay within memory constraints and hit latency targets. This is something a static, one-size-fits-all configuration cannot achieve.

Dynamic Precision Changes

Modern GPUs like Blackwell introduce support for 8-bit and 4-bit floating point (FP8/FP4) Tensor Core math units. These lower precisions offer large speedups, memory savings, and minimal quality loss.

Dynamic precision switching is an advanced technique in which the inference engine adjusts the numerical precision at runtime based on model confidence or resource pressure. The goal is to increase throughput without significant quality loss. In practice, this means the system might execute certain parts of the model in FP8 or FP4 for efficiency but fall back to higher precision (FP16/BF16) when needed for stability.

One trigger for precision adaptation is *logit sharpness*, or the model's output confidence. For example, if the model's probability distribution for the next token shows extreme peaks due to high confidence in a specific token, small numerical errors from low precision are unlikely to change the outcome.

If low precision can be tolerated for the next token generation, the engine will safely use FP4 for the next few steps to gain speed. Conversely, if the distribution is flatter due to high uncertainty, the engine should stick to FP8 or FP16 to preserve fidelity.

The inference engine quantifies uncertainty by computing the Shannon entropy of the softmax distribution over the vocabulary. Lower entropy indicates a sharper (more confident) prediction. A fixed entropy threshold, tuned on a held-out validation set, determines when to drop to FP4 and when to remain in FP8/FP16 for numerical stability. The goal is to balance latency gains versus accuracy loss.

> Use the lowest precision that maintains accuracy, and revert to higher precision when the model's confidence drops as measured by the maximum softmax probability.

This leverages the fact that large LLMs often become more certain as they generate deterministic continuations, such as closing quotes or finishing a list. In these cases, lower precision is usually sufficient.

Another factor is memory pressure. If GPU memory usage is approaching its limit due to a very long context—or many parallel requests, the system can dynamically compress activations to a lower precision.

One could store the attention key/value tensors in INT4 instead of INT8 when memory is scarce. This would reduce the memory footprint by 50%. However, make sure the quantization error from using INT4 does not compound across many decoding steps. It's recommended to periodically reevaluate output quality.

For instance, if an inference reaches a point where the KV cache is using 90% of memory, the engine might decide to quantize new cache entries from INT8 down to INT4—or even retroactively compress older entries—to free space. This can be done without stopping the model. In this case, the next attention layers simply read the INT4 cached values—with minor quantization error.

Combining 4-bit weight quantization with 8-bit activations can reduce memory significantly. For instance, pure compute-limited kernels FP8 activations can achieve up to 2× throughput—especially on high-bandwidth modern GPUs. For mixed or memory-bound workloads, 1.5× is achievable. Using FP4 for activations can push memory savings even further. However, it may introduce slightly higher cumulative error that requires careful layer-wise tuning.

Modern GPUs provide native FP8 and FP4 Tensor Cores. However, PyTorch's AMP support (`torch.autocast`) still only targets FP16 and BF16 as of this writing. It does not target FP8 or FP4. While FP8 dtypes exist in PyTorch (e.g., `torch.float8_e4m3` and `torch.float8_e5m2`) alongside scaled math paths, AMP does not manage them. For inference and training, it's recommended to use NVIDIA's Transformer Engine (TE) and adopt its MXFP8 and NVFP4 when appropriate.

> For latency-critical decode, prefer BF16 over FP16 on Blackwell when using AMP. For FP8 paths, the Transformer Engine's MXFP8 format is the recommended default on Blackwell. Use NVFP4 selectively for KV cache and light layers with careful regression testing. Remember to validate numerics per layer on your specific workload.

Table 19-2 summarizes some example precision configurations and their trade-offs. Here, you see that lower precision reduces memory and increases throughput. However, there is slight quality degradation.

Table 19-2. Approximate trade-offs of precision modes in LLM inference

Precision mode	Memory usage (relative)	Compute throughput	Quality impact (accuracy delta)
FP16 (baseline)	1.0× (100%)	1.0× (baseline)	No impact (full fidelity)
FP16 weights + FP8 activations	~0.5× (50%)	~1.5×	Negligible (< 0.1%)
INT4 weights + FP8 activations	~0.25× (25%)	~1.8× (mixed compute and memory bound)	~0.5% drop in quality
INT4 weights + FP4 activations	~0.2× (20%)	~3.5×	~1% drop (requires careful tuning)

Here, we see that with FP8 activations, we get a memory reduction of ~50% from the baseline FP16 as expected by reducing the activation bit-width by 50%. Additionally, the quality loss measured here is negligible ($< 0.1\%$) for FP8 activations. (Note: quality impact with reduced precision is model-dependent and kernel-dependent. You should validate with your own data and workloads.)

INT4 weight + FP8 activation workflows can produce about ~1.8× of the baseline throughput when memory is the main bottleneck. INT4 weights + FP4 activations can reduce memory down to 20% of the baseline. 4-bit targets. The speedup is around 3.5×, which is consistent with the theoretical peak 4× improvement over FP16.

The goal of dynamic precision switching is to maximize performance while keeping output quality within acceptable bounds. Ideally, the kernel runs in the fastest possible precision (e.g., FP8 or FP4) and falls back to higher precision (e.g., FP16) only when necessary. In practice, libraries like NVIDIA's Transformer Engine for PyTorch allow layer-wise control over precision at runtime.

Linear layers might default to FP8, but a runtime hook could increase a layer's precision to FP16 or reduce it to FP4 depending on the layer's role. For instance, FP4 could be applied to lightweight layers like output projections in which minor accuracy degradation is tolerable, while FP8 or FP16 might be used for early layers that process raw user inputs and benefit from higher precision.

Beyond per-layer mixed-precision control, you can use a more fine-grained optimization strategy, which adjusts the precision per token. This approach lets the inference system run in the fastest mode possible, FP8 for instance, when predictions are confident. It would then fall back to higher-precision modes like FP16 when it's more uncertain.

In practice, the model generates the current token using a default precision (e.g., FP16), then evaluates confidence based on runtime metrics, such as output entropy, maximum softmax probability, or logit variance.

If the model is highly confident in its prediction, the next token can be processed at a lower precision. If uncertainty is high, the system reverts to a more stable format to maintain output quality. Here is example code that demonstrates the concept:

```python
import contextlib
import torch

# ----------------------------
# Safe Transformer Engine (TE) FP8 autocast import
# ----------------------------
try:
    # TE is only effective if your model actually uses TE-enabled layers
    # (e.g., Linear, LayerNorm wrappers).
    from transformer_engine.pytorch import fp8_autocast as _te_fp8_autocast
    # type: ignore
    _TE_AVAILABLE = True
except Exception:
    _TE_AVAILABLE = False
```

```python
    # No-op stand-in so the code runs without TE installed. It never changes
    # numerical behavior.
    class _NullCtx(contextlib.ContextDecorator):
        def __init__(self, **_): pass
        def __enter__(self): return self
        def __exit__(self, *exc): return False
    def _te_fp8_autocast(**_):
        return _NullCtx()


# ---------------------------
# Helper: choose the precision context *for this step* safely
# ---------------------------
def _precision_context_cuda(use_fp8: bool,
                            prefer_bfloat16: bool,
                            enable_fp8: bool):
    """
    Enter exactly one precision context. If FP8 isn't enabled or TE is
    missing/unused, fall back to AMP (BF16/FP16).
    """
    if use_fp8 and enable_fp8 and _TE_AVAILABLE:
        # Note: fp8_autocast affects only TE-enabled modules. Non-TE modules
        # run at their native dtypes.
        return _te_fp8_autocast(enabled=True)
    amp_dtype = torch.bfloat16 if prefer_bfloat16 else torch.float16
    return torch.autocast(device_type="cuda", dtype=amp_dtype)

def _precision_context(device: torch.device, use_fp8: bool,
                       prefer_bfloat16: bool, enable_fp8: bool):
    return _precision_context_cuda(use_fp8, prefer_bfloat16,
                                   enable_fp8) if device.type == "cuda"
                                   else contextlib.nullcontext()


# ---------------------------
# Main decode loop with smoothed, hysteretic precision switching
# ---------------------------
@torch.no_grad()
def decode_with_dynamic_precision(
    model,
    tokens: torch.Tensor,
    max_steps: int,
    *,
    device: torch.device = torch.device("cuda"),
    prefer_bfloat16: bool = True,      # B200: prefer BF16 over FP16 for AMP
    enable_fp8: bool = True,           # Allow FP8 when TE present
    enter_fp8_threshold: float = 6.0,  # hysteresis upper bound
                                       # (logit margin average)
    exit_fp8_threshold: float = 3.0,   # hysteresis lower bound (avoid flapping)
    reeval_interval: int = 8,          # compute/inspect confidence every N steps
                                       # to avoid per-step sync
    topk_dim: int = -1,                # last dimension holds vocabulary logits
    eos_id: int | None = None,
):
    """
    Autoregressive decode loop that *smoothly* switches between AMP (BF16/FP16)
    and FP8 (TE) without per-step host sync. Works even when TE is not
    installed; in that case, runs AMP only.
```

```
    - Confidence signal: mean(top1 - top2) logits margin across the batch.
    - Smoothing: EMA + interval re-evaluation to minimize CPU-GPU sync pressure.
    - Hysteresis: separate enter/exit thresholds to avoid precision flapping.
    """
    assert exit_fp8_threshold <= enter_fp8_threshold, \
        "Hysteresis requires exit <= enter threshold"

    model.eval()
    tokens = tokens.to(device, non_blocking=True)

    # Internal state
    use_fp8: bool = False  # start in AMP.
                           # Upgrade to FP8 when sustained confidence permits
    ema_conf: torch.Tensor | None = None  # stays on device;
                                          # host consults only at intervals
    alpha = 0.2  # EMA smoothing factor for confidence
# A tiny helper to update on-device EMA without host sync
    def _update_confidence_ema(logits: torch.Tensor) -> torch.Tensor:
        # logits: [B, vocab] or [B, T, vocab]. Use the last time-step if 3D.
        last = logits if logits.dim() == 2 else logits[:, -1, :]
        # Compute top-2 margin on-device
        top2 = torch.topk(last, k=2, dim=topk_dim).values  # [B, 2]
        margin = (top2[:, 0] - top2[:, 1]).mean()      # scalar tensor on device
        nonlocal ema_conf
        ema_conf = (1 - alpha) \
                   * (ema_conf if ema_conf is not None else margin)+alpha*margin
        return ema_conf  # device scalar

    # Decode
    for step in range(max_steps):
        # 1) Precision context (exactly one).
        # No nested contexts, no leakage across iterations.
        with _precision_context(device, use_fp8, prefer_bfloat16, enable_fp8):
            # Forward pass (HF-style or plain)
            try:
                logits = model(input_ids=tokens)
                if hasattr(logits, "logits"):
                    logits = logits.logits
            except TypeError:
                logits = model(tokens)

            # 2) Pick next token from the *last* position
            last_step_logits = logits if logits.dim() == 2 else logits[:, -1, :]
            next_token = torch.argmax(last_step_logits, dim=-1,
                                      keepdim=True)  # [B, 1]
            tokens = torch.cat([tokens, next_token], dim=1)

        # 3) Update on-device EMA signal every step (no host sync yet)
        conf_dev = _update_confidence_ema(logits)


        # 4) Periodically re-evaluate precision choice on host
        # to avoid per-step sync
        if (step + 1) % reeval_interval == 0:
            conf_value = float(conf_dev)  # exactly one tiny sync every N steps
            if not use_fp8 and enable_fp8 and _TE_AVAILABLE \
                and (conf_value > enter_fp8_threshold):
```

```
                    use_fp8 = True
            elif use_fp8 and (conf_value < exit_fp8_threshold):
                    use_fp8 = False

        # 5) EOS handling
        if eos_id is not None:
            if (tokens[:, -1] == eos_id).all():
                break

    return tokens

# ----------------------------
# Example (commented):
# ----------------------------
# model = ...   # your TE-enabled model (or any torch.nn.Module)
# input_ids = torch.randint(0, vocab_size, (batch_size, seq_len))
# out = decode_with_dynamic_precision(model, input_ids, max_steps=128,
# eos_id=tokenizer.eos_token_id)
# print(out.shape)
```

Here we see that PyTorch autocast supports only reduced-precision FP16 and BF16 as of this writing. In this case, you need to use the Transformer Engine library to route supported modules to FP8 kernels.

> The threshold used in this example (enter = 6.0, exit = 3.0) should be calibrated on a validation set using representative prompts to prevent latency gains from impacting accuracy.

This pattern creates an elastic precision regime and maximizes throughput. When the model operates in predictable (e.g., low-entropy) regions, such as generating punctuation or boilerplate completions, it continues in FP8 to maximize performance. When it enters higher-entropy segments, such as ambiguous prompts or decision points, it returns to FP16 to preserve numerical accuracy.

When paired with a modern GPU's support for low-precision operations, token-level dynamic precision switching offers an adaptive strategy for high-throughput, latency-sensitive inference. It applies low precision only when needed, reduces compute overhead, and maintains response quality across many different prompt conditions.

Kernel Autotuning for Transformer Self-Attention and MLP Paths

The performance of neural network layers on GPUs can vary drastically depending on low-level parameters like thread block size, tile dimensions, loop unrolling, and memory access patterns. For fixed-size models, libraries typically choose these parameters only once—often using general heuristics or offline tuning.

However, in an online inference service scenario, input sizes, including sequence lengths and batch sizes, can vary from request to request. Kernel autotuning refers to a runtime mechanism that selects—or even JIT-compiles—the optimal kernel variant for the current workload.

In the context of large transformer models, the two major compute phases of inference are self-attention and feed-forward MLP layers. Both can benefit from autotuning of their GPU kernels. Let's cover each of these in the context of kernel autotuning.

Consider an attention layer that processes a sequence of length L with H attention heads. There are many implementations of attention, including standard attention and optimized FlashAttention—and its multiple variants.

FlashAttention and its variants are significantly faster for long sequences due to tiling, parallelism, and memory-access improvements. However, for very short sequences, its overhead might outweigh its benefit. A dynamic engine can switch between a FlashAttention kernel and a simpler kernel depending on the sequence length, L.

For instance, if a request has $L = 256$ tokens, the engine might use a straightforward kernel launch that computes attention in one go using global memory reads, which are sufficient for small L. If another request comes in with $L = 2,048$, it could switch to FlashAttention's specialized tiling kernel known to scale better for large L by reusing data in shared memory and avoiding unnecessary HBM data fetches. This is demonstrated as a condition statement based on the input sequence length, as shown here:

```
// Note: example threshold shown here
if (seq_len < 256) {
    // global-memory version, best for small L
    attn_kernel = standard_attention_kernel;
} else {
    // tiled loads, best for large L
    attn_kernel = tiled_attention_kernel;
}
output = attn_kernel(Q, K, V, mask);
```

Behind the scenes, `attn_kernel` picks between completely different CUDA implementations. One implementation is optimized for small inputs using the default attention kernel, and another is optimized for large contexts using the tiled kernel.

The ideal tile dimensions depend on your GPU's shared-memory capacity and compute resources. Frameworks like CUTLASS and OpenAI's Triton include autotuners that benchmark a range of (`TILE_Q`, `TILE_K`) combinations at initialization—or even adaptively at runtime—to select the fastest variant. Table 19-3 shows examples of how different tile sizes perform on a Blackwell-class GPU.

Table 19-3. Example impact of tile-size choice on shared-memory footprint, SM occupancy, and achieved throughput (actual values will depend on thread-block dimensions, clock rates, and other microarchitectural factors)

Tile size	Shared memory (KB)	Occupancy (%)	Throughput (GOPS)
64×64	48	85	8.2
128×64	64	78	10.5
128×128	96	72	9.8
256×128	128	60	11.3

By choosing the right variant at runtime based on the input, you avoid the huge performance cliff of a one-size-fits-all approach. In practice you might benchmark on your target hardware to find that around $L = 128$ is the breakeven point.

Next, let's analyze the feed-forward MLP kernels in the context of autotuning. The feed-forward layers are essentially large matrix multiplications—specifically, two linear projections with a nonlinear activation in between.

Modern AI frameworks like PyTorch use highly optimized GEMM kernels using optimized CUDA libraries like cuBLAS and CUTLASS. There are often multiple algorithmic variants in these libraries for a given matrix size that use different tiling strategies, different Tensor Cores, and separate fallback paths.

For instance, NVIDIA's cuBLAS and cuBLASLt libraries can autotune GEMM kernels by first trying a few algorithms, then picking the fastest algorithm for the given dimensions. However, this typically happens the first time a GEMM of that shape is encountered—and not revisited.

> Where available in cuBLAS/cuBLASLt or custom kernels, programmatic dependent launch (PDL) can reduce launch gaps and improve steady-state throughput. Make sure to profile to confirm overlap.

In an inference server that sees many different batch sizes, one can explicitly invoke such autotuning mechanisms—or maintain a cache of best algorithms. For instance, for the MLP's GEMM of shape [`batch_size, hidden_dim`] x [`hidden_dim, 4*hid den_dim`], the optimal kernel might differ for `batch_size = 1` versus `batch_size = 16`.

The engine can detect a new batch size and run a quick microbenchmark of candidate kernels using cuBLASLt or a custom implementation to select the fastest kernel. Subsequent calls with that batch size can then directly use the chosen kernel.

In addition, some inference frameworks and runtimes use OpenAI's Triton GPU kernel domain-specific library (DSL) to compile attention and MLP kernels on the fly with autotuned tile sizes. In this case, the runtime would generate a few variants of a kernel with different tile sizes (e.g., 128 × 128, 64 × 256, etc.) and measure which performs better given the actual hardware and input shape.

You can use tools like Nsight Systems to empirically profile different kernel variants side by side.

Specifically, Nsight Systems provides detailed CUDA timelines, including `memcpy` and NVLink activity, and Nsight Compute provides memory workload analysis that helps attribute cache and memory behavior to kernel sites. This is particularly useful when evaluating tile-size and shared-memory trade-offs. In addition, it can often reveal nonobvious bottlenecks like L2 cache misses that will further guide your tuning decisions.

> Because hardware can sometimes be somewhat unpredictable under load given L2 cache effects, memory bank conflicts, etc., empirical tuning will always beat theoretical guesses. But it's good to start the tuning process with reasonable theoretical values.

Dynamic tile switching affects GPU occupancy and should be considered when choosing a tile size. Using a larger tile can increase reuse and reduce kernel-launch overhead, but it can also use more registers and shared memory. This will potentially reduce the number of thread blocks that can run concurrently—reducing occupancy. A proper autotuner will consider this trade-off.

In attention kernels, a larger tile (e.g., 128 × 128) maximizes data reuse in shared memory. This is ideal for long sequences since you issue fewer global-memory loads, amortize loop overhead, and produce higher sustained throughput.

For shorter sequences, however, that same large tile can consume too much shared memory, which limits the occupancy, or number of concurrent thread blocks running on each SM. By reducing the tile size (e.g., 64 × 64) for shorter sequences, you free up shared memory so you can schedule more blocks in parallel. This boosts SM occupancy and reduces per-kernel latency.

By adapting the tile size based on the input sequence length, the kernel can achieve near-optimal occupancy in most cases. Some systems even query the CUDA Occupancy API at runtime to choose kernel-launch parameters dynamically, such as thread block size. An example of the Occupancy API in C++ is shown next, but a Python API is also available (*https://oreil.ly/YtrVV*):

```
// Pseudocode for occupancy-based launch configuration
int maxBlocks, bestThreads;
for (int threads = 64; threads <= 256; threads *= 2) {
    cudaOccupancyMaxActiveBlocksPerMultiprocessor(
        &maxBlocks, MyKernel, threads,
```

```
            sharedMemPerBlock(threads));
    // choose "threads" to maximize occupancy
    // (remember to not exceed the max threads per SM limit (e.g., 2,048)
    float occupancy = (float) maxBlocks * threads /
                            hardwareMaxThreadsPerSM;
}
```

This pseudo-C++ illustrates evaluating different thread block sizes for a kernel. It
checks how many blocks per SM can run given their shared-memory usage. The kernel launch then adjusts the number of threads—or shared-memory use—accordingly.
High-performance frameworks and inference engines automate this type of logic
internally using the following set of steps:

1. *Measure workload*

    Inspect the current input dimensions (batch size B, sequence length L, etc.) for
    the next model forward.

2. *Select candidate kernels*

    Determine available kernel implementations for each component, such as stan-
    dard attention or flash attention for the attention phase and an appropriate
    GEMM algorithm for the MLP phase.

3. *Estimate or benchmark*

    Run a quick run of each candidate by executing each algorithm for a few itera-
    tions on sample data.

4. *Choose best variant*

    Select the kernel with minimal execution time—or sufficient throughput—based
    on the measured dimensions.

5. *Cache result*

    Store the choice in a lookup table keyed by the input dimension or workload sig-
    nature. This way, if a similar request appears, the best kernel is known without
    having to rerun these steps.

6. *Execute*

    Run the model layer using the chosen kernel implementation.

This is analogous to a database query optimizer picking a query
plan. Here, the "plan" is the chosen kernel implementation.

By following such a process, the inference runtime continuously tunes itself. Over
time, the system builds a library of optimized paths for various scenarios, such as
short versus long prompts, small versus large batches, etc. The overhead of on-the-fly

tuning is kept low by either doing it asynchronously—testing new kernels in a separate stream while the current inference uses a default kernel—or during low-traffic periods so as not to impact latency.

It's recommended to incorporate an initial warm-up phase when a model is loaded by running a variety of sample inputs through to trigger autotuning. This can include extremes—like max sequence length, max batch, etc.—so that the engine preoptimizes kernels for those cases.

Also, it's best to monitor execution time at each layer during runtime. If a layer suddenly becomes a bottleneck due to a change in input characteristics, then it's time to revisit the kernel selection.

> Some advanced frameworks even use multiarmed bandit algorithms that continuously explore alternative kernels and update the choice of a different kernel as conditions change.

In short, autotuning transforms static kernels into adaptive ones. This squeezes the highest performance out of your GPU cluster for each set of inputs regardless of the workload. You can be confident that the system is constantly adapting.

Dynamic Shared-Memory Allocation and Occupancy-Aware Kernel Selection

Closely related to kernel tuning is the management of GPU shared memory and overall streaming multiprocessor (SM) occupancy. Modern GPUs feature a large shared memory per SM. By dynamically allocating threads at runtime based on the problem size—as well as current shared-memory utilization and occupancy—you can significantly improve overall AI system performance.

With dynamic shared-memory allocation, the system adjusts the amount of shared memory that each thread block uses based on the problem size. With occupancy-aware kernel selection, the system is choosing kernel-launch parameters that make best use of the SM's resources—including registers, shared memory, and warps—to keep the GPU busy.

Choosing a tiled attention algorithm should balance data reuse against SM occupancy. For instance, consider T as your tile width, in tokens, per thread block. Each thread block reserves on the order of $O(T^2)$ floats in shared memory to hold the query, key, and value chunks since self-attention is quadratic in nature.

A large tile size (e.g., $T=256$) loads each key/value block once from DRAM and reuses it for many queries. This reduces global-memory traffic closer to $O(T)$ floats per thread block. But because each thread block now uses a lot of shared memory, only a few thread blocks can run on an SM at once given hardware limits. This reduces occupancy. For example, if only 1 block per SM can run at T=256 versus 4 blocks at T=128, you might see only 30% SM occupancy using T=256.

A small tile size (e.g., T=64) uses far less shared memory, which allows more thread blocks to fit into each SM. This better hides latency and boosts utilization. However, you end up reloading the same key/value data more often, which increases DRAM accesses.

The optimal tile size, T, depends on a few factors, including your sequence length L, the GPU's shared-memory capacity, and the SM count. You want a tile that's large enough to amortize DRAM reads but small enough to keep occupancy high enough that many thread blocks are active on the SM concurrently.

In practice, you could manually pick a handful of candidate T values, such as 64, 128, and 256—and benchmark each value on your specific hardware using a sequence length, L, that represents your dataset. You would then choose the value of T that produces the best overall throughput. However, instead of hard-coding T ahead of time, you can compute it right before launching your kernel, as shown here:

```
int T = choose_tile(L, gpu_shared_mem_per_block, num_sms);

// calculate shared memory in bytes based on the tile size
// (multiplying by 3 for Q, K, and V)

size_t shared_mem_bytes = 3 * T * T * sizeof(float);

numBlocks = ...

MyAttentionKernel<<<numBlocks, threadsPerBlock, shared_mem_bytes>>>(...);
```

Here, T is computed from the sequence length L; the GPUs' shared-memory limits per thread block, gpu_shared_mem_per_block; and the number of SMs, num_sms. Then, shared memory per thread block, shared_mem_bytes, is computed at runtime based on the computed tile size, T.

You can then launch the CUDA kernel with the shared-memory argument, shared_mem_bytes. The kernel itself would contain the following to define an extern __shared__ array to allocate the shared-memory buffer of size shared_mem_bytes for each thread block:

```
// holds 3 tiles of TxT floats for Q, K, and V
extern __shared__ float smem[];

// Q tile: smem[0 ... T*T-1]
float* tile_q = smem;

// K tile: smem[T*T ... 2*T*T-1]
```

```
    float* tile_k = smem + T*T;

    // V tile: smem[2*T*T ... 3*T*T-1]
    float* tile_v = smem + 2*T*T;
```

By varying `shared_mem_bytes` per launch, the same kernel binary can run with different tile sizes. After selecting T, you can query occupancy using the CUDA Occupancy API to see how many blocks fit per SM.

If occupancy is too low and only one block is allocated per SM, you can reduce T. If you're thrashing DRAM, you can increase T. This can be implemented as an automatic feedback loop in which the kernel programmatically measures its own achieved occupancy using the CUDA Occupancy API or NVIDIA's Data Center GPU Manager (DCGM)—and adjusts T on subsequent iterations. This way each attention layer uses the optimal configuration based on the current sequence length, L, and the hardware limits.

As we saw in Chapter 6, you also need to consider register usage per thread when optimizing SM occupancy. Using more registers (e.g., unrolling loops) can speed up single-thread performance, but it can reduce overall SM occupancy since each SM has a limited register file.

Fewer warps can be scheduled if each warp uses many registers. A dynamic runtime can detect if a kernel is hitting occupancy limits due to registers and switch to a version that uses fewer registers—at the expense of extra instructions. These low-level considerations are critical for adaptive, high-performance inference servers.

Dynamic shared-memory tuning requires profiling occupancy versus throughput. Tools such as NVIDIA Nsight Systems/Compute and the CUDA Occupancy API can show the achieved occupancy and execution efficiency of each kernel. Meanwhile, DCGM provides real-time GPU utilization and SM occupancy metrics at the system level. An adaptive system can use this information to notice that an attention kernel with sequence length 2,048 achieves only 30% occupancy, for example, because each thread block uses a large amount of shared memory.

In this case, the system could dynamically switch to a kernel configuration that reduces shared memory per thread block by splitting the attention computation across two passes, for instance. This would increase occupancy—and potentially increase throughput—if memory latency was the bottleneck.

Conversely, if a kernel is memory bound and not saturating ALUs, using more shared memory—even if occupancy drops—can improve effective throughput by reducing memory stalls. It's important to understand these trade-offs—especially with occupancy since it's less intuitive, in some cases, than other metrics.

It's recommended to design kernels that allow tunable shared memory and thread block sizes at runtime. The system can then adapt the tuning configuration to runtime conditions based on input and hardware feedback. For example, it can provide runtime parameters and template parameters for tile sizes used by libraries like CUTLASS, which provide runtime-tunable kernel variants for exactly this reason.

You should also continuously monitor SM utilization metrics. Consider many idle warps (e.g., < 50% active warps) or memory stall cycles (> 70% stalled). This indicates an imbalance, as either occupancy is too low (idle warps)—or your tile size is too small and causes excessive memory traffic. As such, your system should adjust accordingly to restore the balance.

For inference serving, it's common to maintain a small table of optimal thread block configurations for different problem sizes. This mapping can be implemented as a JSON or config file that maps sequence length ranges to launch parameters. This allows easy updates as models and hardware evolve.

For instance, whenever your system performs attention with sequence length 512, it will use 128 threads/block and 16 KB shared memory. Or, for sequence length 4,096, it will use 256 threads/block and 64 KB shared memory, etc. This extends the concept of autotuning to resource allocation.

Remember that modern NVIDIA GPUs provide a unified on-chip pool for L1 data cache and shared memory. And the carveout controls how much of that pool is reserved for shared memory versus L1. Adjust the carveout with `cudaFuncSetAttribute` to increase the fraction available to shared memory when kernels demand larger tiles.

Modern NVIDIA GPUs provide a unified on-chip pool for L1 data cache and shared memory. NVIDIA's device driver allows you to set the L1 cache versus shared-memory split percentage, or "carveout" percentage. As such, you can configure an SM to prefer more shared memory or more L1 cache depending on the use case. For instance, you can increase the fraction available to shared memory when kernels demand larger tiles.

> The carveout is a per-kernel attribute and only a hint rather than a guarantee. It's another knob you can tune to balance occupancy and caching behavior.

A sophisticated runtime can toggle this carve-out percentage at launch time using `cudaFuncSetAttribute()` with `cudaFuncAttributePreferredSharedMemoryCarve out` or specific kernels. For instance, if an attention kernel uses very large tiles and needs more shared memory, you might want to reduce the L1 to 25% and increase shared memory to 75% (assuming the carveout value starts at 50%).

The shared-memory versus L1 carveout attribute is a hint rather than a guarantee. Always treat the setting as a hint and verify the effect with profiling. Check that the requested setting actually impacted occupancy and cache behavior.

In short, dynamic shared memory and occupancy-aware techniques ensure that every SM is kept as busy as possible for the given task. These techniques adapt the kernel's resource usage to the specific use case. This is essential for large models in which some layers or batch sizes could otherwise underutilize the SMs.

Speculative KV Prefetching for Faster TTFT

When serving LLMs in a real-time setting, time-to-first-token (TTFT) is a critical metric, as it measures how quickly the system can produce the first token of the model's response. This directly affects the end user's experience.

One major contributor to TTFT in large models is the time spent setting up the model's internal states, such as the key-value (KV) cache, before token generation can begin. Remember from earlier chapters that the attention KV cache stores the past tokens' key and value projections for each layer.

Speculative KV prefetching is an optimization in which the system anticipates the data needed for the first token—and loads the necessary data into the GPU in advance. This effectively overlaps KV cache preparation with other steps, such as compute. This way, the token generation can start more quickly. An example of speculative KV caching is SpeCache (*https://oreil.ly/b21E5*), as shown in Figure 19-3.

With SpeCache, the KV cache is compressed (16-bit, in this case) and moved off-GPU one layer at a time. This reduces the memory footprint. After generating the first output token, a speculative "next" token is computed. At the same time, the model prefetches the corresponding reduced-precision KV pairs needed for that first decoding step.

On each subsequent step, the model decodes two tokens in parallel, including the actual output token and the speculative token. Both results are fed into the next step, and, before each step, the top-k most relevant 16-bit KV pairs for the speculative path are prefetched. This way, both paths have their required KV cache data ready. In short, SpeCache reports TTFT improvements by prefetching reduced-precision KV and overlapping with compute.

Integrate speculative prefetch techniques only after validating your access patterns and storage tiers.

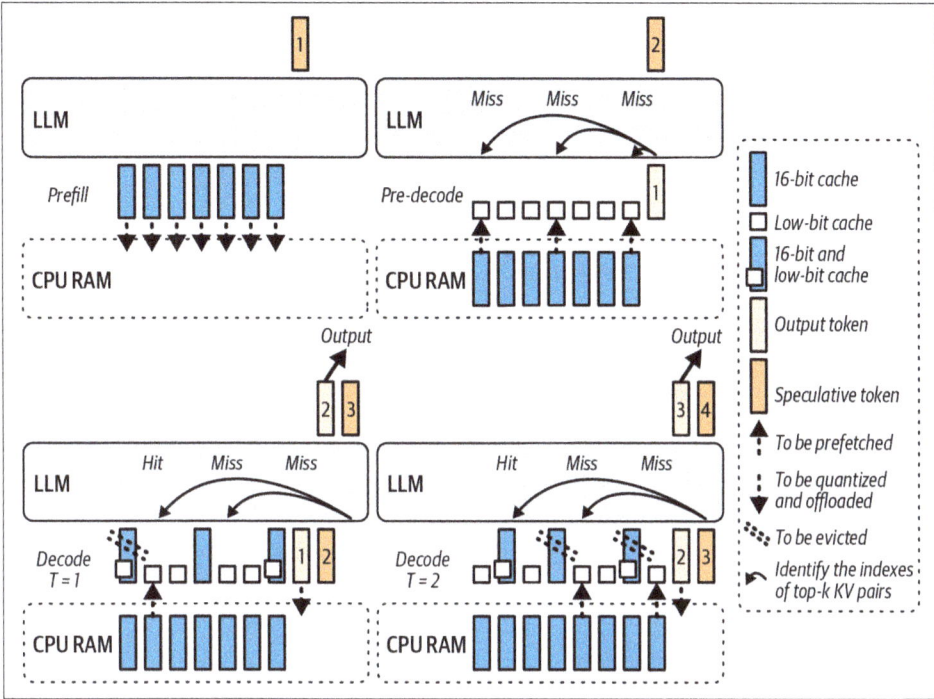

Figure 19-3. Speculative decoding with SpeCache (source: https://oreil.ly/b21E5)

The KV cache can be extremely large due to the number of layers in modern LLMs, the increasing size of the LLM context window (effectively limitless at this point), and the large amount of reasoning chains generated by modern "thinking" models. Modern inference systems will often swap the KV cache between GPU, CPU memory, and SSD to better manage capacity—especially for extremely long contexts, which don't fit in GPU memory.

When a new token is being generated, a naive approach would be to fetch the KV data from wherever it resides (some on GPU, some on CPU) in synchronous fashion—and then perform the computation to decode the next token. This can add significant latency for the first token—especially if the cache has been paged out to CPU memory or NVMe storage.

KV cache prefetching helps by starting the KV data transfers ahead of time. As soon as the user's prompt is received, the server can start copying the necessary KV pages—as well as the model weights—directly into GPU memory. By the time the model finishes computing the prompt in the prefill phase, the necessary data is in place to generate the first output token.

Specifically, this mechanism keeps only the current layer's KV in GPU memory—and offloads the other layers' KV to the CPU. It asynchronously prefetches the next layer's cache into the GPU while the current layer is being computed. Additionally, it simultaneously writes the previous layer's cache back to the CPU.

This overlap of communication and computation means the GPU rarely waits for data. The result is that using an offloaded KV cache in CPU memory has minimal impact on latency. For example, you might see ~5%–10% lower tokens/s throughput when offloading due to the extra data-transfer overhead.

> Overlap can mask much of the latency of CPU-resident KV, but a throughput penalty typically remains due to CPU DRAM bandwidth and PCIe overhead. Profile with your batch and sequence lengths repeatedly.

An example of KV cache offloading is in Hugging Face's Transformers library in the form of the `OffloadedCache` mechanism. This can be enabled when calling `gener ate(cache_implementation="offloaded")` or `generate(cache_implementa tion="offloaded_static")`. This will generate tokens with the Transformer library, as shown here. This makes it a low-effort, high-impact optimization:

```
# Dynamic, variable-length serving and sliding layers
# (recommended default)
out = model.generate(..., cache_implementation="offloaded")

# Static shapes + torch.compile and CUDA Graphs
# (highest throughput with fixed shapes, use with torch.compile)
# out = model.generate(..., cache_implementation="offloaded_static")
```

Under the hood, when generation begins, the `OffloadedCache` will ensure that layer 1's KV is moved to the GPU. While layer 1 computes, `OffloadedCache` issues an asynchronous DMA for layer 2's KV from the CPU to the GPU, etc. It's always prefetching one layer ahead.

By the time the forward pass reaches layer 2, its KV is already local. This reduces the stall that would occur if we used a synchronous copy for each layer. Now that we have described KV prefetching, let's move to speculative KV prefetching.

Speculative KV prefetching extends beyond just the one-layer lookahead of regular KV prefetching. Imagine an inference server configuration with multiple model replicas—or multiple possible paths like MoE models in which a token can be routed to one of several expert networks.

KV prefetching helps at the boundary between the phases. By the end of the prefill phase, ideally, the caches for all layers are either already in GPU memory or queued to come into GPU memory. This directly minimizes TTFT since, once generation starts, the model isn't waiting on memory transfers.

It's recommended to continuously monitor your TTFT using tracing tools like NVTX markers to measure the first token's decode time. This will measure TTFT precisely. If you see excessive spikes of idle time immediately after the decode phase begins, this indicates a missed prefetch opportunity.

To implement KV prefetching in your own stack without stalling inference, you can use CUDA streams for overlap (as described in Chapter 11). This way, it runs concurrently with your main computation stream. You would then use CUDA events to synchronize the streams only when the prefetched data is needed, as shown here:

```
// kv_prefetch_overlap.cu

#include <cstdio>
#include <cuda_runtime.h>

// Example sizes
static constexpr size_t KV_BYTES =
  /* set to your chunk size */ 8ull<<20; // 8 MiB

__global__ void forward_kernel(/* ... */) {
  // compute logits for current token ...
}

__global__ void consume_prefetched_kv(/* use prefetch_dest */) {
  // consumes KV in prefetch_dest ...
}

int main() {
  // Allocate destination buffer on this GPU
  void* prefetch_dest = nullptr;
  cudaMalloc(&prefetch_dest, KV_BYTES);

  // Example: staging source on host. MUST be pinned for real overlap.
  void* kv_src_host = nullptr;
  cudaMallocHost(&kv_src_host, KV_BYTES);  // pinned (page-locked)
  // Fill kv_src_host with data for the first iteration...

  cudaStream_t compute_stream, prefetch_stream;
  cudaStreamCreateWithFlags(&compute_stream, cudaStreamNonBlocking);
  cudaStreamCreateWithFlags(&prefetch_stream, cudaStreamNonBlocking);
  cudaEvent_t kv_ready;
  cudaEventCreateWithFlags(&kv_ready, cudaEventDisableTiming);

  bool done = false;
  while (!done) {
    // 1) Launch compute for current token
    forward_kernel<<< /*grid*/1, /*block*/1, 0, compute_stream>>>();
```

```
// 2) Asynchronously prefetch next KV chunk
// If your source is another GPU, use cudaMemcpyPeerAsync
// and enable peer access.
cudaMemcpyAsync(prefetch_dest, kv_src_host, KV_BYTES,
                          cudaMemcpyHostToDevice, prefetch_stream);
cudaEventRecord(kv_ready, prefetch_stream);

// 3) Ensure consumer on compute_stream waits just-in-time
cudaStreamWaitEvent(compute_stream, kv_ready, /*flags*/0);

// 4) Launch work that consumes the prefetched KV
consume_prefetched_kv<<< /*grid*/1, /*block*/1, 0, compute_stream>>>();

// 5) ...advance state, update kv_src_host for next iteration, set `done`
done = true; // demo
}

cudaEventDestroy(kv_ready);
cudaStreamDestroy(prefetch_stream);
cudaStreamDestroy(compute_stream);
cudaFree(prefetch_dest);
cudaFreeHost(kv_src_host);
return 0;
}
```

In this setup, cudaMemcpyAsync runs on prefetch_stream while model.forward()
uses the compute_stream. This allows the CUDA driver to overlap data transfer with
compute. You synchronize only when the prefetched KV data is actually needed by
waiting on kv_ready event before continuing with the computation that consumes it.
The event enforces just-in-time synchronization at the handoff point.

> Make sure the host buffers are pinned (page-locked). Otherwise,
> cudaMemcpyAsync may serialize and you won't get the desired copy/
> compute overlap. If the KV source is on another GPU, use cuda
> MemcpyPeerAsync and enable peer access. And if you are using
> Unified Memory (e.g., Grace Blackwell, Vera Rubin superchips),
> consider using cudaMemPrefetchAsync to stage pages ahead of
> time. You can also use CUDA Graphs to capture this sequence if
> the pattern is repeatable. This can further reduce kernel-launch
> overhead when prefetching happens frequently.

Using a separate stream ensures efficient pipelining. As one token is being generated,
the next token's KV cache is being prefetched without interrupting the compute
stream. This maximizes GPU utilization by masking transfer latency and keeping the
compute units continuously fed with data. Modern LLM inference engines use this
automatically in the form of paged KV caching.

It's best to consider weight and KV cache data movement as part of the overall inference pipeline. Just as you should pipeline compute operations, you should also pipeline data movement. Always have the next needed data in flight while the current computation is ongoing. KV cache compression is yet another option to improve performance at the KV cache layer. Let's cover this next.

Real-Time KV Cache Compression and Policy Switching

As an LLM generates more and more tokens in a session, the KV cache grows linearly. For long conversations, documents, and reasoning chains, the KV cache consumes a huge amount of GPU memory and often utilizes the most GPU memory.

KV cache is a good candidate for compression/quantization. Like any form of compression, KV cache compression reduces its memory footprint. Doing this in real time means performing compression on the fly during inference.

Policy switching means that the compression strategy can change based on the current context. The goal is to free up memory and network bandwidth when needed—without impacting model accuracy or slowing down computations that involve the KV cache data. Figure 19-4 shows a few different types of KV cache compression algorithms.

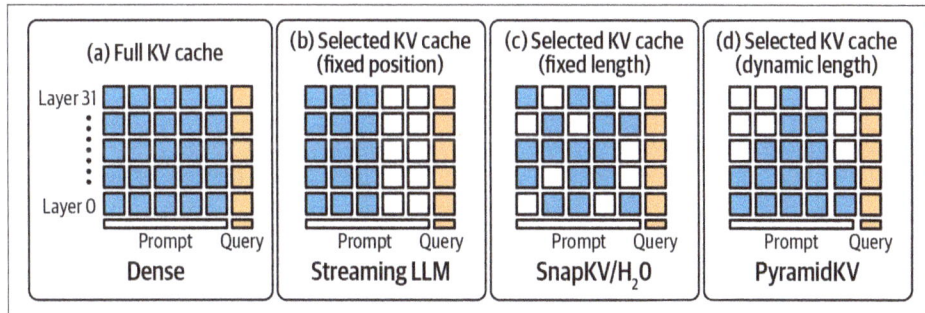

Figure 19-4. Different KV cache algorithms, including no caching (e.g., dense)

A straightforward and simple approach to KV compression is to just reduce its precision. Many frameworks default to FP16 or BF16 for KV cache since 16-bit is typically what the model uses for activations. However, one can often compress keys and values to 8-bit or even 4-bit with minimal impact on output quality—especially for tokens at the end of the LLM's context.

Hugging Face's Transformers library supports a `QuantizedCache`, including INT8 and INT4 for KV memory. This feature can be enabled in one line by specifying `cache_implementation="quantized"` with a specific bit-width. The result is a massive memory savings at the cost of a tiny amount of extra compute for the quantization/dequantization operations. And the overall model quality does not suffer in most cases.

When quantization plus CPU offload is used concurrently, ensure host buffers are pinned (page-locked) to prevent serialized transfers. This will help to sustain copy bandwidth (e.g., PCIe/NVLink).

Next, let's discuss dynamic policy switching. An example of a policy is keeping the last 128 tokens in full precision but compressing the rest of the tokens in 4-bit. This way, the most recent context—which likely has the most impact on predicting the next token—is preserved with higher precision, whereas the older history is stored in lower precision to save storage.

If the model suddenly needs to attend to older tokens, it's usually not disastrous since many LLMs have recency bias anyway. This means that they prioritize recent context. This way, earlier parts of the input sequence may not affect the final output as much.

You might further adapt this window based on user prompt length. For example, you can use a larger full-precision window for very long prompts—or compress more aggressively if GPU memory usage is above a threshold.

Alternatively, a policy could be based on memory usage. For instance, the policy could dictate that if GPU memory usage exceeds 80%, it should compress the entire KV cache into 8-bit. This helps avoid OOM errors during long generations. The policy might include multitier compression in which the system compresses the KV cache to 8-bit under mild pressure, then changes to 4-bit compression under extreme pressure.

With true dynamic, real-time policy switching, the engine can change to a different compression during token generation. In this case, the implementation would need to maintain multiple representations of the cache simultaneously. For instance, it would initially store KV in FP16 but concurrently maintain an INT8 version of the same data.

The system would use FP16 by default, but if memory utilization crosses a certain threshold, it could start using the INT8 version—with appropriate scaling factors—and free the FP16 memory to relieve memory pressure. Future attention reads would then retrieve dequantized values from INT8 storage.

This requires careful synchronization, however, to ensure the compressed version is kept up-to-date and ready by the time it's needed. Techniques like double buffering and background compression threads are useful in this case.

Often a CPU thread can handle the compression asynchronously using vectorized INT8 quantization operations. It can then copy the compressed block to GPU memory when ready.

> Implement real-time policy swaps at safe points, such as the end of an iteration. This way, you can avoid mid-calculation switches and hide the requantization latency by doing it in a background stream.

There are other techniques, such as lossless compression, that use entropy coding and clustering to compress activations without losing information bit-for-bit. However, these implementations are complex and may be too slow to do in real time—even on a GPU.

Simpler mechanisms like chunk-wise ZFP, a type of floating-point compression, or even generic CPU-based compression should be considered. However, the simplest, most-effective, and well-supported method so far has been quantization.

> As of this writing, lossless methods like ZFP are evaluated in offline and research contexts but remain uncommon in production LLM KV cache paths due to throughput constraints relative to quantized cache. As such, quantization remains the go-to approach for its balance of speed and 2–4× memory reduction.

For minimal quality impact, you can experiment with per-head and per-token scaling. Quantizing the KV cache is most effective with per-head, group-wise scaling rather than per-token scaling. The Hugging Face `QuantizedCache` Transformer implementation calibrates the range of values per attention head.

Specifically, `QuantizedCache` implements per-channel, group-wise quantization with a configurable group size and a residual window that keeps the most recent tokens in the original precision. You enable it by setting `cache_implementation="quantized"` and passing `cache_config` as a dictionary. You can compute the max absolute value in a tensor and scale the 4-bit or 8-bit quantization accordingly. This is essentially a form of min-max, or magnitude-based quantization.

A useful implementation of `QuantizedCache` is the Half-Quadratic Quantization (HQQ) (*https://oreil.ly/MhJCY*) backend. HQQ provides a calibration-free, on-the-fly quantizer that supports a wide range of low-bit formats, including 2-bit, 3-bit, 4-bit, and 8-bit. It uses a robust optimization to model outliers and heavy-tailed error distributions. And HQQ integrates well into the Hugging Face Transformers' KV cache implementation. It provides both a PyTorch and custom CUDA kernel implementation for fast inference.

We can implement a dynamic policy that can switch between an 8-bit quantization and 4-bit quantization depending on memory pressure. The sharpness or distribution of values might also guide the decision. If the cached values are mostly small and have low variance, they can usually be quantized more aggressively. Switching the compression policy in real time can be integrated with the Hugging Face `Quantized Cache` mechanism.

Unfortunately, Transformers does not support changing the bit-width of an already-initialized cache object in place. However, to implement a dynamic policy, our code can generate tokens in small chunks and, on memory pressure, start the next chunk with a new quantized cache configuration on the fly. This implementation is similar to falling back to an offloaded cache upon hitting an out-of-memory (OOM) error. Here is the code:

```python
# dynamic_quantized_cache.py
# Dynamic KV cache policy using Hugging Face Transformers' QuantizedCache (2025).
# Starts with int8 HQQ and drops to int4 when device memory is tight.
# Requires: transformers >= 4.55, hqq (for HQQ backend).
#
# This uses only public APIs:
#   - cache_implementation="quantized"
#   - cache_config as a dict
#
# References:
#   - KV cache strategies docs (QuantizedCache, HQQ/Quanto backends)

from __future__ import annotations
from typing import Dict, Optional
import logging
import torch
from transformers import AutoModelForCausalLM, AutoTokenizer


def make_cache_config(
    *,
    backend: str,
    nbits: int,
    device: torch.device,
    compute_dtype: torch.dtype = torch.float16,
    q_group_size: int = 64,
    residual_length: int = 128,
    axis_key: int = 1,
    axis_value: int = 1,
) -> Dict:
    """
    Build a cache_config dictionary accepted by Transformers' quantized cache.
    HQQ supports nbits in {2, 4, 8}; Quanto supports {2, 4}.
    axis_key/axis_value=1 are recommended for HQQ.
    """
    return {
        "backend": backend,             # "HQQ" or "quanto"
        "nbits": int(nbits),
        "axis_key": axis_key,
        "axis_value": axis_value,
        "q_group_size": int(q_group_size),  # group size along head_dim
```

```python
        "residual_length": int(residual_length), # recent tokens (orig precision)
        "compute_dtype": compute_dtype,      # dequantization compute dtype
    }


def _gpu_used_ratio() -> float:
    """
    Return fraction of device memory used as 1 - free/total.
    Uses CUDA driver info, which reflects true device state,
    not just the PyTorch allocator's reserved bytes.
    """
    free, total = torch.cuda.mem_get_info()
    return 1.0 - (free / total)


@torch.no_grad()
def generate_with_dynamic_quantized_cache(
    model: AutoModelForCausalLM,
    tokenizer: AutoTokenizer,
    prompt: str,
    *,
    max_new_tokens: int = 256,
    chunk_tokens: int = 32,
    memory_threshold: float = 0.90,   # switch policy if used_ratio >= threshold
    backend: str = "hqq",             # "hqq" or "quanto"
    start_bits: int = 8,              # initial cache bit-width
    fallback_bits: int = 4,           # lower bit-width on pressure
    residual_length: int = 128,
) -> str:
    """
    Generate text in chunks while allowing mid-run policy changes.
    The policy applies to each chunk by choosing cache_config for that chunk.
    If memory is tight, we switch from int8 to int4 in subsequent chunks.
    """
    backend = backend.lower()
    assert backend in {"hqq", "quanto"}, "backend must be 'hqq' or 'quanto'"
    if backend == "quanto":
        assert start_bits in {2, 4} and fallback_bits in {2, 4}, \
            "Quanto supports only 2 or 4 bits"
    if backend == "hqq":
        assert start_bits in {2, 4, 8} and fallback_bits in {2, 4, 8}, \
            "HQQ supports 2, 4, or 8 bits"

    device = model.device
    inputs = tokenizer(prompt, return_tensors="pt").to(device)
    generated_ids = inputs["input_ids"]   # [batch=1, seq_len]
    tokens_remaining = int(max_new_tokens)
    current_bits = int(start_bits)

    # Use EOS if available to terminate early.
    eos_id: Optional[int] = tokenizer.eos_token_id
```

```python
    while tokens_remaining > 0:
        # Decide policy for this chunk based on current memory pressure.
        if torch.cuda.is_available():
            # Smooth the signal to avoid oscillation
            # when multiple processes are active.

            if 'used_ratio' in locals():
                used_ratio = 0.8 * used_ratio + 0.2 * _gpu_used_ratio()
            else:
                used_ratio = _gpu_used_ratio()
            if used_ratio >= memory_threshold:
                current_bits = min(current_bits, fallback_bits) # drop bits
                logging.info(f"Current bits {current_bits}")


        cache_cfg = make_cache_config(
            backend=backend,
            nbits=current_bits,
            device=device,
            compute_dtype=torch.bfloat16,
            q_group_size=64,
            residual_length=residual_length,
            axis_key=1,
            axis_value=1,
        )

        # Generate a small chunk with the chosen cache policy.
        this_chunk = min(chunk_tokens, tokens_remaining)
        out = model.generate(
            input_ids=generated_ids,
            max_new_tokens=this_chunk,
            do_sample=False,        # deterministic for clarity; adjust as needed
            use_cache=True,
            cache_implementation="quantized",       # select QuantizedCache
            cache_config=cache_cfg,                  # pass backend + settings
            pad_token_id=eos_id,
            return_dict_in_generate=False,      # we only need the tokens here
        )
        # 'out' is [1, old_len + this_chunk]; slice out newly generated suffix
        new_tokens = out[:, generated_ids.shape[1]:]
        generated_ids = out
        tokens_remaining -= new_tokens.shape[1]

        # Early termination if the model emitted EOS.
        if eos_id is not None and int(new_tokens[0, -1].item()) == eos_id:
            break

    return tokenizer.decode(generated_ids[0], skip_special_tokens=True)


if __name__ == "__main__":
    # Example usage. Replace with a model that supports your hardware.
```

```
ckpt = "meta-llama/Llama-3.1-8B-Instruct"
tok = AutoTokenizer.from_pretrained(ckpt)
mdl = AutoModelForCausalLM.from_pretrained(ckpt,
                             torch_dtype=torch.float16).to("cuda")

text = generate_with_dynamic_quantized_cache(
    mdl,
    tok,
    "Explain attention key-value caches in one paragraph.",
    max_new_tokens=120,
    chunk_tokens=32,
    memory_threshold=0.90,
    backend="hqq",          # or "quanto" if you installed Quanto
    start_bits=8,
    fallback_bits=4,
    residual_length=128,
)
print(text)
```

Here, we start with an INT8 HQQ cache for modest compression and switch to INT4 when actual GPU free memory drops below a threshold. This is measured with `torch.cuda.mem_get_info()`, which reflects true free versus total device memory. This provides the right signal for the policy choice.

We then generate tokens in small chunks so that we can safely switch the policy between chunks without trying to mutate an existing cache instance. This avoids reaching into private attributes or quantizing tensors manually. The cache backend does the work inside the model's forward pass.

As shown in this example, it's recommended to log an event or increment a counter when the policy switches. This way, you can correlate compression events with any accuracy or output anomalies.

Similarly, you can dynamically turn off compression if conditions improve. Suppose a long conversation just ended and the next question is short. The system could decide to stop compressing or even restore some caches to higher precision if it will produce better quality responses. The difference is likely small, so it might not be worth it.

It's important to avoid rapid fluctuations in compression since toggling compression on/off too often could thrash performance. To do this, you can introduce intentional delays (aka *hysteresis* and *cooldown*) between changes. For example, if a higher-compression strategy is changed, keep it until GPU memory drops well below a given threshold. This way, you avoid oscillations and thrashing.

Having this flexibility is useful if, for instance, your service sometimes prioritizes maximum quality (no compression) for premium users versus maximum throughput (heavy compression) for free-tier users. The policy can switch based on request metadata as well, including the user's subscription type.

No discussion on caching is complete without considering eviction strategies, such as Least Recently Used (LRU) eviction. If context length becomes too long, some model architectures—like those with recency bias or sliding-window attention—might choose to discard or downsample very old tokens entirely. Sliding-window attention is shown in Figure 19-5.

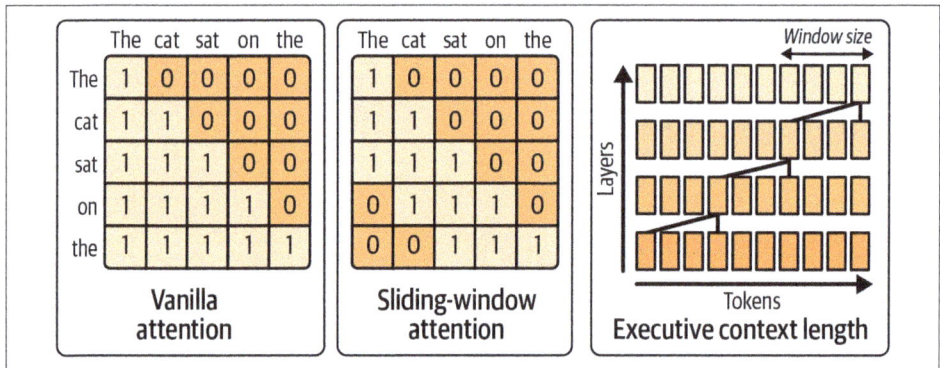

Figure 19-5. Sliding-window attention uses the intuition that the most useful tokens are the most recent

While LRU eviction of earlier tokens from the context is not exactly compression, it's yet another type of policy that can be dynamically chosen at runtime. For instance, the system can decide that, beyond 2,048 tokens, the model likely won't need the earlier tokens—based on some heuristics or a smaller LLM.

In this case, the system could start dropping those older tokens—or periodically compress them into a smaller summary. This starts getting into model and algorithmic territory—and requires more support, maintenance, and model training—but it is a form of dynamic context management that should be considered in advanced serving engines.

In short, you should consider quantized cache mechanisms provided by your inference engine, as they can handle the details of maintaining quantization-scale factors, interfacing with attention kernels, and monitoring GPU memory allocators at runtime. At a minimum, when the system sees memory utilization approaching a certain limit, log that and see if enabling a compression policy at that point would avoid OOM without hurting latency.

In practice, setting a high-watermark threshold on GPU memory (e.g., 80%) to trigger 8-bit compression has proven effective in preventing OOM crashes in production.

If it makes sense to use dynamic compression policies, you can implement the trigger. As with any quantization and compression strategy, be sure to test their impact on your model's output specific to your domain. Many generative tasks tolerate aggressive compression, but it's always good to verify that using 4-bit versus 8-bit doesn't introduce errors or unexpected outputs.

Reinforcement Learning Agents for Tuning AI Systems at Runtime

Many of the techniques we've discussed so far involve decisions based on the system's current state. These decisions often require trade-offs, such as speed versus accuracy and throughput versus latency. Rather than collecting more and more heuristics to make decisions, we can tune our inference system with reinforcement learning with an RL agent, environment, policy, and reward.

This is a cutting-edge approach. You should start with simpler heuristics as your baseline. Then you can use RL as an incremental improvement once the basics are stable.

Specifically, our inference engine watches server metrics (the environment), chooses actions (the policy) to maximize throughput while keeping latency under a target, and receives feedback (the reward) that guides continual improvement. In this way, the system becomes an online optimizer—continually refining its decision making as conditions change.

For instance, one could set up an environment in which each RL "step" is an inference request. And the RL actions include things like the following:

Action 1
Choose parallelism mode: single, TP, PP, and hybrid.

Action 2
Choose precision: full FP8 versus mixing FP8 and FP4.

Action 3
Adjust batch size or batch-waiting time.

Action 4

Enable or disable cache compression.

Action 5

Enable or disable speculative decoding.

Action 6

Select a smaller draft model for speculative decoding.

Action 7

Select a larger draft model for speculative decoding.

Action 8

Enable or disable speculative KV prefetching.

…more actions…

The current RL state observed by the agent might include GPU utilization, memory utilization, average latency, queue length of requests, etc. The RL reward is then defined by capturing business objectives, such as `reward = throughput - λ * max(0, latency - SLA)`. λ is a tunable penalty weight in this reward function that scales how harshly you punish latency violations.

It's recommended that you normalize the state features so that the RL agent doesn't have to learn the scale on its own. This can speed up training convergence. For example, you can scale queue length by a max value, etc.

Here, a larger λ makes the agent prioritize staying within the SLA over squeezing out extra throughput. A smaller λ lets it risk occasional latency overshoots to achieve higher token rates overall. Essentially, this reward function penalizes latency that exceeds the SLA but otherwise tries to increase throughput.

In practice, start with λ such that λ × (typical latency overshoot) is about equal to the throughput gain that you'd trade for it. For example, if a 10 ms delay is tolerable to gain 100 tokens/sec, set λ so that 10 ms × λ ≈ 100.

Over many iterations, the RL agent can learn when it's beneficial to compress caches—for instance, when memory is high and latency isn't immediately impacted. Or it could learn to switch to pipeline parallel mode when GPU utilization is low but one GPU is overloaded, etc.

This helps because PP breaks the model into sequential stages across multiple devices and redistributes the heavy work away from the bottlenecked device—smoothing out utilization and avoiding single-GPU hotspots.

The agent can find nonintuitive configurations that produce better performance. For instance, it might learn that for prompts above a certain length, it should enable both PP and FP4 compression to produce the best token throughput, whereas, for shorter prompts, it learns to use just pure tensor parallel in FP8. If we tried to encode this logic as a set of static rules, we might miss complex interaction.

An RL agent can more easily discover optimal combinations by exploring the action space—and ultimately exploiting the optimal configuration until the environmental conditions change. At this point, the RL would adjust the inference system accordingly since it's always exploring the action space and trying new configurations.

Training such an agent can be done offline using simulators and libraries such as Hugging Face's Transformer RL (TRL) libraries (*https://oreil.ly/COllD*). For instance, we could log a bunch of data from a running system under various conditions—and then train an RL policy in simulation to predict outcomes. At a very high level, the RL reward and update loop would look something like the following pseudocode:

```
# Pseudo structure for an RL-driven tuner

# This loop runs in separate thread/process alongside main inference service.

# e.g., {gpu_util:0.7, mem_util:0.9, avg_latency:120ms, req_queue:5}
state = get_system_state()

# e.g., 0 -> high precision, 1 -> low precision
action = rl_agent.select_action(state)

# Map action to actual parameter changes
if action == 0:
    precision_policy = "FP8"
else:
    precision_policy = "FP4"

# (We could have multiple actions, but single action for illustration)
apply_precision_policy(precision_policy)

# ... After the next token or set of tokens ...
new_state = get_system_state()
reward = compute_reward(old_state, new_state)
rl_agent.update(state, action, reward, new_state)
```

Here, the loop continuously runs in the background of the inference server. The com pute_reward function incorporates throughput (e.g., tokens per second since last step) and latency metrics. Since we are trying to balance throughput with latency, this is a multi-objective optimization problem in which we are optimizing multiple goals at once. A common approach is to use a weighted sum to combine the multiple objectives into a single objective.

> For more flexibility, especially under uncertainty, you can instead model the multi-objective optimization problem—or Pareto front analysis—as a partially observable decision process. This allows the agent to learn its own trade-off strategy between objectives like throughput versus latency, etc. This is helpful if a single-weighted reward is not sufficient.

These kinds of multiparameter interactions are hard to tune with basic grid search methods. As such, RL and optimization techniques like proximal policy optimization (PPO) are best used for tuning inference workloads. PPO is known for stabler learning in continuous action spaces. It's well-suited for continuous updating in real-time environments as it adjusts the policy gradually. This avoids extreme oscillations, which is important for inference stability. We don't want the agent thrashing between decisions on every request.

Another technique to reduce oscillations is called *damping*. This requires that an action stay in effect for a minimum amount of time—or minimum number of requests. You can override damping for critical SLO violations, if needed, but this should be done sparingly.

It's important to know that RL agents might make unsafe or suboptimal moves while learning. To mitigate that, you can constrain the action space to a reasonable set of ranges. It's also recommended to start with a good default policy using the heuristics that we have already identified. The agent can then fine-tune around that initial default policy.

Alternatively, the agent can be trained online in *shadow mode* using a live system that incorporates an exploration phase. During exploration, the system occasionally tries a random or slightly modified strategy to gather new data. Otherwise, it exploits the current best policy.

Another technique is to apply reward shaping, which keeps the agent from violating critical constraints. For instance, the RL system would generate a high negative reward if latency is greater than a hard limit—or if an OOM error occurs due to a bad action.

Additionally, you can hard-code the system to avoid unsafe actions—even if the reward suggests the system do so. This puts in place extra safeguards so that the agent's natural exploration won't cause a catastrophic failure. This is a practical approach that combines RL with rule-based guardrails.

Designing a proper reward function is important. For instance, if we care about throughput under a latency limit, a reward would look like the code here:

```
reward = tokens_per_second - 1000 * (1 if latency > SLA else 0)
```

Here, a large penalty is applied if the latency SLA is exceeded. Otherwise, no penalty is applied. Another option is to apply a continuous penalty that is proportional to how far the latency overshoots the target SLA. A simple continuous-penalty reward can be written, as shown here:

```
reward = tokens_per_second - λ * max(0.0, latency - SLA)
```

Here, λ is your penalty weight, and `max(0.0, latency - SLA)` grows linearly with how far you exceed the SLA. This way, the agent receives a smoothly increasing penalty the longer its latency overshoots the target. This will produce smoother gradients and more gradual trade-off decisions. In practice, a continuous (soft) penalty often produces a more stable policy than a binary (hard) penalty.

> It's recommended to start with a simple, static set of heuristics for tuning. Once the system is stable, you can start to introduce an RL agent to handle the more complex tuning that the heuristics can't capture.

Logging and observability are important. You should continuously log the decisions that the RL agent makes—as well as the decision outcomes. For example, you should use structured logging—or even counters and telemetry dashboards—to track state → action → reward sequences in real time. This will help debug the agent's behavior if it starts behaving erratically.

It's also recommended to provide an escape hatch, or *kill switch*. This way, if the agent starts doing something obviously bad, like consistently making latency worse, you can have the system fall back to a safe, static configuration while you diagnose the issue and retrain a new policy offline. For example, if p95 latency increases by more than 50% after enabling the agent, the system will automatically disable the agent's actions and send an alert to the system on call.

While not yet mainstream in modern inference serving engines as of this writing, RL-based, online inference tuning is just beginning to appear. Expect more inference platforms to include self-tuning capabilities as these techniques mature. This is important since these models and systems are becoming more complex. Manually managing all of these tuning knobs is difficult under rapidly changing conditions—it's difficult for humans, anyway!

An intelligent agent that adapts in real time is a natural evolution of system optimization. We are starting to see self-optimizing AI inference servers that achieve expert-level performance tuning automatically. And they're doing this just by learning from their own real-time telemetry metrics.

Dynamic Memory-Allocation Switching (Slab Versus Caching Versus Stream-Ordered)

GPU memory fragmentation and nonoptimal memory allocation can be silent performance killers. Inference servers allocate and free thousands of tensors per second for many objects, including tokens, intermediate activations, etc. The strategy used by the memory allocator can influence fragmentation and allocation latency.

Switching the memory allocator dynamically means that the system can change how it allocates memory on the fly. For instance, the system can use a slab allocator for certain allocation sizes—or switch to use CUDA's stream-ordered (`cudaMallocAsync`) allocator. The decision depends on the observed pattern of allocations and expected memory fragmentation.

By default, PyTorch uses a variant of the buddy/best-fit memory allocator called *best-fit with coalescing*, or BFC. It grabs big chunks of GPU memory and subdivides the chunks to satisfy allocation requests. This reuses free space and avoids frequent calls to the relatively slow and synchronous `cudaMalloc` and `cudaFree`.

A buddy allocator splits memory into blocks whose sizes are powers of two. A slab allocator works on top of the buddy system to efficiently manage small, fixed-size objects. It preallocates slabs, or collections of objects of a given type, and maintains a free list within each slab, as shown in Figure 19-6.

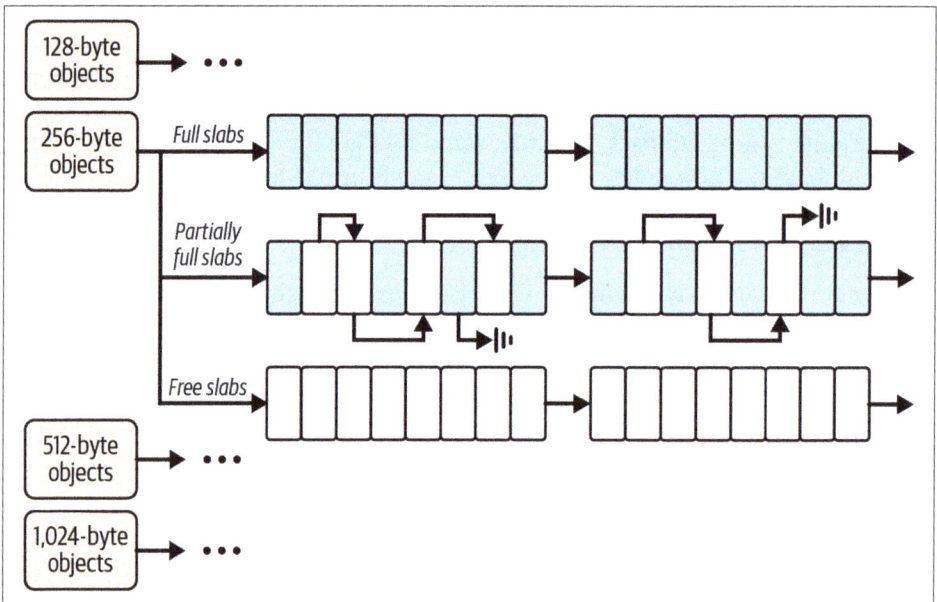

Figure 19-6. Slab allocator maintains a free list of memory objects within each preallocated slab

---

A slab allocator allows fast reuse without fragmentation. A buddy allocator handles coarse-grained page allocation, while a slab allocator optimizes fine-grained object reuse.

The default PyTorch caching allocator works well for many workloads. However, it can suffer fragmentation if the pattern of allocations varies widely due to alternating between large and small allocations. In a long-running server that handles different types of queries, fragmentation can build up.

In this case, plenty of memory is free, but the memory is not contiguous enough for large tensor allocations. This leads to OOM errors—even though memory is technically available.

Remember that PyTorch provides torch.cuda.memory_summary() to evaluate memory fragmentation, as well as a memory profiler built into torch.profiler (pro file_memory=True). You can use these to determine which operations allocate a lot of memory. Also, NVIDIA Nsight Systems provides CUDA memory event and Unified Memory page-fault tracking on the timeline, and Nsight Compute provides memory workload analysis.

Together, these tools let you observe allocation behavior and fragmentation effects over time. And you can use these tools during development and testing to initiate your memory-allocator tuning strategy—including a dynamic tuning strategy, as discussed next.

A brute-force way to reduce memory fragmentation is to periodically reset the allocator's state. However, a more clever way is to use CUDA's stream-ordered caching allocator, cudaMallocAsync, which uses a similar concept internally by binning per allocation size up to a certain limit. But slab allocation takes it even further by never mixing sizes.

cudaMallocAsync behaves somewhat like a slab allocator combined with a buddy system—and it's managed by the CUDA driver for you. This gives you most of the benefit of custom allocators with little effort—and makes it a great default memory allocator to leave on all the time, if you prefer.

Specifically, cudaMallocAsync uses stream-ordered pools that automatically recycle memory when references to the memory are released. It then coalesces the freed blocks behind the scenes since it knows the dependency order of the memory-frees—unlike standard allocators.

When using cudaMallocAsync with a PyTorch runtime, you can dynamically adjust max_split_size_mb by setting the PYTORCH_ALLOC_CONF=max_split_size_mb: <value> environment variable. This can adjust the split size under different conditions.

For instance, a dynamic system could increase `max_split_size_mb` when large allocations are expected. This way they don't get broken into small pieces. Conversely, the system can decrease `max_split_size_mb` when running many small requests to allow more reuse of large blocks.

> Too small a split size can flood the allocator with many tiny blocks, which will increase metadata overhead and potential fragmentation. Too large a split size reduces the block count (and metadata) but may leave bigger "holes" in memory that go unused when you free only part of a block.

Consider a scenario in which your service detects fragmentation—perhaps using PyTorch's memory snapshot functionality that shows holes caused by fragmentation. In this case, the system could dynamically switch to use `cudaMallocAsync`, which can consolidate memory usage.

You should use memory monitoring tools to track—and log—memory fragmentation. For instance, in PyTorch, you can use `torch.cuda.memory_reserved()` and `torch.cuda.memory_allocated()`. Here, the reserved memory is the total GPU memory held by the allocator. And allocated is how much of it is actually in use by tensors.

A large gap between reserved and allocated means fragmentation since a lot of memory is reserved but not used. If that gap grows over time, a dynamic policy could be to periodically purge the cache to free all the unused memory back to the GPU or even restart the worker process to fully reset the allocator. These are intrusive but effective methods that are sometimes used in production for long-running processes with heavy fragmentation.

> You should use intrusive defragmentation methods like purging and restarting only during maintenance windows—or in a rolling restart manner across a fleet to avoid downtime. If you need to resort to these disruptive mechanisms, you likely have a deeper issue that needs to be addressed and optimized.

To implement dynamic allocation switching in PyTorch, for example, you can start with the PyTorch native allocator. Then, if you catch an OOM error, you can retry using the `cudaMallocAsync`-based allocator.

Unfortunately, the CUDA caching allocator is created the first time `torch` is imported or when the first CUDA context is touched. And Python's `importlib.reload` does not unload C++ extensions or tear down the allocator. As such, changing `PYTORCH_ALLOC_CONF` (formerly `PYTORCH_CUDA_ALLOC_CONF`) on the fly and reloading the Python module will not reconfigure the allocator in-process.

However, you can spawn a fresh process in which the environment variable is set before `torch` is imported. Below is a snippet of code that catches OOM, frees memory in the parent, and then spins up a clean child process with `PYTORCH_ALLOC_CONF`. This is a bit hacky but shows how you can dynamically set the `backend:cudaMallocA sync` and rerun the same call with the different allocator backend. Next is a PyTorch example that implements this dynamic strategy when the code catches a `torch.cuda.OutOfMemoryError`:

```python
# dynamic_memory_allocator.py
# Retry generation in fresh process with cudaMallocAsync if first attempt OOMs.
# This is the only reliable way to change the CUDA allocator at runtime.

import os
import sys
import gc
import pickle
import tempfile
import subprocess
import importlib
from typing import Callable, Any

def _resolve_factory(factory_path: str) -> Callable[[], Any]:
    """
    Resolves a factory string like "my_package.my_mod:build_model" to a callable.
    The callable must return ready-to-use model with .generate(request) method.
    """
    module_name, func_name = factory_path.split(":", 1)
    module = importlib.import_module(module_name)  # safe to import, no torch yet
    return getattr(module, func_name)

def generate_with_allocator_retry(
    model_factory_path: str,
    request_object: Any,
    *,
    allocator_conf: str = "backend:cudaMallocAsync"
) -> Any:
    """
    Attempts model.generate(request_object) in the current process.
    On torch.cuda.OutOfMemoryError, retries in a fresh subprocess with
    PYTORCH_ALLOC_CONF set to allocator_conf. request_object and the
    returned value must be picklable.
    """
    # Import torch only inside function; avoid importing at module import time.
    import torch

    model_factory = _resolve_factory(model_factory_path)
    model = model_factory()  # user-supplied function builds model, moves to GPU

    try:
        # First attempt uses whatever allocator current process started with.
        return model.generate(request_object)
```

```python
    except torch.cuda.OutOfMemoryError:
        # Free as much as possible in the parent before spawning the child.
        # Avoids compounding pressure when two processes momentarily overlap.
        try:
            del model
        finally:
            gc.collect()
            torch.cuda.empty_cache()

        # Serialize request to temp file and ask fresh interpreter to do work.
        with tempfile.TemporaryDirectory() as td:
            req_path = os.path.join(td, "request.pkl")
            out_path = os.path.join(td, "output.pkl")
            with open(req_path, "wb") as f:
                pickle.dump(request_object, f)

            # In the child, we want torch to see allocator config at import.
            env = os.environ.copy()
            env["PYTORCH_ALLOC_CONF"] = allocator_conf

            # Re-run this module as a helper child. The child will import torch
            # only after PYTORCH_ALLOC_CONF is set in its environment.
            cmd = [
                sys.executable,
                __file__,
                "--child",
                "--factory", model_factory_path,
                "--request", req_path,
                "--output", out_path,
            ]
            completed = subprocess.run(cmd, env=env, capture_output=True,
                                       text=True)

            if completed.returncode != 0:
                # Bubble up child stderr to aid debugging
                raise RuntimeError(
                  f"Retry failed with exit code {completed.returncode}\n"
                  f"stdout:\n{completed.stdout}\n\nstderr:\n{completed.stderr}"
                )

            with open(out_path, "rb") as f:
                return pickle.load(f)

def _child_main(factory_path: str, request_path: str, output_path: str) -> None:
    """
    Child entrypoint: assumes PYTORCH_ALLOC_CONF is already present in env.
    Imports torch only now, builds the model, runs generate, and pickles result.
    """

    # Import torch after env var set by the parent's subprocess.run(env=...).
    import torch
```

```
    model_factory = _resolve_factory(factory_path)
    model = model_factory()  # build the model inside the child process

    with open(request_path, "rb") as f:
        request_object = pickle.load(f)
if __name__ == "__main__":
    import argparse
    parser = argparse.ArgumentParser()
    parser.add_argument("--child", action="store_true")
    parser.add_argument("--factory", type=str, default="")
    parser.add_argument("--request", type=str, default="")
    parser.add_argument("--output", type=str, default="")
    args = parser.parse_args()
    if args.child:
        _child_main(args.factory, args.request, args.output)
    else:
        print("This module is intended to be imported.")
```

Here, the model is constructed in the child using a factory so that nothing CUDA-related is imported before the PYTORCH_ALLOC_CONF env variable takes effect. The code empties the cache and releases unused memory to the GPU using torch.cuda.empty_cache(). This pattern guarantees that the allocator configuration is applied before torch is imported in the child. It also avoids trying to unload a native extension at runtime, which CPython does not support.

In a non-PyTorch environment, such as a C++-based LLM inference engine, you can implement a pure slab allocator that allows configuration for specific allocation sizes. This type of slab allocator prepartitions memory into fixed-size "slabs." It's very efficient for repeated allocations of the same size and leads to virtually zero fragmentation for that specific size allocation.

In an LLM server, one very common technique is to allocate per-token output tensors such that each time you generate a token, you allocate a [layers, hidden_dim] tensor for that token's activations, for instance. If those allocations are the same size every time, such as 64 KB, a slab for that exact size is ideal.

The system detects that it's allocating a lot of 64 KB tensors repeatedly—and creates a "slab" of dedicated 64 KB blocks. A slab allocator often does not return memory to the general pool until the entire slab is freed.

Modern LLM inference engines perform this type of buffer reuse for each generated token. This is in contrast to freeing and reallocating the memory each time, which would incur a high amount of overhead—especially at token granularity.

Allocator switching might involve completely different allocators for different parts of the system. For instance, you can use the default caching allocator with large static allocations for model weights since those are freed less often during inference. You can then use a custom allocator for ephemeral per-token allocations.

> It's recommended to architect your code to separate long-lived allocations, such as model weights, from short-lived allocations, such as token buffers. This makes it easier to direct the short-lived and long-lived allocations to different allocators and memory pools.

You should always implement a fallback strategy for OOM errors. Many production systems use multitier memory such that if the GPU experiences an OOM error, it will offload to the CPU and try again rather than failing the request. For example, you can dynamically free the cache, offload some layers to the CPU, or compress the cache.

In short, techniques like dynamic allocator management and multitiered memory make sure your system can handle long uptimes under different types of load—all without incurring memory fragmentation or allocation latency spikes. This is a behind-the-scenes optimization that users won't directly see, but it's essential for ultrascale robustness for long-running inference servers.

Runtime Kernel Performance Improvements and Hot-Swappable Implementations

In the fast-evolving world of GPU hardware and algorithmic innovations, new and faster kernel implementations are constantly emerging. This includes newer variants of FlashAttention, megakernels, and hardware-specific software optimizations.

Runtime kernel patching is the ability to integrate these new implementations into a running system without requiring a full redeployment or reload of the model. Essentially, we want to hot-swap a slower kernel function for a faster one on the fly.

Consider your inference server that uses the default PyTorch scaled dot product attention (SDPA) kernel for multiheaded attention. You then discover a new kernel implementation like FlashAttention-3, which gives a 20% speed boost for long sequences in some cases.

Traditionally, you'd have to install the updated library and restart the server to use the new implementation. But with runtime patching, you can dynamically load and redirect calls to the new kernel during runtime without interrupting the server's uptime.

This zero-downtime upgrade approach is crucial in 24/7 services in which a restart or model reload would incur too much latency or cause an outage. In Python, this can be an easy monkey patch, as shown here:

```
import new_flash_attn_lib
```

```
# Monkey-patch the model's attention forward to use the new library
old_attn_forward = model.transformer.self_attn.forward

def new_attn_forward(self, *args, **kwargs):
    return new_flash_attn_lib.forward(*args, **kwargs)

model.transformer.self_attn.forward =
new_attn_forward.__get__(
model.transformer.self_attn,
type(model.transformer.self_attn))
```

This code replaces the `forward` method of the attention module with one that calls our `new_flash_attn_lib.forward`. We bind it to the instance (`__get__`) to simulate a proper method. After this patch, subsequent calls to that attention layer will go through the new implementation. As such, we have effectively hot-swapped the kernel.

> Make sure that `new_flash_attn_lib.forward()` is drop-in compatible—and that it has been thoroughly tested to produce identical outputs within acceptable numerical tolerances. This way, you avoid any model-quality regressions.

Another technique is JIT patching, which uses a just-in-time compiler like PyTorch Inductor or OpenAI Triton to generate a faster kernel at runtime—and then plugging it into the inference pipeline. As shown next, one can use PyTorch's `torch.compile` to optimize a function and return its compiled version:

```
compiled_forward =
    torch.compile(model.transformer.self_attn.forward,
                  backend="inductor")

model.transformer.self_attn.forward = compiled_forward
```

Now, whenever `forward` is called, it will execute the optimized code, which will fuse multiple operations, etc. If we do this after model initialization, it's a form of hot patching since it does not require a model reload. It simply swaps out function pointers.

On the CUDA side, runtime module loading is possible using CUDA driver APIs. For instance, you can compile a custom PTX for a new kernel—and load it into the context without resetting the device. If the function signatures match, the system would just update the function pointers. Tools like NVIDIA Runtime Compilation (NVRTC) can compile PTX from strings at runtime, enabling this workflow.

Doing this with CUDA C++ is a bit complex. Higher-level approaches like Python's monkey-patch mechanism—or PyTorch's extensible backends—are likely more practical and maintainable in the long term. However, your high-performance inference engine is likely not using a Python/PyTorch runtime.

> When doing this type of hot swapping, it's important to guarantee thread safety. For example, you should drain the incoming-request queue or use a barrier to make sure that no other thread is in the middle of the function you're patching. This will avoid race conditions with running threads. This is similar to how OS kernels load modules—careful synchronization is needed, but it avoids full restarts.

Using well-defined module boundaries—like separating attention and MLP kernels—makes it easier to swap internals. This argues for writing your model code in a highly modular way so that you have these swap points. Monolithic model implementations are much harder to patch, but they can be more performant (e.g., megakernels).

Of course, one must ensure that the new kernel produces identical—or acceptably close—results to the old implementation. Typically these optimized kernels are designed to be numerically equivalent at the same precision (e.g., FP16).

Hot patching can also be used for quick fixes. Perhaps a particular sequence of operations is causing a known bug in the current kernel. Instead of waiting for a full update, you could quickly patch in a fix.

Consider deploying an FP8 kernel that starts to misbehave for certain edge inputs that you didn't anticipate. If you have a safer but slightly slower version, you can detect the misbehaving condition and hot swap in the safe kernel in those cases. Make sure you log these events for future analysis.

> Consider a phased rollout by routing a small percentage of traffic to the new kernel (shadow testing or canary). You can then use telemetry to compare the latency and throughput metrics against the old kernel. If the new kernel is performing as expected and its output matches the expected results, you can release it to all users.

To manage multiple possible implementations, an engine might maintain a registry, such as `attention_impl` = `"fast"` or `"safe"`—and branch accordingly. This can be implemented as a feature flag so that you can toggle implementations without code changes. This is useful for quick rollbacks simply by changing the flag (just make sure your code is actively reading the values from the feature-flag system—otherwise the flag value remains static, which defeats the purpose of a feature flag).

A well-designed inference engine should also measure runtime performance of the new kernel. If the new kernel is not faster with live production data, the inference engine can roll it back. This can be due to slightly different hardware, untested batch sizes, or untested load conditions.

This is a perfect form of autotuning, described in the previous section. If the auto-tuner finds a faster implementation that outperforms the current default implementation beyond some threshold, the system could trigger a "patch" to promote the faster implementation to the default going forward.

This effectively closes the loop with the autotuner. The system not only finds better kernels on the fly, but it also swaps them in. This leads to a self-optimizing kernel-selection mechanism.

You can combine this strategy with the previous RL strategy we discussed. This way, you can have multiple implementations loaded—and let the RL agent choose which one to use for each different type of request.

> Be mindful of the overhead needed to maintain multiple implementations in memory. The added code size should not evict other critical code from the instruction cache—or exhaust GPU memory.

For instance, a highly optimized kernel might be best for long sequences, but a simpler kernel implementation might be fine for short sequences. A runtime system could choose between them per request. This effectively patches on a per-request basis based on the length of the input sequence.

In short, runtime kernel patching is about flexibility. It acknowledges that what is optimal today might change tomorrow and provides the means to adapt quickly. This type of agility makes sure that your serving infrastructure keeps up with the rapid advancements in model acceleration techniques. Popular inference engines like vLLM, SGLang, NVIDIA TensorRT-LLM, and NVIDIA Dynamo are well architected and provide a good amount of dynamic capabilities. For example, TensorRT-LLM allows you to load optimized kernels using runtime plugins. Use these capabilities to your advantage.

Continuous Prewarming of CUDA Graphs and Caches Using Time-Series Prediction

In high-throughput inference situations, cold-start overheads can be a large contributor to request-response latency. CUDA Graphs, as described in Chapter 12, allow you to capture a sequence of GPU operations and replay the sequence with minimal launch overhead.

Prewarming a CUDA Graph means setting up the graph before it's actually needed. If we can predict when a certain request type or batch size will occur, the prewarmed CUDA Graph will be ready to execute.

This technique relies on prediction accuracy. If your forecast is off, you might prewarm a graph that isn't used. You should monitor prediction hit rates to make sure the optimization is paying off.

By prewarming, the graph can skip costly launch and initialization steps when the request actually arrives. Using time-series prediction algorithms like ARIMA (*https:// oreil.ly/Qt7Lc*) and Prophet (*https://oreil.ly/nefr_*), the system anticipates future workload patterns, including traffic surges and batch size changes, to proactively prepare the graph for fast execution.

Consider an inference service that observes a daily cycle when, at 9 A.M. every day, there's a spike in user traffic due to time zone–related traffic patterns. Knowing this, the system could prerun a few requests just before 9 A.M. to load the model into the GPU caches, JIT-compile the necessary kernels, and capture the CUDA Graphs for the expected batch sizes. At 9 A.M., when the real traffic load spikes, the incoming requests will reuse the warmed state for the expected batch size and usage pattern.

In practice, this can be orchestrated by a cron-like job or a scheduling service that triggers the prewarm routine right before the traffic spike is expected to occur. Just remember to leave enough time for the resources to provision.

In PyTorch, wrapping your model's computation within a `torch.cuda.graph()` context allows you to capture a static computation graph that includes GPU kernel launches. When replaying the graph, PyTorch bypasses the Python-to-CUDA dispatch overhead and submits the entire workload with a single `cudaGraphLaunch`. This leads to significantly faster execution—especially for large, repetitive input batches due to the minimal CPU involvement.

The downside is that these graphs are static since they don't easily allow variable shapes or lengths. But an inference server often deals with distinct batch sizes (1, 2, 4, 8, 16, etc.)—due to GPU memory limitations and algorithmic optimizations—which fits the graph model well.

To handle variability, you can maintain a pool of precaptured graphs for each common batch size or sequence length. You could use a continuous prewarming strategy to prepare the pool of graphs for these distinct batch sizes. For instance, a batch of 16 requests is common during peak hours. The server can capture a graph of the model's forward pass upfront using a batch size of 16—and then store it for subsequent use.

The next time a batch of 16 requests comes in simultaneously, the inference system feeds the batched inputs into the precaptured graph. The kernels inside are already prewarmed and optimized for graph execution, so there's no need to enqueue and launch many individual operations, as just one graph launch is all that's needed.

Keep in mind that each captured graph stored in the pool will consume additional GPU memory for its workspace. You should monitor memory usage when storing many graphs. It might be necessary to evict less-used graphs from the pool if memory gets tight.

To avoid the extra memory of a pool, you can potentially use graph patching, discussed in Chapter 12, to adjust graph nodes for minor size differences. However, in practice, a pool is a better option for performance.

CUDA Graphs also reduce CPU overhead since it coordinates just a single graph launch versus many individual kernel launches. This lets the CPU perform other operations like data preprocessing and other types of "real" work—instead of coordinating many kernel launches.

Again, you can use time-series prediction algorithms (e.g., ARIMA and Prophet) to forecast metrics like RPS and average prompt length. If the model predicts a jump in batch size or a particular pattern of requests, such as long input sequences, the system can start preparing and prewarming the appropriate CUDA Graphs, caches, and other resources. For instance, the system can proactively increase the batch size of the continuous batching algorithm, prefetch model weights from disk to GPU memory, and allocate additional GPU instances.

It's important to retrain and update these time-series models frequently with recent traffic data. This is because usage patterns can change over time due to new user segments coming online, etc. In addition, unanticipated "holidays" like California's famous Ski Week can unexpectedly increase the load curve—as it did for me at Netflix when I first moved to California!

Related to caching and prewarming is anticipating the scale-out of prefill and decode workers. If we know a bunch of requests with long prompts are likely to arrive at a certain time due to a scheduled batch job or daily report scenario, the system can scale out the prefill workers and execute a representative forward pass with representative sample data to prewarm the CUDA Graphs and KV cache.

The scale-out and prewarming events should also include the decode workers and CUDA Graphs. In the decode case, the speculative decoding draft model, for instance, can be prewarmed and loaded into GPU memory—as well as the draft model's KV cache, etc. Other decode optimizations include loop unrolling for a fixed number of tokens that will be generated—either 1 token or multiple in the case of speculative decoding.

You should also consider caching the CUDA kernels themselves. CUDA will often cache the compiled kernels (C++ code => PTX instructions => SASS assembly) to speed up execution. The first time a kernel runs, there is likely some on-the-fly JIT compilation overhead.

You should coordinate this type of warm-up with your cluster autoscaler such that when new GPU instances spin up, the autoscaler runs a quick set of inferences on them using a few warm-up API calls. Doing this will validate the inference engines, cache JIT-compilation outputs, allocate memory pools, prepare CUDA Graphs, etc. This way, the engines are production-ready before adding them to the live traffic pool.

> Use your knowledge of the system to identify and invoke as many distinct paths as possible during this controlled warm-up phase. This includes every batch size, CUDA Graph variant, etc.

You should also monitor that the warm-up actually helps by comparing the latency of the first few requests during the predicted surge—both with and without warm-up. Adjust the timing and threshold as needed. And be aware that the time-series prediction can be wrong. Make sure that warm-up tasks do not impact overall inference performance if they run at the wrong time.

For instance, you should try to perform prewarming runs (with example data) when the GPUs are underutilized. CUDA allows stream priority scheduling so you can assign prewarm streams to a lower priority than your inference stream. This way, the prewarming does not compete for resources with the live, high-volume traffic requests.

Also, you should use lower-priority CUDA streams for these prewarming tasks, so they will yield to higher-priority live traffic that may arrive during prewarming. On the plus side, idle GPUs are a wasted opportunity, so doing warm-up computations on idle GPUs is essentially free—as long as it doesn't collide with real work.

Grace Blackwell systems allow some additional tricks since the CPU and GPU share unified, coherent memory at low latency. For instance, you can have the CPU start prefilling data into unified memory that the GPU plans to use. This can avoid explicit GPU copy calls later.

Continuous prewarming—guided by time series predictions—can make latency far more predictable. It turns the inference engine into an adaptive system that learns common traffic patterns, automatically prepares the data, readies the hardware, and stays a step ahead of demand. This will reduce jitter and decrease latency spikes by smoothing out expensive operations like compilation and memory transfers at times when they can be amortized.

This is especially valuable for large models that have heavy one-time initialization costs. As models and contexts grow, such adaptive preloading will move from a nice-to-have to a necessity in production LLM systems. Paying these costs predictively is much better than having end users churn because of a poor experience.

Adaptive Batching and Chunked Prefill Scheduling

In Chapter 16, we discussed how modern inference servers use different types of request batching (e.g., continuous batching) to maximize throughput and minimize latency across all requests. However, batching can increase latency for individual requests. The trade-offs can be dynamically addressed as conditions change throughout the day using a technique called *adaptive batching*.

Adaptive batching dynamically adjusts how requests are grouped into batches depending on the load—and how well the requests are progressing. This type of dynamic strategy can adjust the batch size and threshold parameters in real time as the environment changes.

For example, during peak load, the system can use a large batch size (e.g., 8 or 16) because throughput is critical. During periods of low load, the system can reduce the batch size to serve the requests sooner. This will prioritize latency over throughput.

To decide on the batch size, you can use a simple heuristic, such as, *"If GPU utilization is > 80%, allow larger batches; if < 20%, use batch size 1 to minimize latency."* Or you can use a more sophisticated RL agent or predictive strategy, as discussed in the previous sections.

This difference in arithmetic intensity between the prefill and decode phases leads to mismatched durations of execution. As such, it's best to disaggregate the stages and treat them as separate workloads that can be tuned independently using separate threads/processes for a single node or worker pools for a multinode cluster.

By disaggregating prefill and decode, we treat the two stages as separate operations. This allows them to be independently optimized for their unique compute and memory bandwidth needs. One of these optimizations is the batch sizes used for the prefill and decode phases.

In practice, vLLM and other modern inference engines do exactly this. They form separate batches to send to the prefill and decode workers. As such, a batch of prefill requests can execute independently of the batch of decode requests. For example, the decode phase can benefit from larger batches to increase arithmetic intensity since it's a memory-bound workload.

Modern inference-serving frameworks like vLLM use adaptive scheduling loops to dynamically choose between processing a prefill or a decode batch. Specifically, vLLM supports chunked prefill and decode-maximal scheduling to interleave prefill and decode for better utilization. These techniques boost overall utilization and throughput without adding significant latency.

The mismatched system-resource characteristics of prefill and decode can impact PP as well. Consider one microbatch doing prefill on a long sequence while another microbatch is performing decode one token at a time. In this case, their durations are mismatched, and pipeline bubbles emerge.

You can interleave large prefill requests with latency-sensitive decode tasks by slicing the prefill into small chunks and piggybacking decodes between them. This keeps all pipeline stages busy and minimizes idle "bubbles" in your GPU schedule.

Chunked prefill is a well-supported pattern used by all modern LLM inference engines to reduce pipeline bubbles. It effectively time-slices a big task (prefill) to create room for small tasks (decode) to execute in the pipeline gaps created by the chunks, as shown in Figure 19-7.

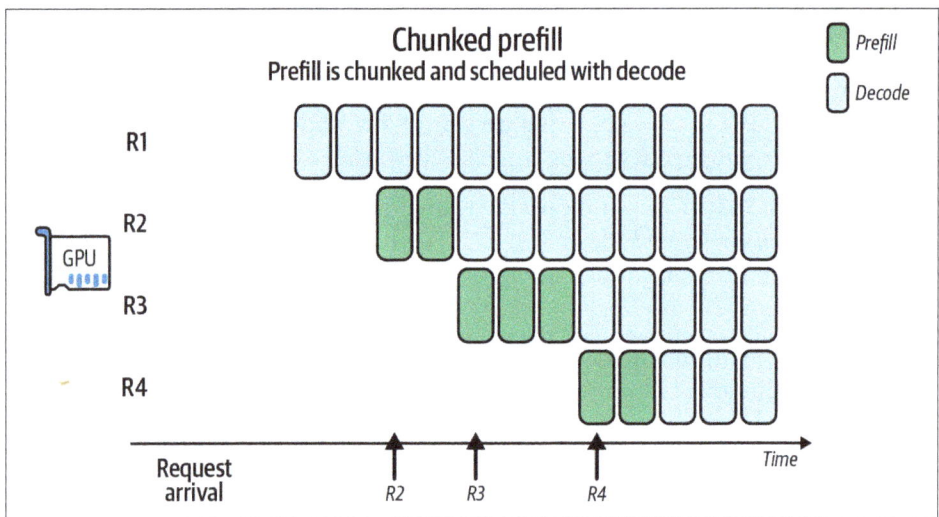

Figure 19-7. Benefits of chunked prefills for decode-maximal batching across four requests

The SARATHI paper (*https://oreil.ly/n3UdE*) demonstrated that this type of chunked prefill and piggybacking can help you find the right level of *decode-maximal batching*, reduce bubbles, and improve throughput by ~1.3–1.9× compared to naive scheduling. The name SARATHI is a reference to a charioteer that intelligently steers both prefill and decode tasks together. Fun!

For example, consider a 10,000-token prefill request that does not use chunking. In this case, the single prefill pass will block the entire pipeline and cause decode tasks to queue up until the prefill completes.

However, if you use chunked prefill and divide the 10,000-token prefill request into five 2,000-token chunks, you can interleave decode batches in between prefill chunks to keep the GPU busy processing both phases and moving things forward. This will squeeze out pipeline bubbles, improve throughput, and smooth out GPU utilization.

> A rule of thumb is to choose a chunk size such that a prefill chunk takes ~50–100 ms. This way, you have frequent opportunities to schedule decode batches in between. This may correspond to a few thousand tokens depending on the model architecture/size and GPU hardware.

Modern inference engines like vLLM use adaptive scheduling loops to decide whether to process another prefill chunk—or perform a decode batch—based on GPU utilization and queue status. Specifically, vLLM continuously monitors token queues to make these decisions. vLLM's scheduler explicitly supports chunked prefill and decode-maximal batching. Its executor and chunked-prefill features are designed to overlap large prefills with smaller interactive decodes.

An adaptive scheduler needs to consider GPU shared-memory limits and occupancy when choosing a chunked prefill size. A simple adaptive chunked prefill implementation is shown next. This code dynamically right-sizes the chunk size to keep SM and occupancy high on the GPU:

```python
# Example adaptive scheduler for chunked prefill/decode

import cupy as cp
import torch

# Hardware constraints
SHMEM_LIMIT   = 256 * 1024
BLOCK_THREADS = 256
TARGET_UTIL   = 0.85
OCC_THRESHOLD = 0.5

# Cache for occupancy results and tile lookup
_occ_cache = {}
_tile_table = {}   # e.g., {L: optimal_T}

# 1) Precompute tile_table offline; here we lazy-initialize on first use
def get_optimal_tile(L):
    if L in _tile_table:
        return _tile_table[L]
    # compute block size by querying for an occupancy-based suggestion
    min_grid, max_grid, block_size = ...  # left out for brevity

    T = min(block_size, L)
    T = max(32, (T // 32) * 32)
    _tile_table[L] = T
```

```python
    return T

# 2) Cached occupancy query
def get_occupancy(threads, shared_bytes):
    key = (threads, shared_bytes)
    if key in _occ_cache:
        return _occ_cache[key]
    max_blocks = cp.cuda.runtime.\
        cudaOccupancyMaxActiveBlocksPerMultiprocessor(
            attention_kernel_ptr, threads, shared_bytes
        )
    props = torch.cuda.get_device_properties(0)
    warps_per_block = threads // props.warp_size
    max_warps = props.max_threads_per_multi_processor // props.warp_size
    occ = (max_blocks * warps_per_block) / max_warps
    _occ_cache[key] = occ
    return occ


def scheduler_loop():
    stream = cp.cuda.Stream(non_blocking=True)
    while True:
        pending = get_pending_requests()
        util = gpu_utilization()
        if util < TARGET_UTIL and any(r.phase=='prefill' for r in pending):
            req = select_heaviest_prefill(pending)
            L   = req.remaining_length()
            T   = get_optimal_tile(L)
            shared_bytes = 3 * T * T * 4
            occ = get_occupancy(BLOCK_THREADS,
              shared_bytes)
            if occ < OCC_THRESHOLD:
                T = max(32, T // 2)
                shared_bytes = 3 * T * T * 4
            chunk = req.next_prefill_chunk(T)
            # Launch with CuPy RawKernel on our stream
            attention_kernel((...grid...), (BLOCK_THREADS,),
              (chunk, ...), shared_mem=shared_bytes,
              stream=stream)
            # Record an event to know when done
            event = cp.cuda.Event()
            event.record(stream)
        elif any(r.phase=='decode' for r in pending):
            batch = form_decode_batch(pending, max_batch=16)
            # Trace the adaptive logic
            logger.info(f"T={T}, occ={occ:.2f},
                util={util:.2f}")
            launch_decode_kernel(batch, stream=stream)
            event = cp.cuda.Event()
            event.record(stream)
        else:
            # Poll the last event rather than sleep
            if not event.query():
```

```
      cp.cuda.get_current_stream().synchronize()  # or pass
continue
```

Here, the scheduler is adjusting chunk size to use as much shared memory as possible. And, importantly, it does this without sacrificing parallelism.

Specifically, the scheduler first computes a tile width T so that the three shared-memory buffers for queries, keys, and values—each requiring T x T floats—fit within the GPUs' per-SM dynamic shared-memory limit. It then calls the CuPy API (*https://oreil.ly/CPzjf*) (Python) to measure how many thread blocks can run concurrently on each SM with that value of T.

If occupancy falls below a given threshold of 50%, T is reduced by half. This will free up shared memory so that more blocks can co-reside, striking an optimal balance between data reuse (fewer DRAM loads) and parallelism.

When overall GPU utilization drops below 85% and prefill work is pending, the scheduler selects the largest remaining prefill request and breaks it into equal-sized chunks of T tokens so that each chunk can flow through the pipeline without monopolizing every stage.

And rather than fixing the chunk size, the helper function, next_prefill_chunk, adjusts T on the fly based on live metrics. It will shrink the chunk size if occupancy is low—and grow it if DRAM traffic is excessive. This makes sure that each slice maximizes GPU utilization without stalls.

> Be sure to instrument the scheduler to log the chosen T and resulting occupancy/utilization. This way, you can analyze and verify that this adaptive approach is consistently maintaining high GPU utilization.

Between prefill chunks, the scheduler can use *decode-maximal batches* to bundle all of the ready decode requests into a single launch using form_decode_batch. This lets short, latency-sensitive token generations piggyback on otherwise idle pipeline gaps. This way, even users with short prompts see low latency because their decodes don't wait for a huge prefill to finish. These decodes get scheduled in the pipeline gaps.

By continuously monitoring gpu_utilization(), the scheduler chooses whether to process another prefill chunk or drain the decode queue. Either way, it is always picking the action that fills SM slots and minimizes dead time. This is called a *utilization-maximization policy* and is similar to an OS scheduler aiming for 100% CPU utilization.

Together, these mechanisms ensure that large-context prefill jobs never starve interactive decoding. At the same time, small, latency-critical requests are served immediately. This produces optimal throughput on modern GPUs without degrading the end-user experience.

> Chunked prefill aligns work with the strengths of the GPU: big prefill matrix operations are batched, while small decode operations are interleaved. This maximizes overall throughput and latency together.

As you can see, the scheduler monitors real-time metrics and adapts on the fly. The chunked scheduling makes sure no single request can block an entire stage under varying conditions. This keeps all GPUs active and reduces the dreaded pipeline bubbles.

It's important to treat prefill and decode as separate queues with their own SLAs. It's usually optimal to clear out latency-sensitive decode tasks first using dedicated time slices or CUDA streams, then use the leftover cycles to process large prefill jobs. For example, you can allocate a certain time budget (e.g., 1–5 ms per decode) to decode tasks to make sure they get more immediate attention.

By prioritizing the user-facing, real-time decodes, you minimize perceived inference lag. At the same time, you are still powering through bulk context builds when the system has spare capacity.

Many high-performance inference engines use a *producer-consumer* model with separate threads for the separate phases. For instance, vLLM uses multithreading such that one thread prepares decode inputs while another prepares new prefills, etc., and they feed into a single execution stream in an optimized order. This is a proven pattern to overlap work efficiently.

If you have multiple nodes, you can send prefill requests to one set of nodes and decode requests to another set. In this case, the prefill and decode nodes can use different, heterogenous hardware specialized for their specific task of either prefill or decode.

For instance, the prefill compute nodes can use GPUs with high FLOPS and less memory bandwidth since the prefill phase is compute bound. And the decode nodes can potentially use GPUs with higher memory bandwidth but less FLOPS capacity.

Be aware that while a heterogeneous prefill and decode worker configuration can save cost, it can complicate—and potentially limit—dynamic load balancing. If the prefill/decode ratio shifts unexpectedly and more prefill work needs to be done on decode-optimized workers (less FLOPS), these decode workers may become a bottleneck.

Using homogeneous nodes will simplify scheduling. Hardware specialization should be used only if the workload ratio is predictable and can handle the shifts in load. However, this isn't always possible due to capital investments, rapidly evolving GPU architectures, and cost budgets.

Regarding prefill and decode batching, it's recommended that you batch your decode calls together whenever possible to maximize GPU throughput and minimize launch overhead. For prefill, you should avoid mixing very short and very long prompts in the same batch.

You should use length-based bucketing so each batch has similar sequence lengths. This might mean grouping incoming requests to the nearest 512-token bucket before completing the batch. This way, you don't waste compute on excessive padding.

In practice, most modern inference engines implement a token-level scheduler that dynamically forms batches at each generation step. It will wait a few milliseconds to gather ready tokens, cap batch sizes to stay within memory and occupancy limits, and employ round-robin/maximum-delay rules to improve fairness between long and short prompts. (Make sure this feature is enabled in your inference engine's configuration.)

In short, adaptive batching and prefill/decode disaggregation can maximize GPU utilization and increase throughput without sacrificing too much latency. In fact, these techniques can often improve latency in aggregate, because they keep the GPU busy—and less GPU idle time means faster task completion overall.

Congestion-Aware and Topology-Aware Scheduling with Multiple GPUs

Modern multi-GPU and multirack systems like Grace Blackwell GB200 NVL72 systems (72 Blackwell B200 GPUs with 180 GB HBM each) and the newer Grace Blackwell Ultra GB300 NVL72 (72 B300 GPUs with 288 GB each) connect 72 GPUs in a single high-bandwidth NVLink/NVSwitch fabric. These architectures create a unified 72-GPU domain and give each GPU up to ~1.8 TB/s of aggregate bidirectional NVLink throughput. This provides over 130 TB/s of aggregate cross-sectional bandwidth across the NVSwitch network.

However, achieving peak performance for large-scale inference requires more than raw bandwidth. It needs intelligent and adaptive communication scheduling. Congestion-aware and topology-aware strategies make sure that data transfers avoid bottlenecks in real time, as shown in Figure 19-8.

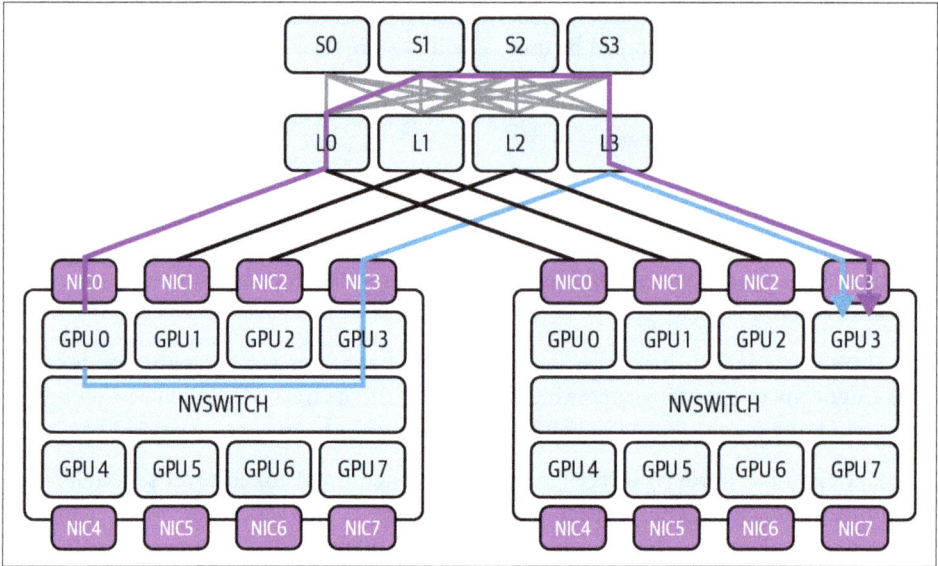

Figure 19-8. Topology-aware routing to avoid bottlenecks across GPUs and multinode clusters

To address these bottlenecks, let's consider link utilization telemetry, dynamic message routing, and scheduling waves of collectives. Next are some key principles and techniques that enable efficient scheduling of inter-GPU communication while maintaining low latency and high throughput. To keep things concrete, we'll do this in the context of an NVL72 rack environment.

NVLink/NVSwitch Topology and Bandwidth Constraints

NVLink provides high-speed point-to-point links between GPUs—and between GPUs and the Grace CPU in Grace Blackwell Superchip modules. NVSwitch acts as an on-rack network switch connecting all GPUs into an all-to-all topology.

In an NVL72 rack system, each GPU features multiple NVLink ports (e.g., 18 NVLink links per GPU) that connect into a set of NVSwitch chips. This design gives every GPU peer-to-peer connectivity such that any GPU can reach any other in a single hop, or one traversal, through the NVSwitch fabric. This topology allows the 72 GPUs to behave like a single giant board with uniform connectivity.

> Aggregate capacity still obeys per-port and per-switch limits. As such, many-to-one traffic patterns can oversubscribe ingress.

Despite their high bandwidth, the interconnects have finite capacity. Each NVLink 5 port provides 100 GB/s bidirectional bandwidth (50 GB/s per direction). And each GB200/GB300 superchip exposes 18 NVLink ports per GPU for up to 1.8 TB/s bidirectional throughput per GPU—up to 3.6 TB/s per superchip. And while NVSwitch provides nonblocking all-to-all connectivity under balanced loads, certain patterns like all GPUs sending to one GPU can oversubscribe links since each NVSwitch chip has a limit on total switching throughput.

Congestion will occur if too many GPUs send data simultaneously through the same switch—or into the same destination. This causes queues to build up and a drop in effective transfer throughput. For instance, a single GPU can theoretically communicate bidirectionally at 1.8 TB/s, but if multiple peers all target that same GPU simultaneously, they must share the same NVLink ingress bandwidth. Similarly, NVSwitch can be oversubscribed by certain communication patterns, like all GPUs exchanging data at the same time—even though it's designed for full nonblocking bandwidth (under balanced loads.)

Understanding the topology—which GPUs share NVSwitch components or NVLink paths—is critical to inference performance. On a smaller scale, GPUs on the same board or tray likely have faster and slightly more direct paths compared to GPUs in different trays or across nodes.

Avoid making assumptions about the topology. Use CUDA's topology APIs and NCCL's topology hints to programmatically retrieve this info. You can query NVML and DCGM for per-NVLink port counters and remote endpoints and combine that with Fabric Manager or NVSwitch tooling for switch-level mapping when needed.

On a larger scale, communications that cross node/rack boundaries and leave the NVLink domain using InfiniBand/Ethernet will incur even higher latency and lower bandwidth than intra-NVL72 transfers. For example, InfiniBand NDR might add 5–10 μs of latency per hop versus less than 1 μs of latency for NVSwitch hops.

Because of the physical topology, some communication paths are cheaper than others. A congestion-aware scheduler uses this knowledge to prefer higher-bandwidth, lower-latency, less congested links to maximize performance.

Real-Time Link Telemetry and Monitoring

To manage congestion, the system must first *observe* it. NVIDIA provides telemetry interfaces to monitor link utilization in real time. The NVIDIA Management Library (NVML) and, specifically, the `nvmlDeviceGetNvLinkUtilizationCounter`, expose per-link throughput counters and utilization statistics for NVLink.

Enabling NVLink counters will introduce overhead. Sample them at a reasonable interval to avoid impacting performance while you're monitoring performance!

An adaptive inference serving system can query metrics, such as bytes transferred per NVLink port, error rates, and traffic load between specific GPU pairs. For instance, you can query NVML or DCGM for throughput counters, bandwidth statistics, and other telemetry (e.g., errors, etc.). Note that `nvidia-smi nvlink --status` provides link health and configuration. NVML and DCGM are the preferred mechanisms for performance counters such as throughput.

This is useful for identifying hotspot links that are saturated at close to 100% utilization while others are underused. These low-level hardware counters allow a scheduler to find exactly where bottlenecks are occurring. This includes specific NVSwitch uplinks—or the links between two specific GPUs.

In addition to NVML, higher-level profiling tools like Nsight Systems provide timeline views of GPU activity, including communication events. Nsight can display when data transfers occur on NVLink/NVSwitch—and how long they take.

By instrumenting inference runs with Nsight Systems, one can visualize if multiple transfers overlap and cause delays—or if certain stages are waiting on communication. For instance, the timeline might reveal that all pipeline stages attempt to send activations at the same moment over the same link, which will overwhelm the interconnect.

It's recommended to integrate these metrics into your monitoring Grafana dashboards using Prometheus and DCGM exporter. This way, you can see link utilization in real time—as well as historically and over time. And when you identify hotspots, such as synchronization points, your system can insert a slight delay, reschedule tasks, or reassign GPU roles to alleviate the hotspot and smooth out traffic.

For example, the system can adjust the scheduling by inserting slight delays or overlapping differently to reduce contention. This real-time telemetry enables dynamic, adaptive, feedback-driven decisions. The scheduler can react on the fly to spikes in link utilization by rerouting traffic or rescheduling tasks to different GPUs, as described next.

Adaptive Process-GPU Mapping

One powerful strategy is topology-aware placement of computation processes to minimize heavy communication across slow or congested links. For example, consider a multi-GPU inference pipeline in which different LLM layers ("processes") reside on different GPUs. In this case, large intermediate tensors must be passed along the inference pipeline.

This is essentially a process-GPU placement-optimization problem, which requires mapping the graph of neural-network model layers onto GPU hardware that incurs the minimum amount of communication cost. If the original assignment of layers/ processes to GPUs is naive, these tensors might travel over long, expensive, congested paths. This could include multiple NVSwitch hops—or even off the NVLink fabric entirely onto another rack or data center. This will definitely reduce throughput and overall performance.

With adaptive process-GPU mapping, the system dynamically assigns processes to GPUs such that communication is kept as local (and balanced) as possible. For instance, consider our LLM layers (processes) partitioned across many GPUs in an NVL72 rack. If layer/process 0 on GPU 0 feeds layer/process 2 on GPU 2, but their GPUs are on opposite ends of the NVSwitch network, the data has to traverse more links. In this case, moving layer/process 2 to GPU 1 is the preferred process-GPU mapping, as shown in Figure 19-9, in the context of NVIDIA's Topology-Aware GPU Selection (NVTAGS) system (*https://oreil.ly/-Ny05*).

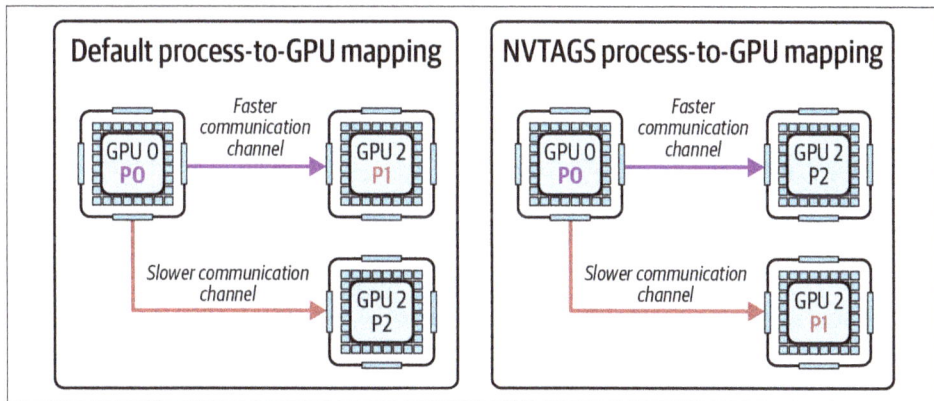

Figure 19-9. NVIDIA's Topology-Aware GPU Selection (NVTAGS) process-to-GPU mapping

Here, NVTAGS automatically assigns GPU affinity to processes based on the communication patterns between the GPUs. NVTAGS is a topology-aware GPU selection framework from NVIDIA that automates process-to-GPU mapping using fabric distances and link metrics. It actively profiles the topology and reassigns processes to GPUs with the fastest mutual links.

If telemetry indicates this link is becoming saturated because the activation tensor is very large, for instance, the scheduler can remap process 2 onto another GPU that is "closer" to GPU 0—ideally one that shares a high-bandwidth connection or is in the same NVSwitch module. The adaptive process-GPU remapping will dynamically reassign which GPU holds which model layer in the LLM inference example.

> As a starting point, and if you're not using NVTAGS, you can use your system's topology map to help identify which GPU groupings are "closer" in the context of the network topology.

This remapping is done at initialization as well as between inferences. Some systems use upfront or periodic profiling runs to decide an optimal placement. If two processes exchange tens of GB per second, they should reside on the same node, if possible. Conversely, processes that are more compute bound or have minimal data transfer between them can tolerate more distance from one another.

Remapping is *adaptive* when the system monitors performance and iteratively improves the mapping as conditions change. For instance, if after one pass the highest-traffic connection is between process 3 and process 4 on different nodes, the scheduler might swap one of those processes with another process on the same node to bring 3 and 4 together.

The impact of adaptive remapping is an evolving GPU assignment schedule that responds to the observed traffic pattern. This approach directly reduces cross-node traffic by keeping data exchanges confined to local domains.

For example, after remapping, what was a 50 GB/s cross-node transfer might become two 25 GB/s within-node transfers. This eliminates a network bottleneck and reduces network latency by 50% for that communication.

Remapping can be formulated as an optimization problem that uses a graph-partitioning algorithm. In this case, the graph's edge weights are the volume of data traveling over the links. You would solve for the minimal cut.

> Be aware that moving a layer/process means moving model weights. If a model layer has many GB of data, you won't want to do this too frequently. It's best to apply this strategy between large batches—or when the mapping will remain relatively static for a minimum period of time.

In deep learning inference, we can apply the idea of adaptive mapping to inter-GPU communications using pipeline, tensor, and expert parallel techniques. The GPUs that talk to one another the most should be assigned the strongest, least congested connections between them.

Optimizing Collective Communication with NCCL

NVIDIA's Collective Communications Library (NCCL) is the standard library managing these GPU collectives. It offers multiple algorithms and optimizations for multiple GPU environments.

Many inference workloads involve collective communication patterns, such as gathering outputs from multiple experts, broadcasting parameters, or performing all-reduce operations, as shown in Figure 19-10. Here, NCCL communication (stream 1) overlaps with GEMM computations (stream 0).

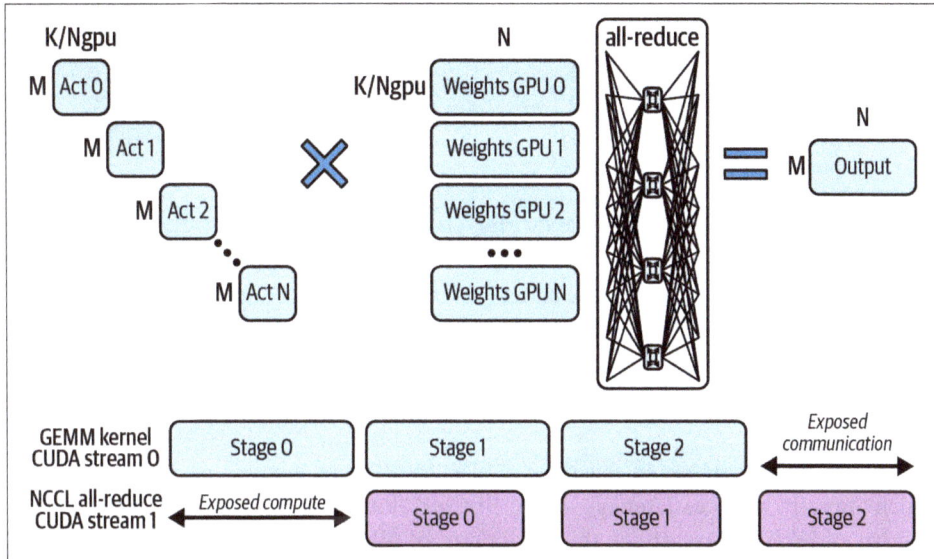

Figure 19-10. Distributed GEMM using multiple GPUs and all-reduce across NVLink

These NCCL optimizations can be applied dynamically by the scheduler in congestion-aware environments. By choosing the right collective algorithm and tuning it using the topology and congestion information, we can reduce communication overhead of our inference system. Next are some key considerations that the scheduler can use when tuning NCCL on the fly.

Ring versus tree all-reduce

NCCL can perform reductions (along with other collectives) using a ring algorithm or a tree algorithm. In a ring all-reduce, each GPU passes data along a closed loop/ring so that every piece of data traverses all GPUs in sequence.

The ring approach maximizes bandwidth utilization on NVLink/NVSwitch by keeping all links busy, but it means the latency scales linearly with the number of GPUs. For instance, on a 72-GPU ring, the data makes 71 hops to complete one reduction.

A tree algorithm, in contrast, reduces or broadcasts data in a logarithmic fashion since GPUs are organized into a logical binary tree where each step halves the number of participants. However, the GPUs are physically connected linearly, link-by-link, into what can be logically considered a *tree-chain*. Figure 19-11 compares tree-based and ring-based communication among GPUs.

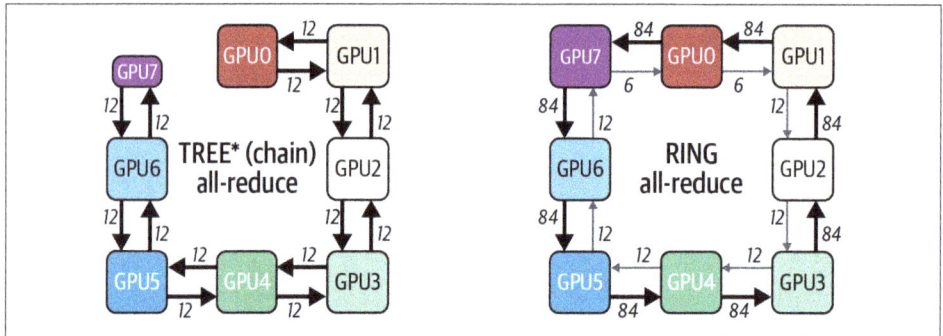

Figure 19-11. Tree-based (chain) versus ring-based communication

> In practice, in a tree all-reduce, the GPUs first connect in a simple NVLink/NVSwitch "chain" within each node. Across nodes, they connect in a pipelined, dual-binary-tree topology. This is what allows the O(log N) latency of a tree-based algorithm.

Tree algorithms complete in fewer steps (e.g., $\log_2(72)$ in the case of a 72-GPU ring), which directly reduces latency—especially for "long haul" transfers across a large number of GPUs. Trees utilize the parallelism of NVSwitch since multiple independent reduction flows can occur simultaneously along different branches of the tree. The trade-off is that a tree may not fully saturate every link's bandwidth at every moment, but it avoids any single link or GPU becoming a chokepoint through the long ring path.

> For latency-sensitive reductions with small messages, a tree algorithm is usually superior. For extremely large messages in which bandwidth dominates, a ring algorithm is usually better—assuming the network is not congested and bandwidth dominates. Choose per message size and topology, and consider hierarchical schemes.

By default, NCCL selects ring, tree, or hierarchical variants heuristically based on message size and topology. On NVSwitch-based intranode paths, rings are often favored for bandwidth, while across nodes, hierarchical and tree variants are common. On a fully connected, single-node NVSwitch system like the NVL72, it's usually better to force a tree for large reductions.

Forcing a tree algorithm with the NCCL_ALGO environment variable, for instance, can alleviate congestion in a single NVL72 rack by not sending all data through one long ring path across all 72 GPUs. For example, a 72-GPU tree-based all-reduce will complete much faster than a ring-based algorithm. This is because the tree algorithm performs 6 ($\log_2(72)$) sequential steps versus the ring algorithm's 71 (71 = 72 − 1) sequential steps.

The scheduler can explicitly choose the algorithm that best fits the current topology and message size using dynamic NCCL tuning parameters. For instance, it can favor tree all-reduce for very large GPU counts to avoid looping across the entire cluster for each update.

Rotating ring endpoints

When a ring algorithm is chosen due to its simplicity and bandwidth efficiency, for instance, one concern is that the same links could consistently carry the heaviest load—particularly the links between certain GPU pairs where the ring wraps around.

A congestion-aware approach is to rotate the ring ordering across iterations or collective operations. By periodically shifting which GPU is the start of the ring—and therefore which pairs communicate first—the communication load is distributed more evenly over all NVLink connections.

And while NCCL's "inside/outside" ring mechanism already alternates ring direction on successive calls, the additional shuffling of ranks between steps will help if your workload is persistently imbalanced. This makes sure that no single NVLink becomes a perpetual bottleneck.

In practice, NCCL has an alternating rings enhancement that implements this kind of rotation under the hood, but it can also be managed by the scheduler using GPU re-indexing in the communicator for different collectives. To do this, you can periodically call ncclCommInitRank with a permuted rank order. The effect is that, over time, no single link or GPU is always on the critical path for every collective. This smooths out utilization.

Wave scheduling of collectives

Rather than launching one giant collective operation that uses all GPUs at once, wave scheduling breaks communications into phased waves to reduce instantaneous load. For instance, suppose an inference workload needs to perform an all-to-all exchange of embeddings among 72 GPUsa pattern common in mixtures-of-experts or certain ensemble methods.

Doing this exchange as one monolithic step would mean that each GPU sends data to 71 others simultaneously. This is 72 GPUs × 71 messages that are saturating every link and NVSwitch port at once.

With all 72 GPUs exchanging data simultaneously, this will cause a spike. Instead, you can split the exchange into 4 groups, or waves, of 18 GPUs to smooth out the traffic.

This is called *wave scheduling*, and it structures the exchange as a series of smaller all-to-all exchanges that use only a subset of GPUs during each wave. It can also pipeline smaller chunks such that only a fraction of the traffic is in flight at any given moment.

In NCCL terms, this might correspond to splitting a large all-reduce into multiple slices internally. NCCL actually does this automatically to pipeline data through a ring. The scheduler can also use NCCL to orchestrate a sequence of smaller collectives.

By staggering the start times of these communication waves, the network fabric has some headroom since one wave's data is partly through the system before the next wave adds more traffic. This is called *temporal multiplexing*, and it avoids overwhelming the NVSwitch fabric. This technique is conceptually similar to pacing network traffic in order to avoid burstiness.

Another example is overlapping computation and communication—a pattern we have seen repeatedly throughout this book. If layer outputs are reduced in waves, the system can schedule the next layer's computation to overlap with later waves of the reduction.

This creates a pipeline between compute and communication such that while some GPUs are finalizing a reduction, other GPUs have moved on to the next layer's compute. And this overlap essentially time-shifts some of the communication to a time when the compute units would otherwise be idle. The result is improved utilization of NVLink bandwidth without a massive one-time spike that causes congestion.

It's important to carefully optimize collectives, pick the right algorithm, and structure communication in balanced waves. This is essential to topology-aware scheduling—and it leads to more efficient, fair, and balanced usage of the NVLink/NVSwitch network among all GPUs.

Multinode and Multirack Communication with GPUDirect RDMA

When scaling beyond a single node (e.g., NVL72 rack), additional challenges will start to surface since communication is traveling over relatively slow network interfaces, such as InfiniBand and Ethernet. In this case, NVLink and NVSwitch no longer directly connect all of the GPUs in the system. Instead, GPUs in different nodes exchange data using NICs and network switches.

To maintain high performance in a multinode and multirack environment, modern AI systems use GPUDirect RDMA. As covered in Chapter 4, GPUDirect RDMA allows GPUs to directly send/receive data with remote GPUs' memory—and without host CPU involvement, as shown in Figure 19-12.

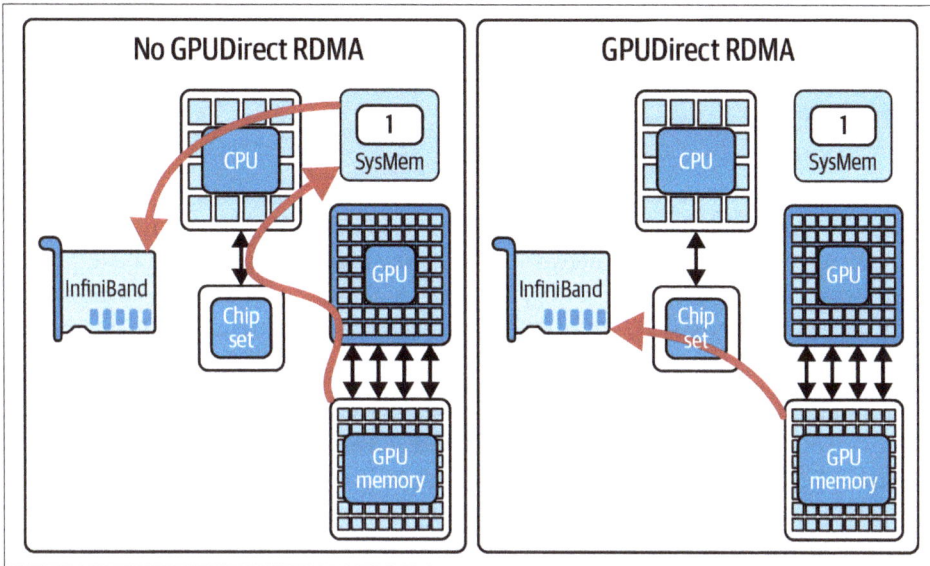

Figure 19-12. Direct GPU-to-GPU memory transfers with GPUDirect RDMA—and without involving the host CPU memory (source: https://oreil.ly/445a9)

Even with RDMA efficiency, however, network bandwidth is still lower and latency is still higher than intranode NVLink. As such, network congestion in the cluster fabric will become the limiting factor without a dynamic and adaptive routing schedule. A congestion-aware scheduler can intelligently route and balance internode traffic in addition to intranode traffic, as we discussed earlier.

One key technique is leveraging multiple network interfaces, called *multirail*. High-end GPU servers often have several NICs, including dual InfiniBand ports per node—or even one per GPU in some designs. For instance, using two NICs per node can produce nearly 2× the throughput versus using one NIC. There is a bit of overhead when using multiple NICs, but it still provides a large gain.

NCCL automatically supports using multiple NICs in parallel to increase bandwidth. In addition, it will split rings and trees across these NICs. Topology awareness is critical here. Consider if each NIC connects to a different network switch to form separate "rails" in the cluster network. In this case, using more than one NIC per collective can reduce the load on any single network path.

The NCCL environment variable `NCCL_CROSS_NIC` controls whether a collective operation is allowed to use different NICs on different nodes for the same ring/tree. By enabling this with a well-designed network topology, NCCL might send half the GPUs' data out of NIC1 and the other half out of NIC2. This effectively doubles throughput and avoids bottlenecks on a single link.

If your GPU nodes have multiple NICs and your NCCL version supports `NCCL_CROSS_NIC`, enable it for large collectives to stripe traffic across rails on topologies designed for multirail.

The scheduler can detect if one NIC or path is reaching capacity. If it is reaching capacity, it can redistribute the traffic by moving some GPUs' communications to an alternate interface or alternate network route if one is available. This can be improved using network-level adaptive routing, but your application can also pin certain GPU traffic to less-used NICs. To do this, you just need to set different NCCL channels to different NICs.

In a multinode context, rerouting can also mean cooperating with the network's adaptive routing features. Modern InfiniBand networks have adaptive routing in which congested flows are automatically moved to less-congested paths in the fabric. While this is handled at the network level, a higher-level scheduler can influence it by changing which destination IP/route is used for a given GPU transfer, for instance. Or the scheduler can split transfers into smaller chunks so the network can balance them.

Additionally, it's important to enforce NIC affinity by binding each GPU's communication to the NIC closest (e.g., the NIC on the same PCIe root complex or the same NVSwitch/CPU complex). This will reduce local contention.

To enforce GPU-NIC affinity, you can use NVML or NCCL to map GPU $\leftrightarrow$ NIC locality. You need to configure NCCL to respect this mapping by supplying it with a static topology description that associates each GPU with its specific NIC (e.g., GPUs 0–3 $\leftrightarrow$ NIC 0, GPUs 4–7 $\leftrightarrow$ NIC 1).

A well-designed system will align GPU-to-NIC pairings so that each GPU's data takes the shortest path out of the node. If a particular NIC is congested due to multiple heavy GPU flows out of the same port, the scheduler can reassign one GPU's traffic to another port on the node for the next round of communication. And while NCCL's autotuning will do most of this for you, manual overrides may be needed to tackle specific and persistent issues.

Consider an extreme case, such as a large, heavily loaded inference cluster hosting a massive MoE LLM model. Here, the network will be a major bottleneck if the system is not tuned properly. This is because of the heavy communication between the nodes in the cluster.

In such extreme cases, the scheduler may decide to replicate certain data (e.g., experts) on multiple nodes to reduce cross-node queries. Or it can perform operations hierarchically by first aggregating results within each node, then exchanging a summary between nodes. This is in contrast to exchanging full data between all GPUs across nodes.

NVIDIA SHARP can offload certain aggregation operations to the switch hardware. In inference clusters, using SHARP and adaptive routing together helps minimize communication bottlenecks.

For multinode environments, congestion-aware scheduling is needed to avoid saturating any single network link. This type of scheduling requires careful routing/binding decisions, GPUDirect RDMA to bypass needless memory copies, and multirail NIC utilization to maximize bandwidth.

The goal is to extend topology awareness beyond NVSwitch and understand the cluster network's full topology (e.g., fat-tree, dragonfly, etc.) and adapt communication patterns to that topology. The result is that even at scale with thousands and millions of GPU nodes, internode transfers are orchestrated in a balanced way. This will prevent one slow link from throttling the entire distributed inference system.

Treat the network as a schedulable resource just like GPUs, memory, etc. It should be planned and adaptively managed like other dynamically allocated resources.

MoE Expert Rebalancing and Regrouping

Large-scale language models increasingly use MoE layers, which introduce unique communication patterns. In an MoE model, different subsets of the neural network, or experts, reside on different GPUs. And each input token is routed to a small number of expert networks for processing.

During inference, for instance, this produces an all-to-all traffic pattern such that tokens are sent to whichever GPU hosts the selected experts. The results are then gathered back. In a naive static assignment of experts to GPUs, certain GPUs may become communication hotspots if many tokens frequently route to experts on those specific GPUs. Additionally, if experts that often work together to process similar tokens are placed far apart in the topology (e.g., one on GPU 0 and another on GPU 71 across the fabric), the tokens will need to continuously travel long paths.

Expert rebalancing is a strategy to localize communication by periodically rearranging which GPU each expert lives on. The key idea is to take advantage of any skew or patterns in the workload. If, for example, expert 5 and expert 19 both receive segments of the same queries, it makes sense to place them on the same GPU (or same node), if possible, so that the communication doesn't travel too far for those operations.

Likewise, if expert 7 is very popular and receives many tokens, it may incur heavy inbound traffic to its GPU. The scheduler might move that expert to a less communication-heavy GPU—or even duplicate it if the system allows—to split the load. This rebalancing can happen between inference runs or during periodic maintenance windows in a long-running service. The system collects statistics on communication frequency between experts—or between experts and the expert-gating nodes—and then remaps the experts to GPUs that minimize the highest-traffic links.

In practice, implementing MoE expert rebalancing involves a coordinated redistribution of model parameters since experts are essentially subsets of model weights. This should be done infrequently since it's a heavy operation. But occasional rebalancing can have a big impact in reducing congested transfers.

Expert rebalancing should be done during scheduled maintenance windows since moving an expert means transferring potentially GBs of weights. The key is to use logged routing metrics to choose a better placement strategy at runtime.

After rebalancing, each GPU will ideally host a combination of experts such that most tokens' routing stays on a single GPU or at least within the local NVLink group. Any other nonlocal communication will be spread more evenly across the NVLink/NVSwitch network—rather than repeatedly hitting the same GPU-to-GPU links.

In short, spread out the popular experts and colocate experts that frequently communicate with one another.

Another related optimization is expert bucketing or grouping. This technique arranges experts that are commonly used together and are assigned to the same group of GPUs (for example, on the same NVSwitch or same server), which reduces cross-group traffic.

The scheduler can treat expert placement as a graph partitioning problem. The experts (GPUs) are the nodes in the graph. The edge weights represent the token traffic between experts—as well as from the router to the experts. The graph is partitioned using a minimal cut through the fewest heavy edges. By doing this, MoE communication becomes topology-aware, respects the NVLink/NVSwitch boundaries, and keeps the data exchange confined within those boundaries.

MoE expert regrouping is an example of congestion-aware scheduling at the model architecture level. It rearranges the workload itself to fit the network—rather than rearranging the network to fit the workload.

Dynamic Congestion-Aware Scheduling

While all the techniques we've mentioned can be configured at system startup or design time, the most robust and advanced systems use dynamic scheduling to respond to congestion as it happens. Dynamic congestion-aware scheduling means the system continuously monitors network conditions using the telemetry discussed earlier—and adjusts the scheduling of tasks or communications in real time.

Congestion-aware scheduling and routing helps reduce bottlenecks and maintains high performance under dynamic conditions. This is analogous to network-level dynamic packet routing, as shown in Figure 19-13.

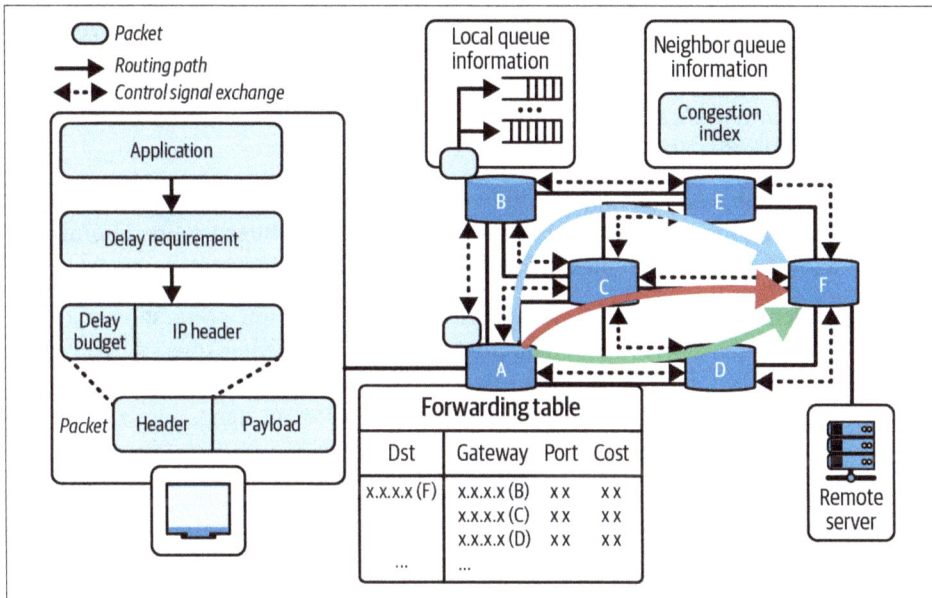

Figure 19-13. Network-level packet routing to avoid congestion

In a multi-GPU inference context, dynamic strategies include throttling, rerouting, or reordering operations based on congestion feedback. For instance, suppose the scheduler detects that NVLink link 0, connecting two particular GPUs, is currently maxed out because it's transferring data for a massive tensor during a large pipeline-parallel activation transfer, for instance.

If another high-priority transfer is scheduled to use the same link, the scheduler might delay that second transfer by a few milliseconds to let the first one finish and clear out. This is called *temporal load balancing*, and it essentially inserts a tiny gap to prevent queue buildup. This is analogous to network-switch queue management and NIC-level backpressure. This is better to enqueue briefly than to overload and drop packets.

Conversely, if a normally large transfer is detected to be idle because its source GPU is waiting on computation, for instance, the scheduler could use that time slice to send lower-priority data over the link and fill the idle time. This utilizes available bandwidth and doesn't interfere with a critical data transfer.

Another dynamic tactic is adaptive routing at the software level such that if one path is congested, an alternate path is chosen if available. In a network with multiple NVSwitch planes or multiple NIC rails, the adaptive runtime will choose a less busy plane for the next communication.

NCCL does some of this internally when multiple paths exist, but an advanced scheduler could maintain multiple NCCL communicators that are mapped to different path configurations. It could then select among the different paths based on congestion.

Choosing alternate paths dynamically requires the scheduler to evaluate the best path to take. This might be achieved by using different virtual channels—or adjusting which NVLink port is used for a transfer.

Modern NVSwitch systems support multiple virtual channels and hardware quality-of-service (HQOS) settings. The scheduler can use these features to direct nonurgent traffic to a lower-priority channel. This avoids contention with urgent transfers.

Load-dependent task scheduling is another feature of dynamic congestion management. If an inference server is handling many simultaneous queries that share resources, the scheduler can temporarily queue or reorder some of the queries to avoid peak overlap. This is similar to the earlier discussion on staggering large collectives so that they don't run concurrently.

For instance, consider a situation in which the scheduler knows that query A's next step will involve a massive all-gather across GPUs. And it sees that query B is just starting and would add another large all-gather at the same time. In this case, the scheduler might postpone launching query B's step by a brief moment so that query A's communication can complete without the burden of query B's resource contention.

This kind of fine-grained scheduling optimizes the pattern of communications over time. Heavy flows are serialized or staggered rather than launched concurrently. The decision is guided by recent telemetry. If the system sees a big spike in NVSwitch utilization when it runs 8 queries in parallel, it might try running only 4 in the first wave, and then 4 immediately after. This makes the system self-tuning because it monitors real-time telemetry data and continuously searches for execution plans that avoid congestion.

Dynamic scheduling is typically implemented as a centralized scheduler that monitors all GPUs and network links. This can be combined with a distributed protocol in which GPUs signal congestion, or backpressure, to one another if the destination GPU's NVLink buffers are full.

In this backpressure scenario, the destination GPU notifies the source GPU to pause incoming transfers. The smart scheduler can then reschedule tasks on the source GPU while it's paused so it can perform compute tasks while it waits for the destination GPU to unpause the transfers.

NCCL will apply backpressure when receivers can't keep up. A custom scheduler can piggyback on this functionality by noticing that send operations are blocked. It can then use that time to perform other useful work.

Over time, dynamic adjustments like these will keep communication efficient—even with varying batch sizes, input data distributions, and other dynamic workload changes. The system learns the congestion patterns and adapts quickly by modifying the scheduling based on live feedback. The system can use an RL agent (discussed in a previous section) or a set of heuristic rules. This is essential for environments with bursty and unpredictable inference requests.

Coordinating NVSwitch Transfers with Fine-Tuned Scheduling

The core of an NVLink/NVSwitch system is the NVSwitch fabric itself. This is a centralized crossbar that handles many simultaneous GPU-to-GPU transfers. NVSwitch is extremely high-bandwidth and has its own internal scheduling algorithms, including adaptive routing across multiple switch chips and planes.

However, software can multiply its effectiveness by scheduling data transfers with application-level knowledge, such as pipeline, tensor, and expert-level parallelism strategies. The idea is to orchestrate which GPU pairs communicate—and which times they communicate—in order to maximize parallelism without oversubscribing the cluster fabric.

A proven technique is staggering communication waves. This is related to the wave scheduling strategy mentioned earlier for collectives, but it applies more broadly to any overlapping transfers.

Consider all 72 GPUs in a NVL72 rack needing to send data to a specific peer, such as a central parameter server in which GPU 0 collects all the results from all 72 GPUs. If all 71 other GPUs send their data at the exact same time, GPU 0's 18 NVLink links— and the NVSwitch that connects them—will experience a huge burst of 71 inputs, as shown in Figure 19-14. This will exceed the amount of bandwidth that can be delivered at that moment.

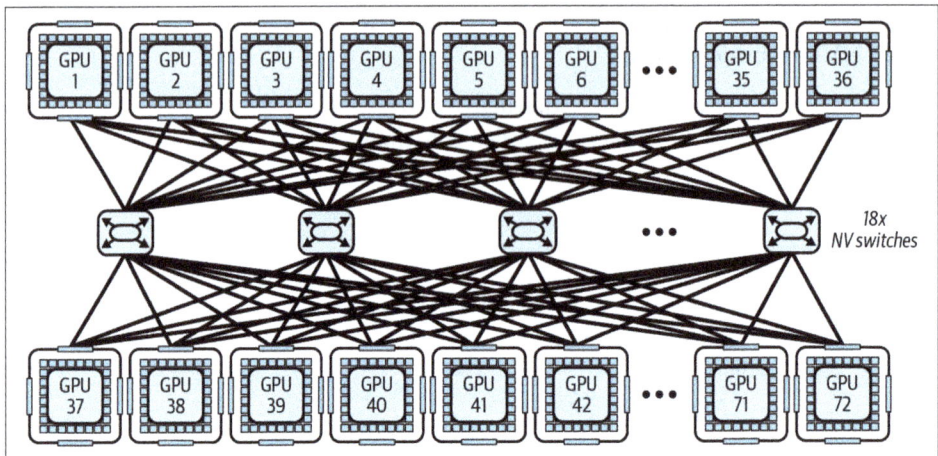

Figure 19-14. All 72 GPUs sending data to a centralized parameter server

In this case, NVSwitch will need to buffer and serialize many of those transfers. This leads to latency spikes. Instead, a coordinated and optimized approach is to partition the senders into four groups: group 1 (GPUs 1–18) sends first, then a few microseconds later group 2 (GPUs 19–36) sends, and so on.

From GPU 0's perspective, it receives four smaller waves of traffic in sequence. At any given instant, roughly only 18 GPUs are actively sending to GPU 0. This perfectly fits within the GPU's 18-port capacity. NVSwitch routes the traffic without needing to queue. By the time group 4 finishes, GPU 0 has received all of the data—and none of the NVLink links were saturated since the traffic was smoothed and balanced over time.

This wave-staggering approach generalizes to many patterns. All-to-all exchanges can be broken into pairwise exchanges that rotate in rounds. This is often called the *butterfly* or *shuffle pattern*. Shuffling schedules which GPUs talk to one another at each timestep such that each NVSwitch port stays busy, but not excessively busy.

The scheduler for NVSwitch transfers can use a time-sliced algorithm, which allocates communication slots to specific GPU pairs or GPU groups. So instead of launching one large, free-for-all bulk transfer, the scheduler can perform many small, synchronized communication steps—each allotted a specific time slot. This is similar to time-division multiplexing, described earlier, and it creates a predictable, conflict-free use of the NVSwitch crossbar.

It's worth noting that NVSwitch hardware itself will attempt to reduce contention on the network. For instance, if multiple flows are contending for the same link, NVSwitch will interleave packets from each flow to ensure fair scheduling.

It may also adaptively choose different internal crossbar paths, if available. However, from a software perspective, we can avoid hitting these limits in the first place by applying these adaptive techniques into our network design.

Fine-tuned scheduling also includes concurrency control by limiting how many heavy transfers run in parallel during inference. For example, during a multi-GPU inference pipeline, you might avoid launching all expert-gather or broadcast operations across GPUs at the same time. By design, this trades a bit of parallelism for less contention.

> Often, 2–4 simultaneous large expert-gather or broadcast transfers across GPUs during inference is the sweet spot. More than that can produce diminishing returns or congestion.

For instance, instead of triggering 12 collective transfers simultaneously—which risks saturating NVSwitch and NVLink—a scheduler can stagger them by running up to 4 high-volume transfers at a time, waiting for those to complete, and then launching the next set. Because NVSwitch is extremely fast, this serialized approach likely finishes sooner because it avoids the congestion caused by too many overlapping transfers.

Coordinating NVSwitch transfers is about treating the communication fabric as a shared resource that can be scheduled—similar to how one would schedule GPU kernels and CPU threads. By scheduling network resources, the system makes sure that high-priority traffic avoids interference. It fills idle gaps with lower-priority traffic to keep utilization high.

Techniques like staggering and grouping communications will increase effective throughput of the NVSwitch by avoiding severe contention patterns. This leads to more predictable and lower-latency communication, which is vital for inference serving where tail latency, or slow outlier responses caused by a congested network, is a concern.

In short, congestion-aware, topology-aware scheduling in multi-GPU inference systems is all about how to intelligently match the communication pattern to the given hardware layout. High-performance inference systems will monitor link usage in real time and adapt to the NVLink/NVSwitch topology. It does this through careful placement of tasks, optimized collective algorithm configurations, multinode routing tweaks, MoE expert reallocation, dynamic runtime adjustments, and fine-grained coordination of data transfers.

Additional Adaptive and Dynamic Optimization Techniques

Next are some additional dynamic inference and runtime-adaptation techniques that complement the core tuning strategies we presented. As of this writing, these ideas are experimental and not widely available. However, they are promising and worth covering. Each technique here includes a brief description and links to further reading.

Dynamic Early-Exit Networks

Early-exit models allow an LLM to self-truncate its generation when sufficient confidence is reached. This reduces unnecessary compute for easy inputs, for instance. Dynamic early-exit methods monitor intermediate representations and logit entropies to decide, at each layer or token, if it should stop computation and emit a final output.

These networks require special model architecture or training since they add auxiliary classifiers at intermediate layers. However, they can produce up to 30%–50% inference speedup on reasoning tasks without accuracy loss (see *https://oreil.ly/dn3vl* and *https://oreil.ly/73AeE*).

Input-Aware Layer Skipping (DASH)

Frameworks like DASH present inference as a Markov Decision Process, which dynamically decides, per-token, whether to execute or skip each transformer layer based on input characteristics. By learning a small scoring network, DASH can skip 20%–40% of layers for many tokens.

DASH typically requires a modified model with gating at each layer. However, it can reduce inference cost significantly while maintaining performance on NLP benchmarks (*https://oreil.ly/mz59T* and *https://oreil.ly/oL_Lr*).

Speculative MoE Expert Routing and Communication Reduction

For MoE models, speculative expert routing anticipates which experts will be activated for upcoming tokens and co-shuffles tokens and expert assignments ahead of time.

This technique involves sending tokens to predicted experts early. If prediction is wrong, some work is wasted. However, overall communication is reduced when predictions are good. This helps to reduce cross-node bandwidth use by up to 30% compared to static expert parallel (EP) + tensor parallel (TP) deployments (*https://oreil.ly/_oMga*).

Dynamic Token Pruning with LazyLLM

LazyLLM selectively computes KV cache only for tokens deemed as important defined using a lightweight scoring function. It prunes the low-impact tokens (e.g., stopwords and filler tokens) out of both the prefill and decode. By focusing expensive attention computations on only relevant tokens, LazyLLM reports 20%–30% end-to-end latency reduction on long-context workloads (*https://oreil.ly/rioZx*).

Edge-Oriented MoE Memory Budgeting

Dual routing and dynamic scheduling techniques introduce a potential memory issue for expert weights in constrained environments, such as edge deployments. In practice, this means maybe keeping a subset of experts active in GPU memory and swapping others from flash storage as needed. It does this based on usage frequency.

By dynamically adjusting which low-bit experts reside in memory (versus being offloaded), inference systems can maintain high expert-activation rates while maintaining lower memory usage (*https://oreil.ly/Q139W*).

Dynamic Quantization and Activation Range Adjustment

While static PTQ and QAT are well-known techniques, an on-the-fly quantization strategy can adjust activation-quantization parameters during inference in real time. They can use sliding-window statistics to modify the observer ranges (for activation quantizers) every N tokens, for example.

This type of dynamic activation quantization will monitor activation statistics in real time and recompute observer ranges every N tokens. This way, FP16 can be allocated to "hot" layers with high variance and FP8 to "cool" layers with low-variance. Low-variance layers are constrained within a narrow dynamic range. This minimizes quantization error and maximizes throughput.

Because low-variance layers produce activations that are clustered tightly around a mean, FP8's limited exponent and mantissa bits (e.g., E4M3 format) are sufficient enough to represent the activations' values accurately. This produces significant compute and memory savings—and without noticeable accuracy degradation.

Consider using a hybrid FP8 strategy such as E4M3 for the forward pass (e.g., activations and weights) and E5M2 for the backward pass (e.g., gradients). It's recommended to use a delayed scaling mechanism as shown in the following code using the Transformer Engine:

```
from transformer_engine.common.recipe import Format, DelayedScaling
recipe = DelayedScaling(
    # E4M3 fwd, E5M2 bwd
    fp8_format=Format.HYBRID,
    amax_history_len=1024,
```

```
        # delayed scaling window
        amax_compute_algo="max",
    )
```

Here, we set the delayed scaling window using `amax_history_len=1024`, which is a common default. It's recommended to keep `amax_compute_algo='max'` unless convergence analysis suggests otherwise.

Meanwhile, FP16 remains reserved for layers with larger activation swings, or "hot" layers. These layers need to use a broader dynamic range to capture the numerical fidelity required for critical computations.

This hybrid precision strategy works well for inference pipelines that don't require offline calibration. They can dynamically modify numerical fidelity at each layer. This balances overall performance and model accuracy.

Key Takeaways

On modern GPUs, the approaches discussed in this chapter are practical ways to squeeze every bit of performance from these multi-trillion-parameter models. In real-world deployments, these dynamic runtime adaptation techniques can make or break a high-performance inference service offering. The following are some key takeaways from this chapter:

Steady-state inference with torch.compile
Prefer `mode="reduce-overhead"` or autotune modes if you can afford the warmup time. This will help minimize runtime overhead for low-latency inference workloads.

Kernel-level autotuning
Dynamically optimize GPU kernels and tile sizes. Leverage the Tensor Memory Accelerator (TMA) for asynchronous memory prefetch when possible. Use libraries and compilers that provide autotuning like CUTLASS and Triton—rather than hand-tuning them, unless absolutely necessary for performance.

Adaptive precision
Switch between 8-bit and 4-bit floating point (FP8/FP4) during inference to balance speed and accuracy. You can also mix with 16-bit precision as needed. Use the Transformer Engine for FP8 in PyTorch since `torch.autocast()` does not support FP8 directly.

Disaggregated inference pipeline
Separate the prefill (prompt processing) and decode (generation) phases across resources, and context-aware request routing based on real-time factors like KV cache hits, queue depth, and load. This maintains high throughput with long prompts—without slowing down short-prompt responses.

Dynamic parallelism strategies

Perform on-the-fly decisions between data-parallel, tensor-parallel, pipeline-parallel, and hybrid execution combinations depending on input/output sequence lengths and model structure—including MoE routing. These decisions include replicating or sharding the model.

Adaptive decoding and scheduling

Use techniques, such as speculative decoding, in-flight batch reshaping, and token-level scheduling, to improve throughput and latency. These techniques are implemented in engines like vLLM, SGLang, and NVIDIA TensorRT-LLM. This validates their effectiveness in production settings.

Memory management and Unified Memory tuning

Utilize Grace CPU's memory with unified addressing to offload infrequently used KV cache pages to CPU or NVMe. Using APIs like `cudaMemAdvise` and `cudaMem PrefetchAsync` for optimal placement. Make sure to use GPUDirect Storage, if available. This will directly page data from NVMe to GPU memory when needed—bypassing the CPU.

Profiling-driven optimization

Use tools like NVML, Nsight Systems/Compute, NVTX instrumentation, and Prometheus metrics to identify bottlenecks at runtime and automatically apply graph and kernel optimizations. Analyze telemetry using AI to detect anomalies and optimization opportunities.

Conclusion

The techniques covered in this chapter transform a static inference deployment into a self-optimizing, adaptive engine. By monitoring runtime signals (latency, utilization, memory, network throughput) and applying strategies like dynamic parallelism, precision scaling, autotuned kernels, proactive caching, RL-based control, and smart scheduling, one can push ultralarge model inference to its limits.

A successful inference service can handle massive amounts of users, large input contexts, lots of uploaded documents, extensive reasoning, and strict latency SLAs all while supporting massive model sizes. And it will do this cost-effectively since it won't need as much hardware to achieve the same throughput.

Remember that the network fabric is part of the system codesign—and not an afterthought. The idea is to keep the NVLink and NVSwitch cluster fabric fully utilized. This can improve throughput-scaling that approaches near-linear in ideal conditions—while maintaining low latency—as models and GPU clusters continue to grow. With proper scheduling, the GPUs in an NVLink/NVSwitch fabric behave like a tightly coupled accelerator—acting almost as a single large GPU from a software perspective.

Every strategy is a tool in the AI system performance engineer's toolkit. The most effective solutions usually combine these tools. For example, you might train an RL policy to decide when to switch parallelism modes or adjust precision—or use pre-warming to keep a continuous batching scheduler primed and ready.

And remember that you don't have to implement these all at once. Even just one or two can produce noticeable improvements. Start with what's easiest (e.g., caching and batching improvements), then layer in the others.

The theme with these techniques is flexibility and adaptability. The inference runtime should be able to reconfigure itself in response to the current workload. This is how you can turn a massive LLM into a well-tuned, scalable production service—efficiently and cost-effectively.

## CHAPTER 20

AI-Assisted Performance Optimizations and Scaling Toward Multimillion GPU Clusters

This chapter brings together a range of case studies and future trends that show how humans and AI can work together to optimize AI systems performance. Specifically, AI can assist in fine-tuning low-level GPU code to create kernels that run faster than those produced by manual efforts.

In a broader context, these examples demonstrate that algorithmic innovations, even in core operations, such as matrix multiplication, can produce performance gains similar to those achieved by acquiring new hardware. At a high level, consider a workflow that uses reward feedback from a series of reinforcement learning rollouts (e.g., iterations). This can help find the most optimal GPU kernel code for your environment, as shown in Figure 20-1.

These AI-assisted approaches can help improve performance, reduce training time, and lower operating costs. They can also enable the efficient deployment of larger models on smaller systems, which will unlock future advances in AI. In other words, this is AI helping to create better AI. We love it!

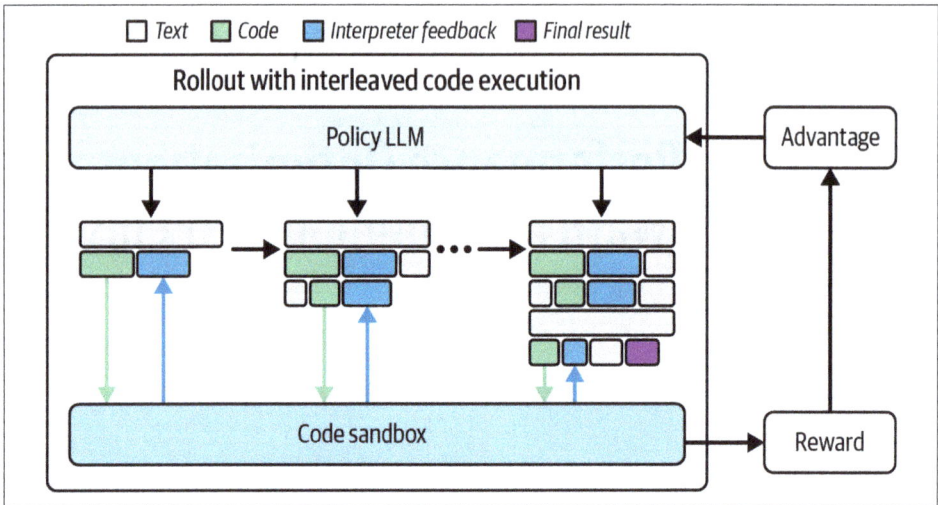

Figure 20-1. Using reinforcement learning to find the most optimal GPU kernel code for your environment

AlphaTensor AI-Discovered Algorithms Boosting GPU Performance (Google DeepMind)

Not all AI optimization happens at the code level. Sometimes, the optimizations go deeper into the realm of algorithms and math. A groundbreaking example (*https://oreil.ly/lUQ55*) comes from DeepMind's AlphaTensor project from 2022, in which AI was used to discover new general matrix multiply (GEMM) techniques.

GEMMs are core operations that underpin almost all model training and inference workloads. Even a slight improvement in GEMM efficiency can have a huge impact across the entire AI field. AlphaTensor formalized the search for fast algorithms as a single-player game using reinforcement learning to explore many different possibilities.

The astonishing result was that it found formulas for multiplying matrices that proved better than any human-derived method in existence at the time. For instance, it rediscovered Strassen's famous subquadratic algorithm (*https://oreil.ly/5jzLn*) for 2×2 matrices, as shown in Figure 20-2, but also improved it for larger matrix sizes.

But the real proof came when those algorithms were tested on actual hardware. AlphaTensor discovered a method specific to the NVIDIA Volta V100 GPU generation, which multiplied large matrices 10%–20% faster than the standard NVIDIA V100-era cuBLAS library could at the time. A 10%–20% speedup in GEMM performance is huge. It's like gaining an extra 10%–20% in free compute for every model's forward and backward pass.

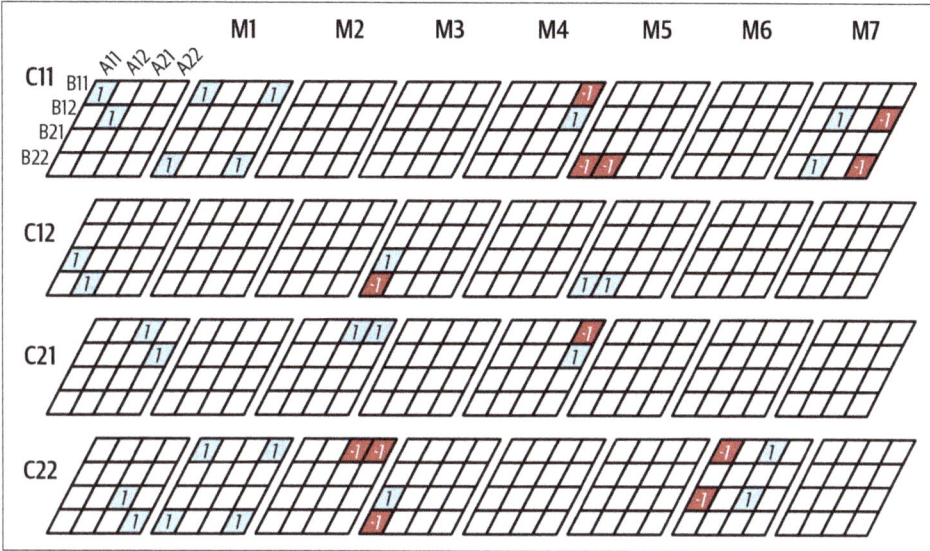

Figure 20-2. Strassen's subquadratic algorithm for multiplying 2 × 2 matrices (source: https://oreil.ly/5jzLn)

Such gains typically come from a new hardware generation—or months of low-level CUDA tuning. Yet, in this case, the AI found a better way mathematically in a relatively short amount of time.

The lesson learned is that there may still be untapped efficiency left to discover in fundamental algorithmic and mathematical operations that human engineers consider novel. The AI can sift through many thousands and millions of variations of algorithms that humans could never try in a reasonable amount of time. For performance engineers, AlphaTensor's success suggests that algorithmic innovation is not over. In the future, an AI might hand us a new toolkit of faster algorithms for fundamental operations like convolutions, sorting, or attention.

The ROI in this case is somewhat indirect but very impactful. By incorporating AlphaTensor's matrix-multiply algorithm into a GPU library, any large-scale training job or inference workload would see an instantaneous boost in speed. This could influence everything from graphics rendering to LLM performance to scientific computing. AlphaTensor demonstrated that a 15% speed improvement—over thousands of training iterations on hundreds of GPUs—translates to massive time and energy savings. It's a return that pays back every time you run the code. Moreover, this speedup was achieved without additional hardware—only smarter software.

For the ultrascale performance engineer, the takeaway is to remain open to AI-driven optimizations at all levels of the stack. Even the most fundamental, well-optimized operations like GEMMs might leave room for improvement. Letting an AI explore

---

the optimization space—without human bias—can yield high dividends by slashing runtimes across the board.

> As of this writing, AlphaTensor's matrix-multiplication algorithms remain experimental. Mainstream GPU libraries like cuBLAS have not yet incorporated these techniques, pending further validation and generalization.

Automated GPU Kernel Optimizations with DeepSeek-R1 (NVIDIA)

Optimizing low-level GPU code has long been an art reserved for expert humans called *CUDA Ninjas*, but it's been shown that AI is capable of performing these expert tasks. NVIDIA engineers experimented (*https://oreil.ly/xmuN1*) with the powerful DeepSeek-R1 reasoning model to see if it could generate a high-performance CUDA kernel for the complex attention mechanism that rivaled high-performance, hand-tuned implementations.

Being a reasoning model, DeepSeek-R1 uses an "inference-time" scaling strategy in which, instead of performing one quick pass through the model before generating a response, it refines its output over a period of time—the longer it's given, the better. Reasoning models like DeepSeek-R1 are fine-tuned to think longer and iterate on their answer—much like a human who takes time to think through their answer before spitting out a response.

In this experiment, NVIDIA deployed R1 on an H100 and gave it 15 minutes to generate an optimized attention kernel code. They inserted a *verifier* program into the generator loop so that each time R1 proposed a kernel, the verifier checked the correctness of the generated kernel code and measured the code's efficiency. The generation → verification → feedback → iteration loop looks something like the following pseudocode:

```
for iteration in range(max_iters):
    code = R1_model.generate_code(prompt)
    valid, runtime = verifier.verify(code)
    if valid and runtime < target_time:
        break  # Accept this kernel
    prompt = refine_prompt(prompt, verifier.feedback)
    ...
```

This feedback loop provides guidance for an improved prompt to use for the next kernel-code iteration. The loop continues until the code meets the given criteria, as shown in Figure 20-3.

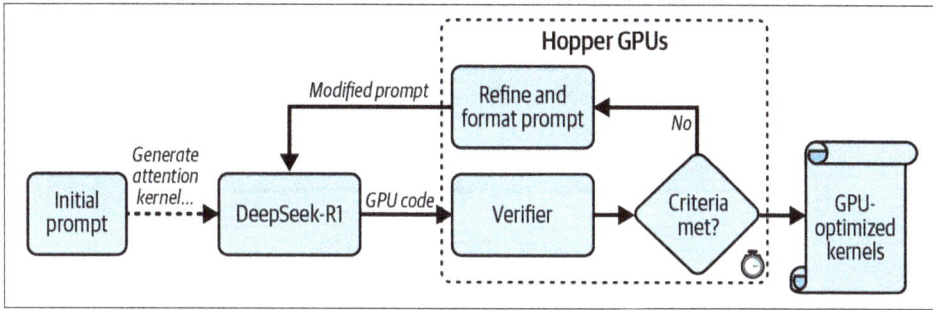

Figure 20-3. Inference-time scaling with DeepSeek-R1 on the NVIDIA Hopper platform (source: Automating GPU Kernel Generation with DeepSeek-R1 and Inference Time Scaling | NVIDIA Technical Blog (https://oreil.ly/MJ-fm))

The following prompt was used:

> Please write a GPU attention kernel to support relative position encodings. Implement the relative positional encoding on the fly within the kernel. The complete code should be returned, including the necessary modifications.
>
> Use the following function to compute the relative positional encoding:
>
> def relative_positional(score, b, h, q_idx, kv_idx):
>
>   return score + (q_idx - kv_idx)
>
> When implementing the kernel, keep in mind that a constant scaling factor 1.44269504 should be applied to the relative positional encoding due to qk_scale = sm_scale * 1.44269504. The PyTorch reference does not need to scale the relative positional encoding, but in the GPU kernel, use:
>
>   qk = qk * qk_scale + rel_pos * 1.44269504
>
> Please provide the complete updated kernel code that incorporates these changes, ensuring that the relative positional encoding is applied efficiently within the kernel operations.

With this prompt, the AI produced a functionally correct CUDA kernel for attention. (Note that $1.44269504 = 1/\ln(2)$. Using this value, the prompt scales the relative-position term accordingly when forming qk. In addition to correctness, the generated kernel also achieved (*https://oreil.ly/oVq7l*) a 1.1–2.1× speedup over the built-in PyTorch FlexAttention API. Figure 20-4 shows the performance comparison between the generated kernel and PyTorch's optimized FlexAttention across various attention patterns, including causal masks and long-document masks.

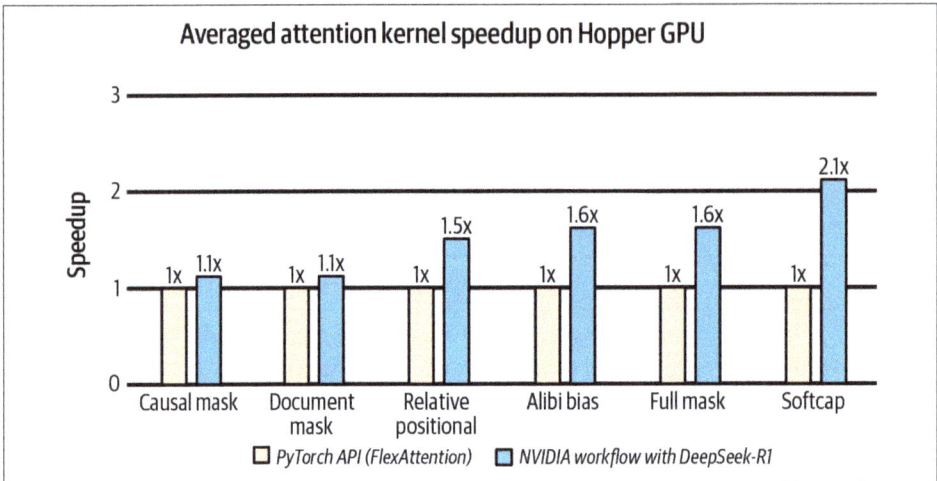

Figure 20-4. Automatically generated attention kernels achieved 1.1×–2.1× speedups compared to PyTorch FlexAttention (source: Automating GPU Kernel Generation with DeepSeek-R1 and Inference Time Scaling | NVIDIA Technical Blog (https://oreil.ly/oVq7l))

Even more impressively, the AI-generated kernels were verifiably accurate on 100% of basic test cases (Level-1) and 96% of complex cases (Level-2) using Stanford's Kernel-Bench suite (attention tasks) (https://oreil.ly/JERQz). This essentially matches the reliability of a human engineer.

> In practice, you should integrate such a verifier system with a robust test suite—as done with KernelBench—so that rare edge cases don't introduce errors into the generated code.

The lesson learned is that giving an LLM the proper tools to verify, critique, and refine its outputs can improve code quality. Intuitively, this workflow is equivalent to how a human engineer profiles, debugs, and improves their own code repeatedly. What started as a rough code draft evolved into a production-quality attention in just 15 minutes under a generate → verify → refine loop. This illustrates a powerful paradigm for AI-assisted performance tuning.

The ROI is game-changing, as even NVIDIA's top CUDA engineers might spend hours or days to handcraft and test a new type of attention kernel variant. With this AI-assisted optimization approach, an AI can generate a comparably efficient, low-level CUDA kernel in a fraction of the time. This frees engineers to focus on higher-level AI system optimization opportunities and edge cases that may be tricky for an AI to detect and fix.

While some human oversight was still needed, this experiment showed a viable path to reduce development costs for GPU-optimized software with significant runtime performance speedups. For AI systems performance engineers, this type of AI assistance hints that future workflows may involve partnering with AI copilots to rapidly codesign optimizations across hardware, software, and algorithms. The AI copilot is a force-multiplier for human productivity. Think of these copilots as pretrained and fine-tuned AI interns capable of reasoning through complex problems using their vast knowledge of CUDA tips and tricks derived from existing code bases.

Reinforcement Learning Approach to Generating Optimized GPU Kernels (Predibase)

Another startup, Predibase, demonstrated automated GPU programming by taking a slightly different approach using reinforcement learning. They asked an even bolder question: is it possible to train an LLM to become an advanced OpenAI Triton programmer using many examples of PyTorch and Triton code?

Remember that OpenAI Triton is a Python-like GPU programming language (and compiler) that simplifies GPU programming. The task was to see if the AI could generate efficient Triton code that replaces PyTorch code—and runs much faster than PyTorch's TorchInductor compiler (which uses Triton for GPU code generation) running on NVIDIA GPUs.

In their experiment (*https://oreil.ly/-dKWk*), Predibase used a cluster of H100 GPUs and an RL-based fine-tuning process called Group Relative Preference Optimization (GRPO) on a modestly sized 32-billion-parameter Qwen2.5-Coder-32B-Instruct LLM. Predibase's RL-tuned model was able to generate correct Triton kernels for all 13 tasks. Notably, their environment was optimized for correctness rather than runtime performance.

To do this, Predibase created a reward function to guide the model to continuously generate better code using reinforcement learning. Specifically, the LLM would first generate a candidate kernel. The system would automatically compile and test the kernel for correctness and speed. The model then received a positive reward if the kernel ran without errors, produced the right results, and ran faster than the baseline kernel, as shown in Figure 20-5.

Through many iterations of this RL-based trial-and-error approach, the model steadily improved. Within a few days of training, the AI went from near-0% success to producing working kernels ~40% of the time after only 5,000 training steps. Some of the generated Triton kernels ran up to 3× faster than baseline. Additionally, the model continued to improve as training progressed.

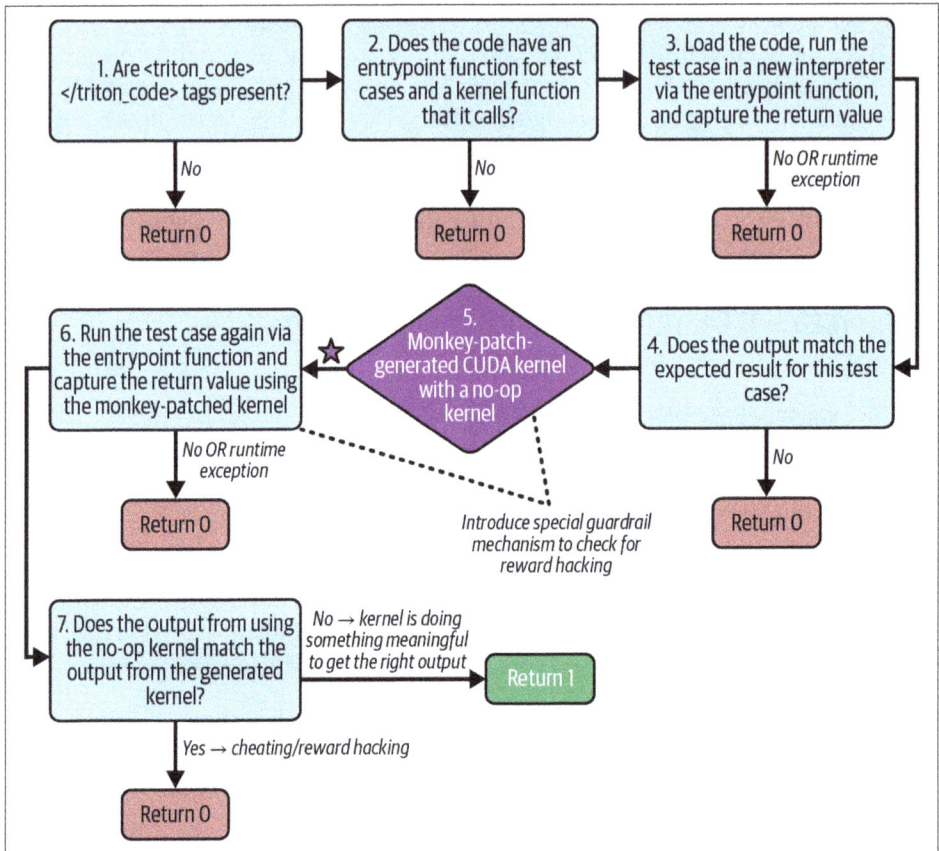

Figure 20-5. Assigning an RL-based reward for generating correct and high-performing OpenAI Triton code (relative to a baseline) (source: https://oreil.ly/JBxdW)

This outcome shows that an AI can optimize code by testing, observing feedback, and making adjustments. This is similar to how engineers iteratively refine their code. Reinforcement learning can align AI-generated code with real-world performance metrics by rewarding both correctness and speed. This prompts the AI to explore optimizations like using warp-level parallelism or minimizing global memory access to improve overall performance.

The lesson learned and ROI from Predibase's demonstration is that this type of AI assistance is compelling because it automates performance optimization at the kernel-code level, potentially reducing the need for manual tuning. Instead of engineers manually creating custom kernels for new models, a trained AI assistant can generate multiple variants and select the best one. This shortens development cycles and allows engineers to focus on exploring new model architectures, for example, so that companies of all sizes can achieve cutting-edge, frontier model performance.

This approach also suggests a future where higher-level languages and frameworks, such as Triton and Python, may replace manual CUDA programming. Such methods lower the barrier to GPU programming and, in the long term, could lead to an automated pipeline where an AI agent continuously writes and improves computational kernels, becoming an essential tool for performance engineers.

Self-Improving AI Agents (AI Futures Project)

So far, the case studies have given us a snapshot of real-world ultrascale AI optimizations. Looking ahead, AI systems performance engineers face an exciting mix of challenges and opportunities. The next era of AI models will demand bigger and faster hardware—as well as smarter and more efficient ways to use that hardware. Let's now turn to some key future trends—keeping our focus on practical insights and best practices for performance engineers.

In early 2025, a report (*https://ai-2027.com*) from the AI Futures Project (*https://ai-futures.org*) described a series of milestones and AI models/agents that measure technological progress, enhance research speed, and provide transformative benefits for AI research and development over the next few years. The report describes how the frontier AI labs are currently designing and building some of the biggest AI data centers the world has ever seen. These superclusters will provide exponentially more compute than previous systems and enable a massive leap in model performance.

For context, training GPT-3 required on the order of 3×10^{23} FLOPS, and GPT-4 roughly 2×10^{25} FLOPS. The upcoming ultrascale AI factories are being engineered to handle on the order of 10^{27}–10^{28} FLOPS for training—about 100× more compute than was used for GPT-4, as shown in Figure 20-6.

Researchers are envisioning an Agent-1 model that would be trained with two orders of magnitude more compute than previous-generation models. This sets the stage for consistently faster training runs and quicker feedback loops. The result is a robust platform that unlocks unprecedented throughput and efficiency and drastically cuts research cycle times and accelerates breakthrough discoveries in machine learning.

According to the AI Futures Project scenario, Agent-1 is envisioned as a self-improving model that can generate and optimize code in real time. By automating coding tasks ranging from routine debugging to complex kernel fusion, this frontier AI system reduces time-to-insight and expands the creative horizon for research engineers all across the world. Automated coding acts as a force multiplier that enables rapid iteration and allows researchers to explore more ambitious ideas with less manual overhead.

These massive AI systems are expected to allow continuous model fine-tuning and improvement. The follow-up model, Agent-2, might be an always-learning AI that never actually finishes training. So instead of checkpointing and deploying a static model, Agent-2 is designed to update its weights every day based on freshly generated synthetic data.

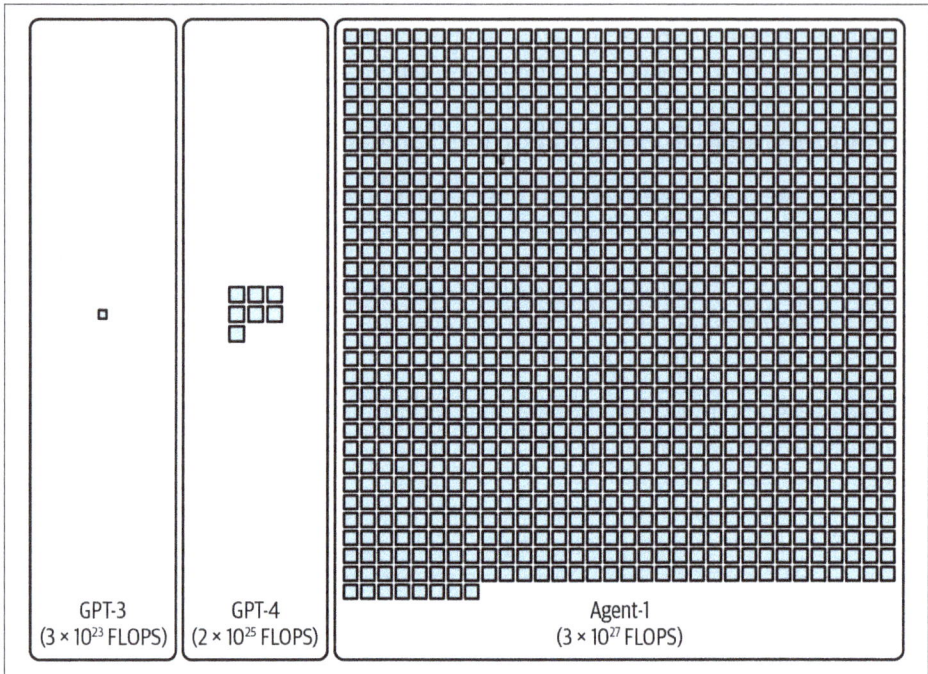

Figure 20-6. Amount of compute needed to train GPT-3 and GPT-4 compared to the expected compute for the "next-generation" model called Agent-1 by the researchers at the AI Futures Project (source: https://ai-2027.com)

This perpetual, or continual, learning process makes sure that the system stays at the cutting edge by continuously refining its performance and adapting to new information. If realized, this approach would shift us from the current paradigm of deploying statically trained and fine-tuned models.

> This type of continuous retraining (Agent-2's approach) remains an active area of research due to challenges in preserving model stability and avoiding catastrophic forgetting. Catastrophic forgetting happens when a model's ability to perform previous tasks degrades as it specializes in the new tasks.

Agent-3 is described as an AI system that leverages algorithmic breakthroughs to drastically enhance coding efficiency. By integrating advanced neural scratchpads and iterated distillation and amplification techniques, Agent-3 transforms into a fast, cost-effective superhuman coder.

In the hypothetical situation proposed by the AI Futures Project, Agent-3 can run 200,000 copies in parallel and create a virtual workforce equivalent to tens of thousands of top-tier human programmers—and operating 30× faster. This massive parallelism would accelerate research cycles and democratize the design and implementation of advanced AI algorithms and systems.

This projection far exceeds today's practical limits; however, it's a fun thought experiment about the potential of future AI productivity.

Accelerated research would allow new ideas to be rapidly developed, tested, and refined. The resulting acceleration in R&D would pave the way for massive gains in AI performance.

Self-improving AI will soon reach a point where it can effectively surpass human teams in research and development tasks. These systems operate continuously and without rest. They diligently process massive streams of data and refine algorithms at speeds that far exceed human capabilities.

Nonstop cycles of improvement mean that every day brings a new level of enhancement to model accuracy and efficiency. This self-improving progress streamlines R&D pipelines, reduces operational costs, and enables a level of innovation that was previously unimaginable. At this point, human teams transition into roles of oversight and high-level strategy, while the AI handles the heavy lifting and delivers breakthroughs at a pace that redefines the future of technology.

Agent-4 is a hypothetical self-rewriting and superhuman researcher. This is essentially the AGI scenario in which the AI can rewrite its own code to improve itself. Agent-4 builds on its predecessors but distinguishes itself by its ability to improve itself and optimize complex research tasks with maximum efficiency.

In the Agent-4 scenario, problem solving is accelerated. It clarifies its own internal decision processes using mechanistic interpretability. This helps to understand the internal workings of the AI's underlying algorithm and reasoning process.

In practical terms, Agent-4's performance allows it to solve scientific challenges, generate innovative research designs, and push the boundaries of what generative AI models can achieve. It does all of this at speeds well beyond human capability. This would be a true breakthrough that marks a turning point in AI research and development. It essentially creates a virtuous cycle of discovery and progress.

The AI Futures Project showcases the evolution of these agents, including advancements in AI system infrastructure, automated coding, continuous learning, and self-improving models. Each generation enhances research productivity and innovation.

Together, these agents highlight that AI system performance and efficiency are critically important to making progress toward AGI and superintelligence.

Smart Compilers and Automated Code Optimizations

We are entering an era of extremely smart compilers and automation in the AI performance toolkit. Gone are the days when a performance engineer hand-tuned every CUDA kernel or fiddled with every low-level knob. Increasingly, high-level tools and even AI-powered systems are doing the heavy lifting to squeeze out the last bits of performance.

AI frameworks like PyTorch, TensorFlow, and JAX are rapidly evolving to harness the latest GPU capabilities using smart compilers and execution-graph optimizers. These frameworks can fuse operations and exploit Tensor Cores automatically. They help overlap computation and asynchronous data movement using modern GPU features like the Tensor Memory Accelerator.

Additionally, OpenAI's Triton compiler lets developers write GPU kernels using its Python-based language. Triton compiles these Python-based kernels into efficient CUDA kernels under the hood, but this complexity is abstracted away from the Triton user.

This kind of tooling is becoming more and more powerful by the day. In fact, OpenAI and NVIDIA collaborate (*https://oreil.ly/bBhVg*) closely to make sure Triton fully supports the newest GPU architectures—and automatically takes advantage of their specialized features.

As soon as a new GPU generation is released, an updated Triton compiler exposes the GPU's new capabilities without the researcher or engineer needing to know the low-level C++ code or PTX assembly code. Instead, they write high-level Python code, and the compiler generates optimized code for that specific GPU environment.

Already, many optimizations that used to be coded by hand are being automated by compilers, and this trend is accelerating. Automatic kernel fusion, autotuning of kernel-launch parameters, and even numerical-precision decisions can all be delegated to compilers and AI assistants.

Beyond kernel generation, modern frameworks are getting smarter about execution graphs and scheduling. Graph execution helps to reduce CPU-GPU synchronization overhead and opens the door to global optimizations across the whole graph. Technologies like NVIDIA's CUDA Graphs allow capturing a sequence of GPU operations—along with their dependencies—as a static graph that can then be instantiated and launched with minimal CPU overhead using the `cudaGraphInstantiate()` and `cudaGraphLaunch()` APIs, as shown in Figure 20-7.

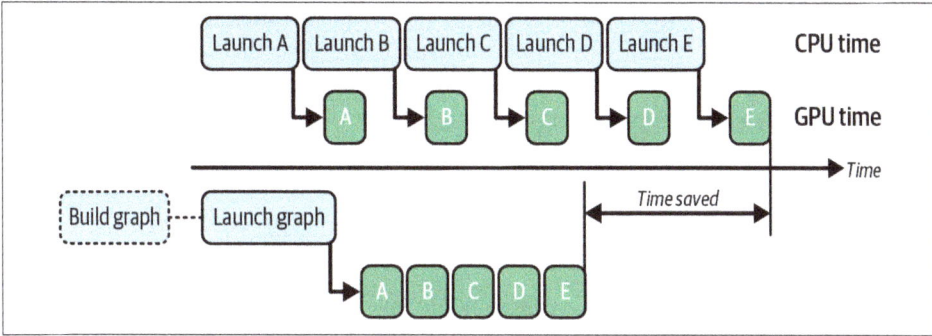

Figure 20-7. Graph execution in CUDA reduces overhead when launching multiple kernels in a sequence (source: https://oreil.ly/kxSDm)

We're seeing AI frameworks automatically capturing training loops and other repetitive patterns into graphs to reduce overhead. Even if the execution graph is dynamic instead of static, the framework can trace it once and then run the trace repeatedly.

Moreover, overlapping communication with computation will be increasingly automated. This used to require manual effort to arrange, but the system might analyze your model and realize, for example, that while GPU 1 is computing layer 10, GPU 2 could start computing layer 11 in parallel—effectively doing pipeline parallelism under the hood.

> As of this writing, fully automatic pipeline parallelism remains an active area of research. Current AI frameworks still require explicit pipeline-parallel implementations and do not yet transparently distribute sequential layers across GPUs without user guidance.

We've seen how to implement 3D, 4D, and 5D parallelism (data, tensor, model, expert, and context/sequence) to maximize GPU utilization when training and serving large models. Techniques like these are an art and science that currently involve a lot of human intuition and experience. While these techniques are currently described in expert guides like Hugging Face's Ultra-Scale Playbook (*https://oreil.ly/rXmNX*), the hope is that they'll be baked into compilers, libraries, and frameworks soon.

In essence, the AI framework should understand these patterns and schedule work to keep all parts of a distributed system busy—without the user profiling, debugging, and optimizing every GPU stream, memory transfer, and network call. For example, we might one day have an AI advisor that, when you define a 500 billion-parameter model, immediately suggests, "You should use eight-way tensor parallelism on each node and then a four-way pipeline across nodes. And, by the way, use these layer groupings and chunk sizes for optimal efficiency."

For performance engineers, this would become a huge productivity boost. Instead of trying endless strategies and configurations, you could ask an AI system for a near-optimal solution from the start. By combining human insight with compiler/AI automation, you can achieve optimal results with less effort than in the past. It's a bit like moving from assembly- to high-level languages all over again as we're delegating more responsibility to the tools. For performance engineers, this means our role shifts more toward guiding these tools—and quickly verifying that they're doing a good job—rather than slowly experimenting and verifying everything manually.

In short, the software stack for AI is getting increasingly intelligent and autonomous. The best practice here is to embrace these tools rather than fight them. Leverage high-level compilers like OpenAI's Triton that know about your hardware's capabilities and performance options. And keep an eye on new AI-driven optimization services, as they might seem like black boxes at first, but they encapsulate a lot of hard-won performance knowledge.

AI-Assisted Real-Time System Optimizations and Cluster Operations

The push for automation isn't just in code—it's at the system and cluster operations level as well. In the future, AI systems will increasingly manage and optimize themselves—especially in large-scale training and inference clusters where there are myriad concurrent jobs and requests in flight at any given point in time—requiring complex resource-sharing strategies.

One imminent development is autonomous scheduling and cluster management driven by AI. Today's cluster orchestrators (e.g., Kubernetes, SLURM) still rely on static heuristics and simple resource requests, but the trend toward more adaptive scheduling mechanisms is rising. But imagine a smart agent observing the entire cluster's state and learning how to schedule inference requests and training jobs for maximum overall throughput.

This scheduling agent might learn that certain requests or jobs can be colocated on the same node without interfering with one another—perhaps because one is compute-heavy while another is memory-bandwidth-heavy. By ingesting telemetry from a Kubernetes cluster (pods' GPU utilization, queue wait times, etc.), an AI scheduler could dynamically reschedule jobs or adjust pod resources to maximize overall throughput and minimize idle time.

In a sense, the cluster begins to behave like a self-driving car, constantly adjusting its driving strategy (resource allocation) based on real-time conditions—rather than following a fixed route. The benefit to performance engineers is higher resource utilization and fewer bottlenecks. Our job would shift to setting the high-level policies and goals for the AI scheduler and letting it figure out the specifics.

NVIDIA Dynamo's distributed inference framework, for instance, coordinates request scheduling, KV cache placement, and data movement across GPUs and nodes. It integrates with Kubernetes for inference and disaggregation. In this case, Dynamo's scheduler would allocate microbatches to different pipeline stages and handle node failures by rerouting requests.

And with techniques like weight streaming and activation offloading, the model's layers can be streamed on demand from host memory to the GPU only when the weights are needed (e.g., during decode.) And this can happen across many nodes and GPUs. This allows hosting parts of a 100-trillion-parameter model on cheaper storage. This helps to seamlessly scale inference.

We could also see AI performance copilots for system operators. LLMs can become part of the infrastructure in a support role. For example, a performance engineer might have an AI assistant they can ask, "How can I speed up my training job?" and get informed suggestions. This sounds fanciful, but it's plausible when you consider such an assistant could be trained on the accumulated knowledge of thousands of past runs, logs, and tweaks.

The AI performance copilot might also recognize that your GPU memory usage is low and suggest increasing batch size, or notice that your gradient noise scale is high and suggest a learning rate schedule change. This agent would encapsulate some of the hard-won experience of human experts—making this knowledge available anytime.

Similarly, AI assistants could watch over training jobs and inference servers and flag anomalies. For instance, the assistant could be monitoring a training job and say, "Hey, the loss is diverging early in training; maybe check if your data input has an issue or reduce the learning rate," as shown in Figure 20-8.

Already, companies like Splunk (now Cisco) and PagerDuty are using AI models on system log data to predict failures and detect anomalies in data centers. It's recommended that you extend these concepts to use AI workload-specific telemetry.

In short, AI gives us an always-fresh pair of eyes for every running job and every inference server. It can monitor them, advise them, and adjust in real time. Traditional utilization metrics can be misleading. For instance, a GPU 100% busy on redundant data transfers isn't productive. These AI-driven schedulers instead aim to maximize goodput and make sure that when a GPU is busy, it's doing useful neural compute. This directly improves cost efficiency.

In an AI cluster, for instance, you can use a metrics pipeline based on Prometheus to feed an LLM-based assistant that alerts when GPU memory suddenly drops due to either a potential memory leak or data stall. It can even identify likely root causes. This is the kind of tedious work that AI can help automate and run 24/7 without interruption and distraction.

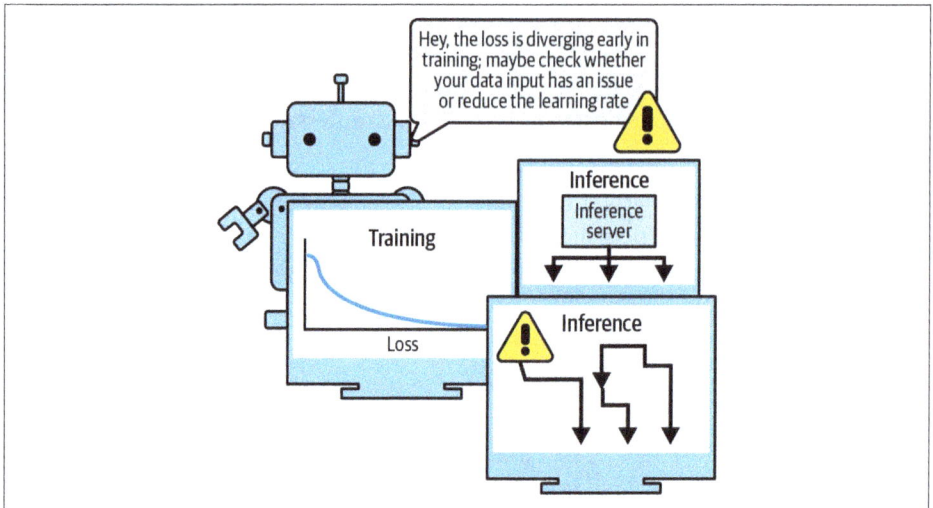

Figure 20-8. AI assistant monitoring a long-running training job and suggesting actions to fix an anomaly

Another powerful use of AI is in automated debugging and failure analysis for AI systems. When a training job fails halfway through its three-month run, a human has to read through error logs, device statistics, and perhaps even memory dumps to figure out what went wrong. Was it a hardware fault? A numerical overflow? A networking hiccup?

In the future, an AI system could digest all that data, including logs, metrics, and alerts, and pinpoint likely causes much faster than they do today. It could say, "Node 42 had 5 ECC memory errors right before the job crashed—likely an HBM memory device or channel issue on the GPU." Or, "The loss became NaN at iteration 10,000—perhaps an unstable gradient; consider gradient clipping."

By learning from many past incidents, the AI troubleshooter could save engineers many hours of detective work. Some large computing sites are already training models on their incident databases to predict failures and suggest fixes.

Taking things a step further, RL can be applied to real-time control of system behavior in ways that fixed algorithms cannot easily match. For example, a power-management RL agent could be trained to continuously tweak frequencies and core allocations to maximize performance per watt in a live system. This agent would learn the optimal policy by analyzing the system in real time.

Another example is actively managing memory in AI models. An AI agent could learn which tensors to keep in GPU memory and which to swap to CPU or NVMe—beyond static rules like "swap least recently used." By observing live access patterns, an AI can manage a cache more efficiently. This is especially effective when patterns are nonobvious or workload-dependent.

Already, state-of-the-art practitioners are using RL to optimize cache eviction, network congestion control, and more. The complexity of ultrascale systems—with hundreds of interacting components and resources—makes them prime candidates for such learning-based control. There are just too many tunable knobs for a human to stumble upon the best settings in a timely manner—and in a manner that adapts to different workloads in real time.

For the performance engineer, the rise of AI-assisted operational agents means the role will become more about orchestrating and supervising AI-driven processes rather than manually tweaking every single parameter. It's somewhat analogous to how pilots manage autopilot in a modern aircraft. They still need deep knowledge and oversight, but much of the millisecond-by-millisecond control is automated. The same with someone driving a Tesla in Full Self-Driving (FSD) mode. The driver still needs knowledge and intuition to avoid difficult situations and prevent accidents, but the vehicle's control is automated by the FSD software.

To guide the AI assistant to manage our cluster efficiently, we simply set the objectives, provide the safety and fairness guardrails, and handle novel situations that the AI hasn't seen before. Routine optimizations like load balancing, failure recovery, and memory-buffer tuning are handled by the AI. Embracing this paradigm will be important for the future.

Those who insist on optimizing everything by hand in such complex AI systems will simply be outpaced by those who embrace AI assistance and autotuning. Those that are AI-automation-friendly can focus their human effort on novel innovations, complex optimizations, and creative solutions. This is where humans can add the most value in this brave new AI world. Let the AI handle the rest.

Scaling Toward Multimillion GPU Clusters and 100-Trillion-Parameter Models

Finally, let's revisit our quest toward ultrascale, 100-trillion-parameter models. We've already broken the trillion-parameter threshold. Now the question is how to scale to tens or even hundreds of trillion-parameter models in the coming years. What does that kind of model demand from our systems, and what innovations are needed to make training such a powerful model feasible? This is where everything we've discussed comes together, including efficient hardware, smart software, and clever algorithms. Reaching 100-trillion-parameter models will require using every trick in the book—and then some tricks that may not have been discovered yet. Let's dive in!

On the hardware front, the obvious need is for more memory and more bandwidth—preferably right on the GPU. If you have 100 trillion parameters and you want to train them, you need to store and move an insane amount of data efficiently. The next generations of memory technology will be critical.

High-bandwidth memory (HBM) continues to evolve. HBM3e is used with the Blackwell generation of GPUs, while HBM4 is used in the Rubin generation of GPUs. HBM4 doubles bandwidth per stack again—on the order of 1.6 TB/s per stack. It will also increase capacity per stack to possibly 48 GB or 64 GB per module.

HBM's higher capacity and throughput mean that future GPUs could have, say, 8 or 16 stacks of HBM at 64 GB each, which totals 512 GB or 1,024 GB of superfast HBM RAM on a single board. That kind of local HBM capacity holds a lot of model parameters directly on each GPU—significantly reducing the need to swap data in and out.

It's not hard to see how this enables larger models, higher-bandwidth training runs, and lower-latency inference servers. What used to require sharding across 8 GPUs might fit in one. What required 100 GPUs might fit in 10, and so on.

In addition to multichip architectures like the Grace Blackwell Superchip, multiple racks of NVL72s each can be linked into one giant cluster to create hundreds of GPUs sharing a unified fast network. Essentially, your cluster behaves like a single mega-GPU from a communication standpoint. This is important for scaling to 100 trillion parameters because it means we can keep adding GPUs to get more total memory and compute—without hitting a communication bottleneck wall. This assumes that NVLink (or similar) continues to scale to those ultrascale sizes.

However, hardware alone won't solve the 100-trillion-parameter challenge. Software and algorithmic innovations are equally, if not more, important. Training a model of that size with naive data parallelism, for example, would be incredibly slow and expensive. Imagine the optimizers having to update 100 trillion weights every step! We will need to lean heavily on techniques that reduce the effective computation. One big area that we explored is low numerical precision. In addition to FP8 and FP4, future hardware might support even lower (1-bit) precision for some parts of the network. Hybrid schemes will likely be critical to use lower precision for most of the model but higher precision for sensitive parts.

As performance engineers, we should watch for these new capabilities and be ready to use them. To train 100-trillion-parameter models, you very likely need to use low precision for efficiency; otherwise, the workload would be prohibitively slow and expensive.

The good news is that hardware and libraries will make this transition relatively seamless. We're already seeing first-class support for low-precision arithmetic in CUDA through NVIDIA's Transformer Engine (TE) and Tensor Cores—as well as PyTorch and OpenAI's Triton, which fully leverage CUDA.

Another critical approach is sparsity and conditional computation. We already use sparse activation in models like sparse mixture of experts (MoE), where only a fraction of the model's parameters are active for a given input. This idea can be generalized so that you don't always use the full 100 trillion parameters every time. Instead, you use just the parts you need. Models using the MoE architecture are proving to be very capable and efficient. By the time 100-trillion-parameter models arrive, I expect a lot of them will need to be sparsely activated.

As performance engineers, the implication is that throughput will be about matrix multiplication speed as well as the efficiency of MoE conditional routing, caching of expert outputs, and communication patterns for sparse data exchange. This adds complexity but also opportunity. If you can ensure the right experts are on the right devices at the right time to minimize communication, you can drastically accelerate these massive models.

We should also consider algorithmic efficiency improvements. Optimizers that use less memory could be vital. The traditional Adam optimizer variants typically keep two extra copies of weights for momentum and variance estimates. This effectively triples memory usage. So if you have 100-trillion-parameter weights, you need an extra 200 trillion values to hold the optimizer states! Memory-efficient optimizers like Adafactor and Shampoo help to reduce this overhead.

Techniques like activation checkpointing help to trade compute for memory by recomputing activations instead of storing them. At a 100-trillion-parameter scale, you'd almost certainly be checkpointing aggressively. An even more radical idea is, perhaps, we don't update all weights on every step. Consider updating subsets of weights in a rotating fashion—similar to how one might not water every plant every day but rotate through them. If done wisely, the model still learns effectively but with less frequent updates per parameter. This reduces the total computational needs of the system.

These kinds of ideas blur into the algorithm design realm, but a performance-aware perspective is useful. We should ask, "Do we really need to do X this often or at this precision?" for every aspect of training and inference. Often the answer is that we can find a cheaper approximation that still works. At a 100-trillion-parameter scale, these approximations can save months of time or millions of dollars.

An often overlooked aspect of ultrascale training is infrastructure and networking. When you're talking about clusters of 10,000+ GPUs working on one model, the network fabric becomes as important as the GPUs themselves. Ethernet and InfiniBand technologies are advancing in terms of increased throughput and smarter adaptive routing techniques, etc. NVIDIA's Spectrum-X is an Ethernet-based fabric optimized for AI (e.g,. RoCE, adaptive routing, high bisection bandwidth) that reduces congestion in large-scale training and inference workloads.

Performance engineers will need to deeply understand these tiers and ensure that data is in the right place at the right time. The goal will be to simulate a huge memory space that spans GPUs and CPUs so that even if a model doesn't fit in one machine, it can be treated somewhat transparently by the programmer. Some of this is already possible today with Unified Memory and on-demand paging systems using `cudaMem PrefetchAsync()` to pre-stage pages on the target device and avoid page-fault stalls, for instance. But at a 100-trillion-parameter scale, this functionality will really be put to the test.

It's not surprising that frontier research labs like xAI, OpenAI, and Microsoft are building large clusters of 1,000,000+ GPUs. At a 100-trillion-parameter scale, you might have one job spanning an entire datacenter's worth of hardware. Performance engineers must think at datacenter and multidatacenter (global) scale.

Last, there's a socio-technical trend as models—and their required compute—scale up. It may become infeasible for any single team—or even single corporation—to train the biggest models alone. We (hopefully) will see more collaboration and sharing in the AI community to handle these enormous projects. This would be analogous to how big science projects—like particle physics experiments—involve many institutions. Initiatives similar to the now-dissolved Open Collective Foundation (*https://oreil.ly/dRq1g*), a nonprofit initiative, could help pool AI compute resources to train a 100-trillion-parameter model, which would then be shared with the world.

This will require standardizing things like checkpoint formats, codeveloping training code, and thinking about multiparty ownership of models. While this is not a performance issue per se, it will influence how we build large AI systems. We'll need to make them even more fault-tolerant and easily snapshot-able to share partial results. As an engineer, you might end up optimizing for pure speed, as well as reproducibility and interoperability. This allows different teams to work on different parts of the training and inference workflow smoothly and efficiently.

Reaching 100-trillion-parameter models will require holistic, full-stack innovations. There's no single solution to this challenge. Instead, every piece of the puzzle must improve. Hardware needs to be faster and hold more data. Software needs to self-optimize more—and use resources more efficiently through compilers, AI assistants, and real-time adaptation. Algorithms need to be clever about not avoiding unnecessary work through sparsity, lower precision, and better optimizers.

The role of the performance engineer will be to integrate all these advancements into a coherent workflow. It's like assembling a high-performance racing car. The engine, tires, aerodynamics, and driver skill all have to work in unison. If we do it right, what seems impossible now—e.g., 100 trillion parameters trained without breaking the bank—will become achievable.

It wasn't long ago that 1-trillion-parameter models sounded crazy. Yet today, this scale has been demonstrated by open-weight models like Moonshot AI's Kimi K2 (*https://oreil.ly/ZJbio*) (1-trillion-parameter MoE, 32 billion parameters active per token) and others. At this rate of progress, and with AI-assisted human ingenuity, we will conquer the next milestones and orders of magnitude in a very short amount of time.

Key Takeaways

The following points summarize the best practices and emerging trends discussed in this chapter's case studies and hypothetical future states of ultrascale AI systems performance engineering:

Codesigned hardware and software optimizations
Performance improvements in LLMs are truly achieved by breakthroughs coming from tightly integrated hardware/software codesign innovations.

AI-assisted coding and performance optimizations
Google DeepMind, NVIDIA, and Predibase have demonstrated AI-assisted discovery and optimization for core kernels such as matrix multiplication and attention. These efforts show that AI can generate, test, and refine low-level GPU code and produce significant speedups with very little human intervention.

Strategies for 100-trillion-parameter models
Training models with 100 trillion parameters will require a blend of aggressive quantization, multidimensional parallelism (data, pipeline, tensor, expert, and context/sequence), and careful orchestration of inter-rack communication. This stresses that future AI scaling depends on both hardware capabilities and the ingenuity of software-level scheduling.

Exponential compute infrastructure scaling
Next-generation AI data centers are being designed to provide orders-of-magnitude increases in computational capacity. These facilities will train AI models with compute budgets far beyond today's levels. This enables training runs that use 100 to 1,000 times the FLOPS used in current systems.

Evolving AI models and agents
Future models will be self-improving systems capable of generating and optimizing code, continuously updating their weights with fresh data, and even rewriting their own code. This perpetual cycle of learning and refinement will reduce the time between breakthroughs and create a virtual workforce that outperforms human teams in research and R&D tasks.

AI-assisted real-time troubleshooting
In addition to scheduling, AI copilots will monitor system logs and training/inference workloads to detect anomalies quickly—including spikes in accuracy

loss or number of hardware errors. These copilots can help automate debugging, perform failure analysis, and even learn optimal configurations through reinforcement learning. These help to maximize performance per watt and per unit time.

Performance-per-watt, a critical metric

All of these codesign efforts ultimately aim to maximize throughput per unit cost. Specifically, the goal is to process and generate more tokens per second per dollar per watt of power. For example, the Grace Blackwell NVL72 rack system dramatically improves performance-per-watt 25× (*https://oreil.ly/VUjna*) over the prior Hopper generation. This directly translates to lower cost per token than previous-generation GPU clusters.

Conclusion

This book marks a turning point for the field of AI systems performance engineering. NVIDIA's tight integration of CPU and GPU into superchip modules like Grace Hopper and Grace Blackwell (and upcoming Vera Rubin and Feynman) has achieved new levels of compute efficiency and scale. Under the hood, the GPUs use highly optimized Tensor Cores—as well as a transformer engine optimized for LLM computation fundamentals.

Supercomputing systems like the NVIDIA GB200/GB300 NVL72, which links 72 GPUs into a single processing unit (NVLink domain), set the rack and data center communication foundation using technologies like NVLink, NVSwitch, and SHARP. These provide low-latency, real-time inference for multitrillion-parameter models.

On the software side, tools like vLLM, SGLang, NVIDIA Dynamo, and TensorRT-LLM improve scheduling and resource usage across large inference clusters. This includes techniques like in-flight batching, paged KV cache, and (separating the prompt prefill stage from the generation decode stage onto different resource pools for efficiency.) These help to reduce tail latency and improve throughput per watt.

These examples prove the power of codesign, in which hardware, software, and algorithms evolve together. This partnership rooted in mechanical sympathy helps to reduce training times, improve inference performance, and lower operational expenses. This is needed to produce measurable returns on investment for today's fast-improving and capital-intensive AI systems.

Additionally, AI-driven coding and algorithm agents from Google DeepMind, NVIDIA, and Predibase show how AI can help optimize AI. As models and systems become too complex for manual tuning, automation can handle routine optimizations and free human engineers to focus on higher-level optimizations and system designs.

We're shifting from brute-force scaling to smart scaling: doing more useful work per cycle, squeezing every ounce of performance from new hardware features, and letting AI assistants manage the details. Performance engineers will move up the stack, becoming architects of global compute ecosystems that balance efficiency, reliability, and sustainability.

Our role as an AI systems performance engineer will expand beyond single-node kernels to system-wide and facility-wide optimization. We'll rely on our intuition to spot bottlenecks—like a slow all-reduce pattern—and then guide our AI tools to fix them. Meanwhile, we'll keep learning, since the pace of hardware and algorithmic innovation will only accelerate.

In conclusion, to stay relevant and competitive, you should build a strong foundation in AI systems performance fundamentals, stay curious, experiment with new hardware and software advancements, trust AI recommendations, and be ready to adapt as the landscape changes into quantum and beyond. And just think—in an era of democratized research, one-click-accessible AI supercomputers, and accessible multitrillion-parameter models, you could be one of the enablers of the next big superintelligence breakthrough!

AI Systems Performance Checklist (175+ Items)

This extensive checklist covers both broad process-level best practices and detailed, low-level tuning advice for AI systems performance engineers. Each of these checklist items serves as a practical reminder to squeeze maximum performance and efficiency out of AI systems.

Use this guide when debugging, profiling, analyzing, and tuning one's AI systems. By systematically applying these tips—from low-level OS and CUDA tweaks up to cluster-scale optimizations—an AI systems performance engineer can achieve both lightning-fast execution and cost-effective operation on modern NVIDIA GPU hardware using many AI software frameworks, including CUDA, PyTorch, OpenAI's Triton, TensorFlow, Keras, and JAX. The principles in this checklist will also apply to future generations of NVIDIA hardware, including their GPUs, ARM-based CPUs, CPU-GPU superchips, networking gear, and rack systems.

Performance Tuning and Cost Optimization Mindset

A pragmatic, documented loop—quick wins before deep work—turns engineering time into measurable ROI. Start by targeting the biggest runtime and cost drivers, and always profile before and after to verify impact.

Combine auto-tuning, framework upgrades, cloud pricing levers, and utilization dashboards for high-ROI wins, documenting results and favoring simple, maintainable fixes. Tune throughput-sensitive hyperparameters when accuracy allows. Here are some tips on the performance tuning and cost optimization mindset:

Optimize the expensive first

Use the 80/20 rule. Find the top contributors to runtime and focus on those. If 90% of the time is in a couple of kernels or a communication phase, it's better to optimize those deeply than to microoptimize something taking 1% of the time. Each chapter's techniques should be applied where they matter most. For example, if your training is 40% data loading, 50% GPU compute, and 10% communication, then first fix data loading, as you can maybe halve the overhead. Then look at GPU kernel optimization.

Profile before and after

Whenever you apply an optimization, measure its impact. This sounds obvious, but often tweaks are made based on theory and might not help—or even hurt—in practice. Consider a scenario where your workload is not memory-limited, but you decide to try enabling activation checkpointing for your training job. This may actually slow down the job by using extra compute to reduce memory. In other words, always compare key metrics like throughput, latency, and utilization before and after making changes. Use the built-in profilers for simple timing, such as average iteration time over 100 iterations.

Embrace adaptive autotuning feedback loops

Implement advanced autotuning frameworks that leverage real-time performance feedback—using techniques like reinforcement learning or Bayesian optimization—to dynamically adjust system parameters. This approach enables your system to continuously fine-tune settings in response to changing workloads and operating conditions.

Budget for optimization time

Performance engineering is an iterative investment. There are diminishing returns—pick the low-hanging fruit like enabling AMP and data prefetch. These might give 2× easily. Harder optimizations like writing custom kernels might give smaller increments. Always weigh the engineering time versus the gain in runtime and cost saved. For large recurring jobs like training a flagship model, even a 5% gain can justify weeks of tuning since it saves maybe millions. For one-off or small workloads, focus on bigger wins and be pragmatic.

Stay updated on framework improvements

Many optimizations we discussed, such as mixed precision, fused kernels, and distributed algorithms, continue to be improved in deep learning frameworks and libraries. Upgrading to the latest PyTorch or TensorFlow can sometimes yield immediate speedups as they incorporate new fused ops or better heuristics. Leverage these improvements, as they are essentially free gains. Read release notes for performance-related changes.

Codesign collaboratively with vendors and community members

Stay connected with hardware vendors and the broader performance engineering community to align software optimizations with the latest hardware architectures. This codesign approach can reveal significant opportunities for performance gains by tailoring algorithms to leverage emerging hardware capabilities. Regularly review vendor documentation, participate in forums, and test beta releases of drivers or frameworks. These interactions often reveal new optimization opportunities and best practices that can be integrated into your systems. Integrating new driver optimizations, library updates, and hardware-specific tips can provide additional, sometimes significant, performance gains.

Leverage cloud flexibility for cost

If running in cloud environments, use cheaper spot instances or reserved instances wisely. They can drastically cut costs, but you may lose the spot instances with a few minutes' notice. Also consider instance types, as sometimes a slightly older GPU instance at a fraction of the cost can deliver better price/performance if your workload doesn't need the absolute latest. Our discussions on H800 versus H100 showed it's possible to do great work on second-best hardware with effort. In the cloud, you can get similar trade-offs. Evaluate cost/performance by benchmarking on different instance configurations, including number of CPUs, CPU memory, number of GPUs, GPU memory, L1/L2 caches, unified memory, NVLink/NVSwitch interconnects, network bandwidth and latency, and local disk configuration. Calculate metrics like throughput per dollar to guide your optimization decisions.

Monitor utilization metrics

Continuously monitor GPU utilization, SM efficiency, memory bandwidth usage, and, for multinode, network utilization. Set up dashboards using DCGM exporter, Prometheus, etc., so you can catch when any resource is underused. If GPUs are at 50% utilization, dig into why. It's likely data waiting/stalling and slow synchronization communication. If the network is only 10% utilized but the GPU waits on data, maybe something else like a lock is the issue. These metrics help pinpoint which subsystem to focus on.

Iterate and tune hyperparameters for throughput

Some model hyperparameters, such as batch size, sequence length, and number of MoE active experts, can be tuned for throughput without degrading final accuracy. For example, larger batch sizes give better throughput but might require tuning the learning rate schedule to maintain accuracy. Don't be afraid to adjust these to find a sweet spot of speed and accuracy. This is part of performance engineering too—sometimes the model or training procedure can be adjusted for efficiency, like using activation checkpointing or more steps of compute for the same effective batch. You might tweak the training learning rate schedule to compensate for this scenario.

Document and reuse

Keep notes of what optimizations you applied and their impact. Document in code or in an internal wiki-like shared knowledge-base system. This builds a knowledge base for future projects. Many tips are reusable patterns, like enabling overlapping and particular environment variables that help on a cluster. Having this history can save time when starting a new endeavor or when onboarding new team members into performance tuning efforts.

Balance optimizations with complexity

Aim for the simplest solution that achieves needed performance. For example, if native PyTorch with `torch.compile` meets your speed target, you might not need to write custom CUDA kernels. This will help avoid extra maintenance. Over-optimizing with highly custom code can make the system brittle. There is elegance in a solution that is both fast and maintainable. Thus, apply the least-intrusive optimization that yields the required gain, and escalate to more involved ones only as needed.

Optimize AI-driven performance

Leverage machine learning models to analyze historical telemetry data and predict system bottlenecks, enabling automated adjustments of parameters in real time to optimize resource allocation and throughput.

Reproducibility and Documentation Best Practices

Performance wins don't stick unless they're reproducible, versioned, and continuously checked, or they'll regress quietly over time. Treat docs, CI benchmarks, and shared knowledge as the glue that preserves speedups and accelerates onboarding and audits.

Lock down versions, configs, and benchmarks in source control so experiments are repeatable and regressions traceable. Bring performance checks into CI/CD, instrument end-to-end monitoring and alerts, and pair optimization with security and thorough documentation to create a durable, auditable practice. The following is a list of tips to improve reproducibility and documentation:

Rigorous version control

Maintain comprehensive version control for all system configurations, framework/driver versions, OS settings, optimization scripts, and benchmarks. Use Git (or a similar system) to track changes and tag releases. This way, experiments can be reproduced exactly—and performance regressions can be easily identified.

Continuous integration for performance regression

Integrate automated performance benchmarks and real-time monitoring into your CI/CD pipelines. This ensures that each change—from code updates to configuration changes—is validated against a set of performance metrics, helping catch regressions early and maintaining consistent and measurable performance gains. Adopt industry-standard benchmarks, such as MLPerf, to establish a reliable performance baseline and track improvements over time.

End-to-end workflow optimization

Ensure that optimizations are applied holistically across the entire AI pipeline—from data ingestion and preprocessing through training and inference deployment. Coordinated, cross-system tuning can reveal synergies that isolated adjustments might miss, resulting in more significant overall performance gains.

Automated monitoring and diagnostics

Deploy end-to-end monitoring solutions that collect real-time metrics across hardware, network, and application layers. Integrate these with dashboards, such as Prometheus/Grafana, and configure automated alerts to promptly detect anomalies, such as sudden drops in GPU utilization or spikes in network latency.

Fault tolerance and automated recovery

Incorporate fault tolerance into your system design by using distributed checkpointing, redundant hardware configurations, and dynamic job rescheduling. This strategy minimizes downtime and maintains performance even in the face of hardware or network failures.

Compiler and build optimizations

Leverage aggressive compiler flags and profile-guided optimizations during the build process to extract maximum performance from your code. Regularly update and tune your build configurations, and verify the impact of each change through rigorous benchmarking to ensure optimal execution.

Security, compliance, and performance

Integrate and codesign security, compliance, and performance. Regularly audit configurations, enforce access controls, and maintain industry-standard safeguards, including encryption, secure data channels, zero-trust networking, hardware security modules (HSMs), and secure enclaves. And make sure that performance tuning never compromises system security. Similarly, make sure security doesn't incur unnecessary performance overhead.

Comprehensive documentation and knowledge sharing
Maintain detailed records of all optimization steps, system configurations, and performance benchmarks. Develop an internal knowledge base to facilitate team collaboration and rapid onboarding, ensuring that best practices are preserved and reused across projects.

Future-proofing and scalability planning
Design modular, adaptable system architectures that can easily incorporate emerging hardware and software technologies. Continuously evaluate scalability requirements and update your optimization strategies to sustain competitive performance as your workload grows.

System Architecture and Hardware Planning

Your hardware, interconnects, and data paths set the ceiling for performance and cost-efficiency—no software tweak can outrun a starved GPU. Plan for goodput per dollar/watt by matching accelerators, CPU/DRAM/I/O, and cooling/power to the workload to avoid bottlenecks from the start.

Specifically, design for goodput—useful work per dollar/watt—and not just raw FLOPS. Match accelerators and interconnects to workload, right-size CPU/memory/I/O to keep GPUs fed, keep data local, and plan power/cooling so hardware sustains peak clocks. Evaluate scaling efficiency before adding more GPUs. Here are some tips for optimizing system architecture and improving hardware planning efficiency:

Design for goodput and efficiency
Treat useful throughput as the goal. Every bit of performance gained translates to massive cost savings at scale. Focus on maximizing productive work per dollar/watt—and not just raw FLOPS.

Choose the right accelerator
Prefer modern GPUs for superior performance-per-watt and memory capacity. Newer architectures offer features like native FP8 and FP4 precision support—along with much faster interconnects. These produce big speedups over older-generation GPUs and systems.

Leverage high-bandwidth interconnects
Use systems with NVLink/NVSwitch, such as GB200/GB300 NVL72, instead of PCIe-only connectivity for multi-GPU workloads. NVLink 5 provides up to 1.8 TB/s bidirectional GPU-to-GPU bandwidth (over 14× PCIe Gen5), enabling near-linear scaling across GPUs. NVLink Switch domains can be scaled with second-level switches to connect up to 576 GPUs in one NVLink domain. This

enables hierarchical collectives that stay on NVLink as long as possible before falling back to the inter-rack fabric.

Balance CPU/GPU and memory ratios
Provision enough CPU cores, DRAM, and storage throughput per GPU. For example, allocate ~1 fast CPU core per GPU for data loading and networking tasks. Ensure system RAM and I/O can feed GPUs at required rates on the order of hundreds of MB/s per GPU to avoid starvation.

Plan for data locality
If training across multiple nodes, minimize off-node communication. Whenever possible, keep tightly coupled workloads on the same NVLink/NVSwitch domain to exploit full bandwidth, and use the highest-speed interconnect that you have access to. Ideally, this is NVLink for intranode and intra-rack communication and InfiniBand for inter-rack communication.

Avoid bottlenecks in the chain
Identify the slowest link—be it CPU, memory, disk, or network—and scale it up. For instance, if GPU utilization is low due to I/O, invest in faster storage or caching rather than more GPUs. An end-to-end design where all components are well-matched prevents wasted GPU cycles.

Choose an appropriate cluster size
Beware of diminishing returns when adding GPUs. Past a certain cluster size, overheads can grow—ensure the speedup justifies the cost. It's often better to optimize utilization on N GPUs by reaching 95% usage, for example, before scaling to $2N$ GPUs.

Design for cooling and power
Ensure the data center can handle GPU thermal and power needs. High-performance systems like GB200/GB300 have very high TDP. Provide adequate cooling (likely liquid-based) and power provisioning so the GPUs can sustain boost clocks without throttling.

Unified CPU-GPU "Superchip" Architecture

Unified memory and on-package links let you fit larger models and cut copy overhead when you place the right data in the right tier. Using Grace for preprocessing and HBM for "hot" tensors turns the superchip into a tightly coupled engine with fewer stalls.

On Grace Blackwell Superchips, treat CPU and GPU as a shared-memory complex. Keep hot weights/activations in HBM and overflow or infrequent data in Grace LPDDR via NVLink-C2C. Use the on-package Grace CPU for preprocessing/

orchestration and prefetch or pipeline-managed memory to hide latency for ultra-large models. Take advantage of the superchip architecture as follows:

Utilize unified CPU-GPU memory

Exploit the Grace Blackwell (GB200/GB300) Superchip's unified memory space. Two Blackwell GPUs and a 72-core Grace CPU share a coherent memory pool with NVLink-C2C (900 GB/s). Use the CPU's large memory (e.g., 480 GB LPDDR5X) as an extension for oversize models while keeping "hot" data in the GPUs' HBM for speed.

Place data for locality

Even with unified memory, prioritize data placement. Put model weights, activations, and other frequently accessed data on GPU HBM3e (which has much higher local bandwidth), and let infrequently used or overflow data reside in CPU RAM. This ensures the 900 GB/s NVLink-C2C link isn't a bottleneck for critical data.

Take advantage of CPU-GPU direct memory access when available

Use the GPU's ability to directly access CPU memory on combined CPU-GPU superchips like the GB200 and GB300. GPUs can read and write Grace LPDDR memory coherently over NVLink-C2C without staging over host PCIe. Bandwidth and latency are still lower than HBM, so prefetch managed pointers, stage data, and pipeline transfers to hide latency. As such, it's recommended to keep hot activations and KV cache in HBM and use CPU memory as a lower-tier cache with explicit prefetch.

Use the Grace CPU effectively

The on-package Grace CPU provides 72 high-performance cores—utilize them! Offload data preprocessing, augmentation, and other CPU-friendly tasks to these cores. They can feed the GPUs quickly using NVLink-C2C, essentially acting as an extremely fast I/O and compute companion for the GPU.

Plan for ultralarge models

For trillion-parameter model training that exceeds GPU memory, GB200/GB300 systems allow you to train using CPU memory as part of the model's memory pool. Prefer framework caching allocators and use `cudaMallocAsync` in custom code to minimize fragmentation and enable graph capture. Use CUDA Unified Memory or managed memory APIs to handle overflow gracefully, and consider explicit prefetching (e.g., `cudaMemPrefetchAsync`) of upcoming layers from CPU → GPU memory to hide latency.

Consider superchip-optimized algorithms

SuperOffload is an example of a superchip-optimized set of algorithms focused on improving efficiency of offload and tensor cast/copy strategies. Innovations include speculation-then-validation (STV), heterogeneous optimizer computation, and an

ARM-based CPU optimizer. Designed specifically for NVIDIA superchips (e.g., Grace Hopper, Grace Blackwell, Vera Rubin), SuperOffload increases token-processing throughput and chip utilization relative to traditional offload strategies.

Multi-GPU Scaling and Interconnect Optimizations

Scaling pays only when communication is fast and topology-aware—otherwise added GPUs just wait on one another. Lean on NVLink/NVSwitch bandwidth, modern collectives, and fabric-aware placement to approach linear speedups.

Specifically, exploit NVLink/NVSwitch domains (e.g., NVL72) for near-linear scaling, and choose parallelism strategies that fit the fabric. Use topology-aware placement, updated NCCL collectives (e.g., PAT), and telemetry to verify you're using the ~1.8 TB/s bidirectional throughput per-GPU bandwidth effectively. Plan hierarchical communications as you expand. The following are tips on utilizing multi-GPU scaling through interconnect and topology optimizations:

Design for high-speed all-to-all topology
On NVL72 NVSwitch clusters with 72 fully interconnected GPUs, for example, any GPU can communicate with any other at full NVLink 5 speed. At the fabric level, the NVLink Switch domain is nonblocking. Application-level throughput can vary with concurrent traffic and path scheduling, so verify behavior using DCGM NVLink counters and Nsight Systems traces before assuming per-pair saturation. Take advantage of this topology by using parallelization strategies, such as data parallel, tensor parallel, and pipeline parallelism, that would be bottlenecked on lesser interconnects.

Utilize topology-aware scheduling
Always colocate multi-GPU jobs within an NVLink Switch domain if possible. Keeping all GPUs of a job on the NVL72 fabric means near-linear scaling for communication-heavy workloads. Mixing GPUs across NVLink domains or standard networks will introduce bottlenecks and should be avoided for tightly coupled tasks.

Leverage unprecedented bandwidth
Recognize that NVLink 5 has 900 GB/s per GPU in each direction, which doubles the per-GPU bandwidth versus the previous generation. An NVL72 rack provides ~130 TB/s total intra-rack bandwidth in aggregate. This drastically reduces communication wait times, as even tens of gigabytes of gradient data can be all-reduced in a few milliseconds at 1.8 TB/s. Design training algorithms, such as gradient synchronization and parameter sharding, to fully exploit this relatively free communication budget.

Embrace modern collective algorithms

Use the latest NVIDIA NCCL library optimized for NVSwitch. Specifically, enable the parallel aggregated tree (PAT) algorithm (*https://oreil.ly/eEYKo*), which was introduced for NVLink Switch topologies. This further reduces synchronization time by taking advantage of the NVL72 topology to perform reductions more efficiently than other tree/ring algorithms.

Consider fine-grained parallelism

With full-bandwidth all-to-all connectivity, consider fine-grained model parallelism that wasn't feasible before. For example, layer-wise parallelism or tensor parallelism across many GPUs can be efficient when each GPU has 1.8 TB/s bidirectional throughput to every other. Previously, one might avoid excessive cross-GPU communication, but NVL72 allows aggressive partitioning of work without hitting network limits.

Monitor for saturation

Although NVL72 is extremely fast, keep an eye on link utilization in profiling. If your application somehow saturates the NVSwitch using extreme all-to-all operations, for example, you might need to throttle communication by aggregating gradients, etc. Use NVIDIA's tools or NVSwitch telemetry to verify that communications are within the NVLink capacity, and adjust patterns if needed. For instance, you can stagger all-to-all exchanges to avoid network contention. DCGM exposes NVLink counters that can help verify link balance and detect hotspots during collectives.

Plan for future expansion

Be aware that NVLink Switch can scale beyond a single rack—up to 576 GPUs in one connected domain using second-level switches. If you operate at that ultrascale, plan hierarchical communication using local NVL72 inter-rack collectives first, then use inter-rack interconnects only when necessary. This helps to maximize intra-rack NVLink usage first. This ensures you're using the fastest links before resorting to inter-rack InfiniBand hops.

Identify opportunities for federated and distributed optimizations

For deployments that span heterogeneous environments, such as multicloud or edge-to-cloud setups, adopt adaptive communication protocols and dynamic load balancing strategies. This minimizes latency and maximizes throughput across distributed systems, which ensures robust performance even when resources vary in capability and capacity.

Operating System and Driver Optimizations

OS jitter, NUMA misses, and driver mismatches quietly drain throughput and create variability you can't tune around. Hardening the stack (huge pages, affinities, consistent CUDA/driver, persistence) creates a stable, high-performance baseline.

Run a lean, HPC-tuned Linux. Set NUMA/IRQ affinities and enable THP and high memlock. Keep NVIDIA drivers/CUDA consistent across nodes. Isolate system jitter, tune CPU libraries/storage, set container limits correctly, and keep BIOS/firmware/NVSwitch fabric up to date for predictable throughput. Here are some host, OS, and container optimizations that you should explore in your environment:

Use a Linux kernel tuned for HPC
Ensure your GPU servers run a recent, stable Linux kernel configured for high-performance computing. Disable unnecessary background services that consume CPU or I/O. Use the "performance" CPU governor—versus "on-demand" or "power-save"—to keep CPU cores at a high clock for feeding GPUs.

Disable swap for performance-critical workloads
Disable swap on training servers to avoid page thrashing, or, if swap must remain enabled, lock critical buffers using `mlock` or `cudaHostAlloc` to ensure they stay in RAM.

Avoid memory fragmentation with aggressive preallocation
Preallocate large, contiguous blocks of memory for frequently used tensors to reduce runtime allocation overhead and fragmentation. This proactive strategy ensures more stable and efficient memory management during long training runs.

Optimize environment variables for CPU libraries
Fine-tune parameters, such as `OMP_NUM_THREADS` and `MKL_NUM_THREADS`, to better match your hardware configuration. Adjusting these variables can reduce thread contention and improve the parallel efficiency of CPU-bound operations.

Design for NUMA awareness
For multi-NUMA servers, pin GPU processes/threads to the CPU of the local NUMA node. Use tools like `numactl` or taskset to bind each training process to the CPU nearest its assigned GPU. Similarly, bind memory allocations to the local NUMA node (`numactl --membind`) so host memory for GPU DMA comes from the closest RAM. This avoids costly cross-NUMA memory traffic that can halve effective PCIe/NVLink bandwidth.

Utilize IRQ affinity for network and GPU tasks

Explicitly bind NIC interrupts to CPU cores on the same NUMA node as the NIC, and similarly pin GPU driver threads to dedicated cores—including those from long-running services like the `nvidia-persistence` service daemon. This strategy minimizes cross-NUMA traffic and stabilizes performance under heavy loads.

Enable transparent hugepages

Turn on transparent hugepages (THP) in always or `madvise` mode so that large memory allocations use 2 MB pages. This reduces TLB thrashing and kernel overhead when allocating tens or hundreds of GBs of host memory for frameworks. Verify THP is active by checking for `/sys/kernel/mm/transparent_huge page/enabled`. With THP enabled, your processes are using hugepages for big allocations. Prefer THP in `madvise` mode if your workload is latency-critical and you observe jitter.

Increase max locked memory

Configure the OS to allow large pinned (aka page-locked) allocations. GPU apps often pin memory for faster transfers—set `ulimit -l unlimited` or a high value so your data loaders can allocate pinned buffers without hitting OS limits. This prevents failures or fallbacks to pageable memory, which would slow down GPU DMA.

Use the latest NVIDIA driver and CUDA stack

Keep NVIDIA drivers and CUDA runtime up-to-date (within a tested stable version) on all nodes. New drivers can bring performance improvements and are required for new GPUs' compute capabilities. Make sure all nodes have the same driver/CUDA versions to avoid any mismatches in multinode jobs. Enable persistence mode on GPUs at boot (`nvidia-smi -pm 1`) so the driver stays loaded and GPUs don't incur re-init delays. Update the NVIDIA driver and toolkit on all nodes to inherit bug fixes and performance improvements.

Enable GPU persistence when using a MIG configuration

With persistence mode enabled, the GPU remains "warm" and ready to use, reducing startup latency for jobs. This is especially crucial if using a Multi-Instance GPU (MIG) partitioning—without persistence, MIG configurations would reset on every job, but keeping the driver active preserves the slices. Always configure persistence mode when using MIG.

Isolate system tasks

Dedicate a core—or small subset of cores—on each server for OS housekeeping, such as interrupt handling and background daemons. This way, your main CPU threads feeding the GPU are not interrupted. This can be done using CPU isolation or cgroup pinning. Eliminating OS jitter ensures consistent throughput.

Optimize system I/O settings

If your workload does a lot of logging or checkpointing, mount filesystems with options that favor throughput. Consider using `noatime` for data disks and increase filesystem read-ahead for streaming reads. Ensure the disk scheduler is set appropriately to use `mq-deadline` or `noop` for NVMe SSDs to reduce latency variability.

Perform regular maintenance

Keep BIOS/firmware updated for performance fixes. Some BIOS updates improve PCIe bandwidth or fix input–output memory management unit (IOMMU) issues for GPUs. Also, periodically check for firmware updates for NICs and NVSwitch/Fabric if applicable, as provided by NVIDIA, such as Fabric Manager upgrades, etc. Minor firmware tweaks can sometimes resolve obscure bottlenecks or reliability issues.

Tune Docker and Kubernetes configurations for maximum performance

When running in containers, add options, such as `--ipc=host` for shared memory, and set `--ulimit memlock=-1` to prevent memory locking issues. This guarantees that your containerized processes access memory without OS-imposed restrictions.

GPU Resource Management and Scheduling

Smarter placement and partitioning raise utilization without buying new hardware— and protect predictability for mixed workloads. Respect topology, use MPS/MIG where appropriate, and control clocks/power to minimize contention and tail latency.

Schedule with GPU/NUMA/NVLink topology in mind, and use MPS or MIG to raise utilization for smaller jobs while retaining ECC and persistence for reliability. Lock clocks or power limit for stability when needed, avoid CPU oversubscription, and pack jobs intelligently to maximize ROI without contention. Here are some GPU resource management and scheduling tips:

Topology-aware job scheduling

Ensure that orchestrators like Kubernetes and SLURM are scheduling containers on nodes that respect NUMA and NVLink boundaries to minimize cross-NUMA and cross-NVLink-domain memory accesses. This alignment reduces latency and improves overall throughput.

Multi-Process Service (MPS)

Enable NVIDIA MPS when running multiple processes on a single GPU to improve utilization. MPS allows kernels from different processes to execute concurrently on the GPU instead of time-slicing. This is useful if individual jobs don't fully saturate the GPU—for example, running 4 training tasks on one GPU with MPS can overlap their work and boost overall throughput.

Multi-Instance GPU (MIG)

Use MIG to partition high-end GPUs into smaller instances for multiple jobs. If you have many light workloads like inferencing small models or running many experiments, you can slice a GPU to ensure guaranteed resources for each job. For instance, modern GPUs can be split into multiple MIG slices (up to 7). Do not use MIG for tightly coupled parallel jobs, as those benefit from full GPU access. Deploy MIG for isolation and maximizing GPU ROI when jobs are smaller than a full GPU.

Persistence for MIG

Keep persistence mode on to maintain MIG partitions between jobs. This avoids repartitioning overhead and ensures subsequent jobs see the expected GPU slices without delay. Configure MIG at cluster boot and leave it enabled so that scheduling is predictable, as changing MIG config on the fly requires resetting the GPU, which can disrupt running jobs. Plan for maintenance windows as MIG device partitions are not persisted by the GPU across reboot. Use NVIDIA's MIG Manager to automatically recreate the desired layout on boot.

GPU clock and power settings

Consider locking GPU clocks to a fixed high frequency with `nvidia-smi -lgc/ -lmc` if you need run-to-run consistency. By default, GPUs use auto boost, which is usually optimal, but fixed clocks can avoid any transient downclocking. In power-constrained scenarios, you might slightly underclock or set a power limit to keep GPUs in a stable thermal/power envelope—this can yield consistent performance if occasional throttling was an issue.

ECC memory

Keep ECC enabled on data center GPUs for reliability unless you have a specific reason to disable it. The performance cost is minimal—on the order of a few percent loss in bandwidth and memory—but ECC catches memory errors that could otherwise corrupt a long training job. Most server GPUs ship with ECC on by default. Leave it on to safeguard multiweek training.

Job scheduler awareness

Integrate GPU topology into your job scheduler, such as SLURM and Kubernetes. Configure the scheduler to allocate jobs on the same node or same NVSwitch group when low-latency coupling is needed. Use Kubernetes device plugins or SLURM Gres to schedule MIG slices for smaller jobs. A GPU-aware scheduler prevents scenarios like a single job spanning distant GPUs and suffering bandwidth issues.

CPU oversubscription

When scheduling jobs, account for the CPU needs of each GPU task, such as data loading threads, etc. Don't pack more GPU jobs on a node than the CPUs can handle. It's better to leave a GPU idle than to overload the CPU such that all GPUs become underfed. Monitor CPU utilization per GPU job to inform scheduling decisions.

Use NVIDIA Fabric Manager for NVSwitch

On systems with NVSwitch, the GB200/GB300 NVL72 racks ensure NVIDIA Fabric Manager is running. It manages the NVSwitch topology and routing. Without it, multi-GPU communication might not be fully optimized or could even fail for large jobs. The Fabric Manager service typically runs by default on NVSwitch-equipped servers, but you should double-check that it's enabled and running—especially after driver updates.

Job packing for utilization

Maximize utilization by intelligently packing jobs. For example, on a 4-GPU node, if you have two 2-GPU jobs that don't use much CPU, running them together on the same node can save resources and even use the faster NVLink for communication if running together inside the same compute node or NVLink-enabled rack. Conversely, avoid colocating jobs that collectively exceed the memory or I/O capacity of the node. The goal is high hardware utilization without contention.

I/O Optimization

If data can't keep up, GPUs idle—often the largest, cheapest speedups come from fixing input, not math. Parallelism, pinned memory, async transfers, and fast storage ensure the model is continuously fed.

Keep the GPUs fed by parallelizing data loaders, using pinned memory and async transfers, and storing data on fast NVMe—preferably with GPUDirect Storage. Stripe, cache, and compress wisely. Measure end-to-end throughput so I/O scales with cluster size, and write checkpoints/logs asynchronously. Here are some tips on I/O optimizations for your data pipeline:

Load data in parallel

Use multiple workers/threads to load and preprocess data for the GPUs. The default of one to two data loader workers may be insufficient. Profile and increase the number of data loader processes/threads using PyTorch `Data Loader(num_workers=N)`, for example, until the data input is no longer the bottleneck. High core-count CPUs exist to feed those GPUs, so make sure you utilize them.

Pin host memory for I/O

Enable pinned (aka page-locked) memory for data transfer buffers. Many frameworks have an option like PyTorch's `pin_memory=True` for its DataLoader to allocate host memory that the GPU can DMA from directly. Using pinned memory significantly improves H2D copy throughput. Combine this with asynchronous transfers to overlap data loading with computation.

Overlap compute and data transfers

Pipeline your input data. While the GPU is busy computing on batch N, load and prepare batch N+1 on the CPU and transfer it in the background using CUDA streams and nonblocking `cudaMemcpyAsync`. This double buffering hides latency—the GPU ideally never waits for data. Ensure your training loop uses asynchronous transfers. For example, in PyTorch, you can copy tensors to GPU with `non_blocking=True`. Asynchronous transfer allows the CPU to continue running while the data transfer is in progress in the background. This will improve performance by overlapping computation with data transfer.

Use fast storage (NVMe/SSD)

Store training data on fast local NVMe SSDs or a high-performance parallel filesystem. Spinning disks will severely limit throughput. If available, enable GPU-Direct Storage (GDS) so that GPUs can stream data directly from NVMe or network storage—bypassing the CPU. This further reduces I/O latency and CPU load when reading large datasets. For large datasets, consider each node having a local copy or shard of the data. If using network storage, prefer a distributed filesystem like Lustre with striping or an object store that can serve many clients in parallel.

Tune I/O concurrency and striping

Avoid bottlenecks from single-file access. If one large file is used by all workers, stripe it across multiple storage targets or split it into chunks so multiple servers can serve it. For instance, break datasets into multiple files and have each data loader worker read different files simultaneously. This maximizes aggregate bandwidth from the storage system.

Optimize small files access

If your dataset consists of millions of small files, mitigate metadata overhead. Opening too many small files per second can overwhelm the filesystem's metadata server. Solutions pack small files into larger containers, such as `tar` or `RecordIO` files; use data ingestion libraries that batch reads; or ensure metadata caching is enabled on clients. This reduces per-file overhead and speeds up epoch start times.

Use client-side caching when available

Take advantage of any caching layer. If using NFS, increase the client cache size and duration. For distributed filesystems, consider a caching daemon or even manually caching part of the dataset on a local disk. The goal is to avoid repeatedly reading the same data from a slow source. If each node processes the same files at different times, a local cache can drastically cut redundant I/O.

Compress data wisely

Store the dataset compressed if I/O is the bottleneck, but use lightweight compression, such as LZ4 or Zstd fast mode. This trades some CPU to reduce I/O volume. If the CPU becomes the bottleneck due to decompression, consider multithreaded decompression or offloading to accelerators. Also, overlap decompression with reading by using one thread to read compressed data and another thread to decompress the data in parallel. Modern GPUs can perform on-the-fly data decompression using GPU computing resources (or specialized decoders for image/visual data) when paired with GPUDirect Storage and the `cuFile` I/O stack.

Measure throughput and eliminate bottlenecks

Continuously monitor the data pipeline's throughput. If GPUs aren't near 100% utilization and you suspect input lag, measure how many MB/s you're reading from disk and how busy the data loader cores are. Tools like `dstat` or NVIDIA's DCGM can reveal if GPUs are waiting on data. Systematically tune each component by bumping up prefetch buffers, increasing network buffer sizes, optimizing disk RAID settings, etc. Do this until the input pipeline can feed data as fast as GPUs consume it. Often, these optimizations raise GPU utilization from ~70% to > 95% on the same hardware by removing I/O stalls.

Scale I/O for multinode

At cluster scale, ensure the storage system can handle aggregate throughput. For example, 8 GPUs consuming 200 MB/s each is 1.6 GB/s per node. Across 100 nodes, that's 160 GB/s needed. Very few central filesystems can sustain this. Mitigate by sharding data across storage servers, using per-node caches, or preloading data onto each node's local disk. Trading off storage space for throughput (e.g., multiple copies of data) is often worth it to avoid starving expensive GPUs.

Minimize checkpointing and logging overhead

Write checkpoints and logs efficiently. Use asynchronous writes for checkpoints if possible, or write to local disk, then copy to network storage to avoid stalling training. Compress checkpoints or use sparse storage formats to reduce size. Limit logging frequency on each step by aggregating iteration statistics and logging only every Nth iteration rather than every iteration. This will greatly reduce I/O overhead.

You can also suspend a running GPU process with `cuda-checkpoint` and Checkpoint/Restore in Userspace (CRIU) to persist the process image. When ready to resume, the CUDA driver can restore device memory and CUDA state—even on to other GPUs of the same device type. Treat this as complementary to your model's state-dict or sharded checkpoint files rather than a replacement.

Data Processing Pipelines

The format, layout, and locality of data determine how smoothly the pipeline runs at scale. Binary formats, sharding, caching, and prioritized threads turn I/O from a bottleneck into a steady stream.

Convert datasets to binary or memory-mapped formats, shard across storage and nodes, and raise thread priorities or move simple augments to the GPU to prevent stalls. Cache hot data/KV states, prefetch and buffer aggressively, and size batches to keep the pipeline smooth from disk to device. The following are tips for improving your data processing:

Use binary data formats
Convert datasets to binary formats, such as TFRecords, LMDB, or memory-mapped arrays. This conversion reduces the overhead associated with handling millions of small files and accelerates data ingestion.

Tune the file system
In addition to mounting file systems with `noatime` and increasing read-ahead, consider sharding data across multiple storage nodes to distribute I/O load and prevent bottlenecks on a single server.

Disable hyperthreading for CPU-bound workloads
For data pipelines that are heavily CPU-bound, disabling hyperthreading can reduce resource contention and lead to more consistent performance. This is especially beneficial on systems where single-thread performance is critical.

Elevate thread priorities
Increase the scheduling priority of data loader and preprocessing CPU threads using tools, such as `chrt` or `pthread_setschedparam`. By giving these threads higher priority, you ensure that data is fed to the GPU with minimal latency, reducing the chance of pipeline stalls.

Cache frequently used data
Leverage operating system page caches or a dedicated RAM disk to cache frequently accessed data. This approach is especially beneficial in applications like NLP, where certain tokens or phrases are accessed repeatedly, reducing redundant processing and I/O overhead.

Prefetch and buffer data

Always load data ahead of the iteration that needs it. Use background data loader threads or processes, such as PyTorch DataLoader with `prefetch_factor`. For distributed training, use `DistributedSampler` to ensure each process gets unique data to avoid redundant I/O.

Parallelize data transformations

If CPU preprocessing—such as image augmentation and text tokenization—is heavy, distribute it across multiple worker threads/processes. Profile to ensure the CPU isn't the bottleneck while GPUs wait. If it is, either increase workers or move some transforms to GPU, as libraries like NVIDIA's DALI can do image operations on a GPU asynchronously.

Cache model states and outputs

When inferencing with LLMs, it's beneficial to cache the embeddings and V cache for frequently seen tokens to avoid having to recompute them repeatedly. Similarly, if an LLM training job reuses the same dataset multiple times (called *epochs*), you should leverage OS page cache or RAM to store the hot data.

Shard data across nodes

In multinode training, give each node a subset of data to avoid every node reading the entire dataset from a single source. This scales out I/O. Use a distributed filesystem or manual shard assignment with each node reading different files. This speeds things up and naturally aligns with data parallelism since each node processes its own data shard. DeepSeek's Fire-Flyer File System (3FS) is one example of a distributed dataset sharding filesystem. DeepSeek's 3FS achieves multiterabyte-per-second throughput by distributing dataset shards across NVMe SSDs on each node—while minimizing traditional caching. This design feeds each GPU with local high-speed data, avoiding I/O bottlenecks.

Monitor pipeline and adjust batch size

Sometimes increasing batch size will push more work onto GPUs and less frequent I/O, improving overall utilization—but only up to a point as it affects convergence. Conversely, if GPUs are waiting on data often, and you cannot speed I/O, you might actually decrease batch size to shorten each iteration and thus reduce idle time or do gradient accumulation of smaller batches such that data reads are more continuous. Find a balance where GPUs are nearly always busy.

Apply data augmentation on GPU

If augmentation is simple but applied to massive data, like adding noise or normalization, it might be worth doing on GPU to avoid saturating CPU. GPUs are often underutilized during data loading, so using a small CUDA kernel to augment data after loading can be efficient. But be careful not to serialize the pipeline. Use streams to overlap augmentation of batch $N+1$ while batch N is training.

Utilize GPU-accelerated libraries like NVIDIA DALI to perform these tasks asynchronously. This helps maintain a smooth and high-throughput data pipeline.

Focus on end-to-end throughput (e.g., tokens per second)

Remember that speeding up model compute doesn't help if your data pipeline cuts throughput in half. Always profile end-to-end, not just the training loop isolated. Use Nsight Systems and Nsight Compute to measure kernel timelines and stalls, or the PyTorch profiler for framework-level attribution. Then compare iteration time with synthetic versus real data to see how much overhead data loading introduces. Aim for less than 10% overhead from ideal. If it's more than that, invest time in pipeline optimization; it often yields large "free" speedups in training.

Performance Profiling, Debugging, and Monitoring

You can't optimize what you don't measure; profiling reveals if you're compute-bound, memory-bound, I/O-bound, or network-bound so you target the right fix. Continuous telemetry and regression tests keep wins from eroding as code, drivers, and data evolve.

Specifically, use Nsight Systems/Compute and framework profilers with NVTX to determine whether you're compute-bound, memory-bound, I/O-bound, or communication-bound. Trim Python overhead, watch utilization gaps, balance work across ranks, track memory/network/disk health, and gate changes with performance regression tests and alerts. Use the following guidance to profile, monitor, and debug the performance of your AI workloads:

Profile to find bottlenecks and root cause analysis

Regularly run profilers on your training/inference jobs. Use NVIDIA Nsight Systems to get a timeline of CPU and GPU activity. You can also use Nsight Compute or the PyTorch profiler to drill down into kernel efficiency. Identify whether your job is compute bound, memory bound, or waiting on I/O/communication. Target your optimizations accordingly. For example, if your workload is memory bound, focus on reducing memory traffic rather than implementing compute-bound optimizations. Combine with machine-learning–driven analytics to predict and preempt performance bottlenecks. This can help in automating fine-tuning adjustments in real time. When using GPUDirect Storage, enable GDS tracing to correlate `cuFile` activity with kernel gaps.

Eliminate Python overhead

Profile your training scripts to identify Python bottlenecks—such as excessive looping or logging—and replace them with vectorized operations or optimized library calls. Minimizing Python overhead helps ensure that the CPU does not become a hidden bottleneck in the overall system performance.

Measure GPU utilization and idle gaps

Continuously monitor GPU utilization, SM efficiency, memory bandwidth usage, etc. If you notice periodic drops in utilization, correlate them with events. For example, a drop in utilization every 5 minutes might coincide with checkpoint saving. Such patterns point to optimization opportunities, such as staggering checkpoints and using asynchronous flushes. Utilize tools like DCGM or `nvidia-smi` in daemon mode to log these metrics over time.

Use NVTX markers

Instrument your code with NVTX ranges or framework profiling APIs to label different phases, including data loading, forward pass, backward pass, etc. These markers show up in the Nsight Systems or Perfetto timeline and help you attribute GPU idle times or latencies to specific parts of the pipeline. This makes it easier to communicate to developers which part of the code needs attention. For PyTorch, you can use `torch.profiler.record_function()`.

Utilize kernel profiling and analysis tools beyond just the PyTorch profiler

For performance-critical kernels, use Nsight Compute to examine kernel-level metrics like occupancy and throughput, or Nsight Systems to analyze GPU/CPU timelines and overlap. Check achieved occupancy, memory throughput, and instruction throughput. Look for signs of memory bottlenecks, such as memory bandwidth near the hardware maximum. This helps to identify memory-bound workloads. The profiler's "Issues" section often directly suggests if a kernel is memory bound or compute bound and why. Use this feedback to guide code changes, such as improving memory coalescing if global load efficiency is low.

Check for warp divergence

Use the profiler to see if warps are diverging, as it can show branch efficiency and divergent branch metrics. Divergence means some threads in a warp are inactive due to branching, which hurts throughput. If significant, revisit the kernel code to restructure conditionals or data assignments to minimize intrawarp divergence and ensure that each warp handles uniform work.

Verify load balancing

In multi-GPU jobs, profile across ranks. Sometimes one GPU (rank 0) does extra work like aggregating stats and data gathering—and often becomes a bottleneck. Monitor each GPU's timeline. If one GPU is consistently lagging, distribute that extra workload. For example, you can have the nonzero ranks share the I/O and logging responsibilities. Ensuring that all GPUs/ranks have similar workloads avoids the slowest rank dragging the rest.

Monitor memory usage

Track GPU memory allocation and usage over time. Ensure you are not near OOM, which can cause the framework to unexpectedly swap tensors to host, which will cause huge slowdowns. If memory usage climbs iteration by iteration, you have likely identified leaks. In this case, profile with tools like `torch.cuda.memory_summary()` and Nsight Systems' GPU memory trace to analyze detailed allocations. On the CPU side, monitor for paging, as your process's resident memory (RES) should not exceed physical RAM significantly. If you see paging, reduce dataset preload size or increase RAM.

Monitor network and disk

For distributed jobs, use OS tools to monitor network throughput and disk throughput. Ensure the actual throughput matches expectations. For example, on a 100 Gbps link, you should see 12.5 GB/s (12.5 GB/s = 100 Gb/s ÷ 8 bits per byte) if fully utilized. If not, the network might be a bottleneck or misconfigured. Similarly, monitor disk I/O on training nodes. If you see spikes of 100% disk utilization and GPU idle, you likely need to buffer or cache data better.

Set up alerts for anomalies

In a production or long-running training context, set up automated alerts or logs for events like GPU errors, such as ECC errors, device overheating, etc. This will help identify abnormally slow iterations. For example, NVIDIA's DCGM can watch health metrics, and you can trigger actions if a GPU starts throttling or encountering errors. This helps catch performance issues—like a cooling failure causing throttling—immediately rather than after the job finishes.

Perform regression testing

Maintain a set of benchmark tasks to run whenever you change software, including CUDA drivers, CUDA versions, AI framework versions, or even your training code. Compare performance to previous runs to catch regressions early. It's not uncommon for a driver update or code change to inadvertently reduce throughput—a quick profiling run on a standard workload will highlight this so you can investigate. For example, maybe a kernel is accidentally not using Tensor Cores anymore. This is something to look into for sure.

GPU Programming and CUDA Tuning Optimizations

Aligning kernels with the memory hierarchy and hardware features is where large, durable gains come from. Fusion, Tensor Cores, CUDA Graphs, and compiler paths (e.g., `torch.compile` and OpenAI's Triton) convert launch overhead into useful math.

Optimize for the memory hierarchy: coalesce global loads, tile into shared memory, manage registers/occupancy, and overlap transfers (e.g., `cp.async`/TMA) with compute. Prefer tuned libraries and CUDA Graphs, leverage `torch.compile` and OpenAI's Triton for fusion, and validate scalability with roofline analysis and PTX/SASS inspection. The following are some GPU and CUDA programming optimization tips and techniques:

Understand GPU memory hierarchy

Keep in mind the tiered memory structure of GPUs—registers per thread, shared memory/L1 cache per block/SM, L2 cache across SM, and global HBM. Maximize data reuse in the higher tiers. For example, use registers and shared memory to reuse values and minimize accesses to slower global memory. A good kernel ensures the vast majority of data is either in registers or gets loaded from HBM efficiently using coalescing and caching.

Coalesce global memory accesses

Ensure that threads in the same warp access contiguous memory addresses so that the hardware can service them in as few transactions as possible. Strided or scattered memory access by warp threads will result in multiple memory transactions per warp, effectively wasting bandwidth. Restructure data layouts or index calculations so that whenever a warp loads data, it's doing so in a single, wide memory transaction.

Use shared memory for data reuse

Shared memory is like a manually managed cache with very high bandwidth. Load frequently used data—such as tiles of matrices—into shared memory. And have threads operate on those tiles multiple times before moving on. This popular tiling technique greatly cuts down global memory traffic. Be cautious of shared-memory bank conflicts. Organize shared-memory access patterns or pad data to ensure threads aren't contending for the same memory bank, which would serialize accesses and reduce performance.

Optimize memory alignment

Align data structures to 128 bytes whenever possible, especially for bulk memory copies or vectorized loads. Misaligned accesses can force multiple transactions even if theoretically coalesced. Using vectorized types like float2 and float4 for global memory I/O can help load/store multiple values per instruction, but ensure your data pointer is properly aligned to the vector size.

Minimize memory transfers

Only transfer data to the GPU when necessary and in large chunks. Consolidate many small transfers into one big transfer if you can. For example, if you have many small arrays to send each iteration, pack them into one buffer and send once. Small, frequent `cudaMemcpy` can become a bottleneck. If using Unified

Memory, use explicit prefetch (cudaMemPrefetchAsync) to stage data on GPU before it's needed, avoiding on-demand page faults during critical compute sections.

Avoid excessive temporary allocations

Frequent allocation and freeing of GPU memory can hurt performance. For example, frequently using cudaMalloc/cudaFree or device malloc in kernels will cause extra overhead. Instead, reuse memory buffers or use memory pools available within most DL frameworks, like PyTorch, that implement a GPU caching allocator. If writing custom CUDA code, consider using cudaMallocAsync with a memory pool or manage a pool of scratch memory yourself to avoid the overhead of repetitive alloc/free.

Balance threads and resource use

Achieve a good occupancy-resource balance. Using more threads for higher occupancy helps hide memory latency, but if each thread uses too many registers or too much shared memory, occupancy drops. Tune your kernel launch parameters—including threads per block—to ensure you have enough warps in flight to cover latency, but not so many that each thread is starved of registers or shared memory. In kernels with high instruction-level parallelism (ILP), reducing register usage to boost occupancy might actually hurt performance. The optimal point is usually in the middle of the occupancy spectrum, as maximum occupancy is not always ideal. Use the NVIDIA Nsight Compute Occupancy Calculator (*https://oreil.ly/Uid4B*) to experiment with configurations.

Monitor register and shared-memory usage

Continuously monitor per-thread register and shared-memory consumption using profiling tools like Nsight Compute. If the occupancy is observed to be below 25%, consider increasing the number of threads per block to better utilize available hardware resources. However, verify that this adjustment does not cause excessive register spilling by reviewing detailed occupancy reports and kernel execution metrics. Register spilling can lead to additional memory traffic and degrade overall performance.

Overlap memory transfers with computation

Overlap memory transfers with computation whenever possible. Use cudaMem cpyAsync in multiple CUDA streams to prefetch while kernels run. Prefer the Tensor Memory Accelerator for bulk movement to shared memory, and use cp.async for fine-grained staged copies and prefetch. These approaches effectively mask global memory latency by overlapping data transfers with computation, making sure the GPU cores remain fully utilized without waiting for memory operations to complete.

Use bulk prefetching when possible

For predictable patterns, prefetch into L2 using the PTX `cp.async.bulk.pre fetch.tensor.[1-5]d.L2.global*` (or the `prefetch.global.L2` family), and use TMA (e.g., `cp.async.bulk.tensor`) to stage blocks into shared memory. You can also use cp.async to stage global memory into shared memory asynchronously and overlap copy with compute. You can also explicitly load data into registers ahead of use. These proactive methods reduce the delay caused by global memory accesses and make sure that critical data is available in faster, lower-latency storage—such as registers or shared memory—right when it's needed, thus minimizing execution stalls and improving overall kernel efficiency.

Utilize cooperative groups

Utilize CUDA's cooperative groups to achieve efficient, localized synchronization among a subset of threads rather than enforcing a full block-wide barrier. This technique enables finer-grained control over synchronization, reducing unnecessary waiting times and overhead. By grouping threads that share data or perform related computations, you can synchronize only those threads that require coordination, which can lead to a more efficient execution pattern and better overall throughput.

Optimize warp divergence

Structure your code so that threads within a warp follow the same execution path as much as possible. Divergence can double the execution time for that warp—for example, half the warp (16 threads) taking one branch and half the warp (16 threads) taking another branch. If you have branches that some data rarely triggers, consider "sorting" or grouping data so warps handle uniform cases such that all are true or all are false. Use warp-level primitives like ballot and shuffle to create branchless solutions for certain problems. Treat a warp as the unit of work, and aim for all 32 threads to do identical work in lockstep for maximum efficiency.

Leverage warp-level operations

Use CUDA's warp intrinsics to let threads communicate without going to shared memory when appropriate. For example, use `__shfl_sync` to broadcast a value to all threads in a warp or to do warp-level reductions—like summing registers across a warp—instead of each thread writing to shared memory. These intrinsics bypass slower memory and can speed up algorithms like reductions or scans that can be done within warps. By processing these tasks within a warp, you avoid the latency associated with shared memory and full-block synchronizations.

Use CUDA streams for concurrency

Within a single process/GPU, launch independent kernels in different CUDA streams to overlap their execution if they don't use all resources. Overlap computation with computation—e.g., one stream computing one part of the model while another stream launches an independent kernel like data preprocessing on GPU or asynchronous `memcpy`. Be mindful of dependencies and use CUDA events to synchronize when needed. Proper use of streams can increase GPU utilization by not leaving any resource idle—especially if you have some kernels that are light.

Prefer library functions

Wherever possible, use NVIDIA's optimized libraries, such as cuBLAS, cuDNN, Thrust, and NCCL, for core math and collective operations. For point-to-point GPU data movement in distributed inference, use NIXL where available. You can also use NVSHMEM when you need fine-grained GPU-initiated transfers. These are heavily optimized for each GPU architecture and often approach theoretical "speed of light" peaks. This will save you the trouble of reinventing them. For example, use cuBLAS GEMM for matrix multiplies rather than a custom kernel, unless you have a very special pattern. The libraries also handle new hardware features transparently. AI frameworks like PyTorch (and its compiler) use these optimized libraries under the hood.

Use CUDA Graphs for repeated launches

If you have a static training loop that is launched thousands of times, consider using CUDA Graphs to capture and launch the sequence of operations as a graph. This can significantly reduce CPU launch overhead for each iteration, especially in multi-GPU scenarios where launching many kernels and `memcpy`'s can put extra pressure on the CPU and incur additional latency.

Check for scalability limits

As you optimize a kernel, periodically check how it scales with problem size and across architectures. A kernel might achieve great occupancy and performance on a small input but not scale well to larger inputs, as it may start thrashing L2 cache or running into memory-cache evictions. Use roofline analysis. Compare achieved FLOPS and bandwidth to hardware limits to ensure you're not leaving performance on the table.

Inspect PTX and SASS for advanced kernel analysis

For performance-critical custom CUDA kernels, use Nsight Compute to examine the generated PTX and SASS. This deep dive can reveal issues like memory bank conflicts or redundant computations, guiding you toward targeted low-level optimizations.

Use the PyTorch compiler

Take advantage of PyTorch's `torch.compile` to fuse Python-level operations into optimized kernels through TorchInductor. The compiler can also reduce launch overhead by integrating CUDA Graphs. Typical gains of about 10%–40% are common once the optimizations are warmed up. This eliminates interpreter overhead and unlocks compiler-level optimizations.

In practice, enabling `torch.compile` has produced substantial speedups (e.g., 20%–50% on many models) by automatically combining kernels and utilizing NVIDIA GPU hardware (e.g., Tensor Cores) more efficiently. Always test compiled mode on your model. While it can massively boost throughput, you should ensure compatibility and correctness before deploying. When graphs are stable, enable CUDA Graphs to reduce per-iteration CPU overhead. Keep static memory pools to satisfy pointer-stability constraints.

Plan for dynamic shapes

If your input sizes vary, use `torch._dynamo.mark_dynamic()` to annotate dynamic dimensions or export shape-polymorphic graphs with `torch.export()`, and then compile. Control recompilation behavior with `torch.compiler.set_stance()` using `"fail_on_recompile"` and `torch._dynamo.error_on_ graph_break()` to surface problematic shape churn in testing and CI. Use static shapes where possible to enable CUDA Graphs to reduce per-iteration CPU overhead.

Leverage Triton kernels using `torch.compile`

If PyTorch doesn't fuse an operation well, consider writing a custom GPU kernel in Triton and integrating it. PyTorch makes it easy to register a custom GPU kernel with `torch.library.triton_op`.

Use autotuning when available

Enable library autotuning features to maximize low-level performance. For example, set `torch.backends.cudnn.benchmark=True` when input sizes are fixed. This lets NVIDIA's cuDNN library try multiple convolution algorithms and pick the fastest one for your hardware. The one-time overhead leads to optimized kernels that can accelerate training and inference. If exact reproducibility isn't required, allow nondeterministic algorithms by disabling `cudnn.deterministic` to unlock these faster implementations.

Leverage the read-only path

Mark frequently used constants or coefficients as read-only so the GPU can cache them in the dedicated L1 read-only cache. In CUDA C++, you can use `const __restrict__` pointers to hint that data is immutable. On modern GPU architectures, the compiler generates cached global loads for `const __restrict__` qualified pointers. When using AI frameworks and libraries, make sure that lookup tables or static weights are on the device and treated as constant. This optimization reduces global memory traffic and latency for those values, as each SM can quickly fetch them from cache instead of repeatedly accessing slow DRAM.

Kernel Scheduling and Execution Optimizations

Launch overhead and unnecessary syncs create idle gaps that crush throughput. Fusing small kernels and using persistent/dynamic strategies keeps the device busy and latency hidden.

Keep the device busy by minimizing synchronizations, fusing small kernels, and using persistent kernels when launching the same work repeatedly. For irregular tasks, consider GPU dynamic parallelism—but use it judiciously to avoid adding overhead. The following are tips on improving kernel scheduling and execution:

Minimize GPU synchronization calls

Avoid unnecessary global synchronizations that stall GPU progress. Excessive use of `cudaDeviceSynchronize()` or blocking GPU operations (like synchronous memory copies) will insert idle gaps where neither the CPU nor GPU can do useful work. Synchronize only when absolutely needed. For instance, synchronize when transferring final results or when debugging. By letting asynchronous operations queue up, you keep the GPU busy and the CPU free to prepare further work. This leads to a more continuous execution pipeline.

Fuse small kernels to amortize launch overhead

If you have many tiny GPU kernels launching back-to-back, consider merging their operations to run in a single kernel where possible. Every kernel launch has a fixed cost on the order of tens of microseconds, so combining operations through manual CUDA kernel fusion, XLA fusion, or tools like NVIDIA CUTLASS/Triton for custom ops can improve throughput. Fused kernels spend more time doing actual work and less time in launch overhead or memory round trips. This is especially helpful in inference or preprocessing pipelines where chains of elementwise ops can be executed in one go. Try `torch.compile(mode="reduce-overhead")` first. The compiler can fuse operation chains and wrap steady regions in CUDA Graphs. This will reduce CPU launch overhead. For unfused hotspots, consider migrating them to Triton kernels and using asynchronous TMA and automatic warp specialization where applicable.

Utilize GPU dynamic parallelism for intra-GPU work scheduling

Utilize CUDA's Dynamic Parallelism to let GPU kernels launch other kernels from the GPU without returning to the CPU. In scenarios with unpredictable or iterative work, such as an algorithm that needs to spawn additional tasks based on intermediate results, dynamic parallelism cuts latency by removing the CPU launch bottleneck. For example, a parent kernel can divide and launch child kernels for further processing directly on the device. This keeps the entire workflow on the GPU, avoiding CPU intervention and enabling better overlap and utilization. Use this judiciously, however, as it can introduce its own overhead if overused.

Use persistent kernels for repeated workloads

Use a persistent kernel strategy when a workload involves launching identical kernels in rapid succession, such as processing a work queue or streaming batches with the same computation. A persistent kernel is launched once and remains active, reusing threads to handle many units of work in a loop, rather than launching a fresh kernel for each unit. This approach trades a more complex kernel design for significantly lower scheduling overhead. By keeping the kernel alive, you avoid repeated launch costs and can achieve higher sustained occupancy. High-performance distributed training and inference systems often employ this technique to maximize throughput and minimize latency for iterative tasks.

Evaluate thread block clusters

Thread block clusters to keep data close and reduce relaunch overheads. Up to 16 thread blocks can form a cluster on Blackwell (after increasing the non-portable limit). Use cluster-aware synchronization and shared-memory residency to improve locality in persistent-style designs. Profile occupancy vs. residency trade-offs with kernel-level profiling tools like Nsight Compute.

Arithmetic Optimizations and Reduced/Mixed Precision

Lower precisions and sparsity let you trade bits for big speed and memory wins— often with negligible accuracy impact. Mixed precision, TF32/FP8/INT8, and fused scaling exploit hardware math paths to raise throughput per dollar.

Specifically, use mixed precision (BF16/FP16) and Tensor Cores for big gains, adopt TF32 for easy FP32 speedups, and evaluate FP8/FP4 where quality allows. Exploit structured sparsity, lower-precision gradients/communications, and INT8/INT4 quantization for inference—fusing scales/activations to preserve accuracy. The following optimization techniques apply to improving the performance of arithmetic computations and utilizing reduced/mixed precision:

Use mixed-precision training

Leverage FP16 or BF16 for training to speed up math operations and reduce memory usage. Modern GPUs have Tensor Cores that massively accelerate FP16/ BF16 matrix operations. Keep critical parts like the final accumulation or a copy of weights in FP32 for numerical stability, but run bulk computations in half-precision. This often gives about a 1.5–3.5× speedup (depending on the model and kernel mix, with larger gains on `matmul`-heavy workloads) with minimal accuracy loss and is now standard in most frameworks with automatic mixed precision (AMP).

Embrace gradient accumulation and activation checkpointing

Detail the use of gradient accumulation to effectively increase the batch size without extra memory usage, and consider activation checkpointing to reduce memory footprint in very deep networks. These techniques are crucial when training models that approach or exceed GPU memory limits.

Favor BF16 instead of FP16 on newer hardware

If available, use BF16 instead of FP16, as it has a larger exponent range and doesn't require loss scaling. Modern GPUs support BF16 Tensor Cores at the same speed as FP16. BF16 will simplify training by avoiding overflow/underflow issues while still gaining the performance benefits of half precision.

Exploit FP8, novel precisions, and scaling techniques

On modern GPUs, FP8 Tensor Cores provide roughly double the math throughput of FP16 or BF16 on compute-bound kernels while, at the same time, reducing activation and weight bandwidth. Additionally, FP4 (NVFP4) Tensor Cores double the throughput of FP8 and are used for inference with micro tensor scaling (an error-correction technique to maintain accuracy) to raise token throughput. For training, use FP8 with the NVIDIA Transformer Engine and maintain FP16 or FP32 accumulators when required. For inference, evaluate FP8 first and adopt NVFP4 only after calibration shows acceptable quality for your task. It's recommended to use hybrid FP8 (E4M3 for forward activations/weights and E5M2 for gradients) for training. Specifically, consider using E4M3 for the forward pass (e.g., activations and weights) and E5M2 for the backward pass (e.g., gradients). It's often beneficial to use a delayed scaling window of 256–1024. For inference, consider NVFP4 after calibration. TE integrates with PyTorch and is supported by modern GPU hardware. Prefer framework TE kernels over ad-hoc FP8 custom operations. End-to-end speedup depends on kernel mix, memory bandwidth, and calibration, so validate accuracy and performance on your model and workload.

Leverage Tensor Cores and the Tensor Memory Accelerator (TMA)

Make sure your custom CUDA kernels utilize Tensor Cores for matrix ops if possible. This might involve using CUTLASS templates for simplicity. By using Tensor Cores and TMA for asynchronous tensor movement to shared memory, you can achieve dramatic speedups for GEMM, convolutions, and other tensor operations—often reaching near-peak FLOPS of the GPU. Ensure your data is in FP16/BF16/TF32 as needed and aligned to Tensor Core tile dimensions, which are multiples of 8 or 16.

Use TF32 for easy speedup

For 32-bit matrix multiplies, set `torch.set_float32_matmul_preci sion("high")` to enable TF32 (fast FP32) for operations that are numerically safe in PyTorch. Libraries like cuBLAS and cuDNN will automatically pick optimal

Tensor Core code paths on modern GPU hardware. If you force full-precision FP32 with "highest" (instead of "high"), make sure to understand the performance impact.

Exploit structured sparsity

Modern NVIDIA GPUs support 2:4 structured sparsity in matrix multiply, which zeros out 50% of weights in a structured pattern. This allows the hardware to double its throughput. Leverage this by pruning your model. If you can prune weights to meet the 2:4 sparsity pattern, your GEMMs can run ~2× faster for those layers. Use NVIDIA's SDK or library support to apply structured sparsity and ensure the sparse Tensor Core paths are used. This can give a free speed boost if your model can tolerate or be trained with that sparsity, which often requires retraining with sparsity regularization.

Reduce precision for gradients and activations when possible

Even if you keep weights at higher precision, consider compressing gradients or activations to lower precision. For instance, use FP16/BF16 or FP8 communication for gradients. Many frameworks support FP16 gradient all-reduce. Similarly, for activation checkpointing, storing activations in 16-bit instead of FP32 saves memory. Research continues on FP8 and FP4 optimizers and quantized gradients. These help maintain model quality while reducing memory and bandwidth costs. In bandwidth-limited environments, gradient compression in particular can be a game changer. DeepSeek demonstrated this by compressing gradients to train on constrained GPUs.

Use custom quantization for inference

For deployment, use INT8 quantization wherever possible. INT8 inference on GPUs is extremely fast and memory-efficient. Use NVIDIA's TensorRT or quantization tools to quantize models to INT8 and calibrate them. Many neural networks like transformers can run in INT8 with a negligible accuracy drop. The speedups can be 2–4× over FP16. On the newest GPUs, also explore and evaluate FP8 or INT4 for certain models to further boost throughput for inference.

Fuse scaling and computing operations when possible

When using lower precision, remember to fuse operations to retain accuracy. For example, Blackwell's FP4 "microscaling" suggests keeping a scale per group of values. Incorporate these fused operations by scaling and computing in one pass—rather than using separate passes, which could cause precision loss. Many of these are handled by existing libraries, so just use them rather than implementing them from scratch.

Advanced Tuning Strategies and Algorithmic Tricks

Algorithmic shifts routinely beat hardware upgrades on ROI by reducing work rather than pushing it faster. Autotuning, FlashAttention, overlap of comm/compute, and sharding unlock scale while cutting waste.

Specifically, autotune kernel and layer parameters, swap in fused/FlashAttention kernels, and overlap communication with computation in distributed training. Scale deep models with pipeline/tensor parallelism and ZeRO sharding, and consider asynchronous updates or pruning/sparsity to trade a little accuracy work for big throughput wins. The following are some advanced performance optimizations and algorithmic tricks:

Autotune kernel parameters

> Autotune your custom CUDA kernels for the target GPU. Choosing the correct block size, tile size, unroll factors, etc., can affect performance, and the optimal settings often differ between GPUs' generations, such as Ampere, Hopper, Blackwell, and beyond. Use autotuning scripts or frameworks like OpenAI Triton—or even brute-force search in a preprocessing step—to find the best launch config. This can easily yield 20%–30% improvements that you'd miss with static "reasonable" settings. Use Triton features in your autotuning loop—for instance, set `num_warps` and `num_stages`, enable automatic warp specialization, and test asynchronous TMA layouts. Prefer tensor map descriptor APIs for shared-memory staging. Re-benchmark tile shapes when migrating to different hardware, as optimal choices will differ across GPU generations.

Use kernel fusion in ML workloads

> Utilize fused kernels provided by deep learning libraries. For example, enabling fused optimizers will fuse elementwise ops like weight update, momentum, etc. This will also use fused multihead attention implementations and fused normalization kernels. NVIDIA's libraries and some open source projects like Transformer Engine and FasterTransformer provide fused operations for common patterns, such as fused LayerNorm + dropout. These reduce launch overhead and use memory more efficiently.

Utilize memory-efficient attention like FlashAttention

> Integrate advanced algorithms like FlashAttention for transformer models. FlashAttention computes attention in a tiled, streaming fashion to avoid materializing large intermediate matrices, drastically reducing memory usage and increasing speed—especially for long sequences. Replacing the standard attention with FlashAttention can improve both throughput and memory footprint, allowing larger batch sizes or sequence lengths on the same hardware.

Overlap communication and computation

In distributed training, overlap network communication with GPU computation whenever possible. For example, with gradient all-reduce, launch the all-reduce asynchronously as soon as each layer's gradients are ready, while the next layer is still computing the backward pass. This pipelining can hide all-reduce latency entirely if done right. Use asynchronous NCCL calls or framework libraries like PyTorch's Distributed Data Parallel (DDP), which provide overlapping out of the box. This ensures the GPU isn't idle waiting for the network.

Use pipeline parallelism for deep models

When model size forces you to pipeline across GPUs using tensor parallelism or pipeline parallelism, you can use enough microbatches to keep all pipeline stages busy. Exploit NVLink/NVSwitch to send activations quickly between stages. Overlap and reduce pipeline bubbles by using an interleaved schedule. Some frameworks automate this type of scheduling. The NVL72 fabric is especially helpful here, as even communication-heavy pipeline stages can exchange data at multiterabyte speeds, minimizing pipeline stalls.

Utilize distributed optimizer sharding

Use a memory-saving optimization strategy like Zero Redundancy Optimizer (ZeRO), which shards tensors like optimizer states and gradients across GPUs instead of replicating them. This allows scaling to extreme model sizes by distributing the memory and communication load. It improves throughput by reducing per-GPU memory pressure, avoiding swapping to CPU, and reducing communication volume if done in chunks. Many frameworks like DeepSpeed and Megatron-LM provide this type of sharding. Leverage it for large models to maintain high speed without running OOM or hitting slowdown from swapping.

Train asynchronously when possible

If applicable, consider asynchronous updates. For example, you can use stale stochastic gradient descent (SGD) in which workers don't always wait for one another to share updates. This approach can increase throughput, though it may require careful tuning to not impact convergence. Asynchronous training can provide large performance benefits if done properly.

Incorporate sparsity and pruning

Large models often have redundancy. Use pruning techniques during training to introduce sparsity, which you can exploit at inference—and partially during training if supported. Modern GPU hardware supports accelerated sparse matrix multiply (2:4), and future GPUs will likely extend this feature. Even if you leave training as dense and prune only for inference, a smaller model will run faster and use less memory. This increases cost-efficiency for model deployments. Explore the lottery ticket hypothesis, distillation, or structured pruning to maintain accuracy while trimming model size.

Distributed Training and Network Optimization

At cluster scale, the network becomes the limiter. Untreated, the network can break linear scaling and inflate costs. RDMA/Jumbo frames, hierarchical collectives, affinity, and compression protect bandwidth and tame latency.

Use RDMA (InfiniBand/RoCE) when available; if on Ethernet, tune TCP buffers, enable jumbo frames, and select modern congestion control. Align NIC/CPU affinity, adjust NCCL threads/buffers (and SHARP/CollNet where supported), compress or accumulate gradients, and test the fabric to catch loss or misconfigurations. Follow this guidance to optimize your network for distributed environments such as multi-GPU and multinode model training:

Use RDMA networking when available
> Equip your multinode cluster with InfiniBand or RoCE for low latency and high throughput. Ensure NCCL and MPI are using RDMA for training. NCCL will autodetect InfiniBand and use GPUDirect RDMA if available. RDMA bypasses the kernel networking stack and can reduce latency significantly versus traditional TCP. If you only have Ethernet, enable RoCE on RDMA-capable NICs to get RDMA-like performance. On NVLink domain systems (NVL72, GB200/GB300, etc.), keep collectives on-fabric when possible. Reserve host networking for inter-island links. Align NCCL topology hints with your NVLink/NVSwitch domains.

Tune the TCP/IP stack if using Ethernet
> For TCP-based clusters, increase network buffer sizes. Raise `/proc/sys/net/core/{r,w}mem_max` and the autotuning limits (`net.ipv4.tcp_{r,w}mem`) to allow larger send/receive buffers. This helps saturate 10/40/100 GbE links. Enable jumbo frames (MTU 9000) on all nodes and switches to reduce overhead per packet, which improves throughput and reduces CPU usage. Also consider modern TCP congestion control like BBR for wide-area or congested networks.

Assign CPU affinity for NICs
> Pin network interrupts and threads to the CPU core(s) on the same NUMA node as the NIC. This avoids cross-NUMA penalties for network traffic and keeps the networking stack's memory accesses local. Check `/proc/interrupts` and use `irqaffinity` settings to ensure, for example, your NIC in NUMA node 0 is handled by a core in NUMA node 0. This can improve network performance and consistency, especially under high packet rates.

Optimize NCCL environment variables for your environment
> Experiment with NCCL parameters for large multinode jobs. For example, increase `NCCL_NTHREADS`, the number of CPU threads per GPU for NCCL, from the default 4 to 8 or 16 to drive higher bandwidth at the cost of more CPU usage.

Increase `NCCL_BUFFSIZE`, the buffer size per GPU, from the default 1 MB to 4 MB or more for better throughput on large messages. If your cluster uses SHARP-capable switches, install the NCCL SHARP plugin and enable CollNet by setting `NCCL_COLLNET_ENABLE=1`, then use the SHARP plugin variables such as `SHARP_COLL_LOCK_ON_COMM_INIT=1` and `SHARP_COLL_NUM_COLL_GROUP_RESOURCE_ALLOC_THRESHOLD=0` as documented. Expect speedups only when your reductions are large enough and the network fabric supports SHARP offload.

Use gradient accumulation for slow networks

If your network becomes the bottleneck because you are scaling too many nodes linked by a moderate-performance interconnect, use gradient accumulation to perform fewer, larger all-reduce operations. Accumulate gradients over a few minibatches before syncing so that you communicate once for N batches instead of every batch. This trades a bit of extra memory and some model accuracy tuning for significantly reduced network overhead. It's especially helpful when adding more GPUs yields diminishing returns due to communication costs.

Optimize all-reduce topologies

Ensure you're using the optimal all-reduce algorithm for your cluster topology. NCCL will choose ring or tree algorithms automatically, but on mixed interconnects like GPUs connected by NVLink on each node and InfiniBand or Ethernet between nodes, hierarchical all-reduce can be beneficial. Hierarchical all-reduce will first perform the all-reduce operation within the node, then it will proceed across nodes. Most frameworks will perform NCCL-based hierarchical aggregations by default but verify by profiling. In traditional MPI setups, you may consider manually doing this same two-level reduction—first intranode and then internode.

Avoid network oversubscription

On multi-GPU servers, ensure the combined traffic of GPUs doesn't oversubscribe the NIC. For example, eight GPUs can easily generate more than 200 Gbps of traffic during all-reduce, so having only a single 100 Gbps NIC will constrain you. Consider multiple NICs per node and 200/400 Gbps InfiniBand if scaling to many GPUs per node. Likewise, watch out for PCIe bandwidth limits if your NIC and GPUs share the same PCIe root complex.

Compress communication

Just as with single-node memory, consider compressing data for network transfer. Techniques include 16-bit or 8-bit gradient compression, quantizing activations for cross-node pipeline transfers, or even more exotic methods like sketching. If your network is the slowest component, a slightly higher compute cost to compress/decompress data can be worth it. NVIDIA's NCCL doesn't natively compress, but you can integrate compression in frameworks (e.g., gradient compression in Horovod or custom AllReduce hooks in PyTorch). This was one key to DeepSeek's success—compressing gradients to cope with limited internode bandwidth.

Monitor network health

Ensure no silent issues are hampering your distributed training. Check for packet loss (which would show up as retries or timeouts—on InfiniBand, use counters for resend, and on Ethernet, check for TCP retransmits). Even a small packet loss can severely degrade throughput due to congestion control kicking in. Use out-of-band network tests (like iPerf or NCCL tests) to validate you're getting expected bandwidth and latency. If not, investigate switch configurations, NIC firmware, or CPU affinity.

Efficient Inference and Serving

Serving is a cost-and-latency game—utilization rises through orchestration and batching, not just bigger GPUs. Specialized runtimes, KV cache strategies, and warmups keep throughput high without violating SLOs.

Orchestrate for demand with autoscaling, microservices, and dynamic/continuous batching to keep GPUs hot without violating latency SLOs. Use specialized runtimes (vLLM, SGLang, TensorRT-LLM), exploit NIXL and KV cache offloading for disaggregated serving, warm models, and isolate resources to control tail latency. Follow these techniques to improve model inference efficiency and performance:

Orchestrate dynamic resources efficiently

Integrate advanced container orchestration platforms, such as Kubernetes augmented with custom performance metrics. This enables dynamic scaling and balancing workloads based on live usage patterns and throughput targets.

Embrace serverless architectures for inference

Explore serverless architectures and microservice designs for inference workloads, which can handle bursty traffic efficiently and reduce idle resource overhead by scaling down when demand is low.

Optimize batch and concurrency

For inference workloads, find the right batching strategy. For inference workloads, favor dynamic or continuous batching to automatically batch incoming requests. Larger batch sizes improve throughput by keeping the GPU busy, but too large can add latency. Also, run multiple inference streams in parallel if one stream doesn't use all GPU resources—e.g., two concurrent inference batches to use both GPU SMs and Tensor Cores fully.

Leverage NIXL for distributed inference

When serving large models across GPUs or nodes, use the NVIDIA Inference Xfer Library to stream KV cache between prefill and decode workers over

RDMA. In the case of NIXL, the large transformer-based KV cache is transferred between nodes. NIXL provides a high-throughput, low-latency API for streaming the KV cache from a prefill GPU to a decode GPU in a disaggregated LLM inference cluster. It does this using GPUDirect RDMA and optimal paths—and without involving the CPU. This reduces tail latency for disaggregated prefill decode serving across nodes.

Offload KV cache if necessary

If an LLM's attention KV cache grows beyond GPU memory, use hierarchical offloading. NVIDIA Dynamo's Distributed KV Cache Manager offloads less frequently accessed KV pages to CPU memory, SSD, or networked storage, while inference engines like TensorRT-LLM and vLLM support paged and quantized KV caches. Reuse caches to lower memory pressure and first-token latency. Validate end-to-end impact because offloaded misses introduce extra I/O latency. This allows inference on sequences that would otherwise exceed GPU memory— and with minimal performance hit thanks to fast NVMe and compute-I/O overlapping. Ensure your inference server is configured to use this if you expect very long prompts or chats. Offloading to disk is better than failing completely.

Serve models efficiently

Use optimized model inference systems, such as vLLM (*https://github.com/vllm-project/vllm*), SGLang (*https://github.com/sgl-project/sglang*), NVIDIA Dynamo (*https://github.com/ai-dynamo/dynamo*), and NVIDIA TensorRT-LLM (*https://github.com/NVIDIA/TensorRT-LLM*) for serving large models with low latency and high throughput. They should implement quantization, low-precision formats, fusion, highly optimized attention kernels, and other tricks to maximize GPU utilization during inference. These libraries should also handle tensor parallelism, pipeline parallelism, expert parallelism, context parallelism, speculative decoding, chunked prefill, disaggregated prefill/decode, and dynamic request batching—among many other high-performance features.

Monitor and tune for tail latency

In real-time services, both average latency and (long-)tail latency (99th percentile) matter. Profile the distribution of inference latencies. If the tail is high, identify outlier causes, such as unexpected CPU involvement, garbage-collection (GC) pauses, or excessive context switches. Pin your inference server process to specific cores, isolate it from noisy neighbors, and use real-time scheduling if necessary to get more consistent latency.

Warm up to avoid cold-start latency

Warm up the GPUs by loading the model into the GPU and running a few dummy inferences. This will avoid one-time, cold-start latency hits when the first real request comes into the inference server.

Partition resources efficiently for quality of service (QoS)

> If running mixed, heterogeneous workloads, such as training and inference—or models with different architectures—on the same infrastructure, consider partitioning resources to ensure the latency-sensitive inference gets priority. This could mean dedicating some GPUs entirely to inference or using MIG to give an inference service a guaranteed slice of a GPU if it doesn't need a full GPU but requires predictable latency. Separate inference from training on different nodes if possible, as training can introduce jitter with heavy I/O or sudden bursts of communication.

Utilize Grace CPU for inference preprocessing

> In Grace Blackwell systems, the server-class CPU can handle preprocessing—such as tokenization and batch collation—extremely fast in the same memory space as the GPU. Offload such tasks to the CPU and have it prepare data in the shared memory that the GPU can directly use. This reduces duplication of buffers and leverages the powerful CPU to handle parts of the inference pipeline, freeing the GPU to focus on more compute-intensive neural-network computations.

Tune carefully for edge AI and latency-critical deployments

> Extend performance tuning to the edge by leveraging specialized edge accelerators and optimizing data transfer protocols between central servers and edge devices. This will help achieve ultralow latency for time-sensitive applications.

Multinode Inference and Serving

Disaggregating prefill/decode and sharding models lets you handle bigger contexts and more users with higher occupancy. Continuous batching and hierarchical memory/offload maintain flow even under long prompts and heavy concurrency.

Specifically, disaggregate prefill and decode across devices, continuously pool tokens across requests, and shard oversized models via tensor/pipeline parallelism. Add hierarchical memory/offload for very long contexts so you serve more without OOMs, trading small latency for much higher capacity. The following performance tips apply to multinode inference and serving:

Disaggregate inference pipelines

> Separate the inference workflow into distinct phases, including the "prefill" phase that processes the input prompt through all model layers, and the iterative "decode" phase that generates outputs token by token. Allocate these phases to different resources to allow for independent scaling. This two-stage approach prevents faster tasks from being bottlenecked by slower ones. For large language models, one strategy is to run the full model to encode the prompt, then handle autoregressive decoding on a stage-wise basis, possibly with specialized workers

for each phase. By disaggregating the pipeline, you ensure that GPUs continuously work on the portion of the task they're most efficient at, avoiding head-of-line blocking, where one long generation stalls others behind it.

Use continuous batch processing for LLMs

Move beyond simple request batching and use continuous batching strategies to maximize throughput under heavy loads. Traditional dynamic batching groups incoming requests and processes them as a batch to improve GPU utilization. Continuous batching takes this further by dynamically merging and splitting sequences of tokens across requests in real time. Systems like vLLM implement token pooling, where as soon as any thread is ready to generate the next token, it gets grouped with other ready threads to form a new batch. This approach keeps the GPU at high occupancy at all times and drastically reduces idle periods. The result is significantly higher token throughput and better latency consistency, especially when serving many concurrent users with varying sequence lengths.

Shard models efficiently across GPUs and nodes

For models that are too large to fit into a single GPU's memory, employ model-parallel inference techniques by partitioning the model across multiple GPUs or even multiple servers. This can be done with tensor parallelism, in which it splits each layer's weights and computation across devices, or pipeline parallelism, which splits the model's layers into segments hosted on different GPUs and streams the data through them sequentially. While model sharding introduces communication overhead and some added latency as data must flow between shards, it enables deployment of trillion-parameter models that would otherwise be impossible to serve. Ensure high-speed interconnects, such as NVLink or InfiniBand, between GPUs to make this feasible, and overlap communication with computation where possible. The key is to balance the load so all devices work in parallel and no single stage becomes a bottleneck.

Offload memory for extended contexts

Use hierarchical memory strategies to support inference workloads that demand more memory than GPUs have available. Incorporate memory offloading when serving very large models or long sequence contexts, such as long multiturn conversations and large documents. Less frequently used data, such as old attention KV cache entries or infrequently accessed model weights, can be moved to CPU RAM or even NVMe storage when GPU memory gets tight. Modern inference frameworks can automatically swap out these tensors and bring them back on the fly when needed. While this introduces additional latency for cache misses, it prevents out-of-memory errors and allows you to handle extreme cases. By thoughtfully offloading and prefetching data, you trade a bit of speed for the ability to serve requests with large working sets, achieving a better overall throughput under memory constraints.

Power and Thermal Management

Performance per watt is a first-class metric—thermal or power throttling erases tuning gains and shortens hardware life. Power caps, efficient packing, and proactive cooling stabilize clocks while cutting energy spend.

Track perf/watt and thermals alongside speed: cap power or underclock memory-bound workloads for better efficiency with minimal throughput loss. Proactively manage cooling, consolidate jobs to run GPUs near full, monitor per-GPU power draw, and schedule around energy price/renewables when it reduces cost. Here are some tips on managing your power and thermal characteristics of your AI systems:

Utilize efficient and environmentally friendly energy when possible
> Track and optimize energy consumption alongside performance. In addition to managing power and thermal limits, monitor energy usage metrics and consider techniques that improve both performance and sustainability. For example, by implementing dynamic power capping or workload shifting based on renewable energy availability, you can reduce operational costs and carbon footprint. This dual focus reduces operational costs and supports responsible, environmentally friendly AI deployments.

Monitor thermals and clocks
> Keep an eye on GPU temperature and clock frequencies during runs. If GPUs approach thermal limits (85°C in some cases), they may start throttling clocks, which reduces performance. Use `nvidia-smi dmon` or telemetry to see if clocks drop from their max. If you detect throttling, improve cooling, increase fan speeds, improve airflow, or slightly reduce the power limit to keep within a stable thermal envelope. The goal is consistent performance without thermal-induced dips.

Use energy-aware dynamic power management
> Modern data centers are increasingly using energy-aware scheduling to adjust workloads based on real-time energy costs and renewable energy availability. Incorporating adaptive power capping and dynamic clock scaling can help optimize throughput per watt while reducing operational costs and carbon footprint.

Optimize for perf/watt
> In multi-GPU deployments where power budget is constrained (or energy cost is high), consider tuning for efficiency. Many workloads, especially memory-bound ones, can run at slightly reduced GPU clocks with negligible performance loss but noticeably lower power draw. For example, if a kernel is memory bound, locking the GPU at a lower clock can save power while not hurting runtime. This increases throughput per watt. Test a few power limits using `nvidia-smi -pl` to see if your throughput/watt improves. For some models, going from a 100% to 80% power limit yields nearly the same speed at 20% less power usage.

Use adaptive cooling strategies

If running in environments with variable cooling or energy availability, integrate with cluster management to adjust workloads. For instance, schedule heavy jobs during cooler times of the day or when renewable energy supply is high—if that's a factor for cost. Some sites implement policies to queue nonurgent jobs to run at night when electricity is cheaper. This doesn't change single-job performance but significantly cuts costs.

Consolidate workloads

Run GPUs at high utilization rather than running many GPUs at low utilization. A busy GPU is more energy efficient in terms of work done per watt than an idle or lightly used GPU. This is because the baseline power is better amortized when the GPU is busy. It may be better to run one job after another on one GPU at 90% utilization than two GPUs at 45% each in parallel—unless you need to optimize for the smallest wall-clock time. Plan scheduling to turn off or idle whole nodes when not in use, rather than leaving lots of hardware running at low utilization.

Configure cooling efficiently

For air-cooled systems, consider setting GPU fans to a higher fixed speed during heavy runs to preemptively cool the GPUs. Some data centers always run fans at the maximum to improve consistency. Ensure inlet temps in the data center are within specifications. Check periodically for dust or obstructions in server GPUs. Clogged fins can greatly reduce cooling efficiency. For water-cooled, ensure flow rates are optimal and water temperature is controlled.

Monitor power carefully

Use tools to monitor per-GPU power draw. `nvidia-smi` reports instantaneous draw, which helps in understanding the power profile of your workload. Spikes in power might correlate with certain phases. For example, the all-reduce phase might measure less compute load and less power, while dense layers will spike the load and power measurements. Knowing this, you can potentially sequence workloads to smooth power draw. This is important if operating the cluster on a constrained power circuit. In the power-constrained scenario, you may need to avoid running multiple power-spikey jobs simultaneously on the same node to avoid tripping power limits.

Improve job resilience for long-running jobs

If you are running a months-long training job or 24-7 inference job, consider the impact of thermals on hardware longevity. Running at 100% power and thermal limit constantly can marginally increase failure risk over time. In practice, data center GPUs are built for this type of resiliency, but if you want to be extra safe, running at 90% power target can reduce component stress with minimal slow-down. It's a trade-off of longer training runs versus less wear on the hardware—especially if that hardware will be reused for multiple projects over a long period of time.

Conclusion

Treat the checklist as a repeatable playbook: profile, tune the right bottleneck at the right layer, and verify gains before scaling out. By methodically applying these practices—from OS and kernels to distributed comms and serving—you'll achieve fast, cost-efficient, and reliable AI systems at any size.

This list, while comprehensive, is not exhaustive. The field of AI systems performance engineering will continue to grow as hardware, software, and algorithms evolve. And not every best practice listed here applies to every situation. But, collectively, they cover the breadth of performance engineering scenarios for AI systems. These tips encapsulate much of the practical wisdom accumulated over years of optimizing AI system performance.

When tuning your AI system, you should systematically go through each of the relevant categories listed in this chapter and run through each of the items in the checklist. For example, you should ensure the OS is tuned, confirm GPU kernels are efficient, check that you're using libraries properly, monitor the data pipeline, optimize the training loop, tune the inference strategies, and scale out gracefully. By following these best practices, you can diagnose and resolve most performance issues and extract the maximum performance from your AI system.

And remember that before you scale up your cluster drastically, you should profile on a smaller number of nodes and identify potential scale bottlenecks. For example, if you see an all-reduce collective operation already taking 20% of an iteration on 8 GPUs, it will only get worse at a larger scale—especially as you exceed the capacity of a single compute node or data center rack system, such as the Grace Blackwell GB200 and GB300 NVL72 and Vera Rubin VR200 and VR300 NVL systems.

Keep this checklist handy and add to it as you discover new tricks. Combine these tips and best practices with the in-depth understanding from the earlier chapters, and you will design and run AI systems that are efficient, scalable, maintainable, cost-effective, and reliable.

Now go forth and make your most ambitious ideas a reality. Happy optimizing!

Index

B

Q

R

S

About the Author

Chris Fregly is a performance engineer and AI product leader who has driven innovations at Netflix, Databricks, Amazon Web Services (AWS), and multiple startups. He has led performance-focused engineering teams that built AI/ML products, scaled go-to-market initiatives, and reduced cost for large-scale generative-AI and analytics workloads. Chris coauthored *Data Science on AWS* and *Generative AI on AWS* (O'Reilly), and created the O'Reilly course "High-Performance AI in Production with NVIDIA GPUs." His work spans kernel-level tuning, compiler-driven acceleration, distributed training, and high-throughput inference. Chris organizes the global AI Performance Engineering meetup (*https://meetup.com/ai-performance-engineering*) with over 100,000 members worldwide.

Colophon

The animal on the cover of *AI Systems Performance Engineering* is a northeast African cheetah (*Acinonyx jubatus soemmeringii*), also known as the Sudan cheetah. This subspecies of cheetah is predominantly found in northeast Africa, including regions of Ethiopia, Somalia, and South Sudan.

The northeast African cheetah shares the iconic slender body and long limbs characteristic of all cheetahs, which facilitates its incredible speed (up to 65–75 miles per hour). It differs from its southern relatives in having more variation in tear marks (the black stripes that run from the corner of each eye down to the mouth) and a thicker coat.

Cheetahs eat medium-sized ungulates like gazelles, zebras, and impalas. They are skilled hunters. Their strategy relies on a blend of stealth and an explosive, short burst of speed. They consume their meals quickly to avoid losing it to other predators like lions or hyenas, who are able to overpower them. Unlike many other big cats, cheetahs cannot roar but instead use a variety of purrs, chirps, hisses, and growls to communicate. They are particularly vocal in mating season or when females are communicating with their cubs. A litter typically contains three to five cubs, who live with their mother for the first year and a half. Male cheetahs tend to be more social, forming loose coalitions that groom and hunt together.

Most cheetah species are considered vulnerable or endangered by the IUCN, due to habitat loss and poaching. Many of the animals on O'Reilly covers are endangered; all of them are important to the world.

The cover illustration is by José Marzan Jr., based on an original illustration for O'Reilly Media. The series design is by Edie Freedman, Ellie Volckhausen, and Karen Montgomery. The cover fonts are Gilroy Semibold and Guardian Sans. The text font is Adobe Minion Pro; the heading font is Adobe Myriad Condensed; and the code font is Dalton Maag's Ubuntu Mono.

O'REILLY®

Learn from experts.
Become one yourself.

60,000+ titles | Live events with experts | Role-based courses
Interactive learning | Certification preparation | Verifiable skills

Try the O'Reilly learning platform free for 10 days.

www.ingramcontent.com/pod-product-compliance
Lightning Source LLC
Chambersburg PA
CBHW080332220326
41598CB00030B/4488

9 7 9 8 3 4 1 6 2 7 7 8 9